UNDERSTANDING COMPUTER SCIENCE

for Advanced Level

Third Edition

About the author

Ray Bradley is a well-published and widely respected author of books on computing and related subjects for those studying GCSE and/or advanced level courses. He began his career in the Engineering industry where he completed an apprenticeship in Mechanical and Electrical Engineering. Later he obtained an Honours degree in Electronic Engineering, specialising in Computer Engineering and Communication systems. After completion of his degree he obtained a post-graduate certificate in education specialising in Mathematics. He has taught for about twenty years split between the state and private sectors, and has been employed in various capacities including the deputy Head of Mathematics at Sandhurst School, and the Director of Electronics and Computing at Tonbridge School. He is currently the Director of Computing and Information Technology at Tonbridge School where he is also the IT co-ordinator responsible for staff training.

Cross-platform integration

Students of computer science may be interested to know how most of this book was compiled. Here is a potted history which gives little indication of the tortuous route which was actually taken.

The text

This was originally created on the Acorn Archimedes and Risc PC computers using Computer Concept's Impression Style DTP package. The text was then exported using the RTF (Rich Text Format) option and imported into Microsoft's Word 6, then exported again using the Word for Macintosh 5.1 export utility. The text, complete with all the original styles and formatting was then used to produce the book on a professional typesetting package.

UNDERSTANDING COMPUTER SCIENCE
for Advanced Level
Third Edition

Ray Bradley

STANLEY THORNES PUBLISHERS LTD.

Dedication
To Sue whose love and patience and understanding were all needed in great abundance to complete a project of this magnitude.

Special thanks are due to:
Jared Prakash
Alex Bone
Sue Bradley

Acknowledgements
Thanks are due to the following for kind permission to reproduce photographs or other material:
Aitch Design Consultancy, p. 569 (Figure 24.7, left); Apple: p. 219 (Figure 11.2(b),(d)), p. 222 (Figure 11.5), p. 563 (Figure 24.2); BostoMatic (UK) Ltd, p. 545 (Figure 23.6(b)); Bull HN Information Systems Ltd, p. 16 (Figure 2.9(b)); Cameron Communications, p. 221 (Figure 11.3(a)); Canon (UK) Ltd, p. 229 (Figure 11.12(a)); Connor Peripherals, p. 269 (Figure 13.5, left); Creative Photography (Leicester) Ltd, p. 545 (Figure 23.7); Epson (UK) Ltd, p. 248 (Figure 12.8(a)); Fast Electronic (UK) Ltd, p. 233 (Figure 11.16); Gildemeister (UK) Ltd, p. 545 (Figure 23.6(a)); Hakuto International (UK) Ltd. 543 (Figure 23.4); Harvard Marketing Services, p. 249 (Figure 12.9); IBM: p. 15 (Figure 2.8), p. 17 (Figure 2.10(b)), p. 217 (Figure 11.1); Intel Corporation, p. 233 (Figure 11.17); Linear Graphics Ltd, p. 257 (Figure 12.16(a)); Logitech, p. 221 (Figure 11.3(c)); Marquardt, p. 219 (Figure 11.2(a)); Mentecaptus, p. 221 (Figure 11.3(b)); Microsoft, p. 562 (Figure 24.1); NEC: p. 15 (Figure 2.8), p. 240 (Figure 12.1); Penman Products Ltd, p. 257 (Figure 12.16(b)); The Royal Bank of Scotland PLC, p. 232 (Figure 11.15); Roland (UK) Ltd, p. 256 (Figure 12.15); Rover Group, p. 549 (Figure 23.13); Science Photo Library: cover, p. 17 (Figure 2.11) Paul Shambroom, p. 550 (Figure 23.14(a)) Jerry Mason, p. 551 (Figure 23.16) Taquet, Jerrican; Sibelius Software, p. 235 (Figure 11.18); Sony Manufacturing Co. (UK) Ltd, p. 546 (Figure 23.9); Tomy (UK) Ltd, p. 550 (Figure 23.14(b)); Viewfinder, p. 223 (Figure 11.7).

Thanks are also due to the following examination boards for kind permission to reproduce examination questions:
Associated Examining Board; Northern Examinations and Assessment Board; Northern Ireland Council for the Curriculum Examinations and Assessment; Oxford and Cambridge Schools Examination Board; University of Cambridge Local Examinations Syndicate; University of Oxford Delegacy of Local Examinations; University of London Examinations and Assessment Council; Welsh Joint Education Committee.

First edition published 1987 by Hutchinson Education
Second edition published 1991 by Stanley Thornes (Publishers) Ltd

Third edition published 1995 by:
Stanley Thornes (Publishers) Ltd
Ellenborough House
Wellington Street
CHELTENHAM GL50 1YW

97 98 99 00 / 10 9 8 7 6 5 4 3

ISBN 0 7487 1979 2

A catalogue record of this book is available from the British Library.

Typeset by Florencetype Ltd, Stoodleigh, Devon
Printed and bound in Great Britain by Scotprint Ltd, Musselburgh

Contents

Preface to the third edition

Computer science – the future

The challenge to new students

In many respects the future has been much better than we had expected! The meteoric rise in power of the latest 64-bit microprocessor chips has been astonishing. The raw-processing power that is now available at a reasonable cost on the top of your desk is something that would literally have been regarded as being in the realms of fantasy when the first edition of this book was being written just over ten years ago. Now we must look even further ahead, and must cast our eyes firmly towards the 21st century for the next batch of even more outstanding and exciting possibilities.

Impressive recent developments in software have been more than a match for the turbo-charged hardware on which this software is currently being run, and users have come to expect quantum leaps in developments as being the norm – in general they have not been disappointed. The predicted slowing down in the development of silicon technology has not yet materialised, and there seems to be few limits to continued developments at the current pace for about another decade. There are other new technologies on the horizon too, which if man can prove to be ingenious enough over the next couple of decades or so, will increase processing speeds and power by very significant factors indeed – far greater in fact than we have seen hitherto. So the future looks like an inspiring challenge for new students on the computer-science frontier. Many of these new hardware and software ideas and developments have been fully integrated into Understanding Computer Science for Advanced Level, and this extensively-revised and enhanced edition reflects much of the innovation and excitement which continues unabated throughout the whole computing industry.

You need vision and imagination

People often ask, 'What's the point of having ever-increasing speed and more processing power?' They might say, for example, that they are completely satisfied with how their word processor performs, and can't see why computers running this software will ever need to go any faster. From their individual and limited perspective they are probably right – but I personally think that at worst they are burying their heads in the sand, and at best they have little vision and even less imagination. Why, for example, have the current generation of word processors *not* got comprehensive *and foolproof* grammar and context-sensitive spelling checkers that can work instantly in *any* language? The Oxford English Dictionary, for example, *is* now available on CD-ROM – but why have we not got this *and* all the equivalent and equally comprehensive foreign-language dictionaries available on our micros at the touch of a button? Why can't we yet get easy access to *all* worldwide databases from our laptop portables? In short – what limits us from having access to most human knowledge on our desktop or laptop computers? This would surely be a laudable aim from an educational point of view? The simple answer is that the computers which the majority of the population regularly use are not powerful enough, are not fast enough, have nowhere near enough memory, and have not got the necessary high-bandwidth communication links available at a sensible cost.

The above single example, chosen from many other possible scenarios looking into the future may sound like some pipedream – but don't forget that's exactly what some of the colour-DTP systems available now, for example, would have sounded like if you had written a technical description of them just a few years ago! Ten years ago the thought of microcomputers working with over sixteen million colours, with resolutions of 1200 dpi *and* having several hundred Megabytes of RAM – plus the ability to print this out in photographic quality to boot – well, quite simply, it *would* have been ludicrous. At *that time* most computers had no colour at all, and eight colours plus a few hundred Kbytes of RAM represented the cutting edge of new technology! However, we will now leave the crystal-ball gazing behind, get off the soap box for a moment, and look in detail at the major changes which have occurred in this new edition.

The third edition

Extensive new material

The third edition of this book has had the most extensive revisions to date, with about 80 per cent of the previous edition being completely updated. Indeed, it has been a lot more work and taken longer to write than the original first edition! An extra 160 pages have been added, and this means that the range of topics covered is considerably broader in scope, and important topics are covered in a lot more depth. There is an extended section in chapter 1 on the planning of both the theoretical and practical work encountered in computing courses at advanced or equivalent level. There is also advice on application-based training, class activities, visits and materials which are suitable for a broad range of computer-science courses.

Low-level language improvements

The material in chapters 4 and 5 on low-level languages has been completely rewritten, and we have introduced BORIS – the Beginner's Optimised Reduced Instruction Set microprocessor – a device which has been invented to enable beginners to appreciate how simple microcomputers work in principle. The second half of chapter 4 takes the reader on from basic microprocessor architecture to the ultra modern multiprocessor-multibus systems used on minis, mainframes and some of the most-powerful micros. Material in chapter 5 now contains more up-to-date examples, and RISC-based technology is covered in more detail which reflects the current important developments in this exciting field.

Greatly enhanced software chapters

Perhaps *the* most fundamental change of all has been the considerable enhancement of all the software-based chapters, and the addition of several new ones. This has markedly enlarged the proportion of the book devoted entirely to software and analysis, thus reflecting the drastic increase in the importance of software techniques in the real world, and in all the modern computer-science-based syllabuses. Recent object-oriented languages such as C++ have also been included and considered in some detail, and the structured analysis and design sections have grown considerably to include popular techniques such as Jackson Structured Programming (JSP), state-transition diagrams, Gantt charts, decision tables and several other methods not included in the 2nd edition. Chapters 6, 7, 8 and 9 now give all readers much greater potential for being able to carry out detailed analysis by using up-to-date methods. Chapter 9 on special-programming techniques has also been revamped and now includes a very detailed explanation of the Mandelbrot set, together with the basic theory of complex numbers to enable students to understand enough about the system to program their own Mandelbrot worlds.

Extended hardware chapters

The old hardware chapter from the second edition has been split into three, and the material in each of the new chapters 11, 12 and 13 has been enhanced and extended to cover all the modern input, output and storage devices, including recordable CD-ROMs, colour laser printers, colour LCD screens on portables, virtual reality input systems such as the data glove, and many other systems too numerous to mention in this preface. Unusually in a book of this nature, technical details have also been included which, although not strictly a requirement of most examination syllabuses, will help curious students and frustrated teachers who are continually being asked to explain how modern devices work.

More detailed file handling

Chapter 16 on files and file handling has been completely rewritten and many new diagrams have been included which help to explain the serial, sequential, indexed and indexed-sequential file structures, together with suitable algorithms for maintenance of these different data structures. Examples making use of the popular high-level data-processing language COBOL completes a more professional approach to file handling in general.

Enhanced work on operating systems

Operating systems have become increasingly sophisticated in the last few years, and chapter 17 on operating systems has been rewritten to reflect the developments in object-oriented systems, concurrency, and other modern trends, but also completely updates the mainframe sections so that what's happening here is dealt with in some considerable detail too.

Up to date systems analysis

A brand new systems-analysis chapter (chapter 18) making use of the many new methods covered in the structured analysis and design chapters, including the use of CASE (Computer Aided Software Engineering), further enhances modern techniques and demonstrates in depth, and with detailed examples, how large-scale projects are tackled. It also draws many parallels with tackling the practical course work which has to be undertaken by most students at this level.

Much extra database material

Chapter 20 on databases has been completely rewritten and extended to reflect the increasing importance of relational databases in many modern computer-science courses. All database models are covered, but relational databases are covered in greater depth, with all three stages of Codd's normalisation looked at in some detail. The modern role of the DBMS has also been extended, and the new WIMP-based database systems are also covered.

Updated applications

All three applications chapters have been updated, and chapters 22, 23 and 24 now include examples making use of up-to-the-minute technology. The importance of the Internet, the latest CD-ROM based systems, multimedia authoring packages, morphing and even autostereograms (looking at the 3-D images in a 2-D picture) have been included to add interest to the work on further computer-based applications.

Global influence of networks

The networks' chapter (chapter 21) has also been considerably updated to include the TCP/IP Internet protocols which, together with systems like ATM look set to mould multimedia-communication systems well into the foreseeable future. As networks are likely to play a pivotal role in the implementation of the information superhighway, this chapter sets the scene to enable students to understand what's going on from a sound theoretical basis to an appreciation of the implications of such extensive global network systems on their future society.

New control material

A new chapter on control systems, chapter 25, has been added. Control is now tackled in some depth from both a hardware and software point of view, and a case-study involving 'Widget testing' serves to demonstrate current industrial practice.

In depth social implications

Due to the tremendous pace of change that has taken place, chapter 26 on social implications now reflects what's been happening recently, and looks in depth at privacy implications, hacking, computer crime, viruses, data encryption and artificial intelligence and launches some of these ideas further into the future.

Examination material

The examination sections have been removed from the end of each chapter and placed in chapter 29 at the end of the book. It was felt that it is often difficult to find whole examination questions which reflect only that work which is covered in a single chapter, and this was frustrating if students attempted to complete the questions without a knowledge of work in some of the other chapters.

Larger glossary and new end-of-chapter summaries

The large glossary at the back of the book has been considerably extended and now contains well over 1,000 definitions. The glossary, together with the *new* end-of-chapter summaries, should make an invaluable contribution and act as extra revision aids for all students.

Substantially extended answers

The answers section to the end-of-chapter exercises has had an enormous increase in size, and now contains well over 45 pages of detailed answers to questions. These enhanced and extended answers, together with extensive page references should ensure that students are guided through the critical thought needed to answer each question.

Finally, while every effort has been made to ensure that all parts of the book are absolutely correct, it's almost inevitable that in a highly technical book of this nature, which contains somewhere in the region of 400,000 words and about 500 diagrams, some mistakes will unfortunately creep through. The author has been extremely grateful in the past to all those who have written in with constructive criticism and pointing out errors, and hopes that future readers will be just as helpful. Not all sections of this book are applicable to all syllabuses, and therefore the author and his students do not make use of every single page on a regular basis. Therefore, unless people are kind enough to write in, a particular mistake may not be found until the next edition is due to be updated.

Take up the challenge

The gauntlet has been thrown down to you by the increasingly sophisticated technology mentioned at the beginning of this preface. When computers become ever more powerful – which *is* inevitable – it will be up to people like you to make sure that they are used wisely and are usefully employed. Let your imagination have full reign, I would expect no less, but make sure that it's for the good of humanity – not to its detriment.

Ray Bradley 1995

Board by board syllabus analysis

Codes for examination boards

AEB – Associated Examining Board
CCEA – Northern Ireland Council for the Curriculum Examinations & Assessment
Hong Kong Examinations Authority
NEAB – Northern Examinations and Assessment Board – **JMB** (Joint Matriculation Board) and **NEA** (Northern Examining Association)
OCSEB – Oxford & Cambridge Schools Examination Board
SCAA – Secondary Schools Assessment Authority
UCLES – University of Cambridge Local Examinations Syndicate
ULEAC – University of London, Examinations and Assessment Council
UODLE – University of Oxford Delegacy of Local Examinations
WJEC – Welsh Joint Education Committee
BTEC – Business & Technician Education Council. There are many relevant BTEC syllabuses – specifically this book will help with many aspects of the **BTEC First Course** modules, is ideal for use with much of the **BTEC National Course**, and is also useful with some parts of the Higher National qualifications in Computing, Software Engineering and Information Technology.
There is also much material in this book which is applicable to **Part 1** of the **British Computing Society** examinations, **first year degree courses**, and the higher (advanced) levels of the **NVQ** and **GNVQ** programmes.

Examination board (Codes are explained above)	Page no.	AEB	BTEC (See notes)	Hong	Kong	NEAB	CCEA	OCSEB	UODLE	ULEAC	UCLES	WJEC	SCAA Score
Chapter 2													
Basic concepts	**9**												
What is a computer?	9	✔	✔	✔	✔	✔	✔	✔	✔	✔	✔	✔	✔
The information rich and poor	9	✔	✔	✔	✔	✔	✔	✔	✔	✔	✔	✔	✔
Technical jargon	9	✔	✔	✔	✔	✔	✔	✔	✔	✔	✔	✔	✔
Data and information	10	✔	✔	✔	✔	✔	✔	✔	✔	✔	✔	✔	✔
Some basic ideas	10	✔	✔	✔	✔	✔	✔	✔	✔	✔	✔	✔	✔
The simplest computer system	10	✔	✔	✔	✔	✔	✔	✔	✔	✔	✔	✔	✔
An expanded computer system	11	✔	✔	✔	✔	✔	✔	✔	✔	✔	✔	✔	✔
Hardware and software	12	✔	✔	✔	✔	✔	✔	✔	✔	✔	✔	✔	✔
Why a digital computer?	12	✔	✔	✔	✔	✔	✔	✔	✔	✔	✔	✔	✔
Generations of computers	13	✔	✔	✔	✔	✔	✔	✔	✔	✔	✔	✔	✔
A modern overview of computers	14	✔	✔	✔	✔	✔	✔	✔	✔	✔	✔	✔	✔
From laptops to supercomputers	14	✔	✔	✔	✔	✔	✔	✔	✔	✔	✔	✔	✔
Microcomputers	14	✔	✔	✔	✔	✔	✔	✔	✔	✔	✔	✔	✔
The laptop computer	15	✔	✔	✔	✔	✔	✔	✔	✔	✔	✔	✔	✔
The minicomputer	16	✔	✔	✔	✔	✔	✔	✔	✔	✔	✔	✔	✔
Mainframe computers	16	✔	✔	✔	✔	✔	✔	✔	✔	✔	✔	✔	✔
Supercomputers	17	✔	✔	✔	✔	✔	✔	✔	✔	✔	✔	✔	✔
Some modern computing ideas	18	✔	✔	✔	✔	✔	✔	✔	✔	✔	✔	✔	✔
Multi-tasking	18	✔	✔	✔	✔	✔	✔	✔	✔	✔	✔	✔	✔
The virtual machine	18	✔	✔	✔	✔	✔	✔	✔	✔	✔	✔	✔	✔
Parallel processing	18	✔	✔	✔	✔	✔	✔	✔	✔	✔	✔	✔	✔
Computer languages	18	✔	✔	✔	✔	✔	✔	✔	✔	✔	✔	✔	✔
Applications	19	✔	✔	✔	✔	✔	✔	✔	✔	✔	✔	✔	✔
Defining a problem	19	✔	✔	✔	✔	✔	✔	✔	✔	✔	✔	✔	✔
The future	19	✔	✔	✔	✔	✔	✔	✔	✔	✔	✔	✔	✔
Chapter 3													
Representation of data	**22**												
The binary system	22	✔	✔	✔	✔	✔	✔	✔	✔	✔	✔	✔	✔
Conversion between decimal and binary	24	✔	✔	✔	✔	✔	✔	✔	✔	✔	✔	✔	✔
Adding binary numbers	25	✔	✔	✔	✔	✔	✔	✔	✔	✔	✔	✔	✔
Subtracting binary numbers	25	✔	✔	✔	✔	✔	✔	✔	✔	✔	✔	✔	✔
Multiplication of binary numbers	26	✔	✔	✔	✔	✔	✔	✔	✔	✔	✔	✔	✔
Division of binary numbers	26	✔	✔	✔	✔	✔	✔	✔	✔	✔	✔	✔	✔
Octal	27	✔	✔	✔	✔	✔	✔	✔	✔	✔	✔	✔	✔
Hexadecimal	27	✔	✔	✔	✔	✔	✔	✔	✔	✔	✔	✔	✔

Examination board (Codes are explained on page xi)	Page no.	A E B	B T E C (See notes)	H o n g	K o n g	N E A B	C C E A	O C S E B	U O D L E	U L E A C	U C L E S	W J E C	S C A A
Ink-jet and bubble-jet printers	255	✔	✔	✔	✔	✔	✔	✔	✔	✔	✔	✔	✔
Thermal wax and dye sublimation	256	✔	✔	✔	✔	✔	✔	✔	✔	✔	✔	✔	✔
Graphics output devices	256	✔	✔	✔	✔	✔	✔	✔	✔	✔	✔	✔	✔
Plotters	256	✔	✔	✔	✔	✔	✔	✔	✔	✔	✔	✔	✔
Photographic computer output	257	✔	✔	✔	✔	✔	✔	✔	✔	✔	✔	✔	✔
Virtual reality helmets	258	✔	✔	✔	✔	✔	✔	✔	✔	✔	✔	✔	✔
Chapter 13													
Storage devices	**261**												
Introduction	261	✔	✔	✔	✔	✔	✔	✔	✔	✔	✔	✔	✔
Primary storage techniques	261	✔	✔	✔	✔	✔	✔	✔	✔	✔	✔	✔	✔
Semiconductor memory	262	✔	✔	✔	✔	✔	✔	✔	✔	✔	✔	✔	✔
Principles of main memory	262	✔	✔	✔	✔	✔	✔	✔	✔	✔	✔	✔	✔
Bits, bytes and nibbles	262	✔	✔	✔	✔	✔	✔	✔	✔	✔	✔	✔	✔
Multipliers	263	✔	✔	✔	✔	✔	✔	✔	✔	✔	✔	✔	✔
How the main memory is utilised	263	✔	✔	✔	✔	✔	✔	✔	✔	✔	✔	✔	✔
Addressing the memory	264	✔	✔	✔	✔	✔	✔	✔	✔	✔	✔	✔	✔
Moving data along the bus	264	✔	✔	✔	✔	✔	✔	✔	✔	✔	✔	✔	✔
Access times	264	✔	✔	✔	✔	✔	✔	✔	✔	✔	✔	✔	✔
Types of semiconductor memory	264	✔	✔	✔	✔	✔	✔	✔	✔	✔	✔	✔	✔
Dynamic and static RAM	264	✔	✔	✔	✔	✔	✔	✔	✔	✔	✔	✔	✔
Volatile memory	265	✔	✔	✔	✔	✔	✔	✔	✔	✔	✔	✔	✔
ROM	265	✔	✔	✔	✔	✔	✔	✔	✔	✔	✔	✔	✔
PROM	265	✔	✔	✔	✔	✔	✔	✔	✔	✔	✔	✔	✔
EPROM	266	✔	✔	✔	✔	✔	✔	✔	✔	✔	✔	✔	✔
ASCII code	266	✔	✔	✔	✔	✔	✔	✔	✔	✔	✔	✔	✔
Extended ASCII code	267	✔	✔	✔	✔	✔	✔	✔	✔	✔	✔	✔	✔
Secondary storage techniques	267	✔	✔	✔	✔	✔	✔	✔	✔	✔	✔	✔	✔
Direct and sequential access	267	✔	✔	✔	✔	✔	✔	✔	✔	✔	✔	✔	✔
Floppy disks	267	✔	✔	✔	✔	✔	✔	✔	✔	✔	✔	✔	✔
Speed of operation	268	✔	✔	✔	✔	✔	✔	✔	✔	✔	✔	✔	✔
Disk formats	268	✔	✔	✔	✔	✔	✔	✔	✔	✔	✔	✔	✔
Higher-density disks	268	✔	✔	✔	✔	✔	✔	✔	✔	✔	✔	✔	✔
Winchester disk technology	268	✔	✔	✔	✔	✔	✔	✔	✔	✔	✔	✔	✔
Drive array systems	269	✔	✔	✔	✔	✔	✔	✔	✔	✔	✔	✔	✔
Large hard-disk systems	270	✔	✔	✔	✔	✔	✔	✔	✔	✔	✔	✔	✔
Disk packs	270	✔	✔	✔	✔	✔	✔	✔	✔	✔	✔	✔	✔
Other types of disk unit	271	✔	✔	✔	✔	✔	✔	✔	✔	✔	✔	✔	✔
Making sense of the stored data	271	✔	✔	✔	✔	✔	✔	✔	✔	✔	✔	✔	✔
Optical drives	272	✔	✔	✔	✔	✔	✔	✔	✔	✔	✔	✔	✔
Reading data from a CD-ROM	273	✔	✔	✔	✔	✔	✔	✔	✔	✔	✔	✔	✔
Magneto-optical devices	274	✔	✔	✔	✔	✔	✔	✔	✔	✔	✔	✔	✔
WORMS	275	✔	✔	✔	✔	✔	✔	✔	✔	✔	✔	✔	✔
Multiple standards of CDs	276	✔	✔	✔	✔	✔	✔	✔	✔	✔	✔	✔	✔
Disk-cache systems	276	✔	✔	✔	✔	✔	✔	✔	✔	✔	✔	✔	✔
Serial and sequential access techniques	277	✔	✔	✔	✔	✔	✔	✔	✔	✔	✔	✔	✔
Magnetic tape - basic principles	277	✔	✔	✔	✔	✔	✔	✔	✔	✔	✔	✔	✔
EBCDIC	278		✔										
Buffers	280	✔	✔	✔	✔	✔	✔	✔	✔	✔	✔	✔	✔
QIC (¼inch) tape streamers	281	✔	✔	✔	✔	✔	✔	✔	✔	✔	✔	✔	✔
DAT & Video	281	✔	✔	✔	✔	✔	✔	✔	✔	✔	✔	✔	✔
Bubble memory	282	✔	✔	✔	✔	✔	✔	✔	✔	✔	✔	✔	
Plated-wire store	282												
Chapter 14													
Data structures	**286**												
Typical operations	286	✔		✔	✔	✔	✔	✔	✔	✔	✔	✔	✔
Linear list	287	✔		✔	✔	✔	✔	✔	✔	✔	✔	✔	✔
Stacks	288	✔		✔	✔	✔	✔	✔	✔	✔	✔	✔	✔
Processing data in a stack	289	✔		✔	✔	✔	✔	✔	✔	✔	✔	✔	✔
Queues	290	✔		✔	✔	✔	✔	✔	✔	✔	✔	✔	✔
Processing data in a queue	291	✔		✔	✔	✔	✔	✔	✔	✔	✔	✔	✔
Arrays	293	✔		✔	✔	✔	✔	✔	✔	✔	✔	✔	✔
Processing data in arrays	295	✔		✔	✔	✔	✔	✔	✔	✔	✔	✔	✔
Linked lists	297	✔		✔	✔	✔	✔	✔	✔	✔	✔	✔	✔

Examination board (Codes are explained on page xi)	Page no.	A E B	B T E C (See notes)	H o n g	K o n g	N E A B	C C E A	O C S E B	U O D L E	U L E A C	U C L E S	W J E C	S C A A core
Chapter 18													
Systems analysis and design	**400**												
What is a system?	400	✔			✔	✔	✔	✔	✔	✔	✔	✔	✔
Systems analysis methods	400	✔			✔	✔	✔	✔	✔	✔	✔	✔	✔
Sound project advice	401	✔			✔	✔	✔	✔	✔	✔	✔	✔	✔
Alternative approaches	402	✔			✔	✔	✔	✔	✔	✔	✔	✔	✔
Systems flowchart symbols	403	✔			✔	✔	✔	✔	✔	✔	✔	✔	✔
A complete systems analysis example	404	✔			✔	✔	✔	✔	✔	✔	✔	✔	✔
Definition of the problem	404	✔			✔	✔	✔	✔	✔	✔	✔	✔	✔
Feasibility study	405	✔			✔	✔	✔	✔	✔	✔	✔	✔	✔
Collecting information	405	✔			✔	✔	✔	✔	✔	✔	✔	✔	✔
General objectives	406	✔			✔	✔	✔	✔	✔	✔	✔	✔	✔
The database	407	✔			✔	✔	✔	✔	✔	✔	✔	✔	✔
Resource file	407	✔			✔	✔	✔	✔	✔	✔	✔	✔	✔
Borrower's file	407	✔			✔	✔	✔	✔	✔	✔	✔	✔	✔
Other information	408	✔			✔	✔	✔	✔	✔	✔	✔	✔	✔
The librarian's perspective	408	✔			✔	✔	✔	✔	✔	✔	✔	✔	✔
The academic departments	409	✔			✔	✔	✔	✔	✔	✔	✔	✔	✔
Potential problems	410	✔			✔	✔	✔	✔	✔	✔	✔	✔	✔
A student's perspective	410	✔			✔	✔	✔	✔	✔	✔	✔	✔	✔
Security	411	✔			✔	✔	✔	✔	✔	✔	✔	✔	✔
Disadvantages	411	✔			✔	✔	✔	✔	✔	✔	✔	✔	✔
Costs	411	✔			✔	✔	✔	✔	✔	✔	✔	✔	✔
Initial conclusions	411	✔			✔	✔	✔	✔	✔	✔	✔	✔	✔
Analysis of the problem	412	✔			✔	✔	✔	✔	✔	✔	✔	✔	✔
General systems analysis methods	421	✔			✔	✔	✔	✔	✔	✔	✔	✔	✔
Testing	421	✔			✔	✔	✔	✔	✔	✔	✔	✔	✔
The bottom-up approach to testing	421	✔			✔	✔	✔	✔	✔	✔	✔	✔	✔
Testing individual modules	421	✔			✔	✔	✔	✔	✔	✔	✔	✔	✔
Debugging tools	422	✔			✔	✔	✔	✔	✔	✔	✔	✔	✔
Testing processed data	423	✔			✔	✔	✔	✔	✔	✔	✔	✔	✔
Data validation	423	✔			✔	✔	✔	✔	✔	✔	✔	✔	✔
Data verification	423	✔			✔	✔	✔	✔	✔	✔	✔	✔	✔
Check digits	423	✔			✔	✔	✔	✔	✔	✔	✔	✔	✔
Modulo 11 example	424	✔			✔	✔	✔	✔	✔	✔	✔	✔	✔
The dreaded bugs	424	✔			✔	✔	✔	✔	✔	✔	✔	✔	✔
Alpha and beta testing	424	✔			✔	✔	✔	✔	✔	✔	✔	✔	✔
Documentation	424	✔			✔	✔	✔	✔	✔	✔	✔	✔	✔
Program documentation	425	✔			✔	✔	✔	✔	✔	✔	✔	✔	✔
Additional information	426	✔			✔	✔	✔	✔	✔	✔	✔	✔	✔
Other forms of documentation	426	✔			✔	✔	✔	✔	✔	✔	✔	✔	✔
CASE	426	✔			✔	✔	✔	✔	✔	✔	✔	✔	✔
Chapter 19													
Electronic logic	**430**												
Introduction	430		✔	✔									
Logic gates	431		✔	✔									
The AND gate	431		✔	✔									
The OR gate	432		✔	✔									
The NOT gate	432		✔	✔									
Why use logic?	432		✔	✔									
Further logic gates	434		✔	✔									
NAND and NOR gates	434		✔	✔									
The XOR gate	436		✔	✔									
Boolean algebra	436		✔	✔		✔							
Switching algebra	437												
Basic laws	437		✔	✔		✔							
Simplifying Boolean expressions	440		✔	✔		✔							
Use of truth tables	441		✔	✔		✔							
Karnaugh maps	441		✔	✔		✔							
Further electronic logic	445		✔	✔									
Decoders and encoders	445		✔	✔									
Further computer arithmetic	448		✔	✔									
The full adder	449		✔	✔									
Parallel addition of binary numbers	451		✔	✔									

Examination board (Codes are explained on page xi)	Page no.	A E B	B T E C (See notes)	Hong	Kong	N E A B	C C E A	O C S E B	U O D L E	U L E A C	U C L E S	W J E C	S C A A	Score
Serial addition of binary numbers	451		✔	✔										
Flip flop circuits	452		✔											
The SR flip flop	452		✔											
The clocked SR flip flop	453		✔											
The JK flip flop	453		✔											
Shift registers	454		✔											
Chapter 20														
Database systems	**458**													
Introduction	458	✔				✔	✔	✔	✔	✔	✔	✔	✔	
Background information	458	✔				✔	✔	✔	✔	✔	✔	✔	✔	
Why make use of a database?	459	✔				✔	✔	✔	✔	✔	✔	✔	✔	
Modelling data	460	✔				✔	✔	✔	✔	✔	✔	✔	✔	
The basic database models	462	✔				✔	✔	✔	✔	✔	✔	✔	✔	
An example structure	463	✔				✔	✔	✔	✔	✔	✔	✔	✔	
The hierarchical database model	464	✔				✔	✔	✔	✔	✔	✔	✔	✔	
Advantages and disadvantages	464	✔				✔	✔	✔	✔	✔	✔	✔	✔	
The network database model	465	✔												
Advantages and disadvantages	467	✔												
The relational database model	467	✔				✔	✔	✔	✔	✔	✔	✔	✔	
Tuples	468													
Normalisation	469	✔				✔								
First normal form	470	✔				✔								
Second normal form	471	✔				✔								
Third normal form	473	✔				✔								
The DataBase Management System	475	✔				✔	✔	✔	✔	✔	✔	✔	✔	
How is the system organised	475	✔				✔	✔	✔	✔	✔	✔	✔	✔	
The DBA	475	✔				✔	✔	✔	✔	✔	✔	✔	✔	
The schema	476	✔				✔	✔	✔	✔	✔	✔	✔	✔	
The data description language	476	✔				✔	✔	✔	✔	✔	✔	✔	✔	
The data dictionary	477	✔				✔	✔	✔	✔	✔	✔	✔	✔	
The file manager	477	✔				✔	✔	✔	✔	✔	✔	✔	✔	
The data manipulation language	477	✔				✔	✔	✔	✔	✔	✔	✔	✔	
The query language	477	✔				✔	✔	✔	✔	✔	✔	✔	✔	
Commercial database applications	478	✔				✔	✔	✔	✔	✔	✔	✔	✔	
Extracting information from database	479	✔				✔	✔	✔	✔	✔	✔	✔	✔	
Use of 4GLs	480	✔				✔	✔	✔	✔	✔	✔	✔	✔	
Mathematical financial functions	481	✔				✔	✔	✔	✔	✔	✔	✔	✔	
Time and date calculations	481	✔				✔	✔	✔	✔	✔	✔	✔	✔	
Wild cards	481	✔				✔	✔	✔	✔	✔	✔	✔	✔	
Reports	481	✔				✔	✔	✔	✔	✔	✔	✔	✔	
The state of the art	481	✔				✔	✔	✔	✔	✔	✔	✔	✔	
Security on the system	482	✔				✔	✔	✔	✔	✔	✔	✔	✔	
Physical security	482	✔				✔	✔	✔	✔	✔	✔	✔	✔	
Storage of data	482	✔				✔	✔	✔	✔	✔	✔	✔	✔	
Preventing unauthorised access	482	✔				✔	✔	✔	✔	✔	✔	✔	✔	
Advantages and disadvantages	483	✔				✔	✔	✔	✔	✔	✔	✔	✔	
Data protection act	483	✔				✔	✔	✔	✔	✔	✔	✔	✔	
The computer misuse act	484	✔				✔	✔	✔	✔	✔	✔	✔	✔	
Chapter 21														
Modern communication systems	**487**													
Introduction	487	✔	✔	✔		✔	✔	✔	✔	✔	✔	✔	✔	
Computer networks	487	✔	✔	✔		✔	✔	✔	✔	✔	✔	✔	✔	
Local area networks	488	✔	✔	✔		✔	✔	✔	✔	✔	✔	✔	✔	
Why make use of LANs?	488	✔	✔	✔		✔	✔	✔	✔	✔	✔	✔	✔	
Using a LAN in practice	489	✔	✔	✔		✔	✔	✔	✔	✔	✔	✔	✔	
Network management software	490	✔	✔	✔		✔	✔	✔	✔	✔	✔	✔	✔	
Problems with networks	490	✔	✔	✔		✔	✔	✔	✔	✔	✔	✔	✔	
Problems of bandwidth	490	✔	✔			✔			✔					
Solutions to bandwidth problems	491	✔	✔			✔			✔					
A solution using software	491	✔	✔			✔			✔					
A solution using other hardware	491	✔	✔			✔			✔					
More sophisticated networks	492	✔	✔			✔			✔					
Network topology	492	✔	✔			✔			✔					

Examination board (Codes are explained on page xi)	Page no.	A E B	B T E C (See notes)	H o n g	K o n g	N E A B	C C E A	O C S E B	U O D L E	U L E A C	U C L E S	W J E C	S C A A c o r e
Typical viral-infection symptoms	602	✔	✔	✔	✔	✔	✔	✔	✔	✔	✔	✔	✔
Practice safe hex!	602	✔	✔	✔	✔	✔	✔	✔	✔	✔	✔	✔	✔
The cost of viral infections	602	✔	✔	✔	✔	✔	✔	✔	✔	✔	✔	✔	✔
Anti-virus software	603	✔	✔	✔	✔	✔	✔	✔	✔	✔	✔	✔	✔
Software piracy	603	✔	✔	✔	✔	✔	✔	✔	✔	✔	✔	✔	✔
Security measures	604	✔	✔	✔	✔	✔	✔	✔	✔	✔	✔	✔	✔
Physical security	604	✔	✔	✔	✔	✔	✔	✔	✔	✔	✔	✔	✔
System security	605	✔	✔	✔	✔	✔	✔	✔	✔	✔	✔	✔	✔
Passwords	605	✔	✔	✔	✔	✔	✔	✔	✔	✔	✔	✔	✔
Cryptography	605	✔	✔	✔	✔	✔	✔	✔	✔	✔	✔	✔	✔
Computers and employment	607	✔	✔	✔	✔	✔	✔	✔	✔	✔	✔	✔	✔
IT in the office environment	607	✔	✔	✔	✔	✔	✔	✔	✔	✔	✔	✔	✔
My best friend's a robot!	608	✔	✔	✔	✔	✔	✔	✔	✔	✔	✔	✔	✔
Computers and privacy	609	✔	✔	✔	✔	✔	✔	✔	✔	✔	✔	✔	✔
The role played by the computer	609	✔	✔	✔	✔	✔	✔	✔	✔	✔	✔	✔	✔
Computers: education, training, home	610	✔	✔	✔	✔	✔	✔	✔	✔	✔	✔	✔	✔
Computers in the home	611	✔	✔	✔	✔	✔	✔	✔	✔	✔	✔	✔	✔
Microprocessor-controlled TVs	611	✔	✔	✔	✔	✔	✔	✔	✔	✔	✔	✔	✔
The thinking machine?	612	✔	✔	✔	✔	✔	✔	✔	✔	✔	✔	✔	✔
Algorithms and religion	613	✔	✔	✔	✔	✔	✔	✔	✔	✔	✔	✔	✔
Chapter 27													
History of computing	**616**												
Early calculating aids	616												
Mechanical calculating aids	617												
From calculating devices to computers	617												
The electrical machine	618												
Major developments in software	619												
Chapter 28													
Computing projects	**621**												
The nature of computing projects	621	✔				✔	✔	✔	✔	✔	✔	✔	✔
Where to begin	622	✔				✔	✔	✔	✔	✔	✔	✔	✔
The marking scheme	623	✔				✔	✔	✔	✔	✔	✔	✔	✔
The written report	623	✔				✔	✔	✔	✔	✔	✔	✔	✔
Project analysis	624	✔				✔	✔	✔	✔	✔	✔	✔	✔
The method of solution	624	✔				✔	✔	✔	✔	✔	✔	✔	✔
Testing the system	625	✔				✔	✔	✔	✔	✔	✔	✔	✔
Documentation	625	✔				✔	✔	✔	✔	✔	✔	✔	✔
Does it work?	625	✔				✔	✔	✔	✔	✔	✔	✔	✔
Presentation	625	✔				✔	✔	✔	✔	✔	✔	✔	✔

General notes

Syllabuses are correct as at 1996/1997 – but you will need to *check carefully* for any changes. From 1998 **all syllabuses will include the Secondary Schools Assessment Authority (SCAA) core** shown in its *final form* in the tables above. **Teaching to this core should begin in September 1996.**

Appropriate 'AS' level syllabuses are usually subsets of the A level syllabuses outlined in the above lists. However, some syllabuses have optional elements, and this means that these topics are studied in more detail. This book contains enough material for all known options. You should note that 'AS' level questions are the *same standard* as the 'A' level ones.

Some boards offer an additional 'A' level special paper (called **'S' level**) in which questions of a more searching nature are provided. I don't recommend that you tackle these papers unless you find *all* the work at 'A' level relatively easy. There is no extra material required, and readers with a full understanding of this book, together with a good appreciatoion of all the practical work they have undertaken at school or college will be more than adequately prepared for the 'S' level paper.

Notes on the SCAA Core

The existing Computer Science common core has been taken into account when the SCAA core was being written. The final version of the SCAA core was published in January 1995, and has been written in *very general terms* such that most boards will still have the opportunity to develop individuality on certain parts of the syllabus. The ticks in the above SCAA column reflect the Author's interpretation of the SCAA core requirements. For example, the SCAA core requires that students understand *the features of contemporary storage methods and devices*, therefore, chapter 13, covering storage techniques has been included in the core. Similarly, a study of *the capabilities of processors* is required, therefore, it has been assumed that the machine architecture and low-level language chapters are needed too. Understanding Computer Science for Advanced Level should cover the material for all current examination boards offering 'Computing' at 'A' level. However, it's up to you to make sure that you keep up to date with contemporary computing methods such as the use of supercomputers for simulation purposes in the automobile industry, for example. This is best done by watching TV programmes and videos as outlined on page 6. Together with your practical experienced gained from using a whole range of applications and the experience from your project work, you should be adequately prepared for virtually any eventuality.

Modular courses

If you are undertaking modular courses then you should check each module carefully to ascertain the parts of the syllabus which are relevant to each module which you have decided to do.

Case studies

Some boards require that you undertake the study of a particular computer application in more depth. You should check carefully if this applies to your syllabus and find out what this work involves.

1 How to make the best use of this book

Introduction

Student and teacher guidance notes

Suggested schemes of work

Put the kettle on, make a cup of coffee, then spend just a few minutes reading this short section on how to make the best use of this book – you'll find it's well worth the effort. Indeed, it's also worth the effort to re-visit this chapter at regular intervals throughout your course to bring important features back into focus.

Extra sections and aids have been designed specifically to help guide students and staff when using this 3rd edition – *the* most important features are as follows.

- Recent **syllabus guides** to **'A' Level** boards and relevant **BTEC** courses.
- A new **course-planning section** to help students, teachers and lecturers.
- A unique **pig system** indicating the degree of difficulty of the work.
- Text is highlighted in **bold** or *italics* to aid readability and *stress* **importance**.
- **Greyed-out text** helps when skimming through the chapters.
- **End-of-chapter summaries** help with revision *and* bring out **key points**.
- There is an up-to-date and **comprehensive glossary** of technical terms.
- A greatly extended *answer section* to **end-of-chapter questions**.
- Recent **past-examination questions** from **'A' level** boards.
- A new **companion volume** containing hundreds of worked examples.

Although you *could* undertake your computer-science course by reading this book from cover to cover – by starting at page one and working your way through in a linear fashion – this is probably *not the most productive* and certainly *not the most interesting way* to proceed. **Different parts of this book can be tackled simultaneously, and the harder chapters can be left out on first reading**. Also, many schools and colleges have different teachers/lecturers who tackle different parts of the course. To help both students and staff plan their courses more effectively, one possible **suggested scheme of work** has been shown in figure 1.1 – it should be referred to constantly when reading the rest of this introductory section.

Figure 1.1 shows both the **theoretical** and **practically-based components** of many computer-science courses. The *important thing to notice* is that the work has been split up into **6 major terms** – namely Christmas, Easter and Summer over a period of *two* years. Chapters 1 and 2 are suggested compulsory reading at the beginning of the course, but options then present themselves for going off at different tangents – by doing this in an effective way, the course can be made more interesting, and long stretches of theory can be avoided – practical work, projects, visits, debates, extra reading and videos etc. can be interwoven with the more theoretical concepts to make a better and more balanced course.

The suggested scheme has particular merit because it *ensures that most of the important work* necessary for the **major practical project** has been covered *before* term 4. For example, using this scheme ensures that, by term 4, students have covered practical DTP systems and CAD packages which are both useful for writing up their projects as they proceed – it ensures that the students have covered the practical work on spreadsheets and databases which is so often needed for their projects – it ensures that they have covered the all-important high-level languages – *and* studied enough about data structures, structured analysis and systems analysis to be useful for the design and analysis parts of their project too.

You should take special note of the **vertical lines** in figure 1.1 which **separate the terms**. For example, *if* you decide to start off with the 'high-level language principles' covered in chapter 6, although chapters 7, 8, 9 and 10 cover all the related work in a logical manner, it is suggested that you should *not* go straight through the chapters

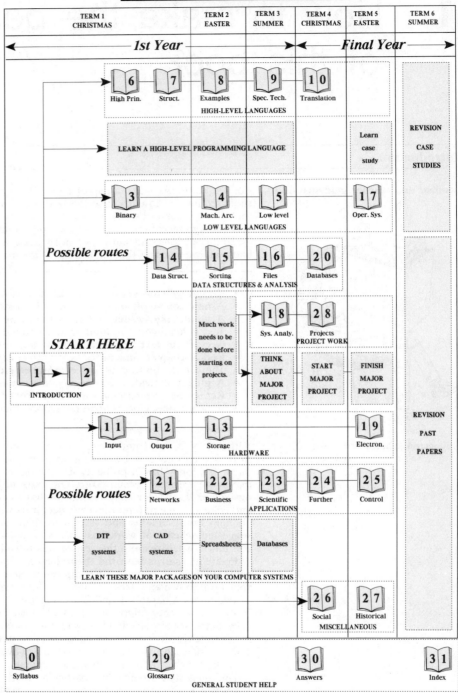

Figure 1.1

in this way – careful observation of the diagram shows that you would have ended up undertaking a level of work more suitable for the Christmas term of the second year! Indeed, parts of chapters 9 and 10 contain **pig ratings** (*more difficult work*). It would be far better, as is suggested in figure 1.1, to tackle chapters 6 and 7, while *at the same time* undertaking the practical work on learning a high-level language such as BASIC, Pascal or C++, for example. Chapters 6 and 7 go hand-in-hand with this more practically-based work. As light relief from learning to program, DTP systems and CAD packages can be covered during this term too. Also, the hardware chapters like 11, 12 and 13 can be tackled independently of the work being covered elsewhere.

The **horizontal lines** (joining the chapters) in figure 1.1 *generally* indicate which chapters *must* be covered before progressing to any of the others. For example, it would be silly to undertake chapters 4 and 5 on low-level languages before tackling any of the binary work in chapter 3. However, the applications-based chapters can be covered in *any* order.

Timing

You should take special note that much work has been covered *early* on in the course (**during the first year**) so that *class time* can be spent on projects during the 4th and 5th terms. Also, and *this comes as a shock to some students* – **there's not much time during term 6 for anything other than revision**! Some 'A' level computer-science examinations are taken in May – this leaves only a few weeks after coming back from the Easter vacation to wrap up the whole course – there really is very little time for learning anything new or covering major topics from scratch – *all learning of the theory, the practical work, case studies and projects must be done within the first five terms.*

Levels of difficulty

As can be seen from figure 1.1, this book has been arranged with some degree of logic – however, due to the more difficult nature of some of the work, certain parts of chapters or indeed whole chapters are best left until later on in the course. In particular, topics like the work on **recursion** in chapter 9, **parsing** in chapter 10, and **normalisation** in chapter 20, for example, should be tackled only when the students are ready and able to do them – indeed, it may be that some of the weaker students should not spend much time on these topics at all. These and other topics of a similar degree of difficulty are often a **pig** to do! A **pig system** will therefore be used to indicate the degree of difficulty of the work. If work is perceived to be difficult for many students then a little pig (one is shown on the left here) will be shown in the margin. It does not mean that you should not understand the work or give up, it's just to reassure you that many students often find these particular sections quite hard.

Essential extras

Computer science covers a very broad spectrum of knowledge, and different hardware and software platforms ensure that no one book is able to cover all the work exactly as it is tackled on your particular systems. Therefore, other source material needs to be available throughout your course. In particular, *you should make sure that* **you have access to**, *and* **experience of**, *all of the materials listed below*.

Applications

At the *beginning* of your course you should learn how to use an application like a **DTP system** or a **top-of-the-range word processor**, together with a **CAD package** that is able to build up diagrams suitable for inclusion in your chosen DTP or word-processor package. (A package like ClarisWorks, for example, which does both functions together is perfectly acceptable.) You should *use these packages at frequent intervals* throughout your course so that you are an **expert** by the time you have to write up your major project report (usually during term 5 or during the Easter holidays if you have a suitable machine at home). Hastily-hand-written documentation is no longer acceptable, and usually indicates lack of planning on the part of the student concerned. Also, if you write up the report using a DTP system *as you are doing the project* then much hassle and time is saved later.

Other packages of primary importance are **spreadsheets** and **database systems**. The only way in which you can truly appreciate these packages is to use them extensively. *It's also most important* that you *program databases* using a suitable **SQL language,** and *program a spreadsheet* using a suitable **macro language**. This work should supplement your work with high-level languages.

You *must* make sure that you have access to *all* the necessary **manuals** and/or **textbooks** (or **videos**) available for use with these basic packages – there are few excuses (other than financial ones) these days, as literally thousands of suitable books, magazines and videos are available for all manner of computer-based applications. Don't forget that libraries often carry suitable books, and if your own library is not up to scratch then make use of a specialist technical library – there is usually one in each county – ask your local librarian if you don't know where it is – books can be borrowed from the technical library via your local library.

High-level languages

I suggest that **you learn one** (or preferably two if you are keen and have the time) **high level language/s in depth**. This *must* be a modern **structured programming language** such as the *latest* versions of **BASIC** or **Pascal**. **C++** may also be used if you are keen to get started on a high-powered language which is easy to use at a basic level, but powerful enough to program the very latest applications. It's also *essential* that you have some experience of using a **compiler** – experience of interpreted BASIC alone will not be sufficient – all versions of the languages mentioned here have compilers available for most machines.

It's also an added advantage if you have access to and can *play around with* other high-level languages such as **FORTRAN 90**, **COBOL** or **Prolog**, for example. Without a computer to test out and run simple programs in these languages, work such as that covered in chapter 8 becomes gut-wrenchingly boring! *Much time can be saved if you are presented with many pre-written procedures* which carry out particular functions in different languages – it's then easy to make small modifications to these procedures which you can easily run on your own machine in a short space of time. You should never forget the famous quote which goes something like this:

'*Tell me and I forget – Show me and I remember – Let me do it and I understand.*'

There is no substitute for practical experience with different languages, even if it's only for an hour or so.

Low-level languages

BORIS – the Beginner's Optimised Reduced Instruction Set microprocessor, together with the other material in chapter 4 will teach you the rudiments of microprocessor systems. Chapter 5 on low-level languages will teach you much more, but *there's no substitute* for **running your own assembly-language programs on the machines which you have at school or college**. Without practical experience on a *real machine* the concepts of low-level languages are much more difficult to grasp – make sure that you have access to an assembler and are able to run simple programs on it – the experience is well worth it and you can more readily appreciate what is going on when you come to read more advanced work on operating systems later in the course.

Using the glossary

Computer science is riddled with jargon – most of which, in my opinion, is justified. Any academically-respectable science must have an extensive technical language or you can't communicate effectively. For example, can you imagine referring to '**non-volatile memory**' as '*The little black boxes with funny legs sitting on the main electronic board inside the computer which do not lose the contents which have been stored inside them when the electricity to the system is switched off*'?

The glossary built up in the second edition has been extensively revised and updated, and now contains well over 1,500 explanations of technical terms. Moreover, terms used within a definition which are themselves defined in the glossary are highlighted in bold type. Make extensive use of the glossary, especially in the early stages of your course. It will also act as a neat way to do an **alternative** form of revision towards the end of your course.

Case studies

Some syllabuses require that you study a particular application or general area of computing in some considerable detail – usually in much more depth than would be expected in a general-syllabus context. For example, the BP refinery at Baglan Bay is the current case study for the O & C and Cambridge Examination Boards. Case studies are published well in advance and appear in the syllabus for your particular course. You should *make sure that you know which case study, if any, you should be undertaking*, and **get any relevant material from the examination boards or nominated agents well in advance** of the examination. It's essential that you check that you have the right syllabus regarding the year in which you take the examination – case studies have often been the same for years and then are suddenly changed – beware, some people have been caught out in the past, there's nothing worse than going into your examination having studied the wrong material – it *has* happened in the past – it *will probably* happen again in the future – **make sure that it does not happen to you.**

Using this book with different courses

Understanding Computer Science for Advanced level has been used on a wide variety of different courses for many years, and the 3rd edition of this book has been considerably expanded to reflect this wider user base. Therefore, you will have to be particularly careful in making sure that you spend most of your time on the material which is very important as far as *your* particular course is concerned, unless, of course, you're interested in expanding your knowledge in other areas of computer science as well. The Board-by-Board syllabus analysis section near the beginning of this book should help considerably, but there is no substitute for checking your *current* syllabus, as changes on a yearly basis could be likely.

The key to an efficient analysis of any course is modularisation. Put simply, is a posh way of compartmentalising your chosen subject into separately-identifi chunks. Fortunately, computer science as a subject can be modularised very e and this makes it particularly easy to identify various sections which are applic Having identified an appropriate topic, the only thing yet to be established is depth in which to study it. This is a slightly more difficult problem, but consider able help is at hand by reading the sub-sections belonging to each chapter in the syllabus-analysis section. For example, if 'Structured Analysis and Design' forms part of your course, then looking in detail at the sub-sections of chapter 7 in the syllabus-analysis section will help you to compare those parts of this topic which are relevant to you. You may find, for example, that JSP or Decision tables are not specifically listed in your syllabus. If it is not clear on these details, then ask your teacher or lecturer if such topics are needed. Some syllabuses are so general that they are not particularly helpful in the detailed lists which they give. Even teachers and lecturers are often not too sure in one or two instances. One can only gain an inkling by studying past examination papers in some considerable detail, but even this would not help if a topic is completely new.

Computer Science is a very open-ended subject, and *you will often find that sub-sections of topics not listed in your syllabus will help considerably when it comes to taking the final examination.* There are so many different ways of tackling similar problems that knowledge of several techniques is often helpful, and you will obviously not be penalised in an examination for knowing something which is not in the syllabus, or for tackling a particular problem in a more-sophisticated or professional manner.

The SCAA core

One of the most recent innovations is the introduction of the SCAA (The Schools' Curriculum Assessment Authority) core for 'A' level, regarding examinations in 1998 and beyond. Being available in 1995, this too has been included in the Board-by-Board syllabus-analysis section at the beginning of this book. This should, however, be nothing to worry about, as computer science has some advantage in this particular area too – we have been working with an agreed inter-board common-core syllabus now for a number of years.

BTEC courses

There is such a huge variety of specialist BTEC courses that it would take up too much space to list all detailed possibilities for which this text would be useful. However, core courses, large parts of which are particularly suited to this book, include *Computer Systems*, *Communication Skills*, *Information Systems*, *Introduction to Programming* and *Quantitative Methods*.

ONC/D, HNC/D and BCS pt1

Students on BTEC ONC/OND and 1st year students on BTEC HNC/HND computer-related courses will also find this book useful, as will students undertaking Part 1 of the British Computer Society examinations.

First Degree

Many students undertaking computer-science degree courses start the course without having undertaken an 'A' level or even a GCSE in this particular subject. Therefore, this book can act as a valuable reference to help students to understand many of the unfamiliar concepts which they will be required to assimilate, often at a lightning-fast pace. Students on degree courses have often found that the approach at 'A' level helps considerably to understand a large number of the fundamental concepts which are being covered in their courses at more advanced levels.

GNVQs

Large numbers of GNVQ courses will be appearing on the curriculum of some institutions, and a number of these courses too should find that large sections of this book are appropriate. Again it would take up too much space to map out all curricular details, but the exercise would be well worth your while if you are undertaking one of these newer courses.

Keeping up to date

You probably won't need reminding that computer science is a rapidly-changing subject. There is, fortunately, a huge core of knowledge that does not change too rapidly, and large sections of this book will be useful for some considerable time to come. However, what changes on an almost-monthly basis is the rapid advancement in microprocessor technology, the new microcomputers which are built around these new processors, and the increased sophistication of the software which such systems can support. The third edition of this book has been completely re-written in all areas which have seen rapid advances, but **it is up to you to keep even more up to date** by reading appropriate **magazines**, the **computer press**, and articles in some of the more-serious newspapers.

The number of computer-based magazines on sale in the newsagents these days testifies both to the quantity and diversity of available material. Although some magazines are not suitable for gaining very much new knowledge, the vast majority of magazines will have articles which make suitable reading material for keeping right up to date. In particular, I have found that the following magazines, newspapers and TV programmes are particularly worthwhile in the context of computer science courses at advanced level.

Useful magazines

Archimedes World	Acorn-based technical information
BYTE	For in-depth technical articles
Personal Computer World	PC-based technical information
Mac User	Mac-based technical information

Useful newspapers

Computer Weekly	Good technical articles
Times, Telegraph and Guardian	Good technical articles

Useful TV programs

Equinox	Excellent technical programmes
Horizon	Excellent technical programmes
Q.E.D	Excellent technical programmes

The above are only a selection – you should always be on the lookout for new programmes which may be of use – *do this by scanning through* the **TV** *and* **Radio** programmes each week and consult the educational TV guides produced by the BBC and ITV.

Most schools and colleges are licensed to video Open University programmes and other programmes too. Find out if your school or college has any suitable video material, and ask your lecturer/teacher to show you some if they are available and if the staff are willing – there are now hundreds of videos and many CD-ROM based training materials suitable for many parts of computer-science courses. Good use of CD-ROMs, videos, newspapers, magazines, manuals and other training material will make the course so much more interesting.

Past examination papers

Computer-science examinations at advanced level have now been going for over 25 years. Unfortunately, only the most-recent papers (about the last 10 years) have any hope of containing questions which are relevant to today's syllabuses. The author used to teach a lot of mathematics at 'A' level, and was always grateful for the vast bank of past-paper questions containing relevant material. However, getting past computer-science papers from different boards will enable you to increase the range of suitable questions and thus build up a sizeable bank. However, even doing this is not quite as good as it used to be – the agreed inter-board common core has meant that some questions on different examination papers are identical – that's life!

Much relevant practice of the *appropriate standard* can be found in the many exercises throughout this book, and hundreds of suitable worked examples can be found in the **companion volume** which will be available after the third edition of this book has been published for the first time. Together with a range of past papers as described above, you should not lack suitable material.

Visits

You should try to visit one or two professional computer-based organisations. Without this experience it's possible to get into a rut where you think that computing revolves around the micros which you have at your school or college. If you can go and see a **mainframe** or even a **supercomputer** in operation then this would be much to your advantage, assuming that you are able to get a proper look and have the system explained properly – it's no good just looking at the box in which the computer is housed – you can easily do this from a book. Remember to build up a bank of suitable questions so that you appear to be intelligent! Also, don't forget to thank your hosts, even if you feel that the visit was not one of the highlights of your year.

If possible try and get your school or college to arrange one or two talks from computer experts in particular fields. At the author's school we have had successful visits from local health authority computer managers, travel agents, banking personnel, engineering companies and professors from universities.

Debates and discussion groups

Although chapter 26 deals with a good number of different social issues, **you will need to do some extra reading to get different views regarding major issues affecting computing** – there are suitable books in most libraries, each containing strong arguments both for and against computerisation. How about choosing a topic and then giving a presentation to the rest of your class, or even better to a larger group of students? There's nothing guaranteed to sharpen up the mind as much as presenting a case for or against some particular argument *in front of an audience*. If you don't do your homework then you will not look particularly impressive – so how about using your DTP systems to present professional-standard OHP (acetate) sheets – they can be produced by a bubble-jet or LASER printer. (Note that *different types* of acetate sheets are needed for each!) How about linking up one of your computers to a projection TV or OHP system if these facilities are available to be used? Use all the technology at your disposal to present the most powerful arguments that you can – these visual aids also act as a prompt if you can see your pre-prepared material on the screen.

If possible arrange full-scale debates on particular subjects like 'Virtual Reality', 'Do computers possess intelligence' or 'Are computers enhancing or detracting from our children's education'. The number of possible topics is endless. **As a computer-scientist you should be able to argue rationally from a position of strength**, *because* you have considerable knowledge about computing. Much argument from non-computer-scientists revolves around irrational fears and prejudices, and is based on misconceptions and lack of knowledge.

Revision

There is *just one* **magic formula** for carrying out effective revision – and that is to make sure that you have worked hard over the entire course beforehand – it's difficult to revise things that you have not learned properly in the first place! Nevertheless, even if you *are* in this unfortunate position, and there are several weeks to go before the examination, all is not lost. What **effective revision** *will enable you to do* is to build on whatever foundation you have built up for yourself, and thus ensure that your chances of getting a better grade are maximised. Specific areas in this book and the accompanying companion volume which are useful for revision are as follows.

Use the syllabus analysis section as a guide to what you are expected to know. However, *this is no substitute for having your own syllabus in front of you.* Changes from year-to-year are likely. Get a *photocopy* of the syllabus and **tick off parts which you have learnt, still understand, and can do**.

Use the **greyed-out text** and the **end-of-chapter summaries** to revise a specific area quickly. Make use of the **glossary** for *extra revision material* – go through the glossary or end-of-chapter summaries by getting a friend to ask you questions, or by covering up the explanations with a piece of paper and asking yourself the questions.

Make use of the **companion volume** which concentrates on **brief summaries of the syllabus**, and backs them up with a **vast range of completely-worked examples**.

Build up a revision schedule over the space of 6 to 8 weeks *before the examination* – integrate this schedule with your other subjects so that you are not overloaded. Make a **list of the topics** which you *don't understand* and get your teacher to go over them or re-read the relevant sections of this book.

Find out early on which are *your* most productive times regarding doing *effective work*. **Do get up early if you can work well first thing in the morning, but don't stay up very late if you can't do productive work at night**. Make sure that you *are* doing effective work by monitoring your progress – if you have spent the last half an hour staring at the wall then stop work and do something else – or do nothing.

Make sure that you tackle **entire past papers and limit yourself to the actual time which you would have been allowed in the final examination**. *Get your teacher or lecturer to mark the work* that you have done under these conditions – this is the *only* way in which you can effectively measure your actual progress regarding your performance in the final examination.

It's not my fault. I didn't ask to be in this book.

The jokes and silly cartoons

There is an extended and enhanced collection of jokes and silly cartoons in this third edition. (Oh no, I hear some of you sigh – well you don't have to look at them if you don't want to!) They are designed to make the book more interesting and amusing, and to promote a happier atmosphere in the classroom when covering work which is often hard going. If you feel that the jokes are bad in this book then you should attend some of my lessons! Reactions to these jokes often range from hilarity to downright nauseating – nevertheless it shows that most students do actually pay attention, even if it's just to tell me how bad they are.

The highlight for me regarding the jokes in this book was when a student who went on to study Computer Science at Cambridge University rushed into one of my lessons and said – 'Sir – I've found a mistake in your book – it's in the glossary'. 'You look up *endless loop* and it says see '*loop endless*' – then you look up '*loop endless*' and it says *see 'endless loop*'. 'That's meant to be one of my jokes' I said. 'Oh no – that's terrible Sir' came the reply – he has never lived it down since.

End of chapter summary

- **This book can be used on a wide variety of different courses at Advanced level.** Make sure that *you know which parts are the most relevant* to your particular course.
- **This book can be used in a large number of different ways.** Make sure that you understand how to make the most efficient use of this book from your point of view.
- **Do tackle the work in this book in the most interesting ways.** Mix complex theoretical topics with practical work and applications.
- **Make sure that you understand your practical project requirements** early on in your course. Plan ahead for this major work and less problems will occur.
- **Make use of the suggested schemes of work** if you feel that this is appropriate for your particular course structure.
- Don't forget that some of the work is a pig – and the **pig-rating system** *can help identify work which students find more difficult* – it might help you through the more-difficult sections to realise that other students find the work tough going too.
- **Do make sure you cover the essential extras** like learning a range of major applications packages, one or two high-level languages, have experience of an assembly language and learn the case-study material if necessary.
- Don't forget to **keep up to date by reading** the specialist computer press, computer magazines, and the technological sections of the more serious press. Also, listen to appropriate TV and radio programmes.
- **Do make use of the end-of-chapter summaries**. These can also act as a useful revision aid – use them like crib cards containing important information.
- **Do make use of the comprehensive glossary** at the end of this book, it will often help if concepts or unfamiliar words need explanation.
- A **visit to computer installations other than your school or college** helps to broaden your outlook.
- **Do undertake an effective and comprehensive revision schedule** in the run up to the final examination.
- **Do read this chapter several times throughout your advanced computer science course**. It will help you to remember efficient ways of organising your work and of using this particular text book.
- *If you need more practice* with examination-type questions, don't forget that a **volume containing worked examples** will be available after the 3rd edition of this book has been published.

2 Basic concepts

Introduction

This chapter is designed to give an introduction to the fascinating world of **computer science** at a *simple level*. It is intended to give a broad overview of many concepts and will act as a base from which the more complex ideas in the other chapters can be developed. The material here is **essential reading** if you have not done any previous computer studies courses, but will act as a useful reminder for those students who are starting out with a wider knowledge base. I suggest that the more knowledgeable students do actually read this work, but they may be able to skim through some of it more quickly. Those who are starting from scratch are advised to take time to absorb the concepts, and undertake the work in the exercise at the end of this chapter – a sound base is needed from which to develop the more complex principles.

What is a computer

A **computer** is basically a **processor of information**. What gives it such tremendous power and versatility is the fact that the information contained in it may be processed in many different forms, with *text, sound, video* and *computer-generated graphics* being just a few common examples. Add to this the fact that a computer is very fast, can make use of the global network to communicate with other information-based systems, and you will start to appreciate just a fraction of the potential of these information-processing machines. At this early stage in your course you should appreciate the importance of what is meant by the term '**information**', and realise that **information** *which can be processed* forms the basis of **knowledge** itself – *these ideas are this fundamental* – a fact not often appreciated by people with little or no computer literacy.

The information rich and poor

In the future there's likely to be a tremendous gap between those people who simply make use of the computer as an effective tool in carrying out their day-to-day tasks, and those who can understand the computer and therefore start to mould the future by applying their own innovative ideas to help develop new and better information technology. There will be an even larger gap between those countries which can develop high technology effectively by applying IT principles, and those which cannot. Countries in the former category have been described as the 'information rich', and countries in the latter category have been described as the 'information poor'. Many people in the more developed countries can and do make use of computers in the normal course of their work, and one has only to look at the millions of people using **applications** such as **word processors**, **DTP** systems and **spreadsheets**, for example, to illustrate this fact. Nevertheless, *most of these people do not understand* anything at all about the systems beyond the immediate application they are using – and this pays tribute to the immense advances that have been made in the last few years in making computer systems much easier to use – once they have been set up properly by people with more advanced knowledge. By undertaking an advanced course in computer science you are already starting out on the road to a fundamental understanding of computers and information technology in general, and should you be successful in your chosen course, will be well on the way to becoming the sort of person who is able to make a valuable contribution to the advanced technological development of IT and computing well into the 21st century.

Technical jargon

As with any technologically-based subject, there is much technical jargon in computing – indeed, I think that 'computer science' might well be favourite to receive the gold award for the most jargon in any single subject – for example, in the mid 1990s there were well over 25,000 technical terms associated with computers – with over 1,500 of them being described in the glossary at the end of this book. To get to grips with computer science you will have to come to terms with many new technical terms, most of which are useful. Computer scientists do have a sense of humour, and some of the jargon is a little ridiculous to say the least, nevertheless, it's only when your technical vocabulary has increased beyond a certain point that you will start to appreciate and therefore enjoy learning more detail.

Data and information

Data is the **raw material** on which a computer operates. When some appropriate **structure** has been applied to the data it becomes **information**. As we have seen above, information can be processed in many different forms, so a simple numerical example will help to explain. Consider, for a moment, the following numbers:

262, 294, 330, 349, 392, 440, 494 and 523.

It is doubtful whether too many readers would be able to guess what the above **data** represents – it is therefore an example of **raw data**, where **structure** has yet to be applied. (In fact the structure has been applied – it's just that most of us don't know what is is yet!)

Suppose that you were told that the above numbers represent the frequencies, to the nearest Hz, of musical notes starting from middle C and spanning one octave. You are then enlightened because meaning has been given to a previously meaningless set of data. **Structure** has been applied and the **data** has become **information**, as shown in the following important relationship.

Information = Data + Structure

The new **information** is now shown pictorially in figure 2.1. You should note that this is not a mathematical formula to be applied in the normal sense, but is simply a way of describing a fundamental concept in computer science. Throughout much of your computer-science course you will unconsciously be applying structure to extract information from data.

Approximate frequency | 262 | 294 | 330 | 349 | 392 | 440 | 494 | 523
(in hertz)   (Middle 'C')

Figure 2.1

A **computer**, under the guidance of a *set of instructions* called a **program**, could be connected up to an appropriate instrument via a **MIDI interface** (see page 235), and be made to play the scale as described by the original **data**. Indeed, had the original data been an entire Beethoven symphony, then this too could be processed in a similar way.

Some basic ideas

From the previous section you have seen how **processing** needs to be applied to some **input data**, and after this **processing** has been accomplished, the **information** can then be **output** from the system. In the previous section you used your brain to carry out the appropriate thought processes, but we now look at some fundamental principles of organising machines to perform similar tasks.

The musical example in the previous section is just one specific case of an infinite variety of scenarios which could have been chosen – *translating a foreign language, drawing a picture, controlling a robot* or *sorting names into alphabetical order* would also have served the same purpose. What makes a computer so versatile is the ability to model the data such that it can represent almost anything. In the past people have become used to machines built to perform a specific purpose – a typewriter can produce neat text – a musical instrument can produce a certain type of sound – an air brush and stencils can produce a professional illustration for a magazine – however, a **computer** can do all of these things, *often more efficiently than the purpose-built devices* just mentioned. How then do we start to think in terms of such generality? How do we begin to organise such a general information-processing machine?

The simplest computer system

Figure 2.2 shows how the general concepts outlined above can represent the basic parts of any information-processing system. The ideas of **input**, **processing** and **output** are fundamental to all modern computer systems.

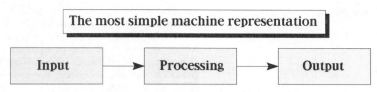

The most simple machine representation

Input → Processing → Output

Direction of data flow is shown by the arrows

Figure 2.2

An expanded computer system

Such ideas might seem simple, and indeed they are, but they help to categorise what's happening in our general information-processing system. You will quickly realise however, that the terms are a little vague to say the least, and will need to be expanded considerably to be of any use. Figure 2.3, for example, shows the next stage up the evolutionary ladder, with the input and output sections expanded to show more detail.

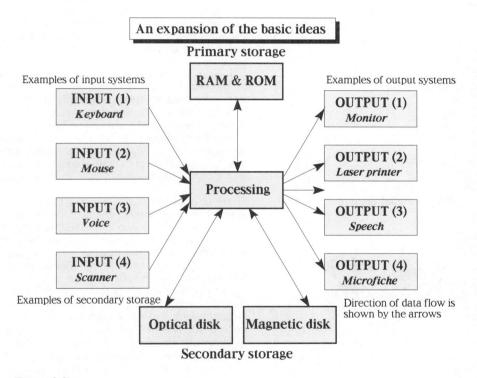

An expansion of the basic ideas

Primary storage

Examples of input systems

RAM & ROM

Examples of output systems

INPUT (1) *Keyboard*
INPUT (2) *Mouse*
INPUT (3) *Voice*
INPUT (4) *Scanner*

Processing

OUTPUT (1) *Monitor*
OUTPUT (2) *Laser printer*
OUTPUT (3) *Speech*
OUTPUT (4) *Microfiche*

Examples of secondary storage

Direction of data flow is shown by the arrows

Optical disk   Magnetic disk

Secondary storage

Figure 2.3

The diagram also shows the addition of the vital **primary storage** or **memory**, which is needed to store the *sets of instructions* that the computer will follow, and the necessary **secondary storage**, which enables the computer to *save information or get information from other sources* such as CD-ROM or floppy disk etc.

Notice that there is a wide variety of methods for getting **data** *into the computer* (the **INPUTS**) and getting **data** *out from the computer* (the **OUTPUTS**). In our expanded diagram only very few of the possible inputs and outputs have been shown. For example, our system has no means of communication via a telephone line or computer network, could not operate a magnetic tape machine and has no means of controlling a robot. Nevertheless, it's the ideas that are important here, all the details mentioned here are covered in great depth in other parts of this book.

We have only come a short way along the road to a generalised machine, but you should already appreciate the need to split up the system into different types of **inputs** and **outputs**, you should appreciate that some complex **processing** is magically carried out by the **central processing unit**, *instructions* held in the **primary storage** are followed, and information can be *saved* and *loaded* from **secondary storage devices** such as **CD-ROM** and **disk**.

Hardware and software

An important distinction is made in computing between the *devices* made up from the *mechanics* and *electronics* which are used to *build the system*, and the *instructions* (the **ideas**) which are used to *control* the system. The **hardware** is easy – it simply means all the equipment and other devices that you can see and touch (literally) – it's *simply the computer equipment*. The sets of instructions called **programs** mentioned earlier are called **software**, and the word 'idea' is more important than might appear at first sight – you can't touch an idea – you can only appreciate the consequences of what that idea conveys. Without trying to be pedantic, *if* the **program instructions** are *written down on a piece of paper* then you are staring at **hardware**! – this is because the **paper** and **ink** which has been used are both things you can touch, and are, therefore, **hardware**. However, it's the ideas and concepts *conveyed by these instructions* which are the software – consider **software** as an **intellectual idea** rather than a physical thing and you won't go far wrong. Of course we would not get very far without hardware – we need a machine to control, we need manuals and instruction books and a whole host of other documentation which usually accompanies **software packages** and **programming languages**. Only about 20% of this book is devoted to hardware – the rest concentrates on software, data structures, applications and implications, as well as large sections of material specifically written to help students with their studies. This ratio in favour of 'software and analysis methods' reflects modern trends in computing, and mirrors what's going on in the real world. Most often it's the software which causes the problems, and a much greater investment now goes into software analysis than was the case hitherto.

To give you some idea of the complexity of current software, Windows NT, one of the windows-based operating systems, has over 4.5 million different software instructions! An **operating system** is the name given to the **software** which is responsible for giving the computer its personality – *it's what makes the fast and powerful hardware much easier for us to use*. Before the advent of easy-to-use operating systems computers were very difficult machines to understand, and used only by specialists such as engineers and scientists. In less than 50 years we have progressed from computers being cumbersome, difficult to use and costly, to being a versatile tool which is accepted and used by tens of millions of people each day.

Why a digital computer?

These days everything seems to have gone **digital** – digital Compact Discs (CDs), digital tuning on radios, digital information received by the TV to display teletext, digital controls on video recorders, washing machines and microwaves, and let's not forget the digital watch which decimated the traditional swiss-watch industry a couple of decades ago. At the heart of most of these devices lies a **chip** which is identical in principle to the *main chips* controlling all of our **personal computers**, but first let's see why digital systems reign supreme.

The common thing regarding all the devices mentioned in the last paragraph is that they are controlled by **electronics**. Now electricity can be controlled in many different ways, but the easiest and quickest way of all is simply to switch the stuff on and off. This has led to a system in which the **two states 'on' and 'off'** are used to represent the **data** and hence the **information**. These simple ideas happen to mirror the **binary** (two state) **system** in mathematics exactly, where a '**1**' can be used to represent '**on**' and a '**0**' can be used to represent '**off**' – this is why a *full appreciation* of the **binary system** is so important to obtain a fundamental understanding about computers.

Line of sight communication link

It might seem a tremendous stretch of the imagination to make the connection between these binary-digit 'ons' and 'offs', and the tremendous variety of things which a computer can do – but that's exactly what's happening in practice. To help explain this most fundamental of concepts I have invented a simple machine called **BASIL – the Binary Apparatus for Sending Intelligent Letters**. BASIL can be used to clarify how information can be sent backwards and forwards between two remote points by making use of binary – the remainder of this book will help to explain the rest of the theory of computers at advanced level!

BASIL is a machine in which eight electric-light bulbs can be independently switched 'on' or 'off' by a group of switches. If a particular bulb is *switched* '**on**' then this represents a '**1**', or if a particular bulb is *switched* '**off**' then this represents a '**0**' as shown in figure 2.4.

We have thus devised a simple way of sending **data**, which, when it's *received and decoded*, becomes **information**. We would need some sort of table, part of which could be as shown in figure 2.5. If this particular table is used it would obviously be relatively simple for anyone to work out the code, but the principles of **data encryption** are covered in chapter 26 for those readers who feel the need to make their data a lot more secure.

'1' indicates that the bulb is 'on' - '0' indicates that the bulb is 'off'

Code for this part of the message is 10001010

Figure 2.4

You may feel that sending data in this way would be tedious in the extreme, taking a long time for even a simple request such as 'Put the coffee pot on' to be sent – and indeed you would be right. However, don't forget the fundamental point about computers mentioned at the beginning of this chapter – these machines are *very* fast.

BASIL light bulbs	Letter of the alphabet
0 0 0 0 0 0 0 0	----
0 0 0 0 0 0 0 1	A
0 0 0 0 0 0 1 0	B
0 0 0 0 0 0 1 1	C
0 0 0 0 1 0 0	D
0 0 0 1 0 1	E

Make use of your own codes for secret messages

Figure 2.5

A high-speed fibre-optic (see page 496) link could transmit about 100 million of these codes each second! At that rate we would be able to send the entire contents of the Encyclopaedia Britannica in just a few seconds – have you just changed your mind about this method of communication? Other operations carried out inside the computer are just as impressive, but you will have to wait until later on in your course to find out more.

Generations of computers

Inside each computer there are tiny devices called **transistors** which carry out these lightning-speed switching operations. Today tens of thousands of these transistors can 'easily' be packed into a **silicon chip** – but this has obviously not always been the case. In the early days of electronic computers, **valves**, as shown in figure 2.6, were used as the switching device. They were quite large, consumed lots of energy, and thus the computers built up using these components took up the space of a very large room – they became known as the **first generation of computers**. Later on the **transistor** was invented, and this smaller and more energy-efficient device led to the **second generation of computers**. They were more powerful, consumed less energy, and took up less space that the first generation machines. (See chapter 27 for more detail.)

A real breakthrough came in the 1960s when several transistors were put into a single package called an **integrated circuit** or **silicon chip**. These became known as the **third generation machines** and were smaller and more powerful again. In the 1970s and 1980s it became possible to pack more and more transistors into a single silicon chip, until in the mid 1990s, it became possible to get well over 1,000,000 in a single-chip device. Computers making use of these latest chips are called **fourth generation computers**. **Fifth generation computers** have been on the drawing board for a number of years, but are discussed elsewhere in this book.

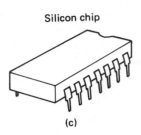

Figure 2.6

A modern overview of computers

In the following sections many ideas are introduced that will be covered in detail elsewhere. However, it's important to get a modern overview of computers in general, and the hierarchy of computer systems in particular. More jargon will be thrown around in this section but it's not important to understand every detail at this stage of your course. Nevertheless, if there are one or two terms you don't understand at all, make use of the glossary at the back of the book.

From laptops to supercomputers

Until recently, computers could easily be classified into **minis**, **micros** and **mainframes** by considering their **size**, **performance** and **cost**. However, today these definitions are not so cut and dried, due to the ever increasing pace of technology. Indeed, in a few years time some of these definitions may drop out of common usage altogether. The manufacturers are not helping by bringing out many terms such as **mini-supercomputers**, **superminis** and **micromainframes** etc. These are obviously terms used to describe the approximate position in the hierarchy to which their products belong. To understand this mass of jargon, *it's still necessary to understand the older definitions* of the terms **minis**, **micros** and **mainframes**. And a guide to the accepted use of these terms now follows.

Microcomputer

This is, quite simply, a computer which uses a **microprocessor** as its *central processing unit*. A **microprocessor** is the name given to the very-complex chip which contains most of the basic systems needed to set up a computer system using this single chip as the central processing unit. Microcomputers are usually the smaller **'desk-top models'** which range in price from a few hundred pounds to well over ten thousand pounds. They are usually accompanied by a single keyboard and printer, have one or two hard-disk drives, and may be connected to a network in the school, college or office.

In the late 1970s the first microcomputers were 8-bit machines. (Although some less-useful 4-bit microprocessors were available earlier.) This meant that their fundamental unit of **data** was *eight* **binary digits**. However, the 1980s saw a tremendous increase in both speed and processing power, and 16-bit and 32-bit microcomputers are now common. We have more recently also seen the introduction of the first 64-bit microprocessor which gives the effective power of a mainframe of the early 1980s! However, if you think that's impressive, in 1994, a company called MIPS brought out the new R8000 64-bit RISC chip which is claimed to have the power of a CRAY YM/P supercomputer. This micro, currently being developed at the time of writing, can perform over 300 million double-precision floating-point operations/sec, and will sell at a very reasonable £110,000. (That *is* reasonable compared to the cost of a Cray!) The term **micromainframe** is sometimes used to describe these very powerful micros with near-mainframe speed and performance – nevertheless, you should realise that it's *not* the same as having an actual mainframe computer – for reasons soon to become obvious as you read the rest of this chapter.

It is still relatively unusual for a microcomputer that we ordinary mortals can afford to be **multi-user** (i.e. *more than one person can make use of it at the same time*), but **multi-tasking** is now very common (i.e. the computer *carrying out several different tasks at apparently the same time*). The very powerful microcomputers tend to be used for powerful applications such as top-of-the-range CAD which requires an enormous amount of processing power, graphics-handling ability and pots of memory. Some typical modern microcomputers can be seen in figure 2.7.

Figure 2.7

The laptop computer

Portable power came of age towards the end of the 1980s. Indeed some of these **laptop portables** now have the same ability as some of the larger microcomputers, and in 1994 Intel's powerful Pentium processor found its way into portables too. 8 or 16 megabytes of main memory, together with a medium-capacity hard disk and coloured monitor is now usual. In addition to this, the laptop portable can have sophisticated communications facilities, made even better by the introduction of the PCMCIA architecture. It's now possible for any person to get important data back to the office via a network or the telephone system from anywhere in the world.

Most of the software that can run on a desk-top micro can be run on a top-of-the-range laptop portable. It is these portables which have revolutionised the way in which many people make use of their computers. If you have a computer available wherever you are, then you are more likely to make use of it. Indeed, in many years time, most computers may be of the laptop variety, perhaps permanently linked to a network via a radio link similar to that used for portable phones, or direct via satellite. It has been estimated that the power of todays supercomputers will be available in a laptop or even a 'pocket calculator' in less than a decade. If you think that this statement is a little far fetched, just ponder for a moment on the facts mentioned earlier in this chapter – a 'computer which used to take up the space of a very large room', can now have the equivalent processing power on a 'piece of silicon 1cm^2 in area, and a few fractions of a millimetre thick'! If you are still not convinced, think for a moment about the computer which fits inside a standard credit card! As a final example, the mathematical processing ability of my Texas TI 85 calculator far exceeds the capacity of the mainframe to which I had access when I took my degree back in 1975!

Some typical laptops can be seen in figure 2.8.

Figure 2.8

Remember the above facts when being asked about the social effects of micro-miniaturisation and computerisation. The microcomputer started off the personal computer revolution, the portable laptop computer will take it many stages further.

The minicomputer

This is a medium-sized computer and can vary in power from a *very large and powerful* **micro** to a **small mainframe**. Indeed, because of the increasing power of minis, the mainframe market has shrunk considerably over the last few years. A minicomputer is often a floor-standing model, although some modern ones now fit onto the top of your desk – but there's not much space left for the coffee pot! A small **minicomputer** might be able to support between ten and twenty users. It is, therefore, ideal for use within a single department within a college or university, or for use in a medium size business. They are really mini versions of the mainframe computer, and this is where the term mini was originally coined.

The mini has been designed with **multi-user access** in mind, and is therefore usually easy to expand up to the maximum possible numbers of users. A schematic diagram of some typical minicomputer facilities can be seen in figure 2.9(a) and a typical minicomputer is shown in figure 2.9(b).

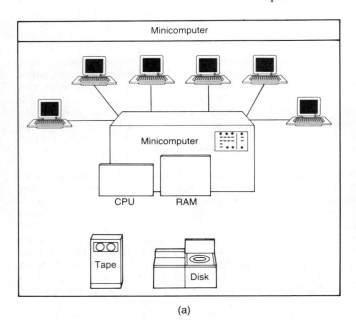

(a)　　　　　　　　　　　　　　　　　　　　　　　　　(b)

Figure 2.9

The ability to upgrade is all important when considering minis. For example, **DEC** (the **Digital Equipment Corporation**) has a range of **VAX computers** which go from a desk top microcomputer to a powerful mainframe supporting thousands of users. This has the added advantage that, when changing from the smaller to the larger machines, you do not have to change operating systems. They all run **Ultrix**, which is DECs version of **Unix**. This makes the VAX a popular machine for companies which need to expand, but don't wish to make fundamental changes to the computer systems which lie at the heart of their operations. Other major players in the market also do similar upgrade paths.

Mainframe computers

These are the *largest* of computer systems (*not necessarily the fastest or most powerful*) – they certainly won't fit on the top of your desk! It is common to have hundreds of simultaneous users on such a system. There is usually a vast amount of **RAM,** and many extra peripherals such as tape and disk machines. A schematic is shown in figure 2.10(a), and a typical mainframe is shown in figure 2.10(b). You should pay particular attention to **mainframe** and *larger computer systems* throughout your advanced level course, because many questions in examinations which revolve around these large machines will not make too much sense if you are mentally locked into the world of microcomputers.

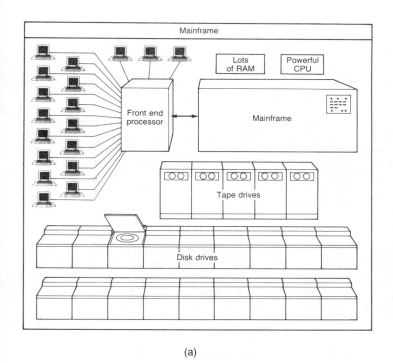

(a)

(b)

Figure 2.10

Supercomputers

These are the **fastest and most expensive modern computer systems**. They are usually not used for normal data processing, but for *intense mathematical calculations* such as forecasting the weather, or super high resolution graphics such as ray-traced images. Nevertheless, for very large systems such as the customs-clearance system in the port of Singapore, all the government departments are linked to a super-computer which is then able to produce all the necessary documentation for clearance in just a few minutes, compared to several days under the older manual systems. There are also many complex scientific and engineering applications which require enormous processing speed and power. One of the latest supercomputers is shown in figure 2.11.

Figure 2.11

Some modern computing ideas

After the above whirlwind tour of different computer types, we will finish off this chapter with an equally fast whirlwind tour of some other major concepts which are useful to appreciate at the beginning of your course.

Multitasking

A **single processor** may have the ability to carry out several tasks at apparently the same time. This process is called **multitasking**. A good demonstration of this ability can be seen on some of the most modern microcomputers when running different software packages in two different windows on the same screen simultaneously. It's obviously not as fast as running each process individually, but is often a great help. For example, you could be writing a letter on a word processor while a database package is searching the database to produce a report. Or you can make use of **OLE** (see page 530) which enables you to transfer data between the two different packages with ease.

The virtual machine

This idea can be considered as apparently having multiple copies of the same hardware. For example, **virtual memory** makes it appear that the machine has more memory than it has actually got by making use of a disk to transfer data to and from the main memory. A **virtual peripheral** might be a printer that can serve several different people simultaneously. If you are to print out your document and the printer is being used by another person, then your file is automatically saved on disk until the printer is free, when it will be automatically printed out as though the printer had been free all the time. You will see the term 'virtual' crop up in many situations. For example, the **VAX** in **VAX machines** mentioned previously, stands for **Virtual Address eXtension** machines. The operating system on this machine is **VMS** which stands for **Virtual Memory System**. This gives an effective '4096 Megabytes of RAM'!

Parallel processing

It is possible for one processor to carry out several tasks as described in the multitasking section, but it's also possible for **several processors** to carry out a **single task**. This can range from a simple multi-processor machine that has a main microprocessor for the running of the programs, and a separate microprocessor for the handling of the peripherals, through to a powerful machine having many processors operating on the same problem in parallel. Much work has recently gone into parallel processing, as it gets over the traditional computer bottleneck of only being able to do one thing at a time. Such systems often make use of **transputers**, and some typical approaches to parallelism are covered in chapter 4.

Integration of these ideas

You will find that systems are being developed all the time which use combinations of the **hardware** and **software techniques** mentioned above. Therefore you may see descriptions such as a '*multi-processor multitasking supermini running a virtual systems architecture*'!

Computer languages

Although we have seen that computers ultimately work in **binary code**, it would be tedious in the extreme if humans had to instruct them in this way too. At a fundamental level *people can instruct the computer in binary*, and this is called **machine code**. However, a more convenient way of carrying out fundamental operations is to replace the binary code by *easy-to-remember instructions* which is called **assembly language**. **Assembly language** makes use of **mnemonics** (*aids to the memory*), where, MUL, for example, might be part of the instruction to MULtiply two numbers together. Both the **machine code** and **assembly-language** methods of programming are known as **low-level language programming**, because they are intimately tied up with operating the machine at a very low level.

It's fortunate that we are able to program computers in much simpler ways, and many high-level languages have been developed. These high-level languages are far removed from the detailed ways in which the machine operates, and are closer to English-like instructions and the ways in which humans like to think. Examples would be languages like **BASIC**, **Pascal**, **Prolog** or **FORTRAN 90**. Such languages can be split up into two major different methodologies called **imperative languages** and **declarative languages**, although others are also considered later in this book.

Imperative languages typify the type in which the programmer gives the computer a set of instructions (called imperatives) which explain exactly how to achieve a result, whereas declarative languages typify giving the computer declarations in which the user has not had to state explicitly how the end result is to be achieved – all will be revealed in time!

Applications

Most of the population would neither want to nor be capable of programming computers in either high or low level languages. It's fortunate, therefore, that specialist companies write their own very complex programs to perform specific jobs such as turning the computer into a **word processor** or **DTP system**, for example. These programs enable non-specialist users to be able to use the computer as a tool without an understanding beyond the system they are currently using. Such useful programs are called **applications packages** or, more simply, **applications**. There are literally thousands of different applications on the market, and more are being developed each day. As computer hardware becomes more high-speed and sophisticated, applications become more powerful and easier to use by all. Much computer literacy is obtained by being familiar with and able to use a variety of different applications packages. In your advanced level courses, it's essential that you are able to use **word processors**, **DTP systems**, **spreadsheets**, **CAD packages**, **databases**, **communications packages** and a variety of others such as **control systems** and **data loggers** if possible.

Computer control of industrial plant and other machinery is also a major area in which computers are currently employed, it varies in range from the control of robots and aircraft, to the control of oil installations in the North Sea. Such systems make heavy demands on the operating systems, and real-time systems are often employed. These real time systems are generally those which have to respond very quickly to external events, and need very high reliability factors too.

Defining a problem

Even with a superabundance of applications and high-level languages, it's still up to individual people to use their talents and initiative to invent new ways of using computers or to improve existing methods. Complex projects have to be managed, and resources such as time and money have to be used efficiently. Much computer science is therefore devoted to organising your thoughts into ways of getting defined outcomes to problems quickly and efficiently. Many graphical techniques of problem solving, together with a huge variety of other computer-based methods are covered later on in the book. Nevertheless, at the most fundamental level you have to write down your solution to a problem in some particular way, and in computing this vital recipe for the solution to a problem is called an **algorithm**.

Many different methods exist for constructing algorithms, including **flowcharts**, **pseudocode**, **structure diagrams**, **JSP diagrams** and **state-transition diagrams** to name but a few. All have advantages for particular types of problem, and by the end of your course you should be able to realise where each one would be most helpful. Some methods are reasonably obvious, such as flowcharts for example. Figure 2.12 shows a very simple flowchart which describes the very last part of an algorithm to turn off the taps when filling the bath.

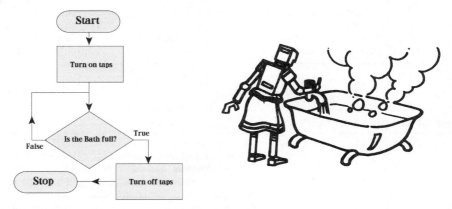

Figure 2.12

Notice that in this particular mode of operation, a machine would spend most of its time whizzing round the loop asking if the bath is full. When it has decided that the bath is full, probably by some suitable sensor attached in an appropriate position to detect the water level, then the taps will be turned off and this particular part of the bath-tub algorithm would be completed.

The future

Most people perceive computer science as being a rapidly changing subject, and in the main they are right. However, many of the basic principles don't change, it's just that the technology used does change at an amazing pace. For example, **hard disks** have been with us now for about 30 years – their principles of operation have changed little, but what *has changed* is a *great increase* in their **speed of operation**, a *vast increase* in their **memory capacity**, *drastic reductions* in their **size**, even more *drastic reductions* in their **price** and a *huge increase* in their **reliability**. Disks with several-hundred-Mbytes capacity would have been a mainframe peripheral device just ten years ago – today they are now common inside portables – tomorrow who knows? – **nanotechnology** (see page 553) might mean that they will fit inside a credit card!

What is revolutionising the entire computer world is the link between **computers** and **communications** – it's not necessarily going to be an overnight explosion, but in ten years time we will probably all wake up to find that it's natural for almost all computers to be permanently connected to a **network**, either via the *phone line* at home, via a *radio link* or *infra-red link* at the office, or via a *satellite link* direct to the computer. This will open up so many business opportunities for the media and computer companies that they will not miss such an opportunity for investing in a multi-billion pound industry. As far as the consumer is concerned, it may mean that we have, at last, access to an almost infinite variety of information systems on a truly global basis, and the dream outlined in the preface could become a reality.

Exercise 2.1

1. (a) Into which three *major* sections can a computer system be split? What benefits are brought about by doing this?
    (b) Which is the odd one out in the following list? (*Use the glossary if necessary*.) **Monitor**, **Keyboard**, **Microprocessor**, **Compiler**, **Printer**, **Paper**.

2. Explain the relationship between **raw data** and **information**.

3. Answer the following questions about the computer system which you have at your school or college.
    (a) List the main types of computers used.
    (b) Which high-level languages are supported?
    (c) List 10 different software packages.
    (d) How much RAM is available?
    (e) What is the name of the operating system in each type of computer?
    (f) If a network is used, what type is it and how many bits/sec can it transmit?

4. Which *electronic components* are used to define each **generation** of computers?

5. Make a list of some of the important characteristics associated with each of the following types of computer: *micro, mini, mainframe, laptop*.

6. What is meant by a **parallel processing architecture**?

7. Explain in principle how a machine as versatile as a computer may carry out all of its tasks by 'simple' manipulation of binary digits.

8. Considering the current rapid changes in technology, suggest some changes (*other than the communications one mentioned at the end of this chapter*) which you feel might lead to differences in the ways in which computers might be used in the future.

End of chapter summary

- A **computer** is a processor of information.
- **Information** = **data** + **structure**
- A *computer system* can be split up into **input**, **processing** and **output** sections.
- The *set of instructions* inside a computer is called a **program**.
- **Software** is the name given to the **programs** which control the computer system.
- **Hardware** is the *machines and materials* like the monitors, printers and paper etc.
- The **binary system** is a *two-state system* on which **digital computers** operate.
- *Any information* can be encoded into **binary form** and manipulated electronically.
- **Electronic digital computers** are built up making use of transistors.
- A **silicon chip** is an **Integrated Circuit** (**IC**) which contains many transistors.
- A 'complete computer' on a single chip is called a **microprocessor**.
- A **microcomputer** is a *small computer* based around one or more microprocessors.
- The **first generation** of computers makes use of **valves**.
- The **second generation** of computers makes use of **discrete transistors**.

- The **third generation** of computers makes use of **integrated circuits**.
- The **fourth generation** of computers makes use of **VLSI integrated circuits**.
- The **fifth generation** of computers employs a different philosophy and is designed around **knowledge-based machines**.
- A **minicomputer** is a medium-sized computer allowing several users simultaneous use via a number of terminals.
- A **mainframe computer** is a very large scale computer often allowing hundreds of users simultaneous access – it usually has a vast array of peripheral devices too.
- A **supercomputer** is the most powerful computer in terms of having the fastest available processors. It's usually used for applications such as forecasting the weather or simulations in the engineering industry.
- **Multi-tasking** enables a computer to *apparently* do more than one thing at the same time.
- A **virtual system** is one which has apparently got more memory or other resources than are actually present.
- **Parallel processing** is the ability to do more than one thing at the same time, often by utilising more than one processor in the same system.
- The **Operating System (OS)** is a huge and complex piece of software which controls the entire operation of a computer.
- **Computer languages** can be split up into **low-level** and **high-level languages**.
- A **low-level language** uses **machine code** or **assembly language** which is near to what happens inside the electronics of a particular machine.
- A **high-level language** is nearer to the natural languages in which humans think.
- Many different high-level languages exist on today's modern computer systems.
- Most computers today work by following an **algorithm**.
- An **algorithm** is a *sequence of instructions to solve a specific problem*.
- Technology changes at an ever-increasing rate and modern methods continually change what we perceive as being possible or practical.

3 Representation of data

Introduction

So much in computing (and indeed in society today) depends on a comprehensive mastery of the way in which data can be manipulated and stored. From the understanding of some of the algorithms used to solve problems in the most sophisticated high level languages, to an understanding of the most intricate detail in an individual chip inside the computer, all depends on a thorough understanding of the way in which binary code in its most simple and advanced forms can be used to represent data.

This chapter will take you from the birth of the binary system and through to many of the ingenious ways of representing and manipulating numeric data types. If you are interested in the way in which the computer actually manipulates these binary numbers, then the sections on binary arithmetic logic in chapter 19 explain how some of the more basic operations are carried out.

The binary system

The **binary system** (also called **base two**) has just two states: usually called **'on'** and **'off'** or '1' and '0'. The reason why this system is so important is that it is the most simple system to implement in practice using the electronic technology available today. It is relatively easy to detect very quickly if a circuit is switched on or off. It would be a much more difficult task to detect levels in between these two extremes. Hence binary is ideal for use in modern electronic digital computers. In fact, if you worked out the optimum base for a computer mathematically, in terms of cost of storing numbers that could be represented in different bases, with complete disregard for what could be built in practice, you would find that a base of two or three (or 2.718 281 828 4 . . . to be exact!) is the ideal. Mathematicians may recognise this number as being e (the base for natural logarithms). Also, a 2-bit code is the minimum necessary to be able to transmit any information. The case for binary, I think, is therefore proved.

To understand the binary system it is useful to think more carefully about a system with which most people will be more familiar, i.e. the **decimal system** or **base ten**. The decimal system of numbers is also known as denary.

When you learnt to count in base ten you would have been told that the symbols to be used are 0, 1, 2, 3, 4, 5, 6, 7, 8 and 9 i.e. ten different symbols in base ten. You would also have been told that the column headings above each number, starting at the right, represent units, tens, hundreds and thousands etc. Therefore the number:

Th	H	T	U
1	0	7	3

would represent one thousand, no hundreds, seven tens and three units, making a number that is called one thousand and seventy three.

In base ten, each column heading to the left is obtained by multiplying the previous column heading by ten i.e. the number representing the base in which we are working. Now consider the **binary system.** Here just two symbols are used: **0** and **1.** Therefore any number must be represented using 0s and 1s only. This time the column headings will be (from right to left) 1s, 2s, 4s, 8s, 16s, 32s, etc. To obtain the next column heading the number is multiplied by two, the base in which we are working. Any column headings in **any number base** can be obtained by starting with the units column and multiplying by the base in which you are working. Therefore, in base sixteen (a number base with which you will soon become familiar), the column headings would be 1s, 16s, 256s, 4096s, etc.

Therefore, in the binary system, the number:

16	8	4	2	1
1	**0**	**1**	**1**	**1**

would represent **one lot of 16, no lots of 8, one lot of 4, one lot of 2** and finally **one unit.** There is no point in inventing a name for such a number unless it is going to be the major system used by everybody. Therefore, we manipulate numbers in binary when doing computing, but convert them into decimal numbers if we wish to have a 'human' idea of the magnitude (size) of the number.

When dealing with number bases it is important not to confuse the base of the number in which we are working. For example is 101, five, one hundred and one, or two hundred and fifty seven? The first answer assumes binary, the second answer assumes decimal and the third answer assumes base sixteen! To get over this problem a useful subscript notation has been developed. If there is any chance of ambiguity then the number base is written at the end of the number as a subscript:

Therefore, 101_2 means base two, or 101_{16} means base sixteen.

If no subscript is used, then it is usual to assume that base ten is being implied. However, in sections where there is no ambiguity as to the base in which we are working, the subscript is often omitted.

It is most important to be able to count in binary. The system is simple as the following example shows.

To start with it is simple to count up in decimal and write down the binary representation of the decimal number as described above:

e.g.　　1 decimal =　　1 binary
　　　　2 decimal =　　1 0 binary　　One lot of 2 and no lots of 1
　　　　3 decimal =　　1 1 binary　　One lot of 2 and one lot of 1
　　　　4 decimal = 1 0 0 binary　　One lot of 4, no lots of 2 and no lots of 1

This sequence is extended in the following table:

Decimal number 10 1	5-bit binary number 16 8 4 2 1	Decimal number 10 1	5-bit binary number 16 8 4 2 1
0	0 0 0 0 0	1 6	1 0 0 0 0
1	0 0 0 0 1	1 7	1 0 0 0 1
2	0 0 0 1 0	1 8	1 0 0 1 0
3	0 0 0 1 1	1 9	1 0 0 1 1
4	0 0 1 0 0	2 0	1 0 1 0 0
5	0 0 1 0 1	2 1	1 0 1 0 1
6	0 0 1 1 0	2 2	1 0 1 1 0
7	0 0 1 1 1	2 3	1 0 1 1 1
8	0 1 0 0 0	2 4	1 1 0 0 0
9	0 1 0 0 1	2 5	1 1 0 0 1
1 0	0 1 0 1 0	2 6	1 1 0 1 0
1 1	0 1 0 1 1	2 7	1 1 0 1 1
1 2	0 1 1 0 0	2 8	1 1 1 0 0
1 3	0 1 1 0 1	2 9	1 1 1 0 1
1 4	0 1 1 1 0	3 0	1 1 1 1 0
1 5	0 1 1 1 1	3 1	1 1 1 1 1

It is tedious to build up a table, but the decimal values and the patterns established above should be understood and remembered. To count in binary we simply start with 00000, to the required number of digits. The units column changes 0, 1, 0, 1 etc. The twos column has two 0s followed by two 1s followed by two 0s etc. The fours column has four 0s followed by four 1s followed by four 0s etc. The eights column has eight 1s followed by eight 0s etc. This system is particularly useful as it is very easy to make a mistake when filling in tables of this nature.

It would be unrealistic to start from 0 if the binary number we wish to obtain is large. In this case the column headings can be used together with a little common sense as follows:

Suppose we wish to express 183 as a binary number:

1. Write down the binary columns until the value of the column heading exceeds the magnitude of the number you wish to convert:

256   128   64   32   16   8   4   2   1

2. Next write down a 1 underneath the maximum number that can be subtracted from your original number. In this case it is 128.

256   128   64   32   16   8   4   2   1
       1

There is one lot of 128 in 183 with 55 left over.

3. Move along to the next binary heading that can be taken away from the remainder of (2) above. 64 is too big and therefore 32 must be taken away from 55. A 0 is written underneath the 64 column (no lots of 64) and a 1 is written underneath the 32 column, as there is one lot of 32 in 55.

256   128   64   32   16   8   4   2   1
       1   0   1

There is one lot of 32 in 55 with 23 left over.

4. The process is continued until the remainder is zero. This will always be the case with **integer** (i.e. whole) numbers. Continuing the above, the final result obtained would be:

256   128   64   32   16   8   4   2   1
       1   0   1   1   0   1   1   1

Therefore $183 = 10110111_2$

The above is obviously one method of converting between base ten and binary. A useful check to see if the answer is correct, and a method of converting between binary and base ten, is to add together all the column headings with a 1 underneath them and see if the sum of these numbers is the same as the original number.

i.e. $128 + 32 + 16 + 4 + 2 + 1 = 183$ (thus confirming that the answer is correct). (Always a good idea in an important examination.)

Conversion between decimal and binary using repeated division

Another popular method for conversion between base ten and binary is repeated division by two. In fact the idea will work for any base: for example, if you were using base eight, repeated division by eight would be used. The method is particularly suitable for computerisation in conjunction with MOD and DIV commands in most versions of the high level language BASIC. (MOD gives the remainder after division and DIV gives the whole number part of the result of a division.)

As an example, consider converting 183 to binary again. A suggested layout is as follows:

2	183 remainder 1	(i.e. 2 into 183 goes 91 times with 1 left over)
2	91 remainder 1	(i.e. 2 into 91 goes 45 times with 1 left over)
2	45 remainder 1	(i.e. 2 into 45 goes 22 times with 1 left over)
2	22 remainder 0	(i.e. 2 into 22 goes 11 times with 0 left over)
2	11 remainder 1	etc.
2	5 remainder 1	
2	2 remainder 0	
2	1 remainder 1	
2	0	

Consider the top part of the above ladder of division sums. Now two into 183 went 91 times with one unit left over. This unit is represented by the remainder at the top of the ladder. Therefore, in the final binary number, this digit represents $2^0 = 1$ (i.e. a '1' in the units column of the answer).

Next we divide by two again. This means that four goes into the original number 45 times with one lot of 2' left over (plus the original unit found above of course). Hence the second remainder means that there is a 1 in the 2s column of the answer.

Continuing the above argument we can see that the answer is the vertical col[umn] of remainders with the least significant bit at the top. The final answer must there fore be this vertical column of remainders read from bottom to top.

$$(1 \times 128) + (0 \times 64) + (1 \times 32) + (1 \times 16) + (0 \times 8) + (1 \times 4) + (1 \times 2) + (1 \times 1)$$

or in binary   1   0   1   1   0   1   1   1

Example

Convert 25 into binary using the method of repeated division by 2.

```
2 | 25
2 | 12    r 1
2 |  6    r 0
2 |  3    r 0
2 |  1    r 1
2 |  0    r 1        Therefore 25 = 110 01
```

On many occasions it is useful to be able to add, subtract, multiply and divide in binary. The following is therefore included for completeness, and to allow people who are rusty to brush up on this topic before proceeding further. However, these topics are obviously included in the computer science syllabus for people who have not covered them before. Plenty of examples are included in the end of chapter exercises.

Addition of binary numbers

The main points to remember are that the answer can only contain 0s and 1s, and that you carry groups of two. Consider the following sum:

```
  1  1  1  0  1  0
  0  1  1  0  1  1  +
-------------------
1 0  1  0  1  0  1
  1  1  1     1
```

All possibilities with two digits are covered in the above sum. The main point to realise is that if the digits you are adding equal 2 then you carry 1 (i.e. one lot of 2 into the next column.)

Example

Add together the following binary numbers: 10101, 101, 110011, and 101101

The layout used in the above example is recommended.

```
  0  1  0  1  0  1
  0  0  0  1  0  1
  1  1  0  0  1  1
  1  0  1  1  0  1  +
-------------------
1 1  1  1  0  1  0
  1  1  1  2  1  2
```

A point of confusion which often arises occurs in the units column. When the digits are added we end up with 4. This is simply two lots of 2, and therefore 2 is carried into the next column. It is permissible to write down 2 even though this number does not exist in binary. This is not a fiddle, it is exactly what would happen in a decimal sum if the units column was so large that you were to end up with say 273. You would write down 3 and carry 27 (i.e. 27 lots of ten into the 10s column).

Subtraction of binary numbers

At least with subtraction we can only have two rows! As long as we remember that when we borrow 1 from the previous column it is really twice as big, there should be no problems. Consider the following example:

```
        0  2
  1  1  X  X  1  1
  0  1  0  1  0  1  -
-------------------
  1  0  0  1  1  0
```

Example

Evaluate 10011 – 1111

```
    0   2̸ 1 2
    1̸   8̸ 0   1   1
    0   1   1   1   1   –
    _____
    0   0   1   0   0            Therefore: 10011 – 1111 = 100
```

No difficulties occur until the third column is encountered. Here we need to borrow a 1 from the previous column. As there is no digit to subtract from in the third column, the third column has to borrow a 1 from the fourth column. Now the fourth column has no digit either, therefore we move along until we find a digit from which to borrow. One is found in the fifth column. Therefore the fourth column borrows 'one lot of 2' from the fifth column. This is shown by making the 0 at the top of the fourth column into a 2. The third column can now borrow 'one lot of 2' from the fourth column. This is shown by making the zero at the top of the third column into a 2 and reducing the 2 at the top of the fourth column into a 1. The sum can then proceed in the normal way.

Multiplication of binary numbers

This is really easy when compared with subtraction. If you can manage the once times table then this is all that is needed!, i.e. we have only to work out 1×0 or 1×1. The multiplication sum is set out in the standard way with 0s being inserted every time you move to the next digit of the multiplying number. However, remember that the adding up of the subtotals has to be done in binary as in the binary addition section.

Example

Evaluate 1010111×1011

```
                1   0   1   0   1   1   1
                        1   0   1   1   ×
        _____
                1   0   1   0   1   1   1
            1   0   1   0   1   1   1   0
    1   0   1   0   1   1   1   0   0   0   +
    _____
    1   1   1   0   1   1   1   1   0   1
    _____
        1   1   1   1   1   1   1
```

It can be seen that the process is quite simple. It may also have been noticed that the original number was simply shifted over to the left, once for the second digit and three times for the fourth. In binary a shift left is the same as a multiplication by two. This is because the digits are written under the new column headings, one place to the left, which are twice as big. This shifting is a process which will be of fundamental importance later on.

Division of binary numbers

Although a little more complex than multiplication, it is still relatively simple. This simplicity stems from the fact that the answer can only contain the digits 0 and 1. The layout is as follows:

Example

Evaluate 11100001 / 101

```
                    1   0   1   1   0   1
            _____
    1 0 1 | 1   1   1   0   0   0   0   1
            1   0   1   .   .   .   .   .
            _____
                1   0   0   0   .   .   .
                1   0   1   .   .   .
                _____
                    1   1   0   .   .
                    1   0   1   .   .
                    _____
                        1   0   1
                        1   0   1
                        _____
                            0   remainder   0
```

The layout is that of a classic division sum. The details of the subtraction processes have not been shown for reasons of clarity. If the above sum had yielded a fractional answer then binary fractions (see later) should be used.

Other number bases

Octal

If the principles of the last few sections have been well understood then it is relatively easy to extend the concepts of the four basic rules to any other number base. However, in computing, only two other number bases are of any importance. These are **octal** (base eight) and more important, **hexadecimal** (base sixteen). In octal we have eight different characters: (0, 1, 2, 3, 4, 5, 6 and 7). The column headings in octal are units, 8s, 64s, 512s etc. Some octal examples now follow:

```
                         2 14                                    1 0 3 7
a.  2 3 4      b.  2 3 6          c.    1 3 6      d. 2 4 6 | 2 6 0 0 3 2
    1 7 +          1 2 7 -              3 4 ×              2 4 6 . . .
    ─────          ─────               ─────              1 2 0 3 .
    2 5 3          1 0 7                5 7 0               7 6 2 .
    ─────                            4 3 2 0               2 2 1 2
      1                              ─────                 2 2 1 2
                                     5 1 1 0               ─────
                                     ─────                   0 r 0
                                       1 1
```

(Not easy to think about! Don't forget that the subtraction is done in base 8.)

Hexadecimal

This number base comes into its own when it is necessary to deal with large groups of binary digits. It is therefore most important that **hexadecimal** (or more simply **hex**) is well understood. All the previous principles of number bases still apply. The only novelty with hex is that we have to use sixteen different symbols. Binary needs two, decimal needs ten and therefore hex needs sixteen. The sixteen different symbols used are:

0, 1, 2, 3, 4, 5, 6, 7, 8, 9, A, B, C, D, E and F

Here A represents ten, B represents eleven and so on until F which represents fifteen.

Some hex examples now follow:

```
                                                                B E 3
                       D 29                                ─────────────
a.  1 2 7      b.  B E D          c.    A 0 B      d. A 7 | 7 C 1 1 5
    5 0 A +          7 0 F -              3 9 ×             7 2 D
    ─────          ─────                ─────              9 4 1 .
    6 3 1          4 D E              5 A 6 3               9 2 2 .
    ─────          ─────            1 E 2 1 0               ─────
                                   ─────────               1 F 5
                                   2 3 C 7 3               1 F 5
                                   ─────────               ─────
```

It must be stressed that not many people would attempt the octal or hex division sums outlined above. It would be far less damaging to the brain to convert to base ten, perform the division and then convert the answer back to the appropriate base. However, division in binary is important because it gives an insight into how the computer might tackle such problems.

Conversion between octal, hex and binary – quick method

Any number base can be converted to any other by first changing it into base ten. To convert binary into hex, first convert binary into base ten and then convert this base ten number into hex using the methods described earlier in this section. However, there is a much quicker method, and this should be used in preference to the long way round. The methods are simple because of the strong relationship between binary, octal and hex.

Each group of four binary digits represents numbers from 0 to 15 inclusive. Each hex digit also represents numbers from 0 to 15 inclusive, and so there is a one-to-one relationship between a hex digit and a group of four binary digits. The principles can be stated as follows:

To change a binary number directly into hex, split up the binary number groups of four digits starting at the right hand side of the number. Next the hex equivalent for each group of four binary digits.

Example

Change $39A4_{16}$ into binary.

| 3 / | 9 / | A / | 4 | (Split up hex numbers) |

1 1 / 1 0 0 1 / 1 0 1 0 / 0 1 0 0   (Binary digits representing hex digit)

Therefore $39A4_{16} = 11100110100100_2$

The principles are very similar for octal. Here three binary digits instead of four are used.

Example

Change 10110011000_2 into octal.

1 0 / 1 1 0 / 0 1 1 / 0 0 0   (Group into 3s from right)

2 / 6 / 3 / 0   (Octal digit for each group)

Binary coded decimal

There are several other types of binary representation which can occur inside computers. One of the most important is called **Binary Coded Decimal.** This is because each decimal digit has its own special binary code. There are several different types of binary coded decimal (**BCD**), but we will consider the most common which is called the **8421 weighted code.**

Let us use the example of representing 3591 in BCD. Each decimal digit is written as it appears in the decimal number, i.e.

3   5   9   1

Each digit is then coded into binary as follows:

3   5   9   1

0011   0101   1001   0001

It is called the 8421 weighted binary coded decimal because each digit is encoded using four binary column headings with weightings 8421 (i.e. a normal binary number). However, you can see that the system is not a number base in the sense that binary, hex and octal are.

As the maximum decimal digit that can occur is 9, the maximum code that can be represented using each of the 4 bits is 1001. This means that 1010, 1011, 1100, 1101, 1110 and 1111 are effectively redundant. Therefore this type of code is inefficient in terms of the numbers that it can store for a given number of digits used.

If you are wondering why such a code is used, then you will see that it comes into its own when binary numbers have to be electronically decoded to operate displays such as those found in pocket calculators. As an example, consider the pure binary and BCD representation of the number 3591 shown above.

i.e. binary for 3591 is 111000000111_2 but BCD for 3591 is 0011010110010001_{BCD}

Each number must be decoded so that decimal digits representing 3, 5, 9 and 1 are presented with the correct codes. In the case of the pure binary number, considerable manipulation will have to be done (i.e. a binary to decimal conversion). However, in the case of the BCD number, all that is necessary is to split the number up into groups of 4 bits, starting from the right, and then to feed the codes directly to the digits as shown:

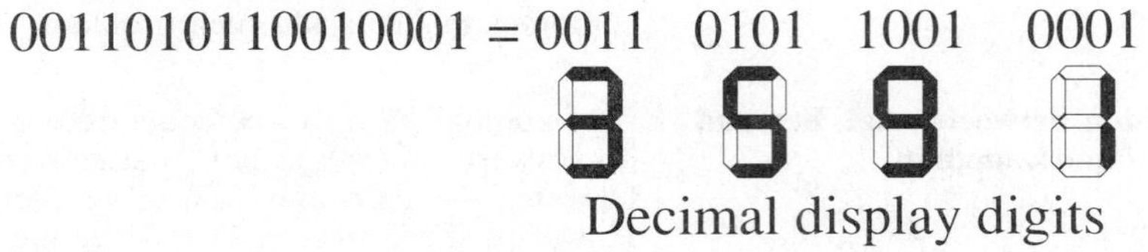

$$0011010110010001 = 0011 \quad 0101 \quad 1001 \quad 0001$$

Decimal display digits

Figure 3.1

The advantages of such a system are, however slightly reduced because arithmetic with such numbers becomes slightly more complicated. For example if 3591 was to be added to 1694 using BCD techniques, then a 'fiddle factor' would have to be applied. The reason for this is quite simple. A carry would not naturally be generated from each group of digits until the code 1111 + 1 (i.e. 16) was reached. As we are really working in a coded decimal system we must generate a carry when ten (i.e. 1010) is reached. To make 1010 into 10000 we need to add 0110 (i.e. add 6). Therefore, to get the 'sums right', we add 0110 to each digit to generate a possible carry. However, it is slightly more complicated as can be seen:

3 5 9 1	0 0 1 1	0 1 0 1	1 0 0 1	0 0 0 1
1 6 9 4 +	0 0 0 1	0 1 1 0	1 0 0 1	0 1 0 0 +
5 2 8 5	0 1 0 0	1 0 1 1	(1)←0 0 1 0	0 1 0 1

(Normal binary addition)

(Add carries if necessary)   1←Carry

(Answer after carries)	0 1 0 0	1 1 0 0	0 0 1 0	0 1 0 1
(Add fiddle factor +6)	0 1 1 0	0 1 1 0	0 1 1 0	0 1 1 0

(Normal binary addition)   1 0 1 0   (1)←0 0 1 0   1 0 0 0   1 0 1 1
(Add carries if necessary)   (1)←Carry

(Answer after carries)	1 0 1 1	0 0 1 0	1 0 0 0	1 0 1 1
(Deduct fiddle factor of +6 from any non-BCD number)	0 1 1 0			0 1 1 0

(Final answer at last!)	0 1 0 1	0 0 1 0	1 0 0 0	0 1 0 1
(i.e. in decimal)	5	2	8	5

Thus confirming that 3591 + 1694 is 5285.

Although the above may seem complicated, some machines are indeed organized in a similar way. Although the arithmetic may seem long and ridiculous, it is relatively easy to do such 'mechanical' operations using electronic hardware in a fraction of a second. The initial conversion into binary and the final conversion back into decimal are also avoided.

Binary fractions

Oh no! not binary fractions. I've only just got the hang of ordinary binary.

The processes introduced in the last few sections can be extended to include fractions with little problem. If you consider the column headings for binary numbers then you will realise that from left to right the column headings get smaller by a factor of two i.e. 8s, 4s, 2s, and 1s. If we continue this process of dividing by two then we get the **fractional headings** 1/2, 1/4, 1/8, 1/16 etc. The **binary point** separates the fractional and whole number part as follows:

32	16	8	4	2	1	.	1/2	1/4	1/8	1/16	1/32
1	0	1	0	1	0	.	0	1	0	1	1

Therefore, the number shown above must be treated in two parts.

1. The whole number or integer part can be treated using the theory of the previous sections: i.e. to find the decimal value we add: 32 + 8 + 2 = 42.
2. The fractional part can be found using a similar method, i.e. 1/4 + 1/16 + 1/32.

It is usual to express these fractions as decimals, therefore we get 0.25 + 0.0625 + 0.031 25 = 0.343 75.
The values are now added together to get 42.343 75.

Therefore 1 0 1 0 1 0. 0 1 0 1 1$_2$ = 42.343 75

It is useful to have a table of some of the more common binary fractions and this is included for your convenience:

Binary fraction	Fraction	Decimal fraction	Binary fraction	Fraction	Decimal fraction
.1	1/2	0.5	.000001	1/64	0.015 625
.01	1/4	0.25	.0000001	1/128	0.007 812 5
.001	1/8	0.125	.00000001	1/256	0.003 906 25
.0001	1/16	0.0625	.000000001	1/512	0.001 953 125
.00001	1/32	0.03125	.0000000001	1/1024	0.000 976 562 5

Representation of negative numbers

Negative numbers are essential, and any computer not capable of dealing with them would not be particularly useful. There are several methods which can be used to represent negative numbers in binary. One of the most common methods used can be explained with reference to a car 'mileometer'. Let us assume that we have a three digit decimal car mileometer as shown in figure 3.2(a).

If we start the car on the starting grid shown, with the mileometer set to 000, then after 23 miles the car mileometer would register 023. This system could record positive numbers up to and including 999 miles. However, the system would break down if we did 1000 miles because the mileometer would read 000 again.

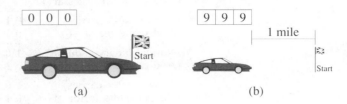

Figure 3.2

Let us now use the same mileometer, but this time invent a way to record negative distance as well. If the car starts off at the grid as shown in figure 3.2(a), then if we set the same mileometer to 000 again, but drive backwards, then after 1 mile the reading would be 999. We can use 999 to represent –1 (i.e. 1 mile in the reverse direction). Of course we could not let 999 represent 999 miles in the forward direction as well, and so our range of numbers in the forward direction would be more limited. The principle of using the mileometer in this way is shown in figure 3.2(b).

Let us now consider a 'binary mileometer'. However, we will call it a **register** as this is the name given to the place where such numbers would be stored inside the computer. For simplicity our register will have just **4 bits, (binary digits).** If we now analyse the possibilities with just 4 bits we get the results in the following table:

	Register number	Decimal equivalent
	1000	–8
	1001	–7
Negative	1010	–6
numbers	1011	–5
	1100	–4
	1101	–3
	1110	–2
	1111	–1
Start here→	0000	0
	0001	+1
	0010	+2
	0011	+3
Positive	0100	+4
numbers	0101	+5
	0110	+6
	0111	+7

If a 4-bit binary number was used in the conventional way, 0000 to 1111 would give us sixteen different combinations of numbers from 0 to +15. Using the above method we still have sixteen unique numbers (–8 to +7) but the range in the positive direction is reduced.

At first sight it may seem difficult to distinguish between positive and negative numbers until you realize that **all negative numbers start off with 1** and **all positive numbers start off with 0.** This method of representing numbers is called **twos complementation** for reasons soon to become obvious.

Before dealing with complementation more formally, a quick method of obtaining the answers is now introduced. It is a method which can be used in preference to the other methods if you are not asked specifically to prove what you are doing.

Twos complement, a quick method

It would be inconvenient to have to draw out a table similar to the above to find the binary representation of a particular negative number. Suppose that we wish to find the twos complement 4-bit representation for –6. From the above table we can see that the answer is: 1010. However, consider the following:

1. Write down the positive binary number using 4 bits, i.e. for –6, we would write the binary number for +6.

Therefore 6 becomes: 0110 using 4 bits.

2. Starting at the right hand side, rewrite this number up to and including the first 1. For 0110 this would mean writing down 1 and 0.

Therefore the right hand two digits only are written down: 10.

3. For the remainder of the number (i.e. all the digits to the left), change the 0s for 1s and 1s for 0s. Therefore the number becomes:

1010 which is the required answer. It's as simple as that!

Example

Write down the twos complement 8-bit representation for –39.

$$\begin{array}{ll} 39 \text{ in binary is} & 0\ 0\ 1\ 0\ 0\ 1\ 1\ 1 \quad \text{Using 8 bits} \\ & \qquad\qquad\qquad 1 \quad \text{Write down number from right,} \\ & \qquad\qquad\qquad\quad \text{up to and including first digit} \\ & 1\ 1\ 0\ 1\ 1\ 0\ 0\ 1 \quad \text{Change all other 0s for 1s and 1s for 0s} \\ \end{array}$$

Hence –39 = 1 1 0 1 1 0 0 1

Besides being able to represent negative numbers in binary, it is possible to subtract numbers by adding the complement, i.e. 59 + (–32) is the same as 59 – 32. Therefore all the electronic circuits designed for adding (see chapter 19) can be used for subtraction as well. It is for this reason that complementation is of such fundamental importance in computing.

Complementation, a more formal approach

Complementation (for the purpose of this chapter) is a way of representing numbers (particularly in binary) that enables us to subtract these binary numbers by using the process of addition i.e. we find the complement of the number that we wish to subtract, then add it to the original number instead.

There are two important methods of complementation.

The radix-minus-one complement

A radix is just the posh name for **base**. Hence if we are working in binary then **radix-minus-one** becomes $2 - 1 = 1$, i.e. the ones complement. To obtain the ones complement of a binary number each digit is subtracted from 1 or inverted.

i.e. the ones complement of 101001 is 010110 (111111–101001)

The radix complement

In binary, this would become the **twos complement** i.e. the method used in the table for the binary mileometer on page 30. To obtain the twos complement we simply add 1 to the ones complement.

i.e. the twos complement of 101001 is 010110 + 1 = 010111

However, don't forget the quick method mentioned earlier.

Examples

(1) Find the radix-minus-one complement of 1011100110000

Answer: 0100011001111   Subtract each digit from 1 or invert each digit.

(2) Find the radix complement of 100110011

Answer: 011001101   Quick method

(3) Use the ones complement method to work out the following subtraction by addition:

101110001 – 101100   (Note the 'fiddle' needed when using this method.)

The ones complement of 101100 is 010011
The ones complement of 000101100 is 111010011

Therefore work out:

$$
\begin{array}{r}
1\ 0\ 1\ 1\ 1\ 0\ 0\ 0\ 1 \\
1\ 1\ 1\ 0\ 1\ 0\ 0\ 1\ 1\ + \\
\hline
1\ 0\ 1\ 0\ 0\ 0\ 1\ 0\ 0
\end{array}
$$

The carry must be   (1)   1 1 1 1   1 1
taken to the other   1 0 1 0 0 0 1 0 0
end and added on!   1 +   (Adding on the carry
                                        ——————   at the other end)
                                 1 0 1 0 0 0 1 0 1

You will often find that 'fiddle factors' such as the above have to be applied to get the right answer. However, for a given number of bits it can easily be shown that by adding round the carry the right answer is obtained in every case.

(4) Use the twos complement method to work out 101110001 − 101100

The twos complement of 101100 in 9 bits is 111010100 (using quick method)

Therefore work out:

$$
\begin{array}{r}
1\ 0\ 1\ 1\ 1\ 0\ 0\ 0\ 1 \\
1\ 1\ 1\ 0\ 1\ 0\ 1\ 0\ 0\ + \\
\hline
1\ 0\ 1\ 0\ 0\ 0\ 1\ 0\ 1
\end{array}
$$

Carry is ignored (1)   1 1 1 1

This time the carry is not taken to the other end, as was the case with the ones complement method. If you think that the twos complement is easier because there is no digit to add on, don't forget that to find the twos complement the ones complement must first be found and then a digit must be added on to get the twos complement! This is the way a machine would do it. However, the twos complement has other advantages over the ones complement:

Consider the representation of zero in both systems:
Using 4 bits the twos complement of 0000 (zero) is 0000
(i.e. 1111 + 1 but the carry is lost), but the ones complement of 0000 (zero) is 1111.

Now consider the representation of −1 in both systems:
Using 4 bits the twos complement of 0001 (+1) is 1111.
But the ones complement of 0001 (+1) is 1110.

Working out a few values each side of zero the following table can be built up:

Number	Ones complement	Number	Twos complement
+ 3	0 0 1 1	+ 3	0 0 1 1
+ 2	0 0 1 0	+ 2	0 0 1 0
+ 1	0 0 0 1	+ 1	0 0 0 1
Zero	0 0 0 0	Zero	0 0 0 0
Zero again (− 0!)	1 1 1 1	− 1	1 1 1 1
− 1	1 1 1 0	− 2	1 1 1 0
− 2	1 1 0 1	− 3	1 1 0 1

We can see from the above table that we have a redundant zero when using the ones complement method. This is one more of the reasons why the twos complement is used in preference to the ones complement.

Explicit sign method

There is one final method that is often used called the **explicit sign method.** It is also called the **sign and magnitude** method. When using ones and twos complement methods the sign of the number was taken care of implicitly when applying the rules for each method. The explicit sign method is very easy to understand; it is simply an ordinary binary number with one extra digit placed in front to represent the sign. Again a '1' is used for negative numbers and a '0' is used for positive.

Example

Express + 13 and −13 using the explicit sign method and 8 bits.

Now 13 in binary is 1101 = 0001101 (using 7 bits for the actual number)

Therefore +13 = 00001101, and −13 = 10001101

Negative binary fractions

These are really a combination of previous methods.

Example

Find a twos complement representation of $-13\frac{5}{16}$ using 5 bits for the integer part and 4 bits for the fractional part.

First the whole number part: +13 = 1101 = 01101 (5-bit integer part)

Next the fractional part: $\frac{5}{16} = \frac{1}{4} + \frac{1}{16}$ = 0.01 + 0.0001

= .0101 (4 bits for fractional part)

Therefore: $+13\frac{5}{16}$ = 01101.0101

Therefore: $-13\frac{5}{16}$ = 10010.1011 (twos complement representation)

Fixed point binary numbers

In the last few sections we have not been too bothered about the number of digits required for the number represented, or the position of the binary point within the number. In practice the registers for holding the numbers are of a fixed length and therefore many compromises will have to be made. The situation can be compared to an electronic calculator. If only ten digits are available on the display, then we can't possibly display an eleven digit number. The size of register will therefore affect the range of numbers which can be displayed. There are methods available to increase this range, but at the expense of one or two other desirable attributes (see later in this chapter).

There are two major types of fixed point representation, **integer** and **fractional.** We will now consider these two systems.

Integer fixed point representation

We will assume an 8-bit register (a sensible choice as many computers work in 8 bits or multiples thereof) and twos complementation will be used throughout. The register is therefore as follows:

*	*	*	*	*	*	*	*

It is important to be able to evaluate the limitations of such a system, i.e. what is the largest number that can be held in the register? What is the smallest? This can easily be worked out by filling the register up with the appropriate bits and having a look to see what happens.

First the maximum positive number: 01111111 i.e. +127

(Don't forget that the sign bit at the beginning must be 0 to be positive in twos complement.)

Next the minimum positive number: 00000001 i.e. +1
(Zero is neither positive nor negative!)

The smallest magnitude negative number: 11111111 i.e. −1
(Don't forget the car mileometer if the above is confusing. See page 30.)

Finally, the largest magnitude negative number: 10000000 i.e. −128

If the above was difficult to understand, you need more practice using twos complement notation.

If we look at the above results then we can see that the **range** of numbers (i.e. from largest to smallest) is + 127 to − 128 inclusive.

It would be more useful to express the relationship in terms of powers of two, because this can then be extended to evaluate the numbers for any register with N bits:

For our 8-bit register $-2^7 \leqslant \text{range} \leqslant 2^7 - 1$

Therefore for an N-bit register $-2^{N-1} \leqslant \text{range} \leqslant 2^{N-1} - 1$

Exercise 3.1

1. (a) Convert the following **binary** numbers into **denary**:
   (i) 1010   (ii) 101000
   (iii) 1111111   (iv) 010100111011
   (b) Convert the following **denary** numbers into **binary**:
   (i) 27   (ii) 128
   (iii) 789   (iv) 176 891

2. Convert the following **base ten** numbers into **binary** making use of the **repeated division method.**
   (a) 13   (b) 127
   (c) 357

3. Work out the following **binary** arithmetic:
   (a) 1000 + 101
   (b) 1011 + 1110
   (c) 10011 + 10011 + 101011
   (d) 1001011 + 100110 + 110111 + 011 + 1101
   (e) 1111 – 101
   (f) 1010 + 101
   (g) 10000000 – 1001100

4. Work out the following **binary** arithmetic:
   (a) 101 × 11   (b) 10110 × 1011
   (c) 101 × 10 × 101   (d) 11010 × 1011
   (e) 10010 / 10   (f) 1001011 / 101
   (g) 1001011101 / 1110

5. Work out the following **hexadecimal** arithmetic:
   (a) 192 + 76   (b) A73 + B412 + 52D
   (c) 170 – 36   (d) BED – ABC
   (e) 127 × 79   (f) CAD × B0D
   (g) 19E / 12

6. Work out the following **octal** (base eight) arithmetic:
   (a) 17 + 234   (b) 2732 – 156
   (c) 123 × 456   (d) 77 / 25

7. Convert the following **binary** numbers into **hexadecimal**:
   (a) 10101011   (b) 10110010
   (c) 11110000   (d) 1001100101010100
   (e) 10110   (f) 1010101

8. Convert the following **hexadecimal** numbers into **binary**:
   (a) 160   (b) 279
   (c) FF60   (d) FBFF

9. Convert the following **octal** numbers into **binary**:
   (a) 160   (b) 275
   (c) 1234   (d) 7531

10. Convert the following **hexadecimal** numbers into **octal**:
    (a) 281   (b) F7BB
    (c) ABCD   (d) 1000

11. Convert the following **octal** numbers into **hexadecimal**:
    (a) 731   (b) 100
    (c) 6661   (d) 7070

12. Represent the following numbers in the BCD 8421 weighted code:
    (a) 101010 (binary)   (b) 746 (octal)
    (c) A4F (hex)

Fractional fixed point representation

Again, twos complementation will be used, but this time the binary point will be in the position shown: (In fact the binary point may be in any desired position within the register.)

| First the maximum positive number: | 0.1111111 |

The best way to describe the above is $1 - 1/2^7$ i.e. $1 - 1/128 = 0.992\ 187\ 5$

| Next the smallest positive number: | 0.0000001 |

This time the number is simply $1/2^7$ i.e. $1/128 = 0.007\ 812\ 5$

| Next the smallest magnitude negative number: | 1.1111111 |

The twos complement of the above is 0.0000001 therefore the number is $-1/2^7$ i.e. $-1/128 = -0.007\ 812\ 5$

| Finally the largest magnitude negative number: | 1.0000000 |

Therefore, the number is –1 (the twos complement of the above number is the same).

As we are dealing with fractional numbers, there will be many numbers (most, actually) that we cannot represent exactly. For example the largest magnitude negative fraction that can be represented is:

1.0000001

The twos complement of the above is

$$0.1111111 = -(1 - 1/2^7) = -(1 - 1/128) = -0.992\ 187\ 5$$

Therefore numbers between this and –1 cannot be represented. The consequences of this are dealt with more fully when **accuracy** and **errors** are dealt with later in this chapter.

Exercise 3.2

1. Change the following **decimal fractions** into **binary fractions:**
   (a) 0.25
   (b) 0.031 25
   (c) 1.5
   (d) 15.375
   (e) 13.5625
   (f) 67.0468 75

2. Represent the following **decimal** numbers using 8-bit **twos complement** representation:
   (a) – 4
   (b) – 13
   (c) – 69
   (d) – 123

3. (a) Represent the following **binary** numbers using **ones complement** 10-bit representation:
   (i) 1001
   (ii) 110111
   (iii) 0110001001

(b) Represent the following **binary** numbers using 10-bit **radix complement** notation:
   (i) 1001
   (ii) 110111
   (iii) 0110001001

4. Represent the following **decimal** numbers using a 12-bit explicit sign representation:
   (a) +128
   (b) –50
   (c) –196

5. Find the **twos complement** representation of the following **real numbers:** (use 8 bits for the **integer part** and 4 bits for the **fractional part)**
   (a) –63.25
   (b) –17.625
   (c) –113.1875

Floating point representation of binary numbers

This is a much more versatile system than fixed point representation. To understand it we need to recall that numbers can be split up into two parts called a **mantissa** and an **exponent.** As an example consider:

$$1.637 \times 10^{60}$$

Here 1.637 is called the **mantissa** and 60 is called the **exponent.** You will recall from your mathematics that such a number means that the decimal point in the mantissa has to be moved 60 places to the right (for a positive exponent). Therefore the equivalent number to the above would be:

1637000000000000000000000000000000000000000000000000000000000000

You will agree that the range is considerably extended! However, the **precision** has been sacrificed. It is usual to make a compromise between the bits used for the mantissa (more precision) and the bits used for the exponent (more range). It is fortunate that it is unusual to require a vast range and to be highly precise.

The term **floating point** is derived from the fact that to build up the final number (as above) the point floats along (it is moved by you!) until it rests in the final correct place.

Let us consider an example which uses a 16-bit register. We will assign 10 bits for the mantissa and 6 bits for the exponent. This is shown as follows:

└─ Binary   10-bit mantissa   6-bit exponent
   point   (Fractional twos complement)   (Integer twos complement)

As can be seen the mantissa will have a 10-bit fractional representation in twos complement, and the exponent will use an integer twos complement representation. Therefore the method will be a combination of the two previous sections on binary fixed point notation, both fractional and integer.

Consider the following number contained in our 16-bit floating point register:

0.101100100 | 000100

The number must be decoded in two parts:

1. The mantissa: 0.101100100 is simply rewritten in the same form.
2. The exponent: 000100 is binary for 4. This means that the binary point in the mantissa has to be moved four places to the right, using the convention that + means move right.
3. Combine the above two stages:

   The final answer is therefore: 01011.00100 i.e. 11⅛

   Therefore: 0.101100100 | 000100 represents 11.125

Example

Using the same floating point representation as above, determine the decimal number for:

1.100110000 | 111100

1. This time the mantissa is a negative number (twos complement and the sign bit is 1). Therefore we will have a negative answer.
   The twos complement of 1100110000 is 0011010000

Therefore, the mantissa becomes –0.011010000

2. The exponent is also negative. Now the twos complement of 111100 is –000100 = –4. Therefore, we move the binary point four places to the left.

Altering the original mantissa we get –0.00000110100.

Now $0.00000110100 = \quad 1/64 \quad + \quad 1/128 \quad + \quad 1/512$

$$= \quad 0.015\ 625 + 0.007\ 812\ 5 + 0.001\ 953\ 125$$

$$= \quad 0.025\ 390\ 625$$

Therefore: 1.100110000 | 111100 = –0.025 390 625

Before dealing with the possible range for such a representation as that above, let us consider a consequence of using such a system.
   Consider the following three numbers represented using our 16-bit register:

(a) 0.100000000 | 000010

(b) 0.010000000 | 000011

(c) 0.001000000 | 000100

Number (a) above is $0.100000000 \times 2^2 = 010.0000000 = 2$

Number (b) above is $0.010000000 \times 2^3 = 010.0000000 = 2$

Number (c) above is $0.001000000 \times 2^4 = 010.0000000 = 2$

i.e. they are all different representations of 2.

This is not a satisfactory state of affairs. Also, if there are leading zeros before the most significant figures in the (b) and (c) representations above, then it is possible that some less significant digits will be lost, thus causing an unnecessary error. For example, if 0.100000101 had been used then this can be represented using (a), but not using (b) and (c) because the last digit would be lost. This would cause a slight difference in the value of the final number. This would not be sensible if it was not necessary to lose this digit.
   To overcome the problems of many different representations of the same number, and to keep results as accurate as possible, a technique called **normalisation** is used.

Normalization (standardization)

The precision of the floating point representations just described depends on the number of digits that can be held in the mantissa. It is a waste if the number is stored in such a way that any precision is lost, given the fixed number of digits that are available.
   For positive numbers, there must be no leading zeros to the left of the most significant bit. This obviously must exclude the sign digit or it would be a negative number!
   Thus (using 10 bits) the number:

0000011111 would be represented in the mantissa as: 0.111110000

The exponent would obviously have to be altered to compensate.
   For negative numbers, there must be no leading 1s to the left of the most significant bit. (If you think about twos complement negative numbers then the '0' becomes the significant bit.) This must obviously exclude the sign bit or it would be a positive number.
   Thus (using 10 bits) the number:

1111100100 would be represented in the mantissa as: 1.001000000

Again the exponent would have to be altered to compensate.

Normalization therefore ensures that the maximum possible accuracy with a given number of bits is maintained and also ensures that only a single representation of the number is possible, i.e. it is a sort of standard form which optimises the way in which the number is stored. It can also be used to detect if an error condition such as **underflow** or **overflow** occurs (see the section on errors later in this chapter).

Examples

Using a 16-bit register (10-bit twos complement fractional mantissa and 6-bit twos complement integer exponent) as before, express the following numbers in normalized form:

(1) 123   **(2)** 0.1875   **(3)** –15/32

(1) 123 in binary is: 0001111011 (10 bits). Therefore the normalized mantissa will be: 0.111101100

The binary point will have to be moved seven places to the right to make the normalized mantissa back into the original number.
Therefore the exponent will be: 7 = 000111

Hence the normalized form for 123 = 0.111101100 | 000111

(2) 0.1875 = 1875/10000 = 75/400 = 3/16 = 2/16 + 1/16 = 1/8 + 1/16

Therefore 0.1875 = 0.001100000 (10 bits). Therefore the normalized mantissa will be 0. 110000000
The binary point will have to be moved two places to the left to make the normalized mantissa back into the original number.
Therefore, the exponent will be: –2. Now the exponent must be represented in twos complement integer notation using 6 bits.
Now 2 in binary (6 bits) is 000010. Therefore –2 = 111110
Therefore the exponent will be: 111110

Hence the normalized form for 0.1875 = 0.110000000 | 111110

(3) –15/32 is a negative number and we therefore need the twos complement of +15/32 to represent it.

Now +15/32 = 1/4 + 1/8 + 1/16 + 1/32 = 0.011110000 (10 bits).
The twos complement of 0.011110000 is 1.100010000. Therefore the normalized mantissa will be 1.000100000.
   The binary point will have to be moved one place to the left to make the normalized mantissa back into the original number. Also don't forget that if the number is negative, when the point is continuously moved to the left, leading 1s and not 0s would have to be introduced.

Therefore, the exponent will be –1. The twos complement of +1 (000001) using six digits is 111111.
Therefore, the exponent will be: 111111

Hence the normalized form for –15/32 = 1.000100000 | 111111

   One thing to notice about all the normalized numbers is the first two digits (the sign digit and the next one) will always be different. This can be used as a check to see if the number is in fact in normalized form.

Range of normalized floating point numbers

As with fixed point it is essential to be able to determine the largest and smallest numbers that a given register combination can hold. The rules in the previous section on normalization should be well understood. To keep the ranges of the numbers to a reasonable level let us consider a 10-bit register which uses 6 bits for the twos complement fractional mantissa and 4 bits for the twos complement integer exponent.

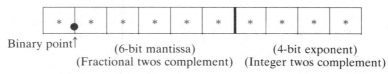

Binary point↑   (6-bit mantissa)   (4-bit exponent)
(Fractional twos complement)   (Integer twos complement)

1. First the maximum positive number. This will need the largest positive mantissa and largest positive exponent.

0.11111 | 0111

The exponent requires the binary point to be moved seven places to the right. Therefore the mantissa now becomes:

01111100. = 124

Therefore the largest positive number is +124.

2. Next the minimum positive number. This will be when the smallest positive mantissa and largest negative exponent occurs.

0.10000 | 1000

Note that (0.00001) would not be a normalized number. The twos complement of the exponent is 1000 and thus the exponent requires that the binary point be moved eight places to the left. Therefore the mantissa now becomes:

0.000000001 = 1/512 = 0.001 953 125

Therefore, the smallest positive number is +0.001 953 125.

3. The smallest magnitude negative number can be found by having the smallest magnitude negative mantissa and the largest negative exponent.

1.01111 | 1000

Note that 1.01111 is the smallest possible negative mantissa in standard form. 111111 is not a normalized number. The exponent requires that the binary point be moved eight places to the left. Therefore the mantissa becomes:

1.1111111101111

Note leading 1s are required for negative numbers. The twos complement of this number is:

0.0000000010001

This number is binary for +1/512 + 1/8192 = 17/8192 = 0.002 075 195 313 (to ten decimal places).
Therefore, the smallest magnitude negative number is –0.002 075 195 313

4. Finally, the largest magnitude negative number occurs with the largest magnitude negative mantissa and the largest positive exponent.

1.00000 | 0111

The twos complement for the negative mantissa is 1.00000.
The exponent requires that the binary point is moved seven places to the right, therefore the mantissa becomes:

10000000. = 128

Therefore, the largest magnitude negative number is –128.

The range for the 10-bit register using a 6-bit twos complement fractional mantissa and 4-bit twos complement integer exponent is therefore:

–128 ≤ negative range ≤ –0.002 075 195 313

+0.001 953 125 ≤ positive range ≤ +124

Working through the above theory you may have lost sight of the fact that zero (000000) is not a normalized number! It does therefore not exist in normalized floating point numbers. To get over this slight problem the computer will normally use the smallest positive number. In the above case this is only 0.001 953 125, a pitiful representation of zero! However, it is usual to have many more digits than 10 to represent floating point numbers, even on the humblest of microcomputers. The smallest positive numbers are, therefore, very small indeed. Less then 10^{-60} is typical.

Further arithmetic with floating point numbers

It will be convenient if we keep to the same floating point representation for all the different examples. This makes it easier to understand the principles involved. Therefore we will use a 12-bit register using an 8-bit fractional twos complement representation for the mantissa, and a 4-bit twos complement integer representation for the exponent.

Addition and subtraction of floating point numbers

First consider the decimal sum: 123.45 + 1.6589. Before you can add the digits together you must line up the decimal points as follows:

    123.45
    1.6589 +
    ‾‾‾‾‾‾

The same principles will apply to binary numbers. We must make sure that the binary points are underneath each other before adding the digits.

Examples

(1) Add together the following normalized floating point numbers and put the answer in normalized form.

$$0.1001000 \mid 0010 + 0.1111000 \mid 0100$$

For the first number, the exponent requires that the binary point is moved two places to the right. Therefore, this number now becomes: 010.01000

In the second number, the exponent requires that the binary point be moved four places to the right. Therefore this number now becomes: 01111.000

Adding these two together:

        0 1 0 . 0 1 0 0 0
        0 1 1 1 1 . 0 0 0   +
        ‾‾‾‾‾‾‾‾‾‾‾‾‾‾‾‾‾
        1 0 0 0 1 . 0 1
        ‾‾‾‾‾‾‾‾‾‾‾‾‾‾‾
        1 1 1

The result is now 10001.01 (Note a quick decimal check 2.25 + 15 = 17.25)

To normalize the result we would need to move the binary point five places to the left. The number would now become: 0.1000101. When written in this form we need an exponent of +5 to make the normalized answer correct. Therefore the exponent will be +5 or 0101.

The normalized answer is therefore: 0.1000101 | 0101

Note, if more digits than are available were needed, then the least significant digits would have to be chopped off or rounded (see section on errors later in this chapter).

(2) Subtract these numbers and give the answer in normalized form:

$$0.1100000 \mid 0001 - 1.0100000 \mid 0000$$

Note that the second number is negative (sign bit is 1) therefore the answer should be positive. For the first number, the exponent requires that the binary point be shifted one place right. Therefore this number becomes: 01.100000

Now the exponent of the second number requires that the binary point is not moved. Therefore, this number becomes: 1.0100000. We can perform the subtraction by adding the complement of this second number. The twos complement of the second number is: 0.1100000

We now line up the point and 'subtract' the numbers:

        1 . 1 0 0 0 0 0
        0 . 1 1 0 0 0 0 +
        ‾‾‾‾‾‾‾‾‾‾‾‾‾‾‾
        1 0 . 0 1 0 0 0 0
        ‾‾‾‾‾‾‾‾‾‾‾‾‾‾‾
        1

(Note decimal check on correct answer +1.5 − (− 0.75) = 2.25 as shown in above sum.)

To normalize the answer we write 0.1001000 and the exponent needs to be +2.

Therefore the normalized form of the answer is: 0.1001000 | 0010

Multiplication and division of floating point numbers

This is one of those rare occasions when something is extremely simple for once. The only thing to remember here is that **double length registers** may be needed to hold the result of a product.

Again consider a decimal analogy:

Suppose we wish to work out $(4 \times 10^2) \times (2 \times 10^3)$

From our mathematics we remember that we can write $4 \times 2 \times 10^2 \times 10^3$
We can multiply the powers of ten by adding the indices. Therefore the sum becomes:

$$(4 \times 2) \times 10^5$$

Therefore we **multiply** the original numbers and **add** the indices. The same can be done with binary floating point numbers as follows:
  Multiply the mantissa of each number and add the exponents.

Example

Put the two decimal numbers into normalized form. Multiply them together and put the answer in standard form. $12 \times 9 = ?$ (Answer should be 108.)

The binary for 12 is 1100. Therefore in normalized form: 0.1100000 | 0100
The binary for 9 is 1001. Therefore in normalized form: 0.1001000 | 0100

Multiply the mantissae:

```
    0 . 1 0 0 1
    0 . 1 1          ×
    ───────────
      1 0 0 1
    1 0 0 1 0        +
    ───────────
0 . 0 1 1 0 1 1
```

Remember the rule for counting up the number of figures after the point in the question, and then making sure that there are the same number of figures after the point in the answer. It works in binary too.

Therefore $0.11 \times 0.1001 = 0.011011$

The normalized form of the above is: 0.1101100 | 1111 (exponent of -1)

Next add the original exponents (The easy part!): $0100 + 0100 = 1000$

Now incorporate this with the normalized mantissa. Note that the sum of the previous exponents will have to be added to the -1 produced from the normalized mantissa. Therefore the new exponent will be:

```
        1 0 0 0
        1 1 1 1+
        ───────
        0 1 1 1        i.e. 1000 + 1111 = 0111 using a 4-bit exponent.
Carry is
lost        (1)
```

Therefore, the new mantissa becomes 0111

Hence the final answer is 0.1101100 | 0111

In pure binary this is $01101100 = 108$

Note that the system can only handle numbers up to $+128$. If we had tried to work out 12×11 then we would have obtained the wrong answer. This would have been a case of **arithmetic overflow** (see later in this chapter).
  Division of floating point numbers is performed in a similar way. The only difference is that the mantissa of the first number is divided by the mantissa of the second, and the exponents are subtracted.

Multi precision

If greater precision is required, then **words** (the collections of binary digits which we have been using) can be joined together to form longer words e.g. two 8-bit words can be joined to form a 16-bit word, thus giving a large increase in the number of significant figures. Such a technique is known as **double precision**. Three words joined together would be **triple precision**. The collective term is simply known as **multi precision.**

Computer-based arithmetic procedures

After wading through many of the previous sections you will be aware of the fact that computer arithmetic in its many forms is a combination of shifts (left and right), adding, adding complements and fiddle factors. It is beyond the scope of this book to go into too much detail for complex computer arithmetic, but some elementary computer-based methods are included in some syllabuses.

The restoring method (binary division)

Let us assume that we are going to work out $39/3 = 13$ in binary. To save us using long groups of names like 'the number which we are dividing by' we will use the correct terminology. In any division sum it is:

$$\frac{\text{Dividend}}{\text{Divisor}} = \text{Quotient, and Remainder (if necessary)}$$

Therefore, in the above sum, 39 is called the **dividend,** 3 the **divisor** and 13 is the **quotient.** There is no **remainder.** We would normally set out the sum as follows:

```
        0 0 1 1 0 1
  1 1 | 1 0 0 1 1 1
        1 1 . . .
        ───────
          1 1 . .
          1 1 . .
          ─────
            0 1 1
              1 1
            ─────
              0 r 0
```

The bits in the quotient will be called **quotient bits**.

Note the number 01 is used as though we are going to start the sum again using 01, and eventually 011. As the 'new dividend' these numbers are called **partial remainders**.

A very considerable amount of insight has gone into the above sum. For example, in the very first part we would mentally ask ourselves if 11 goes into 1. The answer is obviously no because 11 is bigger. However, a computer could not mentally do this and would, therefore, have to do some test on the numbers. One way would be to try the subtraction to see if it worked. If it did not, you could **restore** the dividend and move along to the next group of digits to try again. This forms the basis for what is called the **restoring method.** The method is demonstrated using the 39/3 example again. Let us use an 8-bit integer twos complement representation.

When the divisor (11) is subtracted we will add the twos complement. Now the twos complement of 11 is 101 (must have a 1 in front or it would not be a negative number) Therefore, this number will be added to the appropriate part of the dividend:

	Sign bit		
Start with dividend		0 0 1 0 0 1 1 1	{i.e. 39}
Place divisor under appropriate digits		1 0 1	{twos complement of +3}
'Subtract' i.e. by adding twos complement		───────	
		1 1 0 0 0 1 1 1	{Sign bit negative, did not work}
Restore the original number		0 1 1	{Set quotient bit (1) = 0}
		───────	
Carry is lost	(1)	0 0 1 0 0 1 1 1	{Original number restored}
Shift divisor right 1 place		1 1 0 1	{Note leading 1s for negative no.}
'Subtract'		───────	
		1 1 1 1 0 1 1 1	{Sign bit negative, did not work}
Restore original number		0 0 1 1	{Set quotient bit (2) = 0}
		───────	
Carry is lost	(1)	0 0 1 0 0 1 1 1	
Shift divisor right 1 place		1 1 1 0 1	
		───────	
Carry is lost	(1)	0 0 0 0 1 1 1 1	{Sign bit positive, it worked!}
			{Set quotient bit (3) = 1}
Partial remainder is now		0 0 0 0 1 1 1 1	
Shift divisor right 1 place		1 1 1 1 0 1	
		───────	
	(1)	0 0 0 0 0 0 1 1	{Sign bit positive, it worked!}
			{Set quotient bit (4) = 1}
Partial remainder is now		0 0 0 0 0 0 1 1	
Shift divisor right 1 place		1 1 1 1 1 0 1	
'Subtract'		───────	
		1 1 1 1 1 1 0 1	{Sign bit negative, did not work}
Restore original number		0 0 0 0 0 1 1	{Set quotient bit (5) = 0}
		───────	
Carry is lost	(1)	0 0 0 0 0 0 1 1	
Shift divisor 1 place right		1 1 1 1 1 1 0 1	
'Subtract'		───────	
	(1)	0 0 0 0 0 0 0 0	{Sign bit positive, it worked!}
			{Set quotient bit (6) = 1}

We cannot shift the divisor right any more unless we introduce more digits and a binary point. The above shows that 3 goes into 39 exactly 13 times, i.e. no remainder. If there were a remainder it would be contained in this last number. The answer is obtained by building up the quotient bits shown above as follows:

Quotient bit number   1 2 3 4 5 6
                       0 0 1 1 0 1   i.e. the answer is 13

We will now summarize the above procedure so that an algorithm can be formulated. The following must be read in conjunction with the above working out of the binary sum:

(a) Start at the most significant end of the dividend, i.e. shift the divisor left until the most significant bit of the divisor lines up with the most significant bit of the dividend.

(b) Next subtract (by adding the twos complement) the divisor from the three most significant bits of the dividend (or four for a four figure, five for a five figure divisor etc.).

(c) If the result of the subtraction in (b) is positive put a 1 in the most significant bit of the quotient. If the result of the subtraction in (b) is negative put a 0 in the most significant bit of the quotient

(d) If a 0 was put in (b) we **restore** the quotient by adding back the divisor or shifted divisor. If a 1 was put in (b) then we leave the partial remainder alone.

(e) Next shift the divisor one place to the right and repeat the above process making sure that the 0 or 1 in (c) above is put in the next most significant bit of the quotient.

(f) The only problem is how to know how many shifts right of the quotient we must make. To solve this problem, if we shift the divisor left at the start of the procedure until a 1 appears in the most significant bit of the register, and if we record the number of shifts that were necessary, then this will be the number of shifts right that are necessary.

Consider the following example which reflects what happened during the above process:

We started with a divisor of 3. i.e. in 8 bits: 00000011

Shift left until a 1 appears in the most significant bit i.e.: 01100000 (Note the number must still be positive).

Five shifts left were necessary. Therefore five shifts right were needed in the above problem.

Exercise 3.3

1. (a) Explain the difference between **fixed and floating point** numbers. What are the **advantages** and **disadvantages** of each system?

   (b) Clearly explain the functions that the **mantissa** and **exponent** have in **floating point** number representation.

   (c) Why is **normalisation** necessary when representing numbers in floating point form?

2. Using an **integer fixed point binary twos complement** representation with a 12-bit register, work out the following:

   (a) What is the **maximum positive number** that can be stored?

   (b) What is the **minimum positive** number?

   (c) What is the **smallest magnitude negative number**?

   (d) What is the **largest magnitude negative number**?

3. Using a **fractional fixed point binary twos complement representation** and a 10-bit register, and assuming that the **binary point** is in the position shown:

   * * * * * * * * * *

If **normalization is ignored,** work out the following:

(a) What is the **maximum positive** number that can be stored?

(b) What is the **minimum positive** number?

(c) What is the **smallest magnitude negative number?**

(d) What is the **largest magnitude negative number?**

4. A 12-bit register is split up such that 8 bits are used in **fractional twos complement** representation to represent the **mantissa** and the remaining 4 bits are used as an **integer twos complement** representation for the exponent as follows:

   * . * * * * * * * / * * * *

   Mantissa   **Exponent**

Using the above register represent the following numbers in **normalised** or **standard form**:

(a) + 1   (b) + 9
(c) − 3   (d) − 30
(e) 0.125   (f) −0.015 625

5. Using a **fractional floating point twos complement binary representation** with a 16-bit register, split up into a 10-bit **mantissa** (twos complement fractional) and a 6-bit **exponent** (twos complement integer). Assuming that your answers must be **normalised** work out the following:
   (a) What is the **maximum positive** number that can be stored?
   (b) What is the **minimum positive** number?
   (c) What is the **smallest magnitude negative number**?
   (d) What is the **largest magnitude negative number**?

6. Explain the differences in the techniques of carrying out **addition** and **subtraction** when compared to carrying out **multiplication** and **division** using **fractional floating point binary twos complement representation** of numbers. Make specific references as to how the **mantissa** and **exponents** play their particular parts.

7. Use the **restoring method** for carrying out the following **binary** divisions:
   (a) 48/8   (b) 51/6

Errors in computer arithmetic

In the previous sections the numbers have been carefully chosen so that 'right answers' were obtained when the various methods of arithmetic were being tried out. It must be realised that the number of bits available to perform the arithmetic is limited and therefore errors will occur because the numbers will probably have to be simplified in some way. The representation of the numbers, i.e. fixed or floating point, has a major effect on the accuracy that can be achieved with a given number of digits. Errors that are introduced because of the way that the numbers are represented inside the computer are called **computational errors**. If we are able to understand why these errors occur, then it is often possible to design algorithms that minimize these errors. Other types of errors, e.g. data being entered into the computer the wrong way round, etc., will be treated in other parts of this book.

Let us think of the real numbers in terms of the following graphs. Here we simply have real numbers represented graphically from 0 to 10.

0	1	2	3	4	5	6	7	8	9	10

If we were to zoom in on part of the above range, say from 1 to 2, then we could expand the range between 1 and 2 as follows:

1.0	1.1	1.2	1.3	1.4	1.5	1.6	1.7	1.8	1.9	2.0

We could continue this process further and look at the range between 1.3 and 1.4:

1.30	1.31	1.32	1.33	1.34	1.35	1.36	1.37	1.38	1.39	1.40

The process can be extended indefinitely. Thus we can see that we have an infinite supply of real numbers. Therefore, no computer could possibly represent all of the real numbers even in the small range 1.3 to 1.4! As an example, consider a 3-bit fixed point register. In twos complement we could only represent the following:

011	+3
010	+2
001	+1
000	0
111	−1
110	−2
101	−3
100	−4

If we wished to express 2.75 in the above system then it could not be done exactly. Now 2.75 can be represented exactly in binary as: 010.11. If we chop off the last two digits then we would get 010 (i.e. 2) or if we used a method of rounding up then we would get 011 (i.e. 3).

Therefore, in the above system 2.75 would have to be represented as 2 or 3.

In a real computer the range of numbers would be vast compared with the above representation, and precision would be considerably improved due to the very large increase in digits available. However, the same principles of finding and working out the errors will still apply.

Some terminology used with errors

It is important to define a few terms and concepts used in error analysis before proceeding any further.

1. **Precision**. This is the term associated with the word length (i.e. the number of bits) that is available to represent a given number. As an example consider an 8-bit register. Any number that is contained inside this register can only be precise to one part in 256. The term precision should not be confused with the term accuracy.

2. **Accuracy**. This is a measure of the closeness of an approximation to the exact or true value. This term should not be confused with precision.

An example to clarify the difference between accuracy and precision is as follows: Suppose that we have to represent the number 7 in pure binary using four digits. Seven can be represented exactly (i.e. without error) as 0111.

Next suppose that the fraction 0.10101010101 is to be represented using 8 bits. The number would become 0.1010101. There has been an error introduced in representing the original number.

The second representation above, containing the error is more precise (i.e. 8 bits instead of 4) but it is not more accurate.

3. **Range.** The range is the set of all numbers that can be represented by a particular system. For example, in 4-bit twos complement integer representation the range of numbers would be from –8 to +7 (see page 31). The range can also be expressed as the difference between the largest and smallest values. Therefore –8 to + 7 could also be expressed as a range of $15[(+7) - (-8)]$.

4. **Resolution**. This is simply the magnitude of the difference between the last two adjacent digits or numbers, e.g. for a three–digit decimal representation, the range may go from 000 to 999. Over this entire range the resolution would be 1, because the difference between the last two adjacent integer values is 1.

Obviously for other representations, like floating point, the resolution is not constant over the entire range and varies according to the value of the exponent being used.

5. **Truncation**. Also known as **rounding down**. This is one of the methods for dealing with situations where the precision is not adequate to represent all digits in the number to be stored. As an example suppose we wish to store the decimal number representing π (i.e. 3.141 592 653 . .) but only five digits are available. If the number is truncated then this means that all the digits after the fifth are to be dropped, i.e. the number 3.141 592 653 . . . would be represented in five digits as 3.1415.

6. **Truncation error**. This is the error that results from the use of the truncation process; e.g. if the number 273.1473 is represented as 273.14, then the truncation error would be 0.0073.

7. **Rounding**. This is a method which tries to select a value nearest to the original value of the number. It is the method with which most people will be familiar from mathematics. In the decimal system the following rules would apply:

> If the number after the last digit to be represented is 5 or more, then increase the previous digit by 1.
> If the number after the last digit to be represented is less than 5, then truncate (see above).
>
> e.g. 21.7348 would be 21.735 to five significant figures or 21.73 to four significant figures.

In binary, if the digit after the last digit to be represented is a 1, then increase the previous digit by 1, otherwise leave the previous digit alone.

8. **Overflow**. This occurs when a computation has produced an answer that is too big to be represented in the system. For example, if we had a 4-bit integer twos complement representation then the range is –8 to +7. However, if we worked out 3×5 then this would produce an answer of 15 i.e. a number which is too big to be represented in our 4-bit system. This happens so often with multiplication that double length registers are needed to hold the answer. If the system did not detect that an overflow had occurred, then great errors could easily be made, e.g. in the above example $3 \times 5 = 1111$, the number would be taken as –1 instead of +15!

9. **Underflow**. If an answer that is smaller than the smallest number that can be represented by the system is produced, then underflow has taken place. It is possible to generate an error message but often the system puts the number to zero instead.

10. **Errors introduced from decimal to binary conversion.** Most decimal numbers are converted into binary and therefore, for the majority of numbers, an error will be introduced at this stage before the numbers are even used in any calculations.

Consider the following:

If the decimal fraction 0.75 is converted into binary, then no error occurs because 0.75 can easily be represented as 0.11. However, most numbers are not multiples of binary fractions and will not be able to be expressed exactly, irrespective of the number of binary digits available.

The number 0.1414 using 8 bits would be represented as follows:

0.5	0.25	0.125	0.0625	0.031 25	0.015 625	0.007 812 5	0.003 906 25
0	0	1	0	0	1	0	0

0.1414
0.1250 –   Sum for the previous decimal to binary conversion

0.0164
0.015625

0.000775

Hence 0.1414 = 0.00100100 (8 bits). But 0.00100100 is actually 0.015 625 + 0.125 = 0.140 625.

Therefore 0.1414 has been represented as 0.140 625 in 8 bits. Errors like this happen when most decimal fractions are input to a computer. However, it is usual to have a large number of binary digits and this means that the decimal number is represented to a sensible number of decimal places.

Error classification

There are two important ways in which computational errors can be described. It is really common sense but can be expressed as follows:

1. Actual error = exact value – computed value

Here the **exact value** would be the value obtained in theory without any error, and the **computed value** is the value obtained from the computer after it has been processed, e.g. we might have a decimal to binary conversion error followed by a truncation error followed by a binary to decimal conversion error.

2. Relative error = actual error/exact value

Therefore **relative error = (exact value – computed value)/exact value** (Combining (1) and (2) above)
The actual error could be very misleading, e.g. an error of 0.000001 sounds better than an error of 10. However, it depends on the size of the original number. Hence the need for relative error.

In practice it is likely that we may not know the exact value, and hence we have to use the approximation:

relative error = estimated error/approximate value

This would be used in such examples as: 'If 180 has been given correct to three significant figures what is the maximum relative error?' (see later).

3. Absolute error = |actual error| (Note | | means modulus)

4. Absolute relative error = |relative error| (this is similar to percentage error)

The last two formulae are simply the previous two without any regard to the signs of the error; it is usual in many cases to concentrate on the magnitude of the error.

5. Percentage error = relative error × 100 per cent

Examples

(1) Find the actual and relative error when 1/3 is approximated to 0.333.

Now exact value = 1/3 and computed value = 0.333

Hence actual error = 1/3 – 0.333
                   = 1/3 – 333/1000 = (1000 – 999)/3000 = 1/3000
Therefore actual error = 1/3000

Relative error = actual error/exact value
               = 1/3000 / 1/3 = 1/3000 × 3/1 = 3/3000 = 1/1000

Hence relative error = 0.001

(2) The sum 4.39 + 0.798 is to be worked out using only three significant figures. Find the actual and relative errors if truncation is used.

4.39
0.798 +
———
5.188   (This value is truncated to 5.18)

The exact value is 5.188 and the computed value is 5.18.
Therefore actual error = 5.188 − 5.18 = 0.008
Hence relative error = 0.008/5.188 = 0.001 542

Finding maximum errors

It can be seen from the above that it is simple to calculate each error for a given number if necessary. However, every different number would produce different values for error. It would be more useful to calculate the **maximum error** that **is** likely to occur in a given situation. The same terminology is used, but this time we calculate **maximum actual or relative errors.**

It is important to realize that the maximum actual error that can occur is very simple to work out. For decimal numbers it is simply 'put a 5 in the digit after the required number of places'. As a demonstration we will choose a situation where **rounding** occurs with decimal numbers.

Let the exact decimal number vary over the range 0.120 to 0.130. Also let there be only two figures after the decimal point available to represent the number.

Exact value	0.120	0.121	0.122	0.123	0.124	0.125	0.126	0.127	0.128	0.129	0.130
Computed value	0.12	0.12	0.12	0.12	0.12	0.13	0.13	0.13	0.13	0.13	0.13
Absolute error	0.000	0.001	0.002	0.003	0.004	0.005	0.004	0.003	0.002	0.001	0.000

From the above we can see that the maximum absolute error that can occur is 0.005 so 5 is put in the column after the last digit that can be represented, in this case, the third column. The following patterns for decimal numbers can therefore be established:

Typical decimal number	Maximum absolute error
0.3	0.05
0.72	0.005
0.769	0.0005
0.2856	0.00005

As an example, consider working out the maximum relative errors for the decimal numbers 0.017 and 0.916 when computed to two decimal places:

(a) Actual value   = 0.017
    Computed value   = 0.02
    Max absolute error = 0.005

    Max relative error = 0.005 / 0.017
                        = 0.2941

(b) Actual value   = 0.916
    Computed value   = 0.92
    Max absolute error = 0.005

    Max relative error = 0.005 / 0.916
                        = 0.005 459

The maximum relative error for any given number will therefore increase as the actual number becomes smaller. In the worst case of all the maximum relative error could be 1. The relative error will always be less than or equal to the maximum relative error.

Examples

Find the maximum absolute and relative errors of the following:

(1) 0.072 71 is rounded to four decimal places.
Maximum absolute error = 0.000 05.
Maximum relative error = 0.000 05/0.072 71 = 0.000 687 7

(2) 12.727 is stored to four significant figures.
Maximum absolute error = 0.005.
Maximum relative error = 0.005/12.727 = 0.000 392 9

Exercise 3.4

1. (a) What is meant by **errors** when applied to computer arithmetic?
    (b) Explain the difference between **accuracy** and **precision.**
    (c) What is meant by the terms **overflow** and **underflow**?
    (d) Find the **relative error** when 5/7 is represented correct to three decimal places.
    (e) Find the **actual** and **relative errors** when 2.31×5.82 is truncated to four significant figures.
    (f) Find the **maximum absolute error** when 0.2753 is computed to three decimal places.

2. Find the **worst possible relative error** when 29.1 is subtracted from 108.3.

3. When the numbers 31.8 and 2.16 are added together the arithmetic is to be restricted to only three decimal digits. Work out the possible range of values of the answer and give the answer correct to two significant figures.

4. In the following, **a** can be found by using the formula:

    $$a = (h^2 - b^2)$$

    Now $h^2 - b^2$ can be worked out in the following two different ways:

    (1) $(h \times h) - (b \times b)$ or   (2) $(h + b)(h - b)$

    Work out the relative percentage error when each method is used if the machine on which the algorithms are executed is accurate only to two significant figures.

Non–numeric representation of data

Throughout this chapter we have concentrated entirely on representation of data from a numerical point of view. However, this is only one single aspect of data representation, and non-numeric data types are equally important.

The codes and structures which are used for expressing non-numeric data types are covered in very great detail in many of the other chapters throughout this book – special codes such as **ASCII** and **EBCDIC** are covered in chapter 13, special data structures such as **arrays**, **linked lists** and **trees** etc are covered in chapter 14 and **files** are covered in chapter 16. All these chapters, in conjunction with the chapters on **databases** and high- and low-level languages cover a great deal of non-numeric data forms, and chapter 10 on language translation covers a few extra numeric ones too.

End of chapter summary

- The **binary system** has just *two* stable states – **on** and **off** or **1** and **0**.
- The **binary system** is used in computers because it's easy to represent these two states using electricity.
- The **decimal** or **denary** system is also called **base ten.**
- The **binary system** uses just *two symbols* **{0,1}**
- The **decimal system** uses *ten symbols* **{0,1,2,3,4,5,6,7,8,9}**
- Conversion *between decimal and binary* may be accomplished by using **repeated division.**
- **Binary numbers** may be **added**, **subtracted**, **multiplied** and **divided** using methods *identical in principle* with normal decimal arithmetic.
- **Hexadecimal** (or **hex**) is another name for **base sixteen.**
- **Base sixteen** uses *sixteen symbols* **{0,1,2,3,4,5,6,7,8,9, A,B,C,D,E,F}**
- **Octal** is another name for **base eight** and uses the symbols **{0,1,2,3,4,5,6,7}**
- **Conversion** between **binary**, **octal** and **hex** is trivial because of the relationships between these bases.
- **Binary coded decimal** or **BCD** is a method of coding each decimal digit separately using an 8-4-2-1 weighted binary code.
- **Binary fractions** are a simple extension to ordinary binary numbers. A **binary point** *is used instead* of a **decimal point**.
- **Negative numbers** may be represented in binary using a variety of techniques including **explicit sign**, **ones complement** and **twos complement**.
- **Twos complement** is the *most versatile method* although many other forms which are extensions of this principle exist on real computers.
- **Fixed-point** binary numbers are used to represent **integer** and **fractional numbers**, with limited range but greater precision.

- **Floating point** binary numbers are numbers with **mantissa** and **exponent** parts used to represent a wider range of numbers with less precision.
- A **mantissa** is that part of a number which represent the **digits** in a number.
- The **exponent** is that part of a number which represents the **power** (i.e. the number of places that the binary point has to be moved from it's current position to determine the value of the final number).
- **Normalization** is a method of preventing loss of accuracy and multiple representations of the same number.
- **Precision** is a term associated with the word length.
- **Accuracy** is a measure of how close to a real value we can get.
- **Range** is the difference between the largest and smallest values.
- **Resolution** is the magnitude of the difference between the last two adjacent digits.
- **Truncation** is rounding down.
- **Truncation** errors are errors due to rounding.
- **Overflow** occurs when a number is too big to be represented by the system.
- **Underflow** is when a number is too small to be represented by the system.
- **Actual error** = exact value − computed value
- **Relative error** = actual error/exact value
- **Absolute error** = | actual error |
- **Absolute relative error** = | relative error |
- **Percentage error** = relative error × 100%

4 Machine architecture

Introduction

Many important fundamental concepts will be introduced in this chapter, but the details are kept relatively simple so that the beginner can easily understand the principles involved – here we will be dealing with the internal organisation of the computer at its most basic level. Reading this chapter will enable you to understand the principles of how small microprocessor-controlled computers operate, but the details of how to program these machines, together with real-life examples are covered in chapter 5. **Indeed, you can omit chapter 5 on a first reading of this book, as long as you have read and understood the first half of** *this* **chapter**.

Basic principles

The computer program

Most people should be aware of the fact that what goes on *inside* a computer is a very complex process. One moment your computer might be acting as a DeskTop Publishing system – next it could change to operating a spreadsheet which might be involved in some mathematical modelling – you might then use the computer to log on to an external database via a MODEM – or you might use the computer to look at some photos which have been stored on a CD-ROM system. All these examples of very different tasks have been performed by the *same* machine controlling extra pieces of hardware attached to it.

At the heart of most computer systems is a complex chip called a **microprocessor**. You've probably seen the advertisements on the television which claim that a machine has an Intel processor inside, for example. This is referring to a particular manufacturer who happens to be a large player in the microprocessor-manufacturing business. The purpose of this chapter is to take a *simple look* at how a microprocessor inside a typical computer can perform many different activities like those described in the last paragraph.

Put simply, a **computer program** is a *set of instructions* which tell the computer what to do. This set of instructions, or program, would normally be stored in the computer's main **memory**. It is the job of the **microprocessor** which is controlling the computer to **fetch** a single program instruction from the memory, decide what to do (by **decoding** this instruction), and then carry out any action which might be needed – called **execution** of this instruction. It is the sole task of the microprocessor inside the computer to carry out this **fetch-decode-execute** cycle over and over again operating on different instructions from memory – it does nothing more – nothing less. Often the **fetch-decode-execute cycle** is *shortened* to the **fetch-execute cycle**, because one clock pulse (see in a moment) is used to **fetch** *and* **decode** the instruction, and the next clock cycle is used to **execute** the instruction.

You will also hear the term **CPU** used in connection with the **microprocessor**. The term **CPU** stands for **Central Processing Unit** and refers to the *unit inside the computer which actually caries out the fetching, decoding and executing of the instructions*. However, during your computer science course you will also use the term **CPU** in a much-broader context – on larger computers, for example, the CPU is often used to refer to the **main processing unit** which houses one or more processors and the memory associated with the system.

The electronic clock

The **microprocessor** does *not* have a mind of its own (although if you try to program one you may not be so sure!), therefore, there *must* be something which tells it what to do. You will recall from reading the last paragraph that it is the sole function of a microprocessor to fetch, decode and execute the instructions in memory, and this being a very repetitive task, it's therefore not surprising that something very repetitive is needed to get the microprocessor to carry out these actions. This *repetitive control signal* is derived from an **electronic clock** and these simple ideas are shown in figure 4.1. The other parts of this diagram will be explained in just a moment.

Notice that the **clock** is an electronic system which produces a **train of binary pulses** which are represented by the pattern **01010101** . . . etc. Each 0 – to – 1 – to – 0 transition is called a clock pulse, and represents one cycle of the squarewave shown in the diagram. One pulse is usually needed to **fetch** an instruction from memory – it is then **decoded** automatically by the electronics inside the microprocessor chip – then the next clock pulse *might* cause the instruction to be **executed**. The word *might* is important here, because in real-life systems some instructions are too big to fit inside a single memory location – therefore another clock pulse might be needed to load the next part of the instruction into the microprocessor before it can be executed.

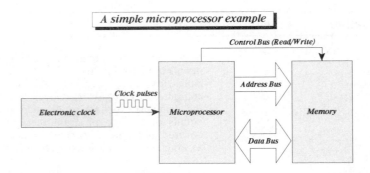

Figure 4.1

The **speed** (*same as frequency*) of the clock is measured in **Hz** (or *cycles per second*). Therefore, you may see statements such as 'an 80586–150 MHz processor' in an advert. This would probably mean that Intel's Pentium microprocessor is being clocked at a rate of 150,000,000 times per second. In turn this means that this particular processor is being told to do things 150 million times a second – as you can see, microprocessors don't hang around!

The *actual process* being carried out by a *single* microprocessor-program instruction would be **extremely simple**, and typically might be a check to see if a number is too big, for example. However, do a few million instructions each second, and we end up with some impressive processing power which has the ability to achieve things like the applications mentioned at the beginning of this chapter.

Computer memory

The concept of computer memory is a simple one – it's just many pigeon holes into which we can store binary data. The idea is shown in figure 4.2(a).

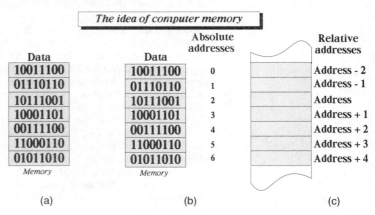

Figure 4.2

Here we have shown only seven pigeon holes, each able to store just **one byte** (**8-bits**) of data. The **data** *itself* may represent **instructions**, **numbers**, **ASCII characters** (see page 266) or a **whole host of different codes** which are limited only by *your* imagination. If we need to refer to one of these numbers inside the memory, then we will need to know *where* this number lives in 'memory lane'. Therefore, each number is given a unique **address**. If we use the decimal system for the sake of simplicity, and if we start at address zero and take it from the top, then we can see that the number 10111001 lives at address number 2, as shown in figure 4.2(b).

In practice millions of pigeon holes would be the norm, and in this book we will often make reference to computer memory as shown in figure 4.2(c). Here the numbers have been replaced by words which symbolise the actual numbers – often the absolute number representing the address itself is of secondary importance.

Data and address busses

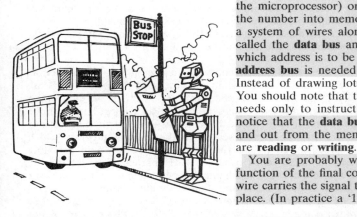

If we need to **read** a number from memory (*copy* the number from memory into the microprocessor) or **write** a number to memory (get the microprocessor to *put* the number into memory) then two obvious extra systems are needed. The first is a system of wires along which the **data** (numbers in memory) can travel. This is called the **data bus** and is shown in figure 4.1. Next we need to tell the memory which address is to be used – therefore, a second group of parallel wires called the **address bus** is needed to carry this information. This is also shown in figure 4.1. Instead of drawing lots of individual parallel wires, large arrows are used instead. You should note that the **address bus** is *one way only* – because the microprocessor needs only to instruct the memory as to which address is to be used. However, notice that the **data bus** is *two way* – this is because the data can travel both into and out from the memory and microprocessor system. It depends on whether we are **reading** or **writing**.

You are probably wondering how the data knows which way to go! This is the function of the final connection which forms part of the **control bus**. This particular wire carries the signal to tell the memory whether a **read** or **write** operation is taking place. (In practice a '1' might mean read and a '0' might mean write.)

RAM and ROM

One big problem with most of the electronic memories used to store user's programs is that the contents of the memory chips disappear *if* the power to the computer is switched off! These types of memory are known as **RAM**, which stands for **Random Access Memory**, though the name is not because of this particular property. When you switch on your computer a program called an **operating system** (see page 370) needs to be *resident in memory* if it is to make sense of what you type in at the keyboard or display on the screen, for example. This program is stored in an alternative type of memory called **ROM (Read Only Memory)** which does not lose its data when switched off. We can *only read* the data from this type of memory – we can't change it (write to it). *Both* types of memory are needed in most computer systems. Memory systems are covered in a lot more detail in chapter 13.

Other input/output

It would be a very boring computer if it were set up just like the diagram shown in figure 4.1. For example, we have no keyboard from which to type in some data, we have no VDU (screen) on which we can see the results of our efforts, and we have no printer to produce some hard copy. A few **embedded systems** have little more than this (see page 582), but most microcomputer and other computer systems need a whole host of extra hardware connected to them to enable the systems to act in the useful ways described earlier in this chapter.

You should already appreciate the concept that *data* can be transferred between the **memory** and the **microprocessor** making use of the **data bus** – it's therefore a simple extension to connect *any device* to the *same* **data bus** and transfer this data

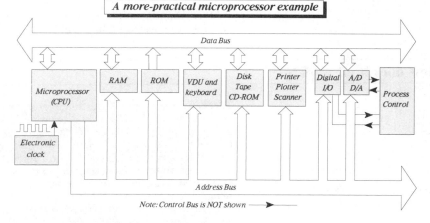

Figure 4.3

in the same way too. Indeed this *is* what is done, and the only difference between putting data out to memory or putting it out to a disk, for example, is the fact that the **address** used for the *destination* of the data is *different*. Each device is **mapped** onto the system so that it *acts as if it were memory*. As far as the microprocessor is concerned, it is simply sending out the data in the same way – the fact that it is being sent to a disk drive instead of a memory location is irrelevant. The hardware inside the disk drive, together with the programs that control the disk make sure that the data ends up in the correct physical place. A more-general concept for our computer system would, therefore, look more like the diagram shown in figure 4.3.

To keep the diagram as simple as possible, several devices have been lumped together in the same box. In practice the disk, tape and CD-ROM system, for example, would be in *different* boxes. However, the principles of these systems are identical.

Memory maps

From the last section we saw how different hardware devices might be **mapped** as though they were different areas of memory. In fact we need to **map** out *all* the areas of memory that are to be used for specific purposes. If this is not done then writing to the wrong area of memory may inadvertently cause chaos. For example, if you intended to print a file, then it would have to be directed to that area of memory which controls the printer. If you sent it to the area of memory which controlled the VDU graphics instead, then the computer screen would probably show nonsense as it tried to make sense of the ASCII characters meant for the printer. This is typical of the sort of thing which may happen when we get a computer crash – one of the programs is doing something that it should not do.

A very simple memory map is shown in figure 4.4. Notice that some of the memory is allocated to **ROM** which contains a **BIOS** (see page 389) program – this means that the computer will be able to do a useful set of things when you switch it on. Other chunks of memory are allocated to the rest of the operating system. This would usually be loaded in from disk when the computer is started up. In practice this operating-system memory would be the place where systems like MSDOS or Windows, for example, would live. There is a little space too for some user programs!

A very simple memory map	
	Addresses (Hex)
Operating System	FFF001 - FFFFFF
User Programs	0F4241 - FFF000
Operating System	010000 - 0F4240
ROM	000000 - 00FFFF

Figure 4.4

More comprehensive memory maps are shown in chapter 17 when operating systems are considered in detail.

How does it all work?

The key to a simple understanding of the above system lies in an appreciation of how a very simple microprocessor would execute an extremely simple program held in the computer's memory. We therefore present **BORIS** – a microprocessor invented for the purpose of this chapter. Real microprocessors are covered in chapter 5, but BORIS is not to be insulted – he contains *all* the necessary elements to carry out his task of running our simple program. By the way – BORIS stands for the **Beginner's Optimised Reduced Instruction Set** microprocessor. In fact, the instruction set is *so* reduced that there are only three instructions – called **LOAD**, **ADD** and **STORE**! BORIS has a few electronic-storage locations inside him called **registers**. These are the places where **binary digits** can be *stored* and *manipulated* – the general layout is shown in figure 4.5. If you imagine each of the bus lines inside BORIS to be

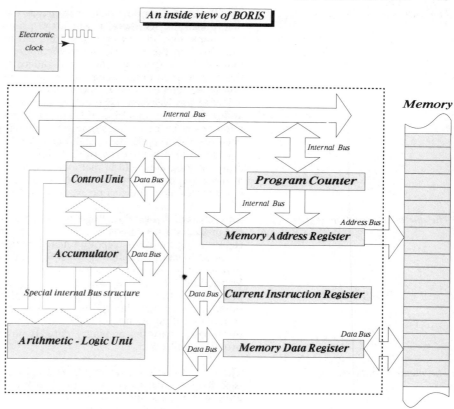

Figure 4.5

similar to railway lines, and the binary digits which travel along these lines to be equivalent to the trains, then the registers are equivalent to the stations in which the trains are allowed to stop.

Before proceeding further we need to know what functions are performed by each of the registers inside BORIS. They are therefore explained in the following sections.

The accumulator

The **accumulator** is used to **accumulate** *results* – hence its name. It is *the* place where the *answers* from many operations are **stored temporarily** *before* being put out to the computer's memory, for example. As with most microprocessors, the accumulator plays a vital role in what's going on for most of the time.

The arithmetic logic unit

The **Arithmetic Logic Unit** or **ALU** as it is often known is the 'brains' of the outfit. The ALU is able to do simple arithmetic on numbers and put the answer into the accumulator. Interested readers who are curious to know *how* arithmetic with binary digits can be carried out by using electronics should look at chapter 19.

The control unit

The **control unit** is literally *in control*. It acts under the direction of the clock, and sorts out all the **internal paths** needed inside the microprocessor to make sure that data *gets from* the right place and *goes to* the right place, it instructs the ALU which arithmetic or logical operation is to be performed, and carries out other operations like deciding which part of the fetch-decode-execute cycle BORIS is in. If you imagine that the clock is like a metronome going tick-tock tick-tock etc., then the control unit is equivalent to the conductor in the orchestra. He or she will make sure that all the different sections of the microprocessor are in time with each other. If this did not happen, then the whole thing would get out of synchronisation and fail to operate properly. Some of the internal connections from the control unit to other parts of BORIS have *not* been shown – it would make the drawing look like a spider's web. Nevertheless, coming back to our railway analogy for just a moment, if the data, address and control busses are equivalent to railway lines, then the control unit would be equivalent to the person who is operating all the points and making sure that they open and close at the right time. The whole network must all be run to a strict timetable – which is dictated by the clock.

The program counter

The **Program Counter (PC)**, or **sequence control register** as it is sometimes known, determines the **sequence** in which the **program instructions** are to be executed. In our simple microprocessor circuit, this will be just *one after the other*. Therefore, we would set up the **PC** to *point to the appropriate part of memory* where the beginning of the program can be found (hence the address-bus connection), then, after the first instruction has been loaded, **increment the PC by 1** so that the *next instruction* to be **fetched** from memory can be accessed very easily.

It was **von Neumann** who first proposed the idea of **having a program in memory**, and then each program instruction being **fetched and executed in sequence**. All operations, even inside the most-complex of microprocessors, still rely on this basic fetch-decode-execute cycle being continually repeated at great speed. Chapter 5 will deal with the added complexity of diverting control to other parts of the program, or to different programs held in memory, and towards the end of this chapter we will look at more-recent ideas which are designed to speed up the process. However, BORIS is a simple beast and has no need of such sophistication.

The current instruction register

This **Current Instruction Register (CIR)** is a place for the **current instruction** (i.e. the instruction which has just been fetched from memory) to live. The binary digits representing the most-recently fetched instruction are held here so that they can be decoded by the instruction decoder in the control unit. It's most important to realise that as far as the microprocessor is concerned, **data** (numbers and letters etc.) and **instructions** *all look the same*. It's up to the programmer to make sure that appropriate instructions are put at appropriate places in the memory. If data intended for other purposes gets interpreted as an instruction by the microprocessor, then the computer will show nonsense because it's attempting to carry out action based on meaningless patterns of binary data. If mistakes occur in the program then these problems will occur.

The memory data register

The contents of the **Memory Data Register (MDR)** holds the **data** that was either **read from** or **written to** the main **memory** – the *last time* that this read/write operation was carried out. You will recall from reading the above that data and instructions all look similar. In fact, the codes used by some instructions are bound to be identical to the codes used for some of the data. However, *if* the instructions are being interpreted correctly, then **instructions** *will* be **transferred to the CIR register** whereas **ordinary data** will *not*.

The memory address register

The **Memory Address Register (MAR)** holds the **address** of the data (or instruction) currently being accessed. It's used to alter the address bus *without* changing the PC.

A simple program

BORIS is going to **execute** (*carry out*) the simple program which now follows. Comments have been added to help clarify what's going on.

        LOAD   A, [10]   ;Load the Accumulator with the no. from memory loc. 10
        ADD   A, [11]   ;Add no. from memory loc. 11 and put result in the Acc.
        STORE A, [12]   ;Store the Accumulator in memory location 12

This program will **LOAD**, into the Accumulator register, the number contained inside memory location **10**, **ADD** this to the number contained in memory location **11** – then **STORE** the result from the **Accumulator** into memory location **12**. Let's suppose, for the sake of argument, that the number 3 lives in memory location 10, and that the number 2 lives in memory location 11. Being an intelligent student, you've already worked out that the answer is going to be 5 – however, let's see how BORIS would go about achieving the same result.

First the **program** itself *would have to be stored somewhere in memory*, preferably not in memory locations 10, 11 or 12, as these have already been used up by storing the data (the numbers to be added) and reserving a place for the answer. For the sake of argument we will assume that the program will be put into memory starting at **Address 100**. Being three lines long, and assuming that the code for each instruction *will* fit into a single memory location (in most real systems it may not), we end up with the important parts of our memory map as shown in figure 4.6(a) and (b).

We have assumed that the contents of all irrelevant memory locations have been set to zero – in practice the contents of these memory locations are of no consequence with regard to this particular program.

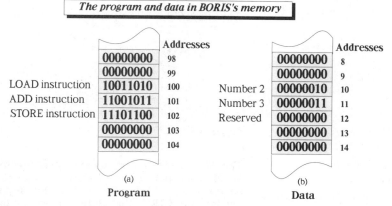

The program and data in BORIS's memory

	Addresses
00000000	98
00000000	99
LOAD instruction 10011010	100
ADD instruction 11001011	101
STORE instruction 11101100	102
00000000	103
00000000	104

		Addresses
	00000000	8
	00000000	9
Number 2	00000010	10
Number 3	00000011	11
Reserved	00000000	12
	00000000	13
	00000000	14

(a) Program   (b) Data

Note: 10011010 is the machine code for LOAD the number from memory location [10]
10011011 is the machine code for ADD the number from memory location [11]
11101100 is the machine code for STORE the result in memory location [12]

Figure 4.6

You will observe that the numbers to be added are contained in memory locations 10 and 11, and are stored using pure binary. However, each program instruction needs a code too. This is usually assigned by the microprocessor manufacturers, and we have just assumed that the codes will be as in figure 4.6. The name given to the code for the instructions when used in this form is called **machine code**.

There is usually some sort of logic to the codes used to represent the instructions, and the BORIS language works along the lines shown in figure 4.7. As can be seen from the diagram, a **unique code** is assigned to each operation, *together with a means of identifying the source or destination of the data*. In each particular case the memory location is contained in the same byte as the code – in practice, more than one byte would be needed for a greater range of instructions and a sensible addressing range.

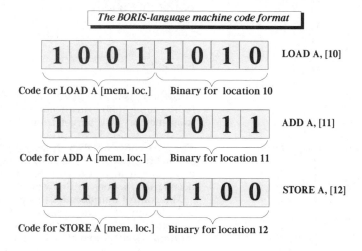

Figure 4.7

Executing the program

If the program which is resident in memory beginning at location 100 is to be executed, then the first stage is to make sure that the **program counter (PC)** *is set to 100*. The idea is shown in figure 4.8(a). You should note that all registers hold binary numbers, therefore, the binary representation for each number is used.

Next the **memory address register (MAR)** is set up to contain the binary code for 100, obtained from the contents of the PC – this is so that the **address bus** can be used to access the correct location in memory and is shown in Figure 4.8(b).

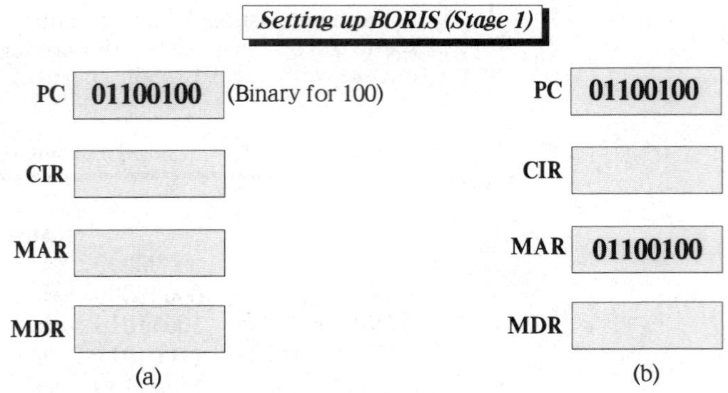

Setting up BORIS (Stage 1)
PC
01100100
(Binary for 100)
CIR
MAR
MDR
(a)
PC
01100100
CIR
MAR
01100100
MDR
(b)

Figure 4.8

The fetch phase for the 1st instruction

The **data** from memory location 100 is now **fetched** and loaded into the **CIR** via the **MDR**. You will recall that BORIS *can't tell the difference* between **data** and **program instructions** – it's all data to him. The only reason why the pattern 10011010 gets put into the **CIR** is that BORIS must assume that the *first thing encountered* in a **program** *will* be an **instruction** – so it's **fetched** from the memory and *interpreted* as such. Figure 4.9(a) shows that the data representing this instruction ends up in the current instruction register.

Setting up BORIS (Stage 2)
PC
01100100
CIR
10011010
MAR
01100100
MDR
10011010
1st program instruction
Addresses
00000000
98
00000000
99
10011010
100
11001011
101
11101100
102
00000000
103
00000000
104
Program
PC
01100101
CIR
10011010
MAR
01100100
MDR
10011010
(a)
(b)

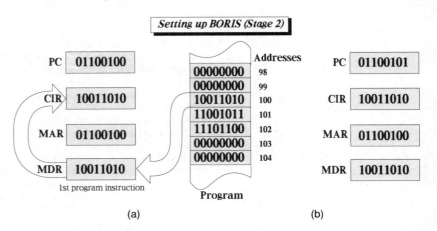

Figure 4.9

The next *vital* step is that the **PC is incremented by 1** to **101** (or the *binary* pattern representing this). This needs to be done so that the *next* **instruction** to be **fetched** from memory will be got from the right place.

The 1st instruction is decoded

The next phase involves **decoding** this instruction. This is done automatically by the instruction-decoder electronics inside BORIS's control unit. The idea can be thought of as shown in figure 4.10. Reader's interested in *how* electronics can be used to decode instructions in this way should look at page 445.

The control unit **decodes** this particular instruction and finds out that this machine code means that *the contents of memory location 10 must be loaded into the accumulator*, therefore, the MAR has to be set up to point to this new memory location. Don't forget that we have made an analogy between the control unit and the signal-box operator on a railway – therefore, the control unit has now set up all the paths (by opening and closing the electronic points) within BORIS so that what is being requested by this instruction can actually be carried out.

Execution of the 1st instruction

Figure 4.11 shows the result of the execution phase of the first instruction.

Eureka! We have, *at last*, carried out enough of these basic operations to load just one number into the accumulator! We have, therefore, **fetched**, **decoded** and **executed** the first instruction. Only another two to go – and we will have managed to add two numbers together and store the result. Now BORIS might appear to be slow – but nothing could be further from the truth – in practice the above operations would

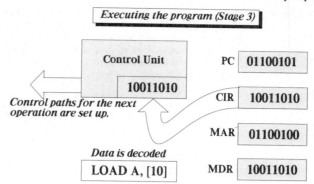

Figure 4.10

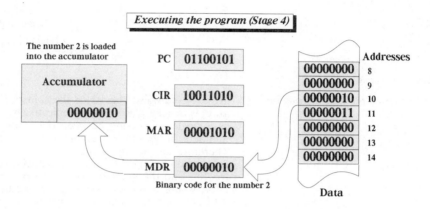

Figure 4.11

take place in just a fraction of a millionth of a second on a typical microprocessor – food for thought – we said that BORIS was not to be insulted!

The fetch phase for the 2nd instruction

We now go through very similar processes again. If you have understood what's been going on, you should find now that the processes become easier to understand.

Don't forget that the **PC** has *already been incremented*, therefore the **MAR** is set to 101 (the contents of the PC) and the data from memory location 101 is loaded into the **CIR** via the **MDR** as shown in figure 4.12(a). As before, after an instruction has been fetched, we automatically **increment the PC**. This action is shown in Figure 4.12(b).

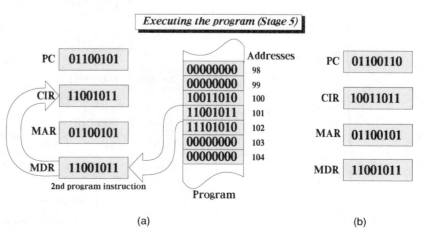

(a)   (b)

Figure 4.12

The 2nd instruction is decoded

The 2nd instruction is now **decoded** as shown in figure 4.13, and found to be an **ADD instruction**. After further decoding the electronic paths are set up so *the number already in the accumulator has the number contained in memory location 11 added to it, and the result is then stored back in the accumulator* – lots of work for the control unit to do here – many levers would have to be pulled in the right sequence to make sure that the binary trains don't go down the wrong track.

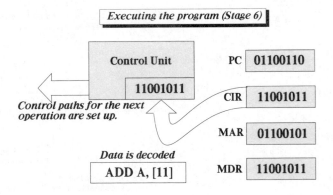

Figure 4.13

Execution of the 2nd instruction

To carry out these operations the control unit instructs the ALU that an ADD operation is to take place. This is indicated by the part of the internal control bus shown as a single connection between the control unit and ALU in figure 4.14. Now the numbers to be added are contained in memory location 102 and the accumulator. Therefore, as shown in the diagram, the first number from the accumulator gets transferred to a register inside the ALU – next the MAR is set to the binary pattern for 102, and the number from memory location 102 is transferred into the accumulator, where it is then combined, by addition, with the first number already in the ALU register, to produce the sum which is then about to be put back into the accumulator, thus overwriting the old contents of the accumulator with the answer. In figure 4.14 the overwriting part of this operation has not been shown.

On first reading, operations like these might appear to be quite complex, but they do give a very good indication of what is actually going on inside a typical microprocessor. Binary digits are constantly being got from memory, manipulated in registers inside the microprocessor, then the results put back out to memory again. In practice there would be a lot more registers than are present inside BORIS, but the principles are very similar.

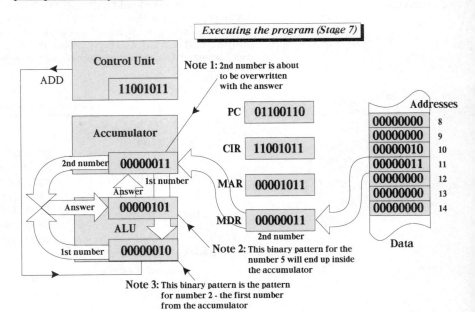

Figure 4.14

   If you have understood fully all the above, then you should now be capable of working out what happens when the final instruction is fetched, decoded, and then executed. See *if you can actually do this* by trying to predict what will happen *before* reading the final section.

The fetch phase for the 3rd instruction

   We are nearly there! The **MAR** is now set to the contents of the **PC**, and the data from memory location 102 is **fetched**. As before, the **PC** contents are *incremented by 1*, ready for the next instruction! These stages are shown in figures 4.15{a) and (b).

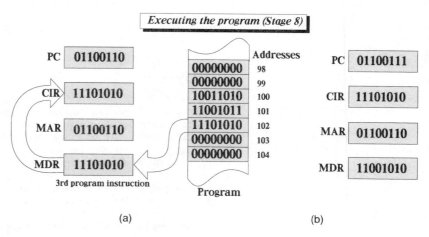

Figure 4.15

The 3rd instruction is decoded

   The final instruction is decoded, and requires that the current contents of the accumulator be stored in memory location 12. This is shown in figure 4.16.

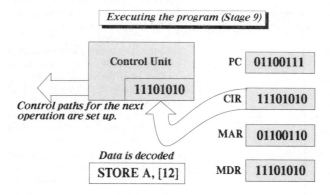

Figure 4.16

Execution of the 3rd instruction

   After being executed, the result of the addition, (binary for the number 5), is stored in memory location 12. This is shown in figure 4.17. We have, at last carried out all the operations necessary to work out 2 + 3! – but wait – this is not the end of the story.
   As stated before, a microprocessor does not have a mind of its own. Therefore, it can't just go to sleep. You will recall that a microprocessor has just one purpose in life – to fetch, decode and execute instructions just like we have been carrying out. The PC has already been set up – so let's go – BORIS will fetch the next piece of data from memory location 103, attempt to decode it, then attempt to execute it – what happens next could be literally anything. The machine which is being controlled by BORIS would certainly crash as BORIS runs through all of the memory desperately trying to do what he 'thinks' is carrying out running the program.
   In practice, any program run in this way would need an instruction which **returns control** back to what BORIS was doing before his program counter was set to 100

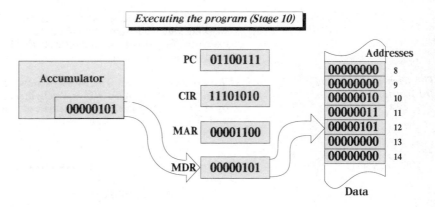

Figure 4.17

and he started to run this particular program.

In a real computer the microprocessor is constantly running programs, even when the machine appears to be doing absolutely nothing. Don't forget that if there is a picture on the screen then the computer *is* doing something. If, when you type in a character at the keyboard it appears on the screen, then the computer must be monitoring activity at the keyboard when a key has been pressed. The computer must also go through a complex program to find out what character was actually typed, then instruct the electronics controlling the video display to put the pattern which represents this particular character on the screen in the right colour etc.

It's important to understand that microprocessors are usually carrying out millions of operations each second – even if this means looping round some program while waiting for something else to happen. The only time that a microprocessor will cease to fetch, decode and execute instructions is when the clock is switched off. This usually happens only when the machine itself is actually switched off.

At switch on, the microprocessor will reset all the circuits, and then execute a program (called booting see page 390) which loads the operating system (see page 370) and gets the computer into a usable state so that normal activities such as loading an application from disk, for example, can be carried out. If the application just loaded happens to be a DTP system as described at the beginning of this chapter, then the microprocessor would jump to the beginning of the DTP-system program which is now resident in memory and fetch and decode the first of the hundreds of thousands of instructions which make the computer act as a DTP system – that's how it's done – and all with a few binary digits – a magnificent human achievement.

Reading chapter 5 will explain how more-complex programs may be carried out, but a fundamental understanding of the last few sections will take the mystery out of computers. If you have fully understood the concepts explained in this chapter, then you are already well on the way to an appreciation of the fascinating and high-speed life of a microprocessor-controlled machine. von Neumann could not have appreciated where his work would lead – I suggest you propose a toast to him the next time you go out for a drink!

Exercise 4.1

1. Explain the meaning of the following terms.
   (a) Microprocessor
   (b) Fetch-decode-execute cycle
   (c) CPU   (d) ALU
   (e) Program counter   (f) Register
   (g) Bus   (h) Memory

2. A microcomputer is clocked at 150Mhz. What is the function of this clock and what type of signal is output from it?

3. Memory forms an integral part of any computer system. In what form is the data stored in memory?

4. There are *three* main different types of bus system external to the CPU, what is the name and purpose of each type of bus?

5. Many different devices such as disk drives, keyboards and printers etc. are simultaneously connected to a system. Briefly explain how it is possible to control many different devices in this way.

6. What is meant by a memory map and why is it necessary to have a detailed memory map for all computer systems?

7. Explain the function of the following sub-systems inside a typical microprocessor.
   (a) Control unit   (b) Accumulator
   (c) Memory data register
   (d) CIR   (e) Internal bus
   (f) Memory address register

8. How is it possible for groups of binary digits to represent operations such as ADD, SUBTRACT or MULTIPLY etc? What is the name given to groups of binary digits when used in this way?

9. How does the microprocessor 'know' the difference between a machine-code instruction and ordinary data?

10. A typical microprocessor has the following instruction set.

LOAD, STORE, ADD, SUBTRACT, DIVIDE, MULTIPLY

Using these instructions as a guide, carefully explain the typical processes that a microprocessor executing some machine code would need to carry out for the computer to work out the cumulative total of five numbers held in consecutive memory locations. State any assumptions that you need to make.

Other architecture systems

This section, although not difficult in itself, may be left out on a first reading of this book. If you have found the work in the first half of this chapter quite difficult, then I suggest that you stop until you've had time to absorb these new ideas. However, if your enthusiasm for finding out about how the very latest microprocessor architectures operate continues unabated, then read on...

BORIS (see page 52) should have given you a fundamental understanding of what basic microprocessors are all about. He has done his job well, but he is slightly outclassed by today's more modern microprocessor architectures! In the remainder of this basic chapter we will bring you right up to date to include the most modern architectures which are poised to take us into the 21st century. We will not be able to study these systems in the detail with which BORIS was covered, but this is not necessary because it's only the principles of these more-complex architectures that need to be studied if you are to gain an appreciation of the trends which appear to be moulding future developments.

The von Neumann bottleneck

You may recall that it was a German called **von Neumann** who first proposed that **program instructions** be *stored* in **memory**, then *single* instructions be **fetched**, **decoded** and **executed** in the ways described at the beginning of this chapter. The performance of systems based on these simple ideas is impressive, but there is a fundamental queueing mentality which is built up due to the physical constraints imposed by the system. The only way to increase the speed of the processing is to speed up the clock rate, or increase the width of the data bus. Both of these techniques have been tried with stunning success, but even greater efficiency may be achieved by having a fundamental rethink regarding the ways in which things are carried out at microprocessor level. The limitation of being able to do just one thing at a time in sequence has come to be known as the **von Neumann bottleneck**. Ways had to be found of getting over this linear nature of processing – ways had to be found of doing more than one thing at the same time, and this is called **parallel processing**.

Single-pipeline processors

One method suggested to improve the situation was that of using what's called a **pipeline architecture**. The name pipeline architecture is appropriate because several things are in the 'pipeline' (metaphorically speaking) at the same time. It's a simple idea – if *you* were working on *three different projects* simultaneously, then you would have *three projects in the* **pipeline**! In a similar way, a specially-designed processor could fetch one instruction, while another was being decoded, while yet another was being executed. The idea can be visualised as shown in figure 4.18.

Notice that by the end of the third cycle, a conventional non-pipelined architecture would have fetched, decoded and executed just one instruction. However, making use of a **pipeline** which has the capacity to do *three different parts of the cycle at once*, we see that by the end of the third cycle the first instruction has been fetched, decoded and executed, the second instruction has been fetched and decoded, and the third instruction has been fetched.

We could obviously make the pipeline 'longer' and therefore process even more data. However, there is a problem – if the next instruction in the queue is *not* the one that is required, then the whole system goes to pot – you have to flush the pipeline, and start again with the instruction which *is* actually required. This is usually

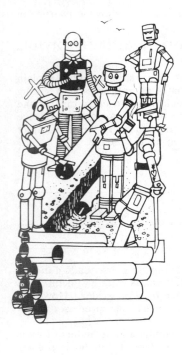

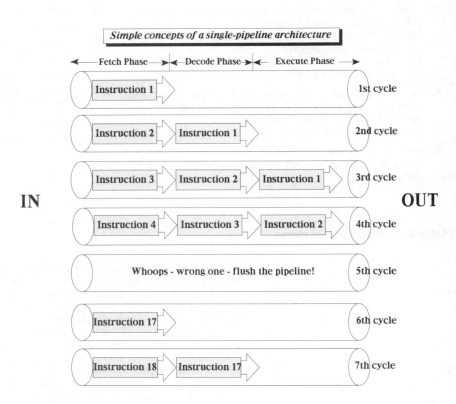

Figure 4.18

as a consequence of a jump instruction – something which most microprocessors are doing all the time. Therefore, although this method does increase the throughput, there are problems due to the nature of most programs. However, part of the art of getting computers to do many different things at the same time is in organising the program structure so that these problems arise less often. Simple techniques of **parallel processing** are covered later on in this chapter.

Multiple-pipeline architecture

If a single pipeline, as shown in figure 4.18 increases the rate at which instructions can be processed, then *more than one* **pipeline** working in parallel could be much better still. *If the instructions being carried out in parallel are* *not connected* in any way (i.e. the result from one instruction being executed is not needed by the next, for example), then execution will take place at a much-faster rate. Some sort of check for instruction dependence would therefore be needed before putting these different instructions into the pipelines.

Array processor architecture

An **array processor** can act on **data structures** called **arrays** (see page 293). In practice this means that an **array of processors** can perform *identical operations* on many different items of data simultaneously. The term **vector processor** is also often used instead of the term array processor. However, as the mathematicians amongst you will realise, a vector is simply another name for a one-dimensional array.

Multiprocessor architectures

Hitherto we have concentrated mainly on improving the performance of a *single* processor, but there are other lucrative lines of thought which enable *different processors* to work together as a team. Although many systems do make use of **multiple processors** in this conventional sense, you should note also that each processor does not necessarily have to be housed inside a different chip – many processors can be built inside the same chip if required, and work is going on in the research labs to get hundreds or even thousands of processors inside the same chip! However, it should be reasonably obvious that *if* this latter method is being employed then *the complexity of each of the processors is relatively simple compared to the latest generation of powerful microprocessors* – silicon technology is nowhere near good enough to get several thousand of these beasties onto a single chip – yet!

I've just been fitted with three brains. It's amazing how I get jobs done much more quickly.

When using multiprocessor architectures we get added complications due to the nature of the possibilities which have now opened up. For example, with a pipeline architecture, the code executed on a particular processor did not have to be modified from the basic type of code which would work on a conventional architecture of the BORIS variety (see page 52) – however, with a multiprocessor architecture we have the possibility that completely different parts of the program can be executed simultaneously. If the original code has been written such that the program can only be executed in a linear fashion (most conventional programs in the past have been), then the multiprocessor architecture will not be used with great efficiency under these particular circumstances.

The greatest efficiency from true parallel processing using a multiprocessor architecture comes only when the original code has been written with this sort of scenario in mind. Much code can be rewritten in this way, and some of the very latest windows-based operating systems software and some applications software are starting to take advantage of new multiprocessor possibilities. Indeed, mainframes and communication systems have been doing this for some time, and the very powerful micros are now starting to jump on the bandwagon.

There are several different philosophies – a common one used on many micros is that of having a few different processors share the same memory, but common too on mainframes and supercomputers is having totally independent systems with shared-message-passing capability. This latter option is also typical of the **front-end-processor systems** which help to organise the complex communications between the many possible users of a mainframe system and the mainframe **CPU**.

The top half of figure 4.19 shows a simple multiprocessor architecture with shared memory. It's easy to appreciate how such a system works because, apart from the scheduling of the processors which is handled by the **operating system** (see chapter 17), each CPU works in identical ways to those in a single-processor system.

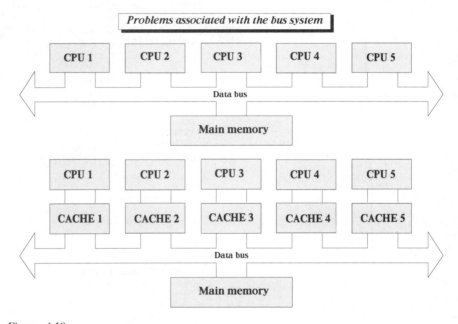

Figure 4.19

Bandwidth and the bus systems

What perhaps is not immediately obvious is the 'strain' imposed on the bus systems when being shared between many CPUs. *Any* **communication system** making use of physical wires, radio waves or fibre-optic links etc. will have physical limitations imposed on it by its physical construction – i.e. the materials out of which it is made, and the electronics which are controlling it, for example. This is not a difficult concept to understand – *your* body has physical limitations imposed on it because of the way in which *it* is made. Your hearing, for example, can't pick up frequencies which are no problem for a dog or a bat – *because* they are built differently.

The **physical limitation** imposed on a typical bus system is measured in terms of the amount of **bits/sec** that can be *transmitted along the bus* and is called its **bandwidth**. A bus system for a micro, for example might be quoted as having a bandwidth of 50 Mbits per second. Now if each processor demands data at a rate of 10 Mbytes per second, then you have a problem – the CPUs are demanding $5 \times 10 = 50$ Mbytes/sec – which is eight times faster (1 byte is 8 bits) than this particular bus is able to handle, due to its maximum-bandwidth limitation.

This problem can be reduced to some extent by transferring data from main memory into a fast **cache memory** (see page 393) – one for *each* **microprocessor**. In this way, many transfers of data between cache and CPU don't use the main bus at all – until data needs to be moved from main memory to cache or vice versa, in which case this may not affect the other four CPUs which are hopefully using their own cache at this particular time. However, if too many processors are added to the system, all sharing the same memory, then beyond a certain break-even point the processing ability of the system will actually go down!

Another way of increasing the bandwidth of a bus system is to increase the bus width. This is now being done in the most modern microprocessor-based systems, with 32 bit and 64 bit data busses now becoming the norm, and no doubt 128-bit data busses will be with us in the near future. As software becomes ever more demanding, and as the variety of plug-in boards such as real-time video processors, real-time sound processors and ever faster CD-ROM-based systems become common place, perhaps only multiple-processor architectures will be able to keep pace, and the bus structures of such systems will have to expand accordingly. Readers who are interested in investigating the detailed relationship between the bus systems and main memory should refer to page 264.

Multiple-bus systems

Instead of building up a 128-bit bus to increase the bandwidth, two 64-bit busses, for example, might actually be better. Although this may not make too much sense at first sight, the better performance of the two separate 64-bit bus systems is due to the fact that in the 128-bit system, only a single bus can be used at any one time – if another processor wishes to get access to the bus, then it must wait until the current processor has finished using it. With the dual 64-bit bus system, two processors may access the bus simultaneously. Obviously extra memory management hardware would be needed so that the processor may switch between one bus system

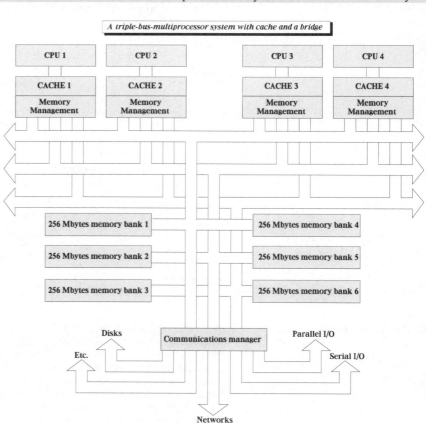

Figure 4.20

or the other according to which bus is not in use at the time. Figure 4.20 shows a four-processor triple-bus system, and includes connections to other bus systems via an intelligent communications controller.

As you can see from this diagram, multiprocessor-multibus systems with appropriate management hardware (and software) can be arranged to provide very significant increases in bandwidth and hence overall speed. However, such systems are currently quite expensive, and a system of the complexity shown in figure 4.20 would be found only in mini or mainframe computers, or in top-of-the range workstations. Nevertheless, with the current price/performance characteristics being achieved, this probably means that such a system may be available inside a pocket calculator before the fourth edition of this book!

Other aids to increased speed

Most readers have no doubt heard of terms like **maths co-processors, floating point accelerators** and a whole host of weird and wonderful additions to make one system more turbo-charged than another. Such systems are are usually referring to extra hardware in the form of extra chips. A maths co-processor, for example, usually plugs into the main board in a microcomputer system such that mathematical operations needed by the main processor can be carried out efficiently and in parallel. Without a co-processor being resident, such operations are often coded in software by making use of complex machine-code routines. These routines can be carried out much more quickly making use of the extra maths hardware, and this in turn means that mathematically-intensive applications such as object-oriented CAD packages (see page 539) can be speeded up by significant factors. However, the extra co-processor will not have the slightest effect on non-mathematical operations, and so can't be regarded in the same light as having a two-processor option of the sort described above.

The idea of co-processors has become so popular that they are actually being incorporated inside the main microprocessor itself, with a corresponding further increase in execution speed due to the closer proximity of the hardware (see page 262). Other processors such as I/O co-processors and network co-processors, for example, use the same ideas to increase the speed of input/output and some networking activity respectively. These co-processors are simply an extension of the parallel-processor architecture idea for very specialist purposes.

Data flow architectures

The natural conclusion to be drawn from parallel processing architectures is that problems may often be solved more efficiently if we split them up into smaller problems that can be solved in parallel. If we are to achieve this greater efficiency then different approaches to the solution of problems present themselves. **Data flow architectures** are just one example of such techniques, and a simple example will be used to illustrate the thinking behind this type of processing. These ideas are similar in nature to the ideas involved when critical-path analysis is covered on page 147.

Example

Imagine working out the cost of decorating a living room having dimensions of length (l), width (w) and height (h). The walls are to be painted with paint costing 20p per square metre, and the ceiling is to be painted with paint costing 15p per square metre. Assuming that there are no doors or windows, the cost of the paint will be:

$$\text{Cost (£)} = \frac{(\text{Wall area} \times \text{Wall cost/m}^2) + (\text{Ceiling area} \times \text{Ceiling cost/m}^2)}{100}$$

where Wall area = $(2 \times h \times w) + (2 \times h \times l)$
and Ceiling area = $l \times w$

A **conventional sequential program** to solve the problem making use of a *single processor* might go along the following lines.

```
Begin
    W_Cost = 20  :Wall cost/m²
    C_Cost = 15  :Ceiling cost/m²
    Input(l,w,h)
    W_Area = (2*h*w) + (2*h*l)
```

```
        C_Area = l*w
        Pence = W_Area * W_Cost + C_Area * C_Cost
        Cost = Pence/100
    End
```

Now consider a **data flow** graph for the above problem. This is shown in figure 4.21.

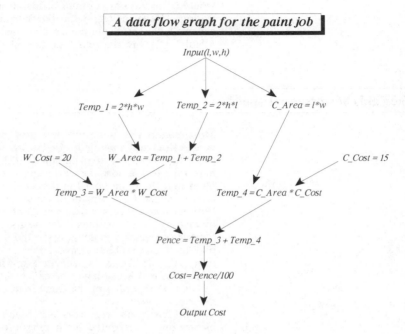

A data flow graph for the paint job

Figure 4.21

Notice that from the above analysis of the problem we have immediately split it up into three sub-problems which consist of working out Temp_1, Temp_2 (temporary storage) and the ceiling area. **All three of these processes can be worked out simultaneously as the data for each part, (l, w and h) is already available.** These three operations can, therefore, be worked out by separate processors at the same time.

You can see from the above how the data flow architecture gets its name – a data flow computation (such as W-Area = Temp_1 + Temp_2) can be carried out according to the data availability and resources (i.e. are there enough processors to carry out the required tasks). The processors would actually be **dynamically allocated** – i.e.

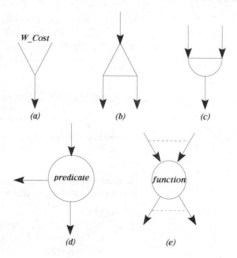

Figure 4.22

allocated as and when necessary. As you can see this is a radical departure from the conventional architecture of the von Neumann variety. Processors of this type are still under development, and work will probably go on well into the next century to develop more powerful techniques.

There are five basic flow nodes which help to show the data-flow model at this level, and these are shown in figure 4.22.

Figure 4.22(a) shows a **constant generator**, with W_Cost (wall cost) from the previous example. Figure 4.22(b) shows a **copy node**. This shows that the data generated by the previous node is copied directly to the next node or nodes. Figure 4.22(c) shows a **merge node**, where the first data to arrive is simply passed on. Figure 4.22(d) shows a **gate node**, where this input is passed on only if a condition is matched. This condition is usually expressed as a Boolean value and is called a **predicate**. Finally, figure 4.22(e) shows a **function node**.

The 'decorating the room' problem is shown as a **data-flow** graph at **operation level** making use of these new symbols in figure 4.23.

There are other parallel-processing architectures under development, but a detailed analysis of them is beyond the scope of this book. However, one other architecture called a **neural network** is covered on page 555. This radically different approach is often used in **AI (Artificial Intelligence)** and pattern-recognition systems.

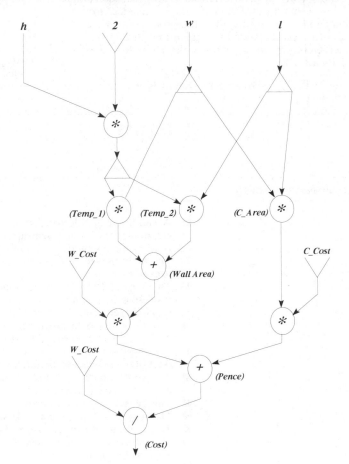

Figure 4.23

Exercise 4.2

1. What is meant by **parallel processing** and why is this exciting development leading to faster computers?

2. **Pipeline architectures** are currently used to increase the effective rate at which a microprocessor can fetch and execute instructions. Explain the principles of **pipelining** and show how this leads to an increased throughput under ideal conditions.

3. What problems are encountered when using **multi-processor systems** when *compared to* conventional single-processor **architectures**?

4. Explain what is meant by the term **bandwidth** when applied to the bus systems inside computers. In what **units** is bandwidth normally measured?

5. Multiprocessor bus systems often have a bus structure with a lower bandwidth than would be needed for optimum continuous use by all of the processors. What *extra hardware* can be added to ensure that this apparently inefficient system can work well? How does this achieve its aim?

6. Name two ways of *increasing* the **bandwidth** capacity of a data bus.

7. Which of the following software would probably benefit from the addition of a floating-point co-processor? Justify your answers.
   (a) Spreadsheet
   (b) CAD package
   (c) Communications software

8. Explain how problems may be split up for solution by using multiprocessor architectures. If the same problems are coded using conventional techniques, why might the performance of these parallel systems not be so impressive?

9. An advert regarding Intel's Pentium processor contains the following:
   (a) 8 k Code cache
   (b) 8 k Data cache
   (c) 64-bit bus
   (d) Superscalar dual-pipeline architecture
   (e) Inbuilt floating-point accelerator
   (f) 100 MHz processor
   (g) Processing speeds of 100 MIPS
   Write a paragraph about each of the above stating what is meant by this particular part of the advert, and how the use of such techniques makes this particular chip a powerful microprocessor in the mid 1990s.

End of chapter summary

- A **computer** is able to carry out a huge variety of different tasks making use of essentially the same **hardware**, but being controlled by different **software**. This is what makes modern computers so powerful and versatile.
- The **main device** *at the heart* of controlling a modern computer is called a **microprocessor chip**.
- The term **CPU** (**central processing unit**) is an *alternative* to the term **microprocessor** in a simple microcomputer, *but* the **CPU** *is also the term used* for a **much-larger processing unit** on **mainframe** or **mini** computers.
- A *very simple* **microprocessor system** would consist of a **clock**, the **microprocessor** itself, and some **memory** to store the program.
- The **clock** provides the signals to instruct the microprocessor to go through the **fetch-decode-execute** or **fetch-execute** cycle.
- The **clock rate** is measured in **Hz** (**cycles per second**) – this dictates the **speed** at which the microprocessor is able to operate.
- The **program** which controls the microprocessor is *stored* in **memory**.
- **Memory** chips *store data* as **binary digits**.
- To get **data into** or **out from** the memory the **data bus** is used.
- To instruct the memory **which location** is to be used in the transfer of data, the **address bus** is used.
- A **bus** is simply the name given to a **parallel group of wires** which are used to carry data. A large arrow is often used to represent these wires on a diagram.
- The **address bus** is **one-way only**, whereas the **data bus** is **two way**.
- A third bus called the **control bus** is used to carry the **control signals** such as the **read/write line** needed by the memory chip.
- Two types of memory are needed in most computer systems – **RAM** and **ROM**.
- **ROM** stands for **Read Only Memory** and is used to contain software such as the **operating system**, for example.
- **RAM** can be used to store the **user's programs** after the computer has been switched on.
- **RAM** is **volatile** – this means that the contents are lost when the power is removed.

- **ROM** *does not* loose its contents when the power is removed – it is **non-volatile**.
- Other devices such as **disks**, **CD-ROM drives**, **printers**, **VDUs** and **keyboards** etc. are **mapped** into the system *as if they were memory*. As far as the microprocessor is concerned these devices are identical to memory.
- A **memory map** of the system *is* needed if we are to avoid inadvertently putting data where it does not belong.
- A **microprocessor** contains special electronic circuits called **registers** which are used as a **temporary store** in which to *manipulate binary data*.
- The **accumulator** is one of the main **registers** used to accumulate temporary results from various operations carried out by the microprocessor.
- The **control unit** acts as an **electronic manager** who makes sure that all the data paths are set up at the correct moments in time.
- The **Arithmetic Logic Unit (ALU)** performs arithmetic and other operations on binary numbers, and puts the answer in the Accumulator.
- The **Program Counter (PC)** keeps track of the address of the next memory location from which the next byte of data is to be loaded (assuming that data is transferred in byte-sized chunks).
- The **Current Instruction Register (CIR)** keeps the binary pattern of the current instruction so that it can be analysed and decoded.
- The **Memory Data Register (MDR)** keeps the binary pattern of the last data taken out of or put into memory.
- The **Memory Address Register (MAR)** contains the address of the most recent memory access.
- Data from memory is **fetched**, **decoded** and **executed** by the microprocessor. This is the sole function of the microprocessor – it can do nothing else.
- The **first byte of data** in a **program** is *assumed to be* an **instruction** – if it's not, then the computer will probably go out of control and the program will produce unpredictable results.
- It is up to the **programmer** of the system to make sure that the instructions are interpreted correctly. A single mistake is enough to cause a simple computer to crash.
- **Microprocessors** have *very simple* **instructions** like **LOAD**, **ADD** and **STORE**. The fact that it can carry out these simple operations at incredible speed gives the computer its great power and versatility.
- **Parallel processing** is the ability of a computer system to undertake more than one task simultaneously.
- **Parallel processing** can be carried out by using **multiprocessors** or special single-processor systems such as **pipeline** and **array processors**.
- A **pipeline processor** is a system which employs the simultaneous fetching, decoding and executing of different instructions.
- An **array processor** can act on different elements in an array data structure simultaneously. It is also called a **vector processor**.
- A **multiprocessor system** is one in which *more than one* main processor is used.
- **Multiprocessor systems** often use **cache memory** to reduce the activity on the main bus systems.
- The **bandwidth** of a bus is its limitation in terms of the maximum number of bits/sec which can be transmitted along the bus.
- **Multiple-bus systems** are used in high-end systems to increase the effective bandwidth of the bus.
- Extra devices such as **maths co-processors**, **I/O co-processors** and **network co-processors** increase the efficiency of specialised parts of the overall system.
- **Data flow architectures** are useful for splitting up problems such that they can be solved by parallel processors.

5 Low-level languages

Introduction

One of the most fascinating things about computers is that no matter how complex they become, or how much apparent intelligence they may exhibit, everything inside them eventually gets boiled down to **binary digits**. The principles of how to control these ingeniously-designed machines at this most basic level will now be covered.

From reading chapter 4 on **machine architecture** you should already be able to appreciate how a **microprocessor** can be used to cycle through a sequence of simple instructions called a program, and from reading chapter 3 on **representation of data** you should also appreciate how the **binary system** can be used as **code** to represent data in many different forms. If you have *not* read these chapters then you are *strongly advised to do so* before continuing with your work on **low-level languages**.

A **low-level language** *is* the language of a *particular* **processor**. It *is* the code for a *particular* **machine** (computer), and is therefore given the name **machine code**. In this chapter we will, therefore, deal with the **binary codes** (called **machine code**) used by the microprocessors to carry out operations at machine-architecture level.

To prevent insanity on the part of the people who program at this low level, different **mnemonics** (aids to the memory) are used to represent the different binary patterns for each machine-code instruction. When using these mnemonics *instead* of the pure machine code, this method of programming is called **assembly language programming**. Few people these days program directly in machine code, as assembly language achieves almost identical results with less effort and far less frustration.

Although a few parts of this section might be heavy going for some students, *it is this work which will enable you to understand the computer at a most fundamental level*. It is knowledge of this chapter which overcomes the view held by the general public that a computer is a strange box which they can sometimes use, but never completely understand. It has been said that "Any sufficiently-advanced technology is indistinguishable from magic". This chapter will enable you to look beyond what's happening on the outside of the computer, and help you to gain an insight into the fascinating micro world happening at incredible speed inside modern microprocessor-controlled systems. It's also not only the key to understanding modern computers, but the key to understanding **embedded systems** (see page 582) such as those found in video recorders, the ABS systems on cars, robot-controlled production lines in automated factories and many other control applications.

Introduction to microprocessors

To appreciate the importance of programming in a low level language we need to look in a little more detail regarding some real-life microprocessor examples. It is only by doing this that you will gain an appreciation of why things are the way they are, and gain an insight into what's likely to be happening in the future.

Since the 1970s chip manufacturers have been coming up with ever more complex **microprocessors** as the technology to build these devices gets more sophisticated. Most manufacturers are obviously in competition with each other and so they try to make sure that their particular family of microprocessors becomes the most popular. **Intel**, for example, produce a range of microprocessors which are *the* current standard inside most **IBM PCs** and **PC compatibles**, and **Motorola** produce a series of microprocessors which are used at the heart of the **Apple Mac**. Other companies, such as **ARM Ltd**, produce **RISC** processors which are successful in **Acorn's** machines.

The obvious major problem with the above situation is that *all of these microprocessors are totally incompatible with each other*. **Low-level-language** software written for one type of processor will *not* work with another. **High-level-language** software is supposed not to be a problem because of portability (see page 103), but in practice there are *many* problems, mainly due to the **operating systems** (see page 369) used by each type of machine. For example, the windows-based operating systems on the three main families of machine mentioned above all behave in very different ways. The term **platform** is often used when referring to a particular series of microprocessor hardware or operating-system software – therefore, you may hear terms like the **Intel platform** or a **Unix** (a popular operating system) **platform**.

As each microprocessor becomes more powerful other possibilities exist to overcome these incompatibility problems. Some computer manufacturers are at last getting together to develop **multi-platform machines** which will enable the *same hardware* to run *software originally designed for other machines*. For example, IBM, Apple and Motorola have developed the Power PC and Power Mac, which are in direct competition with Intel's Pentium, but with the advantage of being able to run IBM compatible *and* Apple Mac software on the *same* machine. Obviously the 'holy grail' of microprocessor technology would be to develop a system which is so powerful that it could emulate any other machine, but billions of dollars are at stake and this Utopian image is unlikely to exist in the near future.

Each individual family of microprocessors attempts to be downwards compatible with the *same* family of microprocessors which has gone before. For example, Intel's range of processors at the time of writing consists of the 8086/88, 80186, 80286, 80386, 80486 and the Pentium (80586). Any low-level software which runs on the earlier processors is supposed to run on all versions of the later processors. Unfortunately, it is this highly laudable aim which is proving to be the thorn in the flesh of many future developments. For example, *if* the latest microprocessor *is* to be compatible with the original microprocessor in the family, then the latest version of the microprocessor will probably have to do some things in ways which may not make the best use of the current technology. This is one of the reasons why the design of such processors is becoming increasingly complex. Nevertheless, the alternative would be to instruct tens of millions of people with the earlier computer systems that they must now throw them away because the latest computers won't run the software – they would have to start again from scratch. This is not a situation which would be acceptable in many business environments, especially when one considers the enormous task of transferring the company data over to the new system when the old ones are working perfectly adequately on their current tasks.

For the immediate future we are therefore stuck with a range of different types of microprocessors and operating systems which make compatibility between different machines a nightmare. It is therefore fortunate for us that *every microprocessor does have much in common with others* in terms of the fundamental ways in which these devices can be programmed. If this were not the case then low-level-language programmers would have to learn how to program again from scratch each time they encountered a different platform! It is to this common base of knowledge that we must now turn for the rest of the chapter, and we will now look at the basic principles of machine code and assembly-language programming.

Each microprocessor has an **internal architecture** which is unique, but fortunately *all* have *common principles* which can be used to understand microprocessor systems in general. For example, each microprocessor has what's called an **instruction set**. This is simply the set of instructions which can be understood by a particular microprocessor chip. These instructions may include some complex ones as is the case with **CISC processors**, or the instructions might be kept as simple as possible to speed up execution time, as is the case with **RISC processors**. (The CISC v RISC processor argument is covered on page 91.)

Basic principles

The set of instructions for each microprocessor will be different, but there are many subsets which are common to all. For example, a logical AND will carry out the *same function* within different microprocessors, even though the actual machine code is almost certainly different for each machine. Therefore, we can study these common subsets and principles to gain an understanding of how all modern microprocessors may be programmed, using specific examples to illustrate the more general concepts.

Instruction sets and mnemonics

Each instruction in the set is usually given a **name** which acts as a **mnemonic**. A few typical mnemonics from one particular set are shown in the table on the next page.

Each **mnemonic** which represents the **assembly-language** (and hence the machine-code) **instruction** is literally an **aid to the memory** – the function carried out by each instruction relates to the mnemonic. The start of the **machine code** (binary 1s and 0s) is also shown in the last column of the table. These **codes** are chosen by the manufacturer for this particular chip to represent these particular instructions. These **binary** (or, more conveniently – **hex**) numbers are called **operation codes** or

op codes for short. Each instruction has a *unique* op code. All the op codes are *not* shown for each of the instructions because the final few digits of the code often relate to the *context* in which a particular instruction is being used.

Mnemonic	Function performed	M/c code
MOV	MOVE data	100010.....
AND	Logical AND	001000.....
ARPL	Adjust requested privilege level	01100011.....
XCHG	Exchange	1000011....

Most programming at **low level** usually involves tasks like 'getting data from memory' in binary form, and 'manipulating the data' in various ways before using it to control hardware connected to the microprocessor chip. Therefore, *the microprocessor is able to perform basic operations on the binary data*. For example, these might be **arithmetical operations** such as those carried out in chapter 3, **logical operations** such as **AND** and **OR** (see page 79), or checking to see if a number has become too big or too small for the system to use – this is done by checking **special bits** called **flags** (see page 78).

Internal registers

Inside each microprocessor chip there are special *electronic circuits* called **registers** (see page 454), which act as a **temporary storage** for the data which is currently being processed. In general, the more modern microprocessor chips have greater quantities of larger-size registers than the early versions, but the principles are still the same. The top-of-the-range Intel 80x86 range of chips, for example, operate on the **register model** or **register set** shown in figure 5.1

Figure 5.1

At first sight **register sets** like these may appear to be a little daunting for the beginner, but stop to think for a moment about the role played by the register set – quite simply it's just a lot of different places into which binary digits can be placed temporarily ready for processing, or a lot of places to store the results after the binary digits have been processed. Viewed in this light the principles are extremely simple – in fact, laying out the registers in an orderly manner as shown in this diagram simplifies things tremendously, because we now have a *mental model* of the registers for this particular range of microprocessor chips.

All the chip manufacturers provide diagrams similar to the above which helps programmers to appreciate the functions which each register can perform. If you look at a few different register-set diagrams you will soon start to see that concepts such as **accumulators**, **flags**, **stack pointers** and **program counters** (called an **instruction pointer** in the above diagram) etc. are common to *most* microprocessor chips.

General-purpose register sets

Many modern 32-bit and 64-bit microprocessors have more general-purpose register sets. For example, the ARM series used in Acorn's machines (see page 92) have fifteen general-purpose registers plus a program counter. The Motorola 68000 chips have general-purpose data and address registers with a program counter, stack pointer and a condition-code register. Although apparently very different from the more-specialised nature of the Intel chip register set, assembly language programming principles are similar on all of these different devices.

There are usually other registers inside most microprocessors, but they are often invisible to the programmer. These registers help the microprocessor with its internal organisation and will therefore not be considered in a chapter which is concerned mainly with assembly-language programming.

Notice that when the Intel range of chips is considered, downwards compatibility *has* been maintained with the older chips in the series by keeping the old registers as parts of the new ones. The new chips still have an accumulator – it's just that it can now hold more bits than the old accumulator could. Indeed, apart from some special-purpose registers, 'size of registers' is one of the main differences between the older microprocessors and the new. Radically different architectures (see page 61) can also make an enormous difference to the processing speeds, but the *principles* of **assembly-language programming** are common on most modern microprocessor systems, be it RISC, CISC, 64-bit or 16-bit. In fact, the early 8-bit micros are generally more difficult to program because of the lack of many of the basic facilities now taken for granted on the more-modern chips.

Memory size and bus systems

In addition to the internal microprocessor architecture, an important feature of modern microprocessor design is the amount of **memory** that can be **addressed** by the processor, and the amount of **data** that can be moved along the **bus system** *at the same time*. The first practical microprocessors for use in computer systems were of the 8-bit variety. (The earlier 4-bit micros were so limited that they were not a practical proposition.) Then came the 16-bit, and currently we have the 32-bit and 64-bit microprocessors. No doubt 128-bit and 256-bit microprocessors will be with us at some time in the future.

The **external address bus** size (see page 264) determines the amount of **physical memory** which a processor can address. A processor with a **32-bit address bus**, for example, will be able to address 2^{32} = **4 Gbytes** (4, 294, 967, 296 bytes) of RAM. Compare this with the older **16-bit address bus** which could only manage 2^{16} = **64 Kbytes** (65, 536 bytes) of RAM. The first generation of **Pentium** and **PowerPC** microprocessor chips have a 64-bit external address bus, and the top-of-the-range **MPC620 chip** has a 64-bit data bus too.

The **external data bus** is equally important as its size relates to the number of bytes that can be sent along it simultaneously, and therefore to the speed with which the data can be transferred from memory to the processor and back again. If a **32-bit data bus** is used then data can be transferred **4-bytes** *at a time*. If the accumulator inside the microprocessor is 32-bits wide, then these four bytes of data may be processed *at the same time* if this is desirable and sensible in the context of what the data represents.

The word **external** is important here as this refers to the connections coming out of or going into the chip. The **internal address busses** and **data busses** *inside* the microprocessors are often of larger size to facilitate super-fast data transfer speeds. For example, the Motorola MP601 PowerPC chip has internal data-bus widths ranging from 32-bits to 256 bits wide.

Memory organisation

As can be seen from the chapter on storage (see page 262), memory can be organised in a variety of ways. With an 8-bit data bus one had little alternative but to set up the memory in byte-sized chunks. However, with the advent of the larger data-bus systems as described above, we can now organise memory such that each location is bigger – 16 or 32 bits, for example. This refers to the **word length** for a particular microprocessor system. Even so, memory is still usually quoted in bytes, irrespective of the physical organisation and bus structure. One reason for this is that it's easier to compare memory size if everything is quoted in bytes – it also sounds good in the sales literature as larger numbers are encountered and the public apparently get more memory for their bucks – 64 Mbytes sounds better than 32 MWords of memory!

Basic assembly-language principles

Before looking at basic concepts such as **modes of addressing** and 'splitting up the instruction set into suitable subsets', we need to look at a **typical format** for an **assembly-language instruction**.

Instruction formats

You will recall that the *whole point of* **assembly language** *is to give the microprocessor instructions to perform manipulations on groups of binary digits*. Suppose, therefore, for the the sake of argument, we wish to **MOVE** the 16 bits of data contained in the **Base-indeX** register (the **BX** register) in figure 5.1, into the **Accumulator** (the **AX** register). To carry out this particular move is simple.

```
MOV AX, BX
```

In this particular instruction the *source* of the data (contained in the **BX register**) is **MOVED** (*copied* actually!) into the *destination* which is the **AX register**. If only it were as simple as this – well it *is* actually, in principle! In fact the more general form of an assembly-language instruction has *four parts* and is expressed as follows.

Label Field	Op Code	Operand/s	Comments
	(Mnemonic)	(Address field)	

Therefore, *if* we were to put a label at the front of our example instruction and then add a *comment*, the simple **MOV AX, BX** instruction might look something like

```
START:      MOV     AX, BX          ;This is a comment
```

The **label field** is *optional*, and is used only for identification purposes or as a place to which program execution may jump, for example. The **comments** are also *optional*, and are totally ignored when the code is **assembled** – changed into machine code ready to be run on the computer (see later). In fact, only the **op code** which is represented here by the **mnemonic** is compulsory, but *most* instructions have some **operands** in the **address field**.

To get the flavour of some typical instructions several different ones are contained in the following short extract from a real 80x86 assembly-language program.

```
PUSH        AX
MOV         AX, WORD PTR a1[ 2 ]
XOR         AX, a2
POP         AX
PUSHF
```

No matter which microprocessor is used, we can split up the instruction set into basic subsets, with most microprocessors having very similar types of instruction subsets. The 80×86 family of microprocessors being considered here, for example, have subsets consisting of **data transfer**, **arithmetic operations**, **bit manipulation**, **string operations**, **program transfer** and **processor control** instructions. Some of these types of instruction will be looked at in detail, but first it's important to understand another concept fundamental to all assembly-language programming – that of different **addressing modes**.

Modes of addressing

Different addressing modes are not difficult to understand – they refer simply to the *different ways in which the microprocessor is allowed to calculate and process the addresses* which represent the source and/or destination for the data. These concepts should become obvious after reading the following few sections.

Register addressing

We have just seen one mode of addressing demonstrated when the contents of the **BX register** were transferred to the **accumulator** (the **AX register**).

On the Intel 80x86 range of microprocessors, this type of addressing is called **register addressing** because the data is transferred from a *source register* to a *destination register*. The idea using this specific example with 32-bit registers is shown in figure 5.2. Well – that's register addressing done! It's not possible to transfer *any*

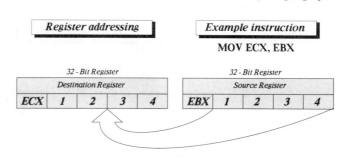

Figure 5.2

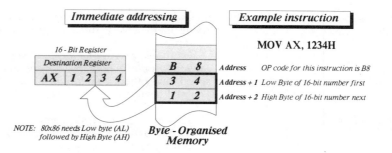

Figure 5.3

register to *any* other, but further information like this can be found in an appropriate assembly-language guide if you need this amount of detail.

Immediate addressing

Immediate addressing is also simple. It refers to the situation where the *data to be used is stored* **immediately** after the **op code** for the instruction i.e. the **operand field** *actually contains the data to be transferred.* Consider the MOV instruction again. If, for example, the *hex* number 1234H is to be stored in the 16-bit accumulator (AX), then 1234H follows **immediately** after the 'MOV AX,' part of the instruction. Therefore, as shown in figure 5.3, we end up with the immediate-addressing-mode instruction MOV AX, 1234H. Note that *two bytes* are needed in memory to store 16-bits as shown in the diagram.

If you looked up the actual **op code** for '**MOV AX**', you would find that it's '**B8**', therefore, 'B83412' is shown for this particular example in the memory locations shown in figure 5.3. Note that the 80×86 microprocessor requires that the *order of the bytes be swapped* from what may seem to be the most logical order. You will find that most microprocessors have some little quirks of this sort! Assembly-language programmers just have to get used to them. After execution of this particular instruction the data which **immediately** follows the op code is transferred into the (AX) accumulator. This method is ideal for getting *constant numbers* into the accumulator very quickly, and with a minimum amount of memory taken up by the Op Code itself. In chapter 25, when **real-time operating systems** are being considered, you will see that *speed* and efficiency of programming are often critical.

Direct addressing

This mode of addressing refers **directly** to a **memory address** and is able to transfer data between this memory location and a register. **Direct addressing** is also often called **memory addressing**. The idea is shown in figure 5.4.

Here the 16-bit number contained *inside the memory locations called 'Address'* is transferred **directly** from the **memory** into the accumulator. Note that we have made use of a **symbolic address** here in the example instruction which is given the name 'Address'. We could have specified the exact address (using hex numbers) of the memory location if we wished, but it is usually very bad practice to do so as we will see later. Note also that the op code does *not* have to be anywhere near the actual address in this case. Therefore, this particular mode of addressing allows you to store data away from the guts of the program details. However, the **op code** for this particular instruction is much longer than that of the immediate-mode-addressing instruction, (look it up in an assembly-language manual if you are interested)

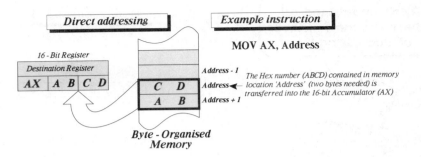

Figure 5.4

and would therefore take up more memory. This might be important if you were trying to fit a very small program into an embedded system (see page 582), for example.

You should now start to begin to appreciate the need for different types of addressing modes – some impose restrictions but are more efficient in terms of storage and speed, and others enable you to access data in different ways. In the next section you will begin to see the power and versatility of different addressing modes.

Indirect addressing

This is the first addressing mode to make use of another register to help specify where the data is to be transferred from. In the 80x86 microprocessor, there are several registers which can be used for this purpose, but we will illustrate this type of addressing by making use of the **BX (Base indeX)** register as shown in figure 5.5. Used in this way, this mode of addressing is called **register indirect addressing**. Here the contents of the BX register is a number called 'Address'. The number inside the BX register is used to *point* to the memory location 'Address' from which the data can be found and loaded into the accumulator.

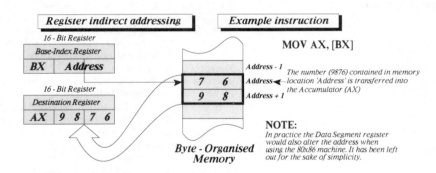

Figure 5.5

Budding 80×86 programmers should note that the DS (Data Segment) register would also be involved in this calculation. However, it has *not been used* in this example because it obscures the simplicity of this addressing mode. It does not matter in practice how many registers might be involved in the actual calculation, as long as you know which ones they are and take this into account. You will recall that all microprocessors are very different, and this is just another example of the type of difference which ensures that all machine code is unique.

Indexed addressing

Indexed addressing is where a number, usually held inside an **index register**, is used in combination with an existing address to determine the final address to be accessed. This sounds a mouthful, but is really very simple too. The idea is shown in figure 5.6. The number in the BX register is added to the number in the DI register to produce the actual address which contains the number to be put in the CX register. This method is ideal for accessing numbers stored in an **array**. The base-index register can be used for the **row address** and the destination index register can be used for the **column address**, for example. The idea is shown in figure 5.7 where, for simplicity, only a single dimensional array is shown. Two-dimensional arrays can be built up by altering the value of the base-index register to point at the memory location in which the next column of numbers would start. As before, 80x86 programmers should note that the DS register would also be used in practice for the calculation of the final address.

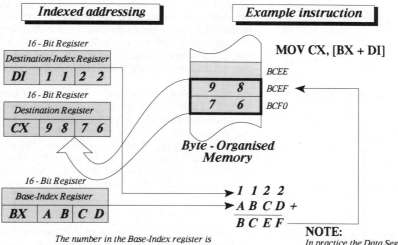

Figure 5.6

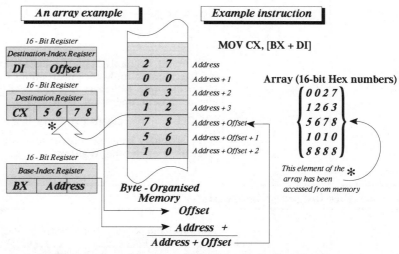

Figure 5.7

Notice how we are just starting to build up useful methods for accessing different **data structures** (see chapter 14). Using assembly-language instructions, other structures such as **queues**, **stacks** and different types of **trees**, for example, may also be built up in similar ways.

Other addressing modes

The **addressing modes** mentioned above are the *most common*. Indeed, most other addressing modes, if they exist on a particular processor, are combinations of the basic addressing modes covered on the last few pages. Any new and powerful processor will probably have a few unique modes of addressing – for example, on the 32-bit 80×86 range of processors there is a scaled-index addressing mode. These new modes usually mean that the low-level-language programmer will be able to do things more simply than would have been the case with the older microprocessors. Indeed, on the new processors, much can now be achieved by more-powerful addressing modes which hitherto would have needed many lines of assembly-language programming to achieve similar results.

In practice, some microprocessors have several different modes of operation. This often modifies the actual addressing modes by the further addition of offsets etc. We have not introduced these added complications when considering the simple modes of addressing in this chapter. For the purposes of computer science at advanced or equivalent level – an understanding of the basic addressing modes outlined in this section is all that is necessary. Any other useful addressing modes for particular processors can be learnt and used in your practical work if needed.

Other important registers

As can be seen from figure 5.1, inside a microprocessor there are usually some special registers dedicated to particular tasks which help the low-level-language programmer considerably. For example, it is possible to alert the program when certain conditions arise such as an **overflow** or a **carry** etc. (see page 44). Each condition may be **flagged** by the processor, either by *setting* (making the digit = 1) or *resetting* (making the digit = 0) different digits *within this register*. A special register used for this purpose is usually called a **flag register** or a **status register**. Part of the 32-bit flag register for the 80386 and 80486 processors is shown in figure 5.8.

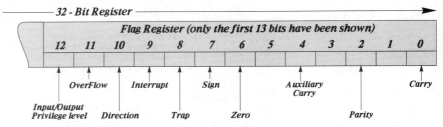

Figure 5.8

Different assembly-language instructions can be used to check the condition of the flag register, and other instructions may be used to set or reset some of the flags. If, for example, the **carry flag** has been *set* because of the result from some particular arithmetic operation, then

    CLC   ;This clears the Carry flag

is the assembly language instruction (with a comment thrown in for free) that would **reset bit 0** of the **flag register**.

Basic assembly-language instructions

Assembly-language programming often involves carrying out operations like those described in the last sections, and then sending control to different routines depending on the results of the various flags. We will now take a more-detailed look at some typical assembly-language-instruction subsets, and look at some typical operations which can be carried out by each of the subsets.

Arithmetical operations

Typical operations are obviously **addition**, **subtraction**, **multiplication** and **division**. However, as you have seen from chapter 3, operations of this sort are not necessarily trivial. Typical instructions for the 80x86 microprocessor set would be as follows.

    ADD AL, BL   ;Add BL to AL and store result in AL
    SUB AX, SP   ;Subtract SP from AX and store result in AX
    MUL BL   ;AL is multiplied by BL and the result stored in
                   ;AX (Note: AX is double the width of AL & BL).
    DIV CX   ;The DX-AX register pair is divided by CX with
                   ;the quotient being placed in AX and the remainder
                   ;being placed in DX

The above simple subset is just a fraction of the available **ADD**, **SUB**, **MUL** and **DIV** commands. The complexity of the operation depends on what is being done –

for example, when dividing two numbers there will probably be an integer answer *and* a remainder. When multiplying two numbers the register length needed for the result is much larger than the register lengths which hold the original numbers. Other factors, including the base used, coding methods, and whether 8, 16 or 32-bit numbers are needed further complicate the issues. Besides being able to do arithmetic on **decimal**, **binary**, and **hex** numbers, modern microprocessors often allow you to do arithmetic in **BCD** (see page 28) too.

Logical operations

The logical operations include **AND**, **OR**, **NOT** and **XOR** etc. These instructions operate in what's called **bitwise mode**. This means that each bit of a register is matched against the equivalent bit in another register when the operation is being carried out. For example, consider the **AND** operation using two *8-bit registers*. The idea is shown in figure 5.9.

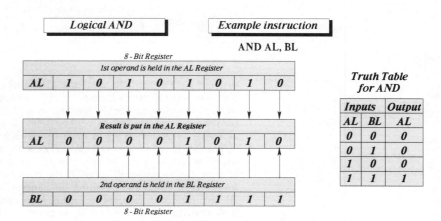

Figure 5.9

The **truth-table** (see page 431) for a two-input **AND** function is shown at the right-hand side of this diagram. Applying these rules to each bit in the AL and BL register produces the result shown in the AL register in the centre of the diagram. It can be seen from figure 5.9 that the original contents of the AL register (one of the operands) is overwritten by the answer which is placed in the same register.

The logical OR operation is also simple and is shown in figure 5.10.

Masking

Note that the bit patterns above have *not* been chosen at random, but to illustrate an important concept in computing called **masking**. When using the logical **AND** and **OR** functions we can create a **mask** which either lets a pattern of bits through, or blocks it with either 1s or 0s. If you consider the *contents* of the **AL register** to be the

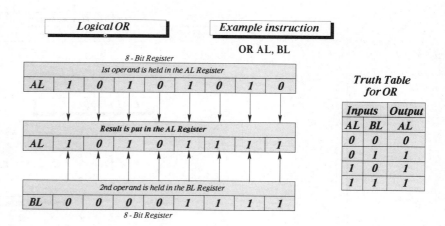

Figure 5.10

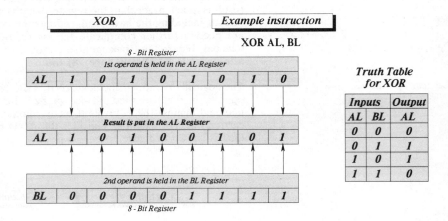

Figure 5.11

original pattern, and the contents of the **BL register** to be the **mask**, then the AND function has let the bottom four bits 'through' and reset the top four bits, whereas the OR function has let the top four bits of the original pattern 'through' and blocked off the bottom four bits by setting them all to 1s. Masking is also used extensively in assembly language to set or reset bits without altering the patterns of other bits.

The **XOR (eXclusive OR)** function is shown in figure 5.11. This function is particularly useful as a check to see if all the corresponding bits in two different registers are the same or different. If the corresponding bits in AL and BL are the *same*, for example, then the resulting bit is **reset**, but if the corresponding bits in AL and BL are different then the resulting bit is **set**.

A register's contents can be **negated** (or **inverted**) by the use of the **NOT** function. This will change all the 0s to 1s and all the 1s to 0s. Therefore, this is one way of finding the **ones complement** of a number (see page 31). Also, if we wish to find the **twos complement** of a number then we can invert it and add 1 – you will recall that this is one method of finding the twos complement of a binary number. However, in the 80x86 range of processors there is a NEG operation which combines these two processes into one, and thus finds the twos complement straight away.

The idea of the NOT function is extremely simple and is shown in figure 5.12.

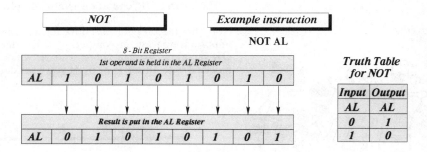

Figure 5.12

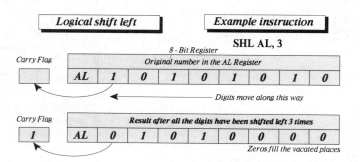

Figure 5.13

Logical shift operations

A **logical shift** instruction **shifts (moves)** each binary digit *left* or *right* and *fills up the vacated spaces with zeros*. The idea for a **logical shift left** is shown in figure 5.13.

A **logical shift right** is very simple too, and is shown in figure 5.14. Notice that a **carry flag** (i.e. *bit 0* of the **flag register** for the 80×86 processor) shown in both of these diagrams acts as a **buffer** to look at the last bit that's 'fallen off' the end.

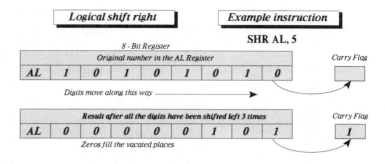

Figure 5.14

Arithmetic shift operations

There are also **arithmetic shift** instructions. These are useful for **multiplication or division** by *powers of two*. The arithmetic implications of these instructions, although simple in concept, need a little more thought. Take, for example, the number shown in the 8-bit AL register in figure 5.15.

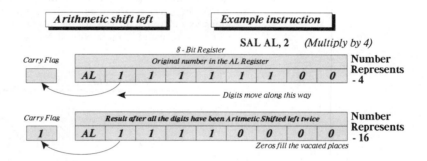

Figure 5.15

This number is the 8-bit twos complement representation of –4 (see page 30). The instruction SAL AL, 2 will **shift** all the digits **left** by *two places* – thus having the effect of **multiplication by 4** (2^2). Analyse the resulting number pattern *after* this operation and you will find that indeed, we have the correct 8-bit twos complement representation for –16, (the answer to –4 × 4). Therefore, an **arithmetic-shift-left** instruction is ideal for **multiplication of binary numbers** by powers of two. However, as is explained in just a moment, you must be careful to restrict the range, or the register will *not* be able to hold the appropriate information to give the correct answer.

A similar analysis with *positive* numbers will reveal that this method works too – again, as long as you *don't go too far and exceed the range of twos-complement numbers that an 8-bit register can hold*. Using an 8-bit register such as the AL register described above, would produce errors outside the range –128 to +127. It is *up to the assembly-language programmer* to use appropriate length registers, and to check, by an analysis of the flag register, if anything has exceeded the appropriate range.

From an analysis of the above you will see that for **arithmetic left shifts** *only*, there is *absolutely no difference whatsoever* from a **logical shift left**. Indeed, although most assemblers provide instructions like SAL shown above, there is usually no difference between the logical (SHL) and arithmetic (SAL) shift left instructions.

The **shift arithmetic right** instruction *is* different as *preservation of the sign bit is necessary to maintain the correct answers for numbers within the appropriate range.* Figure 5.16 shows a typical example where –16 is shifted right two places right, and therefore has the effect of division by 4 (2^2).

You will notice that without provision for maintenance of the sign bit the twos complement representation of the number would change from being negative to being positive – thus giving the wrong answer, even though the length of the register is perfectly capable of storing this number.

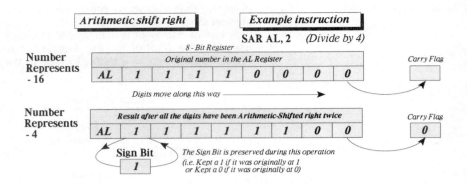

Figure 5.16

Rotate instructions

Rotate instructions have several uses, the most important being that it enables the assembly-language programmer to look at numbers which are too big to be contained in a single register – as some microprocessors allow you to rotate register pairs. This scenario still applies even if the larger 32-bit registers being considered earlier in this chapter are used. An example using a **rotate right** 4-bits instruction is shown in figure 5.17. Instead of the digits 'falling off' the end, they are directed round the path shown by the arrows and re-directed into the other end of the register.

Note that the carry flag in figure 5.16 is acting as a copy of the last digit to be shifted round from the end. However, there may be some instructions available in which the carry flag acts as a 1-bit extension to the register itself. Nevertheless, the ideas associated with the rotate instruction are quite simple to understand, and we will therefore not bother with showing the **rotate-left** instruction format.

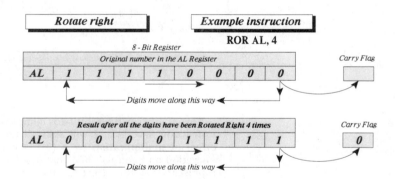

Figure 5.17

Bit set and reset instructions

This useful subset of instructions allows the assembly-language programmer to **set** or **reset** the contents of **registers** or **memory locations** depending on certain conditions, usually associated with the carry flag, for example. Consider the following example taken from the 80386/80486 assembly-language instruction set.

```
SETNO     Data      ;SET contents of the memory location labelled Data
                    ;if there is NO overflow (i.e. O = 0)
```

When programming in assembly language you will quickly realise that the contents of the flag register will change very rapidly, probably after the execution of each instruction! Therefore, this method could provide a convenient means of storing the result at some particular instant in time, perhaps ready for later analysis. In the above case, this would mean that the memory location labelled 'Data' would have the number 01H stored in it *if* **no overflow** had occurred, or the number 00H stored in it *if* there *was* an **overflow** at the time the sample was taken.

You may also need to set or reset some bits inside a register at any point in time. For example, if the carry flag has been set as the result of some particular operation, then **CLC** is usually the instruction to **clear (reset)** it.

Program control instructions

For some of the time a typical assembly-language program will be executed **sequentially**. This means that each instruction, one after the other, is repeatedly loaded, decoded and then executed, as was the case when discussing the simple BORIS microprocessor considered in chapter 4. Nevertheless, there are many cases where we need to control programs in much more sophisticated ways than this, and instructions are therefore needed to divert the flow of the program to different parts depending on the state of some particular condition. These essential and important assembly-language instructions are known as the **JUMP** instructions. There are many different types of JUMP instructions and a few of the more-common types are covered in this section.

Unconditional jumps

This type of instruction *forces program control* to move to some other part of the memory unconditionally. The idea is quite simple and is shown in figure 5.18. Although physically possible, it's *not* usually good practice to specify an absolute value for the address of a particular memory location – it is far better to use a label instead. This practice usually enables us to **relocate** the code more easily (i.e. run it in any part of the memory). **Non-relocatable code** is not usually a good idea because of the *lack of transferability* of the software when run on machines with different memory maps (see page 52).

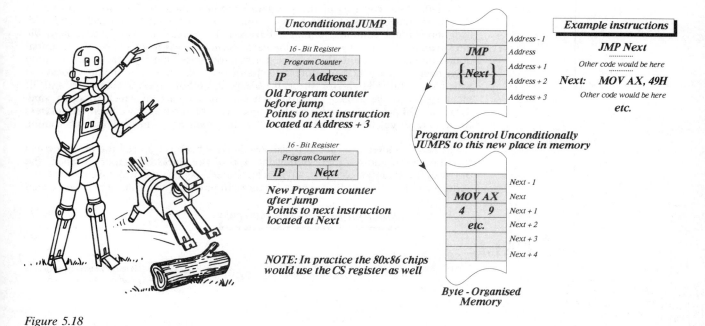

Figure 5.18

Conditional jumps

Many different types of jump commands are usually available, and this variety stems from the multitude of ways in which most microprocessors can **address** *different areas of memory*, and the **conditions** which apply as to whether or not the jump is made. It would take up too much space to demonstrate them all, but it's important to appreciate some typical jump conditions. You will recall that a **flag register** exists to flag different conditions happening inside the processors, so it's not surprising, therefore, to find that the flag register plays a pivotal role in helping to decide if jumps are to take place. Therefore, conditions like – 'jump if no overflow' or 'jump if carry set', for example, are typical of the types of **conditions** which may be used. Some of the jumps for the 80x86 range of processors are shown in the following list.

```
JNO     Next        ;Jump if No Overflow (i.e. the O flag = 0)
JS      Next        ;Jump on Sign bit = 1 (i.e. S = 1)
JCXZ    Next        ;Jump if the CX flag = Zero (i.e. CX = 0)
```

The actual distance over which the jump may take place depends on how many **bytes** are used to hold the **jump address**. For example, *if* **1 byte** is used, then a jump to **+127** or **–128** with respect to the current location could be made. However, *if* a **2-byte** address is used, then we can go to **+32,767** or **–32,768**. (See page 33 if this seems confusing.) Four bytes would be needed to cover the full 4 Gbyte range possible on a microprocessor with a 32-bit address bus.

Stack operations

We'll 'ave this 'ere stack down in a jiffy!

A **stack** is just one example of the *many* important **data structures** (see page 288) which are particularly useful in assembly-language programming. It's being covered here because of its importance in enabling you to understand how **control** may be *passed backwards and forwards between many different assembly-language routines*. It is the last major assembly-language concept to be considered in this chapter before going on to look at some real-life examples.

The examples given in this section will *not* use an actual microprocessor, and will *not* bother with the added complications of memory being organised in byte-sized chunks. Doing this would obscure the simplicity of what is actually happening with the operation of a stack. However, should you wish to write your own working versions of any assembly-language programs making use of a stack, then you will have to look in considerably more detail to see how the system may be implemented on your particular processor. For the purposes of computing at Advanced Level, the principles are more important than the details.

Consider figure 5.19. Let's assume that the *main program* is being executed **sequentially** until the processor gets to the memory location labelled 'Address' in the main memory. This 'location' contains a **CALL** to a sub-routine called 'Start', which lives in a *different area* of the memory. The CALL instruction initiates the following sequence of operations to pass control over to the sub-routine and back again.

First the 'old' contents of the **program counter** (called the **instruction pointer** in the 80×86 range) is stored in a *safe area of memory* called the **stack**. The 'old' program-counter contents contain '**Address + 1**' because this *would have been the next memory location from which the next instruction was to be loaded* if sequential operation had continued. (In practice, for byte-organised memory, the counter would have been set to a higher address to 'jump over' the next few memory locations which store the address for the call.) There is nothing special about the area of memory called the stack – it's simply a convenient place in which to store some data. The **old program-counter contents** *must* be stored because we need this address to be able to get back to the next part of the main program *after* the sub-routine has finished.

The **stack pointer** is a special register which has been set up (by the programmer) to point to the address representing the '**top of the stack**' in memory – where the old program-counter contents have been stored. Again, we will assume that the address can fit into a single memory location. In practice two or more may be needed

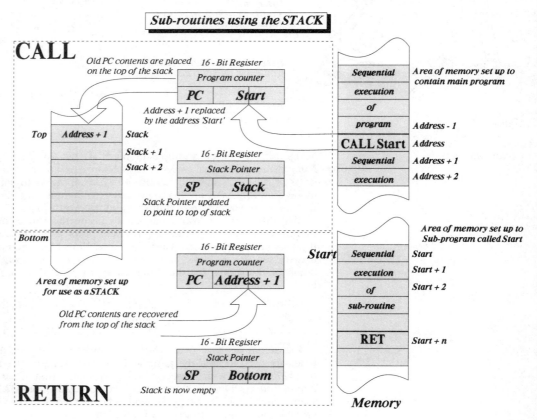

Sub-routines using the STACK

CALL

Old PC contents are placed on the top of the stack

16 - Bit Register

Program counter

PC   Start

Address + 1 replaced by the address 'Start'

Top   Address + 1   Stack

Stack + 1   16 - Bit Register

Stack + 2   Stack Pointer

SP   Stack

Stack Pointer updated to point to top of stack

Bottom

Area of memory set up for use as a STACK

16 - Bit Register

Program counter

PC   Address + 1

Old PC contents are recovered from the top of the stack

16 - Bit Register

Stack Pointer

SP   Bottom

RETURN

Stack is now empty

Sequential   *Area of memory set up to contain main program*

execution

of

program   *Address - 1*

CALL Start   *Address*

Sequential   *Address + 1*

execution   *Address + 2*

Area of memory set up to Sub-program called Start

Start   Sequential   *Start*

execution   *Start + 1*

of   *Start + 2*

sub-routine

RET   *Start + n*

Memory

Figure 5.19

to store this address information. The stack-pointer register itself *can't be used* to hold this address because we may have *yet another* **CALL** to a *subroutine from within the one just about to be executed* (see in a moment). In practice the stack area of memory could be many memory locations in size, and it is the job of the stack-pointer register to keep tabs on the memory location representing the 'top' of the stack. You can see from figure 5.19 that a label 'top' has been assigned to memory location 'stack' to help you visualise these concepts more easily. Also, as the stack obviously can't be of infinite length, another label called 'bottom' is shown which represents the address for the **end** of the stack.

The microprocessor carries on regardless with the fetch-decode-execute cycle (see page 49), but due to the operations described earlier, now happens to be working through the **sub-program** contained in memory locations 'Start', 'Start + 1' and 'Start + 2', etc. *As far as the processor is concerned, there is no real difference between working though the main program and working through the sub-program.* However, when the **RETURN (RET)** instruction is encountered, this terminates the sub-program and initiates the following sequence.

The address from the 'top' of the stack (pointed to by the stack-pointer register), is removed and *placed back inside* the **program counter**. The contents of the stack-pointer register are then updated to show that there is nothing left on the stack. Hence we are now in a position identical to that which existed *before* the original **CALL** instruction was encountered. Therefore, the program can now continue as though nothing special had happened, and therefore continues with the rest of the main routine. Any other routine can be called and serviced in the same way.

Interrupts

Microprocessors spend most of their time jumping in and out of routines in ways similar to those described in the last section. Indeed, much of the time hardware devices (see chapters 11, 12 and 13), will cause **interrupts** to happen. This means that a device such as the keyboard, for example, might need servicing *because* a key has just been pressed. The processor could be notified that an interrupt had just occurred, place the current contents of the program counter onto the stack, load up the address of the routine to service the keyboard, carry out the servicing, then return from the service routine and carry on with what it was originally doing.

Interrupts are probably going on inside the machine many times each second, with the update of the real-time clock being a particularly good example. It's obvious that other interrupts will probably happen when a previous interrupt is in the middle of being serviced, and the stack can also be used to hold the address of the sub-routine which is being executed in identical ways to the example given in the previous section. In this way interrupts may be **nested** (*queued up*) such that higher-priority ones can be serviced immediately. Interrupts are covered in more detail on page 378, but figure 5.20 shows how two interrupts (represented by CALLs to Start and Next) can be serviced by making use of a stack.

As can be seen, the main routine is interrupted when a call is made to the sub-routine called Start. This is identical in principle to the way in which this subroutine was serviced in the last section. However, when dealing with the sub-routine called Start, *another call is made* (called a **nested sub-routine**) from within the sub-routine already being executed. Therefore, the program-counter contents (which pointed to the next instruction to be loaded) is now placed on the new top-of-stack position, and relegates the old program counter contents (the old address to get back to the original calling routine) to second place. The stack pointer register is also updated to show the position of the new 'top' of the stack.

Control is now passed to the new routine called 'Next', and the microprocessor, as before, carries on regardless with the fetch-decode-execute cycle. The 'Next' sub-program is sequentially executed as *no* CALLs are made from this routine (there could have been!), therefore, when the **RET** instruction is encountered, the top of the stack is **popped off** (*not physically removed – see in a moment*), the **program counter** gets updated so that it can now go back and carry on with the *first* sub-routine called **Start**, and the **stack pointer** is altered (again by the programmer) so that the *original address* to get back to the **main routine** is ready when needed (i.e. it's ready for the time when the RET instruction is encountered at the end of 'Start'). In practice, the memory contents would *not* be deleted from the stack, as the stack pointers ensure that the correct addresses are removed from the stack, or over-written by new ones which may be placed onto the stack next time it is used.

Finally, when the RET instruction in the 'Start sub-routine' is encountered, the Program Counter is updated with the next address to be executed within the main routine, the stack is empty, and control then proceeds with the remainder of the main routine. The stack and other data structures are considered in more detail in chapter 14.

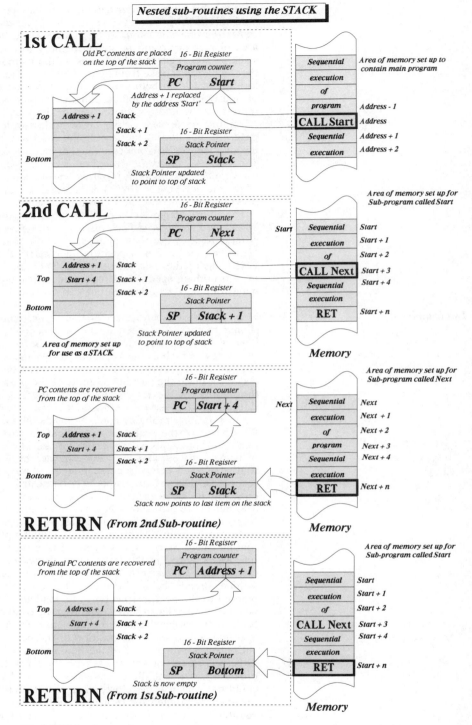

Figure 5.20

That's all there is to it!

If you have fully understood the previous sections then you will have a very good idea indeed of how typical microprocessors go about their business. The modern microprocessor spends all of its time jumping between different chunks of assembly-language code in exactly the ways described in this section. You will also appreciate that what's happening inside is nothing more or less than manipulation of binary digits. It's up to the programmer to decide how these digits are interpreted – it could be arithmetic on numbers, representations of colours on the screen (see page 241), interpreting speech (see page 234) or controlling a robot (see page 550). The power of modern microprocessors is formidable – man's ingenuity in getting binary digits to do almost anything is a remarkable human achievement.

Having understood some of the basic things which can now be achieved with a typical assembly language, we now turn to the last stage in the plot – namely the mechanics of getting an assembly-language program to run on a typical computer system.

The assembler

Basically an assembler is a piece of software supplied by the computer manufacturer that converts the mnemonics into machine code ready for execution on the machine. However, a typical modern assembler does much more than this. Without an assembler program you would have to translate each assembly language mnemonic into machine code by hand!

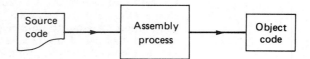

Figure 5.21

Suppose, for example, one line of your program was CLC on a 6502 machine. Then, after looking it up in the manufacturer's manual, you would find that the **op code** for this instruction is 18 hex. Therefore the binary pattern 00011000 would have to be put into the exact memory location inside the computer's main memory; a long and tedious procedure. This process would be called **hand assembly.** In practice on most computers you would be able to enter the codes in hex, but it is still a long, tedious and error-prone task.

The assembly language mnemonics would normally have to be written on a text editor or word processor. The listing of the assembly language mnemonics is called the **source code** or the **source program.** After the assembly process has been carried out we end up with the machine-code program which is called the **object code** or the **object program** as shown in figure 5.21. Note that the syntax of the assembly-language program is not important. What is important is to realise that each instruction produces one unique machine code instruction that will appear in the object code. Also, it is important to realise that on a very small microcomputer several memory locations may be needed to store this instruction because of the restricted word length.

The machine on which the object code will finally run is called the **target machine**. It should be realised that the original source code does not necessarily have to be written on the target machine.

It was mentioned above that if hand assembly were undertaken then we should have to decide exactly where the instructions would be placed in memory. With an assembler, provided it has information about where in the memory to start the object code, it takes care of the positioning of all the code for you. We will now consider the main features of a typical assembler.

Main features of a typical assembler

Besides the obvious features, such as translating the source code into the object code, the main features (not necessarily in order of importance) are:

1.   Enables the user to use **symbolic addressing,** i.e. the assembler will work out the address values for any labels that have been correctly used in the source program. You can give names to specific memory locations where data is to be found.
2.   You can perform arithmetic (often only very simple on a micro), simply by including the appropriate signs in the source code listing.
3.   You can often use different bases for your numbers e.g. base two, eight, sixteen and ten are often supported.
4.   The assembler will alert the user to any errors during the assembly process such as incorrect instructions.
5.   The user can tell the loader program (see later) where parts of the program or data should be in the computer's memory.
6.   The assembler can produce a listing of the source code or object code, together with error messages, formatted to the user's requirements. It is essential to be able to produce a listing with comments so that you can manually work through parts of the program to sort out any bugs.

7.   The assembler will work out all the necessary forward and backward references such as jumps and subroutines, a very painful process by hand!

8.   Enables the user to use just one instruction to define a sequence of other instructions. It then converts these instructions into the equivalent set of machine-code instructions. These are called **macros** (see later).

Some of the above operations, such as defining directives to be used in the source program or allocating areas of memory, are not translated into machine code instructions. These extra instructions are called **assembler directives** or **pseudo-operations** because they are really instructions to the assembler and not actual code to be executed on the target machine.

Different types of assembler

Before going on to the asssembly process it is important to realize that there are several different but important types of assembler available for many computers. They all translate the original source code into the final object code, but some have added facilities. Some of the more important types of assembler are:

1.   **Basic assembler.** Most assemblers go through the source code producing the object code, but will ignore any forward references such as jumps (i.e. it does not know where to jump to until it has got that far in the assembly process!). This is called the first pass. On subsequent passes, the assembler will go through and resolve all the jump addresses to produce the final object code. It will also produce a data dictionary (see page 202).

2.   **Resident assembler.** This is an assembler that runs only on the target machine, i.e. it will only translate the mnemonics into the specific machine code for the processor resident in the particular machine.

3.   **Cross assembler**. Unlike the resident assembler the cross assembler is able to produce the object code that will run on a different machine.

4.   **Macro assembler.** This type of assembler supports macros. Macros define a sequence of instructions with just one other instruction called a **macro instruction.** Every time the macro is encountered within the source code all the necessary machine code instructions are generated. It is not like a subroutine because no branch is executed. Macros are useful because only one instruction has to be changed if a complete new routine is required when the assembler is used. However, using macros can create very long object programs if not used with care.

5.   **Meta assembler.** This is an assembler that can deal with many different instruction sets.

Loaders

A **loader** is a program that takes the object code (i.e. the machine code produced by the assembler) and **loads** it into the computer's main memory in the correct place. There are various types of loader.

1. **Bootstrap loader.** This is a loader that loads itself by using the instructions at the beginning to load the rest of itself! The name bootstrap is a hangover from the days when the expression 'pull yourself up by your own bootstraps' meant to achieve something by your own efforts, or in computing terms to achieve the loading of a large system on the basis of the effort of a smaller one.

2. **Linking loaders.** These are particularly useful as they are able to **link** together programs that have been assembled separately. For example, there may be a library of assembly language routines that can be used by other assembly language programs. An example of a typical routine may be a sort program. The assemblers that are used to produce the object code for a linking must be able to cope with what are called external references. Without this facility an error message would of course be generated.

3. **Relocating loaders.** This type of loader can load the object code anywhere in memory, as opposed to an **absolute loader** which can't. This is obviously very convenient if many programs are being run at the same time on a system. However, the object programs that are produced must be **relocatable code,** i.e. programmers must ensure that no reference to an absolute memory location is used. You can't program with instructions like: STA 0100H for example, i.e. store the contents of the accumulator in memory location 100 hex. These problems can easily be over-

come by using labels rather than absolute addresses e.g. you would use 'STA answer' instead. Using this better method the relocating loader can move your program around anywhere in memory and it will always work.

Writing relocatable code is always the best policy. If a specific memory location is used for input/output purposes then this is also usually referred to by a name. If the manufacturers suddenly decide to update the system (they often do!) then they might decide that the absolute address of this input/output port will change. However, if you have referred to it by a standard name, then your original program should still work satisfactorily because the new operating system software should be able to cope.

An assembly-language example

Practical features of a typical assembly language

The principles covered at the beginning of this chapter are best illustrated by some practical examples. First we will cover the general principles, then give a couple of specific examples making use of some modern microprocessors.

General principles

Having covered a lot of complex and detailed information, it is important to get it clear in your own mind exactly what has to happen when we go through the assembly process, i.e. what do you actually have to do to get an assembly program going? The following section outlines the typical processes that have to be carried out.

1. **The basic idea.** The problem to be solved must be broken down into a suitable form, making use of **flowcharts, pseudocode,** or a **clear set of written statements.**

2. **Coding the problem.** By making use of the **appropriate assembly-language mnemonics,** the code must be written either by making use of a text editor or a **word processor** that can produce **ASCII** text. This code must be combined with all the appropriate **directives** and **interrupts** (see in a moment) that will make it actually run on the target machine.

3. **Assembling the program.** The code produced in step 2 must be **assembled** by making use of an appropriate **assembler** for your particular machine. Such processes are considered in detail for particular machines at the end of this section.

4. **Any errors?** If the assembler produces any errors, then these must be corrected by going back to step (2), changing the **source code,** and **re-assembling.** Errors detected at this stage would include invalid instructions or other **syntax errors.**

5. **Link and add macros that may be needed?** The assembler code is converted into **executable code,** i.e. code that can be run on a particular machine, by the **linker,** and **linked** with any **macros** that may have been called.

6. **Any execution errors?** Even though the program may assemble correctly, i.e. it is syntactically correct, it may not produce the desired results. If this is so then you will have to return to step (2) yet again, find the error, alter the source code, then re-assemble and run again.

It is most advisable to save your program on disk **before running it.** This is because certain errors can cause the machine to crash, thus destroying your program. Such errors are called **fatal errors.**

On many systems there are also debuggers that help you to single-step through assembly-language code as it is being run. Without these useful **utilities** it is often difficult, if not impossible, to see why a program does not produce the desired output. The only alternative would be to do a very tedious **dry run** by hand.

The exact details to be carried out on particular machines may vary, but they are all variations on the above theme. For example, some assemblers may not support macros, and therefore the 'adding the macros' stage might be missed out completely.

The above ideas are summarised in the flowchart of figure 5.22.

Some background information

Before using an assembly language in practice, there are a few important things to understand. This involves the mass of extra help that is usually given to programmers when they use a particular assembler on a particular machine – help with using parts of the operating system, and help with the 'nuts and bolts' of telling the computer exactly what you want it to do.

A few assembly-language instructions by themselves would not normally run properly on a computer. Extra information is required such as 'where the program

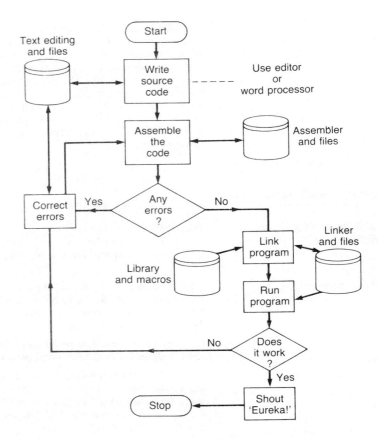

Figure 5.22

will be assembled in memory'. Also, there is usually much help with carrying out common tasks, or help enabling you to get listings of your programs on the printer, etc. To undertake these routine but useful tasks requires an understanding of **directives** or **pseudo-operations**, and **interrupts**. These are briefly covered before looking in detail at the assembly-language examples.

Directives and pseudo-operations

These are operations that *do not form part of the actual program*. Thay are **not assembly-language instructions** in the normal sense, but **instructions to the assembler.** They will not produce machine code that forms part of your program. For example, in the **PC** system, the **END** command tells the assembler when to stop assembling. There are many other uses of **pseudo-ops** and **directives** such as telling the assembler the position in memory at which the code is to start being assembled, or convenient ways to **define bytes** and **words.** Without help such as this, assembly-language programs would be much more tedious and difficult to write. However, remembering such details is best left to the reader when an individual assembly language (or subset of one) is studied.

Calling operating system functions

Often there are many basic operations that need to be carried out. Examples would be putting characters on the screen, getting characters from the keyboard, opening or closing a file, printing a character, or any other of the many chores that might need to be done.

It would be inefficient if you had to write all these routines from scratch, especially if they are already extensively used by the **operating system.** Therefore, most computer systems have ways of calling up the appropriate **subroutines** that reside somewhere in the operating system. This is usually done by making use of **interrupts**, i.e. your program is **interrupted** to **call a subroutine** that resides somewhere else in the computer. After carrying out the required task, control is passed back to your original program .

On the **PC range**, and on the **Archimedes**, both of which will be covered shortly, these calls are carried out by using **software interrupts**. These calls simply let the user have access to routines which save the programmer the bother of having to work out all the instructions that would be necessary to carry out the desired tasks.

It should be realised **the above routines are usually called by name or number,** and *not* by specifying an absolute address within the machine. *This is essential* as it creates code that is *not* dependent on a particular version of the operating system. If a new version of the operating system is produced, the routine may reside at different memory locations, but the names can be used to create a **vector** that directs you to the new place where the subroutine is stored.

Typical examples on the Archimedes would be:

SWI "OS_ReadC"	Read a Character from the keyboard into register R0 using an Operating System Interrupt
SWI "OS_WriteC"	Write a Character from R0 to the screen etc.

In addition to the above, you can often buy **macros** on disk from a third party supplier, or write your own. These would also be able to be **called by name,** as with the above functions and SWIs. However, with **macros, whole chunks of code would be added to your assembled programs,** i.e. for each macro that you call, the instruction to call the macro is replaced by however many instructions are contained within the macro. Note the difference here between this and the other **procedure**- or **subroutine** type calls when dealing with interrupts.

Don't forget that it's quirks like the above that ensure that low-level languages are only applicable to a particular machine, unlike high-level languages which are supposed to be portable.

Some specific examples

In the last part of this section we will show some typical assembly-language programming. **The only way that you can really learn about assembly-language programming is *actually to do some*.** These examples will bring out many important points which are applicable to general assembly language programming. They should, therefore, be gone through with great care.

Although the mechanics of doing things in assembly language are very different indeed from one machine to another, many of the principles are *exactly the same.* For example, although we will 'draw a circle on a 32-bit RISC processor', and then 'set the time on a 16-bit CISC processor', both methods essentially involve exactly the same thing! This might sound very surprising, but in essence, both methods involve putting special numbers into the appropriate registers and then calling one of the standard routines from the operating system. Always bear this in mind. This is why it is more important to learn the principles rather than the particular mechanics of any assembly language process. However, most students want to know how, and therefore we have included two of the three most popular systems found in schools: the **BBC/Archimedes** range of computers, and the many others that are based around the **PC** range and its clones.

In the following examples the code used is *extremely simple,* making use of just a single interrupt call. We will, therefore, omit the usually essential part of developing the program from flowcharts or other methods. Here we are just giving examples of the **assembly processes,** and will keep the actual code used to a bare minimum.

The first example is based on the **ARM 32-bit RISC processor** used in the **Archimedes,** and the second is on the **80x86 CISC processor** used in the original **PC** range of computers. The Archimedes has been chosen because of the number of schools and colleges which now have this machine, and because of its vastly different approach to the actual process of assembly. The PC has been chosen because of its standard approach used on the majority of other machines.

Detailed examples

The Acorn 32-bit RISC processor

The Archimedes computer is based around a powerful microprocessor called the **ARM (Advanced Risc Machine).** This is a **32-bit RISC processor** based on a **pipeline architecture**. It is also interesting to note that the ARM processor fully supports **virtual memory** up to a maximum of 64 megabytes, but this is not implemented on all Archimedes computers.

RISC stands for **Reduced Instruction Set Computer**, as opposed to a **CISC**, or **Complex Instruction Set Computer**, such as the instruction set of the 386 and 486 microprocessors.

The theory of RISC is simple. When typical computer programs are executed, most of the time they are carrying out **simple operations**. It is only rarely that the **most complex instructions** from the machine's assembly language are needed. Therefore, the **RISC philosophy** is to make the more complex instructions up from

The ARM register set

many simpler instructions. If there are not so many different types of instruction, then they are called a reduced instruction set. The system is arranged to optimize the execution of these simpler instructions. The more complex operations will obviously take much longer to carry out on the RISC machine, but overall, the RISC machine could be faster. The other advantage is that it is much simpler to produce the chip during the fabrication stage, and thus you have a very fast machine that is relatively cheap to produce and consumes far less power

The ARM has twenty-seven 32-bit registers, sixteen of which can be accessed at any one time, depending on the mode of operation. In common with many modern processors, the concept of **general purpose registers** is used in the ARM. **R0 to R14 are general purpose registers**, but **R15** is used for the **program counter** and the **processor status register** (flags). However, conventionally, some of the other registers are used for stacks and other special purposes, e.g. R13 and R14 in the following table.

Register name	Typical uses
R0	General purpose
R1	General purpose
R2	
R3	
R4	
R5	
R6	etc.
R7	
R8	
R9	
R10	
R11	
R12	General purpose
R13	Private stack pointe4rs
R14	Subroutine link register
R15	PC and status registers

The ARM assembly process, like the BBC machine before it, is unusual in some respects. This is because there is a powerful assembler built into **BASIC** (Beginner's All-purpose Symbolic Instruction Code). We therefore set up things that would normally be done in other ways from *within BASIC itself.* In this system the '[' is used to differentiate between the start of the assembly language and the end of BASIC, and the ']' sign is used to show the end of the assembly language listing, i.e. after this sign is used you are back in BASIC. Again the details of such systems are best left to a detailed individual study, but are mentioned here because they are necessary if the following programs are to be understood.

As mentioned above, the Archimedes is strange in that some things need to be done from within BASIC. However, don't go away with the idea that you can't call an assembly language program from BASIC with other machines; this is not what is meant. Indeed, on the PC machine you can interface assembly language to a variety of high-level languages and databases. To sum up, on the Archimedes you have to *use* BASIC to get the code assembled.

Two important things done from BASIC are as follows:

1.   **Reserving memory where the assembly-language code is to be stored.** This is done by BASIC statements such as

    100 DIM assembly_code% 500

This is a special form of the DIM (DIMension statement). It is used here to reserve memory from **assembly_code% to assembly_code% + 500,** thus giving you a total of 501 bytes in which to store your assembly language program. The 'assembly_code%' is simply an integer variable which represents the start address of the reserved area in memory. It is necessary to reserve a **safe area of memory**, otherwise unpredictable results might happen. The results could be spectacular (though not very useful) if you assemble your program in the middle of memory which controls the graphics display!

2. Setting the program counter (PC). This is done from within BASIC by making use of the special variable P%. Here P% is literally the program counter (PC). Now, as you know from reading chapter 4, the program counter must be set to point to the first part of your assembly-language program. We have seen from the above that this happens to be at assembly_code%, therefore, the required statement would be:

```
110 P% = assembly_code%
```

The above two lines are sufficient for simple assembly-language programs which are to be run from the locations at which they have been assembled.

The start of any simple assembly-language program on the Arc can therefore be accomplished by using:

```
100 DIM assembly_code% 500
110 P% = assembly_code%
120 [
130 . . . . . . . .
140 . . . . . . . . assembly code goes here . . .
150 . . . . . . . .
160 ]
```

Don't forget that the '[' and ']' signs denote the **beginning** and **end** of the assembly code respectively.

Making passes! When assembling machine code, the assembler must go through converting all the assembly-language instructions into the appropriate machine code ones. However, this is often not possible on the first pass because of some forward references that might be in the code. For example, acting on the results of some test condition, you might have to transfer control to a routine that resides much later on in memory. As the assembler has not got that far yet, it cannot possibly assemble the memory address to which control would have to be transferred. Therefore, two or more **passes** are usually necessary, the **second or third pass** to *resolve all the jumps that were not possible during the first pass*. Very simple programs consisting of a few linear instructions may not need a second pass to assemble the code properly.

On the Archimedes computer, these passes are performed by putting the assembly language code in a BASIC FOR-TO-NEXT loop. In addition to resolving forward references, this FOR-TO-NEXT loop structure works in conjunction with an **OPT** (**OPT**ion) **assembler directive** (see section on directives and op codes). This OPT directive determines various options such as whether a listing will be produced on assembly, or whether any errors that might be generated are to be suppressed, etc. This might sound terribly complicated, but gives the programmer a great deal of freedom to choose what happens during the assembly process. For example,

```
OPT 0 (Binary 0 0 0 0) is
```

No range check, No offset assembly, No errors reported and **No listing produced.**

and

```
OPT 3 (Binary 0 0 1 1) is
```

No range check, No offset assembly, Errors reported and **Listing produced.**

Notice how the **binary pattern** of the number *after* the **OPT command** determines whether or not one of the **four options** is switched **on** or **off**.

As far as simple programs are concerned, you can set the OPT command to a standard default and then forget it. A common setting for most purposes would be **OPT 0** on the **first pass**, and **OPT 3** on the **second**. This would be achieved in practice by using the following:

```
100  DIM assembly_codes% 500
110  P% = assembly_code%
115  FOR pass% = 0 to 3 STEP 3
120     [
```

```
125    OPT pass%
130    . . . . . . . . .
140    . . . . . . . . . assembly code goes here . . .
150    . . . . . . . .
160    ]
170  NEXT pass%
```

Calling the program. The above program structure assembles the code in memory, but we still need to **CALL the machine-code routine** to make use of it. This is carried out quite simply by means of the CALL command, either from within BASIC, or in immediate mode direct from the keyboard. The above program is simply called assembly_code%, although a more descriptive name would usually be used which reflects the operations being carried out by the machine code program. One way to call the above program from BASIC would require the addition of the line:

```
180 CALL assembly_code%
```

This would ensure that the code is called up and executed.

Labels. These are useful for **labelling the start of subroutines** or other parts of your program. They can be used as a **reference for jumps and calls**, as it saves the programmer having to work out **relative jumps** etc. (see earlier in this chapter). In the Archimedes, *labels are denoted by starting with a decimal point.* Some typical labels might be:

```
.start    .finish    .window_definition    and    .floating_addition
```

Comments. It is essential to put comments in assembly language listings, for without them the programs become difficult to read and almost impossible to maintain. In ARM assembler, comments can be put in by the use of the semi-colon. For example,

```
;This would be a comment
```

An example problem. As the Archimedes is a powerful graphics computer, we shall write a typical program making use of some of the graphics software interrupt calls. Simple graphic shapes such as triangles, circles, rectangles, etc. can be drawn very easily. We will develop a simple assembly language program to plot a circle.

The ideas revolve around moving to an appropriate position on the screen, providing the information necessary, then making use of the appropriate PLOT routine. As an example, from BASIC we might use:

```
MOVE x_centre, y_centre
PLOT 153, radius, 0
```

153 represents plotting a filled-in circle using the centre at the current graphics position with the radius given. There are much easier ways, but this method has been used because the number 153 is important if the appropriate software interrupts are to be called using an assembly language routine.

Basically, all we have to do is **load the appropriate registers** with the **appropriate numbers** and **call** the **SWI "OS_plot"**. Three registers are important for this operation. These are R0, R1 and R2, and should each be used as follows:

On entry to the **SWI "OS_plot"** routine

R0	contains	**#4**	(Number 4 represents the **code for MOVE**)
R1	contains	**#640**	(The x_centre coordinate)
R2	contains	**#512**	(The y_centre coordinate)

The following assembly-language code therefore moves the cursor to the centre of the screen:

```
MOV R0,#4          ;#4 is the code for MOVE
MOV R1,#640        ;Get x_centre
MOV R2,#512        ;Get y_centre
SWI "OS_plot"      ;Perform MOVE x_centre, y_centre
```

Note that MOV has nothing whatsoever to do with the BASIC MOVE command; it is an *assembly-language instruction* to **MOVe #4** into the **register R0**, or to **MOVe #640** into **register R1** etc.

Next we have to do the same for PLOT:

```
        MOV R0,#153          ;#153 is the code for solid circle
        MOV RI,#200          ;Get radius
        MOV R2,#0            ;zero must be put in register 2
        SWI  "OS_plot"       ;Perform PLOT 153, x_centre, y_centre
```

In practice we could easily alter the colours etc., but here we will be content with the default colours. The complete routine would therefore be:

```
10    REM>circle
20
30    DIM plot_circle% 500
40    P% = plot_circle%
50    FOR pass% = 0 TO 3 STEP 3
60
70       [
80
90          OPT pass%
100
110         MOV R0,#4          ;#4 is the code for MOVE
120         MOV RI,#640        ;Get x_centre
130         MOV R2,#512        ;Get y_centre
140         SWI "OS_plot"      ;Perform MOVE x_centre, y_centre
150         MOV R0,#153        ;#153 is the code for solid circle
160         MOV R1,#200        ;Get radius
170         MOV R2,#0          ;Zero must be put in register 2
180         SWI "OS_plot"      ;Perform PLOT 153, x_centre, y_centre
190
200         MOV PC,R14         ;Return to BASIC
210
220      ]
230
240   NEXT pass%
250
260   CALL plot_circle%
```

Note: Being a strictly linear sequence of simple instructions, the above program does not actually require more than one pass. However, it is useful to get into the habit of structuring the programs in the above way.

When the above program is RUN (i.e. assembly takes place) with the OPT set to the values shown, you may get the following listing:

```
00009170
00009194
00009194                            OPT pass%
00009194    E 3 A 0 0 0 0 4         MOV R0,#4          ;#4 is the code for MOVE
00009198    E 3 A 0 1 D 0 A         MOV R1,#640        ;Get x_centre
0000919C    E 3 A 0 2 C 0 2         MOV R2,#512        ;Get y_centre
000091A0    E F 0 0 0 0 4 5         SWI "OS_plot"      ;Perform MOVE x_centre, y_centre
000091A4    E 3 A 0 0 0 9 9         MOV R0,#153        ;#153 is the code for solid circle
000091A8    E 3 A 0 1 0 C 8         MOV R1,#200        ;Get radius
000091AC    E 3 A 0 2 0 0 0         MOV R2,#0          ;Zero must be put in register 2
000091B0    E F 0 0 0 0 4 5         SWI "OS_plot"      ;Perform PLOT 153, x_centre, y_centre
000091B4    E 1 A 0 F 0 0 E         MOV PC,R14         ;Return to BASIC
```

The extreme left-hand side shows the memory locations at which the code has been assembled, and the second column is the list of machine code that represents the mnemonics in the next column. Finally, the comments included in the original source listing are also shown.

The 8086 16-bit processor

To contrast with the philosophy of the Archimedes we will now look at a CISC 8086-based processor. This is a 16-bit processor from Intel, and it is interesting to note that any software developed on an 8086 system should be able to run on the much more powerful 80286, 80386, 80486 and Pentium machines, although, obviously, the more powerful 80×86 code will not run on the 8086 if the more advanced features have been used.

The **internal register set** of the 8086 processor is as follows:

Data registers

AH	**AL**	**Accumulator AX** (high and low bytes)
BH	**BL**	**Base BX** (high and low bytes)
CH	**CL**	**Counter CX** (high and low bytes)
DH	**DL**	**Data DX** (high and low bytes)

Pointer and index registers

SP	**Stack pointer**
BP	**Base pointer**
SI	**Source code**
DI	**Destination index**

Segment registers

CS	**Code segment**
DS	**Data segment**
SS	**Stack segment**
ES	**Extra segment**
IP	**Instruction pointer**
FlagS	**Status register**

The **data registers** can be treated as four 16-bit registers or eight 8-bit registers: hence the layout in the above diagram. If the 8-bit registers are used they are called AH, AL, etc. as shown above, or if the 16-bit registers are used, then they are called AX, BX, CX and DX respectively.

The segment registers. These are used primarily to keep the programs and data in **separate segments** of memory. This is a quirk of 8086-based processors. If you are going to learn to program on a PC machine making use of either the 8086/88 or indeed the 186, 286, 386 and 486 based 32-bit machines, then you will have to fully understand how segmentation works. As with the Archimedes system mentioned above, these quirks ensure that low level languages are totally incompatible with one another.

The instruction pointer register. As in the RISC-based processor discussed earlier in this chapter, the 8086 makes use of a **pipelined** architecture (see page 61). Separate parts of the chip fetch the instructions while another part of the chip executes a different instruction at the same time. If the results of one instruction are needed before another has been finished, then the chip will go into a wait state until the result has been worked out (a very short period of time in practice). The instruction pointer register contains the offset of the next instruction to be executed.

The pointer and **index registers.** These registers provide offsets that are used in conjunction with the segment registers to access parts of the memory.

The status register. This contains the flags that indicate the processor status at any particular time.

The assembly process. The features here will make use of **Microsoft's MASM assembler ver 5.1.**

Unlike the Archimedes, the Microsoft version is more standard. However, as with the Archimedes version, you would generate your source code by making use of a suitable editor. On a PC machine you could make use of your usual word processor put into ASCII mode.

From figure 5.22 you can see that there are a number of different files involved in the assembly process. The files required, together with the appropriate MSDOS extensions might be as shown in the following sections.

A very simple program. Setting the time is a standard operation on many micros. As with most low-level languages, operations like this involve loading registers with certain numbers, and then calling the appropriate routine from the operating system.

On the PC system this would involve putting the hours, minutes, seconds and centiseconds (i.e. hundredths of a second) into the registers CH, CL, DH and DL respectively, then putting the code 2D hex into the AL register, and calling the software interrupt number hex 21. The time given by the variables would then be set.

It is necessary to **push** the AX, CX and DX registers (i.e. the 16-bit versions of the accumulator etc.) on to the stack *before* the interrupt is called, and then restore these registers by **popping** the contents off the stack at the end of the procedure. (See page 84 for stack operations.)

We will assume that the variables **hour, min, sec** and **csec** have already been set up. (If you have MASM or an alternative version of a PC assembler, then you could find out how to add routines which would accept appropriate input from the keyboard.) It should be obvious that the variables can take on any of the following values:

$$0 \leq \text{hour} \leq 23$$
$$0 \leq \text{min} \leq 59$$
$$0 \leq \text{sec} \leq 59$$
and
$$0 \leq \text{csec} \leq 99$$

The following 8086 assembly language code forms the backbone of the 'time set' procedure. Note that ';' is used to denote a comment.

```
;
; Procedure to set up the time
;
        PUSH    AX              ;Save registers on stack
        PUSH    CX
        PUSH    DX
;
        MOV     CH,hour         ;Load values for time
        MOV     CL,min
        MOV     DH,sec
        MOV     DL,csec
;
        MOV     AH,2DH          ;Select time option
;
        INT     21H             ;Call the interrupt to set the time
;
        POP     DX              ;Restore the registers
        POP     CX
        POP     AX
```

As with the Archimedes example earlier in this section, the above code would not work in isolation, there would need to be other additions such as directives etc. However, without going into unnecessary detail, we will assume that the above code is complete. The purpose of this exercise is to concentrate more on the assembly process itself.

Assembling the program. The code, together with all the directives etc. which have not been shown, would be saved on disk with an appropriate file name and an extension of **ASM** to denote the assembly source code. If we call the program **Time**, then the file could have been saved as:

Time.ASM

Suppose that you want to assemble the program straight away. At the MSDOS prompt you could simply type the name of the assembler you are using. As you are using MASM, you would type:

C>MASM

You might see a message like the following:

Microsoft ® Macro Assembler Version 5.10
Copyright © Microsoft Corp 1981, 1989. All rights reserved.
Source filename [.ASM]:_

After typing in 'Time', you would get the following response:

Source filename [.ASM]:
Object filename [Time.OBJ]:_

i.e. the computer has come up with the default suggestion of Time.OBJ for the object code. In general, the following files are required by MASM.

The minimum requirement would be:

(a) The **source code** (i.e. the original code created on your editor or word processor),

    e.g.   My_Prog.ASM

(b) The **object code** (the code that will eventually run on the machine; it is produced by the assembler)

    e.g.   My_Prog.OBJ

In addition you ought to have:

(c) A **listing** (i.e. a file which can help you to debug your programs by looking at some hard copy),

    e.g.   My_Prog.LST

In addition you might have:

(d) A **macro file** (if you are using the macro facility),

    e.g.   My_Prog.MAC

(e) An **include file** (e.g. a file containing some important data),

    e.g.   My_Prog.INC

There will also be other options which are too detailed for a first glance at MASM.

Therefore, a complete interactive dialogue for the Time program might be as follows:

On screen action	Notes
Source filename [.ASM]: **Time**	Time is the name of the program
Object filename [Time.OBJ]:	Default object code name
Source listing [NUL.LST]: **Time.LST**	List *is* required
Cross-reference [NUL.CRF]:	
50004 + 324006 bytes symbol space free	Assembly process under way
0 Warning errors	
0 Severe errors	No errors

The assembly process is now complete and you have a copy of Time.OBJ (the object code) and Time.LST (the listing) on disk. However, the object code does not contain executable code, and, as can be seen from figure 5.22, has to go through the **linking** process.

The linking process. The object code must now be translated by the linker into executable machine code. The linker would join together more than one of your programs if necessary, and resolve the external references if possible. It will also produce a listing if you have made this request. The **linker** is a *separate program from the assembler.* You usually have the choice of using the one that is supplied with your assembler, or going for a third party linker with perhaps more sophisticated facilities. For example, one type of linker from Borland enables you to handle 32-bit code for the 80386 and 80486 processors.

After the linking process has taken place, executable code will have been produced, with a file extension of EXE. This is the code that can be run directly as shown below.

Running the linker is very similar to running the assembler itself. Simply type its name from the MSDOS prompt:

On screen action	Notes
C> **Link**	Run the link
Microsoft ® Overlay Linker Version 3.65	
Copyright © Microsoft Corp 1983-1989.	
All rights reserved.	
Object modules [.OBJ]: **Time**	Specify Object code
Run file [Time.EXE]:	Default run file
List file [NUL.MAP]:	No map required
Libraries [.LIB]:	No libraries necessary

You have now created Time.EXE which can be run in the following way.

Running your program. Assuming that it works, this is the easy bit. You simply type the name of your program at the MSDOS prompt, i.e. if you are currently working on drive C, then you would proceed as follows:

    C> Time

Listings of the program would look very similar to those obtained from the Archimedes, i.e. a long list of numbers representing the memory locations, machine code instructions, the assembler mnemonics and the comments etc.

The thing to realise from the above is that the PC 8086 assembler more closely follows all the stages of the general principles outlined earlier in this section. The Archimedes has many similar ideas, but, as you have seen, the actual mechanics of the assembly process is quite different.

The details of the above are not important but you should now appreciate more fully how an assembler can help us to write programs in machine code using assembly language mnemonics and a host of other extra help facilities such as directives, pseudo-ops, listings and symbol tables.

Exercise 5.1

1. What is the difference between **machine code** and **assembly language**?

2. Why do **assembly-language programs** written for one type of machine *not run* on any other? Is it sometimes possible to do this?

3. Explain why **assembly-language instructions** are represented by **mnemonics**, and, making use of a typical example, describe why **four fields** are often used as the format for the representation of many assembly-language instructions.

4. What is the purpose of the following with regard to assembly-language programs?
   (a) **Op code**   (b) **Operands**
   (c) **Comments**.

5. Explain why different modes of addressing are often encountered within a particular assembly language, making *specific reference* to **immediate**, **direct**, **indirect** and **indexed addressing modes**.

6. Some microprocessor manufacturers have gone for a general-purpose register set, while others have kept specific registers. Comment on the advantages and disadvantages which each approach may bring.

7. Sometimes specific registers are often used, even in a more-general-purpose register set. One example is the **flag register**. Explain what is meant by a **flag register** and comment on *four different conditions* which may be brought to the programmer's attention by the use of this register.

8. An assembly-language instruction set may be broken down into major subsets such as the arithmetic, logical and control subsets, for example. Making use of the **arithmetical subset**, explain how two simple one-byte-twos-complement binary numbers may be added together. Your answer should make reference to *where* the original numbers may come from, and *where* the answer may be stored. If the resultant number is *too big* to fit into your chosen register, how would this be handled by the microprocessor?

9. Explain how a **mask** may be used to prevent alteration of the top three and bottom two digits in a one-byte register. How would you then proceed to set the remaining three digits to 1?

10. Carefully explain the difference between an **arithmetic** and a **logical shift operation**. Show, by making use of the 16-bit register in the following diagram, how the contents would be altered by the following operations.

I	I	I	I	0	0	0	0	I	I	I	I	0	0	0	0

(**Note** you should *start each operation using the bit pattern shown above*.)

   (a) **Logical shift left 3** places.
   (b) **Arithmetic shift left 3** places
   (c) **Logical shift right 3** places.
   (d) **Arithmetic shift right 3** places.

11. Explain, with examples, how logical operations such as 'AND' and 'OR' may be carried out making use of registers within a processor.

12. Explain the *difference* between a **conditional** and an **unconditional jump** instruction by reference to a particular assembly-language instruction set with which you are familiar.

13. What is the function of the **stack-pointer register** within an assembly-language program?

14. What is an **assembler**, and why is it desirable to make use of one when programming in assembly language? Outline the main *advantages* from a programmer's point of view when an assembler is used.

15. Why are there different types of assembler? Make reference to the use of **meta assemblers** and **cross assemblers** in your answer.

16. A **loader** is often used during the assembly process – what is it and why is it useful?

17. Explain the terms **macro assembler**, **macro**, and **library routines** with regard to an assembly language program.

18. Give a typical scenario in which a **debugger** would prove *particularly useful* in finding **run-time bugs** in an assembly language program.

19. It's essential to have links between operating-system routines and assembly-language programs. Why is this the case and what advantages are to be found when making use of routines provided by the operating system?

20. If you have an assembler at school or college, make use of it to program the following tasks.
   (a) Read a character in from the keyboard and print it out on the screen.
   (b) Read in some characters in upper case and print them out in lower case.

End of chapter summary

- *All* activity within any computer system is ultimately broken down into **operations** involving **binary digits**.
- **Machine code** is the **binary-digit language** of a particular **machine** (*computer*).
- **Machine code** is *unique* to a particular **processor** (**microprocessor**).
- **Programming** in **machine code** is a *tedious*, *time consuming* and *error-prone* task. **Assembly language** is normally used instead.
- **Assembly language** makes use of **mnemonics** which r*epresent individual machine-code instructions*.
- **Machine code** and **assembly language** are called **low-level languages** because they are close to what's happening inside the computer at a **low** (*fundamental*) level.
- A **mnemonic** is simply an **aid to the memory**. It's *easier to remember* than the equivalent group of binary digits.
- **Assembly language** *will only work on the processor for which it has been designed.* (Assuming that another processor is not being used to emulate it!)
- A particular **family** of **microprocessors** usually characterises the main **hardware** of particular machines. For example, Intel – IBM PC or Motorola – Apple Mac.
- An **instruction set** is the **set of instructions** (*commands available*) for a particular assembly language.
- Instruction sets can be broken down into **major subsets** such as **arithmetical**, **logical** and **control instructions** etc.
- *Each* **assembly-language** instruction is given a *unique* **op code** or **operation code**.
- An **operation code** is the name given to the **binary code** (*machine code*) which represents a particular assembly-language instruction.
- Each microprocessor type will have a **set of registers** which is unique.
- A **register** is a place *inside* a **microprocessor** used for the **temporary storage** of patterns of **binary digits**.
- Some microprocessors have **general-purpose register sets** while others have registers *dedicated* to particular tasks.
- **Dedicated registers** are those such as **stack pointers**, **accumulators, flags** and **index registers**, for example.
- The **address-bus size** *is* important because it affects the *amount* of **external memory** which can be **addressed** by the processor.
- The **data-bus size** *is* important because it affects *how much data* can be transferred between the processor and memory *at the same time*. It thus affects the *speed of* **data transfer**.
- **Memory** is usually addressed in **byte-sized** chunks. This often makes what's going on a little more complex to understand.
- A typical **assembly-language instruction** is usually split up into *four parts* called **fields**, namely the **label**, **op code**, **operands** and **comments** fields.
- Only the **op code** field is *compulsory*, although the **operands field** is also used in most assembly-language instructions.
- The **op code** field contains the **mnemonic** which represents the **operation code**.
- The **operands field** contains the *source* and *destination* information for the data.
- A **comment field** is *ignored by the computer* when the program is run, and is documentation for the convenience of the programmer.
- The **label field** contains a **symbolic address** used for **jumps**, for example.
- A **symbolic address** is where a **label** represents the address of a **storage location**.
- Most microprocessors have some common **modes of addressing**. This refers to the ways in which data can be accessed or transferred in the system.
- **Immediate addressing** is where the *data to be used* follows **immediately** *after the op code* for the instruction.
- **Direct addressing** is where the contents of a memory location can be **addressed directly** from an instruction, usually making use of a **symbolic address**.
- **Indirect addressing** is where the contents of another register contains the actual address to be used for accessing the data, i.e. the instruction gets the address for the data indirectly from this other register.
- **Indexed addressing** is where a number contained in an **index register** is used in combination with some other address or addresses to determine the final address.
- **Indexed addressing** can be used to implement **arrays** and other **data structures** within memory.
- Other **modes of addressing** exist, but are usually combinations of the types already mentioned, and are less important to remember.

■ The **flag register** holds important information regarding the status of activity within the processor. For example, has an overflow occurred?

■ **Arithmetical operations** within an assembly language are instructions like **ADD**, **SUB**, **MUL** and **DIV** etc. which represent the basic arithmetic operations.

■ **Arithmetic operations** can usually be carried out in **binary**, **hex**, **decimal** and **BCD** etc.

■ **Logical operations** are operations such as **AND**, **OR**, **XOR** and **NOT** etc.

■ A **shift operation** can be split up into **arithmetic** and **logical shifts**.

■ A **logical shift** moves the digits **left** or **right** *replacing the vacated spaces with zeros*.

■ An **arithmetical shift** moves the digits **left** or **right**, but the **sign bit** must be *altered if necessary* to maintain the *arithmetical sense* of the number.

■ **Rotate operations** move the digits **left** or **right** within a register, but *feed one end into the other*, *instead* of filling up with zeros or ones.

■ **Bit set** and **reset instructions** enable register contents or memory locations to be set or reset according to various conditions. Individual bits can be altered if **masking** is used, or if the register is designed specifically for this (e.g. the flags).

■ **Masking** is where part of the original data is *protected from alteration* by a particular process.

■ **Program control instructions** contain instructions such as **conditional** and **unconditional** jumps etc.

■ An **unconditional jump** is where **control is passed** to some other part of the program **unconditionally**.

■ A **conditional jump** is where **control is passed** to some other part of the program *only if* a particular condition has been met.

■ A **stack** is an **area of memory** *set up to hold addresses* needed by the processor to **return** to places from where the *sequential operation of the program was interrupted*.

■ A **stack pointer** is a special-purpose register set up to maintain what's happening to the stack.

■ **CALL** and **RETURN** instructions are used to **transfer control** to **sub-routines** contained at different memory locations. *It's up to the programmer to maintain the stack.*

■ A **sub-routine** is the name given to a self-contained part of the program which executes a particular task. It helps to split up the program into smaller modules.

■ An **assembler** is a **piece of software** which *converts* the **assembly-language mnemonics** *into* the **machine code** which will *actually run* on the computer.

■ The **assembler** provides *much* more extra help than just a simple conversion service.

■ The **assembly-language program** is usually built up by *typing the assembly-language mnemonics* into a **text editor** (a simple word processor).

■ The **assembly-language code** from the text editor is called the **source code**.

■ After being **assembled** (*converted into machine code*), the resulting program from the assembler is called the **object code**.

■ The **machine** (or microprocessor) on which the **object code** *is intended to be run* is called the **target machine**.

■ An **assembler** enables **symbolic addressing** to be used.

■ An **assembler** enables **listings** of the program to be produced easily.

■ An **assembler** will help with **trapping errors** within a program.

■ An **assembler** works out all the **jump references** to labels.

■ Most **assemblers** enable **macros** (one instruction replacing a sequence of others) to be used.

■ An **assembler** provides **assembler directives** (or **pseudo operations**) which enable the programmer to achieve a variety of tasks with ease. Examples would be selecting particular modes of operation, defining the start and stop of a macro or assigning values to particular labels etc.

■ A **resident assembler** is one that will *only run* on the **target machine**.

■ A **cross assembler** is able to assemble code to run on a different machine.

■ A **macro assembler** is one which supports **macros**, i.e. it enables a key word (the macro name) to be replaced with a whole section of code if needed.

■ A **meta assembler** is one which can deal with different instruction sets.

■ A **loader** is a piece of **software** which *loads* the **object code** into memory in the correct place.

■ A **linking loader** is a **loader** that is *able to link together programs that have been assembled separately*. This is, of course, useful for getting your own **pre-written** routines and other **library routines** joined together, for example.

- The **assembly-language process** involves the following stages:
  (1) A **clear statement of the problem** using appropriate techniques (see chapter 7)
  (2) **Code the problem** using a **text edito**r.
  (3) **Assemble** the program.
  (4) Correct any **errors** if necessary.
  (5) **Link**, then **add macros** if necessary
  (6) Any **execution errors** will involve going back to stage (2).
- A **debugger** is the name given to a piece of **software** which helps to **debug** (get the bugs out of) your **assembly-language program**.
- A **debugger** often allows you to *step through the program*, and *analyse the contents of registers* etc. **after the execution of each instruction**. Without these utilities it would often be impossible to check what's happening when the **object code** is run.
- Operating system functions (see page 369) may usually be **CALL**ed from *within* **assembly-language programs**. These often enable the assembly-language programmer to carry out mundane tasks such as *reading a character from the keyboard*, for example, **without having to write the code themselves**.

6 High-level-language principles

Introduction

An overview

What a fabulous contribution **high-level languages** have made in the field of computing. Without them we would still be programming computers with **low-level languages** like the **machine code** and **assembly languages** covered in the last two chapters. Without high-level languages the development of the computer would literally be decades behind the current levels of performance, and it is indeed to the last few decades that we must look if we are to understand how current practices in the 1990s have evolved, and how these practices look set to take us into the 21st century – but first, let's see why these high-level languages are so very important.

When humans solve a problem we normally operate in a very different way to the way in which a machine would operate to solve the same kind of problem. It is difficult and unnatural for most people to have to specify how their problems are to be solved in the often-tedious machine-code forms. The further we can get away from the **binary digits** and **registers** used in the computer's architecture the better it will be, especially if the path taken gets us closer to the way in which humans prefer to think. Such human-oriented methods might include **mathematics**, **logic**, **English-like statements,** or indeed *any method that enables us to communicate concisely and elegantly with the computer* without having to 'speak' to the computer in its own primitive low-level language. (Don't forget that the computer's language may be primitive – but what you can achieve with it is not!)

Human or machine oriented?

A **high-level language** is, therefore, a *more-convenient way for humans to communicate sets of instructions to the computer.* High-level languages are often said to be **problem-specific** rather than **machine-specific** languages. However, you must remember that the computer still operates by manipulation of binary digits, and therefore these high-level languages must eventually be **translated** into a form that the machine will be able to understand. A high-level language must be able to be expressed in both **human-readable** *and* **machine-readable** format. This important translation process is covered in detail in chapter 10. Unlike the machine code and assembly languages which depend very much on a particular machine architecture, high-level languages are *meant to be* **portable**. This means that they can be used on different computers with different architectures, but total portability is rarely achieved in practice.

Natural and formal languages

The term **language** is used in *exactly the same way* as it is in French, German or Spanish, for example. However, due to current limitations of computer hardware and software, computer languages are much more restrictive. **Human languages** such as English and French belong to a class of **context-sensitive languages** or **natural languages**. This is because the **meaning (semantics)** of these languages depend upon the context being used, and not just the **legal arrangement (syntax)** of the words. For example, the sentence -

'If fat Fred wins this race I'll eat my hat!'

does not literally mean that the person concerned will eat his or her hat. It has to be taken in the context of a phrase that is often used to express an opinion which, in this particular example, is that in the opinion of the speaker, poor-old Fred has not got very much hope of winning the race. **Computer languages** are **context free** *which means that they are more easy to analyse by machine.* Each line of a program **(set of instructions)** must be **precisely defined** so that it is **unambiguous** – we are still a very long way indeed from being able to talk to a computer system which will allow for all the idiosyncrasies in our context-sensitive languages. **Context-free languages** (i.e. computer-type languages) are also known as **formal languages**.

Software engineering

Over the last few decades computer-based languages have undergone many transformations. *No longer are they simply methods for conveniently communicating with the computer* – the best high-level languages have now become part of a whole new **design philosophy** which embraces what is called **software engineering**. This methodology not only considers how software should be used to solve problems, but the wider and equally-important aspects of **analysis**, **debugging**, **testing** and **documentation**. It is no longer enough in professional systems to simply present the user with a program that works. Not only do the users of our systems deserve and expect continuing support over the years, but the systems themselves have now become so complex that there is *no sensible alternative strategy currently available.*

High-level-language development

It's interesting, enlightening and important to realise that the long path of high-level-language development has been neither straight nor smooth. Political decisions, monetary considerations and circumstance have had just as great an impact on development as advances in methodology! Take the language 'C', for example, although a superb language in its own right, it has proved to be very popular *because* it was intimately connected with **Unix** – which was, and still is, one of the most powerful operating-system platforms. Many languages have come and gone because they were not accepted in tightly-controlled hardware and operating-system environments. You should also realise that people are quite naturally reluctant to re-learn methods just because a different language comes along. This is one of the main reasons why COBOL has reigned supreme for such a very long time – the enormous investment in programs already written and the number of programmers that have been appropriately trained must be astounding. There must be very compelling reasons indeed for the professionals to start again with a new language. It is also important to realise that languages pass through **stages of evolution**. Most languages which have stood the test of time have probably been re-defined (usually by adding new and better features) at least several times.

High-level languages started to be developed in the early-to-mid 1950s when **FORTRAN** and **COBOL** were introduced on **mainframe** computers. (*Most* of the high-level languages mentioned in this chapter *will be looked at* briefly in chapter 8.) It is indeed a tribute to both of these languages that they are still thriving today, unlike hundreds of other languages of much-later origin which have quietly passed away into oblivion. COBOL is still *the* data processing language and FORTRAN 90 is still widely used for engineering and scientific purposes. **ALGOL** was also an important language developed in the 1950s because so many of the more modern languages such as C and C++, for example, are developed from it.

During the 1960s computer technology continued to grow at an amazing pace, and high-level-language development tried to emulate the same lightning-fast progress. Computer scientists of the time had a dream that an all-purpose language could be developed which encompassed all the desirable attributes of COBOL, FORTRAN and ALGOL – but this was never to be – it was far too complex a project for the available level of knowledge and the technology of the time. Also, spurred on by the enormous profits that were being made by the developers of the successful languages, many other special-purpose languages were developed during this decade. One of the several languages to survive this 1960s chaotic-development phase is **BASIC**, which in its latest incarnation is still popular, mainly in a non-professional capacity.

The 1970s saw a swing in the opposite direction. Complexity was out of the window and consistency and common platforms were of paramount importance. **Pascal** is an example of one of the better-structured languages to emerge in the 1970s, and is still going strong today where it has often been used as a teaching language alternative to BASIC. C and FORTH were also developed in the 70s, with 'C' often being referred to as a **middle-level language** because of the comprehensive low-level-language support available from within it.

The 1980s has seen a consolidation of the better methods of the 1970s, and the continuing emergence of fundamentally different methodologies. A better version of **LISP** made this language more predominant than it was in previous versions, and the logical language **Prolog** was developed further. **Object-oriented language methods** were becoming increasingly attractive and this has led to the development of **C++** (a different language to C although most of C is a subset of C++) which is currently *the* most popular programming language for **systems development**. I strongly recommend that all students should have a go at C++ at some stage during their advanced courses – C++ is extremely easy to use for doing basic things, and objects themselves are easily within the scope of competent programmers at 'A' level.

What's going to happen in the late 1990s is obviously impossible to tell, but it looks like the object-oriented methods are helping to solve many of the current problems with complex systems programming. Therefore, until something better comes along, consolidation of this methodology with the best of the rest seems the most-likely scenario.

Generations of languages

Software, like hardware, can be classified into **generations** according to major changes in methodology. Nevertheless, not too many people applied (or even knew of!) these terms until **SQLs** (see page 480) and the like were commonly called **4GLs** or **fourth-generation languages**. The natural question to ask is 'What on earth were the previous three?' Unfortunately, not everybody agrees on all of these definitions!! Nevertheless, it is now more-generally accepted that the following levels of abstraction apply.

Low-level languages like **assembly language** and **machine code** are the **first-generation-languages**. (A bit of an insult to the latest assemblers! – C'est la vie.)

The **second-generation languages** are the **unstructured** high level languages like the *early versions* of *FORTRAN* and *BASIC*. (Some definitions include assembly language as second generation with high-level languages being the third.)

The **third-generation languages** are the **structured** high-level languages like the current versions of *Pascal* and *C*. (Some definitions include all high-level languages as third generation.)

The **fourth-generation languages** are languages with the all-powerful commands like the **SQLs** considered on page 480, or the languages that *accompany* **spreadsheets** and a whole host of other **applications**. Commands such as '**SORT**' are a lot easier than *writing your own sort procedures* using *third-generation languages*. However, *most* 4GLs are very specific in the tasks that they can easily perform.

Fifth-generation languages are languages like **Prolog** (see page 167) which are often regarded as *very-high-level languages*, but **expert systems** (see page 557), often written in Prolog, also belong to this class of language definition.

The terms **4GLs** and the **fifth-generation languages** are a little bit fuzzy to apply as many people in authority often refer to some of these languages as 'so-called 4GLs' etc. The situation is also not helped by manufacturers making wild claims making use of these terms – perhaps it will all be sorted out by the fourth edition of this book!

Although the labels for each generation of language might be slightly fuzzy, *what is important* is to realise that languages have gone through a slow metamorphosis starting with **machine code**, then proceeding through **assembly language** and all the different versions of the **high-level languages**, to arrive at today's extremely-powerful **object-oriented languages** and other equally-successful methodologies (see in a moment).

Different language classes

Over the last few decades hundreds of different high-level languages have been developed, but fortunately it is possible to *categorise* these different high-level languages by consideration of the *main organising principles* used by the designers of the language. The posh term for these basic organising principles is called a '**paradigm**'. There are four different paradigms considered in this book, and the ideas behind them are outlined in the next few sections.

Imperative languages

BASIC, **FORTRAN** and **Pascal** for example, and indeed most conventional high-level languages are examples of what are called **imperative languages** or **procedural languages**. Make a special note of the fact that an **imperative**, for the purpose of computer languages, refers to an **expression of command** – so imperative languages typify those languages in which *sequences of commands* (called **imperatives**) are given. This derives from the English-language grammatical use of the word imperative – denoting the mood of verbs used in commands.

Imperative languages typify telling a computer '**how to do something**' rather than telling the computer '**what to do**'. With an imperative language the programmer writes a *sequence of instructions* which are obediently carried out by the computer. Conventional programming is based to a large extent on **imperative languages**, but this has led to some unfortunate restrictions which are now being overcome by the use of *different* organising principles (**paradigms**).

Declarative languages

Prolog, for example, (**Programming** in **log**ic) typifies a very different approach, (a totally different paradigm) and this is just one of the reasons why it's sometimes called a fifth-generation language or a very-high-level language. When programming using Prolog, problems are expressed in terms of **structured objects** and the **relationships** between them. For example, we could type in the following two 'facts'

```
male (ray_bradley)
owns (ray_bradley, ferrari)
```

which mean that Ray Bradley is a male and owns a Ferrari (I should be so lucky – well, at least I'm male!). Sets of statements (or **clauses** as they are known in Prolog) like those given above can be used to describe relationships. Prolog can then answer questions (or **queries**) about the relationships which have just been defined. For example, typing the query

```
? male (ray_bradley)
```

asks the question 'Is Ray Bradley male?' – and pressing return on the keyboard would cause Prolog to answer (hopefully!)

```
yes
```

Notice that we have written *no loops or selection procedures*, and we have written *no code which tells the computer how to handle the input*. All that is needed are sets of **clauses declaring** the properties of the problem, then we are ready to run the program. For this reason languages which operate in this way are called **declarative languages. Declarative languages** typify the **'what to do'** rather then the 'how to do it' method, and although the above example is extremely simple, it does show how programs may be written in this alternative way. Further examples of Prolog can be found in the chapter on high-level language examples on page 167.

Object-oriented languages

An increasingly important strategy (**paradigm**) is the use of **object-oriented languages**. C++, for example, makes extensive use of **objects** (see page 162), which can be used to great effect in minimising mistakes in extremely complex systems. An **object** is really a single unit which encapsulates *both* **functions** and **data**. Although this does not sound too revolutionary to the uninitiated at this stage, a sizeable chunk of chapter 8 is devoted to the language C++ where these vitally important principles are explained in some detail.

Functional languages

Functional languages or **applicative languages** as they are sometimes known make use of the final **paradigm** (organising principle) to be considered in this book. (There are other **paradigms** and no doubt more will be invented in the future.) **LISP** is an example of a functional language and this type of organising principle involves **parameters** that are *passed to functions* from **expressions** which are being evaluated, and then these **values** are *returned from the functions* to the calling **expression**. Functional programming languages owe much to the ideas of functions borrowed from mathematics, and examples of functional programming making use of LISP can be found on page 169.

General principles of high-level languages

From reading the above you are probably thinking that most languages contain elements of some or all the fundamental paradigms mentioned – and indeed this would be true. For example, **functional programming** from the **applicative languages** is also used in today's **imperative languages** as in Prolog, for example. However, the categorisation in the previous few sections has taken place by considering the *overriding organising principles* on which a particular language is based.

As languages evolve, facilities are added to them which include elements of most of the four basic language classes outlined above – this is indeed the whole point of language evolution – the best of one type of language is often built into another type. You can also obviously simulate *any* organising principle in almost any language, but this is *not the same* as having these structures available to you at the most fundamental levels. Bear these important facts in mind as you progress through a tour of all the languages mentioned in this introductory section.

Recall that the *main purpose* of a high-level language is to enable humans to communicate their ideas to the computer in **human-readable form**, and be a vehicle for turning these ideas into codes in a **machine-readable form**. High-level languages do this by creating **abstract concepts** which can eventually be turned into **machine code** programs. These abstract concepts are usually built up from the basic **character set,** and expressed in terms of special **reserved words** (or **keywords**), **constants** and special symbols etc. (all of these terms are explained very shortly). The **words** (or **tokens**) used to make up the language are used later by the compiler when the time comes to process the language instructions during the **parse phase**. (See chapter 10.) It is in this way that the code gets turned into **machine-readable form**.

High-level language constructs

The basic bricks from which a high level language is built are known as the **high-level language constructs**. In the next few sections when dealing with high-level language constructs **Pascal** will be used for many of the examples. Pascal has been chosen because it is still one of the *most popular and highly respected structured teaching language* used in most universities, colleges and schools, and is a language which has most of the desired attributes for modern programming methods. However, other languages such as **C++** or **BASIC**, for example, will also be used when special points need to be made. When reading the next few sections you should also note that computer-related text will be shown like this.

The syntax and semantics

You will probably be aware that the **syntax** (the *rules and regulations governing the layout* and **keywords** used etc.) of different high-level languages differ from one language to another because different **keywords** and **paradigms** (see page 105) have been chosen by the designers of the language. Nevertheless, high-level languages should *not* be so strange that conventional programmers would have difficulty in understanding what is going on. Therefore, whenever a new language is designed the designers must pay attention to current standards and methods. This is called conformity, and is one of the desirable attributes of all high-level languages (see page 170).

In addition to the **syntax** we must obviously be able to **understand what is meant** by routines written in different languages, or else we would not be able to use them to effectively convey our ideas to the computer. The **meaning** which we attach to the statements and the way in which they are used in the language is called **semantics**.

The character set

All high-level languages need **characters** such as **letters of the alphabet**, **digits** and other **special symbols** etc. which all help to form the **higher-level** concepts which may be expressed by using the language. (All these terms are explained in the next few sections.) A typical **character set** for the **Pascal** language is as follows:

    letters = { a b...y z A B...Y Z }
    digits = {0 1... 9}
    special symbols = {+ − * / := . , ; : = <> < <= >= > ( ) [ ] (* *) ^ ..}
    other symbols = {@ & # $! ... plus other ASCII characters not in special symbols}

Normally *any* **character** available from your keyboard may be used, but often symbols have special purposes in a high-level language. The special symbols used by **Pascal** are shown in the special-symbols set above.

Reserved or keywords

Reserved words (**keywords**) are examples of **identifiers** (see below) which are used by the language to represent words like '**if**', '**function**' or '**else**' etc. Different high-level languages have *different sets* of **reserved words**, but fortunately (remember **conformity**?) many of these are both similar in **syntax** and in the effects which they produce. This is one of the most important reasons for having a general overview of high-level languages. The programmer is *not allowed* to use **reserved words** in any other context. **Pascal** for example, has the following set of **reserved words**:

and	array	begin	case	const	div	do	downto	else
end	file	for	function	goto	if	in	label	mod
nil	not	of	or	packed	procedure	program	record	repeat
set	then	to	type	until	var	while	with	

Identifiers

An **identifier** is a string of one or more characters which *uniquely* **identifies** a data item or element of a program. Examples would be **constants**, **variables**, **functions** and **procedures**, **arrays**, and **records** etc. Other identifiers *can't usually clash* with **keywords**, because the meaning of the language would then be ambiguous. However, BBC BASIC V allows the use of identifiers with 'keyword names' as long as *lower case letters are used*, e.g. **print** would not be confused with **PRINT**. The **standard Pascal identifiers** are as follows, although some versions of Pascal have extra ones.

abs	arctan	boolean	char	chr
cos	dispose	eof	eoln	exp
false	get	input	integer	ln
maxint	new	odd	ord	output
pack	page	pred	put	read

readln	real	reset	rewrite	round
sin	sqr	sqrt	succ	text
true	trunc	unpack	write	writeln

It should be noted that the Pascal **standard identifiers** in the above list are simply placed in alphabetical order. They are usually further sub-divided into **constants**, **files**, **functions**, **procedures** and **types** according to the use to which they are put.

For example, the **functions** sub division would be

abs(x)	arctan(x)	chr(x)	cos(x)	eof(x)
eoln(x)	exp(x)	ln(x)	odd(x)	odd(x)
ord(x)	pred(x)	round(x)	sin(x)	sqr(x)
sqrt(x)	succ(x)	trunc(x)		

Functions

Although most of these are **functions** in the *mathematical* sense, (sin(x), for example), the term **function** should be considered *more generally than this*. In computing read the term **function** as something which *calls up the right subprogram during the compilation stage* (see page 200). **Functions** such as **eof(x),** for example, which determine if an end-of-file has been detected, make a little more sense when viewed in this light.

User-defined identifiers

The user may make up their own identifiers as long as the names do not clash with any **standard identifiers** or **reserved words** in the previous lists, and follow the set of rules (**syntax**) which has been laid down (see in a moment). Examples of user-defined identifiers (**constants** *or* **variables** *in this case*) might be:

balance_of_account   (Note *some earlier versions* of Pascal do not
foregroundcolour   allow the use of the underscore _ character.
perimeter   balance_of_account would not be allowed.)

We obviously can't go round making wild guesses as to what may or may not be valid identifiers in a particular high-level language, so it is therefore fortunate that the complete **syntax** (the grammatical rules for combining the elements we are now considering) for **Pascal** can be expressed efficiently in terms of what are called **syntax diagrams**. These diagrams are simple to use and an example for a **Pascal identifier** is shown in figure 6.1.

Pascal syntax diagram for an IDENTIFIER

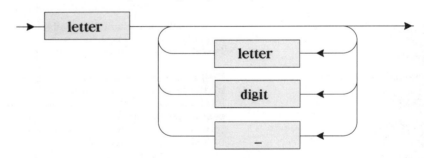

Figure 6.1

By following the arrows, legal identifiers can be built up. You can see instantly, for example, that the identifier

1stnumber

would be *illegal* in **Pascal** as it starts with a *digit* – and this is *not allowed*. By using the syntax diagram you can see that all identifiers must start with a letter, so

Firstnumber, Area_of_circle and monkeynuts

would all be legal. **Syntax diagrams**, together with the **BNF or extended BNF languages** for syntax definition (see chapter 7) convey what is and what is not legal in a particular high-level language. Syntax diagrams will be used extensively where they help illustrate principles throughout this chapter.

Returning to valid identifiers for a brief moment, programmers must often *beware of using very long identifier names*, as many compilers, (see page 200) although allowing the use of long variable names (as with Pascal), might only pay attention to the first eight characters, for example. If you are unfortunate enough to have a version of a high-level-language compiler which does this, then

statement_1, statement_2 and statement_3

would all be the same! This adds to the fun of programming – especially if you like whiling away hours of your valuable time debugging esoteric errors.

Variables

A **variable** is simply the name given to an **identifier** chosen by the user (obviously not clashing with any reserved words or standard identifiers) whose *value is allowed to vary* (change) during the execution of a program. In Pascal, variables must be declared at the beginning of the program by the use of the **reserved word 'var'** and a simple **variable declaration** (which also states the *type* of the **variables**) is shown in the following Pascal example.

```
var average : integer;
    compare : boolean;
```

The **syntax diagram** for a variable is *not shown* in this introductory session on variables as many types of variable are usually expressed in terms of other terminology such as field identifiers and expressions which would also have to be defined. The resulting syntax diagrams would get too large to be useful in helping to understand what is going on at this stage.

Constants

Constants represent things which don't vary such as '46.3' which represents a **numeric constant**, or 'The cat sat on the mat' which represents a **string constant.** *When used in this way* constants are also called **literals**, because they are *represented by their literal value* – i.e. a *value that is used to define itself!* However, a **constant** can also be represented by an **identifier** whose value is not allowed to change (i.e. a constant identifier) during the execution of a program. The **syntax diagram** for a **Pascal constant** is shown in figure 6.2.

Using this diagram and after reading about strings you should be able to see that

+46.3   45   -123   and   Porkpies

are all valid constants.

Pascal syntax diagram for a CONSTANT

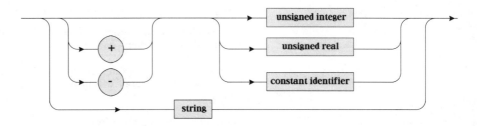

Figure 6.2

Constants have to be declared too at the beginning of a Pascal program, and a typical Pascal **constant declaration** example using (you've probably guessed it!) the reserved word **const** is as follows:

```
const maxnumber = 10;
      teststring = 'Testing 123';
```

Strings

A string is quite literally a **string of characters**. However, the compiler (see page 200) must have a way of knowing when a string ends, as spaces are usually allowed to make up part of the string. Most high-level languages therefore have what are called **delimiters** at the ends of the string, and the syntax diagram for a Pascal string is shown in figure 6.3.

From this syntax diagram you can see that Pascal allows the use of a delimiter within the string *only if* it is followed immediately by another delimiter character. If you want to use Pascal to print out 'I don't like soggy cabbage' for example, then you would use the statement

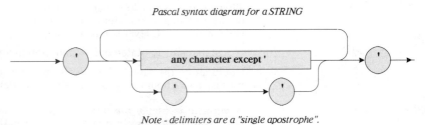

Pascal syntax diagram for a STRING

| any character except ' |

Note - delimiters are a "single apostrophe".

Figure 6.3

writeln('I don''t like soggy cabbage')

Note the *two apostrophes* next to each other inbetween the n and t of don't.

BASIC is unusual in that strings are *explicitly indicated* by the use of a dollar sign ($) on the end of the variable name, and do not have to be **declared** (i.e. explicitly stated either at the beginning or at some point throughout the program).

On the other hand, C++ for example, treats a string as **arrays** of type **char** (char being exactly the same as the numeric data type called char described in the table on page 111), i.e. C++ treats a string as a one-dimensional array of characters (which is what it is!). In C++ we can set up a string as follows:

char My_string[ ] = "This is what is inside the string"

In most versions of BASIC strings are limited to 255 characters, but in C++ and some versions of Pascal they can be much larger than this.

Statements

A **statement** in a high-level language is simply a descriptive phrase which generates one or more machine-code instructions. (Sometimes it's just a single line of program code but it's often more.) Statements are *further classified* according to what they do, and the examples show different statements in **Pascal**, together with the **statement types** assigned to them.

total := x + y + z;

This is called an **assignment statement** because the **assignment operator** ':=' is used to **assign** the value of **variables** x+y+z to the variable called total. Another example is

if number > 999 then writeln('The number just typed in is too big')

This is called a **conditional statement** (also known as an **if then** statement), because the code after the '**then**' part is executed only **if** the given **condition** (in this case number > 999) is true.

There are lots more examples that could be covered but different statement types will be looked at in detail within the section on **basic structures** covered later in this chapter.

Expressions

Programming languages often distinguish between **statements** and **expressions**. For example, '**x+y+z**' is an **arithmetic expression**, but, as we have seen in the last section, when included with an assignment operator, the line of code becomes a **statement**. In Pascal, for example, you can have a**rithmetic**, **Boolean**, **integer** and **real** expressions.

When using **arithmetic expressions** the order of precedence is of paramount importance. For example, x+y/z should be worked out by first dividing y by z, and then adding the result to x. The levels of precedence are used by the compiler (see page 211) so that expressions may be worked out with the minimum use of brackets. In Pascal, the levels of precedence correspond with those in normal arithmetic and are summarised in figure 6.4.

Data types

Different data types are of fundamental importance because they describe the nature of the data. For example, the **integer** and **floating point numbers** considered in chapter 3 are examples of just two different **data types**. Data types are important because they add to the **readability** of the program and make **maintenance much easier** (i.e. if the program needs to be altered at some later stage either by the original programmer or, more usually, by someone else). If a program is easier to maintain and read then it is also likely to be more reliable. With *well-defined data types* both

Precedence Level	Operators
1 (Highest)	*( )*
2	*not*
3	** / div mod and*
4	*+ - or*
5 (Lowest)	*= <> <= > >= in*

Figure 6.4

the **programmer** and the **compiler** (see page 200) can determine much more easily exactly what is going on within a program.

One of the many criteria by which a programming language may be judged (see page 170) is the number of data types that are supported. Some of the older languages which have *not* gone through many stages of development have relatively few data types. However, one of the reasons why languages like C++ and Pascal are so popular is because of the large variety of data types that are supported. Data types may range from the simple **integer numbers** available in most languages, via the **complex-number** types (real and imaginary numbers – see page 180) available in **FORTRAN**, to the advanced **objects** available in **C++**.

Numeric data types

Most modern high-level languages (**BASIC** is one of the exceptions) require that the programmer **declare** the **data types** – either at the beginning of, or at various points throughout the program. This *is so that the* **compiler** *can make sure that the correct variable types are being properly used.* Therefore, if a programmer wishes, for example, to **declare** that he or she is going to use *three numeric variables* called *x*, *y* and *z*, of which *x* and *y* are **integers** and *z* is a **floating point number**, then in C++, for example, this would be done by the following two **statements**

```
int x y;
float z;
```

We are making a small diversion into the C++ language here because the range of numeric data types available is considerable. They are summarised in figure 6.5.

C++ numeric data types		
Name	**Range**	
	From	**to**
char	*-128*	*127*
int	*-32,768*	*32,767*
short	*-32,768*	*32,767*
long	*-2,147,483,648*	*2,147,483,647*
float	3.4×10^{-38}	3.4×10^{38}
double	1.7×10^{-308}	1.7×10^{308}
long double	3.4×10^{-4932}	1.1×10^{4932}

Figure 6.5

Staying with the idea of numeric data types in the C++ language for a moment, as can be seen from the table there are seven different keywords used, and this gives an enormous variation in **precision** and **range** (see page 44).

There are also variations of the above such as **unsigned char**, for example, which gives a range of 0 to 255 instead of –128 to +127. As you can see, this range of numeric data types should prove to be adequate for most purposes. Compare the above range with that which is available in the BASIC language – you can see just one of the reasons why C++ is a more-professional choice of language.

In **Pascal**, variables also have to be **declared**, normally at the *beginning* of the program or in the procedure declaration (although pointer-data types are an exception to this general rule – see page 115). If we wish to achieve the same result in **Pascal** as we did with our integer and real numbers in declarations in C++, then we would use the alternative statements making use of the **reserved word var** as follows:

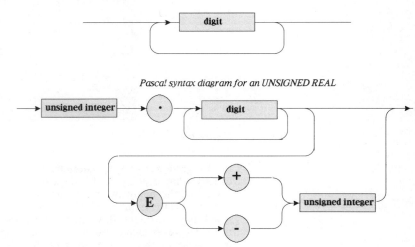

Figure 6.6

```
var x, y: integer;
var z; real;
```

Unsigned **integer** and **real-number** data types in Pascal are defined by the syntax diagrams shown in figure 6.6.

You should be able to work out from the above syntax diagrams that the following are valid unsigned-number formats in Pascal.

178 (unsigned integer) 12.653 (unsigned real) 6.4E-23 (unsigned real)

Other data types

Much of the power of any high level language stems from the *number* of **data types** that it can handle. We have just seen some numeric data types, but other types exist too. For example, **Pascal** has **array**, **boolean**, **char**, **enumerated**, **file**, **integer**, **pointer**, **real**, **record**, **set**, and **subrange** data types, and a version of object-oriented Pascal is now available.

Some languages, such as C++, for example, enable users to *define their own* data types – this leads to more efficient programming as the user is not constantly trying to bend the problem to be solved because they are making use of the limited range of data types which some languages allow. For example, try coding the **multiple-linked-list** and **tree data structures** (see page 297) using Pascal and you will find the job relatively simple. However, try using BASIC, and due to the lack of suitable data types you will find the job considerably more difficult, though by no means impossible. The **Pascal data type** categories are shown in figure 6.7.

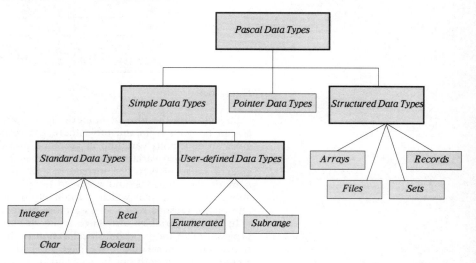

Figure 6.7

Exercise 6.1

1. Explain the *significance of* and the *need for* **high-level languages** in computing.

2. Why is there a need for *so many different types* of high-level language, and what is the difference between the following high-level language types?
   (a) **Imperative** (or procedural) languages
   (b) **Declarative** languages
   (c) **Functional** languages
   (d) **Object-oriented** languages

3. Why is the concept of **software engineering** so important in modern computing?

4. To which **generation** of language do the following belong?
   (a) **Pascal** and *structured* **BASIC**
   (b) 68000 **assembly language**
   (c) **Fortran** and **COBOL**
   (d) **Prolog**
   (e) *Non-structured* **BASIC**
   (f) A spreadsheet programming language

5. Define the following terms in the context of a high-level language giving *five legal examples* of each in a high-level language of your choice.
   (a) Variable
   (b) Identifier
   (c) Reserved word
   (d) Built-in mathematical function

6. (a) What is a syntax diagram?
   (b) Why are syntax diagrams useful for high-level language definitions?
   (c) Name an alternative method of language definition.

7. What is meant by a **data type** in a high-level language and why is it useful to have strictly-defined data types?

8. In a language of your choice *briefly* describe the syntax of the following statements:
   (a) for loop
   (b) while loop
   (c) repeat until loop

9. In a high-level language of your choice make a complete list of the **data types** available to you, and make another list (similar to that shown on page 111) of the **name** and **range** of the **numeric data types** available in the same language.

10. Compare and contrast the use of the following data types
    (a) Boolean
    (b) Integer
    (c) Real
    (d) String

Other simple data types

The **Char (string)**, **integer** and **real-number** data types already considered earlier in this section are examples of what Pascal refers to as simple data types. Other data types consisting of multiple data items such as **arrays** and **files** are called **structured data types** and are considered later. In the remainder of this section we will complete our lightning-quick tour of Pascal's remaining simple data types.

Boolean data types

Boolean data types represent values that can *only be* **true** or **false**. In **Pascal**, **true** is encoded as **1** and **false** is encoded as **0**. Boolean variables are most often combined with the Boolean operators such as **AND**, **OR** and **NOT** (see page 79) to form **Boolean expressions** (or **Boolean conditions**) which take on true or false values. For example, suppose that an integer variable called x has a value of 99 – then (x > 10) would be true. Also, (x < 10) OR (x = 10) would be false as both (x < 10) and (x = 10) are false. It's interesting to note that C++ has no Boolean data type, with the integer values 0 and 1 being used instead. These Boolean conditions are an essential part of the **control** and **selection structures** considered later in this chapter, and are therefore an *essential part* of structured programming techniques.

Enumerated data types

As far as computing is concerned, '**enumerate**' means to *go through a list*. It is not surprising, therefore, to find that **enumerated data types** consist of **lists of data items**. The classic examples make use of 'days of the week', or 'months of the year' etc., but any values (words) may be inserted in the list.

In **Pascal**, we can define an **enumerated data type** (using the **reserved word type**) which represents 'abbreviated months of the year' as follows:

```
type months = (jan,feb,mar,apr,may,jun,jul,aug,sep,oct,nov,dec);
```

The brackets and commas used for separation indicate to the compiler that this is an enumerated data type. Here it is *only possible* for the values '**jan**' or '**feb**' etc. to be *associated with* the **variable** called **months**. Any value not in the list will cause an error. Numbers are assigned with the data items, and in the above example, 0 would be assigned to 'jan', 1 to 'feb' and so on up to 11 for 'dec'.

Take good note of the fact that even though we have different items in the list this is *still* a **simple data structure** because the data items can't be altered during the execution of the program. To add another item to the list would require **re-editing** and **re-compiling** the **source code** (see page 201).

Being an ordered list we can use **Boolean expressions** on **enumerated data types**. For example,

jan < feb   would be   true

this leads to very efficient coding of problems involving, for example, chronological order.

Subrange data types

A **subrange data type** is simply referring to a sub range (i.e. part) of the original range in an enumerated data type. Using the months example again for the enumerated data type, if

```
type months    = (jan,feb,mar,apr,may,jun,jul,aug,sep,oct,nov,dec);
     summer     = jun..aug
     autumn     = sep..nov
```

then summer (being defined as jun, jul and aug) and autumn (being defined as sep, oct and nov) are examples of subrange data types.

Structured data types

All the data types considered so far, as can be seen from figure 6.7, belong to the **simple-data-type category**. However, there are also **structured data types** such as **arrays**, and **files** etc. which can have multiple data items that are related to one another in terms of the definition of the **structure** being used. Pascal has four **structured data types** and these are briefly considered in the next few sections.

Arrays

Fundamental concepts of this important data type are covered in detail in the **data-structures** chapter. However, an array called 'fred' consisting of a *one-dimensional* set of 100 real numbers may be declared in Pascal by use of the following syntax:

```
var fred :array [1..100] of real;
```

Multidimensional arrays are also no problem in Pascal, and a three-dimensional array called 'bert' consisting of a 10 by 10 by 10 matrix of integer numbers can be set up with the following syntax:

```
var bert :array [1..10, 1..10, 1..10] of integer;
```

The only restriction here, as in most high-level languages, is that the array elements must always consist of the same data type, and you are obviously limited by the amount of available RAM. For example, suppose a three-dimensional array containing 100 numbers in each dimension were to be set up where each entry in the array is a real number. Assuming that a real number is stored making use of 4 bytes of memory, (see page 35 where the storage of numbers is considered) then you would need 4 Mbytes of RAM to store this item of data!

Subscripted variables

Reference to any element in an array is usually accomplished by means of a **subscripted variable**. For example, to set the 9th element of 'one-dimensional fred' mentioned above to 3.16 we would use

```
fred[9] := 3.16;
```

To print the last element of three-dimensional bert we could use

```
writeln('The last value of bert is ' , bert[10,10,10]);
```

The part in brackets which is tacked onto the variable name is known as a **subscript** – hence the variable is known as a **subscripted variable**.

Set data types

Pascal allows you to define sets in the normal mathematical sense (i.e. a group of objects belonging to the same set). A set can relate to any user-defined objects from days of the week via letters of the alphabet to colours of the rainbow. For example, when defining a set of upper-case letters we could make use of the **reserved words** **var** and **type** in the following way.

```
type letters = set of char;
var upper_case : letters;
```

The set definition itself, together with the definition of a set of vowels and the generation of a set of consonants takes place in the short program that follows. Note that the sets do *not* have to be ordered (i.e. in the order a..z as defined in the above case).

```
type letters = set of char;
var upper_case,vowels,consonants : letters;

begin
    upper_case := ['A'..'Z'];
    vowels := ['A','E','I','O','U'];
    consonants := upper_case − vowels;
end.
```

As the upper-case consonants are simply the upper-case letters minus the vowels, we have used the operation of set difference ((−) in Pascal) to generate a set with upper case consonants as the elements within it. Note that the operations of **union (+)**, **intersection (*)** and **set difference (-)** (all these set operations having the same meaning as in elementary mathematics) can be used to operate on the sets.

Record data types

Records are looked at in more detail in chapter 16 when file handling is covered. However, suppose we want to set up a list (i.e. an array) containing 500 customer-account records. Let's also suppose that we want the customer number, name and balance to be stored as fields (see page 339) within each record. The following code makes use of the **reserved words type**, **var** and **record**.

```
type account = record
                number : integer;
                name : char;
                balance : real
              end;
var customer : array [1..500] of account;
```

would be one possible way of setting up the system. Here **customer[10]** would be the **record** belonging to the 10th customer, or **customer[20].name** (note the dot) refers to the **name field** (i.e. the actual name) *of* the **20th customer**.

You may be wondering where the syntax diagrams have gone, but the appropriate syntax diagrams have got a little too large to be included here. If you have got access to a Pascal compiler then you can consult the manual if you are interested. The syntax diagram for 'type' would not help too much at this stage to explain further the concept of a record structure.

An important point can now be made which is especially poignant if you are used to programming in BASIC. Notice how much easier it is to handle records when appropriate data types are available from within the language. Record handling *can* be done in BASIC by the use of pointers and string functions, but it's messy compared to having the dedicated structure of Pascal or COBOL for example.

File data types

Files (also covered in chapter 16) are essential to any language and are obviously intimately connected with the record data types described in the last section. A file may be defined in Pascal using the following syntax:

```
var file_name : file of type
```

If we use the same structure as for the record in the previous section then

```
type account = record
                number : integer;
                name : char;
                balance : real
              end;
var customer : file of account;
```

would be one possible way of setting up a file consisting of N records each having the field structure outlined above. The number N here would depend on the disk capacity of the system and does not have to be specified.

Pointer data types

Lists and **pointers** are slightly more complex, but are extensively covered in chapter 14. The Pascal **pointer data type** may be used to set up **linked lists**, **circular lists**, **queues** and **trees** etc. with relative ease. Unlike arrays and sets, pointer data types, like files, do not consist of fixed lists, but may be expanded given the limitation of available memory (or disk space in the case of most files). In this context **files** and **pointers** are called **dynamic data structures**, whereas **arrays** and **sets**, for example, are examples of **static data structures**. A dynamic data structure may have its size altered during the execution of a program, but static data structures can't be altered during execution of a program.

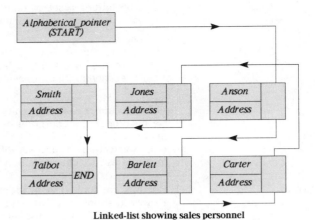

Linked-list showing sales personnel

Figure 6.8

Consider the simple linked list shown in figure 6.8. This shows six sales personnel with the names and addresses shown at each node (see page 304). In practice much more information than name and address would probably be stored. However, as far as programming with pointers is concerned, each element in the list consists essentially of *two* important pieces of information represented by variables. Firstly, there is the **pointer variable** which points to the next element in the list, and secondly, the **referenced variable**, which is the variable which is being pointed at.

Note, however, that the **referenced variable** may be a **structured type** containing *lots of different information*. (For example, it contains a 'pointer', 'name' and 'address' in this particular case.)

In Pascal, **dynamic variables** are treated in a slightly different way to **static variables** and have to be *declared in those parts of the programs which alter them*. This is because these variables can be created and destroyed (by inserting and removing items from linked lists) dynamically, unlike static variables which exist throughout the duration of the program, and use the conventional declaration methods outlined much earlier. The **standard identifier** called '**new**' can be used to create a new referenced variable as follows:

    new(alpha_pointer)

Any pointer name will do, but alpha_pointer has been used to correspond with the linked list in figure 6.8. The variable type will also have to be declared and for this particular example, this can be accomplished by using:

    type alpha_ptr = ^sales

You can see the use of this pointer-data-type definition in the following *part* of a Pascal program. Note that (*comments are like this in Pascal*) and for simplicity an array has been used to hold the information. Note also that the structure is assumed to have been created.

```
type field = array[1..30] of char;
     alpha_ptr = ^sales;              (*pointer to object of type sales*)
     sales = record                   (*sales record data type defined*)
         name : field;
         address  : field;
                                       (*other data could easily go in here*)
         .
         .
         .
         next : alpha_ptr             (*store next pointer with data*)
     end;
var  sales_ptr : alpha_ptr ;          (*sales_ptr declared as data-type pointer*)

procedure read_data(var dummy : field);
    begin
         .
         .                            (*code in here to read the data*)
         .
```

```
            end;
        begin                          (*Main part of program to read the data*)
            new(sales_ptr)             (*New referenced variable called sales_ptr*)

            with sales_ptr^ do         (*Use of pointer in loop*)
                read_data(name);       (*Call read_data procedure to get name*)
                read_data(address);
                .                      (*other data could easily be read here*)
                .                      (* checks for EOF too*)
        end.
```

Creation of the structures in the first place is not difficult, and the pointers can be utilised by making use of pointer variables in statements like the following:

```
sales_ptr^.name := 'Bert Bloggs'
sales_ptr^.address := 'Disneyland'
```

i.e. 'sales_ptr^.name' refers to the name field in the record currently pointed to by the pointer.

When inserting and deleting items from a list then these pointer variables are also most useful as pointers can be swapped or moved around the list with great ease. You are pointed (pun intended!) in the direction of the file handling chapter (see page 338) to investigate this fascinating topic further.

Basic language structures

All **imperative or procedural languages** (see page 105) are made up of fundamental structures which are implemented in each language by certain statements or groups of statements. The most-common structures will now be investigated and typical **flow-chart, Nassi-Schneiderman structure diagrams** and **pseudo-code (high-level-language-like instructions)** representations will be given where this is helpful to explain the concepts involved.

Linear structure

This is the simplest of structures and some might argue that this is no structure at all – but if there were no structure at all, then the statements could go in any order, and this is obviously not so! A **linear structure** is the simplest type of structure and a trivial example where five statements are executed to find the average of three typed-in numbers is shown in figure 6.9.

Control structures

In most high-level languages you can't get very far without making some sort of decision, or repeating linear sequences many times. For example, you may require that a temperature is constantly monitored (see page 586) until a **condition** arises in which the temperature becomes too high – in which case **control** needs to be passed to that part of the program which may shut down the process or switch on a fan. These powerful control structures will now be considered.

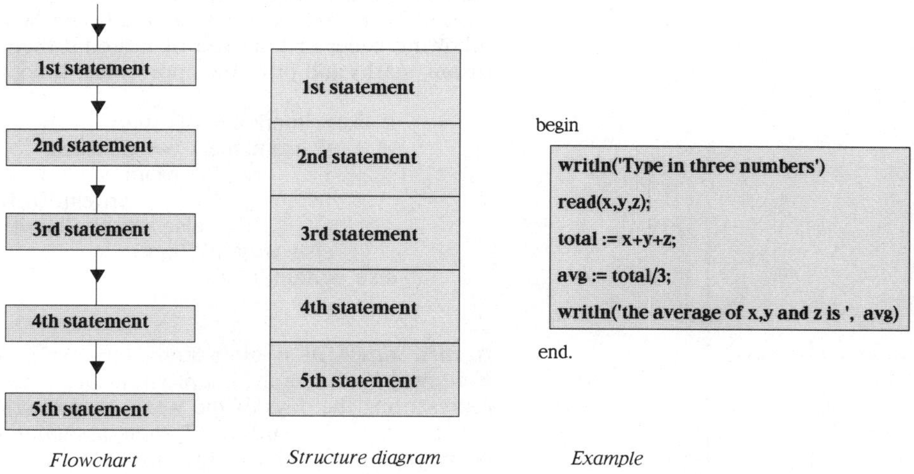

1st statement	
2nd statement	
3rd statement	
4th statement	
5th statement	

```
begin
    writln('Type in three numbers')
    read(x,y,z);
    total := x+y+z;
    avg := total/3;
    writln('the average of x,y and z is ',  avg)
end.
```

Flowchart   *Structure diagram*   *Example*

Figure 6.9

Conditional statements

Decision making in many high-level languages can be made by using the '**if then conditional statements**'. Simple **Boolean conditions** (see page 113) are normally used as a basis on which to make the decisions. For example,

$$temp < 50$$
$$and \ (x < 40) \ or \ (y <> 10)$$

would be typical of the statements used in the decision-making process. If the **expression** or **condition** is true, then control is diverted to one part of the program, whereas if the condition is false then control is diverted to another. A typical example is shown in figure 6.10.

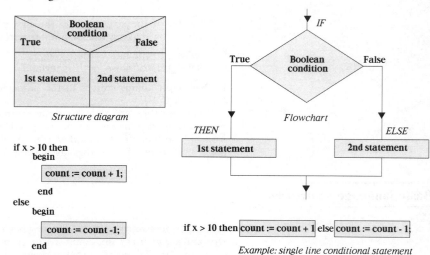

Structure diagram

```
if x > 10 then
        begin
            count := count + 1;
        end
else
        begin
            count := count -1;
        end
```

Flowchart

THEN

1st statement

ELSE

2nd statement

if x > 10 then count := count + 1 else count := count - 1;

Example: single line conditional statement

Example: multiple-line conditional statement

Figure 6.10

As can be seen from figure 6.10, the layout of this conditional statement is quite flexible (there are other variations too). Note also that the assignment-statement parts of the above can, if necessary, be *replaced by multiple line statements or other structures*. If this is the case then the layout on the left is preferable, but for simple conditions the layout on the right is all that is usually necessary. It should also be noted that, in this example, **x** would be called the **control variable** as it is used to control the loop.

Nested if-then statements

Most high-level languages, including Pascal, allow the use of **nested if-then statements**, and we will use a simple example to illustrate these techniques. In the days when the author took his exams you failed if you got less than 40%, 40% to 59% gave you a pass, 60% to 79% gave you a credit, and 80% or more gave you a distinction. The following code, making use of nested-if-then statements, would analyse the marks (exam_mark) and print the appropriate grade on the computer's monitor.

```
if exam_mark >= 40 then
        if exam_mark >= 60 then
                if exam_mark >= 80 then
                        writeln('Distinction')
                    else writeln('Merit')
            else writeln('Pass')
    else writeln('Fail');
```

Case statements

A **case statement** is often more convenient when constants are used for the test condition. For example, if a program was written in which the user types in a number representing the days of the week, then making use of the convention that monday = 1, tuesday = 2...sunday = 7, then, assuming that a variable called day had already been typed in and checked for range, a case statement can be used *instead of* a huge row of if-then-else statements as follows:

```
case day of
     1 : writeln('Monday');
     2 : writeln('Tuesday');
     3 : writeln('Wednesday');
     4 : writeln('Thursday');
     5 : writeln('Friday');
     6 : writeln('Saturday');
     7 : writeln('Sunday');
end;
```

It is a pity that standard Pascal does not allow the use of ranges (as well as constants) for the case labels at the beginning of each line. However, other languages, such as **Modula-2** for example, do not have this restriction.

From reading the above you may be thinking that the case statement is very restrictive and not able to cope with the examination-results type of example considered earlier. However, an extension of the case statement using multiple case labels (conditions) together with some clever programming will show you that this is not so. Consider the following:

```
test = exam_mark div 10;
case test of
0,1,2,3 : writeln('Fail');
4,5 : writeln('Pass');
6,7 : writeln('Credit');
8,9,10 : writeln('Distinction');
end;
```

Making use of the 'exam_mark div 10' part of the first line – this takes the integer examination mark and puts the variable 'test' equal to an **integer value** which is the *result of dividing the exam_mark by 10*. Therefore, for any marks between 0 and 39, test would yield just 0,1,2 or 3, as indicated by the multiple conditions at the beginning of the first part of the case structure. Marks between 40 and 59 after exam_mark div 10 would yield 4 or 5 etc.

The structure diagram and flowchart representation for the examination-mark problem is shown in figure 6.11. It is obviously necessary to keep the nested-if-then-else structures as more-complex conditions and tests making use of different variables are possible. Nevertheless, if the case structure can be used efficiently, it's usually easier to read and understand the final code.

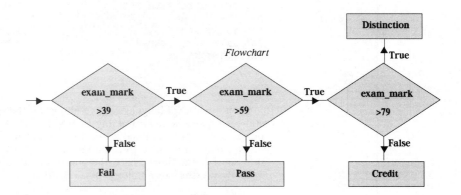

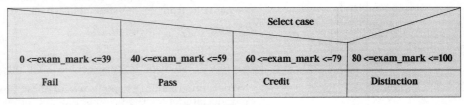

Structure diagram

Figure 6.11

The 'dreaded' goto

The **goto statement** is a statement which might be more usefully described as an 'out-of-control statement' rather than a control statement! Ever since the late 1960s the goto statement (or **unconditional branch statement**) has been considered awful programming style – as misused it often leads to **spaghetti code**. This is not some unique pasta recipe but refers to the control statements getting so tangled up with each other that it resembles a plate of spaghetti.

One of my favourite examples is a BASIC program written by one of my 14-year-old students way back in the late 1970s. (He was not one of the brightest in the set.) The code obviously does not work – but being an advanced-level-standard student you ought to be able to get the program working for him – shouldn't you? It's worth spending ten minutes of your time *if you are not convinced* that gotos can be easily misused.

Assuming that you have some idea of what the program is meant to do, (and that's not totally obvious from the lack of comments and zero documentation), you will probably find it almost impossible to debug. It would be far easier to start again from scratch. Professional programmers can't afford to make a mess of the work they do, especially if other people have to work with them in a team. This is why structured programming (and more-recently object-oriented programming – see page 162) is so very important, and the goto should only be used (if at all) with extreme care.

```
10 PRINT"What number do you want       220 Y = Y -50
   converted to Roman Numerals?"       230 IF Y < 10 THEN 270
20 INPUT Y                             240 PRINT"X"
30 IF Y < 1000 THEN 80                 250 Y = Y - 10
40 PRINT "M"                           260 GOTO 230
50 Y = Y - 1000                        270 IF Y < 9 THEN 300
60 GOTO 30                             280 PRINT"IX"
70 IF Y < 9000 THEN 1000               290 Y = Y - 9
80 PRINT"CM"                           300 IF Y < 5 THEN 330
90 Y = Y - 900                         310 PRINT"V"
100 IF Y > 500 THEN 130                320 Y = Y - 5
110 PRINT"D"                           330 IF Y < 4 THEN 360
120 Y = Y - 500                        340 PRINT"IV"
130 IF Y < 1000 THEN 200               350 IF Y < 4 THEN 360
140 Y = Y - 100                        360 IF Y = 0 THEN 400
150 PRINT"C"                           370 PRINT"I"
160 GOTO 130                           380 Y = Y - 1
170 IF Y < 90 THEN 200                 390 GOTO 350
180 Y = Y - 90                         400 PRINT"IS THE ROMAN NUMERAL
190 PRINT"XC"                              EQUIVALENT TO ";X
200 IF Y < 50 THEN 230                 410 END
210 PRINT"L"
```

Some high-level languages have abolished the **goto** altogether, but in others it can still have its uses, most notably in BASIC and FORTRAN. Nevertheless, the arguments over whether it should go or stay are not over yet. It is probably best to sit on the fence and have the opinion that it should be used very sparingly and only in essential situations where the clarity or efficiency of the program is improved.

In **Pascal**, the goto statement takes on the following form:

    goto label

where label is a number which has a maximum of 4-digits. The label is used by placing it in front of the statement which is the destination for the jump.

    goto 999
    .
    .
    999: Statement to be executed after the goto-999 unconditional jump

When programming making use of these labels, the label must be declared in a label declaration at the beginning of the program (see page 109).

Repetition structures

One of the reasons why computers are so good at what they do is in their ability to **repeat** *sequences* many times. This is also commonly known as **iteration**. Certain fundamental repetition structures are common to most high-level languages and these will now be considered. It should be noted that the syntax of different high level languages varies more widely to some extent when considering these structures, but the same ideas (semantics) are used by all.

While loops

The **while loop**, also known as a **do-while loop**, or **do loop**, checks a **Boolean condition** *before* carrying out any of the statements that would be executed if the condition is true. It should therefore be noted that when 'while loops' are used the statements may *never be executed* if the Boolean expression is false. Compare this with the repeat-until loops in the next section.

As with most structures, the statements shown in the grey boxes in the example of figure 6.12 could also be other structures too, and, as we have seen before, **count** would be called the **control variable**.

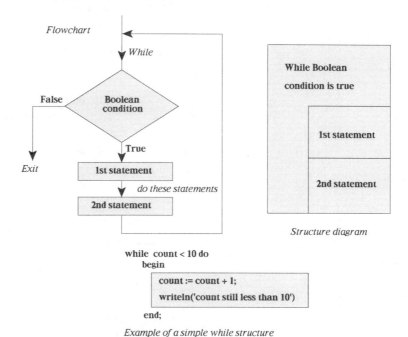

while count < 10 do
    begin

        count := count + 1;

        writeln('count still less than 10')

    end;

Example of a simple while structure

Figure 6.12

Repeat loop

The **repeat loop**, also known as the **repeat-until loop** has the structure shown in figure 6.13. It should be noted that the Boolean condition is not examined until the loop has been gone through once, therefore, with repeat loops *the statements are always executed at least once*, even if the condition is such that the loop is terminated immediately.

For loops

The **for loop** or **for-to-next loop** as it is sometimes known appears in many high-level languages. It is often compiled (see page 201) more easily that the **repeat** or **while** loops mentioned above because of the close relationship between the control variables used and registers in the machine. (An increment, test and branch is all that is necessary to implement this loop in common machine code operations – see chapter 4). This type of loop therefore often executes more quickly in some languages.

With this type of loop the number of repetitions is fixed, and controlled by a variable which is incremented from some minimum to some maximum in integer or non-integer steps. Decrements from some maximum to some minimum are also easily possible. An example of this type of loop is shown in figure 6.14. As with the repeat and while loops, for loops may also be nested.

Between them, **for-to**, **repeat-until** and **while-do loops** cope with most of the situations needed for good structured programming techniques, and indeed the **repeat until** and **while-do** loops can often be interchanged, for example

    repeat loop statements until condition_red

has exactly the same effect as

    while (not condition_red) do loop statements

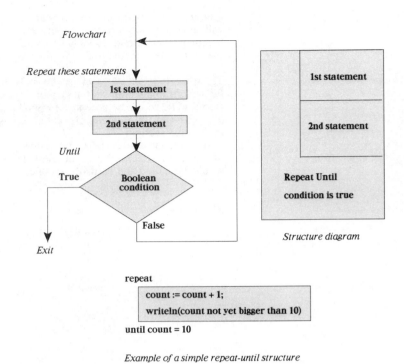

Figure 6.13

Example of a simple repeat-until structure

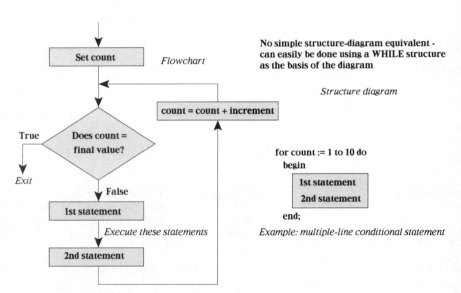

Figure 6.14

You should note that it is *very bad practice* (that will often cause an error) to jump into the middle of one of these loop structures from outside the loop, but it is usually *acceptable* to exit from within a loop structure. The bad habit just mentioned can easily be accomplished by the use of a GOTO or if-then statement, but many languages do provide exit or break statements which allow legal jumps out of the loop from arbitrary points within. Nevertheless, if you can code your algorithms without doing this then the code is usually a lot easier to read.

Pascal *allows* you to **jump out** of a loop but will *not allow* you to **jump into** a loop, unless you are jumping to some other part of the same loop from within.

We have already seen the use of the nested-if-then-else loops, and many other loop types can also be nested. However, you must obey the rules of loops which, simply stated, require that each loop (or structure) is completely embedded within another with no overlapping. Examples of these simple rules are shown in figure 6.15.

Examples of nested-loop structures

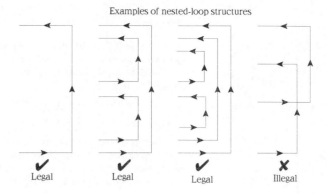

| Legal | Legal | Legal | Illegal |

Figure 6.15

Program sub-structures

You should be well aware of the need to split up larger problems into smaller more-manageable chunks which perform specific tasks (see page 129), and you should also be aware of the need to make use of set-routines many times, if necessary, during the execution of a program. The next few sections concentrate on how a typical high-level language enables the programmer to carry out these essential modularisation principles.

Functions and procedures

One of the main concepts of **structured programming** revolves around breaking up the tasks to be solved into much-smaller subtasks, and therefore the ideas of **functions** and **procedures (or subprograms)** are of fundamental importance. Both functions and procedures can be **called by name**, and this adds to the readability of the overall program. They also prevent the same code being written more than once if it is needed in many different parts of the program. We can thus often shorten the program considerably if these two techniques are extensively used. Other important techniques of programming such as recursion are covered in chapter 9.

A function is often similar in nature to a procedure, but you should understand the important differences between them. These differences stem not only from the uses to which these different techniques are normally put, but from fundamental differences in their operation. A **function** is used in a *similar way* to the **built-in functions** that are available from within the definition of a language, whereas a procedure (see next section) is most often used like a completely self-contained program which performs a specific subtask.

Functions

The end result of a function is that the **function identifier (name)** has a **value assigned to it** *after* the function has been executed. This is *not* the same as that which happens when a procedure or subprogram is executed.

The **built-in functions** that are supplied with a programming language might be functions like the square roots, logs and the trigonometric functions such as sin, cos and tan. All the Pascal built-in functions have been defined on page 108. However, there is no built-in function for working out the hypotenuse (longest side) of a right-angled triangle, for example, therefore, using Pascal, we will invent one ourselves and call it **hypot**. As no function definition for hypot exists from within the language itself, we must obviously define hypot in detail ourselves, and this can be done as follows:

```
function hypot (var side1, side2 : real) : real;
        begin
            hypot := sqrt(sqr(side1)+sqr(side2))
        end;
```

In the above function, two **parameters** (i.e. the variables called side1 and side2 which represent the other two sides of the triangle) are **real numbers** *passed over to the function* from the calling routine. The **value returned** *from the function* (**hypot**) which has been **assigned** its value by the maths expression contained within the assignment statement is also real. We can call such a function from within an expression as follows.

```
longest := hypot(x,y);
```

If you are using Pascal then it is worth noting that only **single simple data types** (see page 112) may be returned from a function.

Functions and factorials

The classic example of a function call is to calculate **factorials**, but before we start on this example just a brief reminder of what is meant by a factorial. A factorial is denoted in mathematics by an '!' (exclamation mark) and has the following definition.

$n! = n \times (n–1) \times (n–2) \ x \ .... \times 3 \times 2 \times 1$ and $0! = 1$ by definition.

For example, $6! = 6 \times 5 \times 4 \times 3 \times 2 \times 1 = 720$

If, as in the following function definition, there are variables which are used within the function (in addition to the parameters that are passed to it) then these variables *must be declared* at the beginning of the function in an identical way to that which we have declared variables at the beginning of the programs.

```
function factorial (n: integer) : integer;
    var count,product : integer;
    begin
      if (n = 0) or (n = 1) then product := 1
            else
            begin
              count := 2;
              product := 1;
              repeat
                product := product * count;
                count := count + 1;
              until count = n+1
            end;
      factorial := product
    end;
begin
    x := factorial(10);         (*Calls the above function*)
    writeln(x);                 (*Intended to show only main program*)
end.                            (*block & function definition*)
```

You should compare and contrast this function definition with the **recursive definition** of factorials on page 186. Both functions and procedures **may be called from within themselves**, and this powerful technique is known as **recursion**.

Scope of variables and constants

The above factorial function looks innocent enough but illustrates a common problem in many high-level languages, especially if different people are working on different aspects of the program. We have introduced two extra variables within the function called **count** and **product**. Now in some languages (Pascal is not one of them) the entire program would be screwed up if 'product' or 'count' happens to be used in other parts too. Mistakes of this nature where variables interact can be a pig to track down, and so the concept of the **scope of variables** has been introduced.

The **scope of a variable** means *that area of the program which recognises it and therefore has access to it*. If, as in the Pascal example above, the variables have been defined from *within* a **function,** then they are called **local variables** as they are *only accessible from within* the **function** or **procedure** in which they have been defined. However, there may obviously be a need for a variable to be accessed both from within a procedure and from other parts of the program (including other functions and procedures). In this case the variables scope is said to be **global**. In **Pascal**, **global variables** are those defined in the **variable declaration** part of the data description section at the *beginning* of the program (see the Pascal program-structure diagram on page 126).

It should be noted that although the term variable has been used above, the concept of scope also applies to constants. Therefore, we talk of global and local constants in the same way as global and local variables. It should be obvious that the *same name* can be used for *many different* **variables** and **constants** *if* they are defined locally.

Problems with one programmer inadvertently messing up other programmer's data and variables have been addressed in much more sophisticated ways when the alternative paradigm (methodology) of object-oriented programming is used. These techniques are extensively used in C++ and are explained in detail on page 162.

Procedures

Only trivial programs are usually written without recourse to **procedures**, and the main body of many highly-complex programs often consists of just a few statements and calls to procedures! Each procedure is known by a different name which hopefully relates to the task which that particular procedure undertakes.

A **procedure** is usually **called** by stating its **name**, and although not essential, it is often necessary to **pass parameters** over to the procedure from the calling routine. These **parameters** are simply the names given to the information *being passed* to (or obtained from – see in a moment) a procedure. After being called, control is passed to the procedure and the statements contained within the procedure are executed (which could include calls to other procedures or functions). When the procedure is finished control is **returned** to the statement *after the one* from which the procedure was called. Don't forget that both procedures and functions can be called recursively (i.e. from within itself).

In **Pascal** a **procedure definition** takes on the following form:

```
procedure tempconvert (var cent : real);
var fah :real;
    begin
      fah := (9*cent/5)+32;
      writeln(cent, 'centigrade is the same as' ,fah, 'fahrenheit');
    end;
```

To call the above simple procedure (which takes a centigrade temperature, converts it to fahrenheit and then prints out the answer with a message) we could make use of the following procedure call:

```
tempconvert(reading)
```

which, if reading = 50, for example, would result in

```
50 centigrade is the same as 122 fahrenheit
```

being displayed on the computer's monitor after the procedure had been executed.

Parameters

One of the most important concepts relating to procedures is in the *passing of information* in *both directions* between the **procedure** and the **calling routine**. We could, for example, pass information to a procedure by making use of a **global variable** (see page 124), but, as we have already seen, this often causes problems if you are not extremely careful regarding variable names used in other parts of the program, or in other procedures.

To examine the mechanism of parameter passing consider the temperature-conversion procedure again, but this time concentrate on the *parameter list* (the part inbetween the brackets) in the following statement:

```
procedure tempconvert (var cent : real);
```

When this procedure is called, in the above case, the value 50 is substituted for the parameter cent, and cent becomes a real variable which has a value of 50 within the procedure.

In this particular procedure, we also want to pass information *back* to the calling routine – the parameter used for this is declared as a **variable** from *within* the procedure definition, in our case, by making use of:

```
var fah   : real;
```

Passing by value and reference

It's good practice to define *all parameters used within a procedure* as being **local**, then they won't inadvertently get mixed up with any other variable that might happen to have the same name in other procedures or elsewhere in the program. If we use a parameter-passing scheme such that the variable used to **pass the value** to the procedure *does not get altered* by the variables inside the procedure, i.e. the value is simply copied, then this is called **passing by value**.

An alternative would be to let the variables inside the procedure be allowed to alter the value of the variable which passed it. Thus the variable used to pass the value has been *referenced and irrevocably altered*, and this method is called **passing by reference**.

Overall program structure

We have seen how structures operate *within* a language, but most high-level programming languages must themselves adhere to a strict overall structure. (BASIC is one of the exceptions, though structured BASIC can be well written if you apply similar self-imposed rules.) Pascal's structure, for example, consists of a **program header**,

Structure of a Pascal program

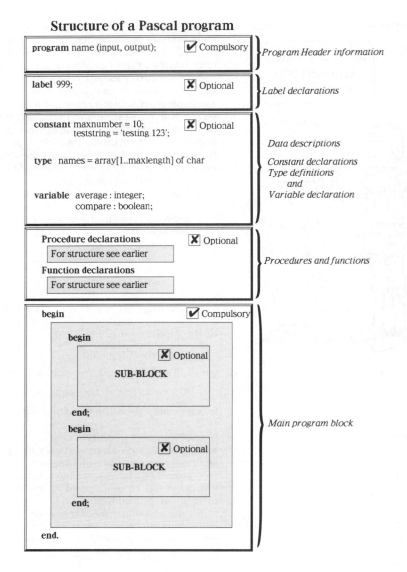

Figure 6.16

label declarations, **data descriptions**, **procedures and functions** and then the **main block** of the program which may consist of many **sub blocks.** The overall structure for a Pascal program is shown in figure 6.16.

In the chapter on high-level-language examples, other structures are considered in detail, most notably COBOL, which is considered on page 155.

We have indeed come a long way from the days when programs were a simple linear sequence of instructions with a few simple loop structures. The structured programming techniques outlined in this chapter have been developed with several decades of hindsight, and represent the best in current structured program techniques. However, this chapter has concentrated on one main **paradigm**, that of **imperative languages**. You should refer to the software-examples in chapter 8 to look at some of the alternative paradigms such as object-oriented programming, functional programming and declarative programming. Nevertheless, do not forget that as languages develop there is a large overlap. For example, even though C++ is an object-oriented language, most of the Pascal features outlined in this chapter are also available in C++. Therefore, the different methodologies are not mutually exclusive, but enhance each other to a great extent.

Exercise 6.2

1. What is meant by the term **enumerated data type**?

2. Using a high-level language of your own choice, explain how **subscripted variables** are used to access the elements within a two-dimensional array.

3. Explain how the **pointer data type** helps to implement structures such as linked lists and trees. (These structures are covered in chapter 14.)

4. What is meant by a **conditional jump** or branch in a high-level language?

5. Compare and contrast the use of the **repeat until** and the **while do** loop structures.

6. Outline the *basic rules* that apply to **loop structures**.

7. Why is the 'goto statement' often outlawed and when is it 'safe' to make use of it?

8. Compare and contrast the use of **nested if-then structures** and the **case structure**.

9. What are the main differences between a **function** and a **procedure**?

10. In a high-level language *of your choice* write some code to work out the area of any circle *making use of a* **function call**.

11. In a high-level language of your choice, show how a **procedure** might be used to to input and work out the average of a list of five **integer** numbers.

12. Explain what is meant by the s**cope of a variable** making sure to use the terms **local** and **global variables** in your explanation.

13. Explain what is meant by **passing by value** and **passing by reference** when programming making use of procedures.

14. Why is it best to have a strict program structure such as that shown in the Pascal example on page 126?

End of chapter summary

- A **high-level** language is a convenient method of instructing the computer in a way that is in *both* **human readable** and **machine readable** form. It is a **problem-specific** rather than a **machine-specific** language.
- A **high-level** language is an example of a **formal language**, whereas most human languages such as English are examples of **natural languages**.
- **Natural languages** are **context sensitive**, **formal languages** are *not*.
- **High-level languages** are *meant to be* **portable**, which means that they should work on many different hardware and operating system platforms. (Different types of computer.)
- **Syntax** is the grammatical rules that govern the layout and use of a language.
- **Semantics** is the meaning that is applied to a language.
- **Software engineering** is the methodology which embraces the **documentation**, **maintenance**, **debugging**, **testing** and **analysis** etc. when using computer languages or other applications to solve problems.
- **Development of high-level languages** has taken place over decades, and has been a slow **evolutionary** process.
- **Languages** can be classed into **five generations**.
- **First generation** languages are machine code and assemblers.
- **Second generation** languages are the unstructured high-level languages.
- **Third generation** languages are the structured high-level languages.
- **Fourth-generation** languages are the SQLs and the like.
- **Fifth-generation** languages are the very-high-level languages like Prolog, and also the languages used to drive expert systems.
- **Languages** can be classified into different main **paradigms** or **methodologies**.
- **Imperative languages** or **procedural languages** typify the 'how to do it' way of programming. Other languages are classed as **non-procedural.**
- **Declarative languages** typify the 'what to do' way of programming.
- **Functional languages** have **parameters** that are *passed to functions* from **expressions** which are being evaluated, and then these **values** are *returned from the functions* to the calling **expression**.
- **Object-oriented languages** are based on objects which represent single units which encapsulate *both* **functions** and **data**.
- The **character set** is the set of **letters**, **digits** and **symbols** used in a language.
- **Reserved words** represent **identifiers** used by the language such as **if** or **then**.
- An **identifier** is a name, often chosen by the programmer to identify variables or special functions, files or procedures etc. It can't usually clash with **keywords**.
- **Keywords** are reserved words which *represent some language construct* such as **PRINT** or **IF** or **COS** etc. They can't be used as identifiers.

- A **syntax diagram** is often helpful when defining the syntax of a language. This pictorial method makes it easy to see if you are conforming to the syntax rules.
- A **variable** is the name given to an **identifier** chosen by the programmer which represents some value that can vary during the execution of a program.
- A **constant** is the name given to an **identifier** which is not allowed to change its value. A **constant** is also called a **literal**.
- A **string** is literally a string of characters (usually bound by delimiters).
- A **statement** is a descriptive phrase in a high-level language which generates one or more machine-code instructions.
- **Expressions** are usually arithmetical but Boolean expression are also common.
- The **order of precedence** determines the order in which arithmetic expressions will be evaluated.
- Different **data types** describe the nature of the data and therefore help maintain the readability of the program.
- **Numeric data** types are **integer** and **real**.
- A **Boolean data type** can only have a **true** or **false** value.
- An **enumerated** data type is one which contains a **list** of data items.
- A **sub-range** data type is a sub-set of an **enumerated data type**.
- **Structured data types** such as files, for example, can have their contents dynamically altered during the execution of a program.
- An **array** is a **data structure** consisting of **one or more dimensions**. A **one-dimensional array** is a **linear list** of **data items,** and a **two-dimensional array** consists of **rows and columns of data**. **Multi-dimensional arrays** are possible in many languages.
- An **array** is usually *referenced* by a **subscripted variable**.
- **Set data types** are **fixed lists of data items** and relate to the idea of sets in maths.
- **Record data types** mirror the **record structure in a file**, but can be set up in other structures like **arrays**.
- **File data types** are **files** stored in main memory or, more usually, on **disk**. They make use of **record data type substructures**.
- **Pointer data types** are the dynamic data types used to implement the **pointer** systems in **linked lists**, **queues** and **trees** etc.
- **Basic structures** within a program refer to linear, control and the repetition structures that are available.
- A **linear structure** is one in which *one statement is executed after another* in some pre-defined order.
- A **control structure** is one in which control can be passed to different parts of the program.
- A **conditional statement** is the **if-then-else** type statement.
- A **case statement** can test for a **multitude of conditions.**
- A **repetition structure** is one of the **while**, **repeat** or **for** structures.
- A **while structure** executes statements *only while a condition is true*. If the condition is never true no statements can ever be executed.
- A **repeat structure** will repeat a set of instructions **until a condition is false**. If the condition is always false the statement will be executed once.
- A **for loop** is used to execute a number of statements controlled by a counter with the **control variable** controlling the count.
- A **function** is a sub-program which is usually called from **within an expression**, and whose **name** acts as an **identifier** which represents the **value** returned.
- A **procedure** is a completely self-contained **subprogram** which may be called from the main program.
- **Parameter passing** means passing values to or getting values back from a procedure.
- **Passing by value** means the **value** of the *variable* used to pass the parameter to the procedure is **not altered**.
- **Passing by reference** means **referring** to the *variable* used to pass the parameter and thus the value of the variable used to pass the parameter **does get altered**.
- Many **high-level languages** require that a **strict program structure** be adhered to. For example, **headers**, **label declarations**, **data description**, **procedure** and **function definitions** and the **main body** of the program are typical in **Pascal**.

7 Structured analysis and design

Introduction

The first part of this chapter is concerned with the all-important initial stages of **structured algorithm design**. We will not be too concerned with specialist algorithms as are covered in the chapters on **sorting** and **searching** for example, nor specifically in making use of any particular **high-level language constructs** as are considered in chapters 6 and 9. Here we will concentrate on the basic techniques of how to convey *your* ideas to *other* people – and even to yourself if necessary. (It often is!) We will be looking specifically at some of the common **diagrammatic and pseudocode methods** used to help solve problems and convey important ideas in a structured way. However, a detailed discussion of the **high-level-language constructs** covered in chapters 6 and 9 is *almost inseparable* from the **diagrammatic methods** used in this chapter, and where necessary we *will illustrate* the solution to some of the problems by making use of **pseudocode** (a made-up computer-like language) or a **typical high-level language**. It should also be well understood that *solving problems on modern computer systems does not necessarily mean writing programs in the conventional sense*, but could also mean making use of **SQLs** as defined on page 480, or other similar **software packages** and **applications** in which **4GLs** and the like play a major part. However, even when these more-modern and **sophisticated tools** are used, understanding how to solve problems and convey ideas by whatever means is still of fundamental importance.

Algorithms

It's also most important to realise that the methods we will use at the beginning of this chapter are equivalent to just a few important pieces in an infinitely-more-complex jigsaw of events that goes into making a satisfactory and complete **software development environment**. This environment is described by the art of **software engineering**, which embraces many aspects of development including the **analysis, debugging, documentation** and **testing** of complete systems. We will also cover the applications of these principles in practice when dealing with the detailed systems-analysis examples covered in chapter 18 – but first let's see what's meant by an algorithm.

A useful **algorithm** is a *step-by-step process* or *sequence of instructions* that can be used to **solve a problem** in a *finite* amount of time.

There's not much point in designing an algorithm that would take an infinite amount of time! For example, a **simple algorithm** to solve the Tower's of Hanoi problem is given on page 187 where the important concept of **recursion** is covered in detail. Nevertheless, even a **supercomputer** working at speeds of 100 million moves/sec would take about 6,000 years to perform this particular task! The philosophers among you should also note that some problems are *not* **computable** – this means that no matter how simple some problems may appear to be to us, they have no solution based on the **algorithmic (step-by-step) approach** of computers, no matter how powerful the computer is likely to be! This fascinating area, developed mainly by a brilliant mathematician called Turing, has long been used as the basis for arguments as to whether computers will ever be able to think, and this is discussed in more detail on page 558. We will now concentrate on computable problems which can be solved in a sensible amount of time by today's **algorithmic computer technology**.

Basic flowcharts

The flowchart is one of the most-basic **algorithmic constructs** (methods for representing algorithms). It has been around for many years and is *still useful* as a precise method of explanation in some circumstances. For example, basic flowcharts are still used in many explanations of Microsoft's **C++ constructs** (this is one of the most-recent object-oriented languages) and as you have probably seen in chapter 6, basic

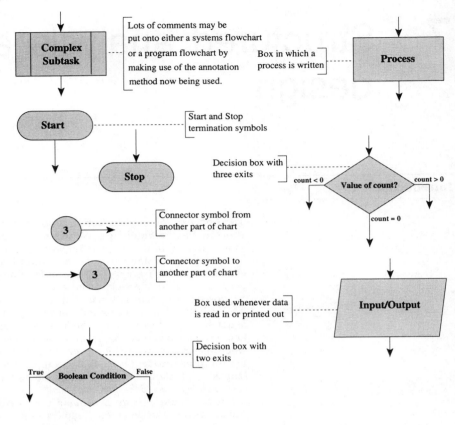

Figure 7.1

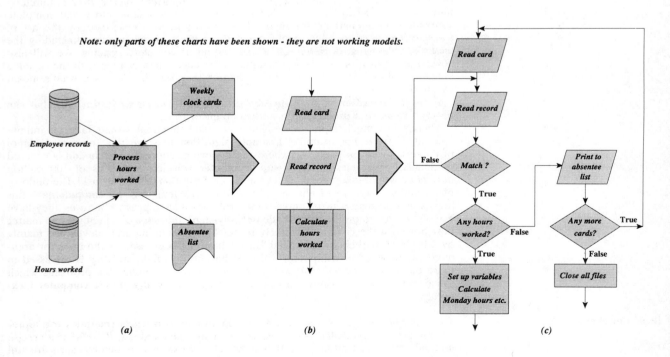

Note: only parts of these charts have been shown - they are not working models.

(a)   *(b)*   *(c)*

Figure 7.2

flowcharts also prove to be extremely effective when explaining the **Pascal-language constructs**. Even so, *the* **main use of flowcharts** today is in **systems flowcharts** as described in chapter 18. Many of the more-basic uses to which flowcharts were put in the past have now been superseded by the use of **structure diagrams** and **pseudocode**. *Over-use of basic-flowchart techniques should be avoided*, as the resulting charts can become unwieldy and counter-productive.

Many programmers (including the author!!) have often constructed the flowcharts *after* the programs have been written! I would not mind £1 for each student I have met over the years who has done the same in their 'A' level project documentation! Flowcharts in this basic form are therefore not adequate for all but the most basic documentation, (such as the language construct explanations mentioned in the last chapter) and are inadequate for professional use when describing complex systems. Nevertheless, the basic flowchart symbols form an important subset of the popular systems-flowchart symbols, and deserve separate consideration.

Systems and program flowcharts

There are **several different forms of flowcharts** with corresponding different symbols and uses. We will start by looking at what are commonly called **program flowcharts**, because they were originally used to chart the detailed workings of programs. The basic shapes used in **program flowcharts** are shown in figure 7.1. Program flowcharts produce far too much detail when a problem becomes large and complex, and the overall structure of the problem is often lost in the mountain of interconnected boxes. They also do not cope easily with systems concepts such as the interrelation of a mass of different types of equipment and processes.

To get over many of the problems just discussed the **systems flowchart** was developed, and figure 7.2 shows how a typical small part of a systems flowchart (on the left) relates to the more-detailed program flowchart (on the right), via an intermediate flowchart which contains a complex-subtask box (shown at the bottom). This is a particularly simple example, and in practice a single box on a **systems flowchart** can often correspond to *many more boxes* on a **program flowchart**.

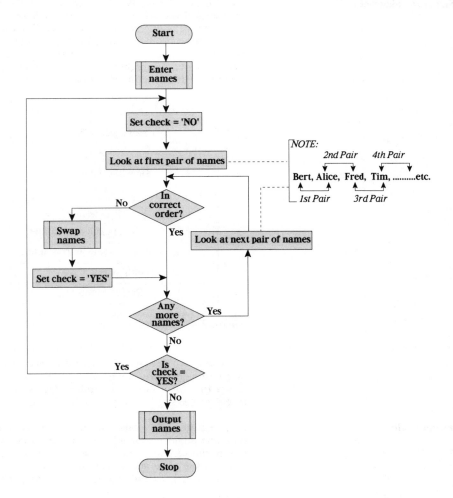

Figure 7.3

A simple flowchart example

A simple **program-flowchart** example is shown in figure 7.3. This particular flowchart shows one method of sorting names into ascending order. Take notice of this method as it will be used as an example to compare *different techniques* of picturing the *same* problem. Notice the correct use of the box shapes, but note also that inputting names, for example, is generally a more-complex task, perhaps involving validation, (see page 231) and perhaps making sure that the correct number of names have been entered. Therefore, although data *is* being input, it is not shown as a trapezium-shaped box, but as a more-complex task involving detail not shown on this flowchart for purposes of clarity. Other routines in the chart have had similar treatment in terms of the shapes of boxes to represent the processes.

Flowcharts of this nature are often taught in elementary mathematics classes, but you should work carefully through the chart if you have not used them before, or have forgotten exactly what to do.

Obtaining the final solution?

You should note that any *useful* method should lead naturally on to the next stage in the development of the solution to the problem. In the case of the name-sorting flowchart shown above, the next stage would probably be to write the code making use of a typical high-level language such as Pascal. A quick look at the flowchart does not really help very much – does it? A longer look at the flowchart might suggest how the **repeat-until** or **while-do structures** covered in chapter 6 map onto this sort of diagram, and it is obviously possible to stare long enough at the flowchart and come up with a sensible structure – *but this defeats the point*. If a diagram is intended to help with the solution to a problem then it's going to have to contribute much more help than is available from a program flowchart as shown above.

Structure diagrams

As with flowcharts, the basic ideas of one type of structure diagram developed by **Nassi and Schneiderman** have already been introduced in chapter 6. If we were to use these ideas *instead* of the **program flowchart**, then the structure diagram for the name-sorting problem could be represented as shown in figure 7.4. Let's pose the same question again – if the next stage in the solution to the name-sorting problem were to write the high-level language code, how long would it take to do this by looking at the structure diagram?

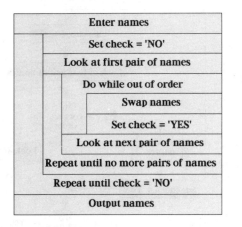
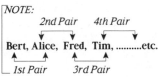

Figure 7.4

As you can see – the structure of the program instantly jumps out without too much thought. Any complex subtask can then be given similar treatment. Don't forget that in professional circles time is money, and any method that can be used to get to the final goal more quickly has an obvious advantage.

Pseudocode

If one of the **main goals** is to produce **code in a suitable high-level language or 4GL**, then one might reasonably ask the question – why not do this straight away? Indeed, *this is the idea* of **pseudocode**. One might also ask – what is the point of flowcharts if pseudocode can get straight to the heart of the matter? When considering examples such as the simple name-sorting techniques just described, then there *is* *not much advantage* in using pictorial methods, if, (and this is sometimes a BIG if), you can visualise what the code will be straight away. Although this seems obvious today, you must remember that structures such as **while** and **case** etc. were *not available* to the early programmers using **second-generation unstructured high-level languages**. It was in this sort of development environment that the program flowchart was first extensively used. With the advent of **third-generation high-level languages, pseudocode** (or **direct coding** in a language such as **Pascal** or **C++** etc.) has become a much more feasible proposition for professional programmers. These languages are now so much more sophisticated than the old languages that with a suitable number of comments the program becomes **self-documenting** as far as other professional programmers are concerned. Indeed you may recall that this is one of the desirable attributes of a language – **readability**.

Some typical **pseudocode** for the name-sorting problem is given below:
(Note pairs of names are as defined in last two sections)

```
Enter names
repeat
    set check = 'NO'
    Look at first pair of names
    repeat
            while names out of order do
                begin
                    swap names
                    set check = 'YES'
                end
            Look at next pair of names
    until no more pairs of names
until check = 'NO'
output names
Procedure definitions for name-swapping could go here
```

Note that the **level of indentation** is of *paramount importance* as it gives a **visual indication of the scope of the loops**. It is easy, for example, to see where the inner repeat-until loop is in relation to the outer repeat-until loop. Note also that while the code is Pascal-like, it has not got the correct syntax for Pascal. (Whoever heard of 'Enter names' as being a valid command except, perhaps, in a 4GL.) It is, therefore, pseudo-Pascal or **pseudo code**. Indeed, code can be **pseudo anything** as long as you make use of **acceptable loop structures**, **a logical layout** and/or **English-like terms**. You should pay much attention to writing pseudocode as it is becoming an increasingly important part of examination questions at this level.

Multiple-decision boxes

As **program constructs** became more sophisticated (for example the introduction of the **case structure** as shown on page 119) it soon became obvious that the basic program flowcharts just described lacked the ability to cope easily with many situations. For example, multiple decisions were particularly clumsy as many decision boxes often had to be drawn. To get over the maximum-of-two-exits problem,

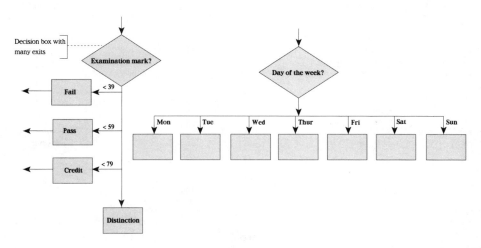

Figure 7.5   (a)   (b)

(or three *if* just one box is used) the alternative forms of decision box shown in figure 7.5 can be used. Figure 7.5(a) shows a multiple-decision box for the examination-mark case structure considered on page 119, and figure 7.5(b) shows a similar alternative for the 'days of the week' case construct shown on page 119.

Design structure diagrams

In the search for different and more informative pictorial methods of communicating algorithms alternative flowcharts called **design structure diagrams** provide yet another approach. Figure 7.6 shows the name-sorting algorithm again, but this time developed using the BS6224 (British Standard) **design structure diagram**. Arrows are not normally necessary in this type of diagram as the structure is arranged such that the flow is exactly as if you were reading a book – i.e. top to bottom and from left to right.

Design-structure decisions

The name-swapping algorithm just considered, consisted only of **while** and **for structure**s, and therefore did not demonstrate the ability of **design structure diagrams** to handle **multiple decisions** – because of this a simple example making use of the BS6244 system is shown in figure 7.7. Note that an *important role* is played by the *small diamond shapes* in this particular type of diagram – if the condition being evaluated is *true* then the *flow is from left to right*, or if the condition being evaluated is *false* then the flow is from *top to bottom*. The examination-mark case structure on page 133 is used again for demonstration purposes.

Top down design approach

We have now analysed the name-sorting problem using four different methods – namely **program flowcharts, Nassi-Schneiderman structured diagrams, pseudocode**

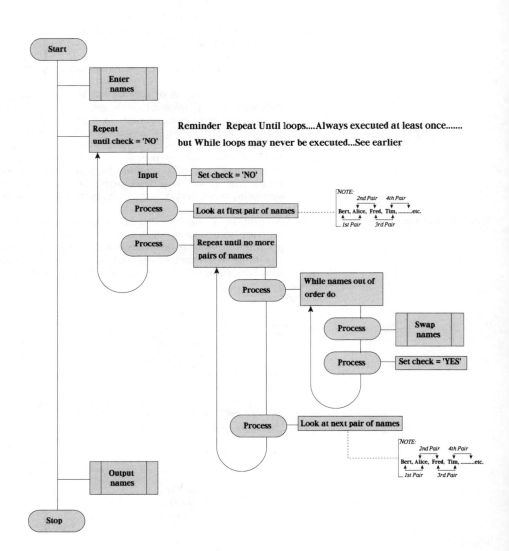

Figure 7.6

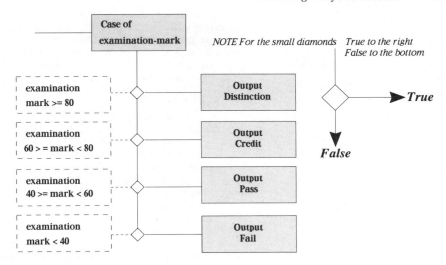

Figure 7.7

and **design structure diagrams**. You can probably now appreciate why pseudocode is so popular! However, each method has it's advantages and disadvantages, and you need to do an appreciable amount of work with each method to appreciate the finer points. Nevertheless, even pseudocode becomes unwieldy and often difficult to develop in many cases, and a method called **Jackson-Structured Programming (JSP see page 137)** is now used extensively in many professional circles to help develop programs by making use of the top-down approach to solving algorithms.

Take it from the top

This method of designing systems *starts off with* the **ideas at the highest level,** and then *progressively works down to* the **lowest level of detail**. This method of analysing a problem revolves around **hierarchical data structures** as described on page 304. Many systems can be described in terms of a hierarchical (family-tree type) data structure and a typical example is shown in figure 7.8.

Figure 7.8

Starting at the top, you can see the **highest-level idea** is the production of a sales report. The *next level* in the **hierarchy** involves data initialisation and generation of the main report headings (notice how we work from left to right along the same level). However, when you arrive at the individual-report-body box, this has a sub level which must be executed before going on to write the cumulative totals. Indeed, for the most-likely scenario of many sales-people records, the bottom level of this structure chart would be repeatedly executed until there were no more records, (we will see how to modify such diagrams for these loops very shortly). Next control would pass to the write cumulative total box. We are then at the end of the second level – and so we return to the top level and the problem has been executed.

The visual advantage of this type of structure diagram is obvious, and is ideal for implementation by the JSP methods to be covered shortly. Notice how easy it is to produce pseudocode from this type of chart as the levels of hierarchy mirror the levels of indentation of the loop structures.

Assuming that many records will be read from a file, some typical pseudocode to match this top-down structure could be as follows:

```
open files
write main headings
repeat
    read sales-person record
    write sales-person sub-headings
    write name and other personal details
    calc. sales figures
    write analysis of figures
    write analysis to record
until end of file
write cumulative totals
```

From the above structure diagram or by using the above pseudocode, a high-level or 4GL language program could easily be constructed.

Bottom up design approach

The bottom-up approach to systems design *starts with* the **lowest levels of detail** and *works up to* the **highest level of the idea**. The **top-down approach** to developing **algorithms** and **systems** seems so obvious that the **bottom-up approach** is *often neglected*. The normal reaction of students who have used the top-down-design approach is to ask 'How on Earth can anyone work *up from the bottom* without knowing what they are working towards?' This seems an understandable attitude until the techniques of bottom-up design are more fully explained. From a programming perspective, **bottom-up design is equivalent to writing modules or procedures first**. This technique is often used when **prototyping** a module before joining it on to the main system. You can then glue the whole system together like bricks which go to make up a wall – but starting from the bottom. Viewed in this light the bottom-up approach seems eminently sensible, although you still obviously need to know what you're trying to work towards. The bottom-up approach does not mean having no plans!

On a more common-sense tack – if you know that certain facilities are not available, then you *will have to write them* irrespective of the overall grand plan. For example, if you are dealing with a high-level language that does *not provide facilities* for manipulation of a particular data structure (such as complex numbers or matrices) then you will need to write typical procedures to carry out these elementary tasks.

In fact the bottom up approach is often used by default as a method of working out parts of the problem while you are trying to work out what should be happening on the whole problem! Although this often happens in practice, especially with students at school – it can hardly be put forward as a whole-hearted endorsement of the bottom-up philosophy.

Of course *the* major problem that a bottom-up approach can generate is in the fitting together of all the pieces into the final jigsaw puzzle – at least with the top-down approach you *can ensure* that all the pieces fit together at the grand-design stage. Indeed, this used to be such a large problem that the bottom-up approach was not really a viable alternative other than for writing procedures.

In chapter 6, where different programming methodologies are considered, you will recall that *one of the major headaches with the development of complex systems was to do with the unintentional interaction between modules of programs*. These modules often interacted with each other in unexpected and very subtle ways, especially if one module which affected many others had to be modified. It was this type of scenario that suggested doom for the bottom-up approach to algorithmic design.

With the more-recent introduction of **object-oriented programming** (see page 162), bottom-up approaches (or variations on this theme) have been revived. You may recall that these objects are not easily messed-up by other programmers' code, so one can develop an enormous number of routines based around objects that could be built up into more comprehensive objects – that could built up into useful procedures – that could be combined into useful utilities – that could be joined onto other utilities – to make up useful programs that . . .You get the idea!!!

A well-balanced viewpoint   You must not forget that the top-down and bottom-up approaches are *not* mutually exclusive. It is not a case of belonging to one camp or the other, but of using combinations of sensible techniques which are appropriate for the problems in hand.

Exercise 7.1

1. Making use of *program flowcharts* solve the following problems. Make sure that suitable annotation is used if clarification of method is needed.
   (a) Read a temperature in fahrenheit and convert it into centigrade making use of the formula $C = 5(F-32)/9$. The process is halted when –999 has been entered.
   (b) Determine the *largest* and *smallest* numbers from a list of ten floating-point numbers, then automatically output the two answers.
   (c) Read in an unspecified number of examination marks where pupils are allowed to score between 0 and 100 inclusive. Make sure that any data outside this range is ignored, and an appropriate message printed out. Work out the average examination mark for the *correct number* of *valid* examination scores, and make sure that your program does not crash *if no marks* are entered.
   (d) Read an unspecified quantity of positive and negative numbers whose range is checked to be between –500 and +500 inclusive. The data is to be terminated by –999. Output how many positive, negative and zero numbers there are in the list.
   (e) Create a basic four-function calculator. The user should enter an operator (+, –, / or *), followed

by the two numbers to be used in the calculation using the convention that the top number or first number in the calculation should be entered first. After checking for a valid operator and performing the correct calculation, the correct answer should be output. The calculations should terminate when a '$' is entered.

2. Making use of *Nassi-Schneiderman structure diagrams*, solve the problems in question (1) again.

3. Write *pseudocode* algorithms to solve the problems in question (1). Make use of the Nassi-Schneiderman diagrams in (2) if you have answered this question.

4. Convert the pseudocode algorithms of question (3) into code in a high-level language of your choice. Execute the code and get the programs working.

5. Compare and contrast the *top-down* and *bottom-up* approaches to solving problems giving convincing examples of where each method would be best suited to the solution of a particular problem.

6. Why have object-oriented programming techniques contributed to the resurgence of the bottom-up approach to algorithmic design?

Other structured analysis and design techniques

Jackson structured programming   This methodology was invented by the famous **Michael Jackson**. Not the pop singer of course, but *the* famous computer programmer when writing his book Principles of Program Design. It is a method which is ideally suited to problems which can be expressed as **hierarchical data structures**, such as those described by the **top-down-approach**. As this includes most of **business data processing**, you can see why this particular method is so popular with students and professionals alike.

Sequence   JSP makes use of **top-down structure diagrams** to *give an indication* of the **sequence of operations** to be carried out. The levels on the structure diagram are important because some operations are made up of a sequence of others. Therefore, in figure 7.9(a), for example, P is made up of the sequences Q, R and S, and in turn S is made up of the sequence T and U. Notice that although this diagram is equivalent to the linear sequence PQRSTU, **structure** has been implied from the **hierarchy** of the diagram and may, for example, imply different procedures representing each box.

Iteration (loops)   The **notation for a loop** or **iteration** is an '***' (asterisk or star) which is normally written in the top right-hand side of the box which represents the iteration (loop structure). We obviously need to know what conditions are in force, and on JSP diagrams this condition would normally be referenced by a number which in turn refers to the actual condition written down in what is called a **condition list**. This saves the JSP diagram from becoming cluttered up. The idea is shown in figure 7.9(b). In this diagram W is repeated until the end of file is reached.

Selection   A **selection structure** is indicated on a **JSP diagram** in a *similar way* to an **iteration**, but this time we may need **more than one box**, and the symbol for selection is different and is indicated by a small '**o**'. Figure 7.9(c) shows a selection structure whereby **Y is executed if the condition is true else Z is executed**. Of course *any number of boxes* could be used with the different conditions terminated by an 'else'.

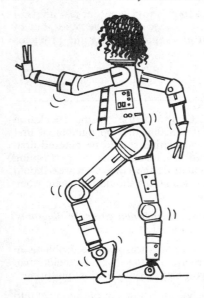

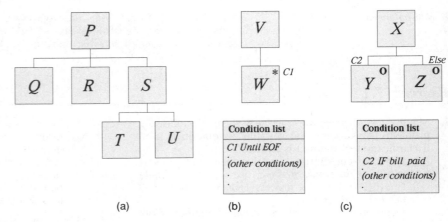

Figure 7.9

When using JSP techniques you *must ensure* that **all the children are of the same type.** In other words, when using JSP diagrams, and when considering any element in the structure as a parent (i.e. an element with sub-structures) the parent should not have children where the **brothers** and **sisters** are mixtures of sequences, iterations and selection structures. (Note that we are using parents, children, brothers and sisters etc. as used in the tree-structure diagrams shown on page 304.) This is not such a restrictive practice as might appear at first sight, as dummy boxes with a suitable comment (see figure 7.10) can easily be inserted to help obey these rules which are designed to making coding the structure easier.

Example using JSP

As a very simple example, let's suppose that we wish to work out some statistics on an unspecified quantity of people's ages to the nearest year typed in by the user. Let the **rogue value** (i.e. the terminating number which is *not part of the data*) be –999. Let's also suppose that the following statistics are required:

The mean (or average) age
The maximum age
The minimum age

A typical JSP diagram for this example is shown in figure 7.10. Note that we could have added *further detail* like how the variables are set up or how the statistics are

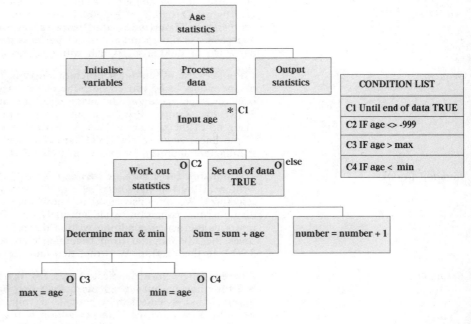

Figure 7.10

output, but these are trivial and have been left out for the sake of clarity – they have been included in the pseudocode that follows shortly. Notice that we have stuck to the rule that all components must only have children who are of the same type – we had to introduce the process-data box and the determine-max-and-min box to conform to these requirements in this particular JSP structure. Note also that the selection boxes at the bottom of the structure have no else part, therefore the simpler version shown in this diagram is acceptable. (There's not much point in drawing an empty box for the do-nothing situation if the condition C2 or C3 is not true.)

There is *very much more* to **JSP** than is indicated in the brief description here, but this will enable you to make use of these useful structure diagrams in your projects as part of suitable documentation if necessary. The real beauty of JSP lies in the next stage – It really *is* a doddle to derive the pseudocode (or most high-level language code) directly from the structure diagram, and the following part of a Pascal program demonstrates this wonderful correspondence between the structure diagram and the final code. JSP really is to be recommended.

```
program statistics(input,output);
var
age, sum, min, max, number : integer;
average : real;
data : boolean;
begin
  sum := 0;
  max := 0;
  min := 500;
  number := 0;
  data := false;
  repeat
    write('Enter age');
    readln (age);
    if age<>-999 then
        begin
          if (age < min) then min := age;
          if (age > max) then max := age;
          sum := sum + age;
          number := number + 1;
        end
    else
        begin
          data := true;
        end;
  until data = true;
  average := sum/number;
  writeln('The average age is ' , average);
  writeln('The maximum age is ' , max);
  writeln('The minimum age is ' , min);
end.
```

Although **hierarchical data structures** (either **top-down** or **bottom-up**) may seem like the best thing since the invention of sliced bread, they do have their limitations in terms of *lack of information* when formulating some problems. For example, does anything go on in parallel with anything else? *How much* information will be transferred between one database and another? However, other methods, developed by Gane and Sarson, start to address these problems and are considered in more detail a little later in this chapter.

HIPO charts

A **HIPO chart (Hierarchical Input Output Processing)** is an IBM structured chart technique which helps analysts to visualise the **overall plan of a project** rather than the detailed coding. The HIPO chart *emphasises the relationships* between the elements of a system. It's the same idea as the normal hierarchical chart, but with extra information regarding the function of each module or program. A simplified example of a HIPO diagram is shown in figure 7.11.

As can be seen from figure 7.11, the HIPO chart is useful for asking questions like 'What does each module do?' and 'What are the inputs and outputs?' On more-comprehensive HIPOs we could obviously include more information, and go into much greater detail. It is often more convenient to make use of a HIPO chart instead of writing down the same information in a long sequence of text.

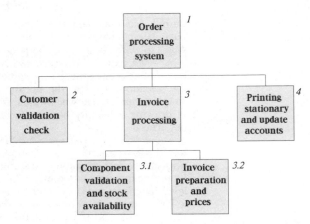

1　Controls all processing and calls the customer validation, invoice processing and delivery note printing system.

2　Receives customer number, performs validation check and credit worthiness of customer. Returns flag to main processing routine.

3　Accepts component numbers as input and calls routines to validate component, access prices and keep a running total of cost and availability of stock.

3.1　Validates component number, access and updates stock file, generates message if component is not available.

3.2　Produces invoice on screen, accepts data and messages from validation routines, accesses price files and updates the invoice on screen.

4　Prints out delivery notes for stores and updates accounts using invoice information.

Figure 7.11

Keeping the **software writing on schedule** is important in the business world. We have already seen how **structured methods** *reduce the time* spent on coding the software, and later in this chapter we shall see how the structured approach helps with the testing too.

Data flow analysis

The hierarchical data structure diagrams, good as they are for showing relationships between software modules and with helping to code programs, can't show many of the data interactions which are going on in many real-life systems. For example, how do we analyse how data gets transferred between different departments in a factory when computers, pieces of paper, people, and perhaps specialist machines such as CNC lathes and robots (see page 545) are involved? How do we cope with a telephone call from New York in our system diagram? How do we include a human messenger as part of the shop-floor flow of data in the factory?

Data flow diagrams

Fortunately there is another useful tool in our 'structured-analysis toolbox' in the form of a **data flow diagram** or **DFD** as it is sometimes known. These methods were developed by Gane and Sarson, and initially used extensively by the McDonnell-Douglas Corporation. Similar methods were also developed by other companies. The **data flow diagram** can be a representation of a **physical system** such as specific people or machines, or it can represent the **logical data flow** which is a device-independent diagram drawn without any reference to the physical characteristics of the system. However, both types of diagram make use of the same four basic symbols which are as follows.

Data flow symbol

The *first symbol* is a simple **arrow** as shown in figure 7.12(a). This simple data flow symbol shows the direction of the flow of data from any source to any destination in whatever form. Therefore, there is no distinction between documents or telephones or disks or any other media.

Process symbol

The Gane and Sarson symbol for processing is shown in figure 7.12(b). We could not care less about the physical device that is actually carrying out the process, so this can represent anything from a person undertaking a process to an automatic stock validation procedure carried out by a computer.

Source or destination symbols

The symbol shown in figure 7.12(c) shows any source or destination which is outside of the system. For example, if a stock-control system is being considered, then the

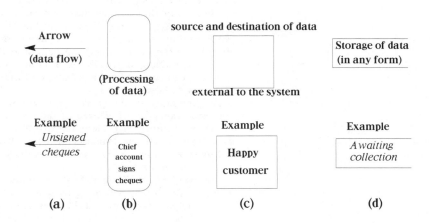

Figure 7.12

store keeper could be drawn making use of this symbol. Other examples might be incoming mail or a department in a factory which makes use of the system.

Data store symbol   This symbol, shown in figure 7.12(d) represents the storage of data in whatever form. So it could be on anything from a computerised CD-ROM drive to a pile of paper.

These symbols are obviously so general that the names which accompany them must be very descriptive of the actual processes which are taking place. Nevertheless, the terminology of these diagrams is so simple that they can be of great use in explaining the system to experts and non-experts alike.

Data flow example   The best way to get an understanding of data flow diagrams is to make use of them. Therefore, we will develop a data flow diagram using a simple example.

Suppose that we wish to analyse what happens in an office where Sue, the accounts clerk, processes requests for the payment of expenses in a company.

A typical scenario would be that an employee brings along a filled-in expenses sheet, then Sue verifies the signature, transfers the information into the computer system, and makes sure that a particular budget is not over spent. If successful, then a cheque

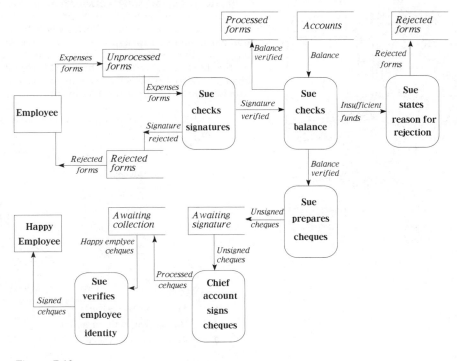

Figure 7.13

must be raised, signed by the chief accountant, then put in a tray ready for collection via Sue – how do we show these typical transactions on a data flow diagram?

A good start to many of these problems is to mirror the actual physical situation which is going on in the office as shown in fig 7.13. The very process of doing this often helps the analyst (and the people in the office) to understand exactly what is going on. Indeed, it is only after doing such an analysis that people often see a better way of carrying out a process that they have been doing without much thought for years.

The first stage in the process is obviously the request from the employee, and so the **employee**, being a **source** of data (in this case bringing the expenses form), is shown in a *source box*. Next the arrow from the employee must show the **flow of data**, (in this case the expense form), ready to be picked up by Sue. Hence we need a **data-flow arrow**, going *from the employee to Sue's in tray*, with **expenses form** written on the arrow.

Now Sue's 'in tray' is a **data store**, and so a **data storage symbol** with unprocessed forms written on it has been used for this purpose. You can see that it is pretty obvious what's happening as this diagram is intended for non-specialists. When some sort of processing takes place, such as Sue checking the signature (i.e. the fact that the expenses form has actually been signed, and signed by an appropriate person), then this takes place in the appropriate shaped box too.

You should have little difficulty in following the logic of a data flow diagram, but there are certain checks that you can do to try and ensure that the system is correct. For example, does each data-flow arrow have a name associated with it? Do all processing components have both inputs and output? Have all the data store components been used?

There are many more sophisticated uses of data flow diagrams but an understanding of the sort displayed in figure 7.13 is all that is necessary at advanced level. They are really useful for describing parts of your 'A' level projects that the other diagrams can't reach.

State transition diagrams

It is often convenient for us to consider a physical or logical object as being in one of a number of different **states**. For example, if we are considering a **physical object** such as a *burglar alarm*, then an **event** could activate this object such that it changes state. The states of a physical object such as a burglar alarm just described could be *disarmed*, *armed but not activated*, and *armed and activated*. An **event** such as a **burglar entering the premises** could cause the alarm to change from *armed but not activated* to *armed and activated*. Another **event**, such as **pressing the reset button** could cause the state of the alarm to be changed to **disarmed**.

Figure 7.14 shows what's often referred to as a **state transition diagram**. This particular example shows what can happen with our simple burglar alarm system.

Note that we have three buttons which, when pushed, cause **events a**, **b** or **r** to happen as defined in figure 7.14. We have allowed *any* button to be pushed from *any* state. For example, if the alarm is in the disarmed state, then pressing reset (r) or the burglar entering the house (b) would *not* cause the state of the alarm to change. By following with your finger on the diagram you can predict which **state transitions** will occur when any **event** happens.

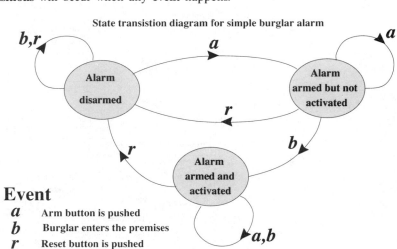

State transistion diagram for simple burglar alarm

Event
a   Arm button is pushed
b   Burglar enters the premises
r   Reset button is pushed

Figure 7.14

The state transition diagram in figure 7.14 referred to **physical objects** which represented the state of an alarm. However, state transition diagrams are not limited to physical objects. Software states (logical states) can be represented too. For example, when a **program** or **job** is being run by an **operating system** (see page 372), the program may be in a **ready state** (i.e. waiting to have some CPU time), or it might be in a **running state** (making use of the CPU). **Events** such as a t**ime-out interrupt** might **flag** the end of the **CPU time slice**, and this event may cause the state of the program to change from 'running' back to the 'ready state' (waiting to be run). Another typical scenario is that a program under the control of an operating system might be waiting for input or output. In this case it will have to be locked out of the cycle which gives it its time slice until the peripheral activity has taken place.

A state transition example

Figure 7.15 shows a typical state of affairs (pun intended!) for the OS problem.

State transistion diagram for operating system processes

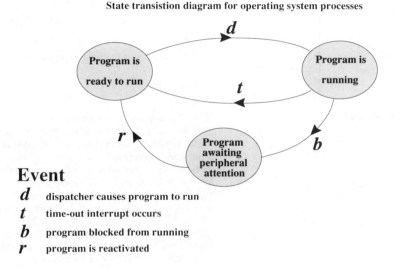

Event

d   dispatcher causes program to run

t   time-out interrupt occurs

b   program blocked from running

r   program is reactivated

Figure 7.15

Each of the three states of a program is shown within the 'circles', and each event, viewed from an operating-system (OS) perspective is shown by the state-transition arrows. The **dispatcher** is part of the **operating system** software which has the job of dispatching (**shown by event d**) the program so that it may be run by the CPU. If the program is going to hog the CPU for a long time then an interrupt will cause it to time out, (**shown by event t**). If a peripheral request is made during the execution of a program then the running of the program is blocked by the operating system, (**shown by event b**). Finally, when the peripheral request has been serviced the program is ready to be reactivated (shown by r). This means that it is ready for a further stint of CPU time when the dispatcher is able to get round to this program again.

State transition diagrams are extensively used in theoretical courses on computer science where mathematical models of computation using the algorithmic approach of computers is considered in detail. These diagrams help to cope with the basics of helping to understand about Turing machines, and thus form a fundamental part of computer science theory. Besides helping with highly advanced theoretical computer science or helping to program a burglar alarm, state-transition diagrams are helpful in developing pattern-recognition algorithms too. For example, suppose we were to design a find-text algorithm for a word processor. Let's also suppose for the sake of argument that we wish to search for the string 'abba'. Now we can go along the text rejecting all characters until an 'a' occurs – lets suppose that this state is represented by Q_1 as shown in figure 7.16. Now we either get a 'b' occurring, in which case we go to the next successful state which we will call Q_2, or we don't get a 'b' occurring, in which case we go back to an unsuccessful state which we will call Q_0, unless it was another 'a', in which case we remain at state Q_1.

This diagram would considerably help towards writing some code that could find the string 'abba'. State-transition diagrams often clarify quite complex situations in which the states of processes or objects are continually in a state of change.

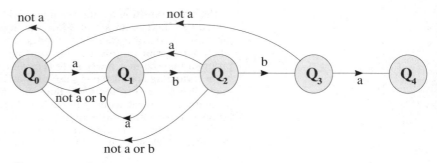

Q_0 Unsuccessful search so far
Q_1 A single 'a' has been found that could belong to the sequence abba
Q_2 An 'ab' has been found that could belong to the sequence abba
Q_3 An 'abb' has been found that could belong to the sequence abba
Q_4 We have found the sequence abba

Figure 7.16

Decision tables

This is a tabular arrangement of conditions and actions arranged as a matrix of rows and columns. There are alternative systems but the most common type of decision table is shown in figure 7.17. The table can be considered as being divided up into **four main quadrants** as shown in figure 7.17(a). In the *top left quadrant* we list the **conditions** or **questions** which are to be involved in the decision-making process, and in the *bottom left quadrant* we list the **actions** that can be taken. Considering the top right quadrant, we put Yes or No in the boxes depending on which conditions are applying in a particular column. In this we are building up rules which are given the numbers 1,2,3 etc, where each rule is determined by the vertical column underneath each of the numbers in the top-right-hand quadrant. Finally, in the bottom right-hand quadrant we list the **actions selected** or the **results** which relate to the rules indicated in the columns above.

You should note that when considering the **conditions selected** by rule number in the top right-hand quadrant, **Y and N** represent **Yes** and **No** respectively, and a '–' means that the condition is **not appropriate**. However, when considering the **actions selected** in the bottom right-hand quadrant, an **X** is used to denote that a particular action **has been chosen**.

A decision-table example

It's a difficult decision to make

Let's suppose that we wish to validate (see page 231) a date in the form **dd/mm/yy**. This is a classic case where a decision table is ideal for making a tabulated list of the conditions and actions. If, like the author, you can't remember how many days are in each month, then you will probably resort to the well-known rhyme.

Decision Rules

	1 2 3 4 5 6 7...
Conditions (Questions)	**Condition entries**
Actions (List of)	**Action entries** (Results)

(a)

Conditions	1	2	3	4	5	6
Date is numeric.	N	Y	Y	Y	Y	Y
1 <= month <= 12	▪	N	Y	Y	Y	Y
1 <= day <= 31	▪	▪	N	Y	Y	Y
month = 9, 4, 6 or 11	▪	▪	▪	Y	▪	▪
day = 31	▪	▪	▪	Y	▪	▪
leap year	▪	▪	▪	▪	Y	N
month = 2	▪	▪	▪	▪	Y	Y
day > 28	▪	▪	▪	▪	▪	Y
day > 29	▪	▪	▪	▪	Y	▪
Actions						
Reject date	X	X	X	X	X	X

(b)

Figure 7.17

*Thirty days has September
April, June and November.
All the rest have 31,
excepting February which has but 28 days clear,
and 29 in each leap year.*

So, putting the above algorithm into action, we can derive the **decision table** shown in figure 7.17(b). To gain an understanding of how the table works, you need to see how the conditions have lead to the production of the rules.

First let's consider rule number 1 which is shown vertically in column (1) in the top right-hand side of the table. Looking at the first condition, if the date is *not* in numeric form, as indicated by the N, (i.e. 6th June 1999 might have been entered) then we **do not accept the date** irrespective of any other condition which may be met. Therefore, if we have already rejected the date on this criterion alone (as shown by the **X** in the action-entries section), then none of the other conditions need apply, as is indicated by the '–' entries for the remainder of rule 1.

Now for rule 2, we are assuming that the date is in the correct numeric form, as indicated by the Y entry in the second column. We must therefore take into account the next condition, namely 'Is the month between 1 and 12 inclusive?'. If it is not, then the month is invalid, we can reject the date (as shown with the X entry at the bottom of column 2) and any further conditions are irrelevant.

For rule 3, if the date is numeric and the month is OK, but the day is outside the range 0 to 31 inclusive, then these conditions are sufficient to reject the date. The process continues in this way until all possible conditions which could be used to reject the date are accounted for. The table would be too long if we considered all the possibilities for accepting the dates!

Linked decision tables

It's often convenient to link several decision tables when solving more-complex problems. When linking tables the action that may be taken may often refer to another table. For example, we could have a list of actions which included Do table 1 or Do table 2 etc. Used in this context the decision tables become part of a larger structured diagram with pointers between the tables.

Linked decision-table example

To illustrate this idea let's consider a simple business in which there are two types of customer. Those *with* an account who can have credit, and those *without* accounts who must pay cash. Let's also suppose that discount is available to credit (*account holding*) customers at the following rates.

	Goods < £100 . . . . . 5% discount
£100 ≤	Goods < £1000 . . . . . 10% discount
£1000 ≤	Goods . . . . 15% discount

Now suppose that the *cash-paying* customer gets a slightly higher rate of discount as follows:

	Goods < £100 . . . . . 10% discount
£100 ≤	Goods < £1000 . . . . . 15% discount
£1000 ≤	Goods . . . . 20% discount

Figure 7.18 shows how the tables may be linked, and how they can form part of a more-comprehensive decision-table diagram. By linking tables in this way the size of each table can be more easily controlled.

Decision trees

Decision trees form another tool in our arsenal of structured-analysis techniques. They are identical to the trees which are used in elementary mathematics to calculate probabilities and are extremely easy to use. We can use the customer status and discount information data in the previous section to analyse the problem again, but this time making use of a decision tree.

As can be seen from figure 7.19, working from the root we can easily see which decisions must be made first. We must decide which condition satisfies any particular situation and then follow the appropriate branch of the tree. Eventually, after all the appropriate conditions have been fulfilled, we will end up at the leaf of the tree where the action to be taken is encountered.

You must not forget that time is also a valuable resource which must be managed effectively if we are to make sure that complex projects are completed on time. All the analysis techniques considered so far have not included the time factor, but the

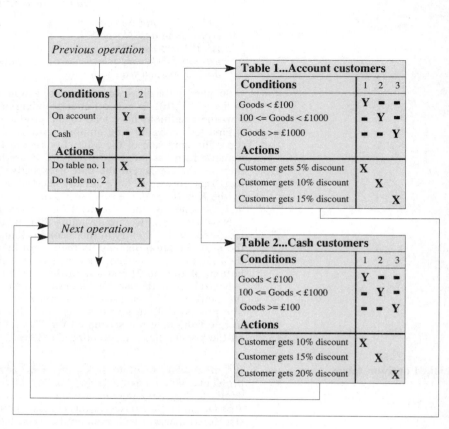

Figure 7.18

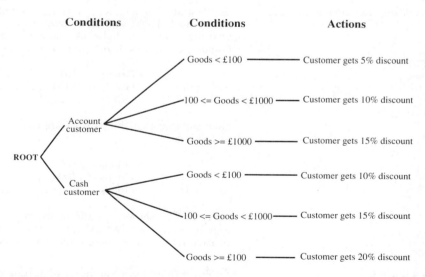

Figure 7.19

Gantt charts and the PERT charts considered in the next section will redress this balance.

Gantt charts

A **Gantt chart** is similar in nature to the specialist calendar charts which display the whole year on a horizontal month-by-month basis. However, instead of an arbitrary year, the actual project-activity time from conception to completion is expressed at the top of the chart, usually in weeks. A typical example is shown in figure 7.20. The information shown here relates to the overall project structure, but other Gantt charts may be used for sub-sections of the project.

Gantt chart

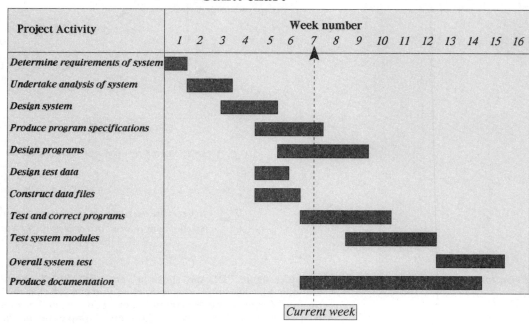

Project Activity	Week number
	1 2 3 4 5 6 7 8 9 10 11 12 13 14 15 16
Determine requirements of system	
Undertake analysis of system	
Design system	
Produce program specifications	
Design programs	
Design test data	
Construct data files	
Test and correct programs	
Test system modules	
Overall system test	
Produce documentation	

Current week

Figure 7.20

Although designed specifically for larger projects, I would advise students to make use of a Gantt chart on their own advanced-level project. You will probably find that you have not got the experience to map out the exact times which will be needed, but you *have* already got the project activities mapped out in detail if you have bothered to do a structured analysis of your project! You can get your lecturer or teacher to help you with the likely project times – you'll be amazed at how much help this will give.

The biggest advantage of producing a **Gantt chart** is that it shows if you are *on schedule*. If one part of the project is taking considerably longer than expected, then you will obviously have to do something drastic or revise the time taken to do the rest of the project activities. This is a sobering thought as the deadline for handing in the project approaches. In industry and business, other activities like employees holidays etc. can also be included on the chart.

Although ideal for planning the simpler projects, a **Gantt chart** is *not sufficient* for an **analysis of the dynamic nature of many large projects**. For example, what happens if an expected utility is not ready? If other project activities depend on this particular piece of software, then these other activities will be delayed too. On complex projects a delay in one critical activity might result in an unacceptable extension to the project time, and usually result in the all-too-familiar over-budget scenario. As large projects often run into millions of pounds or more this is an unacceptable state of affairs. The critical activities need to be identified and appropriate action such as putting more members of the programming team on these activities might be necessary if the overall project is not to go over the scheduled time and budget.

PERT charts

PERT (Program (or **Project**) **Evaluation** and **Review Technique) charts** have been popular for managing large projects ever since the US navy made use of this system way back in the 1950s when the Polaris Submarine project was being managed. The idea is that a project *can be spilt up into* **activities** and **events**.

One of the *problems* with the **top-down approach** considered earlier is that although it breaks up the project into smaller and more-manageable sections, there are no facilities to check if the overall progress of the project is being efficiently managed. Project managers are often required to ask questions like 'What shall we do next?' or 'Can this be done at the same time as that?' or 'We can't get on with X because Y has happened...therefore, what shall we do?' The Gantt or hierarchical charts don't give a visual indication of the interdependence of modules within a project.

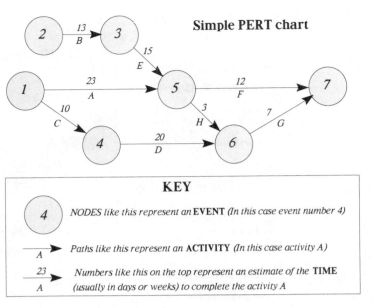

Figure 7.21

Event timing

Consider figure 7.21, this shows a very small PERT chart, but the main ideas are embodied in this simple diagram. Here you can see that the project has been divided up into **7 events** and **8 activities**. Let's concentrate on **event 5** in this system, and let's suppose that this event represents '**Completion of the testing modules**'. Now we can see from the diagram that **event 5** *can't be completed until* **activities A** and **E** have been done. **Activity A** might be '**Construct data files**' which will take an estimated **23** days work, for example, and **activity E** might be '**Design the test data**' which will take an estimated **15 days**. (This assumes that the units of time on the chart are in days.)

Obviously more-complex PERT charts than this would be needed for most projects, but one of the main advantages of using a PERT chart is in the ability to calculate the **critical path**, i.e. **the path which effectively dictates the completion time of the project**. If we analyse the PERT chart shown in figure 7.21, then we can see that the path 2 – 3 – 5 – 7, which takes an estimated time of 13+15+12 = 40 days dictates the time that the project will take, *assuming that everything goes to schedule*. However, everything does not normally run to schedule, and this is where the PERT chart comes into its own. Suppose that activity C is delayed and takes 15 days. The new critical path now becomes 1 – 4 – 6 – 7 which will take an estimated 42 days with the revised time for activity C.

If you are wondering how tedious it would be to manually recalculate these critical paths on a large project, then you need not worry because **PERT computer programs** have been doing this for years. They form an established part of project management and are an extremely effective tool both in the software industry and elsewhere. The above type of software is also known as **CPA** or **Critical Path Analysis**.

Earliest starting times

An added dimension to the PERT chart which helps tremendously with effective project management is 'How early may we be able to start an event or how long may an event may be delayed without endangering the overall project schedule?' This too can be worked out automatically by computer, but figure 7.22 shows a modified version of figure 7.21 in which this new information has been added.

To fill in the extra time information you proceed along the following lines:

Events 1 and 2 can be started instantly, it does not depend on anything that has gone before, therefore, the earliest event times are trivial and are both equal to zero.

Concentrate next on the *top numbers only*. Let's choose event 3, as it is one of the next in the chain. Now there is only one previous event (event 2) and so we simply add 13 (the time taken for activity B) to the zero already established in event 2 to get the next time of 13 which is written in the *top* of event 3. (*Don't forget it's top numbers only for the moment!*) Event 4 can be filled in by using an identical method.

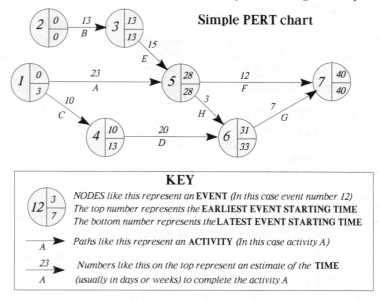

Simple PERT chart

KEY

NODES *like this represent an* **EVENT** *(In this case event number 12)*
The top number represents the **EARLIEST EVENT STARTING TIME**
The bottom number represents the **LATEST EVENT STARTING TIME**

Paths *like this represent an* **ACTIVITY** *(In this case activity A)*

Numbers *like this on the top represent an estimate of the* **TIME**
(usually in days or weeks) to complete the activity A

Figure 7.22

Concentrate now on event 5, but again, *top numbers only*. There are two scenarios:

(1) Activity E.... Preceding time 13 .... Event E time 15.... Total time 28 or
(2) Activity A.... Preceding time 0 ..... Event A time 23.... Total time 23

Therefore, the earliest event time for event 5 must be 28, the largest of these two numbers, *because the 2 – 3 – 5 path will be the critical factor here* for the earliest start time if we are waiting to complete event 5. Proceed in the above manner until all the top numbers have been filled in. Note that the number in the top-right hand side of the final box denotes the minimum amount of time needed to complete the whole project.

Latest start times avoiding delays

Next let's concentrate on the *bottom numbers only*, namely – 'How late can we start an event without delaying the project-completion time?'

For this we start at the end of the PERT chart. If the project is to be completed without delay then 40, being the minimum necessary amount of time must be entered into the bottom box on the last event (event number 7).

Working backwards to event number 6, for example, 7 days would be needed to get from event 6 to event 7, therefore, event 6 must start 7 days before the 40-day deadline *at the latest*. Therefore, the number 33 must be written in this box.

To determine what the latest starting time would be for event 5, for example, use the following scenario:

    (1) Activity F.... Succeeding time 40 .... Event F time 12.... Latest time = 28
or (2) Activity H.... Succeeding time 33 .... Event H time 3..... Latest time = 30

This time we must choose the smallest time being 28 days, as this represents the latest time at which we can start this activity without delaying the project.

All the calculated values for these times are shown in figure 7.22. Even with this simple PERT chart a project manager can start to see the flexibility which may be inherent in some activities. For example, Activity 4 could be started on day 10, or delayed until day 13, but activity 5 must be started on day 28, or the project will be delayed. The *critical path is given by events 2 – 3 – 5 – 7*, and any activities on this particular path can't be delayed.

Exercise 7.2

1. Explain why **Jackson Structured Programming** (JSP) techniques are particularly useful for the production of the source code for many common types of algorithm.

2. Show, making use of suitable diagrams how 'sequence', 'selection' and 'iteration' (loops) are implemented making use of **JSP** techniques.

3. Use a **JSP diagram** to develop an algorithm to read in an unknown quantity of names and examination marks terminated by 'dummy', –99. The names are to be sorted into categories of pass (mark ≥ 40%) and fail (mark < 40%). The algorithm is to produce a list of names of the students who have passed, a separate list of names of the students who have failed – both lists being in order of descending marks. You may assume that a utility exists to sort the names and marks into descending order.

4. Why is a **HIPO chart** sometimes more useful than a conventional hierarchical diagram?

5. Construct a typical **data-flow analysis diagram** for handing in your assignments to be marked by your tutor or teacher. You should allow for marks to be entered into a register and for terrible work to be returned to be re-marked if necessary. You should also allow for a list to be made of students who have not handed in their work!

6. List two or three different types of problem in which a **state-transition diagram** could help with the solution. Use a state-transition diagram to show how a security-lock system can be used to control entry to a computer centre. Use a unique 4-digit code of your choice, and the system should activate an alarm if more than 3 incorrect digits are entered without some form of corrective action taking place. You may assume that a reset button is available if you think that this is necessary.

7. The following **decision tree** shows the delivery charges made by a furniture-manufacturing company. Show the *same information* making use of a decision table.

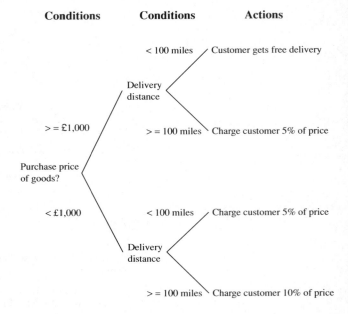

8. What is meant by a Gantt chart and why are they extensively used in project management? Why are Gantt charts less useful for showing the dynamic nature of some projects?

9. What characteristics of project management are best analysed by making use of a PERT chart? Using a simple example explain what is meant by critical-path analysis (CPA).

End of chapter summary

- **Software engineering** is the name given to the **analysis, debugging, testing** and **documentation** of a system.
- An **algorithm** is a step-by-step **sequence of instructions** to solve a particular problem in a finite amount of time.
- An **algorithm** may be expressed in many ways including English-like statements or many different forms of diagram.
- **Basic flowcharts** or **programming flowcharts** are useful to describe relatively simple algorithms in a pictorial way, making use of **termination symbols, processing symbols, input/output symbols, decision symbols** and **connection symbols.**
- More-comprehensive **decision making** is possible making use of the **multiple-output decision** methods.
- **Complex systems** can be described by making use of **systems flowcharts**.
- **Flowcharts** should be **annotated** (*with added comments*) where possible.
- **Structure diagrams** are a useful and often better alternative to the flowchart because they *mirror the structured programming constructs more closely*.
- **Pseudocode** is useful for describing algorithms in a structured way. It makes use of English-like statements which mirror modern structured high-level languages.
- **Design structure diagrams** using British Standard (BS 6224) provide a structured-flowchart style alternative to conventional charts and structure diagrams.

- **Hierarchical structure diagrams** help set out simple algorithms or help with the visualisation of an overall program or project.
- The **top-down approach** to project design means splitting up complex problems into easier and easier subtasks until each subtask is of manageable proportions.
- The **bottom-up approach** to project design involves using pre-written routines and procedures which can be used to construct a more comprehensive system.
- **Jackson Structured Programming (JSP)** techniques take hierarchical diagrams a stage further by including the concepts of **sequence**, **iteration** (*loops*) and **selection**.
- It is often *very easy* to produce **pseudocode** from **JSP** or **structure diagrams**, but *not so easy* from **flowcharts**.
- A **HIPO chart** is a **structure diagram** specifically to *emphasise the relationships* between the elements of a system but with *added annotation*.
- A **data flow diagram** makes use of **data flow symbols**, **processes symbols**, **source or destination symbols** and **data store symbols**. It is ideal for showing how data moves around in *virtually any environment*.
- A **state transition diagram** is useful for representing **physical or logical objects** which can be in a variety of states. An **event** causes the *state of an object to change*.
- A **decision table** consists of **conditions** and **actions**, **condition entries** and **action entries**. **Numbered rules** are derived which give the conditions under which appropriate action is taken.
- **Linked decision tables** often help to reduce the size of a decision table to make its use more manageable.
- A **decision tree** is a tree structure consisting of conditions which must be executed to arrive at an appropriate action.
- A **Gantt chart** is a static time-management chart useful for visualisation of an overall project.
- A **PERT (Project Evaluation and Review Technique)** chart is a **dynamic time and resource management chart** which enables **time-critical paths** to be calculated.

8 An overview of high-level languages

Having read through chapters 6 and 7 you should now be well placed to appreciate the **evolution and development** of **high-level languages** in a *more general context*. You should appreciate the need for **structure**, the need for **efficient analysis and coding**, the need for **self-documentation**, and the need for the many other **desirable facilities** that go into making up modern high-level languages. You have already seen that high-level languages belong to **different classes** such as **imperative, declarative** and **object-oriented**, for example, and should also be aware of the differences between the **generations of languages**. As systems become ever more complex, the need to strive for **absolute correctness** is now one of the most fundamental and demanding problems that needs to be solved by computer scientists – but unfortunately, at the moment, we are a long way from being able to achieve this for very complex programs – either theoretically or in practice. Finally, you should now also be wise enough to appreciate that it's not possible nor desirable to develop a single language which would be able to cope with the huge variety of different problems, ranging, for example, from control of a chemical plant to dealing with the accounts for millions of customers who belong to a large clearing bank.

All the above introductory work has already been covered elsewhere, so we will now concentrate on looking at particular examples of different high-level languages, and see how they have evolved over the years to get to the current state of play in the mid-to-late 90s. **Major languages** such as **Pascal**, **FORTRAN 90**, **COBOL85** and **C++**, for example, are considered in some detail, but other, less prominent but nonetheless important languages are covered more briefly.

Student activities

Throughout this chapter you will find a range of **student activities** *relating to the different languages* being considered. They have been designed to be simple enough to be carried out within a short space of time. *If* your school or college has a compiler for any of these languages then you should use it, if possible, to carry out the suggested activities. Brief answers for each activity using the language concerned can be found in the answers section at the end of this book.

FORTRAN 90

FORTRAN (or **Fortran**) stands for **FOR**mula **TRAN**slator (or **Formula Tran**slation). It is *the* **mathematical** and **scientific programming language**. The FORTRAN language is to mathematics, engineering and science, what the COBOL language is to the business or data-processing community. A huge variety of mathematical and scientific applications and utilities written in FORTRAN have been built up over many years, and *it is probably this above all else that makes the language so convenient* for use by both engineers and scientists – it has most of the built-in facilities and functions to solve their type of problems in ways which are efficient and relatively easy for scientists and engineers to understand.

The FORTRAN language was one of the *first* high-level languages to be developed way back in 1954. Being over 40 years old, it has gone through several incarnations, the most recent of which is called **FORTRAN 90**. As its name implies, this new version is intended to be a language for the 1990s. Unlike the older versions such as FORTRAN 77 or FORTRAN IV, for example, many new and powerful facilities have been included giving FORTRAN 90 a hitherto unheard of ability to process *non-numerical information* in powerful ways too. It has retained all the advanced mathematical-processing abilities of the older versions, but has been

considerably enhanced in the areas in which FORTRAN was originally lacking. However, FORTRAN 90's advanced mathematical features are already being extended! For example, direct use of the **parallel-processing architectures** as described on page 62 is an attractive proposition for any mathematically-intensive language, and work is currently going on in this area where it has proved to be ideal for complex matrix manipulations which FORTRAN handles with ease. However, *until all computers can handle parallel processing*, the portability of Fortran programs would be considerably reduced if they were written in this way, unless a mechanism exists for switching between the two modes.

One of the *outstanding features of FORTRAN* has been it's **portability**. FORTRAN avoided differences in graphics and operating systems etc. by *not* providing any sophisticated input/output facilities in this particular area. (That's one way of doing it!) Third-party vendors tended to produce input/output/graphics interfaces to FORTRAN programs for their particular machines. Therefore, if you wanted to produce a stunning display with 3D graphics to impress your friends, FORTRAN would do all the analysis and number crunching, and then pass the data over to routines which control the graphics display – quite a clever idea really.

FORTRAN handles **complex numbers** with ease. (Not hard numbers! – but numbers with *real and imaginary parts* as used in the Mandelbrot set shown on page 180). FORTRAN also has a vast array (excuse the pun) of **MATRIX functions** for manipulating matrices including **addition**, **subtraction**, **multiplication**, **inverse**, **deter-minants** and **transpose** etc. We *could* program *all* of these functions from any other competent language, but it's *far easier* and *very much faster* if the language supports them in the first place – this is one of the reasons why FORTRAN has reigned supreme in this field. Indeed, the three-dimensional wire-frame image manipulation capabilities making use of transformation geometry can easily be implemented using FORTRAN – and together with a **vector display** of the type described on page 245,

Simplified structure of a FORTRAN 90 program

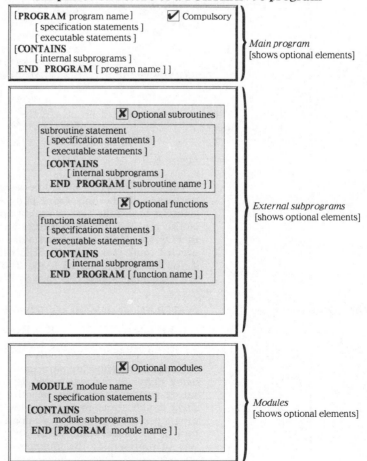

Figure 8.1

scientists and engineers are easily able to move complex 3D-wire-frame images around the screen in real time.

In fact wire-frame images and transformation geometry make a challenging project at Advanced level – assuming of course that you don't mind learning the fascinating topic of transformation geometry itself, which is not too difficult and can be found in modern 'A' level mathematics texts. If you don't have a FORTRAN compiler then you can write all the matrix-manipulation commands from scratch in a language like BASIC, for example, but you will probably have to **compile** the source code and use a *very fast* machine – especially if you wish to be able to manipulate a complex image without having time to make three cups of coffee before it's finished drawing the next scene.

FORTRAN 90 program structure

Figure 8.1 shows the **structure** of a *typical* **FORTRAN 90** program. Note that the square braces [ ] show which elements are optional (most are!). As can be seen from the diagram, *only the main-program module is compulsory*, and even here it's only compulsory to have the keywords END PROGRAM! However, without many of these optional elements the resulting FORTRAN program would be very trivial indeed (see the example in a moment). Most of the pre-written programs available to engineers and scientists would be considerably more complex than this, and many run into tens of thousands of lines of code. There is a huge investment in FORTRAN both in terms of time and money – and this is one of the reasons why FORTRAN has remarkable staying power.

A *very simple* FORTRAN program for working out the square root of a positive number, together with a trap to eliminate the possibility of entering negative numbers could be designed from the Nassi-Schneiderman structure diagram of figure 8.2.

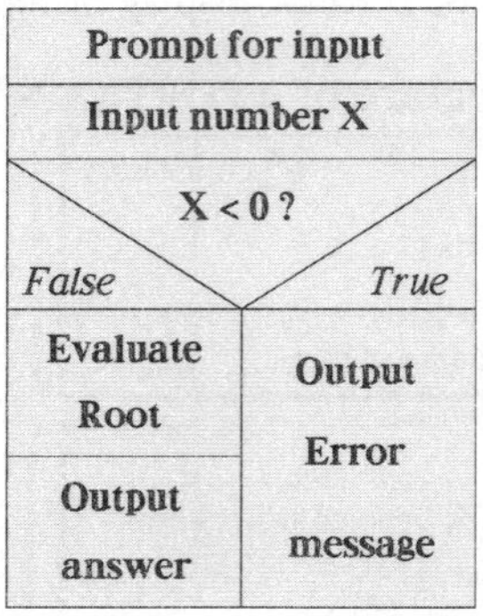

Prompt for input

Input number X

X < 0 ?
False   *True*

Evaluate Root	Output Error
Output answer	message

Figure 8.2

A *very* simple FORTRAN program

```
PROGRAM Square_Root
REAL::x,ans
WRITE (*,*) "Input a positive number:"
READ (*,*) x
Sign: IF x < 0 THEN
    WRITE(*,*) "Can't do negative numbers"
    ELSE Sign:
      ans = SQRT(x)
      WRITE (*,*)"The square root of: ", x,"is",ans
    END IF Sign
END PROGRAM Square_Root
```

The above program should be reasonably easy to understand for computer-science students, with the only weird part being (*,*) which is instructing the FORTRAN compiler to use the *current* **output unit** and the *default* **conventions** for input/output. Notice also that the **IF construct** has been used *rather* than a simple **IF statement**. In FORTRAN 90 a **construct name** (**Sign:** in the above example) is used in a way which I think makes the IF-THEN-ELSE parts far easier to understand, especially if you have many nested loops. The other parts of the program consist only of a few **executable statements** such as WRITE, READ and one to work out the answer.

FORTRAN 90 variable types

FORTRAN 90 supports the following variable types.

I – Integer	R – Real	Z – Complex
C – Character	S – Character string	L – Logical

Complex variables are *particularly useful* in **engineering** and **science**, as *they model many things in the real world*. If complex variables had been used in the above square-root program, then negative numbers could have been typed in too. With slight modifications to the program, if –2, for example, had been typed in, then the program could be made to respond with the *two* different answers for the square root of –2, which would be (0 , 1.41421356) and (0 , –1.41421356). This is just one way of representing the numbers (0 + i1.41421356) and (0 – i1.41421356), and, if you are an 'A' level or higher-standard mathematician, you will realise that when either of these two complex numbers are multiplied together the result would be –2. We did say that FORTRAN was mathematical!

FORTRAN 90 keywords

FORTRAN 90 has a very powerful set of over 100 intrinsic procedures which are available to the programmer and which act like functions. To get just a little of the flavour, a small subset has been chosen and is shown in the following list.

Name	Brief explanation
CONJ(Z)	The *CONjugate* of a complex number.
CLOG(X)	*LOG* of a Complex number X.
DCOS(X)	*COSine* of X in Double-precision.
DOTPRODUCT (Vector_A,Vector_B)	*Dot-product* of two vectors.
MATMUL(Matrix_A,Matrix_B)	Multiply two *matrices* together.
TRANSPOSE(Matrix)	Work out the *transpose* of a matrix

FORTRAN 90 *is* indeed the tops for mathematical work, and the number of array-related functions is enormous. However, it's ironic to note that *all* the above functions – and *many others* are now available on my Texas TI-85 calculator! Indeed, my TI-85 calculator can easily solve simultaneous equations in 10 unknowns by using matrix methods – a feat which needed a mainframe when I was a student! It's amazing what embedded microprocessor systems can now do (see page 582).

Student activities – FORTRAN 90

You will find that all of these examples can also be done using the older FORTRAN 77 compilers.

(1) Write a program to input a series of positive integer numbers and work out the average. Use a rogue variable value of –999.

(2) Write a program to multiply two 3 × 3 matrices together and output the answer. Use real numbers only.

COBOL

COBOL (COmmon Business Oriented Language) is the *workhorse* of the **business and data processing world**. The language was originally designed by a group in the USA called CODASYL (the COnference on DAta SYstems Languages), being made up of representatives from government agencies, computer manufacturers, universities and other interested parties. Work was finally completed in about 1960 and COBOL compilers have been produced in one form or another ever since. COBOL has become *the* standard business language and *is ideally suited for data processing where large volumes of business-type data and files have to be handled efficiently*. However, the **mathematical processing capability** is *strictly limited* to the more mundane arithmetic processes that are used in accounting. The syntax of COBOL varies slightly between COBOL, COBOL 85 and COBOL II, but the general ideas are the same.

COBOL structure

The language is made up of many English-like statements which were originally used so that non-specialist computer users would have some idea of what is going on. This verbose language is therefore effectively **self documenting**. The English-like analogy was taken several stages further, such that **statements** were referred to as **sentences** and *many* **sentences** were grouped together to form a **paragraph**.

Figure 8.3 shows a simplified structure of a COBOL program, which would be *almost useless* without most of the optional elements present! It consists of four main divisions called the **identification, environment, data** and **procedure divisions**. The functions of each of the four divisions, together with some tongue-in-cheek examples, are explained in the following sections. These will gradually build up into part of a COBOL program which deals with a garden-gnome computer file-handling system for the famous Fothergill, Sprogitt & Greendish chain of garden centres.

Identification division

This first section of a COBOL program identifies the program and contains *just* one paragraph which is called the program-ID. – it *must* specify the name of the program, but may *optionally* be used to specify the author of the program, its intended purpose, and any other information which can be added as comments if required. An identification division for our garden-gnome example might be as follows. Note that an asterisk (*) denotes the start of a comment in COBOL.

Simplified structure of a COBOL program

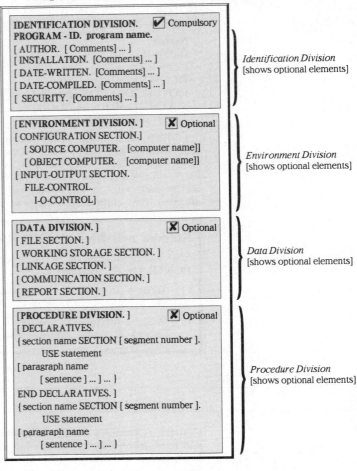

Figure 8.3

Identification division

```
IDENTIFICATION DIVISION.
PROGRAM-ID.           Gnomes.
AUTHOR.               FotherGill and Greendish.
DATE-WRITTEN.         16/12/95.
DATE-COMPILED.        16/12/95.
SECURITY.             Top secret!.
*Program to interrogate garden gnome file
```

Environment division

The second part of a COBOL program contains the **environment division**. It consists of *two sections* called the **configuration** and **input-output** sections. Together these specify the *type of computer* on which the program is to be compiled and run, and the *peripherals* that will be required such as the **input** and **output units**. An optimistic environment division for the garden-gnome program might be as follows.

```
ENVIRONMENT DIVISION.
CONFIGURATION SECTION.
SOURCE-COMPUTER.
    CRAY Y-MP/832.
OBJECT-COMPUTER.
    CRAY Y-MP/832.
```

Data division

The third part is the **data division** and it *describes the data* used by the programs. For example, the **variables** to be used, a *detailed description* of the **files** and the *organisation* of the **storage requirements**. This is a little more involved and will therefore be treated in more detail in the example that follows.

Procedure division

The final part of the program is the procedure division. This is basically the **main guts of the program**, and will therefore not be considered any further in this introduction, but an example follows later on in this chapter.

A simple COBOL example

It's interesting to look at just one or two of the file-definition features in a simple COBOL program, and we will continue to use the garden gnomes as an example. Although the following might appear verbose, compare it with the *very primitive* file handling facilities usually available within BASIC, for example. When dealing with the **data structures** in chapter 14, or the **files and file-handling** sections in chapter 16, it is *far easier to implement all of these techniques* by using a language such as **COBOL**.

One nice thing about COBOL is that it mirrors very closely what would naturally be done by using common sense – after all, it *is* intended to be an English-like language. Let's assume that we have a manual-cataloguing system up and running in the garden centre where the garden gnomes are catalogued in a book as shown in figure 8.4. Notice that hair colour (head), body colour and beard colour, along with the names, stock description, quantities and price are all present.

Fothergill, Sproggit and Greendish - famous garden-gnomes catalogue

Cat. number	Name of gnome	Description			Stock quantities			Price
		Head	Body	Beard	Max.	Min.	Actual	
DLF 1	David	Brown	Red	Black	150	50	98	22.50
JIP 1	Jared	Black	Blue	Brown	300	100	276	25.00
KJD 1	Kevin	Red	Grey	Grey	250	75	43	15.60

Figure 8.4

We will assume that the manual stock-catalogue layout shown in figure 8.4 will be mirrored exactly on the computer system using COBOL. Now file handling (see chapter 16 for more detailed analysis) is COBOL's forte, and the relationships between the data are very efficiently described by making use of **different levels**.

The stock catalogue itself would represent the **file** (in practice there would be other files such as customers, suppliers and accounts, for example). Notice that a typical stock catalogue entry (one for each gnome) naturally splits up into **5 major categories**, namely, **catalogue number**, **name**, **description**, **quantities** and **price**. *Each entry* for a *single gnome* represents a **record**, and the *five major categories* represent different **fields** within a record. Notice that the description and stock quantities contain sub-fields, namely, 'head', 'body' and 'beard' belonging to the description, and 'max.', 'min.' and 'actual' belonging to the stock quantities. COBOL allows us to code this structure for the file as follows, but *additional information* is needed before the code can be used.

```
DATA DIVISION.
FILE SELECTION.
FD GNOME-STOCK-FILE
   LABEL RECORDS OMITTED
   DATA RECORD is GNOME.
01  GNOME.
     02  CAT-NUMBER.
     02  NAME-OF-GNOME.
     02  DESCRIPTION.
          03  HEAD.
          03  BODY.
          03  BEARD.
     02  STOCK-QUANTITIES.
          03  MAX.
          03  MIN.
          03  ACTUAL.
     02  PRICE.
```

The **different levels** are assigned a number with **01** being assigned to the **record** gnome (i.e. for each entry in the original catalogue). **02** is assigned to the **fields**, and **03** is assigned to the **sub-fields**. (You can go up to level 49!)

A COBOL compiler would now be able to deduce the structure, but does *not* yet know the type of data which is contained within each field or sub-field – which is the *additional information* referred to above. In COBOL there are *three different types of field*, namely **numeric**, **alphabetic** and **alphanumeric** (plus variations on these fields which we will *not* use here). Each field is described in COBOL by what's called a **picture**. A picture is a simple concept – an alphanumeric field, for example, is described to the compiler by using the word PICTURE followed by a letter X, followed by the number (within brackets) of alphanumeric characters which will appear within the field. Therefore, if we are describing the 4-character-catalogue-entry system for the garden gnomes, where entries consist of three letters followed by a single digit, (e.g. KJD1 or JIP1), then this would be described as PICTURE X(4).

Alphabetic fields are described by the word picture and the letter A, and numeric fields are very slightly different – they are described by the word picture and then a number of 9s are used to represent digits in an integer numeric field. Other variations of this theme are possible, but we will limit ourselves to the garden-centre example.

Figure 8.5 shows the number of characters for each field and sub-field within the stock-file catalogue, together with the field data description explained above.

Data needed for the COBOL-PICTURE definitions in the Gnome file

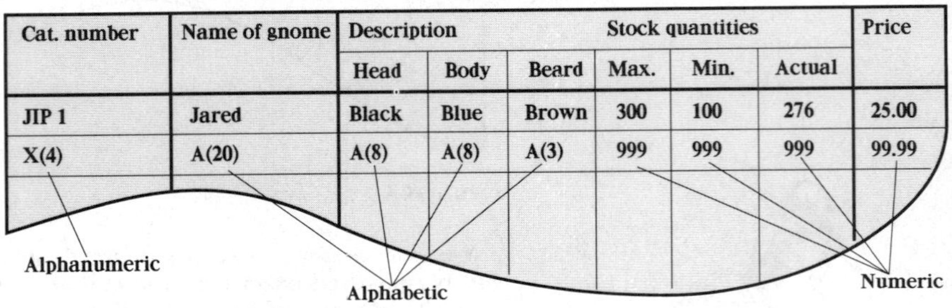

Cat. number	Name of gnome	Description			Stock quantities			Price
		Head	Body	Beard	Max.	Min.	Actual	
JIP 1	Jared	Black	Blue	Brown	300	100	276	25.00
X(4)	A(20)	A(8)	A(8)	A(3)	999	999	999	99.99

Alphanumeric

Alphabetic

Numeric

Figure 8.5

Using the information in figure 8.5, together with the file structure already built up in the previous DATA DIVISION, the COBOL garden-gnome program now looks something like the following.

```
DATA DIVISION.
FILE SELECTION.
FD  GNOME-STOCK-FILE
    LABEL RECORDS OMITTED
    DATA RECORD is GNOME.
01  GNOME.
    02  CAT-NUMBER              PICTURE X(4).
    02  NAME-OF-GNOME           PICTURE A(20).
    02  DESCRIPTION.
        03  HEAD                PICTURE A(8).
        03  BODY                PICTURE A(8).
        03  BEARD               PICTURE A(3).
    02  STOCK-QUANTITIES.
        03  WS-MAX              PICTURE 999.
        03  WS-MIN              PICTURE 999.
        03  ACTUAL              PICTURE 999.
    02  PRICE                   PICTURE 99V99.
```

(Note that the 'V' in the last definition shows the position of the decimal point.)

Notice how easy it is to describe data structures for business-type problems. Have a look at the ways in which your version of BASIC at school or college handles files – there is no comparison with the ease with which the files can be described, and with the self-documenting aspects of looking at programs such as the one shown above – COBOL wins hands down, as of course, it should!

A complete COBOL example

COBOL contains all of the structures necessary to be regarded as a good structured language, and COBOL's input output facilities are very impressive. As COBOL is intended for business use, a very simple program to add VAT at 17.5% to a number and print it out is shown as follows.

A Very-simple COBOL program

```
IDENTIFICATION DIVISION.
PROGRAM-ID.         VATMAN.
AUTHOR.             BRUCE WAYNE.
DATE-WRITTEN.       16/12/95.
DATE-COMPILED.      16/12/95.
SECURITY.           TOP SECRET!.
*Program to calculate VAT-inclusive price
*

ENVIRONMENT DIVISION.
CONFIGURATION SECTION.
SOURCE-COMPUTER.
    CRAY Y-MP/832.
OBJECT-COMPUTER.
    CRAY Y-MP/832.
*
DATA DIVISION.
WORKING-STORAGE SECTION.
01  PRICE-IN         PICTURE 99999V99.
01  VAT-RATE         PICTURE 99V9.
01  PRICE-OUT        PICTURE 99999V99.
*
PROCEDURE DIVISION.
VAT-CALCULATION-SECTION.
ACCEPT PRICE-IN.
ACCEPT VAT-RATE.
MULTIPLY VAT-RATE BY PRICE-IN GIVING PRICE-OUT.
DISPLAY "The cost of" PRICE-IN "and VAT @" VAT-RATE "% is" PRICE-OUT.
STOP RUN.
```

That's all there is to multiplying two numbers together – well, we did say COBOL is verbose! To be fair, much of the above is optional, but COBOL *is* superb for business data processing, and an example like the above gives you little indication of COBOL's true power. As with the other programs in the section, for an advanced-level student the overall structure should be simple to understand. The only extra part which needs a little explanation is the **WORKING-STORAGE section** which describes *data which is not associated with files*. The level number 01 has been used here, but in **older COBOL compilers the number 77 is often used**.

COBOL keywords

COBOL is a verbose language and has about 400 keywords (at the last count). Can you imagine trying to remember all of these! To keep with the style in which this chapter is written, and to get a flavour of COBOL, a small subset of keywords are shown in the following list.

Name	Brief explanation
DELETE	Removes a record from a direct-access file.
INDEXED BY	Indicates an index associated with a table.
OCCURS	Helps to define a table – like the decision tables, for example, shown on page 144.
OPEN	Prepares a file for opening.
PAGE	Helps to make sure that the printout starts on the next page.
PERFORM	Perform specified paragraph the number of times indicated.
SEARCH	Helps to implement a table look up.
USING	Helps to indicate an external file that is to be sorted.

Student activities – COBOL 85

You will find that all of these examples can also be done using the older COBOL compilers.

(1) Write a program to input a price from the keyboard, then work out and print out the VAT inclusive price by adding VAT at 17.5%.

(2) Write a program to work out the compound interest on a sum of money for a specified number of years. Both the years and the interest rate are to be entered from the keyboard.

Other language examples 1

Pascal

Pascal was developed by Nicholas Wirth at Zurich in Switzerland in 1968, and was completed and operational by 1971. The roots for Pascal were therefore laid down much later than FORTRAN and COBOL, for example. The name **Pascal** *is in honour of* the famous French mathematician **Blaise Pascal** who died in 1662. He developed one of the earliest calculating machines which was the first to use the concepts of input, output and processing (see page 11). Pascal is derived from the **ALGOL language** which was also popular in the 1960s, but Pascal itself *has evolved into* languages such as **Ada, Modula-2 and Modula-3**. As you can see – the relationship between many high-level languages is highly incestuous! It's also enlightening to note that languages themselves are usually quite stable, with variations on a theme lasting for tens of years – a fact not common in other areas of computing.

Pascal is a **general-purpose easy-to-use programming language** which has been *widely adopted by academic institutions* for teaching students **structured-programming** techniques. One reason for this is that Pascal was originally designed for teaching and for expressing algorithms in an efficient structured way. Pascal has already been extensively used throughout the rest of the book, and is the main language used when the principles of high-level languages are discussed in chapter 6. Therefore, *you have already studied Pascal* in much-greater depth than could ever be achieved by just a few pages in this chapter. Pascal or Pascal-like pseudo-code is also used extensively in other chapters on data structures. Also, don't forget that some of the latest versions of Pascal are now object oriented, and these are worth having a look at too.

Pascal program structure

The **detailed-program structure for Pascal can be seen in figure 6.16 on page 126**. Notice that Pascal, just like COBOL, for example, forces you to declare variables used at the beginning of the program. Compare this with languages like BASIC, for example, where variables do *not* have to be declared. Without variable declarations anyone reading the program has a more difficult job to work out what is happening. If variable declarations are forced onto the programmer in this way, then the programs become more readable and self-documenting. Due to the constraints placed on the programmer in this way, it is actually quite difficult to write a badly-structured Pascal program.

There have been several versions of Pascal since the standard version was introduced in 1971. One of the versions, with added features in the string handling, files and graphics areas is **UCSD Pascal** (University of California in San Diego). **Turbo Pascal** for the PC platform is also currently quite popular.

As students should be more familiar with Pascal than most of the other languages considered in this section, the student activity which now follows is a little more difficult than the simpler activities for the other languages.

Student activities – Pascal

You will find that all of these examples can also be done using the older Pascal compilers.

(1) Write a program to sort 20 numbers into descending order using any method that you wish. (See chapter 15 if you get stuck.)

(2) Write a program to calculate factorials which includes an output indicating the time, in centiseconds, taken by the computer to complete the task. (See chapter 9 if you get stuck.)

ALGOL

ALGOL, the **ALGOrithmic Language**, started to be developed by a committee in 1958 for scientific, mathematical and engineering purposes. The name ALGOL derives from the fact that this language expressed programs in terms of **algorithms**. (Don't they all!) The first version was called ALGOL 58, but a better version, commissioned in 1962 came to be known as **ALGOL 60**. We are not going to study ALGOL in detail here, but simply *mention it because of its tremendous historical importance*. **ALGOL was the spur behind the development of languages like Pascal, Ada and Modula-2**, and another *spin off* from **ALGOL in 1972 was the language C, and hence the C++ language of today** – covered in detail in a larger section later on in this chapter.

ALGOL was *the first* highly-**structured programming language**, and must, therefore, feature in any overview of high-level language development. It was the first language to introduce the ideas of **block structure**, was the first to introduce **procedures** *with* **parameter passing** (see page 125) *and* **local variables**, and was the first to introduce **recursion** (see page 185). ALGOL was also the first language to introduce the **BNF** (Backus-Naur Form) method for **describing syntax**. The BNF system is covered in detail in chapter 10, but you may have seen it used to describe the syntax of high-level languages, SQLs, other 4GLs and macro languages in your computing manuals. For example, the **Pascal 'if statement'** may be described, using BNF, as follows.

> <if-statement> ::= if <condition> then <statement> [else <statement>]

You may have noticed that the **square braces []**, shown in the above definition, have already been used in this chapter to denote **optional elements**, – you have already been using some BNF definitions without realising it! Of course, in the above if-statement definition, the terms <condition> and <statement> would have to be defined using BNF too – but we will not concentrate on this aspect here.

Algol 68 was later developed as a more-powerful language, but, unusually in a high-level language development context, was not simply an extension of Algol 60.

There are still Algol compilers in use today, but the language never became popular in its own right.

BASIC

BASIC – or **Beginner's All-purpose Symbolic Instruction Code** has also been through many stages of metamorphosis. Originally designed in the 1960s by J.G. Kemeny and T. Kurtz at Dartmouth College in the U.S.A., specifically to enable non-specialist students to learn how to program the computer in simpler ways compared to the high-level-language heavyweights like COBOL, ALGOL and FORTRAN, which were the only sensible alternatives around at the time. The *early versions* of **BASIC** were designed specifically for use in a **time-sharing environment** (see page 381). In those days there were no micros, and so students learnt to program by using teletype terminals (there were no VDUs either!) connected to a mainframe.

The BASIC language is usually **interpreted** rather than **compiled** (see page 200), which means that students did *not* have to learn how to create source code in a text editor, did *not* have to compile the source code to create the object code, did *not* have to link the object code with any library files, and then did *not* have to run their programs via a separate process. Students could simply type in the code, and get an 'immediate' response from the computer. More importantly, an 'instant' response to any errors made by the students was the order of the day, together with the ability to 'instantly' correct the error and try again. This created a revolutionary jump in the user-friendliness of learning to program for the first time, and was known as **conversational mode** for obvious reasons.

BASIC was not without its critics, and has probably been *the* most **controversial language** in the history of high-level languages to date. Computer-science students today find this criticism difficult to understand, but it was entirely justified when considering the early versions of the language. The early versions of BASIC were about as unstructured as you could get, and forced most programmers into extremely-bad habits. (See the spaghetti code on page 120.)

More-recent versions of BASIC have redressed the balance somewhat, but **it is still possible to write bad programs**, *because* **BASIC does not impose any structure** on the part of the programmer. It's up to the programmer to write the programs in a structured way if he or she so desires to do – unfortunately, some students don't desire to do! – and this is why BASIC still has its critics even today. However, with good discipline, and an excellent version of BASIC like BBC BASIC version V on the Acorn range of machines, it's possible to write programs with excellent structure. As to variable declarations, BASIC still does not insist, but comments can be used in appropriate places to get over this particular objection.

One of the other problems with BASIC is its portability (or *lack of*). Different versions like Acorn's BBC BASIC V, or Microsoft's Visual BASIC, for example, are very different in syntax especially when it comes to things like graphics and sound. Therefore, BASIC has not been chosen by professional programmers who have to make sure that their systems work on multiple-platform machines. BASIC is also grossly inadequate when undertaking operations on files and many other data structures. Nevertheless, BASIC is popular in educational institutions like schools, and some very sophisticated and elegant programs can be written using this language.

Student activities – BASIC

You will find that all of these examples can also be done using any BASIC interpreter or compiler.

(1) Write a program which analyses a sentence of characters, then prints out the number of words, vowels and consonants.

(2) Write a program which puts 200 red squares on the screen in a grid being made up of 20 squares across and 10 squares down. The number of graphics units used for each square and the distance between the squares should be appropriate for the screen size being used.

Object-oriented programming

C++

OOPs, I've dropped all my objects

What makes OOP different?

In this section we will spend a little longer investigating the importance of the language C++, and look in more general terms at the important concept of **object-oriented programming**.

There have been several important high-level-language-development stages, but **Object-Oriented Programming (OOP)** is probably *the* most-important and most recent one after the **structured programming development techniques** of the late 1970s and 1980s. After reading chapter 7 you should know that structured programming techniques were introduced to make programs more comprehensible, and thus easier to modify and develop. However, as systems have become ever-more complex, even structured-programming techniques are cracking under the strain, especially in the complex **systems programming** environment. *Don't* get the wrong idea – **structured programming** *is still very important* and is here to stay – it's just that *more* is needed. Structured programming techniques *are still an essential part of object-oriented programming*, but in addition to these more-conventional techniques, there are some powerful new concepts to be added to your arsenal of ideas. The programming language C++ has been developed with object-oriented programming in mind, and it's the "++" part which differentiates it from C, for example, which is a well-structured language which does *not* support these object-oriented techniques. Although C++ is not the first (**Smalltalk** came before C++ and is still popular) or the only object-oriented programming language, it will be used to illustrate these concepts as it is by far the most popular language for **systems** and **application programming**, and looks well set to serve as the main systems-programming language into the 21st century.

Although **C++** *is* a superset of **C** (or C is a subset of C++), there are some important differences in the emphasis which is put on certain techniques, or the ways in which programming different structures is carried out. Things that might be frowned upon or are uncommon in C are common in C++ and vice versa. Therefore, if you are hoping to learn C, then *don't bother* – go straight ahead and learn C++. However, if you have already learnt C, then apart from having to undo some of your pre-conceptions, you should be well able to go straight to the heart of object-oriented programming without having to learn all the relevant syntax of C++ before proceeding.

Object-Oriented Programming (OOP) provides *all* of the usual programming structures (including, unfortunately, the dreaded goto!) which are available in most advanced 3GL programming languages, but in addition **other fundamental concepts** have been introduced. One of *the* most fundamental ideas addresses the problem of programmers inadvertently messing up things that they shouldn't. Consider, for example, a team of programmers working on a large project (typically $\geqslant$ 50,000 lines of code). Suppose also that a wonderful routine has been written by some members of the team which deals with the input and output (I/O) parts of the project. Now it may have taken six months to perfect this large and complex routine, and after extensive testing no known bugs exist within the system.

Let's now suppose that someone alters the specification, (they always do!), such that different data needs to be handled in addition to the original spec. A typical conventional-language-based scenario would be to tinker with the existing code so that it can accommodate the revised specification – but this often has unforeseen effects, especially in large and complex systems. The simplest of alterations to a small part of the code might cause very subtle changes and unforeseen actions to occur within other parts of the program. If this happens, then the complete module of the original program which used to work is now totally screwed up, with the consequent need to modify it yet again, and go through all of the testing a second time. It would be far better if the original tried-and-tested code could be used in the new system *without alteration*, or, better still, the language specification be designed so that this is no longer a big problem. This is the essence of object-oriented programming.

The above scenario is not only typical, *on complex systems its almost inevitable!* Although it *is* possible to use conventional languages such that the above effects are minimised, all too often projects are late due to these sorts of reasons. Object-oriented languages are designed to get over these problems by the creation of structures which make it very difficult to mess up things inadvertently that are already working well, and it does this by using a variety of techniques such as **data encapsulation** and **inheritance** etc. which are explained in the next few sections.

Classes and objects

Fundamental to C++ is the idea of **classes** and **objects**. Although **classes** and **objects** can be regarded as theoretical concepts which relate to the most-abstract of **data structures**, in practice it is best to start considering them as relating to some physical classes and objects found in the real world. This gets over the mystique of these new principles and is useful because these programming concepts can and indeed often do relate to real-world objects and classes.

A **class** can be thought of in the same way as its normal use in English. For example, the 'teachers in your school or college' or the 'food served in a local restaurant' would represent different types of class, with each class being characterised in some particular and in these cases obvious ways. **Objects** are simply **members of classes** – for example, each **teacher** in your **college** is an **object**, because they are **members of the class** which we have just defined as '**teachers in your college**'. Stilton cheese might be an object of the 'food served in a local restaurant' class. One of the advantages of using classes in this way is that data structures can mirror the real world more closely than is possible with procedurally-based languages. However, choosing your classes and objects is not always so obvious, at least until you have built up some experience with OOP methods.

A **class** is defined by certain characteristics which are exhibited by objects belonging to that class. However, each object of a particular class may and often does exhibit

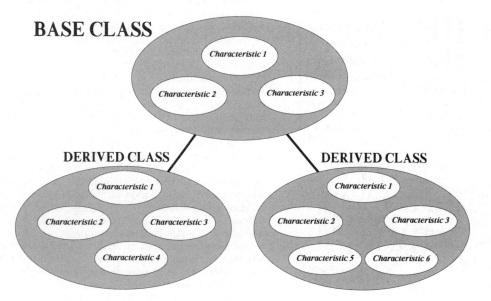

Figure 8.6

other characteristics. For example, each teacher in your college will probably belong to many different classes such as 'the family', 'the malt whisky association' or 'the local tiddlywinks club' for example, and exhibiting these extra characteristics does not mean that they are no longer teachers at your college. These ideas are shown in a more general form in figure 8.6. Here, to be a member of the **base class** means exhibiting three special characteristics which we have arbitrarily called 1, 2 and 3. However, we have also shown two different **derived classes**. Note that each derived class, being derived from the base class, exhibits, in addition to any other characteristic that may be present, the three characteristics of the base class we called 1, 2 and 3.

Inheritance

We have just seen that the original class is called the **base class**, and any classes derived from the original in this way are called **derived classes.** This leads to an important concept in **OOP** called **inheritance**. You can easily see from figure 8.6 that derived classes have inherited all the characteristics associated with the base class, and have added some new characteristics of their own. You will recall that an important idea associated with OOP was that existing structures can be used *without modification* to achieve different outcomes. **Inheritance** *is* one of the methods used in OOP whereby suitable work already completed can be added to by the derived class inheriting the characteristics of the base class with additional characteristics added.

Public and private

It is a natural reaction for those new to OOP to think that all the above could be achieved in conventional programming by clever use of procedures or sub-routines – but this would be missing the point. In C++, for example, special **data structures** called **classes** together with the idea of **public** and **private** data associated with each class provide the necessary mechanisms whereby programmers are forced into using this powerful idea of inheritance. By using such mechanisms and all the associated data structures it is very difficult to accidentally alter the code so that previously-tested routines are messed up. Programmers hell-bent on breaking the rules could obviously destroy any formalised mechanism – but in C++ this is difficult to do accidentally. Even with the most carefully structured conventional programs, it is very easy if not inevitable to accidentally create chaos on very large systems.

Data encapsulation

Another important feature of OOP is **data encapsulation**, which means that the **objects** contain **both data and functions**, unlike more-conventional programming techniques which deal with the data and the functions which may operate on the data entirely separately. In OOP the data itself *is as important* as the functions which operate on the data. With conventional programming techniques, although data can be **global** or **local** (see page 124), most data can be accessed and modified with relative ease. In OOP, data can typically *only be accessed* through the object which was designed to operate on that particular data. You access the data by what's called a **member function** of the object containing the data. In this way each object has total control over its own data, and it's therefore less likely that other routines or modifications will inadvertently alter the private data.

These ideas are far more fundamental than would appear at first sight. In a conventional procedurally-based language, the whole analysis of a problem is of paramount importance and usually involves carrying out sequences of operations using functions. For example, read a string from the disk, test to see if it contains a sub-string, if a particular sub-string is found then branch to a particular procedure to process it and re-save the data to disk. *Little or no attention has been paid to the data itself*, and making use of these older methods means that data plays a subservient role to the procedures which operate on it.

Data has a much-more important role in object-oriented programming. Here vital data that may have to be accessed from many different parts of the program forms part of the object which controls the data (see the real-life analogy in a moment). In conventional programming if the data is altered in any way, then *all routines* which need to have access to the data will have to be altered too. With the concept of **data encapsulation**, if the data is altered in any way, then only the object that controls the data and gives access to it needs to be altered. Therefore, modifications and alterations can be done much more quickly and efficiently. Moreover, all members of the programming team do not even have to know that this part of the program has been altered, because they are simply asking this routine to supply them with the appropriate information, not manipulating it themselves.

One other point worthy of note is that when objects are used in OOP they retain any variables used throughout the duration of the program. This may not sound revolutionary, but compare this to the use of procedures or sub-routines in a conventional language, where local variables are lost once the procedure or sub-routine has been executed. Making a variable global would obviously get over this problem, but this would make it more easy to mess up these variables inadvertently from other procedures. You can see that OOP scores well in this area too.

As can be seen from the above, C++ is bringing programming into the systems world in the conventional sense. This means that parts of the program can be considered as a black box, which responds to your request for information and passes back the appropriate information without the need to understand what is going on inside. System methods have helped in many walks of life such as electronic systems or biological systems – they are now helping programming through the use of OOP.

A C++ example

Although it is not appropriate to go into much detail here, I strongly recommend that you spend some time playing around with C++ if you have access to a suitable compiler. The ideas expressed above will then become more obvious, and you will gain a tremendous insight into the way in which systems and applications are being programmed in the foreseeable future.

An example of an extremely simple **C++ class definition** now follows. Note that // denotes the start of a single-line comment in C++.

```
#include <iostream.h>

    class electronic_component      //Electronic component object
{
    private:
        int man_number;             //Manufacturer's component number
        int ss_number;              //School stock component number
        float cost;                 //Cost of component
    public:
        man_number = m_num;
        ss_number = ss_num;
        cost = c;
        void setup_part(int m_num, int ss_num, float c)
        {                           //Set up data definition
        }
        void display_part( )
        {                           //Display-on-screen data definition
            cout << "\n Manufacturers number " << man_number;
            cout << "\n School stock number " << ss_number;
            cout << "\n Cost of component " << cost;
        }
};
    void main( )

    {
    int dummy;
    electronic_component component1;
                                    //Define object called component1
                                    //which belongs to the class
                                    //electronic component
    component1.setup_part(1234, 1735, 1.23);
                                    //Set up data
    component1.display_part( );
                                    //Display data
                                    //Display data
        cout << " \n Please type in an integer number to terminate ";
        cout << "\n";               //Enter an integer number to clear
        cin >> dummy;               //the display and return
    }
```

The above function can be thought of as part of a simple electronic-component-stock-control system which allows the user to set up the special stock numbers which describe the electronic components, or look at a particular component number on screen. The routine is so simple that all items in stock would have to be typed in and held in memory! Nevertheless, this simple example shows some important concepts in C++ and OOP in particular.

The above code shows how a class called 'electronic_component' is set up. It consists of just three characteristics, namely 'manufacturers number', 'school stock component number' and 'cost'. The main part of the program (as with normal C) consists of the code at the end after 'void main ( )'. This function defines an object called component1 (i.e. a component with this name) which is of the class electronic_component. The data declaration at the beginning of the main function can be compared with simpler data declarations such as '**int part1**' – which declares to the C++ compiler that you wish to make use of an integer variable called part1. One of the most-powerful features of C++ classes is that *you can define your own data types*, then make use of them in any way that you wish. Most languages give you a range of data types such as integer, floating point, string, complex etc. but the C++ object-oriented programming language lets you define your own – with all the benefits that this flexibility is likely to bring.

Let's suppose, for the sake of argument, that you wanted to **add together** two **complex numbers** (numbers with real and imaginary parts as used, for example, in defining the mandelbrot set (see page 180)). Unlike FORTRAN, many languages, including C++ , do not support variables of type complex. Now it's possible to get round this restriction making use of a number of techniques such as defining a complex (in the number sense!) procedure to add the real and imaginary parts, passing over parameters to them, and receiving data back from them. You could, for example, use something like the following in BASIC.

```
complex_add(x,y)
```

However, it would be far easier if, after defining a suitable data type, you could use the *normal* arithmetic operators in expressions like:

```
complex_z = complex_x + complex_y
```

The C++ language enables you to do exactly this. You are limited only by your imagination and programming expertise in the number of data types which can be dreamt up. Defining sophisticated and specialised data types often leads to enormous simplification in the readability and structure of the program.

Data hiding and member functions

The private and public parts of the above class definition ensure that private data or functions if necessary are **hidden** from *normal* view. (The term *normal* here means accessible from outside the class.) This helps to prevent inadvertent tampering with data or misuse of functions via other routines which should not accidentally alter the data or make use of these functions. All the public functions in the above class definition are accessible from outside the class. This concept of **data hiding** is another important concept in object-oriented programming. Only **member functions**, i.e. functions which are a *member* of a particular class can have access to the private data or functions within their own class.

A real-life analogy

It is interesting to see how the principles of OOP mirror real life to some extent, and the 'teacher objects' considered earlier will act as an example. Although one could consider the base class of teachers, at secondary and tertiary level teachers tend to be subject specialists such as geographers or physicists. Therefore, taking our OOP analogy further, we could create classes of Geography teachers, Physics teachers, and Maths teachers etc. We will now look at a typical interaction between the objects of different classes.

If we were to model the school by conventional programming techniques, this would probably mean storing all the data on pupils such that each object (teacher) has global access. This means that each teacher, regardless of subject would access any data via their own routines. Maths teachers, for example, would have access to geography data and could accidentally alter it. However, taking the OOP approach, and applying the principle of **data encapsulation** described earlier, if a maths teacher, perhaps also being the tutor of a particular pupil, wishes to know how his or her student is doing in geography, then he will ask the geography teacher, who will then access his or her own files and interpret the data in a way that the maths teacher can understand. Note that the maths teacher has not had access to any of the geography teacher's data – it is the geography teacher who has rummaged in the data structures, messed around with their own functions and data and extracted the required result. It does not matter that the maths teacher did not know where to find the geography data, or how to access it, all that was necessary was to ask the appropriate geography teacher who did all of the necessary processing. In object oriented programming the ideas are similar with access to private data being controlled in a similar way to our teacher example just considered.

If you consider that all the teachers in the school will keep their own data functions and data in whatever form, and other teachers can only gain access to the data by asking the right person, then you will begin to appreciate one of the main principles in object-oriented programming methodology.

Disadvantages of OOP

Although OOP is *the* current way forward in the foreseeable future, there are some disadvantages. One of the main ones is increased program size. (One of the reasons why some of the new operating systems are several Mbytes long?) If a program is larger then it may take longer to execute than similar functions carried out making use of conventional programming techniques. However, with computers becoming ever faster and more complex, and with pots of RAM now becoming the norm, these are small prices to pay considering the considerably-reduced development time and increased reliability of the software.

Student activities – C++

You will find that all of these examples can also be done using any C++ compiler.

(1) Write a program which accepts a number, then displays the square root of that number.

(2) Write a program to enter a character, followed by a number representing the number of times the character just entered is to be repeated on the same line. Your program should then print out the required number of characters.

Other language examples 2

Prolog

Prolog stands for **Pro**gramming in **Log**ic, or '*Programmation Logique*' as they say in France at the University of Marseille where the language was originally developed by Monsieur Colmerauer and his team back in the 1970s. Along with **LISP** (page 169), these currently represent *the* two languages which are most popular for **Artificial Intelligence** or **AI** (see page 554) applications. You may recall that Prolog belongs to a set of languages which have been labelled **fifth-generation** languages. Put simply, this means that it is yet a further stage removed from what's happening inside the guts of the computer at the most fundamental machine level. Prolog was developed from a branch of mathematics called first-order predicate calculus, and LISP was developed from lambda calculus, a special sub-set of the more general predicate calculus. The mathematics of predicate calculus deals with **symbolic logic** – the sort of language in which propositions are made and inferences are proved to be true or false – it's probably the language in which Spock thinks on the Starship Enterprise!

Prolog *is a declarative language*, which means that we no longer have to concentrate too much on the detail of **how to** solve problems, but concentrate more on the **descriptive side** of defining *relationships*, then asking appropriate questions – Prolog is then expected to figure out the response to these questions by an analysis of the database which is automatically built up by the relationships which the programmer has just defined. However, for most Prolog programs there will be *some* **imperative** or **procedural** elements – we are still some way off from being able to use totally declarative languages with no reliance on procedurally based ideas which are common in all other languages.

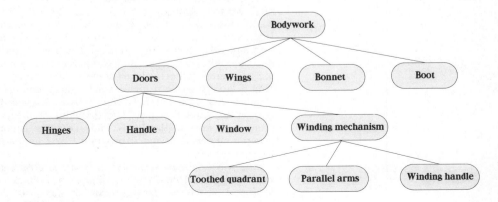

Figure 8.7

The above ideas are typical of the type of thinking that lies behind **knowledge-based systems** or **expert systems** (see page 557) – this is because the programmer can be concerned more with the knowledge held in the database rather than specifically thinking up the algorithms which will be used to extract subsets of this knowledge. Therefore, if a medical database, for example, is built up making use of Prolog, then Prolog's facilities are ideal for enabling the programmer (and hence the end users of the system) to extract medical facts based on complex relationships describing the possible symptoms of an illness.

Prolog is wonderfully simple for expressing hierarchical and list-type data structures. For example, consider a tree structure (see page 304) for parts of a typical car as shown in figure 8.7.

These ideas are identical to those associated with a family tree – so consider, just for a moment, the **parent** called 'Bodywork' and the *four* **children** called 'Doors', 'Wings', 'Bonnet' and 'Boot'. In **Prolog** this structure could be represented as follows:

    Bodywork(Doors, Wings, Bonnet, Boot)

These ideas can easily be extended so that the entire structure could be coded, and for figure 8.7, this can be accomplished with the following line of Prolog.

    Bodywork(Doors(Hinges, Handle, Window, Winding_mechanism(
    Toothed_quadrant, Parallel_arms, Winding_Handle)), Wings, Bonnet, Boot)

The above can be regarded as a simple 'bodywork database' for a car – it's a database because that's how prolog treats this data structure – and it's simple because we don't have the space to build up a database of the complexity needed to mirror the parts in a real car. As you will have guessed, there are much more sophisticated ways of defining the structure of the car database than typing out an incredibly long line as implied above, but this is best left to a more detailed study of Prolog if you have a suitable compiler. MicroProlog *is available* for most computers including Acorn's Archimedes, the PC, its clones and the Apple Mac ranges.

You will probably be amazed to realise just how much data in real life can be massaged to mirror the natural structure of trees, and a good Prolog programmer would probably be able to change just about any given data into the form of a list or a tree structure. Anything from books in a library via the timetable at your school or college to the information contained in a sporting almanac could all be encoded in Prolog as a set of complex tree structures. It is this which enables Prolog to act as a **knowledge-based system** in which the base of knowledge could be organised facts about almost any topic under the sun. The ability of Prolog to interact with the structure (database) and to do efficient searches based on complex criteria makes this declarative language a joy to use compared to programming the same functions in a procedural language such as BASIC, for example. With appropriate procedures to hide the end user from the complexities of predicate calculus then user-friendly knowledge-based systems can be established relatively easily – it's worth a try if you have the time.

It would take up far too much space to look into too many languages in the above detail, so snippets from other languages will now be covered in the next few sections. You are obviously not required to remember too much detail, but reading the following will add to your knowledge of the development of languages, and will allow you to impress the examiners with your knowledge of languages in general.

Ada

Ada is derived from **Pascal**, but has a considerable number of enhancements. The final version, sponsored by the U.S. Department of Defense, and developed in conjunction with industry and academic institutions, was presented in 1980. Interestingly enough, it was not until the development of Ada that computer scientists and other academics did very much work on the development of what makes one computer language good compared to another – and these complex questions are answered subjectively to some extent in the very last section of this chapter. Ada is a very modern high-level language compared to some of the others in this chapter, and *is named in honour of* **Ada Augusta Byron**, the **Countess of Lovelace** (known as Lady Lovelace, and daughter of the poet Lord Byron), who did much pioneering work in the 1800s. Lady Lovelace is considered to be the *first* computer programmer, and designed programs for Charles Babbage's mechanical computers (see page 617).

Ada was originally designed for **systems programming**, (i.e. developing things like applications etc.), and had the unique advantage of combining **real-time** (see page 586) and **structured programming**. It was also ideal for programming **embedded systems** (see page 582) – hence the interest from the Department of Defense for real-time-missile-control applications and the like. Being able to handle events in real time, Ada also has applications in handling **concurrent events** – i.e. it's useful in modern **parallel-processing** applications. Nevertheless, Ada has become more of a general-purpose language than was perhaps originally intended, and, perhaps reassuringly, is now being used to program embedded systems in vending machines, cars and other non-military applications.

LISP

LISP, along with **Prolog** (page 167) represents the cutting edge for programming **AI** (**Artificial Intelligence**) systems, however, the original version of LISP was the first of these languages to be developed way back in the late 1950s (that's not a misprint!) at MIT – the Massachusetts Institute of Technology in the USA – not bad for a fifth-generation language to be developed back in the 1950s! Unfortunately, the machines of the day were not good at running LISP programs, and it was not until the advent of greater processing power that LISP programming became generally available. LISP is ideal for defining and manipulating data structures such as those found in lists and trees in chapter 14 – indeed, this is where LISP gets its name – **LISP** stands for **LISt Processing**. Consider a list data structure with nodes (see page 298) in the form of a binary tree as shown in figure 8.8.

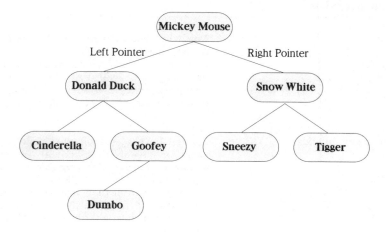

Figure 8.8

The concept of a **pointer** (see page 289) is an important one in **LISP**, and the left-hand and right-hand pointers are used to good effect in the **binary tree** of figure 8.8. On page 330 a system of 'sorting' names into alphabetical order is given by using a simple rule to insert the data into a **binary tree**, and using an **inorder traversal** mechanism to read back the data. Building up such data structures using languages such as BASIC, for example, is a little tedious, however, using LISP, both definition and manipulation of data structures in the form of trees and lists are simple. Making use of LISP we could print out the Walt-Disney characters in alphabetical order as shown in the next couple of sections.

First we need to define a *set of* **functions** which will make up the **node data** – in this context a **node** consists of just *three items* – **a data item** like 'Mickey Mouse', for example, along with the **left** and **right-hand pointers** which, in LISP, are curiously known as CAR and CDR respectively. CAR is a LISP function which finds the beginning of a LIST and originally was an acronym for Content of Address Register. CDR is a LISP function which finds the end of a LIST and this was an acronym for Contents of Decrement Register. (We did say that LISP was developed back in the 1950s – this old-style terminology has remained to this day.) The following code consists of three **defined functions** called build_node, left_subtree, right_subtree and node_data.

```
(defun build_node (data left right)
    (list left data right))
(defun left_subtree (tree)
        (car tree))

(defun right_subtree (tree)
        (caddr tree))
```

```
(defun data (tree)
    (cadr tree))
```

To print out the data in alphabetical order the following function can be used.

```
(defun print_binary_tree (tree)   (cond
    ((null tree) nil)
    (t (print_tree (left_subtree (tree))
        (print (data tree))
        (print_tree (right-subtree tree)))))
```

Although quite simple once you get used to it, you can see why an alternative acronym for LISP has been thought up – Lots of Infuriating Spurious Parenthesis!

A final overview

Much has been covered in this chapter, many languages have been briefly introduced, and together with the work covered in chapters 6 and 7, students should now have a good idea of the spectrum of high-level language development. In this final section we will try to bring these ideas together so that students are able to formulate strategies in their own minds regarding arguments for and against language developments which have taken place and still are taking place.

Why so many languages?

As you have seen from the beginning of this chapter, the 1960s were the boom years for software development – **all future strategies were developed from the base languages developed during this period**. Before the advent of the micro, bigger and better was the order of the day, and the mainframe and mini hardware manufacturers got rich on their increasingly lucrative share of the markets. Software developers tried to jump on the same bandwagon – all trying to strive for the ultimate language which would replace all other languages. PL/1 was probably the only serious contender for this utopian title, but the compilers were so big and clumsy, were so full of bugs, and the language was so difficult to learn that computer scientists have given up trying to develop an all-things-to-all-people language in the foreseeable future.

Criteria for language evaluation

We are, therefore, left with a variety of languages, each suitable for specific purposes, of which a general-purpose language is only yet another specific example! Don't forget that general-purpose does not mean that the language can do everything. Therefore, we have developed languages which are good at scientific and engineering applications such as FORTRAN, are good at data processing such as COBOL, are good teaching languages such as Pascal, or are good system's programming languages such as C++, for example.

How then, do we evaluate the effectiveness of one language compared to another? How do we decide which language to use? How do we decide which language would be the most efficient for a particular job? All these questions and many other of a similar nature need answering – unfortunately, these questions are complex ones. Much computer science beyond advanced level answers these types of questions in considerable detail, and during the development of Ada, for example, a wealth of suitable evaluation material was produced. However, this is beyond the scope of this book, and here we will concentrate on just a few general points.

It's relatively easy to generate some suitable criteria which can be used for direct comparisons, but far less easy to be totally objective about how these criteria can be applied in practice. For example, **input and output facilities** would be an obvious candidate – but, as we have seen in this chapter, some languages, such as FORTRAN 90, for example, have third-party software which considerably improves this area. It's rather like having a brilliant spreadsheet with no graphics capability – bolt on a graphics application and the combination might be dynamite, completely nullifying the initially-justified criticism. However, if difficulties like this are put to one side, and ignoring some of the subjective opinions which are bound to be present in our simple-analysis techniques, then the list shown in Figure 8.9 would make a reasonable starting point. It is not in any particular order of preference.

Some generally accepted criteria for language evaluation and comparison

Is the language well structured?
> In terms of *modularity*.
> In terms of the *data types* supported.
> In terms of the *control structures* supported.

Is it complex or relatively easy to use and understand?
> In terms of being *powerful*.
> In terms of *expressiveness*.
> In terms of *comprehensibility*.

Is it self documenting?
> Variable declarations etc.
> Is documentation sufficient to reduce maintenance problems?

Are good run-time diagnostics available?
> Debuggers – how easy is it to debug programs?

Are the input and output facilities good?

Is ther a good base of pre-written utilities or library functions?
> Mammoth *FORTRAN and COBOL libraries*.
> Huge C and *C++ libraries etc.*

Are compilers available over a wide range of hardware and software platforms?
> For, *PCs, Power PCs, Apple Macs, DECs, Suns* etc.
> Different *Mainframe* and Mini computers.
> *Unix, Windows, MSDOS,* Windows NT, *System 7 RISC-OS* etc.

Is the transferability (portability) good?
> Do major modifications have to be made when going across platforms?

Speed of execution?
> Fast or snail's pace? – use appropriate *benchmarks*.

Is it good for teaching purposes?
> Is good structure *imposed* on the students?

Can it cope with real time systems?

Can it cope with parallel processing?
> Using *real parallel processors?*
> Or simply multi-tasking?

Is the language general purpose or designed for a specific purpose?
> *Artificial intelligence*
> *Data processing*
> *General purpose*
> *Scientific, engineering or maths* applications
> *Systems programming*
> *Text processing etc.*

Figure 8.9

An example using Pascal

Suppose we wish to undertake a *brief and informal evaluation* of the **Pascal language**. We could work through the following list, perhaps awarding ticks on a scale of 1 to 5 (with 5 representing excellent, against each of the criteria).

Is the language well structured?

Modularity: ✔✔✔✔
Well block structured e.g. headings, compulsory declarations, data descriptions, procedures with local and global variables, functions, supports recursion, main body for program.

Data types: ✔✔✔
Loses marks on lack of proper support for strings. Pascal supports Arrays, but does not support variable-length Arrays. Boolean, Char, Enumerated, File, Integer, Pointer, Real, Record, Set and Subrange data types etc. are all supported, and later versions including UCSD Pascal do support random-access files (see chapter 16).

Control structures: ✔✔✔✔
Most of the structures needed such as 'conditionals', 'if-then' and 'nested if-then', 'case', 'goto', 'while', 'repeat', 'for' etc. However, some non-uniformity exists because 'while' and 'if' statements require 'begin-and-end' pairs, but 'repeat' statements do not.

Complex or easy to use?

Powerful: ✔✔✔✔

Powerful is a relatively subjective judgement, it depends on what you are trying to do. Different users will have different perceptions of the power of a language depending on the subset of instructions which they use most frequently. Overall, Pascal is regarded as being quite powerful, with the exception of its limited file-handling techniques. However, more objective judgements are discussed in the bench-marks section at the end of this chapter.

Expressiveness: ✔✔✔

Expressiveness can be interpreted as fitness for the purpose for which it was intended – in terms of allowing programmers to *express themselves* in ways which are appropriate to the job in hand. For example, when adding the numbers B to A and putting the result *back in* A, then Pascal would use the following syntax.

    A := A + B

The ':=' part is better than a plain '=' because 'A = A + B' is algebraic nonsense as far as most students are concerned, therefore, the ':=' sign could remind the student of this fact. Indeed when Boolean operators are used '=' is used instead because this has a more literal meaning. Compare these differences with the syntax from a language like BASIC, for example, which is far less expressive.

Comprehensibility: ✔✔✔✔✔

In terms of *comprehensibility* Pascal scores very well indeed. The block-structured nature of the language combined with the fact that it was originally designed to enable students to be able to understand the teaching of algorithms more effec-tively, makes this a relatively simple language to learn and use.

Self documenting: ✔✔✔✔✔

For a language to be successful it should communicate its meaning to other users as well as the programmers. The problems of maintenance and extension are far more easily solved if a programming language, together with suitable comments is self documenting. The structure and comprehensibility of Pascal together with comments fulfils this requirement quite well.

Good run-time diagnostics: ✔✔✔✔✔

This depends to a large extent on the compiler which accompanies the language. Most Pascal compilers have good run-time diagnostics which include trace routines which display helpful messages.

Other important factors

Input-output facilities: ✔✔✔

Input output facilities are not brilliant compared to some of the other first-class high-level languages such as COBOL for example.

Good base of utilities: ✔✔✔

Pascal suffers a little from not having a vast arsenal of library utilities like those which accompany FORTRAN or C++, for example.

Compilers – range of platforms: ✔✔✔✔✔

All popular machines have Pascal compilers, therefore Pascal covers a huge range of platforms. Also, the code generated by Pascal compilers is usually efficient in terms of being relatively short and fast to execute.

Transferability and portability good: ✔✔✔✔✔

Transferability is excellent. As with all languages, apart from operating-system specific commands making use of Windows, for example, most Pascal programs will run on all platforms. Several extensions to Pascal exist, but most people now have the latest versions which include all the extensions to the original versions. Pascal also goes further than many languages in making some of its features machine inde-pendent.

Speed of execution: ✔✔✔✔

This is probably the most subjective topic, as execution speed obviously depends on what your computer has got under the bonnet. There is little data available regarding the speed of particular languages, and therefore most people rely on various benchmarks as explained in the next section.

Good for teaching: ✔✔✔

This language was designed with teaching in mind – you won't get much better. However, in some peoples' opinion Pascal is regarded as being over simplified, and this often leads to unnecessary complications when trying to program more advanced features which other more-complex languages would naturally support.

Real time?: ✔

Few languages have been designed to cope with the demands of a real-time system. However, you should note from page 587 that real time, in the true sense of the term, does not necessarily mean a fast response. Nevertheless, it is in the context of responding to very fast events that this rating has been given.

Parallel processing: ✔✔✔

A version of Pascal called **Concurrent Pascal** is available in which code can be split up for solution by machines which are capable of carrying out this facility. Making sure that code written for parallel machines works with a single-processor machine increases portability.

General or specific?: ✔✔✔

You can't easily give a tick rating one way or the other based on these criteria – it is usually just one or the other! However, Pascal is quite versatile and therefore scores reasonably well in this area too.

In the final section of this chapter we will take a brief look at more objective ways of evaluating actual performance parameters for a particular language or system.

Benchmarks

A **benchmark** is simply a well defined task which people have dreamt up to get the computer to perform 'standard' operations, then measure either the speed or some other important parameter. *Assuming that the hardware on which the language is being run is identical*, then languages could be compared on by writing various algorithms in identical ways (if possible) in different languages. Obviously different benchmarks would be needed for testing different aspects of the language, and speed of execution would also depend on other factors such as the compiler used.

Typical benchmarks might involve testing how long it takes to go round various loop structures, working out mathematical algorithms like calculation of factorials, a measurement of the precision with which numbers might be stored, and the time taken to manipulate various well-defined data structures.

You will no doubt come across benchmark terms like **Dhrystones**, **Whetstones**, **Khornerstones** (and maybe even the Blarney stone!), and the computer press seem to invent new benchmarks each week. Basically, Whetstones are tests for floating point operations (see page 35), Dhrystones are tests for determining the number of times particular programs with a mix of instructions may be run each second, and Khornerstones are a measure of CPU input/output capability.

Exercise 8.1

1. Most languages can be used to express the solution to a problem as an algorithm. Why, therefore, does it matter in practice which language is used?

2. FORTRAN 90 is particularly suited to mathematical, scientific and engineering problems. There are obvious technical reasons for this, but other factors play an important part too – outline both the technical, historical and practical reasons why FORTRAN 90 often reigns supreme in these areas.

3. Many languages such as Concurrent Pascal, FORTRAN 90 and Ada, for example, support true parallel processing. What is meant by true parallel processing and why might this compromise the portability of these languages in the short term?

4. Languages such as C++ are inherently suited to parallel processing. Why is this?

5. Write a **BASIC** program which simulates the tossing of two coins 100 times, making use of the computer's random-number generator utility. Print out a table which indicates the number of head-and-tail combinations at the end of the simulation.

6. Write a **BASIC** program which acts as a spell checker for single-word data entered by a user. Your maximum dictionary size should be no more than 10 words!

7. Write a **FORTRAN** program to analyse the distance travelled from the Earth of a stone thrown vertically into the air. A printout is to be arranged which gives the stone's distance from the ground at 0.1-sec intervals until the stone returns to Earth. You may assume that $g = -9.81$ m/sec^2, that the initial velocity (U) of the stone is 3 m/sec and it is thrown from a height of 10m. The formula governing the motion of the stone is $S = Ut + \frac{1}{2}gt^2$ where t is the time in seconds, and S is the height above the ground in metres.

8. Write a **Pascal** program which generates the first 25 numbers in the Fibbonacci sequence 1,1,2,3,5,8 etc. (i.e. the next number is the sum of the previous two).

9. Write a **Pascal** program to convert a date typed into the computer in the form dd,mm,yyyy into the form Day, Month and Year. i.e. 16,12,1951 would get converted to 16th December 1951. You should do a simple validation on the date if possible. If you have time do a more complex validation (i.e. don't allow 31,4,1991), but don't include any leap-year validation unless you are a masochist.

10. Choose a high-level language (*other than* **Pascal**) with which you have some familiarity. Carry out a subjective analysis of the language based on the criteria shown on page 171.

End of chapter summary

- High level languages have *evolved* over many years, with specific **classes** and **generations of languages** being applicable to a variety of purposes.
- The need to strive for **absolute correctness** is a *long-term aim* in the development of high-level languages.
- *No single language* is able to cope with the huge range of modern-day requirements – **specialist** and **general-purpose languages** have therefore been developed.
- Hundreds of high-level languages have been developed but relatively few have stood the test of time – some of the best have now been going in one form or another for over forty years.
- A **general-purpose language** is *not* one which is designed to solve all problems, but one which has been **designed to solve a wide variety of problems** with varying degrees of success.
- **Languages** have also been designed for **specific purposes** such as business data processing or scientific and mathematical problem solving, for example.
- **FORTRAN 90** is a language primarily based around helping to solve numerical problems in mathematics, science and engineering.
- **FORTRAN** is an acronym for **FORmula TRANslator** or **Formula Translation**.
- **COBOL 85** (and **COBOL II**) are the latest incarnations of **COBOL** – *the* primary language for **data processing** in the business community.
- **COBOL** is an acronym for **COmmon Business Oriented Language**.
- **Pascal** is a well-structured general-purpose teaching language, and is named in honour of the mathematician Blaise Pascal who invented an early type of calculator.
- **ALGOL** stands for **ALGOrithmic Language**, and was one of the first block-structured languages to be developed. Algol is still used today but is also the root from which other languages such as **Ada** and **Pascal**, for example, have been developed.
- **BASIC** stands for **Beginner's All-purpose Symbolic Instruction Code**. It was originally developed as a simple unstructured teaching language, but is more respectable and powerful in its latest incarnations.

- **C++** is an example of a different programming methodology called **object oriented programming**. It has become the de-facto standard for modern systems programming. (If you're wondering why it's called C – it was the language to be developed after A and B!)
- **Prolog** stands for **PROgramming in LOGic**. It is a fifth-generation declarative language developed from first-order predicate calculus and is used extensively for AI applications.
- **Ada** is a language named in honour of Lady Ada Augusta Byron who is regarded as the first computer programmer. This relatively modern language is ideal for real-time and embedded systems, and is used extensively by the military.
- **LISP** stands for **LISt Processing**. Along with Prolog this language is extensively used in AI applications.
- The *effectiveness* and *efficiency* of a language can be **subjectively evaluated** by **suitable criteria**, and **objectively evaluated** by using suitable **benchmarks**.
- Suitable criteria for subjective evaluation would be – **Is the language well structured? Is it complex or relatively easy to use or understand? Is it self documenting? Are good run-time diagnostics available? Are the input and output facilities good? Is there a good base of pre-written utilities or library functions? Are compilers available over a wide range of hardware and software platforms? Is the transferability (portability) good? Speed of execution? Is it good for teaching purposes? Can it cope with real time systems? Can it cope with parallel processing? Is the language general purpose or designed for a specific purpose?**
- A **benchmark** is a task dreamed up to test some specific aspect of a computer. An example would be speed of floating point arithmetic.

9 Special programming techniques

Introduction

Part of the *art of programming* involves a detailed knowledge of a range of standard techniques which will enable you to use the computer as an efficient analysis tool. These techniques are powerful because they exploit the fact that a computer can be used to create simple and elegant solutions to certain types of complex problems. Some of these techniques are a little difficult to understand on first reading, but is is well worth spending a few hours wrestling with this type of problem to understand what's involved. Your patience and concentration will be amply rewarded if you can eventually understand enough to program making use of these powerful techniques.

If you've ever wondered how computers are used to produce stunning graphics such as those found in the Mandelbrot set (see page 181), the beautiful landscape patterns that are produced by fractals, or even in coping with the unpredictability of chaos, then buried inside such computer simulations are often specific algorithms based on the simple ideas of **iteration** and **recursion**.

Student activities

At frequent intervals during this chapter **you will be asked to stop and think about various points** *before* **going on to read the next section**. You will be given a set of practical questions which ask you to perform activities which check that you have understood what you are reading. Carrying out these activities will enable you to get appropriate practice in developing algorithms, and are thus very useful for your 'A' level examinations and projects too.

Iteration

Iteration is easy to understand – it simply means **repetition**. Iteration is easily carried out on a computer, because computers are in their element when things are repeated over and over again. We have seen, for example, how software gives us ample scope for **looping (repeating)** in the form of FOR-TO-NEXT, REPEAT-UNTIL and DO-WHILE loops, and so it is these sort of structures that are needed to perform this most-basic of computer operations. The *art of problem solving* making use of iteration lies with **establishing patterns** within certain problems (often the most difficult bit!), *expressing these patterns as* **algorithms**, and then *coding* them using a **suitable language**. Although there are thousands of different examples that could be chosen to cover these techniques, one or two common examples will illustrate the sort of processes which, if you can master them, will considerably improve your programming skills.

A simple example

Iteration forms a large part of **computer modelling** *because* programmers may use the computer to solve problems in ways which would be most inefficient if carried out manually. It may not matter too much if the computer takes hours or even days to produce a result – the alternative of making such calculations by hand would be unthinkable. In this chapter, use will be made of typical BASIC-language pseudocode, but programming making use of any other high-level or macro language such as those found in a **spreadsheet** *for example, would be just as effective.*

Square roots

Let's suppose that we wish to find the square root of a number N, by making use of an **iterative method**. (I know that you can push the button on your calculator, or type in a single line in BASIC and get the answer, but how do you think the calculator is working it out? – this is just a simple example which is *used to demonstrate an* iterative method.) Other examples giving you extra practice can be found in the exercise at the end of this chapter.

The bisection method

This is an example of a very simple **iterative method** borrowed from **numerical analysis** in mathematics. It is one method for *finding the root of an equation*, and we will use it to find the positive square root of a positive number. We will illustrate the principle with a concrete example, then develop an algorithm suitable for computer solution. The concrete-example stage mentioned here is more important than you might at first think – for most people it is often necessary to manually work through a method to fully understand how to develop a suitable algorithm.

Suppose we want to find the square root of 2 – another way of specifying the same problem is to find the positive root of the equation $x^2 = 2$. (Don't forget that a quadratic equation of this sort would have two roots, as +1.414.. and –1.414.. are both square roots of 2.)

The method is easier to understand if we rewrite this equation as $f(x) = x^2 - 2 = 0$.

If we draw a graph of $x^2 - 2 = 0$, then it would be as we have shown it in figure 9.1(a). Now let's just concentrate on the positive root, as shown in figure 9.1(b).

By common sense, we can see that an intelligent couple of first guesses would be $x = 1$ and $x = 2$. 1 is too small, and 2 is too big. Therefore, the actual root lies somewhere inbetween 1 and 2.

We need to develop a mechanistic way to arrive at the above obvious conclusion, for less obvious numbers. (Try finding the root of 187256 in your head if you're not convinced.) Now you will see from figure 9.1(a) that a clever way to see if a guess is too small or too big is to plug in the value of our guess into $f(x)$ and examine the sign of the result. Guesses too small will produce $f(x)$ negative (below the x axis), and guesses too large will produce $f(x)$ positive (above the x axis). Don't forget that our ideal answer, the exact root of 2, is where the graph *actually crosses* the axis.

For example,   1st guess will give $f(1) = 1^2 - 2 = -1$ (Negative sign)

and   2nd guess will give $f(2) = 2^2 - 2 = +2$ (Positive sign)

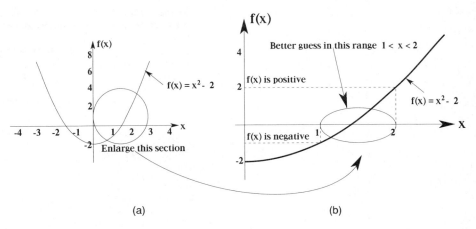

(a)   (b)

Figure 9.1

Next we make a guess *exactly half way* between our previous two best guesses (hence the name **bisection** method), and carry out the above test again to see if the next guess would be between 1 and 1.5 (in which case we guess 1.25), *or* between 1.5 and 2 (in which case we guess 1.75). We then carry on with the same processes and tests until we get *near enough* to the answer.

Before developing this method any further, let's just concentrate on the overall principles we are trying to establish. Here *we have developed a method which can be applied again and again so that we get nearer and nearer to the solution to the problem*. **This is the whole idea behind iterative modelling** – such techniques are ideal for solution by computer programming.

The following table shows the above bisection method to finding the root of 2 applied manually (i.e. by using a calculator and writing down the intermediate stages).

Starting values		Next approximation (guess)	New values
$x_1 = 1.0$	and $x_2 = 2$	$x_3 = 1.5$	x_1 and x_3
$x_1 = 1.0$	and $x_2 = 1.5$	$x_3 = 1.25$	x_3 and x_4
$x_1 = 1.5$	and $x_2 = 1.25$	$x_3 = 1.375$	x_3 and x_5
$x_1 = 1.5$	and $x_2 = 1.375$	$x_3 = 1.4375$	x_5 and x_6
$x_1 = 1.375$	and $x_2 = 1.4375$	$x_3 = 1.40625$	x_6 and x_7
$x_1 = 1.4375$	and $x_2 = 1.40625$	$x_3 = 1.421875$	x_7 and x_8
$x_1 = 1.40625$	and $x_2 = 1.421875$	$x_3 = 1.4140625$	etc.

We could go on forever, but that would be irrational (mathematical joke!). We therefore need to decide when to stop, and it's usual to decide on a particular number of decimal places. You would usually go on until no changes take place in the decimal place in which you are interested, therefore, if we wish to know root 2 to 3 decimal places, for example, the above method would need to be taken a little further.

Student activity 1

An algorithm using the bisection method to find square roots.

You have now seen the detailed principles of the bisection method. Build up a suitable structure diagram showing this method of solution which must include the following.

(1) It allows the user to enter a positive number.

(2) It terminates the iterative procedure after a suitable period.

Test your algorithm manually using root 2 as an example.

A possible structure diagram for the above method is shown in figure 9.2.

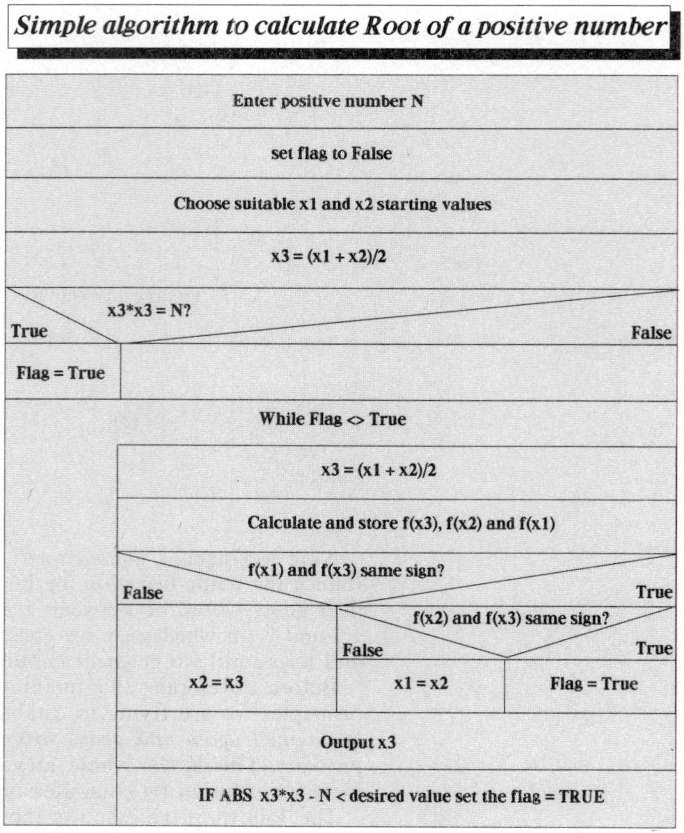

Simple algorithm to calculate Root of a positive number

Enter positive number N

set flag to False

Choose suitable x1 and x2 starting values

x3 = (x1 + x2)/2

x3*x3 = N?   True   False

Flag = True

While Flag <> True

x3 = (x1 + x2)/2

Calculate and store f(x3), f(x2) and f(x1)

f(x1) and f(x3) same sign?   False   True

f(x2) and f(x3) same sign?   False   True

x2 = x3   x1 = x2   Flag = True

Output x3

IF ABS x3*x3 - N < desired value set the flag = TRUE

Figure 9.2

Note that this is not the only solution, and some readers may find a more elegant one. Nevertheless, it is typical of what might be required to answer an examination-type question, or to solve a small section of your project work.

Student activity 2

An algorithm using the bisection method to find square roots.

Using the algorithm described above, or making use of your own algorithm, write some suitable code in a high-level language of your choice, and test the code by getting the computer to print out values of x until the iterative procedure is halted.

A program (using BBC BASIC V) follows shortly. The program could be made more elegant, and better starting values could be found. Also, if the numbers get very large, then the BASIC compiler can't do integer arithmetic with enough precision to cope with parts of the tests. Nevertheless, keep the numbers to less than 100 million and the method works quite well!

Don't forget that the whole point of this exercise is to demonstrate an iterative procedure in which **a loop is executed a number of times until some condition is met**. Although the bisection method usually converges on the answer reasonably quickly, it illustrates very well how a relatively small amount of code can be used to solve a problem in a way which would be extremely tedious without the use of programmable devices such as calculators or computers. This example has illustrated just one particular method, but there is a whole branch of mathematics and computer science called **numerical analysis** – this relates to using the computer in these sorts of ways to solve problems which are often quite difficult to solve using conventional analytical techniques. Modern calculators these days work out the solutions to many different forms of equations by using different numerical methods.

```
INPUT N
flag = FALSE
x1 = 1 : x2 = N
x3 = (x1+x2)/2
IF x3*x3 = N THEN flag = TRUE
WHILE flag <> TRUE
   x3=(x1+x2)/2
   fx1=x1*x1-N:fx2=x2*x2-N:fx3=x3*x3-N
   IF((fx1>0) AND (fx3>0)) OR ((fx1<0) AND (fx3<0)) THEN
         IF ((fx2>0) AND (fx3>0)) OR ((fx2<0) AND (fx3<0)) THEN
            flag = TRUE
         ELSE
            x1=x3
      ENDIF
   ELSE
      x2=x3
   ENDIF
   PRINT "Guess so far is";x3
   IF ABS(x3*x3-N) < 0.001 THEN flag = TRUE
ENDWHILE
PRINT "Answer is ";x3
```

Fractals

As a complete change from the above root-solving problem, we will now take a look at producing some patterns making use of **iteration** and **fractal** techniques. **Fractal geometry** has been described as the '**Geometry of Nature**' – this is an apt definition because *it's possible to describe intricate shapes* such as **trees**, **clouds**, **mountains** and **valleys** etc. in ways *which bear an uncanny resemblance to the real thing*. Indeed, if you were not told that some of these objects had been created mathematically, you would probably think that you were looking at real pictures created by an artist or photographer. The basic concepts of **fractal geometry** were developed around the 1920s when a French mathematician called Julia proposed some extensions to what mathematicians call measure theory. However, it was not until the application of these techniques through the use of computers that much widespread excitement was generated. In 1982, **Benoit Mandelbrot**, a mathematician working for IBM Research at Yale University, discovered that incredibly beautiful patterns could be produced from relatively simple **iterative** rules. It is to this fascinating topic that we now turn to illustrate the processes of iteration still further. You may have to spend just a few minutes learning a little extra mathematics, but the effort is well worth it for the satisfaction of creating your own worlds on the screen of the computer.

Complex numbers

First we will need to take a very brief look at what's meant by a **complex number** – an unfortunate choice of word, as the basic ideas are really quite simple. **Complex numbers** are *numbers with two parts* – an **imaginary part** and a **real part**. Imaginary is also an unfortunate term as real problems can be solved making use of these imaginary numbers. Complex numbers can be represented on a *special graph* called a **complex plane** or **Argand diagram**, in which the real parts are plotted horizontally on the x axis, and the imaginary parts are plotted vertically on the y axis. The real part of the number is written normally and the imaginary part of the number is prefixed by using the letter 'i' (i for imaginary). Therefore, a typical number might be written as (2 + i3), and this is represented by the dot shown in figure 9.3(a). As far as computing is concerned, *we can view this particular* **complex number** *as a* **vector (2,3)**, and this is why the vector (2,3) has also been shown in this diagram.

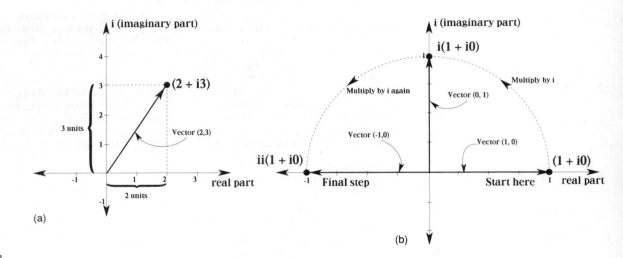

(a)

(b)

Figure 9.3

At this stage you may well be wondering about the difference between a co-ordinate like (x,y), for example, and a complex number like (x + iy) – well, as far as the *plotting* of the co-ordinate is concerned there *is no difference* – a property which we will soon be using with remarkable effect. Nevertheless, there must be something mysterious about these complex numbers, and their unique properties come from the way in which i is defined. Now **i** can be thought of as an *operator* which, when applied to a vector using multiplication, *turns the vector through 90° anticlockwise*. Therefore, if we start off with the real number +1, for example, shown by the complex number (1 + i0) or the vector (1,0) in figure 9.3(b), then after multiplying this by i, the original horizontal vector rotates by 90° and ends up facing upwards. The resultant new vector (0,1) now represents the complex number (0 + i1).

Next consider what happens if we multiply the complex number (0 + i) by i again – this operation moves the upwards-facing vector by a further 90° until it now faces left – the complex number for this new position is given by (−1 +i0). Now the imaginary part (the coefficient of i) of this latest complex number is zero, and therefore this represents the ordinary number −1 in the 'real world'.

Now here comes the exciting part – we started off with +1, we then multiplied by i to get i, and then multiplied i by i again to get −1. This means that $i^2 = −1$. So what, I hear you ask? Well, if $i^2 = −1$, this means that $i = \sqrt{−1}$ – a magical number which had eluded mathematicians for centuries. To be able to get a number which, when multiplied by itself produces a negative number was revolutionary – you are reminded that there is no ordinary number, positive or negative which has this remarkable property.

As far as we are concerned, for the purposes of the arithmetical work covered in this section, **complex numbers** *may be treated like* **ordinary numbers**, *except for the fact that* **when i^2 is encountered, it should be replaced by −1**. For example, if we want to multiply (2 +i3) by (1 + i2), then this can be done by multiplying the brackets out using the usual rules of algebra as follows,

$$(2 + i3)(1 + i2) = 2 + i4 + i3 + i^2 6 = 2 + i7 - 6 \quad \text{(Don't forget } i^2 = -1\text{)}$$
$$= -4 + i7$$

hence the answer to this particular multiplication problem is −4 + i7.

The only other thing that we need to know is how to work out the magnitude of a complex number. Now the **magnitude** is given simply by the **magnitude** *of the* **vector** which represents it. Therefore, the magnitude of (2 + i3), for example, will be given by the length of the hypotenuse of the right-angled triangle whose other lengths are the horizontal and vertical dimensions given by 2 and 3 in figure 9.3(a). A simple application of Phythagoras is all that is needed. If, for example, we let Z represent a more general complex number (x + iy), then the magnitude of Z is represented by

$$|Z| = \sqrt{(x^2 + y^2)}$$

There is very much more to the theory of complex numbers, but we have already learnt all we need to know. Having covered the relevant details we can now to get down to the business of producing some interesting patterns by using **iteration**.

The Mandelbrot set

The Mandelbrot set (in this case for a squared function) is governed by the following equation,

$$Z_n \rightarrow Z_{n-1}{}^2 + \lambda$$

where Z and λ are *both* **complex numbers**.

Now the **iterative nature** of this problem should pose no difficulty whatsoever for computer-science students – it's identical in principle to the techniques covered when dealing with roots in the last section. For example,

choose a suitable value of Z (say Z_1) and a suitable λ (see in a moment)
put Z_1 in the formula $Z_2 \rightarrow Z_1 + \lambda$ which gives the new value for Z_2
put Z_2 in the formula $Z_3 \rightarrow Z_2 + \lambda$ which gives the new value for Z_3
put Z_3 etc.

Apart from the special case of no change, in general, there are *two types of behaviour* exhibited by the above iterative processes – either the value of Z_n approaches infinity, or the value of Z_n approaches some constant. If the value tends towards infinity then it is said to **diverge**, but if it tends towards a constant then it is said to **converge**. *Any point* that **converges** to a particular value *belongs* to the **Mandelbrot set**, but any point that **diverges** to **infinity** lies *outside* of the **Mandelbrot set**. The enormous fascination with this topic lies not with looking at the numbers within the set itself, but with an exploration of the boundary between the two sets – we look in detail at the patterns produced on the edge of the Mandelbrot set, which gives

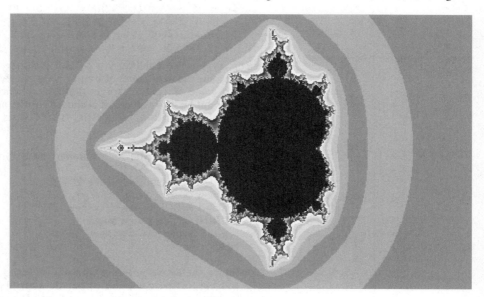

Figure 9.4

rise to intricate patterns of literally infinite detail – *you* will soon be writing an algorithm to generate the patterns shown in figure 9.4, but colour is needed to appreciate the beauty.

The *boundary* of the **Mandelbrot set** is an example of a **fractal**, other common examples are **Julia sets** and **Sierpinski triangles** – because fractals literally contain infinitely complex amounts of detail, they can be used to describe the infinitely-complex characteristics of many shapes such as plants and trees found in nature.

In it's most basic form, the Mandelbrot set can be investigated by starting off with a value of $Z_1 = 0 + i0$, then putting this value into the above equation with a suitable value of λ (see in a moment). We then stop the process according to the rules outlined in the next paragraph, then start the whole process again from scratch using different values of λ. It is these values of λ which give the co-ordinates of the points to plot.

Now the clever part comes by a consideration of what's happening to Z for different vales of λ as these iterations proceed. If the value of Z_n converges we plot the points in black, but if the value of Z_n diverges, we colour the original points by considering how slowly or how quickly Z_n approaches infinity. If it does not take too many iterations for $|Z_n|$ to become large then it's rapidly increasing, or if it takes ages for $|Z_n|$ to get to a large value then it is slowly increasing, and is therefore plotted in a different colour. In practice all we have to do is to count the number of iterations, test for some arbitrary magnitudes – and assign colours accordingly.

Development of the iterative algorithm

You are going to develop this algorithm in several parts. The suggestions inside the boxes will guide you through in relatively short and easy stages. Try not to look at the section of text following each box until after you have attempted the work!

Student activity 3

An algorithm to multiply the complex numbers.

On page 181 you have seen how complex numbers may be multiplied together. Using a suitable high-level langauge of your choice, write an algorithm which performs the following.

(1) Sets up $Z = x + iy$, and $\lambda = p + iq$

(2) Uses the equation $Z \rightarrow Z^2 + \lambda$ to compute the next value of Z

(3) Puts the whole lot inside a loop to investigate whether or not $|Z|$ converges or diverges using $p = -2$ and $q = 2$

The following procedure works out multiplication of complex numbers as described on page 181. What we have to do is simple – if we let $Z = x + iy$, and let $\lambda = p + iq$, then the new Z will be

$$
\begin{aligned}
Z \rightarrow Z^2 + \lambda &= (x + iy)(x + iy) + p + iq & \text{(Put in the values of Z and } \lambda) \\
&\rightarrow x^2 + 2ixy + i^2y^2 + p + iq & \text{(Multiplying out the brackets)} \\
&\rightarrow x^2 + 2ixy - y^2 + p + iq & \text{(Don't forget that } i^2 = -1) \\
&\rightarrow (x^2 - y^2 + p) + i(2xy + q) & \text{(Collect real and imag. parts)}
\end{aligned}
$$

This gives us the real '$(x^2 - y^2 + p)$' and imaginary '$(2xy + q)$' parts of the *new Z* which then become the *new values* of x and y respectively – this will then be used to calculate the next value of Z. Don't forget that λ, and hence the values of p and q will remain the same until a new value of λ is chosen for the next set of iterations.

A suitable algorithm, using BBC BASIC V, is as follows

```
x_old = 0:y_old = 0
INPUT "Please type in p followed by q ", p,q
FOR count = 1 TO 10
  x_new = x_old^2 - y_old^2 + p
  y_new = 2*x_old*y_old + q
  MagZ = SQR(x_new^2+y_new^2)
  PRINT x_new,y_new,MagZ
  x_old=x_new:y_old=y_new
NEXT count
```

Running the above program with $p = -2$ and $q = 2$, you will probably find that $|Z|$ gets too big for the computer to handle after about 5 or 6 iterations! Therefore, in the final program we will have to test for $|Z|$ becoming large very rapidly, and stop the arithmetical processes before it has time to generate an error on the computer.

The complex plane

Figure 9.5

In the above example you were given p and q in a rather arbitrary fashion. However, *typical values for p and q which lie between – 2 and +2* give a **good picture to investigate**. Therefore, if we are to colour these points using the arguments stated in the last section, then the complex plane shown in figure 9.5 needs investigation.

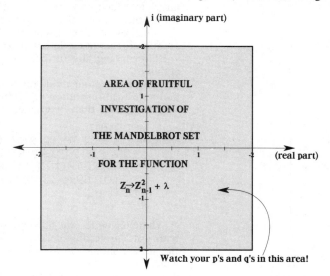

The resolution chosen is up to you, and depends upon the graphics capability of your system, but high resolutions would be needed if great detail is to be seen. Nevertheless, you can get the iterative algorithms working with with far less resolution, and this is what I would suggest doing during the initial-development phases. Techniques such as simplifying the underlying number of iterations necessary so that algorithms may be developed more quickly should be remembered when you are undertaking your project work. One strategy for the Mandelbrot problem would be to sweep values of p from –2 to +2 in suitable steps, and then repeat this procedure for each value of q from –2 to +2, again using suitable steps. Now this could represent a huge amount of calculation. For example, if we take 500 steps from –2 to +2 in each direction, then this means that we go through 250,000 tests for convergence and divergence, with each test possibly taking up to about 50 iterations each, giving typically over 12½ million calculations and tests – unless you have a fast computer, there will be plenty of time for coffee while you are waiting for the results.

The last thing to do before *you* develop the algorithm to cycle through the p's and q's in the above area is to suggest a suitable colour scheme. You will recall that the time taken to whizz off or escape to infinity is used to determine a suitable colour for a chosen starting point. Now suppose that you choose a 16-colour mode, black has already been reserved for the convergent numbers, therefore, this leaves us with 15 colours for the rest of the diagram.

As a measure of speed of escape to infinity we can simply count the number of iterations needed to get past some particular value. Therefore, we can assign 15 different values on the way to infinity.

One common colour-assignment technique is to count the number of iterations (times round the loop calculating new values of p and q), and assign a colour

---

Student activity 4

Graphics preparation for the Mandelbrot Algorithm.

Choose a suitable graphics mode on your computer with sufficient resolution and colours. I would suggest just 16 colours at first. In a high-level language of your choice write the following.

(1) Map out the complex plane onto your screen graphics area (i.e. actual values of p and q needed to fill up most of the screen).

(2) Vary the values of p and q from –2 to +2 and plot dots to verify that this is happening.

(3) Assign a different colour to any area of the screen based on the values of p and q. (You can choose any criteria you wish.)

accordingly. For example, if you were in a 64-colour graphics mode then once round the loop could be assigned colour one, twice round the loop colour two and so on until 64 times round the loop would get colour 64. Don't forget that each time round the loop we must check for the magnitude of the complex number becoming too large, in which case we exit with the value to determine the colour. Also, don't forget that some values might change very slowly, in which case it's best to limit the number of times round the loop. Applying this method without thought to a 16-million colour mode could be a little time consuming!

Before going any further carry out the graphics-preparation activity in Student activity 4.

Using a 16-colour mode on Acorn's RISC PC with a horizontal resolution of 1600 and a vertical resolution of 1200, and assigning just two different colours according to p being less than or greater than 0, we get the following code.

```
MODE 102
FOR p = -2 TO +2 STEP 0.01
  FOR q = -2 TO +2 STEP 0.01
    IF q>0 THEN GCOL 0,2 ELSE GCOL 0,4
    PLOT 69,(p+2)*200,(q+2)*200
  NEXT q
NEXT p
```

Whatever code you have produced should fill up a large portion of the screen with dots, preferably so close together that you can't easily see them. Portions of the screen should be assigned different colours according to your chosen criteria, which in the above case are very simple indeed. It's important to note that the origin of the complex plane used to view the Mandelbrot set is in the middle of the picture, but the origin of your graphics screen is likely to be the bottom-left-hand-side of the VDU. Therefore, although appropriate values of p and q must be used in the mathematical analysis, 2 has been added to each to map the complex plane so that it moves along two and up two and can be viewed on the screen. Next we have to multiply the co-ordinates by some large value (200 in the above program) so that the area of the plot is large enough to be seen in the screen.

Student activity 5

The final Mandelbrot Algorithm

(1) Produce a structure diagram for the complete Mandelbrot plot.
Use p an q from –2 to +2 in steps of 0.01, and 64 different colour-assignment tests. Test for the magnitude of Z getting bigger than 1E5 and stop the iterative procedure if this is true.

(2) Code the above algorithm in any suitable high-level language. Decrease the step size during the development stages if necessary.

(3) Enjoy the patterns on the screen of your computer.

You are now ready to program your Mandelbrot algorithm. You need to use the graphics program developed in the last section to sweep out the appropriate area of the screen, the complex-number-multiplication algorithm to evaluate new values of x and y for the complex number Z, and use the colouring algorithm based on how many iterations (loop counts) are needed for Z to whiz off to infinity. Best of luck – don't forget that much of the initial thought has already been done, and don't cheat by looking at the answers first.

A suitable algorithm is shown as follows.

```
Initialise variables
FOR p = -2 TO +2 STEP size
  FOR q = -2 TO +2 STEP size
    Initialise iteration count
    WHILE Absolute value(Magnitude of Z) < Max AND iteration count <64
      X = x^2 – y^2 + p
      Y =  2*x*y + q
      Magnitude of Z = Square root of(X^2+Y^2)
      set next values of x and y from newest values of X and Y
      increment iteration count
    ENDWHILE
```

```
            Choose suitable graphics colour based on iteration count number
            PLOT point at graphics position with appropriate scale factor
            Reset the variables x and y to zero
         NEXT q
      NEXT p
```

A program written in BBC BASIC V for the Archimedes, based on the above pseudocode algorithm is as follows.

```
      MODE 40
      MagZ=0
      x_old = 0:y_old = 0
      FOR p = -2 TO +2 STEP 0.01
        FOR q = -2 TO +2 STEP 0.01
          Loop=1
          WHILE ABS(MagZ) < 100 AND Loop <64
            x_new = x_old^2 – y_old^2 + p
            y_new =  2*x_old*y_old + q
            MagZ = SQR(x_new^2+y_new^2)
             x_old = x_new:y_old=y_new
            Loop = Loop + 1
          ENDWHILE
          GCOL Loop
          PLOT 69,(p+2)*200,(q+2)*200
          x_old=0: y_old=0: MagZ=0
        NEXT q
      NEXT p
      PRINT "DONE"
```

The above code is a very basic shell. There is room for considerable improvement, and adding routines to investigate interesting parts of the complex plane are common additions. Similarly, there is no provision to save the picture which could have taken some time to complete. It is left to the reader to develop the algorithms further if desired, or to make use of some suitable screen-saving utility. Hours of practice with your programming skills will be amply rewarded.

Recursion

Recursion is a vitally important topic as it represents part of the ultimate dream of being able to produce lots of results with the minimum of coding. By the continued repetition of the same group of instructions one can produce staggering graphics effects or work out mathematical equations which would involve long and tedious coding by other methods. These are just two of the many hundreds of possible applications of recursion. Others can be found in the chapter on data structures.

Recursion and factorials

As an example, consider the working out of factorial 10, using the mathematical notation 10!

Now 10! is defined as $10 \times 9 \times 8 \times 7 \times 6 \times 5 \times 4 \times 3 \times 2 \times 1 = 3\ 628\ 800$

Similarly N! would be defined as

$$N \times (N - 1) \times (N - 2) \times (N - 3) \times \ldots \times 3 \times 2 \times 1$$

You will also need to remember that 0! and 1! are both defined as 1.

Suppose that we had to construct an algorithm to evaluate a factorial. We could proceed in several different ways:

1.   Write down the function explicitly!

No one who still retains 'all their marbles' would code the algorithm in this way as it would involve longer and longer expressions for larger and larger factorials. This method will therefore not even be considered.

2.   It does not take much imagination to see that a simple loop would be more efficient and could be accomplished using pseudocode as follows:

```
Assign value to N
Set up initial conditions
    count := 2
    product := 1
Test for special case
    IF N = 0 OR N = 1
        THEN factorial (N) = 1 in which case we STOP
        ELSE continue with the next part

        REPEAT
            product := product x count
            count := count + 1
        UNTIL count = N + 1
factorial (N) = product
```

Whenever the above routine is needed we could insert the above loop into the algorithm to evaluate a factorial. The method could also be tidied up a little by using a **defined function** (see page 124), and passing over the appropriate parameters to the routine .

3.   This time we will apply a **recursive definition** to the problem of evaluating a factorial. Consider the following:

```
DEFINE MODULE factorial (N)
    IF N = 0 OR N = 1
        THEN factorial = 1
        ELSE work out factorial = N × factorial (N – 1)
END MODULE
```

The above is all the code that is required. The reason is that the module calls itself at line four. A recursive routine is therefore simply one that calls itself.

Consider an example using the above code to work out 4!

	Notes:
MODULE factorial (4)	Module entered with N = 4
IF N = 0 OR N = 1 THEN . . .	
ELSE work out 4 × factorial (3)	Module calls itself with N = 3
[Routine working out 4 × factorial (3)]	
MODULE factorial (3)	Module entered with N = 3
IF N = 0 OR N = 1 THEN . . .	
ELSE work out 3 × factorial (2)	Module calls itself with N = 2
[Routine working out 4 × 3 × factorial (2)]	
MODULE factorial (2)	Module entered with N = 2
IF N = 0 OR N = 1 THEN . . .	
ELSE work out 2 × factorial (1)	Module calls itself with N = 1
[Routine working out 4 × 3 × 2 × factorial (1)]	
MODULE factorial (1)	Module entered with N = 1
IF N = 0 OR N = 1 THEN factorial (1) = 1	Factorial (1) 'evaluated'
ELSE . . .	
[Routine working out 4 × 3 × 2 × 1]	

You can see from the above that the routine begins by working out 4 × factorial (3). However, factorial (3) is then worked out by the routine calling itself. Therefore, when factorial (3) is worked out, the routine is then working out 4 × 3 × factorial (2). The routine then calls itself to work out factorial (2) etc.

A Pascal function can be used in a similar way to the above as follows:

```
PROGRAM factorial (input,output)

VAR number: integer;

    FUNCTION factorial (N: integer): integer;
        BEGIN
            IF N = 1 OR N = 0 THEN
                BEGIN
                    factorial := 1
```

```
                        END
                    ELSE
                        BEGIN
                            factorial := N * factorial (N–1)
                        END
            END;
```

The above FUNCTION could be called from the main Pascal program as follows:

```
    BEGIN (* work out factorial*)
        WRITELN('Input number to be used for the factorial calculation');
        READLN(number);
        WRITELN('Original number', number, 'factorial', number, 'is', factorial
        (number));
    END.
```

Example using recursion

One of the classic examples of recursion is in the development of an algorithm to solve the Towers of Hanoi problem.

The problem can be illustrated using the apparatus shown in figure 9.6.

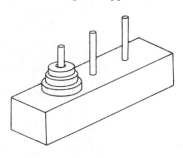

Figure 9.6

There are three vertical poles over which discs with holes in the centre are placed. Initially the discs are placed such that the largest one is on the bottom, progressively leading up to the narrowest one on the top of the pile. The object of the game is to transfer the discs, one at a time, on to another pole to end up in the same order. The difficulty obviously arises from the rules of the game which are as follows:

1.   Only one disc can be moved at any time.
2.   After each move, all discs must be on the poles (you can't hide one in your pocket!)
3.   No disc may be placed on top of a disc which is smaller than itself.

It is essential when dealing with recursive algorithms to be able to visualize how the overall problem can be split up into sub-problems. These sub-problems may then be solved by the application of the same algorithm again and again, but obviously with different parameters being passed on every time the original algorithm is recursively called.

Firstly, it is obvious that no matter how many discs are involved, the problem must ultimately be broken down into the movement of just one disc. Therefore, there must be a routine that carries out this simple move. The routine to do this is as follows:

Move (source, destination)

The source will be the pole from which to get the disc and the destination will be the pole which is to accommodate the disc.

Now it is also obvious that the source and destination will change, according to which disc is to be moved and when. Therefore, we need some method of constantly swapping over the source and destination throughout the algorithm.

Although the problem seems to be very complicated, it is an excellent example of how recursion can provide the solution quite simply, and very elegantly. Consider the following:

Let us assume that the left hand pole is to be the source pole i.e. the pole on which the pile of discs is originally placed, and the middle pole is to be the destination pole for the final pile of discs. Given this information it is obvious that the right hand pole can be regarded as a temporary store for the discs until they are needed.

First we will assume that we have just three discs on the pile. The classic solution to the above problem is simple and consists of just three stages:

(a) Move the top two discs from the left hand pole to the right hand pole, making use of the poles as a temporary store when necessary.
(b) Move the remaining disc on the left hand pole to the middle pole.
(c) Move the two discs on the right hand pole back on the middle pole making use of the poles as a temporary store when necessary.

The above algorithm should be quite obvious. The only way that you can get the biggest disc from the bottom of the pile on the left hand side on to the bottom of the pile on the middle pole is to make sure that the rest of the discs are not in the way of this move i.e. they form a pile on the right hand side! This is in fact part (a) of the above algorithm. Part (b) is simply the disc that remains on the original pole being transferred on to the final pole. The final part transfers the other discs back on top of the bottom disc on the middle pole.

Suppose that we started with four discs. This time, we would have to remove the top three discs from the left to the right for part (a) of the algorithm. If we had N discs, then we would have to move (N − 1) discs from the left to the middle for part (a) etc.

We can therefore generalize the three major steps as an algorithm for N discs (moving the pile from the left to the middle) as follows:

(a) Move (N − 1) discs from the left hand pole to the right hand pole using poles for temporary stores where necessary.
(b) Move the remaining disc from the left pole to the middle pole.
(c) Move the (N − 1) discs from the right hand pole on to the middle pole using the poles as a temporary store when necessary.

What the above algorithm does is to split up the problem into simpler sub-problems. These sub-problems are almost identical in nature to the main problem. For example, with four discs, the problems involve moving a pile of three discs. With three discs, the problems involve moving a pile of two discs etc.

To understand how the parameters such as source and destination need to be swapped is a little more difficult. We will therefore manually work through an example using three discs, and the above algorithm as a skeleton:

Let C = Largest disc, Let B = Medium disc, Let A = Smallest disc
Let 1 = Left hand pole, Let 2 = Middle pole, Let 3 = Right hand pole.

Start   A | | | We should end up with . . .   Finish | A |
         B | | | B |
         C | | | C |
        ───────   ───────
        1   2   3   1   2   3

Manual operations to be carried out:
Note: The level of indentation is vitally important.

Transfer: means 'Thinking what to do' and Move: means 'actually moving the disc'. Each time a sub-problem occurs the whole routine is called again.

```
Transfer 3 discs from 1 to 2.                (Main problem)
(set N = 3, source = 1, dest = 2 and temp = 3)
(These values are set up by the user)
  .  Transfer 2 discs from 1 to 3            (Sub-problem)
  .  (set N = 2, source = 1, dest = 3 and temp = 2)
  .  (dest and temp swapped)
  .  .  Transfer 1 disc from 1 to 2.         (Sub-problem)
  .  .  (set N = 1, source = 1, dest = 2 and temp = 3)
  .  .  (dest and temp swapped)
  .  .     Move 1 disc from 1 to 2 . . . . . . . . . . . . . . . . .
  .  .     (source = 1 dest = 2)
  .  .
  .  .
  .  .
  .  Move 1 disc from 1 to 3 . . . . . . . . . . . . . . . . . . . .
```

```
A |   |
B |   |
C |   |
─────────

B |   |
C | A |
─────────

  |   |   |
C   A   B
```

```
. .
. .
. .
.    Transfer 1 disc from 2 to 3              (Sub-problem)
.    (set N = 1, source = 2, dest = 3, temp = 1)
.    (source and temp swapped)
.        Move 1 disc from 2 to 3 ...................
.
.
Move 1 disc from 1 to 2  ......................
.
.
Transfer 2 discs from 3 to 2                (Sub-problem)
(set N = 2, source = 3, dest = 2, temp = 1)
(source and temp swapped)
.    Transfer 1 disc from 3 to 1            (Sub-problem)
.    (set N = 1, source = 3, dest = 1, temp = 2)
.    (dest and temp swapped)
.        Move 1 disc from 3 to 1 ...................
.
.
.
.
.    Move 1 disc from 3 to 2 .....................
.
.
.
Transfer 1 disc from 1 to 2                 (Sub-problem)
.    (set N = 1, source = 1, dest = 2, temp = 3)
.    (source and temp swapped)
.        Move 1 disc from 1 to 2 ...................
```

Coding the problem:

1. Identify the number of discs to be moved (supplied by the user).
2. IF N = 1, THEN move the disc from the source to the destination.
3. IF N > 1 THEN
    (a) Call routine to move (N – 1) discs (supply N, source, temporary_store, destination).
    (b) Move 1 disc from source to destination.
    (c) Call routine to move (N – 1) discs (supply N, source, temporary_store, destination).

N, source, temporary_store and destination can be supplied (in the correct order) so that the routines that make the actual move know the current poles which are acting as the source, temporary_store and destination.

Consider the following Pascal-like pseudocode which defines a procedure called Transfer:

```
PROCEDURE Transfer (N, source, destination, temporary_store : integer)
  IF N = 1
    THEN
      BEGIN
        Move (source, destination)
      END
    ELSE
      BEGIN
        Transfer (N – 1, source, temporary_store, destination)
        Move (source, destination)
        Transfer (N – 1, temporary_store, destination, source)
      END
END;
```

To make the procedure easy to use, the source, temporary_store and destination will be assigned integer numerical values of 1, 2 and 3 respectively which would represent the pole positions as follows:

i.e.   If we have to move a disc from left to right
then   1 would be the source
       2 would be the temporary_store
and   3 would be the destination.

N.B. When the routine is called, a pair of parameters are swapped to accommodate the different poles that act as a source, destination and temporary_store throughout the problem. This is of fundamental importance in understanding this recursion algorithm and an example follows:

Every time the original procedure is to be called the parameters are:

Transfer (N, source, destination, temporary_store)

Suppose that N = 3, source = 1, destination = 2 and temporary_store = 3.

NOW IF
  Transfer (N – 1, source, temporary_store, destination)
  calls the procedure then
       (i)   N would become 2
       (ii) source would remain the same, i.e. source = 1
       (iii) temporary_store is swapped with destination,
             i.e. temporary_store = 2
and   (iv) destination is swapped with temporary_store, i.e. destination = 3.

Make sure that you understand the above principle well before doing the following dry run. Failure to appreciate how the parameters are swapped will result in failure to understand this recursive algorithm.

Dry run:
The following routine is not long. It looks quite long because of the many comments to explain carefully each stage.

User will supply the parameters N = 3, source = 1, destination = 2 and therefore, temporary_store = 3.

We will start off by calling the procedure transfer with the above parameters:

```
Transfer (N, source, destination, temporary_store)          A
(* source = 1, dest = 2 and temp = 3 *)                     B
(* transfer 3 discs from 1 to 2 *)                          C


IF 3 = 1
  THEN
    BEGIN
      [Code not executed as N <> 1]
    END
  ELSE
    BEGIN
      Transfer (N – 1, source, temporary_store, destination)
      (* Routine calls itself recursively *)
      (* N – 1 = 2, source = 1, dest = 3, temp = 2, temp and
         dest swapped *)
      (* transfer 2 discs from 1 to 3 *)
      IF 2 = 1
        THEN
          BEGIN
            [Code not executed as N <> 1]
          END
        ELSE
          Transfer (N – 1, source, temporary_store, destination)
          (* Routine calls itself recursively *)
          (* N – 1 = 1, source = 1, dest = 2, temp = 3, temp and
             dest swapped again *)
          (* transfer 1 disc from 1 to 2 *)
          IF 1 = 1
            THEN
              BEGIN
                Move (source, destination)            B
                (* Move 1 disc from 1 to 2 *)         C    A
              END
```

```
              ELSE
                 BEGIN
                    [Code not executed as N = 1]
                 END
              END
           Move (source, destination)
           (* move 1 disc from 1 to 3 *)
           (* note parameters are now as at the beginning of the
              'IF 2 = 1' loop *)
           (* i.e. N – 1 = 2, source = 1, temporary_store = 2
              and destination = 3 *)
           Transfer (N – 1, temporary_store, destination, source)
           (* Routine calls itself recursively *)
           (* N – 1 = 1, source = 2, dest = 3, temp = 1, source
              and temp swapped *)
           (* transfer 1 disc from 2 to 3 *)
           IF 1 = 1
              THEN
                 BEGIN
                    Move (source, destination)
                    (* Move 1 disc from 2 to 3 *)
                 END
              ELSE
                 BEGIN
                    [Code not executed as N = 1 *]
                 END
              END
     Move (source, destination)
     (* Move 1 disc from 1 to 2 *)
     (* note parameters are now as at the beginning of the
        'IF 3 = 1' loop *)
     (* i.e. N = 3, source = 1, dest = 2, temp = 3 *)
     Transfer (N – 1, temporary_store, destination, source)
     (* Routine calls itself recursively *)
     (* N – 1 = 2, source = 3, dest = 2, temp = 1, temp and source swapped *)
     (*i.e. transfer 2 discs from 3 to 2 *)
     IF 2= 1
        THEN
           BEGIN
              [Code not executed as N <> 1]
           END
        ELSE
           BEGIN
              Transfer (N–1, source, temporary_store, destination)
              (* Routine calls itself recursively *)
              (* N–1 = 1, source = 3, dest = 1, temp = 2, temp and
                 dest swapped *)
              (* i.e. transfer 1 disc from 3 to 1 *)
              IF 1 = 1
                 THEN
                    BEGIN
                       MOVE (source, destination)
                       (* Move 1 disc from 3 to 1 *)
                    END
                 ELSE
                    BEGIN
                       [Code not executed as N = 1]
                    END
                 END
     Move (source, destination)
     (* Move 1 disc from 3 to 2 *)
     (* note, parameters are now as at the beginning of
        the second 'IF 2 = 1' loop *)
     Transfer (N – 1, temporary_store, destination, source)
     (* Routine calls itself recursively *)
     (* N – 1 = 1, source = 1, dest = 2, temp = 3, temp and source swapped *)
     (* i.e. transfer 1 disc from 1 to 2 *)
```

C	A	B

C		A
		B

		A
	C	B

A	C	B

	B	
A	C	

```
                        IF 1 = 1
                          THEN
                            BEGIN
                               MOVE (source, destination)
                               (* Move 1 disc from 1 to 2 *)
                            END
                          ELSE
                            BEGIN
                               [Code not executed as N = 1]
                            END
                          END
                      END
                  END
```

```
A
B
C
```

If you worked your way through that and understood it, then you should have a deep insight into recursion, and a terrible headache! It is remarkable how much work can be carried out with such a small amount of code. The above only uses three discs, but you can do several more if you program the computer to do it.

The final program is quite simple. All it needs is a routine to print out the moves as it goes along. The following routine simply prints out the source and destination of each move. However, you should be capable of programming some good graphics to make the output attractive on your machine.

Final routine including very simple output

```
PROGRAM recursion_example (input,output);

VAR N : integer;

PROCEDURE Transfer(N, source, destination, temporary_store : integer)

PROCEDURE Move (source, destination : integer);

(* This simple procedure writes out to the screen the moves made by the
computer * )
BEGIN
   Writeln ('Move disc from', source, 'to', destination);
END;

IF N = 1
  THEN
    BEGIN
       Move (source, destination)
    END
  ELSE
    BEGIN
       Transfer (N − 1, source, temporary_store, destination)
       Move (source, destination)
       Transfer (N − 1, temporary_store, destination, source)
    END
END;

BEGIN

( * This is the main calling routine * )

   WRITE ('Please enter the number of discs. . .');
   READLN (N)
   WRITE ('Please enter the source pole. . .');
   READLN (source)
   WRITE ('Please enter the destination pole. . .');
   READLN (destination)
   IF source = 1 AND destination = 2 THEN temporary_store = 3
   IF source = 2 AND destination = 3 THEN temporary_store = 1 ELSE
   temporary_store = 2

   Transfer (N, source, destination, temporary_store)

END
```

The original problem was devised by the monks of Hanoi. In fact they had a total of 64 discs on their model! Indeed they believed that by the time the problem was solved the end of the world would have arrived. However, I should not worry too much about this because it has been calculated that even if the monks worked out the perfect algorithm, and moved one disc every second, then it would take over 600 000 million years to complete the solution!

You could now develop an algorithm to solve the Towers of Hanoi problem using a computer, but first, let us think how long it would take the computer to solve the problem:

Suppose that we could make 100 000 000 moves every second (a very fast computer!)

Moving at one disc per second would = 600 000 000 000 years
Moving at 100 000 000 discs per second = 600 000 000 000 / 100 000 000
                                        = 6000 years!

I suggest that you limit the number of discs to a little less than 64 if you wish to try out the program!

Monte Carlo methods

This is nothing to do with the famous car races at Monte Carlo! It is the name given to a technique which can be used for finding areas under a graph by making use of **random numbers**, or in fact **pseudo random numbers**, that are generated inside a computer.

Consider the graph $y = x^2$ as shown in figure 9.7.

Suppose that we wish to find the area under this graph between the limits $x = 1$ and $x = 2$.

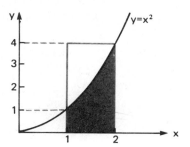

Figure 9.7

Consider the rectangle shown in grey in figure 9.7. We can see that values of x range from 1 to 2 and values of y range from 0 to 4. If we 'zap' (excuse this highly technical term!) this area with random co-ordinates then some of them will lie in the shaded area we wish to calculate, and some will lie above the shaded area in the remainder of the grey rectangle. If we choose many random co-ordinates then the proportion of them lying in the shaded area will give this shaded area as a proportion of the entire rectangle.

It is relatively easy to calculate the area of a rectangle (even without a computer!) and so an approximation to the shaded area can be made by the following:

$$\text{Area} = \text{Area of rectangle} \times \frac{\text{Number of random co-ordinates in shaded area}}{\text{Total number of random co-ordinates}}$$

It is easy to determine if a random co-ordinate is in the shaded area by checking to see if the y value is less than or greater than x^2. If it is in the shaded area then it is called a hit, or if it is not in the shaded area then it is called a miss.

To sum up the procedure for the above example is as follows:

(1) Generate a random number x between 1 and 2. (2) Generate a random number y between 0 and 4. (3) Calculate the corresponding value of y, from $y = x^2$ for this particular function. (4) Check to see if $y < x^2$. If it is then a hit is obtained or if not then a miss. (5) At the end of the required number of random numbers work out:

$$\text{Area} = \text{Area of rectangle} \times \frac{\text{Hits}}{\text{Misses} + \text{Hits}}$$

Generation of pseudo random numbers

We can see from the above that it is necessary to have a source of random numbers inside the computer. The theory of generating good random numbers is long and complex but it is relatively easy to generate what are called **pseudo random numbers**. In fact these are numbers with a pattern, i.e. the numbers will repeat themselves over and over again. In fact on some computers you can even set the seed of pseudo random numbers to go through exactly the same cycle each time the program is run. This is very useful for checking to see if statistical simulations etc. are working properly. Imagine trying to track down a bug in your program when the data keeps changing!

A pseudo random number is one in which the cycle of numbers repeats itself. The trick is to make this cycle so long that no one actually notices! In practice this means making the cycle length long compared with the number of random numbers that is likely to be encountered in any one application.

We will start off by using some techniques to generate a short cycle length, and then go on to more sophisticated methods reproducing very long cycle lengths.

There are many simple methods of generating random numbers, but all of them suffer from various faults eventually. For example, it may be a small cycle length, or it may be that the procedure being used is fine until a certain number happens to come up, and then the procedure breaks down. An example of a simple procedure is called the mid-product method.

Mid-product method

This method involves multiplying two numbers (called **seeds**) together, and then taking a specified number of digits out of the middle of the product. (Hence the name mid-product.) Finally the set of digits extracted from the middle of the product is used in conjunction with the second seed to produce the second pseudo random number. The process is then repeated as shown in the following example.

Example

Starting with the seeds 1833 and 9899, and using the middle four digits of the product, generate 10 pseudo random numbers.

Seed 1	Seed 2	Product	Pseudo random number
1833	9899	18{1448}67	1448
9899	1448	14{3337}52	3337
1448	3337	04{8319}76	8319
3337	8319	27{7605}03	7605
8319	7605	63{2659}95	2659
7605	2659	20{2216}95	2216
		etc.	

It would appear from the above that a satisfactory sequence of 4-digit random numbers is being obtained. Try writing a program starting with different seeds and print out many random numbers. You will find that for some choice of seeds the cycle length is short, and if you are unlucky enough to hit on 0000 as your four middle digits then the system collapses because all the random numbers from this one on will be 0000. Hardly a random sequence.

There are other simple methods but all pale into insignificance compared with the following types of methods using modulo arithmetic. One such method is as follows:

The linear congruential method

First a resumé on **modulo** arithmetic for those who may not be familiar with the term. Modulo arithmetic is often known simply as clock arithmetic because when you start to learn about it a clock can be used to explain the system easily. Consider the square clock shown in figure 9.8(a).

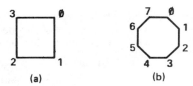

(a)   (b)

Figure 9.8

There are four numbers in modulo 4, namely 0, 1, 2 and 3. You count by moving round the clock in a clockwise direction: i.e. 0, 1, 2, 3, 0, 1, 2, 3, 0, 1, etc. That is the principle of modulo arithmetic. As another example consider modulo 8 as shown in figure 9.8(b). Here we can count as 0, 1, 2, 3, 4, 5, 6, 7, 0, 1, 2, 3, etc.

To perform arithmetic is simple. Consider the following:

What is 2 + 3 in modulo 4?

Start counting round the modulo 4 clock and you will find that 2 + 3 = 1.

It would not be convenient if we had to draw clocks every time and it is relatively simple to deduce what the answer is going to be once the principle is well understood.

Suppose that we want to find 2 + 3 mod 4. It is basically the remainder after division of the original number by 4. Hence:

    2 + 3 = 5.   Now 5/4 = 1 remainder 1. Therefore 2 + 3 = 1 mod 4

or in modulo 9

    8 + 4 = 12.   Now 12/9 = 1 remainder 3. Therefore 8 + 4 = 3 mod 9.

The linear congruence formula is expressed as follows:

$$R_{n+1} = (a.R_n + i) \bmod m$$

The formula states that the pseudo random number R_{n+1} can be obtained from the previous pseudo random number R_n, by multiplying it by a (a multiplier), and adding i (an increment), in modulo m.

It is most important that sensible values of m, a and i are chosen. If not the sequence produced can be far from the best possible.

The principles of choosing these numbers are beyond the scope of this book, but it does not stop you being able to use the above formula.

We have seen from the modulo arithmetic above that there are four possible remainders in modulo 4 (i.e. 0, 1, 2 and 3) and eight in modulo 8 etc. Hence if we choose modulo m (as in the above formula) then there will be m possible remainders. This effectively defines the maximum length of the cycle. We therefore will have to choose a large value for m. It is convenient when trying to generate random numbers to choose m to be 2 to the power of an integer, as this significantly reduces the processing time. As m must be as big as possible, the power of two is often chosen to be the maximum number that the computer's word length can hold (i.e. this would be $2^8 - 1 = 255$ for an 8-bit micro. (The cycle length would obviously be more in practice, as 256 is not large enough. This can be achieved by using multiple bytes.) However, to make sure that this maximum cycle is achieved, the values of a and i must be chosen with the following restrictions borne in mind:

All of a, i, and the starting value R_n must be less than the modulo m.

Also a, i, and the starting value R_n must be greater than or equal to 0.

The maximum cycle length occurs when a lies between $\sqrt{m}$ and $m - \sqrt{m}$.

A full treatment of the above can be found in one of the seven volumes by Knuth called *The Art of Computer Programming, Vol 2. Seminumerical algorithms*.

Example

Generate 10 random numbers using the linear congruential method with a starting value of 8029, a value of a = 37, a value of i = 19 and using modulo 65535 (16-bit word length).

n	R_n	$aR_n + i$	$R_{n+1} = (aR_n + i) \bmod 65535$
1	8029	297092	34952
2	34952	1293243	48078
3	48078	1778905	09460
4	9460	350039	22364
5	22364	827487	41067
6	41067	1519498	12193
7	12193	451160	57950
8	57950	2144169	47049
9	47049	1740832	36922
10	36922		

Computer queueing simulations

After ploughing through random number generation let us see how it can be put to good use.

There are many occasions when computers can be put to good use for simulating the likely outcome for possible decisions that can be made in a business. For example, suppose that it is proposed to build a new petrol pump forecourt It is essential that customers are not kept waiting for too long before being able to use the pumps. Similarly, it would be bad policy to install many expensive pumps if they are never going to be used at anywhere near full capacity. It is possible to use a computer to simulate the sit-

uation that is likely to occur at the pumps if a different number of pumps is installed. One of the major advantages of such a system is that parameters such as number of pumps, customers arriving per minute, number of cashiers etc. can all be altered to see the likely outcome on the queue. Hence the name **queueing theory.**

Statistics and probability play an important role in queueing theory. For example, it is most unlikely that the number of customers arriving each minute will be in rectangular distribution i.e. it is unlikely that 0, 1, 2, 3 etc. customers per minute will arrive with equal probability. In this example let us assume the following distribution:

Table 1

Number of customers arriving per minute	0	1	2	3	4	6	7
Probability	0.10	0.23	0.30	0.20	0.10	0.05	0.02

Notice how all the probabilities add up to 1.

During the computer simulation we will make use of a pseudo random number generator which can generate random numbers in the range 0 to 1 inclusive and use to generate appropriate scaled numbers (see page 197). When a number is generated, we will compare it with the above table to determine the nearest match. This will then set up the number of customers arriving during that minute of the simulation.

Next it is important to realise that not all the customers are served in exactly the same amount of time. Let us also suppose that (based on previous experience of similar systems), a customer will be served according to the following distribution:

Table 2

Customer self service times at the pumps to the nearest minute	1	2	3	4	5
Probability	0.30	0.25	0.2	0.15	0.10

Finally, there is the time taken to pay for the petrol and the buying of sweets etc. in the garage forecourt shop. For this we will use the following distribution:

Table 3

Customer service time at the kiosk to the nearest minute	1	2	3	4
Probability	0.60	0.30	0.07	0.03

It is also found that if a customer has to wait too long before being able to get to the pumps, then he or she will go away and not buy any petrol at all. Let us suppose that the probabilities of the customer going away is given as follows:

Table 4

Number of cars in queue for the pumps	0	1	2	3	4	5	>5
Probability of leaving	0.0	0.1	0.2	0.4	0.7	0.9	1.0

i.e. a one in 10 chance of the customer leaving if there is one car waiting in the queue etc.

Let us consider simulating the situation for one hour, but having a print-out of the state of the pumps, queues, etc. every minute. First let us define some variables:

time	a variable that is incremented every 'minute', and controls the entire simulation.
pumps	the number of pumps available in the simulation.
cashiers	the number of cashiers available to take the money.
new_cust	the number of customers arriving in one minute (from Table 1).
cust_pumps	the number of customers at the pumps.
cust_kiosk	the number of customers at the kiosk.
cust_waiting	the number of customers waiting in queue.
cust_left	the number of customers who have left without being served.
cust_pump_time	time taken for customer to use the pump (number between 1 and 5 given in Table 2).
cust_kiosk_time	time taken for customer to be served at kiosk (number between 1 and 4 from Table 3).
prob_leave	the probability of a customer leaving given the number in the waiting queue (Table 4).

We will assume that the forecourt is initially empty and that all the variables reflect this at time = 0 minutes.

At time = 0 we will generate a random number that simulates the number of customers entering the garage, based on the distribution given in Table 1.

To generate a random number for a given probability distribution is simple. As an example, consider the following:

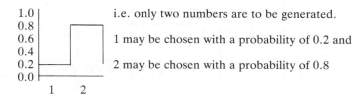

i.e. only two numbers are to be generated.

1 may be chosen with a probability of 0.2 and

2 may be chosen with a probability of 0.8

Now the numbers will all be equally likely in the range 0 to 1 inclusive. We can therefore generate a number in this range and modify it to the above range using:

LET random_number = RND(1)   : generates random number in range (0,1)

IF random_number < 0.2 THEN number = 1   : generate number 1 with probability of 0.2

IF random_number > 0.2 THEN number = 2   : generate number 2 with probability of 0.8

IF random_number = 0.2 THEN do again   : generate another random number.

We can see that generating the distributions is simple, and will therefore assume that procedures have been written that will return the appropriate numbers and times etc.

    i.e. on the increment of each time slice the following number will automatically be generated:

    new_customers: The number of new customers entering the garage in the current minute.

Similarly, when a customer arrives at the pumps or the kiosk:

    cust_pump time: The time taken for each customer to serve themselves at the pump

and cust_kiosk time: Time taken for customer to be served at the kiosk.

will automatically be generated.

A typical scenario can be seen in the flowchart of figure 9.9.

The flowchart assumes that the time taken for the computer to execute the required simple calculations is negligible and therefore all processes that are time dependent are checked with great rapidity. By the time the algorithm has worked through to the 'has time incremented by box one' then the time will either not have incremented by one, or will be very shortly after the actual increment.

An extra point that is not clear from this initial flowchart is the fact that each new customer will have new variables uniquely assigned.

i.e. for the first customer to arrive at the pumps the variable

    cust_pump_time(1) must be generated using the distribution of Table 1.

Similarly, when customer two enters the kiosk then

    cust_kiosk_time(2) will have to be generated from Table 3 etc.

We can see that when a customer has been served at the kiosk then his variable may be returned to the system for future use i.e. if customer five has been served then the variables associated with this customer are no longer needed and can be reassigned when necessary to a new customer.

We therefore literally use a queueing system where the variables can be held in an array:

    new_cust(1), new_cust(2), new_cust(3) etc.

The size of the array will have to be estimated and indeed during early simulations may cause the system to crash if its dimensions are exceeded.

The flowchart given in figure 9.9 is only really a start to point you in the right direction. For example, we have assumed that the customer service time at the kiosk

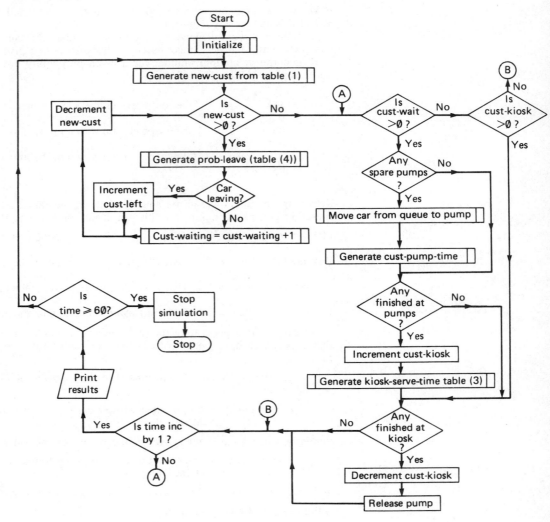

Figure 9.9

can be taken from the distribution shown in Table 3. However, it might be more realistic to assume that in addition to the above information, it would be desirable to introduce a factor that increased this time as a function of the length of the kiosk queue. Also, many readers may not agree with the approach that deals with the assigning of the probabilities to see if a customer leaves or not before the queue has effectively moved to the pumps. However, this is one of the problems with modelling real life situations. Many simulations usually have to be carried out, often testing them against real data obtained in practice, to see if the accuracy of the results obtained is satisfactory. If not, and the discrepancy is too large, then the reasons will have to be established and the parameters changed accordingly until satisfactory results have been obtained. Only when this process has been carried out can the simulation be used to good effect to produce results that may be relied upon for the analysis of future trends.

It is a relatively simple matter to develop the basic algorithm further so that it may be perfected and the appropriate high level language code written. However, even this simple example gives you a good idea of how a simulation is tackled, and is considerably more complex than most examples you would find in an A-level examination. Perhaps it is a good idea for a project. It is also fun to make some sort of graphic demonstration so that the users are presented with an animated picture on the screen of what is going on. Also, it is possible to 'fiddle' the simulation so that it is not carried out in real time. This is obviously essential for many applications, but for the car and garage, it simply gives you a good deal of fun watching the screen operate at super high speed!

Exercise 9.1

1. An **iterative modelling technique** states that if x_n is an approximation to the square root of a number N, then a better approximation x_{n+1} may be found by using the formula

$$x_{n+1} = \frac{1}{2}\left(x_n + \frac{N}{x_n}\right)$$

   Write a program in a high level language of your choice to evaluate $\sqrt{5}$ to five decimal places. (Note that $\sqrt{5} = 2.23606798$.)

2. An approximation to π may be found by using a **Monte Carlo method**. A clue is to draw an inscribed circle (one that just touches each side of the four sides) inside a square, and use the ratio of the points that fall inside the circle to those that fall inside the square to derive a value for π. Write a program in a high-level language of your choice to estimate π by this method. How accurate can you get?

3. With thought it is possible to code many different algorithms making use of **recursive** or **iterative** procedures. Outline some of the advantages or disadvantages of each approach.

4. Making use of a **recursive** function, and using pseudocode or a high-level language of your choice, write a program to input an integer, then print out *all integers* less than this number down to 1 e.g. *if 3 is input then 3, 2 and 1 are printed*.

5. Making use of a **recursive** function, and using pseudocode or a high-level language of your choice, write a program to sum all the integers up to a maximum of n, where n is typed in by the user e.g *if n=5 then sum = 1+2+3+4+5 = 15 etc.*

6. Making use of a **recursive** function, and using pseudocode or a high-level language of your choice, write a program to input a string of characters and then print them out in reverse order e.g. *'kit cat' would become 'tac tik'*.

7. You are to **simulate** customers arriving at Barry Ramsden's fish-and-chip shop, and work out the possible state of the queue at one-minute intervals over a 2-hour period. The following two tables show the number of arrivals at any given minute, and the probability of serving a given number of customers in a given amount of time.

   The number of customers arriving each minute is as follows.

Cust/Min	0	1	2	3	4	5
Probability	0.20	0.25	0.25	0.15	0.10	0.05

   With a full staff, the chippy can serve the following number of customers in any given one-minute period.

Cust. Serv	1	2	3	4	5
Probability	0.35	0.25	0.20	0.15	0.05

   Barry Ramsden never wants more than 6 people in the queue at any one time. Does he have a sufficient number of staff?

8. Explain how a computer might be used to generate **pseudo random numbers**. Why is it not possible to generate completely random numbers?

End of chapter summary

- **Iteration** is the technique of repeating things by looping.
- **Iteration** may be carried out by making use of **REPEAT-UNTIL**, **DO-WHILE** and **FOR-TO-NEXT** constructs, for example.
- Complex problems can often be solved using a *minimum amount of code* and **iterative techniques**.
- Many *examples of iteration* can be drawn from **numerical analysis**, **computer modelling** and **simulation**, fractals and autostereograms, for example.
- **Recursion** is a technique where appropriate code may be arranged to call itself. This means that many steps may be coded where each step makes use of a result from the previous step.
- Recursive procedures are elegant and efficient in terms of code, but often take up more memory than iterative techniques.
- **Monte Carlo methods** generate an approximate solution to a problem by making use of pseudo-random numbers.
- **Pseudo random numbers** are sequences of numbers where the sequence is incredibly long such that to all intents and purposes they appear random.
- The **linear congruential** and **mid-product methods** can be used to generate pseudo random numbers.
- **Random numbers** are often used to control **queueing** and other types of computer **simulations**.

10 Translation of high-level languages

Introduction

He says he understands

This chapter looks at some of the ways in which languages are transformed into a form that can be run on a computer system, and some of the methods that are used to check to see if the rules of a language have been obeyed and applied correctly.

Anyone who uses a computer system must be using some form of language to control it. Therefore, a study of language itself is fundamental to the study of computer science. However, this topic is not an easy one and is therefore not covered in great depth at this level.

It is the job of the computer language to interface with the computer user in such a way that the hardware of the computer system is completely disguised. In this way, the user does not see the hardware of the machine, but a COBOL or Pascal computer.

We mentioned at the beginning of chapter 6 that computer languages are not like natural languages such as English but are a class of **formal languages.** Even so, many of the techniques of language analysis that are used in natural languages can be used to help define the formulation and manipulation of computer languages.

First, it is obvious that the statements that constitute high level languages can in no way control the computer at machine code level. For example:

    PRINT TAB(3,7) "Good Morning."

This does not bear very much relationship to the processes that go on inside the machine to cause the string 'Good Morning.' to appear on the output device at the desired tab position. Therefore, some method of **translation** is needed that must act upon code such as that shown above, to produce the desired machine code that will perform this operation. In fact the general name for all the software that translates source code into the code that can be run directly on a machine is a **translator**. The situation can be summarised in figure 10.1.

Figure 10.1

The code that is input to a translator is called the **source language** and the code that is output from the translator is called the **object** (or **target**) **language**.

The three common forms of translators are **compilers**, **interpreters** and **assemblers**. However, assemblers have been covered in detail in chapter 5.

An **interpreter** is a translator that goes through the processes of translation every time the program is run. Indeed **line interpreters** such as those found running some versions of BASIC translate one line of the program at a time. If the lines happen to be inside a particular loop structure then, if the loop is to be executed 1000 times the lines must be interpreted 1000 times! This means that all the stages of translation, including checking, will have to be gone through many times. This is the main reason why most interpreters are very slow.

A **compiler** is a translator that goes through the translation process only once. The object language is then saved and next time the program is run it does not have to be **recompiled**. Although compilers are very much faster than interpreters, if the source language has to be modified then the whole program must be recompiled. This means that they are not as convenient as interpreters for program development and debugging.

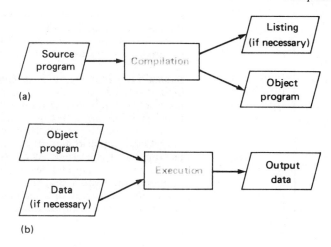

Figure 10.2

The processes of **compilation** and **execution** can be seen in figure 10.2(a) and figure 10.2(b) respectively. Figure 10.2(a) shows the source program, i.e. BASIC, Pascal, COBOL, etc. being **compiled**. The details of this compilation process will be covered shortly. A different compiler would be needed for each high level language that is to be run on the machine. A large machine may have many different high level language compilers. Besides producing the **object program** a listing of the **source program** is often required at this compilation stage.

Figure 10.2(b) shows the object program being executed by the CPU, i.e. this is a machine code program that is resident in the computer. If the object program needs any additional data, such as files, they would have to be presented to the system so that the object code could act on them to produce the desired output from the computer system.

Compilation

It should be obvious that the compiler must be a very complex piece of software. Indeed most compilers on large computer systems take many years to write.

The **compilation process** can be split up into several stages. These are:

    1. Lexical analysis   2. Syntax analysis   3. Code generation

Lexical analysis

Lexical analysis is the first stage of compilation. A **lexical analyser** is a part of the compiler program that breaks up the input to the compiler into chunks that are in a form suitable to be analysed by the next stage of the compilation process.

For example, if different peripheral devices have been used to input a program into the computer system then it is the job of the lexical analyser to standardise these different source codes into a form that would be identical for the next stage of the compilation process. For example, if two identical programs were to be run on a computer, but one program was stored on disk and the other on magnetic tape, then the codes that represent these programs may be slightly different. The lexical analyser ensures that these codes are changed into a form that is the same for each peripheral device that may be used to input source programs into the system.

When the strings of characters representing the source program are broken up into small chunks, these chunks are often known as **tokens.** The source code has therefore been **tokenized.** It is usual to remove all redundant parts of the source code (such as spaces and comments) during this tokenization phase. It is also likely in many systems that **key words such** as ENDWHILE or PROCEDURE will be replaced by a more efficient, shorter token.

It is the job of the lexical analyser to check that all the key words used are valid and to group certain symbols with their neighbours so that they can form larger units to be presented to the next stage of the compilation process. This is due to the fact that the characters of the source program are taken one at a time. Characters such as + or × are known as terminal symbols in their own right, but other characters such as P, R, 1, N and T may have to be grouped together to form the token for the **reserved word** PRINT.

As errors can be detected during this first phase of compilation, facilities to generate an **error report** must also be provided.

Syntax analysis

Syntax analysis is the stage of compilation which determines whether the string of input tokens form valid sentences etc. At this stage the structure of the source program is analysed to see if it conforms to the context-free grammar for the particular language that is being compiled. This stage would also include finding out if the correct number of brackets have been used in expressions, and determining the priorities of the arithmetical operators used within an expression. This is also called **parsing** and it is carried out by that part of the compiler that is called the **parser**.

The syntax of any high level language is expressed as a set of rules. For example, in Pascal the **syntax diagram** is often used. This is simply a convenient way of expressing the syntax of a language (syntax definition). For example, in Pascal, the syntax diagram for an **identifier** is shown in figure 10.3.

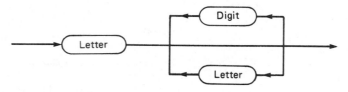

Figure 10.3

From figure 10.3 it is easily seen that A, H7, ASS31 and ABC12U are all valid identifiers but 1B, 17 and 17BY14 are not, as they all start with a number. Other forms of syntax definition using the Backus Naur form will be developed later in this chapter. As errors in syntax can be generated during this syntax analysis phase then the ability to print reports is also necessary. It is also at this stage that a **dictionary is** generated. This is simply a list kept by the compiler of the variables used by the program, the variable types such as numerical, integer, real, complex or logical, and the place in memory at which these variables can be found. All the information stored in the dictionary will be needed later when the object program is run. The details of syntax analysis will be covered shortly.

Code generation

Code generation is the final phase of the compilation process, where the code specific to the target machine is generated. As the code is **machine code** then it is usual for several machine code instructions to be generated for each high level language instruction.

As a simple example, consider the following line in a BASIC program:

LET length = 2*(sidel − side2) + 4*(side3 − side4)

Now LET is actually redundant and would therefore have been removed during the lexical analysis stage. Therefore we would have:

length = 2*(sidel − side2) + 4*(side3 − side4)

The variables side1, side2, side3, side4 and length will have been created in the dictionary mentioned earlier during the syntax analysis stage. The dictionary will contain the variable name, the variable type and where in memory this variable can be found so that it can be loaded by the machine code program.

Therefore, for the above line, in the dictionary used by the compiler you may have:

Variable name	Variable type	Memory location
length	Numeric	F B F F
side1	Numeric	F C 0 6
side2	Numeric	F C 0 D
side3	Numeric	F C 1 4
side4	Numeric	F C 1 6

As well as building up tables such as the above, routines from the system library may often have to be called up. Functions such as square roots or sine will be needed so often that the machine code to deal with them is stored in the system library.

If we now imagine some fictitious assembly language with mnemonics ADD, SUBTRACT and MULTIPLY etc., then the following assembly language code might be generated for the single line of BASIC.

```
LOAD        side1
SUBTRACT    side2
MULTIPLY    2
STORE       temp
LOAD        side3
SUBTRACT    side4
MULTIPLY    4
ADD         temp
STORE       length
```

In the above assembly language program **temp** is simply a location used by the computer to store a **temporary** answer during a calculation. In fact machine code would be produced by the compiler but a list of hex or binary numbers is not so enlightening as the above for showing the principles of how the object language is generated.

Often the code produced by such methods is not the best that could be obtained. This is a consequence of trying to construct machine code from a high level language. It is often possible to make more efficient machine code by carrying out a process which is called **optimisation**.

It is still very unlikely that even the best optimisers can produce code that would be as good as hand-optimised code. However, most times the final product would not be worth going to these extraordinary lengths.

Methods of syntax definition

One of the advantages of being the **user** of a language is that even if you don't understand all of the language, you can try bits out to see if they work and let the interpreter or compiler throw error messages at you if necessary. There is no such luck if you have to write the language or the compiler in the first place! Therefore, formal methods have to be developed to describe the syntax of a language completely before it is written and implemented.

One of the most common methods for defining syntax was developed by John Backus and was originally called the **Backus normal form.** However, it was later pointed out that it was not normal from a mathematical point of view and so became known as the **Backus Naur form.** This gave recognition to the work of Peter Naur who did much work using this syntax definition to define the ALGOL language. The letters BNF are an abbreviation for Backus Naur Form and will be used whenever necessary.

Any language (such as BNF) which is used to describe the syntax of a computer language is known as a **meta language**.

BNF notation

The BNF notation is quite simple and involves a list of statements which define symbols that represent the language.

At the start we will define the symbols: ::= to mean: 'is defined by'

Hence LHS ::= RHS

would be read as the 'left-hand side' is defined by the 'right-hand side'.

::= is known as a **meta symbol**.

The second important meta symbol is | which means 'OR'.

For example:

LHS ::= A | B

would be read as the 'left-hand side' is defined by A or B.

The third part of the notation involves the use of 'corner braces' < and >. These braces are used to define what are called **meta variables** or **syntactic variables** (or even metasyntactic variables!).

This sounds horribly complex but consider the following simple example:

<hexdigit> :: = 0 | 1 | 2 | 3 | 4 | 5 | 6 | 7 | 8 | 9 | A | B | C | D | E | F

Therefore a 'hexadecimal digit' is defined by 0 or 1 or 2 etc.

<hex digit> is known as a **meta variable**.

The symbols such as 0,1,2,3, etc. in the above example are known as **terminal symbols**.

Once a meta variable has been defined it can then be used to form the next part of a more complex definition of the syntax of the language.

For example to define an integer we may use:

<digit>   ::= 0 | 1 | 2 | 3 | 4 | 5 | 6 | 7 | 8 | 9

<integer> ::= <digit> | <digit><integer>

An integer is defined by a digit or a digit and an integer.

Groups of definitions such as this are known as **productions.** From these productions we can see that an integer can consist of as many digits as necessary.

There are more meta symbols, but the above three are sufficient to define many of the simple syntax structures of a language. We will not concern ourselves with any more of these symbols at this level.

Methods of syntax analysis

Having defined how to use BNF, we can now see how the parsing (syntax analysis) stages can be carried out. The parsing process breaks down the original sentence written in the language to see if it is legal or illegal. A sentence is simply a part of a language such as a single line in a BASIC program.

To give an example of the parsing process we will consider a simple example using car registration numbers. This also goes to show that non-numerical sentences are just as important.

Consider the following productions:

Rule 1   <car registration>::= <letter><digit><digit><digit>
<letter> <letter> <letter>
|<letter><letter><letter>
<digit > <digit> <digit> <letter>

Rule 2   <letter>::= A | B | C | D | E | F | G | H | J | K | L |
M | N | P | R | S | T | V | W | X | Y |

Rule 3   <digit>::= 0 | 1 | 2 | 3 | 4 | 5 | 6 | 7 | 8 | 9

We will now parse the 'car registration number' B463YKL to see if it is legal.

B   4   6   3   Y   K   L
<letter> <digit>   <digit>   <digit>   <letter> <letter> <letter>
<car registration>

Productions used
Rules 2,3,3,3,2,2, and 2
Rule 1

As each of the above forms one of the valid definitions of <car registration> (from Rule 1) we can see that the syntax analysis has been successful.

Another method is by means of a parse tree and this is shown in figure 10.4.

Figure 10.4 shows that it is possible to start off with the production <car registration> and end up with legal terminal symbols B463YKL. If the registration number had been B463UKL then the parse would have failed because we would have ended

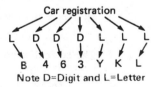

Car registration

L   D   D   D   L   L   L

B   4   6   3   Y   K   L

Note D=Digit and L=Letter

Figure 10.4

up with an illegal letter 'U'.

We will now look at a more computer-based example using a simplified conditional branch from the BASIC language.

Consider simple statements such as IF test < 20 THEN 400.

If we now formally express this type of statement using BNF notation we get something along the following lines:

Rule 1   <conditional branch statement>   ::= <line number> IF <condition>
THEN <line number>

Rule 2   <condition>   ::= <variable><relation><constant>

Rule 3	<line number>	::=	<integer>
Rule 4	<integer>	::=	<digit> | <digit><integer>
Rule 5	<digit>	::=	0|1|2|3|4|5|6|7|8|9
Rule 6	<variable>	::=	<letter> | <letter> <integer>
Rule 7	<letter>	::=	A|B|C|D|E|F|G|H|I| J|K|L|M|N|O|P|Q| R|S|T|U|V|W|X|Y|Z
Rule 8	<relation>	::=	< | > | = | < = | > = | <>
Rule 9	<constant>	::=	<signed integer> | <integer>
Rule 10	<signed integer>	::=	+ <integer> | – <integer>

One can see how the definition of even this simplified form of conditional branch can become complex very rapidly. For example we have only very simple variables such as A or B7 etc. and have not even considered the use of strings. Good compiler designers certainly deserve one's admiration for the sheer enormity and complexity of their task.

We can now apply the above productions (rules) to see if the following BASIC statements are valid.

(a)   250 IF X < 20 THEN 400

                                                                      Productions applied

250	IF	X	<	20	THEN	400	
<line number>	IF	<letter>	<relation>	<integer>	THEN	<line number>	3,7,8,4 and 3
<line number>	IF	<variable>	<relation>	<constant>	THEN	<line number>	6,9
<line number>	IF		<condition>		THEN	<line number>	2
		<conditional branch statement>					1

Therefore we have a valid conditional branch statement, i.e. one which has passed the syntax analysis stage.

If you think that it might have been a wild guess to go straight to <line number> at the beginning and not to go via <digit> <integer> <line number>, it was done because the compiler would have found the key words IF and THEN and tried to see if the statement was a conditional branch.

(b)   270 IF 30 > X THEN 400

                                                                        Productions applied

270	IF	30	>	X	THEN	400	
<line number>	IF	<integer>	<relation>	<letter>	THEN	<line number>	3,4,8,7,3

The parse has already failed as <condition> can never be obtained using any of the rules. This is because a <condition> cannot start off with an <integer>. There are no rules above that can turn an <integer> into a <variable>. Therefore this second statement has failed the syntax analysis stage and is an invalid statement.

The parse tree for statement (a) can be seen in figure 10.5(a) and the parse tree for statement (b) can be seen in figure 10.5(b).

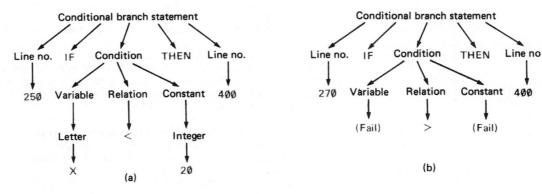

Figure 10.5

Methods of parsing

It can be seen from the above that under certain conditions it may easily be possible to end up with an ambiguous parse. You will also recall that one of the essential requirements of a computer language is that it is unambiguous. Therefore methods that can't produce ambiguous languages must be used. One simple method is to start at the left hand side of the statement to be parsed and replace each element by the appropriate meta variable. We then proceed in the same way always working from the left, and always replacing multiple meta variables with a more comprehensive meta variable where possible. This simple technique of working methodically from left to right is called **canonical parsing**.

Consider the following simple examples to show how canonical parsing works.

1. A decimal number may be defined using BNF notation as follows:

		Production number
<decimal number> ::=	<point><number> | <number><point><number>	1
<number> ::=	<digit> | <number> <digit>	2
<digit> ::=	0|1|2|3|4|5|6|7|8|9	3
<point> ::=	.	4

Using a canonical parse we can see if the following is a valid decimal number:

3.142   Production used

3	.	1	4	2	
<digit>	.	1	4	2	3
<number>	.	1	4	2	2
<number>	<point>	1	4	2	4
<number>	<point>	<digit>	4	2	3
<number>	<point>	<number>	<digit>	2	2
<number>	<point>	<number>	2		2
<number>	<point>	<number>	<digit>		3
<number>	<point>	<number>			2
	<decimal number>				1

The sequence of productions applied is shown in the last column. It is not possible to generate any other sequence if canonical parsing is used.

2. Sometimes the language definition may not be satisfactory, as in the next set of productions:

<expression> ::=	<variable> | <expression> <operator> <expression>
<operator> ::=	+ | * | ↑
<variable> ::=	W | X | Y | Z

Consider the 'expression' W * X + Y ↑ Z

Applying a canonical parse:

W	*	X	+	Y	↑	Z
<variable>	*	X	+	Y	↑	Z
<expression>	<operator>	X	+	Y	↑	Z
<expression>	<operator>	<variable>	+	Y	↑	Z
<expression>	<operator>	<expression>	+	Y	↑	Z

We can see without proceeding further that W * X + Y ↑ Z would be evaluated from left to right thus not obeying the normal rules of precedence, i.e. a successful canonical parse would have taken place with the + taking priority over ↑. Thus the original definition of the language must be changed.

A new set of productions could be:

<expression> ::=	<term> | <expression> + <term>
<term> ::=	<factor> | <term> * <factor>
<factor> ::=	<primary> | <factor> ↑ <primary>
<primary> ::=	<variable>
<variable> ::=	W | X | Y | Z

Let us now perform a canonical parse on W * X + Y ↑ Z again:

Step							
1	W	*	X	+	Y	↑	Z
2	\<variable>	*	X	+	Y	↑	Z
3	\<primary>	*	X	+	Y	↑	Z
4	\<factor>	*	X	+	Y	↑	Z
5	\<term>	*	X	+	Y	↑	Z
6	\<expression>	*	\<variable>	+	Y	↑	Z
7	\<expression>	*	\<primary>	+	Y	↑	Z
8	\<expression>	*	\<factor>	+	Y	↑	Z
9	\<expression>	*	\<term>	+	Y	↑	Z
10	\<expression>	*	\<expression>	+	Y	↑	Z

We can see that \<expression> * \<expression> is not defined and therefore the parse has failed at this point. We now backtrack to step 5.

5	\<term>	*	X	+	Y	↑	Z
6	\<term>	*	\<variable>	+	Y	↑	Z
7	\<term>	*	\<primary>	+	Y	↑	Z
8	\<term>	*	\<factor>	+	Y	↑	Z
9			\<term>	+	Y	↑	Z
10			\<expression>	+	Y	↑	Z
11			\<expression>	+	\<variable>	↑	Z
12			\<expression>	+	\<primary>	↑	Z
13			\<expression>	+	\<factor>	↑	Z
14			\<expression>	+	\<term>	↑	Z
15			\<expression>				

Here we can see that \<expression> ↑ anything is not defined. We therefore backtrack to step 13.

13	\<expression>	+	\<factor>	↑	Z
14	\<expression>	+	\<factor>	↑	\<variable>
15	\<expression>	+	\<factor>	↑	\<primary>
16	\<expression>	+		\<factor>	
17	\<expression>	+		\<term>	
18		\<expression>			

There at last! We can see how the definition of the language forced ↑ to be evaluated before being added to the rest. Similarly * took precedence over +.

Parse trees

A **parse tree** or syntax tree is another method of determining whether an expression is ambiguous or not. If two trees can be drawn for the same expression then the expression is ambiguous. Consider again the examples described above.

1.   First definition. W * X + Y ↑ Z

The parse tree is as follows:

```
                                    <expression>
                <expression>        <operator>                      <expression>
<expression>    <operator>    <expression>    +    <expression>    <operator>    <expression>
<variable>          *         <variable>            <variable>         ↑          <variable>
    W                             X                     Y                             Z
```

However, it is easily possible to end up with a completely different parse tree:

```
                <expression>
<expression>    <operator>                          <expression>
<variable>          *         <expression>    <operator>                          <expression>
    W                         <variable>          +          <expression>    <operator>    <expression>
                                  X                          <variable>          ↑          <variable>
                                                                 Y                             Z
```

As it is possible to draw two completely different syntax or parse trees and still end up with a valid expression, then the language definition is ambiguous, as was found out by parsing in the last section.

2. However, using the second language definition: W * X + Y ↑ Z

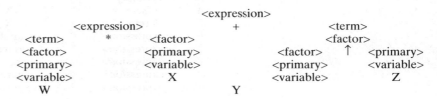

This time we have a unique parse tree. Try and devise another making sure that you stick exactly to the improved language definition!

Exercise 10.1

1. (a) Why is a **translation** process necessary when computer languages are used?
    (b) Name **three** common types of translator.
    (c) Explain the **major** differences between the three types of translators outlined in (b).

2. The **compilation** process can be broken up into **three** main stages:
    (a) **lexical analysis**   (b) **syntax analysis**
    (c) **code generation**.
    Outline why these three stages are necessary and give an example for each of the above stages using a language of your choice.

3. When using a **compiler** the following terminology is often encountered:

    Object program, source program, tokens, parsing, dictionary, terminal symbols, optimisation.

    Write at least one sentence on each of the above parts to show that you fully understand the meaning of each term.

4. Backus Naur form is one method of defining syntax. Using a high level language of your choice show (by being as detailed as you can), how BNF notation can be used to define the following:
    (a) **Identifier**   (b) **String**
    (c) **Unsigned real number.**
    Give **two legal** and **two illegal** examples of syntax for **each** of the above.

5. Define the syntax of parts (a), (b) and (c) in question (4) making use of **syntax diagrams.**

6. Consider some typical telephone directory entries:

    Hopkins A.B.C., 32 Relbridge Close....Pembury 123456
    Williams Rev, F.V., 1 Davidson Road.....Brighton 78152

    It can be seen that each entry is split up into two fields as follows:

    Surname | [title] | initials, | [number] | street |.....
    ..... | town | telephone number

    The attributes in brackets are optional, i.e., we could easily have:

    Blogg B.C., Oak Farm   . . . . .Ashford 253

    Devise a set of productions using Backus Naur form which, when applied to typical telephone entries, will determine the legality or otherwise of the entry.
      By making use of a canonical parsing method apply the productions you have devised to show that:

    Brown Y., 271 Kingsway   . . . . .Exeter 736442

    is legal and

    Zoe P.J., 274   . . . . .Bognor 817325

    is not.

Parsing arithmetical statements   It makes the design of compilers easier if the arithmetic expressions are presented to the compiler in what is called **reverse Polish notation.** This form of notation will now be investigated.

Polish notation

Polish notation was developed by Jan Lukasiewicz (you can easily see the reason why it is called Polish notation!). Polish notation is also known as **prefix notation** because each operator precedes its operands. To appreciate this notation fully the concept of a **stack** (see chapter 14) should be understood.
  For example, instead of writing X + Y, +X Y is written.

+X Y is interpreted as follows:

You have two numbers X and Y. The operator which precedes the numbers tells you what to do with them. Therefore, in the above case, the numbers must be added together.

Hence +3 5 = 8

Polish notation has the advantage that there can be no ambiguity in the way that an arithmetic expression can be worked out. It also needs no parentheses to separate the different parts.

Another form of notation called **reverse Polish** (or **postfix**) **notation** is very similar in principle and also forms a parentheses-free notation. However, this time reverse Polish notation is particularly suited to computerised methods because of the ability to deal with such expressions easily by using a **stack**.

An example will make things clearer. We may write down a 'normal' arithmetic expression as follows:

$$(3 + 5) \times (9 - 7)$$

This is called **infix notation** because all the operators are inside the expression. To work this out we apply the rules of precedence, i.e. brackets, exponentiation, multiplication and division.

$$(3 + 5) \times (9 - 7) = 8 \times 2 = 16$$

If we were to work out this problem using a low level computer language then we would have to go along the following lines:

LOAD	3
ADD	5
STORE	temp
LOAD	9
SUBTRACT	7
MULTIPLY	temp
STORE	result

However, let us consider the logical order in which a sum such as this should be worked out:

$$(3 + 5) \times (9 - 7)$$

Get the number 3 (1st part) and then get the number 5 (2nd part).
Add them together (3rd part).
Get the number 9 (4th part) and then get the number 7 (5th part).
Subtract the above (9 − 7) (6th part).
Finally multiply the number from the 3rd part by the number from the 6th part (7th part).

Now consider using reverse Polish. Using reverse Polish or postfix notation we would write:

3 5 + 9 7 − ×

This leads to the following very simple rules for evaluating such expressions:

1. The next symbol encountered must be loaded on to the stack if it is an operand, i.e. a number or variable which is to be operated upon.

2. If the next symbol to be encountered is an operator, i.e. +, /, − etc. then carry out the required operation on the top two items in the stack. The result of this operation must be left on the top of the stack.

For the above numbers we get:

Stack contents

Part (1) 3 is an operand . . . .(Put on stack) . . . .   [3] top

Part (2) 5 is an operand . . . .(Put on stack) . . . .   [5] top
  [3]

Part (3) + is an operator . . . .(Perform operation on top two numbers in . . . . . .   [8] top
stack and leave the result on the top of the stack)

Part (4) 9 is an operand . . . .(Put on stack) . . . .   [9] top
  [8]

Part (5) 7 is an operand . . . .(Put on stack) . . . .   [7] top
  [9]
  [8]

Part (6) − is an operator . . . . . .(Perform operation on top two numbers in stack . . .   [2] top
and leave the result on the top of the stack) . . . . .   [8]

Part (7) × is an operator . . . . . .(Perform operation on top two numbers in stack . .   [16] top
and leave the result on the top of the stack)

We now read the answer from the top of the stack.

The above is not really a weird and wonderful set of rules; it is simply the way that the expression would be logically worked out. This corresponds with the logical order of working out the sum.

In fact reverse Polish notation is more natural than the usual infix notation with which we are all so familiar. Some calculators use reverse Polish notation as their normal mode of operation as it does away with the clumsy brackets so often needed in lengthy calculations.

Conversion between infix and reverse Polish notation

One novel way of converting from infix to reverse Polish makes use of trees. If the algebraic expression is written down as a binary tree then, if a **postorder traversal** of the tree is undertaken (see page 307) and the nodes visited are written down, the result is the original expression converted to reverse Polish.

As an example consider the following infix algebraic expression:

$$X = A * B + C/D$$

The binary tree for this expression is shown in figure 10.6. Note to form the binary tree we simply put the '=' sign as the root node. The left-hand side of the expression (simply X in this case) forms the left-hand subtree and the right-hand side of the expression forms the right-hand subtree. The lowest precedence operators (i.e. +, − etc.) form the next level of the tree. The tree is continually formed in this way

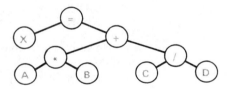

Figure 10.6

until the terminal symbols form the leaf nodes of the tree.

If we now visit each node using the postorder traversal method (see page 307) then we get the following list:

X   A B*C D /+ =

It is easy to remember that **postorder traversal** of the tree is required, as reverse Polish is the same as **postfix notation**.

Notice that, in these examples, with the equals sign at the root node, the **right-hand subtree becomes the required reverse Polish notation expression**, and the X, being the left-hand subtree, is equivalent to it.

As another example, convert the following into reverse Polish notation:

$$X = 3 * (A + B + C) − (F − G)/5 + 2 * (D − E)$$

The binary tree for the above expression is shown in figure 10.7. Figure 10.7 may seem a complex tree but it is really easy once you get used to the principles involved. For example, concentrate on the grey part of the tree. This shows how it was formed by the author.

First the '=' sign was put at the root and the left-hand side easily dealt with.

Next the first '−' sign in the expression was chosen. This acts as a root for the next subtree.

Therefore the left-hand side of this subtree becomes the part of the equation on the left of this minus sign and the right-hand side of this subtree becomes the part of the equation to the right of the minus sign.

Note: We did not *have* to choose the minus sign. The '+' sign between the 5 and 2 would have done just as well as this is a low precedence operator. The other '+' signs are within brackets, which have the highest precedence.

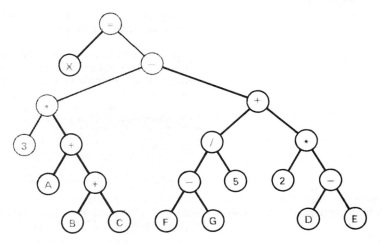

Figure 10.7

If we next consider the part of the equation to the left of the minus sign then this forms a subtree the root of which is the '*' sign i.e. the lowest precedence operator.

3 is to the left of this '*' sign and therefore forms the left-hand subtree.
(A + B + C) is to the right of this '*' sign and therefore forms the right-hand subtree.
We continue in this way until all the terminal symbols have been arrived at.

If we now do a postorder traversal of the right-hand subtree we get the reverse Polish expression which is:

$$3\ A\ B\ C + + * F\ G - 5/2\ D\ E - * + -$$

If you think that the above looks messy don't forget that it was the logical way that the sum would have been worked out. Also don't forget that reverse Polish notation is used because it is ideal for solution by a low level language making use of a stack. Therefore, it is a simple matter for the computer to evaluate it. Also, and most importantly, once the expression has been converted to reverse Polish the computer has only to scan the expression once to evaluate it. Compare this with how many times it is necessary to scan the original expression containing the brackets. The compiler may eventually change the expression into reverse Polish notation so that the code to evaluate the expression is the most simple and efficient. This is so that the programmer may program using the more familiar infix notation. We therefore need an algorithm that will convert infix to reverse Polish notation.

First let us remind ourselves of the normal mathematical rules of **precedence**:

Operators		Normal precedence
Unary +, & ()	Unary +, – & brackets	Highest
↑	Exponentiation	Very high
* & /	Multiplication and division	High
+ & –	Addition and subtraction	Low
=	Equals sign	Lowest

In fact >, <, <=, >= and <> have the same precedence as '='.

Also, the logical operations 'NOT', 'AND' and 'OR' have decreasing orders of precedence even lower than the '=' sign shown in the above table. However, to keep matters simple only the signs used in the above table will be used in the examples that follow.

In many high level languages, where a unary minus occurs (–7 or –3 etc.) we usually have to enclose this in brackets. In high level languages we must not use expressions like X = A * –B. We must rewrite it as X = A * (–B). The brackets then make sure that B is multiplied by –1 first. However, this is only another way of assigning unary '–' and unary '+' the highest precedence as shown in the above table.

If you are confused by the term unary minus, it simply means a '–' sign used with a single operand, as opposed to the binary minus such as 8 – 6 which is used with two.

Unary '+' and unary '–' will also be left out of the examples that follow.

It is usual to assign numbers to the precedence of an operator from 0 (representing lowest precedence) to a number representing the highest precedence. Therefore:

Operator	Precedence
() & ↑	3
* & /	2
+ & -	1
=	0

Developing the algorithm to convert from infix to reverse Polish notation

The basic process that must go on when converting from infix to postfix is quite simple, i.e. the operator must be taken from the place inside the two operands and be placed post (i.e. after) the two operands. For example:

X + Y must become XY+

This is all very easy with a simple equation, but obviously gets much more complex depending on the complexity of the original infix expression. The following will take a lot of concentration, but if worked through very carefully considering each point, the final algorithm should make sense.

Consider now the more complex infix string:

V + W ↑ X * Y/Z

First we read the variable V (i.e. an operand). We output this to the postfix string.

Situation so far:	Infix string	Postfix string	Stack
	V + W ↑ X * Y/Z	V	(empty)

Next we read the operator (i.e. + in this case). Now V must be the preceding operand but we must now find out what other operand is to be used with V. Therefore we must save this addition until we have found this out and placed it in the postfix string. The + is therefore saved on the stack.

Situation so far:	Infix string	Postfix string	Stack
	+ W ↑ X * Y/Z	V	+ (top)

Next the variable W is read. We output this to the postfix string:

Situation so far:	Infix string	Postfix string	Stack
	W ↑ X * Y/Z	VW	+ (top)

The operator ↑ is read. However, ↑ has a higher priority than + (the last operator on the stack) therefore the W belongs to the exponentiation and not the plus. The ↑ is therefore saved on the stack so that we can find the other operand to go with it.

Situation so far:	Infix string	Postfix string	Stack
	↑ X * Y/Z	VW	↑ (top)
			+

Next the variable X is read. This is output to the postfix string:

Situation so far:	Infix string	Postfix string	Stack
	X * Y/Z	VWX	↑ (top)
			+

Next the * is read. However, this has a lower priority than the operator currently at the top of the stack. Therefore, the X variable must be the one that belongs to the exponentiation. Therefore the exponentiation is output to the postfix string.

Situation so far:	Infix string	Postfix string	Stack
	* Y/Z	VWX↑	+ (top)

The next character in the infix string is * (as shown above). Before the exponentiation messed up our train of thought we were trying to find the second operand for the addition. We must therefore return our thoughts to looking for this second operand. It is obvious from looking at the infix expression that it is the whole of the right-hand of the expression, i.e. W ↑ X * Y/Z. Let's see if this works out.

We have just read the multiplication operator. This is compared with the addition operator on the stack. Now since this multiplication has a higher priority than the addition operator the W ↑ X part must be the first operand for the multiplication. We must now look for the second operand for this multiplication. The * sign is therefore placed on to the stack while the search takes place:

Situation so far:	Infix string	Postfix string	Stack
	*Y/Z	VWX↑	* (top)
			+

The next character to be read in is the variable, Y. This is therefore output to the postfix string:

Situation so far:	Infix string	Postfix string	Stack
	Y/Z	VWX ↑ Y	* (top)
			+

Next the operator / is read. Now this has the same priority as the * operator at the top of the stack, therefore the * sign can now be output to the postfix string:

Situation so far:	Infix string	Postfix string	Stack
	/Z	VWX ↑ Y *	+ (top)

As the / operator has a higher priority than + at the top of the stack, the / operator is saved on the stack:

Situation so far:	Infix string	Postfix string	Stack
	/Z	VWX ↑ Y *	/(top)
			+

Finally Z is read and output to the reverse Polish string:

Situation so far:	Infix string	Postfix string	Stack
	Z	VWX ↑ Y * Z	/(top)
			+

As there are no more characters to be read the contents of the stack are output to the string. First the / operator:

Situation so far:	Infix string	Postfix string	Stack
		VWXY * Z/	+(top)

And finally the + operator:

Situation so far:	Infix string	Postfix string	Stack
		VWX ↑ Y * Z/ +	(empty)

The algorithm is summed up in the flowchart shown in figure 10.8. From figure 10.8 we can see that the algorithm shown in the flowchart also copes with brackets within the expression. Try using the flowchart with the following:

$$(A + B)/(C + D)$$

Note that (as before) spaces have been shown within the expression simply to clarify the expression. These spaces do not count as a space until the end of the equation is encountered.

Using the flowchart you should obtain the following postfix (reverse Polish) string:

Symbol being considered	Postfix string	Stack	
(		(	
A	A	(	
+	A	+ (	Note + has higher priority than left brackets already on the stack. This is because the expression within the brackets must be evaluated first.
B	AB	+ (	
)	AB+		Note top of stack removed
/	AB+	/	
(	AB+	(/	
C	AB+C	(/	
+	AB+	+ (/	
D	AB+CD	+ (/	

```
)              AB+CD+        ( /
               AB+CD+          /
               AB+CD+/                    Note stack empty
```

Therefore postfix string is AB+CD+/

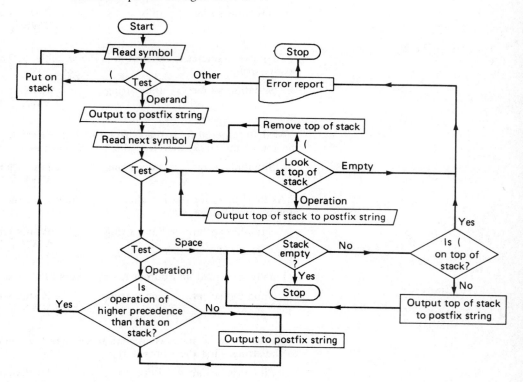

Figure 10.8

You should confirm that this is the answer that would have been obtained if a binary tree structure had been used to obtain the postfix string.

One of the things that may cause confusion with the above happens when the '+' operators are encountered. When working through the flowchart one is presented with the question: 'Is operation of higher precedence than that on stack?'

One's immediate reaction is that the answer is yes. However, if you think about it, if the top of stack contains a '(' then any operator coming after it must have a higher precedence so that the expression within the brackets can be evaluated. Of course if another '(' was encountered this would be entered on to the stack in the standard way.

After ploughing through the above you should have a good idea of some of the basic principles that are involved when translators have to convert the source language into the object language for both arithmetical and non-arithmetical processes.

Exercise 10.2

1. Convert the following expression into **reverse Polish**
   (postfix) expressions:
   (a) P*Q + (R – S)*T
   (b) (M + N) * (O – P)
   (c) W + X × Y / Z
   (d) (x + y/z) / (u – v)

2. Convert the following **reverse Polish** expressions into
   infix (normal) form:
   (a) A B + C ×
   (b) X Y Z / S × T + –
   (c) x y + r s – x t / * *
   (d) A B + 3 F G – H / * K F G – * – –

3. By making use of an appropriate stack, show how the
   following **postfix** arithmetic would be evaluated:
   (a) 9 3 – 2 /
   (b) 12 9 – 16 20 – *
   (c) 11 3 2 ↑ + 7 6 3 / – /

End of chapter summary

- Natural languages are languages such as English or French etc.
- Computer languages belong to a class known as formal languages.
- **Natural languages** are context sensitive.
- **Formal languages** are *not* context sensitive and are **unambiguous**.
- A **source language** is the high-level code written by the computer programmer.
- An **object language** is the code in a form that the machine can understand.
- A **translator** is needed to convert a **source language** into an **object language**.
- The three most common types of translators are called **assemblers**, **interpreters** and **compilers**.
- **Assemblers** convert **assembly-language mnemonics** into **machine code**.
- **Interpreters** convert each line of the source code into the object code as the program is being run. This gives a better interactive environment but is slower.
- A **compiler** converts the entire source code into machine code so that it can be run on the machine without further translation. However, error correction is tedious.
- The **compilation** process can be split up into three sections – **lexical analysis**, **syntax analysis** and **code generation**.
- The **lexical analysis** phase breaks up the source code into logical chunks ready for the next stage of analysis. The resulting chunks are often called **tokens**.
- A **token** represents the *smallest independent part of a program* which has some meaning such as a key word or variable etc.
- The **syntax analysis** phase determines if the string of input tokens passed via the lexical analysis phase *forms a valid sentence*.
- A **dictionary** is generated during the *syntax analysis phase*.
- A **dictionary** is simply a list of variables etc. used by the compiler.
- The **code generation** phase generates the machine code from the information passed over from the lexical and syntax analysis phase – the dictionary is also consulted.
- Further **optimisation** can often be achieved by the use of special software.
- **Backus Naur Form** (BNF) is one method used to *describe formally the syntax* of a language.
- A **meta language** is the name of a *language used to describe the syntax of another language*.
- A **meta symbol** is the name given to the symbols in a meta language.
- **BNF meta symbols** are '::=', ' | ', '<' and '>'.
- **Extended BNF (EBNF)** includes the symbols [ ] to denote options, { } to denote repetition, and ( ) to denote group components.
- In **BNF**, literals are plain and **meta-variables** are in angle braces.
- In **ENBF meta variables** are plain and **literals** are put in quotes.
- Syntax analysis is known as **parsing**.
- **Parsing** breaks down a sentence to see if it is legal.
- Productions are the names given to the **rule definitions** which define syntax using the BNF and EBNF systems.

- Parsing can be carried out by hand using common sense or **parse trees**.
- **Canonical parsing** is a *general rule enabling a machine to carry out parsing* in a methodical way.
- **Parsing arithmetical statements** is often carried out by using **reverse Polish notation**.
- **Polish notation** is prefix notation i.e. **+ X Y**.
- **Infix notation** is **'normal'** notation i.e. **X + Y**.
- **Reverse Polish notation** is **postfix notation** i.e. **X Y +**.
- **Reverse Polish notation** is a *parenthesis-free notation* and can be easily manipulated by a **data structure** called a **stack**.
- **Post-order traversal** of a **binary tree** *converts infix to reverse Polish*.

11 Input devices

Introduction

The variety of computer-input devices currently available is remarkable. From the humble keyboard in its many different forms, via pen-based input on the latest **PDA**s (**Personal Digital Assistants**) to the still (but not for too long) illusive *reliable* form of voice recognition system – man's ingenuity for coming up with new ways for data entry never ceases to amaze. Advanced level students are required to have a thorough knowledge of the implications of input devices for computer systems, and be able to make reasoned choices from the vast range available, but they are *not* usually required to remember any of the technical details of operation. However, as with the chapters on output devices and storage devices, in the author's opinion it *is* desirable to understand a few technical details at a simple level, or devices like the mouse, for example, become just a magic box, and students may use an inappropriate input device due to lack of technical knowledge regarding its performance. For example, a hand-held scanner is most unlikely to be appropriate for inputting high-quality photos – due to its lack of resolution and consistency of scanning. Students at Advanced level are also usually curious to know how things work, even if it's only at a relatively simple level – so *some* technical details *are* included in this chapter – mainly to satisfy insatiable curiosity about how ingenious modern devices function, and to overcome the problems mentioned above.

Although this chapter will concentrate on **computer-input** devices or **computer-input peripherals** from a **hardware** perspective, you should not forget the part played by a formidable array of software, and this aspect is extensively covered in the system-software and other software and application-based chapters.

Peripherals

A computer **peripheral** is the name given to equipment on the periphery of the computer system. Devices such as **disk drives**, **VDUs**, **printers** and **keyboards** are therefore examples of peripherals. In this chapter we will concentrate almost exclusively on **input peripherals**, with the other peripherals such as printers and disk drives etc. being considered in chapters 12 and 13.

The word **peripheral** was easier to interpret in the early computer systems. Indeed, all peripherals *were* on the **periphery** of the system and housed in separately-identifiable boxes, with the **main processor** boards housed in a separate box too. With **mainframes** and many **minis,** as can be seen from figure 11.1, this *is* still usually the case, but with **micros** the term can't be so literally applied. For example, some

Figure 11.1

tower systems might house a hard disk, floppy disk, CD-ROM drive and a tape streamer in the same box that houses the main processor.

Most portable computers now have integral liquid-crystal-display screens, and some even have printers, faxes and modems housed in a box with a footprint no larger than an A4 piece of paper. Nevertheless, the word **peripheral** *is still the correct term to use* when talking about computing devices other than the main processor board, its associated electronics and main memory.

The keyboard

This has been *the* standard input device for a great number of years, and will certainly be around in one form or another in the foreseeable future. The standard computer keyboard is similar in layout to that of the old typewriter keyboard, and is based on the QWERTY design (look at the keys along the top row). Computer keyboards usually have extra keys called **soft keys** or **function keys**, **control keys**, **escape keys** and some **other special-purpose keys**. In addition it's also usual to have a numeric keypad incorporated for fast entry of numeric data. The QWERTY layout is *not* the most efficient in terms of speed of typing or ergonomics (see in a moment). In fact, it was designed to slow down typists so that the mechanical arms operating the keys on the old-style typewriters were less likely to jam!

Ergonomic keyboards

Alternatives to the keyboard?

The key (pun intended!) method of data entry for many years has been to make use of a standard keyboard, but this has unfortunately led to health problems in recent years, namely **RSI** or **Repetitive Strain Injury**. This mainly affects **data-entry operators** who use the keyboard for prolonged periods. It does not usually affect computer programmers (and authors!) who normally spend half of their time making coffee and wondering what to do next – instead of typing in data at a frantic rate of knots as would be the case for a typical secretary or data-entry clerk.

Government legislation is currently limiting the amount of time that can be spent at the keyboard (and VDU see page 240) without a break, but more **ergonomic designs** of keyboard have been manufactured to help get over these health problems. Figure 11.2(a) shows a V-shaped keyboard for the PC called the KBC 5500 Ergonomic keyboard. It still has the standard QWERTY layout, but has a large resting area for the palms of the hands. Note also that the V-shape leads to a more natural position for the hands. The next step up the ladder is the **Adjustable Keyboard** for the Apple Mac shown in figure 11.2(b). Although it may look like somebody has dropped the keyboard on the floor and shattered it into several pieces, people who have used this type of keyboard for extended periods don't want to go back to the conventional system. However, when yours truly the author went to make use of one of these split keyboards – tragedy struck a blow for all you two or three-fingered typists out there – you have to cross your hands over the break in the keyboard if wish wish to continue your self-taught-high-speed two fingered typing! Perhaps I won't be buying one after all – at least not until I have time to learn to type properly! However, most designs do allow you to put the keyboard back into ordinary mode, so it's not quite so bad.

A radical alternative to the 'ordinary' keyboard is the **Maltron keyboard** shown in figure 11.2(c). *This design is ergonomically very sound indeed*, and people who have become used to this type of keyboard seldom want to change back to the conventional layout. Earlier designs of the Maltron used non standard layouts of the keys, but the later designs have stuck with the QWERTY layout and have thus become more popular. RSI sufferers are often cured completely by using this particular Maltron keyboard technology.

Other types of keyboard exist with a much smaller number of keys. For example, the Quinkey system which uses combinations of 5 keys has proved to be a possible alternative. Using this method it is claimed that non-typists can quickly master data entry, and be entering data at a faster rate than would have been possible with a conventional keyboard, even after just a few hours of use. This is useful for beginners, but is again not useful where professional data entry is required for the reasons stated above. Nevertheless, this type of keyboard *is used* in situations where a conventional keyboard would be inappropriate. It is possible, for example, to mount the few keys onto a joystick – in this way the operator could control a craft such as a car or a plane, while at the same time be typing at the 'keyboard' with the fingers of the same hand! One eccentric computer journalist travels the world on a solar-powered tricycle typing his reports as he goes along using one of these specialist 'keyboards' integrated into a control-stick for his craft!

More-recent developments in **handwriting recognition** have meant that the conventional keyboard can now be dispensed with altogether. The Apple Newton computer, for example, shown in figure 11.2(d), uses a **pen (stylus)** with which the user writes on the 'screen' using his or her normal handwriting. (Pen-based input technology is considered on page 222). Although this is ideal for pocket-sized organisers and casual

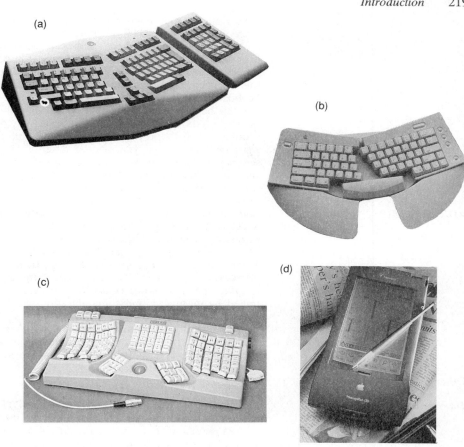

Figure 11.2 (a), (b), (c), (d)

data entry, there is, however, a dilemma here – if you can't type then there is no problem, but there are millions of people (the author included) who can now type *much faster* than they can write with a pen. So the ergonomically-unsound standard QWERTY keyboard is mightier than the pen for many users. Nevertheless, the Newton and similar computers were not designed to replace laptops or desk-based machines, and computers with real handwriting recognition capability are a break through in a technology, which, when coupled with a supportive WIMP environment, can produce an extremely efficient method for carrying out many common tasks. For example, a simple message could be written with the pen, instantly changed into a proper type face then faxed to a remote destination – a boon for busy business people on the move, and typical of the modern communication methods which will probably dominate the portables market in the next decade. However, I think that the only thing that will get anywhere near to removing the keyboard (but even this won't remove it altogether) is perfect voice recognition – most of us can talk *very much faster* then we can write or type – but a completely reliable form of this technology together with a large vocabulary and recognition of many different voices is still a little way into the future.

Basic keyboard operation

A keyboard is *not* just a group of switches, inside there are some sophisticated electronics which process what is happening at the keys *before* passing the information on to the computer. However, most PC-type keyboards work in similar ways. Whenever a key is pressed this causes an electrical signal to be generated which can be detected by a microprocessor that lives inside the keyboard. It is the job of this microprocessor constantly to scan the keyboard many times each second, process the electrical signals generated by the keys and change them into suitable code. Each key has two unique codes associated with it, (one for being pressed and the other for being released). Therefore, the microchip can determine which key has been pressed, when the key has been pressed, when it has been released, and, therefore, for how long it has been pressed. Most readers will probably be familiar with the auto-repeat function on most computers – especially, for example, if you happen to have leant on the keyboard and suddenly got a couple of hundred identical characters put into your DTP document!

When a valid keyboard code has been received for an appropriate amount of time it is stored in a **buffer** inside the keyboard. An **interrupt** (see page 378) is then requested and it is then the job of the **operating system** (see chapter 17) to service this interrupt, read the code generated by the keyboard electronics, then change the keyboard code into **ASCII** (see page 266) so that the processor can understand which key has been pressed. Note that when using this method, the *same keyboards* can be used on different international systems, only part of the operating system (usually a utility called the keyboard driver) would have to be changed (and obviously the signs on the keys) if you wanted different-language characters to appear on the screen. The processor will also be **flagged** (see page 78) if any of the special keys such as '**CTRL**' or '**ALT**' have been pressed, as different actions are often required if these keys are pressed *in addition* to the 'normal' alphanumeric keys.

VDU terminals

Sometimes the keyboard is integrated with a VDU and housed in the same unit which is then referred to as a **terminal**. In its simplest form (known as a **dumb terminal**), all that can be accomplished is the sending of characters to a mainframe or mini and displaying the characters returned from the system. However, most modern terminals have some sort of processing capability, as they usually contain a microprocessor. Indeed, the most recent trend is to make use of a **microcomputer** *running suitable* **terminal-emulation software**, so that local processing ability is determined by the micro, and communication with the host computer is determined by the software.

More recently **distributed processing** (see chapter 21) and the use of networks have meant that there are now fewer terminals operating in the way described in the last paragraph, but large campus-wide systems are still found running in this mode.

Other data-input methods

Touch screen

One variation based on a conventional VDU is the touch-sensitive screen. An example is shown in figure 11.3(a). Here the user of the system can point at a menu on the screen with their finger, and thus cause some desired effect to happen. Detection of the pointing device is made by monitoring infra-red beams which criss cross the screen of the conventional monitor just in front of the glass. Some beams are horizontal, and others are vertical, and two beams might typically be intercepted – the vertical one giving the x ordinate and the horizontal one giving the y ordinate. By combining these two the position of the pointer can be determined, and could thus cause some appropriate action to be taken if this were desirable in this context.

A touch-sensitive screen is a popular method of input for non-specialists, and is particularly suitable for choosing from menus in shopping malls, theme parks, museums and any other similar type of venue where the public needs to find out information in user-friendly ways.

Light pen

These new light pens are brilliant for doing your homework in the dark

This is a device for enabling a person to draw a picture or write on the screen of a computer by making use of a special pen which detects light from the screen. The idea is shown in figure 11.3(b). On page 241, raster displays are explained in detail, and from this you should appreciate that an electron beam scans the computer screen from the top to the bottom about 50 times each second or more. The light pen does not emit light itself, but detects the presence of the path of the electron beam underneath it due to the increased brightness experienced by the pen when the electron beam passes. Because of the precise timing of the raster displays, the dot will be at a particular point at a certain time interval after the screen has started to be refreshed, therefore, by measuring the time between the start of the screen refresh and the pick up by the light-sensor inside the tip of the pen, the exact position of the pen can be determined. If the exact position is known, then a line can be drawn on the screen which mirrors the exact path which is being taken by the light pen.

Such a system is usually ideal for art and CAD packages and provides a unique way of interacting with the computer screen. Relatively thin lines can be drawn, but the actual thickness can obviously be determined by the resident software controlling the system.

The mouse

From being a novelty to becoming one of *the* most prolific attachments – not bad within the space of a few years! Mice come in all shapes and sizes, with buttons varying in number from one to three – to a numeric keypad riding on the back of the mouse. Of course the mouse has increased in popularity due to the more user-

(a)

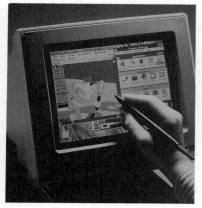

(b)

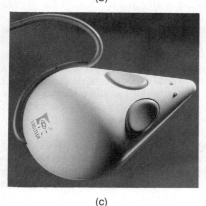

(c)

Figure 11.3 (a), (b), (c)

Mice with no tails!

Mice with no balls!

The track ball

friendly GUI operating systems such as windows, but few micros are now sold without some sort of mouse attached as standard. A typical mouse in shown in figure 11.3(c).

The conventional mouse converts its movement into positional information by using a rotating ball which is held underneath the device. As can be seen from figure 11.4, this ball causes two small shafts to rotate, one shaft recording movement in the x (W-E) direction, and the other recording movement in the y (N-S) direction. Therefore, if you were to move the mouse in a perfect horizontal direction, the shaft recording movement in the y direction would not rotate.

The movement of each shaft is encoded into a series of pulses by using a mechanical or optical system such as that shown in figure 11.4. A small turn of either shaft by just a few degrees causes a pulse to be produced which can be processed by the electronics so that the frequency of the pulses from each encoder can be processed by the computer. If no pulses are detected then the mouse is stationary, or if many pulses/sec are detected then the mouse is moving quickly. Together with the direction of movement of the shaft, a mouse pointer on the screen can be caused to move in the appropriate direction and by an appropriate distance.

An extra button (or buttons) on top of the mouse can be used to provide additional information to the computer. For example, when the pointer is over an icon a mouse button may be pressed so that action dictated by the type of icon being pointed at can be caused to happen. In addition to a simple press of a button sometimes **double-clicking** (*clicking a button twice within a short space of time*) or **dragging** (*pressing and holding down a mouse button while the mouse is moved*) give different effects to a single click of a button. Typical actions might be cataloguing a directory, pulling down a menu, drawing a line in a CAD package or marking a block of text in a DTP system ready to apply a style change.

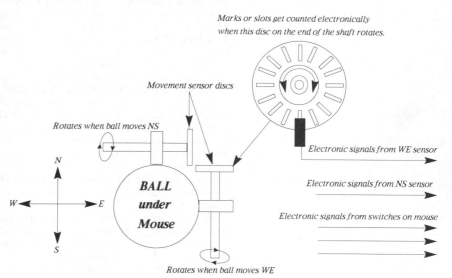

Figure 11.4

The mouse derives its name from the fact that it has a tail, (the wire connecting it to the computer), and the device itself can be thought of as the body of the mouse attached to the tail. The term was first used at Xerox's research centre in Palo Alto (USA) and was made internationally famous by Apple. However, it's now possible to get an **infra-red mouse**. This device is identical in principle to the species just described, but the wire link is replaced by an infra-red beam, and works rather like the remote-control unit in a TV. So we now have mice without tails!

One disadvantage of the modern mouse is that it picks up biscuit crumbs, bits of pickled onions and the like from the mouse mat which makes the ball inside the mouse stick. A recent development makes use of a beam which is transmitted to and reflected back from a special mat or the table top. Movement can be detected without the need for a rotating ball, and hence the system is more reliable.

The track ball is used on many portables, but the touch pad and 'nipple' in the centre of the keyboard are also popular alternatives. Many people find the touch pad particularly effective, and at the end of 1995 this was becoming the de-facto standard

Figure 11.5

for portables. A finger is placed on the pad and movement of the finger causes the pointer to move on the screen in the direction of motion. This idea can be seen in figure 11.5. Many portable computers are now being produced in which the **track ball** is integrated into the keyboard in a similar way to the Mac Power Book.

Pen-input methods

The Apple Newton, shown in figure 11.2(d) is an example of a computer which makes use of **pen-based-input** techniques. Although these techniques have been available on several larger computers for a number of years, Apple is the first computer that can *analyse handwriting as it is written,* (i.e. in real time) *and cope with joined-up writing.* Previous versions of this technology such as the Amstrad **Personal Digital Assistant (PDA)** required that single letters representing words were written one letter to a box – which made for a very unnatural form of input. In fact the term personal digital assistant or PDA is now being commonly used for organiser-type computers with pen-based-input technology, fax capability and the rest of the gismos which usually accompany these machines.

There are several techniques available to detect the position of the pen, but most revolve around the use of a modified **LCD screen** (see page 245). Pressure applied with the **pen** on this special screen causes different currents to flow depending on the x and y positions of the pen. Some computers need special pens which generate electromagnetic fields, but others, including the Apple Newton, have displays that do not require special pens – the tip of your finger would produce shapes on the screen if you happen to loose the **pen (stylus)** provided. By monitoring the currents produced by the action of the pen, the processor can work out where the pen is in relation to an origin on the screen.

The next stage can be compared to drawing with a **pixel-based** art package (see page 566) using a mouse. As the pen is moved across the screen, tiny **pixels** which correspond most closely with the positions which the pen has touched have their colour changed. On a monochrome screen this might correspond to black pixels on a green background. As the pen is moved then more pixels are turned on as shown in figure 11.6.

The real-time analysis of hand writing can be disconcerting, and the Newton has a user-controlled variable time delay which prevents your handwriting from being instantly turned into typed text. If desired you can wait until the end of the message and then ask the computer to perform the analysis.

A specialised windows environment causes different effects to happen according to the icons or words on menus underneath the pen. For example, if it is put into a letter-writing mode, then the computer will mirror the pen's actions in exactly the same way as the magic pads did which you probably all used when you were children (i.e. the type of pad where you could draw a picture, then make it disappear so that another may be drawn in its place). If the pen is then raised and place over a special area, this might, for example, instruct the computer to interpret what has just been written and change it into a type-face of the desired **font**. (See page 524.) If the text has been successfully interpreted (see in a moment) then the screen will look as if the message had been typed in instead of hand written – and all without a keyboard – magic!

Obviously some text may not be recognised correctly, and as the analysis is performed, systems will usually make an intelligent guess from an internal spell-check dictionary. The user can then point with the pen to replace a word or, if it is not in the dictionary, you have the option of adding it. Errors may be corrected by

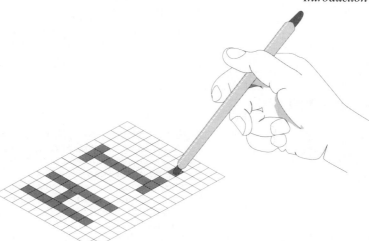

Figure 11.6

The graphics tablet

Figure 11.7

The concept keyboard

a variety of methods. For example, if a cross is drawn over an existing word, then special software inside the computer could interpret this as meaning that the word is to be deleted. The system learns as it goes along and so the recognition process gets better with time.

Pictures (or any scrawl) can be saved 'as is' by instructing the machine to save the image in bit-mapped mode rather than as ASCII codes with an appropriate font. In this way you could save your *actual* handwriting, although this does seem to be defeating the object of the exercise somewhat – this mode is intended for doodles.

Utilities for tidying up shapes etc. make useful additions to what these organisers and communicators can do. For example, if you make a bad attempt at drawing a circle you can instruct the Newton to make your scrawl into a perfect circle. In this way drawings compiled on the screen can be made to look quite professional. The potential for new and innovative ideas on these special breed of machines over the next few years would seem to be tremendous.

Pen-based input is not confined to the **PDA**s described in the last section – professional engineers and artists often make use of pen-based input techniques as a more natural input mechanism compared to the mouse. A **graphics tablet** would normally be used for these specialist purposes and a typical one is shown in figure 11.7.

The graphics tablet is very similar in operation to the special screens described in the PDA section, but the drawing obviously comes out on the computer screen instead of on the tablet over which the stylus is writing. Software which accompanies the graphics tablet, usually in combination with the **art** or **CAD software** being used on the machine at the time determine the range of facilities which will be available. For example, on some models the hardware and software is able to detect 120 different pressure levels with the stylus, and this can be mapped into 120 different thicknesses of line – thin if little pressure is applied – to very thick if lots of pressure is applied. A typical resolution for a graphics tablet is about 1/100th inch, which is easily enough to cope with the most minute movement of the human hand.

An alternative input device called a **puck** usually accompanies most graphics tablets. This device, also shown in figure 11.7 has buttons somewhat similar to a mouse, and a window through which cross-hairs can be viewed. Unlike a mouse, if the puck is picked up and moved to a different position on the tablet, the cursor will move to a different position on the screen. This is because the puck does not rely on a rolling-ball mechanism, but its position is detected by the graphics tablet itself. In this way the tablet mirrors the screen much more closely, and the artist or engineer can think of the tablet as the piece of paper on which he or she is working.

Concept keyboards bear little resemblance to the standard QWERTY keyboards described earlier. The idea is similar to the graphics tablet shown in figure 11.7. Indeed, *most* **graphics tablets** can be used as **concept keyboards**. A special overlay relevant to a particular application is placed on top of the pressure-sensitive pad. A typical overlay might be for a CAD package such as Autocad, and contain a vast array of useful menu selections. If you poke your finger on top of the appropriate part of the pad, the sensors inside the pad will translate the co-ordinates to the computer and thus appropriate action may be taken which relates to the item on the menu which has just been pressed. The stylus can also be used to prevent the tip of your finger from wearing out!

Optical input methods

OCR

Optical Character Recognition (OCR) is *not* solely to do with the recognition of handwriting or conversion of typewritten documents into computer-based text via a scanner. Similar techniques have been used in the mini and mainframe computer environment for many years. These ideas are used extensively in service industries such as banking, gas, electricity, water supply and mail-order companies, for example. These companies might choose to produce an invoice on a computer which is then sent out to the customer. When the customer pays the bill, the *same* invoice is fed into a machine which can read characters on it which might represent the customer's account number, for example. In this way the cashier who is carrying out the transaction does not have to type in any details regarding the customer, it has automatically been read by the machine which has scanned the invoice, and translated the customer-account number into a form which the machine can understand. When a document, such as the invoice quoted in the above example, has been used in this way, it is called a **turnaround document**. This is because the document (called the source document), which was originally produced by the computer, has been **turned around** and *fed back* into the computer at some later date.

The electricity boards are, however, going one stage better – it *is* now possible to electronically read special meters via the mains cables to the house. Although the water and gas boards obviously can't do this, it's possible to link up all utilities via the telephone systems so that special water or gas meters could also be read. This obviously presupposes that each house would have a telephone system. Nevertheless, it could be possible for data to be transmitted via satellite systems to each house, and a small transmitter could relay back the meter readings – this is not crystal ball gazing – computers linked to **radio networks** (see page 504) are available now.

Characters on documentation can also be used to collate different documents into some sort of order, or be used to update files automatically as they are read from the OCR peripheral machine. A typical machine is shown in figure 11.8(a), and a typical document containing characters which can be read by the machine is shown in figure 11.8(b).

High speed machines such as the one shown in figure 11.8(a) are capable of reading several thousand characters per second, and are thus capable of handling huge quantities of documents per day. Cheques are handled by the clearing banks using methods (see page 231) which are very similar in principle.

Mark sense reader

Most students are only too familiar with this method of optical input – it's the method by which multiple-choice examination questions are automatically marked by computer. However, there are many other uses for this type of system such as

(a)

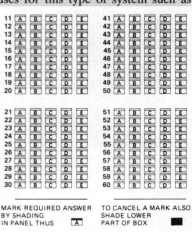

(c)

(b)

Figure 11.8

patients ordering their food from a hospital bed, or waiters placing an order in your favourite restaurant, for example. Part of a typical multiple-choice answer form is shown in figure 11.8(c). An HB pencil is used to make a mark on a specific area of the paper, then, when the document is fed through the mark-sense reader at a later stage, the light being reflected from the pencil marks is at a different level from the light being reflected from a space where there is no pencil mark, and this gives the computer the ability to determine the appropriate responses.

OCR machines typically read examination-type documents at speeds of a few hundred documents per minute. This means that it takes much less than 1/100th of a second to read in your examination responses which you have probably sweated over for about an hour. Further food for thought is that it would take a mainframe considerably less than 1/100th of a second to mark your entire paper – then *you* have to wait months for the results but that's life!

Bar codes

Most people will be familiar with **bar codes** since they appear on products ranging from tins of baked beans to library books. A typical bar code is shown in figure 11.9(a).

(a)

(b)

Figure 11.9

I can't get used to these new codes... I wish drinks still had proper names like 'Harvey Wallbanger'

As can be seen from figure 11.9(a) a bar code consists of varying thickness vertical lines that represent **a unique code** for the product. There are several different types of bar code in circulation but the European Article Number (EAN) shown in figure 11.9(a) is the most common for food and other goods in the UK, and the Universal Product Code (UPC) shown in figure 11.9(b) is the most common for items of grocery and other goods in the USA.

In both the EAN and UPC systems there are three different widths of bars and each character is represented using two bars and two spaces.

A device called **a bar code reader** or **optical wand** is moved over the surface of the bar code (in either direction) and the data is recorded in the computer or a portable hand-held device.

Although you would not be asked to quote such detailed information in an examination, it is infuriating not to be able to decode the bars on the side of the cans and so the principle of the EAN system will now be explained.

The system appears a little complex at first sight. However, this is necessary due to the fact that the system has to be operated under quite arduous conditions as the optical wand is passed over the bar code in either direction at many different and inconsistent speeds. If the code is not instantly recognized by the reading device then an error signal must be generated so that the operator attempts to read the bar code again.

The EAN consists of 12 codes grouped together as two lots of six, separated by a centre pattern and guard bits at each end. The arrangement of Pedigree Petfoods Ltd's code for Whiskas Supermeat with Pilchard (courtesy Moggy Wyatt of Camberley) is shown in figure 11.10(a).

The bar code is split up into 15 regions plus an initial number not coded in bars that represents the country of origin. Each character is represented by two bars and two spaces, and each character position is split up into seven segments. A typical seven-segment two-space-two-bar code character is shown in figure 11.10(b). If this is decoded assuming that white is '0' and black is '1' then we obtain the code 1110010 which could represent 0. The reason that it could represent zero is that there are three types of coding system called set A, B and C. To decode the bar code properly you need to know which set of codes is being used. The codes which represent the second set of six digits (i.e. the numbers at the right-hand side of figure 11.10(a)),

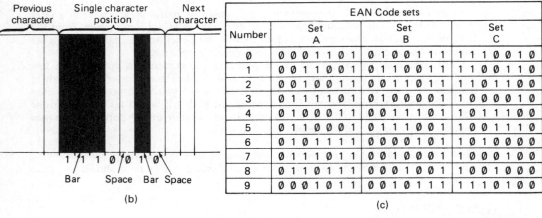

Previous character	Single character position	Next character

1 1 1 0 0 1 0
Bar   Space   Bar Space

(b)

	EAN Code sets		
Number	Set A	Set B	Set C
0	0 0 0 1 1 0 1	0 1 0 0 1 1 1	1 1 1 0 0 1 0
1	0 0 1 1 0 0 1	0 1 1 0 0 1 1	1 1 0 0 1 1 0
2	0 0 1 0 0 1 1	0 0 1 1 0 1 1	1 1 0 1 1 0 0
3	0 1 1 1 1 0 1	0 1 0 0 0 0 1	1 0 0 0 0 1 0
4	0 1 0 0 0 1 1	0 0 1 1 1 0 1	1 0 1 1 1 0 0
5	0 1 1 0 0 0 1	0 1 1 1 0 0 1	1 0 0 1 1 1 0
6	0 1 0 1 1 1 1	0 0 0 0 1 0 1	1 0 1 0 0 0 0
7	0 1 1 1 0 1 1	0 0 1 0 0 0 1	1 0 0 0 1 0 0
8	0 1 1 0 1 1 1	0 0 0 1 0 0 1	1 0 0 1 0 0 0
9	0 0 0 1 0 1 1	0 0 1 0 1 1 1	1 1 1 0 1 0 0

(c)

EAN code sets for left-hand side of barcode	
First Number	Combinations of sets shown in Fig 11.10(c)
0	A A A A A A
1	A A B A B B
2	A A B B A B
3	A A B B B A
4	A B A A B B
5	A B B A A B
6	A B B B A A
7	A B A B A B
8	A B A B B A
9	A B B A B A

(d)

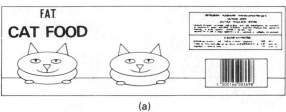

(a)

Figure 11.10

are always coded using the C set. The codes for each set A, B and C are shown in figure 11.10(c).

The arrangement for the six digits on the left is more complex, and depends on the number at the beginning of the bar code. Set A, or a combination of set A and set B is used to code this first sequence of six digits. The combinations are shown in figure 11.10(d).

As an example of decoding a bar code, consider the cat food bar code shown in figure 11.10(a). A larger version is shown in figure 11.11. The first number at the left-hand side is 5. Hence we use the ABBAAB system for decoding the first six digits as indicated in figure 11.10(d).

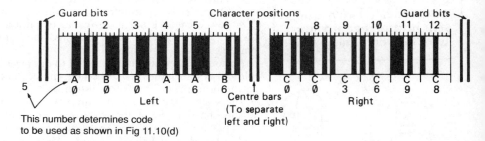

Figure 11.11

The first digit uses the A set and is 0001101 i.e. 0
For convenience the decoding process is set out in tabular form below:

Digit number guard bit	Set used	Binary representation	Number
1	A	0001101	0
2	B	0100111	0
3	B	0100111	0
4	A	0011001	1
5	A	0101111	6
6	B	0000101	6

centre pattern			
7	C	1 1 1 0 0 1 0	0
8	C	1 1 1 0 0 1 0	0
9	C	1 0 0 0 0 1 0	3
10	C	1 0 1 0 0 0 0	6
11	C	1 1 1 0 1 0 0	9
12	C	1 0 0 1 0 0 0	8
guard bit			

Using the above figures together with the 5 at the beginning we get:

5   000166   003698

Fortunately the numbers are usually written at the bottom of the bar code as it would not be easy for a human operator to go through the above process.

Such systems are used in supermarkets to perform a variety of functions such as looking up the details and price of a product so that this can automatically be fed into a checkout terminal printer, i.e. the customer would get a detailed itemized account such as:

ITEM		£. p
Baked Beans	500g	0.48
Sausages	496g	1.23
Oven Chips	1kg	0.98
Whiskas Supermeat	405g	0.43
	TOTAL	3.12

Thank you for shopping at our wonderful fully computerised store.

In some supermarkets an optical wand is not necessary as the product can be put into an automatic **laser scanning mechanism**. In fact in this case the customer can simply place the items on to the conveyor belt and the machine can automatically scan the goods and produce the bill.

Both types of system (laser and optical wand) would be linked to the store computer (the checkout is effectively a computer terminal) and could therefore be used to take control of stock levels automatically and re-order when necessary. Such a computer terminal is known as a **point of sale (POS) terminal.**

There are also a great deal of 'behind the scenes' operations that could go on as a result of bar codes being used in the retail trade. Not only can they help to give up-to-date information regarding stock levels, and therefore help with purchasing, but they can also be used to help maintain a huge database (see page 475) for an entire chain of stores. The business can then extract statistics such as which are the best selling lines nationwide, which goods sell best in a particular area, or which goods are not selling as well as they should. It can even go one stage further and have automatic links with the companies that manufacture the cans, and the companies that produce the labels. Such systems can easily be put into operation with the introduction of the new **FDDI national and international networks** mentioned on page 496.

In addition to the bar codes, the current generation of POS terminals can deduct money directly from people's bank accounts. Such methods using 'switch' cards are common, but some systems go one better so that the actual transaction appears on one's monthly bank statement. These systems are generally known as **EFTPOS** or **Electronic Funds Transfer at the Point Of Sale.**

At the other end of the price scale, users with home micros can now purchase inexpensive bar code readers together with software than can produce bar codes on a printer. These are also useful in education for demonstrations to students, computerising the school library system, or even to produce a system of stock control in the school shop.

In addition to the conventional bar-code systems, it's now possible to have a new system in which the goods have a radio tag placed on them. ICL has developed a radio-based system which can automatically detect the goods without them being removed from the supermarket trolley. Therefore, all you have to do is walk through the checkout and the bill is added up automatically – plus any goods which some people may have put inside their pockets by mistake! A tiny aerial inside the tag which either replaces or accompanies the bar code responds to the radio signals being emitted from the checkout control system. At the moment the system's too expensive for practical purposes, but no doubt it will get cheap enough to install in the next few years.

Non-specialised font OCR

We have seen in the last few sections how **specialised fonts** can be used on **turn-around documents** such that the text is easily readable by machine, and how fast input of data is possible by making use of these **OCR** methods. However, more recent systems, especially on **microcomputers,** are attempting to read **normal type-written text** and indeed **normal joined-up handwriting** (see page 222). Although the speed of data entry is not in the same league as the turnaround documents intended for **batch** use (see page 224) on a **mainframe**, these systems are proving to be increasingly useful as their reliability improves.

The distinction between **machine-readable** and **non-machine-readable** documents is becoming *less* distinct with the advent of some **OCR** systems. One type of **OCR** system which is becoming a more-common option on **flat-bed scanners** (see page 229) is the ability to read a page of pre-typed text into the computer in a form which can be understood, i.e. *not* simply a **bit-mapped image** (see page 252), but in a form where the scanned characters are replaced by **ASCII codes** in the computer's memory – which means that the text may be processed as though it had been manually typed in on a word processor. The ability to be able to do this is obviously a tremendous advantage because of the phenomenal amount of data already available in pre-printed form. Without this sort of system the user has no option but to get a typist to re-type the entire text into the computer system manually – a daunting task if the text to be entered is vast.

Initially, if a scanner is being used, then there is little option other than to scan the document in **bit-mapped** form, but the clever part comes next in attempting to interpret the meaning of the text. The first problem is to sort out the lines of text, and the white spaces inbetween the lines give a simple clue as to how each base line is derived. If the text being scanned is in a known font, then the task is made easier because the computer system can compare the dark scanned patterns (representations of the letters) with the known patterns for that particular font. With plain text and no fancy variations such as **bold** or *italics* (this book would not do too well!), the degree of correlation between scanned text and stored patterns can be remarkably high. However, splodges and other marks on the printed sheet being scanned will obviously mess up the system.

If the text being scanned is not in a known font, or if the computer does not have a set of patterns with which to compare, then some systems give you the option of a learn mode. Characters to be scanned are guessed by the computer and confirmed by the user of the system. As the learning progresses the computer should get better and better at predicting what each letter should be, due to the fact that the patterns are becoming more refined because of the constant updates based on the learning that is taking place. The early OCR systems were awful, with the learning process taking so long that it would have been quicker to type in the text being scanned! The correlation was also so low that half of the characters were unsuccessfully recognised. However, **neural networks** are potentially ideal for this purpose (see page 555), and are currently being developed further in the laboratories – some are even starting to be incorporated into recent OCR scanning systems.

Variations on the techniques used in the last paragraph are employed when trying to scan hand-written documents. At the time of writing there has been some considerable success in this field, but the cheaper software packages are still not good enough to please the most discerning of secretaries. Nevertheless, as explained on page 222, the Apple Newton computer can now learn and therefore read joined-up writing. As long as the handwriting being scanned is not too badly written, then there are probably going to be systems in the not-too-distant future which will cope satisfactorily – it's certainly a better option than manually typing in the text.

You will recall that we can achieve a high degree of correlation with interpretation of type-written text, but less degree of correlation with hand-written text. This implies that there will be characters which are impossible to read, or ones that will be misinterpreted by the software. This is indeed the case and most software that is available will either replace the character with a wild card such as # or ~ (i.e. characters which are unlikely to appear in the text and which can be searched for by the word processor very easily) or make an intelligent guess at what the word should be by using a spell checker and grammar checker in the conventional way.

Scanners

The ability to scan a document (e.g. the OCR mentioned earlier) or a picture into a computer is now taken for granted. However, the types, quality and cost of these scanning devices vary tremendously from small **hand-held scanners** costing about

£100, to A3 size scanners working at 1200 dpi using in excess of 16 million colours – which can cost in excess of £150,000.

A more typical scanner would be a **flat-bed scanner** capable of working with an A4 document as shown in figure 11.12(a), and the principle on which all these scanners operate is shown in figure 11.12(b). Most of these devices (with the exception of the hand-held scanners) are used rather like a photocopier, where the picture or document to be scanned is placed face down onto a glass surface and covered by a lid.

A powerful light inside the scanner is used as a source to reflect light from the image on the document which is being scanned. This thin tube of light *slowly traverses the image*, and thus, a beam of light the width of the page is diverted onto a bank of photocells by a system of rotating mirrors, which is similar in principle to those shown in figure 11.12(b). These mirrors rotate so that the light beam is correctly directed at the bank of photocells, irrespective of the many different positions of the light source passing under the document during the scan. A lens then ensures that a sharp image is presented to the photocell bank. For simplicity only a single beam of light representing a single pixel at a particular instant in time has been shown in this diagram. You should appreciate that you are looking at the scanner from the side, and have taken a slice through the device to have a look inside it. Therefore, the eventual path taken by this particular beam of light would represent a vertical stripe of pixels from the top to the bottom of the page being scanned.

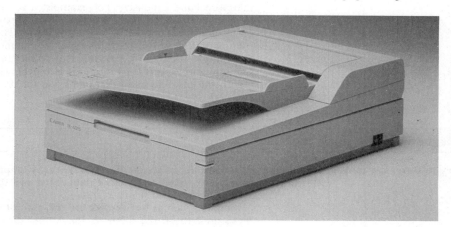

(a)

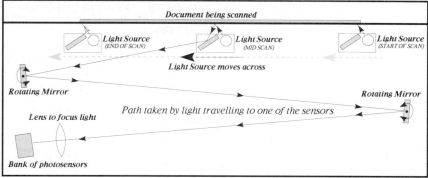

Figure 11.12

(b)

Side view of Flat-Bed scanner showing just a single light path

First let's consider a **grey-scale image** (i.e. **shades of grey from black to white**). Different levels of light will be reflected from different parts of the picture depending on whether they are white (lots of light being reflected), black (little or no light being reflected), or somewhere inbetween. Therefore, each photocell in the bank will experience a signal from the reflected light whose strength depends upon the amount of light being reflected. These light levels are obviously **analogue** in nature (see page 577), and therefore some sort of A to D conversion must be made so that binary signals may be sent to the computer system's memory. It is common to represent these black and white (monochrome) images considered here as being represented by 256 grey scales, thus requiring an 8-bit (2^8) A to D converter chip.

A typical scanner might have 300 dpi (dots per inch) resolution, which means that 300 photocells per linear inch in the photocell bank would be needed. Therefore, if we were to scan an A4 page which has a width of about 8¼ inches, then 300 × 8.25 or just under 2500 different photocells would be needed to produce the necessary 2500 pixels across an A4 page. Therefore, each square inch on the page is split up into about 90,000 (300 × 300) squares if this typical resolution is being used. If a 256-grey scale is used then one byte of memory would be needed to store each pixel. An A4 page is about 11¾ inches long and 8¼ inches wide, therefore, about 11.75 × 8.25 × 90,000 bytes would be needed to store a 256-grey level A4 page. This works out at just over 8Mbytes of memory.

If a **colour scan** is needed then the above process must be repeated 3 times – *once* using a **red filter**, a *second time* using a **green filter** and a *third time* using a **blue filter**. This produces three monochromatic images which, when combined, produces a coloured image in the ways described in chapter 12 when monitors or VDUs (see page 242) are being considered. An A4 coloured image would thus need about 24Mbytes if 24-bit colour is used (see page 242) – and this is only at 300dpi! Good though this is, professional quality publications require higher resolutions so that no difference can be seen between a scanned image and an original photograph. If 600 dpi is used, for example, then over 100 Mbytes would be needed for this single very-high-quality A4 coloured image! However, compression techniques can often be used to reduce this final figure to something more realistic (see page 563).

The special machines that manipulate and process these high-quality images are therefore quite expensive. For example, a company in Tunbridge Wells which helps to produce the luxury-liner brochures for companies like P&O, produce the brochures on machines with about 11 Gbytes of RAM. These are obviously specialist machines running special software, as this amount of memory is currently beyond the addressing capability of the 80×86 generation of 32-bit chips. However, with the advent of the Pentium and PowerPC 64-bit chips (see page 71) – this is not going to be a problem – with the possible exception of paying for it!

Magnetic media input methods

Key-to-store, key-to-disk, key-to-tape   These are the methods that have virtually eliminated punched cards and paper tape as modern viable methods of data entry into the computer. The principle of such a system is shown in figure 11.13(a).

Methods such as **key-to-disk** are the natural successors to card and tape input, as these used to be the methods for getting data into machine-readable format. You could actually consider a card punch as a key-to-card input system. In fact the general term for all such systems would be **key-to-store** as it is possible to type data in at the keyboard and store it on any desired medium, magnetic or otherwise, as shown in figure 11.13(a).

The need for such systems arises from having to convert the data from large numbers of **source documents** into machine readable format. Key-to-disk, key-to-tape, key-to-floppy and key-to-cassette systems are all available.

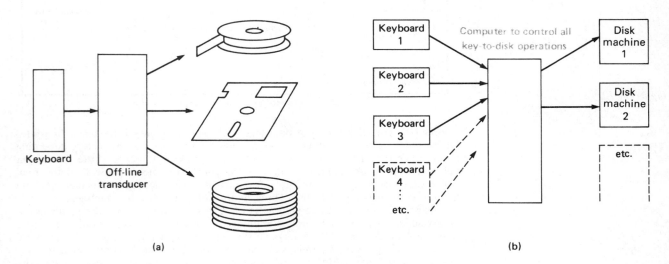

(a)   (b)

Figure 11.13

It is important to be able to prepare data for **batch entry** into large computer systems because it would be inefficient to tie up a high speed computer CPU with such a slow task. Batch entry methods are those where the data to be entered is **off-line** as opposed to **direct entry methods** where the data is entered from a terminal **on-line**. **On-line** means under the control of the computer and off-line means under the control of some other device such as a key-to-disk encoder. The data is therefore transferred on to the magnetic medium ready for high speed entry into the computer system at some later stage. Many large systems have multistation key-to-disk systems where it is possible to have many operators typing data on to the key-to-disk system simultaneously. On such systems a minicomputer might be employed to supervise and control the entire operation including verifying the data before being entered into the main system. The principle of such a system is shown in figure 11.13(b).

Verification of data is checking data to see if any errors such as words being mistyped has occurred. Such a process involves a different operator typing in the same data again. The machine then checks the data in memory with that currently being entered .

Another important concept is **data validation.** This is where the data is checked to see if it is sensible in the context for which it is intended, e.g. a source document might contain the age of a person as being 361 years. If this is 'correctly' typed in and verified then it would get past the checks. However, the data validation process could be set to a sensible age limit that would detect such an error. Similar validation checks could be made to ensure that letters are not typed in when numbers are expected etc.

Magnetic ink character recognition (MICR)

One of the best examples of MICR is the line of characters that appears at the bottom of bank cheques (see figure 11.14(a)). The special characters form the numbers which represent the cheque number, branch number (sorting code) and customer account number. These characters are designed to be read by humans and also by a special machine called an **MICR reader**, hence the slightly weird shape of the numbers. A picture of a typical MICR reader is shown in figure 11.14(b).

Special ink is' used that can be magnetized by passing the characters through a magnetic field before the cheque is read by the **MICR** reading head inside the machine. The system of characters is known as the **E13B** font and only 14 different characters are available. These are the characters 0 to 9 and four special symbols.

There are no alphabetic characters available. The advantage of the MICR process for banks is that enormous numbers of cheques may be cleared quickly and the system is capable of reading the characters even if the numbers on the cheques have been folded. Further MICR information representing the amount of the cheque is put on by the banks after the cheque has been cashed, to aid the processes which are carried out at a later stage. Without such machines, the major clearing banks would not be able to maintain a system of clearing all cheques within just three days.

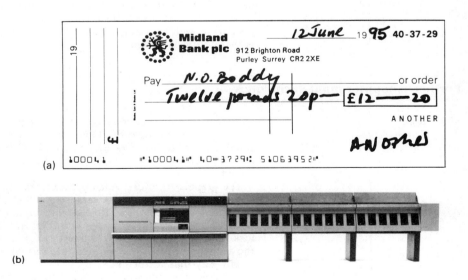

Figure 11.14

(a)   (b)

Figure 11.15

Electronic funds transfer (EFT)

There are very few large banks without EFT machines outside. These machines are generally known as **cash terminals, teller machines, automatic cash dispenser machines, or financial transaction terminals**. A typical terminal is shown in figure 11.15(a) and a typical cash card complete with magnetic strip is shown in figure 11.15(b).

These machines act as a 24-hour banking service which offers facilities to customers such as withdrawals and deposits. The customer has to insert a plastic card with data such as account number and credit limit (the maximum amount that can be withdrawn each day) magnetically encoded on to it. A **personal identification number (PIN)** which acts as a password must then be typed in. After the password has been typed in and accepted by the computer the customer may choose from a range of services consisting typically of balance enquiry, statement request, withdrawal and, in some cases, deposits.

In fact the cash machine outside the bank is only a very small part of the complete EFT system now in operation. Much more grandiose schemes are being developed here and in the USA. Instead of an encoded magnetic strip or stripe it is now possible to incorporate a microchip inside the card. Much information could be stored inside this chip and updated each time it is plugged into the EFT machine. Cards that incorporate microchips are known as **smart cards** and will become more widespread in the 1990s. The computers inside the latest version of these smart cards can be programmed to self-destruct if the wrong password is entered too many times!

EFT facilities are not limited to cash dispenser machines. Businesses are using EFT to transfer money electronically from one business to another.

As well as smart cards it is possible to get smart keys, i.e. door keys with microchips inside them. Such keys can form the basis of security systems in industry and some high-tec hotels (see page 604). Information regarding who has entered what door and when can easily be logged by the computer system, which is linked to all the doors. If the system is used in conjunction with a digital keypad at the point of entry, then a password (which can be changed at any time by the central computer system) as well as a key, would be needed to gain entry and a very secure system is therefore established.

Further computer-input techniques

Video input

Having a **video signal** connected to a computer system is not new, but the variety of things that can now be done with this signal is getting pretty exciting. With a suitable **interface** it is now easy to plug in a **standard video signal** from a **camcorder** or a **TV receiver**, and then display the picture within a **window** on the computer's screen.

The **graphic (resulting video picture)** can usually be displayed in real time (i.e. as a moving image), or you can capture a still at exactly the right moment in time. The resultant **graphic** can then, for example, be imported into an **art package** for further processing, be used as an image in a **DTP** frame, saved as a **still photo** on an **optical disk** or sent via the telephone line to a colleague who is far away. Being digitised, the image is then in a computer-data format – which may obviously be processed in any way that you wish.

A whole new industry has been built up around processing video images on the computer, and a powerful computer with the appropriate hardware attached can now act as a professional editing suite for making excellent-quality videos at a fraction of

Figure 11.16

the cost of using more-conventional equipment. A typical system from Fast is shown in figure 11.16.

Video recorders can be remote controlled by the computer, do assemble and insert edits, colour correction, time-base correction and variety of other useful processing can be carried out. Video processors and special-effects units for producing wipes and fades can now be replaced with a suitable computer system. Titles and other graphics can be superimposed onto any video image, and colour-separation overlay (CSO) can easily be achieved. Making use of the CSO technique it is possible, for example, to create effects which make it look like Superman is flying over New York, when in actual fact, he is lying down on a blue background, and a moving video image of New York has been used as a backdrop for his image which is super-imposed on it. Most people are already aware that powerful computers can produce stunning surrealistic images, which, when coupled with real-time video control will produce a whole new arsenal for the next generation of professional and amateur film makers.

Non-linear editing

A more-recent development for video processing is called **non-linear editing**. Traditionally one or two video recorders are used as the source to provide material that is to be recorded in sequence onto a 3rd video recorder. However, it's now possible to store a couple of hours video on large optical CD-ROM drives, and edit the lot in one go. The computer stores all the instructions necessary for the entire video production, and then goes through the process of putting the whole thing in the correct sequence onto a single video recorder. The amount spent on computer kit is probably saved by having to have fewer video recorders and effects processors etc. It can all be done by a powerful PC-type computer.

Figure 11.17

Video communications

Video input makes it possible to turn your PC into a **video phone**, and some companies (including IBM and BT) are now manufacturing the technology to do exactly this.

A small video camera built into the screen surround relays your image to the person at the other end of the phone via the **modem** (see page 500) in your computer, and a similar arrangement transmits the recipient's image back to your computer. The audio signals are obviously sent by microphone. Figure 11.17 shows this system in operation. Technology such as this obviously has much to offer the commercial market, especially in the field of **video conferencing**. Companies can set up meetings with 'eyeball-to-eyeball' communication between people who are not in the same room, building, or even the same country – and all because the computer can handle **video input**. However, much use has to be made of compression techniques if acceptable non-jittery video images are to be transmitted over a standard telephone line in real time.

Speech input

The real-time analysis of speech is still illusive, but is obviously one of the goals to be achieved if people are to eventually interface with a computer using their most natural mode of communication. To a human, speech is a deceptively simple means of communication, but to a machine it's extremely complicated due to the vast variety inherent in human speech. Not only are there different ways of saying exactly the same thing, there are different languages, different dialects within the same language, different sounds within each dialect, and even the same people can sound quite different on different days because they might have a cold, for example. Such a system is obviously going to be fraught with difficulty, unless we can find some common characteristic on which to perform some sort of analysis.

One method is to undertake an analysis of speech by breaking up the sound into what are called **phonemes**. Using this method one can analyse (and produce) acceptable speech by stringing together the many basic sounds which can be made by humans using their vocal chords. However, even when this method is perfected, there are usually problems relating to the actual spelling of the text, especially in a language like English, for example, in which the spelling of a word sometimes bears little relationship to how it sounds.

It's also important to remember the principles covered in the earlier chapters on computer languages. It was mentioned that natural languages, such as English, for example, are context sensitive. Therefore, words like 'there' and 'their', which sound exactly the same phonetically, will have to be interpreted in different ways by the computer. Humans use the context-sensitive nature of language without thought, and it is this which enables us to understand a foreigner, for example, trying to speak English – due to the large amount of redundancy contained within a language like English, we are able to get the gist of what is trying to be said. Therefore, if a computer is to correctly interpret what's being said, then it too must cope with context sensitivity, in addition to the huge number of problems outlined above.

Even if we can correctly interpret the sound in a context sensitive way, we have the additional human problems of making false starts, uttering words which we then instantly alter, and speaking, for example, against a background of noise such as traffic, a radio or other people chatting. Our brains automatically filter out what we don't want to hear, and we use facial expression and other body language to help rectify our far from faultless modes of conversation.

After reading the above one might be tempted to throw ones hands in the air and give up. However, tremendous progress has been made, and many different research projects are going on around the world. Computer models of the human vocal and auditory systems have been simulated on powerful computers, mathematicians are frantically working on sound analysis and pattern recognition, and computer scientists are developing algorithms which are getting more successful. I am sure that one day it will be possible to communicate with a computer using a natural form of speech.

I'm running Windows and I still can't hear anything

Listen for windows

Although **speech input** is still very much in its infancy, **Listen For Windows** was introduced for the PC in 1993. This can recognise a vocabulary of just over 400 words, and is mainly intended for **command-driven voice control**, *not* for speaking text into a word processor. Although 400 words does not seem many, it is clearly ahead of other systems, but still way behind the hundreds of thousands of words which will be the ultimate goal.

Virtually all current voice-recognition systems require that the computer go through a learning session with the people who will operate it. The early systems such as those found on the BBC computer in the mid 1980s restricted speech in ways that made communication with the computer very unnatural. Words had to be spoken separately and very carefully. Listen For Windows, being a later-generation product is very much more sophisticated, allowing for a more-natural mode of speech in which the words can be joined together as in normal conversation. However, the down side of this is that the system takes longer to learn the words than for the single-word-at-a-time systems.

Sound input

Sound from a *variety of sources* (e.g. microphone, DAT, CD etc.) can now be stored and processed with ease making use of today's modern microcomputers. A special **digitiser board** is necessary to convert the **analogue signals** (see page 577) which represent the sound, into **digital signals** which the computer can understand. The device which carries out these conversions is called an **A-to-D converter** and is covered on page 577. If 16-bit A to D converters are used then, assuming the sampling rate is sufficient, CD-quality sound will be input ready for processing.

Sound sampling

Sound input (**sound sampling**) takes up pots of memory, with 40kbytes/second of memory being typical. At this rate it would take nearly 8Mbytes to store a 3-minute pop song. However, computers are rarely used simply to replace a tape recorder – the advantage comes with the computer's ability to processes the sound in an infinite number of ways. For example, an old scratchy record could be digitised, then all the scratches (represented by very sharp peaks on the sound graph) could be removed. The digitised information can then be recorded on a CD ready for mastering a new batch of scratch-free recordings.

Computers with fast A to Ds attached can act as spectrum analysers for the recorded sound thus replacing very expensive specialist equipment. This allows engineers to obtain a frequency spectrum of the sound which could help them to design better acoustics for buildings etc.

Sound effects

In the theatre the computer has become part of the standard kit for producing sound effects, digitised sound effects can be precisely queued, or a quadrophonic sound stage can be controlled giving the audience the illusion that aircraft are buzzing round the theatre, for example. Effects such as these are difficult to control by manual means.

MIDI

MIDI is a special standard which was originally developed to link electronic keyboards (of the **musical** variety!) together. **MIDI** stands for **Musical Instrument Digital Interface**. As is the case with most things electronic, the addition of a computer can considerably enhance functionality, and much special software for controlling these keyboards from the computer has been developed.

MIDI is being considered here because it *is* a special form of computer input. Musicians are able to play on these MIDI-equipped electronic keyboards (or any other device connected up to the MIDI interface such as a guitar or clarinet, for example) and the music being played appears on the screen. The system is not without its problems, the biggest of which is that most musicians are not robots (but some robots are musicians! see page 550) and therefore what appears on the screen might not be quite that which was intended. However, wrong notes can be edited out, and any other attribute of the system may be changed too.

With a suitable system such as Sibelius as shown in figure 11.18, professional standards of music capture and consequent printing are easily possible.

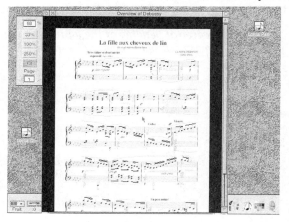
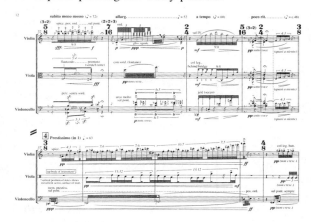

Figure 11.18

Virtual reality input

Virtual Reality or **VR** provides the current state-of-the-art in computer input. Appropriate hardware devices like the **data glove** shown in figure 11.19 could enable a user to interact with his or her virtual environment by pointing a finger or operating a virtual control panel. For example, the image of an imaginary control panel can be projected into the users eyes via a helmet that is worn on his or her head (see page 258). The human hand wearing the data glove could produce a virtual hand in the computer's memory which is also projected into the eyes of the user. By moving the real hand the virtual hand can mirror the operations, and be used to operate a virtual control on the virtual panel. People at NASA have already programmed such systems to play virtual musical instruments or to pick up virtual tools and do virtual work.

The data glove

The data glove contains fibre-optic cables, some LEDs and a special tracking mechanism which is able to determine the position of the glove within a specified 3-D Cartesian coordinate system (usually a room).

For simplicity the body of the glove on the hand has not been shown, and the fibre-optic sensors are only one per finger. However, the principles are all here – the amount of light being detected from the LED (detector not shown) via the fibre-optic link depends upon the degree of bending of the finger joint. Therefore, this system can detect if a finger is straight (pointing), or bent – it can also detect the degree of bending too. If multiple fibre-optic and LED arrangements were put on each finger, then more-sophisticated movements can obviously be detected. A separate system called **Polhemus** (part of which is shown at the top of the hand), relays positional-information regarding the hand (or VR helmet – see page 258) back to a system which is completely separate from the fibre-optic network inside the glove. The data glove has found many practical uses, and one system which has been developed translates sign-language for the deaf into script on the computer – now that's computer input!

Current conventions dictate that certain movements of the hand will cause the software controlling the virtual environment to react in a particular way. For example, point with the index finger of one hand, (you could have a data glove on each!) and you might move within the virtual world in the direction in which you have just pointed. This sort of technology has been used as an interface to control robots in hostile environments. For example, with the appropriate output devices, it would be possible to get a mechanical hand to mirror the action of a virtual hand, which in turn is being controlled by a real hand inside the data glove. The mechanical hand could belong to a robot who is defusing a bomb! Being telepresent in this situation is a far safer experience than being actually present.

The data glove is probably the most commonly known example of VR input, but whole-body suits have been wired up in similar ways to enable humans to react with machines in ever more sophisticated ways. With the vast increase in microprocessor power over the next ten years VR systems will become more sophisticated and realistic. For example, transducers (see page 580) already exist to apply pressure so that the user experiences g force, and hence torque or the feeling of picking up some weight within the virtual world, and heat pumps are being used to give feelings of hot and cold – the mind boggles. People have already started working on brain-wave monitors and limited success with these systems has meant that people can 'think about' turning machines on and off – and it actually happens. It is reasonably trivial to get a trained person to control brain-wave activity in simple ways,

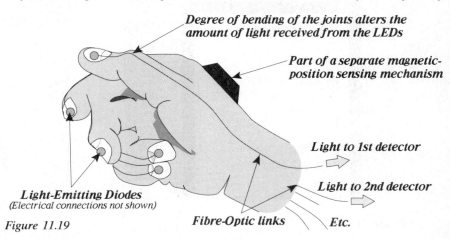

Degree of bending of the joints alters the amount of light received from the LEDs

Part of a separate magnetic-position sensing mechanism

Light to 1st detector

Light to 2nd detector

Light-Emitting Diodes
(Electrical connections not shown)

Fibre-Optic links

Etc.

Figure 11.19

monitor this activity via EEG electrodes placed on the scalp, and get the person to 'think' about activating a machine. This is a far cry from the film 'Fire Fox' in which Clint Eastwood stole a thought-controlled Russian fighter plane – but who knows what we can expect in the future?

Smells

This is currently an underdeveloped form of input, but is rapidly gaining popularity in industry with the development of new software techniques. In the second edition of this book it was predicted that computers would probably be giving their opinions on the Beaujolais Nouveau! Although we are not quite at this stage yet, 1994 has seen the development of computers which can sort out different varieties of Champagne by 'sniffing' the contents of the glass. The system operates using the principles of **neural networks** (see page 555), coupled with appropriate input transducers (see page 580), and provides a very reliable means of sorting out fake Champagne from the real thing. The system has been praised by leading wine-tasting experts and should open up whole new avenues in the fight against forgery in industries like food, drink and perfumery. You may also like to link this little gem of knowledge with the smelly-vision section of chapter 12 where smells are generated as a computer output.

Other forms of input

There are literally hundreds of other more-specialist ways of entering data into a computer system, for example, **light levels**, **pollution levels**, **currents** and **voltages**, **pH measurements** and the like can *all* be **monitored automatically** and **logged** by using a suitable range of *input transducers*. However, this area of computing is so vast that it is considered in a separate chapter on **computer control**. All the necessary input techniques for physical quantities such as those just described are covered in chapter 25.

Exercise 11.1

1. Choose *one or more* appropriate methods of data entry for the following situations or applications – in each case fully justify your answers.
   (a) Marking multiple-choice examination scripts.
   (b) CAD.
   (c) Cyberspace – virtual reality.
   (d) Retail outlet.
   (e) Production of CD-ROM based texts from *existing* books.
   (f) Getting quality coloured images into a DTP system.
   (g) Production of sheet music from a music keyboard.

2. Why have **ergonomic keyboards** recently increased in popularity?

3. Explain a typical use for **OCR** with **turnaround documentation**.

4. Explain how a **concept keyboard** might be appropriately used in a children's nursery.

5. What is EFTPOS, where is it used, and what advantage does it have over conventional methods of transferring funds?

6. Write *brief* notes on the following topics.
   (a) Different types of computer keyboards.
   (b) Using the mouse and track-ball as a computer input device.
   (c) The graphics tablet as a computer-based input medium for artists.
   (d) Computers as alternatives to video-editing equipment.
   (e) Getting a computer to give its opinion on the Beaujolais Nouveau.

7. Explain what is meant by **terminal-emulation software**. Why is this still needed when very powerful microcomputers are available in abundance?

8. When perfected, **voice input** will obviously lead to the *demise* of the **keyboard**! Make up *two convincing arguments* – one *for* and one *against* this idea.

9. **PDA**s are beginning to change the face of sub-notebook computer design. Find out about recently developed PDA systems and comment on some likely possible future scenarios for this particular technology.

10. **Bar codes**, **magnetic stripe cards** and **smart cards** can all be used as a means of *gaining access* to a **secure building**. Comment on which system would be the most effective, stating reasons for your answers. Name three other measures which could be taken which would enhance security still further when used in combination with your chosen system.

11. Comment on the *likely differences* in **computer-input techniques** regarding office **PCs** and **mainframe** computer installations.

12. When a document is scanned it might be in what's called **bit-mapped image** form. What is meant by this statement and what would have to be done to the text to get it into a form which could be understood by the computer?

13. A system's analyst has been asked to suggest ways of getting computer input from severely-disabled people with very limited movement capacity. For example, a nod of the head or the movement of a big toe etc. Suggest several ways in which this particular type of computer input may be transferred into a system whereby the disabled person could make use of a specialised word processor.

End of chapter summary

- An **input**, **output** or **secondary-storage** device is called a **computer peripheral**. **Input peripherals** are devices for getting data into a computer system.
- The term **peripheral** is still appropriate even though in modern micros many of these peripheral devices are likely to be housed in the *same unit* as the main processor.
- The standard **QWERTY keyboard** is still the most common manual data-input device, but new forms of **ergonomic keyboards** are helping to reduce **RSI.**
- **RSI – Repetitive Strain Injury**, caused by long uninterrupted use of the keyboard.
- **Non-QWERTY keyboards** are available *and useful* for special purposes, but are *unlikely* to supersede standard and **ergonomic keyboards** in the foreseeable future.
- **Terminals** are often used in the **mainframe** and **mini** environment as a means of communicating with the main processor. The main components are a VDU and keyboard. Terminals range from **dumb terminals** through **smart terminals** to **intelligent terminals**. **Micros** can also have **terminal-emulation software** loaded which achieves the same job.
- **Touch screens** enable users to point at the screen with their finger, usually at an icon or word. With appropriate software loaded this causes some action to take place.
- **Light pens** enable users to draw pictures on the screen by using an appropriate pen connected to the computer. This can also act as a pointer-input device.
- The **mouse** is currently the *most popular* pointing device for input on **desk-top micros**, but is also becoming standard equipment due to extensive use of **windows**.
- **WIMPS (Windows Icons Menu Pointer)** are now the most-common form of **GUI (Graphical User Interface)**.
- The **infra-red mouse** needs no connecting cable to the computer as the signals are sent to the machine making use of an IR beam.
- **Track balls** are commonly becoming an *alternative* to the **mouse** for input, especially for **portables** where they are built into the keyboard.
- **Joysticks** are still a common form of computer input, especially with computer games and software such as flight-simulators where they are often integrated into a control panel called a **yolk** (i.e. with some of the flight controls built in).
- **Pen-input** methods are a common input technique on **PDAs (Personal Digital Assistants)**, and provide an alternative to the keyboard for entry of small amounts of data. It is now possible to input joined-up handwriting using these techniques.
- **Graphics tablets** are used in conjunction with a **stylus** or **puck** to input graphical information. They are ideal for **art** or **CAD** applications.
- **Concept keyboards** are useful for **specialist-data input** ranging from primary schools to complex CAD packages.
- **OCR (1) (Optical Character Recognition)** is used extensively in **batched-based turnaround documentation**. It enables characters (usually in **human-readable** form) to be input into the computer system. Used for *fast* data input.
- **OCR (2) (Optical Character Recognition)** is used to enter **pre-typed** or **neatly-hand-written documents** into the computer. A **bit-mapped image** is usually produced by a **scanner** which then gets interpreted by comparison with known patterns. Some current systems are often *slow* and *unreliable*.
- **Mark-sense readers** are devises designed to read marks, usually made with an **HB-pencil**. A common example is the **multiple-choice-exam** script marking system.
- **Bar codes** are now commonly found on all types of consumer goods, food and books etc. They can be read easily by **bar-code readers (optical wands)** or **LASER scanners** as found at many supermarket **EFTPOS** terminals.
- **EFTPOS Electronic Funds Transfer at the Point Of Sale**.
- **Key-to-disk** and **key-to-tape** machines are sometimes used to build up **disks** and **tapes** ready for use on **mainframe-computer** systems. They save tying up the main machine when vast amounts of data needs to be entered for **batch processing**.
- **MICR (Magnetic Ink Character Recognition)** uses the **E13B font** found at the bottom of **bank cheques**. It is used by the bank's clearing-house system.
- **EFT** These are **teller machines**, **cash terminals**, **hole-in-the-wall machines** etc. which accept credit and cheque cards for obtaining cash and other transactions.

- **Scanners** are the devices that convert images (and text) into bit-mapped images so that the image or text can be loaded into a computer system in bit-mapped form.
- **Hand-held scanners** are lower quality scanners with more-limited resolutions and smaller scanning areas.
- **Flat-bed scanners** vary in size from small A5 to A3 models or larger. The large high-resolution 24-bit colour scanners are expensive and much memory is needed to store the image produced from the scanner.
- **Video input** is a means of **digitising** a **video signal** from a camcorder or VTR so that it may be processed by a computer system. Input for art packages and DTP images are common using this method, but video phones, powerful editing suites and video processors for the film industry are now available at reasonable cost.
- **Video editing** is now possible using a computer system instead of vast array of more-specialist electronic equipment.
- **Sounds** can be input into a computer system by making use of an **A to D converter**. The **digitised sound** may then be processed in a variety of ways including special effects or scientific analysis.
- **Voice input** is still a long way from the ideal, but is becoming more common for command-based input with a limited vocabulary. Currently about 500 words.
- **MIDI input** from a suitably equipped **musical instrument or keyboard** can be used to input data about **music** into a computer. The music may then be printed out on a printer.
- **Virtual reality systems** may use *special* input devices such as the **data glove**.
- Inputting **physical quantities** such as pH, light intensity, and voltage etc. are covered in chapter 25 on computer-control.

12 Output devices

Introduction

The extraction of data in whatever form from a computer system is of obvious fundamental importance, and this chapter is therefore devoted to these essential **output peripheral devices**. As with the computer-input-devices chapter, students undertaking computer science courses should be fully aware of the hardware from a *performance and usefulness point of view*, but are *not* usually expected to remember any of the technical details. Nevertheless, some technical details are included here as understanding a few of these helps considerably. For example, an understanding of bit mapped graphics, which is required in most syllabuses, is enhanced considerably with a little knowledge of Raster displays. Advanced level students are also usually curious, and many interesting modern developments would remain a complete mystery if no technical details were included at all. Most students wish to know at a simple level how colour LCD displays on the latest portables work, for example, and therefore this chapter goes slightly beyond the conventional syllabuses by giving simple and clear answers to the sort of hardware questions most often asked by the students in the classroom at this level.

Computer monitors

Some time ago the *only* **output peripheral** on a computer system was a printer which had upper-case only characters! Next came low-resolution computer screens and the versatile dot-matrix printers and plotters – but in the last ten to twenty years the variety of output devices has become vast, ranging from **COM** via **voice** to **photo-CD-ROM** to name but a few. However, today the **computer screen** is probably *the* most-common form of output, and is used on all but a very few of the current computer systems. The **computer screen** is more correctly called a **monitor**, but the term **VDU (Visual Display Unit)** and **monitor** are interchangeable. The term **computer display** is also sometimes used. Being *the* most prolific form of output, monitors will therefore be considered first.

Basic principles

Gone are the times when you simply went out and asked for a **computer monitor**. Do you need TTL RGB, analogue RGB, Hi-res, Low-res, colour or monochrome? Do you need CGA, EGA (nobody in their right mind would want these types anymore!) – or perhaps you might need VGA, SVGA, XVGA, multi-sync, non-multisync, low radiation, touch-sensitive – the list of features is enormous.

Figure 12.1

Figure 12.1 shows some high-quality modern monitors, but let's look at the basics first, and get to the bottom of the details concerning the ever-growing complexity and terminology associated with computer monitors.

The LCD screens found in portables will be covered shortly, but most **monitors** for **desk-top microcomputers**, **mainframes** and **minis** are based around a **CRT (Cathode Ray Tube)** similar to that found in your TV sets. However, *this is where the similarity ends*. Most people don't sit just a few inches away from their TVs, thus lower-quality tubes can be used when it comes to domestic sets. Due to this short-viewing distance and the fact that very small text (compared to the screen size) must be easily readable, computer monitors tend to have a much-higher quality screen than a conventional TV. (This is just one of the reasons which explains why you can buy a good-quality large television for just a few hundred pounds, whereas a good large monitor costs a few thousand.) In practice this means that the tiny dots which make up the picture on the screen are much closer together. You will thus see adverts which say that a monitor has a 0.28mm dot pitch, for example, which refers to the distance between the dots. The smaller this distance the better quality the monitor.

Raster scanning

The early computer screens were low-resolution-text-only **monochrome** (i.e. white on black or black on amber etc.) models. However, the ideas are still very similar, where a single electron beam scans from the top to the bottom as shown in figure 12.2. Each time the electron beam passes a point on the screen this causes the phosphor dots on the screen to glow for a short period of time, and by turning the beam on and off very quickly as the picture is scanned, an illusion of a picture (or text) can be made to appear on the screen. This method, whereby dots are generated line by line on the screen, is known as a **raster scan**. Notice that in figure 12.2 the electron beam starts off at the top left-hand side, then scans across the screen line by line. The beam is very quickly returned to the left hand side at the end of each line, and this is known as flyback period – the picture is thus blanked off during flyback. Similarly, when the beam reaches the bottom of the screen, another flyback period and blanking gets it back to the start at the top left again.

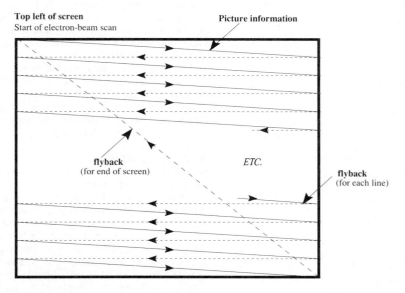

Top left of screen
Start of electron-beam scan

Picture information

flyback
(for end of screen)

ETC.

flyback
(for each line)

Figure 12.2

Figure 12.2 shows what is called a **non-interlaced raster scan**. This mode of operation is common in computer monitors, but **interlaced raster scanning** where the screen is constructed as two separate parts called fields is also available, and is the system used in domestic TV sets.

TTL colour monitors

The next generation of monitors were **colour**, and are based on the fact that most colours (when using light) can be made up by a mixture of just **three primary colours** namely **Red**, **Green** and **Blue** (hence the term **RGB monitor**). Artists should note that colour mixing making use of light is *not the same* as with paints. Figure 12.3(a) shows a Venn diagram which represents the three **primary colours**, together with

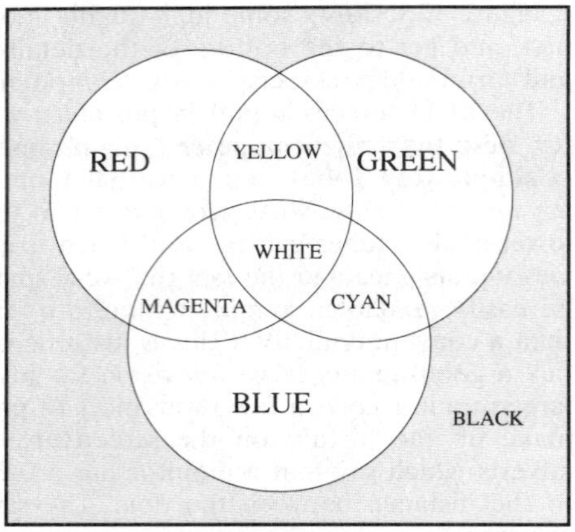

COLOUR	THREE GUNS		
	R	**G**	**B**
BLACK	**0**	**0**	**0**
BLUE	**0**	**0**	**1**
GREEN	**0**	**1**	**0**
CYAN	**0**	**1**	**1**
RED	**1**	**0**	**0**
MAGENTA	**1**	**0**	**1**
YELLOW	**1**	**1**	**0**
WHITE	**1**	**1**	**1**

(a)   (b)

Figure 12.3

the other combinations which can be obtained by having the primary colours switched completely on or off. As three primary colours are used, colour monitors need **three electron guns** inside them, and each gun illuminates the Red, Green or Blue phosphors on the screen. (This is why colour monitors are so much more expensive than monochrome ones.) A clever arrangement of dots in groups of threes (called triads), similar in idea to the Venn diagram, creates an illusion of a single colour. As each triad of dots is so close together, at normal viewing distances you can't distinguish between them – hence you are fooled into thinking you are seeing a single colour. Other systems making use of stripes instead of dots are also available.

The early colour monitors had simple electronics inside them based on TTL logic. This meant that the guns could only be switched completely on or off, and hence a choice of just 8 colours was available. (Poetic licence enables us to call black and white colours.) These systems were typical of what was then available on computers such as the old BBC micro. Figure 12.3(b) shows a truth table in which the colours and corresponding bits needed to control the colour are mapped out. It can be seen that just **3 bits** are needed for the colour information which controls each triad of dots on the screen. Each bit is used to control one of the three electron guns.

Eight colours is not over exciting, and ingenious interweaving methods gave the illusion of more. However, the more-expensive **analogue RGB** monitors allowed many more colours than this.

Analogue colour monitors

Analogue monitors were the next step up this evolutionary scale, and this monitor technology allowed the electron guns (and hence the intensity of the R, G and B components) to be infinitely variable. This is great as far as the monitor is concerned, but unfortunately the system can mop up pots of computer memory. For example, if we allowed just two-bits per R, G and B component, then 2^6 or 64 colours would be possible, but we would need 6 bits per **pixel** instead of the original 3 for the eight-colour mode. Note that a **pixel** is the name given to a **picture element,** and refers to the smallest **logical element** used for building up a picture in a particular graphics mode. For example, if you have a 200×640 graphics mode, then you have exactly this many (128,000) pixels. There does not necessarily have to be any relationship between the number of triads-of-dots on the actual screen, although you could obviously not display more pixels than the screen has triads, even if your computer was capable of doing so. A pixel is therefore a **logical rather** than a **physical unit**, although *if* there is a one-to-one correspondence between **pixels** and **triads** in a particular mode, then a single pixel would represent a single triad on that particular colour monitor, and the logical and physical units would be the same.

24-bit colour graphics

Today 256 colour modes are common for 'normal' computer work, but the highest-quality graphics workstation and computers used for professional art and photography utilise over 16,000,000 colours. This number is convenient because it is derived from assigning 1 byte to each colour R, G and B. Therefore, we have 24-bits assigned to the colours leading to the often-used term **24-bit colour graphics.** You should appreciate that with 24 bits available, 2^{24} or 16,777,216 colours are now possible. This is easily enough for *photo realism* and the most demanding *professional film* *and video graphics.* It has therefore become the standard on many top-of-the-range machines, and is also available too on micros which pride themselves on their graphics capability such as the Apple Mac, for example. You may also hear the term **32-bit** CMYK (see page 526) graphics, but this does *not* apply to the addition of any further colours. It refers to conventional 24-bit colour *plus* a control for the black (key) level.

Returning to the memory problem – if 24 bits are assigned to each graphic element, and assuming that you are driving a very-high-resolution display of say 1200 × 1600, then you will need an astonishing 1200 × 1600 × 24 = 46 Mbytes just for a single coloured image – and this says nothing of the processing power needed to alter it! Although the memory for such graphics is usually built into a special board called a display adapter, needless to say, until RAM gets cheaper and more plentiful, most microcomputers are content with fewer colours and less resolution. This also explains why very-high resolution images are often monochrome, or 24-bit graphics images are often not of the highest-resolution modes. Nevertheless, only ten years ago we thought that 8 colours were good, who knows – in the next ten years 24-bit graphics will probably become the standard. There's not that much point getting better because the human eye is not capable of resolving more colours or greater resolutions on normal-size monitors.

Graphics cards and different types of monitor cause a dilemma for software writers. Do you stick with the older systems or do you go for the more-modern ones with the consequence that your software no longer works on the older machines? In 1987 the VGA standard was introduced by IBM which is currently the base standard for normal computer work, but this can't last forever. Graphics and monitor standards are a very messy area of computing and one which causes constant problems with compatibility. Upgrades usually involve both a change of monitor and graphics card.

Multiscan monitors

It's essential that the picture is presented to the user at a rate which is fast enough to prevent flicker. If the picture is presented at about 35 times/sec then the flicker would be terrible – 50 Hz or 50 times/sec is acceptable, and faster rates are preferable. Without working out the maths, if you wanted a graphics mode of say 800 × 600 at a refresh rate of 56 Hz, then the monitor must be capable of a 35.2 kHz horizontal scan rate (frequency at which the lines are drawn). However, for a higher-resolution mode, say 1024 × 768, then if interlacing is not used, a rate of 48.7 kHz is necessary.

Different modes and refresh rates imply different scanning frequencies for the raster scan mechanism, and multisync or multiscan monitors (unlike domestic TV sets) can cope with these different scanning frequencies. **Multiscan** or **multisync** monitors are now common for medium and high-resolution graphics work, but you get what you pay for. The higher-scanning-frequency monitors, capable of getting the highest resolutions are more expensive than the slower scanning monitors.

Graphical display methods

All the methods considered so far in the monitor section have made use of **raster displays** (i.e. generating the dots line by line), and the most-common method for displaying graphics on these types of monitors is known as **bit mapping**.

1 bit/pixel monochrome

For simplicity let's start with a monochrome display in just two intensities – on and off. Let's also suppose for the sake of argument that there are 200 vertical lines (dots) and 640 horizontal dots. (Far less than this will actually be shown in the diagrams!) We require on-off information regarding 200 × 640 = 128,000 pixels. If we make use of 128,000 bits of memory, where each location might be 1 if a pixel is to be on, or a 0 if the pixel is to be off, then these **128,000 bits** in memory contain a **bit map** of what should be going on on the screen. By *continually referencing* each **bit** in the **map** at the appropriate time, the electron beam in the raster-scanning mechanism can be switched on or off. By storing the appropriate map in memory (**video RAM**) then the corresponding picture or text is displayed on the screen. See figure 12.4.

8 bits/pixel monochrome

Next let's choose a 256 grey-level 'monochrome' screen. It is convenient to assign one byte of memory to each pixel in this case because a byte is all that is necessary to describe 256 levels of grey from black (00000000 – min) to white (11111111 – max).

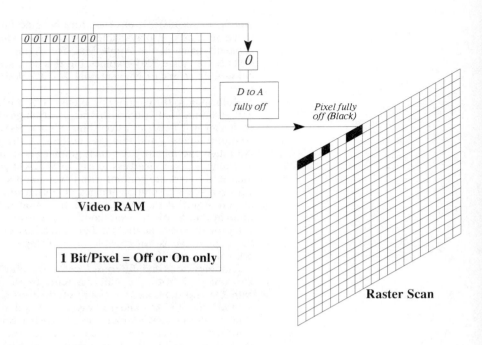

Figure 12.4

An analogue monitor would obviously be needed here and the digital values stored in the memory map are used to control the intensity of the gun via a D to A converter (see page 577) on the graphics board. Although bytes are being used here the system is obviously still the same and is therefore still called a bit-mapped system. The idea is shown in figure 12.5.

Character graphics

At this point it is worth contrasting this with a system that is called memory mapping or **character graphics**. Under this alternative system the extended ASCII codes for each character are held in memory, one character per byte. These codes are then

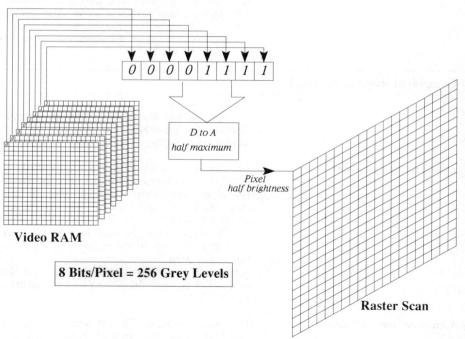

Figure 12.5

sent to the graphics display or special monitor not as a bit-mapped image but as the ASCII code. Hardware inside the monitor then converts these codes into the appropriate characters to be displayed on the screen. This idea is similar to the character graphics generator inside a normal TV set if **teletext** is being used. The codes being received are received by the set and the appropriate raster-scan patterns are generated by a special teletext chip inside the TV. Teletext is an example of character-based graphics generation.

Meanwhile, back at the bit-mapped camp, we can easily introduce colour by assigning in effect three different bit maps of the type described for the 256 grey scale display. One map would be for **red**, one for **green** and one for **blue** (**RGB**). For the 24-bit graphics described earlier, each red byte would control the red gun, each green byte would control the green gun and each blue byte would control the blue gun in ways identical to the way in which the 256-grey level bit-map controlled the display in the previous section.

Vector graphics

Most graphics computers make use of **bit-mapped images** described in the last few sections. However, some systems make use of what's called **vector graphics**. In this system a **line (vector)** is drawn directly on the screen by the electron beam. You can imagine it to be rather like the plotter output (see page 256), but the vector would obviously have to be refreshed at a fast rate or the line would disappear. It's unlikely that the computer would be able to cope with the constant and demanding refreshing on this type of screen, and so a **buffer** is used continually to drive the display electronics.

The picture is usually based on a system of co-ordinates and characters are generated by special electronics inside the display. As with many computer images, most of the picture is probably static, and so the processor only has to pass that part of the image which has changed since the previous picture was drawn over to the display electronics.

Other display technologies

LCD displays

The amount of energy needed for a raster CRT display is very significant, and far in excess of that which could be supplied from the batteries in a portable computer. You may think that the few hours battery life on a typical portable is not long, but hang a CRT on the end and the battery would probably last a few minutes!

Backlit LCD displays

The term **LCD** stands for **Liquid Crystal Display** and is based on the development of a technology that has been used in small calculators for a number of years. A liquid crystal is one in which the molecules can be in a state which is *part liquid* (freely moving about) and *part crystal* (fixed). This state exists at just a few degrees above the melting point of some special materials. By using an *electrostatic field* it is possible to make the *rod-shaped molecules* line up with each other, and this modifies the optical properties of the material from the original state. Figure 12.6(a) shows how the rod-shaped molecules in the material may be twisted by increasing the action of the electrostatic field (charge).

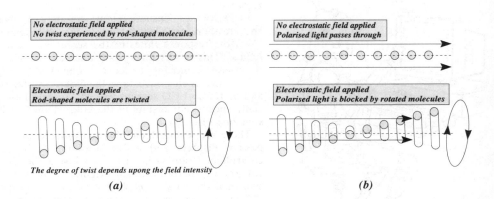

Figure 12.6

The whole secret of this display method lies in the fact that polarised light (light shining in one plane only) will either pass through the crystals if the plane of polarisation is chosen correctly and the crystals are not twisted, or will be attenuated (cut down or cut out completely) if the degree of twist of the molecules is sufficient. Therefore, little or no light will be let through from the fluorescent panel behind the display if the plane of polarisation is at right angles to the light. The LCD display is made from a huge matrix of these crystals – all of which are individually controllable by applying the appropriate degree of charge. Figure 12.6(b) shows how polarised light may be attenuated by the liquid crystals. However, you should note that the method just described assumes a backlit display. Cheaper portables often rely on the properties of reflected light which gives an inferior display which can't be used in bad lighting conditions. In these types of display ambient light is reflected off a reflector which occupies the same position as the backlit plane in the backlit display.

Colour LCD displays

LCD colour displays operate on the same backlit principles, but with three coloured filters for each pixel placed at strategic points on the screen producing the red, green and blue components. By increasing the degree of twist on the R, G and B components, and by making sure that the dots are very close together (see CRT displays) it is possible to fool the human eye into thinking that it is seeing a single dot of some composite colour. For example, figure 12.7 shows how bright yellow would be produced by attenuating all of the blue but none of the red and green light.

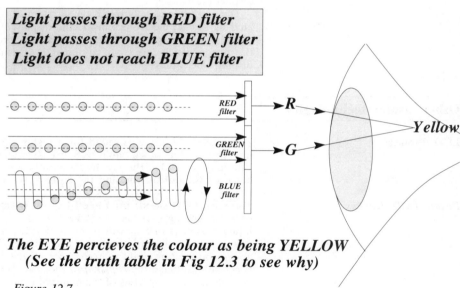

Light passes through RED filter
Light passes through GREEN filter
Light does not reach BLUE filter

The EYE percieves the colour as being YELLOW
(See the truth table in Fig 12.3 to see why)

Figure 12.7

Figure 12.7 is obviously not to scale, and in practice the R, G and B components of the light would be minuscule compared to that shown in the actual diagram. However, it illustrates the principles quite well.

LCD displays consume minute amounts of power compared with the CRT displays and are therefore ideal for use in portable computers. However, compared with the CRT, the response times of the screen are relatively slow, with 50 or 100ms being typical. This is why cheap portable screens often can't react to the speed at which the mouse is moving, or leave a 'comet tail' in the wake of the mouse pointer.

We have seen above how the liquid crystal state is quite temperature sensitive, and therefore LCD screens will not tolerate large changes in temperature, with especially spectacular results in the cold. (Don't stick your portable in the fridge – use someone else's!)

There are several technologies available and you will often come across the terms **passive displays** and **active displays**. Active displays are best as more charge controllers (transistors) are used inside the display (one for each pixel) and the colours are therefore much brighter. However, they are considerably more expensive than the passive displays used in the cheaper portables.

You may also come across the term **supertwist** when looking through technical literature on portable computers. This is referring simply to the technique of rotating the molecules through 270° instead of 90° which provides for a display with greater

clarity. Double supertwisted displays where the interaction of two supertwist molecules gives an even better display are also on the market, and no doubt other developments will enhance the displays for portables even further.

The future of LCD displays

Liquid crystal technology has developed at an amazing pace in the last few years, and manufacturers are reasonably confident in getting a 20-inch colour display developed by the mid 1990s. If successful, then LCD displays could not only be useful for the portable market, but for energy-saving larger displays too. For example, the **FLCD** (The Ferroelectric Liquid Crystal Display), will not need refreshing, and will therefore consume much less power. This could be essential for the lap-top market as battery-supply time is currently a major concern.

Touch-sensitive screens

The technology of this type of monitor has nothing to do with the internal guts of the system, (i.e. CRT or LCD), but is usually carried out as an add-on to an existing monitor. What makes a touch-sensitive screen different is the addition of a matrix of infra-red beams which criss-cross the front of the screen at right angles. If a finger is pointed at the screen then some of these infra-red beams will be broken – some in the vertical and others in the horizontal direction. This interception of the beams can be converted into a co-ordinate and thus the system can easily determine the position of the finger on the screen.

It should be relatively obvious that a special program is usually used in conjunction with the pointer information from the infra-red display which together enable the user of the touch-sensitive screen to point a finger at the screen and cause some pre-determined action to happen.

Projection TV output

A projection TV takes an RGB signal from the computer, and via a complex system of electronics and optical lenses projects an image of the computer screen on a much-larger cinema-type screen. The most expensive projection TVs are now capable of quite high resolution modes with screen sizes of several square meters. They are ideal for use in lecture theatres when audiences of several hundred people have to watch the computer screen simultaneously.

On a more modest scale, a normal OHP (OverHead Projector) as found in most classrooms can be turned into a projection system for a computer by placing a special LCD device on top of the projector where the transparency would normally be placed. Although not anywhere near as sophisticated as the projection TV in terms of resolution or colours available, an acceptable medium resolution display for a group of 20 to 25 people can be satisfactorily carried out by making use of this technology.

Smelly vision

Although still in its infancy, some centres are now successfully experimenting with the production of smells in association with computer generated graphics and video. For example, the Museum of Perfumery at Bourton on the Water in Gloucestershire, England, has a demonstration which shows an image of an orange while at the same time spraying orange-smelling chemicals into the room. The most difficult problem to solve is obviously completely dispensing with the smell before another is needed. When smelly vision is used in conjunction with computer-generated graphics, sounds and lights you obviously have the potential for a spectacular advertising launch of virtually any product. The link to **virtual-reality** systems is an obvious one too.

Monitors and their uses

Most displays today are usually colour, but it must not be forgotten that monochrome displays are still useful in many circumstances. For example, if you are writing COBOL programs for a large bank then you are unlikely to need a colour display, as most of the work that you do is based around text. Word processors and some DTP systems for newspaper production need only monochrome monitors too. It's bad enough having to pay about £5,000 for a very high resolution 30 inch monitor for specialist CAD or typesetting without having to pay for the extra expense of colour if this is not needed.

Modern CAD packages demand the highest resolution monitors, and the art packages used by the film and advertising industry demand 24-bit colour graphics on top of this too. Therefore the most expensive top-of-the-range monitors are found in this sort of industry. Most microcomputers now have colour monitors as standard, as the consumer obviously expects at least 16 or preferably 256 colours on the current generation machines. (How else would you be able to enjoy the games during the coffee break?)

For portables, LCD displays are the only current monitor technology with a power consumption low enough to be driven from batteries. However, portables for use outside the office present special problems, especially as the LCD screens are sensitive to temperature. LCD displays are essential in the sub-notebook and PDA (see page 222) range of miniature computers, and have been modified slightly to accommodate the increasingly popular pen input.

Hard copy

Printers

After computer monitors the printer is probably the next most common form of output, and the output from *any* printer is known as **hard copy**. Printing technology in the last few years has made very significant progress, and what used to be regarded as acceptable just a few years ago is now only suitable for **draft copy**. The all-important company image is paramount in today's competitive environment.

During the 1980s the dot matrix printers ruled supreme, but laser printers and bubble-jet printers have now been pushing hard as the main contenders for the most-common form of output from microcomputers. Nevertheless, the dot-matrix printer is still very common and is still much cheaper than laser printer technology. It has therefore not yet been confined to the ever-growing heap of computer technology which has rapidly become out of date.

Dot matrix printers

Dot matrix printers, or indeed any printer that prints just *'one character'* at a time is known as a **serial printer**. (This term should be compared with the terms **line printer** and **page printer** considered elsewhere in this chapter.)

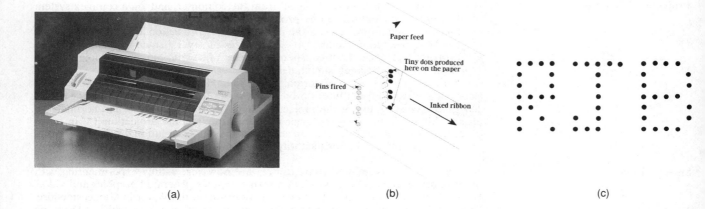

(a)   (b)   (c)

Figure 12.8

Dot matrix printers work by firing a *matrix* of tiny pins, usually arranged in rows, through a ribbon similar to that found in a typewriter. The older dot matrix printers had just 9 pins, but 24 pins are now the most common number available. Figure 12.8(a) shows a typical modern dot matrix printer, and for the sake of simplicity, the mechanism for a 9-pin dot matrix printer is shown in figure 12.8(b).

The tiny pins are fired by activation of electromagnets which force the pins to make an impact on the paper through the ribbon, thereby making a tiny dot on the paper. The mechanism containing the pins is called the **print head**. As the head is moved across the page the pins are fired in the desired combination to produce the correct effects. Figure 12.8(c) shows how the letters 'RJB' would be produced with just 9 pins. Notice that not all 9 pins are used for capitals, because two are reserved for the descenders which form the parts of the letters below the line (as with a 'g' or a 'p', for example).

Dot matrix printers are much more versatile than older printing techniques such as those found in typewriters and daisy-wheel printers. The hard copy, being made up of lots of tiny dots, can give a tremendous range and number of styles and different sized letters, or effects. For example, **bold**, <u>underlined</u>, *italic*, double height or condensed modes of text are easily possible by altering the pattern of dots. However, it is the ability of the dot matrix printer to produce **graphics images** which has really put this printing technology in an enviable position in the cheap-printer market. A typical speed for a dot matrix printer is a few hundred characters per second, although speeds of 1,000 cps or more are possible on the more expensive models.

There are two distinct modes of operation when it comes to printing characters on a dot-matrix printer. They can either be printed as a graphic, which obviously gives you an infinite variety of styles, but this is painfully slow – taking up to a few minutes to print a single A4 page of text in a high-resolution graphics mode (300 or 600 dots per inch). The second mode of operation is to pass ASCII characters (see page 256) down to the printer and get the character generators inside the printer to generate the appropriate patterns of dots. This is a much faster mode of operation, but with a limited number of styles dictated by the printer. Control codes are usually sent to the printer to change styles or put the printer in *italics* or underlined mode etc. It is often possible to purchase a font card which plugs into the printer to enhance the range of text styles that are available. The method used to print standard fonts on most dot-matrix printers is called **bit-mapped fonts** and this is described in detail later on in this chapter.

The biggest disadvantage of the 9-pin first generation of dot matrix printers is their poor quality of output compared to conventional typewriters, and the amount of noise that these printers make. However, the advent of 24-pin technology and using techniques such as double strike have largely got over the quality problem. When special techniques such as these are used to produce better quality output the resultant hard copy is often known as **NLQ** or **Near Letter Quality**. Letter quality refers to the quality obtained from daisy wheel and conventional typewriters. Some of the modern dot matrix printers are now considerably quieter than the previous generations, and acoustic hoods can be purchased to cut down the noise even further. However, 24-pin printers are extensively used in offices for the production of invoices and other communications where good quality is important but the highest quality is not of paramount importance.

Line printers

The **line printer** has been around for many years, although improvements in performance and a reduction in size have characterised later models. A typical line printer is shown in figure 12.9(a). The line printer is the printing device that is most common with large mainframe computer installations, where vast amounts of computer printout are required at high speed. As the name implies, text is printed 'one line at a time'. One type of print mechanism consists of many hammers and a **drum.** The characters are embossed on the edge of the drum as shown in figure 12.9(b). In fact this type of line printer is often referred to as a **drum printer** or **barrel printer.**

The drum (barrel) revolves at high speed so that each character can be presented underneath the hammer in a fraction of a second. The carbon paper is then passed between the drum and the hammers as shown in the diagram. An example is the best way to understand the mechanism of printing. Suppose the text 'A LEVEL COMPUTER SCIENCE' is to be printed on a line printer. The whole line of text

(a)

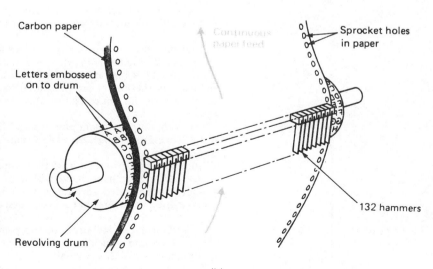

(b)

Figure 12.9

would be produced within one revolution of the drum. Let us assume for convenience that the As appear under the hammer first. The net result would be:

A

i.e. an 'A' in the appropriate first position of the text. There are no Bs in the text to be printed so no hammers are activated while this letter is under them. However, when the Cs are encountered, the text printed will be modified to one A with three Cs. The principle is as follows:

Text produced within one revolution of the printer drum:

Letter currently under the hammer

```
A                                                    A
A                C                   C        C       C
A        E  E    C           E       C  E     CE      E
A        E  E    C           E       CIE      CE      I
A      L E  EL   C           E       CIE      CE      L
A      L E  EL   C     M     E       CIE      CE      M
A      L E  EL   C     M     E       CIE N C E        N
A      L E  EL   C O   M     E       CIENCE           O
A      L E  EL   C O M P     E       CIENCE           P
A      L E  EL   C O M P    E R      CIENCE           R
A      L E  EL   C O M P    ER SCIENCE               S
A      L E  EL   C O M P TER  SCIENCE                T
A      L E  EL   C O M P U T E R SCIENCE             U
A      L E V E L COMPUTER  SCIENCE                   V
```

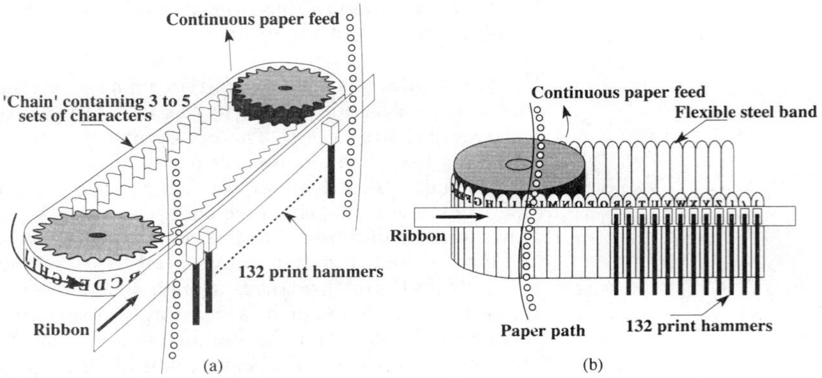

Figure 12.10

Many line printers have alternative print mechanisms to the drum such as **chain** or **band.** These mechanisms are shown in figure 12.10(a) and figure 12.10(b) respectively.

The chain mechanism simply revolves as shown in the diagram and hammers strike the paper through ribbon when the appropriate character is under them. To speed up the printer's operation several sets of characters are printed around the chain. In this way the letters are presented to the hammers several times during a single revolution of the entire chain. This type of line printer is also known as a **chain printer.**

On both systems (chain and drum) 132 hammers are usually employed giving the full 132-width printout. With the drum-type line printer over 2000 lines per minute are possible.

The band-type printer whose mechanism is shown in figure 12.10(b) utilizes either a steel or polyurethane band with the characters embossed on to it. This type of printer has the added advantage that it is possible to change **character fonts,** i.e. the style of the characters that are embossed on to the band.

Laser printers

This is *the* current favourite among printers, and is rapidly becoming the norm in many office and educational environments due to its excellent standard of print quality, high reliability, virtually silent running and rapidly-reducing cost.

Laser-printing technology is based around the guts found in standard photocopying machines, and the basic principle of operation can be seen in figure 12.11. Indeed, the only difference between a standard small photocopier and a laser printer is that

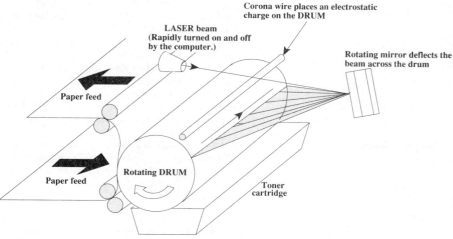

Figure 12.11

the laser printer has been modified to accept input from a computer rather than a sheet of paper placed inside a typical photocopier.

As can be seen from figure 12.11, a **laser beam** is **modulated** (switched on and off or changed in intensity) by the computer, whilst at the same time a multi-sided mirror is rotated to distribute the beam of light in a line across the specially-coated drum. The drum is coated with **organic chemicals** such that it becomes **conductive** when illuminated by light.

The **corona wire** shown in figure 12.11 is typically carrying several kV (ouch!) which charges up the drum as the surface passes by this highly-charged wire. In the regions of the drum which are *not illuminated by the light* the chemicals *do not become conductive* and therefore this part of the drum retains its charge. However, where the light has struck an area of the drum the chemicals become conductive and therefore these parts loose their charge. After one line of dots have been drawn then the drum contains one line of an image made up of charged parts where the light has not struck and uncharged parts where the light has struck the drum. As the drum rotates the next line of dots is produced in the same fashion.

As the drum rotates the charged parts of the drum (representing black) attract black powder called **toner** from the **toner cartridge**, but the parts of the drum which are not charged (representing white) do not attract any toner. In this way the toner is attracted only to those areas (groups of dots) which represent the black part of the image.

The next part of the operation is to get the toner off the drum and onto the paper. This is done by giving the paper a higher charge than the drum so that the charged particles of toner are attracted to the paper. This mechanism is not shown in the diagram.

Finally, the paper is **heat treated** so that the toner is fixed and does not fall off the paper when the paper looses its charge. Again for reasons of clarity this heating process is not shown in the diagram of figure 12.11.

Even the cheapest laser printers have a resolution of about 300 dpi (dots per inch), and 600 dpi is now standard. Although some laser printers can produce up to 1200 dpi, 800 is around the limit that can be seen with the naked human eye (i.e. without the aid of a magnifying glass or microscope). Sometimes 2400 dpi is used for professional typesetting, but 300 or 600 dpi easily matches the quality required for the typical office, which is one of the reasons why these machines have become so popular.

It is the laser printer which has been the leading light (pun intended) in the strive towards desk-top publishing (DTP see page 523). Without the quality and reliability of the laser printer you would have to send the disk away to be printed by the professionals – a costly and time-consuming operation.

Laser printers are classed as **page printers** because they print *one page at a time*. (Nevertheless *you* will realise that the image is produced one line at a time or even one dot at a time inside the machine – a little knowledge is a dangerous thing!). Typical laser printer speeds are between 6 and 12 pages per minute, although increases in this speed as the technology progresses will be inevitable.

Laser printers are obviously quite memory hungry. The image, being made up of lots of tiny dots, has to be stored somewhere before it can be printed. For example, a typical A4-size piece of paper is about 11¾ × 8¼ inches, giving a total area of about 97 in². If we are working at 600 dpi then we would need 600 × 600 = 360,000 dots for each square inch on the page. An A4 600 dpi document would therefore require about 4 Mbytes to store the image if no special techniques were being used. An A3 laser printer would obviously require over 8 Mbytes to store an image of twice these A4 dimensions, although compression techniques can reduce this figure considerably.

As with dot-matrix printers, laser printers can either print text as a graphic or by sending appropriate codes to the printer. There are two basic systems in operation for the production of text, namely **bit-mapped** and **outline fonts**. We will cover bit-mapped fonts first as these are the easier of the two systems to understand.

Bit-mapped fonts

We have already seen how **bit mapping** has been used to great effect in computer monitors. The principles here for **bit-mapped fonts** are identical. Each character to be formed is made up by considering it to consist of a matrix of tiny squares in which a **bit** (represented by one square) is either **on** or **off**. The idea is shown in figure 12.12.

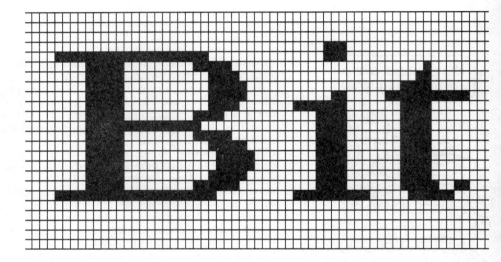

Figure 12.12

Figure 12.12 shows the word 'Bit' written in the **Times font** at **36pt** blown up on a grid so that you can see how each character is formed as a **map of bits** which relate to the grid. A single bit controls each square and the state of each bit determines whether or not the pixel is on or off.

A **map** *needs to be held for* **each font and font size** that will be supported by the printer. In this way ASCII codes can then be sent to the printer which represent style and font size, followed by the codes which represent the letters themselves. For example, after the appropriate control-code sequence representing style etc. the codes 42 hex, 69 hex and 74 hex would be sent representing 'B', 'i' and 't' respectively. As a limited number of maps are available this method of producing fonts is limited. A typical printer making use of bit-mapped fonts would probably have about ten different fonts each of which may have about 6 different point sizes. However, it is this method which *considerably speeds up printing* when making use of dot-matrix printers, as the character generators inside the printer are being used instead of the computer having to work out where all the dots should be.

Outline fonts

A more versatile method of text production is to make use of what are called **outline fonts** or **true-type fonts**. Instead of using bit-mapped images, mathematical relationships define the attributes of these particular fonts. It's *identical in principle* to the difference between **pixel (bit mapped) art packages** and **object-oriented CAD packages** (see page 539).

Page description languages

Outline fonts are more versatile because large numbers of bit-mapped images do not have to be held in memory to obtain a large numbers of font sizes. The instructions or mathematical definitions describing the outline of each type of font can be sent to the printer by means of a **page description language** such as **PostScript** or **HP PCL** (Hewlett-Packard Printer Command Language). However, more recently it's been possible to drive the laser-printing mechanism directly by using a **video signal** to drive the laser beam rather like the electron beam in a CRT display (see page 241).

As each character in a *particular* font is **mathematically similar** to the *same character* in many different point sizes, (different sizes of character), then all that is needed is the font outline definition together with information relating to its increase or decrease in size. Being similar, all angles etc will be the same, and only lengths will increase or decrease in proportion to the size of the letter. The idea is shown in figure 12.13. Assuming that the original text is the original size, then an increase from 72pt to 300pt gives an enlargement of about 416%. Note, however, that the shape of the font is identical, with all the angles governing the serifs (little feet at the bottom) being the same, and the radii of the 'B' being relative to the height.

Note that whichever mechanism is being used to define the fonts, the medium on which the final characters are presented *must be* a **bit-mapped image** made up of dots, due to the mechanical characteristics of the laser printer, dot-matrix printer or CRT screen. Nevertheless, outline fonts are the ones most commonly used because of their versatility, and **anti-aliasing** (little grey areas) is often used to make a more pleasing appearance (apparently less jagged edges as far as the human eye is concerned) when being presented on a CRT screen or printer.

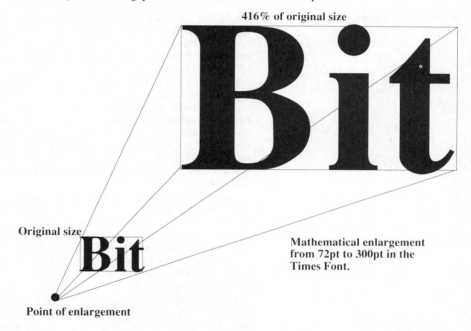

416% of original size

Original size

Mathematical enlargement from 72pt to 300pt in the Times Font.

Point of enlargement

Figure 12.13

With outline fonts the language which describes each character is of paramount importance. A language such as **PostScript** is usually contained in a ROM within the laser printer itself, or the computer will directly translate the **outline fonts** into the language which the printer understands.

It's enlightening to consider a typical PostScript file which would be necessary to print 'The cat sat on the mat'. The following extract is just the last 20 lines of the 284 lines which are needed to do the job on an Acorn Archimedes driving a PostScript laser printer. You can see the actual text just a few lines from the bottom end of the file!

```
EndPage
%%Page: 2 2
%%PageBoundingBox: 23 28 572 814
231 7990 0 100 60 110 StartPage
-0.5 0 MT 64 (RAM::RamDisk0.$.TextStory    17:51:08 27-Sep-1993
                                              Page 2) SS

1 0 MT 0 ( locktolinespace off;) SS
2 0 MT 0 ( ruleaboveoffset 0pt;) SS
3 0 MT 0 ( rulecontrol 6;) SS
```

```
4  0  MT  0  ( vertrulewidth 1pt;) SS
5  0  MT  0  ( ruleleftmargin 57.5pt;) SS
6  0  MT  0  ( rulerightmargin 467.7pt;) SS
7  0  MT  0  ( shortcut 459;) SS
8  0  MT  0  ( tabs vertrule 56.7pt,vertrule i55.9pt,170.1pt,vertrule
                             255.1pt,269.3pt,vertrule 354.3pt,36) SS
9  0  MT  1  (l) SS  0  (8.5pt,vertrule 467.7pt}The cat sat on the mat) SS
EndPage
%%Trailer
end
%%Pages: 2
```

Page description languages contain mind-bogglingly tedious and complex sets of commands, but enable the production of superb fonts to the highest standards. They include descriptions of the fonts to be used, margins on the page and lines or other shapes that may need to be drawn. Languages such as PostScript are complete languages in their own right, and if you are mad enough you can write your own PostScript commands to make your printer perform amazing feats not supported by your DTP systems.

Producing a coloured image on paper

Producing a **coloured image on paper** is *very different* indeed from the methods used to produce a coloured image on a computer monitor, for example. As we have seen earlier in this chapter, a computer monitor uses what's called the **primary additive colours** – namely **red**, **green** and **blue.** This is because when *light* representing each of these colours is *added*, the eye perceives almost any other colour if the RGB components are mixed in the right proportions. However, when looking at a picture on a piece of paper, a very different mechanism is in operation. Light does not emanate from the paper! – here we view the picture by a *reflection of ordinary* (assume daylight is ordinary) *light* from the page. The material on the page absorbs parts of the white light (i.e. it **subtract**s parts of the daylight coming in), and the eye perceives whatever colours are reflected after the others have been absorbed (subtracted). Making use of these facts, printers have developed a model (called the **CMY model**) based on the three **subtractive primary colours** called **cyan**, **magenta** and **yellow.**

Using cyan, magenta and yellow inks or toner it's possible to create other colours. For example, cyan and yellow makes green, all three makes black, or none at all makes white (assuming that you are printing on white paper!). In addition to these base colours, by using clever combinations of masses of dots printed close together, an optical illusion can be created in which the eye is fooled into thinking that it is observing a continuous colour of a different hue. For example, a less-saturated red could be made up from red dots with an increased amount of white space in between. The effect would make the eye perceive that the colour is pink.

Although in theory black is produced by the addition of all three 'inks', in practice it is found that a 'better black' is produced by having a black ink or toner just like that which would be present in a black-and-white printer. Therefore, a new colour model called **CMYK (Cyan**, **Magenta**, **Yellow**, and **Key** (black)) has been developed for the best results. It is this CMYK model that's used for many modern laser, thermal and ink-jet printing devices. The CMYK model is used as the basis for 32-bit colour graphics.

Colour laser printers

If you've understood how a black-and-white laser printer works, and you've understood the principles of the CMYK subtractive colour printing process, then you could probably explain the principle of a colour laser without reading further! A colour laser is identical in principle to a black-and-white laser, but the paper is processed four times – *once* with **cyan toner**, a *second time* with **magenta toner**, a *third time* with **yellow toner** and a *final time* with **black toner**.

It's important to appreciate how the coloured image is produced, and how this relates to the memory requirements of the printer. It's different to what happens on the screen because pastel shades and lighter shades of grey are not made up by turning down the intensity of an electron gun as is the case with a monitor, but in printing dots further apart to get more white space in between. For example, if a light grey is required, then black dots are simply printed further apart. If a coloured image is required then cyan, magenta and yellow dots are printed with appropriate spacing in between. This means that it's only necessary to have a single bit (not a byte) for each colour toner controlling each dot on the page. This means that far less memory is needed than would be the case for producing the equivalent coloured image on the screen. This is important because laser printers have to store an entire page before printing it out, unless you drive the drum directly with a video signal, as is done from the Archimedes range of computers, for example. A numerical example is carried out in the exercise at the end of this chapter.

It's possible to feed the paper backwards and forwards four times, but a serial arrangement with four separate electrostatic systems, four separate toner cartridges and four separate toner-removal systems could process the same paper serially but making one pass only. Needless to say, with four times the guts of a standard black-and-white laser, the price of a colour laser is about three or four times higher than that of a standard laser printer – even so, drastic cost reductions have meant that less than £10,000 is now required for a typical 300 dpi A3 colour laser in the the mid 1990s. Even so, this is not cheap, and ordinary mortals have to make do with less expensive technology such as that found in ink-jet and bubble-jet colour printers.

Ink and bubble jet printers

Ink-jet printers have evolved with several variations on a theme, namely – **liquid ink-jet**, **phase-change ink-jet**, and **continuous flow ink-jet** technologies to name but a few which are in current production. Each of these technologies will now be covered very briefly. Some ink-jet printers make use of **liquid-inkjet technology** – this makes use of the fact that *tiny droplets of ink can be squirted onto the page* under the application of an appropriate electrical signal. This squeezing process can either be carried out by the application of heat (expansion of the ink) or pressure (caused by a piezo-electric crystal), and these simple ideas can be seen in figure 12.14. These printers are also known as **bubble-jet printers**.

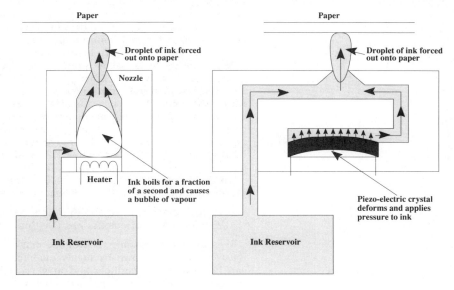

Figure 12.14

The first method shows a system in which the ink is heated up very quickly by a coil or resistor. Just a few msec or less quickly vaporises a small quantity of ink and a bubble forms, thus forcing a droplet of ink out from the nozzle. The capillary action makes sure that the ink does not come out of the nozzle under normal circumstances. The second method is very similar in principle, and shows a piezo crystal in its deformed state ejecting a droplet of ink from a similar nozzle. When no voltage is applied to the piezo crystal no extra pressure is applied to the ink and again capillary action keeps the ink in the tube – the smaller reservoir next to the piezo crystal fills up again when the voltage to the crystal has been removed.

Phase-change ink jet technology relies on the fact that some inks *change phase from a solid to a liquid* when heated up and melted – the ink then solidifies again when cooled down as it reaches the paper, and is then further processed by being pressed onto the paper by cold-fusing rollers.

Continuous-flow technology continually squirts ink from the nozzle whether it's needed or not! To save it splatting out all over the page the ink is charged up electrostatically and then diverted back into a reservoir or allowed to be sprayed onto the page according to the magnitude of a voltage on deflection plates through which this squirt of ink is passing. It operates rather like the deflection of an electron beam in a raster scan computer monitor – however, the stream of ink is being deflected instead of the electron beam.

You may be wondering why there is such as plethora of different mechanisms and methods regarding non-laser colour printing technology. The main reason is that manufacturers are constantly trying to find smaller, cheaper and faster ways to produce colour printers. Indeed, they have been very successful indeed over the last couple of years, and reasonable quality colour printers are now available for just a couple of hundred pounds – something which would have been unthinkable just two or three years ago, and it's all due to these new and varied methods of shooting ink out of a nozzle.

Thermal wax and dye sublimation

One of the problems with some ink-jet or bubble-jet printers is that if ordinary paper is used then the ink either goes into globules on the paper or soaks through and spreads out. Some of the technologies are able to use ordinary paper but others need special paper to get the best results. The use of special paper makes printing with some of these technologies more expensive per sheet than with ordinary paper. A couple of other methods exist for colour-printing technology, but you already know enough to appreciate the modern range of colour output peripheral devices.

Further output devices

Graphics output devices

Plotters are machines that are widely used to produce graphics output, as they can automatically draw pictures. They range in complexity and price from single-colour, single-pen plotters capable of drawing very slowly on to A4 sheets of paper, to very large (the size of a small room) multicolour high speed systems, capable of producing top quality graphics at very high speeds.

Most plotters work on the principle of a mechanical arm arrangement that holds a pen which can be moved across the page. The paper can be positioned on a flat bed (**flat bed plotters**), or arranged so that it revolves around or passes over a drum (**drum plotters).** The pen mechanism moves in both the X and Y directions on the flat bed type plotters but needs only to move in the Y direction on the drum-type plotters, as the movement of the paper over the drum causes the X movement. Both types of plotter cause effective movement of the pen in both the X and Y directions and are therefore known as **X-Y plotters.** A flat bed X-Y plotter is shown in figure 12.15(a), and a drum-type X-Y plotter is shown in figure 12.15(b).

The major advantages of the graphics output produced on plotters over the graphics produced on devices such as dot matrix printers are:

1.   Continuous lines, the thickness limited only by the pen.
2.   Hundreds of colours possible, limited only by the ink.

It is therefore possible to produce diagrams of perfect quality that would previously have been drawn by highly qualified draughtsmen. What is more, the copy can be produced accurately and at very high speed. Speeds of over 100 cm per second are possible on large, high quality flat bed plotters.

(a)

(b)

Figure 12.15

Plotters are usually classed into two categories: **digital and incremental. In a digital system** the plotter requires information regarding the exact X-Y coordinates of the pen, such as move to position 12026,10973. However, in the **incremental system** the plotter is supplied with relative coordinates, such as move 300 positions to the left of the current position.

In most high quality systems an arrangement is made for more than one pen to be used without having to stop the plotter and change the colour. This is achieved by such methods as a carousel of about eight pens, which can be rotated so that the desired colour pen is automatically placed in the drawing position. If more colours than the maximum are desired then another pass over the plotting area will have to be made after the appropriate pens have been inserted into the carousel.

Inexpensive graph plotters costing several hundred pounds or less are also available for connection to microcomputer systems. Although quite slow in comparison with the expensive machines, and usually being limited to A3 paper or less, the quality of output is very good indeed.

Another type of plotter that is often used with microcomputers is the **turtle type**. A typical plotter of this type is shown in figure 12.16(b). It is a device that can hold one or more pens that move around under the control of the computer. It is usually attached to the computer by means of an umbilical cord. High quality printing is possible and the device is not limited to standard size pieces of paper.

Although primarily designed for pictures, plotters can produce any shape (i.e. text of any style). In fact many plotters have their own character generator chips so that standard sizes of text may be plotted simply by sending the appropriate ASCII code to the plotter. However, used in this mode, the plotter is obviously very slow compared with the standard printing devices for producing text.

As any style of text may be printed it is also possible to produce text that looks like handwriting. Signatures are also possible! Typical outputs from X-Y plotters are shown in figure 12.16.

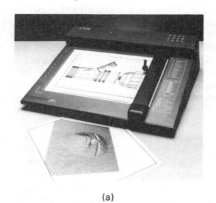

(a)

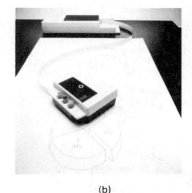

(b)

Figure 12.16

Photographic computer output (microfilm and microfiche)

It is possible to store a massive amount of information if it is drastically reduced in size before being printed on a suitable medium. Both text and graphics can be condensed in size so that large amounts of output are obtained within a very small area.

Computer output on microfilm (COM) is a technique of reducing documents in size and photographically printing them so that they can be conveniently read at a later stage by someone with telescopic eyeballs or, more conveniently by a special machine.

A typical **COM recorder** is shown in figure 12.17(a) and a typical **COM reader** is shown in figure 12.17(b). The COM process is ideally suited to taking large amounts of information stored on a computer and printing it out in a form that is convenient to store in a limited amount of space. Such systems are ideal for use in places such as libraries. As it is also possible to store pictures the system is also widely used to store data that would normally be found in a typical book. The system is even being used to store criminals' finger prints for police record systems.

There are two systems which are in common use: **microfilm** and **microfiche**. Microfilm is simply a roll of 16 mm film and microfiche is a rectangular photographic card on which many **frames** (pages of information) can be stored. Microfiche is derived from the French word *fiche* which means file or card. The popularity of microfiche

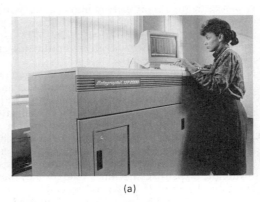
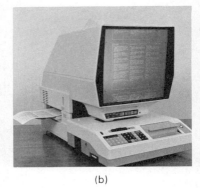

(a)

(b)

Figure 12.17

has increased tremendously as the space taken up by a filing cabinet of microfiche documents is equivalent to hundreds of filing cabinets for storing the same data in normal printed form. However, more recently 270 sheets of information per card has become the norm. There is also the new **Ultrafiche** system that can cope with 1000 pages per card!

One possible way of running a COM system is for the data requiring printing to be displayed on a special VDU screen and then photographed. It is possible to photograph a screen at a time passing the film serially through the machine, or to use a special machine adapted for the microfiche format. Typically about 80 screens of information are stored on a single card. Either way the system is very fast. It is possible to photograph over 120 000 characters per second using high speed cameras.

The film produced is sometimes processed in the same machine or else sent to a separate processing machine. Having got the first copy it is easily possible to run off thousands of other copies by making use of film duplicators.

The data to be printed out on **microform** (the collective term for microfilm or microfiche) is often first stored on a magnetic medium such as disk or tape. The disk or tape can then be fed into the recording machine off-line. It is also possible on alternative systems for the computer to feed the information directly (i.e. on-line) into the recorder.

Most systems used to read microfiche documents are based on manual methods of data retrieval i.e. the operator first finds the appropriate microfiche and places it into the COM reader. After the correct card has been placed into the machine the operator then places the reading head over the appropriate part of the microfiche and the frame is displayed on the COM reader screen.

Other systems are now becoming available that can automatically retrieve and display information on microfiche. Each microfiche (and frame) is given a unique number which, when typed into the computer controlling the COM reader, initiates a search and display program. However, this system is several orders of magnitude more expensive than the manually operated COM reader. As more companies are now using COM techniques to store and retrieve information the techniques are becoming more cost effective compared with other means of mass storage of information. It is now actually less expensive to use microfiche techniques than to use ordinary paper! Add to this the considerable reduction in weight together with the reduced postal charges to send data through the post and you will realize why COM techniques are becoming very popular.

BEEP BEEP BEEP

VR helmets

VR (Virtual Reality) helmets are devices worn over the head which project images into the eyes by using small computer screens extremely close to the eyes. It is, therefore, basically a **head-mounted CRT display**. There is, in fact, a big difference between displaying a picture on a normal screen, and displaying a picture close to the eyes. NASA found that if the field of vision was increased such that the angle of the extreme edges of the visual field is greater than about 60 degrees, then people began to feel as if they were part of the picture. They feel as if they are being projected inside the virtual world portrayed by the computer-generated image. The nearest thing we can get to this effect without an actual VR helmet is to visit a theme park such as Futuroscope at Poitiers in France, where enormous screens project images such that it feels as though you are actually part of the action.

Although great for arcade games, there are many more serious uses of the head-mounted display. For example, after a CAT scan, (Computer-Aided Tomography), a three dimensional picture of a human body can be built up. Instead of trying to view this through the two-dimensional medium of a conventional computer monitor, a surgeon can put on his or her VR helmet and feel as if they are walking around inside the patient. They could move their head and see views of some cancerous tumour, for example, from different angles. In combination with the data glove (see page 236), surgeons can interact with the computer generated images, perhaps by grabbing hold of a virtual organ and moving it out of the way.

VR helmets are also of educational value on training courses. Imagine a garage mechanic who has not seen some particular process before. He or she could put on a single-eyed version of a head-mounted display, and look at a video of what to do in one eye, whilst actually carrying out the process using the other eye to observe what they are actually doing. The possibilities are endless, and both the surgeon and garage mechanic examples are not figments of my imagination, but are actually being carried out in practice.

Exercise 12.1

1. Outline the *important differences* between **computer monitors** and standard **domestic TV sets**. Why are there so many different types of computer monitor, and why are the good ones relatively expensive?

2. What's meant by the statement '24-bit colour graphics'?

3. A *bit map* of the screen can be associated with the **video RAM** used inside the computer. Explain the principles behind the operation of this system.

4. Compare and contrast CRT and LCD computer monitors making sure that you cover the advantages and disadvantages of each system.

5. What is a touch-sensitive screen and where might the use of one be advantageous?

6. Printing technology has changed drastically over the last few years. Briefly outline major developments from the typewriter through to the latest colour laser printers.

7. What's the difference between a **bit-mapped font** and an **outline font**?

8. Why are **line printers** still popular on mainframe computers?

9. Explain how the **CMYK model** is used to produce a colour print?

10. How much *memory* would be needed inside a colour laser printer if an **A5 24-bit colour image** is to be output at 300dpi with *no compression*?

11. How do you think that the computer's ability to print high quality documentation has changed the face of the printing industry?

12. Is it likely that laser printers will eventually take over the role of plotters? Explain your answer.

13. Why are **microform** and **microfiche** still popular?

14. Outline likely *main output peripherals* for use in the following situations.
    (a) A firm of high-quality architects.
    (b) The producer of a glossy magazine.
    (c) A school secretary.
    (d) A library information system.
    (e) A EFTPOS terminal.

15. Explain the need for **compression** *with regard to the output of images* on a **printer**. What advantages would the same techniques have if applied to sending information over a network or telephone system?

16. Devise and discuss *suitable* forms of **computer output** for use with people who have the following disabilities.
    (a) Blind.
    (b) Blind *and* deaf.

End of chapter summary

- An **output peripheral** is used to *display output* from a computer system.
- A **computer screen**, **VDU** or **monitor** is the most common form of output.
- **VDU** stands for **Visual Display Unit**.
- **Computer monitors** need to be high quality *due to the short viewing distance*.
- **Multisync monitors** are needed to display the highest resolutions without flicker.
- Most **desktop monitors** are based on **CRT** (Cathode Ray Tube) displays.
- **TTL colour monitors** are capable of displaying *eight colours only*.
- **Analogue monitors** are needed to display a *vast range of different colours*.
- Most **CRT displays** are based on the raster scan system.
- **Colour monitors** have *three electron guns* called R,G and B, representing the colours Red, Green and Blue respectively.
- A **pixel** is a **logical picture element**, usually representing the *smallest element* (dot) which makes up a picture.

- **24-bit colour graphics** can represent *16,777,216 different colours*.
- **Bit-mapped displays** map **video RAM** onto the **monitor display screen**, the number of pixels determines the resolution and the number of bits/pixel determines the grey scales or number of colours.
- **Character graphics** use character generators inside the display to change ASCII code into suitable characters in a similar way to the teletext displays.
- **Vector graphics** is an alternative to bit-mapped-raster-display images – vectors are drawn directly onto the CRT screen.
- **LCD (Liquid Crystal Displays)** are most common in portables but are breaking into the large monitor markets, especially for projection TVs.
- **LCD displays** may be **passive** or **active**, with the more-expensive active displays giving the brightest results.
- **Touch-sensitive screens** are 'normal' screens with the addition of a range of sensors to detect a 'finger' position when pointed at the screen.
- **Projection TVs** project computer and other images onto very large screens.
- **OHP output devices** allow computer screens to be projected with the use of an OverHead Projector as found in many classrooms.
- **Computer generated smells** are still in their infancy, but are finding their way into advertising and product launches etc.
- **Virtual reality helmets** project an image which makes the user of the system feel that they have been projected into the picture.
- **Hard copy** is the term used for the computer output from printers.
- **Serial printers** print just one character at a time.
- **Dot matrix printers** print characters made up from a matrix of tiny dots, usually 24 pins firing through an inked ribbon.
- **Dot matrix printers** can use **character graphics** or **bit-mapped fonts** which can be printed as a graphics image.
- **Laser printers** have become the standard for most high-quality output in business and industry, but they are seriously challenged by some ink-jet printers, especially at the cheap end of the market.
- **Laser printers** are usually 300 dpi, but 600 dpi is common and 1200 dpi is also available.
- **Bit-mapped fonts** map the shape of each font onto a matrix of dots suitable for the printer.
- **Outline fonts** *mathematically define* the fonts shape, but obviously have to be converted to a bit map when the characters are finally printed.
- **Increases in printer processing power** (or on-board computer power) are making *outline fonts* more attractive.
- **Page description languages** such as **Postscript** define each and every attribute of the layout on the printed page.
- **Laser printers** are an example of **page printers** because they print a page at a time.
- **Line printers** print a line of characters at a time. They are used mainly in a mainframe environment.
- **Impact printers** make use of **hammers** or **pins being fired** – they tend to make a noise.
- **Non-impact printers** such as **lasers** or **bubble jets** are virtually silent in operation.
- **Coloured images** are produced on paper using the **CMYK model**. This should be contrasted with the RGB model used for computer monitors.
- **Ink-jet** and **bubble-jet printers** make use of various technologies. They are examples of serial non-impact printers.
- **Photographic output** from the computer is called **COM** or **Computer Output on Microfilm**.
- **Microfiche** is used extensively to store vast amounts of textual and pictorial information which can be read without a computer using a microfiche reader.
- **Voice output** is relatively common in specialised situations where a pre-set vocabulary is acceptable, e.g. phone banking.
- **VR helmets** or head-mounted CRT displays are ideal for viewing computer worlds in three dimensions – you feel as though you are actually there.

13 Storage techniques

Introduction

Computer storage techniques have made tremendous progress in recent years, and this chapter covers the principles of all major storage media from **magneto-optical devices** via **SRAM** and **DRAM** to **RAID** and **tape streaming**. As with the chapters on computer input and output devices, students are expected to have a complete understanding of what is available and where these devices may be used most appropriately, but students on many courses are *not* expected to understand any great technical detail. However, some detail has been included at a simple level to enable a better understanding of these devices, to enable the most-common questions usually asked in the classroom to be answered, and indeed to satisfy the understandable curiosity of most students who have progressed to this level.

Primary storage techniques

The computer's memory organisation may be split up into *two* main parts – **primary storage techniques** such as the **semiconductor memory chips** found *inside* the computer, and **secondary storage** techniques such as the **disks** and **tapes** connected as **peripherals** – this chapter is also split into these two sections.

The primary requirement of main memory is **speed of operation**. This is because it is this type of memory which holds the **immediate instructions** used in the **fetch-decode-execute cycle** (see page 49). As the speed of the **main processors** and **micro-processors** increases dramatically, *memory speed limitations have become a major problem* in the restriction of the overall performance of modern computer systems, and faster memory is an ongoing technical requirement. An alternative name for **primary** or **main storage** is **Immediate Access Store (IAS).**

It's amazing, but the limitation of the speed of light will eventually become a significant factor in limiting computer design. Within the current realms of scientific understanding, electrical signals can't travel faster than light, which is about 300,000 km/sec, or 300,000,000 m/sec. Let's suppose, for the sake of argument, that the effect of an electrical signal, travelling at the speed of light, has to travel along a piece of cable just 1 metre long. The time taken for the signal to get from one end to the other would be:

$$1/300,000,000 = 3.3 \times 10^{-9} \text{ sec.}$$

In practice, it would be slightly slower than this. Although this is reasonably quick by any standards, this unfortunately would mean that a very fast processor would have to wait for this information while it was travelling along the wire! A *very* fast processor (faster than the current generation of top-of-the-range PC chips) will sooner or later be capable of executing one instruction and require another in less than 1 nano second. Therefore, we have to make sure that the signal paths between main memory and the processor are considerably shorter than the one metre described above, and this is why some of the fastest computers such as the Cray (see page 17) are designed in a circular arrangement.

It is indeed fortunate that the actual distances involved in the CPUs *are* considerably less than one metre, but the above illustrates the point that current technologies are approaching some awkward theoretical limits – the only current way known to increase the speed of operation is to reduce the distance that the signals have to travel. This is one of the reasons why chips are becoming smaller, and just one of the reasons why the **cache memory** (see page 393) located inside the microprocessor chip itself is considerably faster than memory external to the processor chip.

Semiconductor memories

Semiconductor memories are based around materials which have an *electrical conductivity* roughly half way between that of a **conductor** and an **insulator** – hence the name semiconductor. By doping these semiconductor materials with other materials, and by making use of precise manufacturing methods, it's possible to build up a device called a **transistor** which forms the basis of the units inside these chips. Each transistor acts as a switch (or as a store for charge) which can either be on or off. It is the *state* of each transistor (or group of transistors) which represents the **state of a binary digit inside the computer**. Indeed, any physical device which can be in one of two states may represent a memory cell, and man is constantly striving for new technologies which will give a better memory performance.

There are several different technologies available and some under development, (see **nano technology** on page 553), but in the mid 1990s **semiconductor chips** are still the *main devices* used for high-speed main memory inside a computer. This is because they are *relatively cheap* to make (compared with other technologies), have a *relatively high capacity* (in terms of the number of bits that can be fitted into a single chip), and are *easy to integrate* into electronic computer systems.

Principles of main memory

Fortunately, all main memory devices can be viewed as a *matrix* of tiny **cells**, the state of which represents a binary digit (on or off). The term **memory cell** is therefore used to represent the *smallest physical unit* of any memory device, and is effectively a **one-bit store**. However, even with one bit, we can see the need to have a **control line** attached to this simple device which enables the computer to **read** the contents of the cell (*find out what digit is located inside*) or **write** a number to the cell (*put a new number inside*). The idea is shown in figure 13.1(a).

One bit of memory is not quite sufficient for today's modern computers, and so groups of cells are arranged in various ways to build up a sensible-size storage unit. The most common method is to build up **rows** and **columns** of **cells** as shown in figure 13.1(b).

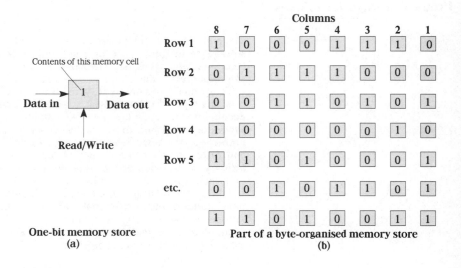

One-bit memory store
(a)

Part of a byte-organised memory store
(b)

Figure 13.1

Figure 13.1(b) shows a simple arrangement of what would be termed an 8-bit memory chip because each **row** (called an **address**) is made up of 8 cells into which **8 binary digits** or **1 byte** of information could be stored. If there happened to be 1024 rows in which 8 bits could be stored then the chip which is organised in this particular way would be called a **1024 x 8-bit memory chip**. However, as it can also store 8 lots of 1024 bits then it can also be referred to as an **8k-bit chip**.

Bits bytes and nibbles

Memory chips are categorised both by their **capacity** (e.g. 8 kbits) and by their **internal organisation** (e.g. 1024 x 8-bits). Therefore, we could have 256 k, 1 M or 16 M-bit capacity chips for example, but the internal **organisation** could be **bit** (1 binary digit), **nibble** (half a byte or 4 bit), **byte** (or 8 bit such as that shown in figure 13.1(b)), or **word** (1 byte, 2 byte etc.) orientated. Figure 12.5 shows video RAM organised for 256-grey-level graphics using memory arranged internally as 1 bit.

It is worth remembering at this stage that the terms k (kilo), M (Mega), G (Giga) and T (Tera) do not have precisely the same meanings as used in other branches of science, but refer in computing to the **nearest binary multiple**. Therefore, 1 kbyte of memory is actually 1024 bytes, giving us 24 bytes more than you might think from the words actually being used. Although this is not too impressive, think for a moment about having 1 Gbyte of memory. This is sometimes referred to as 1,000 Mbyte but actually means $1024 \times 1024 \times 1024 = 1,073,741,824$ bytes which is about 74 Mbytes more – a number not to be sneezed at!

Multipliers

As computers get faster and memory gets larger the standard units such as kbytes and Mbytes etc. are rapidly being used up. With this borne in mind, the table shown in figure 13.2 may be helpful in extending your knowledge of multiples which will hopefully last you for some considerable time. **Tbytes** of **secondary storage** are now quite common on larger computer systems, and even if one considers the humble micro – if a single CD-ROM can store in excess of 600 Mbytes of information, and a micro can address 160 CD-ROMs via a suitable SCSI (see page 575) interface, then this gives 160×600 Mbytes = 96 Gbytes of storage available to a microcomputer in the mid 1990s.

Notice that in the following table **smaller letters** are used to denote **multiples < 1**, and **capitals** are used to denote **multiples > 1**. However, although technically incorrect, it is usual to use a small k for Kilo – that's life!

Name	Abbreviation		Multiplier number
atto	a	1×10^{-18}	0.000 000 000 000 000 001
femto	f	1×10^{-15}	0.000 000 000 000 001
pico	p	1×10^{-12}	0.000 000 000 001
nano	n	1×10^{-9}	0.000 000 001
micro	μ	1×10^{-6}	0.000 001
milli	m	1×10^{-3}	0.001
Kilo	k	1×10^{3}	1,000
Mega	M	1×10^{6}	1,000,000
Giga	G	1×10^{9}	1,000,000,000
Tera	T	1×10^{12}	1,000,000,000,000
Peta	P	1×10^{15}	1,000,000,000,000,000
Exa	E	1×10^{18}	1,000,000,000,000,000,000

Hi, Milli...remember me? . I'm Mic Ro...and this is my son Peta...he's een a real Tera today!

Figure 13.2

How main memory is utilised

It is fortunate that most of the decoding necessary to extract information from a semiconductor memory chip is carried out electronically inside the chip itself. From an external point of view, the computer supplies the chip with a number called an **address**. This refers to the **address** (number) *in memory lane* at which a particular bit or group of bits reside depending on internal memory organisation. In figure 13.1(b), for example, if **address 3 (being row 3)** is being considered, then if a **read operation** were carried out then the number revealed would be **00110101** corresponding to the group of binary digits which makes up the **byte** of information living in row 3.

The **address** is supplied to the memory chip along the **address bus**, and the **data** being put into or taken out of the memory chip is supplied or received along the **data bus** (see page 51). The microprocessor would determine whether a **read** or **write** operation is to be carried out by the state of one of the lines going to the memory chip.

Not all memory is organised in the same way internally or makes use of the same number of bits. However, from a **software programmer's point of view**, *all that is necessary is to read data from or write data to the memory by specifying an address, and knowing how the memory is organised in terms of bytes.*

Addressing the memory

Different amounts of memory can be addressed by the processor depending on how many lines are available on the address bus. With just 8 bits available, only 2^8 or 256 bytes of memory would be possible. Even on the most humble of microprocessor chips used in computer systems 16 bits is common for the address bus giving 2^{16} or 65,536 bytes (64 kbytes) as the maximum main memory size. This is why the early micros were usually limited to 64 kbytes of main memory.

On the current generation of 32-bit micros 2^{32} gives us 4096 Mbytes or 4 Gbytes of main memory. This is easily enough for the most discerning animation and video fanatic, and some processor chips have therefore included only a 24-bit address bus which gives a main memory of 2^{24} or 16 Mbytes. If you have attempted to upgrade your RAM in the last year or two then these numbers should start ringing bells as to why your machine might be limited to a maximum of 16 Mbytes of main memory.

Some 64-bit micros are now available and *if* all 64 bits are available on the address bus then a staggering 2^{64} or 1.8×10^{19} bytes of main memory would then be possible. This would be right at the top end of our extended table, and would be unrealistic not just because of the enormous size, but because of the cost. At mid 1990s prices an extra 4 Mbytes of RAM costs about £150. If we desired 1.8×10^{19} bytes of RAM then this would cost us a cool £4,000,000,000,000 – less bulk quantity discount of course! – a sum far in excess of the GNP for many countries! However, these minor irritations of cost can be overcome to some extent by the use of virtual memory as described in the operating-system chapter on page 381. When **virtual memory** is used very large and fast hard disks act as an extension to RAM, hence the need for these larger processor addressing ranges.

Moving data along the bus

The size of data bus is important too, as this affects the speed at which a quantity of data may be shifted around inside the computer. The early micros had just 8 bits available, thus a single byte could be moved around at any moment in time. However, micros with a 16-bit data bus can move twice as much data in the same time as two bytes can travel along the wider data bus simultaneously. Similarly a processor with a 32-bit wide address bus can move data at 4 times the rate of an 8-bit data bus processor. The latest MPC601 PowerPC chip has some internal 256-bit data buses!

Access times

The access time of a memory chip is particularly important, because it affects the speed at which the processor can be allowed to go. The **access time** is simply the time taken for the electronics inside the memory chip to access the required cells, and then place the data on the data bus ready to be transmitted to the CPU. In practice the time taken to get data from a memory chip and put data into the chip is often the same, but if not, then the read access and write access times would be quoted separately.

Types of semiconductor memory

A typical **static RAM** (see in a moment) memory chip would probably have an access time of about 40 nsec, thus enabling data to be extracted from it at a rate of about 25,000,000 words/sec. (Don't forget that a word refers to how many bits can be extracted from the chip at the same time.) If you need the speed but have not got the required word length, then this is where one-bit internally-organised chips come into their own, simply line up 64 of these 1-bit chips in parallel, and you have a 64-bit word available in <40 nsec – magic.

First let's consider **RAM**. This is an acronym for **Random Access Memory** which means that *the time taken to access the data does not depend on the location at which it is stored*. Random access in this context should be contrasted with the **serial-access** mechanisms on a tape, for example, where the amount of time taken to read the data *does* depend on its position on the storage media.

Dynamic and static RAM

There are two major types of **read/write RAM** called **static RAM** and **dynamic RAM**. **Dynamic RAM** (or **DRAM**) is made up from transistors which store the state of a binary digit as a charge built up on a transistor. This method is the most popular because of its ease of manufacture and hence its cost effectiveness. However, it is more complex to operate than static RAM because the stored charge leaks away very quickly and gets lost if it is not topped up at frequent intervals, which currently means every few msec! This means that extra electronics have to be put into the system to carry out these operations, but this is hardly of any consequence to the users of such systems. What is of consequence is that due to this topping up cycle the speed of access for dynamic RAMs is considerably slower than the speeds with which one can access static RAM. Dynamic RAM access speeds are currently between 100 and 200 nsec – this being typical in the mid 90s. However, it is too expensive to have Mbytes of the faster static RAM as the mainstay of most microcomputers.

Static RAM (or SRAM) is more expensive to produce as more transistors are needed for the storage of each byte. However, **static RAM** *does not have to be topped up*, as the data is stored by monitoring the state of a transistor being used as a switch, rather than a charge-storing mechanism as is the case with dynamic RAM. In the operating systems chapter you will see on page 393 that **static RAM** *is ideal for* **cache memory** – which often increases the performance of computer systems by several orders of magnitude.

Volatile memory

Both **SRAM** and **DRAM** are **volatile**. This means that if the power is removed from the system then all the binary data stored in the memory chips would be lost. This should be compared to the non-volatile nature of magnetic or optical storage media such as disks, which retain the data for a considerable period of time, usually measured in tens of years.

The problems of volatile memory can be overcome by the use of **Uninterruptible Power Supplies (UPS)**, which are effectively batteries connected to the computer system which are constantly charged up from the mains under normal operation, but come into their own and provide the necessary power when a mains failure occurs. It's possible to have relatively cheap battery backup which would allow you to save the data in the event of a failure of power, or relatively expensive uninterruptible power supplies which effectively means having your own power station hooked up to your micro, mini or mainframe. Obviously the more expensive systems are used in places like hospitals where emergency generators would automatically cut in if a mains failure were detected. A big battery is usually needed to provide the power between the generators coming on line and the actual failure of the mains, but this time can be simply a matter of seconds.

ROM

Some programs, such as those parts of the **operating system** (see page 390) which start up the machine *must not be lost* even when the power to the system has been removed for extended periods of time. A special chip called a **ROM (Read Only Memory)** is ideal for this purpose as it is non-volatile. However, its contents have to be programmed by the manufacturer of the chips and they *can't be changed*. Brave operating system designers often commit their operating systems to a ROM chip as this saves having to load the operating system from disk each time the machine is switched on. However, as you will appreciate by reading chapter 17, no operating system is ever bug free, and this means that software patches (bug fixes) would have to be loaded from disk until a new version of the operating system is available on ROM.

ROM-based operating systems are ideal for portable computers as the amount of power saved by not having to load the operating system from disk is considerable. It is also very convenient on desk-top versions too, especially if the operating system is working well. Operating systems are also quite large, and the saving in RAM by having the operating system ROM is also a considerable benefit.

Languages too are sometimes committed to ROM, especially BASIC in some of the educational microcomputers. However, any software could be stored in this way and the term used to denote the fact that the **software** is *permanently and unalterably embedded* in the ROM chip is called **firmware**. This is to distinguish from the terms **hardware** and **software** which have been defined elsewhere in this book. A rather cheeky term is to refer to the people who operate the computers as **liveware**!

One philosophical point to bear in mind here is that **ROM is also RAM**! This is because the *definition* of RAM refers to the access times to retrieve any data and not to its volatility or otherwise. **ROM is random access too**. Nevertheless, people have lived with this definition for years, and the only people to suffer are the students trying to understand the system!

One final point about ROM is that it's not used only in computers, but is extensively used in **embedded microprocessors** and **control systems** such as those found in a variety of equipment from cruise missiles to the control of domestic microwave ovens. These aspects of ROM are covered in the chapter on computer control systems (see page 585).

PROM

It's a nuisance having to get the manufacturers to program the chips for you, especially if you are ordering less than a few thousands chips as the price per chip becomes prohibitive. Therefore, developers wanted a way to test out read-only chips without having to manufacture fully-blown ROMS. The answer to their prayers was the **PROM** or **Programmable Read Only Memory**. A special machine can be used to program the ROM, and this is a considerably cheaper option than getting the chip manufacturers to build up a special mask – which is a necessary and expensive stage during the programming of a ROM. Once the PROM has been programmed it behaves in an identical way to the ROM. However, unlike the ROM where a mask is produced, PROMs are not suitable for mass-production methods.

EPROM

Although **PROM**s are better suited to development work, if a mistake is made then the chips have to be thrown away. A better method for development would be to have a system where the contents could be erased and the chip could be programmed again from scratch if necessary. This is indeed what can be done when using an **EPROM**. A very cost effective machine can program the system, usually under the control of a standard microcomputer. However, if the contents are to be erased then UV (ultra-violet light) is shone through a special window in the top of the chip, and after a few minutes the contents are erased. Because daylight contains UV radiation, after programming an EPROM the window must be covered up or the data could be erased in a relatively short space of time.

EPROMs are not as permanent as ROMs or PROMS, and the data would be lost after a number of years even if the window is covered up. About ten years is the current norm and this is obviously not usually a problem, as the computer designed to take the EPROM has probably been superseded by the next fifteen generations of machines – nevertheless, if permanent data storage is required, then an EPROM would not be suitable for the job.

RAM, ROM and EPROM, when plumbed into the architecture of a computer system behave as if they are all RAM. (Which they are!) The only difference being that you can't alter the contents of the ROMs under the control of the computer. It is usual to have a memory map of the system which shows how the memory is allocated to the operating system software and user programs. Memory maps are extensively covered in the operating systems chapter on page 392, and so here we will concentrate on how data stored inside the memory chips relates to something useful.

ASCII code

The need to communicate information from one computer system to another is of paramount importance. Therefore, a common code used on all systems is needed if any sense is to be made of the masses of binary digits inside a computer's main memory. The **ASCII code** was developed for this purpose and is an acronym for the **American Standard Code for Information Interchange**. Being a code for communications as well as data representation, the ASCII code is made up not just of letters of the alphabet and numbers etc. but of simple **communications protocols** such as ACK (acknowledge) and ENQ (enquiry). Figure 13.3 shows the ASCII character set and is an invaluable reference for trying to decode the contents of memory or disks by hand. (Nevertheless, most sane people would probably make use of a memory or disk-sector editor which does the decoding automatically.)

ASCII code table

Basic ASCII Character codes for IBM and Compatibles (All codes 0 to 127 are shown.)

000 Null	001 SOH	002 STX	003 ETX	004 EOT	005 ENQ	006 ACK	007 BEL	008 BS	009 HT
010 LF	011 VT	012 FF	013 CR	014 SO	015 SI	016 DLE	017 DC1	018 DC2	019 DC3
020 DC4	021 NAK	022 SYN	023 ETB	024 CAN	025 EM	026 SUB	027 ESC	028 FS	029 GS
030 RS	031 US	032 SP	033 !	034 "	035 #	036 $	037 %	038 &	039 '
040 (	041)	042 *	043 +	044 ,	045 -	046 .	047 /	048 0	049 1
050 2	051 3	052 4	053 5	054 6	055 7	056 8	057 9	058 :	059 ;
060 <	061 =	062 >	063 ?	064 @	065 A	066 B	067 C	068 D	069 E
070 F	071 G	072 H	073 I	074 J	075 K	076 L	077 M	078 N	079 O
080 P	081 Q	082 R	083 S	084 T	085 U	086 V	087 W	088 X	089 Y
090 Z	091 [	092 \	093]	094 ^	095 _	096 `	097 a	098 b	099 c
100 d	101 e	102 f	103 g	014 h	105 i	106 j	107 k	108 l	109 m
110 n	111 o	112 p	113 q	114 r	115 s	116 t	117 u	118 v	119 w
120 x	121 y	122 z	123 {	124 |	125 }	126 ~	127 ■		

Extended ASCII Character codes for IBM and Compatibles (Only codes 128 to 169 are shown.)

								128 Ç	129 ü
130 é	131 â	132 ä	133 à	134 å	135 ç	136 ê	137 ë	138 è	139 ï
140 î	141 ì	142 Ä	143 Å	144 É	145 æ	146 Æ	147 ô	148 ö	149 ò
150 û	151 ù	152 ÿ	153 Ö	154 Ü	155 ¢	156 £	157 ¥	158 fi	159 fl
160 ó	161 í	162 ó	163 ú	164 ñ	165 Ñ	167 ª	167 º	168 ¿	169 ⌐

Figure 13.3

Extended ASCII

In the early computer systems the ASCII code consisted of just 128 characters as shown at the top of figure 13.3. This is because the 8th bit was used for **parity checking** (see page 511). However, when being used inside computers, parity was not really necessary and the top bit in the byte was wasted. It was a good idea to make use of this top bit, thus releasing a further 128 characters giving a total of 256 overall. This has led to what is now known as the **Extended ASCII** character set.

ASCII data in memory

The early micros using just 8-bits for the data bus and memory organisation had a very tidy relationship with the ASCII code. Each address in memory stored just a single character. However, as the address bus grew larger, memory became organised in 16-bit and 32-bit chunks. This means that more than a single byte can now be stored in an individual memory location, with 4 bytes being possible on a 32-bit system or 8 bytes on a 64-bit system etc. However, the memory addresses are often byte-oriented, even in multiple-byte systems, and the habit of referring to the memory in byte-sized chunks has remained to this day in most microcomputer-based machines. On large mainframes and minis the situation is often different.

Secondary storage techniques

Although speed is still a very important criterion, the main objectives when dealing with secondary storage are **data integrity** and **mass storage capability** coupled with **low cost**. **Auxiliary** or **backing store** are *alternative names* for **secondary storage**. Magnetic media such as **disks** and **tapes** have ruled supreme for the last twenty years, but are now being seriously challenged by the new writable **optical** and **magneto-optical** technologies. However, we will deal with magnetic technologies first, as these will still be around for some considerable time to come.

Direct and sequential access

Secondary storage techniques can be split into two broad categories. The first relates to **direct-access** storage techniques. This refers to the ability to go to the data you wish to access *without* having to read through all previous data. The second is **sequential-access** storage techniques where all previous data has to be gone through in sequence until you get to the item of interest. The most common form of **sequential-access** media is obviously magnetic tape. It's *important to distinguish between* **direct** and **sequential-access devices**, as the *characteristics* of each device give rise to very different methods of **data processing**, as can be seen from handling **data structures** called **files** which are covered in chapter 16.

Floppy disks

These are the smallest of magnetic disks and have become the norm for use on microcomputer systems and for software distribution. However, in the next few years the software distribution stakes are likely to see a considerable challenge from the CD-ROM based systems which allow you to try before you buy (see page 273). The early floppy disks were 8 inch or 5¼ inch, and stored a relatively low volume of data. The latest 3½ inch disks have now gone through several stages of meta-

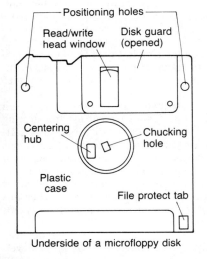

Underside of a microfloppy disk

(a)

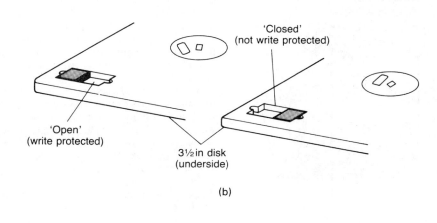

(b)

Figure 13.4

morphosis to get to the current state of 1.4 Mbytes or up to 4 Mbytes depending on the type of drive. The earlier versions of floppy disks were single sided, but today's versions are invariably double sided, meaning that two head assemblies are needed – one for the top surface and one for the bottom surface of the disk. Nevertheless, the principles of data storage on these magnetic disks are essentially the same, with the disk surface having to be **formatted** into **tracks** and **sectors** (see in a moment).

A typical 3½ inch disk is shown in figure 13.4, and the write-protect tabs prevent data from being accidentally overwritten by inadvertent use of the disk. Floppy disks rotate at about 360 r.p.m. and, unlike the hard disks in the next section, the read/write heads (see figure 13.4) are in constant contact with the surface of the disk whenever data is being written to or read from the disk – hence a floppy disk will only revolve in the drive during a read or write operation.

Speed of operation

When data is stored on the disk it must be in a form such that a computer can identify where the data is, and be able to retrieve it quickly. Obviously, being a mechanical system, the longest retrieval time would be governed by a single rotation of the disk such that the desired data is underneath the head (see figure 13.4). If a rotational speed of 360 r.p.m. is typical, (6 revs/sec) then 1/6th sec or about 170 msec would be the worst time needed to find the data, assuming that the head could move in and out to the appropriate part of the disk in time. The average time (called rotational latency) is obviously half this, and this is what is inevitably used to determine the final figure in the sales literature. The actual time would obviously be a combination of the rotational latency, the seek time (moving the head to the data), the settling time (the head getting its act together) and the read/write time (the time taken for the data transfer to take place). Needless to say this is slow compared to the more-expensive forms of secondary storage.

Disk formats

If a computer is to be able to find the data stored on the magnetic surface of a floppy, then some sort of recognizable pattern to the stored data is needed. This pattern is made up of concentric circles called **tracks**, which are then further subdivided into many parts called **sectors**. The process of putting these tracks and sectors onto the disk, along with other vital information is called **formatting**, and is explained in more detail on page 270 when large-disk systems are being considered.

High-density disks

Most floppy disks have 80 tracks, with a density of about 96 tracks per linear inch of the surface (going from the outside to the middle), but the amount of data which can be stored on a typical disk has increased over the years. For example, if you double the rate at which the data is written to the disk for a given disk speed, then you have doubled the amount of data which can be stored on that disk. However, the area on the surface of the disk which represents a binary digit has halved, and therefore the surface of the disk needs to be of a higher quality. Such techniques are known as **double-density**, although **quad-density** disks are now available.

Wither the floppy disk?!

Apart from an increase in the quality of disks that are needed, another disadvantage in the quest for ever-higher storage capacity is the generation of multiple standards. Obviously the lower-density disk drives will not be able to read data from the high-density floppies. We have therefore created a vast range of different disk-formatting standards, and this says nothing of the different number of operating-system standards too. It all makes converting even the simplest data from one system to another a nightmare. It has been known for users to log onto a remote mainframe computer simply to transfer data between two different microcomputer systems!

A couple of Mbytes is no longer regarded as adequate secondary storage – even for small microcomputer systems. Nevertheless, floppies are useful for transferring small amounts of data between compatible systems, and for the distribution of software. It is not unusual today to purchase software distributed on several (sometimes many) floppy disks, together with a utility to install the system onto your local hard disk or network. With the increasing use of graphics and high-quality images, the long-term future of the floppy is probably not very bright – for example, a full colour 24-bit high-resolution image could easily munch up 16 Mbytes of memory. Thus this single image would not be able to be transferred between two compatible systems on the current generation of highest-density floppies.

Winchester disk technology

Winchester disk drives or **Winnies**, as they are affectionately known, were developed by IBM as an alternative to the large disk drives and packs (see page 270) used on mainframe computers. These small hard-disk drives have revolutionised the

Figure 13.5

microcomputer industry since they first appeared in the early 1980s. The magnetic surface of the disk is no longer floppy (as was the case with floppy disks), but is now contained on a rigid disk, or more likely a stack of rigid disks as shown in figure 13.5.

The mechanics of Winnies are much more precise than inside the humble floppy – hence the extra expense. The surface of the disk drive is housed in a hermetically sealed unit (which keeps out all the dust, grit, tomato sauce, biscuit crumbs and smoke particles etc.) and this enables the tracks to be much closer together and a higher recording density to be used. The disk rotates continually (even when data is not being written to or read from the disk), and the read/write heads float on the surface of the disk due to the Bernoulli effect. This is not an illness, but the lift caused by the aerodynamic effect of the rotational speed and the proximity of the head to the surface of the disk. A parking area is usually provided for the heads when no read/write activity is taking place.

The rotational speed of a Winnie is typically 10 times that of a floppy and is thus about 3,600 r.p.m. Regardless of the increased packing density, a ten-fold increase in data retrieval rate is obtained just by rotational speed alone.

The early small hard disks had modest capacities of about 5 Mbytes, but today's 'small' hard disks have typically a few hundred Mbytes, with the most recent having capacities in excess of 1 Gbyte. This is adequate for the current range of micro-computers, especially when you consider that you can have a good number of different drives simultaneously on line. The size of these hard drives has been reduced considerably from 14 inch in their original generation, to the current generation of ¼-height 3½ inch disks which fit snugly inside portables, and are capable of storing several hundred Megabytes of data.

Typical access speeds for the current generation of small hard disks is a little less than 20 msec, and a data-transfer rate of about 5 Mbits/sec is common. The total capacity of a disk will obviously relate to the total number of surfaces, the number of tracks/surface, the number of sectors/track and the number of bytes/sector.

Disk array systems

Hard disks *will* eventually crash. Therefore, even if you are careful, you will lose the hundreds of Mbytes of precious data on your hard disk sooner or later – hopefully later! Good backup procedures will hopefully mean that you have not actually lost your data, but there is an inconvenient period during which you have to replace the useless hard disk with a new one, and replace the data, perhaps via a network link or a tape streamer. It would be nice if the system could be made to carry on regardless (well almost) during a hard-disk crash, and often a second drive with a mirror-image of the original can be switched over immediately in the event of such an unfortunate occurrence. Such a system is known as a **drive array**, and the acronym **RAID** has been coined by some people which stands for **Redundant Array of Inexpensive Drives**! This is because, when used in this particular configuration, there is no advantage to having the second drive (i.e. it's effectively redundant) until a catastrophe occurs. RAID systems are usually accompanied by software which gives you the option of using them automatically in the event of a drive failure as described above, or using the two (or more) drives as a file-server configuration on a network. RAID systems for network file-server and drive-failure fail-safe applications typically have total storage capacity in excess of 100 Gbytes. No doubt we will see Tbyte systems in the very near future.

Large hard-disk systems

We will now concentrate on the very large hard disk systems which are the bastion of **secondary storage** for **mainframe computer systems**. The Winchester disk drive systems were developed from these larger hard-disk drives now being discussed, and many of these principles can be applied to the Winchester disks on a smaller scale.

Disk packs

A **hard-disk pack** is an *assembly of hard disk surfaces* (called **platters**) which can be *removed* from a large **hard disk drive**. Figure 13.6 shows a typical disk-pack assembly in which 6 platters (disks) are used to create 10 useable surfaces onto which data can be recorded. (The very top and very bottom surfaces are not used.)

As with the Winchester drives considered earlier, the disks rotate at about 3,600 r.p.m. and the heads float on the surface of the disks due to the Bernoulli effect (see page 269). However, unlike the Winchester drives which park the heads on an unused part of the surface of the disk when the disk is not in use, the head assemblies on the large hard-disk systems usually completely remove themselves from the disk surface. This allows these disk packs to be interchangeable with others. This versatility also makes this type of machine expensive, because disks prepared on one machine have to work with all the others, whereas a Winchester drive can't be removed from its own hermetically-sealed enclosure.

A modern disk pack, as shown in figure 13.6, has about **200 tracks** *per* inch (measured from inside to out) of **recordable surface**, but only the inner and outer-most tracks have been shown in the diagram for the purposes of clarity.

Disk-pack arrangement showing how a cylinder is generated

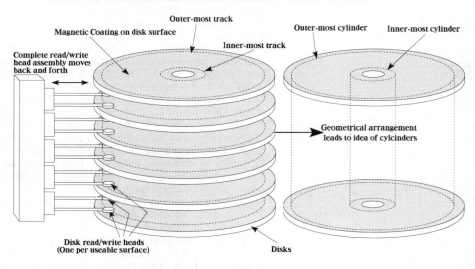

Figure 13.6

It's most important to note that the *entire head assembly can move in and out, thus causing all the heads to move in and out at the same time*. This naturally leads to a fundamental data storage idea associated with disks which is called a **cylinder**. For the case of the **six pack** (nothing to do with beer, unfortunately!) shown in figure 13.6, there would be **about 200 cylinders**, where *each cylinder* consists of **10 tracks**, because there are ten heads. Disk packs on large mainframe installations have about 11 disks per pack giving about 20 usable surfaces.

The diameter of a large disk surface is about 14 inches. Now assuming that the hole in the middle takes away a couple of inches, and assuming that the extreme outer and inner edges of the disk can't be used, you end up with about 11 inches of useable surface, or about $(11 \times 200) = 2,200$ tracks per surface. If you have an 11-disk pack, then this would be equivalent to 20 useable surfaces which gives us **44,000 tracks** in the disk pack.

Figure 13.7 shows a single useable surface of a disk pack as viewed from the top. A single track has been shown which contains 256 sectors. The sectors making up each track are separated by small gaps as shown in the right-hand side of the diagram.

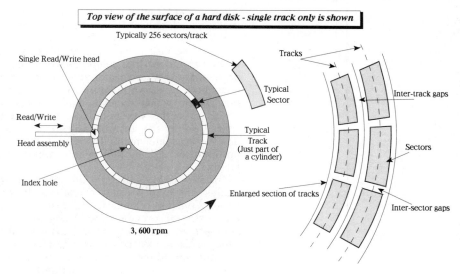

Figure 13.7

Assuming for the sake of argument that our disk pack can store 512 bytes/sector, then for 44,000-track system described in the last paragraph, the disk would hold $512 \times 256 \times 512$ which gives us 5,767,168,000 or about **5 Gbytes** per pack.

The exchangeable disk pack described above is just one of a variety of formats for large hard disks, but, in general the principles of storage are all very similar. Some disk drives, like the Winchesters described earlier are fixed in the machine and therefore can't be removed. These fixed-disk machines, being sealed, can often work to much finer tolerances, and can therefore store more data than the removable disk packs mentioned in the last paragraph.

Alternative head arrangements are possible, and some very expensive drives have one read/write head per track so that the head assembly does not have to move at all. These are called fixed-head disks and the access times are extremely fast. You don't have to wait for the heads to move in or out to the right cylinder, it's simply a matter of waiting for just the right moment when the disk position is such that the correct sector is underneath the head. At 3,600 r.p.m., the average access time for this particular disk would therefore be about 3.3 msec (the time taken for half a revolution to take place). Other disk drives, where the heads have to move to the right track have access time in the order of 20 to 30 msec.

Other types of disk unit

Sometimes you will get just a *single* **disk platter** inside a suitable container which fits into the disk machine. Obviously the top and bottom surfaces *are* the only ones available and are therefore used for recording data in this case. These particular disks are called **disk cartridges**, and are available on both large and small systems.

Making sense of the stored data

The **concentric-circular-track** arrangement as outlined above is the *most* obvious, but a **single spiral track system** is an alternative method that's used in **optical drives** (see page 272). The concentric-track arrangement is used on *all* **hard** and **floppy-disk formats**, and so any data that is stored on the disk can be directly accessed by knowing the address of the track (track number) and the address of the sector (subdivision of a track as shown in figure 13.7). If the arrangement has multiple surfaces, then a cylinder number, surface number and sector number arrangement is used instead – as track-number alone would *not* be enough to uniquely identify any specific data on a multi-platter system.

As a magnetic disk drive is a **constant speed device**, (3,600 r.p.m. for a Winchester, for example), astute readers will have noticed that the track length on the outside of a disk is considerably longer then the track length on the inside of the disk, but there are the *same number* of sectors in a track. As with floppies, the packing density of the data is therefore varied so that the inner-most tracks have the bytes packed much more densely than the outer tracks. This is indeed wasteful of space on the outer edges, but it makes the system considerably simpler to operate because each sector, regardless of its position on the disk, is always under the head for the same length of time, and hence the data transfer rate is constant regardless of the sector's position. As the disk rotates with constant speed the data transfer rates at the outer edges would be much greater if this variable-packing-density system were not to be used. Indeed, on CD-ROMs, the data packing density *is* the same and the rotational speed of the CD is varied to compensate.

While the disk is whizzing round it's obvious that *some form of* **identification** is needed to instruct the computer where the **beginning of a track** or **cylinder** is – we need to know where sector zero begins on each track, for example. Sometimes, an index hole, as shown in figure 13.7 is used, together with an electronic optical-detection system which shines a light through the hole. This physical marking of the boundary in this way is called a **hard sector**. In other systems, the operations are carried out by the software which electronically puts an ID onto the surface of the disk – if this later method is used it is called **soft sectoring**. These ID numbers are put onto the disk by the program which carries out the **formatting** (see next paragraph).

The *process* of setting up the disk such that the **tracks**, **sectors** and **IDs** etc are ready to be used is called **formatting**. It is also the job of the formatting program to map out any damaged areas of the disk's surface that may be found during this setting up process. After being formatted the disk will contain its **cylinder** (if appropriate) or **track** numbers, **sector** numbers and **control data** (see in a moment) which helps the system to be able to **read** and **write** files on the disk.

Extra **control data** is usually recorded onto the surface of the disk which is used only by the disk-drive-interface controller, and refers to the ways in which the formatting of the tracks and sectors etc are mapped onto the system – for example, the number of sectors per track and the number of bytes per sector etc. This information, together with the track and sector numbers mentioned above, enables the operating-system software to be able to locate data items on the disk **randomly** – being able to do this opens up many extra possibilities for file handling over and above those available for serially-based systems (see page 352).

The *minimum amount of data* that can be **read from** or **written to** a disk at any one time is a **sector**. Even if just a single byte of data were to be altered, the complete sector containing that data would need to be rewritten. This is because there are **CRCs** (see page 512) made on the data to ensure its integrity. If small amounts of information such as logical records which have a number of bytes much smaller than the physical sector size being used on the disk are being used, then **blocking** (in ways identical to that of tape) helps to make sure that less physical space is wasted on the disk in these circumstances.

Larger chunks of data, much larger for example, than a single sector on disk, need to be 'glued' together to form a larger unit which is called a **cluster**. Therefore, to store a file of data as a cluster, we would have to know about which tracks and sectors etc are **allocated** to the **files**. A **map** of this information can be stored on the disk along with all the other data, and this is usually referred to as a **File Allocation Table** or **FAT**. To cut a long story short, the ideas are very similar to the **linked-list data structures** covered in chapter 14. The file allocation table helps us to form the hierarchical directory structure shown on page 489. The FAT is covered in more detail in the operating-system chapter on page 391.

You now know a considerable amount about how data is stored magnetically onto a disk. In general the drives are getting smaller, the access times are getting shorter, and the price of the drives is getting cheaper. The 4 Gbyte storage capacity and 10 msec access times available on some top-of-the-range Winchester drives in 1995 far outstrip the large hard disk drives which were available on mainframe computers during the 1980s. However, optical disk technology, to be covered in the next section, is beginning to make a huge impact too.

Optical drives

Drastic price reductions in the last few years have made CD-ROM drives common, and with tens of thousands of CD-ROM titles available during the early 1990s, (there is even a CD-ROM of CD-ROMs!) the CD-ROM drives and magneto-optical drives (see page 274) look set to dominate the computer industry for some considerable time. It's not hard to see why – low cost, superior quality, robustness and greater storage capacity, plus the ability to store conventional audio and video images as well, all conspire to make these secondary-storage devices the serious **multimedia** (**audio** + **video** + **computer data**) contender for the foreseeable future.

Although the mechanism for reading data from a CD-ROM drive is very different from reading data on a magnetic disk, the track is still split up into sectors. The word track here is correct because, unlike conventional magnetic disk drives, *a single track*

spirals from the outside of the CD to the inside. The *speed* of the CD-ROM drive is *varied* to compensate for the different rates at which the head would be moving past each sector, and thus each sector can have the same packing density. This should be compared with the methods used for conventional magnetic disks where the speed of the drive is kept constant but the packing density varies (see page 271).

A conventional CD has the equivalent of about 600 tracks per linear inch of disk surface (from the outside to the middle – but don't forget that it's actually a single track!), and at current recording densities this single spiral track can store about 600 Mbytes, which is equivalent to several hundred thousand pages of textual information. A typical CD-ROM disc is about 12 cm in diameter and made out of a poly-carbonate material onto which a fine coating of aluminium has been deposited. A **LASER** beam (**L**ight **A**mplification by the **S**timulated **E**mission of **R**adiation) is used to detect the presence or absence of pits which have been burned into this surface at the writing stage by a more-powerful laser used by the manufacturer. **Mini-format** (8 cm) **CDs** have been developed too, and these are currently being put into some portable computers.

Reading data from a CD-ROM

To read data from the surface of a disk requires revolving the disk and reflecting a laser beam off the surface as shown in figure 13.8. Figure 13.8 is obviously a simpli-fied diagram as any physicist carefully checking the optical paths taken by the laser beam will be able to tell! However, it does illustrate, in principle, exactly what's going on. Laser light, produced by a laser diode is reflected off the reflective material on the underside of the CD-ROM disc. When the *original* CD master was being recorded (i.e. *not* the system shown in figure 13.8) a laser beam is switched on and off very rapidly by the electronics which is acting as a modulator. If the laser beam is on – it burns away the surface and what's called a pit is produced (as viewed from the top), or if the laser is switched off – then no pit is produced, and this is called land! Therefore, the surface of the disc is made up of a single spiral track of **lands** and **pits** which represent the binary digits being recorded, a protective layer is then used to coat the disc.

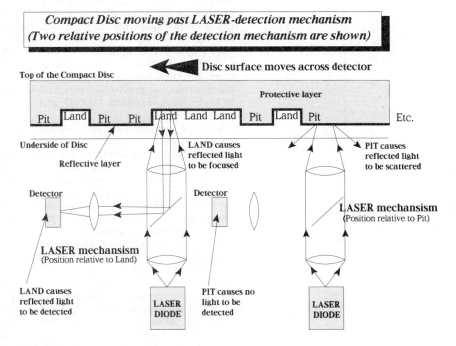

Figure 13.8

A lower-power laser in the CD-ROM machine on your computer at home then shines laser light at the land and pits *from the underside of the disc* as the track on the disc is being moved over the detector. If **land is encountered**, then *the system causes the beam to be focused onto a light detector*, which in turn can produce a suitable electrical signal. If, however, a pit is encountered by the same beam at some later stage (as shown on the *right* in figure 13.8), then the geometry and polarisation characteristics of the materials and reflectors being used cause the beam to scatter, instead of being focused as before. Therefore, in **the case of a pit**, *no reflected light is picked up by the detector*, and hence no electrical signal is produced. In this way the binary digits represented by the constantly-changing patterns on the underside of the CD are turned into binary digits.

Some students at this stage may well be attempting to guess whether a land or a pit represents a binary one or a zero – in fact it's neither! Even worse – it's the length of the pits which are important and a **binary one** is actually represented by a *transition* **from a land to a pit** OR the *transition* from a **pit to a land**. (That's not a typing error!) The actual coding methods employed are quite complex (this is an understatement!) due to the error checking routines that are built in to increase reliability, but needless to say groups of binary digits can be extracted from the system once the data has been decoded.

The first-generation CD-ROM based systems used the drive technology found in a conventional compact disc player. However, the speed of data retrieval (although quite adequate for audio playback) was too slow for the extraction of computer data (mainly high-res graphics), and so faster drives with up to four times the conventional speed have considerably improved this situation. A Quadraspin drive in 1994, for example, would have a typical data-transfer rate of 614 kbytes/sec, which is a considerable improvement over the standard CD-ROM drives which have transfer rates of only 150 kbytes/sec – to do this it spins at a speed of 2120 r.p.m. However, this is still considerably less than the data-transfer rates obtainable from Winnies. Another problem stems from the single continuous spiral track – it's great for a high storage density, but the access time is obviously going to be slower than for magnetic disk. This indeed proves to be the case, where access times are typically between 200 and 400 msec.

A typical CD can store about 600 Mbytes of information, but due to the complex encoding methods mentioned earlier, not all of this space is available for user data. Although it sounds like a lot – it's relatively small for a vast number of moving coloured images of the sort needed to display a 2 or 3 hour video movie. IBM are currently developing a system using a much more expensive **blue laser light** than the conventional cheap **red laser light** used at the moment. The wavelength of blue laser light is about half of that for red, and thus an area about one quarter of that needed for the red laser light is actually used. This means that four times the quantity of data can be stored on a blue-laser CD-ROM drive. In fact IBM have actually increased this to five times normal making use of some additional techniques. This means that a massive 3 Gbytes of data may be stored on later generations of CD-ROM drives making use of blue laser light. Even so, the **HDCD (High Density Compact Disc)** has been released, and this, using conventional red lasers with better mechanisms, has produced a much higher storage density of 3.7 Gbytes, and conforms to Gold Book standard. HDCD and blue lasers will push this limit much further to over 20 Gbytes.

Current systems have also involved the heavy use of **compression techniques** to apparently pack yet more data onto the disc. Indeed, compression techniques are being used extensively not only on optical drives, but also on conventional floppy and hard-disk drives as well, *and* in the transmission of computer data over networks and conventional telephone lines. Some of the ideas of compression, especially where pictorial information is being considered, are quite simple. For example, instead of sending the absolute values for each pixel in a picture, we send only information regarding *change* that has occurred. Therefore, if we are transmitting a picture of a beach on a beautiful summer's day, then if the sky is the same-colour blue all over, then only a few bytes are needed to code the fact that the information is identical for large parts of the picture.

In trying to compress strings of textual information, we can often apply compression techniques too by analysing patterns and replacing chunks of text with tokens which represent larger strings. For example, the larger spacing between the paragraphs on this page require a few hundred ASCII characters – a wasteful one character representing each space. This could, for example, be compressed by sending a single 'space character' followed by a number which represents how many spaces are present. Decompression routines would then analyse the compressed text and expand it so that normal software such as a word processor or DTP system could interpret it properly. Other, more sophisticated compression techniques are covered on page 563.

Magneto-optical disks

As the unlucky ones amongst you who have placed your disks on top of hi-fi speakers will know only too well – the data on ordinary floppies and removable hard disks can be destroyed by external magnetic fields at room temperature. If, instead of using conventional ferrite-based materials for storing the magnetic patterns on the surface of a disk, special alloys are used in which the crystals contained inside the alloy can be altered by a magnetic field *only if* they are heated up to a suitable temperature, then you have a system which is far less susceptible to external magnetic fields.

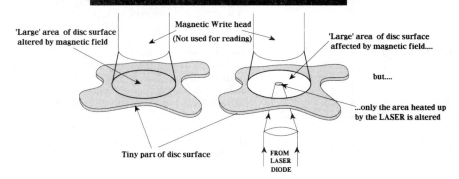

Figure 13.9

Now if a laser beam is used to produce the required heating effect then a very small area, represented by the tiny dot of laser light on the disk surface, can be altered by a conventional magnetic head as shown in fig 13.9. This area is far smaller than the area which would have been affected by the same magnetic head on a conventionally-based ferrite magnetic disk surface. As the area affected is much smaller, a greater packing density can be achieved if this method of altering the crystals is used. Indeed, several hundred Megabytes can be fitted onto a conventional-sized 3½ inch disk, compared to just a few Megabytes using the ferrite-based technologies described in the last few sections.

The crystals on the surface of this type of disk would normally be distributed at random, but when a laser beam heats up a local part of the disk past the critical temperature (known as the Curie point) then the crystals can be lined up easily if they are placed in a suitable field produced by a conventional magnetic head. When the local area of the disk is cooled then the crystals in the altered area remain in alignment, and can thus be used to represent a bit of information. Different alignment directions are used to represent a binary 1 or 0.

To read back the data from this disk a laser beam of less intensity (otherwise the data will be destroyed!) is reflected from the surface of the disk . Where no data is stored the light will be reflected at random because the crystals in the special alloy are randomly distributed, but where a laser beam and magnetic head has previously altered the surface of the disk, a special light-detecting sensor can pick up the light which is reflected from the aligned crystals. Polarisation is used to determine the difference between a binary 1 and 0.

These devices are called **magneto-optical drives** because **optical** (laser beams and light sensor) and **magnetic** (the magnetic write head) methods have been used to produce the data patterns on the surface of the disk. Purely optical methods (a laser beam reflected from the disk and picked up by a light sensor) are used to read the data. The speed of writing and reading data on a typical magneto-optical drive at the time of writing is very similar to standard Winchester times, thus turning in a performance of about 10 to 20 msec. The storage capacity is also comparable to that of the largest Winnies, and drives of a few Gbytes are easily obtainable. However, when the expected 5Gbyte, 10Gbyte and larger drives become available in bulk, CD may begin to lose its position as the cheapest mass-storage device per megabyte available on most systems. **Magneto-optical drives** tend to be of the *removable* **disk-cartridge** type, although *much smaller versions*, comparable in size with the 3½ inch floppies (and in almost identical containers) are called **floptical disks**.

WORMs

This is nothing to do with the species of underground **WORM** – but an acronym for **Write Once Read Many** times. Standard CD-ROMs are obviously read-only devices, but one type of CD is manufactured in which a gold reflective layer is placed under opaque dye. A special drive is needed which carries out the actual recording by making use of lower-power lasers, but get it right first time – as you can't alter the disk once it has been written to. These systems are obviously ideal for long-term backups of important data which are never likely to change. Various formats are supported, and the cost-effective nature in terms of cost per byte of data storage is second to none. However, the original cost of the recorder is about 20 times that of a conventional CD-ROM drive.

Multiple CD standards

How do you decide between **CD, CD-DA, Photo CD, CD-I, CD-R** or **CD-ROM-XA** etc? – all are variations on how data can be stored and/or used on a Compact Disc! A brief explanation of each now follows, but no doubt other standards will appear in the future. Originally, Philips, Sony and Microsoft all agreed on what's called the **High-Sierra** standard for CDs, and this was further split up into a number of **coloured books** all dealing with different standards. Some examples now follow.

CD or CD-DA

This is an easy one – the original **CD (Compact Disc)** is a 4¾ inch disk developed by Philips during the early 1980s. Although designed originally for audio, other information such as text is stored on this type of disc. (If it were not you would not be able to get a clever CD player to display the title of your favourite album!) You will also see the term **CD-DA** which refers to **Compact Disc Digital Audio**, an alternative name to distinguish the conventional audio-based CDs from the variety of CDs such as those listed below. CD-DAs can store just over 72 min. of audio sound track for hi-fi reproduction. This standard is known as the **Red Book** of the High Sierra standard.

CD-ROM

CD-ROM is the technology developed specifically for use by computers. A special standard defined by the International Standards Organisation called ISO 9660 shows how data is to be stored on this type of disc, and is a standard which has been generally accepted by many different manufacturers. This is the basic format used by the majority of CDs which distribute information in forms such as encyclopaedias and databases etc. The current standard for CD-ROMs is known as the **Yellow Book**.

CD-I

CD-I stands for Compact Disc Interactive. It is designed to enable text, audio and video to be processed and displayed on a normal TV screen. It has its own embedded-microprocessor system inside the CD-I box, which includes a special operating system. The current standard for CD-I is known as the **Green Book**.

Photo CD

Photo CD is yet another system, developed by Kodak, which supports the transfer of photos or slides etc. onto CD. This is a stunning way to view your photographs if you have a high-resolution monitor, and also allows you to transfer the images to disk, and hence to process them in any way that you wish. Indeed, this is one way of storing personalised photos for inclusion in DTP and art-package systems. Some systems which read conventional CD-ROMs are Photo-CD compatible.

CD-ROM-XA

The **CD-ROM-XA** has been designed to take advantage of the **Memory eXtended Architecture** of the **PC**. It enables text, audio and video to be used simultaneously. This is an *extension* of the **Yellow-Book** standard.

CD-R

This stands for **Compact Disc Recorder**, and enables the user to **record** on **CD-ROM**. This allows the user to master a CD-ROM or create backups for large amounts of data. The formats of recording vary, and can use many of the techniques listed above.

MPC

Special **Multimedia CDs** – called **MPCs (Multimedia Personal Computer)** are now available, this is not referring to a CD standard as such, but to the type of computer needed to run the system. These run on **PCs** which have been upgraded to multimedia standard. *These systems are covered in greater detail in the multimedia section in chapter 24 on further-applications.*

Disk-cache systems

Before going on to study serial and sequential methods of access, we pause for a brief period to look at a method of making the disk access appear to be faster. Throughout the last few sections of this book you have been constantly bombarded with data regarding disk-access time. Impressive though these figures might sound, the fastest drives available hitherto will still need a few msec to access any data and load it into your computer. Hopefully, you will recall that the data for the RAM-based memory systems nearer the beginning of the chapter had typical access speeds in the order of a few nsec. Therefore, even the fastest access drives currently available are around 1,000,000 times slower than RAM. Therefore, a bright idea is to take a slice of the data on disk, (the larger the better), load it into some convenient RAM, then fool the applications into thinking that data is obtained from a super-high speed disk. This is the idea behind a **disk cache** system.

Now this sounds all very well in theory, but there are problems – the main one being how do you know which areas of the disk are likely to be the ones which are needed next? Nevertheless, good guesses can be made, based on assumptions such as assuming that the data near to the data being accessed is the next data that is

needed. Implementation of such a system is obviously similar in practice to the idea of virtual memory systems covered in page 381. However, this time, instead of disk pretending to be memory, memory is pretending to be disk! Although the system may sound a bit hit and miss, in practice astonishing increases in performance can be obtained because most data *is* actually close to the data which is currently being accessed. Disk drives are now also being manufactured with their own **on-board cache** to save having to use up any of the RAM inside your computer system.

Whenever the term cache is being used it always implies that things are being speeded up in some particular way by the use of faster memory elements, but the differences can be a little confusing. For example, on page 393 we have seen how the much-faster SRAM memory is used instead of DRAM memory to act as an interface between the CPU and DRAM. All or parts of programs currently being used by the CPU can be cached and run at higher speed, thus giving an increased performance. Indeed, many modern CPUs now have some on-board cache (i.e. inside the chip itself) to speed up things even further. Under these conditions we are increasing the memory speed by making use of the fastest RAM available. However, when disk cache is being considered, there's not much point using SRAM, as even relatively-slow DRAM is faster than the typical access speeds by several thousand times. Any old memory will therefore do for disk cache, but only the fastest and most expensive memory will do for the much higher speed memory cache.

Serial and sequential access techniques

Serial and sequential-access storage techniques are *not* dead. They are still used *extensively* for **batch processing** on **mainframes** and **minis**, (see page 371), and are also used *extensively* for **backup purposes** on **microcomputers**. Also, as can be seen when carrying out the work with files covered in chapter 16, many techniques developed from tape-based machines are often used today on *direct-access media* such as disks as well. We will, therefore, first take a look at the *large* tape machines as used on mainframe computer systems.

Basic principles of magnetic tape

The basic *principles* of recording data onto magnetic tape are *quite simple*, but the incredible recording densities now available using modern recording techniques on the latest tape machines make the mechanics and electronics of these devices *anything but* simple. You can easily visualise the simple principles involved from considering a single **recording head** as shown in figure 13.10.

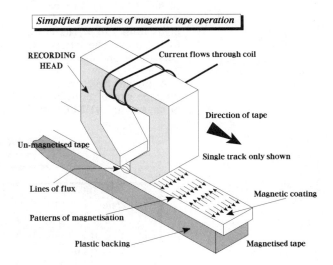

Figure 13.10

This head is acting as an electromagnet to induce lines of flux (magnetic lines of force) into the magnetic coating on the tape. The resultant patterns on the surface of the tape consist of particles (e.g. chrome dioxide or metal etc.) whose arrangements are lined up one way or another within this magnetic material which is attached to a plastic (or other suitable) backing. As the tape passes by the magnetic recording head, tiny patterns of magnetism are left in the surface of the tape which bear a relationship to the electrical signals which were passing through the head at the time, and these in turn bear a relationship with the original binary **data** being **written** onto the tape. We have said 'bear a relationship' here because the actual data-encoding methods are not so trivial, and a knowledge of these methods is beyond what is needed at 'A' level.

When the tape is being **read**, the tape passes under the head and the flux patterns previously recorded onto the tape induce tiny voltages into the **reading head** which in turn induces a current into the coil. Depending on the encoding methods used, the characteristics of this current can be analysed and the original patterns of flux deduced. This can in turn be decoded to give the original binary data recorded onto the tape. To give you some idea of the precision here – making use of more-sophisticated methods than would be implied from reading the above section, it's now possible to record several hundred thousand bits/cm^2 on tape, giving a recording density of about 6,250 bytes/ linear inch of tape. Tape speeds are in the order of 200 inches/sec, and 3,600 feet of tape is typical of what can be fitted onto a single reel.

From reading the above paragraph and looking at a typical machine, the first thing to realise is that these reel-to-reel machines are built like battleships! They are large and incredibly reliable, and have data transfer rates and storage capacities which are impressive, even by today's standards. Couple this with the relatively low cost per byte of storage (typically 0.00003p/character) compared with most other systems, and you can begin to appreciate that these tape systems will still be around well into the 21st century.

As with most hardware devices there are a number of totally-incompatible systems around, but ½-inch tape with 9 tracks is one popular system used on mainframes. One head/track will be needed as *all 9 tracks are recorded simultaneously*. This means that if a character is to be written to tape, then it is *written across the tape* making use of all 9 heads.

EBCDIC

The **EBCDIC** code (Extended Binary Coded Decimal Interchange Code) is one of the codes used for IBM tapes, and indeed other IBM peripheral units too. You have *already met* the **BCD code** in chapter 3, and so if you extend these ideas a little you get EBCDIC! EBCDIC is a code which makes use of **zones** and **digits** in ways similar to those used on the old punched cards. Part of the EBCDIC code for upper case letters only is shown in the table of figure 13.11.

You will hopefully recall from your knowledge of **BCD** that *4-bit pure binary numbers* are coded so that they can represent **decimal digits** very simply. In the table of fig 13.11, 4-bit binary numbers are coded so that they represent characters very easily. **Characters A to I** are *coded* with a **zone number of 12** (1100) *and* with **binary digits from 1 to 9**. Therefore 'E' is represented by 12 and 5, or the code 1100 0101, for example. The letters J to R are coded using zone number 13 and binary numbers 1 to 9, and finally the letters S to Z are coded using zone 14 and binary numbers 2 to 9.

Applying these principles to the actual layout showing just a *very-small* part of the tape would result in the EBCDIC bit patterns shown in figure 13.12 – the string of characters '**BEEFBURGER**' is used for the data and assuming the following.

> **EBCDIC code as used on a 9-track IBM reel-to-reel magnetic tape unit**

	EBCDIC Code				EBCDIC Code				EBCDIC Code		
	Zone		Digit		Zone		Digit		Zone		Digit	
A	1 1 0 0		0 0 0 1	**J**	1 1 0 1		0 0 0 1		1 1 1 0		0 0 0 1
B	1 1 0 0		0 0 1 0	**K**	1 1 0 1		0 0 1 0	**S**	1 1 1 0		0 0 1 0
C	1 1 0 0		0 0 1 1	**L**	1 1 0 1		0 0 1 1	**T**	1 1 1 0		0 0 1 1
D	1 1 0 0		0 1 0 0	**M**	1 1 0 1		0 1 0 0	**U**	1 1 1 0		0 1 0 0
E	1 1 0 0		0 1 0 1	**N**	1 1 0 1		0 1 0 1	**V**	1 1 1 0		0 1 0 1
F	1 1 0 0		0 1 1 0	**O**	1 1 0 1		0 1 1 0	**W**	1 1 1 0		0 1 1 0
G	1 1 0 0		0 1 1 1	**P**	1 1 0 1		0 1 1 1	**X**	1 1 1 0		0 1 1 1
H	1 1 0 0		1 0 0 0	**Q**	1 1 0 1		1 0 0 0	**Y**	1 1 1 0		1 0 0 0
I	1 1 0 0		1 0 0 1	**R**	1 1 0 1		1 0 0 1	**Z**	1 1 1 0		1 0 0 1

Figure 13.11

½ - inch tape format used on large reel-to-reel machines

```
9          Parity  9              1 0 1 1 0 1 0 0 0 1     9
8                  8              1 1 1 1 1 1 1 1 1 1     8
7                  7              1 1 1 1 1 1 1 1 1 1     7
6                  6              0 0 0 0 1 0 0 0 0 0     6
5          9 tracks 5            1 0 0 1 0 0 0 0 0 0     5          9 tracks
4                  4              1 0 0 1 0 0 0 0 0 0     4
3                  3              0 1 1 0 1 0 1 1 1 0     3
2                  2              0 0 1 0 0 1 1 0 0 1     2
1                  1              1 1 1 1 0 0 0 1 1 0     1
```

R E G R U B F E E B

Direction of tape

Beginning of tape marker

ID

Beginning of tape

In practice information would be stored in blocks as shown in figure 13.13

Figure 13.12

(1) Track 9 is used for **parity** (see page 510) and **even parity** has been set.
(2) Track 1 represents the LSB of the EBCDIC digit data.
(3) Track 8 represent the MSB of the EBCDIC zone data.

As the direction of tape is usually from left to right, then the word BEEFBURGER appears to us to be the wrong way round! Nevertheless, you should be able to appreciate how the EBCDIC patterns are now represented on the tape.

Although the above illustrates the coding principles quite well, in practice it would *not* be efficient to code the data in one continuous stream as implied by the above scenario. It is rare for tapes to whizz from one end to the other – they are more likely to be used to read in some data, then wait until the next part is needed, then move along again – when you see a mainframe computer operating a tape, they seem to be constantly stopping and starting – it certainly makes them look more impressive!

When a tape stops there will need to be a **gap** in which *no data has been recorded*. (You can't read data under the head if the tape's not moving, it would be like trying to expect some music from your cassette in pause mode!). Now **data processing** usually involves writing **records** to **files** (see page 338), and therefore it would seem to make sense if a single record were the unit of data in which to write to the tape in one go. However, given the current packing densities of 6250 bytes/inch, and given that a typical gap in which a high-performance machine would be able to stop is about 0.25 inch, recording some typical records just one at a time would result in the situation shown in the diagram of figure 13.13(a). Consider a simple calculation – for a typical name, address and telephone-number record consisting of about 100

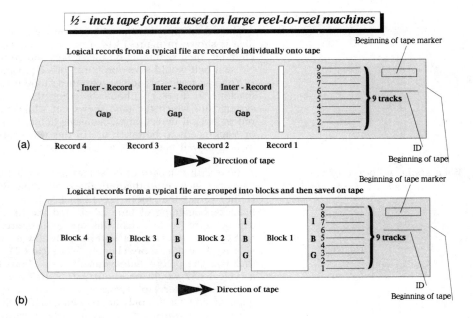

Figure 13.13

characters, the amount of tape taken up would be 100/6250 = 0.016 inch. So we have 0.016-inch records with 0.25-inch gaps! Clearly this would waste most of the space on the tape.

It would be far better to group a whole series of records into a **block**, such that the ratio of the used tape to unused tape is more sensible. If we bunch many **logical records** from the file together so that they form a **physical record** for the tape machine which is called a **block**, then the blocks may be saved on tape as shown in Figure 13.13(b). The resultant gaps in between the blocks are known as **inter-block gaps** or **IBGs**.

Buffers

Secondary storage devices such as disks or tapes, for example, are usually interfaced to the operating-system software by using areas of memory called **buffers** (see page 383). This means that the larger chunks of data which we have called blocks can match the available buffer size, so that efficient transfer between the tape and computer can take place. Each block shown in figure 13.13 represents a physical record on the tape machine, and all data within a particular file would be stored in this way. However, extra **header information** would usually be required at the *beginning of the tape* for tape identification purposes, and, as is very likely, *if* more than one file is to be stored on a particular tape, then **file header information** which identifies the file will be needed too.

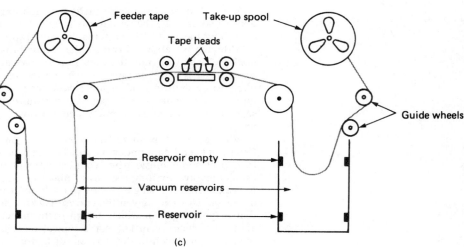

(c)

Figure 13.14

The actual tape drive mechanisms for this type of machine are impressive, and the idea is shown in figure 13.14. Can you imagine moving at a speed of just over 180 km/hour, then slamming on the brakes and stopping within a space of ¼ of an inch!! No seat belt would save you here – it's equivalent to driving into a solid brick wall.

You can now start to see why these tape machines are so impressive. To stop the machine so quickly without shredding the tape to bits, use is made of a reservoir system into which the tape spews out while one end is held at a dead stop. Infrared or optical detection mechanisms detect when more tape needs to be wound on or slack needs to be taken up. In this way there is virtually no tension on the tape as it is moved backwards and forwards.

What about the future of tape?

A tape with a length of 3600 feet and a machine with a recording density of 6250 bytes per inch could theoretically store about $3600 \times 12 \times 6250 = 270,000,000$ bytes. (Don't forget that there are 12 inches in a foot.) However, because of the IBGs, headers, beginning of tape labels and the like, the maximum amount of data that can be stored is less than this optimum figure. Nevertheless, at about £50 for this reel of tape, the cost per byte is fairly low at just 1.85×10^{-5} pence! Only CDs are able to store data more cheaply. A typical CD can store about 600 Mbytes, and one that you can record onto yourself costs about £20. Therefore, the cost per byte of a typical CD would be about 3.07×10^{-6} pence per byte. Nevertheless, with data transfer rates for tape typically in excess of 1,200,000 bytes/sec – even the fastest quad-speed CDs are only approaching half of this. With the unthinkably large mountains of data which already exist on tape, we can't easily write off tape – they will be around for a considerable number of years yet.

QIC tape streamers

A large tape machine of the sort described above would look silly sitting next to your micro. Indeed, even if you could afford one, the machine probably wouldn't fit through your bedroom door! You have to put up with some inconvenience if you want data transfer rates in excess of 1 Mbyte per second from a tape recorder! Therefore, smaller tape formats and physically very much smaller machines exist for microcomputers. A typical machine makes use of a cartridge tape where tiny reels of tape are mounted inside a cartridge housing as can be seen in figure 13.15. As the tape is ¼ inch wide, these systems have become known as **QICs** or **Quarter Inch Cartridges**. Typically, QIC systems enable you to back up 120 or 250 Mbytes on a single tape, but some tapes are capable of storing up to 8 Gbytes.

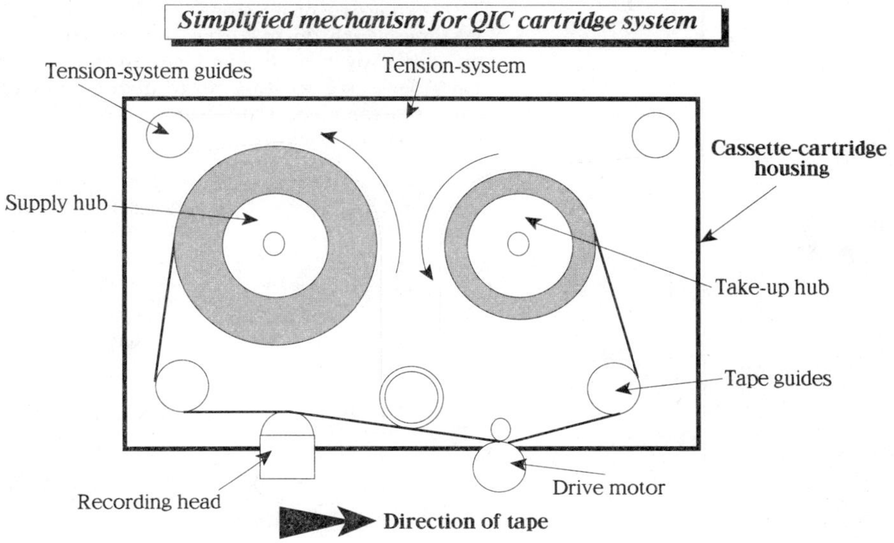

Simplified mechanism for QIC cartridge system

Figure 13.15

These smaller machines based around a micro would also be used in very different ways too. The large tape machines on mainframes are extensively used for **batch processing** (see page 371), but the smaller tape machines on micros are used almost exclusively for the purposes of **backup**. Because of this backup role, these tape machines are also known as **tape streamers**. SCSI tape streamers are also available in 525 Mbyte versions.

The requirement for speed is *not* important here, the tape is not being used as a data-processing system, as speeds of only about 15 inch/sec are typical on fast high-quality machines. Recording densities at the high end of the range would be about 200 bytes/inch. Different standards of tape systems exist, but usually a maximum of 32 tracks are fitted onto a ¼ inch tape! Instead of whizzing through the tape reading all 32 tracks simultaneously, these small cassette machines read just a single track at a time. The tape moves backwards and forwards so that different tracks can be read next time the heads pass by.

You should note that there are no inter-block gaps of the sort that were available on the large tape machines. Indeed, even if there were it would do no good because the tape streamer drive is not sophisticated enough to stop in time anyway! Therefore, what usually happens is that a massive amount of data (in micro terms) is recorded in a single session. It is usual to leave a tape streamer going over night as half an hour to an hour of recording time might be needed to back up your hard disk. It is also usual for the **hierarchical directory structure** (see page 356) of the hard disk to be recorded *along with the data* on the tape, so that sense can be made of the data on the tape when backed-up files may need to be recovered – it's a tedious and slow process, but much less tedious *and* cheaper than losing all the data on your hard disk as the result of a crash.

DAT and video

DAT, or **Digital Audio Tape**, and ordinary **VCR (Video-Cassette Recorder)** tapes are also used for **file-backup** purposes.

DAT uses a recording system similar to that of video in that a group of rotating heads, as shown in figure 13.16, produce tracks across the tape rather than longitudinally. It does all this by ditching the linear-track recording systems encountered earlier, and replaces it with a helical track system. (In fact this is where the video-tape name VHS comes from – Vertical Helical Scan). You will recall that the larger tape machines go at a high speed – if the DAT or video cartridge went at the same speed your favourite movies would only last a few minutes! The vast increase in speed comes from the fact that the heads themselves rotate very quickly across the tape, and thus the speed between the tape and the head is as though the head was stationary and the tape moving by quickly – a very clever but extremely complex system.

DAT is quite reliable, as are top-quality VCRs, but ordinary video tapes, not being designed for computer data, can be a little unreliable because of drop out. This means that some metallic particles on the coating of the tape might be missing. Use expensive professional-quality tapes and there should not be a problem. Some systems which do make use of ordinary VCRs for backup, record the data five or six times over to try and get over any potential drop-out problems. With DAT cartridges able to store up to about 8 Gbytes, and the price of DAT machines and tape streamers becoming more cost effective, these should be used in preference to VCRs for backup.

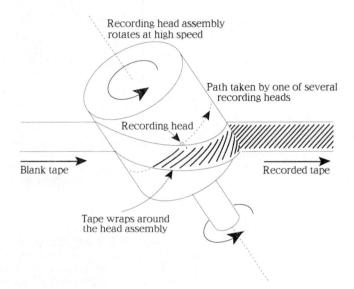

Figure 13.16

Other secondary storage devices

To complete our tour of available methods for storing data we will look at a couple of other systems which, although less well known, do have a role to play in specialist applications.

Bubble memory

Bubble memory is available as memory on a chip, but instead of making use of silicon, it makes use of a thin coating of magnetic material on a garnet crystal. This device was to be an alternative to some of the semiconductor and disk-based systems considered earlier in this chapter, but is now only used in niche markets because it has been ousted by extremely impressive developments in all the other technologies. One big advantage of bubble memory (besides being the small size of a chip) is that it is **non-volatile**. Access times are not as good as DRAM and this has probably led to the downfall of this device. A typical access time for bubble memory is about 4 msec, and typically about 125 Kbytes can be stored on a single chip. It is, therefore, ideal for **embedded systems** (see page 582) of the sort found in applications by the military.

Plated-wire store

This is a derivation from the old core store which used to be inside some of the older computers when the author was in his nappies. It is a form of magnetic storage whereby the data is stored on a thin film coated on the surface of a wire. Now you may feel that the author has lost his marbles in even mentioning such a system that the majority of people have not even heard of, however, as with the bubble memory mentioned above, it is actually quite popular in embedded systems used in aircraft in-flight (black-box) recorders, spacecraft and satellites. This type of memory is not as susceptible to harm from radiation, and is therefore ideal for some critical military applications. Access times vary but 250 nsec is typical, but these devices are especially useful because they are extremely robust, consume zero power when not being used, and are, therefore, non-volatile.

There have been several reasons for going into some detail regarding a huge variety of storage techniques – you are now well aware of the huge variety of different devices, and you are also aware of the vast differences in the current performance which is available from such systems. This knowledge, together with a knowledge of the other two hardware chapters on input and output devices, can be used to good effect when making decisions regarding what form of hardware is most appropriate in given data-storage situations.

Exercise 13.1

1. Describe three ideal characteristics of **primary storage**.

2. Explain the concepts behind **primary storage**, commenting on the importance of *memory capacity*, *word length* and *access times*. Make specific reference to the width of the address bus and data bus in your explanation.

3. Why should **primary storage** have *very-fast* access times?

4. **RAM** and **ROM** is now included in most systems – explain typical uses for each. Are there any systems in which RAM only or ROM only would be used?

5. Some memory is **volatile**. What is meant by this statement and what can be done to overcome this problem?

6. What is **SRAM** and where is it most-frequently used?

7. What is a **memory map** and why are memory maps used?

8. What is an **EPROM** and in what situation is it most frequently used?

9. What is **ASCII** and why was it developed?

10. What is **auxiliary** or **secondary** storage?

11. Categorise **secondary storage** into its *two* main modes of operation.

12. Outline some of the typical problems that might be encountered when data needs to be moved from one computer system to another.

13. Why are the data-storage capacities of hard disks and floppy disks of the same physical size so different?

14. What limits the amount of data that can be stored on a hard disk, and what limits the computer's ability to quickly access the data stored on a typical disk?

15. **Optical disks** are proving to be a versatile storage medium for software distribution – what has made them so popular and versatile?

16. What are the current *limitations* of a typical CD-ROM drive? What is being done to overcome these limitations?

17. Why are there so many different standards of CD-ROM systems?

18. Magnetic disk is currently the *fastest* available backing store. Given this fact, why is it necessary to have **disk-cache** memory?

19. Tapes were one of the first secondary storage media for computers. Why are they still necessary as part of a modern computer system?

20. Why are **buffers** often used when interfacing disk drives and tapes to computers? Explain the difference between **physical** and **logical records** in your answer.

21. Tapes on micros and mainframes tend to to be used for very different purposes. Outline *the* major uses of tapes when using these different systems.

End of chapter summary

- **Primary storage** relates to the main memory inside a computer. On modern computers this usually refers to **semiconductor-memory chips**.
- **Immediate Access Storage (IAS)** is an alternative name for **primary storage**.
- **Secondary storage** refers to storage making use of **peripherals** such as **disks** and **tape** etc.
- **Auxiliary** or **backing store** are alternative names for secondary storage.
- The *most important* requirement for **primary storage** is **speed of access**.
- **Semiconductor** memory chips are electronic devices made from materials which have a conductivity roughly half way between that of an **insulator** and a **conductor**.
- **Main memory** can be thought of as being made up of a **lot of tiny pigeon holes** into which **binary digits** may be stored.
- **Memory** can be organised in **bits**, **bytes** or **words** (multiple bytes), but the **size of the main memory** is usually specified in **bytes**, *irrespective* of the physical organisation.

- The **size** of memory (primary and secondary) is usually specified in **kbytes** or **Mbytes**, but **Gbytes** and **Tbytes** are now becoming increasingly common. Other useful multiples are to be found in the table on page 263.
- **kbytes** mean **kilobytes** or **1,024** actual bytes.
- **Mbytes** mean **Megabytes 1,024 × 1,024** or **1,048,576** actual bytes. **Gbytes** are $(1,024)^3$, **Tbytes** are $(1,024)^4$ etc.
- An **address** is a **unique number** which relates to a 'single' pigeon hole which holds one or more binary digits (usually 8) in memory.
- The **address bus** is the **parallel group of wires** along which the binary codes which represent the address travel.
- The **data bus** is the **parallel group of wires** along which the binary code representing the data travels.
- The **control bus** is the **parallel group of wires** along which the binary codes representing control information such as **read/write** to memory can travel.
- The **access time** is the time taken for data to be written to or read from memory.
- **Semiconductor memory chips** come in two basic forms – **RAM** and **ROM**.
- **RAM** stands for **Random Access Memory**, the **access time** does *not* depend on the position within the memory which holds the data.
- There are two types of **RAM** – **static** and **dynamic**.
- **DRAM** stands for **Dynamic Random Access Memory**. It is the *most common* type of **semiconductor memory** used in today's computer systems. Unfortunately, because data is stored as charge, the contents need topping up at very frequent intervals which is called **refreshing** the memory. **DRAM is the cheapest** primary-storage system.
- **SRAM** stands for **Static RAM** – a system which does *not* have to be refreshed – it is **faster that DRAM**, *but* **more expensive**. It is often used as **cache** memory.
- **Cache memory** is the **fast memory** used to hold the *most-frequently-needed instructions* being used by the processor.
- **Volatile** is the term used to describe the fact that the contents of memory will be lost *if* the power to the system is removed. **DRAM and SRAM are both volatile**.
- **Uninterruptible Power Supplies (UPS)** *can overcome* some of the difficulties associated with **volatile RAM**.
- **ROM** stands for **Read Only Memory**. Data is programmed by the manufacturer of the chip and *can't be altered* by the user of the computer.
- **ROM** *is still an example of* **RAM** because access time does not depend on storage position – **PROM** and **EPROM** are also examples of **random access memory**.
- **ROM** is usually used to hold **operating systems**, **programming languages** or for **general programs** when using **embedded microprocessor systems**.
- **PROM** stands for **Programmable Read Only Memory**. A special machine can be used to program this chip – it is cheaper than ROM for lower quantities.
- **EPROM** stands for **Erasable Programmable Read Only Memory**. This device can act as a ROM, but can be programmed and erased by the user using a special machine and UV light respectively.
- **ROM**, **PROM** and **EPROM** are all *non volatile*.
- **Memory maps** map out how ROM and RAM etc are to be used in a system.
- **ASCII** stands for the **American Standard Code for Information Interchange**. One of the international standards for exchanging mainly textual information.
- **Extended ASCII** uses the **top bit** *normally* reserved for **parity**, and thus produces an 128 additional codes.
- The *most important* aspect of **secondary storage** is **data integrity** and **mass storage capability**.
- **Direct access** and **serial access** characterise *two different types* of **secondary-storage techniques**.
- **Direct access** refers to devices such as disks where data can be accessed directly, without having to read any other stored data.
- **Serial access** refers to devices such as tape where direct access is *not* possible.
- **Floppy disks** make use of a **magnetic surface** on which the data is stored in the form of **tracks** and **sectors**. The disk inside the case is literally floppy.
- **Track (floppy disk)** – a set of **concentric circular paths** going across the surface of the disk. These **tracks** (*and* **sectors**) form the basis of a **pattern** which *uniquely defines* how the data can be stored on the disk.
- **Sector** – each **track** of a magnetic disk is split up into a *uniform number of smaller parts* called **sectors**.
- **Magnetic disks** have to be **formatted** (initialisation of the track and sector pattern plus control data) *before* they can be used to store the data.

- **High density disks** such as **double-density** or **quad-density** increase the amount of data that can be stored on a disk. However, the quality of the magnetic material used on the surface of the disk needs to be higher.
- **Winchester disks** are **hard-disk-drive systems** housed in a hermetically-sealed environment. Often a stack of disks form a single drive with multiple heads.
- A **hard disk** is the general name given to systems similar to **Winchester disks**.
- The *speed of data transfer* and the *storage density* of **hard disks** are much higher than those of floppy disks.
- **RAID** is an acronym for **Reduced Array of Inexpensive Drives**. It is an array (two or more) of different drives intended for **extra security** or **file-server** applications.
- **Large hard disk** systems are the 14-inch hard drives used on mainframes.
- **Disk packs** refer to the removable packs used in the large drives on mainframes.
- **Disk packs** are often multiple-platter devices.
- A **cylinder** is the unit of storage obtained from a consideration of the natural cylinder shape generated by the heads on multiple-surface drives.
- **Disk packs and Winchesters** have the data on the disk addressed in terms of **cylinders, surface number** and **sector**.
- **Disk cartridges** (1) are single-disk versions of large disk packs on a mainframe.
- **Disk cartridges** (2) are the names given to the removable hard disks on micros.
- **Formatting** is the name given to the **initialisation process** of *preparing a disk ready to receive stored data.*
- **The sector is** the smallest unit of data that can be written to or read from a disk.
- **Blocking** (disks) is used to make storage of data on a disk more efficient.
- A **cluster** is the name given to several sectors.
- A **FAT** is a **File Allocation Table** – it is stored on disk and holds an 'information map' of where each file has been allocated space on the disk.
- **The FAT** is an example of control information which is stored on a disk at the time of formatting.
- An **optical drive** is the name given to CD-based systems in which the data is read by a beam of light called a laser.
- **Laser – Light Amplification by the Stimulated Emission of Radiation.**
- **Lands** and **pits** are the *different levels on the surface of a CD* after the data has been burned in by the **laser**.
- **CD – Compact Disc.** The 12 cm polycarbonate disc used for storing audio and other types of information such as computer data and video.
- **Magneto-optical drives** are disk drives which operate on *both* **magnetic** and **optical** principles. Data is *written to the disk* by means of a **magnetic head** and a **laser**, and *read back from the disk* by a **laser** in a similar way to that of a CD.
- **WORM**s are **Write Once Read Many** times drives. They are **special CDs** which can be written to *once only* by means of a special recorder machine available to users.
- There is a large variety of CD-ROM standards including **CD, CD-DA, Photo CD, CD-I, CD-R** and **CD-ROM-XA**.
- **Disk cache** systems make use of RAM as a mirror-image of some parts of the disk. It helps to give an apparently vast increase in disk-access speeds.
- **Magnetic tape** is used in a variety of formats, the most expensive of which can be found on **mainframe computers** being used for **batch processing**.
- One common tape format is **9-track ½-inch tape** as used on mainframes.
- The **EBCDIC code** is a *popular alternative* to **ASCII** and is used on IBM tapes and other machines.
- **EBCDIC** is an acronym for Extended Binary Coded Decimal Interchange Code.
- **Logical records** to be stored on tape are **blocked** for increased data-storage capacity and efficiency.
- **IBG**s are the **Inter-Block-Gaps** between blocks on a tape.
- The **blocking factor** is the number of logical records per block.
- A **buffer** is **an area of memory** used as an efficient interface to convert blocks to logical records and back again.
- **Smaller tape formats** such as **QIC**s and **DAT** are extensively used on micros for backup purposes.
- **QIC – Quarter Inch Cartridge.** A 20 to 32-track system depending on type.
- **DAT – Digital Audio Tape** is also used extensively for backup of disk.
- **Bubble memory** – non-volatile memory used in embedded applications.
- **Plated-wire store** – non-volatile memory which is not as susceptible to radiation – it is therefore used by the military, in aircraft, in satellites and space ships.

14 Data structures

Introduction

A study of data structures is fundamental to the study of computer science at A-level. A fundamental understanding of the structure of data leads to a greater awareness of how computers can be used to process data, and this naturally leads to the development and testing of efficient algorithms to carry out these basic operations.

Typical operations carried out on data structures

There is nothing difficult about the most common data structures. The concepts are derived from day-to-day business operations. Indeed, it is from these non-mathematical data processing businesses that much of the terminology is provided. For example, if you run a business, then it is a natural operation to **add data** to your files. Therefore, **ADDITION of data** such as 'customer name and address' is a natural data processing operation. Similarly, a customer may have to be deleted from your accounts. **DELETION of data** is, therefore, another of these naturally occurring **business transactions**.

Each common operation is summarised in the following list. The only slightly strange term is **'traversing'.** This simply means **going through the set of data** and, usually, undertaking some process on the way. Such a process might be generating a list of the names and addresses of all your customers who are to receive an invitation to the annual dinner!

List of common data processing operations

The following are the most common data processing operations to be carried out on basic data structures.

> Traversing the data (i.e. processing the data held in the list)
> Addition of data
> Deletion of data
> Sorting of data into some order
> Searching for a specific item of data
> Merging different sets of data

Computer science students should easily be able to carry out any of the above operations with manual or computerized filing systems. However, what we are most interested in doing, is finding *efficient* ways of carrying out the above operations when large amounts of data are involved. **This is the fundamental importance of data structures**.

As with the operations themselves, there are many **naturally occurring data structures.** For example, businesses have always had **lists,** have always stored things in **alphabetical** or **numerical order,** or have always had their own ways of doing things, given the nature of their particular business problems.

What are the most common data structures

Data structures allow us to carry out all the above data processing operations efficiently. To illustrate how this may be so, we will look at **lists, stacks, queues, arrays, trees,** etc. as these are the most common data structures. As this chapter develops, you will realize that these data stuctures too derive from many day-to-day business operations. For example, a queue is exactly the same as a queue in a shop, and a tree is exactly the same as the 'tree structure' or 'hierarchy' that is normally found in a business or a family tree. Therefore, typical things to be tackled would be how to **delete** data from a **linked list,** how to **add** data to a **hierarchical** data structure, etc.

The **efficiency** spoken of above is usually measured in terms of **how much time a particular operation takes.** For example, what is the average time to find a random item of data from a data structure containing 50,000 items? The other measure of efficiency is **how much memory is taken up** on the computer. However, this is a lot less important than it used to be, as many megabytes of RAM are now common.

Searching, sorting and merging are covered in other chapters. Here, we will look in detail at the first three techniques mentioned above. In most cases, simple examples will be given, **algorithms** will then be developed, and **pseudocode** examples given at the end of each section. In the more complex cases, **dry runs** are also included. After reading through this and the other relevant chapters, you should have enough experience to develop and code your own algorithms, write some appropriate pseudocode, then code these ideas using a high level language that you have chosen.

In fact, the writing of pseudocode is now becoming very popular in computer science examinations at A-level. **It is worth spending much time on this work as it forms a major part of many syllabuses.** When working through any textbook you will find that different authors will do things in slightly different ways. However, there is no substitute for applying a mass of common sense to the problems, as the underlying principles are often not very difficult.

What students do find most difficult is to be consistent about terminology, and meticulous in their testing of the algorithms. It does not matter too much about what you call the pointers or lists, etc. What is important is that you explain what you are doing and *write enough comments* in the psuedocode to enable your teachers and examiners to work out exactly *what* you are doing.

You must make sure that the **algorithms work for all possible cases**. If there is some case for which your algorithm will not work, then say so. It is often the case in an examination that you are asked to state any assumptions that you have made. It is a good idea to do this even if you have not been asked.

The exact ways in which these data structures are processed depends on the software which you have. Some high level languages enable you to maintain pointers with far greater efficiency than does a language such as BASIC.

Linear list

The following description may seem a little long winded considering we are only going to talk about six numbers! However, some important concepts will be introduced which will be assumed without explanation for the more complex data structures that follow.

One of the most simple forms of data structure is a **linear list.** In fact a linear list can be thought of as a **one-dimensional array.** It is easier to consider data structures by means of simple examples rather than to introduce them as complex mathematical relationships. As an example of a linear list consider the following sales figures for the month of March for five different sales personnel selling Bradbury's chocolates:

Bradbury's chocolates: March sales figures	
Salesperson	**Sales** **(thousand boxes)**
Smith	2.3
Jones	1.9
Anson	6.4
Talbot	5.0
Bartlett	3.9
Carter	0.0

This list of numbers forms what is called a linear list, i.e. 2.3, 1.9, 6.4, 5.0, 3.9 and 0.0. If you were presented with the raw data 2.3, 1.9, 6.4, 5.0, 3.9 and 0.0 then it would be meaningless in itself, until the structure given by the above table was applied to it. When we do this the data becomes information, i.e. 3.9 means that salesperson Bartlett has sold 3900 boxes of Bradbury's chocolates in the month of March.

The above linear list is not in any particular order. It would be possible to rearrange the data so that other information could be more easily obtained from it. For example we may want to know who sold the most chocolates and who did next best. In this case the rearrangement shown in figure 14.1(a) would be most appropriate. Other information might be found more easily if the names of the people were in alphabetical order. In this case the arrangement shown in figure 14.1(b) would be convenient.

All these arrangements of the data still form a linear list, but some are more useful than others for extracting certain information. In this chapter we will see ways

of extracting information such as that shown in figure 14.1, without having to physically move the data around in the way that we have shown. To be able to do this
we must refer to the data within the list in a very general way that is suitable for
representation on a computer.

Salesperson	Sales (thousand boxes)	Salesperson	Sales (thousand boxes)
Anson	6.4	Anson	6.4
Talbot	5.0	Bartlett	3.9
Bartlett	3.9	Carter	0.0
Smith	2.3	Jones	1.9
Jones	1.9	Smith	2.3
Carter	0.0	Talbot	5.0

(a)   (b)

Figure 14.1

The linear lists we have just considered contain only six sets of information. In
general a linear list may have N sets of information where N >= 0. Let us give a
general name to each element. S might be a good choice representing sales. Each
item in a linear list is referred to as an **element.** We can use a subscript to uniquely
identify each element (sales figure) as follows:

If we assume the original list 2.3, 1.9, 6.4, 5.0, 3.9, 0.0 then:

$$S_{(1)} = 2.3, S_{(2)} = 1.9 \text{ and so on until } S_{(6)} = 0.0$$

Data is stored inside computers as a linear list. In fact the use of the subscript to
uniquely identify each element within the list corresponds very closely to the address
used for the storage locations inside the computer. In fact it is convenient if we
think about the values of each element as being put inside a box whose address is
given by the subscripted element as follows:

Linear list S

$S_{(1)}$	2.3
$S_{(2)}$	1.9
$S_{(3)}$	6.4
$S_{(4)}$	5.0
$S_{(5)}$	3.9
$S_{(6)}$	0.0

A general element within the list can be referred to as the ith element.

Hence if i = 3 then we are referring to the 3rd element which is $S_{(i)} = S_{(3)} = 6.4$

A set of related variables such as those in the above linear list is also known as
a **vector S of size N**. The name derives from the fact that in mathematical terms a
vector is simply the name for a **one-dimensional array**, i.e. a list.

As can be seen from figure 14.1(b), a linear list may often be in some convenient
order such as alphabetical. However, if we wish to **add** an item of data into the
middle of the **list,** then all the data *after* the item to be inserted would have to
be moved to make way for the new item of data. Similarly, if we were to **delete**
an item of data from a **linear list,** then there would be a **free space,** and all the items
of data after the item that has just been removed would have to be moved up.

It would be possible to develop algorithms to do this, but they would not be used
in practice, and are very inefficient if large amounts of data are involved. It is far
better to concentrate your efforts on understanding the **pointer systems** to be introduced in the next few sections. These show how new, **more sophisticated data
structures enable us to insert and delete items of data without having to move any
of the existing data.**

Stacks

A **stack** is one of the methods used to insert and delete items from a linear list.
Other more sophisticated methods will be considered later in this chapter. The
concept of a stack is of fundamental importance in computing as it is used in so
many different applications. The principle of a stack is illustrated in the following
example:

Consider the numbers in the list 23, 54, 10 and 90. When talking of a stack we will refer to the **top** of the stack or the **bottom** of the stack and so the numbers will be set out vertically, to reinforce this point visually.
The list now becomes:

23
54
10
90

If we now add a number (such as 77) to the stack it is **pushed** on to the top of the stack. The stack now becomes:

77
23
54
10
90

The words '**pushed** on to the top of the stack' is the phrase used with stacks to indicate that an item of data has been added to the stack.

If an item is to be removed from the stack then it is said to be popped off the stack. Using this system the last number in is always the first number out. This sytem of storing numbers in a list is called a **LIFO stack (Last In First Out)**. A LIFO stack is often compared with a pile of plates in a canteen. After washing up the plates the last plate will be placed on to the top of the stack. The next plate to be used will be taken from the top of the stack, i.e. a LIFO stack.

Any reader familiar with machine code programming will realise that often PUSH and POP are included in the assembly language mnemonics exactly for this purpose.

Reading the above gives the impression that when an item is pushed on to the top of the stack all the other items of data are pushed down one. Although this is conceptually correct, in practice a stack would be built up in the computer's memory using a **pointer system.** A pointer is simply a number used to point to an item of interest, it may be used to point to the memory location inside the computer which indicates the top of the stack. Used in this way it is called a **stack pointer**. Let us assume that we have 6 memory locations as shown in figure 14.2.

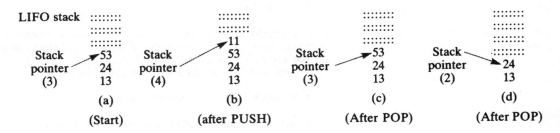

Figure 14.2

These six memory locations are shown as dotted boxes and will represent our LIFO stack. Only three items of data 13, 24 and 53 are currently on the stack. The numbers were placed on to the stack in the order shown, and hence 53 will appear at the top of the stack. The stack pointer will therefore be pointing at the memory location containing the number 53 as shown in figure 14.2(a). Let us now suppose that a new number, 11, is pushed on to the stack. The situation now becomes as shown in figure 14.2(b). If the next operation is a pop then the number 11 will be popped off the top of the stack giving the situation shown in figure 14.2(c). Finally if another pop is carried out we get the situation shown in figure 14.2(d).

If the stack becomes empty or full then an error message would have to be generated. Such techniques might set the stack pointer to − 1 so that the next pop operation could report an error. Languages such as Forth or techniques of evaluating **reverse Polish notation expressions** (see page 209) make extensive use of stack operations such as those shown above.

Processing data in a stack

To implement a stack system in memory is relatively simple. The algorithms in this section perform the operations **PUSH** and **POP** on memory called **STACK.**

In the **pseudocode algorithms,** the following terminology will apply:

Stack_Pointer	=	variable used to indicate the current top of the stack.
Maximum	=	used to determine when the stack is full up.
Minimum	=	used to determine if the stack is empty.
Data	=	item of data to be **pushed** or **popped**.
STACK	=	general name for the stack contained in memory.
STACK(Stack_Pointer)	=	subscripted variable representing the data at the current stack pointer, i.e. it is an **identifier** for data on the stack.

The above are parameters that are passed over to generalized stack maintenance procedures **called PUSH** and **POP**.

Pseudocode to PUSH a new item of data on to the top of the STACK

The code is relatively obvious; the only thing to check is that there *is actually room* to put another item of data on the top of the stack. If this is not possible, then an **error message** must be generated as **an overflow** has occurred.

The procedure assumes that an array **STACK(N)** has already been set up, and the procedure is to be called by using:

    PUSH(Stack_Pointer, Maximum, Data)

The actual **pseudocode for the PUSH procedure** is as follows:

```
PROCEDURE PUSH(Stack_Pointer, Maximum, Data)
                            (*Check if the stack is already full*)
    IF Stack_Pointer = Maximum THEN
    PRINT No room on the stack
    EXIT PROCEDURE
    ELSE
                                (*Push data item on to stack*)
    SET Stack_Pointer = Stack_Pointer + 1
    SET STACK(Stack_Pointer) = Data
    ENDIF
END PROCEDURE
```

Pseudocode to POP an item off the STACK

Here it should be obvious that the stack cannot **overflow** from this operation. However, there might be no items of data on the stack, in which case, we cannot remove any more data.

The pseudocode procedure is to be called by using:

    POP(Stack_Pointer, Minimum, Data)

The actual **pseudocode POP procedure** is as follows:

```
PROCEDURE POP(Stack_Pointer, Minimum, Data)
                            (*Check if the stack is already empty*)
    IF Stack_Pointer = Minimum THEN
    PRINT The stack is already empty
    EXIT PROCEDURE
    ELSE
                            (*POP data off of stack and adjust pointer*)
    SET Data = STACK(Stack_Pointer)
    SET Stack_Pointer = Stack_Pointer − 1
    ENDIF
END PROCEDURE
```

If the stack was not empty, then the procedure is exited with **data** containing the **information that was at the top of the stack.**

Queues

A **queue** is very similar in principle to the operation of a stack and indeed is often called a FIFO stack (First In First Out). The principle of operation of a queue is exactly the same as the principle of a normal queue waiting to be served in a shop, i.e. the first in the queue would be expected to get served first and therefore be the first out. Hence the name **FIFO stack**. To implement the queue in memory uses the techniques demonstrated in figure 14.3.

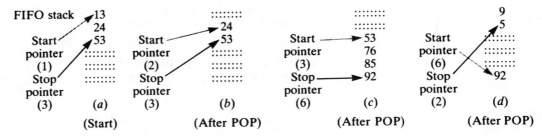

Figure 14.3

The start position shown in figure 14.3(a) shows three numbers in the queue. Number 13 is at the head of the queue as indicated by the **start pointer** and 53 is at the end of the queue as indicated by the **stop pointer.** 13 was placed first in the queue and has therefore been waiting longest. However, the number 13 has not physically moved. It has remained in its position at the top of the queue.

Figure 14.3(b) shows what happens when 13 is popped off the queue (i.e. the number 13 has been **served**). Notice again that the data does not move, it is the pointers that have been altered.

If three more numbers 76, 85 and 92 are pushed on to the queue and then another number is popped off we end up with the situation shown in figure 14.3(c). Any data added to the queue must now be put into position number 1 and the pointers altered accordingly .

Figure 14.3(d), shows the situation after three more numbers have been popped off and two more numbers 9 and 5 have been added. A **circular list** arrangement has therefore been established using these pointers i.e. when you have run out of space at the bottom you simply start again at the top.

Queues are particularly easy to implement in practice (it is a simple matter of updating the two pointers) and are useful, together with random numbers and statistics, to produce simulations of real life queuing systems such as simulating how many petrol pumps are necessary in a garage forecourt, given that customers arrive at a particular rate and should not be kept waiting too long (see page 195).

Processing data in a queue

In this section we show a couple of **pseudocode algorithms** to **INSERT** an item of **Data** into a **QUEUE**, and to **DELETE** an item of **Data** from a **QUEUE**.

In the **pseudocode algorithms.** the following terminology will apply:

Start_Pointer	= variable used to indicate the start of the queue.
Stop_Pointer	= variable used to indicate the end of the queue.
Size	= variable that represents the size of the queue (i.e. how many data elements are contained in the queue).
Data	= item of data to be pushed or popped.
QUEUE	= general name for the queue contained in memory.
QUEUE(Pointer)	= subscripted variable representing the data at the current pointer position i.e. an **identifier** for the data in the queue.

The above are parameters that are passed over to generalized stack maintenance procedures called **INSERT** and **DELETE**.

Procedure to INSERT some data into a queue

As with the stack, we must ensure that **overflow** does *not* occur. Therefore, we will have to test for this condition on entry to the INSERT procedure. The checking to see if the queue is full is slightly more complicated:

The first case shown in figure 14.3 is easy, i.e. we can simply state:

IF the **Start_pointer** = 1 AND the **Stop pointer = Size, then the queue is full.**

However, this will not work for the other cases. Observation of the conditions in figure 14.3 (b), (c) and (d) will show that the condition:

IF the **Start_Pointer** = **Stop_Pointer + 1 THEN** the **queue** is also **full.**

These two conditions are, therefore, used to check if the queue is full at the start of the INSERT procedure.

When the queue is empty this will be indicated by setting the start pointer to 0. (Note that location zero does not exist in the queue.)

In the following we assume that a queue, **QUEUE(N)** has already been set up. The procedure will be called by using:

INSERT(Size, Start_Pointer, Stop_Pointer, Data)

The actual pseudocode for insertion of data is as follows:

```
PROCEDURE INSERT(Size, Start_Pointer, Stop_Pointer, Data)
                                                      (*Is queue full?*)
    IF Start_Pointer = 1 AND Stop_Pointer = Size
        OR Start_Pointer = Stop_Pointer + 1 THEN
      PRINT Queue is already full
      EXIT PROCEDURE
    ENDIF
                                         (*Check to see if queue is empty*)
    IF Start_Pointer = 0 THEN
                                                   (*Initialize queue*)
        SET Start_Pointer = 1 and SET Stop_Pointer = 1
                                    (*Queue not empty, update pointers*)
      ELSE
        IF Stop_Pointer = Size THEN
        SET Stop_Pointer = 1
                                      (*Put stop pointer back to beginning*)
      ELSE
        SET Stop_Pointer = Stop_Pointer + 1
                                              (*Update stop pointer*)
      ENDIF
    ENDIF
      QUEUE(Stop_Pointer) = Data
                                             (*Store Data in queue*)
  END PROCEDURE
```

Proceedure to DELETE some data from a queue

As with the stack system, we must ensure that underflow does not occur, i.e. we cannot remove an item of data from an empty queue. Also, if the queue becomes empty after an item of data has been removed, we must ensure that the start pointer is set to zero, as this would be needed by the INSERT procedure shown above to initialize the queue.

Testing if the queue is empty is easy, as is the extraction of the data. However, we must ensure that when only one item is originally in the queue, we set the start pointer to zero as described above.

The procedure will be called by using:

DELETE(Size, Start_Pointer, Stop_Pointer, Data)

The actual pseudocode for deleting from the queue is as follows:

```
PROCEDURE DELETE(Size, Start_Pointer, Stop_Pointer, Data)
                                                   (*The queue is empty*)
    IF Start_Pointer = 0 THEN
      PRINT The queue is empty
      EXIT PROCEDURE
    ELSE
                                                    (*Queue not empty*)
      Data = QUEUE(Start_Pointer)
                                    (*Get data from the front of the queue*)
      IF Start_Pointer = Stop_Pointer THEN
        Start_Pointer = 0
                                        (*Only one item was in the queue*)
        Stop_Pointer = 0
        EXIT PROCEDURE
      ENDIF
                                    (*More than one data item was in queue*)
      IF Start_Pointer = Size THEN
        Start_Pointer = 1
                                      (*Put start pointer back to beginning*)
      ELSE
        Start_Pointer = Start_Pointer + 1
      ENDIF
    ENDIF
  END PROCEDURE
```

Arrays

An array is simply an ordering of data elements so that information may be extracted from them. In the case of the linear list shown earlier, we saw an example of a **one-dimensional array.** More complex data structures can be expressed by making use of two- (or more) dimensional arrays. An example will help clarify the situation.

We will again use Bradbury's chocolates, but this time we will represent the sales figures for the first six months of the year. The following table should be self explanatory:

Bradbury's chocolates: First half-year sales figures						
Salesperson	Sales (thousand boxes)					
	Jan	**Feb**	**Mar**	**Apr**	**May**	**Jun**
Anson	4.7	3.8	6.4	4.6	0.0	4.3
Bartlett	5.1	0.0	3.9	3.7	4.1	3.9
Carter	3.9	4.8	0.0	4.0	5.3	4.7
Jones	0.0	2.8	1.9	3.1	2.6	0.0
Smith	0.9	1.7	2.3	1.5	1.2	2.7
Talbot	4.2	3.6	5.0	0.0	3.4	3.8

The size of an array depends on the number of **rows** and **columns.** In the above case we have a 6×6 **array.** If we again use S to represent the elements then a double **subscript notation** is used to uniquely identify each individual element within the array. As an example consider the following:

$S_{(1,2)} = 3.8$ i.e. Anson's February sales figures.
$S_{(3,4)} = 4.0$ i.e. Carter's April sales figures.

Each element within the array is referred to by $S_{(row, column)}$. This is the convention that is always used.

As mentioned above, the process can be extended into further dimensions. Although more difficult to draw, one could easily imagine a set of sales figures for the whole year set out as above in a **two-dimensional array.** The next year's sales figures could be set out as another two-dimensional array. We can imagine it to be behind the previous year's (i.e. in the third dimension). The system could then work as follows:

$S_{(1,2,1)}$ $=$ 3.8   Anson's February sales in the 1st year;
        i.e. $S_{(Anson, February, 1st year)}$
$S_{(3,6,4)}$ $=$ 8.7   Carter's June sales in the 4th year.

Three and more dimensions may be difficult to imagine or draw out but it is very easy to use them simply by writing down what each dimension means. Most high level languages support many more than two- or three-dimensional arrays, but it should be remembered that a massive amount of memory can be consumed for large multidimensional arrays e.g. a five-dimensional array containing 10 elements in each dimension would need:

$10 \times 10 \times 10 \times 10 \times 10 = 100\ 000$ locations (assuming that each number could be stored in just one memory location).

Arrays must be represented inside the computers as a linear list (i.e. a one-dimensional array). Don't forget that the nature of primary storage is simply a linear list. To represent an array in the computer's memory requires **mapping** each element of the array on to the corresponding **locations** which will store the array. The idea is as follows:

Consider the simple 3×4 array with an identifier T.

$$T = \begin{pmatrix} 10 & 21 & 37 & 31 \\ 35 & 22 & 14 & 66 \\ 13 & 82 & 26 & 94 \end{pmatrix}$$

Using **row-by-row mapping** we get:

	(1,1)	(1,2)	(1,3)	(1,4)	(2,1)	(2,2)	(2,3)	(2,4)	(3,1)	(3,2)	(3,3)	(3,4)
T	10	21	37	31	35	22	14	66	13	82	26	94

Using **column-by-column mapping** we get:

	(1,1)	(2,1)	(3,1)	(1,2)	(2,2)	(3,2)	(1,3)	(2,3)	(3,3)	(1,4)	(2,4)	(3,4)
T	10	35	13	21	22	82	37	14	26	31	66	94

It is the above sort of processes that have to be tackled by the computer when you use a **dimension statement** in a high level language such as BASIC.

For example, the statement: DIM T(3,4) would be the information that the computer uses to reserve an area of memory using methods similar to those shown above. If you refer to an element in the array such as T(2,1) then the computer knows exactly where that element can be found.

The above methods are often useful when programming in a low level language (see page 77) as no such help with array structures is available. We therefore have to devise our own system for accessing the stored information. This can be done in the following ways:

The only things that we know about the elements in the array are the row and column numbers. Similarly the only things we know about the memory locations are the first location and the number of locations needed, i.e. the number of elements within the array.

We next have to choose to map either row-by-row or column-by-column as demonstrated above.

The absolute addresses of the memory locations are usually irrelevant and so we will use the label MEMstart to indicate the start of the array in MEMory. The address of an element such as T(R,C) will be denoted by ADD T(R,C), i.e. the ADDress of the element of T in the Rth Row and Cth Column.

Let us assume row-by-row mapping. Taking some typical examples of where the data would be stored, we can build up the following picture of the data structure in memory:

Memory location			Array element	Data
Base address	+	Offset	T(R,C)	
MEMstart	+	0	T(1,1)	10
MEMstart	+	1	T(1,2)	21
MEMstart	+	2	T(1,3)	37
MEMstart	+	3	T(1,4)	31
MEMstart	+	4	T(2,1)	35
MEMstart	+	5	T(2,2)	22
MEMstart	+	6	T(2,3)	14
MEMstart	+	7	T(2,4)	66
MEMstart	+	8	T(3,1)	13
MEMstart	+	9	T(3,2)	82
MEMstart	+	10	T(3,3)	26
MEMstart	+	11	T(3,4)	94

From the above patterns we can establish a general expression to indicate where in memory a general element T(R,C) would be stored, i.e. to find ADD T(R,C).

We must use the R and C numbers in the **array element** column to generate the offset from the base address called MEMstart. Concentrate on the C numbers in the array element column of the above table. You will notice that the numbers form a cycle (1,2,3,4), (1,2,3,4) etc. Also you will notice that these C numbers conveniently go up in steps of 1, although to generate a suitable offset we really need to use $(C - 1)$. Hence $(C - 1)$ will form part of our final expression:

$$\text{OFFSET} = ????? + (C - 1)$$

The unknown part of the offset expression must be some function of R. Now R must not contribute anything to the first four addresses as 0,1,2 and 3 from the $(C - 1)$ part do this already. Hence when $R = 1$ we need 0 generated for this unknown part. When $R = 2$ we need 4 generated or when $R = 3$ we need 8 generated. The function $4(R - 1)$ will generate these numbers, i.e. $R = 1$ we get 0, $R = 2$ we get 4 etc.

Combining these two expressions we get:

$$\text{Offset} = 4(R - 1) + (C - 1)$$

A few tests will confirm this expression:

T(1,1) Here $R = 1$ and $C = 1$ Therefore offset $= 4(1-1) + (1-1) = 0+0 = 0$
T(2,3) Here $R = 2$ and $C = 3$ Therefore offset $= 4(2-1) + (3-1) = 4+2 = 6$
T(3,4) Here $R = 3$ and $C = 4$ Therefore offset $= 4(3-1) + (4-1) = 8+3 = 11$

Confirm that these answers agree with those given in the original table.
Hence the memory address at which an element T(R,C) would be stored is:

$$\text{ADD T(R,C)} = \text{MEMstart} + 4(R - 1) + (C - 1)$$

If we were to study several different sizes of arrays having M rows and N columns then you would find the following general form of the above for row-by-row mapping:

ADD T(R,C) = MEMstart + N(R–1) + (C–1) (where N = number of columns)

or for column-by-column mapping:

ADD T(R,C) = MEMstart + M(R–1) + (C–1) (where M = number of rows)

Processing data in arrays

Arrays are also useful in **high level languages.** As with all **data structures**, the usefulness is reflected by the needs of the business or application which is to make use of the data. As an example, consider a firm of four computer consultants. They all have their own customers, but make use of the same computer system for processing their transactions. Let the names of the consultants be Bradley, Faithfull, Prakash and Whyte.

You could have **four different arrays** called **Bradley, Faithfull, Prakash and Whyte.** Suppose we treat these as one-dimensional arrays, each having ten elements (not much room for expansion but it makes the diagrams simpler!). Then these could be represented as follows:

Data structure 1			
Bradley	**Faithfull**	**Prakash**	**Whyte**
1 Cole	1 Brasier	1 Luscombe	1 Dixon
2 Collis	2 Greenwood	2 May	2 Patrick
3 Gray	3 Jordan	3 Moon	3 Phelps
4 Pegden	4 Sidders	4 Godden	4 Saggers
5 Tonkin	5 Widgery	5	6
6 Williamson	6	6	6
7	7	7	7
8	8	8	8
9	9	9	9
10	10	10	10

Therefore, **Faithfull**(2) would refer to the customer Greenwood who has Faithfull as computer consultant.

The above data structure is only one of many possible arrangements when making use of arrays. For example, CUSTOMER and CONSULTANT might be a better alternative as follows:

Data Structure 2	
Customer	**Consultant**
1 Brasier	Faithfull
2 Cole	Bradley
3 Collis	Bradley
4 Dixon	Whyte
5 Godden	Prakash
6 Gray	Bradley
7 Greenwood	Faithfull
8 Jordan	Faithfull
9 Luscombe	Prakash
10 May	Prakash
11 Moon	Prakash
12 Patrick	Whyte
13 Pegden	Bradley
14 Phelps	Whyte
15 Saggers	Whyte
16 Sidders	Faithfull
17 Tonkin	Bradley
18 Widgery	Faithfull
19 Williamson	Bradley

In the above structure, CUSTOMER(7) would refer to Greenwood, which in turn would refer to CONSULTANT(7) which gives Faithfull, Greenwood's consultant. Finally, a pointer system which points to the location in a customer array can be set up. Each of the three consultant's pointers points to the start address of the position in the array where the information is stored. Extra information regarding the number of clients that each consultant has is stored along with the pointer information. One representation is as follows:

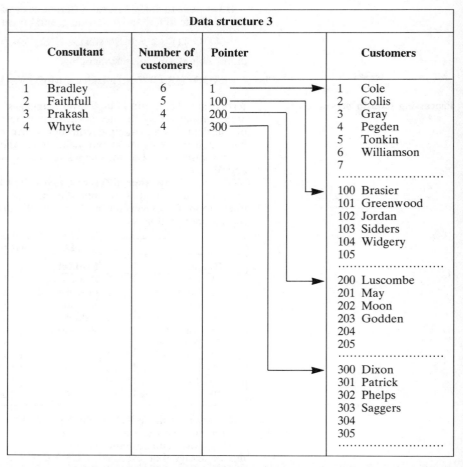

The above structures all have their advantages and disadvantages. The usefulness of each depends on how information contained within the data structure needs to be accessed. For example, what would be the case if the customers wanted to swap consultants? In data structure 1 it would be a simple case of altering one item of information. If each consultant wanted to process all their clients separately, then data structures 1 or 3 would be best. If the office has to process all the consultant's accounts each month, then data structure 2 would be a good idea. But what if the accounting systems were different for each consultant etc.?

Arguments such as the above have to be weighed up when implementing data structures on a computer. As stated at the beginning of this chapter, it is the business applications which dictate the most efficient ways in which to store the data.

Pseudocode to process data held in an array

As an example, take another look at the data structure 3 for the computer consultancy service. Suppose that we wish to process the monthly bills for Whyte. Then this can be done quite simply in the following way:

The terminology in the pseudocode algorithm is as follows:

Start_pointer = pointer set to the start of the consultants list in the array CUSTOMERS .

C = **Consultant number,** i.e. Prakash = 3, Bradley = 1, etc.

N = **Number of Customers** derived from associating the position of the consultant with the number of their customers.

(*Set start pointer to beginning of list*)

Start_Pointer = **Pointer(C)**

(*Deduce the end of the list*)

Stop_Pointer = **Start_Pointer** + N

(* Process customer information*)

FOR count = Start_Pointer TO Stop_Pointer
   PROCESS CUSTOMER(count)
NEXT count

Addition and deletion of data is considered in great detail **when dealing with linked lists and trees** in the next few sections. As with the **linear list** (which is really a one-dimensional array), addition and deletion of data involves moving many data items and becomes ineffficient for huge amounts of data.

Linked lists

In a linked list the structure of the data does not necessarily reflect the way that the data is stored in the computer's memory locations. A linked list uses the highly important concept of pointers. A **pointer** is simply a number stored in memory that points to the location where another item of data is to be found.

Again consider the original example about the Bradbury's chocolate sales people. The original list was not in any particular order. We then rearranged the list so that the sales performances could be analysed and then rearranged the list yet again into alphabetical order of names. However this was achieved by completely rearranging the relative positions of the data as shown in figure 14.1.

If we make use of pointers then the data need not be moved at all to extract exactly the same information. The idea is as follows:

Bradbury's chocolates: March sales figures				
Salesperson	Memory location	Sales data	Alphabetical pointers	Best salesperson pointers
Smith	1	2.3	3	3
Jones	2	1.9	5	4
Anson	3	6.4	6	5
Talbot	4	5.0	2	1
Bartlett	5	3.9	1	2
Carter	6	0.0	4	6

The absolute values of the memory locations where the sales data is stored are unimportant and have therefore just been called 1,2,3,4 etc. for convenience. The alphabetical pointers point to the memory location which holds the next item of data in the alphabetical list.

If we read off the alphabetical pointers from top to bottom we get 3 (the location where Anson's figures are stored), 5 (the location where Bartlett's figures are stored) etc. We get a list of the sales data in alphabetical order without having to physically rearrange the data in such a way. The situation is shown in figure 14.4(a). Figure 14.4(b) shows the same idea for the best salesperson pointers.

The lists are simply called **linked lists** because they are linked together by pointers.

An important point to realise from the diagrams below is that each of the boxes represents a **record**. A record is simply a set of related data. If the record contains more than one item of data (as is the case with Anson and 6.4) then the record is said to be split up into **fields**. The example we have just considered could have two

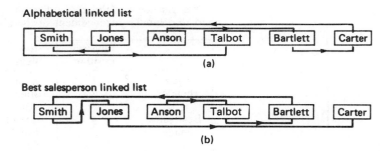

Alphabetical linked list

| Smith | Jones | Anson | Talbot | Bartlett | Carter |

(a)

Best salesperson linked list

| Smith | Jones | Anson | Talbot | Bartlett | Carter |

(b)

Figure 14.4

fields: one containing the surname Anson and one containing the data 6.4. However, we could include the year's sales figures, in which case there would be 13 fields to the record: one containing the surname Anson, and 12 others containing the monthly sales figures for January to December.

The way that the records are split up into fields is entirely the responsibility of the programmer and will be considered in some detail in the chapter on **file handling.**

It would be sensible to choose an item of data within the record to be the one that describes that record most conveniently. In the case of our example the name Anson would seem a sensible choice. Hence the field Anson will become what is known as the **key field.** The sales data associated with this key field will not be shown.

For the purposes of this chapter we will now consider the record to be one big chunk of data together with some pointers to form specific linked lists.

It is usual when considering data structures to represent the records in similar ways to that shown in the following example. The details of the records are unimportant as we are mainly concerned with the pointer structure. Used in this context the record is often called a **node** or a **cell.**

Node or cell representing Jones's data and pointers	Key field	Alphabetical pointer	Best sales pointer
	Jones	1	6

Note that the above pointers are **actually stored with the node data,** and must, therefore, reflect where you go after visiting the node Jones.

For example, **Jones's alphabetical pointer is now 1**, because the **next person** after Jones in the alphabet is **Smith**, who is **stored at memory location 1**. Similarly, **Jones's best sales pointer is 6**, because, **after Jones**, the **next best sales person is Carter**, who lives at **memory location number 6.** This way of using the pointers will be used in the next table, where each row of the table reflects the node structure within the list.

The above node is the Jones node using a combination of the pointers. You may have as many pointers as necessary.

To make use of such a list the computer must know where the list starts. A separate pointer known as the **start pointer, start cell** or **header** (head of the list) is used. This is simply another memory location or, for the purposes of this chapter, another box. Similarly, as the end of the list must also be known, it is usual to have a **finish pointer**. Again this will simply be a number in a box. Often in practice the last pointer in the list would be set to zero or some other suitable symbol to indicate that no data follows.

The complete list for the March sales together with the headers and end pointers is shown in figure 14.5.

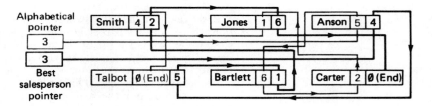

Figure 14.5

You can see that the above diagram gets a little unwieldy due to the many arrows and so a tabular arrangement of the above is often used as follows:

	Physical position	Key field	Alpha pointer	Best sales pointer
Alpha	1	Smith	4	2
header	2	Jones	1	6
3	3	Anson	5	4
Best sales	4	Talbot	0 (End)	5
header	5	Bartlett	6	1
3	6	Carter	2	0 (End)

Important note: The **alphabetical and best-sales pointers in the above table are not to be read from top to bottom.** They must be followed through by threading your way from the start pointers (headers) and working through the list. In this way you should see how this new representation generates all the same numbers that were used in the original list on page 297. The table above is simply a more convenient tabular arrangement of the information given in figure 14.5. It also gives the information in a more convenient form for programming, as it shows the pointer information in each record.

Altering records in linked lists

In the above examples we have not considered the possibility that data will have to be added to, or deleted from the list. **One of the biggest advantages of linked lists is the ability to make additions or deletions without having to move any other items of data around.** The only parts of the list that change are the pointers.

No attention has been paid to the fact that it is highly likely that there will be more memory left. The end pointers (0 in our examples) refer to the end of data, they do not necessarily refer to the end of memory. In fact it is usual to have a pointer that points to the next free storage location and this pointer will therefore be known as the **free storage pointer**. The idea is shown in figure 14.6.

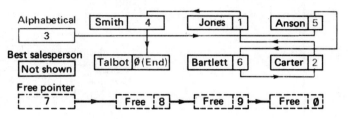

Figure 14.6

Deleting data from a linked list

Suppose that we wish to delete the salesperson called Smith. We can do this by altering the pointers as shown in the diagram of figure 14.6. Again only the alphabetical pointers will be shown. Figure 14.7(a) shows before deletion and figure 14.7(b) shows after deletion. Note the way in which the pointers have been changed:

1. Jones pointer is altered to point to Talbot. This leaves the Smith node free to be added to the list of free nodes, i.e. Smith now becomes the new free node.
2. The pointer of this new free node is now altered to point to where the free storage pointer is pointing.
3. The free storage pointer is now altered to point to the new free node, i.e. the node that used to be called Smith is now first in the free node list.

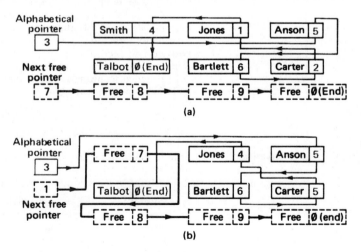

Figure 14.7

It can be seen that slight modifications to the above algorithm would be necessary if the data to be deleted was the first or last in the list. In such cases it is a simple matter to check for this and alter the header or the last free pointers accordingly.

Similarly, one could easily develop algorithms to insert a node into any part of the list. Again you would have to consider the case of the new node to be inserted somewhere in the middle of the list as slightly different from the data to be inserted at the beginning or the end of the list.

Adding data to a linked list

As an example we will start again with the original list and insert another salesperson called Cummings. The before and after pointer situations are shown in figure 14.8.

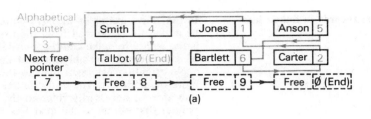

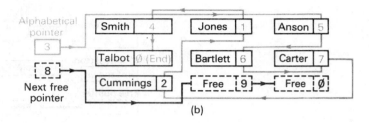

Figure 14.8

The procedure goes along the following lines:

1. Determine where in the list the node is to be inserted. This is obviously in between Carter and Jones.
2. Store data at the position indicated by free storage pointer.
3. Alter free storage pointer to point to next free location.
4. Alter Carter's pointer to point to Cummings.
5. Alter Cummings' pointer to point to Jones.

Again slight modifications will be necessary if the data is at the beginning or end of the list, or if no storage space is available, in which case the free storage pointer would have been set to zero by the previous operations. One could build up a complete set of algorithms to deal with each possible set of circumstances and then incorporate them all into a flowchart to maintain this data structure. It is only necessary to understand the principles on which these data structures are based, unless you wish to incorporate them into a program. In such cases you will be forced to write the algorithms and flowcharts anyway!

In practice to insert items of data in the way described above would require such techniques as following the pointers and checking to find the exact place for insertion. Once found (probably using string comparisons on the key fields) you make a note of the pointers for the data just before the place you are inserting so that stages (4) and (5) above then become a relatively simple matter.

Processing data in a linked list

Linked list systems can be processed by making use of the algorithms shown in the next section:

The following terminology will apply:

Pointer	= variable used as a pointer to each node.
start	= address of start pointer
finish	= address of finish pointer
LIST	= general name for the list contained in memory.
LIST(Pointer)	= Subscripted variable representing data at *current node* pointed to by *pointer*, i.e. the **identifier** for a specific item of data.
LINK(Pointer)	= Subscripted variable used as an **identifier** for the current pointer data, i.e. the number which is used as the link pointer (see traversing a linked list for explanation).

Traversing a linked list

The following pseudocode shows how a typical linked list may be traversed. As traversing the list is usually done for some specific reason, we will print out the data contained at each node.

The following procedure assumes that a list called **LIST(N)** has already been set up. In addition to this, one easy way to set up the **link pointer system** is to establish *another list identical in structure to the first*, but this one contains the **link pointers** and will therefore be called **LINK(N)**. It is easy to visualize as shown in figure 14.9.

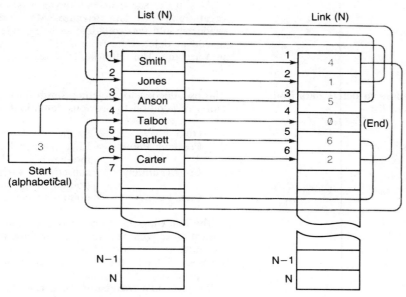

List (N)   Link (N)

Start
(alphabetical)

Figure 14.9

Procedure to print out all the data in a linked list

By referring to the diagram of figure 14.9 you should see that the following pseudocode is all that is necessary to print out the entire list.

```
PROCEDURE PRINT(start, finish)
    Set Pointer = start              (*Point to beginning of list*)
    REPEAT
        PRINT LIST(Pointer)          (*Node information printed out*)
        SET Pointer = LINK(Pointer)  (*Set pointer to new link*)
    UNTIL Pointer = finish           (*Last node printed out*)
END PROCEDURE
```

Notice that we passed the parameters about the start and finish pointers to the procedure. The same procedure could then be used for different pointers such as 'best sales', 'alphabetical', etc.

If the data consisted of just the names of the salespersons, and if the start pointer was put equal to the 'best sales' pointer, then a list would be obtained of the 'best sales' people in descending order. Of course the figures and anything else could also be printed out if this formed part of the data for each record.

Procedure to search for an item of data in a linked list

To **search** a linked list is just as easy. For example, we might want to print out all the information connected with *Talbot*:

If Data = Talbot, the pseudocode for *finding and printing out Talbot's information* could be as follows:

Note in the following case, **Data = Talbot**
When **Pointer = 0**, we are at the **end of the list**

```
PROCEDURE SEARCH(Start, Data)
    SET Pointer = Start                  (*Point to beginning of list*)
    REPEAT
        IF Data = LIST(Pointer) THEN     (*Match found*)
            Print out the data at node
            EXIT PROCEDURE
        ELSE
            SET Pointer = LINK(Pointer)  (*Set pointer to new link*)
        ENDIF
    UNTIL Pointer = 0                     (*Last node*)
    PRINT Information can't be found      (*No match*)
END PROCEDURE
```

As you can see from the above, it is relatively easy to write procedures to interrogate linked list data structures. Many other examples could be developed and the reader should feel confident in being able to do so. It is slightly more complicated to add or delete data from a linked list, as the free pointers also have to be taken into account. The following is an example of one way of deleting data from a linked list.

Procedure to delete data from a linked list

The pseudocode for deleting Smith from a linked list is as follows:
Note: In addition to previous definitions, in the following case:

Data	=	Smith
Previous_Pointer	=	Link pointer from *previous node* (see explanation in a moment) .
LINK(Pointer)	=	subscripted variable used as an **identifier** for the Link pointer in the same way as before (see last algorithm).
Free_Pointer	=	pointer to the *next free node*.

The following should be read in conjunction with figure 14.7, as this gives a visual indication of what is actually happening. Don't forget that as we go through the list, we must keep a note of the previous node's pointer because, if we find the node we wish to delete, then the previous node's pointer becomes important in the deletion process.

We must **first traverse the list, checking the data at each node to see if it is the one to be deleted**. To **delete a node from a linked list** requires **altering the pointers from the previous node to point to the node after the node to be deleted.** We must also allocate the **freed node** to the **next free pointer list**. As shown in the diagram, we will assume that the freed node will go at the beginning of the free node list. The swap routine in the algorithm will swap any pointers that are necessary.

The following situation is slightly more complex if the node to be deleted happens to be the first node in the list, or the last node in the list. This is allowed for in the pseudocode algorithm which follows.

In the following algorithm, if Data = Smith, then it should carry out the processes shown in figure 14.7. Again it is assumed that **LIST(N)** and **LINK(N)** have already been set up, and are being used in exactly the same way as shown in figure 14.9. The only difference is that we now have a free pointer system as well, and are keeping a note of the previous node's pointer.

The actual pseudocode algorithm for delete is as follows:

```
PROCEDURE DELETE(Start, Free_Pointer, Data)
    Pointer = Start                        (*Point to beginning of list*)
    Previous_Pointer = Start               (*No previous pointer yet*)
                                           (*Main procedure for node deletion and
                                               adding to next free list*)
    REPEAT
      IF Data = LIST(Pointer) THEN         (*Node for deletion is found*)
        IF Previous_Pointer = Start AND Pointer = Start THEN
                                               (*lst node to be deleted*)

          temp = Free_Pointer
          Free_Pointer = Previous_Pointer
          Start = LINK(Pointer)
          LINK(Pointer) = temp
                        (*lst node deleted and assigned to free list*)
          EXIT PROCEDURE
        ENDIF

        IF  LINK(Pointer) = 0 THEN          (*Last node to be deleted*)
          temp = Free_Pointer
          LINK(Previous_Pointer) = 0
          Previous_Pointer = 0
          Free_Pointer = Pointer
          LINK(Pointer) = temp              (*New end of list set up,
          EXIT PROCEDURE           deleted node assigned to free list*)

        ENDIF                               (*Middle node to be deleted*)
        temp = Free_Pointer

        LINK(Previous_Pointer) = LINK(Pointer)
        Free_Pointer = Pointer
```

```
            LINK(Pointer) = temp                    (*Middle node out of list and
                                                        assigned to free list*)
          EXIT PROCEDURE
       ELSE                                       (*Update pointers for next node*)
          Previous_Pointer = Pointer
          Pointer = LINK(Pointer)
       ENDIF
    UNTIL Pointer = 0                             (*Node not in list*)
    PRINT Node requested has not been found
  EXIT PROCEDURE
```

In practice the above algorithm would need to check if the initial list was empty, and, if merged with an algorithm to add data to a linked list, would have to have slight modifications. Again the reader should be able to add to and modify the above procedure to carry out a variety of tasks.

Circular or ring lists

In the last example we have seen the use of **end pointers** to indicate the end of a list. Such an example occurred when following alphabetical pointers through the records. Instead of terminating the list with either a zero or some other suitable character we can arrange a pointer to point back to the beginning of the list. A **circular list** using such a pointer system for the March sales of Bradbury's chocolates would be as follows:

	Physical position	Key field	Alpha pointer	Best sales pointer
Alpha	1	Smith	4	2
header	2	Jones	1	6
3	3	Anson	5	4
Best sales	4	Talbot	3 (New pointer)	5
header	5	Bartlett	6	1
3	6	Carter	2	3 (New pointer)

Note that the end of data pointers (they used to be zero) are now pointing to 3 as Anson heads both the alphabetical and best sales lists. The table should be compared with the table for the simple linked list on page 298. The advantage of using a circular list over the simple linked list is that we are able to investigate the nodes as many times as we please by literally going round in circles! Note that we still need the alphabetical and best sales pointers or we would have no indication of where each list starts. Similarly we would still need the free storage pointer to indicate where extra data is to be stored.

Two-way linked lists

It is often desirable to be able to go both in the forward and backward directions by making use of pointers. As an example consider our alphabetical salesperson list used many times in the last few sections. As well as having a list of alphabetical pointers, a **two-way linked list** would also have reverse-order alphabetical pointers. This enables us to go both backwards and forwards in the list with ease. A two-way circular linked list system using both forward and backward pointers on the alphabetical and best sales lists for March would be as follows:

	Physical position	Key field	Alpha pointer	Reverse alpha pointer	Best sales sales pointer	Reverse best sales pointer
Alpha	1	Smith	4	2	2	5
header	2	Jones	1	6	6	1
3	3	Anson	5	4	4	6
Best sales	4	Talbot	3	1	5	3
header	5	Bartlett	6	3	1	4
3	6	Carter	2	5	3	2

Using a two-way linked list (circular or simple) enables us to quickly go both ways in the list to search for data and to make lists in either forward or reverse order. However, the process is relatively slow compared to other more sophisticated methods if large amounts of data are stored, and if random data must be sought quickly. The linked list system is ideal for listing out large amounts of related data such as alphabetical order or sales figures. Other pointer systems could be set up to indicate length of service to the company, age etc.

Tree structures (hierarchical data structures)

Often data does not conveniently fit into a list structure, and other structures such as the **hierarchical data structure** shown in figure 14.10 are often used. Such a data structure would be useful for storing items of data in the automobile industry. In such a system an alphabetical listing of all the component parts of the car would be less efficient compared to representing the system as a hierarchical data structure as shown in the diagram.

The complete data structure is not shown as it would be impossible to fit such a vast quantity of information on to a single page. However, a typical path is shown to obtain information about a toothed-quadrant gear which is used to wind the car window up and down.

First the appropriate car file is located, i.e. the manufacturer, model and year would determine this. Next the mechanical section is chosen because the winding mechanism for the window is mechanical. Going down the hierarchy we chose bodywork, doors, winding mechanism and finally toothed quadrant.

Many data structures in real life, from family trees to a fully structured program (i.e. split up into simpler modules and these modules are then split up into submodules etc.) can be represented as hierarchical data structures.

A hierarchical data structure is called a **tree** (compare it with a family tree). Each part of the tree that contains data is called a **node** (in the same way that we used the term for lists). Much terminology from trees are used to describe various parts of the structure. For example the 'most important' i.e. the node at the beginning of the tree structure is called the **root node.** Car would be the root node for the tree structure shown in figure 14.10. The lines that connect the nodes are called **branches.**

Consider the root node of the structure in figure 14.10. You will see that there are two branches leading to the mechanical node and the electrical node. Car is called the **parent node** and mechanical and electrical are called **children nodes**. Now mechanical and electrical are the children of car but mechanical is the parent of engine, fuel system, gearbox and clutch, suspension and bodywork etc.

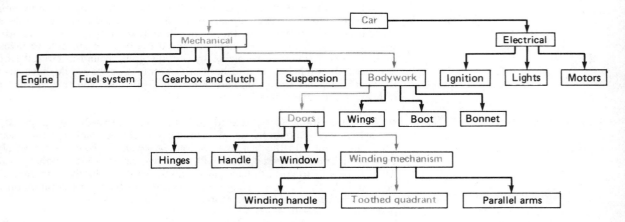

Figure 14.10

Each part of the tree that consists of parent and child nodes (such as mechanical) is called a **subtree**. Similarly bodywork would be another **subtree**.

At the bottom of a tree we end up with a child node that has no children. This is termed a **leaf node** (imagine them to be the leaves on the top of the tree when the tree structure is turned upside down such that the root is at the bottom). **Leaf nodes** are also known as **terminal nodes**.

As can be seen from the tree structure of figure 14.10 some parents have a number of children. Therefore the relationship between these children would be that of brother or sister. **Brother** and **sister nodes** are said to be on the same **level** of the subtree.

Tree structures are often used for storing vast amounts of data, such as are found in **databases**.

To represent a tree structure on the computer extensive use is made of **pointers**. It is usual to start at the root node then follow the pointers through to find the particular item of interest.

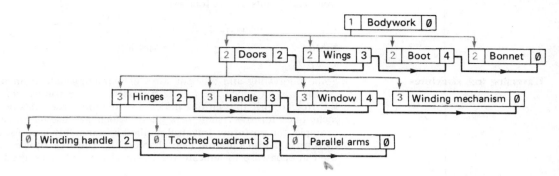

Figure 14.11

Each node has pointers indicating any other nodes on the same level and to point to any subtree that may exist for that node. The general form of a node will therefore be as follows:

| Subtree pointer | Data associated with this node | Pointer to same level nodes |

For simplicity let us consider the Bodywork subtree shown in figure 14.10. This is reproduced with pointers in figure 14.11.

Although such data structures are convenient for quickly locating data related in this way, it is more complex to add and delete nodes compared with linear lists. It is usual to implement some form of stack (see page 288) so that the route through the tree can be retraced back to previously visited nodes.

The zeros used in the above tree indicate the end of list in exactly the same way as those used for linked lists.

Binary trees

These are special types of tree where the parent is only allowed to have a maximum of two children. **Binary tree structures** are implemented using pointer systems in similar ways to the node pointers used with linked lists. The node structure for a typical node in a binary tree diagram would be as follows:

| Left pointer | Data to be contained in the node | Right pointer |

The main point to note is that each node in the structure contains left and right pointers. Either of these pointers may be set to indicate the end of the structure. As an example, consider the following list of names:

Poon   Derry   Smith   Ashton   Wray   Taylor   and   McCulloch

We may wish to store the data using < or > together with the first letter of the name, i.e. Poon > Derry because Poon comes after Derry in the alphabet.

Let us suppose that Poon is the root node. This would be as follows:

Poon

Now Derry is the next item to be added. As Derry < Poon, Poon's left pointer is used to point to Derry. The structure now becomes:

Poon

Derry

Smith is next and as Smith > Poon, therefore, Poon's right-hand pointer points to Smith as follows:

Poon ———→ Smith

Derry

Ashton is next. As Ashton < Poon, we follow Poon's left-hand pointer and arrive at Derry. As Ashton < Derry we make Derry's left-hand pointer point to the new node Ashton. The tree is now as follows:

Poon ———→ Smith

Derry

Ashton

In a similar way all the other nodes are added to build up the complete binary tree. The results are as follows:

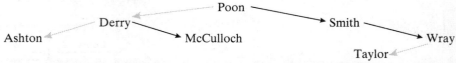

Traversing tree structures

Some interesting and efficient ways of extracting data from tree stuctures depend on the way in which the tree is **traversed** i.e. the routes which are taken through the tree to visit the various nodes in a definite order. There are several standard techniques for traversing trees all of which are useful for specific purposes. For example, the **postorder traversal** method is commonly used for converting from **infix** to **reverse Polish notation** (see chapter 10). The tree shown in figure 14.12 will be used in each case to indicate the traversal method being used.

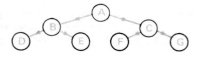

Figure 14.12

For each method the nodes will be listed in the order in which the tree has been traversed. A simple three-stage algorithm is also given in each case. In each case the definitions are **recursive** (see page 185). As far as we are concerned, this means that they can call themselves. For example, if the left-hand subtree is to be traversed, then the three-stage algorithm will call itself to perform the traversal of this subtree. It may seem very complex, but the process is really very simple.

Preorder traversal

1. Start at the root node
2. Traverse the left-hand subtree
3. Traverse the right-hand subtree

As this is the first example it will be explained in detail. Performing stage (1) of the algorithm the list becomes:

A   i.e. write down the root node

Part (2) involves traversing the left-hand subtree. Now we effectively call the routine again because we want to perform a **preorder traversal** of this left-hand subtree.

Part (1) of this second level then starts at the new root node. As the root node of the left-hand subtree is B then this is listed. The list now becomes:

A B

Part (2) involves traversing the left-hand subtree, but this time it is simply a terminal node D. We therefore add D to the list and it becomes:

A B D

Part (3) involves traversing the right-hand subtree. This is again a terminal node E. The list now becomes:

A B D E

We have now performed part (2) of the original set of instructions. We therefore proceed to part (3) which states traverse the right-hand subtree, i.e. the subtree with the root node C, and the definition now recursively calls itself again as above. The complete list for a preorder traversal will therefore be:

A B D E C F G

Inorder traversal

1. Traverse the left-hand subtree
2. Visit the root node
3. Traverse the right-hand subtree

Applying the recursive definition to the tree in figure 14.12 we get the following list for inorder traversal:

D B E A F C G

1.   Traverse the left-hand subtree
2.   Traverse the right-hand subtree
3.   Return to the root node

Applying the recursive definition for postorder traversal we get the following list:

   D E B F G C A

The names **preorder, inorder** and **postorder** are obtained from the position in which the root node is visited with respect to the other operations. In the preorder traversal it is visited during the first stage (1), in the inorder traversal the root node is visited in the middle, stage (2), and finally in the postorder traversal the root node, stage (3) is visited at the end.

Examples

(1) As an example of the application of traversal methods, consider the binary tree shown at the beginning of the binary tree section consisting of seven different names, i.e.

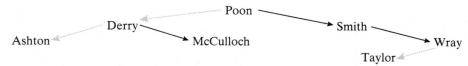

The tree was originally constructed using the standard < and > tests on letters of the alphabet. If we perform an inorder traversal on the above tree we get:

   Ashton, Derry, McCulloch, Poon, Smith, Taylor and Wray

We have produced an alphabetical list of the data contained in each node.

(2) As another example of how these traversal methods can be used, consider the INFIX (see page 210) algebraic expression: $X = 3 * Y + (Z \uparrow 2 - Z)$. This may be expressed as a binary tree as shown in figure 14.13. (You may wish to come back to this example when you understand its significance more readily.)

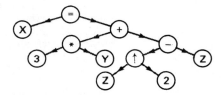

Figure 14.13

To convert this to reverse polish we traverse the right-hand subtree using postorder traversal, listing the nodes when this part of the traversal is complete. The **reverse Polish expression** can be found in seconds when you have had some practice. However we will build it up slowly to illustrate the traversal method.

We traverse the **right-hand subtree**. The root node of this subtree is the + node. Now this can't be written down in one lump and so we apply the algorithm again (the recursive definition).
Traverse the left-hand subtree. The root node of this subtree is now the * node. Hence applying the algorithm again we traverse the left-hand subtree. We have finally arrived at a terminal node which is 3. Hence the expression becomes:

   3

Traverse the right-hand subtree (which is simply the Y). Hence the expression becomes:

   3 Y

We now return to the root node of the subtree which is *. Hence the expression becomes:

   3 Y *

Next we return to the root node which is + and traverse the right-hand subtree. In this way the rest of the expression can be built up as follows:

$$3 \: Y * Z \: 2 \uparrow Z - +$$

Processing data in trees

We will now develop a method for traversing a tree structure using **preorder traversal**. Make sure that you have understood what is meant by preorder traversal, and make sure that you are familiar with the **stack data structure** covered earlier in this chapter.

Pseudocode to traverse a tree using preorder traversal

First, a brief reminder of **preorder traversal**:

1. Start at the **ROOT** node
2. Traverse the *left-hand* subtree using **preorder** traversal
3. Traverse the *right-hand* subtree using **preorder** traversal

As we are traversing the left-hand subtree we shall have to come back to the root of the subtree eventually so that the right-hand subtree may be traversed. The **STACK** will be used as a **temporary store** in which to place the addresses of the nodes which must be visited on our return journey. We must, therefore, *initially* set the STACK to zero. In the following algorithms we have made use of a stack, but will not check to see if the stack will overflow. These techniques have already been covered earlier in this chapter, and will only make what we are trying to do appear more complex. You can easily add these checks at a later stage when the tree traversal algorithms are working for simple sets of data.

Having undertaken a preorder traversal of the tree shown in figure 14.12, you will recall that, as each node is visited it must be processed. As an example, in the algorithm we are developing, the *process* that will be carried out will be to *print the data contained at each node*. We should, therefore, end up with the same sequence of letters: **ABDECFG** after working through the final pseudocode algorithm.

When proceeding down the left-hand path of the tree, as well as processing each node visited as described above, we must push any right-hand child nodes that we find onto the top of the stack. This process must continue until we get to a **leaf node**, whereupon this leaf node is processed. To progress down the subtree we must follow the **Left_pointers.** We will know we have hit a **leaf node** because, at this stage, **Left_pointer = 0**.

After reaching a leaf node we must backtrack by **popping** the address of the stack. However, each time we remove an address from the stack we must check to see if it is zero. If it is, we have finished, if not, we assign our pointer to this new address from the stack and must then go through the same process again with the new pointer from the stack as our new starting point.

In the **pseudocode algorithms,** the following terminology will apply:

Pointer	= variable used as a pointer to each node in the tree.
STACK	= a stack implemented as described earlier in this chapter.
STACK(Stack_Pointer)	= subscripted variable used as an identifier for the data on the stack pointed to by the current stack pointer.
PUSH and **POP**	are used as described in the section on stacks.
ROOT	= root node of the tree.
TREE(Pointer)	= subscripted variable used as an identifier for the data at the node pointed to by the current pointer.
Left_Pointer	= pointer to left child of **TREE(Pointer)**
Right_Pointer	= pointer to right child of **TREE(Pointer)**

It is assumed that **STACK(N)** and **TREE(N)** have already been set up.

We must start at the root of the tree, and therefore the **Pointer** must be **SET** *initially* to the **ROOT**.

If we arrange the following algorithm carefully, then the STACK should be empty only at the start and when the *complete tree* has been traversed.

The final pseudocode algorithm can be developed as shown:

```
PREORDER(ROOT)                          (*Initialization of pointers and stack*)
    SET Pointer = ROOT
    Stack_Pointer = 0
    REPEAT

                                        (*Get data and pointer info from node*)
```

```
            PRINT TREE(POINTER)                (*First time node has been visited*)
            IF Right_Pointer <> 0 THEN              (*Deal with right child node*)
              Stack_Pointer = Stack_Pointer + 1
                STACK(Stack_Pointer) = Right_Pointer        (*PUSH onto STACK*)
            ENDIF
            IF Left_Pointer <> 0 THEN        (*Set pointer to traverse left subtree*)
              SET Pointer = Left_Pointer

            ELSE                                       (*Arrived at a leaf node*)
              SET Pointer = STACK(Stack_Pointer)             (*POP off STACK*)
              Stack_Pointer = Stack_Pointer - 1
            ENDIF

          UNTIL Pointer = 0                              (*Top of stack is empty,
                                                          tree has been traversed*)

      END PROCEDURE
```

To help you understand the above algorithm, consider the following **dry run** with the data from figure 14.12.

Note that *each node is called by its contents,* A, B, C, D, etc. Note also that **Ra** denotes the **Right_Pointer of Node A** and **Le** denotes the **Left_Pointer associated with Node E**, etc. A and B are simply the pointers to these nodes, i.e. if we are dealing with the root node, then the pointer must be at A.

Dry run for **preorder traversal** using the above **pseudocode algorithm** with the **data** from **Figure 14.12**:

Pointers			Stack_Pointer	Contents of stack	Processing results	Comments
L	Ptr	R				
La	A	Ra	0	–	–	Initialization
La	A	Ra	0	–	A	Processing carried out on root node
La	A	Ra	1	Ra	–	Save right child on stack
Lb	B	Rb	1	Ra	–	Update pointers
Lb	B	Rb	1	Ra	B	Processing carried out on node B
Lb	B	Rb	2	Rb Ra	–	Save right child on stack
Ld	D	Rd	2	Rb Ra	–	Update pointers
0	D	0	2	Rb Ra	D	Processing carried out on Node D Note Ld and Rd = 0
0	Rb	0	1	Ra	–	POP off stack
0	E	0	1	Ra	–	NB. pointer been set to E (i.e. RH-pointer of B)
0	E	0	1	Ra	E	Processing carried out on Node E NB. Le and Re = 0
0	Ra	0	0	–	–	POP off stack
0	C	0	0	–	–	NB. Pointer been set to C (i.e. RH-pointer of A)
Lc	C	Rc	0	–	C	Processing carried out on node C
Lc	C	Rc	1	Rc	–	Save right child on stack
Lf	F	Rf	1	Rc	–	Update pointers
0	F	0	1	Rc	F	Processing carried out on node F Note Lf and Rf = 0
0	Rc	0	0	–	–	POP off stack
0	G	0	0	–	G	Processing carried out on node G
0	0	0	0	–	–	Main pointer = 0 Algorithm is therefore terminated

Pseudocode to traverse a tree using inorder traversal

First, a brief reminder of **inorder traversal**:

1. Traverse the *left-hand* subtree using **inorder** traversal.
2. Visit the **ROOT** node.
3. Traverse the *right-hand* subtree using **inorder** traversal.

The ideas are obviously very similar to those when carrying out the **preorder traversal** earlier. However, inorder traversal is a little more tricky. Even so, after following through the dry run given after the algorithm, you should be able to understand the ideas.

As before, 'Pointer' will be used to direct the processing of data. This time however, we will carry on down the 'left-hand side of the tree' pushing each node on to the stack, and continuing in this way until we reach a leaf node, in which case this is the 'root' of the left-hand subtree, and the data at this node will therefore be processed.

We then backtrack to the root node of the left-hand subtree, popping each item off the stack until the stack is empty. However, when popping an item off the stack, if a right child is found, this must then be processed by calling the original algorithm again, but this time with the pointer set to the new Right_Pointer instead of the root.

It should be noted that recursion is used in the following algorithm, i.e. the procedure calls itself (see page 185).

In this **pseudocode algorithm,** as before, the following terminology will apply:

Pointer	= variable used as a pointer to each node in the tree.
STACK	= a stack implemented as described earlier in this chapter.
STACK(Stack_Pointer) =	subscripted variable used as an identifier for the data on the stack pointed to by the current stack pointer.
PUSH and **POP**	are used as described in the section on stacks.
ROOT	= root node of the tree.
TREE(Pointer)	= subscripted variable used as an identifier for the data at the node pointed to by the current pointer.
Left_Pointer	= pointer to left child of **TREE(Pointer)**
Right_Pointer	= pointer to right child of **TREE(Pointer)**
PROCESS	= part of the algorithm which may call itself. It has therefore been written as a separate procedure.

The pseudocode algorithm is as follows:

```
PROCEDURE INORDER(ROOT)              (*Initialization of pointers and stack*)
   SET Pointer = ROOT
   Stack_Pointer = 0
   PROCESS                           (*Call the process procedure shown below*)
END PROCEDURE

PROCEDURE PROCESS
   REPEAT
      Stack_Pointer = Stack_Pointer + 1          (*Push data on to stack*)
      Stack(Stack_Pointer) = Pointer             (*Update pointer to get
                                                     to next node*)

      Pointer = Left_Pointer

   UNTIL Left_Pointer = 0      (*Arrived at leaf node as left pointer = 0*)
   PRINT TREE(Pointer)                           (*POPS node off the stack*)
   Pointer = STACK(Stack_Pointer)
   Stack_Pointer = Stack_Pointer - 1
   REPEAT                                   (*Process the data in the node*)
      PRINT TREE(Pointer)
      IF Right_Pointer <> 0 THEN             (*Traverse right-hand subtree?*)
         Pointer = Right_Pointer
         PROCESS                            (*Recursive call to this procedure*)

      ELSE                                      (*POPS node off the stack*)
         Pointer = Stack(Stack_Pointer)
         Stack_Pointer = Stack_Pointer - 1
      ENDIF

   UNTIL Left_Pointer = 0
END PROCEDURE
```

Dry run for the **inorder traversal** using the **data** from **figure 14.12**:

	Pointers		Stack_Pointer	Contents of stack	Processing results	Comments
L	Ptr	R				
La	A	Ra	0	–	–	Initialization
La	A	Ra	1	A	–	Push data on to stack
Lb	B	Rb	1	A	–	Update pointers Lb <> 0
Lb	B	Rb	2	B A	–	Push data on to stack
Ld	D	Rd	2	B A	–	Update pointers Ld = 0
Ld	D	Rd	2	B A	D	Process data
Lb	B	Rb	1	A	–	Pop data and update pointer
Lb	B	Rb	1	A	B	Process data Lb<>0 Rb<>0
Le	E	Re	1	A	–	Update pointers
*** Procedure calls itself to traverse right-hand subtree ***						
Le	E	Re	2	E A	–	Push on to stack
–	0	–	2	E A	–	Update pointers
						No processing as node does not exist!
Le	E	Re	1	A	–	Pop off stack
Le	E	Re	1	A	E	Process data Re = 0
La	A	Ra	0	–	–	Pop off stack
La	A	Ra	0	–	A	Process data La <> 0
Lc	C	Rc	0	–	–	Update pointers
*** Procedure calls itself to traverse right-hand subtree ***						
Lc	C	Rc	1	C	–	Push on to stack
Lf	F	Rf	1	–	–	Update pointers Lf = 0
Lf	F	Rf	1	C	F	Process data
Lc	C	Rc	0	–	–	Pop off stack
Lc	C	Rc	0	–	C	Process data Rc <> 0
Lg	G	Rg	0	–	–	Update pointers
*** Procedure calls itself to traverse right-hand subtree ***						
Lg	G	Rg	1	G	–	Push data on to stack
–	0	–	1	G	–	Update pointers
						No processing as node does not exist
Lg	G	Rg	0	–	G	Process data Rg = 0
Lg	G	Rg	0	–	–	Pop off stack

END CALL

END CALL

END CALL

END Original PROCEDURE

Pseudocode to traverse a tree using postorder traversal

Having gone through the last two traversal methods in great detail, it is left to the reader to develop the final method. The method is a little more complicated than the previous two algorithms. (Teachers take note: it makes a great assignment!)

Networks

Networks are data structures that allow more complex interconnections than are possible using linked lists or trees. An example of a network is shown in figure 14.14.

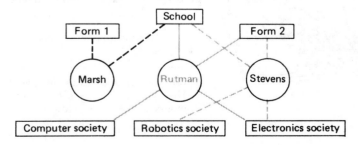

Figure 14.14

For simplicity the network shows just three pupils of a school together with two forms and three school societies. From the network the relations between the various nodes can be seen. For example, Marsh is a member of Form 1 but belongs to no society. Rutman is a member of Form 2 and belongs to the computer and electronics societies etc.

Network data structures have been used extensively in the implementation of **database systems** because of the vastly increased flexibility over the more limited hierarchical data structures. They are difficult to maintain (i.e. difficult to modify because of the spider's web of pointers) and techniques known as **relational structures** (see page 467) are rapidly becoming more popular. However, these will be covered in more detail in the section on databases.

Hash tables

We have seen how data may be stored in lists and trees, and how data may be represented in memory as a linear list. The previous methods are good for finding data that has structure such as a hierarchy, but not so useful for storing and accessing data in more **random** ways. Suppose that we have a table consisting of 10,000 elements (initially empty) as shown in figure 14.15(a).

Suppose now that we run a club with no more than 1000 members each with a five-digit secret membership code. The problem is, how do we map the membership code (the key field) to these 1000 storage locations in the table? One method that gives very quick access to the stored data is called **hashing**.

We must first think up a **hash (or hashing) function.** This is simply a **set of rules that, when applied to the five-digit key field, generates the appropriate address in the table.**

Addresses	Membership number	Hashing function	Addresses
1 ::::::::::::::::::	1 2 3 4 5 26		1 ::::::::::::::::
2 ::::::::::::::::::			
3 ::::::::::::::::::	8 7 2 1 3 370		26 ::number 12345:::
4 ::::::::::::::::::			
5 ::::::::::::::::::	0 2 3 1 1 722		370 ::number 87213:::
.			
.	7 6 2 8 9 522		
.			522 ::number 76289:::
			722 ::number 02311:::
998 ::::::::::::::::::			
999 ::::::::::::::::::			999 :::::::::::::::::
1000 ::::::::::::::::::			1000 :::::::::::::::::

(a)   (b)

Figure 14.15

You can consider the hash function to be a pointer that is used to point to the location where the appropriate data may be found. A generalised hash function is used in the following way:

Address = hash function (key field)

As an example, let us consider the following hash function:

Hash function   =   key field is squared, then take **right-hand three digits** and finally **ADD 1**

Consider the member who has a secret membership code number of 12345. Applying the above hashing function we get:

Original number	Number squared	Right-hand three digits	Right-hand three digits ADD 1
12345	152399025	025	26

Therefore, the address of membership number 12345 = 26.

The above is shown in figure 14.15(b) together with the three other membership numbers worked out below.

Original number	Number squared	Right-hand three digits	Right-hand three digits ADD 1
87213	7606107369	369	370
02311	5340721	721	722
76289	5820011521	521	522

One disadvantage of hashing functions is their ability to generate the same address within the table for different key fields. This is termed a **collision.** From the above it should be reasonably obvious that collisions will occur if the last digits in the membership number are the same. As an example, consider the following three membership numbers:

Original number	Number squared	Right-hand three digits	Right-hand three digits ADD 1
83123	6909433129	129	130
95123	9048385129	129	130
07123	50737129	129	130

We can see that all three unique membership numbers have generated the same address at which to store the data. One method to get over this is to make use of an **overflow table.** The idea is shown in figure 14.16.

We can see that as membership number 83123 was first, it occupied the free loca-

Membership number	Hashing function	Addresses	Overflow table
1 2 3 4 5	26	1 ::::::::::::::::::::	::number 95123::*
			::number 07123:::
8 7 2 1 3	370	26 ::number 12345:::	::::::::::::::::::
			::::::::::::::::::
			::::::::::::::::::
8 3 1 2 3	130	130 ::number 83123::*	
9 5 1 2 3	130		
0 7 1 2 3	130		
0 2 3 1 1	722	370 ::number 87213:::	
7 6 2 8 9	522	522 ::number 76289:::	
		722 ::number 02311:::	
		999 ::::::::::::::::::	
		1000 ::::::::::::::::::	

Figure 14.16

tion 130. Now the next number to generate this address is 95123. This is then stored in the overflow table which is linked to the original address 130 by a pointer system. The * at the end of the data indicates that an overflow table exists or, if it is already in the overflow table, then it indicates a pointer that points to the next entry in the overflow table.

Devising the hashing functions

In the above section we said 'think up a hashing function'! In fact there are thousands of different possible functions, some of which are more suitable than others for particular applications. It is usual to try and get an even distribution of data throughout the table. This is because a bias towards one end or the other would produce more collisions than necessary. Several standard methods for choosing hashing functions have been developed and are as follows:

Methods using modulo arithmetic

A common method used to generate addresses uses the **modulo** function. This is convenient as it enables us to generate the exact number of addresses easily and quickly. For example, if we had just fifty locations in store, then MOD 50 would produce the numbers 0 to 49 from any **numeric field.** Similarly if we had 1000 memory locations then MOD 1000 would produce the numbers 0 to 999 for any memory locations then MOD 1000 would produce the numbers 0 to 999 for any numeric field. Hence a general hashing function using modulo arithmetic might be of the form:

Address = (Key field)MOD N + 1

We have stressed that this is for numeric fields. However, it can be applied to nonnumeric fields if an appropriate coding method is used. As an example, let us assume that we use an alphabetic key field consisting of five letters. We could use the ASCII code (see page 266) for each number and build up the numbers that can be used in the hashing function.

Example

Non-numeric field	=	F R E D
ASCII numbers	=	70 82 69 68
		(ASCII code for F in decimal is 70 etc.)
Numeric equivalent	=	70826968
Addresses (MOD 1000)	=	968

Hence FRED would be stored in location 969.

Radix conversion

You will recall from page 31 that a **radix** is simply the name given to a number base. Any base greater than base ten can be used and hence we will use base thirteen in our example.

Example

Let the original key be 2 3 1 6.

We assume that the above number is in base thirteen and proceed to convert it into base ten. If a base < ten is used you may get high digits that would be impossible in that base!

$$1 \times 13 \uparrow 3 + 1 \times 13 \uparrow 2 + 1 \times 13 \uparrow 1 + 1 \times 13 \uparrow 0 \qquad \text{(Column headings in base 13)}$$

$$\begin{array}{ccccccc} 2 & & 3 & & 1 & & 6 \\ 4394 & + & 507 & + & 13 & + & 6 & = & 4920 \end{array}$$

If the range of addresses is too large (as will probably be the case above) then it is usual to **truncate** the number to the required number of digits. Thus if three digits were required in the above example, then 2316 would generate the address 920.

Mid-square method

Another popular technique is to **square** the **key field** and take N digits out of the middle of the result.

Example

Suppose that we are dealing with a four-digit key field. The maximum number of digits that this can generate when squared is eight. i.e. $9999 \times 9999 = 99980001$

Therefore a number which, when squared, does not generate eight digits, is packed with leading zeros.

Let us choose to take the middle four digits out of the squared number.

The key field 1210 would generate the following address:

$$1210 \times 1210 = 01464100$$

Therefore the middle four digits = 4641, which is the required address.

Exercise 14.1

1. Explain what is meant by the following terms:
   (a) Linear list
   (b) Circular list
   (c) Stack (LIFO and FIFO)
   (d) Queue
   (e) Array

2. (a) Explain the terms:
      (i) Linked list
      (ii) Pointers
      (iii) Two-way linked list
   (b) Design an algorithm to delete a node from a linked list.

3. What is a tree structure and why is it of fundamental importance in computing?
   Briefly explain and give examples of the following terms when applied to a tree structure:
   (a) Subtree
   (b) Node
   (c) Terminal node, child node, parent node, sister node and root node.
   (d) Give two examples of data that would naturally lead to a hierarchical structure.

4. A binary tree is a special type of tree structure. Outline the conditions that must be obeyed for a tree to be a binary tree and give an application of a typical binary tree structure.

5. There are various ways of traversing tree structures. These include:
   (a) Preorder traversal
   (b) Inorder traversal
   (c) Postorder traversal
   Using the following tree structure write down the order in which the node data would be listed using the three traversal methods described above.

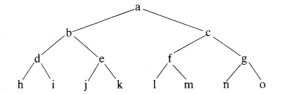

6. What are the main differences between a **network** data structure and a **tree** data structure. Which would be the most appropriate structure for a database and why?

7. (a) What is meant by a **hash table**? Give an example by making use of a suitable hashing function of your own choosing.
   (b) What is meant by an **overflow table** when using hashing functions. What happens when the overflow table overflows?

8. Describe a suitable data structure that could be used to implement a directory on a disk. You must make sure that your directory can cope with file extensions, i.e. files of the type PASCAL.SORT1 would represent a program SORT1 which is an extension of the Pascal directory.

The following ideas can be used for more practice in writing algorithms for data structures. They are of a similar degree of difficulty to the examples given in this chapter. With suitable extensions they could form the basis of an A-level project. You will also have to develop the code to set up the appropriate data structure in the first place.

9. Using a suitable high level language, develop algorithms and produce code to solve the following problems.
   (a) Create a binary tree using the names of people in your class. Choose a suitable root node (i.e. someone whose name is roughly in the middle of the alphabet) and create the tree as shown on page 305.
   (b) Perform an inorder traversal and check that the names come out in alphabetical order.

10. (a) Devise the code necessary to input an INFIX string and build up a suitable tree structure as shown on page 307.
    (b) Perform a postorder traversal and check that the expression comes out in the correct 'reverse polish' form.

End of chapter summary

■ A **data structure** is a *logical way* of organising data.
■ The *most common* **data-processing operations** are **traversing data**, **addition** and **deletion** of data, **sorting**, **searching** and **merging**.
■ A **linear list** is a **one-dimensional array** data structure.
■ A **linear list** is also known as a **vector**.
■ A **stack** is an area of memory set up as a temporary storage of data.
■ A **stack** has a logical **top** and **bottom** which represent the places at which *beginning* and *end* of the data can be found.
■ Stacks are implemented by **pointers** which point to specific areas of memory.
■ A **pointer** is simply a *data element* that *indicates the position* of *some other data element*. (e.g. the data element that points to the top of the stack).
■ **Push** is the term used to indicate that data has been *placed on the stack*.

■ **Pop** is the term used to indicate that data has been *removed from the stack*.

■ A **LIFO stack** is a **Last-In-First-Out stack**.

■ A **FIFO stack** is a **First-In-First-Out stack** or a **queue**.

■ An **array** is a **two-or-more dimensional set of data**.

■ The **data** *inside* two-dimensional **arrays** can be mapped onto memory locations by using **row-by-row** or **column-by-column** mapping.

■ **Linked lists** make use of *one or more* **pointers** assigned to different functions such as alphabetical or increasing-numeric etc.

■ **Circular or ring lists** may be set up by appropriate pointer systems.

■ **Two-way linked lists** allow data to be traversed in both directions.

■ A **tree structure** is a hierarchical data structure.

■ The **root node** is at the 'base' (top!) of the tree.

■ A **node** refers to a **specific data item or items** (which may include pointers too).

■ A **parent node** has other *sub-ordinate nodes* called **children nodes**.

■ A **leaf node** is a child node with no further children.

■ **Brother** or **sister nodes** are *nodes which have the same parent*.

■ A **sub-tree** consists of parent and child nodes which form just a part of the main tree structure.

■ A **terminal node** is the same as a **leaf node**.

■ A branch is the name of the route taken from a parent to a child node.

■ **Binary trees** are trees in which a *maximum of two children per parent* is permitted.

■ There are *several methods* of **traversing tree structures**, namely **pre-order**, **in-order** and **post-order traversal**.

■ **Pre-order traversal** visits the root, left-hand sub-tree, then right-hand sub-tree.

■ **In-order traversal** visits the left-hand sub-tree, root, then right-hand sub-tree.

■ **Post-order traversal** visits the left-hand sub-tree, right-hand sub-tree then the root.

■ 'Sorting' into order can be accomplished by using **in-order traversal** of an *appropriately set up* **binary tree**.

■ **Infix** may be *converted to* reverse Polish (**post fix**) by using **post-order traversal**.

■ **Networks** are *partially or fully interconnected* **data structures**.

■ **Relational data structures** are considered in the databases chapter.

■ **Hashing** is a technique for random access of stored data.

■ An address is generated by applying a hash function to a key element within the data – bank-account number, for example.

■ **Modulo arithmetic methods** are popular for devising suitable hashing functions.

■ **Radix conversion** and the **mid-square** methods are also other popular hashing techniques.

15 Sorting and searching facilities

Introduction

Much data processing is concerned with **sorting** and **searching data.** Sorting data requires putting the raw data in some predetermined order which might be alphabetical if the data is a set of words, or it might be ascending or descending order if the data is numerical. Search means finding a specific item of data from a list of data.

The techniques used for these processes depend very much on the way in which the data is stored, and on particular aspects of the hardware. Is the data in main memory? Is it on disk or is it on tape? Can all the data fit into main memory at the same time? Factors such as these, together with considerations such as speed and efficiency with respect to length of time taken and amount of memory used, all play a part in deciding the most efficient sort or search algorithms to use.

There are very many sort and search algorithms. All we can do in a book of this size is to look at the more commonly used methods.

Sorting

When working through the following algorithms you will find it most useful to write down the numbers on separate pieces of paper and move them around as the algorithms proceed. In this way the author has found that students' understanding of the different sorting techniques is improved.

The following list of numbers will be used in all the algorithms. The algorithms can then be more easily compared and understood.

   27, 48, 13, 50, 39, 77, 82, 91, 65, 19, 70 and 66
                 ↑

Throughout the algorithms we will talk about the elements in the above list. We will also talk about **lower elements** and **upper elements.** Suppose we consider number 77 in the above list, shown by the ↑ sign under the number 77. All the elements **before** 77 (i.e. 27, 48, 13, 50 and 39) are called the lower elements. Similarly all the elements **above 77** would be called the upper elements.

Insertion sort

This is the simplest sort algorithm and so will be considered first.

1. Start with the second number (48 in the above list). You will see why in a moment.
2. Compare the above number with all the other lower elements and **insert** the number in the right place.
3. **Repeat** the above two stages, but moving the third, fourth, and fifth etc., **until** the last number has been considered in stage (1).

Using the above algorithm the list is sorted into **ascending** order.

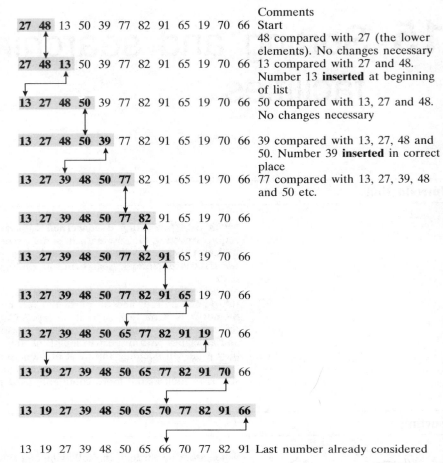

Comments

27 48 13 50 39 77 82 91 65 19 70 66   Start

48 compared with 27 (the lower elements). No changes necessary

27 48 13 50 39 77 82 91 65 19 70 66   13 compared with 27 and 48. Number 13 **inserted** at beginning of list

13 27 48 50 39 77 82 91 65 19 70 66   50 compared with 13, 27 and 48. No changes necessary

13 27 48 50 39 77 82 91 65 19 70 66   39 compared with 13, 27, 48 and 50. Number 39 **inserted** in correct place

13 27 39 48 50 77 82 91 65 19 70 66   77 compared with 13, 27, 39, 48 and 50 etc.

13 27 39 48 50 77 82 91 65 19 70 66

13 27 39 48 50 77 82 91 65 19 70 66

13 27 39 48 50 77 82 91 65 19 70 66

13 27 39 48 50 65 77 82 91 19 70 66

13 19 27 39 48 50 65 77 82 91 70 66

13 19 27 39 48 50 65 70 77 82 91 66

13 19 27 39 48 50 65 66 70 77 82 91   Last number already considered

We will now analyse the above in more detail to produce a solution to the **insertion sort** problem.

First let us introduce some terminology:

Let **current position** indicate the number (initially set to N(2)) for comparison purposes.

Let **pointer position** indicate the number that is being compared with the above.

The argument will go along the following lines:

Set up the current and pointer positions.
Repeat the following:
    Compare all the elements in the list below the current pointer UNTIL N(pointer_position) > N(current_position) in which case we INSERT and MOVE the elements as shown in lists in the examples.
Or UNTIL N(pointer_position) = N(current_position) in which case no inserts or moves will be necessary.
    Increment the current_position and RESET the pointer_position,
UNTIL the current_position is the maximum position in the list.

Using Pascal and assuming the numbers are stored in an array called N we get the following from the above description of the problem:

```
current_position:= 1;
REPEAT
    current_position := current_position + 1;          (* Set up pointers *)
    pointer_position := 1;
    WHILE pointer_position <= current_position DO
      BEGIN
        IF N[pointer_position] > N[current_position] THEN
                                                    (* Insert necessary ? *)
            BEGIN
              temp := N[current_position];        (* Insert and move routine *)
```

```
                    FOR count := current_position DOWNTO pointer_position + 1 DO
                       BEGIN
                          N[count] := N[count - 1]
                       END;
                    N[pointer_position] := temp;
                 END
              pointer_position := pointer_position + 1;          (* Move pointer *)
           END;
        UNTIL current_position = maximum;
```

A working version would obviously have to include declaring the variables, reading in the data and printing out the sorted list. A complete working version using the above Pascal code is as follows:

```
PROGRAM insert sort (INPUT, OUTPUT);
VAR current_position, pointer_position, maximum, temp, count: INTEGER;
N: ARRAY [0..12] OF INTEGER;
BEGIN
  maximum := 12;
    FOR count := 1 TO maximum DO
      BEGIN
         WRITELN('Please type in number ', count);
         READLN(N[count]);
      END;
    WRITELN('Original list of numbers is');
    FOR count := 1 TO maximum DO
      BEGIN
         WRITELN(N[count]);
      END;
    current_position := 1;
    REPEAT
      current_position := current_position + 1;          (* Set up pointers *)
      pointer_position := 1;
      WHILE pointer_position <= current_position DO
        BEGIN
           IF N[pointer_position] > N[current_position] THEN
                                                          (* Insert necessary? *)
              BEGIN
                 temp := N[current_position];        (* Insert and move routine *)
                 FOR count := current_position DOWNTO pointer_position + 1 DO
                    BEGIN
                       N[count] := N[count - 1]
                    END;
                 N[pointer_position] := temp;
              END;
           pointer_position := pointer_position + 1          (* Move pointer *)
        END;
    UNTIL current_position = maximum;
    WRITELN('Sorted list');
    FOR count := 1 TO maximum DO
      BEGIN
         WRITELN (N[count])
      END;
END.
```

Bubble sort

Another popular method is called the **bubble sort.** The name derives from the fact that the sorted item **floats** to the top of the list like a bubble in water.

Again we will use the twelve numbers N(1), N(2), to N(12) as before:

N(1)	N(2)	N(3)	N(4)	N(5)	N(6)	N(7)	. . .	to	N(max)
27	48	13	50	39	77	82	91	65	19	70 and 66

The algorithm for the bubble sort is as follows:

1. Start with the first pair of numbers in the list and compare them i.e. compare N(1) with N(2).
2. If N(1) > N(2) then **swap.** i.e. N(1) becomes N(2) and N(2) becomes N(1). If

a swap was necessary then make a note of it.

3. Go on to the next pair and repeat stages (1) and (2) until the last pair of numbers in the list have been compared.

4. If a swap (1 or more) took place then repeat the entire procedure. If no swaps took place then END.

The above algorithm when applied to our set of numbers produces the following results:

First pass

Comments
Start

27 48 13 50 39 77 82 91 65 19 70 66   (27 compared with 48. No swap necessary)

27 **48 13** 50 39 77 82 91 65 19 70 66   (48 compared with 13. Swap necessary)**

27 13 **48 50** 39 77 82 91 65 19 70 66   (48 compared with 50. No swap necessary)

27 13 48 **50 39** 77 82 91 65 19 70 66   (50 compared with 39. Swap necessary)**

27 13 48 39 **50 77** 82 91 65 19 70 66   (50 compared with 77. No swap necessary)

27 13 48 39 50 **77 82** 91 65 19 70 66   (77 compared with 82. No swap necessary)

27 13 48 39 50 77 **82 91** 65 19 70 66   (82 compared with 91. No swap necessary)

27 13 48 39 50 77 82 **91 65** 19 70 66   (91 compared with 65. Swap necessary)

27 13 48 39 50 77 82 65 **91 19** 70 66   (91 compared with 19. Swap necessary)**

27 13 48 39 50 77 82 65 19 **91 70** 66   (91 compared with 70. Swap necessary)**

27 13 48 39 50 77 82 65 19 70 **91 66**   (91 compared with 66. Swap necessary)**

27 13 48 39 50 77 82 65 19 70 66 91   (last two numbers have been compared)

Swaps were necessary therefore another pass is needed:

Second pass

27 13 48 39 50 77 82 65 19 70 66 91   (27 compared with 13. Swap necessary)**

13 **27 48** 39 50 77 82 65 19 70 66 91

etc. etc.

After the second pass the numbers become:

13 27 39 48 50 77 65 19 70 66 82 91

Swaps were necessary so a third pass is needed:

After the third pass we get:

13 27 39 48 50 65 19 70 66 77 82 91

We proceed with as many passes as necessary until no swaps are recorded. In which case the list of numbers would be:

13 19 27 39 48 50 65 66 70 77 82 91

Notice that all the lower value elements are floating to the left and all the higher value elements are floating to the right. Hence the name bubble sort.

In the cases where swaps were necessary it is useful to indicate that this has happened by using what is called a **flag**. This is simply an indication that at least one swap has taken place. This is useful in the following algorithm because if the flag has been set then swaps were necessary and the routine must be entered again. The flag must obviously be reset at the beginning of every pass.

The pseudocode algorithm for the bubble sort would therefore be as follows:

```
REPEAT the following:
    Reset a flag to zero.
    COMPARE all pairs of numbers and swap if necessary.
    IF a swap occurred set a flag,
UNTIL flag is not set.
```

The main Pascal code to achieve the above is shown (shaded grey), together with the input and output procedures for our 12 numbers:

```
PROGRAM bubble (INPUT, OUTPUT);
    VAR temp, count, flag, maximum, pointer: INTEGER;
    N: ARRAY [0..12] OF INTEGER;
    BEGIN
        maximum := 12
        FOR count: = 1 TO maximum DO
            BEGIN
                WRITELN('Please type in number', count);
                READLN(N[count]);
            END;
        WRITELN('The original list of numbers is');
        FOR count := 1 TO maximum DO
            BEGIN
            WRITELN([count]);
            END;
    REPEAT                                        (*Main routine*)
        flag := 0;
        FOR pointer := 1 TO maximum – 1 DO
            BEGIN
                WHILE N[pointer]>N[pointer + 1] DO
                    BEGIN
                        temp := N[pointer + 1];
                        N[pointer + 1] := N[pointer];
                        N[pointer] := temp;
                        flag := 1;
                    END;
            END;
    UNTIL flag = 0;

        WRITELN('Sorted list');
        FOR count := 1 TO maximum DO
            BEGIN
                WRITELN (N[count])
            END;
    END.
```

Note that although the flag has been set to zero, this will not terminate the REPEAT UNTIL Loop unless the flag was not set to 1 i.e. the loop will be executed at least once (see page 121) and more times if the flag is set after the swap has taken place .

Shell sort

One of the problems encountered with previous sort methods is that numbers being compared may only move a small distance, and therefore usually require a greater number of movements to get to their desired destination. Donald Shell proposed a method that enables numbers to be moved by much larger distances initially, thus getting over this problem to a large extent.

Shell's method is most easily illustrated by means of an example.

As before, we will assume that the numbers are stored as N(1), N(2), N(3), N(4), . . . N(max). In this example, as in the previous ones in this chapter, we will use the same set of numbers to illustrate the sorting method. i.e. we will use the twelve numbers 27, 48, 13, 50, 39, 77, 82, 91, 65, 19, 70 and 66.

There will be several passes through the data, and the number of passes will depend on how many data items are present. Larger lists of numbers will require more passes. The passes are often arranged by choosing a number whose value is the nearest integer to max/2, where max is the number of elements in the array N. In the above case, we have 12 numbers, and so the number to be used will be max/2

which gives 12/2 or 6. We will call this number d, as it represents the distance between elements which form subsets of the data. To illustrate the idea, consider carrying out this process on our twelve numbers:

The first pass

The first subsets of data are formed using d as follows:

N(1) goes with N(7)   As d = 6,   N(1) is grouped with N(1 + d) or N(7)
N(2) goes with N(8)   N(2) is grouped with N(2 + d) or N(8) etc.
N(3) goes with N(9)
N(4) goes with N(10)
N(5) goes with N(11)

finally,

N(6) goes with N(12)   as N(6) is grouped with N(6 + d) or N(12)

We have, therefore, formed 6 subsets of data, with each subset containing just two elements. If there had been 16 numbers in the original list, there would have been 8 subsets of two elements each, or if we had 100 numbers, there would have been 50 two-element subsets so formed. For an odd number of elements, 11, for example, d = 5 and hence 6 subsets would be formed. N(1), N(6) being the first, N(2), N(7) being the second, up to and including the final subset of N(6), N(11).

   Each subset in the above list is sorted separately. On the first pass this is obviously not a difficult operation as there are only two elements in each list! Therefore, a simple insertion sort will suffice, which in this case boils down to comparing and swapping if necessary.

   If we now consider our original set of numbers:

N(1) N(2) N(3) N(4) N(5) N(6) N(7) N(8) N(9) N(10) N(11) N(12)
27   48   13   50   39   77   82   91   65   19   70   66

Sorting out the numbers in each subset as described above, after the first pass, we end up with the following new set of numbers:

N(1) N(2) N(3) N(4) N(5) N(6) N(7) N(8) N(9) N(10) N(11) N(12)
27   48   13   19   39   66   82   91   65   50   70   77

Although all the subsets have been sorted, we only notice any change with two sets of numbers, as all the others were already in the correct order. N(4) has been swapped with N(10), and N(6) has been swapped with N(12).

The second pass

We next make d the nearest integer value to max/4. For our twelve numbers, d = 3.
   The second set of subsets now formed is, therefore, as follows:

N(1) goes with N(4), N(7) and N(10)   as d = 3, N(1) is grouped with N(1+d), N(1+2d) etc.
N(2) goes with N(5), N(8) and N(11)

and

N(3) goes with N(6), N(9) and N(12)   as N(3) is grouped with N(3+d), N(3+2d) etc.

Each subset is now sorted separately, using an insertion sort, for example. Not forgetting that we are now starting off with the numbers obtained from the output of the first pass, this process carried out on the data obtained from the first pass is as follows:

Aftr sorting each subset, the result from the second pass would be:

N(1) N(2) N(3) N(4) N(5) N(6) N(7) N(8) N(9) N(10) N(11) N(12)
19   39   13   27   48   65   50   70   66   82   91   77

The third pass

We now make d the nearest integer value of max/8. For our twelve numbers d = 1.
   In fact, the Shell-sort process will always end up eventually with d having a value of 1. As d = 1, we are now sorting the whole set of data! Now I hear you ask 'What's the point of sorting the whole set of data, when we could have done this in the first place?' Well, the whole point is that the previous operations have made the file relatively well ordered, whereas if we had done a straight insertion sort, for example,

on the original set of data, then more comparisons would have been needed. (Assuming the data did not start off in the unlikely event of being well ordered.)

The final data, after an insertion sort is obviously:

N(1)	N(2)	N(3)	N(4)	N(5)	N(6)	N(7)	N(8)	N(9)	N(10)	N(11)	N(12)
13	19	27	39	48	50	65	66	70	77	82	91

Unbelievable as it might seem, if you plug the twelve original numbers into an insertion sort then 22 swaps are necessary. Going through the Shell sort, using the same data and using the *same insertion sort techniques* at all the appropriate stages requires only 14 swaps, for the reasons given below. You can imagine the savings on larger sets of data. In fact, even better results can be obtained by choosing different values of d. However, an analysis of techniques such as these is beyond the requirements of an 'A' level course.

An efficient algorithm needs to be found to sort all sets of data simultaneously, or the program will become large and unwieldy for larger lists of numbers. We can also use the amazing fact that, while sorting, if we encounter a pair of elements in the proper order, then we may stop the sorting process and go on to the next. This is a major time saver and is one of the reasons why the Shell technique wins on speed even though the 'same' insertion sort technique has to be applied to the whole data set during the last pass. For interested readers, it was Gale and Karp who established this fact, which you can demonstrate for yourselves by working through the methods in conjunction with the Shell-sort algorithm shown below. As before in this chapter, numbers written down on pieces of paper help a great deal with understanding of these algorithms.

The loop structure in the algorithm ensures that the data is processed using the appropriate subsets as shown on the previous pages. Two variables, i and j are used for this purpose. On the first pass, i has values ranging from 7 to 12, and j has values ranging from 1 to 6. Hence, you can see how the elements N(1) and N(7), N(2) and N(8) etc. up to N(6) and N(12) are sorted in pairs.

On the second pass, we effectively have 3 sets of data, each with 4 elements. However, each data set is being sorted 'simultaneously' by using an insertion sort technique. Carefully work through the algorithm and you should see how i and j vary to control comparisons in each subset of numbers. For example, N(1) and N(4) from the first subset are compared and swapped if necessary, then N(2) and N(5) from the second subset up to N(3) and (N6) from the third. Next we work round again to compare N(4) with N(7), the second pair from the first subset, then N(5) and N(8) etc. Note that if no swaps are necessary then we go on comparing the next pair in a subset using the above method. However, if swaps are necessary, then we have to compare the element with the lower elements in the list as happens in a normal insertion sort. But don't forget as stated above, when we encounter a pair that is in the correct order we may go on to the next pair in the next subset as we were doing before a swap took place. This is continued until d = 1, when the entire list is treated as a normal insertion sort, again with the proviso that we may stop and go on to the next elements if we encounter a pair that are already in the correct order. The part of the algorithm which moves us on to the next pair of elements, sets j = 0 if no swap is necessary, thus getting out of the current sorting process.

The main pseudocode for the Shell-sort algorith is as follows:

```
BEGIN
    maximum = 12            (*Set up for the 12 numbers in the example*)
    d := maximum DIV 2           (*Set up initial distanced. 6 in our case*)
    WHILE d > 0 DO
      BEGIN
        FOR i := d+1 TO maximum DO
          BEGIN
            j := i–d
            WHILE j > 0 DO
              BEGIN
                IF N(j) > N(j+d) THEN
                  BEGIN
                    SWAP( N(j), N(j+d) )
                    j := j–d            (*Produces correct value of j for comparison
                                            with lower elements, or j value to jump out
                                                        of WHILE loop*)
              END
        ELSE
```

```
                         BEGIN
                           j := 0                    (*Stop sorting if two elements found in
                                                                        correct order*)
                         END
                       END
                    END
                 d := d DIV 2                         (*Set up d for next pass*)
               END
     END

     PROCEDURE SWAP ( N(j), N(j+d) )
          BEGIN
            temp := N(j)
            N(j) := N(j+d)
            N(j+d) := temp
          END
```

Quick sort (partition sort)

This is another sort routine that is based on exchanging data. However, as its name implies, it is very quick for long lists of numbers (see later) compared with the other methods so far considered, although looking at the following algorithms it seems anything but quick!

The method works by splitting the list first into **two sublists,** and then quick sorting each sublist, then each sublist is split up into two separate sublists and is again quick sorted.

The quick sort algorithm is as follows:

1. Split the list up into two sublists: To do this proceed as follows:
   Set up two pointers (one at each end of the list), i.e.

27   48   13   50   39   77   82   91   65   19   70   **66**
*

(left pointer)   (right pointer)

Let there be a reference number denoted by X, and let the number be put in brackets to emphasise this. Also let the reference be the first number in the list, i.e.

(27)   48   13   50   39   77   82   91   65   19   70   **66**
X*

Compare the two numbers indicated by the pointers and swap if necessary: 27 is compared with 66. No swap necessary as 27 < 66.

Move the pointer not associated with X towards X one place, i.e.

(27)   48   13   50   39   77   82   91   65   19   **70**   66
X*

                                          (pointer moved towards X)

Compare the two numbers: 27 < 70 therefore no swap.

Move the pointer not associated with X towards X one place, i.e.

(27)   48   13   50   39   77   82   91   65   **19**   70   66
X*

                                          (pointer moved towards X)

Compare the two numbers: 27 > 19 therefore swap, i.e.

19   48   13   50   39   77   82   91   65   **(27)**   70   66
*   X

Note the reference number has now been moved due to the swap.

Move the pointer not associated with X towards X one place, i.e.

19   48   13   50   39   77   82   91   65   **27**   70   66
*   X
                                          (pointer moved towards X)

The above processes are repeated until the pointers coincide.

Each stage of the process is shown as follows:

												Comments
19	**48** *	13	50	39	77	82	91	65	(27) X	70	66	Swap
19	(27) X*	13	50	39	77	82	91	**65**	48	70	66	Move pointer
19	(27) X*	13	50	39	77	82	**91**	65	48	70	66	Move pointer
19	(27) X*	13	50	39	77	**82**	91	65	48	70	66	Move pointer
19	(27) X*	13	50	39	**77**	82	91	65	48	70	66	Move pointer
19	(27) X*	13	50	**39**	77	82	91	65	48	70	66	Move pointer
19	(27) X*	13	**50**	39	77	82	91	65	48	70	66	Move pointer
19	(27) X*	**13**	50	39	77	82	91	65	48	70	66	Swap
19	**13** *	(27) X	50	39	77	82	91	65	48	70	66	Move pointer
19	13	(27) X*	50	39	77	82	91	65	48	70	66	

Left sublist   **Right sublist**

At the last stage in the above procedure the pointers have coincided. The sublists are represented by the elements on each side of the reference number X.
The reference number itself is in the correct position.
The above statement is confirmed by noting the very important points that:

(a) All elements in the right-hand sublist are > 27.
(b) All elements in the left-hand sublist are < 27.

This means that each sublist can be treated independently of the others and will enable us to call the same algorithm **recursively**.
Before going on to stage two let us consider the routine to carry out the above operation while it is still fresh in our minds. The following Pascal-like pseudocode performs the above operation of splitting the list into two sublists.

First some terminology:

We will store our list of numbers to be sorted in an **array** called N and refer to the individual numbers by subscripts i.e. N_1, N_2 to $N_{maximum}$.

Let N[left_pointer] refer to the number in the list being pointed to by the left_pointer. Let N[right_pointer] be the number in the list referred to by the right_pointer.

Let reference number (X in the above case) be represented by ref_number.

Let 'left' be the left-hand end of the list (i.e. left would be 1 and right would be maximum initially).
Let 'right' be the right-hand end of the list.

```
BEGIN
    left_pointer := left;
    right_pointer := right;
    REPEAT
        IF N[left_pointer] > N[right_pointer] THEN
            BEGIN
                Swap over numbers and reference number;
            END
        ELSE
            BEGIN
                Adjust pointers;
            END
    UNTIL left_pointer = right_pointer;
END.
```

A complete Pascal procedure called splitup will be used in the final routine. It is developed from the above pseudocode and is as follows:

```
PROCEDURE splitup(VAR left, right, left_pointer, right_pointer, ref_number
  :INTEGER);
  BEGIN
    left_pointer := left;
    right_pointer := right;
    REPEAT
      IF N[left_pointer] > N[right_pointer] THEN
        BEGIN                          (* Swap numbers and ref_number *)
          IF ref_number = left_pointer THEN
            ref_number := right_pointer
          ELSE
            ref_number := left_pointer;

          temp := N[left_pointer]
          N[left_pointer] := N[right_pointer];
          N[right_pointer] := temp;
        END
      ELSE
        BEGIN                              (* If no swap adjust pointers *)
          IF left_pointer = ref_number THEN
            BEGIN
              right_pointer := right_pointer - 1;
            END
          ELSE
            BEGIN
              left_pointer := left_pointer + 1;
            END;
        END
    UNTIL left_pointer = right_pointer;
  END.
```

The above procedure produces a list with the left_pointer, right_pointer and ref_number coinciding. The left sublist (if there is one) is to the left of the reference number and the right sublist (again if there is one) is to the right of the reference number.

Carrying on with the original method:

2. Repeat the above procedure for each sublist.
    In practice we would now store one of the sublists so that it can be sorted later. Therefore, store the left sublist and sort the right sublist:

											Comments
[19 13]	27	50	39	77	82	91	65	48	70	66	
Stored	27	(50) X*	39	77	82	91	65	48	70	66	Move pointer
		(50) X*	39	77	82	91	65	48	70	66	Move pointer
		(50) X*	39	77	82	91	65	48	70	66	Swap
		48 *	39	77	82	91	65	(50) X	70	66	Move pointer
		48	39 *	77	82	91	65	(50) X	70	66	Move pointer
		48	39	77 *	82	91	65	(50) X*	70	66	Swap
		48	39	(50) X*	82	91	65	77 X	70	66	Move pointer
		48	39	(50) X*	82	91	65	77	70	66	Move pointer
		48	39	(50) X*	82	91	65	77	70	66	Move pointer

48	39	**(50)**	**82**	91	65	77	70	66	Move pointer
		X*	~						
48	39	**(50)**	82	91	65	77	70	66	Move pointer
		~							
		X*							
48	39	**(50)**	82	91	65	77	70	66	
		~							
		X*							

New left sublist   **New right sublist**

The numbers 27 and 50 are now in the correct positions.

19	13	(27)	48	39	(50)	82	91	65	77	70	66
		OK			OK						

Left sublist   New left sublist   New right sublist

Note also that the sublists are independently positioned so that no elements need be taken out of any separate sublist to be put into another. This enables us to treat each sublist as an independent unit and to determine its position in relation to the other sublists.

Each sublist must be processed in this way until all the sublists contain just a single number in which case the entire list is sorted.

The principle of a **stack** (see page 288) may be used to help carry out the above operations. Using this principle we push information regarding a sublist on to the stack and pop it off again when the sorting algorithm needs to be called. All that is necessary is to keep a count of the number of elements in each list and the number of lists on the stack. The number of elements in each list together with information about the position of the list can be achieved by storing left- and right-hand pointers for each sublist.

These are the pointers referred to as 'left' and 'right' in the original procedure.

All that is necessary is to write the routine that controls the stack and ensure that the right parameters are passed over to the main routine to split up the list into two sublists.

The following is a summary of the state of the list after the splitup routine has finished with it:

```
(Left sublist) . . .      X . . .            (Right sublist)
       ↑                   ↑                       ↑
     left              left_pointer              right
                       right_pointer
                       and ref_number
```

If the left-hand sublist contains more than one element then it should be stored. The following condition checks to see if two or more elements are present in the left-hand sublist. Therefore:

IF (ref_number – 1) – left >= 1 THEN store the left-hand sublist.

The right-hand list is then processed in the same way until the right-hand list contains only one element.

Therefore it is processed all the time that the following condition is true:

IF ((right) – (ref_number + 1)) >= 1 THEN process right-hand sublist
using the splitup procedure.

Once the right-hand list has been fully processed we then pop a list off the stack and process this new list.

To control the stack we shall use a variable called stack.

If stack = 0 then the stack is empty.

The stack will be used to store two variables leftpointer(stack) and rightpointer(stack), where stack is a number that indicates the number of lists on the stack, i.e.

leftpointer(1)   = points to the left-hand element of the first list on
                    the stack and
rightpointer(1)   = points to the right-hand element of the first list
                    pushed on to the stack.

leftpointer(1) and rightpointer(1) would be the parameters to be pushed on to and popped off of the stack, and are the same parameters called 'left' and 'right' that are needed by the splitup routine, i.e.

```
        left    :=   leftpointer[stack];
        right   :=   rightpointer[stack];
```

is needed on entry to the splitup routine.

The complete stack management routine would also have to take into account the fact that there may not be any elements in the left-hand or right-hand sublists.

For example if there were no elements or only one element in the right-hand sublist then we simply pass the left-hand sublist over to the splitup routine.

If there were no elements or only one element in the left-hand and right-hand sublists then we would have to retrieve a list from the stack (if it was not empty) and process that list.

The following pseudocode forms the main routine which also controls the stack:

```
REPEAT
  BEGIN
    set flag to zero              (* flag used as a test to bypass some of the
                                       following routines *)
    IF (right sublist contains one element or less) AND
    (left sublist contains more than one element) THEN
      BEGIN
        set up left sublist pointers to be passed on to splitup procedure
        set up reference number
        set flag to one
      END;
    IF (flag is zero) AND (left sublist contains one element or less) AND
    (right sublist contains one element or less) AND
    (the stack is not empty) THEN
      BEGIN
        pop a list off the stack to be passed on to splitup procedure
        decrement stack pointers
        set up reference number
        set flag to one
      END;
    IF (flag is zero) AND (left sublist contains more than one element) THEN
      BEGIN
        store the left sublist onto the stack
        increment stack pointers
        set flag to one
      END;
    IF (flag is zero) AND   (there is more than one element in the right
    sublist) THEN
      BEGIN
        set up right sublist to be passed onto splitup procedure
        set reference number to left
        set flag to one
      END;
  END
UNTIL (flag is zero) AND (stack is empty)
```

A Pascal routine based on the above pseudocode is as follows:

```
REPEAT
  flag := 0;
                                                (*Main testing and control*)
    IF (right - (ref_number + 1) <= 1) AND
    ((ref_number - 1) - left > 1) THEN
      BEGIN                               (* Set up left-hand sublist for splitup *)
        right := ref_number - 1;
        ref_number := left;
        flag := 1;
      END;
    IF (flag = 0) AND (right - (ref_number + 1) <= 1) AND
    ((ref_number - 1) - left <= 1) AND (stack > 0) THEN
      BEGIN
        left:= leftpointer[stack];              (* Retrieve list from stack *)
        right := rightpointer[stack];          (* and set up list for splitup *)
        stack := stack - 1;
```

```
                ref_number := left;
                 flag := 1;
              END;
          IF (flag = 0) AND ((ref_number − 1) − left >= 1) THEN
              BEGIN
                stack := stack + 1;              (* Store left-hand sublist on stack *)
                leftpointer[stack] := left;
                 rightpointer[stack] := right;
              END;
          IF (flag = 0) AND (right − (ref_number + 1) >= 1) THEN
              BEGIN
                 left := ref_number + 1;          (* Set right-hand list for splitup *)
                 ref_number := left;
                  flag := 1;
              END;
               splitup(left, right, left_pointer, right_pointer, ref_number);
       UNTIL (flag = 0) AND (stack = 0);
```

A complete Pascal program follows. This enables the user to type in our original 12 numbers and, after processing the numbers using splitup and the main control routine above, prints out the 12 numbers in ascending order:

```
    PROGRAM quick (INPUT,OUTPUT); VAR left, right, left_pointer, right_
    pointer, ref_number, maximum, count, temp, stack, flag: INTEGER;
            N: ARRAY[0..50] OF INTEGER;
            leftpointer: ARRAY[0..50] OF INTEGER;
            rightpointer: ARRAY[0..50] OF INTEGER;
        PROCEDURE splitup(VAR left, right, left_pointer, right_pointer,
    ref_number: INTEGER);
    BEGIN
        left_pointer := left;
        right_pointer := right;
           REPEAT
             IF N[left_pointer] > N[right_pointer] THEN
                 BEGIN
                 IF ref_number = left_pointer THEN
                    ref_number := right_pointer
                 ELSE
                    ref number := left_pointer;
                    temp := N[left_pointer];
                    N[left_pointer] := N[right_pointer];
                    N[right_pointer] := temp;
          END
        ELSE
        BEGIN
           IF left_pointer = ref_number THEN
              BEGIN
               right_pointer := right_pointer − 1;
              END
           ELSE
              BEGIN
               left_pointer := left_pointer + 1;
              END;
           END;
        UNTIL left_pointer = right_pointer;
    END;

BEGIN
    maximum := 50;
    FOR count := 1 TO maximum DO
        BEGIN
           WRITELN('Please type in number', count);
           READLN(N[count]);
        END;
    WRITELN('Original list of numbers is');
    FOR count := 1 TO maximum DO
        BEGIN
```

```
                              WRITELN(N[count])
                      END;
                  stack := 0;
                  flag : = 0;
                  left := 1;                                (* set up initial conditions *)
                  right := maximum;                         (* and split up first list *)
                  ref_number:= 1;
                  splitup(left, right, left_pointer, right_pointer, ref_number);

                  REPEAT
                      flag := 0;
                                                            {*Main testing and control*}
                      IF (right – (ref_number + 1) <= 1) AND
                      ((ref number – 1) – left > 1) THEN
                          BEGIN                             (* Set up left-hand sublist for splitup *)
                              right := ref_number – 1;
                              ref_number := left;
                              flag := 1;
                          END;
                      IF (flag = 0) AND (right – (ref_number + 1) <= 1) AND
                      ((ref_number – 1) – left <= 1) AND (stack > 0) THEN
                          BEGIN
                              left := leftpointer[stack];           (* Retrieve list from stack *)
                              right := rightpointer[stack];         (* and set up list for splitup *)
                              stack := stack – 1;
                              ref_number := left;
                              flag := 1;
                          END;
                      IF (flag = 0) AND ((ref_number – 1) – left >= 1) THEN
                          BEGIN
                              stack := stack + 1;           (* Store left-hand sublist on stack *)
                              leftpointer[stack] := left;
                              rightpointer[stack] := right;
                          END;
                      IF (flag = 0) AND (right – (ref_number + 1) >= 1) THEN
                          BEGIN
                              left := ref_number + 1;       (* Set right-hand list for splitup *)
                              ref_number := left;
                              flag:= 1;
                          END;
                      splitup(left, right, left_pointer, right_pointer, ref number);
                  UNTIL (flag = 0) AND (stack = 0);
                  WRITELN('Sorted list');                   (* flag = 0; hence list sorted *)
                  FOR count := 1 TO maximum DO
                  BEGIN
                      WRITELN(N[count]);
                  END;
              END.
```

In practice better methods of using reference numbers that are placed at random (or better still the median) in the list, produce even faster results. However, these techniques are beyond the scope of computer science at this level.

If you run the various sorting routines that we have covered, then for the 12 numbers used in our examples you would notice that the quick sort is not appreciably quicker! However, the larger the number of elements in the list the faster quick sort becomes in comparison to most other methods. In practice one must consider when the extra work of forming another sublist outweighs the sorting of that sublist by some other technique.

As an example, it can be shown that for a bubble sort:

$$\text{run time} \propto N \uparrow 2$$

For a quick sort:

$$\text{run time} \propto N \log_2(N)$$

If the value of N is large then quick sort is very fast compared with other techniques. Also the initial arrangement of the data drastically affects the time taken. In fact the worst case for the quick sort is data that is already sorted!

Tree sort (tournament sort)

There are several different types of **tree sorting** techniques but the **tournament sort**, making use of a **binary tree** (see page 305), is a popular choice for examinations.

The name tournament sort derives from the fact that the system is exactly the same as in a knockout tournament for a game such as tennis. As an example consider the players:

Bill, Dave, Carol, Emma, George and Fred

Let us assume for convenience that if the initial letter of a player's name appears alphabetically before that of his or her opponent then the player will beat the opponent.

In the first round of the competition Bill will play Dave, Carol will play Emma and George will play Fred.

The winner of each match goes on to the next level in the binary tree as follows:

Bill		Carol		Fred	
Bill	Dave	Carol	Emma	George	Fred

There is now an odd number of players and so we will apply the rule that the player in the right-hand of the tree will play the winner from the other match, unfair I know, but the algorithm will work irrespective of who is seeded, and we are not playing real games of tennis anyway!

Therefore Bill will play Carol and Fred will sit out the semi-final. The situation is now as follows

	Bill			Fred	
Bill		Carol		Fred	
Bill	Dave	Carol	Emma	George	Fred

Finally, Bill plays Fred and Bill therefore becomes champion of the tournament.

		Bill			
	Bill			Fred	
Bill		Carol		Fred	
Bill	Dave	Carol	Emma	George	Fred

Bill is now the root node and has therefore been placed at the head of the list. Bill can now be removed from the root node and placed at the head of an alphabetical list.

Note that Bill would appear at the root node irrespective of who had played who or who had been seeded.

After Bill is removed from the root node a dummy (Z in our case) which is equivalent to ZZZZZZZ as far as the comparison of names in the tournament is concerned is placed in the tree. The binary tree now becomes:

		Z			
	Z			Fred	
Z		Carol		Fred	
Z	Dave	Carol	Emma	George	Fred

The tournament is now replayed with the following final result:

		Carol			
	Carol			Fred	
Dave		Carol		Fred	
Z	Dave	Carol	Emma	George	Fred

Notice now that Carol is the root node and therefore is removed and placed after Bill in the list.

The sorted list now contains Bill, Carol.

The next phase after Carol is removed would be:

		Z			
	Z			Fred	
Dave		Z		Fred	
Z	Dave	Z	Emma	George	Fred

The tournament would be replayed with the following result:

Dave

Dave   Fred

Dave   Emma   Fred

Z   Dave   Z   Emma   George   Fred

The sorted list then becomes:

Bill, Carol, Dave.

We proceed in the above way until the whole tree consists of Zs in which case the list produced is sorted.

More efficient ways of minimising the need to compare Z with Z can be developed.

There are many more algorithms for sorting data into order. However, many examples together with programs to implement them have been given in the first half of this chapter. As a lot of pages have been dedicated to the practical sorting routines it is left to the reader to develop an algorithm and code for the tree sort should it be desired.

During the first part of this chapter we have considered methods that are ideal for **internal sorting,** i.e. sorting using the computer's main store. Other methods making use of backing store are called **external sorting** techniques. These will be mentioned in the chapter on files and file handling.

Exercise 15.1

1. Explain why it is often necessary to sort the data in a computer file.

2. (a) Describe in detail, an algorithm for sorting integers into ascending order.
   (b) Write a routine making use of pseudocode to execute your algorithm.
   (c) Test your algorithm by making use of the following data:
   5, 9, 7, 3, 0, 5, 2, 1, 1, 8, 4, 10.

3. Explain briefly the principles of the following sort routines:
   (a) **Insertion sort**
   (b) **Bubble sort**
   (c) **Shell sort**
   (d) **Quick sort**
   Why is it necessary to have so many different sorting methods?

4. By making use of a suitable algorithm based on a bubble sort technique, show how the following data would be manipulated into its final ascending order:
   7, 3, 9, 1, 4, 8, 1, 2.

5. What type of data would be best to test **sort** algorithms?

6. How would you carry out sorting of data files too large to fit into the computer's main memory? Illustrate your answer by means of a diagram.

7. On many occasions, the length of time taken to sort data into order depends on the initial ordering of the data. Making use of the following sets of data, and sorting into descending order, comment on the effectiveness of three different sort algorithms of your choice.
   (a) 2, 5, 3, 1, 4, 8, 6, 9, 0, 5
   (b) 0, 1, 2, 3, 4, 5, 5, 6, 8, 9.
   (c) 9, 8, 6, 5, 5, 4, 3, 2, 1, 0.

Searching techniques

The second major topic in this chapter is that of **searching**, i.e. searching through lists of data until one or more items of data that match some specified criteria can be found. In most practical systems we will probably be searching for some item of information that is contained in a **key field.** The enquiry will probably want the other data associated with this key field to be printed out also. However, during the following algorithms we will assume that only one item of information is associated with any search. The techniques of coping with the other information associated with the key field are already well established in other parts of this book. Also, it is likely that the information to be searched will be contained on media such as disks or tape. The techniques to deal with this type of application will be dealt with in the chapter on files and file handling.

In the solutions given to the following search techniques we will simply search through a list of numbers contained in the computer's main memory. The compilation of these lists is unimportant and therefore the list of numbers will simply be stored in an array called N. Hence the items in the array will be referred to as N[1], N[2], N[3], etc.

Search techniques are compared by considering the average number of comparisons that must be made to get to the desired item of data. This is referred to as the **search length**. If, for a certain list of data, an average of 250 comparisons must be made before an item of data is located, the search length would be given by 250. Another often quoted parameter would be the **search time**. This is simply the average time taken to search for a given item of data. Obviously, this would be intimately connected with the search length and the hardware being used. However, the search length will just be a function of the algorithm that is being used. We will now consider some of the more common algorithms.

The linear search

The simplest search technique would obviously be to examine each element in a list one by one until the desired element has been found. This is the method where the list is sequentially examined until the information required is obtained. Not much thought needed for this one!

The following pseudocode should be quite obvious:

```
BEGIN
   READ required search criteria
   count := 1
   flag := 0
   WHILE there is more data in the list to be read DO
      BEGIN
         READ element in list
         IF criteria satisfied THEN WRITE information and set flag
         increment count
      END;
END.
   IF flag is not set WRITE no match found in the list
```

The following Pascal program enables the user to find how many integer numbers of a particular size occur in a list of 20. The main algorithm is shown, and the other code is to enable the user to type in 20 numbers for test purposes. In the chapter on files and file handling these numbers will be stored on disk files.

```
PROGRAM linear_search (INPUT,OUTPUT);
   VAR count, test, flag : INTEGER;
   N: ARRAY [0..20] OF INTEGER;
   BEGIN
      FOR count := 1 TO 20 DO
         BEGIN
            WRITELN('type in number', count);
            READLN(N[count]);
         END;

      WRITELN('Please type in the search criteria');
      READLN(test);
      count := 1;
      flag := 0;
      WHILE count < 21 DO
         BEGIN
            IF test = N[count] THEN
               BEGIN
                  WRITELN('criteria matched');
                  WRITELN(N[count]);
                  flag := 1;
               END;
            count := count + 1;
         END;
      IF flag = 0 THEN WRITELN('Sorry, no match found');
   END
```

The **linear** or **sequential search** is certainly not very efficient. If the item of data to be found is at the end of the list then all previous items must be read and checked before the item that matches the search criteria is found. No structure was applied to the data in this simple case.

If there is only one item of interest that is required in the list then the search length can easily be worked out by considering the following argument.

If there were only three data items in the list then it could take one, two, or three, comparisons to find the required item of interest. Therefore, the average search length would be given by:

Average search length = (1 + 2 + 3)/3 = 2

Hence if there were N data items in the list the average search length would be:

Average search length = (1 + 2 + 3 + 4 + ... + N)/N

Using arithmetic progressions it can easily be shown that:

as 1 + 2 + 3 + 4 + ... + N = N(N + 1)/2

then,

average search length = N(N + 1)/ 2N = (N + 1)/ 2

If the data has been sorted (see beginning of this chapter) then much faster techniques for searching can be used.

Structured search techniques

The following methods rely on the data being sorted before it is searched. The techniques of adding and deleting data to such ordered lists and trees were covered in chapter 14. Here we will just concentrate on searching the specified data structures.

The binary search

This is more efficient than the linear search, but requires the data to be in order. The idea is very simple and is as follows:

First compare our search criteria with the middle (the median) number in the list, or one number away from this middle number if there is an even number of numbers.

Consider the following ordered list:

2   3   4   7   12   18   (23)   29   31   37   38   49   53
————left-hand list——   ——right-hand list——

If we compare the desired number with 23 (the middle number in the list) then:

If a match occurs we have completed the search else:
If the desired number is less than the middle number then search the left-hand list else:
Search the right-hand list.

The techniques used to search the left-hand and right-hand list can also be a binary search. Hence the algorithm will call itself **recursively**

As an example of a binary search consider finding the number 3 in the above list.

Index	1	2	3	4	5	6	7	8	9	10	11	12	13	Comments
	2	3	4	7	12	18	23	29	31	37	38	49	53	
	2	3	4	7	12	18	(23)	29	31	37	38	49	53	INT((1 + 13)/2) = 7 i.e. N(7) = 23
	2	3	4	7	12	18	(23)	29	31	37	38	49	53	3 < 23: left-hand list chosen.

_____ left-hand list _____   _____ right-hand list ____

| | 2 | 3 | 4 | (7) | 12 | 18 | | | | | | | | INT(1 + 6)/2 = 4 i.e. N(4) = 7 |
| | 2 | 3 | 4 | (7) | 12 | 18 | | | | | | | | 3 < 7: left-hand list chosen. |

___ left ___   __ right __

| | 2 | (3) | 4 | | | | | | | | | | | INT(1 + 3)/2 = 2 i.e. N(2) = 3 |

Number 3 found: Therefore stop search.
Only three comparisons were needed in the above case.

If we assume that the original list is simply integer numbers in an array called N, then we can set up pointers to indicate the left- and right-hand numbers of each list.

The algorithm can therefore be developed as follows:

```
maximum := number of elements in the array.    (*Set up initial conditions*)
left := 1
right := maximum
middle := INTEGER{(left + right)/2}

READ search criteria
```

```
PROCEDURE split (left, right)                    (*Perform binary split*)
WHILE (flag is not set) AND (middle >= 1) AND
(middle <= max) DO
    BEGIN
      middle := INTEGER{(left + right)/2}
      IF N[middle] = search criteria THEN
        BEGIN
          print out the search criteria
          set flag
        END
      ELSE
        IF search criteria > N[middle] THEN
          BEGIN
            left := middle + 1
          END
      ELSE
        BEGIN
          right := right - 1
        END;
      split (left, right, test)              (*Binary-split called recursively*)
    END;
```

A complete Pascal program to perform a search on twenty numbers using the binary split now follows. The main algorithm is shown, and the twenty numbers to search must be typed in order. If not, one of the sort procedures shown at the beginning of this chapter will have to be used.

```
PROGRAM binary_search (INPUT, OUTPUT); VAR right, left, maximum,
middle, test, flag, count: INTEGER; 15: ARRAY [0..20] OF INTEGER;
PROCEDURE split_up (VAR left, right, test: INTEGER);
    BEGIN
      WHILE (flag = 0) AND (middle > 1) AND (middle < maximum) DO
        BEGIN
          middle := TRUNC((left + right)/2);
          IF test = N[middle] THEN
            BEGIN
              WRITELN('match found', N[middle]);
              flag := 1;
            END
          ELSE
            BEGIN
              IF test > N[middle] THEN
                BEGIN
                  left := middle + 1;
                END
              ELSE
                BEGIN
                  right := middle - 1;
                END;
            END;
            split_up(left, right, test);
        END;
    END;

BEGIN
    maximum := 10;
    left := 1;
    right := maximum;
    flag := 0;
    middle := TRUNC((left + right)/2);
    FOR count := 1 TO maximum DO
      BEGIN
        WRITELN('Please type in number', count);
        READLN(N[count]);
      END;
    WRITELN('Please type in search number');
    READLN(test);
```

```
                    split_up(left, right, test);
                    IF flag = O THEN
                    BEGIN
                        WRITELN('Sorry, no match found in the list');
                    END;
                END.
```

The binary search is obviously much more efficient than the linear search although it must be remembered that the data to be searched must be in order.

To get an idea of the maximum search length for a binary search consider the following:

Suppose we wish to find the number 3 in the following lists by applying the binary search algorithms already well established:

1 (3)
Two elements would require just one comparison
1 3 (5) 6 .... 1 (3)
Four elements would require just two comparisons.
1 3 5 6 (8) 9 12 19 .... 1 3 (5) 6 .... 1 (3)
Eight elements would require three comparisons.
1 3 5 6 8 9 12 19 (23) 26 27 35 37 39 40 41
1 3 5 6 (8) 9 12 19
1 3 (5) 6
1 (3)
Sixteen elements would require comparisons.

The above, together with the next few results are summarized in the table:

Number of elements in list	Maximum number of comparisons
2	1
4	2
8	3
16	4
32	5

This suggests a logarithmic relationship. If we use logs to base two then:

$\log_2 (2) = 1$
$\log_2 (4) = 2$
$\log_2 (8) = 3$
$\log_2 (16) = 4$ etc.

Therefore, in general, for N elements we require a maximum of $\log_2(N)$ comparisons.

Hence for a binary search, MAXIMUM SEARCH LENGTH = $\log_2(N)$.

Exercise 15.2

1. A linear or sequential search involves examination of each element within an array. This can be very slow if the desired elements are near the end of a long list. A better method is to make use of a binary search. This involves storing the data in order as a binary tree. Show how it is possible to search and find any element in a list of 1000 by examining at most only ten of the elements.

2. Devise a search algorithm based on the binary search principle in question (1). Develop a pseudocode algorithm and hence develop a program using a language of your choice.

End of chapter summary

- **Sorting** and **searching** are *fundamental data-processing operations.*
- There are various sorting methods including the **insertion sort, bubble sort, shell sort, quick sort** and **tournament sort**.
- The **insertion sort** splits the list to be sorted into lower and upper elements and a special number, starting at the second element. The special number (pivotal position) is compared with all the lower elements and numbers are inserted into the right place. The pivotal position is then moved one place right and the whole process is repeated until the pivotal position becomes the last number.
- The **bubble sort** starts with the first pair of numbers in the list, they are compared and swapped if necessary. If a swap is necessary this fact is flagged. The next pair of numbers are then compared and the process is repeated until the last pair of numbers in the list are compared. If swaps were necessary the whole process is repeated.
- The **shell sort** method chooses a number which is nearest to max/2 where max is the max number of numbers in the list. This number represents a distance d between elements which are to be compared. On the first pass the pairs of numbers produced in each set are compared and swapped if necessary. The second pass assigns a value of distance d = max/4. Therefore, we end up with larger subsets which are sorted separately. The third pass makes d = max/8, etc. We continue until d = 1, in which case the whole list is sorted.
- The **quick sort** algorithm splits up a list into two sublists, pointers are used and moved to indicate pairs of data to be compared and swapped. If a swap is needed then a reference number is moved towards the other pointer. This process is repeated until the two pointers coincide. After the above process the two sublists are independent and will no longer interact with each other. They can therefore be sorted separately and the algorithm can be called recursively.
- The **tree sort** can be thought of as a sort of tennis tournament (hence the alternative name). 'Players' can play each other and a binary tree is built up until the 'winner' becomes the root of the tree, in which case they are removed, placed at the head of the list and the data is replaced with a dummy Z. The process is then repeated with Zs being used instead of the name of the 'player' who has been removed. When Zs appear all through the final tree the list is sorted.
- **Searching** involves scanning a list until data matching the specified criteria has been found.
- The **linear search** is simply examining each element in the list until the appropriate one is found.
- The **binary search** relies on the fact that the data is sorted before it is searched. The middle or median number in the list is examined and if the criteria is less than that being examined the left-hand sub-list is sorted, again by using a binary search.

16 Files and file handling

Introduction

A **file** is such an *important* **data structure** that this entire chapter is devoted to it. Few activities take place in computing without reference to a file – be it a **database file**, a **word-processor file** or indeed any other **application-based** or **program-based file**. One often hears a huge variety of terms like 'file allocation table' (see page 391), a 'COBOL file', 'file-management utilities', 'file names', 'file servers', 'file types' and 'file maintenance', for example – but the thing which *all* of these terms have in common is that they are all usually referring to **data structures for external storage systems** such as **disks**, **tapes**, or **CD-ROMs**. Although it is easily possible to create and process files entirely within memory, one advantage of file data structures is that they are designed to cope with vast amounts of data in a single structure – typically many Mbytes, but often several Gbytes or even larger – for much of the time complete files are not able to be fitted into the available amount of RAM on the majority of computer systems.

It's *most important* that you have read and understood **chapter 14** on **data structures**, and also have an appreciation of *some of the work* covered in **chapter 15** when **sorting and searching techniques** are discussed in detail. Many of the principles and concepts built up in this chapter rely on work that has been covered in these and previous chapters.

What is a file?

A **file** is *logically organised* (see in a moment) **as a collection of records**, and *usually* contains **related information** – a file is, therefore, **a collection of related information** stored on some suitable storage medium. Such concepts are not difficult to understand, as most people would use similar terms in the everyday sense of the words – the ideas of 'customer files', 'criminal-record files' or 'stock files', for example, would be understood by the majority of people. These terms have literally been

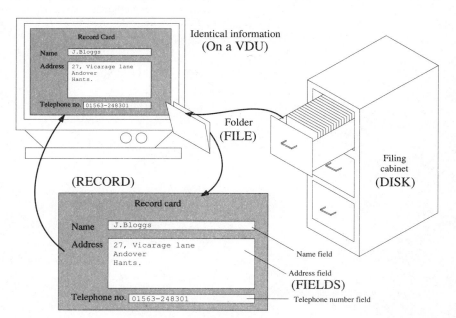

Figure 16.1

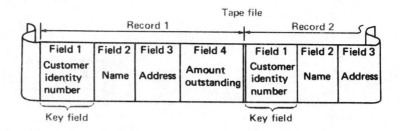

Figure 16.2

borrowed from office terminology where files (folders containing information) are stored in filing cabinets in ways similar to those shown in figure 16.1.

These days, however, more and more data in the form of files are being stored on computer disks and tape. **Throughout this chapter we will be looking in detail at the anatomy of these files, and the ways in which the** *data* **stored within these files can be processed efficiently**.

A file's **logical organisation** relates to the ways in which it is **logically** broken up into smaller self-contained units called **records**. For example, if we are dealing with a customer file, then *each customer* would probably have their *own record*, shown as a record card in the case of figure 16.1. On the other hand – the **physical organisation** of a file refers to the ways in which *the file is physically stored on a disk or tape* – it deals specifically with the ways in which the information is **mapped** onto the **physical blocks** and *eventually* onto the **tracks** and **sectors** (see page 270) on a disk, for example. However, this physical organisation can be forgotten about for the time being, as we will cover it in more detail towards the end of this chapter.

Each **record** usually contains information *which has been further split up into smaller logical units* called **fields**. Figure 16.1 shows a record card with three separate fields, namely 'customer name', 'address' and 'telephone number'. Many students have little experience of using magnetic tape, but it's easy to visualise what's happening here too by considering figure 16.2. In this diagram we can see that this **customer file** has been split up into 'customer identity number', 'name', 'address' and 'amount outstanding' fields. The only problem with tape, as we shall see later, is that all the records have to be cycled through until you get to the one which you need, and this could sometimes take a long time (in computer terms of course), but *don't dismiss tape as a viable and efficient file-storage and data-processing medium* on large systems, **it is often very efficient, fast** *and* **cost effective if used in the correct ways**.

Of course, a **field** is *not* the smallest item of data within a **file**, as the contents of most fields are further sub-divided into **characters**.

Logical file organisation

There are *several different types* of **file organisation**, each being efficient in its own way for certain types of operation, and each more or less efficient – or indeed impossible to use with different types of secondary storage media. **Four main types of file organisation** are shown in the following list, (although alternative names are sometimes used) and each type is explained in the next few sections.

(1) **Serial access**.
(2) **Sequential access**.
(3) **Direct access**.
(4) **Indexed sequential**.

You may come across other file organisations such as indexed or binary search for example – these variations on the above themes are covered later in this chapter.

Serial access files

When this type of file organisation is used **each record is stored one after the other with no regard to any logical order**. *In other words – each record is stored one after*

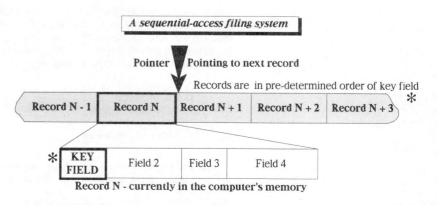

A serial-access filing system

Pointer   Pointing to next record

Records are not in any pre-determined order

| Record N - 1 | Record N | Record N + 1 | Record N + 2 | Record N + 3 |

| Field 1 | Field 2 | Field 3 | Field 4 |

Record N - currently in the computer's memory

Figure 16.3

I've lost my favourite Des O'Connor album..(sob), it's on one of these tapes somewhere...(sob)

Sequential access files

the other in a higgledy-piggledy way. Files organised like this are often the inevitable consequence of day-to-day operations such as reading raw statistical data or collecting data from questionnaires and the like. Serially-organised files therefore usually consist of unprocessed records waiting for some operation such as **sorting**, for example, to be carried out. However, *if the same processing* has to be carried out on *all records* then serial-access files are just as efficient as any other method.

To *access data within a serial file* the concept of a **pointer** must be well understood. Pointers have already been covered in some detail in chapter 14 when *other* **data structures** are considered, and therefore it's not too surprising that pointers are used within files as well. A file *is* just another example of a data structure – albeit usually implemented on an external device. Figure 16.3 shows a serial-access file in which the pointer has been placed at the beginning of the next record, marking the next position within the file ready for reading.

Most high-level languages have mechanisms for **pointer** and **file manipulation**, but *few have the sophisticated file-handling facilities of* **COBOL** (see page 156). Pascal, for example, is limited to **serial or sequential access files only**, and the facilities in most versions of BASIC are literally – just as basic! It is, however, *essential* **that you have some high-level programming experience of file-handling** – programming by making use of a 4GL database language only would give you insufficient insight into what's going on at a fundamental level. To this end there are several examples developed in this chapter which can be further developed into complete working systems in appropriate high-level languages of your choice.

This file-access method operates on *a file which has already been put into some pre-determined* **sequence**. For example, it might be 'ascending order of bank-account number', 'alphabetical order by name', or 'ISBN number' for books, for example. It is usual for the *field associated with the sort order* to be termed the **key field**, and this idea is shown in figure 16.4.

This file must have been sorted into order using techniques similar to those covered in chapter 15. However, *if the file to be sorted is too big to fit into available RAM,* then **other techniques**, *covered later in this chapter* can easily be used.

A sequential-access filing system

Pointer   Pointing to next record

Records are in pre-determined order of key field

| Record N - 1 | Record N | Record N + 1 | Record N + 2 | Record N + 3 | *

| KEY FIELD | Field 2 | Field 3 | Field 4 |

Record N - currently in the computer's memory

Figure 16.4

Sequential files are extremely efficient for **batch processing** (see page 371) operations such as working out quarterly service bills for water, electricity and gas, for example. If the information in a sequential file needs to be updated (see later in this chapter), then it is very *efficient* to make use of a **sequential file** *if* the **amendments file** or **transaction file** *is also in the same order*. It should be noted that *if* **magnetic tape is being used, then serial** or **sequential file organisations are the** *only* *two options* **available**. Even so, it *is* possible to implement such file systems in more efficient ways *if* they are used on a direct-access storage medium such as disk.

A direct-access filing system

Direct-access storage - logical address	Field 1	Field 2	Field 3	Field 4	
Address N - 1	Field 1	Field 2	Field 3	Field 4	
Address N	Field 1	Field 2	Field 3	Field 4	← Calculated by hashing
Address N + 1	Field 1	Field 2	Field 3	Field 4	
Address N + 2	Field 1	Field 2	Field 3	Field 4	
Address N + 3	Field 1	Field 2	Field 3	Field 4	

Record at address N is currently in computer's memory

Figure 16.5

Direct access files

A **direct-access** file (also called a **random-access** file) means that *it's possible to directly access a record without* having to sequentially or serially go through any previous records. Conceptually, *instead of visualising the system as a long list of records* – as in the previous two sections, a direct-access file can be thought of as an **array-type** data structure (see page 293). The idea is shown in figure 16.5. As can be seen from the diagram, **this method relies on the fact that each record is referenced by a unique address on the particular storage medium**. Therefore, *only* **direct access media** *such as disks* **are suitable for this method of access**. You should take particular note that it's possible to put the pointer at any address *without* the need to sequence through any of the previous addresses.

The *addresses for the locations of each record do not have to be contiguous*, and can be calculated by a variety of methods including **hashing** (see page 312), or methods making use of **hierarchical** or other data structures such as the **binary search**, for example, shown on page 333. **Hashing** *is the most direct* and therefore the **quickest** of the record-location methods. Eventually, the calculated address would have to be mapped onto the physical device such as the disk or CD-ROM, and this is covered in more detail when physical records are covered on page 357.

Indexed sequential files

This system *organises the file into some* **sequential order**, usually based on the **key field**, very similar in principle to the sequential files explained earlier in this chapter. However, it is *also possible* to *randomly* (i.e. *without* having to sequence through all the records which appear before the one you want) *access* the **records** by using a separate index file as shown in figure 16.6. The example shown here has a file in which the **key field** is breakfast cereals, together with the names of the people who eat these particular cereals for breakfast.

For example, if the people who like Coco Pops need to be processed, (or a person who likes Coco Pops needs to be found) the index file is searched for the Coco-pops entry, a **pointer** *from* the **index file** is followed to find the *first* Coco-pops record, (Digby in this case) and finally **other pointers** are followed until the *end* of the **Coco-Pops list** of records is encountered (given by Issac in the above sequential file because the next entry points to Shreddies, which is alphabetically beyond Coco Pops).

It is possible to set up more than one index in an indexed-sequential file if this is thought desirable, but the **primary index** is the one in which the **sequential order of the file** was *first established*.

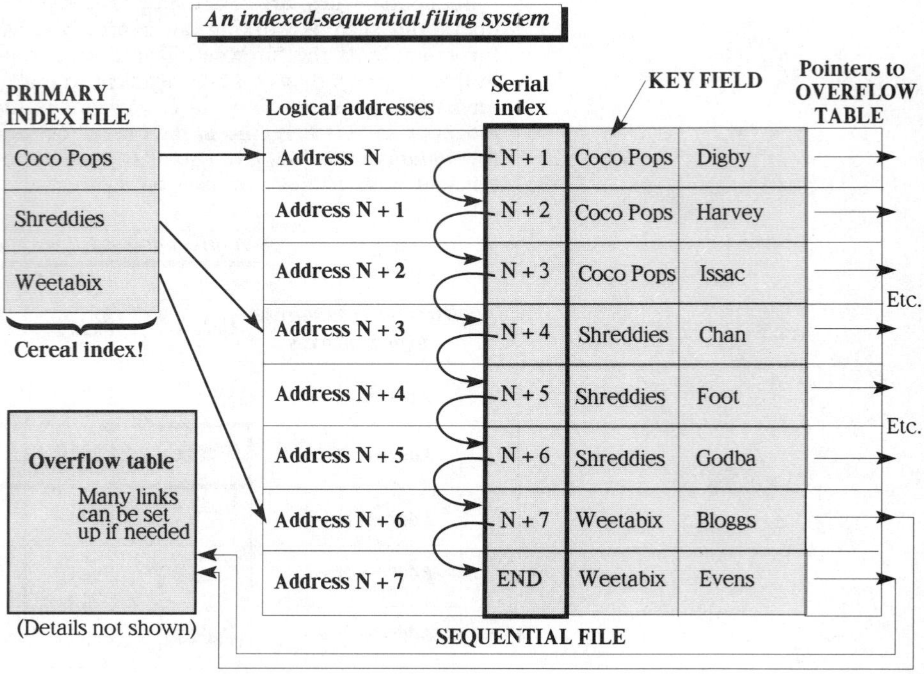

Figure 16.6

One major disadvantage with **sequential files** on **serial-access media** such as tape is that *a complete rewrite of the entire file* has to be done if a new record needs to be added (see page 349). However, with an **indexed-sequential file on disk**, this is *not* the case – *any new addition can be put into an* **overflow table** as shown in figure 16.6, and the pointers pointing to the overflow table can be set in ways similar to those when dealing with **linked lists** in chapter 14. As shown in figure 16.6, each record has an extra field (normally invisible to an application) which points to an overflow table if it needs to be used after the initial file has been created.

After many updates the pointer arrangements are bound to become very messy, the overflow table will fill up and it's usual to run a program which would **merge** (see page 351) the **overflow table** with the **main sequential file** to produce a **new indexed-sequential file** *ready to start afresh* with a **new overflow table**. The techniques for this merging process are covered later in this chapter.

Why an index is useful

At this stage some students might feel that *searching an index file* for an entry is *not* very much different to *searching the actual file* for an entry – however, in practice, nothing could be further from the truth. It's interesting to calculate, for example, how many comparisons would be needed, on average, to find a record of interest *if an* **index** *is used*, compared to the number of comparisons that would have to be made on the same size file *if no index* (i.e. a **sequential file**) is used. Obviously these are only average figures, but it does give a good indication of the enormous difference. The general idea is shown in figure 16.7, and is explained as follows.

Figure 16.7 shows a typical large file with 1,000,000 records. Without any index at all, to find any record of interest would, therefore, on average, take about 500,000 comparisons. You can see that this method would be slow, even on disk! However, suppose that we now have just a single index in which there are 1,000 entries, roughly equally spaced over the entire range of the file. To search for an entry in the index would take on average 500 comparisons. Now assuming that the main file is split up into 1,000 equal parts, one part for each index entry, then each part can be assumed to have, on average, a sub list of 1,000 records. Now again on average, a further 500 comparisons would be needed to find the item of interest in this sub list of the sequential file. This makes **1,000 comparisons needed altogether, compared to the original 500,000 comparisons needed without an index**. Therefore, on average, a single index in this particular example has increased the search speed by a factor of 500! You can now see why the addition of an index is extremely useful.

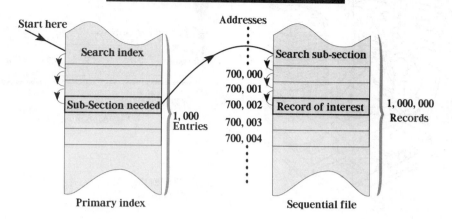

Figure 16.7

It should be obvious that *this file-handling system can only be implemented on* **direct-access storage media** too, because some parts of the systems rely on the fact that you can go straight to a logical address without having to stop and investigate any previous addresses on the way.

Operations with files

Files must obviously be **created** in the first place, usually need **updating** at regular intervals, might have to be **merged** with other files, or individual records might have to be **amended**. New records might have to be **added** or old records **deleted**, or the contents of a file might have to be **sorted** into a different order. Files have to be **searched** for specific criteria and often have to be **backed up** for security purposes. Typical operations like these will now be looked at in a little more detail, together with a brief description of some algorithms to tackle some of these jobs.

The *ways in which files can be processed* **depends to a large extent on the file organisation** *and* **on the storage media on which the file is to be held**. For example, if we are updating a file on tape, then one or more tape files usually act as the input/s, and another (*different*) tape file *must* act as the output – similar methods can also be used on disk, but direct access methods such as indexed-sequential would need to be updated in different ways again, as the index-pointer mechanisms will need to be maintained in ways similar to those shown in chapter 14. We will first look at processing data in serial and sequential files.

Processing data with serial and sequential access files

These methods are *predominantly* used for **tape-based systems**, but can also be used efficiently on disk systems for some types of operation. Don't forget also that some high-level languages such as **Pascal**, for example, treat *all files* **as if they are on tape-based systems** – even when they are on disk!

File creation

Any **data structure** needs to be **created** in the first place, and a **file** is obviously no exception. Let's suppose, for the sake of argument, that we wish to **create a file called 'Students'** *consisting of* student **names** and **initials**, *together with the grades* for each of *five* compulsory subjects – being **Maths, Programming, Analysis, Electronics** and **Systems**. The mark for each subject is an **integer** value from *0 to 100* inclusive. The **name field** is to be **20 characters long** containing the surname, followed by the **initials field** consisting of **5 characters**, being **initials** separated by **full stops**. A typical record would therefore be as shown in figure 16.8.

We have already seen how to create file record definitions in **COBOL** (see page 157), and a typical one for the student's file could therefore be as follows.

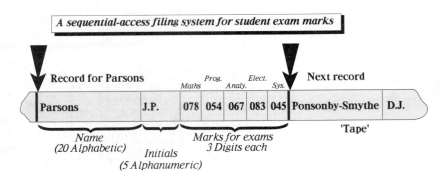

Figure 16.8

```
01  STUDENT.
    02  NAME.
        03    SURNAME     PIC X(20).
        03    INITIALS    PIC A(5).
    02  MARKS.
        03    MATHS       PIC 999.
        03    PROG        PIC 999.
        03    ANALYSIS    PIC 999.
        03    ELECT       PIC 999.
        03    SYST        PIC 999.
```

COBOL would also have to know that this is a **serial-access file**, because, unlike BASIC and Pascal, for example, COBOL *can* cope with direct-access files too – and this is easily achieved by using the **environment division** (see page 156). Note that COBOL does *not* differentiate between serial and sequential files when it comes to the file definitions. A typical environment-division definition is, therefore, as follows.

```
ENVIRONMENT DIVISION.
INPUT-OUTPUT SECTION.
SELECT STUDENTS ASSIGN TO "A:STUDENTS.DAT"
* Assigns file called students to drive A
* with a suitable secondary filename for Data files.
ORGANISATION IS SEQUENTIAL.
ACCESS MODE IS SEQUENTIAL.
```

Writing data to a file

To *create a file* we must first **write** some information to it. In most high-level languages, including COBOL, BASIC and Pascal, for example, a command called '**OPEN**' (or a variation on this theme) is used to **open up a file** for reading or writing. Similarly, when *all file activity has finished* it is usual to **CLOSE** all the files. **Opening** a file prepares a file for processing – it usually involves operations like automatically positioning the pointer at the beginning of a file, for example, which is usually transparent to the programmer. Similarly, **closing** a file ends all the connections between the file and a particular program. Closing a file for the first time will write an **end-of-file marker (EOF)** which is a special character/s that indicates to the system that there is *no more data* in the file after the record which has just been read. The **EOF marker** is useful when reading data from files, as you don't need to know how many records are in the file – all that is necessary is to loop until the EOF is reached.

Let's suppose that we are going to **create the file**, and *at the same time* **enter data regarding the students names and examinations marks** – this is not necessarily the most efficient way to proceed, but it keeps things extremely simple *and illustrates all the appropriate principles* for creating a file and writing some data to it. Let's also assume that a dummy-data entry for surname of "ZZZ" will be used to terminate the proceedings. A structure diagram for the procedure division is shown in figure 16.9.

A complete COBOL program, based on the environment and data divisions in the previous sections, together with the procedure division outlined in the above Nassi-Schneiderman diagram now follows.

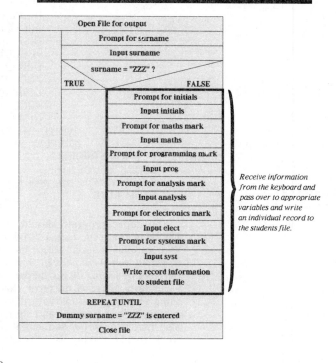

A structure diagram for writing the students' records in the student-examination-mark file.

Figure 16.9

```
IDENTIFICATION DIVISION.
PROGRAM-ID.    STUDENTS.
AUTHOR.        KING KONG.
*
ENVIRONMENT DIVISION.
INPUT-OUTPUT SECTION.
FILE-CONTROL.
    SELECT STUDENTS ASSIGN TO "A:STUDENTS.DAT"
    ORGANISATION IS SEQUENTIAL
    ACCESS MODE IS SEQUENTIAL.
*
DATA DIVISION.
FILE SECTION.
FD  STUDENTS.
01  STUDENT.
    02  NAME.
        03  SURNAME     PIC X(20).
        03  INITIALS    PIC A(5).
    02  MARKS.
        03  MATHS       PIC 999.
        03  PROG        PIC 999.
        03  ANALYSIS    PIC 999.
        03  ELECT       PIC 999.
        03  SYST        PIC 999.

*
PROCEDURE DIVISION.
FILE-WRITE.
    OPEN OUTPUT STUDENTS.
    PERFORM UNTIL SURNAME = "ZZZ"
        DISPLAY "Please enter the student's surname"
        ACCEPT SURNAME
        IF SURNAME NOT = "ZZZ"
```

```
                                    DISPLAY "Initials"
                                    ACCEPT INITIALS
                                    DISPLAY "Maths mark?"
                                    ACCEPT MATHS
                                    DISPLAY "Programming mark?"
                                    ACCEPT PROG
                                    DISPLAY "Analysis mark?"
                                    ACCEPT ANALYSIS
                                    DISPLAY "Electronics mark?"
                                    ACCEPT ELECT
                                    DISPLAY "Systems mark?"
                                    ACCEPT SYST
                                    DISPLAY "Done"
                                WRITE STUDENT
                                DISPLAY SURNAME "'s record has been written to file".
                        END-PERFORM.
                        CLOSE STUDENTS.
                        DISPLAY "File has now been created and closed".
                        STOP RUN.
```

The above program should be relatively easy for students to interpret. After it has been run a file called 'Students.DAT' exists on drive A (one of the hard disks), and contains a serial-access file of the students and grade information *in the order in which they were entered from the keyboard*. You should take special note that *for the sake of simplicity* **no validation routines were used** when the marks were entered – similarly, there is **no error checking of any sort** to handle the situation if something should go wrong with data entry or with writing the data to the file – this is extremely bad practice and should *not* be emulated in your 'A' level projects! Note also that if a *proper* **sequential access file** is required then the **serial file** will have to be **sorted** making use of methods such as those shown in chapter 15 or later on in this chapter.

Once a file has been created you will probably want to interrogate it – there's not much point in creating it otherwise! Again, the concepts are common to most high-level languages, and assuming that the file has been opened for reading, a command called **READ** (or a variation on this theme) can be used to extract data from the file.

Reading data from a file

Files are usually read by programs *other than those* which created them. You must also appreciate that *there's no magical structure which has been stored along with the data on a tape or disk*. Therefore, **the program which reads the file needs to know which data structures were used when the file was created.**

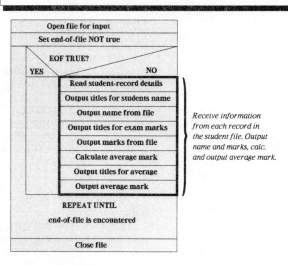

A structure diagram for reading data from the student file, then calculating and outputting the average mark

```
            Open file for input
            Set end-of-file NOT true

                      EOF TRUE?
            YES                        NO

                        Read student-record details
                        Output titles for students name
                        Output name from file
                        Output titles for exam marks
                        Output marks from file
                        Calculate average mark
                        Output titles for average
                        Output average mark

                    REPEAT UNTIL
                end-of-file is encountered

            Close file
```

Receive information from each record in the student file. Output name and marks, calc. and output average mark.

Figure 16.10

Whichever high-level language is being employed, the original structure used *must* be explicitly stated again. With this information the program which reads the data then knows what patterns of data to expect on the disk or the tape, and the data will be interpreted correctly. Suppose, for the sake of argument, we now wish to read information about all the students from the student's file created earlier in this section, print out the student's names and examination marks, calculate the averages, and then output these too. A structure diagram for the procedure division is shown in figure 16.10, and a complete COBOL program based on the above analysis now follows.

```
IDENTIFICATION DIVISION.
PROGRAM-ID.    READ-STUDENTS.
AUTHOR.        GODZILLA.
*
ENVIRONMENT DIVISION.
INPUT-OUTPUT SECTION.
FILE-CONTROL.
    SELECT STUDENTS ASSIGN TO "A:STUDENTS.DAT"
    ORGANISATION IS SEQUENTIAL
    ACCESS MODE IS SEQUENTIAL.
*
DATA DIVISION.
FILE SECTION.
FD STUDENTS.
01    STUDENT.
    02  NAME.
        03  SURNAME     PIC X(20).
        03  INITIALS    PIC A(5).
    02  MARKS.
        03  MATHS       PIC 999.
        03  PROG        PIC 999.
        03  ANALYSIS    PIC 999.
        03  ELECT       PIC 999.
        03  SYST        PIC 999.
*
WORKING-STORAGE SECTION.
01    EOF-FLAG  PIC X.
        88  EOF         VALUE IS "F".
        88  NOT-EOF     VALUE IS "T".
01    AVERAGE           PIC 999V99.
*
PROCEDURE DIVISION.
FILE-READ.
OPEN INPUT STUDENTS.
SET NOT-EOF TO TRUE.
PERFORM UNTIL EOF
    READ STUDENTS
        AT END
            SET EOF TO TRUE
        NOT AT END
            DISPLAY "Student name"
            DISPLAY NAME
            DISPLAY "Examination marks"
            DISPLAY MARKS
            COMPUTE AVERAGE = (MATHS + PROG + ANALYSIS + ELECT +
                                                            SYST)/5
            DISPLAY "Average mark is" AVERAGE
            DISPLAY
END-PERFORM.
CLOSE STUDENTS.
STOP RUN.
```

Notice the use of the **EOF (End of File) variable** mentioned earlier in this section, and see *how it has been used to terminate the loop when the end of file has been detected*. The extended read statement READ...AT END.... NOT AT END acts as an 'IF-THEN with EOF check' type statement when reading files in COBOL. Notice also that displaying (outputting) NAME will display the sub-fields NAME *and*

INITIALS, and displaying MARKS will display *all* of the sub-fields in this group, namely, 'Maths', 'Prog', 'Analysis', 'Elect', and 'Syst' – another nice feature in COBOL.

A more sophisticated example of data processing

Having created a serial-access file and read back the data, we will now concentrate on slightly more realistic and sophisticated data processing. Complete COBOL programs take up a lot of space, therefore, *only the* **procedure divisions** will be given *if* **COBOL** is to be used in an example, and often just a COBOL-like-Pseudocode algorithm only will be given. It is left to the reader to develop these into fully-working COBOL or other high-level language programs of their choice.

Searching

Searching a file is of obvious fundamental importance and carrying out these processes in practice is relatively trivial. All that is necessary is to sequence through the file, record-by-record, until the required match is found *or* until the **end-of-file** (see last section) has been reached – in which case, tough luck, there is no match! The search criteria may be simple, such as a 'customer name', for example, or it may be more complex involving a combination of **Boolean operators**. (Matching criteria strung together with ANDs, ORs, NOTs or other Boolean operators.)

Using the student-examination file created in the last section, we might, for the sake of argument, want to identify all those students who have marks below 40% in any examination, and then inform them that they must retake this/these particular exam/s again before the start of the next term if they wish to carry on! And on a more-positive note, identify all those students who have passed, congratulate them and notify them accordingly. To keep you on your toes regarding different forms of structured analysis and design, a **JSP diagram** (see page 137) is used to express the guts of this particular algorithm, and is shown in figure 16.11.

A typical algorithm using **COBOL-like pseudocode** for the procedure division follows shortly. Note that some procedures, such as the ones shown inside the dotted lines have been **modularised**, (coded once only and called up when needed). In COBOL, the word 'PERFORM' followed by the name of the procedure to be performed acts as a procedure call. These procedures have not been covered in detail, as they contain relatively trivial code and should easily be able to be worked out by most readers. It should also be obvious that these procedure definitions would also be needed for the following programs to work in practice.

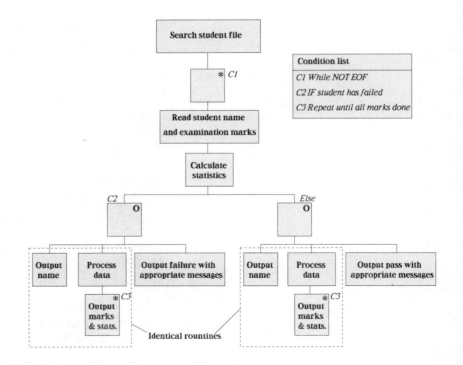

Figure 16.11

```
OPEN INPUT STUDENTS.
SET NOT-EOF TO TRUE.
PERFORM UNTIL EOF
    READ STUDENTS
        AT END
            SET EOF TO TRUE
        NOT AT END
            PERFORM STATISTICS-CALCULATIONS
            IF FAIL is TRUE
                PERFORM WRITE-HEADINGS-AND-NAME
                PERFORM PROCESS-DATA
                PERFORM OUTPUT-MARKS-AND-STATISTICS
                PERFORM FAIL-PROCEDURE
            ELSE
                PERFORM WRITE-HEADINGS-AND-NAME
                PERFORM PROCESS-DATA
                PERFORM OUTPUT-MARKS-AND-STATISTICS
                PERFORM PASS-PROCEDURE
END-PERFORM.
CLOSE STUDENTS.
```

Obviously the middle parts contain *many* lines of code, *but these are of little consequence to a chapter on* **file handling**. Most readers should be able to develop the above pseudocode into code in a high-level language of their choice.

Updating records

Updating a file involves things like **addition** of a new record, **insertion** of a new record, **changing information** *within* an existing record, or the **deletion** of a particular record. With **serial or sequential-access files** some of *these operations are not as trivial as might appear at first sight*.

Don't forget that we are currently dealing with files as though they are stored on tape. Therefore, *we can't just pop a record in at some point within a sequential file without* **physically moving** *all of the other records out of the way* to make space for the new one. The idea is shown in figure 16.12.

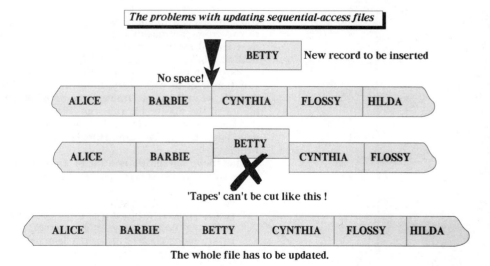

The problems with updating sequential-access files

The whole file has to be updated.

Figure 16.12

Inserting records

If you *imagine* that the **files are physically on tape**, as shown in figure 16.12, then you will easily appreciate the principles involved. Don't forget the fact that some files in large computer systems will be on tape, and some versions of languages like BASIC and Pascal arrange their file handling like this, even though they are on disk.

Whenever you make use of a cassette tape recorder at home, for example, *if you are going to record anything from an existing tape* then **one tape must act as the master** and **another tape must act as the copy**. You *can't* have the *same tape* simultaneously recording something from itself and onto itself! With this borne in mind,

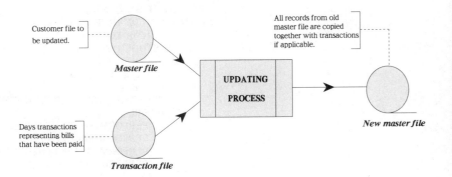

Master file — Customer file to be updated.

Transaction file — Days transactions representing bills that have been paid.

UPDATING PROCESS

All records from old master file are copied together with transactions if applicable.

New master file

Figure 16.13

it should be relatively obvious that the same principles must apply to altering records on a serial-access medium, or a serial or sequentially organised file structure on a direct-access medium.

Whenever a record needs updating – even if it's only a single record – then the entire file will need to be rewritten! However, don't forget that these ideas should not be alien – if you add just a 'single full stop' to the middle of a large word-processor document, for example, – then the whole document will have to be saved again – things are not so daft as they might originally sound.

On systems where *many transactions* may have taken place (such as 3,000 customers paying their electricity bill, for example), it's usual to build up these transactions on a *separate* **transaction file** which is then **sorted** into a *suitable* **sequential order** – perhaps by customer number. At the end of the day, for example, this **transaction file** is then *used to update* the **master file** (also sequentially organised in the same way) so that a **new master file** is produced which contains the latest information. The idea is shown in the systems flowchart of figure 16.13.

The updating process shown in figure 16.13 would consist of reading the sequentially organised files by getting the first record from the master file and comparing it with the first record in the transaction file, and, if a match is found, update and copy the results to the new master file, or, if no match has been found, copy the record from the master file without alteration to the new master file, then get the next record from the master file and carry on with the processes until all records in both files have been processed. There is an added complication if a brand-new record exists within the transaction file that was *not* present within the master file, and this situation is dealt with in the following code. Also, if the transaction file runs out of records, we still have to transfer the remaining master-file records to the new master-file, or, if the master file runs out of records and there are still some records left in the transaction file (obviously new customers) then the remainder of this file will need transferring too – unfortunately it all makes for a more-complex-looking algorithm.

The above paragraph is a bit of a mouthful, therefore **an algorithm** to carry out these transactions using **COBOL-like pseudocode** has been developed as follows.

```
OPEN MASTER-FILE for INPUT
OPEN NEW-TRANSACTION-FILE for INPUT
OPEN NEW-MASTER-FILE for OUTPUT
READ MASTER-FILE-RECORD INTO MASTER-RECORD
READ TRANSACTION-FILE-RECORD INTO TRANSACTION-RECORD
* Need to get first records from each file
* Working records are called MASTER-RECORD and TRANSACTION-RECORD
WHILE NOT END-OF-MASTER-FILE AND NOT END-OF-TRANSACTION-FILE
    IF KEYFIELD-MASTER-RECORD < KEYFIELD-TRANSACTION-RECORD
        *No update necessary for this record
        WRITE MASTER-RECORD TO NEW-MASTER-FILE
        READ MASTER-RECORD INTO MASTER-RECORD
    ELSE
      IF KEYFIELD-MASTER-RECORD = KEYFIELD-TRANSACTION-RECORD
        *Update the record before writing
        PERFORM UPDATE procedure
        WRITE MASTER-RECORD TO NEW-MASTER-FILE
        READ MASTER-FILE-RECORD INTO MASTER-RECORD
```

```
              READ TRANSACTION-FILE-RECORD INTO TRANSACTION-RECORD
          ELSE
              KEYFIELD-MASTER-RECORD > KEYFIELD-TRANSACTION-RECORD
              *New record to be added
              PERFORM NEW-RECORD procedure
              WRITE NEW-RECORD TO NEW-MASTER-FILE
              READ TRANSACTION-FILE-RECORD INTO TRANSACTION-RECORD
          END-IF
       END-IF
    ENDWHILE
    WHILE NOT END-OF-MASTER-FILE
       * Transfer any remaining master-file records to new master file
       WRITE MASTER-RECORD TO NEW-MASTER-FILE
    ENDWHILE
    WHILE NOT END-OF-TRANSACTION-FILE
       * Transfer any remaining transaction records to new master file
       * New record/s to be added and transferred to new master file
       PERFORM NEW-RECORD procedure
       WRITE NEW-RECORD TO NEW-MASTER-FILE
       READ TRANSACTION-FILE-RECORD INTO TRANSACTION-RECORD
    ENDWHILE
    CLOSE MASTER-FILE TRANSACTION-FILE NEW-MASTER-FILE
```

That was a bit of a mouthful too! As you can see, **updating a serial file is no trivial matter!** If you are brave enough you may wish to code the above pseudocode algorithm into a high-level language of your choice. Don't forget that all of these techniques *can be done on disk too* – it's no use saying you can't do it because you don't have a tape system!

Deleting records

We could easily have included records for deletion into the above algorithm. Instead of assuming automatically that all new records would be added, we could simply *not copy* the record across if instructed to delete it. That was easy!

Merging files

This is typical of many transactions that take place in the data-processing industry. For example, it may be that two master files need to be merged into one larger file. In fact, *this is the way that sorting can be accomplished* if the file is **too big** to fit into available RAM. The file can be split up into two, or indeed any number of smaller files such that these smaller files will fit into RAM. Each of the files is then sorted and written as a new sequential file.

The next stage of the process is to **merge** two of the files *using techniques almost identical to those shown in the updating process earlier* – in fact, the process is slightly simpler as no processing has to take place. The two files are simply interrogated sequentially and output to produce a single new master file. This new master file is then combined with another of the tapes in an identical way, to produce an even-newer master file consisting of three of the original tapes, if necessary. The process then continues until all original sorted tapes have been merged onto a single master file. The only limitation is the amount of data which can be fitted onto a single tape – and that's quite a lot of data (see page 280).

Generations of files

One *advantage* of serial and sequential file processing is that *after any updates* you *still have* the **original files intact**. This may not sound too revolutionary, but consider the situation for a moment and you will realise that it's possible to backtrack in

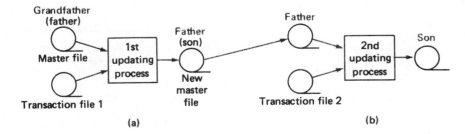

Figure 16.14

some cases of error! It is often useful to be able to do this whereby the original files are kept as well as the new files. This leads to the idea of generations of files, and the concept is shown in figure 16.14.

The **original master file** is renamed the **father file** when a **new master file** (called the **son**) has been produced from it. Similarly, when the **son** is used to produce *yet another* **new master file**, the **son** *becomes the* **father** and the *original father* therefore becomes the **grandfather file**. We could go on with great-grandfather files but we have to stop somewhere otherwise the world would be full of tapes. Three generations is usually the norm, with the grandfather file being 'killed off' when the great grandson is born. Euthanasia *is allowed* when serial or sequential files are being used!

When to use serial and sequential files

After reading the above your immediate answer might be to say never! Nevertheless, such file organisation *is ideal* for **large-volume batch production** of data. Such methods are still extensively used on mainframes today *because* they are extremely cost effective and efficient for many data-processing tasks.

Don't forget that serial access files have a role to play too – not only in acting as an input queue to some particular processing task, but they can be used in their own right when carrying out the **same process** to *all records within a file* – in this case the records do not have to be in any particular predetermined order.

Direct- or random-access files

Direct-access or random-access files are only supported by direct access media such as magnetic disks or magneto-optical disks (see page 274) for example. However, it should be remembered that *all sequential and serial accessing of files,* as carried out in the last few sections, *can be carried out on disk-based files too.*

You may (or may not if you found the work difficult!) be pleased to know that the principles of **direct-access files** are **very similar** to those covered in chapter 14 when **linked-lists** were being studied. **Updating, inserting** and **deleting data** in a **linked list** is similar to **updating, inserting** and **deleting records** in direct-access files.

Instead of the **logical positions** in a **linked list** being *mapped onto* **physical memory locations**, the **logical addresses** within a **direct-access file** are *mapped onto* **physical locations** on the **storage devices**. The ability to do this with an external storage device opens up more possibilities for more flexible arrangements regarding file handling. For example, we can make use of **hashing** for very fast recovery of arbitrary data from a direct-access file – no longer do we have to serially search the file until we get to the record of interest.

We need to devise a suitable **hashing** or **hierarchical algorithm** (e.g. a **search** as shown on page 312) to calculate the address at which the record is going to be placed in our direct-access file. (It's then up to the system software to translate this logical address into a physical address on the disk, as can be seen on page 272.) The **logical-record-address numbers** that we have calculated from the algorithm would

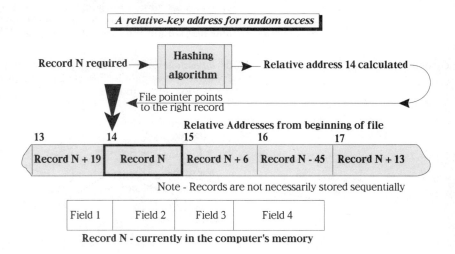

A relative-key address for random access

Record N required → Hashing algorithm → Relative address 14 calculated

File pointer points to the right record

Relative Addresses from beginning of file

13	14	15	16	17
Record N + 19	Record N	Record N + 6	Record N - 45	Record N + 13

Note - Records are not necessarily stored sequentially

Field 1	Field 2	Field 3	Field 4

Record N - currently in the computer's memory

Figure 16.15

usually refer to a **relative address**, this being a number which represents how far the record is 'in' from the beginning of the file. The idea is shown in figure 16.15.

The **COBOL language**, for example, *allows access* by what's called a **relative key**, and, *if* this technique is to be used, the file-control section of the environment division might have something similar to the following.

```
ENVIRONMENT DIVISION.
INPUT-OUTPUT SECTION.
FILE-CONTROL.
    SELECT STUDENTS ASSIGN TO "A:STUDENTS.DAT"
    ORGANISATION IS RELATIVE
    ACCESS MODE IS RANDOM
    RELATIVE KEY IS RECORD-NUMBER
```

We have stated on many occasions that **COBOL** is *the* data-processing language – after getting this far in this chapter you can now start to see why.

Fixed and variable length records

Hitherto we have implied that each record within a file is of **fixed length**. This makes life much easier, because the computer can more easily process the data in record-size chunks which are *all the same*. It is possible to set up a system whereby the records are all of a **variable length**, and although this does save some storage on the secondary storage media being used, the added complexity of the system is often not worth the bother. A more-complex pointer system would be needed, and data regarding the length of a record may have to be stored along with the actual data within each record. On some systems, such as the **relational database systems** covered in chapter 20, it is a requirement of **normalisation** (see page 469) that all records be of fixed length. It's so much easier and often more efficient for the systems to be organised in this way.

Updating records in direct-access files

The **updating** processes here are *not* too difficult to understand. A record is read from the disk, processed in some particular way, then rewritten to the *same* logical storage address. These concepts are, in fact, easier to understand (though not necessarily easier to implement in practice) than the serial and sequential file systems considered earlier. You will probably recall that hitherto in this chapter we have either **opened a file for input**, *or* **opened a file for output**. You will also recall that it was *not possible* on a **serial** or **sequential system** to have the *same file doing both*. (Remember the cassette-tape example!) When **updating** a **direct-access file**, *the file must be* **opened for both input** *and* **output**. Again, when using COBOL language, the same file may be opened for input and output simultaneously.

Inserting a record

Insertion could be a simple case of *calculation of an address* from the *key field* by **hashing**, but, as was seen on page 312 when hashing functions are considered, *if a clash occurs* then some sort of **overflow structure** will need to be maintained to insert the record in an alternative place. There are a variety of methods for being able to do this, with a flag indicating whether a space is occupied or free being one option. For example, in **COBOL**, a particular *file-status code* indicating an error is returned if an illegal attempt (i.e. an insert not an update) is made to write a record over the top of one which already exists. It is up to the programmer to trap this error, then make alternative arrangements for putting the record somewhere else.

Deleting a record

Notice that **record 'deletion' was not an option** in **serial-access file systems**! If we wanted to delete a record it simply meant that we did *not* copy the record to the new master file! Nevertheless, some implementations of **sequential files** *based on disks do* allow for additions and deletions to be made by means of an overflow table similar to the type used when the indexed-sequential files were being considered. Merging of the overflow table and main file would then have to be done at some later stage. However, back to the direct-access files – deletion *can* easily be accomplished when using this file type. Record deletion is simply a case of having some indication that the space occupied by the deleted record can now be returned to the pool of available space – the methods are very similar indeed to those shown when linked lists were covered in chapter 14. **It is not usual or necessary to delete the physical record** – we could not care less whether a sector on a disk, for example, contains irrelevant data or just groups of zeros which may indicate that it is empty. The record is only **logically deleted** – this means that the old data remains there until it's overwritten by something new. Some systems would be organised such that deleted data would simply remain unused, until some clean-up utility reclaiming this space was run at a later stage.

When to use direct-access files

Direct-access files are really the *only sensible option* for **interactive systems** which deal with **on-line queries** where a response time would be expected within seconds. These file systems are the only ones with the appropriate speed necessary, especially if the database (file) is very large. Also, with direct-access files, **on-line transactions from menu-driven systems** within a WIMP environment is an attractive option for more user-friendly systems. If *very quick response* is needed then *only* a **direct-access file** will do.

Processing data in indexed-sequential files

These ideas are extremely simple when applied to direct-access file handling, and are identical in principle to looking up an index in this book. If you have the name of the topic in which you are interested – say nano technology, for example, you look it up in the index, find the page number, then go *straight to* the *right place* in a **sequentially-organised file** – i.e. the sequential pages of this book. Just like this book, these indexed-sequential files have all the advantages of sequential batch-processing organisation, together with a fast-access mechanism by making use of an index. The initials **ISAM** are often used in this context, and stand for **Indexed Sequential Access Method**.

It's of paramount importance to realise at the outset that the *sequential nature* of **indexed-sequential files** *are not subject to the restrictions of ordinary sequential files* such as those found on tape, for example. With an **ordinary sequential file** the file is **literally stored sequentially** on the storage medium. This means that you can't insert or delete records *without having to reorganise the entire file* in the ways described earlier in this chapter. However, with an **indexed-sequential file**, as was shown in figure 16.6, the **overflow table and pointer system** makes it possible to update the records without a rewrite.

It's also important to realise that sequential processing *is* extremely fast for **batch-processing-type activities**. For example, if you are processing the monthly-payroll program in alphabetical order of employee, then there's not much point in using a direct-access file, and hence calculating each logical address by hashing – by dealing with the problem **sequentially**, the next record required would be the one currently after the record being processed in the sequential list. However, if a particular employee has a query on his or her salary, for example, then you do need to go directly to the required record, and in this case you could follow a suitable index system. Therefore, assuming that appropriate and efficient indexes are created, **this system capitalises on the benefits of both sequential and random access**. In practice, for the reasons just stated, indexed-sequential files are *the* most popular in the data-processing industry. It is normal to have a **separate file for the data** and a **separate file for the index**.

COBOL, for example, maintains all of these systems in ways which are reasonably transparent to the programmer, and the following slice of an environment division from a typical COBOL program deals with a file that can be accessed both sequentially and randomly.

```
ENVIRONMENT DIVISION.
INPUT-OUTPUT SECTION.
FILE-CONTROL.
    SELECT STUDENTS ASSIGN TO "A:STUDENTS.DAT"
    ORGANISATION IS INDEXED
    ACCESS MODE IS DYNAMIC
    RELATIVE KEY IS RECORD-NUMBER
```

The keyword **dynamic** in the above COBOL code indicates that the **indexed file can be accessed** *both* **sequentially and randomly**. The **organisation** must be specified as **indexed** (meaning indexed-sequential in COBOL) or the file will be assumed to be sequential. Note also how statements such as those given in the above code adds to the self-documenting aspects of COBOL.

Another advantage of indexed-sequential mode is that the software which controls the system ensures that only those records which are occupied take up space on the disk. This should be contrasted with direct-access files where much space is taken up with empty records and overflow areas waiting to accept data in places which have been calculated by the hashing algorithm.

Creating an indexed-sequential file

One method of creation involves creating a **sequential file** in ways identical to those shown earlier on in this chapter, then *reading the records* from this **sequential file** and *writing them*, together with an **index**, as an **indexed-sequential file**. We have already seen how to produce a sequential file in some detail, and COBOL provides several other facilities to enable index files to be built up using the principles just described. However, the detailed analysis and creation of such an index making use of a language such as COBOL is beyond the scope of this book.

Updating, inserting and deleting

Once the index has been built up in the ways described in the last section, other routines to update delete and insert records, for example, can be devised. Don't forget, however, that there are *two types* of access mechanisms – **sequential** and **random**. Therefore, *different algorithms* would have to be developed for updating by these different mechanisms. Again, COBOL would help considerably by automatically coping with some of the work for us. For example, if an indexed-sequential file is to be accessed sequentially, as long as the environment division specified that the **file type was indexed**, *and* that **access was sequential**, then the algorithms already established for accessing data in a sequential file would work – this saves an awful lot of work.

To access records randomly from an indexed-sequential file using COBOL involves a special form of read statement together with assigning a key field within the program. The computer searches the index for a key which is the same as the key-field in the program, and, when found, the record can then be read directly (randomly) from the data file which is associated with the index. The modified form of read statement also includes what to do if the desired key is invalid.

General terminology associated with files

It is not appropriate at 'A' level to consider detailed algorithms for random updates of indexed-sequential files making use of the more advanced COBOL features. Nevertheless, you should now have a very good idea of all the principles that are involved, and realise that languages like COBOL, for example, provide all the necessary infrastructure to create, interrogate, delete and insert records both sequentially and randomly on multiple indexes when using indexed-sequential files.

Other terminology associated with files from a more-general point of view is covered in this section. For example. There are several different types of file whose names have been coined from the *context in which they are used*, rather than from any fundamental file-organisation principles like the sequential or direct-access methods considered earlier. We now investigate some additional commonly-used terms.

Data files

All files are **data files** – because all files eventually contain just a sequence of digits stored as data! However, this is *not too helpful*, and so extra terminology is used to distinguish between files used for different purposes. Most of the files referred to since the beginning of this chapter are all examples of data files, because **data files** *can more usefully be described* as a **file of related data in which the data has been organised in some particular way** – usually in the form of **records** and **fields**, and arranged by a *file-access method* such as **sequential** or **random**, for example. In any examination assume that this is the definition which is required, but *data files* also have more specific meanings when used in more specific contexts. For example, a table which contains the values from DATA statements in the BASIC language is also called a data file.

Backup files

When using serial or sequential-access files, together with the grandfather-father-son principle, it is possible to recover from many different error situations. However, when using direct-access files, records can inadvertently be overwritten, with no means of recovery. Therefore, copies of the files should be made at frequent intervals and these copies are called **backup files** for obvious reasons.

Scratch files

This is a **file which contains temporary data**. For example, suppose that a sequential file has been created with the sole purpose of being used as a source file to generate an indexed-sequential file (see page 354). When the indexed-sequential file has been created then there is no need for the original sequential file. The original file was simply a temporary file or a **scratch file**.

Indexed files

This name is often used to denote a file which has **multiple indexes**. Such systems are more-common in **database applications** and in the context of system software such as operating systems, for example.

Hashed files

This is just an alternative name for a file which is accessed by means of a suitable hashing function. It is no different to the direct or random-access files considered in this chapter.

Binary search

This is an alternative file-access mechanism and is based on searching for the address of a record in ways identical to searching a binary tree which are covered on page 334.

Hierarchical files

Most modern operating systems today enable the user to structure files so that their organisation is **hierarchical**. This is exactly the same idea as the **hierarchical (tree)** data structures covered in chapter 14. In the early days of disk-operating systems the user was restricted to a single directory in which all files were listed. Manually finding files on such systems was a slow and painful process, and the concept of hierarchical directories was borne.

Figure 16.16 shows a typical directory-structure with which most windows-based operating-system users will be familiar. It shows just a tiny fraction of the directory structure of one of the author's hard disks. As an example, the route to the file containing the very drawing at which you are looking (figure 16.16) has been shown. Follow through the route which starts at the root (base directory) of the structure. (Don't forget that it's called the root because the structure is an upside-down tree in which the top part forms the root.) The path name for the drawing file called 'root' is

C:\Publishing\Stanley\ALevel\3rdEd\Files\Root

Notice that some of the directories have been labelled slightly differently to make the diagram easier to understand. Stanley Thornes, for example, is too many characters for a directory name in most systems and so, in practice, it is called Stanley. The path name illustrated above takes this into account. Different operating systems have slightly different notation, but the ideas are the same.

Without a hierarchical structure of the sort described above, thousands of files would have to live in the same directory – together with all the limitations which this would impose regarding file names. It's not possible, for example, to have two file names which are identical within the same directory. I have an admin directory for school, an admin directory for each of the publisher directories, an admin directory for business and several admin directories for other purposes. If they were all in the same directory then the only way of getting over the problem would be to make use of extensions to the file names such as Admin.sch for school and Admin.sta

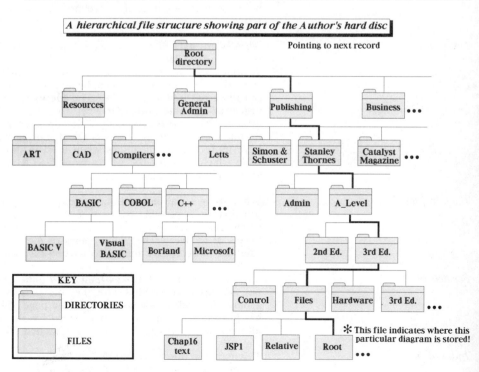

Figure 16.16

for Stanley Thornes publishers, for example. This is an extremely messy way of file organisation and the hierarchical-file structures offered by today's modern windows-based operating systems make life very much easier.

You should note that it is only possible to have an actual **file** (i.e. an **object** containing things like a **word-processor document**, or an **application** for example) as a **leaf node** in the system. All **parent nodes** are **directories**, not files. In most windows-based systems it is usual to have different file types for each application, and thus each file type can have unique icons assigned to them. In this way it's easy to identify a file by simply looking at the picture.

The link to the physical organisation of files

Hitherto in this chapter we have *concentrated entirely* on the **logical organisation** of files from a *programmer's point of view*. Nevertheless, it will be obvious to most readers that all the data being processed, irrespective of the file-organisation methods being used, will have to be stored on some suitable media such as magnetic disk or magnetic tape, for example. No well-rounded overview of file handling on modern computer systems would thus be complete without this final link in the chain being investigated. During the next section we will, therefore, take a brief look at how data eventually gets put onto or read from the storage media – be it tape, magnetic or optical disk, or CD-ROM. In fact, you will probably be quite surprised that, *given the variety of secondary-storage hardware that it's possible to interface to a computer* system, **the way in which the system software treats them all is remarkably similar**. It should be noted that the next section should also be read in conjunction with the storage-devices covered in chapter 13, where the physical attributes of the disks and tape being used in the next section are explained in more detail. All the principles about to be discussed can be applied to all storage media such as disks and tape, but a specific example will make things far easier to understand. At the end of this example we will then show *why* all these ideas can be applied to any system.

As serial and sequential files were handled first, we will first take a look at an *example* of a **tape-based system**. However, don't forget that *these are general principles being established here* so don't think that this section is irrelevant!

Blocks of data

As you will have gathered from reading chapter 13, tape systems on large computers bear little resemblance to the audio tape machines used at home. Unfortunately however, like the audio and video-tape systems which *are* used at home, computer-based tape formats too come in a variety of incompatible formats. Nevertheless, many of the *principles* of storing data on tape *are similar*, irrespective of the format being used. We will now concentrate on *typical* relationships between the **logical-files** considered earlier in this chapter and the **physical blocks of data** on the tape.

A mainframe tape example

Figure 16.17 shows a typical ½-inch-wide 9-track tape format, as is found on many mainframe computers. This particular format would probably make use of the EBCDIC code (see page 278), but different 7-bit codes are also sometimes used. As can be seen from the top of the diagram, just part of the tape is being used to *store* a **logical file** – it might be one of the **serial** or **sequential files** created by COBOL programs considered earlier in this chapter. This large file has been considerably expanded so that only a small section of it can be seen on the second level of the diagram. Now the file is so big that it obviously can't be dealt with all at the same time, therefore, the tape has spilt up the file into **physical records** (nothing to do with the logical records in the file), which are called **blocks**. However, on some systems, as in the system shown in figure 16.17, a physical record can be made up of several physical blocks – it simply depends on the type of system being used.

It's most important to realise that a **physical record** (or block or *group* of blocks depending on the system being used) *is the size of the chunk which is used by the hardware to transfer data in and out* of the system – *this is what is meant by a* **physical record**. It is literally the chunk of data that gets taken in or spewed out to the tape machine in this particular case.

If, as is likely *because of the relative sizes*, several **logical records** fit into a **physical block**, then the number of logical records that can be fitted into the block is called the **blocking factor**. Therefore, in figure 16.17, a **blocking factor of 4** has been used because **4 logical records**, as shown on level 3 of the diagram, have been **fitted into a single physical block**. *If one logical record* fits into a **single physical block** then **blocking** *would not need to be used*, and the blocking factor would be equal to 1.

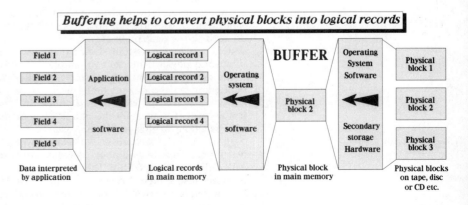

½ - inch tape format used on large reel-to-reel machines

Figure 16.17

It should be obvious that some gaps (i.e. bits of the tape not containing logical data) will inevitably appear on the tape. This means that not every inch of the tape can be used to store useful information, and so the amount of data on the tape is less than would appear from a calculation of bit density times length. Nevertheless, blocking helps to save waste space on the tape. Much space would be wasted if a single logical record of length considerably less than a single physical record was stored in the space occupied on the tape by a single physical record.

Buffering

Buffering is used to *convert* the **physical blocks** or **physical records** *into* the **logical records** used by the **application software**. It is usually the function of the **operating system software** to *carry out these operations* automatically. The idea is shown in figure 16.18. Logical blocks on the storage device (tape in this case) are transferred into an area of main memory called a buffer. The operating system software (i.e. appropriate add-on device drivers for the hardware being used), then convert the data into the logical records needed by the application. This is usually transparent

Buffering helps to convert physical blocks into logical records

Figure 16.18

to the application. The application simply saves or loads the records in this format, and the buffer, operating-system software and hardware interface takes care of how the logical records are mapped onto the hardware device being used.

These ideas are important, because they can be applied to any secondary storage device. It's up to those parts of the operating system which control the interface hardware to make sure that the data gets put onto the storage device in an appropriate format. In this way **any device, even those yet to be invented, can be mapped onto any application software** – magic!

Only a single buffer has been shown above, but it's often usual for the operating systems to employ double-buffering (see page 384) if a faster speed of response is required. This simply means that one physical block can be interrogated whilst another is being loaded or saved by using a second buffer area in main memory.

Disk-based systems

We could have started off this section with a different scenario regarding a typical disk, being made up of tracks and sectors as described in chapter 13. However, we would then have suggested that a **block** of data from the disk, mapped onto **sector** and **track addresses** (or cylinders in the case of larger disks) can be read into an area of memory called a buffer. We would then go on to suggest that it's the job of the disk interface part of the operating system to map these physical blocks held in memory into the logical records also held in memory, so that a logical record can be used by an application or appropriate high-level language. We would have ended up with a diagram identical in principle to that of figure 16.18.

Other systems

As you can see from the above, **blocks of data are buffered into the system and interpreted by the operating-systems software**. Therefore, apart from the obvious restrictions of the physical media such as not being able to operate an indexed-sequential file on a tape, for example, the whole process is transparent to the application or language being used. The idea of blocks of data and buffering apply from the fastest of mainframe tape drives to the humblest cassette-based tape streamers. As can seen from chapter 13, the physical formats and physical methods of storage and retrieval are very different for each type of secondary-storage device, but the principles of **block-data transfer** and **buffering** allow us to work with them all. Mapping physical records or blocks to logical records is done in this way for all secondary storage media, and file handling is thus made much simpler from a user's point of view.

File maintenance

Students at this stage of their course should need no reminding of the need for backup and other general file maintenance. It's inevitable that systems will crash – eventually. As more and more companies rely on computerised information processing the need to maintain a backup policy is essential. On larger systems complete disks will be backed up as a matter of course, and archives of tapes kept in separate buildings. But on microcomputers too it's essential that important parts of your hard disk are backed up, or the complete hard disk is tape streamed (see page 281). Other systems such as RAID (shown on page 269) can be of tremendous advantage in keeping your computer data on files in tact.

The drive-you-mad car company

In examinations (fortunately for many students!) there is usually little time to develop any but the most simple of algorithms relating to file processing. All the principles talked about in this chapter can be covered in general, and questions on these general principles are often accompanied by an example regarding some file-type-data-processing system, usually pulled out of a hat, which the student has obviously *not* seen before. The student is then expected to come up with some reasonably-sensible data structures in the limited amount of time available.

The drive-you-mad car company example can be considered with this scenario in mind, and covers work which might typically be expected under examination conditions. The actual example is obviously longer than would be expected from a half-hour examination question, but this is so that many appropriate questions can be covered. You will find many more exam-type questions in the companion volume.

Example

The drive-you-mad car company is a car hire firm which operates a fleet of three main types of car. There is an executive model (rather expensive but would easily impress the girlfriend/boyfriend), a medium priced family saloon and a budget priced small economy car.

The Drive-You-Mad
Car Company

At present the firm runs a manually operated system with three card index type files and some books. These files are simply referred to as A, H and S. A contains the cars AVAILABLE for hire, H the cars already on HIRE and S contains cars that are out of action because they are being SERVICED. Within each card index there are three different colours used to sort out the executive (exec), family (fmly) and budget (budg) cars. These are green, pink and blue respectively.

At the beginning of each day the manager goes through the cards to establish which cars are needed for that day's hire. The cards are arranged in chronological order so that the cars to be used that day are at or near the front of the pack. A list of possible future bookings is also included with the card so that double booking is not possible. If a customer books in advance, then the name and address of the customer, together with the type of car booked and the dates are recorded in the hire-bookings book. If a customer books a car and wishes to drive it away immediately, then the name and address is again entered on the appropriate page in the bookings book.

The car hire firm has several branches and is considering expansion. However, it is not envisaged that there will ever be more than a total of 1000 cars. It should be possible to book in advance any type and quantity of cars on a daily basis for any number of days.

First consider the existing manual system.

The information on each card consists of the following:

	Example	Future bookings	
		Date	Number of days
Type of car	Executive		
Registration number	M 463 YKL	19/12/95	3
Mileage	38 971	30/12/95	6
Mileage at last service	35 120		

The mileage is updated every time that the car is returned from a hire commitment and the cars are serviced every 5000 miles if possible. The cards are often in a tatty condition because the figures written on them are often rubbed out and changed. When the card becomes too tatty it is replaced.

Design a satisfactory system that could be implemented on a digital computer. You must explain in detail the files that you propose to use, and the detailed structures of **two** of these files. Also, give an example of how a typical transaction using these files might take place.

What other functions (not mentioned in the question) could be performed by the introduction of the system that you have proposed?

Solution

You may think that the following solution is very long winded for a 30 or 40 minute exam question. However, 75 per cent of the following text explains the approaches that can be used.

First notice that you are not asked to design the entire system in detail. That amount of work would rate as a complete project and not a half-hour examination question! Note also that you are asked only to give details of **two** particular files and **one** particular transaction example.

When starting complex problems such as the above it is always a good idea to get an overview of the existing system, with special reference to the way in which data can be moved around from one 'file' to another. Figure 16.19 shows the three manual files A, H and S.

Some possible transactions to be considered are:

Transaction	Consequence
(a) The purchase of a new car:	Add new record to file A
(b) A car is hired:	Car is removed from file A and placed in file H
(c) A car is returned:	Car is removed from file H and placed in file A
(d) A car is scrapped:	Car removed from file A and discarded
(e) A car is removed for a service:	Car is taken from file A and placed in file S
(f) A car has been serviced:	Car is taken from file S and placed in file A

file A: Cars available for hire; file H: Cars on hire; file S: Cars in for service

In essence the manual system consists of nine files: one executive, one family and one budget file for each of the available, hired and service categories. When using

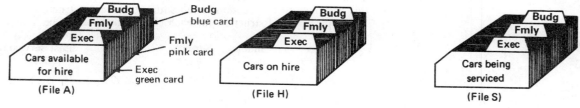

Figure 16.19

a computer, it would not be physically necessary to move the data (entire card) from one file to the other. It would be more efficient to set up flags to indicate if the car was available for hire, was actually hired, or was in for a service. It would make the situation easier to manage, plus increase the access speed, if there were three separate files for each of the categories; executive, family and budget. In this way, it is only necessary to consider the data structure of one of them. The other two are set up in an identical manner.

First consider the information to be contained in a typical field. As there will be three separate files, one for each type of car (exec, fmly, budg), it is not necessary to identify the type of car as this will be implicit from the file in which it is located. The key field could therefore be the car registration number; mileage and last service mileage will also be needed. The most complex task is to arrange the future booking for each car. This will have to be thought out in some detail.

Future booking. The computer will have to keep a table of which cars are booked on each day and future bookings. It is not necessary to book a specific car, only a specific type of car. Therefore, the system can be considerably simplified. All that is necessary is to make sure that there are not more than the available number of each type of car booked on a particular day.

It would be possible to hold the number of cars of each type in a simple array. If a new car is requested on a particular day then this array must be consulted before the booking can be confirmed. As booking can be carried out in advance, there will have to be a number of these totals, one for each day. The system could work as follows:

	1	2	3	4	5	6	7	8	9	10	11	12	13	14	15
Exec	12	8	7	1	2	2	1	1	1	1	1	0	0	0	0
Fmly	45	13	4	0	5	4	2	0	0	0	0	0	0	0	0
Budg	76	52	25	13	8	1	0	O	0	0	0	3	0	0	0

Max exec = 100; Max fmly = 230; Max budg = 350

The current day could be numbered as day 1 (i.e. from 0700 to 0659.59). At the beginning of each day, all the totals for that day would have to be updated. The future days will then be numbered as 2, 3, 4, 5, 6 etc. so that a car booked from day 1 for five days will increment the day 1, 2, 3, 4 and 5 totals by 1.

The above table shows that for the current day, there are already 12 exec cars, 45 fmly cars and 76 budg cars on hire. Or, in three days time (day 4) there are already 13 budg cars booked.

At the beginning of each day, the computer must update the above array so that over booking does not occur. Day 2 will then become day 1 etc. All the figures in the above array will shift left with the passage of time.

Underneath are the variables Max exec etc. that show the total number of cars that the company owns.

As far as the record is concerned, all that is necessary is to have a flag that is set if the car is available for hire; another flag could determine if it is in the service department. These flags will be altered when a car is hired or returned.

The company will have to establish how far in advance it would be sensible to accept bookings, so that the dimension of the array can be deduced. It would seem unnecessary to have a large array as most of it would be empty. However, it must also be possible, perhaps by some alternative method, to make sure that a booking could be established months in advance if necessary. A separate file could be used for this purpose if this was felt to be necessary.

The company's policy of making sure that the last car returned should be the last one to be used again can easily be established by the use of a circular list i.e. when the last car in the list has been hired, you are automatically referred to the first car in the list. We will therefore need to set up a system of pointers in each file, and this will have to be accommodated within the record structure.

A typical record structure for each car could therefore be as follows:

Reg. No.	Available flag	Service flag	Mileage	Last service mileage	Next free pointer
M 463 YKL	1	0	38 971	35 120	003

(1 = YES, 0 = NO)

If the above record is in the exec file then it would indicate that the executive car M 463 YKL was ready for hire, had done 38 971 miles and was not due for a service. The next free pointer indicates that the next exec car that is to be hired can be located at record number 003 within the exec file.

File structure. Having considered the information that is to be contained in each record, we can now consider the file structure. As there is a maximum of only a few hundred cars in each file, then complex accessing methods, to gain super fast access to each record, are not necessary. A sequential access method using the pointer system hinted at above would produce a response within a few seconds which is easily enough for this application.

Circular list. To maintain the circular list principle, there must be a header pointer (pointer to the beginning of the list), and a tail pointer (pointer to the end of the list). If a new car is added, then this can be inserted after the tail so that the new car becomes the tail. If the head and the tail become coincident, we have run out of cars! Also, when the car at the tail end of the list has been hired, the car at the head of the list will be the next one to be chosen (circular list).

Pointer systems. Apart from the header and tail pointers, there will need to be a freespace pointer within each file. Any car that is scrapped can then have its record removed, and the space returned to the free-space stack.

As an example, consider the exec file (the other two are identical in principle) the beginning of which might be as follows:

Record number	Reg. No.	Available flag	Service flag	Mileage	Last service mileage	Next pointer
1	M 463 YKL	1	0	38 971	35 120	025
2	K 768 TDF	0	0	12 987	10 090	003
3	L 342 MBN	0	0	46 981	45 003	123
4	L 234 VTY	0	1	10 234	5 178	067
.						
.						
226						
.						
.						
350						

Available header = 1   Hire header = 2   Service header = 4

From the above table you can see that in the exec file, M 463 YKL is the first car available should an exec car be required for hire. If it were needed immediately, then this would be removed from the available list and placed on the hired list. This can simply be achieved by updating the available header. Similarly, the car at the end of the on hire list (given by the on hire footer pointer) can be altered accordingly. Note that the data has not been physically moved (as was the case in the manual system), pointers have simply been altered. The above situation with regard to the pointers is shown in figure 16.20. Figure 16.20(a) shows the pointers before hire of the car in record 1, and figure 16.20(b) shows the situation after hire.

If the car was to be booked in advance, then the appropriate checks must be made and, if the car is available, a booking confirmed by incrementing the appropriate element in the matrix. Also, the names and addresses of the customers must be entered into the customer record so that bookings can be confirmed on arrival of the customers to pick up the cars.

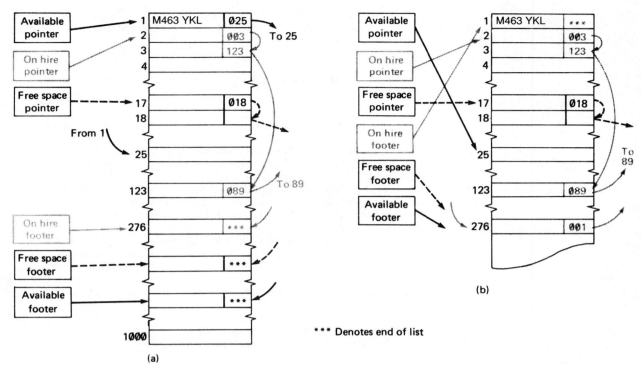

Figure 16.20

Customer name and address file. Let us now consider the customer name and address file (i.e. the information usually contained in the booking book under the manual system). This will simply be a record of the names and addresses of the customers together with the dates of hire and the type of car hired. It may be a good idea to store this in chronological order i.e. in date order. This would mean that if a car is hired on 16/12/95, then this would be the way in which a customer can be traced. This file would get very large if no data was ever deleted from it. We must therefore establish company policy on how long it wishes to keep old records. They must be kept for some time in case of enquiries over payments or police enquiries etc. Perhaps it would be an idea to keep them on disk for a few weeks, then back them up to tape and keep them for a few months or a year if necessary.

We now assume that all customers' names and addresses are to be stored on disk. Also, a flag can be set to indicate whether or not the car has been taken, and if it has whether or not it has been returned. If both of these flags are set then, on the appropriate scan of the disk, the record may be removed and archived to tape in the way described in the previous paragraph.

Structure of the name and address file. Although occasionally it may be necessary to interrogate the files in other ways (such as for a police enquiry) the main point of the file is to give a rapid response to the car hire salesperson in the showroom when a customer comes in to book a car, or to pick up a car that has been booked previously. Therefore, a file with fast access by date, and reasonably rapid access by customer name within that date, would be ideal. It would be a good idea to have a separate file for each date. In this way, access by date would be almost instant. It may be necessary to have two or three months ahead on disk, and the old files (again in chronological order) archived to tape. If a car is to be booked for more than two or three months (very unlikely at the prices that will have to be charged to recoup the cost of the new computer system!) then this will have to be considered as a special case.

Let us consider a typical date: 22/11/95.

As this file will be called 22/11/95 then the date need not be stored in any of the records. A typical record structure for this file would therefore be as follows:

Surname	Initials	Address
Bradley	R.J.	My address

Type of car	Reg. No.	Hire from	Hire to	Car taken	Car returned	Damage?
Exec	M463 YKL	22/11/95	16/12/95	1	0	0

(1 = Yes, 0 = No)

The record structure is simple. Let us now consider the file structure:

Customer name and address file structure. It is unlikely, but a maximum of 1000 enquiries may have to be dealt with in any one day. This would assume that all cars were booked out on a particular day, and no cars were being serviced. It will be usual for there to be a morning rush and therefore many enquiries based on surname and initials will have to be dealt with quickly. Now access to the date is very quick as a separate file is used for each day. It therefore only remains to sort out the structure of each date file.

With up to 1000 names possible, it would take too long for a serial file arrangement i.e. one record after the other with no regard to order. Also, if several enquiries are to be made at the same time from different terminals then the search time would be particularly slow. One possible method would be to implement a pointer structure that is based on a binary tree. The idea can be seen in chapter 14 on page 305.

Using this system, we could set up a hierarchical data structure for the initial letters of the surnames as shown in figure 16.21.

When a particular initial letter is encountered, then a simple serial access list for

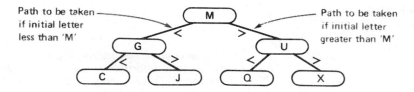

Figure 16.21

each group of surnames beginning with the same letter should be adequate.

To summarize the above, to locate, insert or delete a record on the computer:

(a) Load appropriate date file.
(b) Search binary tree for initial letter of surname.
(c) Serially search sublist for surname and initials match.

How do these files interact? To explain how the system will operate, consider the following scenario:

1.   At the beginning of each day (just before the showroom opens) the computer does various housekeeping facilities, such as archiving unwanted date files and setting up the variables for date and the pointers. This will be known as initialising the system.

2.   During the morning the cars that have been left overnight are checked in by the car cleaning staff, visually checked for damage, and have the new mileage recorded on a special data capture form designed for data entry into the system.

3.   When the data is entered into the computer system the computer will adjust the appropriate flags (e.g. no damage) and check if any cars need a service, as follows:

Mileage >= Last service + 5000

If a car is in need of a service then, when the car is taken off the on hire list and is put on the service list, a suitable printout is provided so that the service manager can arrange schedules.

4. When customers come to pick up a car the showroom salesperson will ask them if they have booked. If so, he or she will initiate the search for the surname and initials on the current date file. If the customer has not yet booked, then the sales-

person will check if a car is available (by getting the computer to check the current totals in the array). If a car is available, the computer will insert the appropriate record in the current date file by searching through the binary tree structure until the appropriate place for the insertion of the record is found.

5. If a customer requires a future booking, then the appropriate date file is loaded, and modifications made to the records in an identical way to that described for a current date booking.

6. When a car has been returned from the service department, the appropriate data is fed into the computer and the flag changed so that the car may be added to the footer of the available for hire list. Of course, all the appropriate pointers must be altered in a similar way to that described at the beginning of this example.

7. If a car is scrapped, then the appropriate record is deleted and returned as free space to the system.

With all the above operations it is likely that an appropriate printout will be necessary, such as customer receipts, cars to be serviced and the number of cars needed for a specific day.

We have now described a brief outline of the possible ways in which some files may be set up to computerise the drive-you-mad car company. The example also asked you to describe a typical transaction that might take place using these files. We will now develop a possible flowchart to show how a car may be booked and taken away immediately .

The part of the algorithm to perform this operation is shown in figure 16.22. Figure 16.22 assumes that the system has already been initialised. It would be likely that this routine would be called from a main menu.

One major point that has not been covered above is that it has been assumed that several terminals would be able to access the files at the same time. This is possible on most systems, but care should be taken when any data is being recorded on a file i.e. if the header pointers are being altered then no other user should access the system during this critical time. However, once the new pointers have been established, the next user may use the next record in the list.

The final part of the question asks what extensions to the system do you see as possibilities. Some of the most obvious attributes not mentioned in the example concern the accounting procedures. No mention was made about how customers would be billed for the hire and how receipts are produced. It would be easily possible to include some sort of accounting procedure, possibly by an extension of the customer name and address record, as this has all information necessary

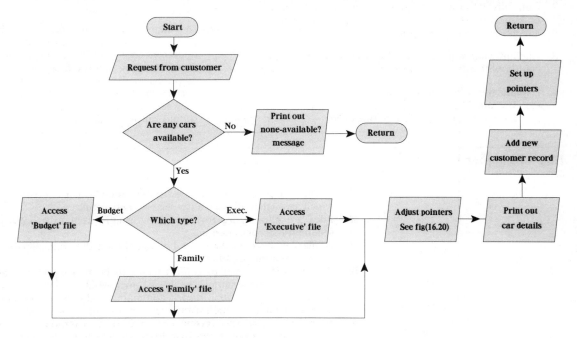

Figure 16.22

(i.e. type of car and number of days, customer name and address) to produce the required bill.

Other obvious things that could easily be produced are a variety of statistics relating to the running of the business such as graphs of the number of cars hired, type of cars and branches hiring the most. Similarly, an analysis of profit could easily be worked out. Such systems would obviously not be carried out at the same time as the on-line enquiries, but would be carried out overnight in a batch-type mode of operation.

Exercise 16.1

1. Define the following terms associated with computer files.
   - (a) **Character**
   - (b) **Field**
   - (c) **Record**
   - (d) **File**

2. Compare and contrast the following file-organisation methods.
   - (a) **Serial access**
   - (b) **Sequential access**
   - (c) **Direct access or random access**
   - (d) **Indexed sequential access**

3. Carefully explain the following terminology associated with files.
   - (a) **File creation**
   - (b) **Updating**
   - (c) **Merging**
   - (d) **EOF**

4. The idea of a **pointer** is of paramount importance. What is a pointer and how is it used in association with file data structures?

5. What is a **key field**?

6. What is meant by the following?
   - (a) An **index**
   - (b) An **overflow table**
   - (c) A **linked list**.

7. Carefully describe a sequential file updating process making sure to refer to the master file, new master file and transaction file in your explanation.

8. Explain what is meant by a **hashing algorithm** in association with reading data from a file.

9. Explain the following terminology.
   - (a) **Backup files**
   - (b) **Hashed file**
   - (c) **Hierarchical file**
   - (d) **Scratch file**.

10. Describe the difference between **logical** and **physical records**, making use of the term **blocking factor** in your explanation.

11. What is meant by the term **file maintenance**?

12. Why are **buffers** often used when accessing files?

13. Using a suitable **high-level language**, write a program which reads positive and negative integers from a serial-access file, then copies the positive numbers into one output file and the negative numbers into another output file, both of which are serial access. You may assume that the files can be held in memory.

14. *Two files* contain data in *sorted order*. Each file is able to be loaded into the computer separately. However, the combined sorted file is too big to fit in memory. Describe a method that could be used to produce a large file containing all data sorted into order.

15. A hamburger restaurant produces a sequential-access file for each transaction made at the till. The item code followed by the quantity is entered, one after the other, for each item sold, e.g. the entry 2,3 might mean that 3 cheeseburgers have been sold because 2 might be the code for a cheeseburger . Write a program which interrogates the file and prints out, in order of code, how many of each item have been sold. State any assumptions you may make.

16. In a high-security system **data integrity** is of paramount importance. Data is already validated on entry, but two operators create the same information in two separate files. Assuming that the files are organised sequentially as pure text files, devise and test an algorithm which **verifies** the files by seeing if there are any differences between the two files. If the verification fails the system should output a suitable error message.

End of chapter summary

- A **file** is a collection of **related information** which is processed as a single unit which is further divided into records and fields.
- **Files** are **data structures** which are usually used to process information on a **secondary-storage medium**.
- A **file** can be considered to be organised either **logically** or **physically** in the form of **records** or **blocks**.
- A **record** is a *subset of a file* which can be **treated as a single-unit** of *related information*. For example, each customer would probably have a single record.
- A **field** is a *subset of a record* containing a **single unit** of information such as 'customer name', 'amount outstanding' or 'age', for example.
- A **logical record** is a **record viewed from a programmer's point of view**. It is the record created by the high-level programming language or application.
- A **physical record** or **block** (sometimes a group of blocks) is the unit used by

the secondary storage medium being used – it usually contains *several* **logical records**.

■ A **logical record** is **mapped** *onto* the **physical record** by the **operating system software** and **interface hardware** for the secondary storage media being used.

■ **Logical file organisation** can be *split up into four main different methods*, mainly, **serial**, **sequential**, **direct** and **indexed-sequential**.

■ **Serial files** are organised such that there is **no pre-determined order to the records**. Often a serial file is the inevitable consequence of data collection before processing takes place.

■ **Sequential files** are organised so that the *records are arranged in order of* **key field**.

■ A **key field** is the *field chosen to identify a* **record**.

■ **Serial** and **sequential file organisation** are *the only two structures that can be used with magnetic-tape systems*, but they can be used efficiently on disk-systems too.

■ A **direct or random-access file** is one in which *it is possible to get to the record of interest without having to go serially or sequentially through any others*.

■ An **indexed-sequential file** is one in which a *sequentially-organised file on a direct-access medium* can be accessed by means of **one or more indexes**.

■ Typical **operations with files** involve the **creation**, **updating** by **altering**, **adding** or **deleting** data, **merging** with other files, **searching sorting** and **backing up**.

■ **Creation of a file** involves using a **high-level language** or **application** to *create an appropriate data structure* such as sequential or random access for example.

■ **Updating** involves changing information in a file by altering one or more records.

■ The **addition or deletion of records** when using **serial or sequential files** *involves a complete re-write of the original file*.

■ **Insertion and deletion** of data on **serial or sequential files** involves the use of **three files** – a **master file**, a transaction file and a **new master file**.

■ The **master file** is the **original** (unmodified) **copy of the data**.

■ The **transaction file** contains details of the **amendments**.

■ The **new master file** contains **copies** of the **original master-file records** *together with the amendments necessary from the transaction file*.

■ Several generations of files are usually kept for security purposes. These three generations are referred to as **grandfather**, **father** and **son** files.

■ A **son file** is the *newest generation* **master file**.

■ A **father file** is the **old master file** *used to produce the* **son file**.

■ A **grandfather file** is the **oldest generation of master file** from which the **father file** was produced. The grandfather file is ditched after a great-grandson has been produced.

■ **Merging files** is the process of *joining two* **sequentially-organised files** record-by-record *transferring them in the correct order* to the **new master file**.

■ **Sorting of very large files** can be carried out by sorting separate subsets of the large file, then *joining them together* by making use of a **merging procedure**.

■ A **direct** or **random-access file** *accesses records by means of a* **hashing function** or **hierarchical data method** such as a **binary search**, for example.

■ **Hashing functions** *generate a range of addresses* which provide **relative keys** for *accessing the data by reference to* **an address**.

■ **Direct** or **random-access files** can *only* be supported on **secondary storage media** with *direct-access capability* such as **disks**.

■ A **relative key** is a system whereby **logical records** can be **directly accessed** by reference to the first record in the file, which is usually labelled record zero or one.

■ An **indexed-sequential file** is accessed by means of *one or more* **indexes** *held as separate* **data structures**.

■ The **index** in an indexed-sequential file needs to be built up by the programmer or application such as a database, for example.

■ Many **high level languages**, such as **Pascal** and **BASIC**, for example, have *limited file handling capabilities*, but the **COBOL language** is *rich in a huge variety of file-handling techniques*.

■ The **algorithms** designed for file handling *rely heavily* on **algorithms** *developed to maintain* **linked-list data structures**, and the **algorithms** for **sorting** and **searching**.

■ A **data file** is the name given to a file organised in ways considered in this chapter. The name is used to distinguish these files from other common file types.

■ A **backup file** is a direct copy of an existing file made for security purposes.

■ A **scratch file** is a file containing temporary data which is deleted after it has served its purpose.

■ **An indexed file** is the name sometimes used for an index-sequential file with multiple indexes.

■ **A hashed file** is the name sometimes used to denote a direct-access file which is accessed by a hashing function.

■ **A hierarchical file** is the name given to the file structure often associated with hierarchical directories in modern WIMP systems.

■ A **block**, *often* the same as a **physical record**, is a **unit** used by the operating-system-hardware interface to **transfer a chunk of data to or from the secondary storage device** being used.

■ **Blocking** is the term used when *more than one* **logical record** *fits into* a **block** or **physical record**.

■ The **blocking factor** is the number of logical records which fits into a physical record or block.

■ **Buffers** are used to help map the physical records and blocks used by the hardware to the logical records used by the high-level language and applications software.

■ **Blocks and buffers** enable any secondary storage device such as tapes, disk and CD-ROM, for example, to be treated in very-similar ways.

17 Operating systems

Introduction

To a novice the **operating system** is probably the least important part of the computer – but nothing could be further from the truth. Many computers have now become so easy to use that beginners do not even realise that there is such a thing as an operating system – this is mainly due to the fact that, on many microcomputers, it is the job of modern **operating-systems software** to present the user with an easy-to-use front end. Most people are now very familiar indeed with **GUI**s such as **Windows**, and even small children, for example, can point with the mouse and draw a coloured picture on the screen. These simple operations belie the fact that programs of enormous complexity called operating systems are controlling such operations at the most fundamental level inside the machine.

The background to the development of operating systems is an interesting one, and goes back to the very early days of computers. The first computers were very difficult beasts to control. Each **machine-code program** (see page 70) had to be keyed in by hand, making use of a bank of binary switches called the **front panel**. This was a tedious and error-prone task. To gain an appreciation of this task, you must realise that there were no programs to read data from a keyboard or disk, indeed there were no computer screens or disk! – and the output from the computer was normally in the form of a bank of lights, or simple data typed out on a **teletype** (an old-style mechanical machine). Even the programs to control the teletype had to be loaded in by hand. It was no small wonder that the operators of these tedious and error-prone systems ever saw the potential of the computer under these awful circumstances.

As the electronic hardware improved, computers got faster and faster at running through their programs, but this increased speed was severely limited by the constant and often time-consuming intervention of **human operators** carrying out many mundane tasks such as loading new programs or stopping the computer if something went wrong. (It often did!) An *automatic* **system** was needed to release the **operator** from most of these tasks, and it was against this background that the very first **operating-system** software was developed. (You should now realise why they're called operating systems.) In the early days of computers there were no minis or micros, and so the original operating systems were developed for **mainframe computers**, and even today, the mainframe operating systems of the 70s are still influencing state-of-the-art microcomputer operating-system designs during the 90s.

The mainframe background to the development of operating systems is an important one to understand, because it's only against this background that one can appreciate the different types of operating systems such as **batch processing** or **time sharing**. Such terms seem to have little relevance for the many non-specialist users who operate in the single-user-microcomputer environment. Indeed, most micro users will probably equate operating systems with DOS – Microsoft's Disk Operating System – but this was developed much later when 8 and 16-bit microcomputers were state-of-the-art technology. (The early 1980s.)

Given such a complex background, we will spilt up operating systems into separate parts – the first considering mainframes and minis, in which we will cover the types of operating systems available – and the second, concerned mainly with micros where we will look at the detailed implementation of some typical operating systems. The final part will be concerned with networks, which is often the bridge between the micro and mainframe world. Fortunately, many basic concepts of operating systems are *common to all three sections*, and the chronological consideration of mainframe systems will enable you to understand more easily the present-day micro systems, as much of the current technology is borrowed from these earlier mainframe ideas.

Basic concepts

The variety of machines on which operating systems are designed to run is huge, anything from a single-user microcomputer through a multi-user minicomputer via a global network to a powerful supercomputer – all are controlled by different types of operating systems. It is indeed fortunate that *all* these systems have many fundamental concepts in common, and these will now be investigated further.

Exploiting the hardware

All operating systems are designed to fully exploit the hardware on which they are to be run. It is the operating-system software which tames the raw electronic power of modern computers, and makes these computers useable by people other than specialist engineers or scientists. A useful analogy can be drawn between the operating system software designed for a computer, and the software (music) on a typical compact-disc hi-fi system. The hi-fi system by itself represents raw electronic power, but put in a CD containing your favourite software, and a complex box of electronic wizardry transforms your lounge into an orchestral hall or a rock-concert venue. You forget about the electronics and enjoy the music. So it is with a computer system – pop in the operating system and you forget about the electronics, but are put in touch with a **virtual world** containing an environment which transforms your computer into a useful and worthwhile tool. No longer do you have to worry about how to write a character on the screen, how to output some data to the printer or how to load and save files regarding the disk drive – the operating system handles all these and many other tedious but essential tasks, leaving you to use the computer in much more creative ways more suitable to human thought, productivity and leisure. However, before getting too carried away, it's wise to remember that all that has changed your hi-fi system from raw electronic hardware into an art form is some software (data which represents the music), and all that transforms your computer into a complete environment is a **computer program**. But this is where the analogy comes to an end – even though operating systems *are* simply computer programs, most will rate among the most-complex programs ever devised by man. **Multiple Virtual Storage (MVS)** for example, developed for **IBM mainframes**, is currently one of the most complex operating systems in existence – it gives each user a maximum **virtual memory** (see page 381) space of up to 32Gbytes, and can support thousands of users. Given that operating systems themselves are among the most-complex things that man has ever conceived, this gives you some idea of the magnitude of this enormous and fascinating human achievement.

An operating-system perspective

The **operating system** is concerned directly with interfacing to the computer's architecture (see page 49). You can think of an operating system in diagrammatic form as a layer which **is on top of** or **wrapped around** the **hardware** of the computer system. However, much of the time non-specialist users of the system will not interact directly with the operating system software, but via some application package such

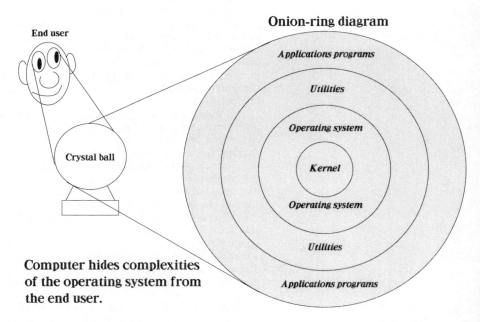

Onion-ring diagram

End user

Crystal ball

Applications programs

Utilities

Operating system

Kernel

Operating system

Utilities

Applications programs

Computer hides complexities of the operating system from the end user.

Figure 17.1

as a spreadsheet for example. We can regard these application packages as yet another layer in our diagram placed between the end user and the operating system. This is indeed what happens, as the application package translates the user **I/O** (short for **Input/Output**) into commands which the operating systems understands, then the operating system translates these commands via machine-code routines contained in the operating system into a form which the hardware of the computer understands. Figure 17.1 shows what's sometimes referred to as an **onion-diagram** representation, as it resembles peeling off layers of an onion to get to the middle. Although our diagram is a simple one, and different computer systems have slightly different representations, the **kernel** (the *inner-most ring*) represents things like the the **software** which controls the **device drivers** – which drive the **electronic devices** such as the **disk-controller chips** – or **software** which contains the **network-communication protocols** *if* the operating system supports communications with a computer network (most do). For example, the popular **TCP/IP protocols** (see page 509) are embedded in the **Unix-operating-system kernel**. In the very centre of the ring we could have drawn an even-smaller circle representing the computer hardware.

The ring marked **utilities** contains many software routines such as those for saving files to disk for example, or useful utilities which help the programmer who is writing applications programs. Useful utilities (programs) might include those for re-drawing windows in a **multitasking** environment if the user has clicked over an icon with the mouse. There are an enormous number of sub-programs written for most operating systems, and without these programs, applications programmers would have to re-invent the wheel each time they wanted to write to a disk, read a character from the keyboard buffer, or any other of the thousands of chores that have to be carried out during the normal operation of a computer. In a nutshell the operating system contains all these often-used routines consisting of the detailed step-by-step instructions to carry out the management of all the memory and peripherals etc controlled by the computer.

Mainframe computers – batch operating systems

You will recall from the introduction that the first operating systems were originally designed to alleviate the need for time-consuming human intervention. The early systems were **serial** in nature in that they undertook just **one task at a time**.

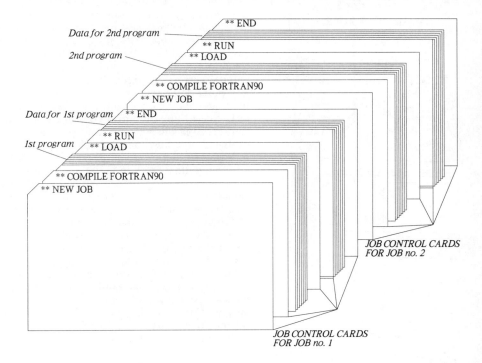

Figure 17.2

So operating systems concentrated on getting many jobs done one after the other as quickly as possible. These **serial operating systems** were known as **batch operating systems**, because they tackled a batch of jobs (**programs to be run**). It was the job of the **computer operator** to make sure that the **batch** of programs, usually submitted on the old **punched cards** were put into the computer system in the right order, and other cards, containing **instructions to the operating system**, were placed inbetween the **jobs**. This was the way that most mainframes operated in the early 1970s, and an understanding of this is useful, not just from an historical perspective, but from the point of view of making some aspects of operating systems more easily understandable today – it is far easier for you to see where computers are going if you know where they have been in the past.

A typical sequence of jobs for a **batch-processing system** at a university might have included running several Fortran programs for engineering students, a few COBOL programs for business-studies students and running some machine code programs for computer-science students. You should realise that these students in the 1970s (of which the author was one!) did *not* sit down at terminals and type in their programs, but prepared the **source code** (see page 200) on special card-punch machines. They would then take their pile of cards to the computer centre – being careful not to drop them all on the floor! – then submit the cards to the receptionist at the computer centre main desk. If you were lucky the results of your computer program would be available the next day, and if you were unlucky the only message out of the computer was a syntax error at line 10!

The computer operator used to prepare the **batch** of cards in a similar way to that shown in figure 17.2, then place the entire pack into the computer-system's card reader machine. The computer's operating system would then take over, ensuring that the correct **compilers** were used for **translating** the **source code** into the **object code** for the **target machine**. (See page 201 if that was gobbledygook!)

Job-control languages

JOB CENTRE

Here's your new job card... now don't mess it up this time!

A **Job-Control Language (JCL)** was (and *still is* in modern computer systems) used to control the jobs being run, and **job-control cards**, containing the job-control-language instructions, used to be inserted by the computer operator to specify things like the peripherals needed by the job, the beginning and end of the job, what compilers would be needed, and might also be used for accounting purposes. Don't forget that mainframes were and still are expensive machines – if you use just a few seconds of CPU time then you have to pay for it! Job-control languages are *still used* in the same context, but the commands are now typed into the system from a terminal instead of being submitted on cards as in the earlier systems.

To gain a better understanding of batch operating systems you need to appreciate the advantages a batch-processing system offers when compared to no operating system at all. Let's assume that a FORTRAN program is being run – when the computer encounters the first job-control-language command, this will automatically cause the FORTRAN compiler to be loaded from the correct magnetic disk or tape. (Note the human operator no longer has to do this.) Next the **source code** is **compiled**, and if no errors are encountered, the **object code** is placed in the computer's memory at a point determined by the operating system. The object code could then be automatically run, which might, for example, cause data to be read from some tape or disk, cause some output to be printed or **spooled** (see page 373), and then continue to proceed in this manner until the program is finished. The operating system would probably time how long it takes the program to execute, and intervene if necessary to terminate the program. A typical reason for termination might be caused by the program getting stuck in an **infinite loop**, which has resulted from a **logical error** on the part of the programmer. After this typical scenario the next program in the batch would be automatically started. Although the chain of events has been simplified, you can see that the mainframe computer is being utilised much more efficiently under the control of the batch-processing operating system. Without the operating system the computer operator would have had his or her work cut out just to make the above sequence of events happen manually. A computer without an operating system is no longer a feasible proposition.

The computer operator would usually have an **operator's console** which is the name given to a special **terminal** into which the computer operator could type instructions to terminate a job, or get a progress report on what is happening at any moment in time. From this operator's terminal the computer operator could interrupt what is happening inside the computer at any moment in time, whether or not the computer was in the middle of a job.

Batch processing today

After reading the above you might think that compared to modern **multitasking windows environments** (see page 388) batch processing operating systems belong in the middle ages. However, think more carefully about problems such as processing thirty million tax demands, or working out statistics from the national census data! These and many other problems of similar and much-smaller magnitudes naturally lend themselves to batch processing, and although the input is no longer controlled in quite the same way, you should appreciate the need to process large amounts of data in a batch. This need will be with us for the foreseeable future.

The strive for greater efficiency

The first operating systems were wonderful compared to none at all, but it quickly became obvious that in certain areas considerable improvements could be made. For example, if a program requested some output on a line printer (see page 249), then this process was very slow indeed compared to the speed at which the central processor could operate. Valuable CPU time was wasted while waiting for output on slow peripheral devices. One way round this problem was to **SPOOL** (**S**imultaneous **P**eripheral **O**utput **O**n **Line** – though nobody uses this mouthful!) the data to a tape or disk. This means outputting the data to a relatively fast peripheral, fooling the program into 'thinking' that it has printed extremely quickly, thus enabling the CPU to get on with the next task in hand. This **spooled** data was then **despooled** (i.e. sent to an actual printer) at some later stage, either under the control of the main computer or a separate computer system. In this way the average throughput of the mainframe system was significantly increased.

Accounting and accountability

Mainframes are expensive pieces of kit, and in the early operating systems any program could reek havoc – and often did! There was nothing to stop students from printing out 5,000 Snoopy cartoons if that's what they wanted to do – if the computer operator was having his or her coffee and did not notice what was happening, then valuable resources could be deliberately or accidentally abused. To get over these problems users of the system could be allocated **levels of priority** which would prevent access to certain resources including **the allocation of time**. The computer operators, having the highest priority level, would still be able to print out as many Snoopy cartoons as they wished, but ordinary mortals would be prevented from unauthorised access to designated parts of the computer, having their jobs automatically terminated by the operating system without the need for human intervention. From the computer operator's point of view this was the biggest break through in operating-system technology, as it allowed them to have their tea and coffee breaks in peace!

With so many complex operations being carried out *without* the need for human intervention, it is essential to have some sort of **log** produced by the computer on the **operators terminal**. This is a list of **statistics** such as the jobs done, the times at which these jobs were started and finished, the resources which have been used, and any errors which may have occurred in a job or with the system etc during a shift. (Mainframe computers are often used 24 hours a day, seven days a week.) Information such as this can be used to monitor the effective performance of the system, and be used for **accounting purposes** such as generating the bills for the people who have made use of the system, or generating statistics about who has been using the system and when. Big Brother is *definitely* watching!

Multiprogramming

Hardware development continued at an amazing pace, and CPUs became ever more powerful and faster compared to the slower peripheral devices. We have already seen how **spooling** helped to solve the very-slow-printer problem, but even the much-faster tape and disk machines were starting to look pedestrian compared to the 'warp-speed' capabilities of the CPU. An analysis of how a typical CPU spent its time would probably show that typically over 95% of time was 'wasted' in waiting while accessing peripheral units. Only the fast **RAM** was keeping up with the CPU (however, in the mid 90s this too has become a major problem – see page 261), and this suggested an alternative strategy. If more than one **job (user program)** was resident in the machine at the same time, then the CPU could switch between **jobs** while it was waiting for a peripheral device such as a disk or tape. Why not have many user programs all resident at the same time? The only limitation was the amount of memory needed to store all the user programs and their data. And so the **multiprogramming operating system** was born – and this is the point where operating systems started to get more sophisticated and very complicated. Nevertheless, these ideas were so successful that multiprogramming-operating-system principles now form the basis of the most modern windows environments in the 90s, but with much more interaction between the users and the computer too.

Multitasking

To prevent multiple copies of the *same* application **programs or compilers** etc being loaded into the machine when requested by several different users, the *same program or application* can be shared between the different **tasks** being undertaken by each user. Such a system is known as a **multitasking operating system**. Therefore, you could easily have several different programs all multitasking in which case you have a multiprogramming-multitasking operating system. However, the term **multitasking operating system** is often used to mean the same thing – when the term multitasking was coined to describe *what's happening on the latest microcomputer operating systems*, nobody noticed that the same term meant something slightly different in the mainframe computer environment! Most modern multitasking operating systems are, therefore, actually multiprogramming-multitasking operating systems, and multitasking on micros means the same thing as multiprogramming.

Batch multiprogramming

To keep matters simple, let's continue our chronological development of operating systems and consider the multiprogramming ideas applied only to batch systems. Thus batches of programs are submitted and put into the computer's 'in tray'. It is the job of the **multiprogramming operating system** to decide which programs to load into memory and when. The actual loading of these programs into memory causes significant **memory management** problems, and deciding which programs to load and when to run them is called **scheduling**.

First consider the two typical scenarios shown in figure 17.3. Figure 17.3(a) shows a program which has a very high calculation content. This maths-intensive program, probably trying to solve some of the mysteries of the Universe, might monopolise the mainframe CPU for 99.9% of the ten minutes that it takes to run. The CPU *is* being efficiently utilised, which *is* one of the major objectives of this exercise, but is this efficient in terms of the throughput of jobs? – perhaps 150 other jobs could have been run in the time taken for this single program to execute.

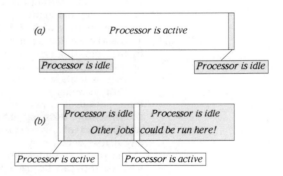

Figure 17.3

Figure 17.3(b) shows a program with intensive-peripheral activity. The CPU is not utilised very efficiently because time is wasted in waiting for other activities to take place. Other jobs could be run during the spaces indicated on this second part of the diagram. Getting the operating system to assign **priorities** to each of the jobs helps to get over these problems (see page 376). However, which jobs should be run? Will they fit into available memory? When loaded will they be the processor-intensive or the peripheral intensive jobs? If one job is not loaded what is to guarantee that it will be loaded next time round? Who decides on these levels of priorities? You've guessed it – the operating system! Conflicting demands are therefore being made on the designers of operating systems and complex **algorithms** need to be implemented if efficient **scheduling** and **memory management** are to take place. Add to this the problems of **security** and **protection of information**, plus the **management of all the other resources** such that these conflicting demands are kept to a minimum, and you will *start to get a very limited idea* of the horrendous problems involved in designing multiprogramming operating systems on mainframe computers.

Scheduling

A simplistic idea of **scheduling** can be gained from considering just three **jobs**, each of which have been split up into equal CPU and peripheral-time requirements as shown in figure 17.4(a).

Look first at the top of this diagram which shows how the three jobs would be tackled in a simple serial fashion, with each job waiting for the previous job to completely finish. We will use 100% as the time taken for these three jobs to complete

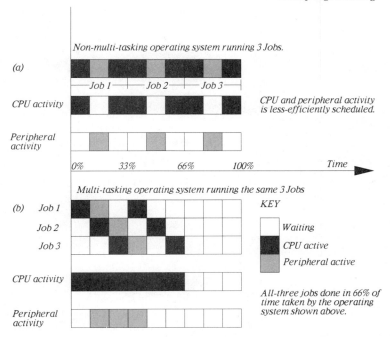

Figure 17.4

execution in this non-multiprogramming environment. Now consider the bottom half of this diagram. This shows the same three jobs, but this time with a multi-programming operating system. As can be seen from the bottom of figure 17.4, Job 1 is executed immediately, while Jobs 2 and 3 are put in the **queue** (i.e. they are kept waiting). When Job 1 is waiting for a peripheral device, Job 2 is run by the CPU while Job 3 is still kept waiting. These processes continue in this way until all three jobs are completed. Although this is a contrived problem, compare the CPU and peripheral-utilisation parts of the diagram for the multiprogramming (figure 17.4(b)) and the non-multiprogramming (figure 17.4(a)) operating systems. You can see that the effective throughput of the three jobs has been made very significantly quicker when multiprogramming has been used, and both the peripherals and CPU have been utilised more efficiently. Note that the CPU has not done any less work, it is just that the scheduling has been improved with a corresponding increase in efficiency. If you can carry out 33% more tasks during any one day, then the computer system will be making a lot more money for its commercial operators.

Managing multiprogramming

We will now look at some of the methods associated with multiprogramming environments. To keep things simple we will *not* consider the use of **virtual memory** (see page 381) or **multi-processors** (see page 62) unless specified later. If several **programs** (often called **tasks** or **processes** in the context of a multiprogramming-operating-system environment) are resident in main memory at the same time, it is the job of another program called the **dispatcher** to set up the main processor's **program counter** (see page 54) so that the main processor can change between the different **tasks**. When dealing with operating systems the term 'task' is a better one to use than '**program**' because not only can it refer to a user's program in the normal sense, but to the start of a new **job** (see page 371) in a **batch environment** or when a new user logs on in a **multi-user interactive environment**.

Queues

A common method (see **time sharing** on page 381) to prevent any one **task** monopolising the main processor's time, is to **interrupt** the **task** after a set period of time has been used up. At this moment the dispatcher will then suspend the operation of the task and go on to the next, putting the task just suspended into a **queue**. It is unlikely that this sequence of events would carry on for very long before one of the tasks themselves **interrupts** this smooth running by requesting a peripheral device such as a disk or printer, or perhaps an error is generated by one of the tasks thus requiring termination of that particular task.

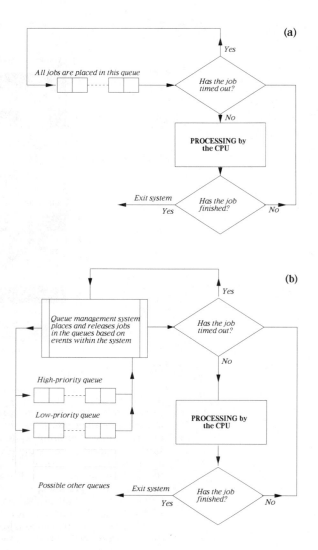

Figure 17.5

Figure 17.5(a) shows how such a queue is managed in diagrammatic form. Note that a **task** is either continually switched between the processor and the queue, or exits under certain conditions such as natural termination of the program or an error condition. The single **FIFO data structure** (see page 290) or **queue** implied in figure 17.5 is *not* the most efficient because this assumes that all tasks in the queue are waiting for processor time. If one of the tasks is halted because of an **I/O request**, then this request may not have been completed before the task gets to the beginning of the queue again. Therefore, it's efficient to implement more than one queue – one for those tasks which are waiting for attention, and another for tasks which are waiting for I/O to be completed. This idea is shown in figure 17.5(b).

Priorities

In practice, multiple queues are established for most operating system designs. One advantage of a **multiple-queue** design is that this is one method of assigning **priorities** to different tasks. **High-priority tasks** can be routed to one queue, while **low-priority tasks** can be routed to another. Multiple levels of priorities can also easily be implemented using this method. Don't forget also that *without* **virtual memory**, (see page 381) all tasks must be resident in RAM simultaneously. This is wasteful if some of the tasks in RAM are not in a ready state, and this problem can be overcome by ushering some of the tasks out to a queue established on a disk. This is often known as the suspended queue and consists of tasks that can be loaded back into RAM at some later stage. We can now envisage a scenario where a large number of tasks are in a great variety of different **states**. For example, a task could be in RAM and ready to go, in RAM and waiting for I/O, on disk and ready to go, or on disk and waiting for I/O. It is the job of the operating system to maintain all the **data structures** (see chapter 14) necessary to deal with all these different tasks and states. **State transition diagrams** are used in advanced courses on operating-system design to get an overall appreciation of what is happening, and a very simple example is given on page 143 in the structured analysis and design chapter where state-transition diagrams are considered in more detail.

Concurrency problems

You saw in figure 17.4(b) how a **single processor** could operate in a multiprogramming environment. If we had *more than one* processor then each **task (job)** could be run in the same way, but more importantly, **tasks** could also be **overlapped**, i.e. more than one task *is* actually being carried out **simultaneously** or **concurrently**. This is an excellent idea, but creates some difficult problems to solve. You should be fully aware of the need to modularise programs (see page 135), as this makes for more-understandable code. However, when larger programs are spilt up into sub-programs and run as separate tasks in a **multi-processor multiprogramming environment**, then problems regarding synchronisation may occur, depending on the order in which the operating system decides to carry out the tasks. On page 65 you will see how restructuring the problems can lead to efficient utilisation of multiple processors, but with an operating system of the type now being considered it's quite different, because programmers are not writing their programs with optimisation from an operating-system viewpoint borne in mind! There are many systems in operation to get over these problems, but **optimisation of scheduling** is one of the most complex problems in operating system design. The detection and correction of operating-system errors in such an environment require gargantuan efforts, as it is almost impossible to reproduce the set of events which may be causing a very subtle error to occur.

Deadlock

Not only must the **queues** of such **tasks** be managed, but so too must the **resources** that are allocated to these tasks. A **resource** in this context can be more easily understood if you consider it to be a **printer**, or a **disk** or **tape** (i.e. **files**) etc. Life would be easy for operating system designers if there were an infinite number of these resources, as each task requesting a resource would be allocated the next one available. Due to the finite number of resources in a system, and the large number of concurrent tasks running, tasks usually have to wait until a suitable resource is free to be used.

From reading the above you might think that all that is necessary is to assign a resource to a task whenever it needs it. Unfortunately, life is not this simple. Consider, for example, the case where the **resource** happens to be a **file** which is to be **updated** (*not* simply read) by two different **tasks**. Task 2, for example, should *not be able to use* the resource (particular file) *if* task 1 already has it. If task 1 and 2 were allowed to update the file at the same time then the resulting data would probably lose its **integrity** (a posh way of saying it could get messed up). However, if task 1 were to update followed by task 2, or task 2 were to update followed by task 1, then there would be no problems as both the changes would have been recorded properly. Therefore, a system of **locking** has been devised whereby a resource can be **locked out** while it is in use by any task. This is often referred to as **mutual exclusion**, and for the reasons just outlined it is a desirable property in multiprogramming operating systems. Similar problems requiring **locking** would also be needed if the **resources** were a **buffer** (see page 358) or **main memory**. On more sophisticated operating systems many different types of locks are implemented to preclude certain subsets of tasks from gaining access to the resources under different sets of conditions.

There are other strategies for resource allocation such as 'a task holding on to a resource until it has been allocated another one', and other policies such as 'not being able to remove a resource from a particular task that needs it'. (Essential in the case of the file resource considered above.) Nevertheless, all current strategies have their problems, one of which is called **deadlock**. Deadlock is when a resource requested by one task is being held by another, and this other task will not release the resource requested because the requesting task is holding onto the one that it wants!

Figure 17.6 shows this problem which is often referred to as a **circular wait** state because, without intervention by the operating system, the two tasks would go round in circles requesting resources that will never be released. Various strategies have therefore had to be implemented for preventing most cases of deadlock, for detecting if deadlock has occurred, and for overcoming deadlock if it has occurred – just another one of the million-and-one things that a modern operating system has to do!

Starvation

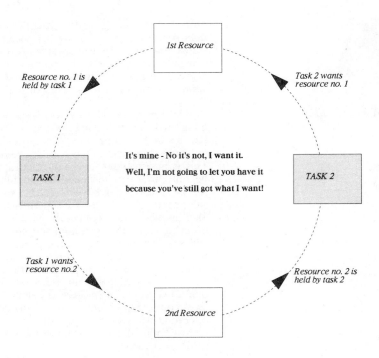

Figure 17.6

One can imagine the scenario whereby a resource is *never* allocated to a particular task. The task might happen to be in a low-priority queue and the resource is being continually used by higher-priority tasks. In the extreme the low-priority task would never come out of the computer system! Therefore, the operating system must prevent tasks being starved of resources so that tasks are carried out in a sensible amount of time.

Interrupts

One of the principle reasons why many of the techniques described above can be used is because of the ability of devices and programs to **generate interrupts**. For example, if the printer was busy printing out some information held in its **buffer** (see page 358) then it could carry on doing this under its own steam until it had run out of data to print. The **peripheral device**, in this case the printer, could then **generate an interrupt**, thus indicating that it needs more data, the CPU could then **service this interrupt**, and then go back to what it was doing before being rudely interrupted!

Simple interrupts are considered in the section on microcomputer operating systems (see page 394) – *here we will concentrate on interrupts from a mainframe and minicomputer perspective.* You should appreciate that mainframe interrupts are much more sophisticated because the operating system can usually preempt what should happen to carry out many tasks efficiently, rather than 'mindlessly' carrying on with what it was doing before the interrupt occurred. It is usually implied that on **mainframes** *all* multiprogramming operating systems are **preemptive multiprogramming operating systems**.

Interrupt priorities

There are many devices that may cause an interrupt in a large computer system. For example, the operator may wish to stop the current program from being run, a printer may run out of paper or the electronics that detect an imminent power failure may initiate routines to save all the current work in the few fractions of a second before the system dies of power failure. The very last example must obviously be dealt with before any of the other interrupts even though it may not be the first interrupt that occurs. It must also be immediately dealt with even if the computer is currently in the middle of servicing another interrupt. Priorities will therefore have to be assigned to the interrupting devices so that the most important interrupts can be serviced first.

Also, interrupts may be split up into different categories. If a hardware device such as one of those described above causes the interrupt, this is an **external interrupt**. There may be a fault in a program such as syntax error or arithmetic overflow. This would be **a program fault interrupt, error interrupt** or **program error trap**.

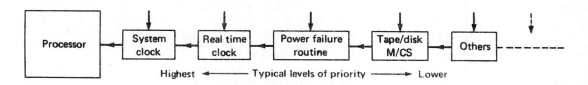

Figure 17.7

Highest ◄──── Typical levels of priority ────► Lower

The current program may simply run out of time as it may get stuck in an infinite loop. This would be an example of a **timer interrupt**.

The external interrupts on a large computer system are usually wired so that the CPU is presented with interrupts at **different levels**. These are the levels of priority assigned to devices that are wired to each of these levels. Each level may be **enabled** or **disabled** (often referred to as **armed** and **disarmed**) by both hardware and software. The situation can be imagined as shown in figure 17.7.

Each device on a particular level has the same priority. Therefore if two devices on level 3 cause an interrupt the first to happen gets priority. Each level of interrupt may be totally disabled so that even if an interrupt did occur the CPU would not take any notice of it.

The interrupt need not necessarily be totally disabled. For example, the interrupt may occur, but the fact that the interrupt has occurred could be registered, i.e. a bit could be set to let the processor know that an interrupt has occurred ready for when the processor can get around to dealing with it.

It is useful to show systematically the sort of thing that can happen when several devices with different priorities are causing interrupts. Let us assume, for simplicity, that there are just four devices on the system. Device number 1 has the highest priority and device number four has the lowest priority. The following diagram shows how the CPU's time would be allocated in dealing with a typical chain of interrupts:

Interrupting devices				CPU	Notes
Device	Device	Device	Device	Main task	(Note * means that the device has requested an interrupt. The * is cancelled after the interrupt has been serviced. M means that the CPU is engaged in carrying out its main task.)
4	3	2	1	MMMMMM	
–	–	–	–	MMMMMM	
–	–	–	–	MMMMMM	
*	–	–	–	444444	Device 4 receives processor attention
*	–	–	–	444444	
–	–	–	–	MMMMMM	Device 4 finished, main task reinstated
–	–	*	–	222222	Device 2 receives attention
–	*	*	–	222222	Device 3 ignored (lower priority than 2)
–	*	*	–	222222	
–	*	–	–	333333	Device 3 gets attention now 2 has finished
–	*	–	–	333333	
–	–	–	–	MMMMMM	Main task reinstated as no more interrupts
–	–	–	–	MMMMMM	
–	–	*	–	222222	Device 2 gets attention
–	–	*	*	111111	Device 1 overrides device 2 service routine
*	–	*	*	111111	Device 4 gets totally ignored for the moment
*	–	*	–	222222	Device 2 reinstated
*	*	*	–	222222	
*	*	–	–	333333	Device 3 gets attention even though 4 was first
*	*	–	–	333333	
*	–	*	–	222222	Device 2 now being served
*	–	*	–	222222	
*	–	*	–	222222	
*	–	–	–	444444	Device 4 at last
*	–	–	–	444444	
–	–	–	–	MMMMMM	Main task reinstated
–	–	–	–	MMMMMM	
–	–	–	–	MMMMMM	

It should be very clear from the above exactly how the processor deals with the priorities that have been assigned to the various devices. To cater for differing needs each day it is usual to be able to redefine the priorities that have been assigned to a particular task. For example, a job may not be the most efficient one to run in terms of processor time but it may be the most important (e.g. the computer operator's pay cheque program!).

The CPU keeps track of what is happening by setting a bit inside a register called the **interrupt flag register.** If a bit is set to '1' then this could be a device for flagging the various conditions (imagine a little man jumping up and down waving a flag shouting 'device 3 needs attention'). In this way it is possible to know which devices are currently interrupting. This therefore means that the CPU can stop servicing an interrupt if a higher priority one comes along. This would be done in exactly the same way as the original main task was tackled, by saving the contents of the registers on the stack, etc. Each time an interrupt has been serviced then the interrupt flag in the interrupt flag register can be reset so that the device may interrupt again if necessary.

Finally, when all the interrupts have been cleared, the original last contents of the registers pulled off the stack would be the conditions for carrying on the main task.

It was mentioned that it is possible to disable interrupts via software control. This can be done by having what is called an **interrupt enable/disable register.** This is another register inside the CPU where bits control how interrupts in the system will be carried out. For example, we may have a bit inside the interrupt enable/disable register that controls device 3. It may be arranged so that if this bit is set to '1' then interrupts from device 3 (indicated by the state of the device 3 flag) will be handled normally. If this bit was set to zero, then interrupts from device 3 could be ignored.

The system could work as follows:

If device 3 has its interrupts enabled and if device 3 is causing an interrupt then service it.

If device 3 has its interrupts disabled then ignore any interrupts caused by device 3's interrupt flag being set.

Memory management

If many different jobs are to be resident in the computer's main memory at any one moment in time, then it is vital that the operating system prevents the programs from interfering with each other. When different programs are sharing the same memory in a computer there will always be the potential for one program to accidentally address the memory space occupied by another. If this were allowed to happen then the programs may get corrupted with potentially disastrous results.

You will recall from the section on **scheduling** that much of the time is spent on **I/O** activities, with the processor being idle for significant periods of time. Therefore, it is the task of the memory-management system to pack as many **jobs** into the main memory as is possible. In a non-multitasking (i.e. single-user) environment you can imagine a simplistic scenario where the memory is basically split up into two sections – part for the operating system itself, and the rest for user-program space. The user's program would thus be running in an area of memory **partitioned** off from the operating system. This partition is fixed as there is only a need to run a single program.

Fixed partitioning

The simple **fixed-partition** idea could also be applied to **memory management** in the more complex **multiprogramming environment.** Appropriate-sized fixed partitions could be set up in memory, and the jobs loaded into an appropriate partition when one becomes available. These partitions could all be of the same size, or there could be a various number of different-sized but fixed partitions. The advantage of this system is that the algorithms for allocating users' programs to the partitions are relatively simple. An important point to realise here is that all programs designed to be run in a **multiprogramming system** must be **relocatable.** You will recall from the **machine-code** section on page 89 that it is bad practice to write programs that write to specific memory locations. If any program is to run in *any* partition you should now see why this is so important.

The **disadvantage** of **fixed partition-memory** is that long **queues** can build up at the same time that much valuable memory remains unused, because many programs don't happen to fit into a particular size partition. Also, the programs that are occupying the partitions might be doing so very inefficiently. For example, if the smallest partition size is 500k, then a 20k program will 'occupy' all of this partition, thus preventing 480k of memory from being used effectively all the time that this program remains in memory. Also, by having a finite number of fixed partitions you are placing an arbitrary limit on the number of tasks that the system can handle at any one time. Due to these **severe limitations, fixed partition systems are not used** very often – if at all.

Variable partitioning

A better, though much-more-complex method of partitioning is to **dynamically allocate** the **partitions** as and when necessary. This is called **dynamic memory partitioning**. When a task is loaded it is allocated an appropriate amount of memory. You might think that we have now reached a situation where memory is being utilised very efficiently – however, when a particular task is finished and another task needs to take its place, then it is most unlikely that the two tasks are of the same size, therefore, a **hole** is produced in the memory which starts to become fragmented. This might not seem too bad, but as time progresses, more holes appear throughout the memory and we eventually get to a stage where the memory is being used very inefficiently indeed. Therefore, from time to time, the system has to **compact** all the tasks by swapping them around until we are back to the situation similar to that when the system started up.

The major **disadvantage** of **dynamic partitioning** is that this **compaction** process is very tedious and time consuming. You will recall that we are trying to utilise the CPU with maximum efficiency. Clearing out the memory and other housework chores such as compaction do not rate as efficient if they do not contribute to the fast throughput of the system in general.

Virtual memory

The next bright idea was to split up the **memory** into relatively-small sections called **page frames**, but *in addition to this*, spilt up the **user programs** into **pages** so that *each page of the user programs occupies exactly the same space as a page frame in memory*. So what, you might ask! If we had spilt up the memory into smaller sections in the first place, and allocated as many sections as needed to each user program, then the problems with partitioning would not have occurred! This is true to a small extent, but here comes the really clever part – why bother to have *all* the user's program resident in the memory at the same time? If the program consists of a large chunk of code, then only a fraction of this code is ever needed to execute the current sub-set of instructions being carried out – most of the program is lying dormant in memory waiting for its big moment. It's rather like the guy in the orchestra who plays a few notes on the triangle half an hour into the main symphony. There's not much point in him being there for the first half hour – he might as well be in the pub down the road! It would be disconcerting for the audience to watch the orchestra as the musicians kept getting up to go out to the pub, (unless they went too!), but this analogy with a virtual-memory system is a good one.

There is also an immense spin-off from this **virtual-memory** method in that each user program can be of enormous size – they do not have to fit into the available RAM of the computer. Therefore, a computer with an actual 50Mbytes of RAM could be simultaneously working on a dozen programs, where each program happens to be 20 Mbytes long, giving a virtual RAM of 240Mbytes.

There must be some disadvantages of the system too, and indeed there are. Some of the time the code is executed without any problems, but a branch instruction to some page of code which is not resident in RAM means that the operating system will have to load this new page. However, the operating system is not clairvoyant – how does it know which page to remove from RAM? The page just removed might be the next page that is needed. In virtual-memory systems the worst case scenario is when pages of code are continually being put into RAM and then taken out again. This **unfortunate phenomenon** is known as **thrashing**. In bad cases, the **virtual-memory** operating system can spend more time removing and reloading pages of code than it spends executing the program.

As you can see from the previous sections, the problems of efficient scheduling and memory management are not trivial, and the operating systems have become more complex by using combinations of these systems to optimise both resources and CPU time to get the maximum amount of work done in the minimum amount of time. With each new generation of operating system more efficient algorithms have been developed in a heuristic way with all the benefit of hindsight from previous operating-system's development. This is one of the main reasons why computers are becoming so fast. (The other is that the electronics inside are much more powerful too.)

Time sharing systems

In the previous sections we have been considering operating systems essentially from a batch-processing point of view. Fortunately, most of the principles covered apply equally well to most of the other types of operating systems. Still sticking with main-frames and larger computers for the time being, we will now take a look at the developments of the **alternatives** to **batch processing**.

After reading the above you should appreciate that batch processing, although efficient in terms of getting vast volumes of work carried out in the minimum time, does not give the user of the system any instant feedback. The author well remembers submitting Fortran IV programs on punched card during the morning, then eagerly collecting the output after tea in the evening, only to find that there was a syntax error in the program. The offending card would then have to be replaced and the job re-submitted the following day. What an awful scenario for maintaining any degree of enthusiasm for the job in hand. What was needed was a system in which the user could sit down at a terminal, type in their program and get a response within a few seconds. Any error could then be corrected and the program instantly re-run. In other words, what was needed was exactly what people today take for granted with their single-user microcomputer. But don't forget – we were using a mainframe computer, *not* a micro – these had yet to be invented, and even if they had been, several hundred people were still itching to get their programs run on a mainframe – so this problem had to be solved anyway.

Interestingly enough, it was in this sort of environment that **BASIC** first came to the fore. This language, originally being **interpreted** instead of **compiled** (see page 200), was ideal for what was to be called a **conversational mode of operation**. What was needed was an **operating system** that could respond to hundreds of people sitting down at terminals running these sorts of programs. (Programs could also be compiled from these terminals but we will stick with interpreted BASIC as it makes **time sharing** much easier to understand.) It might seem an impossible feat to achieve, but an analysis of what, typically, was happening at each terminal makes it feasible. Most people would be typing in their programs – a painfully-slow operation compared to the speed with which a CPU can react. Even if programs were being run, most likely or not they had an error generated which meant that the student at the terminal spent the next few minutes trying to work out what was wrong. In other words, it was very unlikely that many people would be carrying out much processor-intensive activity at any one time, and even if they were, you would simply get the operating system to limit the amount of time it spent with these particular people.

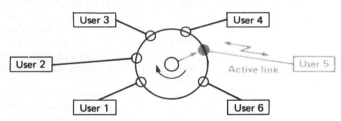

Figure 17.8

The technique was to get the operating system to scan all the terminals that were on line to see if anything needed doing. If not, it simply went on to the next terminal, then the next, and the next until it came round to the original terminal again. Each time the processor allocated time to a user this was known as a **time slice**. The speed of the system compared to what was actually happening at each terminal meant that most requests were dealt with within a few seconds. A mechanical analogy of time sharing is shown in figure 17.8.

Most people are familiar with the term time sharing from taking holidays abroad in villas which are rented for a few weeks of the year, but a better analogy with the computer would be a super-being teacher who is able to quickly whizz round the class sorting out the pupil's problems when they have their hands up. If the teacher acted quickly enough then each pupil would be under the mistaken illusion that they are getting the attention of the teacher all the time. So it is with the computer. Most of the time all the students sitting at the terminals would be under the illusion that they are the sole user of this **multi-user operating system.** Because each person is allocated a small time slice of the computer's time, this type of system is called a **time sharing operating system**.

It's important to realise that a new set of objectives now present themselves, no longer are we trying to utilise CPU time to the maximum, but a **more-important objective** in a **time-sharing operating system** is to **maximise the speed of response** for individual users. When you realise that some mainframes were running batch and time sharing operating systems simultaneously, with all the compromises and

Here's one for you... and one for you...

conflicting conditions, you start to realise what mind-boggling complexities these operating systems start to represent.

Protection of information

Whenever different users have access to the *same* system there is a need to protect against the misuse of information and resources. Users of the system are usually given access via a set of user IDs and passwords. There will be many different types of user all with different levels of privilege ranging for example, from the computer operator who has access to almost anything, down to a first-year student user at a typical university who only has access to their own files and any software which has been placed in the public domain. It is usual for each user to have read/write access to his or her own files, but only read access to the public files. Extra security can be implemented by having hardware-only access to certain parts of the system. i.e. a certain terminal would have to be used to carry out special functions on the computer system. Most terminals within the building would not have this sort of status.

Security has been extensively covered in the network (see page 513) and database (see page 482) chapters and will, therefore, not be repeated here. However, operating system security *is* of paramount importance – if the operating system is not secure then neither is the data held by the computer system controlled by it.

Multiprocessor systems

Most of the systems considered so far have had one thing in common – a **single processor**. In the search for ever more speed and increased reliability, a natural and sensible suggestion is to **add more processors** to the system. There are several different philosophies currently in operation. The first is **true parallel processing** as discussed in detail in the computer architecture chapter (see page 62). Here the problems are formulated in such a way that different parts of the same problem are passed over to different processors for lightning-speed execution. The other type of **multiprocessing**, still common in the mid 90s, is to get a **multiprocessing operating system** to control two or more independent processors by **efficient scheduling** of the work such that the result is similar to having **two or more separate computers**. These processors can either share the same memory or have independent memory allocated to them. Besides getting an increased throughput, another spin-off from this type of multi-processing just discussed is a significant **increase in reliability**. If a fault occurs in one part of the system, then a reduced-efficiency service can be carried out by the other part of the system which is still working. This obviously increases the reliability as a slower response is much better than no response at all.

Direct Memory Access (DMA)

In all the operations carried out so far, any I/O transfers have been carried out under the control of the main processor. Input or output has been accomplished in one of two ways – either being initialised by the main processor, or the processor being forced to carry out an I/O operation because of an interrupt. In the latter case the processor suspends its operations and comes back later to what it was doing. In both of these cases it is the processor which has to carry out an intensive series of operations to get the data transfer actually to take place.

In a modern operating system there is now a third option, called **Direct Memory Access** or **DMA**, and this technique, started on mainframe computers, is now also available on some micros. Basically, the main processor can instruct a **specialised microprocessor** called the **DMA controller** to transfer a block of memory to another part of memory or to disk, for example, then forget about the actual data transfer until the DMA controller informs the processor that the data transfer has finished taking place. The difference here is that the main processor does *not* have to concentrate on the data-transfer operation itself, and does *not* have to suspend any task activity while this data-transfer operation is taking place.

The **DMA microprocessor** has to **synchronise exactly** with the **main processor** as the same **data**, **address** and **control busses** (see page 51) are being used by both systems. This inevitably means that either the DMA controller or the main processor will have to wait *if* the bus is being used by the other device. Nevertheless, although the main-processor is actually slowed down a little, clever timing between the two devices ensures that this method of operation gets the data transferred much more quickly than would have been the case if the DMA controller had not been used. On some more-sophisticated systems, the DMA controller can input from and output to a variety of peripheral devices making use of their own I/O busses separate from the main-processor/s busses.

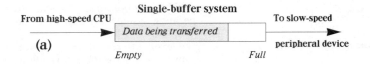

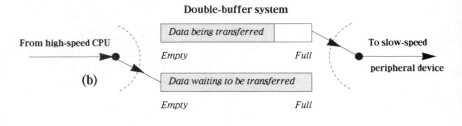

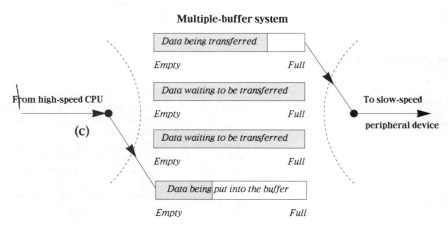

Figure 17.9

Input/output buffering

We have already seen some of the problems caused by the differences in speed of operation of the fast processors and the very slow peripherals. One method of overcoming these problems is to make use of a **buffer**. This is simply **an area of memory** allocated to storing information while it is waiting to be transferred. Without any buffering the main processor would have to wait while a relatively-slow I/O process is taking place. Figure 17.9(a) shows how a single-buffer system would operate. However, when the buffer is empty, time is wasted while a request is made to the main processor to fill it up again if necessary.

A better system is to make use of double-buffering as shown in figure 17.9(b). Here two buffers are used alternately, with the processor filling up the empty one while the contents of the other is being transferred. In some situations, even double-buffering is not man enough for the job, and so multiple-buffering can be used to increase the throughput as shown in figure 17.9(c). However, **double-buffering** is still *the most commonly used system*. Buffers can also be used to help avoid deadlock (see page 377) as the physical output device is not actually locked out under these conditions, but the data is transferred to memory and spooled later (see page 373).

Front-end processors

On large mainframe systems, the transfer of data to and from the outside world is a horrendous problem. The design of a comprehensive strategy for transferring data to and from the enormous number of peripheral devices and terminals attached to the mainframe is a complete science in itself. We have already seen how **buffering**, **DMA systems** with possible **extra I/O busses**, **multiple processors** and **multiprogramming** can increase the workload of a computer system, but the actual transfer of data to the peripherals, and to the hundreds (or possibly thousands) of terminals connected to the system needs a more radical solution. The radical solution to this I/O problem is to put another **more-specialised computer** (often a **minicomputer**) to work on tackling this problem. Figure 17.10 shows the general idea. A new computer, called a **front-end processor** is placed at the **front end** (i.e. the communication-with-the-outside-world end) of the mainframe computer so that the communication

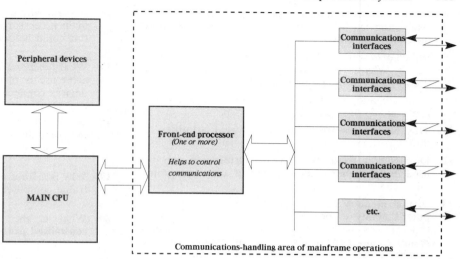

Figure 17.10

channels to the outside world go into one end of this front-end processor, and communication with the mainframe comes out at the other end.

On smaller minicomputers you can often get away with just a simpler **communications controller**, but only a front-end processor can cope on mainframe systems. Indeed, on **very large mainframes** and **supercomputers,** there is often a need for several front-end processors, *and* communications controllers placed inbetween the front-end processors and the real world to deal with a variety of data coming in via networks, the telephone, and various other systems.

Distributed processing

Hitherto we have considered how to increase the power of a **centralised facility** (i.e. a mainframe or mini computer running all the jobs.) However, recent advances in microcomputer design (see the next section) have meant that **distributed processing** is now becoming increasingly important. **Distributed processing** means *many separate computers all doing their own thing, but with an efficient means of communication between them* so that effective, fast and efficient co-operation is possible. These ideas are so important that an entire chapter is devoted to networking, both from a software and hardware point of view. **Network operating systems** are mentioned at the end of this chapter for completeness, but this vitally important topic is covered separately in chapter 21.

After reading the first half of this chapter you are now in a much-better position to appreciate that **multi-processor multiprogramming operating systems** supporting both **batch** and **interactive** modes of operation are common on mainframes. Several hundred users could be on-line to the mainframe computer while many other tasks are being processed in a batch. This is often going on 24-hours a day, seven days a week. You should now be in a position to appreciate the difference between fully-blown mainframe operating systems such as MVS mentioned at the beginning of this chapter, and those operating systems found in the more-humble micro.

Exercise 17.1

N.B. *All questions* in this exercise refer to **mainframe** or **large minicomputer operating systems**. Exercise 17.2 at the end of this chapter will concentrate on operating systems from a microcomputer's perspective.

1. Briefly describe why an **operating system** is needed for any computer.

2. List three *different types* of operating system used on mainframe or minicomputers.

3. With the aid of a suitable diagram explain how the operating system links an application program to the hardware in a computer system.

4. It is often said that the operating system provides a virtual world for the computer user. Explain what is meant by a virtual world and why this description is apt.

5. Explain how a computer operator on a mainframe computer *interacts* with the operating system, giving some indication of a typical brief session.

6. Explain what is meant by the term **batch processing**.

7. **Multitasking** and **multiprogramming** are often used on large computers. Explain what is meant by these terms.

8. In a **multiprogramming operating system** efficient **scheduling** can be used to increase productivity. Show how this may be so.

9. **Interrupts** form an important part of operating system design. Why are they so important and how are they used in a large operating system?

10. Compare and contrast hardware and software interrupts, giving *two* examples of each type.

11. Why is it necessary to assign **different priorities** to different interrupts?

12. Discuss how **fixed** and **variable partitioning** may be used in the **memory management** of a multiprogramming operating system.

13. **Virtual memory** has enormously extended the computer's ability to process a greater number of large tasks at the same time. Explain what is meant by **virtual memory** and how it gives a great increase in the number of tasks that can be tackled 'simultaneously'.

14. What is meant by the term **thrashing** in the context of an operating system?

15. Explain how **time sharing** can be used for giving many users access to a computer system, and how it can be used as a means of implementing a multiprogramming system.

16. Explain why it is a good idea to have *more than one* main processor in a large computer system, and how this could help with increased reliability.

17. What *functions* of an operating system ensure that efficient use is made of the vast number of peripheral devices connected to the main computer.

18. The **DMA controller** helps to make certain aspects of the computer execute more quickly. What is meant by DMA and how does it help in this way?

19. Why is a **front end processor** needed on a large mainframe computer system?

20. What is the difference between **distributed** and **centralised processing**?

21. Why do you think that **centralised processing** was considered to be more important in the 70s and early 80s, but **distributed processing** is increasing in importance in the 90s?

22. List two different methods used to help protect against unauthorised access to information on multi-user or

---

From reading the previous **mainframe** sections you might well be tempted into thinking that the operating systems inside your microcomputer must be quite simple – unfortunately they're not, especially the latest multitasking-windows versions, and even multi-processor-multitasking operating systems have now been written for the most-powerful micros. Nevertheless, let's take a chronological trip though the relatively short history of the microcomputer operating system, and see how it has evolved in the 80s and 90s, lately borrowing much from mainframe operating system techniques. You will see that many events shaped current operating-system philosophy – and they're not all technical ones!

Microcomputer operating systems

The **microprocessor** (see page 14) was invented in the early 1970s, and although 4-bit micros were developed first, it was the advent of the 8-bit microprocessor which heralded the start of the personal computer revolution. Many machines were built up around the Z80 and 6502 chips. For example, the 6502 chip was used in the educationally-famous BBC Microcomputer, and the early BBC machines had just 32k of memory! These early machines gave people the first opportunity to have a computer processor all to themselves, and this was wonderful compared to time-sharing on a mainframe or minicomputer. The original **operating systems** were obviously **single user**, and very simple indeed compared to the operating systems found on the mainframes during the same period. The very early machines had no disk drive facilities, and programs were loaded and saved via a domestic audio tape recorder. The operating systems – or often just part of the operating system (see page 265), being very small, could be stored inside a **ROM** chip, so that data would not be lost when the power to the machine was switched off. This nicely got over the problems of hand loading any code into the computer to start the machine, and was a tremendous break through in user friendliness.

Later versions of this technology were improved and the advent of the **floppy disk** meant that the unreliable audio tape recorders could be dispensed with. Probably the most famous of all the microprocessor chips, used in the first **IBM PC**, was **Intel's 8086 (and 8088) 16-bit chips**, which, together with **version 1** of **MS-DOS**, introduced in 1981, launched what was to become the most famous and formidable (in terms of sales *not* sophistication) Disk Operating System to date for micros. MS-DOS was to dominate the microcomputer market for the next ten to fifteen years, and in 1994 MS-DOS had over 40 million users worldwide. MS-DOS version 1.0

was extremely primitive by today's standards – it did not even have any support for hard disks. Therefore, in 1983, when IBM introduced the PC XT, MS-DOS 2.0 was released with hard-disk capability. This basically added the facility of **hierarchical directory structures** (see page 356).

The next ten years were to prove quite remarkable in the development of microprocessor technology, and this resulted in a string of chips being developed with considerably more power than the old 8-bit models. The original 8086, having a 20-bit address bus (see page 51) could address 2^{20} (1,048,576) or 1 Mbyte of RAM. The **IBM PC AT**, introduced in 1984, used the 80286 16-bit processor, but this has a 24-bit address bus which allows it to address 2^{24} or 16Mbytes of RAM – but MS-DOS 3.0, despite enhancements such as **networking** in version 3.1, and some other upgrades, was still basically the same as the earlier versions, and did not take any advantage of this extra-memory capacity.

With the advent of the **PS/2** machines from IBM, many of which ran the 80386 32-bit chips which had a 32-bit address bus, the addressable memory capacity of the PC was now a considerable 4096 Mbytes. However, MS-DOS version 4 (released in 1989) still only allowed you to have a paltry 640kbyte of addressable RAM, and this became known as the MS-DOS brick wall! In 1981 640kbytes was considered large, but when the PS/2 was released in the late 1980s this was a pathetic amount of memory for a front-line business microcomputer.

At last, versions 5.0 and 6.0 (released in the early 90s) allowed the users of MS-DOS to take full advantage of the memory potential of the more-powerful chips. Also, although parts of DOS were still looking positively antiquated, these latter versions allowed for a bolt-on windows option which ran on top of DOS. Nevertheless, MS-DOS based systems have stood the test of time, and the later versions will probably be around for some considerable time yet. It does not make good sense to write off a perfectly good system just because 'much better' ones are available – *if* the present system meets the needs of your business or industry. Even so, it's human nature (and considerable pressure from sales personnel!) to want the best of what is available, otherwise we would still all be using 8-bit micros.

It is a sensible question to ask why MS-DOS has ruled supreme when so many 'more sophisticated' operating systems are now to be found in abundance. The millstone (or gold mine!) around Microsoft's neck is that they needed to maintain compatibility with the old 8086 code if they were to keep their millions of customers happy. To do this, any software which ran on the old system will have to run on any of the new systems too. The microprocessor machine code (see page 70) had to contain a subset of code which was totally compatible with the early 8086 processor. Millions of businesses all over the world had spent enormous amounts of money on buying and developing MS-DOS-based software. They would not be too happy about having to start again from scratch, even though from a technical point of view this was the most obvious and easy solution. The other key to the success of the IBM PC was that the **BIOS** (Basic Input/Output System – the software which changes data from a **logical structure** to a **physical structure** (see page 357)) was readily clonable by third-party manufacturers. Therefore, many **IBM clones** were built – all based around the **Intel architecture**, and capable of running the same operating system – namely **MS-DOS**. However, this BIOS was defined in 1978 – and is a limiting factor on some of the later machines today! Recently, attempts to re-define BIOS standards are being carried out by several different consortiums of software and hardware manufacturers.

With the relatively new 32-bit 386 and 486 processors (short for 80386 and 80486) now in full swing, new and more-powerful operating systems were, at last, being developed in the late 80s and early 90s. No longer could manufacturers ignore the ease-of-use of the **windows environment** which was so predominant on other modern machines such as the Apple Mac. Therefore, Microsoft and IBM jointly developed **OS/2**, a **multitasking windows environment** that would exploit more fully the latest 32-bit microprocessor technology. So the break from MS-DOS had begun, but many other players in the market were now jockeying for position in this multi-billion pound industry. Unfortunately, the alliance between Microsoft and IBM broke down, with each company going their different ways. IBM developed **OS/2 version 2**, Microsoft developed **Cario**, now called Windows 95, and **Unix**, a powerful **mainframe operating system** which looks set to provide a huge challenge in the microcomputer market. However, there were over 200 versions of Unix in 1982, and currently groups of interested manufacturers are trying to cut these down to about two!

Recent microcomputer operating systems

It's important to realise that the 32-bit and recently-introduced 64-bit microprocessors have become so powerful, that you *can* now have **virtual memory multi-programming/multitasking operating systems** (see page 381) as found on mainframes just a decade ago. These new processors really do give you mainframe power on your desk – although you obviously would not have the peripherals and through-put capability of the large mainframe computers. Nevertheless, these new processors give the end users power which would have been unthinkable just a few years earlier, and the microcomputers based on the most-sophisticated of chips with the latest generations of operating systems are commonly referred to as **work-stations**, being a term to imply a really-beefy micro. However, the term **workstation** is also used in the context of a PC being connected to a network (see at the end of this chapter).

You must understand the relative difference between mainframe and microcomputer users with regard to operating systems. Take **multiprogramming** for example – on a **mainframe**, multiprogramming would be used for increasing the throughput of work in a way similar to that described on page 374. On a micro, although one could arrange things in the same way, **multitasking** comes into its own because you can **run different packages simultaneously**. You can draw a picture with your CAD package, then pop it into a frame in your DTP package. Without multitasking you would have to save work on disk, load up the new package and import the data in the old-fashioned way. OLE has made life even easier (see page 530).

Convergence of operating systems

The new generation of 64-bit chips such as Intel's **Pentium** (actually it's the 80586 but you can't copyright a number, therefore Intel gave it a name) and the new **RISC** chips with even more power has opened up some unique possibilities, and developed some incredible new alliances. These chips are so advanced that it is now technically possible to emulate the older machines with a speed that is so fast that the old software runs faster than it would have done on the original native hardware. In addition to this, the more-modern software can make full use of the new chip technology. If this can be done, then who is going to complain? In early 1994, Apple brought out a **Power Mac** and IBM brought out a **Power PC**. *Both* these machines are based on the Power PC chip and should be able to run each other's software at very respectable speeds, often considerably in excess of the speed that the native hardware could run them in the previous generation of machines. Intel's dominance of the PC market is therefore threatened, and several other companies are now using incredibly powerful 64-bit microprocessors to run extremely sophisticated computers. The **Pentium** and its derivations (**CISC- or so-called CRISC based technology**) versus the seemingly more-promising **RISC-based technology** (see page 91) will be a battle that will rage for several years to come.

The end result of all this development should be affordable desk-top computers which can run a whole host of **different operating systems**, including MS-DOS. **OS/2 Version 2.1** has been released as has **Windows NT**. Apple, IBM and Motorola have also developed their **Power Open system** for the Power-computer hardware described at the beginning of this section.

Object-oriented operating systems

Object Oriented Programming (OOP) is explained on page 162, and these modern and exciting techniques have been applied to operating system design in operating systems such as **OS/2 2.x**. These techniques are clearly in line with the philosophy of multiple-operating system machines. All the operating-system 'components' can be considered as **objects** in exactly the same sense as an **object** in **OOP**. Using these **objects**, a **bottom-up approach** to operating-system design can be considered. Part of OOP philosophy can be compared to having a load of bricks from which you can build up a system – very powerful objects can be built up quickly by **inheriting** the characteristics from **existing classes** of objects. This means that tried-and-tested code can be utilised *without modification*, even though you may want a slightly different function to be carried out. The unmodified object's characteristics can be inherited by a new object class, which has all the characteristics of the old class plus some other characteristics of your own choosing. Object-oriented-programming techniques are *ideal for programming very complex systems*, as the system-development time is considerably reduced, and the likelihood of success is far greater than with conventional-programming techniques. These ideas are explained in more detail using the language **C++** on page 162. One of the first object-oriented operating systems, due to be released in the mid 90s is code named **Taligent**, a joint venture between IBM and Apple, but Microsoft and others are also producing object-oriented operating systems too.

In the past, many parts of the operating system had to be written directly in the appropriate **assembly language** (see page 71). However, C has now become a standard for much system-software writing, and the latest versions of many operating systems are written in C. The more-recently introduced **C++** is now one of the de-facto standards for writing modern operating systems, other systems software and applications, and has been purpose-designed for **object-oriented-systems programming**.

You will appreciate that we have now come full circle – the microcomputer operating systems are now in some respects similar in standard to mainframe-operating-system complexity. With operating systems being extremely complex programs, these object-oriented programming techniques are the current way of coping with this mind-numbing complexity.

Microcomputer operating system principles

Having been taken through the increasingly frantic turmoil of the last two decades, we will now look at the operating system principles inside micros, exactly what it is that they do, and some examples of how recently-introduced systems carry out their tasks. However, we will *not* concentrate at all on the different types of operating systems in this microcomputers section, as these have already been covered in detail in the section on mainframe computers. As MS-DOS is still the most popular current system, MS-DOS 6.0 will be used as an example for helping to explain many of the operating-system principles. On page 370 the onion-diagram concept was introduced, and the onion diagram for MS-DOS 6.0 is shown in figure 17.11. As you can see from figure 17.11, MS-DOS 6.0 has been split up into 4 separate parts and each will now be considered in more detail.

Basic Input/Output Systems (BIOS)

How does an **operating system** in a typical micro go about **handling** the mass of data transfers involving, for example, **mice, trackballs, disks, keyboards, monitors** (screens) and **communication devices** such as the **serial port** or **network cards**? Obviously we are communicating in a complex way with a variety of different hardware **devices** at an electronic level (i.e. the hardware as shown in the centre of the onion diagram – in this case, the computer architecture based around Intel's processor.) Without an operating system it would be almost impossible for most computer users to write programs to carry out these fundamental tasks.

In most operating systems these programs have been written by the manufacturer to help the computer user control all the various **devices**. In MS-DOS, for example, these are the **device drivers** which form part of the operating system at a fundamental level, and have extended the capabilities of the BIOS (see in a moment). Each **device**, such as the **keyboard**, has a separate **device handler**. This means that from a programmer's point of view all the devices look similar, and a change in

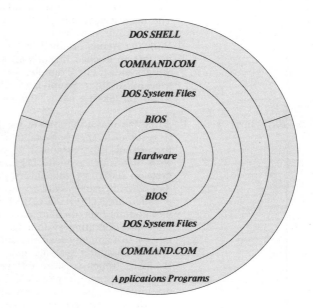

Figure 17.11

device-driver name will re-direct the data to the appropriate device in hardware terms. On an MS-DOS machine only the disks are slightly different in operation and are investigated a little further in a moment.

DOS system files

The DOS system files, supplied on disk, form part of the operating system which is loaded into the computer after it has been switched on (see booting in a moment). These files are combined with the parts of the BIOS already in ROM and RAM (see page 265), to form a much-more comprehensive operating system. Utilities then add to the capability of the operating system still further. These and other types of files considerably extend what the operating system can do.

Booting the system

Whenever a computer system is switched on, it needs to follow a **programmed sequence of events** such as **checking that all the hardware is working and searching for any special start-up instructions**. It is the job of that part of the operating system permanently resident inside the computer (in ROM) to make sure that *other* parts of the operating system are **loaded** into memory and **started up** properly.

Getting the computer started up after switching on is called **booting the system** or more simply, **booting**. It comes from the term 'to pull yourself up by your own boot straps', which means building up your capability from virtually nothing by using what you know already to increase your capability yet further. This is exactly what is happening inside a computer during the switch-on sequence, because more-complex parts of the operating system are being loaded in by the other parts, thus creating a more-sophisticated system that is capable of doing very much more. At the instant you switch on your computer it can do very little – almost nothing at all. After running the boot files and loading the operating system, it has been transformed into a powerful and useful system. It has pulled itself up by its own **boot straps.**

There are a couple of different philosophies around at the moment. The first is to supply *all* of the operating system on a **ROM** chip, as is used for example, in the **Archimedes** computers and many portables too. This method has the advantage that no RAM is taken up with storing operating system software – some of which is quite large and could run to several Mbytes or more for the very latest systems. It is also useful in portable machines because the computer is ready to go after switching on. Nevertheless, the disadvantage is that future upgrades to the operating system require that the set of ROMs be replaced – not a job for the average computer user, and more expensive than the alternative methods. Even so, bug fixes are sometimes supplied on disk to fix bugs even when the entire operating system *is* stored in ROM. These modules are put into RAM and become part of the new operating system.

The second, more-common method, is to supply a very small part of the **operating system** in **ROM**, then supply the rest of the operating system on **disk** (which can be installed on an internal hard disk for convenience if required). This is the technique used by most manufacturers and that used on mainframe computers too. The biggest advantage is that upgrades to the system are trivial – a new disk is all that is required to iron out any bugs or provide a more-recent version of the system. With the trends outlined in the first part of the microcomputer section, you should be able to deduce that it's an advantage to be able to run different types of operating system. For example, Unix may be required for one job, while MS-DOS is used for another. Supplying both systems on disk makes this sort of flexibility easier to obtain making use of the same computer hardware.

Customisation of the system

After the operating system has been loaded then the computer is ready to be able to respond to the user's input in the normal way, but in addition to this, it is useful to customise the computer to your personal requirements. For example, you might wish that your favourite DTP system be automatically loaded, together with a few **desktop tools** like calculators, or clocks and calendars for displaying the time and date. This is usually carried out by what is called an **auto-boot** file. In MS-DOS this is called an AUTOEXEC.BAT file, but CONFIG.SYS plays a major part too. Such files contain lists of commands to instruct the computer to go through a set sequence after the operating system has been loaded and fully installed. It saves the user having to manually load the software each time the machine is switched on.

Most computer systems make use of **battery-backed-up RAM** (also called **CMOS RAM**) in which to store different **default** conditions for the machine at switch on. This enables a variety of different customised functions to be carried out so that the machines can be tailored exactly to each user's requirements. However, this function can also sometimes be carried out by default parameters being stored on a disk file.

Command.COM

Once the operating system has been booted satisfactorily, there needs to be some way for the user to communicate with it. Part of the COMMAND.COM file is the **command interpreter** for MS-DOS, so called, because it **interprets commands** typed in by the user. (Other parts of **COMMAND.COM** run the boot file (**AUTOEXEC.BAT**) and provide extensions to the BIOS). A prompt (A> or C> being typical in MS-DOS), indicates that the computer is ready to accept an operating-system command from the keyboard. 'DIR', for example, would list the files in the currently-selected directory, or '**DOS-SHELL**', would start the shell (see in a moment). In fact, not all commands are held in RAM after boot up, and **FORMAT** is an example of an **external command** which is classed as a **utility**. Typing a command such as 'FORMAT A:', for example, after loading the appropriate program from disk, causes the appropriate operating system sub-programs to be run which carries out the formatting process of a floppy disk drive A, or returns an error if it is not possible to do so – you may have forgotten to put the disk in the drive! Saving and loading programs would be two other common examples of typical operating system interaction with the user via the command processor.

Simplified view of disk operations

When a file is saved to disk, for example, it is the operating system which has to carry out the tasks needed to accomplish this operation. The **operating system** will analyse the filename you have given it, and assuming a hierarchical directory structure (see page 356), that the filename is valid, and that no file with the same name exists within the target directory, then the operating system will add your chosen name to the list of files within the target directory. Note that this is *not enough* to cause the actual data to be saved on disk, it is just a new label which is added into a table called the **File Allocation Table** or **FAT**. Next the FAT has to be checked for information regarding which **cluster**/s is/are ready to receive the data, and which **tracks** and **sectors** on the **disk** (see page 271) make up these clusters. If these operations are successful, then the appropriate data is transferred from RAM via the BIOS (see page 389). As many clusters as are necessary can be allocated provided that the disk is not full. When the **file-writing** operation has been successfully completed, the **FAT** is updated to prevent overwriting this information when the next save operation is carried out. Reading the data back is similar in principle with the **directory** and **filename**, and information contained in the **FAT** being used to retrieve the data. These ideas can be seen in figure 17.12.

The diagram is a *simplified* view of what actually happens in a typical system. It takes no account of the many things that could go wrong when carrying out operations like these in practice. Such errors might be a recently-corrupted disk surface or an error in the transmitted data (see page 510). In addition to this we have not

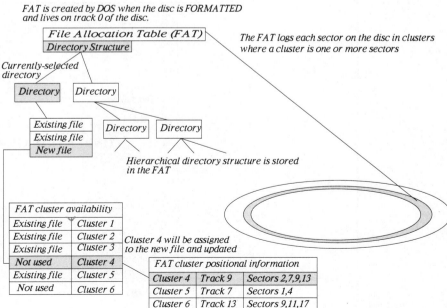

Figure 17.12

covered aspects such as, 'Has the user attempting to gain access to the file got sufficient privilege to do so?' – a real problem in multi-user mainframe and network-operating-system environments.

Other types of error might be caused by mistakes in the user programs. For example, some **assembler code** (see page 87) attempting to address non-existent RAM, or a **Prolog program** attempting an **arithmetical operation** which results in **overflow** (see page 44). Even when running an application program which generates user-friendly messages, it is the **operating system**'s job to pass the appropriate information over to the application program. A real operating system would have to cope with all of this and much much more. By now you should be appreciating what a complex task it is to design modern operating systems!

In addition to the BIOS and Command.COM etc. there are many **utilities** such as the formatting program already mentioned, others are available for producing **statistics** such as **disk size** or the **amount of RAM** available etc. Useful utilities are also supplied by third-party software writers.

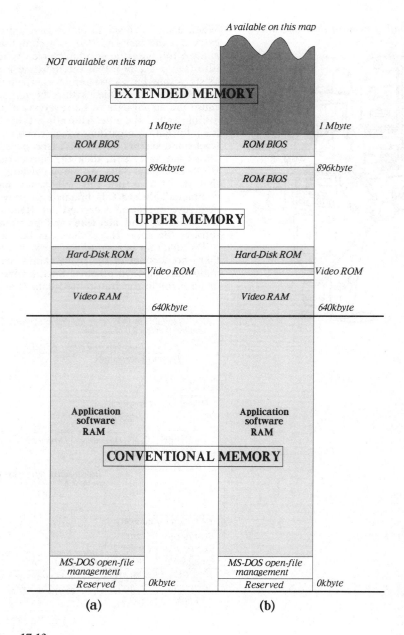

Figure 17.13

The DOS shell

Until recently, typing in terse commands was the only way to communicate with the operating system. However, with the latest versions (MS-DOS 4.x +) there is an option to load a **shell** which gives users of MS-DOS a much more user friendly **GUI**. Just as on the Apple Mac, DOS users can now see folders which represent directories, and point with the mouse to carry out fundamental operations. The shell also provides a multitasking environment, which means, at last, that DOS is interacting in a way which is similar to all of the other common **WIMP**-based operating systems.

Memory maps

We have already seen that in all modern microcomputers some of the **memory (ROM)** is taken up with parts of the operating system. Much of the **BIOS**, for example, is usually permanently resident in ROM.

Other parts of the **operating system** can be loaded and placed in whatever locations are decided upon by the manufacturer (within available **RAM** limitations). Software like the **disk controller** or **display adaptor software,** for example, will need to go somewhere, and memory is also needed for important essentials such as the **stack** (see page 84) or **printer spooler** (see page 373) if one has been implemented. Anything that is added such as a **network interface card** must also have an appropriate part of the memory allocated to the **network operating system software** (see page 396).

To prevent the chaotic situation whereby **applications** and **utilities** could overwrite important areas of operating-system memory, it's necessary for all those concerned to have an *exact* idea of where all the operating system and applications software is to be located inside the memory of the computer system. This is accomplished by means of a **memory map,** and a typical one for the earlier versions of MS-DOS is shown in figure 17.13(a). The first 640Kbyte is referred to as 'Conventional memory' and the remainder up to the 1Mbyte-processor limit is often called 'Upper memory' as can be seen from figure 17.13.

Expanded memory was the first technique used to get over the 640kbyte MS-DOS barrier, but this was a bodge – a 64kbyte block called a page frame could be switched in and out in 16Kbyte sections into an area of upper memory. Later versions of MS-DOS used extended memory, which is real useable RAM beyond the 1Mbyte-earlier-processor limit. This **memory map** is used by version 5.0 and 6.0 of MS-DOS and at last makes full use of the 386 and 486 processor's capabilities. The expanded memory map for this system is a simple extension as shown in figure 17.14(b). However, many software fixes had to be done to keep some older software 'happy' and 'thinking' that it was still running under the old memory maps.

Note that different operating systems will obviously have different memory-map layouts within the same computer hardware. **NETBIOS**, for example, would be needed if the PC was to be operated on a **LAN** (see page 487).

Cache memory

As is explained on page 265, there are two main types of semiconductor (RAM) memory. **Dynamic RAM** (a wee **DRAM**!) is fast (current access times are in the order of 70 nsec 10^{-9} sec) and is the relatively inexpensive memory used for the vast majority of RAM. There are many different-speed RAM chips, but the faster they

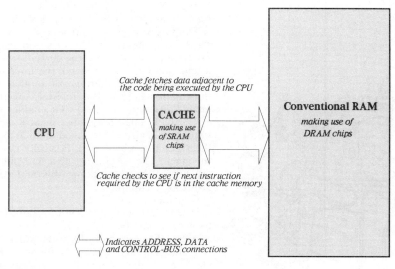

Figure 17.14

are the more expensive they become. However, **Static RAM** (or **SRAM**) which does not need to be refreshed, is faster still, (current access times about 20 nsec) and can be used to maximum advantage if placed inbetween the main memory (DRAM) and the processor as shown in figure 17.14. When used in this way, the memory in between the processor and main memory is called **cache memory**. SRAM is not used for all of the RAM because it is more expensive than even the most expensive dynamic RAM. Although today's memory chips, byte for byte are a lot less expensive that they used to be, the goal posts keep moving due to the increasing expectations of the users of microcomputers, and the increasing power available from the microprocessor chips. A few years ago 1Mbyte of RAM was acceptable. Today 16Mbytes is not uncommon, tomorrow – who knows? Therefore, RAM cost is still an issue.

If you analysed exactly what a typical processor spent its time doing, then you would probably find that much of the time would be taken up with execution of a **linear sequence** of **machine-code instructions**, or in dealing with instructions which are near to the ones currently being processed. With the speed of today's processors the time taken to get an instruction from memory, even though it is only a tiny fraction of a second, significantly holds up the processor's ability to get things done. Therefore, if the **most-likely-used instructions** are held in **cache memory**, then the time taken for the processor to act upon these instructions is very much reduced, due to the **static RAM**'s faster speed. In the majority of cases the increase in speed over a machine without **cache** can be very significant, and most modern microcomputer operating systems and computer architectures now have cache memory as a standard feature. A typical size of **external cache** (see in a moment), on a microcomputer might be anything between about 8k and 256 kbyte.

In the last two paragraphs we have been talking of cache mounted on the mother board (i.e. main-processor board) of the computer. However, you should also appreciate that the same techniques are used to even better effect (due to the incredibly close proximity) inside the actual microprocessors. For example, the top-of-the-range Intel's 80486 chip has its own 8k of cache memory *inside* the microprocessor itself. Because the paths between the **internal cache** and the **main processor registers** (see page 53) are so small (just a few mm or less), this memory is even faster than the **external cache** referred to above.

Simple interrupts

Interrupts have been considered from a **mainframe perspective** on page 378. However, they are extensively used on micros too, although *not (yet!)* the more-complex preemptive types mentioned on page 378. Here we consider the principles of simple interrupts on a typical microcomputer system.

The CPU will normally be happily getting on with its business of running programs until it is rudely interrupted by some peripheral device. It literally has to stop what it is doing and find out what device is causing the interrupt. It will then have to jump to the routine which has been written to handle this particular interrupt and then, when the interrupting device has been satisfied, the CPU will get back to what it was originally doing.

We shall start by having a look at how the CPU of a small computer system handles interrupts in the way described above.

The interrupt may occur at any time. Therefore the processor could be in the middle of any operation. The processor will finish executing the current machine code operation and then stop the current task. As each machine code operation takes only a few millionths of a second, the interrupting device can usually wait that long.

Inside the CPU there is yet another register called the **interrupt register.** It is the information held in this register, together with the information from the **interrupt enable/disable** (see later) that enables the CPU to take the desired action.

The CPU must remember what it was doing and so the program counter and all important registers are saved in an area of memory reserved for such purposes called the stack (see chapter 5). Basically most of the CPU registers can be pushed on to the stack. The CPU must now find out which device is causing the interrupt. There are several ways of doing this and one way is to use what is called a **vectored interrupt** technique.

Consider figure 17.15.

In this particular case the **interrupting device** supplies a number that is then added to a fixed number as shown in the figure. This combined number then forms the address of the memory location which contains the jump address where the routine to handle the interrupt can be found. This may sound a mouthful but it is a particularly clever way of enabling the interrupt handling routines to be placed anywhere in memory.

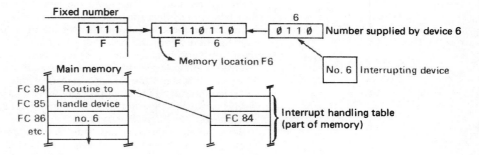

Figure 17.15

The numbers inside the memory locations which are used as pointers to the places where the interrupt handling routines can be found are called **vectors**. In computing, a vector is simply a pointer, i.e. an address that will be used to point to some other area in memory. This is why this method of handling interrupts is known as **vectored interrupt handling**. Consider a simple example:

Let us suppose that we have five devices that could cause an interrupt. We therefore need five different interrupt vectors. Let us also assume that these vectors will be stored in memory locations 1001 to 1005 inclusive as shown in figure 17.16.

Let us also assume that each interrupting device will supply the number 1, 2, 3, 4 or 5. Now suppose device 3 has caused the interrupt, then 3 is combined with the base address of the vectors (1000) to make 1003. The program counter is therefore set to 1003.

The computer will now fetch, decode and execute the instruction at location 1003. This is a **jump** instruction that points the computer to the routine which will handle interrupting device number 3. The interrupt is now being handled and at the end of the interrupt routine a **return from interrupt** instruction will be encountered. This will cause the CPU to return to its original task that it had left when the interrupt occurred. This is achieved by popping all the registers off the stack and restoring the original contents of the program counter.

The interrupt has now been serviced and the computer has resumed its original task and is now ready for another interrupt should one occur.

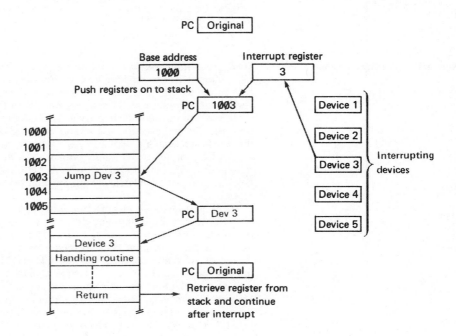

Figure 17.16

One of the ideal things about the above method is that if the interrupting device, and hence the interrupt handling routing, have to be changed, all that is necessary is to change the contents of a single memory location (the pointer) to point to the new location where the new interrupt handling routine can be found. The system is therefore very versatile and easy to update should its needs change.

From reading the above it may seem that servicing an interrupt is a long process. However, this is not the case. An interrupt can usually be serviced in a few millionths of a second. Indeed the computer can service an interrupt so quickly that the operator who is using the computer will not even notice that the program he or she is currently working on has been interrupted.

Some small computers have interrupts happening many times each second. For example, it is possible to organize the keyboard so that whenever a character is typed in, the processor is interrupted to deal with it.

Handling errors

Undertaking an advanced computing course will certainly bring home the fact that computers go wrong quite frequently, especially when inexperienced users are experimenting. Therefore, much effort goes into aspects of operating-system design which try to prevent a complete crash of the system in many preventable circumstances. It would be silly, for example, if a **disk-sector error** on a floppy caused a **major crash** with loss of all data, when the operating system could have detected this, **flagged** the error to the user, then returned control to the user who could rectify the situation by changing the disk, and finally re-saving the data. There is usually an enormous number of conditions which are intercepted by the operating system and appropriate error messages are produced. However, occasionally, even the operating system gets 'confused' and a fatal crash might take place.

Errors can sometimes be **detected** *and* **corrected** by the operating system. For example, by using a method such as **checksums** or **parity** (see page 510) an error might have been detected during the transmission of some data from memory to a disk. A re-try could be requested and the re-transmitted data might pass the check and be saved successfully. The computer user would probably be blissfully unaware that an error had even occurred. However, if after trying several times the transmitted data is still in error, then a likely **hardware fault** has been detected (for example, the dog has started to chew up the disk cables behind your desk!) and an **error message** would then be generated by the operating system.

Operating systems are so complex that it's not possible to make sure that every single eventuality is catered for. All that can be done is to strive towards a 100% perfect system – but never actually achieve it. Nevertheless, the reliability of today's operating systems is very high, with **real-time control systems** being among the most reliable (see page 586), (e.g. computer control of aircraft etc. reaching reliabilities in excess of 99.9999%).

Network operating systems

Having common operating systems on stand-alone computers is a tremendous advantage when it comes to transferring data between different machines, as the disk on one computer may be read by other computers – assuming that the same type and version of the operating system is used. Even though the single-user-microcomputer enthusiast might be able to survive independently at home, in business and education, the sharing of information and other resources is essential. As the concept of the Earth becoming a global village comes ever closer, good communications, and especially computer communications will be an increasingly important part of business and leisure activities. Both physical and **radio networks** (see page 506) are now beginning to play an increasingly important role in the **distributed processing** environment.

There is little point storing hundreds of copies of the same application software on local hard disk inside many different **PCs**, if the same software can be got quickly from a **file server** on a **local network**. The ability to share expensive resources such as **colour laser printers** via a **printer server,** a **modem** via an appropriate **modem server** or to share **multiple stacked CD-ROM databases** (see page 561), and the unquestionable advantage of **electronic mail** communications between all machines make networking a vital ingredient for any company or educational institution which has more than just a few microcomputers. Also, and just as important, is the fact that microcomputers are being used as intelligent terminals to mainframes, or using **LANs**, **MANs** and **WANs** to connect to mainframes which act as information providers. **Network topology**, **hardware** and **communications protocols** are considered in great detail in the networks chapter on page 487. However, the need for part of the **operating system** to be able to deal with network communications is an obvious one, and will be dealt with here for completeness of this operating-systems chapter.

DOS-based workstations

As we have used MS-DOS for the main examples in the micro-operating system section, we will again show how an MS-DOS-based machine can be used on a network from an operating system perspective. The networking software used in these examples will be Novell's Netware, because this looks like being the most popular choice in the mid 90s for linking IBMs, Apple Macs, Sun, DEC and Hewlett Packard workstations etc, and will also support Acorn's Archimedes and RISC PCs if running on the Ethernet system (see page 509).

If using a **DOS-based machine** as a **workstation** on a **network** then it is necessary to have some additional hardware called a **Network Interface Card** (**NIC**), and some additional **network software**. MS-DOS is then booted up (see page 390) at the work-station from an internal hard disk, or a local floppy disk, or from the **file server** on the network *if* the Network Interface Card has a remote boot **PROM** (see page 265) fitted. On early versions of DOS, this network software stole 66k of the valuable 640kbyte of RAM that was available! (see memory map in figure 17.13), but on MS-DOS versions 5.0 and later, this is no longer the case.

You can imagine the **network operating system software** as **another layer** in the **onion diagram** of figure 17.11, and it is also referred to as a **shell**, just like the bolt-on windows options. Two programs called IPX.COM and NETx.COM are the programs that have to be loaded after DOS has booted up. They are usually run by the boot file AUTOEXEC.BAT (see page 390). These network-software programs contain the information that is needed by the workstation to communicate with the network. IPX.COM, for example, contains the data necessary to implement **layers 3 and 4 of the ISO-OSI model** (see page 506). The NIC contains the drivers necessary to interface with **level 2** of the **OSI model**. NETx.COM is another program that interacts with DOS by running on top of DOS to create a **network operating system environment** for the user of the workstation (i.e. the user can then make use of the network as another disk-filing system).

It is to be appreciated that we now have several places on which to save data – local hard disk, floppy disk and the network. Conventionally, drives A to E are reserved for the local hard and floppy disk, while drives F to Z are usually reserved for the network or CD-ROM drives. Once set up in this way the network can often be transparent to the user of the system, but it should be obvious that certain **logging-on** procedures must be gone through before having access to information on a network that is common to perhaps hundreds of computers. It is usual to have to supply a **user ID** and a **password** to gain access to the system, and problems of this nature are covered in great detail in the networks chapter.

Real-time operating systems

In the operating systems considered so far it did not matter too much if a job was delayed or if a task was carried out two seconds later rather than sooner. However, there are situations in which such a delay would be unacceptable, or even fatal. A typical but deadly example of a **real-time operating system** would be found in the embedded processor in a guided missile. Suppose, for example, that you happen to be on the deck of a warship which unfortunately is in the path of an incoming missile. You may have just 15 seconds before impact, and you launch your anti-missile missile guided by the real-time operating system. The missile just launched would have to lock onto the incoming missile and destroy it. You would not appreciate the electronics inside the missile dithering for a few seconds while the operating system decides what to do!

The above example is rather drastic, but illustrates a typical example of the situation in which real-time operating systems are used. However, **real-time does not necessarily mean fast**, and although it is essential to use a real-time system where speed is of the essence, as long as the operating system can respond and process the appropriate data before some outside process could suffer, then you have what is literally a real time system. Suppose, for example, that a computer system was controlling the amount of liquid in a tank. Suppose also that the water valve must be turned off within a 1 minute period of a signal being transmitted from the **sensor** (see page 580). If the computer system responds within say 45 seconds, and the water is safely turned off, then this is a real time system, even though it is painfully slow. However, it must be said that most real-time systems *do* refer to the systems where a fast response is needed.

The majority of real-time operating systems go hand-in-hand with **process control** such as missile guidance or controlling a chemical factory etc. Therefore, these systems will be considered in much more detail in chapter 25 on process control.

Exercise 17.2

1. Explain how more-powerful microprocessor chips have had an enormous impact on the way that micro computer operating systems have developed.

2. Explain how **multitasking** would probably be used in the context of a single-user micro computer operating system.

3. It is now possible to run **different operating systems** on the same micro. Why is this an added advantage over a single operating system?

4. What is meant by an **object-oriented operating system** and why are they becoming important?

5. What is a **BIOS** in terms of a typical micro operating system?

6. **Boot files** are often used to start up a computer. Explain the function of the boot file and why some manufacturers do not commit their entire operating system to ROM.

7. Explain how a typical micro operating system would handle saving a file to floppy disk.

8. What is meant by a **memory map** in connection with a micro computer operating system and why is it so important?

9. Explain the function of an **interrupt** and how an interrupt may be serviced in a typical microcomputer environment.

10. **Cache memory** can be used to increase the amount of work done by a computer in a given time. Explain the function of cache and how it achieves its aim.

11. The **WIMP environment** is much more user-friendly. Why?

12. After booting the operating system it is often useful to **customise** a computer to the exact requirements of a particular user. How is this done and why is this useful?

13. How can an operating system detect that an **error** has occurred when going about its normal tasks? Give an example of an error that could be detected by the operating system.

14. If a micro computer is to be used as a **workstation on a network** then vital software and hardware must usually be added to the system. What two things are normally needed over and above the basic operating system and hardware of the micro computer?

15. Over the last ten years one or two operating systems have dominated the market. Why is this so and why is the situation rapidly changing in the 90s?

16. What **extra precautions** are necessary when a network operating system has been installed in a micro computer connected to a network?

17. Why is it possible for a novice user to not appreciate that an operating system exists inside a computer, even though the operating system is probably the most important piece of software?

18. What problems are encountered in attempting to transfer data between two different computers running different operating systems? How could a network help in overcoming some of these problems?

19. The early micro computer operating systems fitted inside a few kbytes of RAM, but some of the latest operating systems take up many Mbytes. Why is it not possible to guarantee that these complex operating systems found inside today's computers work properly? What do the companies do to help out customers when faults are found?

20. An enormous amount of progress has been made in operating systems design in the last ten years. What do you think might happen in the next ten?

End of chapter summary

- An **operating system** is a **complex piece of software** needed to harness the power of a computer system and make it *much* easier to use.
- **Onion diagrams** conveniently display relationships between the operating system and other software (and hardware) in pictorial form.
- **Batch processing systems** used on mainframes were the first operating systems, and are still popular today for running **batches of jobs.**
- **Job-Control Languages** (**JCL**s) control batch-operating systems.
- Operating systems help **allocate resources, decide on priorities** and do much housekeeping such as helping to produce **logs** and **accounts**.
- A **multiprogramming operating system** can run **more than one program 'simultaneously'**. Literally simultaneously if there are **multiple processors**.
- **Multitasking** is the term used to denote different tasks being run by the same program, e.g. two users using the same word processor on a mainframe. However, it's also often used to mean **multiprogramming**, especially on microcomputers.
- **Multiprogramming** is *equally applicable* to **batch** or **interactive** modes such as **time sharing**.

■ Efficient **scheduling** is necessary in a multiprogramming environment.

■ Assignment of **priorities to tasks** helps manage multiprogramming environments by building up efficient **queues of tasks** waiting to be processed, but **concurrency** problems can lead to **deadlock** or **starvation**.

■ **Interrupts** can have **different levels of priority** *assigned by the* **operating system** or **hardware**. These help manage the computer in efficient ways.

■ Large amounts of RAM need efficient **memory management** and this can be achieved by fixed or preferably **variable partitioning**. The most modern systems **dynamically allocate memory** or use a **virtual memory** environment.

■ **Virtual memory** means that jobs can be **partially stored in RAM**. It gives the effect of having *more* RAM than is physically available.

■ **DMA** enables a specialised piece of hardware to carry out data transfer between memory and peripherals.

■ **Buffering** helps to match the speed of the slower peripheral devices to the fast speed of the main processors. **Double buffering** is normally used.

■ **Front-end processors** are used in large computer systems to help deal with the complex communication problems with the mainframe computer.

■ **Distributed processing** is becoming increasingly important due to the drastically increased power of micro computers and the increasingly common and powerful networks. Sometimes different computers on the network can share the same task.

■ **Microcomputer operating systems** have become increasingly sophisticated due to the enormous power increase of the microprocessors.

■ **MS-DOS** is the *most popular* micro computer operating system to date, but many new operating systems are now in a position to become the dominant force of the 90s.

■ **Object-oriented operating systems** are now being written in C++ to make these incredibly complex systems more comprehensible and easy to manage.

■ The new generation of microcomputers (**64-bit microprocessors**) are now becoming so powerful that older operating systems can be run under **emulation** at speeds in excess of those available on the older purpose-built hardware.

■ **Boot files** are used to get the **main operating system up and running**, and to **customise** the computer for individual use.

■ **Memory maps** are used to show how the operating system and other software is distributed throughout RAM.

■ **Cache memory** (fast **SRAM**) is used to increase the speed of instructions currently or about to be executed.

■ The **operating system** can be used to **detect a variety of errors**, some of which it is possible to correct. Even fatal errors should be handled such that the computer does not crash if possible.

■ **Networking capability** may be added to a micro by adding a **network interface card** and some **network operating system software**.

■ **Shells** may be added in the onion diagram to show how network or windows operating systems may be added on to existing systems.

■ A **real-time operating system** is one that can respond at a speed which is sufficient to process data required by an external source.

18 Systems analysis and design

Introduction

This chapter is **essential reading** – not only because of its paramount importance in developing your overall understanding of systems in general – but also because it contains vital material which you should read *before* starting any serious work on **computer-science-based projects**. *It covers the art of developing systems* – either by using a range of application packages and utilities – including the use of 4GLs, SQLs and Macro languages, or by writing your own software in either high-level or low-level languages. This chapter enhances and extends the material covered in chapter 7 where **structured analysis and design** techniques were first encountered. It *assumes that you have already gained a detailed knowledge* of **structured-programming techniques, Gantt charts, PERT charts** and a whole range of other **structure-diagram principles**. It will *also assume* that you have a general knowledge of the facilities that are available in typical languages such as **BASIC**, **Pascal** or **C++** etc. – these high-level language principles are covered in chapter 6. If you apply the techniques learnt in this chapter to your project work, you will increase the likelihood of a successful project and thus maximise your chances of getting a good grade.

What is a system?

Throughout this book you will encounter many different types of system – for example, microcomputer systems, electronic systems, control systems or information systems. In this chapter we will look at systems in a much broader context – indeed, entire organisations can be regarded as a system. In business and industry computers are used to help control, model, inform, analyse, and act upon all types of information from the shop floor to the boardroom. We therefore take a macro view of systems in this chapter – which can model anything from small companies via large institutions to multi-national organisations. However, these grandiose views will often be tempered with sound advice applicable to computer-science-based projects at advanced level, as this is often the only opportunity which students have of demonstrating their systems analysis and design knowledge in some detail.

Systems analysis methods

Systems analysis and systems design have changed considerably over the last few years. This has been necessary for a variety of reasons, not least of which is that computer systems have now become so complex, that new methods are needed to make these projects more manageable, especially during the software-development phases. The tools available to help deal with both system-design and system-management problems have considerably improved, and the tools to help debug complex systems are now much more sophisticated. In fact, the testing, debugging, documentation and customer-support phases have all assumed much greater prominence in the new order of things. Systems analysis and design is also intimately tied up with what's become known as software engineering. **Software engineering** is the term now often used to denote a whole cycle of software development – being made up of the **analysis**, **testing, debugging** and **documentation** phases, and this is considered in more detail later in this chapter.

   Systems analysis and design deals with the problems of helping us to understand how to analyse and design general solutions to major projects in an effective way – helping to understand how to apply computer techniques to the solution of these problems if possible – helping to manage teams of people who are working on the same project – and to nurture the project through the testing, debugging and documentation phases until the final implementation phase has been achieved. However, even this is not the end – customers expect continued support for expensive products – it's part of the job of **systems analysts** and **software engineers** to ensure that the software and hardware can change to meet the ever-growing needs of the customer as time progresses. Systems analysis and design is all this – and much more!

The classical methods developed for analysis and design involve a set of rules to follow which are known as the '**system life cycle**'. Although these 'rules' are now open to much-greater flexibility (see in a moment), they still form a suitable starting point for getting a *general idea* of how major-projects can be approached. A typical system life cycle, together with some examples of the sort of activities which take place at each stage of the cycle is shown in the following list.

---

(1) Detailed definition of the problem
Without a detailed definition of the problem we are trying to solve, people are often unsure of what it is they are trying to achieve.

(2) A feasibility study
A preliminary investigation is essential to determine whether a project is technically and economically feasible. Some projects may not be suitable for computer solution – it's best to realise this before a great deal of work has been started!

(3) Collecting information about the proposed system
Assuming that the project is feasible, much information needs to be collected – the system's requirements can then be determined in more detail, and a more detailed estimate of likely costs is undertaken.

(4) Analysis
An analysis of the problems using techniques such as the top-down approach, and making use of other structured methods now follows.

(5) Design of the system
Detailed design and coding (if necessary) of all the sub-sections of the project – followed by testing and debugging.

(6) Implementation and evaluation
Installing and testing the overall system, further debugging and testing until it all works as expected. Staff training takes place during this phase.

(7) Maintenance
Making sure that the system continues to function correctly, and correcting bugs that may come to light after extensive use in the field.

Sound project advice!

Too rigorous an interpretation of some of these rules has led to certain problems, and this was reflected quite clearly in the ways in which many computer-science projects at 'A' level have been tackled in the past. For example, after the detailed specification was developed this was often set in a tablet of stone. The success of the entire project was then measured in relation to this original spec.

In the real world things are very different – customers' needs change as projects are being developed, and good ideas – often evident only after considerable work has been done on a project, are used to *modify the original specification* if this proves to be more efficient, cost effective or of great benefit to all concerned. This more-flexible approach has proved to be effective, especially in a modern and constantly-changing computing environment. Unfortunately, pupils at school or college could easily abuse such a system – unscrupulous students might think that they can modify virtually any aspect of their specification *if* they find some parts of their project to be too difficult, tedious or uninteresting. Nevertheless, putting laziness and lack of motivation aside for one moment – it *is* far more efficient to make **agreed modifications** to specifications whose outcome results in an overall improvement to the system. Modern techniques now reflect this philosophy.

Some of the basic techniques have already been started in chapter 7, but you must remember that the *whole point* of **structured programming** and the use of **structure diagrams** and the like is to provide a methodical way of working which will *keep errors to a minimum*, and hopefully work towards the elimination of errors altogether. Having worked through the structured-analysis sections of chapter 7, you often get some students who are impressed with the methods discussed, but then go back to their old habits of trying to develop algorithms inside their heads! For students working on their own this is often possible – but it's *not* desirable.

The very nature of the majority of work tackled on computer-science courses, is, of necessity, quite simple compared to the standards of project tackled in industry. You should note that this is not intended to be a derisory comment, but is a statement of fact. It is only when you have spent hours each day for months or even years working on systems with a team of other programmers that you can begin to understand the need for **good documentation, communication, consistency** and **style**. You *must* view the **software-engineering approach** used in this chapter with the above ideas and comments borne in mind, or it may all seem such a pointless exercise. At the other end of the spectrum are those students who meticulously apply what they have learnt to a comprehensive analysis of their projects. This professional approach has often resulted in near-perfect and in some cases absolutely perfect (100%) grades being awarded to these students for the project component of their advanced level courses. You would do well to bear these facts in mind.

Alternative approaches

Other philosophies exist too – **prototyping**, for example, is one of these alternative approaches. Sometimes it's very difficult to specify exactly what's required. This might sound a little strange, but customers often don't know what they want until someone shows them something to get their minds on the right track. This is not too surprising as many customers are *not* computing experts. One problem with the classic-system-life-cycle approach is that it takes a long time to get anything tangible from the

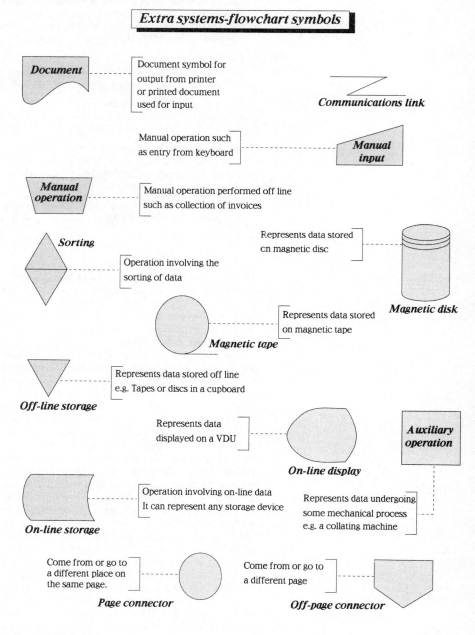

Figure 18.1

system which the customer can actually look at and make some valid contributions. Therefore, if prototyping is used, some front ends can be 'knocked up' quickly and dummy files written to act as a simple simulation of what the real system might be like. If the customer can then see something concrete in front of them, they can then start making good suggestions and the systems can be further developed and refined. Prototyping can help the experts too – it's not only computer-illiterate people who don't know what they want! Prototyping can also be used on sub-problems.

Systems flowchart symbols

Before starting on a large systems-analysis example, you will need to add some further flowchart symbols to your 'flowchart-symbol toolbox'.

You have already studied a range of **flowchart symbols** shown in figure 7.1, and the extra **systems-flowchart symbols** shown in figure 18.1 can be used in addition to the basic symbols. You can buy special templates in the shops which help you to draw the appropriate shapes in your notes, or you can set up a library in your CAD package (if none exists already) which you can then use to draw the diagrams for your project write up.

A simple example

These symbols are very easy to use, and make certain types of processes very easy to understand. Let's suppose that we wish to describe pictorially the processes whereby data is manually entered at the keyboard from a document, validated (see page 231), and then saved to disk if no errors are found, but a report generated if errors during this validation process occur. A systems flowchart for these operations could be as shown in figure 18.2.

The standard symbols used for systems diagrams are often enhanced by the users of the systems, and the increase in flexibility mentioned earlier can certainly be applied to these systems diagrams too. Users will often invent extra notation *if* this helps to make the processes more clear. For example, if a smoke sensor forms part of the diagram, then why not draw a picture of a smoke sensor? The output from the device can still be shown to activate whatever procedure by an appropriate arrow, and a picture of this device will make the diagrams easier to understand. In a similar way, networks of microcomputer terminals are often shown with 3d-images of real computers. In short, if you can make the concepts clearer by the addition of a few other symbols then it's often a good idea to do this. The advent of clip-art libraries has made this far easier to do than has been the case in the past.

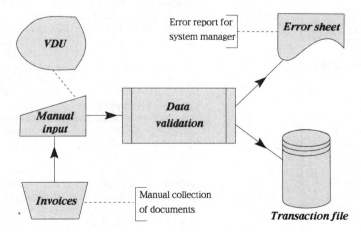

Figure 18.2

The computerisation of Corpus Crumbly College library

Systems analysis and design are most easily covered by considering an example which should be familiar to most students – that of computerising a school, college or university library. This example has been chosen because the ideas being discussed, and the aims to be achieved should not be alien to any student – all have experienced using a library – but most have probably not analysed the possible computerisation of such a large system in detail, or considered the repercussions which it could have on the organisation of an entire educational establishment! We will now consider such a computerised library, and use it to discuss systems' principles in considerable detail. But first let's look at some background information.

A complete systems analysis example

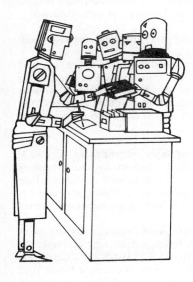

Corpus Crumbly, a large, long established and *very* traditional college has a fine library with a massive collection of just over 350,000 books, many of which can be lent out to the students and staff of the college. The library has had a fine reputation for several hundred years, but has recently lost much credibility due to antiquated methods and organisation. A manual booking system involving filling in handwritten cards and placing them (preferably in the right place!) within a cardboard index inside a shoe box is currently being used. Recent losses of books have been at an unacceptably high level, and books and periodicals are often mislaid due to the ineffective system for borrowing and returns. The system of searching for books in the library using a manual card index is also a slow and tedious process, and students and staff spend many unproductive hours searching for information. The old librarian who knew where most things could be found has, unfortunately, passed away. Some prominent academics have abandoned the library altogether in favour of the easier-to-use library systems elsewhere, and this has been a blow to the pride of the college.

A new librarian has just been appointed who wishes to drag Corpus Crumbly into the 21st century. She intends to do this by introducing new technologies into all aspects of the library in which it can be shown to have proven benefit to both the staff and students. Some academic staff are sceptical of any new technology, and see the introduction of computers into the library as an unacceptable intrusion into a seat of learning which has served the students well for the last 400 years! Nevertheless, the new principle of the college is embarrassed by the way in which the Corpus Crumbly library is run compared to other similar colleges, most of which have already gone some way to installing new technology. *You* are to be placed in the role of **systems analyst** who has been charged with the task of upgrading the library and steering the project through to a *successful* conclusion – best of luck – you will need it!

Student activities

At frequent intervals during this library-computerisation example **you will be asked to stop and think about various points** *before* **going on to read the next section**. *If you take time out to do this you will gain a lot from the experience* and start to realise the thought processes needed for good systems analysis. It's very useful practice for your 'A' Level projects too, as it mirrors the correct procedures.

The **classical system life cycle** will be used as the basis for investigation of this problem, so we will start to define the **information requirements** of the system.

Definition of the problem

This is obviously computerisation of the library – however, there's a little more to it than this! What do we mean by computerisation of the library? Part of the problem involved loss of books, therefore, efficient **security** and **booking systems** are of obvious paramount importance. If you are to use a computer for borrowing and returns, then you will need a **database of the books contained within the library** – a massive and expensive undertaking. Most modern books have **bar codes** on them, but Corpus Crumbly will obviously have many books which are too old for this form of coding – the staff would rightly object to having a bar code stuck onto an original work! Don't forget also that there are *other resources* in the library besides books – **periodicals, newspapers**, articles written by academic staff, specialist college literature produced in house and also **videos, CDs** and **cassettes** etc. What about the links between the main library and the smaller departmentally-based libraries throughout the college? Collectively these departmentally-based libraries account for a further 80,000 books and other resources such as videos etc.

There will be supplementary considerations which are of obvious importance when new technologies are introduced, and spin offs in other directions may become apparent. For example, if a **security system** for access to the library is needed to prevent theft, are there *other security systems* already based around the college – if so, should we make use of the *same* **keys** or **card-entry systems** etc. Does the catering department have a **card** or **key system** for purchasing food? – if so, could the *same cards or keys* be used in the library to pay fines or operate the proposed new **photocopiers** or **laser printers**? We have only mentioned security and booking so far – yet you have already seen that possible interaction between the library and other systems within Corpus Crumbly may be used to advantage. *Take a note about how the introduction of new technology may affect things which at first sight would not have been apparent* – how many students would have guessed a possible link between the library and catering departments? – this is one of the reasons why an organisation such as the educational institution being considered here needs to consider its systems in the wider perspective mentioned earlier – this is systems analysis at its innovative best – the art of the possible versus economic, political and other considerations.

There are many other library-specific considerations too. For example, much vital information can be found by making use of CD-ROM-based systems. This includes Books in Print, British Library bibliographies, and a whole host of other material from newspapers and encyclopaedias to information on global exploration. What about all of the administration which is carried out by the librarians? For example, ordering of new books and periodicals, dissemination of information to the college, stock taking, fines, lists of people with books on loan, blacklisted people not allowed to use the system, who has got a particular book etc? What about connection to external databases for further information? There is already an extensive computer-based network around the college – it would seem sensible if students could interrogate the library-system databases from anywhere within the college at any time of the day or night providing that the student has access to a suitable terminal and has the necessary authority. What about interrogation of the system from home via a modem? This facility would be extremely useful for any holiday work carried out by the students. The list of useful facilities will probably grow with continuing new developments and ideas, and should always be subject to an open-ended review from time to time. *You will recall that good systems analysis should allow for systems to grow as customers' needs change*, and you have now seen some relevant examples.

Student activities – 1

You now appreciate the problem.

(1) How would you go about starting to tackle the problem of computerising the Corpus Crumbly library?

(2) Write down some major points which you think are important at this early stage.

(3) Do you think that the problem is technically and economically feasible?

(4) Who do you think needs to be consulted?

Feasibility study

A fully-blown feasibility study is a little less important here than would be the case in industry or commerce when different major projects are being considered. For example, it's obvious that the system *is* feasible as many other libraries throughout the country have already computerised similar systems. Off-the-shelf library systems such as **BookShelf** or **Alice**, for example, might provide most if not all of the system's requirements. Such systems are already extensively used within many schools, colleges and universities. Systems analysts should not have their eyes closed to existing practice within other institutions.

In industry similar arguments apply. For example, *many systems problems may be solved by the application of standard packages* such as **databases, spreadsheets** and **network systems**. However, some projects are of a more open-ended nature, they may involve computerisation of systems which have not been done before, or involve projects in which their is little relevant experience. *In these cases it's essential to have an extensive feasibility study undertaken or much money and time could be wasted.* Such detailed analysis would be carried out by a team of experts who have proven experience in a particular field – for example, it might be control of a chemical plant, analysis of a financial institution or the setting up of a large medical-system database for the NHS. In industry and commerce many projects are often undertaken simultaneously, so other constraints such as prioritisation of projects needs to be considered. Projects are usually prioritised by considering the likely results relating to which projects are the most feasible, and which projects will bring in the largest economic benefits most quickly to the company.

As far as the library example is concerned, *we will assume* that the requirements are both **technically and economically feasible**.

Collecting information

To help draw up a broad set of objectives many members of staff and students need to be consulted. This is usually done by interview, perhaps by filling in some questionnaires, and the formation of one or more committees would be used to investigate major areas of concern. Unlike the competitive industrial and commercial markets, librarians are usually only too pleased to show others what they have achieved, and visits to other libraries would therefore be an invaluable source of extra information. The following areas would probably make a good starting point.

(1) General objectives.
(2) The database.
(3) The librarians' perspective.
(4) The academic departments' perspective.
(5) Students' perspective.
(6) Security.

Overseeing all of the areas above would be the overriding consideration of cost. Can the college afford to implement the system in one go, or is a phased implementation more likely? If the implementation is to be phased, what are the priorities? We will now consider each of the above areas in more detail.

Student activities – 2 General objectives

Staff, students and librarians have been consulted and have given their opinions.

(1) Write down some of the objectives which you think are important at this early stage.

(2) What benefits do you see from computerising the library?

(3) Are there any other aspects due for consideration at this stage?

General objectives

After some detailed consultation with interested parties, and observation of similar systems in practice, general objectives can be developed. The following is typical of what the users of the new system at Corpus Crumbly might expect to gain.

(a) **A greatly improved service** – information ought to be instantly available regarding what resources such as books, periodicals and videos etc. can be borrowed, who has which resource, and reservations should be handled with greater efficiency. This information is to be extended to include all departmentally-based resources throughout the college.

(b) **Real-time system** – when a book or other resource is returned it should be *instantly available* to be borrowed again, unlike the old manual system where delays of up to a day or even longer used to be the norm.

(c) **On-line interaction** – students should have access to information 24-hours a day from *any* suitable terminal on campus, or via a modem from outside the college. Information from other sources such as CD-ROM should be available via the networks and telephone system if possible.

(d) **Better stock security** – the system should be able to have total control over all aspects of the issuing of books and other resources. It should exclude blacklisted borrowers, be able to manage the fines system, and provide accounting facilities and statistics regarding many different aspects of the usage, abusage and financial management of the system.

(e) **Better physical security** – the system should provide a warning if books or other resources are about to be stolen from the library, and should only allow access to staff and students with appropriate authority at specified times of the day and night, and at specified days and weeks during the year.

(f) **Time saving** – the computer system should carry out mundane routines automatically. This will release staff so that they can spend more time helping the students and staff at Corpus Crumbly.

(g) **A more-polished image** – The image of the college should be considerably enhanced by the increased efficiency of the library.

You should now start to see the enormity of the task ahead. You will also realise that we will only be able to summarise major categories during the rest of this chapter. However, such a system has all the impact of a real system because it *is* a real system. Nothing of major importance has been left out, and the above list indicates what are typical requirements for a large and modern library. However, specific libraries might require further additions, for example, specialist materials for disabled people, music CDs, geological collections etc. – the list is limited only by the needs of the local community, finance, and the imagination of the people who design the systems – i.e. you!

At all stages you must be aware of the economic implications of what you are proposing, be aware of the technical feasibility of the proposals too, and be aware of the potential resistance from users who might undermine what you are trying to do! Don't forget that there are influential academic staff who don't want computers in the library – it does not matter that they don't understand enough to be able to appreciate the benefits of the system, it's your job to convince them of the benefits or at least neutralise their opposition if this is possible – politics plays a large part in the development of many systems – a point well worth noting.

Student activities – 3 The main database

Concentrate on the information that will need to be held in the main database.

(1) What information might be needed regarding the resources such as books, videos and CDs etc. held in the library?

(2) What information might be needed regarding the borrowers? Don't forget to cater for a variety of different students and staff.

The database

Besides security, this is *the* most fundamental area as the success or failure of the system will be judged by the efficiency with which this database of books and other resources is implemented and maintained, and by the ease with which users of the system will be able to gain the considerable benefits proposed.

A **relational database** (see page 467) will probably be the most efficient way to implement such a system, as mundane tasks such as 'borrowing a book' will affect both the 'borrowers' and 'book' (resources) files. Typically there would be a requirement for a *library catalogue of all the resources* which we will call the **resource** file – we have not called it the book file because resources other than books are to be included within it too.

Resource file

This *is essentially the* **cataloguing information**, i.e. the detailed information about each resource held on the library catalogue. Typical information for **individual catalogue fields** (not necessarily in any order of importance) might be as follows.

Field	Remarks
Title	
Author(s)	
Edition	
Series	
Accession number	Number relating to multiple-copies of the same resource.
Resource status	i.e. Reference, available, on loan, requested etc.
Subject	e.g. Science, Engineering etc.
Level	GCSE, 'A' Level, Undergraduate, Postgraduate etc.
Key words	Key words relating to subject content.
Media	Book, CD-ROM, computer disk, map, slide, video etc.
Remarks	Free-flowing text field for notes of any description
Dewey classification	Number system used to help categorise books.
Location	Corpus Crumbly or departmental positional information
ISBN	International Standard Book Number.
Bar-code number	
Library number	Special Corpus Crumbly reference number.
Date	Acquisition date.

Borrowers' file

This information will relate to the students and staff at the college, and their relationship with the Corpus Crumbly library.

Field	Remarks
Staff/student no.	Unique Corpus-Crumbly ID for the college
Name	
Address	Several fields may be required
Post code	Might need alternatives for students who live abroad
Telephone number	
Borrower category	Several different **staff** and **student** categories

Date of registration	
Department	Main department to which staff or student belongs.
Sub. Dept 1	Subsidiary department for use of departmental libraries
Sub. Dept 2	
Sub. Dept 3	
Books on loan	Links to books on loan.
Borrower's status	Blacklisted, owing fines etc.
Balance	Amount owed by the borrower to the library.
Requested 1	A field to enable users to remotely request resources
Requested 2	
Requested 3	
Requested 4	
Requested 5	
Remarks	Free-flowing text field for notes of any description

Other information

There is a whole host of other potentially-useful information. For example, a file of book publishers with links to the database. Much other information is covered in the relevant sections where the library is considered from the perspectives of different staff and student users of the system.

It's essential that some sort of simplified manual-backup for booking and returns is set up as it's inevitable that the computer will go down at some stage. The main and departmental libraries must continue to perform a basic function under these unusual conditions.

Besides the cost of developing the database or purchasing a proprietary database, there is the cost of the enormous task of entering information regarding several hundred thousand books. Typically companies will charge between 25p and 50p for entering data regarding a single book. The cost of this data-entry marathon alone will therefore be in excess of one hundred thousand pounds! If secretarial staff were to undertake this operation, then allowing a few minutes for the entry of a single book, the operation would take about $(350,000 + 80,000) \times 3$ minutes which is about 21,500 hours, or about 10 person years! – assuming that one person were to enter the data 8 hours a day, five days a week with no holidays. There is also a possibility of downloading information on modern books from existing CD-ROM databases.

Student activities – 4 The librarians' perspective

Concentrate on the view of the systems from the point of view of the chief librarian and the other assistant librarians who run the system.

(1) Make a list of the day-to-day tasks that the system will need to be able to perform.

(2) Make a list of the specific administrative functions.

(3) Are there any extra useful functions which can be performed?

The librarian's perspective

All the main functions performed by the librarians need to be listed so that the system will be able to cope with them. Some of the functions (not shown in any particular order of importance) could be as follows.

On a day-to-day basis the librarian will probably need to

(a) Enquire about a borrower by name or number.
(b) Issue books and other resources to students and staff.
(c) Use automatic generation of stamp dates.
(d) Accept books and other resources back into the library.
(e) Be able to make reservations.
(f) Search the database on *all* fields using many different filters.
(g) Modify any of the borrower's details.
(h) Add new borrowers or delete old ones.
(i) Modify any of the catalogue resource records.
(j) Create new catalogue entries.
(k) Access the borrower's account records (for fines and other charges).
(l) Print out details from a variety of queries.
(m) Control the security system (i.e. reset the alarm if it goes off).
(n) Produce standard letters to be sent to students and staff.

Specific administrative tasks might include

(a)   Statistics regarding overdue books and other resources.
(b)   Financial information regarding the library.
(c)   Ordering of new books.
(d)   Books taken out for repair.
(e)   Help with stocktaking.
(f)   Save standard queries for future use.
(g)   Print out reservations.
(h)   Labelling of new books.
(i)   Dealing with requests from/to other libraries.
(j)   Automatic ordering of periodicals and other resources.
(k)   Automatic accounting and billing procedures.
(l)   Helping with circulation of material to relevant staff and students.

Extra useful functions might include

(a)   Statistics regarding readers' borrowing habits.
(b)   A notice-board system for disseminating library information.
(c)   Integration of the software with standard packages such as spreadsheets, word processors and databases etc.

The above lists are not exhaustive, and no doubt many other functions may be dreamt up – you will recall that a major objective of the system is continued development – there are bound to be many good ideas not listed above, and technical innovations yet to be invented. The system should be flexible enough to cope with the constant updates likely to happen over the next few years. One of the points of the earlier exercises where information was gathered from a variety of staff and students would be to collect a selection of good ideas which might enhance the system if they are technically and economically feasible.

Student activities – 5 The academic departments

Consider the use of the library from the point of view of a typical academic department.

(1)   List typical features that may be required by each department.

(2)   What extra technical problems might there be here?

(3)   Are any political problems likely?

(4)   What advantages might there be for these departments?

(5)   Are there any disadvantages?

The academic departments

Each academic department within Corpus Crumbly will have its own perspective of the main library, and the relationship between it and the main library. Corpus Crumbly has the following academic departments.

Biology	Business studies	Chemistry	Classics
Computing & IT	Divinity	Drama	Economics
Electronics	English	French	Geography
German	History	Japanese	Mathematics
Music	PE	Physics	Politics
Spanish	Technology		

Most have their own libraries which are run with varying degrees of efficiency from manual booking systems to the 'haven't got a clue about what books we have or where they are' syndrome!

There are several camps within the college regarding grouping of departments, but the technical departments are particularly keen on the '**key word**' searches that could be set up in the main database. For example, type in 'nano technology', and books or periodicals in either the main library or *any* departmental library in which this fascinating topic is listed should be flagged – i.e. brought to the attention of the user who is searching the database. However, most heads of department don't relish the idea of typing in thousands of key words – a potential area of friction which will have to be borne in mind! It's possible to get CD-ROMs containing huge volumes of information regarding books in print, and it might be possible to find a system in which someone else has already done the donkey work. However, there is no substitute for extending the key word systems to add local flavour, and if the task can be accomplished over a period of years then the benefits will be enormous.

The facilities needed by the departmental libraries are identical in most respects to the facilities required by the main library, however, a few other specials might come to light.

(a) Extra length borrowing periods for students within a department
(b) Very-long borrowing periods for staff within the department.

These requirements might be able to be linked to the main database by using the borrower category and departmental information held in the borrowers' file.

Potential problems

Most departments will probably relish the idea of having someone else look after their library, but access to the books and other resources is a potential problem because they are housed in physically-different locations around the campus, and in rooms which may be locked at times when the main library is open. Staff are naturally reluctant to have an open-access policy at all times, and it's likely that books will have to be reserved if the departmental library is closed.

Some staff will probably feel threatened by the introduction of the new technology. Eventually the manual methods of searching will be removed – this may put off some staff from using the system. Staff training and a sympathetic approach will be needed. Nevertheless, the many perceived advantages of the new system must not be held back to cater for a few educational dinosaurs.

Student activities – 6 A student's perspective

This is the easiest section for students to answer. What do they want from the main and academic department libraries?

(1) List the features which would be useful from a typical student's perspective. (Be realistic!)

(2) What advantages would there be for the students?

(3) Are there any disadvantages of the new system?

A student's perspective

All the features covered hitherto will obviously benefit the students, but extra benefits would include the following.

(a) Unlimited access to appropriate library details via the computer network.
(b) Access to library information 24 hours per day.
(c) Far easier searching for information.
(d) E-mail can be used to communicate with the librarian.
(e) E-mail can be used to flag students when books are available.
(f) CD-ROM and external database searches will add to the considerable arsenal of available methods of research.

Some students may also feel threatened by the system, and much information and publicity will need to be undertaken if the transition from the manual system to the automatic system is to be a smooth one. The whole point of computerisation should not be to alienate the students, but to provide the mechanisms whereby the

---

Student activities – 7 Security

You must consider the physical security of the resources from the point of view of both buildings and day-to-day pilfering.

(1) What systems might be useful for the physical security of the buildings such as the main library and departmental libraries?

(2) What could be done to overcome the pilfering problems?

(3) Are there any disadvantages of the new system?

library can become a more productive environment for both work and pleasure. The success of this system would hopefully be measured in terms of a very significant increase in productive and pleasurable student and staff activity when using the library.

Security

The physical security of the building is important as the library is open for long hours, and at present any member of the public can walk into the building when the library is open. With the old system it's difficult to distinguish pilfering by students or staff from pilfering by members of the public.

Some sort of door where entry and exit is controlled either by a swipe card, a smart card or a smart key (see page 604) would be useful. Access would then be granted only to those students and staff with an appropriate pass. This pass could be the same one used for all financial and security transactions within Corpus Crumbly college. This is to include access to the academic department libraries too.

A smart key or card system could be programmed such that entry by appropriate personnel is controlled by the system. For example, academic staff might have a smart key which gives them access to their particular departmental library at any time of the day or night, 365 days a year. (They're a dedicated lot at Corpus Crumbly!) However, students may only gain access to libraries during term time at specific times of the day or evening. Different types of student may have different privileges which may change according to their age and status.

Disadvantages

The smart key could also be the same device used to book resources from any of the libraries, and to pay for fines if necessary. (Cash can be credited on the microchips inside these keys.) If a student is blacklisted then his or her key is nullified as far as the main library is concerned. The students could also be prevented from entering other installations within the campus including selected departmental libraries.

The smart key system offers many advantages, but some students and staff may feel that big brother is watching over them. To some extent this is true – the whole point of this system is to control access! However, students and staff must be reassured that the information-gathering potential of such a system is not to be misused. For example, it's possible to create a reasonably detailed account of the whereabouts of particular students including the times that they enter and leave particular buildings. Although it's technically possible to do this – it's not what the system has been designed to do. Students and staff will need reassurance that no software exists to perform interrogations of this sinister kind.

Costs

Typical smart-key systems cost in excess of one thousand pounds per door for entry and exit. Typical smart keys cost about ten pounds each, and all students and staff in the college will need to be issued with one.

The specialist security system for tagging books such that alarms are activated if books are being removed that have not been borrowed officially (i.e. stolen!) costs about £20,000 per system.

Initial conclusions

That's the end of the information-gathering stage. We have been reasonably brief compared to the detailed information and opinion gathering which would have to be undertaken in practice, especially in terms of detailed costings. However, as you can see, computerisation of the library system is not a trivial matter. Readers of this book should now be well aware of what happens during the information-gathering stages of a typical system life cycle. You should ensure that the shorter problems that you tackle with your computer-science projects are done with equal thoroughness.

It is at this stage that the potential advantages and disadvantages of the system become clear. For example, **are the benefits to be gained from such a system sufficient to make the cost of the system acceptable?** *This is probably the last stage at which we can sensibly withdraw from the project* without incurring any significant expense of developing software, purchasing hardware, and setting up the database. However, don't forget that there has already been a considerable sum spent on the systems analysts fees!

The final decisions will obviously be financial. It is the job of the systems analyst to declare all the pros and cons of the system in an objective way, so that the managers of Corpus Crumbly can weigh up the potential benefits versus the cost of the system. Don't forget that such a complex system can be phased over a number of years, and this would probably be the most likely scenario in practice.

Analysis of the problem

We will assume that the go ahead has been given, or we won't have anything to analyse! Having seen what is needed, we now have to analyse the best ways of solving the problem. **We need to split up the problem into major subsections**, produce some sort of schedule, and start to plan for the transition from the manual to the automatic system.

Student activities – 8 Analysis of the problem

You must now split up the project into major subsections so that a team of people can be assigned to different tasks.

(1) What structured analysis methods would be most useful here?

(2) How would you manage the time aspects of this project?

(3) Suggest a set of suitable modular activities for computerisation of the Corpus Crumbly Library.

How on earth do we estimate the time that will be needed for this project? Past experience is probably the best yard-stick to use, but what happens if the project has never been done before? Let's suppose, just for the sake of argument, that the library system being considered here had *not* been done before – the only alternative is to break up the system into smaller parts (already needed for modularity), then analyse the time that would be necessary for each part. This is more useful than may appear at first sight. For example, if we are to set up a relational database which deals with just under half a million records for the resources file, where each record has just under twenty fields – then this sort of activity is not unique. Now *it does not matter* if we are setting up a library database or a database dealing with 'Outer-Mongolian snow rabbits' – people have set up databases of this size before – how long did it take to do? – the library system will probably take a similar amount of time.

On most projects tackled in industry and commerce there is often a project deadline – usually yesterday! Systems analysts will have to estimate the resources that will be needed to complete the project by the due date – and point out any unrealistic project deadlines to the management. It is also the job of the systems analyst to make sure that agreed deadlines are actually met.

Unfortunately, software products are notoriously difficult to plan and predict. We always assume that things will go to plan, and when they don't – panic sets in and corners often tend to be cut. Most readers will be well aware of the media hype which accompanies major releases of new packages and operating systems – most readers will also be aware of the fact that many systems don't appear by the due date, and often contain quite serious bugs when they finally do come out! It's against this sort of background that **software engineering techniques** (see later) are being developed which help refine our solutions to these potentially disastrous problems.

Coming back to our library systems, we will therefore concentrate on modularisation and scheduling, before getting down to the 'nitty gritty' of analysis in more detail.

Mapping out progress

Let's suppose that the project deadline to implement the entire Corpus Crumbly system has been set at twelve months. (This is not unrealistic.) The Gantt chart shown in figure 18.3 might reflect a potential solution to some of the problems. This chart shows only the most brief of details, but gives an idea of the relationship and scheduling between different parts of the project. The marker shows some arbitrary point three months into the project, but, as can be seen from the chart, by this time the resource database has been completely designed and is still undergoing tests, but the borrowers' database has been design and tested. The librarians' utilities are about to be designed, tested and added to the existing software.

Notice that a further three weeks at the beginning of the project is allowed to develop more-general ideas further. It should also be noticed that in this particular project there is considerable flexibility about when activities take place. For example, the physical security system is almost a separate issue, and does not relate to any software functions on the system at all. This activity could, therefore, be started at any time so long as the system was installed and tested before much staff training

Corpus-Crumbly library system progress chart

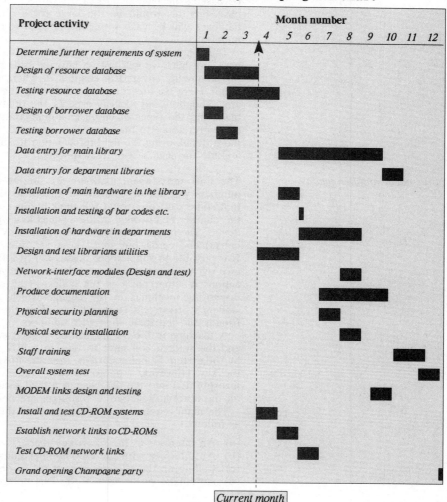

Figure 18.3

had been undertaken. There are other parts of the project which are more critical. For example, the librarians utilities such as new-book labelling routines or fines calculation etc. can't be undertaken until all the basic database software is up and running.

If some parts of the system, such as the main database or data entry routines, for example, were late, then this would probably delay the 'Grand opening Champagne Party'. However, if other more minor parts of the systems were delayed, such as the MODEM link, for example, then this would *not* delay opening the most important parts of the system. **Software** such as **PERT charts** (see page 147) could be used to identify if certain parts of the project were getting to the stage of delaying the overall schedule. Extra person-power could then be put onto these critical parts of the project if finances allowed.

More detailed analysis

The Gantt chart shown in figure 18.3 can, if desired, be further subdivided. If too much detail is shown on the main chart then overall project impressions get lost in a sea of horizontal bars which become meaningless. Similarly, if we undertook a top-down-approach diagram for the whole project it would become unacceptably cumbersome. The Gantt chart has split the project up into an acceptable number of major subdivisions, therefore, individual top-down-approach diagrams can be used for each part of the project.

There is neither the space in the chapter (there's probably not space in the whole book!) nor the time to cover the design of such a system in detail. Therefore, we will concentrate on just one part of the project as an example of the sort of techniques that can be used.

The borrowers' database

This is one of the major parts of the project around which many other modules will be based. The biggest part of the project would be the main catalogue-index database, but this would be too large for a quick example, therefore the borrowers' database will be used instead, and even this will be subdivided and only partially undertaken.

There are several phases to be considered in the design of this relational database, but here we will not go into the pros and cons of different database types as this is already covered in chapter 20 where database design is considered in more detail. Here we are concerned only with the design of the user interface, including any validation and security aspects, the relationships with the main catalogue database, and the types of end-user administrative functions which need to be carried out by reference to the borrowers' database. We now look at these aspects in a little more detail, using the field information for the borrowers' file given on page 407 as a guide for each section that follows.

Staff/student number facility

The staff and student numbers are unique to Corpus Crumbly college, but these numbers will not necessarily be known to the students – if they were it's obvious that some students would tell their number to others. Therefore, it's proposed that the number be encoded inside a **smart key** which can be used with a special reading device. The idea is identical in principle to ATMs (hole-in-the-wall machines outside banks) and cards, but smart keys are *more reliable and robust* than swipe cards. It is possible to supplement possession of a key with a PIN number, and this would give even-greater security. As the smart keys will be used to carry out cash transactions in other parts of the college, (the chips inside are charged up by special dispensing machines in the college which accept £10 notes) *and* gain access to student's private quarters, it's less likely that students will lend their keys to their friends *and* tell them their PIN numbers.

A machine in the library will be needed into which the smart key can be placed, and the student will have to type in a PIN number. If the PIN number is verified by the system as being correct, then the holder will be assumed to be the owner of the key. However, a photo of each student and member of staff could easily be incorporated into the database as a final security check, and this could be displayed on the librarian's screen as resources are being booked out.

The main requirements for this part of the borrowers' database will therefore be as follows.

(a) An interface to the smart-key reader.
(b) An interface with the PIN number numeric key pad.
(c) Calling up the student or staff photo on screen.
(d) Automatic verification of the PIN number in relation to the key number.

Some problems

You may not think that standard information of this sort would cause any problems – but this is not so! Extensive computerisation of administration within Corpus Crumbly means that *this information already exists on other databases throughout the college.* There needs to be much thought put in to avoid possible duplication of existing information in the library system. Can we establish links with these other databases? The advantage of the current administrative system is that it is already being efficiently kept up to date by the administrative staff – it would seem to make little sense to get the librarians to update the same information in a different set of files – this would lead to potential sources of extra errors, and be a tedious chore which is totally unnecessary.

Multitasking (see page 374) within WIMP environments is now commonplace, therefore, it would be a relatively easy solution to separate the general administrative information such as the addresses of the students from the main library database. The address and other administrative information regarding a student can be called up on the screen if needed from the administration database, and viewed within a different window on the same screen. It should be realised that address, post code, telephone number and date of registration would not normally be needed for run-of-the-mill transactions.

It may be possible to hot-link (make use of hot keys) the two systems so that a single key press is all that is needed to call up the appropriate administrative file when needed. However, the administration database might contain information which the management do not wish the librarians to see, therefore, some sort of access level security system (see page 482) would need to be implemented if this proposal were to be acceptable. Therefore, time would have to be allowed for modifications to the administrative database to be carried out. You will see the advantage of planning a campus-wide computer system at the same time, but this is rarely possible in practice.

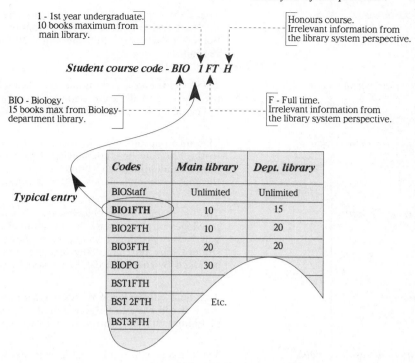

Figure 18.4

Borrower category

There will probably be different categories of borrower with **students** and **staff** being an obvious starting point. However, different types of student may need to be considered, with undergraduates and post-graduates being treated differently, and thus each category might have different departmental and main-library privileges. For example, a 1st-year undergraduate biologist might be able to borrow 10 books from the main library *because* he or she is an undergraduate, but might also be able to borrow 15 books from the biology-department library *because* he or she is a biologist.

These different categories can be generated automatically from the administrative department's computer as these files will store course details for each student. For example, a full-time 1st-year honours biology student might be registered with a course code of BIO1FTH. A simple table could then be set up on the library system's computer showing the relationship between course codes and privileges derived from these course codes. The start of a simplified table is shown in figure 18.4.

Tabular information like that shown above may be as simple or as complex as required. For example, *all staff* may have unlimited access and borrowing capacity from the main library. Particular staff members of departments may have unlimited access to their own departmental library, but more-limited access or no access at all to other departmental libraries. If all 1st year undergraduates have a 10-book (or 10 resource) capacity with respect to the main library, then only the year digit from the course-code string would need to be analysed and the table would be considerably simpler. If different courses allow different resources to be borrowed from different departments, then additional entries will be necessary. Also, a tabular arrangement would allow groups of students on certain combined-honours courses to book out resources from other relevant departments. For example, people on an electronic-engineering and physics course might be able to borrow books from the electronics, physics and mathematics department libraries.

A more-complex tabular arrangement than that shown in figure 18.4 would be necessary for varied booking arrangements, but would be ideal for solution by relational-database methods (see page 467). An administrative utility would therefore need to be programmed which would analyse all the course codes for students, and automatically update the library-database files with the appropriate information. This program would probably be run just before the beginning of each academic year.

Department

This field can be filled in automatically by analysis of the course codes held for the staff and pupils. It would probably belong to the same utility that derives the borrower's limits for each student from the same course codes mentioned in the last section.

Subsidiary departments

These fields enable additional borrowing limits for combined-honours courses which involve several different departments. The course codes for these courses would be indicated in some way in an enlarged version of the table shown in figure 18.4.

Books on loan

This information does not need to be typed in, but should obviously be available to the librarian or student when browsing through the borrowers' file. The Corpus-Crumbly identification number can be used as a flag to extract the information from the main catalogue index if this is required either on the screen or on a printer.

Borrower's status

This is an important field because it will be used as a flag to help determine the privileges on the system. For example, if a borrower has been blacklisted, then there will be no privileges at all, even though the borrower's limits for this particular student may not have been exceeded. The borrower's status field will need to be accessed by the main catalogue system whenever a resource is requested.

Balance

This field can be used to store information regarding fines, or costs for books lost etc. – it will have to be accessible by the administration department for the purposes of billing students who have left or been expelled!

Requested resource fields

These additional fields enable a student to request up to five additional resources (subject to their individual maxima not being exceeded) from any terminal within the campus, or via a modem from outside the campus. This system is particularly useful when the library is closed. If the resources are available and the relevant conditions have been satisfied, then the librarian will physically reserve the appropriate resource at the beginning of the day on which the main library is next open. If a resource is available and has been requested, then a flag should be set in the main catalogue index file to indicate that this resource has now been reserved. This flag will lock out other students from trying to book the same resource from a remote terminal while the library is still closed. The status field in the main catalogue index is intended for this purpose.

Remarks

This is simply a free-flowing textual field into which the librarian may add comments. It may also be possible to store recent E-mail communications here, or hot link (use a hot key) to a separate E-mail system.

Password protection

As can be seen from the above, there will be several different types and categories of users who should be allowed access to different parts of the system. For example, a student should have access to his own borrower's record. However, he or she should *not* be able to change the status of any field except the five requested-resource fields. Indeed, it is not necessary for students to be able to see all of the fields in their borrower's file if this is thought undesirable. The librarian, for example, might wish to keep the remarks field private. (However, the student *may* have a legal right to see it if they wish to via the data protection act! (see page 483)). No student should be able to see anybody else's borrower's record.

The librarians should have complete authority to alter any data or any field within the library database, but it should be remembered that only the DBMS administrator (ie the DBA) (see page 475) should have the authority to alter any of the structure within the database. Administrative staff will need authority to read and update the fields which contain financial information, and all students will need to have read-only access to the cataloguing files.

Finally, it may be that Corpus Crumbly gives outsiders special permission to use the system as a reference library, in which case these individuals would have a restricted access to the system facilities, with no booking or other privileges. Multiple-level password protection of this kind has already been covered in the database section on page 482, and will therefore not be repeated here.

Further detailed analysis

Some sort of visualisation of the interaction between the different elements of the borrowers database is now needed. A suitable diagram is shown in figure 18.5. The detail shown in this diagram contains *no more information* than was presented in the previous few pages, but it *does* allow us to collect our thoughts and appreciate the tasks ahead more easily. For example, it reminds us that critical data is shared between several databases, and relational updates will therefore be needed. It has also gathered together routines which may be considered as belonging to certain categories. For example, administration or security.

There is neither the time nor the space to consider the design of the complete borrowers' database in detail. Therefore, we will take just one area to show what might typically happen in the next stage of development. We have, at last, started to reach the stage where small parts of the system can be developed in detail. **You would do well to pay attention to the amount of detailed thought that has gone into this project** *before* **any coding has actually taken place – apply similar principles to your own project work**. However, this does not stop you from prototyping some parts of the system, especially the user interfaces and menu systems etc.

The course-code utility

Let's now concentrate on the utility (module) which extracts the course-code information from the administrative department's database, and builds up the information given in the privilege table. There will probably be the need for a couple of options here – first a complete update of all students' details at the beginning of an academic

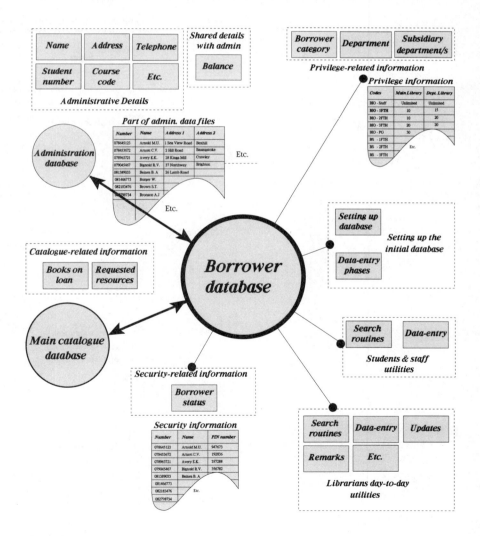

Figure 18.5

year, and secondly a need to update an individual student without referring to all the rest. This is necessary if a student joins Corpus Crumbly mid term. In essence, the module will need to carry out the following processes for each student.

(a) Accept student name/s as an input. (From keyboard or file.)
(b) Extract student number and course code from the admin. database.
(b) Examine course code and extract relevant information.
(c) Match up to privilege statistics.
(d) Build up entry in privilege table in borrowers' database.

Extraction of number/code

To determine if a whole batch of students is to be processed, or if we simply wish to process a single student, then some sort of menu choice will be needed. Either way, we don't want to tie up the administration department's computer for long, and so a file of student numbers and course codes could be saved on the library-computer's disk, and then the utility can use this as the source of information.

Figure 18.6 shows a systems flowchart for the first part of this module. If we are using the multiple-student utility, then at the end of this routine we end up with a file of student number and course code information. Errors – such as the possibility of a name not existing etc. can be echoed on screen or printed out if several names are generated from longer lists of students being processed at the same time.

The borrowers'-database software now has a file of information containing the course code for each student who has access to the library. Note that not all the detail has been shown on this particular flowchart. For example, to get access to the administration database, the librarian would have to log on and go through some

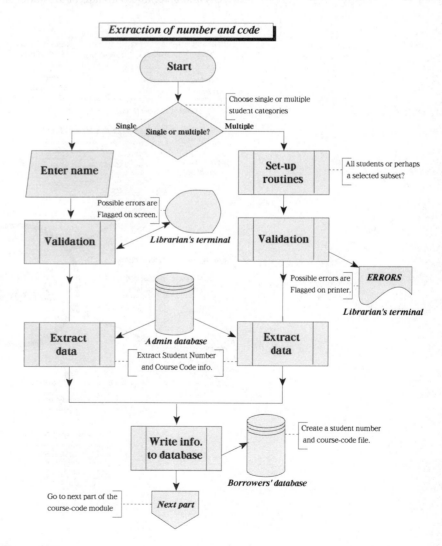

Figure 18.6

Book allocation								
Department	Codes	Year	Main Library	Departmental Libraries...........				
				BIO	BUS	CHE	CLA	Etc....
Biology	BIO1	1	5	5	0	5	0	
	BIO2	2	5	10	0	5	0	
	BIO3	3	10	15	2	10	0	
	BIOP	PG	30	30	5	10	2	
	BIOS	Staff	UL	UL	5	10	5	
Business Studies	BST1	1	5	0	5	5	5	
	BST2	2	5	0	5	5	5	
	BST3	3	10	0	10	10	10	
	BSTP	PG	30	2	20	5	0	
	BSTS	Staff	UL	5	UL	5	5	
Chemistry	CHE1	1	5	5	0	5	0	

UL = Unlimited
PG = Post Grad.

Figure 18.7

password procedures. **We are now into a reasonable depth of analysis, but much more detail needs to be obtained before coding or database design can take place**.

Also, in practice, there would have to be very broad *agreement* between all the people who are writing the different routines as to the exact formats of the shared data. This is considered in chapter 20 when data dictionaries are discussed.

The privilege statistics

Information needs to be held in the system regarding the policies of different departments, and the policy of the main library regarding the number of books that can be leant out to different categories of students and staff. Corpus Crumbly has no agreed blanket policy, therefore, each department's information can be found by using a look-up table. A file can be set up matching the course code with the privilege level for each library. The systems analyst has suggested a more-uniform booking policy to simplify this stage of the proceedings, but traditionalists at the college will not have their lending policies dictated by a computer system! Therefore, we are stuck with an ad-hoc system which will have to be implemented by the computer. Each department has specified the maximum allowed number of books from a departmental library for students undertaking particular courses, and this could, in principle, be stored in a look-up table as shown in figure 18.7.

The table should be self-explanatory. For example, from the part of the table that can be seen, it has been shown that a second-year biology student is able to borrow 5 books from the main library, (the standard second-year undergraduate ration), is able to borrow 10 books from the biology-department library, and due to an arrangement with chemistry, is able to borrow 5 books from the chemistry department library too.

Simplifications could be made to this look up table if analysed in certain ways, and it has been left to the reader to suggests some possible simplifications, not forgetting that some staff still refuse to accept a coherent booking-out policy for all libraries within Corpus Crumbly. Next we need to provide a routine which produces the above table. However, this is not shown in this brief analysis.

Coding

The next stage would be to provide a routine which reads the student number, looks up the course code, matches it within the above table and then produces the relevant information for the borrower category field. Don't forget that it is this field which contains the information regarding the maximum number of resources that can be booked out by each student or member of staff from each library within Corpus Crumbly. There are 22 academic departmental libraries plus the main library, therefore, 23 different items of information could be stored within this field. It may

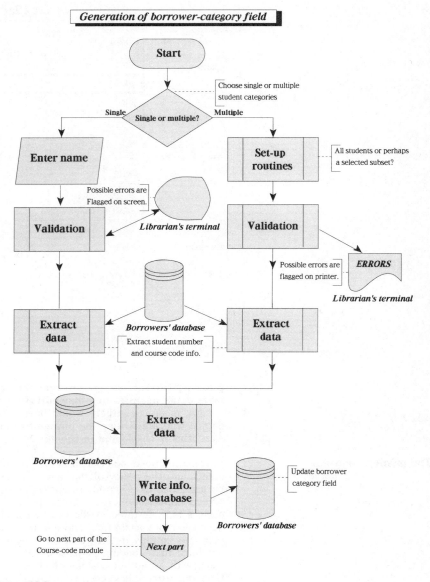

Figure 18.8

be that a 46 character field could be used where each of two subsequent characters
from the beginning of the field represent the 'numeric' information contained in a
single row of the look-up table. The routine for constructing this field for all the
students could therefore be as shown in figure 18.8.

Notice that some of the routines are starting to look similar. Take a brief glance
at the diagrams and you would think that they are the same! This should be seized
upon in practice so that procedures within modules might be able to be called up
and used elsewhere. After the above has been carried out we have the borrower
privileges automatically sorted out from reading a file from the administrative-depart-
ment's computer.

We have only looked at a small part of the library system. Much co-ordination
needs to be put into making sure that each person in the team is pulling in the same
direction, and frequent meetings are needed if misunderstandings are to be kept to
a minimum. However, the next stage would be to go further into detail of the solution to the problem.

You should note that coding does not necessarily mean jumping into a high-level
language of your choice, but could be a combination of any coding methods involving
SQLs, 4GLs or other suitable methods. In this particular case, where relational-
database software would probably be used, writing code by using an SQL-type

language (see page 480) would almost certainly be the way to solve the Corpus-Crumbly library problems. Nevertheless, reading the systems flowcharts gives us an instant idea of what we are trying to achieve in a reasonable degree of detail.

Assuming that the database structure had already been created, then queries and saving of new information based on these queries can easily be established.

General systems analysis methods

We will now leave the Corpus-Crumbly library database system as it has served its purpose in guiding us through part of a typical system life cycle. However, you will recall from the beginning of this chapter that there are other vital areas, including testing and debugging, and methods for helping to cope with these problems within systems analysis and design will now be covered in more detail.

Testing

The **testing** of programs and systems is *immensely important* because more businesses and virtually the whole of industry are increasingly putting their trust in computer-based systems. We have seen at the beginning of this chapter a reasonably detailed systems analysis involving splitting up a major problem until just before the detailed coding and testing phases were necessary. We will now *concentrate on* **individual software modules** (single procedures or groups of procedures), detailed **data validation** and **verification** techniques, and the techniques necessary to ensure that these modules play an effective and constructive part in more comprehensive programs that are then ready to be used in larger systems. You are again reminded that this sort of testing can also be applied to 4GLs and other application-based command and control languages.

The bottom-up approach to testing

As well as helping to understand problems at the design stages, modularisation also helps with testing too, and it is to the smallest modules that we must look to begin our testing and evaluation cycle. Unlike the analysis of the system in the first place, the **bottom-up approach** *is* the most successful when **testing a system**. If the bottom-up approach is used then **individual modules** can be tested for syntax and **logical errors** (i.e. errors in the logic of the program) *without the extra hassle* of having to interact with other modules in the system. Another advantage of modularisation gained by the use of the **bottom-up approach** is that several areas of the project may be **developed concurrently** (i.e. at the same time). This is especially useful if modules will never interact with each other.

When completely-tested new modules are added to old ones any errors generated are most likely to be due to the interaction of the latest module with the rest. Indeed, while developing the modules themselves it's often a good idea to cut them down to the **smallest operational units possible** (i.e. the smallest chunk of code that does anything useful) and get this single piece of code working. You can then build up from this single working unit by adding more code and then retesting. As for the modules, any new errors in the progressively-larger code are *most likely* to be located in the code that has just been added.

Although the above might all sound a little tedious (especially if a **compiler** rather than an **interpreter** is being used), it is worthwhile contemplating the empirical formula

$$\text{debugging time} = \text{programmer time} \times (\text{number of lines})^2.$$

Thus, to ensure **minimum debugging time** – *keep the number of lines in each separate module to a minimum*, as the time taken to debug the code is proportional to the square of the number of lines of code. The constant of proportionality called **programmer's time** depends upon how good a programmer is. A whiz-kid programmer, for example, would have a much shorter value for programmer's time than the average programmer. If you are still not convinced of the need for modularity and the testing of very small sections of code, think about the software engineering philosophy which is intended to be most useful in larger systems. Then think about what a large software system actually means – for example, Microsoft's Windows NT operating system has over 4.3 million lines of code! Think about developing a system of this complexity and there should be no arguments against any of these methods which help to keep the bugs to the absolute minimum.

Testing individual modules

Devising a successful test strategy for any module involves making sure that *each* **condition** or **option** is fully tested. There are a number of things to be considered in detail. First the *program itself* needs testing to ensure that the **syntax** is correct.

These **syntax errors** are obviously detected by the compiler during the **compilation** stage, but it is not unknown to have errors in the compiler itself! Don't forget that few items of code are perfect, and this includes compilers. For example, it's possible to get a 'syntax error' in a complex line of code where none exists! If this is the case, then you have no alternative but to restructure a small part of the code so that the compiler is 'happy', and inform the compiler software writers that a bug exists in their code. Finally, even though a program may be syntactically correct, the **logic** must also be extensively tested. It is likely that the programmer may have sent control to the wrong part of the program or a wrong termination condition for a loop has slipped through, for example.

Debugging tools

Testing the logic of a program involves *running* the program (with **dummy data** if necessary) and checking to see that the expected specifications are met. If, for example, the wrong output is produced, then the programmer must **debug** (*find and correct the bugs or errors*) the system, often by making use of **special utilities** such as **debuggers** or **debugging tools** which are designed for this purpose.

A **debugger** is a **special piece of software** which is run along with the program being tested. A typical scenario would be to put a **break** (or **halt**) in the program at a salient point which needs investigation. A **string of statistics** regarding the **status of the program** at the particular point where program execution is halted can easily be produced. Typical statistics might be a list of the names and values of all the constants and variables currently being used by the program.

Often **debuggers** are *built into* the **compiler software**. For example, in Microsoft's Visual C++ object-oriented programming language (the visual part refers to windows options) there are debugging facilities already built in. A special debug option must be included in the program during the compilation phase, which in turn makes use of a special library file which helps with the actual debugging.

A *common option* in many **debugging utilities** is the inclusion of a **trace** routine. This **traces the progress** of the program giving a suitable indication as to *where the program is* at any moment in time during the execution phase. For example, in the C++ compiler quoted above, it is possible to get the debugger to print out a list of messages chosen by the user and inserted in the source code by using the keyword TRACE. The C++ compiler is quite clever in that it keeps two versions of the source code – one for debugging purposes and the other for the release version of your program. In this way you don't have to edit out all of the trace statements before the final release of your masterpiece.

Trace routines are ideal for tracking down bugs like getting stuck in **endless (or infinite) loops**. For example, if, during the execution of a program, the message:

> Starting statistical analysis section

is put on the screen, and if after the fifth cup of coffee it is still there, then it's worth investigating the logic of your procedure which is calculating these statistics.

Another example from Microsoft's C++ compiler is the use of an ASSERT macro. Termination of the program can be caused after an assertion (such as whether a **Boolean variable** is **true** or **false**, for example) is made. However, these are but two examples of the huge variety of **diagnostics** available to professional programmers using C++.

Students are well advised to make extensive use of these debugging techniques when carrying out their own project work. Even if you are using BASIC then there are trace options available and there is nothing to stop you printing out messages, listing the variables or halting the program at any time during compilation or interpretation of the program. Part of the project write up involves testing what you have done, and *marks are often thrown away because this phase is badly carried out and documented*. It's all too easy to say 'It seems to work', but this will not get you very many marks in the evaluation section.

On very complex systems it would normally be the job of a different team of programmers to write all the testing and debugging procedures. For reasons stated at the beginning of this section, testing and debugging is taken extremely seriously in the software industry, and often involves more effort than is involved in the writing of the original software! Indeed, when large systems have been shipped to the customer, then 90% of programming effort goes into **maintenance** (i.e. the software is updated at some later stage to iron out bugs that have come to light, or to change the system slightly in terms of the changing needs of the business).

Testing your claims!

It's most important that any claims made in the literature promoting your software are verified. For example, if you have just written a module which should sort up to 10,000 names into alphabetical order – then check that it does exactly that!

Testing the processed data

It's important to realise that you *can have* a **program** which is *entirely correct* but which is *unacceptable* because it does not ensure the **integrity (correctness)** of the **data** being processed. It's not much point having a perfect working program which does its job badly.

Data validation

If your module accepts or produces data then it should be **checked for limits** and/or **range** if necessary. For example, if typing in a person's age, then 473 years old is an unlikely entry. Similarly a £6,000,000 water bill is an unlikely output for a domestic customer. There may be a **limited range** of integer numbers such as the number of tickets booked in a theatre – it would be silly to allow a booking of 350 seats for the same performance in a 250-seat theatre, for example. Don't forget also that a **blank entry** (i.e. simply pressing the return key) may be unacceptable input and cause problems with your software if it is allowed to get into the system unchecked.

Data validation is the process of getting the computer to check to see if the data is **valid** *(sensible in the context in which it is being used)*. As can be seen from the above paragraph, this also includes checks for completeness (i.e. has all relevant data been entered). It is particularly easy to validate data when using specialised database languages, as special facilities are often available. If data is not valid then the input would not be accepted by the system.

Other checks are implicitly carried out by the **data types** (see page 110) being used. For example, if a **number** is expected then a **string** would be rejected. If an **integer numeric data type** is being used then a **real number** would be rejected.

Other methods of checking data integrity such as **checksums**, **hashing** and **CRCs** etc. are more concerned with checking the integrity of a **batch of data** such as that found in a **file** or a **packet of information** transmitted on a network, and are therefore covered in other parts of this book, but similar methods can be applied to the entry of simple data such as account numbers, for example, and are considered in a moment.

It's essential to use data validation techniques wherever possible, even though this makes the coding considerably more complex. Indeed, on professional projects, the data validation and other checking procedures are often the most complex parts of the program. Nevertheless, if computer systems are to gain the respect of business and industry, then this important aspect should not be overlooked.

Data verification

Data validation, important though it is, *can't detect all errors*, and in sensitive areas such as the military or top-security databases, **verification** is often used. **Verification** is a means of checking to see if the data being entered is likely to be correct. For example, has 'Mr Clarke' been entered instead of 'Mr Clark'? – There's no way that a computer can tell if Clarke should have an 'e' on the end or not, unless Mr Clark gets it right in the first place! It would be *impossible* for example, to validate a *new* name and address. (Although it would obviously be possible to validate an *existing* address being entered for security purposes, as the data being entered could be compared to a list of suitable names and addresses already held by the computer system.)

The practice of carrying out **data verification** is really quite simple – if, for example, it's essential that names be spelt exactly as they appear on a sheet of paper, then *independent entry* by **two different operators** can produce two **independent files**. These duplicate files are then compared, and any difference between the files can be used to flag an error. One operator can check to see who has entered the wrong data and rectify the situation before the incorrect data is used in the system. With *two different people* entering the *same data* the **integrity (correctness)** of the data is considerably increased – but the system is *obviously not* infallible.

Clerical errors such as **transcription errors** (i.e. errors in **copying (transcribing)** the data from a sheet of paper into the computer, for example) can be reduced to a minimum if **data verification** is used, but this is often too expensive for day-to-day activities – the wages bill, for example, would be doubled! Alternative methods of automatically detecting errors during the data entry phase have therefore been developed, and one common method is covered in the next section.

My name's **Robert**
...not **Robot!**

Check digits

Masses of numeric data being entered by a tired operator pose horrendous problems for the designers of the input routines. It is common for long numbers to be entered with an incorrect digit, and even more common for two digits to be transposed (64154701 being entered as 64154071, for example). However, it's possible to considerably reduce the possibility of these all-to-frequent **transcription errors** by making use of what are called **check digits** as shown in the following example.

Example using modulo 11

Suppose, for example, we are dealing with a system in which the integrity of the customer bank account number is important. Let's also suppose that we want to generate an 8-figure number such that it could be quickly and automatically checked for **integrity** on input to the system. Instead of assigning random or sequential account numbers, the following standard method is often used:

Let the first seven numbers be   6   4   1   5   4   7   0

Assign a weighting   8   7   6   5   4   3   2

(Digits 2 to 9 only – start at two from right to left – use digits again if needed.)

Multiply number by weighting   48   28   6   25   16   21   0

Add numbers in previous row $48 + 28 + 6 + 25 + 16 + 21 + 0 = 144$

Do a modulo 11 division (see page 194) $144/11 = 13$ remainder 1

The check digit 1 should now be added to the number so that the valid account number becomes:

6   4   1   5   4   7   0   1

Now, when this number is entered into the system, the same check is performed on the first 7 digits. Therefore, suppose the number was incorrectly entered as:

6   4   1   5   4   0   7   1

Carrying out the check-digit algorithm as above:

6   4   1   5   4   0   7   (1)

8   7   6   5   4   3   2

$48 + 28 + 6 + 25 + 16 + 0 + 14 = 137$

Modulo eleven check = $137/11 = 12$ remainder 5 which is the wrong check digit.

Therefore 64154071 is an invalid number.

Techniques like this, although obviously not foolproof, drastically increase the chances of the detection of transcription errors at the most crucial stage – that of being input into the computer system.

The dreaded bugs

Unless programs are trivial, then **no system or program can ever be guaranteed to be error free**. It's just that the user has not yet come up with the exact sequence of operations necessary to make the program crash. It is not unusual for programs to perform error free for months or even years, and then to crash because of an unforeseen set of circumstances. Worse than this, it is *not currently possible* to prove that programs are correct. Mathematics is not yet advanced enough to be able to determine the correctness of complex systems, nor are our computers fast enough yet to go through every conceivable path in a complex system. All you can do is to follow a sensible strategy that will keep errors to a minimum.

Alpha and beta testing

The worst people to test software are the people who wrote it! This is because they know how it *should be* used, and are therefore less likely to do unexpected things with it. It's usual to get reasonably-tolerant people to help with the first stages of testing in house, and this is known as **alpha** (the first stage) **testing**. After successful alpha testing some trusted customers are often given the opportunity to try out the software, knowing that it might (will!) contain some bugs – this is called **beta testing**. After successful beta testing has been carried out, the software is released, usually with a version number of 1.0. However, sometimes, even after extensive beta testing, there are still major bugs in the systems – the author thinks that version 1.0 released to the customers should be called gamma testing! After many different versions, when software is almost bug free – that's the time to release a completely-new version and start the process all over again!

Documentation

There's not much point in having a fancy error-free and completely working program if it is not accompanied by appropriate **documentation.** *Without a detailed technical specification and supporting documentation* to show how the program was developed then the program is probably *not in a position* to be **maintained effectively** by other people. As time progresses and the needs of the system change, without the ability to be maintained properly the software will become outdated and useless. It has been estimated that well over 90% of programming activity in industry is in updating existing software, and billions of pounds are being spent each year on **software maintenance.** With this borne in mind, suitable documentation to accompany the programs is of paramount importance.

What constitutes suitable documentation? This all-important question obviously depends upon the system we are documenting. For example, the documentation accompanying a project written in a typical third-generation (3GL) language (see page 105) would be vastly different from the documentation which is needed for a user manual. The following section lists typical subsections for common 3GL scenarios.

Program documentation

This documentation is designed to allow a professional programmer to modify the program at some later stage. It's *absolutely essential* that some form of documentation accompanies the source code in the form of suitable **comments**. Without suitable comments *effective* **software maintenance** becomes very difficult if not impossible to achieve. You must never forget that software maintenance is just as important as all the other stages in the cycle of the development of systems. (See CASE at the end of this chapter.)

The following is typical of **internal documentation** (documentation inherent in the structure of a program) which should provide sufficient information for effective maintenance of a procedure or sub-routine in a typical 3GL. **You should pay particular attention to this section – and you would do well to mirror this philosophy in any programming project which you undertake – or to go back and modify any programs that you are thinking of handing in for your advanced level project**.

A statement of purpose

It's essential that the *purpose* of any sub-routine or procedure be *explicitly stated* at the beginning of the code. For example, in the language 'C' (and still available in 'C ++'), comments at the start of a procedure might take on the following form:

```
/* The purpose of this procedure is to accept data representing the 4
   coloured bands on a resistor, validate these entries, reject them if necessary,
   then calculate the tolerance and ideal resistance values ready to be used by
   the plotting routine.

    */
```

Don't forget that **comments** are *ignored* by the compiler, and therefore do not contribute any extra object code or require any extra execution time.

Use meaningful variable names

Most 3GLs now provide suitable means of using more descriptive variable names. Gone are the days when 'I', 'V' or 'R', for example, would do for variable names. It might be far better to use 'Current_mA', 'Voltage_V' and 'Resistance_kohms' if this is more appropriate. In this particular example you have dramatically increased the information content by making it obvious what the variables represent, and have included the units of measurement as well.

In addition to the use of meaningful variable names it is also useful to include a **list of the variables** *in the appropriate part of the code* (in *addition* to any **declarations** imposed by the syntax of the language). In the resistor example quoted above, a suitable variable list might be:

```
*/ Inputs:    Band_1          Colour representing first digit
              Band_2          Colour representing second digit
              Band_3          Colour representing multiplier
              Band_4          Colour representing tolerance
    Outputs:  Not_valid       Boolean flag set true if data is invalid
              Resistor_value  Number representing the resistance value
              Tolerance       Number representing tolerance limits
    */
```

From the above you can see that four unvalidated variables representing colour are input to this procedure and two validated numeric values are calculated which are to be used by another part of the program. A third variable acting as a flag will terminate the routine if necessary.

Any other sub-routines or procedures which may be referenced (only subordinate routines need be considered) should also be listed. In the above case we might need to make a reference to the procedure which plots the actual picture of the resistor along with its values *if* this is called from *within* the routine currently being considered.

Additional information

In professional circles it is usually necessary to add the author's name and the date on which the final code was completed. In addition to this a catalogue of modifications to the system might also be necessary. A typical entry for our resistor example might be:

```
/*  Author:        Mike Rofarad
    Date:          16/12/94

    Modifications
    Date: 17/04/95  (Version 1.1)
                    Tolerance validation routines now include 20% (No
                    band 4)
                    Resistors.
    Date: 30/05/95  (Version 1.2)
                    Program modified to include 5-band resistor types.
*/
```

You would be well advised to use similar techniques in your advanced-level projects.

Don't go overboard

You must *not* put too much documentation into your program or else it will obscure the overall logic, thus cancelling out the effectiveness of the structured approach. As a guide don't comment on every single line of code, but put larger comments at the beginning of procedures or parts of the program which carry out specific tasks.

Other aids to readability

Don't forget to make extensive use of indents to emphasise the structure of the program. However, when the program is being maintained it is often very difficult to manually modify these indents and it's easy to get mixed up, especially if the program is a complex one. On more-sophisticated systems automatic indenting attempts to get over these problems.

Further systems help

In this chapter we have concentrated on documentation from a programming perspective. We have also seen an enormous number of diagrammatic methods for helping with the structured approach to systems and programming design. However, there are currently a large number of software packages in existence which help significantly with drawing, maintaining and analysing these diagrams. These are commonly known as **diagramming tools**, and the group of software to which they belong is collectively known as **CASE**.

CASE

CASE, or **Computer Aided Software Engineering** is relatively new compared to the more-established technologies such as CAD and CAM, or, more recently CIM (Computer Integrated Manufacturing). However, to the software developer, CASE is just as exciting and has huge implications for the future of software development. At the time of writing the third edition of this book, CASE consists of many different software development tools, most acting in isolation of each other. Just like CAD and CIM, CASE is aiming towards a totally integrated project-support environment for software development engineering. CASE tools can be found in areas as diverse as analysis and design of systems, testing, maintenance, programming, prototyping, business systems, planning and many others.

We have looked at many different methods of analysis and design. For each method considered there are appropriate software tools to aid the design process. For example, **PERT**, **4GLs**, **editors**, **compilers** and other **utilitie**s are but a few of the many **software packages** currently available to help develop software-based projects. The following list contains just some of the major categories where specialised software development programs already exist. Many others are beyond the scope of a book at this level.

Category	Examples
Analysis and design tools	Data flow analysis
Project management tools	Scheduling (PERT)
Programming tools	4GLs, Application generators
Tools to help with testing and debugging	Data generation programs
Documentation tools	DTP systems, CAD
Prototyping tools	Modelling and simulation

The next stage currently under development is to integrate all the above (and very much more) into the *same environment*, similar to that found in a modern database management system (DBMS). In this way software development engineers will have a complete set of tools which will help them to develop a project from initial conception, via specification, development, testing, documentation and maintenance. Indeed, it is hoped that the powerful simulation software will be able to carry out checks on the design and analysis phase before any code has actually been developed. It is also hoped that the necessary code will not be produced by hand, but be automatically developed *and tested* by the system. The degree of automation pointed to by these new systems is of breathtaking proportions, and already there are code generators that can produce the code for major chunks of large projects. Many of these methodologies are based on the object-oriented approach considered in detail in chapter 8.

As with all complex systems there are usually some disadvantages, and as stated in chapter 8, OOP (Object-Oriented Programming) suffers from the fact that much-larger programs are produced by this method than would have been the case if hand-optimised code had been used. Nevertheless, with machines becoming faster and memory becoming more plentiful, this disadvantage is usually of little consequence compared to the much-greater degree of automation and the faster development time. Couple this with the fact that fewer staff are needed and less expensive mistakes are made, and you have a winner until something better comes along. Don't forget that software development is an evolutionary process, and CASE is just the latest in this evolutionary cycle that has been going on for about 50 years.

You can see from the above that we have only just touched on the future potential of software engineering. You should see that it's not just about writing programs, but is about the development of a new and extremely complex environment that will be necessary if the enormous complexity of tomorrow's software is to be developed in a sensible period of time. It is likely that those companies which do not fully embrace this software engineering ethos will not be able to produce complex code in a cost-effective manner or in a sensible time scale. In addition you should also see why the term software engineering has been used – a whole new branch of computer science has been produced which embraces many methodologies from previously unconnected branches. Keep a lookout for development of Computer Aided Software Engineering, it will bring a whole new meaning to the term CASE study!

Exercise 18.1

1. What is meant by **the classic system life cycle**, and why has it been necessary to modify our view of this model with the hindsight of years of systems experience?

2. Why has **prototyping** become important in the context of systems design?

3. Why are program flowcharts insufficient for describing systems? What flowcharts are used instead?

4. Draw a systems flowchart representing possible solutions to the following problems. (A macro view should be taken of each system – i.e. not too much detail.)
   (a) Logging and control of entry to a building by use of a swipe card and pin.
   (b) Checking to see if students are present by using a computerised registration system (i.e. an electronic book for your lecturer/teacher!). Assume that it's linked by radio to the school's centralised database.
   (c) Booking theatre tickets at a computerised box office.
   (d) Helping to manage the arrivals, collation and distribution of newspapers and periodicals which arrive at a local newsagents each day. Your system should help with the lists needed by the delivery boys and girls.

5. Establish a set of suitable objectives that you think might be important if attempting a systems analysis of the following problems.
   (a) A small general-practice surgery (i.e. medical doctors).
   (b) Creating a database of software for a school running multi-platform machines over a network.
   (c) Controlling the central heating system for a large building which is split up into zones for the purpose of heating.
   (d) Creation of a notice-board system of the sort which displays the 'flight-arrivals and departures' at Heathrow. Your system should be designed for a school or college where the principle and other teachers can broadcast notices and pictures to all parts of the campus.

6. For the systems outlined in question (5), outline possible disadvantages the introduction of such a system might have in the short term.

7. In each of the systems outlined in question (5) discuss possible security problems and outline your plans for overcoming them.

8. For the systems outlined in question (5), discuss whether you would use an application package, or write your own software. Give reasons for your decision.

9. For the systems outlined in question (5), discuss how you would proceed to test some salient part of the system.

10. Briefly describe what aids are available to systems analysts and programmers developing systems of the sort described in question (5).

11. Discuss what is meant by checksums, hashing and CRCs when applied to data validation.

12. What is the difference between data validation and data verification – give some examples.

13. Discuss the types of documentation that would be necessary for each of the systems outlined in question (5).

14. What is meant by CASE, and how is this system helping to cope with the increasingly complex software development phases of projects?

End of chapter summary

- A **system** can be regarded from a systems analysis point of view as being anything involving a collection of people, organisations, hardware and software etc. which has been assembled for a particular purpose.
- **Systems analysis** involves a detailed study of a proposed or existing system to determine the **information requirements** of the system.
- **Systems design** involves designing a system which will meet a particular specification in terms of hardware and software, personnel etc.
- **Systems analysis and design** involves finding the solutions to major projects in an effective and efficient way.
- The **system life cycle** is one method of providing a set of rules which, if followed, provides an effective systems-analysis framework. However, it's not the only method, with **prototyping** being one alternative strategy.
- The **system life cycle** is usually made up of a **detailed definition of the problem**, a **feasibility study**, **collecting information**, **analysis**, **design**, **implementation**, **evaluation** and **maintenance**.
- A **feasibility study** is a check to see if the problem is economically and technically feasible for solution by computer.
- The **analysis and design** phases make use of a variety of **structured analysis** and **design** principles.
- **Computer-science-based projects** carried out by advanced-level students should make extensive use of the techniques covered in this chapter.
- **Prototyping** involves making a mock-up of parts or all of the system so that better methods of implementation may be found.
- **Prototyping** and the **system life cycle** can complement each other if applied and used sensibly.
- The **software-engineering approach** can be of great help when working out typical software requirements.
- **Systems flowchart** symbols help express systems ideas in the form of a flowchart.
- **Software engineering** is a systematic approach to the design of software involving **analysis**, **testing**, **debugging** and **documentation** of software.
- **Analysis of software** usually involves **top-down techniques** (see page 135).
- **Testing of software** involves splitting up large programs into smaller modules. The **bottom-up technique** is most appropriate for software testing.
- The **bottom-up approach** involves testing **syntax**, **logical errors**, individual modules, groups of modules, sub systems etc. until the complete system has been debugged and tested.
- A **debugger** is a special **utility** which helps to test software by providing **statistics** regarding **the state of the software** at various stages of development.
- **Trace routines** are often built into debugging software.
- A **trace routine** helps to establish what's happening as a program sequences through its instructions.
- **Diagnostics** is the general name for debugging tools and many other utilities which help to find and correct **bugs** in the system.
- A **bug** is a mistake in the system or program (or an **undocumented feature** if it does anything remotely useful!).
- **Maintenance** is the name given to the phase of correcting bugs or updating the software after it has been released.
- **Test data** should be such that the limits claimed by the specification are achieved in practice. As many different conditions should be tested as is possible.
- It's essential that the **integrity of data** (correctness) within a system has been thoroughly tested.

- **Data validation** checks to see if the range of data is sensible for its intended purpose.
- **Checksums**, **hashing** and **CRCs** etc. can be used to check the **integrity of batches** of data.
- **Data verification** checks to see if the data is likely to be correct by using an alternative source of reference.
- **Verification** is often the only means of checking original **transcription errors**.
- **Check digits** are often useful for reducing the likelihood of mistyping things like account numbers etc.
- **Modulo arithmetic** is often used as a means of providing the check digit.
- **Few systems are error free** – it's just that nobody has found the error yet.
- **Alpha testing** is in-house testing, preferably by people who did not write the original software.
- **Beta testing** is testing of software by a few customers before the software is put on general release.
- **Documentation** is an essential feature of software engineering. Without adequate documentation software will cease to be useful over a period of time.
- Both **technical** and **user** documentation are necessary.
- **Technical documentation** helps future analysts and programmers to modify or update the system.
- **User documentation** is effectively the instruction manual for the users.
- **Technical documentation** is usually for **internal consumption** only.
- **Program documentation** is that part of the **technical documentation** which describes **how the programs operate**. It includes **comments**, **lists of variables**, **author's name, date of last modifications** etc.
- More-recent methods of software development have involved the use of **CASE tools**.
- **CIM** – An acronym for Computer Integrated Manufacture.
- **CASE** stands for **Computer-Aided Software Engineering**.
- **CASE** involves the use of specialist software packages specifically designed to help **systems analysts** and **software engineers** to do their job more efficiently.
- **CASE systems** are becoming more integrated, and systems which will help out with the development of the entire system life cycle should be with us in the near future.

19 Electronic logic

Introduction

Modern digital computers are constructed making use of many integrated circuits or ICs. A typical IC is usually housed in a package similar to that shown in figure 19.1.

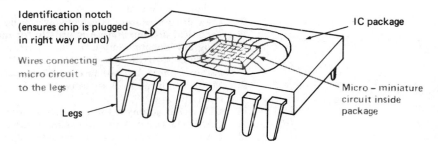

Figure 19.1

The legs on the integrated circuits are used to feed the signals from the micro-miniature circuits inside the device to the outside world. Because of the technology used to make them, **integrated circuits** are also known as **silicon chips**, **micro chips** or simply **chips.** One important device inside these chips is a tiny electronic component called a transistor. Each transistor acts as a switch that is capable of switching electronic signals on and off millions of times a second. It is this that accounts for the fantastic speed of modern digital computers.

These micro chips are called integrated circuits or ICs because the circuits inside them are collections of increasingly smaller and more sophisticated devices, that have been integrated into a single package. The progress over the last few years has been astounding. In 1957 the single transistor was constructed. In 1963 eight transistors were manufactured on a single integrated circuit. In the early 1980s the figure possible was over a quarter of a million and in 1995 it's well over a million.

The terms SSI (small scale integration), MSI (medium scale integration), LSI (large scale integration), VLSI (very large scale integration) and even SLSI (super large scale integration) are often used.

The following definitions can be used as a guideline:

SSI	Less than	10 transistors per integrated circuit
MSI	10 to about	500 transistors per integrated circuit
LSI	500 to about	20 000 transistors per integrated circuit
VLSI	20 000 to about	100 000 transistors per integrated circuit
SLSI	Greater than	100 000 transistors per integrated circuit

The above definitions vary from one manufacturer to another and should be treated as average numbers. As far as we are concerned, the transistors form the main components inside the chips and are used extensively in one form or another to make up the **logic gates** inside these chips. An important point to realise is that besides micro-miniaturisation, getting many transistors on to such a small chip is a major factor in the reduction of the cost and the increase in speed of modern digital computers.

Logic gates

A logic gate is a circuit designed to perform specific functions such as AND, OR and NOT. Logic gates can operate on different systems of logic, but throughout this text we will use the binary positive logic system where '0' represents 'OFF' and '1' represents 'ON'.

The best way to describe a logic system is by using what is called a **truth table.** A truth table is a tabular layout which shows the relationship between the output from a logic circuit and all possible inputs to the circuit. Both the outputs and inputs are expressed in terms of 0s and 1s. Consider the logic circuit shown in figure 19.2(a). In one popular system of logic, '0' is approximately 0 Volts, and '1' is approximately +5 Volts.

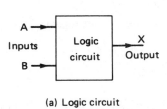

Inputs		Output
A	B	X
0	0	0
0	1	1
1	0	1
1	1	0

(a) Logic circuit   (b) Truth table

Figure 19.2

Figure 19.2(b) completely describes the function that the logic circuit will perform. This is the truth table for this logic circuit. Letters at the beginning of the alphabet such as A, B and C are often used to denote inputs, and letters at the end of the alphabet such as X, Y and Z are often used to denote outputs. The truth table is interpreted by reading across the rows as follows:

When the inputs 'A' and 'B' are both at '0' the output 'X is at '0' (first row)

When 'A' is at '0' and 'B' is at '1'   then 'X' is '1'   (second row)

When 'A' is '1' and 'B' is '0'   then 'X' is also '1'   (third row)

Finally, when both 'A' and 'B' are '1'   the output 'X' is '0'   (last row)

From the above we can see that the output goes to '1' whenever the inputs are different. Hence the function of this circuit could be to detect when two signals (A and B) are not equivalent. Logic gates are simply logic circuits designed to perform specific functions. Each logic gate has a special symbol to distinguish it from others. These functions and symbols will now be investigated.

The AND gate

The circuit symbol for an AND gate together with the truth table is shown in figure 19.3.

A	B	X
0	0	0
0	1	0
1	0	0
1	1	1

Two-input AND gate

Truth table for two-input AND gate

Figure 19.3

It should be noted that many more than two inputs are possible. However, the principles are the same and these slightly different types of gates will be covered later.

The AND gate derives its name from the fact that we get an output of '1' only when **both** of the inputs A AND B are at '1'.

The symbol for the AND operation is denoted by '.'

Hence A.B is read as A AND B. This provides us with a very convenient short-hand notation as we shall see very soon.

The output 'X' from the AND gate may therefore be written as: X = A.B

You will find that it is permissible to omit the '.' Hence the expression X = A.B becomes: X = AB. Here the AND function is implied.

The OR gate

The circuit symbol for an OR gate together with the appropriate truth table is shown in figure 19.4.

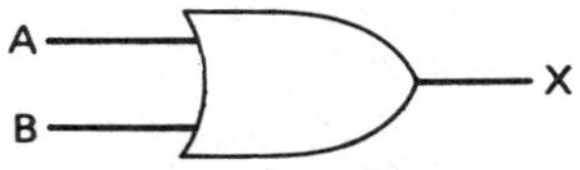

A	B	X
0	0	0
0	1	1
1	0	1
1	1	1

Two-input OR gate

Truth table for two-input OR gate

Figure 19.4

The OR gate derives its name from the fact that we get a '1' output whenever the inputs A or B or both are at '1'. Because this function includes the case where **both** inputs are '1' it is often known as the **inclusive** OR gate.

The symbol for the OR operation is '+'. Thus the shorthand way of writing A OR B is: A + B

The output from the OR gate may therefore be written as: X = A + B

The NOT gate

This gate is the simplest because it has only one input and one output. The circuit symbol for the NOT gate together with the truth table is shown in figure 19.5.

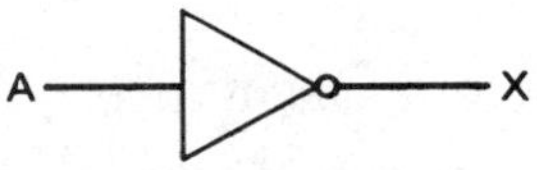

A	X
0	1
1	0

NOT gate

Truth table for NOT gate

Figure 19.5

A simplified truth table is necessary because for one input we have only two possible states i.e. '0' and '1'.

Because the output is always the **inverse** of the input, that is a '1' in gives a '0' out, or a '0' in gives a '1' out, the gate is also known as an **inverter**.

The symbol for the NOT operation is denoted by '‾' Hence the shorthand way of writing NOT A is: $\overline{A}$

Why use logic?

Before dealing with more complex logical functions and Boolean algebra, let us first see why it is necessary to invent functions such as AND, OR and NOT, and to go to all the trouble of trying to get thousands of them inside a tiny micro chip in the first place.

We will consider the very simple function of adding together just two binary digits. The situation is shown as follows:

		Sum 4	Sum 3	Sum 2	Sum 1
A	(digit one)	1	1	0	0
B+	(digit two)	1+	0+	1+	0+
sum	(answer)	0	1	1	0
Carry (if necessary)		1 . . . Carry			

We will now design a simple circuit to add together the two binary digits A and B, and produce the correct answer which we have called sum. The circuit will also produce a carry if necessary. In figure 19.2 we considered a hypothetical logic circuit with two inputs 'A' and 'B', and one output 'X'. In figure 19.6(a) we consider a very similar situation, but this time the circuit will function as a **binary adder.** The binary adder has two inputs: 'A' and 'B', and two outputs: 'sum' and a 'carry' which we will call 'S' and 'C' for convenience.

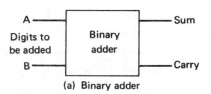

A	B	S	C
0	0	0	0
0	1	1	0
1	0	1	0
1	1	0	1

(a) Binary adder (b) Truth table for binary adder

Figure 19.6

The truth table for the binary adder can be filled in very easily by observing what happens in each of the four sums. For example, the first row of the truth table simply states that for sum 1, when both A and B are 0, then the sum is 0 and the carry is also 0. The next three rows are filled in by considering sums 2, 3 and 4.

Now consider the output columns of the truth table:

Let us concentrate on the S (sum) column. We can clearly see from the truth table that:

S is 1 if A is 0 AND B is 1 OR A is 1 AND B is 0
(note the choice of the words AND and OR)

We can write the above statement in shorthand notation:

$S = \overline{A}.B + A.\overline{B}$

NOT A and NOT B can be derived from A and B by using two NOT gates as shown in figure 19.7 (a).

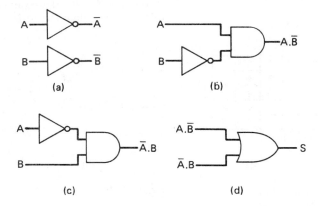

(a) (b)

(c) (d)

Figure 19.7

$A.\overline{B}$ means A AND (NOT B) being fed into a two-input AND gate as shown in figure 19.7(b).

$\overline{A}.B$ means (NOT A) AND B being fed into a two-input AND gate as shown in figure 19.7(c).

Finally, if we feed the outputs $A.\overline{B}$ from figure 19.7(b) and $\overline{A}.B$ from figure 19.7(c) into a two-input OR gate we have generated the expression $\overline{A}.B + A.\overline{B}$. This is the expression for the sum S and is therefore one of the outputs that is needed from our binary adder.

Next consider the C(carry) column of the truth table. Here we can easily see that:

C is 1 only when A AND B are both equal to 1

In shorthand notation:

C = A.B   A simple AND gate with A and B as inputs

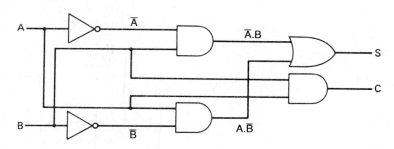

Figure 19.8

The complete binary adder circuit has now been designed and the final connections are shown in figure 19.8.

The above method is not the most efficient and indeed will be considerably improved upon when we have covered more sophisticated logic gates. However, it does illustrate how logic gates such as AND, OR and NOT can be usefully combined to perform functions that are needed inside computers. The circuit just described is called a **half adder**. It is not able to cope with adding several binary digits (a much more useful task). These slightly more advanced techniques will be covered later in this chapter.

Example

Design a logic circuit that can be used to detect whether two input signals A and B are the same.

From the 'X' column in the truth table of figure 19.9(a), we can write down the logical expression as follows:

$$X = \overline{A}.\overline{B} + A.B$$

(NOT A) AND (NOT B) can be generated using two **inverters** and a two-input AND gate as shown in figure 19.9(b). A AND B can be generated using a simple AND gate. Finally, the outputs from these two circuits can be fed into a two-input OR gate. The final circuit is shown in figure 19.9(c).

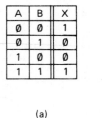

A	B	X
0	0	1
0	1	0
1	0	0
1	1	1

(a)

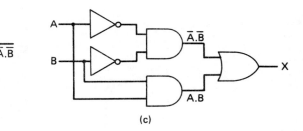

(b)   (c)

Figure 19.9

Further logic gates

Any logic function can be simulated using the AND, OR and NOT functions described in the previous sections. However, for reasons of efficiency and economy, several other very useful gates exist.

NAND and NOR gates

The NAND gate is a combination of an AND gate followed by a NOT gate. Hence the name NAND (Not AND). The idea, together with the symbol for the NAND gate is shown in figure 19.10(a) . The truth table for a NAND gate is shown in figure 19. 10(b)

Similarly the NOR gate is a combination of the OR and NOT gates. The symbol and truth table for the NOR gate are shown in figure 19.10(c) and figure 19.10(d) respectively.

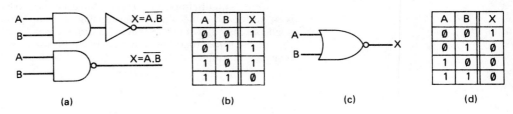

Figure 19.10

You may be wondering why it is necessary to have NAND and NOR gates, besides the obvious reasons such as being able to replace an AND gate followed by a NOT gate with a single gate. The main reason is that any function can be simulated by using NAND gates only or NOR gates only. This may seem rather surprising, but suppose that we had NAND gates only, and wanted to build up a NOT gate, an AND gate and an OR gate:

1. **A NOT gate**. This is quite simple. If you study the truth table for a NAND gate as shown in figure 19.10(b), then you will realise that if both inputs are '0' then the output is '1', or if both inputs are '1' then the output is '0'. Hence if we join the two inputs together as shown in figure 19.11(a), then we have built a NOT gate!

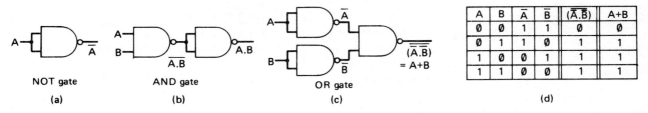

Figure 19.11

2. **An AND gate**. Simply connect one of our custom-built NOT gates on the output of a NAND gate, then we have a NOT NAND (i.e. an AND) gate. This is shown in figure 19.11(b).

3. **An OR gate**. This is slightly more difficult but the technique will soon become obvious after completing De Morgan's law when dealing with Boolean algebra later in this chapter. The circuit necessary is shown in figure 19.11(c). You can understand that it works by considering the truth table shown in figure 19.11(d). This has been filled in just by understanding how a NAND gate works. The first four columns should be quite obvious. The next column is obtained by performing a NAND operation on columns 3 and 4. If you consider the output in the last column with the original inputs A and B. then you will realise that the result is exactly the same as the OR truth table shown in figure 19.4(b). Therefore we have built an OR gate from three NAND gates.

I can imagine that by now some of you are wondering where the efficiency and economy mentioned earlier have gone! Indeed it looks as if we need three gates just to produce a simple OR gate! However, to understand why the author has not gone completely bonkers, you need to know just a little more about chips that contain logic gates.

Suppose we do an analysis of some logic functions similar to the ones that have been done earlier in this chapter, and end up with the circuit shown in figure 19.12(a). Now if you want to build up this circuit you would require a chip that contains NOT gates, a chip that contains AND gates, and a third chip that contains NAND gates. These chips have four gates of each type inside and cost the vast sum of 25p each! Therefore you will need a grand total of 75p. Now if we use NAND gates only, we can simulate the NOT gate using one NAND gate, the AND gate using two NAND gates, and the NAND gate using just one NAND gate!

The circuit using NAND gates only is shown in figure 19.12(b). A single chip contains four two-input NAND gates and we have therefore produced the entire circuit for 25p instead of 75p. A very significant saving and we have only four gates in the entire circuit.

Another equally important reason for using NAND gates only or NOR gates only is to be found at the manufacturing stage of chip production. Each tiny gate inside a silicon chip is formed by manufacturing a precision mask. If all the gates in the chip at the same, then the same mask can be used over and over again, thus cutting costs significantly.

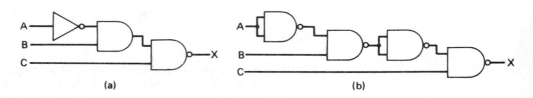

Figure 19.12

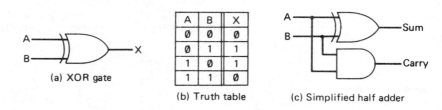

(a) XOR gate

A	B	X
0	0	0
0	1	1
1	0	1
1	1	0

(b) Truth table

(c) Simplified half adder

Figure 19.13

The XOR (eXclusive OR) gate

This is the final gate of any significance. It is manufactured because its output appears so often in computing. The symbol for the XOR gate together with the truth table are shown in figure 19.13.

If you study the truth table carefully then you may recognize it as the exact requirements for the sum output from our binary adder shown in figure 19.6(b). Hence the sum output can be generated much more easily using a single XOR gate. The simplified circuit of the **half adder** is shown in figure 19.13(c).

A glance at the truth table for the XOR gate will also reveal that you only get an output of '1' when the inputs are different or **not equivalent**. For this reason the XOR gate is also known as a **non-equivalence gate**. The symbol for the XOR operation is '⊕'. Hence A XOR B is written as A ⊕ B.

Boolean algebra

After reading the above section you will realise that before any circuit can be designed and built we almost always end up with an expression something like:

$$X = \overline{A}.B + A.\overline{B}$$

In fact you have already been doing some Boolean algebra without realising it. The above is an expression in Boolean algebra! Boolean algebra is named after the mathematician George Boole. It is a form of algebra that helps us deal with truth tables and enables us to simplify expressions of the type covered in the first few sections of this chapter.

We shall be dealing with Boolean algebra in a very informal way. In fact the way that it is going to be explained will make the pure mathematicians of the past turn over in their graves, or at least come and haunt the author! However, for A-level computer science we have to be able to understand how to use it. We are not interested in the mathematical axioms behind its development. Therefore, before we start covering some of the 'rules', I will introduce you to a very simple subject called **switching algebra.** It may not be the most elegant, but it is certainly very easy and makes Boolean algebra simpler to understand, even the more complicated parts.

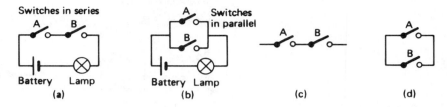

Figure 19.14

Switching algebra

If you can understand how to switch on a light then you are well on the way to a comprehensive mastery of switching algebra. First the basic concepts of AND and OR using switches are explained. Consider the circuit shown in figure 19.14(a). In this circuit the lamp will light up only if both switches A AND B are switched on.

Let '0' represent the switch when it is 'OFF' and let '1' represent the switch when it is 'ON'. Therefore two switches in **series** represent an AND function.

Consider the circuit shown in figure 19.14(b). In this second circuit the lamp will be switched 'ON' if either A OR B OR both switches are on. Therefore two switches in **parallel** represents the OR function.

Remember: Series means 'AND'; parallel means 'OR'.

It is inconvenient to have to draw out the lamps and it is even more inconvenient to draw out the batteries! Therefore the equivalent circuits are shown in figure 19.14(c) and figure 19.14(d). They are to be considered as logically the same as the circuits with the switches and lamps as before.

Most of you will probably be wondering why we are doing all this. The answer is very simple. It enables us to verify the rules of Boolean algebra easily by considering the equivalent switching circuits. It works as follows:

Suppose that we wish to simplify the Boolean expression: $X = \overline{A}.B + \overline{A}.\overline{B}$

$\overline{A}.B$ means two switches in **series**
OR means in **parallel** with, and
$\overline{A}.\overline{B}$ means two switches in **series** again

(Note $\overline{A}$ means that this switch will be closed when A is open, or this switch will be open when A is closed, i.e. the **inverse** of A.)

Now the circuit for two switches called $\overline{A}$ and B in parallel with another two switches $\overline{A}$ and B is shown in figure 19.15(a).

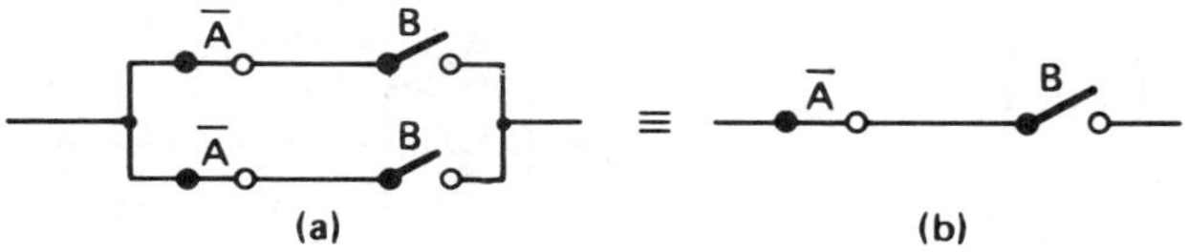

Figure 19.15

A little common sense will tell you that to produce exactly the same effect you only need the circuit shown in figure 19.15(b). Therefore one of the parallel branches is redundant. Two switches in series is simply $\overline{A}$ and B. Therefore the original Boolean expression will simplify to $X = \overline{A}.B$ Hence:

$X = \overline{A}.B + \overline{A}.B$ simplifies to $X = \overline{A}.B$

This is an example of an expression that has been simplified using switching algebra, i.e. common sense. You will realise the need to simplify expressions. The above result needs only one two-input AND gate. The original expression needed two two-input AND gates and a two-input OR gate.

Basic laws of Boolean algebra

Some of the more important rules of Boolean algebra will now be stated and the switching circuit can be used to verify that each rule is correct. The names derive from mathematics; it is useful to remember them so that you can quote the rules you are applying to simplify more complex expressions (see the examples at the end of this section).

1. Commutative laws

a) A + B = B + A

b) A.B = B.A

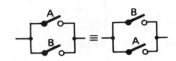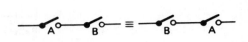

2. Associative laws

a) A + (B + C) = (A + B) + C

b) A.(B.C) = (A.B).C

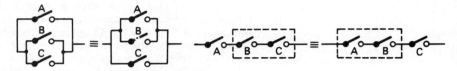

3. Distributive laws

a) A.(B + C) = (A.B) + (A.C)

b) A + (B.C) = (A + B).(A + C)

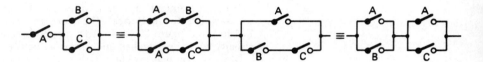

4. Tautology laws

a) A.A = A

b) A + A = A

5. More tautology laws

a) A + $\overline{A}$ = 1

b) A.$\overline{A}$ = 0

6. Absorption laws

a) A + (A.B) = A

b) A.(A + B) = A

7. Common sense number 1 (Note: 0 means 'open circuit' and '1' means 'short circuit')

a) 0.A = 0

b) 1 + A = 1

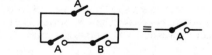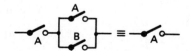

8. Common sense number 2

a) $1.A = A$ b) $0 + A = A$

9. Common sense number 3

a) $\overline{0} = 1$ b) $\overline{1} = 0$

10. Double complement laws

a) $\overline{\overline{A}} = A$

11. De Morgan's law

This is a very powerful law in Boolean algebra and will be treated slightly differently. Instead of using switching algebra we will use truth tables. The two basic forms of the law are as follows:

a) $\overline{(A + B)} = \overline{A}.\overline{B}$ b) $\overline{A.B} = \overline{A} + \overline{B}$

Consider law (a) first: We build up a truth table for the left-hand side and make up a column so it contains $\overline{A + B}$. Next we build up a truth table for the right-hand side of the expressions and build up a column so it contains $\overline{A}.\overline{B}$.

The two truth tables are as follows.

A	B	$\overline{A}$	$\overline{B}$	$\overline{A+B}$	$\overline{A}.\overline{B}$
0	0	1	1	1	1
0	1	1	0	1	1
1	0	0	1	1	1
1	1	0	0	0	0

Same

A	B	$\overline{A}$	$\overline{B}$	$\overline{A.B}$	$\overline{A}+\overline{B}$
0	0	1	1	1	1
0	1	1	0	0	0
1	0	0	1	0	0
1	1	0	0	0	0

Same

Notice that the last two columns in each truth table are identical, thus verifying that both parts of the expressions are the same.

The easiest way of understanding De Morgan's law (which the author always remembers as the 'get notted law'), is as follows:

NOT the individual terms. Change the sign. Then NOT the lot.

Consider the following example:

Start with . . . . $\overline{A} . \overline{B}$

NOT the individual terms to get . . . . $A . B$

Change the sign (AND becomes OR) .. . . $A + B$

NOT the LOT . . . . $\overline{A + B}$

(Note: A and B could themselves be more complex logic expressions. These logic expressions may be treated as if they were letters (see example on page 447).

Hence after applying De Morgan's Law to $\overline{A}.\overline{B}$ it becomes $\overline{A + B}$ (i.e. law (b) above).

Before doing some examples of Boolean algebra let us go back to the problem of understanding how to build an OR gate using NAND gates only:

We start with the expression X = A + B (a simple OR gate)

By applying De Morgan's law we get X = $\overline{\overline{A}.\overline{B}}$

This is 'NOT A' and 'NOT B' being fed into a NAND gate. Hence we can simulate an OR gate using three NAND gates as shown in figure 19.11(c).

Simplifying Boolean expressions

Most people who are familiar with the rules of normal algebra will realise that some of the laws of Boolean algebra are identical. Therefore:

A . (B + C) = A . B + A . C is the same in both systems of algebra

It is as though the + sign was the same as addition and the . sign the same as multiplication. This is one of the reasons why these signs have been so wisely chosen. However, it must of course be realised that A + A = 2A is meaningless in Boolean algebra. Also, there are many Boolean algebra rules which make nonsense in normal maths, e.g.

A + A + A + A = A is nonsense in normal algebra

However, remember the rules and make use of the switching analogies put forward, and you should find this one of the most easy and enjoyable topics at 'A' level.

Examples

(1) Simplify A + B + $\overline{A}$ + $\overline{B}$

Solution: A + B + $\overline{A}$ + $\overline{B}$ = (A + $\overline{A}$) + (B + $\overline{B}$)   Associative laws

$\phantom{Solution: A + B + \overline{A} + \overline{B}}$ =   1   +   1   Tautology laws

Therefore A + B + $\overline{A}$ + $\overline{B}$ = 1

(2) Simplify A.B.C + $\overline{A}$.B.C + A.$\overline{B}$.C + A.B.$\overline{C}$

(NOTE: one extra technique that is very useful and only implied in the previous rules is that you can use some parts of an expression more than once. This can easily be verified by thinking of the parallel arrangements of switches that it is possible to have. If A + A = A, then there is no reason why we could not write A + B = A + A + B. The reasons why we would want to do this can be found in this example.)

For the purposes of this example we will label each part of the original expression. You will probably mentally do this when you tackle similar questions yourself:

$\quad$ (1) $\qquad$ (2) $\qquad$ (3) $\qquad$ (4)

A.B.C + $\overline{A}$.B.C + A.$\overline{B}$.C + A.B.$\overline{C}$

Part (1) of the expression will be used three times (see note above). The new equivalent expression is written out again:

$\quad$ (1) $\qquad$ (2) $\qquad$ (1) $\qquad$ (3) $\qquad$ (1) $\qquad$ (4)

A.B.C + $\overline{A}$.B.C + A.B.C + A.$\overline{B}$.C + A.B.C + A.B.$\overline{C}$

We now make use of factorization (as in normal algebra). We factorize parts (1) and (2), parts (1) and (3) and finally parts (1) and (4). Writing out this factorized form of the above expression we get:

$\quad$ (1) & (2) $\qquad$ (1) & (3) $\qquad$ (1) & (4)

B.C.(A + $\overline{A}$) + A.C.(B + $\overline{B}$) + A.B.(C + $\overline{C}$)

The reasons for using parts of the expression more than once should now be obvious. The factorized form has yielded three new parts which we can simplify. All the terms of the expression in brackets simplify to 1 using the tautology laws. Finally, using common sense rule number 2a, we get the following simplified expression:

B.C + A.C + A.B

This is about the simplest form in which the original expression can be written. It is a considerable simplification which would lead to a considerable reduction in building a circuit should this function need to be realised in practice.

(3) $(\overline{A.\overline{B}} + \overline{\overline{A}.B} + A.\overline{B})$

$(A.B + \overline{A}.\overline{B} + A.\overline{B} + \overline{A}.\overline{B})$ Using part (1) twice

$(\overline{A}.(B + \overline{B}) + \overline{B}.(A + \overline{A}))$ Factorize

$\overline{A} + \overline{B}$ Tautology laws

$\overline{A.B}$ De Morgan's law

The last stage may not in some people's opinion be a simpler expression than the previous line. Unless you were asked to show that the expression was equal to a specific simplified form, then either answer would be acceptable.

Use of truth tables

On many occasions it is a very long and tedious process using the above techniques to verify if a relationship such as:

$$\overline{A}.\overline{B}.\overline{C} + \overline{A}.\overline{B}.C + A.\overline{B}.\overline{C} + A.\overline{B}.C = \overline{B} \text{ is true}$$

One possible and highly useful method is to construct truth tables in the following way.

A	B	C	$\overline{A}$	$\overline{B}$	$\overline{C}$	$\overline{A}.\overline{B}.\overline{C}$	$\overline{A}.\overline{B}.C$	$A.\overline{B}.\overline{C}$	$A.\overline{B}.C$	$\overline{A}.\overline{B}.\overline{C} + \overline{A}.\overline{B}.C + A.\overline{B}.\overline{C} + A.\overline{B}.C$
0	0	0	1	1	1	1	0	0	0	1
0	0	1	1	1	0	0	1	0	0	1
0	1	0	1	0	1	0	0	0	0	0
0	1	1	1	0	0	0	0	0	0	0
1	0	0	0	1	1	0	0	1	0	1
1	0	1	0	1	0	0	0	0	1	1
1	1	0	0	0	1	0	0	0	0	0
1	1	1	0	0	0	0	0	0	0	0

Next compare the last column ($\overline{A}.\overline{B}.\overline{C} + \overline{A}.\overline{B}.C + A.\overline{B}.\overline{C} + A.\overline{B}.C$) with the $\overline{B}$ column (5th one along). You will find that the patterns of 0s and 1s are identical. Therefore the above expression is the same as $\overline{B}$.

This method is also a powerful tool as an aid to simplifying Boolean expressions. One can immediately see from the last column of the truth table that the simplified expression is $\overline{B}$.

Karnaugh maps

Karnaugh maps are one of the most useful aids to simplifying certain types of Boolean expressions. It is worth spending an hour or so learning how to use them because expressions of the type:

$$\overline{A}.\overline{B}.\overline{C}.D + \overline{A}.B.\overline{C}.D + \overline{A}.B.\overline{C}.D + \overline{A}.B.C.\overline{D}$$

can be simplified with ease in very few moments. Further you will find that the probability of getting the right answer is greatly increased. This is because the likelihood of making mistakes using the truth table method is quite high unless you are very careful, and it is very easy to take a couple of sides of paper using the rules of Boolean algebra if you do not happen to apply the most appropriate rules at each stage.

As with all instant wonder methods there is a small price to pay. It involves you sitting down and bearing with the author while you wade through the most weird set of instructions that you have probably encountered to date. However, stick to it, it is well worth the effort. The result may even mean doing part of an examination question in about two minutes when it was intended that most candidates should take about 10 to 15 minutes!

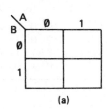

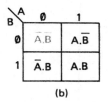

Figure 19.16

A Karnaugh map is simply a convenient tabular arrangement of a Venn diagram with which most people will be familiar from their GCSE mathematics lessons. However, you do not have to realise this to be able to use them with speed and efficiency. No 'A' level computer science syllabus requires you to be able to prove what you are doing. The methods are already well established in computing and electronics.

Consider the arrangement of four cells shown in figure 19.16(a). This is a simplified form of the arrangement shown in figure 19.16(b).

The numbers along the top of the boxes represent A. Therefore '0' means '$\overline{A}$', and '1' means 'A' in the simplified form shown in figure 19.16(a). The numbers down the left-hand side represent B. Therefore '0' represents '$\overline{B}$' and '1' represents B. We can therefore uniquely identify each cell. Using this notation, the top left-hand cell would be called $\overline{A}.\overline{B}$. This is because A is '0' from the numbers at the top AND B is '0' from the numbers at the side. Figure 19.16(b) shows the names of all the cells.

We now consider four variables instead of two. The arrangement is shown in figure 19.17(a), and the names of the cells are shown in figure 19.17(b).

If we choose the third cell from the left on the top row then we can see that both A AND B are 1 (from 11 at the top), and both C AND D are 0 (from the 00 at the side). Hence the name of this cell is $A.B.\overline{C}.\overline{D}$

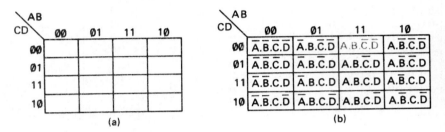

Figure 19.17

You are probably wondering why the numbers along the top and down the side go in the order: 00, 01, 11, 10. This is a consequence of the way in which this type of Karnaugh map works. The derivation of these numbers is fascinating. **Gray code** is a code where only one digit changes at any one time. This is a particularly good practical application of Gray code and this particular code is called **mirror reflecting Gray code**.

To derive these numbers consider the following:

Start with   0   (This is the simplest
                    1   2-bit Gray code)

Reflect the above numbers in an imaginary **Mirror line**

                    0   (Original numbers)
                    1
—————————————— **Mirror line**
                    1
                    0   ('Reflected' numbers)

Next add 0s above the mirror line and 1s below the mirror line to complete the 2-bit Gray code.

We then get   0   0
              0   1   (This is the 2-bit Gray code used for
              1   1   the 4-variable Karnaugh maps)
              1   0

The process can be extended indefinitely. Therefore for a 3-bit code we start with the 2-bit code and reflect that in the mirror line and add the 0s and 1s as before:

              0   0   0
              0   0   1   (Original 2-bit Gray code)
              0   1   1
              0   1   0
——————————————— **Mirror line**
              1   1   0
              1   1   1   (Reflected 2-bit Gray code)
              1   0   1
              1   0   0

Hence if you wanted a 6-variable Karnaugh map then the numbers across the top and down the side would be: 000, 001, 011, 010, 110, 111, 101, and 100.

If you ever have to use any type of Gray code then this one is certainly easy to remember.

How to use Karnaugh maps

We will start by considering a 4-variable Karnaugh map and the problem of simplifying the following Boolean expression:

$$\overset{(1)}{\overline{A}.\overline{B}.\overline{C}.\overline{D}} + \overset{(2)}{\overline{A}.\overline{B}.\overline{C}.D} + \overset{(3)}{\overline{A}.\overline{B}.C.\overline{D}} + \overset{(4)}{\overline{A}.B.C.\overline{D}}$$

Consider the following 4-variable map:

CD \ AB	00	01	11	10
00	0	1	0	0
01	0	1	0	0
11	0	1	0	0
10	0	1	0	0

To fill it in we proceed through the above expression from left to right.

From part (1) we get $\overline{A}.\overline{B}.\overline{C}.\overline{D}$, therefore a '1' goes into the 0100 cell. This is the '1' in the cell on the top row of the map.

From part (2) we get $\overline{A}.B.\overline{C}.D$, therefore a '1' goes into the 0101 cell. This is the '1' in the cell on the second row on the map.

The other two 1s are filled in using the third and fourth parts of the Boolean expression.

When you have finished with all the terms, 0s are put in all the other cells.

To read the answer requires concentrating on the part or parts of the map that contain the 1s. If we draw a 'sausage shape' around these parts then it helps to make them stand out. Look carefully at the range of A, B, C and D covered by this

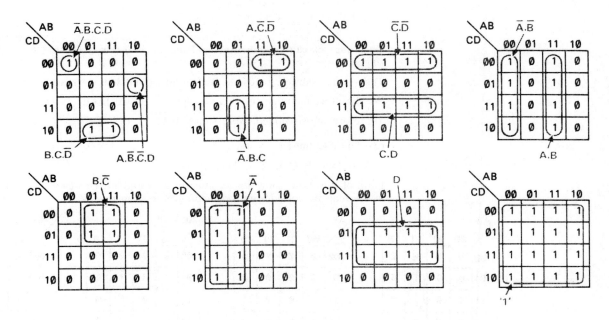

'sausage shape'. If a variable covers both the '0' AND the '1' state then it can be 'forgotten'.

C can be 0 AND 1 because the vertical range of the 'sausage' covers C being both '0' (in the top two rows of cells) and '1' (in the bottom two rows of cells). Therefore, the final expression for this 'sausage' will not contain C.

Similarly, D covers both 0s (top and bottom row of cells) and 1s (middle two rows of cells). Therefore, the final expression for this sausage will not contain D.

However, because the horizontal range of the sausage does not go very far (it only covers one cell), the As do not cover both 0s and 1s and therefore A will be contained in the final expression for this sausage shape. Similarly, the range of 0s and 1s for the B are not covered and therefore Bs will be in the final expression.

To sum up: Cs and Ds do not matter, but 'A must be 0' AND 'B must be 1'.

Therefore the simplified expression is: $\overline{A}.B$

The above might seem a little complicated on first reading. However, after a few practice goes you will find reading the maps as easy as they are to fill in. To help you become familiar with reading Karnaugh maps the examples at the bottom of page 443 are included. Make sure that you understand them well before proceeding any further.

All of the above examples are valid simplification areas. Notice that the numbers of cells in each sausage shape are multiples of binary powers i.e. $2^0 = 1$, $2^1 = 2$, $2^2 = 4$, $2^3 = 8$ etc. You cannot simplify sausage shape cells that contain any other multiples (i.e. 3, 5, 6, 7, 9, 10, 11 etc.).

Cells can be used more than once if this aids simplification (just as expressions in the original Boolean algebra can be used more than once).

Examples

(1) Simplify the following logical expression:

$$\overline{A}.\overline{B}.\overline{C}.\overline{D} + \overline{A}.\overline{B}.C.D + A.\overline{B}.C.D + \overline{A}.B.\overline{C}.D + \overline{A}.\overline{B}.C.\overline{D} + A.\overline{B}.\overline{C}.D + \overline{A}.\overline{B}.\overline{C}.D$$

First draw the map and fill in the 1s for each part of the above expression.

	A B			
C D	0 0	0 1	1 1	1 0
0 0	1	0	0	0
0 1	1	1	1	1
1 1	1	0	0	0
1 0	1	0	0	0

Two sausages can be drawn around the 1s. Two sets of 'Four 1s' can therefore be ringed.

The vertical sausage reads $\overline{A}.\overline{B}$. The horizontal sausage reads $\overline{C}.D$

We therefore combine the two sausages to get $\overline{A}.\overline{B}$ OR $\overline{C}.D$

Therefore the simplified expression will be $\overline{A}.\overline{B} + \overline{C}.D$

(2) Simplify the expression:

$$A.B.D + \overline{B}.C.D + \overline{C}.D + \overline{A}.B.C.D$$

Parts of this expression do not contain all variables. However, it is still easy to fill in the map by considering the reading process in reverse.

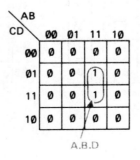

A.B.D

(a)

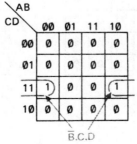

$\overline{B}.C.D$

(see rules of symmetry below)

(b)

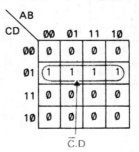

$\overline{C}.D$

(c)

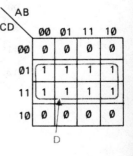

D

(d)

For example, A.B.D are the two cells shown in figure 19.18(a)

$\overline{B}$.C.D are the two cells shown in figure 19.18(b) (see rules of symmetry in the next section) and finally, $\overline{C}$.D are the four cells shown in figure 19.18(c)

We now combine these three patterns of 1s together with the 1 from part (4) of the expression and end up with the map shown in figure 19.18(d).

The larger the sausage shapes that can be drawn the better (assuming that they conform to the binary power rule and obey rules of symmetry discussed below).

Combining all three sausages together with the single '1' we get the simplified expression:

$$A.B.D + \overline{B}.C.D + \overline{C}.D + \overline{A}.B.C.D = D$$

Rules of symmetry for Karnaugh maps

In addition to the binary powers mentioned earlier, we can imagine that the maps can be folded in such a way that they form a cylinder, or be folded so that all four corners can touch one another. This can aid simplification and some of the possible ways are shown below:

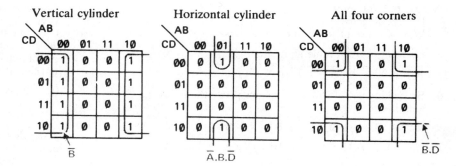

Three- and two-variable Karnaugh maps

Four variables were chosen in the previous examples because if the shapes and sizes of the maps are kept the same then it makes learning the principles easier. However, it is possible to have any number of variables. A 2-variable map and a 3-variable map are now shown together with some simplification of expressions within these different shape maps:

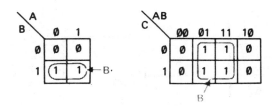

Further electronic logic

Now that you are 'experts' at formulating Boolean expressions from truth tables, and then simplifying them using Boolean algebra or Karnaugh maps, let us see some practical use for this considerable amount of theory.

Decoders and encoders

The terms **encoders** and **decoders** have the following meaning:

An **encoder** is a device that changes data into a form that is usually ideal for entry into a machine. A good example is the keyboard which has to change data from a form that we can understand (the letters on a keyboard) into a form that the machine can understand (often ASCII code).

A **decoder** is a device that changes the code back into its original form that can be regarded as information. For example, the changing of the internal computer codes into a form that prints recognisable letters and numbers on a printer. A decoder (for the purposes of this chapter) is a device, containing a matrix of logic gates, that selects one or more output channels according to the combination of input signals present.

Exercise 19.1

1. What do you understand by the term VLSI? How has this and other technology led to the micro-miniaturisation of vital computer system components?

2. Why are **logic chips** so important to modern day electronic computers?

3. Draw out the truth table for the following **two-input** gates:
 (a) AND gate
 (b) XOR gate
 (c) NOR gate
 Draw out the truth table for a four-input NOR gate.

4. Show that 'AND', 'OR' and 'NOT' gates can be constructed out of:
 (a) NAND gates only
 (b) NOR gates only
 Why is it useful to be able to do this?

5. By using a truth table show that:
$$\overline{X.Y} + X.\overline{Y} = (\overline{X} + \overline{Y}) + (\overline{X + Y})$$

6. By making use of Boolean algebra prove the following identities:
 (a) $\overline{A}.B + A.\overline{B} = \overline{(A + \overline{B}).(\overline{A} + B)}$
 (b) $B.C + A.D = (B + A).(B + D).(A + C).(C + D)$
 (c) $X.Y + X.Y.Z + X.\overline{Y} = X$

7. Simplify the following Boolean expressions:
 (a) $A.\overline{C} + B.\overline{C}.D + A.\overline{B}.C + A.C.D$
 (b) $B + \overline{A}.\overline{B} + A.C.D + A.\overline{C}$
 (c) $\overline{A}.B.C + A.B.\overline{C} + A.B.C + \overline{A}.B.\overline{C}$

8. Draw a truth table for the folowing:
$$X = \overline{A}.\overline{B}.C.D + \overline{A}.B.\overline{C}.D + \overline{A}.B.C.D +$$
$$A.\overline{B}.C.D + A.B.\overline{C}.D + A.B.C.D$$

 (a) By using a Karnaugh map or otherwise, simplify the above expression
 (b) Draw the logic circuit of the simplified Boolean expression making use of NAND and NOR gates only.

9. Given that X = 01011001 and Y = 11001001

 Show that the result of X AND Y, NOT X, and X NOT-EQUIVALENT Y.

10. (a) Show that the Boolean expressions $\overline{(A.(B + C))}$ and $\overline{A} + \overline{B}.\overline{C}$ are equivalent. Justify each step of your answer.
 (b) Four binary signals, A, B, C and D are used to define an integer in the range 0 to 15.
 A combination which represents a decimal digit satisfies at least one of the following criteria:

 (i)   A is 0
 (ii) B, C are the same, but different from A
 (iii) B, C are both 0

 Write down a Boolean expression for **each** condition and hence a simplified expression for a combination which represents a decimal digit. State, with reasons, which of the three conditions if any, is redundant.

 (c) Hence or otherwise, draw an efficient logic diagram, using AND, OR and NOT elements, to detect if the four binary signals represent a decimal digit.

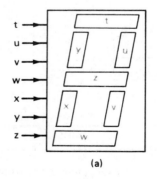

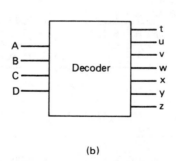

Number	Inputs				Outputs						
	A	B	C	D	t	u	v	w	x	y	z
(0)	0	0	0	0	1	1	1	1	1	1	0
(1)	0	0	0	1	0	1	1	0	0	0	0
(2)	0	0	1	0	1	1	0	1	1	0	1
(3)	0	0	1	1	1	1	1	1	0	0	1
(4)	0	1	0	0	0	1	1	0	0	1	1
(5)	0	1	0	1	1	0	1	1	0	1	1
(6)	0	1	1	0	1	0	1	1	1	1	1
(7)	0	1	1	1	1	1	1	0	0	0	0
(8)	1	0	0	0	1	1	1	1	1	1	1
(9)	1	0	0	1	1	1	1	1	0	1	1

(a)   (b)   (c)

Figure 19.19

Example

As an example consider a typical situation which occurs in practice and is consistent with the second definition above.

A seven-segment LED (light emitting diode) display needs a 7-bit code to drive it as shown in figure 19.19(a).

The LED can display codes from 0 through to 9 inclusive by lighting the different bars of the seven-segment display shown in figure 19. l9(a). To light up the top bar we make sure that it is a '1'. Thus if we wanted the number 'three' to appear on the display, t, u, v, w and z would all have to be made equal to '1'.

It is inefficient to use seven output lines from the computer as 2^7 =128 different codes could be generated using these. Only four lines are needed to generate 10 unique codes. A maximum of 2^4 =16 codes could be obtained using four lines. A decoder is therefore necessary to change the codes from the computer to the codes that are presented to the seven-segment display. The decoder is used as shown in figure 19.19(b).

If we call the outputs t, u, v, w, x, y, and z, and the inputs A, B, C and D, then we can draw up a truth table as shown in figure 19. l9(c). Note that the truth table is very easy to fill in. As an example consider the top row. When A, B, C and D are all zero the number input to the decoder is therefore zero. To get zero on the seven segment display we must light up bars: t, u, v, w, x, and y. These letters are therefore '1', and only z remains off and is therefore '0'. The remaining rows are filled in using similar considerations.

The next, and most important point to realise, is that the remaining input codes (i.e. 10 to 15 inclusive) have no bearing whatsoever on the operation of the circuit. We therefore **don't care** what happens as the input codes can never go into these states. Our bars will only need to light up when the unique codes 0 to 9 are used. We can make use of these don't-care conditions when simplifying the final logic functions. It effectively means that we can use these don't care conditions to help make our 'sausages' bigger in the Karnaugh map. The don't care conditions are shown in the maps as DC.

Consider the Karnaugh map for the t output:

CD \ AB	00	01	11	10
00	1	0	1	1
01	0	1	1	1
11	DC	DC	DC	DC
10	1	1	DC	DC

From this map we can see that all cells with the exception of 0100 and 0001 have a '1' inside them! If this situation arises, then there is a useful way to arrive at a sensible answer much more quickly.

Instead of using the map to gather together the 1s, use it to gather together the 0s and then we have the **inverse** of the correct answer.

In the above case the inverse of the answer is $(\overline{A}.B.\overline{C}.\overline{D}) + (\overline{A}.\overline{B}.\overline{C}.D)$

Using De Morgan's law we can modify this to $\overline{(\overline{A}.B.\overline{C}.\overline{D}) . (\overline{A}.\overline{B}.\overline{C}.D)}$

Therefore $t = (A + \overline{B} + C + D).(A + B + C + \overline{D})$ (De Morgan's law applied to each of the brackets, and taking the inverse to get the right answer.)

Therefore the logic circuit for decoding the t output from the A, B, C and D inputs is as follows:

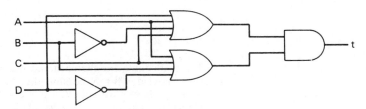

All of the other outputs (u, v, w, x, y and z) are treated in a similar way. Working out the solutions and logic circuits forms one of the questions in the end-of-chapter exercises.

Encoders

Example

Have you ever thought of doing a survey of what people think of your school or college dinners? If you designed a survey form then it might be along the following lines:

Dinner quality survey form
Please pencil in the box alongside the most appropriate comment:
☐ Cordon Bleu standard ☐ Very good ☐ Good ☐ Average ☐ Below average ☐ Disgusting ☐ It can seriously damage your health

Let us assume that we are going to design a device that reads a special mark sense card like the one above. This mark sense card will be passed through an optical scanning mechanism. The data from the scanning mechanism is to be fed into our device so that this data can be **encoded** into the form that will be fed into the computer for analysis. Hence the term encoder. There will be seven separate '0' and '1' type signals produced when the device scans a card. Also, there will be a 'no signal' condition when no choice has been made in the column. **To considerably simplify the situation only one mark may be made in the column at any one time** (i.e. nobody is allowed to think that the dinners are average and disgusting at the same time!). These eight signals are to be fed into the computer as pure binary code on a group of three wires.

Let us label the outputs from our device X, Y and Z (i.e. the three wires to be fed into the computer) and let us label the inputs to our device (i.e. the outputs from the scanning mechanism that reads the card) a, b, c, d, e, f and g to represent the seven columns on the card. The situation is shown in figure 19.20(a).

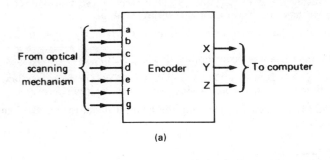

(a)

(Comment)	Inputs							Outputs		
	a	b	c	d	e	f	g	X	Y	Z
(No holes punched)	0	0	0	0	0	0	0	0	0	0
(Cordon Bleu)	1	0	0	0	0	0	0	0	0	1
(Very good)	0	1	0	0	0	0	0	0	1	0
(Good)	0	0	1	0	0	0	0	0	1	1
(Average)	0	0	0	1	0	0	0	1	0	0
(Below average)	0	0	0	0	1	0	0	1	0	1
(Disgusting)	0	0	0	0	0	1	0	1	1	0
(Damage Health)	0	0	0	0	0	0	1	1	1	1

(b)

Figure 19.20

The truth table for the scanning mechanism is shown in figure 19.20(b).

If we consider the X column then we get: $X = d + e + f + g$. Similarly for the Y and Z columns we get: $Y = b + c + f + g$ and $Z = a + c + e + g$.

Hence the circuit for the encoder is as follows:

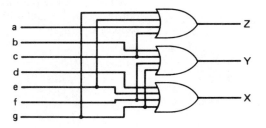

Further computer arithmetic

The full adder

Earlier in this chapter we designed a binary adder which we called a **half adder** circuit (see figure 19.6(a)). The circuit was then considerably simplified when the XOR gate was introduced, figure 19.13(c). We now extend these principles to cater for more complex arithmetic operations.

Consider the following binary sum:

```
0  0 [0] 1  1
1  0 [1] 1  0  +
─────────────
1  1 [0] 0  1
─────────────
      1 [1]        . . .   Carry in from previous column
```

Consider the middle column of the sum contained in brackets. In this column we have had to deal with a carry in from the previous column as well as a carry out to the next column with which we have dealt before. Therefore if we are to add together groups of binary digits we need to be able to deal with **three inputs.** The two binary digits to be added plus a carry from the previous column. This is the difference between a half adder and a full adder. The **full adder** is able to cope with all three inputs.

Let us call the carry from the previous bit P. Therefore the full adder will have three inputs: A, B and P. and two outputs: S and C for sum and carry. The truth table for the full adder is therefore as follows:

Inputs			Outputs	
A	B	P	S	C
0	0	0	0	0
0	0	1	1	0
0	1	0	1	0
0	1	1	0	1
1	0	0	1	0
1	0	1	0	1
1	1	0	0	1
1	1	1	1	1

```
        A        (Two binary digits
        B +      to be added)
       ─────
        Sum
       ─────
(C)arry    (P)revious carry
to next bit
```

Consider the S column of the truth table:

$$S = \overline{A}.\overline{B}.P + \overline{A}.B.\overline{P} + A.\overline{B}.\overline{P} + A.B.P$$

If you tried to simplify the above expression using a Karnaugh map then the following would happen:

```
         AB
  P\   00  01  11  10
   ┌───┬───┬───┬───┐
 0 │ 0 │ 1 │ 0 │ 1 │
   ├───┼───┼───┼───┤
 1 │ 1 │ 0 │ 1 │ 0 │
   └───┴───┴───┴───┘
```

However, consider the following:

$$S = \overline{A}.B.\overline{P} + A.\overline{B}.\overline{P} + A.B.P + \overline{A}.\overline{B}.P \quad \text{(rearrangement of the above expression)}$$

Therefore:

$$S = \overline{P}.(\overline{A}.B + A.\overline{B}) + P.(A.B + \overline{A}.\overline{B}) \qquad \text{(a) (factorizing)}$$

Let us now reconsider the expression for the 'sum output' from the half adder. If you recall this was shown to be:

$$S = \overline{A}.B + A.\overline{B}$$

It was further shown that this was also the output from an XOR gate, page 436. Now the symbol for the XOR operation was $\oplus$. Hence we can write the following:

$$S = A \oplus B$$

Now here comes the clever part. Consider what happens when you 'multiply out' the following brackets:

$$(\overline{A} + B).(A + \overline{B}) = \overline{A}.A + \overline{A}.\overline{B} + A.B + B.\overline{B} = A.B + \overline{A}.\overline{B}$$

(As $\overline{A}.A$ and $B.\overline{B}$ are both 0 from the tautology laws)

Therefore we may write:

$$
\begin{aligned}
A.B + \overline{A}.\overline{B} \quad &= \quad (\overline{A} + B).(A + \overline{B}) \\
&= \quad \overline{(A.\overline{B})}.\overline{(\overline{A}.B)} \qquad \text{(De Morgan's law on each bracket)} \\
&= \quad \overline{(A.\overline{B} + \overline{A}.B)} \qquad \text{(De Morgan's law using the whole expression)} \\
&= \quad \overline{(A \oplus B)} \qquad \text{(Using XOR)}
\end{aligned}
$$

Notice two major points:

1. The expression on the left-hand side of the above is the same as the last expression in brackets in equation (a) above.

2. The expression on the right-hand side of the above is simply NOT an XOR function.

Hence we may rewrite equation (a) above as:

$$S = \overline{P}.(\overline{A}.B + A.\overline{B}) + P.(A.B + \overline{A}.\overline{B}) \qquad \text{(a)}$$
$$S = \overline{P}.(A \oplus B) + P.\overline{(A \oplus B)}$$
$$S = P.\overline{(A \oplus B)} + \overline{P}.(A \oplus B) \qquad \text{(b) (rearranging above)}$$

Now here comes the very clever part:

If you stare long enough at the right-hand side of equation (b) you will realise that this itself is an XOR function in $(A \oplus B)$ and P (i.e. let $(A \oplus B)$ be some other variable Q. Then the expression becomes $P.\overline{Q} + \overline{P}.Q$. This can be written as: $P \oplus Q$ or more conveniently $Q \oplus P$.

Therefore we may write equation (b) above as:

$$S = (A \oplus B).\overline{P} + \overline{(A \oplus B)}.P \qquad \text{(rearranging)}$$

Therefore: $S = (A \oplus B) \oplus P$

After having worked your way through the above you may not be able to see the wood for the trees. It is enlightening to draw the circuit so that we have a picture of what is happening. The circuit for the final equation is simple and is as follows:

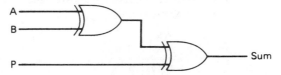

The point to note in the above diagram is that we effectively have two half adders, or at least the sum parts of them at that moment. The first adds together A and B to produce the sum of these two digits and the second adds together this sum and the carry from the previous bit. The sum output from the first half adder and the carry from the previous bit are therefore used as inputs to the second half adder.

But what about the carries? If you look carefully at the truth table you will see that a carry is generated only when a carry is generated by the first half adder or

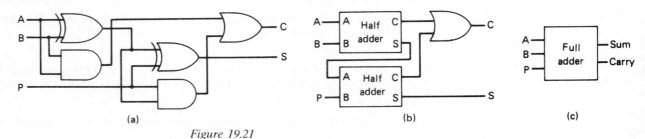

Figure 19.21

a carry is generated by the second half adder (i.e. the condition for two or three 1s in the A, B and P columns). We therefore connect the two carry outputs into a two-input OR gate. The circuit now becomes as shown in figure 19.21(a). This circuit is able to add together two binary digits A and B together with the carry from the previous bit. It produces the sum output and the carry to the next bit. It is called a **full adder**. The complete circuit is shown in figure 19.21(a). It is usual to put the half adder into a box and label it accordingly. This is shown in figure 19.21(b). The entire full adder circuit is now also put into one box. This is shown in figure 19.21(c).

Multi-digit numbers

The full adder is the basic building block of more advanced multiple-digit binary adders. There are two basic ways in which groups of binary numbers may be added together: numbers may be added serially or in parallel. We will first consider parallel addition as it is easier.

Parallel addition of binary numbers

The principle is shown in figure 19.22(a). Here the individual digits are presented so that each digit has its own full adder. Thus if two 8-bit binary numbers are to be added together you would need eight full adders. For simplicity only 4-bit numbers are shown in figure 19.22(a). In addition to the full adders you would need two 4-bit registers (a register is the name given to a place specifically reserved for storing the numbers) for holding the original numbers, plus another register to store the answer. This parallel adding arrangement is shown in figure 19.22(b). Parallel addition is very fast compared to serial addition. However, serial addition requires only one full adder irrespective of the number of digits to be added. As was mentioned at the beginning of this chapter micro chips are now becoming more sophisticated and very inexpensive. Therefore the extra hardware needed for parallel addition is of little consequence. As a result of the speed and the relatively inexpensive hardware, parallel addition is by far the most popular method.

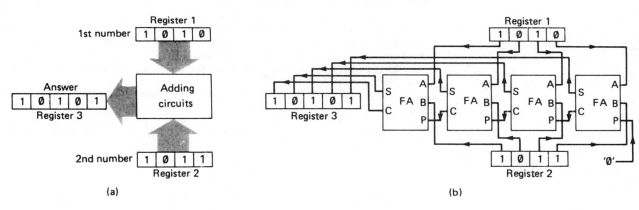

Figure 19.22

Serial addition of binary numbers

This method requires the same number of registers as parallel addition, but only one full adder is required. As each digit shares the same full adder, the carry through to the next bit must be remembered, because next time round it becomes the carry from the previous bit. This is relatively easy as a circuit called a **flip flop** can be used to store the carry for the required amount of time. This circuit is also called a delay line store for the same reason and will be considered later in this chapter.

The arrangement for **serial addition** of two 4-bit numbers is shown in figure 19.23. Note that the carry is input to the temporary storage circuit so that the next time round it appears at the output of this temporary store to become the carry from the previous bit for the next pair of digits to be added. We have twice talked of 'the next time round'. What happens is that the operation of the circuit depends upon **shift registers** (see later) i.e. the first two digits are added and then all the digits are shifted along (see the data direction in the above diagram) so that the next pair to be added are presented to the full adder. The carry presented to the second pair of digits was the one generated from the first pair. The process is then repeated until all the digits have been presented to the full adder circuit. Note the directions of the shifting operation in each register including the answer shift register.

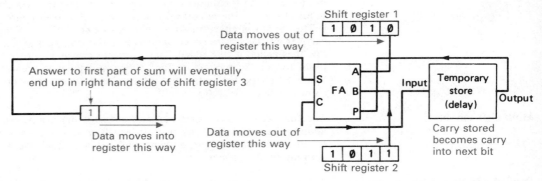

Figure 19.23

Flip flop circuits

The S-R flip flop

The delay line store in the above serial addition circuit is only one of the many hundreds of uses to which many different types of **flip flop** circuits can be put. The basic action of some types of flip flop will now be described.

Consider the two cross-coupled NAND gates shown in figure 19.24(a). This is the simplest type of flip flop circuit and is called an S-R flip flop. The inputs are labelled S and R and the outputs are labelled Q and $\overline{Q}$ for reasons soon to become obvious. The Q and $\overline{Q}$ outputs will become obvious first, as this simply means that they are the inverse of each other i.e. if Q = '0' then $\overline{Q}$ = '1' etc.

We are now dealing with a brand new type of logic circuit. It is called a **sequential logic circuit** because the new outputs depend not only on the present inputs but on previous inputs as well! The truth table for the S-R flip flop is shown in figure 19.24(b). This can be verified by putting the inputs to the desired values and seeing what happens to the outputs.

Let us assume that the initial state of the flip flop is such that Q is '1' and $\overline{Q}$ is therefore '0'.

If both S and R are made equal to '1', then by investigating the circuit of figure 19.24(a) you can see that the outputs do not change i.e. the flip flop remains in its current state.

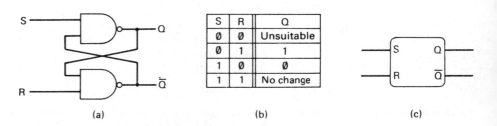

S	R	Q
0	0	Unsuitable
0	1	1
1	0	0
1	1	No change

(a)   (b)   (c)

Figure 19.24

Now if S is made '1' and R is made '0' then Q changes to '0'. The flip flop has been **reset** (i.e. the Q output is made equal to '0') by the action of R going to '0'. Hence the R input is named **reset**.

If both S and R are made equal to '1' again then the outputs do not change. This is consistent with S and R being made equal to '1' above.

If S is made '0' and R is made '1' then Q changes to '1'. The flip flop has been **set** i.e. the Q output has been made equal to '1' by the action of S going to '0'. Hence the S input is named **set**.

Finally, if both S and R are made equal to '0' you get an unsuitable state. Try it using the circuit of figure 19.24(a). You will find that Q and $\overline{Q}$ are both 1!

Summary of operation of the S-R flip flop

We can see from the above analysis that both inputs (**set** and **reset**) are normally held at '1'. The Q output is set (1) if S is briefly made 0, or the Q output is reset

(0) if R is briefly made 0. A negative pulse (101) is usually used to make these conditions happen.

We can see that the output (Q) can be forced into any required state (0 or 1). This state can then be held indefinitely by making the S and R inputs '1'. In this way the S-R flip flop can be used as a 1-bit store. The logic gate configuration is usually ignored and the S-R flip flop is represented by the box shown in figure 19.24(c). It is such a circuit that could act as a store in the serial addition section earlier.

The clocked S-R flip flop

In many applications the above S-R flip flop is not in the most convenient form. Inside a computer system we need to determine very precisely when an operation is to take place. For example, if we are going to use the flip flop to store a bit of data then it is usually important that this operation takes place at the exact moment when the data presented to the flip flop is valid. The arrangement shown in figure 19.25(a) can be used to overcome these problems.

The OR gates on the input to the standard S-R flip flop enable S and R to be changed without affecting the circuit until you decide to enable the device by making the **clock input go low**. This only needs to go low momentarily and is therefore called a **clock pulse**. You can therefore decide the exact moment to cause the change to happen. The truth table for this arrangement is unchanged in principle but it must be realised that the outputs do not change until the clock pulse goes low.

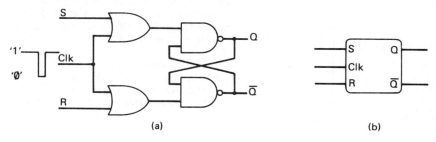

(a)   (b)

Figure 19.25

In most computer systems you will find that much of the logic inside the computer is controlled by what is called the **system clock.** This is a device that produces a square wave of usually a few million cycles per second. It is used to ensure that the data transfers taking place inside the computer happen at exactly the right moment. The symbol for the clocked S-R flip flop is shown in figure 19.25(b).

The J-K flip flop

One of the main disadvantages of the S-R flip flop is the unsuitable condition mentioned earlier. This can be overcome by the use of some additional logic as shown in figure 19.26(a).

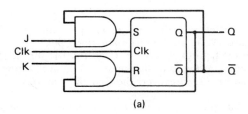

(a)

J	K	Q
0	0	Unchanged
0	1	0
1	0	1
1	1	Toggle

(b)

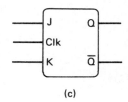

(c)

Figure 19.26

The truth table of the J-K flip flop can be built up in exactly the same way as the truth table for the S-R flip flop (see section on S-R flip flop) and is shown in figure 19.26(b). The logic symbol for the J-K flip flop is shown in figure 19.26(c).

Summary of operation of the J-K flip flop

If both J and K are held at '1' then on application of a suitable clock pulse, the Q output will change state. Therefore if J and K were held indefinitely at '1', on application of successive clock pulses the Q output would produce the pattern 1,0,1,0,1,0, etc. If the output changes in this way it is said to **toggle**. This name derives from the 'ON-OFF' toggle switch used in electronics.

If J is '1' and K is '0' then on application of a clock pulse Q goes to '1'.
If J is '0' and K is '1' then on application of a clock pulse Q goes to '0'.
If both J and K are held at '0' (the unsuitable condition in the S-R flip flop) then the Q output will remain unchanged. Obviously the $\overline{Q}$ output is simply the inverse of the above operations.

More sophisticated logic circuits are often used in combination with those just described to produce different effects such as the data being transferred when the clock goes low instead of high, and circuitry is often used to prevent undesirable effects when J-K flip flops are connected together to form **shift registers** or **counters.** Often extra circuitry is provided to enable the flip flop to be **preset** or **cleared** using alternative input signals. This is most useful if a register has to be set up to a specific state when the system is switched on. The details of these circuits are not important in an A-level computer science course. However, these more advanced J-K flip flops perform their final operations in exactly the way described by the truth table and logic symbols in figure 19.26. In addition you may have (P)reset and (C)lear inputs. The use of these will be shown in the next section.

Shift registers

We can use several J-K flip flops described above to produce a **shift register**. A shift register is used on many occasions such as serial addition (see earlier in this chapter) or fundamental operations within the central processor (see chapter 5 on machine architecture). It is also used when bits have to be transmitted serially (i.e. one bit at a time). The basic idea for a J-K flip flop type shift register is shown in figure 19.27.

Note that the P and C inputs are the preset and clear facilities talked about earlier in the last section. The data presented to the J and K inputs on the first J-K flip flop (left-hand side) will always be the inverse of each other in this application and therefore an **inverter** (NOT gate) will be used as shown. The operation of the shift

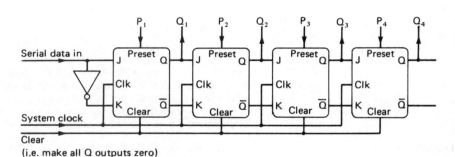

Figure 19.27

register is as follows:

The data (ls and 0s) to be fed into the register are presented one bit at a time to the input shown in figure 19.27. The appropriate clock pulse is applied and the data at J is transferred through to Q_1 (see truth table for J-K flip flop).

The next bit of data is now presented to the input and on application of the clock pulse is transferred through to Q_1. However, the first bit that was at Q_1 now gets transferred through to Q_2 etc.

In this way up to four bits presented serially at the input may be stored in the shift register shown in figure 19.27.

The shift register may be preset to any desired values by presenting the appropriate data at the P_1, P_2, P_3 and P_4 inputs. Similarly, the entire shift register may be **reset** to 0000 by applying a signal to all the clear inputs simultaneously.

It is a relatively easy task to transfer these four bits of data to a parallel circuit as they are all available on Q_1, Q_2, Q_3 and Q_4. A circuit such as this can therefore be used as a **serial to parallel data converter**.

Binary counters

A counter is a device that is usually used to count the number of times that a particular event happens. It is usual in computing to count clock pulses. When a certain number of clock pulses has occurred then the output from the counter can be used to initiate the desired activity.

There are very many types of counter but a simple 4-bit binary up counter (it counts up in binary as opposed to counting down) can be set up using J-K flip flops as shown in figure 19.28.

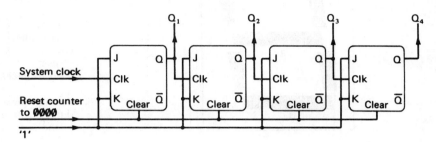

Figure 19.28

It can be seen that both the J and K inputs of each flip flop are held at '1'. This means that the output of each flip flop will **toggle** (see truth table for J-K flip flop).

The Q output from a J-K flip flop is used to clock the next J-K flip flop. As this Q output toggles (goes 0,1,0,1,0,1 etc.) then a satisfactory clock pulse is therefore produced.

To set up the counter initially the **reset** inputs are used to ensure that the outputs from the counter (Q_1, Q_2, Q_3 and Q_4) are all set to zero.

On application of the first clock pulse to the input (left-hand side) of this circuit, Q_1 goes to '1'. It was initially '0' and the J-K is in toggle mode.

This means that the output of the counter (Q_4, Q_3, Q_2, Q_1) after the first clock pulse is: 0 0 0 1

On application of the second clock pulse, Q_1 goes to '0' (it was '1'). This action of Q_1 going to zero clocks the second J-K flip flop. Therefore Q_2 goes to '1'.

This means that the output of the counter (Q_4, Q_3, Q_2, Q_1) after the second clock pulse is: 0 0 1 0

On application of the third clock pulse Q_1 goes to '1'. But this action does not produce a clock pulse for the second J-K. A clock pulse is a high to low transition. Therefore the Q_2 output remains at '1'.

This means that the output of the counter (Q_4, Q_3, Q_2, Q_1) after the third clock pulse is: 0 0 1 1

If we analyse the next few clock pulses in the same way as above we can easily see that the output of the counter is binary numbers starting at zero and going up in magnitude one at a time, i.e. we have designed a 4-bit **binary up counter**.

As only four bits are available the maximum number that can be stored is 1 1 1 1 or 15. The next clock pulse would produce 0 0 0 0 and the cycle would be repeated. However, this process of counting can be extended to more bits by adding more J-K flip flops.

We have only just started to look at some of the more advanced logical operations, but you are now in a position to study more advanced texts on the fascinating micro-miniature and high speed world of digital electonics inside computers.

Exercise 19.2

1. A seven segment display is shown in the following diagram:

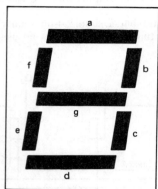

Each of the seven segments is to be driven from a four-digit BCD input labelled A, B, C and D. Assuming that the segments could be driven from the outputs of logic gates, design a BCD to seven-segment decoder (see chapter 3 if you have forgotten about BCD).

2. What is meant by a **flip flop**? How can such a circuit be set up to act as a memory element within a computer system?

3. Why is a **half adder** so called? Using the half adder as a starting point design a logic circuit to produce a **full adder**. How can four full adders be used to add together two 4-bit binary digits so that the sum may be produced? What are the advantages and disadvantages of the **parallel** method of addition over the serial method?

4. What is meant by the term **shift register,** and why are shift registers important in computing? Show how a shift register may be constructed out of flip flops, and explain its operation.

5. Show how a **binary counter** may be constructed by making use of flip flops. How is it possible to make the counter count down instead of up?

6. Develop a logic circuit that can be used to compare two 3-bit binary numbers. If the numbers are called X and Y, then your circuit should be able to detect if X = Y, X > Y or X < Y. Label your outputs (E)qual, (M)ore or (L)ess.

7. A 3-bit binary code is to be used to transmit information from point A to point B. As a check on the information received, a parity bit is to be added to the 3-bit binary number. If odd parity is to be used, develop a circuit which can be used to add the parity bit at the transmitting stage and a separate circuit which can be used to check parity at the receiving stage.

8. A **multiplexer** is a logic circuit which can switch different inputs to the same output. The idea is shown in the following diagram:

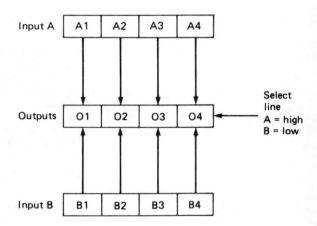

If two 4-bit binary numbers are input to the multiplexor and a select line (for inputs A and B) can be high or low, design a multiplexor circuit using logic gates such that the A inputs are switched to the output when the select line is **high**, and the B inputs are switched to the output when the select line is **low**.

End of chapter summary

- A **logic gate** is an electronic circuit specially built to perform logical functions such as AND and OR etc.
- A **logic gate** is defined by means of a **truth table**.
- A **truth table** shows the *relationships* between all possible **inputs** and **outputs**.
- An **AND gate** has a *'logical one' output only when all inputs are at logical one*.
- An **OR gate** has a *'logical one' output when any of its inputs are at logical one*.
- A **NOT gate**'s *output* is the *opposite of its input*.
- **Logic gates** can be connected together to perform a variety of logic functions. It is these building bricks which make up the heart of a digital computer.
- A **NAND gate** is **NOT** and **AND gate**.
- A **NOR gate** is **NOT** and **OR gate**.
- An **XOR gate** is an **OR gate** which *excludes the inclusive situation* where all inputs are one (i.e the output is zero when all inputs are one).
- An **XNOR** gate is **NOT** an **XOR gate**.

- *Any other logic gate* can be built up from **NAND gates only** or **NOR gates only**.
- **Boolean algebra** helps simplify combinations of logic gates.
- **Commutative laws** A+B = B+A or A.B = B.A
- **Associative laws** A+(B+C) = (A+B)+C or A.(B.C) = (A.B).C
- **Distributive laws** A.(B+C) = (A.B)+(B.C) or A+(B.C) = (A+B).(A+C)
- **Tautology laws** A.A = A or A + A = A
- **More tautology laws** A + $\overline{A}$ = 1 or A.$\overline{A}$ = 0
- **Absorption laws** A + (A.B) = A or A.(A+B) = A
- **Common sense (1)** 0.A = 0 or 1 + A = 1
- **Common sense (2)** 1.A = 1 or 0 + A = A
- **Common sense (3)** $\overline{0}$ = 1 or $\overline{1}$ = 0
- **Double complement laws**
- **De Morgan's law** $\overline{(A + B)}$ = $\overline{A}.\overline{B}$ or $\overline{A}.\overline{B}$ = $\overline{A + B}$
- **Karnaugh maps** help to simplify Boolean expressions in the form of AND functions strung together with OR functions (i.e. A.B.C.D + A.B.C + B.C etc.)
- Use *rules of symmetry* to help simplify Karnaugh Maps.
- Use **mirror-reflecting grey code** to generate numbers on the sides of the maps.
- **Grey code** is a **binary code** in which *transitions from one state to the next involve only one digit*.
- An **encoder** changes data into a form suitable for machine-readable input.
- A **decoder** changes data back from its original encoded form.
- A **half adder** adds together two binary digits and produces an output and carry.
- A **full adder** is similar to a half adder but can also cope with a carry from the previous bit.
- **Parallel** and **serial addition** of binary numbers can be carried out with an appropriate circuit made up out of **full adders**.
- A **flip flop** is an electronic circuit making use of **sequential logic**.
- **Sequential logic** involves **feedback** from the output to the inputs of gates – the output *no longer depends solely on the present combination of inputs*.
- An **S-R flip flop** is a **Set-Reset flip flop**.
- The **J-K flip flop** is a basic building block used in **shift registers** and **counters**.
- A **shift register** can accept **serial data** and *convert it* into **parallel data** form.
- A counter is an electronic circuit built out of **flip flops** which can be set to any desired count – it usually operates in binary.

20 Database systems

Databases have improved considerably over the years. As micros have become more powerful, and **networks** more prolific, we are able to apply very sophisticated database concepts that used to be possible only in the mainframe-computer-system environment. New software packages have meant that ordinary users can now produce elaborate databases with WIMP-based front ends that would have taken a team of skilled systems programmers months to complete. As usual in computer science, most people start to take all these things for granted, and often forget to appreciate what tremendous progress has actually been made. In this chapter we will have a detailed look at the **fundamental database models** which have made all this tremendous progress possible, and then go on to examples of current practice using modern database systems.

Before starting this chapter you should realise that some of the technical details appropriate to many parts are covered in other chapters such as **file handling** and **data structures**. It is also necessary that you are fully conversant with systems analysis and its associated topics. **It is *not recommended* that you read this chapter before becoming familiar with these other basic concepts**.

Databases are so important that a significant proportion of this book is devoted to their use, and, even though a database is only an application in the normal sense of the word, its use permeates into all corners of an organisation. If not properly set up and maintained, then the company that tries to makes use of it could literally be in desperate trouble. If, however, the database is well thought out, well set up and efficiently maintained, it could easily give the managers of the company the information they need to take informed decisions at the appropriate times. Databases range from smaller packages found on micros, to enormous large-volume transaction systems connected to mainframe computers via high speed links. It is no longer unusual for large multinational companies to have a single database containing literally Tbytes of important information. Indeed, when mainframes holding vast databases link together with sophisticated communication systems, then you have started to realise the potential for a vast and very sophisticated global-information system of which the Internet is starting to give us a flavour.

Background information

Before the advent of the ideas behind a modern database, it was common for different divisions within a business to run most of their affairs independently. If we were to go back and consider a typical company at that time, then different departments such as sales, marketing, accounts and production, for example, would probably have run their affairs on their own separate manual or computerised systems. It's likely that there would have been much **duplication of data**, and little opportunity for automatically passing information between their totally **incompatible systems**. To transfer data they would probably have to **physically re-type the data** into one of the different computer systems again, or write out separate forms for each department if the system operated manually.

If management wanted an overall view of the company, they would have to **collate lots of different information** from many disparate departments before the appropriate statistics could be obtained. This process was often **too laborious** to be considered, and thus vital information in the decision-making process could be lost. Even apparently commonplace information such as 'how many customers live in the South East of England?', for example, would probably have been beyond the capability of most of the older computerised and manual systems – unless this particular question had been anticipated and pre-programmed when the original system was conceived. It is against this sort of unsatisfactory background that the modern database ideas were born.

Put simply, a **database** is a '**collection of interrelated data**' – rarely (perhaps on a simple micro system) just a single file, but more often it's a **collection** of **several or many files**. In addition to these basic files which can be **modelled** in a variety of ways, there would be some **program** or a **set** of **programs** to carry out efficiently operations such as **data entry**, and generate **queries** which can extract a variety of information specified by the user of the system. At the most basic level, an 'address book', or even a 'list containing telephone numbers', could be regarded as examples of *very simple* databases. However, in this particular chapter, we will be taking a look at the very powerful **database management systems (DBMS)** and, in particular, at the **hierarchical** and **network** databases. We will, however, take a **special look** at the **relational databases** which are now available on modern computer systems – these relational databases have become the most versatile and popular type of database due to the increased computer-processing power that is now available at a sensible cost. When databases are undertaken within the **DBMS environment,** then computerisation **should** ensure that the database is much more convenient to operate. The DBMS should also ensure that it's more efficient to enter and extract the data than was the case with the older manual or computerised systems based on files which had no interaction capability. Indeed, a properly constructed and well-maintained database should be such that the **overall usefulness** of the system is far greater than the sum of its parts. Databases usually change over a significant period of time, and as the needs of an organisation develop, so too must the flexibility of the computerised database structures used to model the company.

We will look at some of the facilities offered by typical modern database systems, and look at the **setting up** and **maintenance** of these systems. Examples will also be given so that you will gain an idea of many of the typical processes involved. Throughout this section you should always appreciate what facilities are being offered – it will help you to answer more general applications questions during your examinations.

The **advantages** and the **disadvantages** of making use of such systems should always be borne in mind too, and although there are very many advantages, you must make sure that you are always aware of the potential pitfalls – never forget the true saying:

To err is human, but to really foul things up you need a computer!

This is particularly true when it comes to constructing a huge database on which a company may well rely for its day-to-day operation – the database administrators in industry today have an awesome responsibility.

Why make use of a database?

It is very much easier to make use of a 'proprietary database system' than to attempt to program a similar 'set up' from scratch making use of an appropriate high level language. The database system takes care of all the complex file handling and pointer manipulation that is necessary to build up a speedy and efficient system, and handles all the user interfaces such as the menus etc with ease. In conjunction with other specially written languages such as **DMLs** or **SQLs**, the database system copes easily with the numerous and involved **queries** that are often requested by the users of such systems.

A modern database also allows **applications** and **high-level languages** to link to the data in such a way that the **structure of the database** is transparent to the application. This has led to powerful **integrated systems** being set up and used in many businesses. An 'integrated system' means that it's easy to pass information from one system to another without having to manually transfer the data. Indeed, if well set up, then this transfer process should also be automatic and transparent to the users of the system. In this way lengthy delays within an organisation are avoided. Many databases also allow external programs and routines to be called from within the database. In this way it is possible to 'bolt on' the most sophisticated user generated routines that can customise the database to the exact requirements.

If the company mentioned in the background-information section earlier had an **integrated database system**, this would mean that information could be shared between different departments easily. Moreover, with an appropriately set up system, each department would have a view not too dissimilar from that which they had when they operated independently! When viewed from a departmental perspective, each department has a unique view which relates only to the way the database is set up for them. Therefore, the marketing perspective of the database is very different from the sales perspective of the same database, even though they share some common information. These ideas are simple, and are represented in the Venn diagram shown in figure 20.1. You can see that all the data which belongs to a specific set are labelled in their own 'data worlds'. However, each data set will

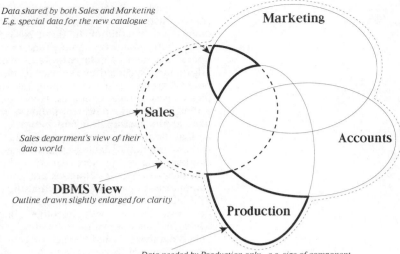

Data shared by both Sales and Marketing
E.g. special data for the new catalogue

Marketing

Sales

Accounts

Sales department's view of their
data world

DBMS View
Outline drawn slightly enlarged for clarity

Production

Data needed by Production only - e.g. size of component

Figure 20.1

overlap with other data sets from different 'data worlds' – it is in this way that much data duplication is avoided. You should note also at this stage that much data can't be viewed from unauthorised places. For example, it would not be desirable for marketing, sales or production to have access to information regarding employees' salaries. This sort of information would therefore live in that part of the database to which only the accounts department would have access.

We will start off the main work in this chapter by having a look at the **logical data structures** on which a database depends, and taking a look at the **theoretical models** which describe how the data within the database are related at a **fundamental level**. These models show how data is **linked** or **related** to other **data** inside the database. Most of the structures can be expressed in the form of diagrams, although the **relational databases** make use of **tables**, and some databases may use a combination of several of these techniques.

Modelling data

An often-used term in database design is the **relationship**. The idea behind a relationship is exactly the same as the **mathematical relationships** which you may have covered in your elementary mathematics courses – but if you've forgotten, or did not cover them in the first place, the ideas are very simple and are summarised in figure 20.2. In database theory, this relationship is often described as a **link**, a **dependency** or some sort of **association** between two **entities** – all these terms are defined very shortly.

When considering the different database models the ideas connected with **relationships** will crop up quite often, as the association between different data items is fundamentally important. An understanding of the above **relationships** will help considerably, especially when trying to explain why things can or can't be accomplished easily when a particular database model is being used, and hence will help you to make a choice which relates to which particular model might be most appropriate in different situations.

When undertaking **database design**, **any concrete or abstract occurrence represented within the database** is usually called an **entity**. In a database at your school or college, for example, **you** would be regarded as an **entity** because you are important from the school's point of view – you are effectively a 'customer' and the 'product' you're receiving is hopefully a good education. With most of the work undertaken at this level, an **entity** can be regarded as being the same as a **record**. Therefore, your record within the school or college database uniquely defines you in terms of the information which the school or college is holding. We can then go on to give any **entity named attributes** – and simplifying matters again, these attributes which together constitute the entity can be regarded as being the same as the **fields** within a **record**.

Sometimes it's not possible to have one entity without the existence of another. For example, in a **tree data structure** it's **not possible** to have a **child** without a **parent**. In a database, for example, it would probably not be sensible to have an order in existence without a customer, and this sort of constraint can be built in at

The mathematical idea of a relationship between entities is simple

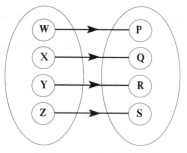

One-to-one relationship

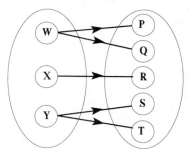

One-to-many relationship

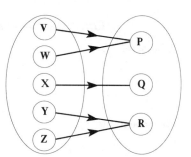

Many-to-one relationship

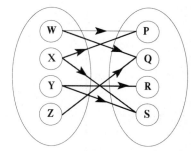

Many-to-many relationship

Figure 20.2

the database-design stage. This particular data relationship is called **dependency**, and defines a relationship in which the existence of one entity is entirely dependent on the existence of another. Specifically this sort of dependency is an important consequence of data being modelled with the **one-to-one** and **one-to-many relationships**, which can be confirmed by looking at the top half of figure 20.2 – take away any entity on the left of these diagrams, and the ones mapped from it on the right hand side cease to exist. The main things of importance when dealing with relationships are the **direction** of the **relationship**, as shown in figure 20.2, and the **associations** (i.e. the **types of connections** between the entities such as **one-to-one** or **many-to-one** etc.) of the relationship which are also shown in figure 20.2.

We can show all the **relationships** mentioned in the last section, and the **entities** and **attributes** just introduced on special diagrams. There are several different types of diagrams in existence, but some simple ones are shown in figure 20.3. Here you can see the **relationships** and **dependencies** between the **database entities** 'Component', 'Order' and 'Customer' for a typical component supplier. Figure 20.3(a) shows a diagram in which the **entity dependencies** are outlined, and figure 20.3(b) shows two simplified **entity relationship** or **ER** diagrams.

If the entities in figure 20.3(b) were expanded to show the format of the information contained within, then the attributes could also be shown.

In figure 20.3(a) the **relationship** between the component and order is **many-to-many** because a single order can include a large number of components, or a single component may be included on a large number of orders. The path between order and customer, however, is a **many-to-one relationship**, because one customer may have many orders, but a single order obviously can't have many customers. Diagrams such as these often help to clarify the relationships between entities. In figure 20.3(b), the relationship 'consists of' is a many-to-one type as an order may consist of many components, but a component can't consist of many orders. Most of the diagrammatic representations are common sense, but you **do** have to think **very carefully** about the **entities, relationships** and **attributes** to draw them properly – indeed, **this is the whole point of using them** – not to explain the obvious, but to map out how data is related in some detail, especially in terms of the direction of the mapping.

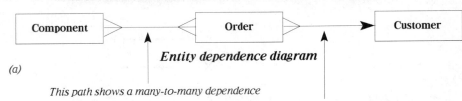

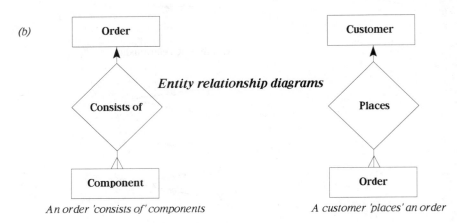

(a) *Entity dependence diagram*

This path shows a many-to-many dependence

This path shows a many-to-one dependence

(b) *Entity relationship diagrams*

An order 'consists of' components

A customer 'places' an order

Figure 20.3

The basic database models

A **database model** is simply a model of the various ways in which the data within a database may be **structured**, i.e. its **logical structure**, and *not* the way that it is stored on any particular storage medium. (Don't forget that the way that the data is actually stored is referred to as the **physical structure**, and this is covered on page 357.) You have already covered many **data structures** in chapter 14, and understanding the work from chapter 16 means that you are already well on the way to an understanding of all the database models – no kidding!

In chapter 14 we looked in detail at **linear lists** and **linked lists, stacks** and **arrays** etc. and you should, therefore, know that **logical data structures** such as these enable **pointers** (or **links**) to be maintained such that the information stored can be navigated quickly, and the data processed efficiently. You should also note that the term **data model** need not apply just to databases, but to any formally defined structure which represents data, usually at the logical level. Although there are others, the three main types of **database models** to be covered at advanced level are as follows.

> **Hierarchical database model**
> **Network database model**
> **Relational database model**

Traditionally, the **hierarchical** and **network data models** allowed very fast, but more limited access to data contained within the database. They were ideal for specific queries of the sort that were carried out most often. These impressive speeds were, therefore, ideal for on-line transactions where certain information was needed quickly from a vast amount of data. On the other hand, the **relational database** was good at dealing with the '*ad-hoc*' query, but was quite slow in comparison with the other two models. (Note *ad hoc*, for our purposes, means 'any old query' that the user might wish to dream up – like the 'South of England' example described earlier.)

On microcomputers, the most extensively used of the above three models is the **relational database**, however, the much-faster **hierarchical** and **network databases** found on many mini and mainframe computers also allow some powerful **relational**

Data to be used for a comparison of database-modelling methods

Surname	First name	Town	Account Number	Balance (£)	Interest (£)
Desmond	Carol	Tonbridge	0135	1,500.67	120.53
Lewis	Sheila	Brighton	0267	1.75	0.14
Lewis	Sheila	Brighton	0078	160.34	12.82
Mills	Kevin	Croydon	1016	12,786.00	1,022.88
Mills	Kevin	Croydon	1143	9,430.45	754.44
Mills	Kevin	Croydon	1209	172	13.76
Norton	Sindy	Bromley	1016	12,786.00	1,022.88
Manning	Brian	Chatham	1782	16,897.21	1,351.77

Figure 20.4

capabilities. As is usual in computer science, much development goes on, and the rules get changed to a certain extent. More recently, the versatility and power of a relational database has been brought to mainframes with a vengeance. The latest relational databases for some of the largest mainframes are approaching the speed of the fastest hierarchical and network database models. As the techniques get refined over the next few years, these relational-database speeds are likely to be in excess of the other techniques. It seems, therefore, that in the foreseeable future, **very high speed, powerful relational databases** will rule, from the humble micro, up to and including the largest mainframes and supercomputers. Powerful companies such as IBM have also put their full weight behind such projects to ensure that this will be so! We will now look at each model in detail.

An example structure

A very simple generalised data structure will help to give an instant impression of the data structure used for each model, but to make life easier, after introducing the concepts we will use just **one small data set** to illustrate how the **three different database models** can be visualised and therefore compared. The data for this simple model will consist of the surnames, first names and towns of people who have accounts in a small building society. An alphabetical list of just a few of the account holders is shown in figure 20.4. As you can see, some customers have more than one account, and Kevin Mills from Croydon has actually got three! In fact, one of Mills' accounts is a joint-business account which he shares with Sindy Norton, who is a co-director in the Mills & Norton company – look out for how these aspects of the data set are handled when using the different database models.

The data contained in the table of figure 20.4 can be handled in a variety of ways, but let's suppose, for the sake of argument, that we wish to split up the information

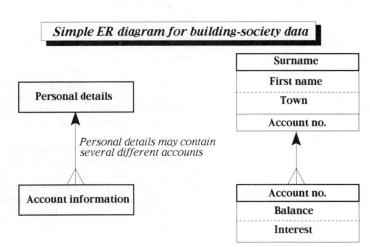

Simple ER diagram for building-society data

Figure 20.5

in the above table into **two different entities** – being a **personal-information entity** with attributes '**Surname**', '**First name**' and '**Town**', and an **account-information entity** being made up of the attributes '**Account number**', '**Balance**' and '**Interest**'. A simple dependence diagram for this structure is shown in figure 20.5.

In the next few sections we now concentrate on the three main models outlined earlier. Don't forget that one of the requirements is to compare and contrast these models as we are progressing through the work.

The hierarchical database model

The logical structure of a **hierarchical database** is not surprisingly based on a **hierarchical data structure** (see page 304), and typical general examples can be seen in figure 20.6.

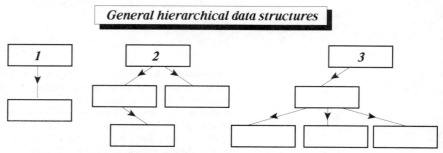

Three different hierarchical structures

Figure 20.6

You should be very familiar with these types of data structures – they're identical to that of the **tree structures** covered in chapter 14, and the hierarchical structure making use of the building-society table on page 463 is shown in figure 20.7. All these structures mirror the **parent-child** or **superior-subordinate** relationships which are typical of those found in a family tree. The **nodes** in the building-society structure correspond to particular instances of **entities** in the hierarchical database, and the sub-sections of a node, such as surname, first name and town etc. correspond to examples of particular **attributes** – in this case attributes for the personal-details entities.

The hierarchical database model is ideal for modelling the **one-to-many relationships** between **entities** found naturally in many organisations, and it's obviously ideal for **one-to-one relationships too** – which are just a special case of the one-to many relationships. Another example already established is considered when storing all the parts that go into the making of a car. The root node could be the car itself, which could then be split up into further sub-systems consisting of engine, gearbox and body, etc. The body could then be further split up into doors, bonnet and boot etc. This diagram is shown in chapter 14 on page 304 when **hierarchical data structures** were considered in detail. You may be surprised at how many real-life data structures can be modelled hierarchically, and the speed with which data can be found is remarkably fast. You should also notice that, for a hierarchical data structure, *each entity can only have one owner*, therefore, other types of relationship can't be modelled using a hierarchical database. Note too that the **hierarchical data structure** is just a **particular case** of the more **general network data structure** to be considered in the next section.

A **hierarchical database model** would be a database that has been set up based on a **hierarchical data structure**. **Links** or **pointers** would be established in the ways already covered in chapter 14, which enable *very fast* searches and processing of data items based on these naturally occurring structures. A typical example of a hierarchical database system is **IMS/VS** – the Information Management System / Virtual Storage database found on many IBM mainframes. However, better facilities are offered with the later version **IMS/R**, the **relational** version of IMS.

Advantages and disadvantages

When choosing a particular database model, the designer must always be aware of the limitations imposed on the users by the structure which he or she has chosen.

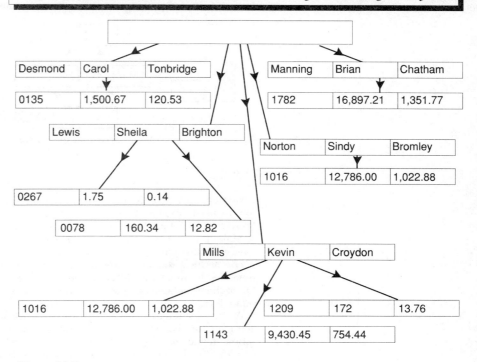

Figure 20.7

For example, if a database is implemented making use of a hierarchical database model, then if a parent within the structure is deleted – all the children are forced to be deleted too. This may be an advantage, in which case this particular operation is efficient and very quick, or it may be a disadvantage, in which case some other database model should have been chosen to represent the data more realistically. In a similar way, we can't add a record to a hierarchical database that has no parent. This may not be an inconvenience, or it may be a disaster. More specifically, when representing the building-society data, the shared account between Mills and Norton is represented as two separate nodes – this will cause potential problems when updating balance etc. It's up to the database designer to make sure that he or she knows what the future requirements will be, and this is usually determined by extensive systems analysis. Later we will see how different database models might be able to cope with these problems.

The network database model

You should note that this refers to the **logical structure** of the **database** and *not* to the use of a database over a computer network. (The use of networks is covered in chapter 21, and the use of **any type** of database over a network presents additional problems due to **multi-user access**.) So, not forgetting that a network database model has nothing to do with physical networks, figure 20.8 shows some generalised network structures.

Any **record**, or **node** in a **network structure** can be accessed from starting at the **root node**. However, there is usually a much more complex **pointer (link)** system to maintain than was the case when using the simpler hierarchical data structure. Notice that unlike a hierarchical data structure, when using a **network data structure**, a **record** can have **multiple owners**, except of course, for the root record.

This is a little like the *impossible situation* where a child node can have many parent nodes, but it's much more sensible to think of it as a 'supplier-customer' relation. For example, one supplier may have three or four customers, but it's also possible for a customer, (one of the child nodes of the original supplier), to be a supplier to other

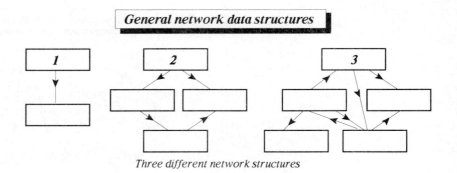

Three different network structures

Figure 21.8

customers *including* the one which originally supplied them – this scenario would be impossible to express as efficiently with a hierarchical data structure. Note also that there may well be alternative routes to get to some data items.

Making use of a network data structure to model the building-society data from page 463, this particular network data structure is shown in figure 20.9.

Hierarchical database models are ideal for **one to many** and **many-to-many relationships** between the different **entities** held in the database. In both **network** and **hierarchical databases**, records in one file may **point** to the locations of records in other files.

A set of standards was set up for **network databases** by CODASYL. This is an acronym for the **COnference on DAta Systems Languages** – an American organisation made up from interested parties which originally developed **COBOL**. CODASYL defined extensions to **COBOL's DATA division** (see page 157), so that it's possible to set up records which are related by **links**. This means that you can **sequentially access non-sequential** information very quickly by following the pointers. The DBTG (DataBase Task Group) of CODASYL has also brought out new proposals in the last couple of years.

Examples of network databases are **DBOMP**, the **DataBase Organisation and Maintenance Processor** and **IDMS**, the **Integrated Data Management System**. Both of these systems operate on **mainframe** computer systems.

Advantages and disadvantages

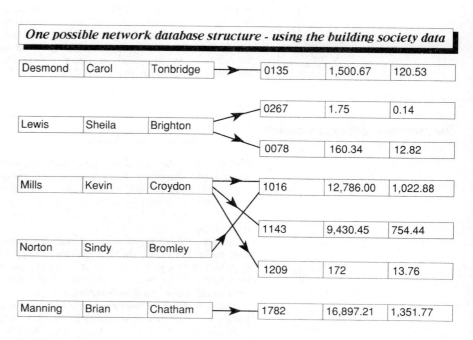

Figure 20.9

As with the hierarchical database model, all the relationships between the entities must be defined at the time when the database is designed. Also, there are one or two extra complications which involve maintaining the database. For example, with a hierarchical database, if a record is deleted which involved pointers to others records then these records too would also be deleted. However, with a network database model, pointers can go to other records which may not need to be deleted. Therefore the maintenance arrangements are complicated by the more-complex data structures involved.

The relational database model

Due to the primary importance and popularity of the **relational database**, we will be looking in much more detail at this particular system. Even though the **network** and **hierarchical** database models are still **extensively** used, at some time in the future it's most likely that all database models will be relational – at least until somebody comes up with a better idea.

The **relational database** is unusual insofar as it's **not** a structure based on the idea of a structure diagram together with a suitable pointer system, and therefore we can't possibly show some generalised relational-database structures as we did with the other two models. However, it's interesting to note that whatever database structure is used, it will eventually have to be mapped onto a **conventional file structure** (see chapter 16) so that it can be stored on a suitable secondary storage medium. We will now go straight into a specific relational-database example using the building-society data on page 463. One possible layout of this data is shown in figure 20.10.

One possible relational database structure - using the building society data

Surname	First name	Town	Account Number
Desmond	Carol	Tonbridge	0135
Lewis	Sheila	Brighton	0267
Lewis	Sheila	Brighton	0078
Mills	Kevin	Croydon	1016
Mills	Kevin	Croydon	1143
Mills	Kevin	Croydon	1209
Norton	Sindy	Bromley	1016
Manning	Brian	Chatham	1782

Account Number	Balance (£)	Interest (£)
0135	1,500.67	120.53
0267	1.75	0.14
0078	160.34	12.82
1016	12,786.00	1,022.88
1143	9,430.45	754.44
1209	172	13.76
1782	16,897.21	1,351.77

'Personal' relational table

'Account' relational table

Figure 20.10

As you can see, in this case we have a collection of two tables which match the ways in which the data was originally split up in figure 20.5. The organisation of the database in this sort of way is known as a **schema**, and the above schema, although chosen by a common-sense method, is **not** a particularly good one! The reasons for this are soon to become obvious – but first let's introduce some new terminology.

Each **table** is made up of **rows** and **columns** which represent a special idea called a **relation**. Using terms which have been previously defined in this chapter, a **relation** is, therefore, a **set of entities** which have the **same attributes**. Each entity in the 'Personal table', for example, has the same attributes 'Surname', 'First name', 'Town' and 'Account number' as described by the column headings in the table. It's usual to make the connection between these tables and the **records, fields** and **files** with which we are all more familiar (see chapter 16). Each **entity** in a **table** usually corresponds to a **record** in a **file**, and each **attribute**, being a sub-section of a **record**, must therefore correspond to a **field**. Finally, the **relation** or **table** itself usually corresponds to a **file**. In a relational database, **relations** are **now defined in terms of**

these special two-dimensional tables, or, putting it simply, a **table is literally a relation**. You should note at this stage that the term 'relation' as defined here should **not be confused** with the term 'relationship', as used in many other contexts throughout this chapter.

Each **column** must have a **unique** name like 'Surname', and 'Town', for example, just like fields in a record must also have a unique name – nevertheless, column names can be used again in other tables, and this will prove essential when we need to establish links between the different tables a little later. It's important to realise that the order in which the entities are entered into the tables is of no consequence whatsoever. Whenever we need to establish a **new set of data** from a **relational database**, a **brand-new table is produced** by the relational-database system which matches the new requirements. In other words a new file of information is produced each time.

Don't forget that we used some ordinary common sense to arrange the two tables. However, in the relation which we have called 'Personal', we have implied that 'Surname' is important, because that's the principle way by which each **entity** within 'personal' is intended to be identified. **Surname** is therefore called the **primary key** for **personal**, and, by a similar argument, **Account number** would be the **primary key** for **Account**. Nevertheless, **there is a major problem here** – a **primary key is intended to be a unique identification** for a **particular record**, entity or row. It should, therefore, act as a unique **identifier** for **each row of information** within a table. In practice, surname would **not be sufficient** because it's probably not going to be unique. It would usually be far better to use account number – but, as the more astute readers will have seen, for joint accounts this is not unique either! Oh dear! Problems like this are sometimes a little awkward to sort out, and a more-efficient arrangement of the tables would be needed to solve them. This process of efficient arrangement of the tables is called **normalisation**, and is explained in detail on page 469. For the moment we will ignore these potential pitfalls, and carry on working with unnormalised data for the purposes of introducing the rest of the terminology.

A **shorthand notation** has been developed for representing these tables by making use of the attribute names in a simple list. Using this shorthand notation the **primary key** is indicated by <u>underlining</u> the appropriate attribute. The shorthand notation for the relation called 'Personal', for example, would therefore be as follows.

Personal (<u>Surname</u>, First name, Town, Account number)

As you can see from the above, each attribute (column heading) is contained in a named list, separated by commas, with the primary key underlined and the name of the relation (table) to the left of the brackets. The **primary key** does not have to be the first column in the table as the order does not matter. Using the same techniques, the shorthand notation for the relation called 'Account' would be represented as follows.

Account (<u>Account number</u>, Balance, Interest)

These and many other ideas for the **relational database** were first proposed by Edgar Codd back in the 1970s. His ideas put database systems on a sound theoretical basis, which has also had spin offs in other computer-science fields such as **Artificial Intelligence** (**AI**) and **natural language analysis**. Codd was a mathematician who worked for IBM, and it's therefore not surprising that some modern-mathematical ideas have come over in his **relational database models**. For example, Codd called a **row** from a **table** a **tuple**! – and this is the term which is often used today – in fact it's the preferred term in more advanced computer-science courses. It's used in preference to the word 'row' which may or may not be anything to do with a relation. If you are wondering why the strange name '**tuple**' is used, then reading the next section on 'tuples' will help to explain. If you're not curious you may skip over the section!

Tuples

In this chapter we have defined a **relation** as being represented by a **2D-table** – this is, in fact, **exactly the same** as the definition of a **relation** using more formal mathematical theory – minus the very complex set-theory terminology that would be used to back up these ideas. Consider the following.

You should all be familiar with the idea of a set – for example, the 'set of hex digits' consists of 0 to F inclusive, and the 'set of months' would consist of January to December inclusive. Therefore, making use of some typical abbreviations, we can write out these sets as follows.

Hex digits = {0,1,2,3,4,5,6,7,8,9,A,B,C,D,E,F}

Months = {Jan, Feb, Mar, Apr, May, Jun, Jul, Aug, Sep, Oct, Nov, Dec}

Relating this to our database theory, the **entity** months, for example, can have any of the **attribute values** listed in the above set. No problems so far! The more rigorous mathematical definition of a relation also takes into account the **range of possible values** that each **attribute** may have, and this is obviously useful for database systems too. In mathematics 'sets of permitted values', like those shown in the above examples, are called **domains**. We can easily denote a domain by a single letter, therefore, D_M might represent the domain of months, or D_H might be used to represent the domain of hex digits.

You have all done enough computer science to realise that **domains** and **sets** are **very important concepts** and exhibit strong connections with database ideas. For example, using the building-society data from the tables in figure 20.10 – we could denote the domain of 'all possible Surnames' as D_S, the domain of 'all possible First names' as D_F, 'all possible Towns' as D_T and 'all possible Account numbers' as D_A. Mathematically, we can express the relation 'Personal' as being a **subset** of

$$D_S \times D_F \times D_T \times D_A$$

which defines **all possibles values** for each of the rows that we can have in the relation we call 'personal'. The 'x' sign in the above domain does not mean multiplication, but is called a Cartesian product, and is from a branch of mathematics called relational algebra. A **Cartesian product** means the set of all ordered pairs, and the following example will make this concept quite clear.

If A = {Tom, Dick, Harry} and B = {1,2} then the cartesian product, A x B would be the set of all possible values of ordered pairs that each two-attribute row may take on.

A × B = {(Tom,1), (Tom,2), (Dick,1), (Dick,2), (Harry,1), (Harry,2)}

We obviously could not have all possible combinations occurring in practice, or else unrelated people would be allowed, for example, to have the same bank account number – this is why the words 'subset of' were used when we mathematically defined 'personal' a moment ago.

If we take a particular 'row' at random from the relation called personal, such as

(Norton, Sindy, Bromley, 1016)

for example. Then we can represent this, or any other 'row' more generally as

(X_S, X_F, X_T, X_A).

Codd called this a 4-tuple, because an 'n-tuple' is the correct mathematical term for a row, consisting of n attributes, extracted from a relation defined in terms of the Cartesian products of the individual domains as described above, but the term 'tuple' is now generally used in preference to the term 'n-tuple'. Furthermore, X_S means that this particular attribute belongs to domain D_S, and X_F belongs to the domain D_F etc.

Now you are probably thinking that all this mathematical theory is an awfully long-winded way of expressing the obvious – but you are possibly not aware of the fact that there are branches of mathematics called 'tuple relational calculus', and 'relational algebra', which take relational-database theory far beyond that which we have outlined here. In fact, these important mathematical theories form most of the groundwork on which many relational-database ideas depend, including the powerful relational queries, normalisation (see in a moment) and most other things which we will take for granted throughout the remainder of this chapter.

Relational databases are very powerful **because** they are formed on the basis of a very sound mathematical reasoning. Codd's mathematical theories of relational-database systems have built up some extremely potent ideas, which, in recent years, have ensured that the entire database market has moved towards his ideas of relational database models. The hierarchical and network databases considered earlier have no mathematical footing – they have been built up from *ad hoc* and heuristic techniques. Another area of computing in desperate need of the full mathematical treatment is determination of absolute correctness of algorithms – but this has yet to be developed. Relational calculus and relational algebra are the theories which gave the relational database its name – and you now know why the term tuple is used!

Normalisation

In 1970, Edgar Codd defined certain **constraints** (i.e. defined certain limits and conventions) that **relations** in a **relational database** should obey. If a database conforms to these constraints then it is said to be **normalised**, or is in **normal form**.

Normalisation is a way of ensuring that the data is processed more efficiently in a relational database, and any *ad hoc* query can be processed.

Normalisation simplifies the **relational tables** by reducing the **relations** to their **simplest forms**, and therefore making these relational tables easier to handle. Each entity should be represented by just one table in the database, but the problems are usually associated in deciding **which entities** to use, and **what attributes** each entity should have. After normalisation, maintenance of the database should be less hassle, and queries (see later) should be able to be carried out more quickly. It should also eliminate the need to restructure the entire database when new and unexpected demands are made of the system, and should preserve relations when any changes are made. For example, in this chapter we have already seen how it might **not be possible** to represent a relationship between different data items easily – if at all, and we have also seen how **deleting** some items of data may cause others to be **unintentionally** deleted too. Normalisation involves some additional data duplication, but this is a small price to pay for the power and versatility of the relational database model.

There are **five normal forms (plus lots of others too!)**, although **not all of them are commonly used**, and only the first **three** are of any importance to many systems analysts. However, for the purposes of work at advanced level, you need only to be able to appreciate that there are **three major stages of normalisation**, and be able to carry out these important processes on simple tables **in the right order**.

An example

A new data set, more suited to those of you who like eating, will be used to show the processes of normalisation, and this is outlined in figure 20.11. This data refers to the orders for delivery of cakes and pies etc. for a local baker. The local baker has been carrying out these processes for years, but now wishes to computerise the system. Figure 20.11 is typical of the sort of information which may be given to the delivery person and held in the baker's computer system. However, in its current form, it's not arranged in ways which allow for efficient processing by using a relational database. It has not yet been normalised to conform to Codd's set of rules.

Data to be used for carrying out the normalisation processes

Order no.	Acc. no.	Customer	Address	Date	Item	Quantity	Item price	Total Cost
7823	178	Dick's cafe	27 Nights close, Tonbridge	16/7	Bakewell Tart	20	0.15	12.35
					Danish Pastry	13	0.20	
					Apple Pie	45	0.15	
4633	562	Harpers	12 The drive, Tunbridge Wells	16/7	Danish Pastry	120	0.20	24.00
2276	167	Pie Crust	3a, High Sreet, Maidstone	17/7	Apple Pie	130	0.15	56.50
					Cherry Pie	100	0.18	
					Steak Pie	30	0.50	
					Danish Pastry	20	0.20	
1788	032	Sloggers	17 Maple avenue, Maidstone	18/7	Apple Pie	15	0.15	12.25
					Danish Pastry	50	0.20	
7120	289	Dibble & Son	The pound, Tonbridge	18/7	Apple Pie	20	0.15	7.50
					Chocolate Log	3	1.50	

Figure 20.11

Don't misunderstand what's happening here – we're not trying to tell the delivery person that they must have the data in a different form to that which they find useful. In fact we can easily print out the data in **any** form, including the form shown in figure 20.11 if this is desired. We are simply restructuring the data for efficient analysis.

First normal form

The first stage of **normalisation** is to make sure that any **attributes** (fields) with **multiple** (or repeating) **values** are removed so that the **records (entities** or **rows)** are **all the same length**.

Fixed-length records (see page 353) are far easier to deal with than variable-length ones – the results of queries, for example, will be obtained much more quickly if the computer system does not have to look and see where a particular record ends. To remove a repeating group is quite simple – we first identify it (or them), then eliminate the repetition by putting this group (or groups) in an **alternative relation** (table).

As an example, carefully consider the baker's data in figure 20.11. Looking at the first entity for order number 7823, we can see that the 'Item', 'Quantity' and 'Item-price' attributes **all** contain multiple-value entries. So what! – the three different types of cakes ordered by Dick don't seem to be causing too much harm – but what if Dick's cafe wanted 103 different items? Would the 'item attribute' (don't forget that it's only a single field in a record!) be able to cope? I doubt it. We need to alter this **relation** so that all **records (entities)** are **of the same length**, and the only possible way to do this is to remove the offending data from the original table and put it somewhere else. Harper's looks OK at the moment, as there's only a single item, but it's still a problem because tomorrow it might contain repeating values like all the the others.

Where do we put all the data that has been removed? – we invent a further relation which relates the 'order number' to the cakes which have been purchased. This new relation will be made up from the offending parts of the original table. The results of these operations can now be expressed as two separate tables, and these two **relations**, which are given the names '**Orders**' and '**Items purchased**', are shown in figure 20.12, – they are now said to be in **first normal form**. Alternatives are available in which repeating groups can be catered for, and some advanced relational databases allow attributes to specify relations themselves! This means that a single attribute can refer to a whole table, and this is ideal for the emerging **object-oriented relational databases**. It's important to note that there must be some sort of link between these two tables, and this is shown by the Order-number attributes being repeated in each table. If this linking is not done then the **tables** would **not** be **related** to each other.

The **shorthand notation** for these two tables in **first normal form** is as follows.

Orders (<u>Order no.</u>, Acc. no., Customer, Address, Date, Total cost)

Items purchased (<u>Order no.</u>, Item, Quantity, Item price)

First normal form for the bakery data

Order no.	Acc. no.	Customer	Address	Date	Total Cost
7823	178	Dick's cafe	27 Nights close, Tonbridge	16/7	12.35
4633	562	Harpers	12 The drive, Tunbridge Wells	16/7	24.00
2276	167	Pie Crust	3a High Sreet, Maidstone	17/7	56.50
1788	032	Sloggers	17 Maple avenue, Maidstone	18/7	12.25
7120	289	Dibble & Son	The pound, Tonbridge	18/7	7.50

Relational table for orders

Order no.	Item	Quantity	Item price
7823	Bakewell Tart	20	0.15
7823	Danish Pastry	13	0.20
7823	Apple Pie	45	0.15
4633	Danish Pastry	120	0.20
2276	Apple Pie	130	0.15
2276	Cherry Pie	100	0.18
2276	Steak Pie	30	0.50
2276	Danish Pastry	20	0.20
1788	Apple Pie	15	0.15
1788	Danish Pastry	50	0.20
7120	Apple Pie	20	0.15
7120	Chocolate Log	3	1.50

NOTE: These two columns show relational information

Relational table for items purchased

Figure 20.12

Second normal form

As this process is carried out **after** the first normal form, this obviously assumes that you have already got your data into the first normal form before you start! So, in addition to this requirement, the second normal form states that all the **attributes** in an **entity** must be **functionally dependent** (have a **unique association**) with the **primary key** for the purposes of identification.

This posh term called **functional dependency** means that there must be **only a one-to-one dependency** (see page 461) for **each attribute** mapped **from** the **primary key to the attribute** – in other words, **each attribute must be uniquely identified just by making use of the primary key** – if this is not the case, then it's not in second normal form. Therefore, to test for **functional dependency**, we have to test each particular attribute in turn, and check that only a one-to-one dependency exists with respect to the **primary key**. If, for example, we have a **primary key** of '**order number**', then we know that **each order number is uniquely associated with just one** 'total cost'. You can't have several different total costs in an order! **Don't think about this the wrong way round** and try to associate a **total cost** with an **order number**, because many different orders may have the same total cost – get this vital one-to-one dependency the wrong way round and you will become very confused indeed – you will begin to think that the desired functional dependency does not exist!

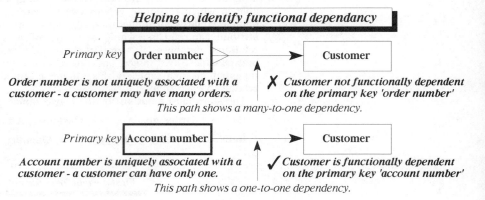

Helping to identify functional dependancy

Primary key | Order number ⟶ Customer

Order number is not uniquely associated with a customer - a customer may have many orders.

✗ *Customer not functionally dependent on the primary key 'order number'*

This path shows a many-to-one dependency.

Primary key | Account number ⟶ Customer

Account number is uniquely associated with a customer - a customer can have only one.

✓ *Customer is functionally dependent on the primary key 'account number'*

This path shows a one-to-one dependency.

Figure 20.13

This whole idea sounds awfully complex, but let's look at another example. Consider the first-normal-form data for the bakery at the top of figure 20.12, and examine the **relationship** between the **primary key** we called '**order number**' and '**Dick's cafe**' as a specific example of the attribute '**Customer**'. We now proceed along the following lines. An entity-dependence diagram between 'order number' and 'customer' is shown at the top of figure 20.13 – because 'Dick's cafe' is able to place many orders, the customer name does obviously **not** have a unique association with order number. Therefore, the one-to-one dependency (the condition for being **functionally dependent**) has **not been satisfied** for this particular attribute at least, and the data in the relational table for 'Orders' is, therefore, **not yet** in **second normal form**.

Changes must therefore be made, and we can, in this particular case, change the **primary key** from '**Order number**' to '**Account number**'. Now the **customer is uniquely associated** with **account number**, and the diagram at the bottom of figure 20.13 demonstrates this functional dependency. Therefore, **if** we invent a new relation called 'Customers', the required functional dependency can be achieved by extracting the 'Account number', 'Customer name' and 'Address' from the original relational table (top of figure 20.12). The table for this new relation to be called 'Customers' is shown in figure 20.14.

As you can see from this new table at the top of figure 20.14, the account number uniquely determines the customer, and the account number uniquely determines the address, therefore, in this particular table, **all these attributes** are **functionally dependent** on the new **primary key**, and therefore this **relation** is now said to be in **second normal form**.

The data which has been removed is shown in the relation (table) called 'Order' at the bottom of figure 20.14. However, we need a link from 'Customers', and 'account no.' serves this purpose admirably. Looking in detail at this new table, we see that the primary key called 'order' uniquely determines 'account no.', 'date' and 'total cost'. Therefore, **this table too is now in second normal form**. The shorthand form for these two new tables is as follows.

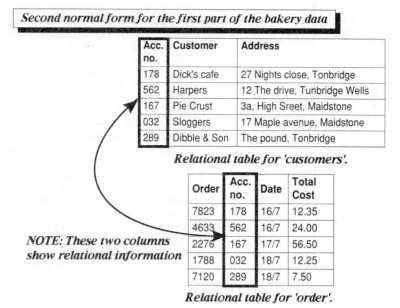

Second normal form for the first part of the bakery data

Acc. no.	Customer	Address
178	Dick's cafe	27 Nights close, Tonbridge
562	Harpers	12 The drive, Tunbridge Wells
167	Pie Crust	3a, High Sreet, Maidstone
032	Sloggers	17 Maple avenue, Maidstone
289	Dibble & Son	The pound, Tonbridge

Relational table for 'customers'.

Order	Acc. no.	Date	Total Cost
7823	178	16/7	12.35
4633	562	16/7	24.00
2276	167	17/7	56.50
1788	032	18/7	12.25
7120	289	18/7	7.50

NOTE: These two columns show relational information

Relational table for 'order'.

Figure 20.14

Customers (Acc. no., Customer, Address)

Orders (Order no., Acc. no., Date, Total cost)

You should note that sometimes it's necessary to include more than one attribute in the primary key in order to achieve functional dependency. **If the primary key does** contain **more than one attribute**, then **functional dependence** is **relative to all attributes** contained within the **composite primary key**, and this particular situation happens in the next part of this example.

Finally, we have to operate on the other first-normal-form relation for the bakery shown at the bottom of figure 20.12. Now this table illustrates a common problem which we have not yet encountered – it's **much more difficult** to choose a suitable **primary key**. For example, if we chose 'order no.', then there is no unique association with either 'item', 'quantity' or 'price'. If we choose 'item' to be the primary key, there is no unique association with 'order number' and 'quantity' – and 'quantity' and 'price' are even less-likely candidates for the primary key! The way out of this dilemma is to choose a **primary key** which has **more than one attribute**.

If, for example, we create a **composite primary key** consisting of the attributes **'order no.' and 'item'**, then this new primary key can be used to establish functional dependency very easily. For example, consider a 'Bakewell tart' belonging to order number 7283. In this case the **quantity (**of '7283-Bakewell tarts') is now functionally dependent on the composite primary key, because order number 7283's Bakewell tarts are uniquely associated with the quantity 20.

The **item price is** obviously functionally dependent on **item**, but **not** on the 'order no. and item' composite primary key, because many different composite primary keys will be associated with the item price. Therefore, to rectify this final problem, a small table consisting of item as the primary key will be needed. Note that the attribute item provides the necessary link between these two tables, and order number acts as the link to the previous tables. We will not bother to show these two new second-normal-form tables in full, as they are defined completely by the standard shorthand notation as follows.

Part order (Order no., Item, Quantity)

Item (Item, Item price)

We have, therefore, established **four relations** for the bakery data, **all** of which are now in **second normal form**.

Third normal form

Don't forget that we must make the assumption that all tables are already in second normal form, so, given this obvious requirement, Codd's third normal form states that there should be no **functional dependencies (unique associations)** existing between **attributes** (or groups of attributes) that could **not** possibly be used as an alternative to the **primary key**.

One of the things which Codd's third normal form helps to eliminate is unintentional deletion of data, and a simple example will help to explain. Consider figure 20.15(a). We already know that each **attribute** in this **entity** must be **functionally dependent** on the **primary key**, for if this were **not the case**, then the relation would **not** be in **second normal form**. However, **all these attributes** could be used as **alternative primary keys** – simply because of the **very strong relationship** between them. Forget for the moment that 'surname', for example, might be duplicated, and therefore be a possible bad choice primary key, it's the idea of the very strong relationship that counts. For example, the surname could determine the account number, or the address could also determine the account number. Here there should be no particular deletion problem as deletion of any one of these attributes would surely require the deletion of the rest. However, for attributes that could **not** be used as **alternative primary keys**, we do have a considerable problem which must be eliminated, and this is demonstrated in the following section.

Next consider figure 20.15(b), again we already know that each **attribute** in this **entity** must be **functionally dependent** on the **primary key**, for if this were **not the case**, then the relation would **not** be in **second normal form**. But, in addition to this **functional dependency**, let's suppose that there happens to be another functional dependency between some other **non-identifying attributes** (i.e. between **attributes** that could **not possibly** function as **alternatives** to the **primary key**). This particular functional dependency is shown by the arrow next to the cross. Because the attribute 'supplier' is functionally dependent on 'component' – elimination of the 'product' will cause the supplier to be eliminated too! This might prove to be disastrous **if** this particular supplier happens to supply the same component for other products! If this type of relationship exists then it's called a **transitive dependency**.

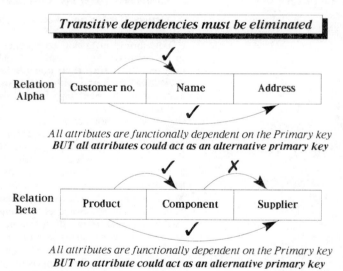

| **Transitive dependencies must be eliminated** | | |

| Relation Alpha | Customer no. | Name | Address |

All attributes are functionally dependent on the Primary key
BUT all attributes could act as an alternative primary key

| Relation Beta | Product | Component | Supplier |

All attributes are functionally dependent on the Primary key
BUT no attribute could act as an alternative primary key

Figure 20.15

If this sort of thing happens in a relational database then the relation can be split up yet again into different relations, and one possible change is shown in figure 20.16. Here we can see that elimination of the original product will **not** cause the supplier to be eliminated, and this would ensure that the data is now in third normal form.

Returning to the first two tables of the bakery problem, we can see that all attributes in the table at the top of figure 20.14 could be used as alternative primary keys, and therefore this relation is already in third normal form. The table at the bottom of figure 20.14 contains no non-identifying attributes. Therefore, we must check to see that there are no functional dependencies (unique associations) existing between them. A careful examination of the 'account no.' 'date' and 'total cost' will

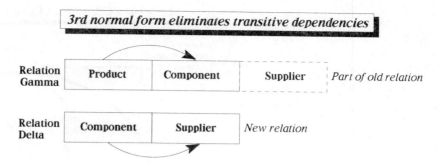

Figure 20.16

reveal that none of these are functionally dependent on each other, and therefore no alterations are necessary. Therefore, **this particular table is already in third normal form**. The remaining two tables, shown in shorthand form on page 473, are also no problem. Therefore, **all tables** are actually in **third normal form**. More practice with third normal form is given in exercise 20.1 at the end of this chapter.

That's all there is to normalisation!

The database management system

Having looked in some detail at the hierarchical, network and relational models used to structure data from the logical point of view, we now go on to look at the crucial role played by the **DataBase Management System** or **DBMS**. The DBMS is basically lots of very complex software which **controls all aspects** of database management. For example, a **database** will need to be **defined** (using techniques very similar to those we have already covered in this chapter), it needs to be **created**, efficiently **maintained** and **managed**, it needs to be **accessed**, **interrogated** and **backed up**, and **queries** need to be made in which information can be extracted for **reports** – and this is just a flavour of some the functions carried out by a modern **DBMS**. It also provides the **interface** between the data and the users – for example, it would prob- ably allow you to create powerful WIMP-based systems that enable non-specialist users to easily enter data into the system or to carry out standard queries. It allows you to interface a variety of high-level languages via suitable language extensions and provides **multiple levels of security** etc. Together with an **SQL**, or **Data Query Language (DQL)**, it provides management with a powerful analytical tool which can handle most aspects of their data-processing business, because the **database** literally **is** their business. The general idea of a typical database management system is shown graphically in figure 20.17.

How is the system organised?

As can be seen from figure 20.17, a **DBMS** provides the necessary **links** between the **data** stored on magnetic disk or other suitable secondary storage medium, and the external **software interfaces** such as **applications programs** etc. As you can see from the diagram, the **database management system** also provides an appropriate **interface** between other **applications** which might want to make use of the data in the database system.

For example, a high level language may wish to use the facilities of the **DBMS** so that it can store and retrieve data for its own particular applications. Modern versions of **COBOL**, for example, have been extended to include special commands which deal specifically with databases.

The DBA

A person called the **DataBase Administrator** or **DBA** (shown by the very special user D in figure 20.17) will be in charge of the database design and maintenance. He or she is the 'big-boss person' and will set up a **database schema** which is the **grand design** of the **overall database**. This design or schema would make use of the **data models** covered in the first half of this chapter.

This DBA is in a very powerful position and has great responsibility. He or she will need extensive knowledge about the nature of the business, and also about the particular company concerned. It's the DBAs responsibility to maintain the database, and this involves operations like altering the structure of the database as the business expands into new areas. You should note that it does not involve the entry of data

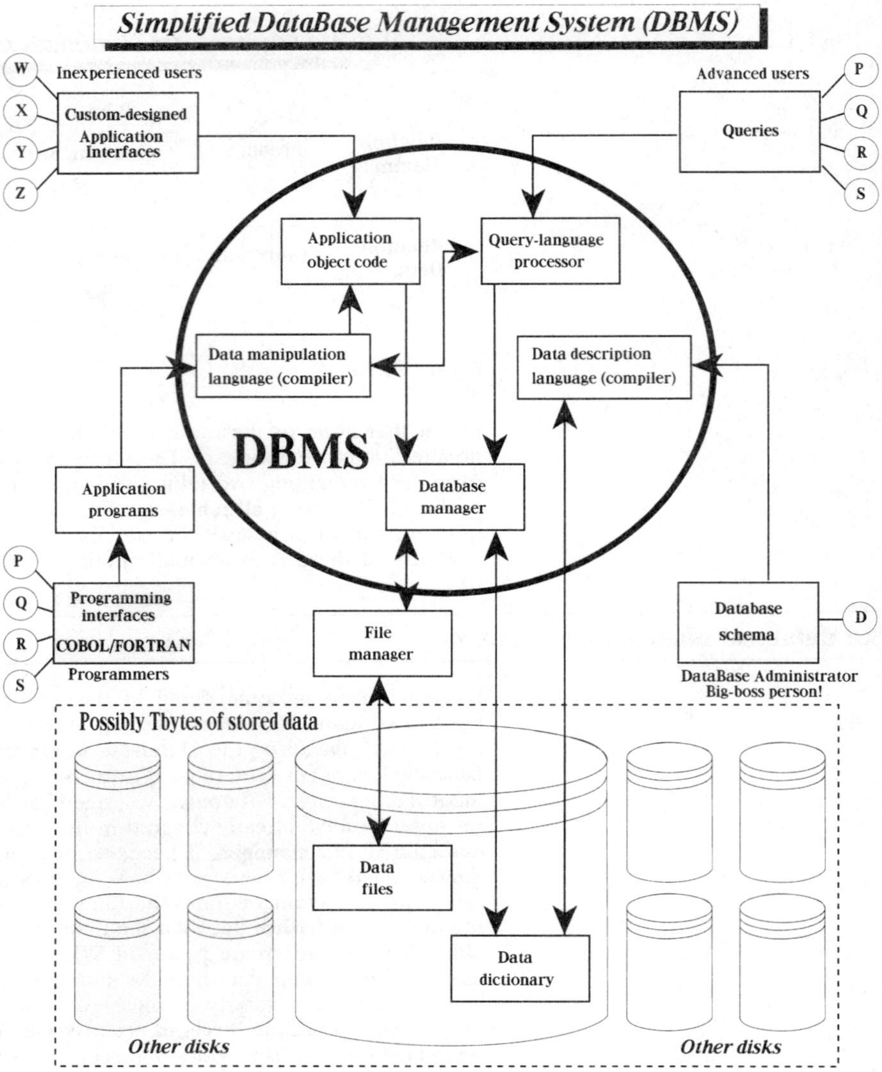

Figure 20.17

itself, except, perhaps, for test purposes. Ordinary data entry would be carried out by the inexperienced users shown in figure 20.17. As the DBA is able to do *anything* to the database, they are given the **highest level of security** possible. The **database management system (DBMS)** would allow the **database administrator** to set a password as soon as the creation of the database is underway, because if this is *not* done then anybody might be able to gain unauthorised access to the data.

The schema

The definition of the entire database or **schema** can be thought of as being viewed from several different **levels** called **subschema**. The first level is the **conceptual level**, which describes the data as seen by the **application** that is making use of the DBMS. (i.e. this could be thought of as the problem level, as it is dealing with problems in the real world). The **second level** is called the **logical level**. This describes **how** the relationships will be represented in the **logical structure** of the database. Finally, the **third level**, called the **physical level**, describes how the data will be stored on the **physical media** such as **primary** or **secondary storage** devices.

Data description language (DDL)

Many of the above **subschema** would also be split up into further **subschema** with defined roles such as 'which users will have access to which data' making use of the ideas shown at the beginning of the chapter in the Venn diagram figure 20.1. Another common problem for the DBA is to define the system in such a way that different users can't update the same data at the same time, as this may obviously compromise data integrity. The **database schema** would by modelled by the DBA with the help of a special language called the **Data Description Language** (DDL) or the **Data Definition Language** (also DDL!) . For example, the **DDL** will help the **DBA** to define the logical structure of the database, which is then used to construct tables which are held in the **data dictionary**.

The data dictionary

The **data dictionary** can be regarded as a **description of the database itself** (not the actual data – that is held in the **data files**), and would help to **map** the **logical database** onto the **physical-level** storage devices, help sort out who has access to what data for security purposes, and help with any validation such as checking to see if the data actually exists, and in making sure that adequate schemes are in operation for recovery in the event of errors such as disk crashes or fire. The data dictionary can be thought of as containing data which describes the data, and therefore enables the DBA to maintain overall control of the system.

The file manager

As you will appreciate from reading chapter 17 on operating systems, the **file manager** would be that part of the **operating system** which allows physical access to the data stored on the disks in this particular database example. Therefore, this manages access to the data at the physical-level subschema. The file manager interfaces the data stored on disk with the software requesting particular data. Therefore, the logical structures used at the higher levels of file management would be identical to those covered in chapter 16 when files and file-handling techniques were looked at in some detail. You should note that **there are no special methods of storing files other than those covered in chapter 16**, and it's the job of the **DBMS** to **convert** the **data** presented by the **users**, via the **schema**, via the **logical-file structures** such as **indexed sequential**, for example, via the **buffering systems** mentioned on page 358 and eventually to the **physical** ways in which the **bytes of data** are **actually stored** on the **secondary storage media**.

Data manipulation language (DML)

The **Data Manipulation Language** (DML) provides a comprehensive set of features to allow modification to the data contained within the database. Some of the facilities provided by the DML are intended only for the DBA, but other facilities such as the query language (see in a moment) allows all users to carry out common operations such as retrieving and modification (if they have appropriate security clearance) of data. You should realise that large database systems will probably have multiple users, and updates obviously can't be carried out on the **same record** at the **same time** by **different** users. Therefore, a process called **record locking** is used whereby a record in the process of being updated is **not** available to other users during this period.

There are two current types of DML supported by most DBMS, and these are related to the procedural (**imperative**) and non-procedural (**declarative**) language types as typified in chapter 6 on high-level language principles. You may recall that 4GLs (see page 105) typified the non-procedural DML types, and it's these which allow users to access data in very easy ways. However, as described in the high-level languages chapter, no language is an island unto itself, and most DMLs have aspects of each. Advanced users would build up their own algorithms enabling them to use the database in innovative ways, but the inexperienced users would make do with the simpler aspects of the DML to retrieve data in standard ways. You should not forget that the programmers or the DBA could write their own code which can then be called up as a macro by inexperienced users of the system.

The query language

Part of the facilities provided by the DML enable the end users to execute queries, and this is specifically referred to as a query language. In some systems the DML and the query language are one and the same thing. It is the job of the query processor in the DBMS to take the queries written by the users and to change them into a form that can be used inside the DBMS to activate the interface with the other systems described above. The query processor must also communicate with the DML so that appropriate queries produced from the high-level languages or other applications may be converted into the application code necessary to communicate with the database manager at the appropriate level – follow the arrows in figure 20.17. Specific examples of queries are covered in the practical section when different systems are looked at later on in this chapter.

Commercial database applications

Having looked in detail at the theory of different data structures and large commercial database systems, we will, for the remainder of this chapter, concentrate on using powerful **databases** on **microcomputers**. Most of the theory covered so far is still applicable to these smaller systems, but we will now take a specific look at database systems from the end-user point of view. For example, figure 20.18 shows a typical WIMP-based front end to a database system at the author's school.

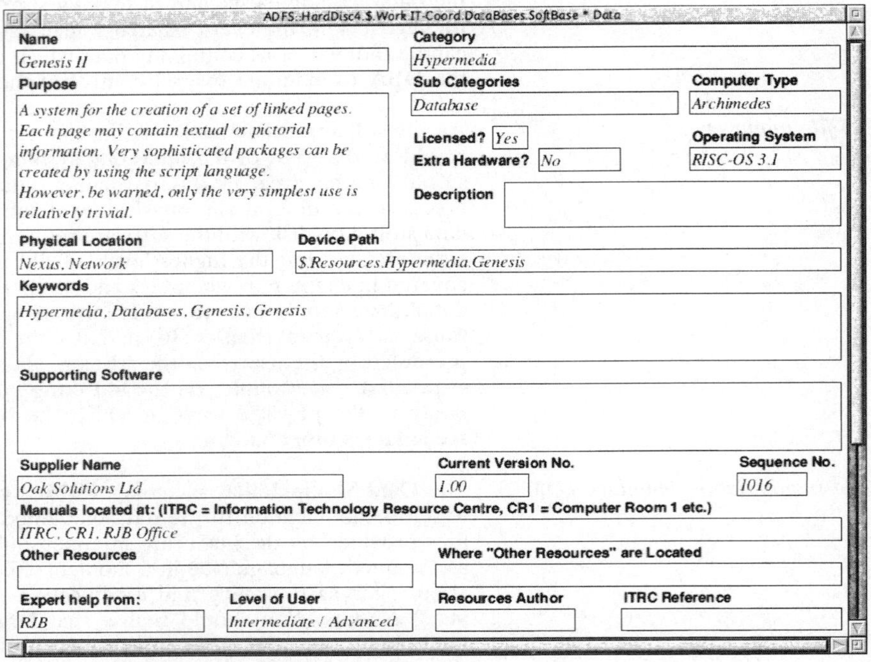

Figure 20.18

Here you can see part of a system set up for helping pupils to interrogate software which is available for use at the school. There are two ways of using the system, but this one shows the full complement of available Boolean fields (see page 113) at the bottom of the record, not usually seen unless specifically requested. This particular system has been implemented making use of a relational database called Squirrel II running on Acorn's RISC PC workstations over an Ethernet network from a special Database file server.

The next few sections will outline some of the facilities available in modern database systems like Squirrel and SoftBase on the Acorn machines, or dBase IV, Access or Paradox on the IBM PCs, but other systems on the Mac are just as powerful.

From reading the work in this chapter you will appreciate that we have taken a snapshot view of what an inexperienced user would see if he or she ran the software database. Here the term 'inexperienced user' means one who is only able to view and extract information from the system. They would have many facilities for interrogation and reporting, but have no facilities to be able to alter any of the actual database, either in terms of its structure, or of the data contained in it. To do this you would have to log on as a system manager to the appropriate database file server, where you would then be placed in the role of the DBA.

You should appreciate that figure 20.18 shows a **custom-designed application interface** (see page 590). However, as we have seen in this chapter, the **HCI** bears little or no simple relation to the **logical** and **physical data structures** used by the database system. In the system shown in figure 20.18, the **entire screen** corresponds to a **record**, the layout of which is simply for the convenience of the user. Each white 'box' within the screen corresponds to a **field** within a record. The data in this record (whole screen) mirrors the data in a **single row** or **tuple** from a **relational table**, and therefore corresponds to the single entity from a relation. Part of the relational table (actually printed as a report) is shown in figure 20.19.

As we have seen, to build up a proper **relational database**, we would have to **normalise** the data and produce other tables constructed by similar means. In practice, **when ordinary users are using the system, even though relational databases are being used, you don't have to make use of the relational capabilities**. It is this fact that enables the man in the street to go and buy a micro, and then set up an address-book database, for example, with little or no knowledge of what he is doing.

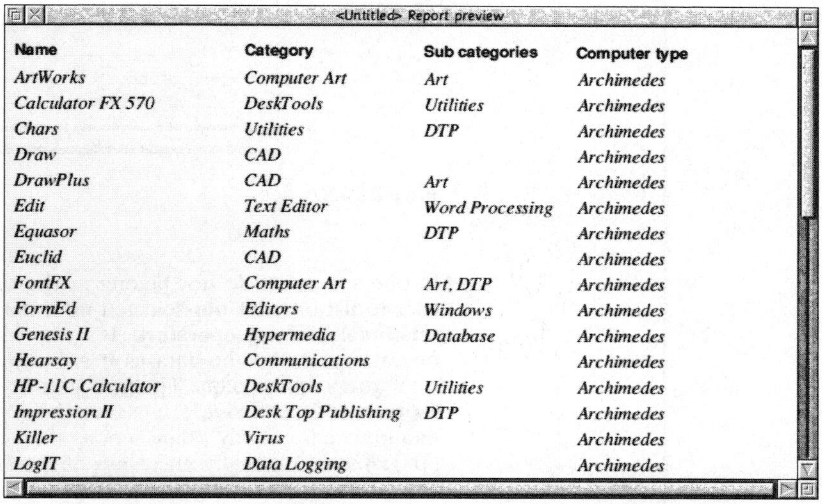

<Untitled> Report preview

Name	Category	Sub categories	Computer type
ArtWorks	*Computer Art*	*Art*	*Archimedes*
Calculator FX 570	*DeskTools*	*Utilities*	*Archimedes*
Chars	*Utilities*	*DTP*	*Archimedes*
Draw	*CAD*		*Archimedes*
DrawPlus	*CAD*	*Art*	*Archimedes*
Edit	*Text Editor*	*Word Processing*	*Archimedes*
Equasor	*Maths*	*DTP*	*Archimedes*
Euclid	*CAD*		*Archimedes*
FontFX	*Computer Art*	*Art, DTP*	*Archimedes*
FormEd	*Editors*	*Windows*	*Archimedes*
Genesis II	*Hypermedia*	*Database*	*Archimedes*
Hearsay	*Communications*		*Archimedes*
HP-11C Calculator	*DeskTools*	*Utilities*	*Archimedes*
Impression II	*Desk Top Publishing*	*DTP*	*Archimedes*
Killer	*Virus*		*Archimedes*
LogIT	*Data Logging*		*Archimedes*

Figure 20.19

The software database shown in figure 20.19 has been set up in this way, and is thus purely a 'record-card' system with no relational features whatsoever. Professional companies with very large amounts of data being accessed and altered by hundreds of users can't afford to work in this way. However, even though the software database would probably benefit from being treated as a relational database – the current version of the software used to build it does not support relational updates, only relational queries – roll on Squirrel version III! Nevertheless, all the powerful searching facilities, complex queries and reports can be undertaken, whichever type of database is being used, and these concepts will now be looked at briefly in the next few sections.

Extracting information

A database can take the information from the data files and, given a set of **relational operators**, (see in a moment), can create new **files** or **reports** containing information based on any **matching criteria**. This means that a database gives you a totally *ad hoc* ability, i.e. you can extract virtually any information (assuming it's there), given that you can define what you want in terms of '=' **'AND'**, **'OR'**, < and > etc. A typical set of relational operators is shown in figure 20.20.

The results of these operations would usually return a **true** or **false** value, or be used as a flag in which to choose a record or otherwise. As you can see from the examples column within the table, it is also usual to have the **set operators** such as **Union (OR)**, **Intersection (AND)** and **Difference** etc. (**Difference** means the values

Relation	Symbol	Examples
'Equals'	=	Teacher = 'Bloggs'
'Less than'	<	Name < 'Cooper'
'Greater than'	>	Quantity > '3'
'Less than or equal to'	<=	Pay <= '30000'
'Greater than or equal to'	>=	Tax >= '40'
'Like'	LIKE	Surname
'Matches'	MATCHES	Name LIKE %BLOGGS%
'Lies between'	BETWEEN	Student BETWEEN 'Tan' AND 'Tuson'
'Not set'	NULL	IQ is NULL

Figure 20.20

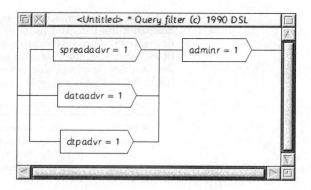

Figure 20.21

in one set which do not belong in the other set.) A typical **query** would allow the user to **list** or **print out** selected information from the database making use of these **relational** and **set operators**. It's also usually possible to perform **count** and **sum** operations etc on the data as it is being extracted.

A **query** is the name given to one or more commands written in a **Data Query Language**. It effectively tells the database how the data it is processing is to be manipulated and any other actions that should be taken. The **Data Query Language (DQL)** would actually make use of the **Data Manipulation Language DML** and the **Data Description Language DDL** to access the physical data within the database.

One nice feature about the Squirrel database software mentioned earlier is that it allows you to define queries pictorially from within the WIMP environment. It uses the convention that **AND** means 'in series' and **OR** means 'in parallel', just like the switching-algebra conventions used on page 437. For example, in my staff training database at school, if I wanted to find out which members of staff (teaching staff) had made a reservation for an advanced course on spreadsheets (spreadadvr), advanced databases (dataadvr) or advanced DTP systems (dtpadvr), but which had **also** booked a 'use of computers in admin' course (adminr), then this query, shown in figure 20.21, can be made.

Use of 4GLs

Figure 20.21 provides a much-easier HCI than the conventional SQL language. The **Structured Query Language** (e.g. a **4GL**) to achieve the same result would be

```
SELECT teaching_staff
FROM SCSI::RJBOffice.$.Work.Databases.Staff.StaffTrain
WHERE (dtpadvr = 1 AND adminr = 1) OR (dataadvr = 1 AND adminr =
                          1) OR (spreadadvr = 1 AND adminr = 1)
```

assuming that you wish only to select the name of the teaching staff from the database. This instructs the system to SELECT teaching staff (the name of the field specifying the teacher's name) FROM SCSI etc which is the name of the secondary storage device and file path, WHERE the Boolean condition matches the chosen criteria. This is a classic example of the difference between a typical custom-designed application interface for inexperienced users, and the SQL languages used as a programming language in its own right. Notice that the above query is declarative in nature, although advanced users may use the imperative nature of the SQL to provide their own more-advanced facilities.

An example of a feature for more advanced users that might be available in a typical 4GL could be that you wish to delete all the records of customers who have not had any transactions with the company for the last ten years, the procedure as defined by the data query language might be as follows:

```
for   CUSTOMERS;
if highest of INVOICES DATE < 01/01/85 then
delete records
else
delete records in INVOICES with (DATE<01/01/84)
end
end
```

The above procedure will search the customers' INVOICES held in the database and determine if the **highest value** for the **date field** selected from the records within a related file have a value that is **less than** the **target date**, if so, then the record will be deleted. However, there may be transactions older than this date with customers that also have more recent transactions. The second part of the above procedure will delete just the old parts of the customers records without deleting any later information.

As you can see, learning a query language could take a long time. The rest of this section will therefore concentrate on what sort of things can be done without going into the actual details of doing them.

Some other functions

Many of the **mathematical functions** found on a scientific calculator are automatically available from many databases, i.e. **sin**, **cos** and **tan**, **square roots**, **logs** and many others are able to be used in conjunction with numerical data. In addition to the mathematical functions, there may be specialist **financial functions**. For example, '**future values**' and **interest** etc may also be available. There is also usually a wealth of **statistical functions** such as **mean** and **variance** etc. The user is, of course, often able to set up any function that they desire by defining it themselves.

Time and date calculations

As shown above, calculations can be made on information contained in the form of date. It is also usual to provide the ability to give similar functions with time. Both American and British systems for date can be catered for.

Wildcards

The ability to search a database is of paramount importance, and much effort would be put into constructing the procedures to search the database. To help out there would probably be a system which makes use of what are known as **wildcards**. There could be several different types of wildcards in a typical system, but typically an * '**asterisk**' could mean 'any number of characters'. Therefore, if you wanted to search for all names beginning with 'BRAD' you might use the following procedure.

```
for CUSTOMERS with LAST NAME = 'BRAD*'
list records
end
```

The above would make sure that names like – **Bradbrooke, Bradbury, Bradley, Bradford, Bradshaw** and **Brady** would all be included in the output from the above search. Other wildcards might be '**?**' to represent a single character.

Reports

A **report** can be generated as the result of a **query**. It is usually possible to format the output to the user's requirements. This output can usually be directed to the screen, the printer or a file. As with the searches, it would be usual for non-technical users to have a set of pre-defined reports which they use for the day-to-day operation of the database. However, the **database administrator** or other **power users** (users with sufficient knowledge and privilege) can also define their own unique reports. Many **utilities** such as '**pre-defined templates**' make report generation relatively simple. Also, as with the import facilities described earlier, there are usually many formats in which data can be exported to other normally incompatible systems by making use of the report generators. Data could be imported into word processors, spreadsheets, transmitted over networks or transported to other systems such as mini and mainframe computer systems.

The current state of the art

Typical systems around at the time of writing include the **DB2 (Database 2) DBMS** system developed by IBM for use on its large mainframe computers. This database is fully relational and uses most of Codd's relational data models. It allows many users to have access to many databases by using standard SQL procedures. It's also possible to embed **SQL commands** in languages such as **COBOL II**, **FORTRAN 90** and yes, even **BASIC**! In addition to this, SQL is also supported by **APL** and the **system/370 assembly language**. These systems are also supported on most IBM **operating systems** from the powerful **MVS/370** mainframe, (**Multiple Virtual Storage**, see page 381 for virtual storage systems), via **DOS** and the latest **OS/2** and **Windows 95** operating system for IBMs 32-bit 286, 386 and 486-based and Pentium based 586 microprocessors.

You should now appreciate the task in front of the database administrator! You should also now fully appreciate why extensive systems analysis would be necessary over a period of many months. It should be obvious that no single person would be able to cope with such extensive computerisation by themselves, and therefore a team of computer specialists would work on the problems over an extensive period.

You will remember that, at the beginning of this chapter, we said that databases can permeate through an entire company. You should now see why.

Security of the database system

There are two different aspects of security to consider; the **physical security** of the data, i.e. the disks on which it is stored etc. and the **prevention of unauthorised access**. This section can be read in conjunction with similar sections regarding security starting on page 513 and page 604.

Physical security

This means recovering from errors if a disk gets corrupted, or making sure that most of the database can be restored in the event of a fire etc.

If one of the disks containing the database becomes corrupted then there should be facilities to recover the database so that a minimum of information is lost. The amount of information lost will depend on the frequency with which the database is backed up. This will in turn depend on the volatility of the data contained in it. Typical backups might be made daily, weekly, monthly or at intervals which particularly suit the organisation and database

Security of data

The backed-up data must be stored such that it can't become corrupted through heat or external magnetic fields etc. It should preferably be stored in a fire-proof container in a different building. However, there are other alternatives – having a complete backup computer system in another building, or some other techniques involve making use of **RAID** or **tape streamers** (see page 269). However, the storage and fire security precautions are similar for all such systems.

The obvious must also not be overlooked. Don't forget that the disks or tapes etc could literally be stolen from the room in which they are stored. Therefore, the room must be locked and the personnel who are allowed access to the main computer room, or access to the micro containing the database must have a high level of security.

Preventing unauthorised access

This is the security which is **used to prevent illegal access** to the data by unauthorised users or hackers. This is normally under the control of the **database management system** and the system is set up by the **DBA**.

Some systems allow you to set several different levels of security and typical ones are shown in the following table of figure 20.22.

Security type	Level	Typical actions
Highest	1	DBA only - access to all functions and data
High	2	Access to all options except administrion of database
Medium high	3	View, enter and delete all records, can define and run reports. Able to import and export data to other systems. Define, run and save their own reports.
Medium	4	View, enter and delete some records, can define and run some reports but not save them.
Medium low	5	Various levels of view security and write security depending on the job description of the user.
Low	6	As for 5, but with even lower priority
Very low	7	View low security records only. Can't change any data but may be able to run a few reports.

Figure 20.22

Although the security levels sound like the temperature settings on an oven, their use is quite simple. You are only able to do things to the data that has been allowed by your level of security. If for example, the **view security** of a **particular field** had a security rating of **medium**, then anyone with **medium**, **medium high**, **high** and **highest** security levels would be able to observe the data. The **medium low, low** and **very low** security people would not be able to see it. These levels of security are usually defined as the database is being created by the DBA.

Sensitive data may also be encrypted as described in chapter 26 on page 605. If the key accompanying the data is long, then it's virtually impossible to crack the codes and read the data.

Every action such as reading, updating and deletion etc. can have *different* security levels assigned to them on data in a particular field. Therefore, you can usually specify which fields are visible or invisible to a particular user, and what type of access the user can have on each file. This information can then be used by the system in a form of look-up table when requests are made by the different users. Databases have to have sophisticated levels of security as many different people can have access to the same database. You would not, for example, want the catering manager to have access to everybody's salary information. However, they may well have a high security level on a field which relates to the restaurant bill for the month. The amount of money in this field might well be related to the salary field by showing up as a debit from the salary cheque.

Disadvantages of using a database

We have already covered many of the possible disadvantages of using databases throughout this chapter. Even so, you must not loose sight of the biggest potential danger of all. That of a **catastrophic failure**. This is the sort of failure that happens when a disk sector gets physically damaged and important data (possibly containing some of the important pointers etc.) is lost. Major contingency plans for recreating as much of the database as possible must be put into action. There must be an appropriate **emergency plan** that is worked out during the systems analysis phase. This must include how the business or organisation is to operate while the system is down (i.e. while the hardware is being mended and the database is being restored). Suitable backup procedures such as those described in this chapter must obviously be carried out. Fatal errors will always occur and must be allowed for by good planning.

Data protection act 1984

Having read through this chapter, and in conjunction with chapter 21 on data communication systems, you should now be in a position to appreciate fully the consequences of storing information in computer systems. The potential for the misuse of such data is enormous. Computer crime (see page 600) can have some very tempting rewards for unscrupulous people, or, quite simply, genuine mistakes can be made. These are usually in the form of human error, or, when it's not possible to completely validate and verify the data entered into the system. It is, therefore, fitting to end the major database chapter with a brief look at a recent Act of Parliament that sets out to legislate for the conduct of people and organisations who hold personal data about individuals – this is called the **Data Protection Act** and was in **full force from late 1987**. The statements of good practice in the 1984 Act are as follows:

(1) *The information to be obtained in personal data shall be obtained, and personal data shall be processed, fairly and lawfully.*
(2) *Personal data shall be held only for one or more specified and lawful purposes.*
(3) *Personal data held for any purpose or purposes shall not be used or disclosed in any manner incompatible with that purpose or purposes.*
(4) *Personal data held for any purpose or purposes shall be adequate, relevant, and not excessive in relation to that purpose or purposes.*
(5) *Personal data shall be accurate and, where necessary, kept up to date.*
(6) *Personal data held for any purpose or purposes shall not be kept longer than necessary for that purpose or those purposes.*
(7) *A data subject shall be entitled*
    (a) *at reasonable intervals and without undue delay or expense*
        (i) *to be informed by any data user whether he holds personal data of which that individual is the subject; and*
        (ii) *to access any such data held by the data user; and*
    (b) *where appropriate, to have such data corrected or erased.*
(8) *Appropriate security measures shall be taken against unauthorised access to, or alteration, disclosure, or destruction of personal data and against accidental loss or destruction of personal data.*

One of the ridiculous things about the Data Protection Act is, that at the time of writing, none of the above protection is available to people who have the same information stored about them on paper in filing cabinets! The Data Protection Act of 1984 just applies to data held on computers. However, it must be appreciated that the potential for the misuse of data held in computers is vast compared with the same data held in filling cabinets. Even so, this does not help the people who have the wrong credit rating stored on a piece of paper in the bottom of a locked filing cabinet!

The Computer Misuse Act

Another legal milestone was introduced when the **Computer Misuse Act** recently came into being. For the first time **hacking** and other such criminal activity became illegal. Before the advent of this particular act the only criminal offence being committed by someone who broke into a computer system was theft of electricity!

Exercise 20.1

1. What makes a **database very much** better than an unrelated collection of files holding information on a computer system?

2. Write down the **type** of **relationship** that exists between the following entities.
   (a) Car   Driver
   (b) Car   Registration number
   (c) Bank account   Customer
   (d) Mother   Children
   (e) Brother   Sister

3. Using a **hierarchical database structure**, show how it might be possible to model the books in a library. Would this be an efficient structure? Why would a **network structure** probably improve the situation?

4. Show how a typical **hierarchical database structure** might be used to model the pupils in a school or college.

5. Why is a **relational** database very different indeed from the **hierarchical** and **network** databases?

6. Define the following terms in relation to a relational database.
   (a) Attribute   (b) Entity
   (c) Relation   (d) Primary key
   (e) Tuple   (f) Normalisation

7. What is meant by the terms **functional dependency** and **transitive dependency**? Give an example of each.

8. What is meant by a **variable-length record**, and why is it best **not** to make use of variable record lengths in a **relational database**?

9. Consider the following data which shows a **single student record**.

Pemburyshire College of Advanced Technology				
Student name Nick Codswallop			Student ID 317256	
Address 123 Oak Road, Seven Oak Green, Welligton MN12 6TH				
Home phone number 081-278-162251				
Company Southern Sewage				
Company phone number 0903-356-198726				
Subject code	Subject name	Grade	Teacher	Department
DENCS1a	Computer science	A	RJB	Computing
DENEL1c	Electronic systems	B	DLF	Electronics
DENPH1b	Physics	B	RIL	Physics
DENMA1d	Mathematics	A	NJL	Mathematics
DENHM1c	Higher mathematics	B	TAG	Mathematics
DENTE1a	Technology	A	AJH	Technology
DENGE1e	General studies	E	DEB	English

Derive a set of **tables** to show the above data in 1st, 2nd and 3rd normal form. There is a potential problem with the data as shown above. What is it, and what data could be added to overcome this problem?

10. Describe the difference between a declarative SQL used to define a query and a typical user-friendly HCI to achieve the same result with inexperienced users.

11. Outline the essential security measures to be undertaken when setting up a database in a large company.

12. Use a database system which you have at school or college to set up a database listing the names and subjects taken by the students in your class. Use an SQL to make a report containing each student under all the different subject headings which are taken by the students, e.g. a heading of 'Maths' followed by all who take maths, followed by a heading of 'Computer Science' followed by all those who take computer science etc.

End of chapter summary

■ A **database** is a collection of related information, organised such that efficient data processing may be carried out on the data contained in it.

■ It's possible to arrange a **centralised database** so that *each department* in an office or factory etc. *has its own specific view* of the data contained in a large database.

■ Large databases form the hub of many companies, with the information contained within the database vital for many different aspects of the business.

■ A **relationship** is a **link**, some sort of **association** or some **dependency** between two or more **attributes**.

■ **Relationships** can be of the type **one-to-one**, **one-to-many**, **many-to-one** or **many-to-many**.

■ An **entity** is any concrete or abstract occurrence defined in a database and can be regarded as a **record**, e.g. customer record or criminal record!

- An **attribute** is part of a **record**, and can be regarded as being the same as a **field** within a **record**.
- A **dependency** can be regarded as a **particular relationship** in which the **existence** of one thing **depends** upon the **existence** of another.
- An **association** is the type of connection between entities and usually defines one of the standard relationships.
- An **entity dependence diagram** shows the relationships between entities in terms of how the existence of one depends on the existence of others.
- An **entity relationship diagram** shows the relationships between entities, the relationships are usually placed in diamond-shaped boxes.
- There are several different types of database including **hierarchical**, **network** and **relational databases**.
- A **hierarchical database** is modelled on a **tree structure** in which *each parent can have many children*. It is therefore ideal for one-to-many relationships.
- A **network database** is modelled on a partially or fully interconnected structure in which pointers may operate in a variety of modes. Unlike the hierarchical database, each record can have multiple owners.
- A **relational database** is a database built up around **relations**.
- A **relation** is basically a **two-dimensional table** where **rows (tuples) represent logical records**, and **column** entries represent the **attributes** of a particular entity.
- A **table** in a **relational database** corresponds to a **file**.
- A **record** in a **relational database** is referred to as a **tuple**, and corresponds to a **row** from a **relational** table.
- **Tuple** is used instead of 'row' because it's the **correct term** from the tuple relational calculus and relational algebra – the **theories** on which **relational databases** depend.
- The set of **all possible values** that an **attribute** may take on is called a **domain**.
- **Relations** or **tables** may be written in **shorthand notation** with the **primary key** underlined.
- The **primary key** is the key by which the **relational table** is **best identified**. It's often the first column in the relation, but this need not be so.
- The **primary key** should **uniquely identify each record** if problems of duplicates are to be avoided.
- A **primary key** may consist of **more than one attribute** if this helps to establish functional dependency. It's often necessary to have to do this.
- **Relational databases** may be **normalised** by application of **Codds rules.**
- **Normalisation** is a s*et of rules developed by Codd* which result in more efficient data organisation, more efficient storage and the simplification of the database.
- The **first normal form** states that any attributes with multiple or repeating values are removed so that all entities (records) are the same length.
- The **second normal form** states that **all attributes** in an **entity** must be **functionally dependent** on the **primary key**.
- **Functionally dependent (on primary key)** means that there should be a unique association between the primary key and the attribute. Thus the primary key should be able to identify uniquely an attribute if functional dependency exists.
- The **third normal form** states that there should be **no functional dependency** existing between **attributes** or groups of **attributes** that could **not** be used as an alternative primary key, i.e. there should be no **transitive dependencies**.
- A **transitive dependency** means that if A is dependent on B, and B is dependent on C, then A is dependent on C also. This often has to be avoided if unnecessary data deletion is to be avoided.
- A **DBMS** is a **DataBase Management System**.
- A **DataBase Management System** is a very powerful piece of software which helps to design, build and maintain a database.
- A **schema** is the name given to the *logical definition of a database*.
- A **subschema** defines a *specific sub-section of a database* that a particular program, for example, might use.
- A **DDL** or **Data Description Language** is used for describing **data** and the **relationships** between data in a database.
- A **DML** or **Data Manipulation Language** is used for manipulating data within a database – i.e. **updating**, **deleting** or **creating** etc.
- The **data dictionary** contains data about the 'data in the database'.
- The **file manager** is part of the OS which helps to map the logical file structures onto the physical storage devices.
- The **DBA** is the **DataBase Administrator**. This is the person who is responsible for the design, implementation and maintenance of the database. (Note: *not* usually the same as the people who enter the actual data!)

- An **SQL** is a **Structured Query Language** – this enables queries to be carried out efficiently by writing simple or complex programs.
- **QBE**, or **Q**uery **By Example** is an alternative to **SQL**.
- **Databases** are usually created by using **specialist applications packages** and *information can be extracted from a database* by means of a **query**.
- A **relational operator** is used to help specify **queries** in a database.
- The **relational operators** are : '=', '<', '>', '<=', and '>='.
- The **set operators OR**, **AND** and **NOT** also help to define database **queries**.

21 Modern communication systems

Introduction

Anyone who has not yet heard of the term **information superhighway** must be living on a different planet. The term is a 'catch all' for the marrying together of several different technologies such as the *telephone systems*, *satellite systems*, *computer networks* and *multimedia*, together with an appropriate set of new **software** and **hardware** facilities, and a large number of **information providers** and **bulletin-board** systems. It is rather an appropriate term to describe the revolution which started to happen just five or ten years ago, but which has now gathered such terrific momentum, due to recent innovations in **compression techniques**, the ever increasing **digitisation** of the **telephone networks**, the tumbling prices of the equipment needed to connect to such systems, and the growing popularity of major national and international interconnected networks such as the **Internet**.

Today we have the remarkable ability to communicate with anybody else at any time, and in virtually any place. Via satellite systems we can communicate from a car travelling in a London high street, to a ship sailing in the South Pacific ocean. We have the ability to send speech, pictures and computer data over any of these links. When (*not if*) the **superhighway** gets sufficiently developed, many homes will have interactive two-way communications to this vast web of networks, and the use of the TV at home will take on many new dimensions. This chapter looks in detail at some of the systems that have championed this communications revolution. In particular we will look at the implications for the connection of computers to these sophisticated communication systems.

Computer networks

Computer networks are categorised according to how they are organised, the ways in which they are used, and the distances over which they can operate. There are three main categories, although alternative names are also in common use. The first type of network we will consider in this chapter is called a **LAN** – which stands for **Local Area Network**. As its name implies this typifies a 'small' network operated *locally*. The term 'small' is obviously relative, as hundreds of computers may be connected up via a LAN. The term LAN can more usefully be quoted in relation to the *length of the cabling which the network can support*, with about *1 km or 2 km* being a maximum length for a typical LAN. Each part of the LAN will usually be under the exclusive control of the educational, business or industrial establishment operating the system.

Next in the hierarchy comes a **MAN** or **Metropolitan Area Network**. These typify the more recent **FDDI networks** (see page 496) where fibre optics are used, and the range of a typical MAN is about *10 km*, hence the term **MAN**. Finally, **WANs** or **Wide Area Networks** make use of *public lines* such as the **national** and **international computer** and **telephone networks** provided by the telecommunications companies such as British Telecom or Mercury, and can thus reach the parts that the other networks can't reach. These *global networks* are sometimes known as **LHNs** or **Long Haul Networks**, but the preferred term **WAN** is more extensively used. A network that is capable of supporting voice, video and computer data, is called an **ISDN** or **Integrated Services Digital Network**. **ISDNs** are normally implemented using digital technology at each stage of the network.

Increasingly sophisticated methods of connection have become possible over the last few years, because the telephone networks are changing from the old style analogue system to the new style high speed digital technology. WANs can make use of the standard telephone system, but, as is more likely in the case of high speed computer communications, use special dedicated lines. Satellite, land-based and underwater links are all now very common. Nevertheless, a combination of many different types of network is now common. For example, a MODEM might be used to access a computer via the standard telephone line, but the computer being accessed might then access other systems which will probably use high-speed network links. Interconnectivity is the name of the game in a modern communications system.

Local area networks

A **LAN** refers to the connection of computers in a **local area** such as a *school*, *office* or *factory* – these may be in the same building, or, just as likely, involve connection of computers in several different buildings on the same site, or at different sites relatively close to each other – bearing in mind the maximum length of an individual network is usually limited to about 500 m, 1 km or 2 km depending on geometry. However, it's common on larger sites to have *several* **LANs** interconnected by the use of **bridges or routers**. In this way, two **LANs** connected via a **bridge**, for example, will give you double the cable length.

A *simple* **local area network** or **LAN** would probably consist of just a few computers sharing some resources, and a typical one is shown in figure 21.1.

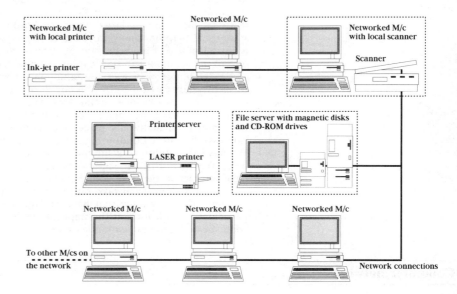

Figure 21.1

In such a system each computer connected to the network is often referred to as a **terminal** or a **workstation**, (not to be confused with the same term used to denote a high-end micro). The **file server** is usually a *high performance micro* with several large drives, often giving several Gbytes of capacity and perhaps a few CD-ROM drives too. The **printer server** such as the one shown allows all networked machines to have access to a laser printer in this particular case. However, it's possible to have access to *other servers* such as **teletext servers** (see page 533), or servers which allow all the micros to have access to an external network via the **public telephone system** or X-25 system (see page 508) etc. It's also very common to set up file servers containing different databases. Printing jobs sent to the printer server would be **queued** if necessary (i.e. more than one thing needs to be printed), and the work is usually **spooled** (see page 373) and sent to the printer when it's free. Notice that a network does *not* prevent **local resources** such as local **disks**, **scanners** and **printers** etc being used. The microcomputer workstations can often work totally independently of the network by using their *own resources*, use the network *instead of their own resources*, or use a *combination of both* simultaneously.

Why make use of LANs?

There are many reasons for making use of networks as opposed to having many independent microcomputers or workstations. The networked computers can make more efficient use of common resources such as **applications software**. This saves the bother of having to store the software on many different disks for each machine – a nightmare scenario for network managers.

The network also gives you the powerful facilities of communication between different computers. For example, you can easily set up **electronic mail** systems (see page 535) and **bulletin boards**, can make use of **facsimile systems** (i.e. scanning a document and transmitting the contents around the network), can carry out **distributed transaction processing** (i.e. workstations have access to and help control parts of the network system) and access central **databases** etc. We have also seen how relatively expensive resources such as laser printers can be shared between several people. A network of machines will usually be cheaper to operate than the equivalent number of machines each having the same facilities (i.e. printers, disks and software etc.). It also means that a manager can easily maintain all the software if it happens to be on a single centralised-distribution system. How about sharing the processing of some complex problem between several machines on the network? There are many different possibilities.

Using a LAN in practice

To make use of a network the user would have to **log on** to the **file server**. On more sophisticated systems, this may mean logging on to a powerful **mini** or **mainframe** computer. The **file server** is an appropriate name because this is the machine on which the users' **files** are stored, then **served** out to the users when necessary. It is also usual to store **applications** such as **DTP systems**, **spreadsheets** and **databases** etc. on the same or a different file server. This saves having multiple copies of the same application on each networked machine.

There would normally be a **security system** whereby each user would have access only to that part of the file-server disk on which their particular files are stored. In addition to this they would probably have **public access** (i.e. **read-only access**) to **utilities** and **packages** used by everybody. Such security is normally implemented by a **password system**, and some suitable **data structure** which helps to *identify which areas of the disk belong to which user.*

One system for user allocation is based on the relationship between a hierarchical directory structure (see page 304), and the user names given to the users of the network system. For example, just a small part of one of the file-server disks on one of the Ethernet networks at the author's school running Acorn's RISC OS network filing system is shown in figure 21.2.

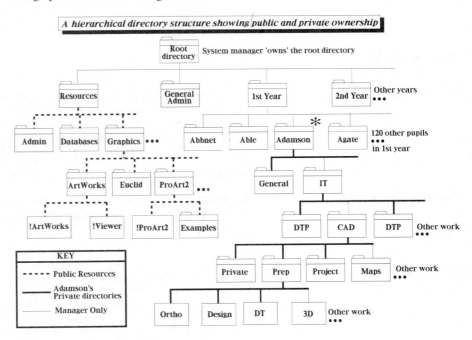

Figure 21.2

Users on this particular system are assigned such that they are mapped onto the above directory structure. Take, for example, the student called **Adamson** in the **1st Year**. He would be *assigned a user ID* called **1stYear.Adamson**. When he logs onto the system he 'jumps into' the directory structure at the point shown by the * in figure 21.2. As far as Adamson is concerned, the **parent directories** *do not logically exist*, and the system will not allow him to see them. However, all the **children**

directories which are subordinate to Adamson's own '**root**' directory are all owned by him, and are managed as though they were on a local hard disk system.

Other students such as **Abbnet** and **Able**, for example, *can't see any* **brother** or **sister directories**, therefore can't go up the hierarchical structure, and therefore *do not* have access to other peoples' work. All users are managed in the above way, and the entire file server would have about 700 student users, all with their own root directories arranged 'as they please' – with just a little friendly guidance from the head of Computing and IT! As you can see, even a typical school-based file server can have a horrendous number of actual directories.

To enable **all users** to have access to resources such as **art packages** and **DTP systems** etc. a **directory** called '**Resources**' is created in which all **applications** and **utilities** are *hierarchically arranged in ways identical* to the 'users' directories' described in the above paragraph. However, all these directories are on **public access**, and therefore available to all who have successfully logged onto the network. There are two types of public access – **read** access and **write** access. Obviously all applications are read-only access or else any user could delete or alter all the files!

Network management software

As you can imagine, it would be too complex for the ordinary user to decide where all the resources are located, from which network and file server certain utilities or applications may be found, and on which disk all their files etc will be stored. To make life easy for the network users, computer manufacturers have developed sophisticated **network operating systems**, (**NOS**) and provide extra utilities for helping to manage the network. Most of these operating systems now provide a user-friendly **HCI** by making many of the difficult operations transparent to the users of the system.

In addition to the above, the **network manager** (the person in charge of the network) will usually provide an 'in-house front end' to the system so that people in the local educational or industrial establishment can do their day to day operations more easily. This may include logging on and making sure that the user is always guided round the network resources in a sensible way. For example, an icon called 'Resources' lives on the icon bar of networked machines at the author's school. Clicking over this icon with the mouse brings up a window in which directories with names such as Admin, Graphics and DTP etc can be seen. If a student wanted a pixel-based art package, for example, then they open the graphics directory, go into the ProArt2 directory and load the ProArt2 pixel-based art-package software.

Practical problems

Under normal conditions, once the user has logged onto the system, there would theoretically be little difference between using the local area network, and operating on local (i.e. inside your own machine) hard or floppy disk drives. However, problems often occur when many machines are being heavily used *at the same time* – this is due to the mass of computer data that has to be transmitted over the same wires. There is often an appreciable delay between requesting a particular operation and getting the appropriate response. This is particularly true with powerful 32-bit or 64-bit microcomputers running complex software on some *inexpensive* networks such as the older Econet system from Acorn. The problems occur due to the **limited bandwidth** of the network system, and this is explained in the next section.

Problems of bandwidth

Bandwidth is a *physical limitation* of any practical communication system – it is to do with the range of frequencies which can be transmitted and received over a communications link. To understand bandwidth, it's best to start with a simple analogy. The human ear, for example, can only hear frequencies in the approximate range of 20 Hz to 20 kHz depending on age. As you get older the higher frequencies tail off. The bandwidth of the human ear is therefore said to be between 20 Hz and 20 KHz. These limitations are imposed because of the unique way in which human beings are built. Other animals, such as bats, for example, have a totally different bandwidth because they are built differently. In a similar way, transmission systems such as networks have a limited bandwidth due to the ways in which *they* are built, and the *materials* from which they are made.

The lower the **bandwidth** of the system, the cheaper it is to produce, but the rate at which data can be transferred is usually slower. It's rather similar to a motorway in the rush hour. If too many cars are trying to get from point A to point B, then there will be traffic jams, and the traffic will take a long time to get through. However, on a computer network, the traffic would be bytes of computer data, and instead of a traffic jam occurring, the computers would keep getting signals that the network is busy. They would have to wait for a free slot before they could send more data. If many computers are trying to send and receive information at the same time, then there will be many clashes and the effective data transfer rate for each computer will be small. More expensive higher-bandwidth systems will cope much better. It's rather like having many more lanes on the motorway, more cars can be sent along the lines at the same time.

An understanding of the **bandwidth limitations** of different network connections is *essential* to an understanding of what can be done in practice when using **LANs** and **WANs**. For example, a simple **E-Mail** connection might be very satisfactory on **low-bandwidth links**, but **full video conferencing** would *not* work over the same link – you would need a **much-higher bandwidth** to cope with the increased amount of information in the video signal which needs to be sent very quickly (more bits/sec) if you are to use the system in real time.

Solutions to limited bandwidth

Inexpensive computer networks (such as those found in some schools) will often have a lower bandwidth. One possible solution would be to upgrade the network to one with a much higher bandwidth and hence a higher data transfer rate. However, this is obviously expensive, so there have been many ingenious ways of making local area networks apparently work at a faster rate. Some of these methods are now described.

Solution using software

One such method is to make use of special software which solves specific problems. For example, if 25 students are trying simultaneously to load a word processor from a **file server** on a **network**, then all the machines are competing against each other to load the same software! There will be a bottleneck as the same software gets sent to each machine in turn. However, consider this different approach – under the control of the teacher, it would be possible to provide an instruction which loads the word processor into each machine on the network simultaneously. This means that, instead of clashing, each machine accepts the same data at the same time. As far as the 25 students are concerned, they have loaded the software into their machines much more quickly. However, it should be obvious that the actual data transfer rate has not been increased, the network has merely been utilised more efficiently.

There would still be a problem if all the machines wanted simultaneously to load different software, but some of the worst bottlenecks in educational establishments occur when a class comes into the computer room and are told to load large applications from a network file server. In many cases the class would all be using the same software. There are many occasions where self-inflicted problems like the above can be overcome by the sensible use of some specially written software. However, there are also some other methods which make use of extra hardware.

Using other hardware

One of the objects of a local area network is to share common resources. One solution is to store all software on local hard disks. However, if each machine is to have a hard disk, this would defeat some of the object of having the network in the first place. A compromise is to have an intelligent hard disk controller connected as a

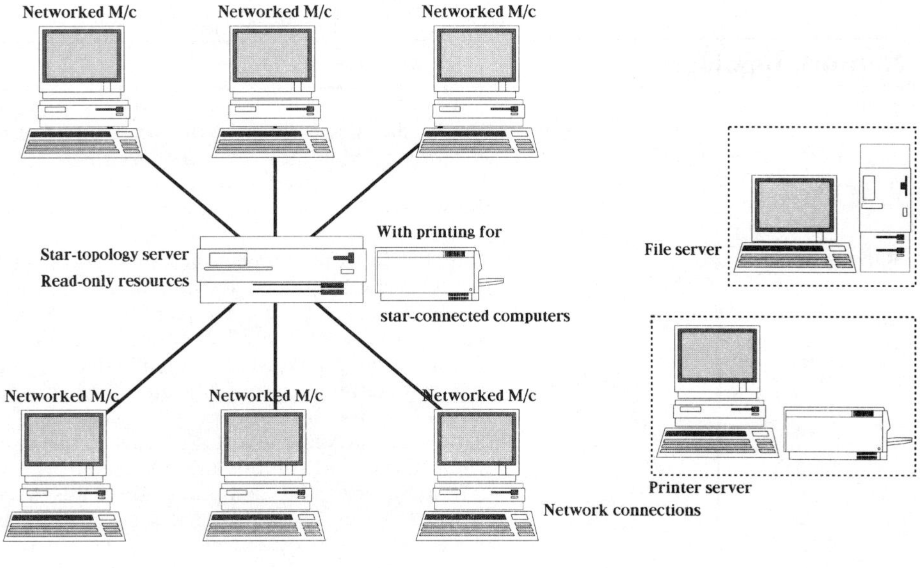

Networked M/c   Networked M/c   Networked M/c

Star-topology server
Read-only resources

With printing for

star-connected computers

File server

Networked M/c   Networked M/c   Networked M/c

Printer server

Network connections

Figure 21.3

star network (see later) serving a limited number of computers. S.J. Research have developed such a system for the Acorn range of computers, it is called NEXUS, and the principle of operation is shown in figure 21.3.

As can be seen from the above, it is almost the same as running two networks simultaneously – the conventional network system shown in grey, and the **star topology** intelligent disk controller 'network' shown in black. Using such a system, it is possible for the *resources* such as **applications software** to be loaded from the **intelligent disk controller**, and the user's **files** to be loaded from the **conventional file server** shown on the right in the diagram. Instead of each machine having its own hard disk, a hard disk is shared between several machines on the network. (A maximum of twelve is allowed in this particular system.) Under normal conditions, this gives each machine the apparent speed of having its own hard disk. Even under heavy use, it's relatively quick, and obviously does not depend on whether the network is busy or not.

More sophisticated networks

Most large industrial users and universities would not be too concerned about saving a few thousand pounds to compromise the speed and efficiency with which they can communicate between computers. Therefore, much higher bandwidth systems would be employed. There could well be very powerful mini or mainframe computers that form the **central node** of the network, and very high speed computer communications over the network may be possible. For example, Cambridge University have higher speed X25 links (see page 505) which connect the remote colleges with their main computer. The modern computer centre is on a separate site in the town centre, and houses a powerful IBM mainframe. The students live in a variety of colleges on separate sites throughout the town. They use many different types of computers such as IBM PCs, Archimedes and Apple Macs etc. However, the one thing that most computers have in common is a serial data communications port called the RS 232 (or RS 423) and these are covered on page 576 in chapter 25. These different computers can be linked via their serial ports to special boxes which then link to the faster X25 system. Besides being able to run local programs on the individual computers, you can run **terminal emulation software** which changes the computers into **terminals** on the mainframe. This means that some students can interact with the powerful mainframe from their own study. If they do not have a link in their study, then they are able to use some of the many public computers which are linked to the mainframe in a similar way. However, the University is currently installing more powerful networks based on the FDDI fibre-optic system and these will be covered later in this chapter.

In addition to the above, some workstations may well have one or more Winchester disks attached to it. This gives an added powerful local processing ability. You would, therefore, get the best of both worlds – a powerful stand-alone computer system, and a high speed computer network allowing fast transfer of software with only a very short delay linking you to the mainframe, other computers or perhaps the **Internet**.

Network topology

This is the name given to the ways in which the **networks** are physically *organised in terms of how they are wired together*. It is also known as **network architecture**. The name is derived mainly from the ways in which the data is distributed along the network to each of the computers connected to it.

Star networks

The star-network connection can be seen in figure 21.4. The central resources for the network would be located at the 'centre' of the star. (*Note that the physical wiring need not be laid out like this – it's the connections that are important.*) Each workstation would be connected to the central **computer** or **file server** by means of its own *unique* link. With a high speed computer controlling the **central node** then *very fast* communication with all machines would be possible. The **bandwidth** of the network is also less of a problem because data for one machine only is being sent down each of the single lines. This is the system which is most often made use of when many workstations are connected to a mainframe computer.

If there are many computers then this would be an expensive option. However, it also has the advantage that security is high. This is because no workstation can interact with any other without going via the central node computer. With sophisticated software security can be *very tight* indeed. However, star networks do have some disadvantages, if one of the links becomes severed then the computer which

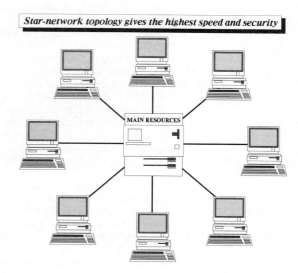

Figure 21.4

relies on that link would become permanently disconnected. With some other network topologies it would be possible to route the data such that communication would still be possible.

Bus networks

The **bus network** is shown in figure 21.5. As you can see it has a *common cable* which, on some networks, is terminated at each end, either inside a computer or by a special box as shown in this diagram. (The size of the box is obviously exaggerated!) One or more of the stations on the network acts as the file server and controls the hard disks which are used for all the common resources and the users' files.

The most prolific example of a bus system is called **ETHERNET**. This is a network with a single co-axial cable. It was developed jointly by Rank Xerox, the Digital Equipment Corporation (DEC) and INTEL. It is one of the main networks used for the interconnection of IBM PCs or any other machine with an Ethernet interface card – i.e. virtually all machines. **Ethernet** is *ideally suited* to the **business**, **educational** and **industrial** environments, giving relatively good transmission rates of 10 Mbits/sec. Ethernet is found in many universities, and has at last become cheap enough to install in many schools.

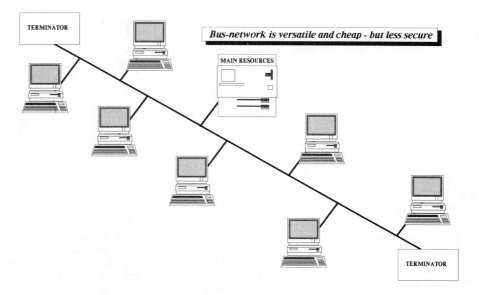

Figure 21.5

The bus network is cheaper to operate than the star network because, for a large number of computers, there is much less cable. However, bus type networks can never be totally secure as the data for one workstation must pass many others. Under normal operation this should not be a problem, but if very clever hackers are determined to illegally interrogate the packets (see page 512) of data as they go by, then there is little to stop them. It's much more difficult to hack a star network because you don't ever see data that is intended for other machines. **Encryption,** (see page 605), offers the best possible security on any highly sensitive bus network.

If a bus network is being very heavily used, then, because everybody is sharing the same communications link, the response will be slow unless the **bandwidth** of the network is quite high – however, with **modern compression techniques** *it's possible to load large windows-based applications within an acceptable number of seconds,* and with a network that's not being heavily used the speed is comparable with a hard disk.

The bus network is also less reliable than the star network, which is not too surprising considering that it's a cheaper alternative. If, for example, there is a fault in the network cable then all the machines will be unable to use the network. On a star network there is a much larger redundancy built in. If one cable has a fault then it does not affect all the other workstations connected to the central node.

Ring networks

As with the bus systems, **physical ring networks,** as shown in figure 21.6, are *less secure* because data intended for a particular machine may have to pass by other machines to get to its destination. Neither the ring nor the bus network is as secure as the star network. One of the first types of ring network was the **Cambridge ring**. This was developed at Cambridge University. In this network one station on the ring is the originator of a message which gets sent to the next station along the line. If the message is intended for this station, it is received, else the signal is boosted by a **repeater** and sent onto the next station. This situation continues until the correct station receives the message. A special station on the network called the **monitor** would provide power for the repeaters. This means that if an individual computer is disconnected from the network, then the messages are still sent round. However, it has been considerably improved upon, and better **token-ring** systems (see page 498) have now been developed.

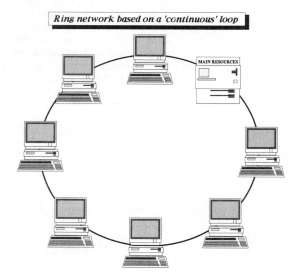

Ring network based on a 'continuous' loop

Figure 21.6

Interconnection of LANs

Many business sites or educational campuses, for example, may have established a number of *separate* **LAN topologies**. It would be useful if these different types of networks, or even a number of networks of the same type could be **interconnected** so that *information may be shared* as if they were all joined together as one larger homogeneous network. Similar principles apply as the networks get much larger, in which case more sophisticated interconnection devices are needed to route the more complex network information to the appropriate destinations.

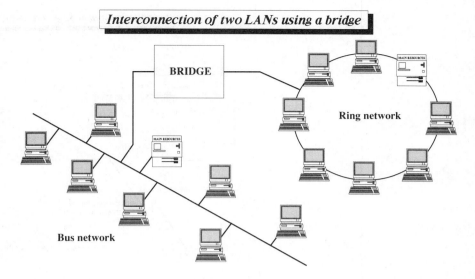

Figure 21.7

A device called a **bridge** is one means of connection between two networks which make use of the same **logical protocols** (see page 506), but might use different **physical protocols** such as a ring and a bus for example. The idea is shown in figure 21.7.

The **bridge** will look at the **electronic packets of information** (see page 505) and determine if the information needs to be passed on to the other network or not. **Intelligent bridges** are also available in which the station numbers of different machines could be used to determine which machines can have access over the bridge – this is useful for network security purposes. The more complex the differences between the networks become, and the more sophisticated the requirements for security and routing etc get, then the more sophisticated these interconnecting bridge devices need to be. A **router**, for example, is used on more sophisticated networks. These **routers** have the ability to connect different physically and logically organised networks, they can often work out the optimal routes, and are generally more 'aware' of the network because of the more sophisticated processing that can be carried out inside them – they can even work out the most cost-effective routes. If the networks are to be connected over long distances, as is the case in the next section, then the interconnection devices are called **gateways**.

Types of network media

The **physical topologies** outlined in the last few sections may be implemented using a wide variety of network-transmission **media**. For example, many networks use **copper cables** such as **coaxial** (*similar to your TV-aerial lead at home*) or **twisted pair** (two copper cables literally twisted together), but others make use of **fibre optics**, land-based **radio** and **microwave** links, **satellite** links or even **infra-red** and **laser** links.

WANs are *usually a combination of many of these systems*. For example, if you are making use of the **Internet** from a LAN-based workstation at college, your data might start off at a respectable rate of knots by going along the college's 10 Mbit/sec coaxial cable Ethernet network until it gets to the external **file server**, which may then link it via a **MODEM** along a *standard* **telephone line** (ordinary thin wire) to your local Internet service provider. Depending on the type of MODEM, and whether any compression facilities are available, your data might then have to crawl along this line at a pedestrian 2400 bit/sec. Your friendly UK-provider might then have an X-25 **packet-switched-network** link to a **mainframe** installation. Going through this part of the network, your data might travel along the higher-bandwidth cable at a rate of 64 kbit/sec. Let's say for the sake of argument that to satisfy your request the mainframe installation might have to contact a **supercomputer**, in which case there might be a 100 Mbit/sec **fibre-optic link** inbetween these two monster computers. This whole scenario is shown in figure 21.8.

It's important to appreciate the sheer number of *different* **physical** and **logical** (see page 492) **topologies** over which your data has to pass, and to understand that the number of **logical** and **physical transformations** between different **protocols** (see page

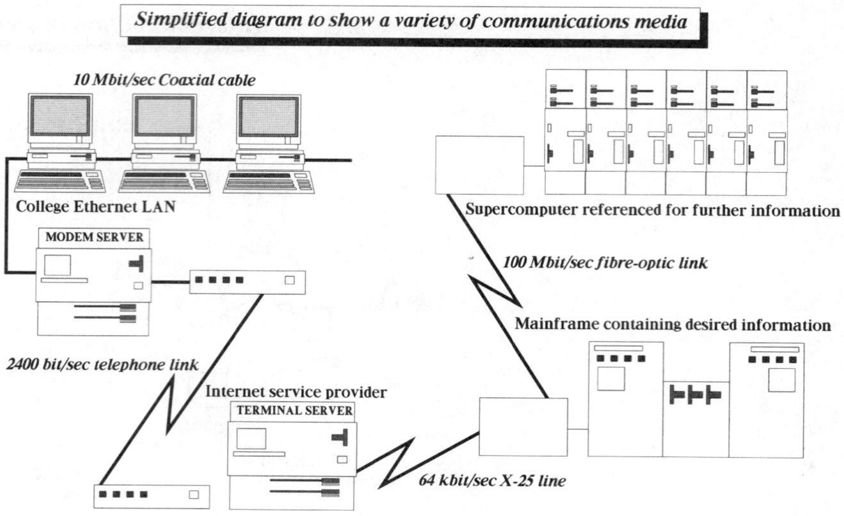

Figure 21.8

506) that is taking place is literally staggering. Eventually your message will be decoded and activate the appropriate software at the host's computer – then it has to go through the reverse procedure to get back to your PC connected to your network back at the college – it's amazing that the entire system works at all!

The **types of media** used in practice and the **data transfer rates** that can be achieved are of *fundamental importance to the performance of the network*. For example, the college system is capable of loading applications from the file server simply because of the relatively high speed 10 Mbit/sec **Ethernet** coaxial cable. If you tried to load the same software from the **mainframe** computer, because of the 2400 bit/sec weakest link in the system, the software would take over 4,000 times as long to load. For example, if it takes 10 seconds to load a DTP system from the file server – it would take just over 11 hours to load it from the mainframe!

The **superhighway** is a very complex beast, and the complexity of the national and international communication networks is mind boggling. In fact the complexity is so great that some scientists have likened the combined international communication networks to a huge **neural network** (see page 555) which has a 'mind' of its own, and some believe that it could eventually exhibit some of the properties predicted by chaos theory – a fascinating topic to brush up on if you have a spare month or two.

Laser links

A novel idea for creating a data link between two buildings can be seen in figure 21.9. Here a **laser beam** (coherent light beam) is used to transmit the data between two different buildings.

The distance between the buildings can be up to a maximum of 20 km, but it is usually considerably less than this as the quality of data communications can be adversely affected by the weather. You may also be interested to know that **infra-red links** are also used to link machines together *inside* the same building. This saves having to have cables underneath the floor or round the walls etc. It's rather like using the remote control with the television – one unit controls the data sent to the others in similar ways.

Fibre-optic networks

Some of the highest data-transfer rates are possible by making use of the **fibre optic networks** that are currently under continuous development. Also if you make use of ordinary or coaxial cable, then these can suffer from electromagnetic interference. Fibre optic cables, being used to transmit light, do not suffer from these problems. There has been an enormous amount of money put into the development of fibre optic networks, and recently they have become cheap enough to develop high-bandwidth cost-effective LANs and MANs. At the time of writing the **FDDI (Fibre Distributed-Data Interface)** system has become the standard. A single network can have a length of up to 100 km, and transmit data at a rate of 100 Mbits/sec. This is 10 times faster than the fastest cable-based systems. You can appreciate that 100 km would be a very extensive LAN! Therefore, these fibre optic links are sometimes referred to as a **MAN (Metropolitan Area Network)**. The second version, called

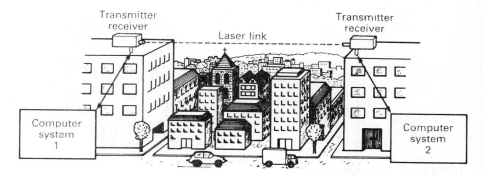

Figure 21.9

FDDI II is already being developed with even higher data transfer rates of up to 1 Gbit/sec predicted.

These fibre optic networks are similar to the ring networks described earlier in this chapter. However, they often work on a more complex dual-ring system which can get over problems such as an entire break in the fibre optic network! To appreciate how a network is able to do this, consider the diagram shown in figure 21.10.

You can imagine the dual ring to be both carriageways of the M25 motorway. If one of the links became severed in both directions (i.e. the same as a break in the fibre optic cable), then you could, theoretically, drive the other way round the motorway to get to the other side of the blocked link. This is exactly how the computer data would be routed round the two-ring fibre optic network. It would take a long time in your car, but a very short time indeed for the light signal to travel round 100 km of cable.

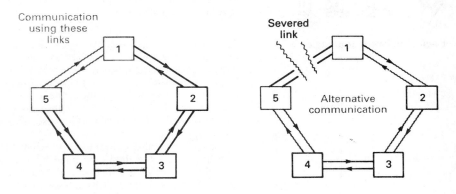

Figure 21.10

The UK Atomic Energy Authority at Harwell has an **FDDI network** in operation. It's fast enough to connect an IBM mainframe, some DEC VAXs and two CRAY II supercomputers! **Bridges** are used to connect this network to **Ethernet** and **token ring** (see page 498) systems.

The **bus, star** and **ring** networks mentioned earlier are some of the most common for LANs. However, other types of topology exist and are shown in figure 21.11. The **mesh network** of figure 21.11(a) is common for long distance networks.

You can imagine each node on the network to be a computer in a different town or part of the country. Indeed, one of the earliest WANs was **ARPAnet**. This was started off by the American government's Department of Defense, and was called the **Advanced Research Project Agency**. This was a **packet-switched** (see page 505) **mesh network** that originally linked the United States cities of Seattle, San Fransisco, Los Angeles, Dallas, Houston, Atlanta, St Louis, Minneapolis, Milwaukee, Chicago, Detroit, Cleveland, Pittsburg, Cincinnati, Boston, New York, Philadelphia and Washington. However, it's much bigger now!! Even the UK now forms part of former ARPAnet system, and the older ARPAnet system now forms part of the global **Internet** system.

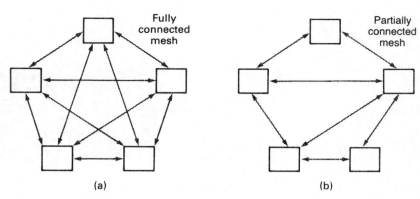

Figure 21.11

If you made use of ARPAnet, then your computer was known as a **host**. This was to distinguish it from the computers at the **nodes** which control the network which were known as **node computers**. The destination computer was also known as a host, and these names have stuck and are now internationally recognised terms. An alternative name for the **mesh network** is a **distributed network**.

A mesh network may be **fully interconnected** as shown in figure 21.11(a), or, more likely, **partially connected** as shown in figure 21.11(b). For links between cities, between military systems, and other systems where high reliability is important, fully connected mesh networks are sometimes used because there is a large amount of redundancy built in. For example, if the link between two computer systems is severed by a bomb (back in the 1970s the Defense Department was keen to survive being nuked!) then the data can still pass between the two disconnected computers via several other paths.

Logical network topologies

This applies to that way in which the networks **logically** operate, and not to the physical connection of the wires as covered in the last few sections – a **token-ring network,** for example, need *not necessarily* be wired up as a **physical ring network**. With a little thought it should be obvious too that not all computers can transmit data over the network at the same time, or the data will clash and get mixed up and corrupted. There *is* an exception to this rule if some types of **radio networks** are used, and this aspect making use of a **broadband network** is covered later in this chapter.

Some system must therefore be established which either gives each machine a turn at sending the data (see page 503), or allows a free for all in which messages are sent *ad hoc*, and, if a clash is detected, they are re-transmitted. Don't forget that no single machine should be allowed to hog the network bandwidth for very long, and some sort of sharing of the system bandwidth must obviously be devised.

Token ring system

One method of sharing out the network bandwidth between all the machines is called a **token-ring network**. An electronic **token** is the name given to a *message* which contains a number of bits that are passed around a network as a packet. Each station may 'grab hold of' a token, and thereby gain control and send data along the network. When the token is released, it may be grabbed by another machine. A typical token ring system would operate at about 4 Mbits/sec, however, the latest token rings go up to about 16 Mbits/sec.

Wide area networks

As can be seen from the **Internet/ARPAnet** example mentioned earlier, a wide area network is unlikely to be organised in the same way as a local area network. For a start, many different types of powerful computers would probably be interconnected by means of special land-based and satellite links. As lots of different computers are talking to each other, then a **communications protocol** (i.e. set of rules) must be established. Many details must be sorted out, and agreements must be made on how the information is to be transferred. (See **ISO OSI model** later.)

Unlike the centralised control of the resources in a local area network, a wide area network is more likely to have **completely distributed control**. In such networks, the control lies with the computers at the individual nodes. At these **node computers** the **communications protocol** is established, and they efficiently control the flow of data between different computers and networks at local, national and international level. *Very high bandwidth* **fibre optic** cables are now being installed between these links handling very high volumes of data.

Most of the operation of even the most sophisticated wide area networks is transparent to the user. Once they have logged onto the system, as with the local area networks, it is just like using a computer with it's own local resources. Therefore, most of the advantages and disadvantages of LANs also apply to WANs. It's just that the phone bills are a lot bigger!

Some basics of communication systems

Before getting embroiled in the detail of network communication protocols, we will digress to have a brief look at some of the basics of communications. An understanding of some of these principles will help to unravel some of the mysteries of modern computer-communication systems.

Back to basics

The simplest type of communication system is called **simplex**. This allows the transmission of data in *one direction only*. Such a system would not be that practical for normal communication between computers. The next stage up from simplex is called **half duplex** – this means the transmission of data in *both directions, but only in one direction at any one time*. Finally, **full duplex** means the *simultaneous transmission of data in both directions*. The ideas are shown in figure 21.12.

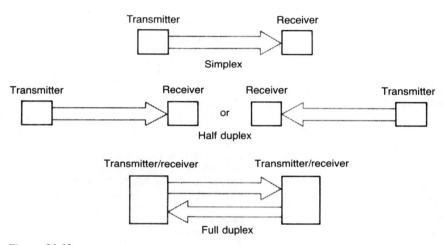

Figure 21.12

Many networks control the flow of data by having special electronic devices that switch the direction of data flow (i.e. half duplex), or control the data over full duplex links. *If* computers had been invented *before* the **telephone system**, then the world of communication systems would probably have been designed in a very different way. In fact, as the old **analogue telephone systems** *get* replaced by the new digital ones – this *is* exactly what's gradually happening. The original telephone system was designed to transmit speech with a relatively small bandwidth of 300 Hz to 3400 Hz. Speech, unlike computer data, is an **analogue signal** (see page 577). Therefore, if computer data is sent over a normal telephone line, it's not surprising that some method is needed to change the computer data into the sort of electrical signals that the telephone line is expecting – i.e audio. Different tones are used, and this is why you can hear the data if you route it through to a suitable loudspeaker system, or simply dial up and listen to a fax line on a normal phone. (Don't do it for very long!)

Most computer data is represented by one or more **bytes**. Inside the computer these binary digits would be transmitted in parallel, making use of a parallel bus system, as was the case when studying computer architecture in chapter 4 . Using this extremely fast method of communication means that there is one wire for each bit – a 64-bit machine, for example, would need at least 64 parallel wires to transmit its data from one place to another. **Parallel transmission** is therefore *not practical*

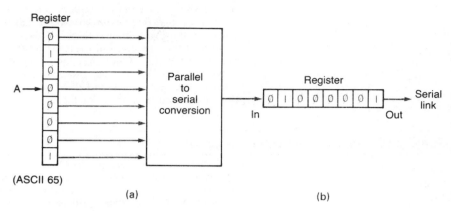

Figure 21.13

for **long distance communication**. (Note that under these circumstances, long distance means more than a few metres!) This parallel bus system is therefore only practical for internal computer connections or for the connection of local peripherals.

For cost effective communication over long distances, **serial transmission** must be used. This means that each byte of data would have to be changed from **parallel** to **serial** form before being transmitted over a single wire or line. Figure 21.13(a) shows a typical example where the ASCII code for the letter 'A' is in parallel form. Figure 21.13(b) shows the same data changed into serial form, ready to be transmitted over a serial link. In practice, some extra digits may be added so that checks can be done on the **integrity** of the data being received (see page 512). Synchronisation problems also have to be solved by the addition of some extra information – these problems are covered in a little more detail later on in this chapter, and when **computer interfacing** is studied in chapter 25 on control-systems .

Baud rates

The rate at which the data can be transmitted is measured in **Baud**. (This is after **Baudot** who did a lot of work with signals.) **One Baud is simply one bit/sec**. However, because extra information as mentioned in the last paragraph may be transmitted along with the data, the actual '**information Baud rate**' may be lower than the **Baud** rate at which the network is transmitting. This sounds complicated, but is quite obvious. If ten bits are used to send a single byte of data, then the actual transmitted Baud rate might be 10 bits/sec. However, as only one byte of data has actually been sent, the information transmitted is only at a rate of 8 bits/sec.

Common Baud rates for transmission of computer data over a *standard* **telephone links** are 1200, 2400, 4800 and 9600. If you do the sums then you will realise that this is pathetically slow. It's enlightening to compare this with the Ethernet LAN Baud rate of 10,000,000 bits/sec! Using the conventional telephone system is slow because it was designed for the transmission of speech and not computer data. We can't increase the data transfer rate because of the limited bandwidth already mentioned. However, **compression techniques** are being successfully used to get a real increase in the information transmission rate over a given bandwidth link.

MODEMs

If we make use of the standard telephone system, then it's the job of a special piece of hardware called a MODEM to turn the computer data into a suitable type and level of signal ready for transmission. *Another* MODEM at the other end of the line would perform the reverse process, i.e. it would receive the signals, then convert them back into a suitable form to be fed into the computer system.

These ideas are shown in figure 21.14. On sophisticated high speed links, **MODEMs** would not be used, as the networks are already designed to accept high speed digital communications. The name MODEM comes from the words **MOdulation** and **DEModulation**. These are the electronic terms for changing a signal into a form suitable for transmission (**modulation**), and then changing it back again into its original form (**demodulation**). Therefore, the transmitting MODEM acts as a **modulator** and the receiving MODEM acts as a **demodulator**.

Similar principles apply to the transmission of data using **microwaves** from **satellites**, and **land-based microwave** or other radio **links**. The land-based microwave links are, however, limited to line-of-sight transmissions where the receiver must literally be visible from the transmitter, as was the case with the LASER link shown in figure 21.9. In all of these systems the computer data must be changed into a suitable form

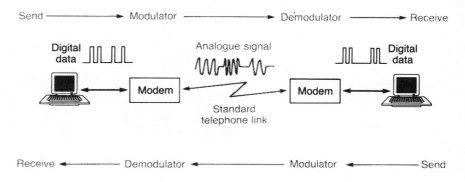

Figure 21.14

to be transmitted over the appropriate link. The methods of modulation that are used vary from one system to another, but some common methods are now investigated.

The ideas of modulation

High frequency radio waves are used to transmit signals over land-based or satellite-based microwave links. We use this radio wave as a **carrier**, which means that the radio wave will literally carry the data which is to be sent. However, it's not like riding on the back of a horse! Instead, some characteristic of the radio wave is varied in sympathy with the data to be transmitted. Consider the radio signal shown in figure 21.15(a).

Here we have a high frequency sine wave. In practice the frequency would be very high – for microwave communication we are sending signals in the region 10 GHz (i.e. 10,000,000,000 cycles/sec!). As this is the wave that will carry the signal to be sent, it is called the **carrier**, or **carrier wave**.

Let's suppose that we wish to transmit the serial binary signal as shown in figure 21.15(b) at the top of the diagram. This 'data signal' is called the **modulating signal**, because it is being used to modulate the carrier. For the sake of argument, let's also suppose that we decide to change the **amplitude** of the **carrier** wave so that it varies in sympathy with the data in the binary signal to be transmitted. The unmodulated carrier (i.e. with no information being sent) is shown in figure 21.15(a), and the effect of the amplitude-modulation process on the carrier wave for this particular binary signal is shown in figure 21.15(b). As the **amplitude** of the carrier wave has been altered, this process is known as **amplitude modulation**.

If the **frequency** of the carrier is altered, then this would be called **frequency modulation**, or if the **phase** of the carrier is altered then this would be called **phase modulation**. The results with the same modulating signal are shown in figure 21.16. Figure 21.16(a) shows the effect of frequency modulation, and figure 21.16(b) shows the effect with phase modulation.

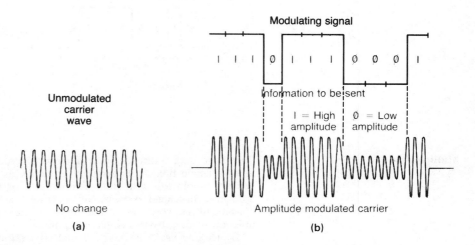

Figure 21.15

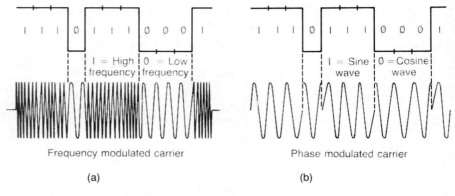

I = High | 0 = Low
frequency | frequency

Frequency modulated carrier

(a)

I = Sine | 0 = Cosine
wave | wave

Phase modulated carrier

(b)

Figure 21.16

The above types of modulation were shown using a digital data signal. However, they work just as well, and are extensively used with analogue signals – they are the methods of modulation used everyday in TV and radio transmissions, and most readers will be familiar with the terms AM and FM on their radio sets.

There are other methods of modulation which are particularly suited to digital signals, and some of the principles are shown in figure 21.17. These would include **pulse code modulation, pulse position modulation** and **pulse duration modulation**. The most important thing to appreciate is that some characteristic of the carrier signal is altered in sympathy with the data that is being sent. At the other end of the line the process is reversed, so that the original signal can be reconstituted ready to be fed into the receiving computer.

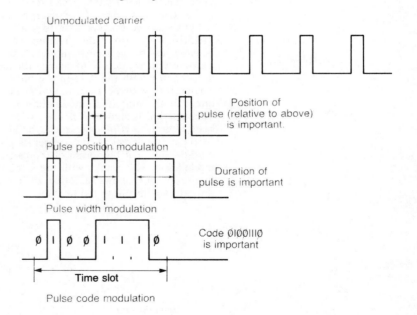

Unmodulated carrier

Position of
pulse (relative to above)
is important.

Pulse position modulation

Duration of
pulse is important

Pulse width modulation

Code 0I00III0
is important

Time slot

Pulse code modulation

Figure 21.17

Multiplexing

In all the data transmission systems considered so far, only one signal can be sent over a single link at its original frequency at any moment in time. Such systems, usually employing data transmission rates of up to about 10 Mbits/sec, are often known as **baseband systems**. Networks such as Ethernet are, therefore, examples of 'baseband' networks, as all the ability of the network is taken up by a single transmission of data from a single computer.

By making use of techniques such as **multiplexing**, it's possible to send different data down the same wires or communication link simultaneously, or, apparently simultaneously. Analogue as well as digital data can often be sent. Various clever

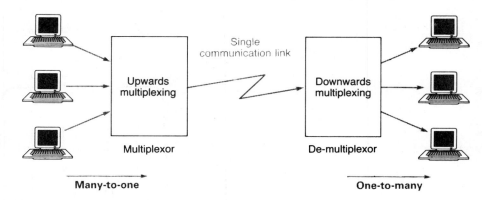

Figure 21.18

methods of getting over this single channel limitation are now considered. The process of sending many signals together over a single line is called **multiplexing**. The basic ideas of upward multiplexing (i.e. many signals going onto one line) and downward multiplexing (getting the signals back again) can be seen in figure 21.18.

Some simple techniques of multiplexing are covered in the next few sections.

Time division multiplexing (TDM)

This is the simplest method, and is basically the same as the methods considered hitherto. In this mode the **transmission time** is split up into *tiny* **slices**. A signal to be transmitted sends some data, then, after the system has given all the other signals a turn, the original signal gets another turn. The entire system continues to operate in this way.

This may sound very slow, but if the bandwidth of the system is quite high, then the turns can be taken at such a high rate that all the signals look as if they are being transmitted at exactly the same time! As an example, it's possible for many people to have simultaneous conversations down the same piece of wire if time division multiplexing is used. If the rate at which the turns are taken is sufficiently high, then nobody notices any difference. They all think that they have exclusive use of the line. Although done electronically, a mechanical system making use of switches can be seen in figure 21.19. This makes time-division multiplexing very easy to understand. Many **digital packets** (see later) of information are sent through networks in a similar way. i.e. first one packet and then the next etc. It can therefore be seen that similar principles are used on high speed digital networks.

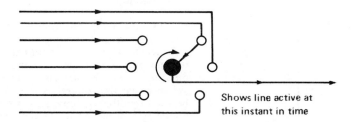

Shows line active at this instant in time

Figure 21.19

Frequency division multiplexing (FDM)

You already know that carrier waves can be used to transmit data over a link. Now it would be possible, by using a different carrier frequency, to send two or more different signals simultaneously down the same link. They would not interfere with each other because the carriers are separated by a suitably large frequency. The frequency spectrum for sending three different modulated signals over the same link in this particular way is shown in figure 21.20.

You can see that a wider bandwidth is needed to send more signals over the link. (This should relate quite well to common sense and to what was discussed earlier in this chapter). These are known as **broadband networks**. At the other end of the line the carrier signals are separated by using electronic filters to filter out the appropriate carrier wave. The original signal is then extracted by the demodulation process.

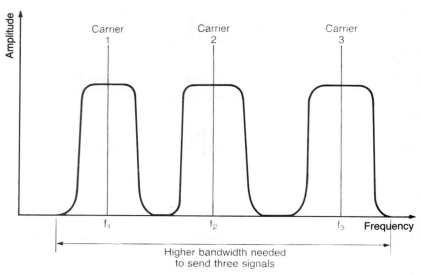

Figure 21.20

An example of a broadband network is the system developed by WANG computers. Here each machine on the network would need a MODEM capable of transmitting and receiving the appropriate radio signals. The bandwidth, and hence the information transmission rates of these networks are much higher than the baseband networks mentioned earlier. There is nothing strange about frequency division multiplexing. It's the same ideas that are used when you tune into some radio stations. The act of turning the tuning knob on the radio selects an appropriate carrier frequency. (The frequency at which the radio station is transmitting.) The radio set then demodulates your selected carrier wave so that you can hear the original signal (i.e. the music or speech for your selected station).

Although broadband networks are being used, the digital **ISDN networks** offer a much greater potential for the future, and even many radio networks are now packet switched.

Network switching

The next few sections on network-switching techniques are important if you are to appreciate the fundamentally different ways in which computer networks route their data compared to the simpler ways in which a standard telephone system would route its data.

Circuit switching

If the normal telephone system is made use of, then the method of switching between one computer and another is likely to be that of **circuit switching.** This means that a dedicated physical electrical path has to be established between the two computers for the duration of the time that this particular path is needed. (Until somebody puts the phone down!) This means that with **circuit switching** *the line is in use all the time* that the computers are likely to need to communicate, and can't therefore, be used by other systems during this time. You have also seen that the normal telephone system has an inadequate bandwidth for fast computer communications, and so this method would not be used for a dedicated fast computer link, unless there is no alternative – e.g. the connection of a MODEM from most private houses, for example. There are also several other disadvantages of using the normal telephone system. Without extra specialist equipment, it's not possible for one computer to communicate with more than one other computer at the same time. In addition to this, the time taken to route the call on a standard telephone line is unacceptably long, (i.e. to dial the number and wait for an answer) in computer terms, although tone dialling is now considerably better than the old pulse-dialling systems still in operation in some parts of the country.

Message switching

A better solution is to make use of **message switching**. This means that a permanent higher-bandwidth line is installed between two node computers. A typical network topology would be a partially-connected mesh network as shown in figure 21.21(a). It would be usual for the computer that wishes to communicate with another to set up the message with a **header** that contains the address of the destination computer. The idea is shown in figure 21.21(b).

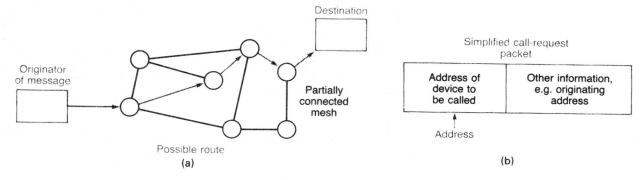

Figure 21.21

The message will be sent off in an appropriate direction and, when it is received by the next computer, the header information will be inspected. If it is not for the inspecting computer to deal with then it will be transmitted again in a direction that will get the message nearer to the destination computer. In other words, the computers at each node are acting as **routers** and will pass the message on in the appropriate direction until it gets to its destination. One of the main things to realise is that these dedicated lines are only occupied for the relatively short duration of the message – they are then instantly available to deal with other traffic on the network. Unlike the circuit switching method where the line is tied up for the entire duration of the computer session. The **node computers** (i.e. the computers at each node) would be powerful enough to respond in **real time** to all the messages that are being received, but you should note that not all messages are dealt with immediately, they are often buffered (see page 384) in a queueing system. The node computers would probably be powerful minicomputers or even a mainframe, but no doubt they will be replaced by extremely powerful micros when these become available.

You should now be able to see the difference between **message switching** and **circuit switching**. In circuit switching, a direct link is established between the two computers for the duration of the session, and can't be used for other traffic. In message switching, the messages are routed via various node computers until they reach their final destination. There is no mechanical switching involved as the dedicated high speed links between each node computer already exist. Message switching is therefore much more suitable than circuit switching for high speed computer links. However, if infrequent connections making use of low bandwidth lines are all that is needed, then this would be a more economical option for the small user. The message-switching lines are quite expensive to rent, but there is no appreciable delay in the connection from one computer to another, except for the slight delay while the node computer decides on the appropriate route.

Packet switching networks

The **message switching** method can get slowed down if the messages to be sent are very large, and other systems are queueing up to use the line. It would be far easier to manage if the size of a large message is chopped up into smaller parts. If this is done then large messages can be sent as several smaller messages. These smaller chunks are called **packets,** and the resulting system is known as a **packet switching network**. If the packets are all the same size, then this would enable efficient storage management and switching at the node computers. It would also enable other messages to be inserted into the middle of messages that were already being sent. As far as the users are concerned, they get an apparent increase in the speed of the network, but, as we have seen before in this chapter, it's simply better management of the available resources. Packet switching networks making use of the X25 protocol are now *some of the most common* means of communication between computers over WANs. The splitting up of messages into packets does introduce some extra complexity, but the processing power of the node computers is such that this added complexity is outweighed by the increased throughput of the data over the network. **JANET**, the **Joint Academic NETwork** that connects British universities, and more recently SuperJANET are examples of large packet switching networks that have been established in the UK and which are now part of the **Internet** system. An ideal connection for the packet switching network would be the higher bandwidth links, and the fibre optic links mentioned earlier would give the fastest performance.

Packet switching is an important concept. It's used not only for cable and fibre optic links, but for land-based radio and satellite links as well. As an example of a satellite link, consider a satellite that is geostationary on the equator over the Atlantic. This could be used to link North America and some of Europe. The host computer sends a message up to the satellite which is some 36,000 km above the Earth. The satellite then broadcasts to all the ground stations. The messages would then be passed on by the appropriate ground station after the header had been decoded. To save clashes over satellite communication links there is a more complex communications protocol. However, this is beyond the scope of this book.

Radio networks

It's interesting to note that packet switching networks have also been established by making use of radio links. Indeed, some radio communications are now undertaken using packet switching techniques. One of the original systems was the ALOHA (Hawaiian for HELLO!) systems developed to interconnect the Hawaiian island to a central computer system. An interesting historical footnote here is that the mighty Ethernet system itself was developed from the original Hawaiian ALOHA network. Radio systems are now being taken very seriously indeed elsewhere, and will probably lead to the idea that all computers can be connected permanently to a network, either by an infra-red link near to a suitable connection point, or, more conveniently, by a radio link similar in principle to the portable-phone system. The consequences of such systems are far reaching. It will, for example, be possible to be virtually anywhere in the world and still have connections to the Internet from your portable, via a suitable radio link. In the preface we lamented that it's not yet possible to have access to all human knowledge at any time and in any place – this may be the first step towards this ultimate goal.

Buffering

You will appreciate from reading the last few sections that interconnection of networks with very different baud rates needs to be carried out in practice. **Buffering** is therefore used to match the differing speeds of the various systems used in a network. It is effectively a block of memory which can hold the data to be transmitted if the line is busy, or if data has to be taken in and sent out at different rates. The ideas are identical in principle to the buffering systems covered in the operating-systems chapter 17 on page 384. **Buffering** is also sometimes carried out at the board level on the PCs, and new Ethernet interfaces have become available which assemble **Ethernet frames** (see page 512) at the *same time* as sending other frames.

International network standards

Before the advent of internationally agreed standards, companies were often at the mercy of the large manufacturers. Indeed, it was often not possible to get information from one system to another because each manufacturer had their own different protocols. The technical information required was often hard to get, and there was little co-operation between competing companies. It was against this unsatisfactory background that the **International Standards Organisation (ISO)** began working on a set of manufacturer-independent network communication protocols (i.e. a system to allow different networks and machines to communicate with each other). From reading the first half of this chapter, you should already appreciate the enormity of their task.

The OSI model

The **ISO OSI model** is the **International Standards Organisation Open Systems Interconnection model**. (An **open system** is simply a system that supports the **OSI standards**.) It is used to define the ways in which different computer networks may be connected to each other. Without standards such as this, it would be impossible to work towards the idea of a **global communications network**.

The ISO OSI model forms the basis of all the interconnections for most of the modern **packet switching networks**. These special **network protocols** are needed to make sure that the enormously complex data communications between different systems is manageable. You will be aware that, throughout your computer science course, the concept of **structure** is *very important* e.g. **structured programming, structured models** and **structure diagrams** etc. The ISO OSI model is therefore a comprehensive **structure** for **data communications**.

As you can imagine, trying to form a standard for the interconnection of different communication systems is no easy task. The model therefore simplifies things to some extent by breaking down this huge task into **seven different sub-tasks**. Each

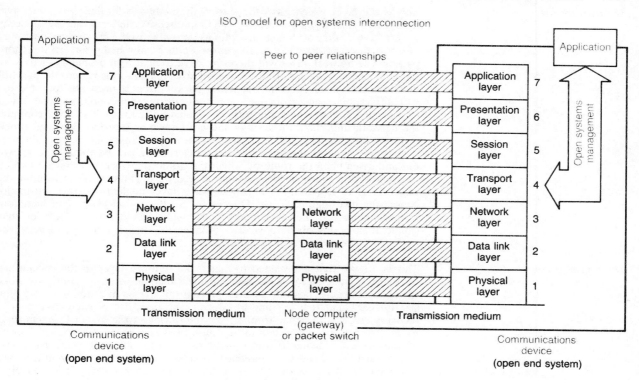

Figure 21.22

sub-task goes progressively from the most fundamental aspects such as where the wires are to be connected (called the **physical level**) right up to the **application layer** which gives high-level support for **applications** making use of the network. Each layer is shown in figure 21.22. The first three layers are concerned with the details of the actual networks being used. You can imagine it to be similar to trying to route the post on a railway system. The individual letters are bundled together and then, according to where they have to go, they are joined onto different engines and sent down the most appropriate routes to arrive at their destination. The brief details of each layer are as follows.

The physical layer

This is the specification of the electronic and mechanical connections, i.e. which wires go where, and what types of electrical signals will be used. It's therefore the environment for the **physical** systems which carry the streams of data between different points in the network. This layer therefore provides the interface between the data and the actual hardware connections such as plugs and sockets. For example, **V.24** is one of the specifications for the connection of devices to **MODEMS**.

The link layer (data-link layer)

This layer provides for transfer of data between two devices that are connected together, e.g. perhaps on the same **LAN**. It allows data to be transferred in such a way that it's possible to detect any errors in the transmission, and also provides synchronisation.

The '**X25 level 2**' is an example of a common **network link layer**. This specifies how the information is to be transmitted in the form of a **frame** e.g. bits to specify where the data is to go, and **CRCs** (see page 512) for **error detection**. The generalised idea of a data-link frame is shown in figure 21.23.

A simple data-link layer frame			
Sending and receiving node addresses	Type of frame e.g. Ethernet or control etc.	Computer data which is being transmitted	Checksum data
Address Fields	*Control Field*	*Data Field*	*Error-control Field*

Figure 21.23

The network layer

This is the layer which gives the system the ability to be linked to other types of network so that a much larger more comprehensive network can be made up, i.e. we are now dealing with communications across networks by routing, switching and other methods of connection. The information is now being sent in the form of a packet. The **network layer** will therefore have to deal with problems such as routing the data and making sure that the packet sizes match – this is because the different networks may have different maximum packet sizes. It must also be able to cope with different messages from one computer to many others, and from many computers to a single computer by some form of sequenced delivery. The node computers in the network undertake these tasks and are known as **Interface Message Processors** or **IMPs**. Internet uses IMPs to route data messages across some parts of the network.

A simple analogy for one type of packet routing can be thought of as working out and assembling the route by which the 'train' (network layer packet) will travel to get from the source to the destination, e.g. we might start off at Edinburgh, and, on our way to London, the network packet layer might route the information via Newcastle, Darlington, York, Doncaster, Sheffield, Leicester, Northampton and Luton. In practice there are many more sophisticated routing methods than the simple analogy described above. The '**X25 level 3**' defines one type of **network layer packet** protocol which is in common use.

The transport layer

This is a layer that is designed to match the **network layer** to the **session layer** to be covered in a moment. It will provide functions such as trying to work out the **cheapest route**, possibly by **multiplexing** the signals. It determines the optimum size for each unit that is going to be sent, and may also provide some extra **error recovery** etc. It is designed to make the interfacing of the higher levels much easier to do. It is needed as the data to be transmitted may go over several different types of network each having its own characteristics. It therefore provides data communication facilities through a **standard interface**, irrespective of whether the data has come from a specific type of LAN or any other system. It effectively takes whatever is thrown at it and assembles it into a more-reliable form for the higher layers. The bottom three layers are effectively hardware dominated, and the top three layers are effectively software dominated. The transport layer is the 'piggy in the middle'.

The session layer

The **session layer** undertakes the **management of communications sessions** between two different systems. It deals with things such as synchronization and requesting permission to send the data etc. This is the first level at which you do not have to get involved with any of the communications systems elementary methods such as network characteristics. Full-duplex communication is possible at this level. Notice how we are progressing up the ladder from raw binary digits towards the end user of the system, i.e. the **lower four layers** are **communication-systems oriented**, and we are now progressing into the **top three layers** which are **applications oriented**. This is what the OSI model is all about.

The presentation layer

The **presentation layer** deals with how the 'information to be represented' is **presented**. It should be reasonably obvious that the way in which the individual characters and numbers etc are stored will vary from one manufacturer to another, and from one system to another, with ASCII and EBCDIC being just two particular examples. There may even be special protocols for creating characters which represent pictures. In addition to this, different node computers might handle their **syntax** in different ways. However, the **presentation layer** will provide the appropriate **transfer** to the agreed '**transfer syntax**', i.e. the syntax that all the communication systems will understand no matter who manufactured them. For example, there might be three types of syntax involved – one for the environment that is sending the data, one for the transfer environment and a third for the environment which is going to receive the data. The presentation layer would cope with all of these types of problems.

The application layer

This is the *highest level* of the **OSI model** and defines the interface through which the users' **applications** (or **programs**) gain access to the communications services. Such typical facilities would be **file transfer** and **message handling**, but there may also be more specific facilities offered by specialised applications. For example, **databases, viewdata systems, teleconferencing systems** and **distributed data processing systems** would all have there own **architectures** (or **structures**). The application layer will provide support such that these applications can make use of the other layers previously defined. It is this particular layer that makes it easy to write software for the global directories involved on the Internet system, for example.

TCP/IP

One of *the* most important sets of communication protocols in operation today is **TCP/IP** standard. This stands for the **Transmission Control Protocol / Internet Protocol**. This is basically a set of protocols which support connectivity between LANs and WANs, and seems to have become the *de facto* standard. These protocols have evolved from the original **ARPAnet packet-switched system** mentioned earlier in this chapter. As the name implies. this system forms the primary mechanisms whereby data is sent over the global Internet network. **TCP/IP** is also embedded in the **kernel** (see page 370) of the Unix operating system.

There are many other protocols, with RIP, SAP and Watchdog, being just three other examples. However, you may be wondering why they all exist if the OSI standard was meant to be the system to which everybody conforms? The fact is that all (most in practice) these other standards *do conform* to the ISO OSI model, and the *relationships* between **OSI model** & **TCP/IP**, for example, are shown in figure 21.24

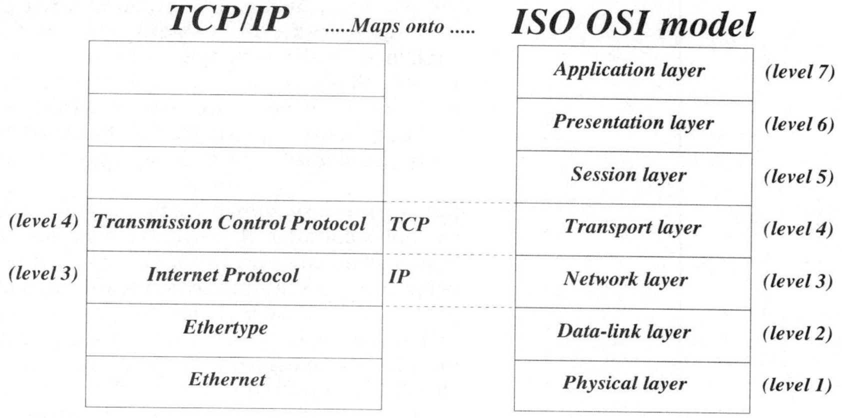

TCP/IP .....*Maps onto*			*ISO OSI model*	
			Application layer	*(level 7)*
			Presentation layer	*(level 6)*
			Session layer	*(level 5)*
(level 4)	*Transmission Control Protocol*	*TCP*	*Transport layer*	*(level 4)*
(level 3)	*Internet Protocol*	*IP*	*Network layer*	*(level 3)*
	Ethertype		*Data-link layer*	*(level 2)*
	Ethernet		*Physical layer*	*(level 1)*

Figure 21.24

As you can see, the **Internet Protocol (IP)** conforms to *level 3* of the **ISO/OSI model**, and **TCP** conforms to level 4. **TCP/IP** is, therefore, an example of a system of protocols which conform to the **network** and **transport layers** of the **ISO OSI model**. These protocols might sit on top of an Ethernet environment as shown in the diagram. The *Ethertype* in this diagram refers to the type of data in the field such as an **Internet Packet** or a **NetWare packet**, for example, and the *Ethernet* physical layer is the guts of the **Ethernet** system. What goes on the top layers depends on the operating system and applications that are being used. In practice other systems for error checking etc would also be included, but, for the sake of simplicity, these are not shown in the above diagram.

Asynchronous Transfer Mode (ATM)

One other **packet-switching** system which is gaining in popularity is **ATM** or **Asynchronous Transfer Mode**. **ATM** is popular because it supports a very large range of different data types including **computer data**, **voice data** and **video data**, and is thus a *very flexible system* for implementing parts of the **information superhighway**. In the ATM system packets of data are referred to as **cells**, and each ATM cell is 48-bytes of data plus 5 bytes of header information containing, for example, cell destination information to be used at the **nodes** which route the data over the networks. **Multiplexing** (see page 502) on this particular system is carried out at this **cell** level. Another plus for the ATM system is that it has proved to be more reliable than some of the other systems which have been used in the past, and ATM is currently being developed for use in LANs too. ATM, together with the an appropriate optical or cable network defines the physical and data-link layers (layers 1 and 2) of the OSI model.

Errors

It has been mentioned at frequent intervals that error checking goes on around most networks. It's obviously important that the messages arrive without any errors, and while it's obviously not possible to guarantee this, it is possible to reduce the probability of error by various mechanisms that will be discussed in the next section. The errors arise from interference on the network. This is usually in the form of electrical noise, but the end result is that some bits get corrupted and binary zeros get turned into binary ones etc. or the complete message is so unrecognisable that you can't make any sense of it!

There are very sophisticated methods for **detecting** *and* **correcting** errors when transmitting data over communication links, but these often involve a large amount of extra data to be sent. However, when using most networks, it's usually enough just to be able to detect that an error has occurred – if an error is detected then the packet of data can be re-transmitted. Two of the most common error checking techniques make use of **parity** and **cyclic-redundancy checks.** Both methods are explained in the next few sections. However, because most students find it unbelievable that you can receive a corrupted message, and then change it back to what it should have been, we have included an example using two-dimensional parity. Although more sophisticated methods are used in practice, this shows how it's physically possible to correct a corrupted message.

Parity

Parity is a very simple method of checking the **integrity** of received data. As an example, consider the ASCII codes for the message, 'A very thick fog'. Normal ASCII characters do not make use of the most significant bit of each byte that is being used to send the data. Figure 21.25 shows the decimal and binary codes using just seven bits each. (Don't forget that a space is also a character.)

If these digits are transmitted using just seven bits, then there is no check that the received message is the one that was sent. We can, however, make use of the eighth bit to perform a parity check on the pattern of bits representing each character. This eighth bit is called a **parity bit**. There are two methods, but we will consider **even parity** first.

	Decimal	Binary (no parity)	Binary (even parity)	Binary (odd parity)
A	65	0 1 0 0 0 0 0 1	0 1 0 0 0 0 0 1	1 1 0 0 0 0 0 1
	32	0 0 1 0 0 0 0 0	1 0 1 0 0 0 0 0	0 0 1 0 0 0 0 0
V	86	0 1 0 1 0 1 1 0	0 1 0 1 0 1 1 0	1 1 0 1 0 1 1 0
E	69	0 1 0 0 0 1 0 1	1 1 0 0 0 1 0 1	0 1 0 0 0 1 0 1
R	82	0 1 0 1 0 0 1 0	1 1 0 1 0 0 1 0	0 1 0 1 0 0 1 0
Y	89	0 1 0 1 1 0 0 1	0 1 0 1 1 0 0 1	1 1 0 1 1 0 0 1
	32	0 0 1 0 0 0 0 0	1 0 1 0 0 0 0 0	0 0 1 0 0 0 0 0
T	84	0 1 0 1 0 1 0 0	1 1 0 1 0 1 0 0	0 1 0 1 0 1 0 0
H	72	0 1 0 0 1 0 0 0	0 1 0 0 1 0 0 0	1 1 0 0 1 0 0 0
I	73	0 1 0 0 1 0 0 1	1 1 0 0 1 0 0 1	0 1 0 0 1 0 0 1
C	67	0 1 0 0 0 0 1 1	1 1 0 0 0 0 1 1	0 1 0 0 0 0 1 1
K	75	0 1 0 0 1 0 1 1	0 1 0 0 1 0 1 1	1 1 0 0 1 0 1 1
	32	0 0 1 0 0 0 0 0	1 0 1 0 0 0 0 0	0 0 1 0 0 0 0 0
F	70	0 1 0 0 0 1 1 0	1 1 0 0 0 1 1 0	0 1 0 0 0 1 1 0
O	79	0 1 0 0 1 1 1 1	1 1 0 0 1 1 1 1	0 1 0 0 1 1 1 1
G	71	0 1 0 0 0 1 1 1	0 1 0 0 0 1 1 1	1 1 0 0 0 1 1 1

(a)   (b)   (c)

Figure 21.25

Even parity

Using this method you simply count up the number of 1's in the data to be sent and, *if even*, the **parity bit** is set at **zero**. If the number of 1's were *odd*, then the parity bit is **set** to **one**, and this, therefore, makes the number of 1's in the data to be sent even again. Therefore, after the parity bits have been added, there is always an even number of 1's in each byte of data that is being sent. The new codes for the message, including the parity bits are shown in figure 21.25(b).

At the receiving end, a check would be made on each byte, and if there are an even number of 1's then the data is assumed to be correct. If an odd number of 1's has been received, then the data is in error.

Odd parity

The ideas are similar to even parity. The only difference is that the number of 1's in each byte is made odd by setting the appropriate value of the parity bit. The message ready to be transmitted using odd parity is shown in figure 21.25(c).

Is parity any good?

It's not any good for sending complex packets across networks, but at a simple level, the probability of receiving the correct message must obviously be higher if parity is used. Using a single-bit parity method means that we can detect if the message received is incorrect, and demand a retransmission if this proves to be the case.

More sophisticated techniques exist to correct errors in messages, and although this highly theoretical topic can take up a whole book in itself, a simple example should convince you that this is easily possible. The main idea is to send extra redundant information along with the message which can be used as a check on integrity and as a mechanism for the correction process. If, for example, we use two-dimensional parity we can sometimes receive a message containing an error, then actually correct it! The ideas are shown in figure 21.26.

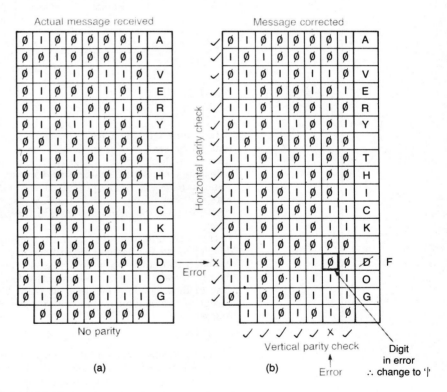

Figure 21.26

Even parity checks have been done on the message vertically as well as horizontally. Figure 21.26(a) shows the message with the parity bits added. Let's suppose that a bit gets changed and the message received is 'A very thick dog'. Now if this message was received then a dog psychiatrist might be called for! However, after the parity checks have been done, we have detected an error in the position shown in figure 21.26(b). As we are using a binary code, then if a digit can be identified as being wrong, then all that has to be done is to change it! We therefore have the ability to correct a message after it has been received.

It's obvious that parity checking could not cope with multiple errors. If two digits were changed then the parity checking would not show up any errors at all. It's also unfortunate that, with modern communication systems, when errors occur, the data is likely to become too corrupted for parity to be of any use. Most of the time the messages are transmitted and received free of errors, then, if a burst of noise occurs on the line, much of the message that was being transmitted at that time is corrupted.

There are many more sophisticated checking procedures available, but these are beyond the scope of an 'A' Level course. Even so, the most important thing to realise is that if an error is detected in the received message, then all that is necessary is to re-transmit the original message, and this is what's normally done in the majority of situations. Therefore, a more efficient way of error detection is required, and this is covered in the next section.

Cyclic Redundancy Checks (CRC)

Often the packet of data sent around the network will have a **Cyclic Redundancy Check (CRC)** carried out on the information associated with it. For example, the CRC information for an Ethernet packet is shown in figure 21.27.

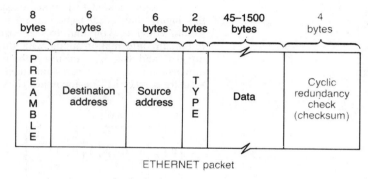

ETHERNET packet

Figure 21.27

In addition to the CRC, you can see the source and destination addresses, the data to be sent, and there is also some synchronisation information. The CRC is used as a check on the **integrity** of the data at the receiving computer. A **cyclic-redundancy check** is a **mathematical method** which, when applied to the data using some *suitable algorithm,* provides some **extra digits** that can be transmitted along with the original data. When the data has been received, the *same algorithm* can be used to see if the digits derived are the same as the additional digits in the CRC check.

There are different CRC methods ranging from simple techniques similar to those developed for the **hashing algorithms** on page 312, to more complex ones which are designed to detect the largest possible range of likely errors that will occur when data is transmitted over modern networks – with success rates in excess of 99.999%. One of these modern methods, used for CRC checks on the X.25 lines mentioned earlier in this chapter makes use of a standard 16-bit polynomial **generator G(x)** as follows:

$$G(x) = x^{16} + x^{12} + x^5 + 1.$$

Coding this as a sixteen-bit binary number is simple, it would be represented inside a register as 10001000000100001 (i.e. 1 lot of x^{16}, 0 lots of x^{15}, right down to 1 lot of x^0). Now you probably think that the quadratics and cubics which you cover in maths are complex enough, but the data from the **message** to be sent is fed into yet another polynomial called a **message polynomial, M(x),** which for a simple 4-bit message consisting of 1011 might be:

$$1011 \rightarrow M(x) = 1x^3 + 0x^2 + 1x^1 + 1x^0$$

$$= x^3 + x + 1$$

The above polynomials are then processed in a variety of ways by multiplication and division, to end up with a **quotient polynomial Q(x)** and a **remainder polynomial R(x)**. Look back at page 41 if you have forgotten about the terms **quotient** and **remainder**. In fact, if you're good at long division, then it's dead easy to divide polynomials, and a simple example for unrelated data is as follows.

$$x^2 + x \overline{\smash{\big)}\ \begin{array}{l} x + \qquad\qquad \text{Remainder } x + 1 \\ x^3 + x^2 + x + 1 \\ \underline{x^3 + x^2 +} \\ \quad 0 \quad\ \ 0 \quad\ \ x + 1 \end{array}} \qquad\qquad G(x) \overline{\smash{\big)}\ \begin{array}{l} Q(x) + \text{remainder } R(x) \\ M(x) \end{array}}$$

Here you can see that the answer to the polynomial division sum

$(x^3 + x^2 + x + 1)/(x^2 + x)$ is x with a remainder of $(x + 1)$.

Now in a real CRC example, the **remainder polynomial R(x)** is used to produce the **bits** for the **CRC check**. By examination of the coefficients of the remainder polynomial – 1 lot of x^1 and 1 lot of x^0 in the above arbitrary example – the CRC bits are generated and inserted into the end of the message. At the receiving end the same procedure is followed, and the CRC bit pattern is checked to see if it conforms to the bit pattern calculated at the transmitting end.

Originally CRC checks were not often used as they are complex to carry out in practice. However, it's now easily possible to do all of the above mathematical manipulations totally in hardware, (such as division of the binary numbers representing the coefficients of the polynomials), and with the current processing power of microprocessors, it takes very little time indeed to carry out these mechanistic but tedious techniques. CRC checks making use of the polynomial methods generate a very compact number of bits compared to other methods. Because of the *very high* **error-detection rates** and the *very low* **overheads** in terms of extra bits transmitted with the data, **CRC checks** are *used extensively* in all modern communication systems.

Security on computer networks

One of the potential problems of extensive computer networking is that of security. **Distributed data processing** poses extra problems for security not present in stand-alone systems. There are several aspects of security to consider.

Hacking

A **hacker** is the name given to a person who breaks codes and passwords etc to gain unauthorised entry into computer systems. Unfortunately, the challenge of breaking into systems for some people is irresistible, and, therefore, protective measures must be taken by the designers of network systems. There are also other hazards which affect the security of data, these include loss of data through interference and sophisticated electronic methods to gain access to unauthorised information. The risks can be categorised as follows.

Prevention of access to buildings

Many security systems ranging from **code locks**, via **magnetic stripe cards** to combinations of both of these systems are put at the entrances to buildings housing computers which have access to the network. Being developed are systems such as **retina scans**, **palm prints** and **voice recognition**, and these are covered in other parts of this book. However, many problems still have to be overcome before these other systems are in common operation. Whatever system is used it is usually linked to the main computer so that access to buildings may be monitored by the security system. Visitors to high security installations will often have to be booked into the buildings and given special badges that they have to wear for the duration of their visit. The fact that they are actually in the building could also be logged on the main computer system. At the end of a set period of time the main computer could help to make sure that all personnel have left the high security areas.

Passwords to log on

Once into the building, a system of **password protection** would be in operation. To log on to the system each person would be allocated a **special password**. There would probably be many categories of users ranging from ordinary employees who have to make use of the system for their day to day work through to users who have complete control over what can be done with any information contained in the files that are accessed over the network. For a more detailed description of defining the types of users refer to the database security system on page 482. In addition to these passwords it may be necessary to have a **key** which will be needed to **physically unlock the system**, i.e. make sure that power is applied to the computer that is being used for access.

Location of specific workstations

There may be extra security by providing the highest levels of access from a limited number of computers. You can imagine there to be an 'inner sanctum' into which people have had to pass to get physical access to certain terminals. The highest levels of users may only be able to access certain sensitive parts of the system from these terminals. In the most sensitive installations there would probably be closed circuit security cameras constantly monitored by security personnel. Therefore, even if some of the passwords were known, the hacker would have to gain access to an inner part of a high security building to be able to make use of them. Passwords would also be changed at frequent intervals.

Protection of transmitted information

This might sound a little like the activities that would be carried out by 'James Bond', but it's now possible to get sensitive electronic equipment that can monitor the electromagnetic fields that are radiated from systems carrying computer data. When electrical signals travel down a cable, there is an associated electromagnetic field which radiates a weak signal that can be picked up by using sensitive electronic detection apparatus.

To get over these problems would involve the screening of the cables so that these electromagnetic fields are not able to be picked up. It's interesting to note that fibre optic communications, making use of light instead of electrical signals, do not radiate these fields. Laser beams are also relatively safe. Radio transmissions however, especially via satellite, are most vulnerable to these types of interference.

As it's virtually impossible to guarantee that these electromagnetic fields could not be picked up, one way to get over the problem is to make use of some sophisticated **encryption techniques**. This means that the data is not sent by making use of standard ASCII in the normal sense, but has some algorithm applied to the data which scrambles the signals to be transmitted. The data must then be unscrambled at the other end of the communication system. Provided the encryption codes are not known by the hacker, it would be virtually impossible to crack the codes. Indeed, it has been calculated, that by making use of some sophisticated **encryption techniques**, it would take a supercomputer longer than the universe has been in existence to crack some of these codes – the details of which are covered on page 605.

Electrical interference

One must not forget the fact that the data may not be lost through malicious interference from human beings, but from noise that might affect the signals. These could be electromagnetic interference from many sources such as cars, power stations, radio and TV broadcasting and electrical distribution systems etc. These affect the integrity of the data as what is being received might not be that which was sent. These types of problems are overcome by making use of error detection systems such as **CRCs** and **parity**, and these are explained on page 512.

Physical damage

Finally, there is the physical security of the system. For example, data may be lost through fire, flood or any number of natural hazards. In addition to this there may be faults in the systems such as a disk becoming corrupted or a power cut etc. All these events can be catered for by making appropriate backup procedures and ensuring that these backups are stored in different locations to the originals.

Exercise 21.1

1. What's the difference between LANs, MANs and WANs?

2. Outline some advantages of using a WAN for a local business. Are there any disadvantages? Explain.

3. Outline the problems of limited bandwidth communication channels.

4. Outline some systems for getting over low-bandwidth networks in a college computer-room environment.

5. Different physical network topologies give LANs different operating advantages. Outline some of the advantages and disadvantages of different systems.

6. Why is there such a large proliferation of different communications systems when considering WANs?

7. Outline the role played by a MODEM in the connection of computers via a WAN system such as the Internet.

8. Define some of the following terms associated with modern communication systems.
   (a) Parallel and serial transmission
   (b) Baud rate and information transmission rate
   (c) Modulation
   (d) Multiplexing
   (e) Message switching
   (f) FDM
   (g) CRC
   (h) FDDI

9. Outline the basic differences between packet-switching networks and the conventional telephone lines in terms of routing information.

10. What's the difference between a baseband and a broadband network?

11. Why is the OSI model for networks important, and why does it not limit vendors from coming up with a variety of network protocol standards?

12. What effect is the standardisation of international communications likely to have on the way computers operate in the future?

13. Why is the physical layer of the ISO OSI model different to the rest of the layers?

14. Why is the TCP/IP protocol important in the 1990s?

15. Outline a couple of different methods for the detection of errors on a network. Why are the *error correction* routines little used in practice?

16. Outline some of the potential hazards that can be encountered when managing a network.

End of chapter summary

- A **network** is a *communication system* which allows the transfer of data between different computer systems.
- **Local Area Network** or **LAN** – a network usually confined to **one building** or **several buildings on the same site** – under control of the local management.
- **MAN** is an acronym for **Metropolitan Area Network** – usually implies several networks working together over a wider area (perhaps up to a few hundred km). The term was coined due to the much more capable FDDI systems now in operation.
- **WAN** – **Wide Area Network** – usually implying **national** or **international communications** making use of public communications systems.
- **LHN** is an acronym for **Long Haul Network** – an *alternative name* for a **WAN**.
- **ISDN** stands for **Integrated Services Digital Network** – it is a digital service which can handle audio, video, and computer data on the same line.
- A **file server** is a computer used to *distribute files* over a **network system**.
- **Computers** *connected to distributed processing systems* such as networks are often referred to as **workstations** or **terminals**.
- **Microcomputers** *running appropriate software* can act as **terminals** or **workstations** on a network.
- **Terminal emulation software** is sometimes used to convert a microcomputer into a terminal suitable for network communications with another computer.
- **Networks have advantages** including efficient sharing of common resources and the ability to set up electronic mail, for example.
- **Networks have disadvantages** such as slow response time if the bandwidth is low and usage is high.
- A network in which the workstations carry out their own processing, and help to control the resources on the network is called a **distributed processing system**.
- A **printer spooler** or a **printer server** accepts data from *any station* on the network and directs it to a **printer(s)** connected to the **spooler**.
- **Logging on** means identifying yourself to a file server or main computer on the network so that you can gain access to a set of resources.
- A **network manager** is the person responsible for maintaining the network – he or she would have the highest level of security possible.

■ The **bandwidth** of a network is the *maximum rate at which it's possible to transmit data* – e.g. Ethernet is about 10 Mbits/sec, FDDI is about 100 Mbits/sec.

■ The **bandwidth** of a system is *determined by physical attributes* such as the material out of which the cables are made, and the performance of the 'interfacing electronics', for example.

■ **Intelligent hard disk controllers** are often shared by a small group of machines on a network to overcome bandwidth limitations.

■ **Network topology** is the name given to the physical attributes of a network in terms of how the cables are routed etc.

■ A **star network** has separate cables going from the central file server or computer to each workstation. This is the best system in terms of security and speed of operation.

■ A **bus network** has a *single cable linking all computers in a 'straight line'*. There is usually an appropriate terminator at each end.

■ A **ring network** has the wires at each end joined so that a *complete ring of cable* linking the systems together is formed.

■ Some networks, such as **Token Ring**, for example, do not necessarily have to be wired up as a physical ring network.

■ **Laser** links can be used to connect networks together where line-of-sight communication is possible.

■ **FDDI** stands for **Fibre-Distributed-Data Interface** – this is a network in which signals are sent in the form of pulses of light via a fibre-optic cable. It has a very high bandwidth indeed, with 100 Mbits/sec being typical.

■ **ARPAnet** is an example of an *extensive national and international network* which has now grown into the **Internet** system.

■ Networks are useful mechanisms for getting different types of computer system to talk to each other.

■ **Simplex** is the transmission of data in *one direction only*.

■ **Duplex** is the transmission of data in *both directions* – but *only one at a time*.

■ **Full duplex** is the *simultaneous two-way transmission* of data.

■ The **Baud rate** is the number of bits/sec.

■ The **information baud rate** may be slightly less than the actual **transmission baud rate** because of added data acting as a check on integrity, e.g. **parity** or **CRCs**.

■ **Serial transmission** is the transmission of data along a single wire or radio link.

■ **Parallel transmission** is the simultaneous transmission of a number of different binary digits by separate parallel paths (e.g. by using a bus).

■ If data is to be transmitted over a link such as the standard telephone system or radio link then it needs to be **modulated**.

■ **Modulation** means changing the signal into a suitable form for the medium over which it is being sent.

■ **Demodulation** means extracting the original data signal from the modulated signal.

■ A **MODEM** performs both the MOdulation and DEModulation functions.

■ A **carrier** is the name given to the signal which carries the data over a transmission link such as a satellite link, for example.

■ Different methods of **modulation** exist including **Amplitude Modulation** (AM), **Frequency Modulation** (FM), **Phase Modulation**, **Pulse Position Modulation**, **Pulse Code Modulation** and **Pulse Duration Modulation**.

■ **Multiplexing** is a system whereby many signals may be transmitted over the same link. A **broadband network** is needed.

■ A **broadband network** is one in which different frequencies can be used to transmit information simultaneously – a **baseband network** can only transmit one signal at a time.

■ **TDM** is **Time Division Multiplexing** – this system allocates each signal a slot of time.

■ **Frequency Division Multiplexing** allocates different **carrier** frequencies to different signals.

■ **Circuit switching networks** are systems like the normal telephone system where a specific line is routed from A to B and is dedicated but not necessarily used all of the time (e.g. two people might be stuck for what to say but the line is still being used).

■ **Packet switching** is where packets of information are routed from A to B by whatever route is convenient at the time. If a packet is not actually being sent at a particular moment in time, then another packet from a different computer may be sent.

■ The **ISO OSI model** is a *well-structured internationally agreed communications protocol* for network systems.

- The **ISO OSI model** contains **seven different layers** ranging from how applications make use of the system to how the physical wires are connected.
- The layers of the **ISO OSI model** are the **physical layer**, the **link layer**, the **network layer**, the **transport layer**, the **session layer**, the **presentation layer** and the **application layer**.
- **TCP/IP** stands for **Transmission Control Protocol/Internet Protocol**.
- **Transmission Control Protocol** is an example of the **transport layer** of the ISO OSI model.
- **Internet Protocol** is used by the Internet system and is an example of the **network layer** of the ISO OSI model.
- **ATM** stands for **Asynchronous Transmission Mode**.
- **Asynchronous Transmission Mode** is a reliable method of sending **computer data**, **voice** and **video data** over a **packet-switching network**.
- **Parity** is a simple method of checking the integrity of received data.
- **Even parity** involves an *even number of 1's* in each byte.
- **Odd parity** involves an *odd number of 1's* in each byte.
- **Two-dimensional parity** can sometimes correct a corrupted message.
- A **CRC – Cyclic Redundancy Check** is one method of checking data integrity – it usually works on mathematical processing of polynomials, and is very efficient in terms of high rates of error detection and low overheads.
- **Hacking** is a constant problem and **password** systems are usually set up to counteract this threat.
- **Data encryption** can increase the security in sensitive systems.

22 Business and commercial applications

Introduction

This is the first of *three chapters* covering the vast topic of **computer applications**. In the late 20th century it has become true to say that there is virtually no aspect of life which has not been affected in some way by computer science – from the television pictures that you watch at home, the newspapers that you read in the morning, the trains on which you travel to get to work, and most of the organisation at work itself has been drastically altered by the use of information technology. The only type of person who could put their hands on their heart and say that they have not been affected in some way by computing would be a self-contained hermit who grows all his or her own food, has no money, and does not communicate with the outside world! – and even he or she would be able to observe a world which has been affected by IT – one would only have to observe an aircraft, for example, flying overhead.

There are literally many thousands of computer applications, with more being invented each and every day. No single person could be expected to appreciate this enormous expanse of knowledge, and it's therefore fortunate that for the purpose of your examinations, and indeed life in general, that it's necessary only to have an appreciation of the more common ones. This general appreciation of important applications leads to a high level of computer literacy. Not many people would bother, or even want to have a knowledge of the 'nuts and bolts' of all the applications, even if it were physically possible to do so. Experts tend to specialise in their own particular areas, or learn new applications as and when it becomes necessary.

What is *very important* is to have an appreciation of various high-profile applications, and to get a good grasp of the advantages and disadvantages that there would be when using computers and other computer-based equipment in particular application areas. *There is no substitute for actually using a particular application, even at an elementary level, and in your studies of computer science you should be given ample scope to do so.* But never forget that there are alternatives to using computers – always keep this in the back of your mind when using a computer for a particular task, this will always help you to keep things in perspective.

In recent years there has been a tendency for any high-tech gadget based on a microprocessor to be regarded automatically as being useful. This is not always the case, and things sometimes get used for their ability to impress friends and colleagues, or simply to boost ones image. For example, do you really need that personal organiser that translates what you type into Chinese! It might impress your friends down the pub, but, in general, that's about all the use that it might be to you. However, if a business dealt regularly with the Chinese community, then a word processor that could translate from English into Chinese, or a real-time language translator over a video phone *would* have some real advantages. As you can see from this example, knowing what is available is not enough. You must also learn where it would be appropriate to use the new technology. The next few chapters on computer applications should familiarise you with many of the current important business and commercial applications, *and* show typical situations in which each application could be put to efficient and cost-effective use.

Why make use of computers at all?

Ever since the American census of 1880, the need for processing data by machine became obvious. The problem then was that the mass of data acquired from the 1880 census would not be analysed before the 1890 census was due to be taken! A competition to find a solution was held, and Herman Hollerith won with his invention of a 'tabulating machine' (see page 618). This meant that the data, entered on punched cards, could be collated and analysed much more quickly.

Technology has come a long way in the last hundred years, but the ideas behind using it are still much the same – we should make use of computers and associated software if it saves time, and hence saves money, or is able to do something which would be quite impossible by manual means. This would include working with great precision and speed, doing highly complex calculations, or doing boring and repetitive or dangerous tasks that are unacceptable if they are being carried out by human operators. When undertaking a study of the many different application areas, you should also bear in mind the effects that the introduction of the technology has on the people that are being replaced. Obvious candidates here would be a reduced workforce or a workforce in which the skills needed are vastly different from those necessary when the processes used to be carried out manually, and this important topic is covered in detail in the social-implications chapter on page 607.

The topics that follow consider several common business applications of computers. However, it would be wrong to consider each application in isolation from the others, and indeed other applications in the engineering and scientific fields. Often some of the greatest advantages from using computers come when the integration of all these systems is considered. From a management level this is possibly the greatest advantage of all – i.e. *the ability to have instant information about many different aspects of your business available whenever you need it.* However, you will not be able to build up this vital overall picture without an analysis of what each individual application can do. Also, the nature of the business will decide which particular applications are important. You must, therefore, keep an open mind when dealing with each application area.

Word processing

Text processing

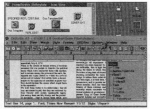

Figure 22.1

There can be few businesses that operate successfully without correspondence. Therefore, **word processors** are playing an important role in the office and many other business environments. In the past a word processor used to be a dedicated machine specifically set up for this single task. Although some of these may still be used (e.g. for complex mathematical and technical type setting), the term 'word processor' is now used almost exclusively to mean the special software which turns a 'microcomputer' or a 'computer terminal' into a system which gives it a text-processing capability.

A **word processor** is, therefore, an **applications package** which gives the user of the computer the ability to process documents in ways which are much more efficient than by hand or on a typewriter. *Its greatest advantages are the ease of editing (changing the text), the ability to see a document on the screen before it is printed out, and the keeping of copies as text files on disk which can easily be recalled for later use, or sent electronically (electronic mail) to any part of the world via a suitable communications network.* These applications packages are very common on micros, minis and mainframes, and can usually be accessed from the local resources or, via a computer network.

The word processor has indeed come a long way in the past few years. The early versions were simply editors where the operator had to remember ghastly control-character sequences to carry out all the basic operations. (A few specialised ones are still no better!) Today, however, it would not be unusual to have large A4-shaped high-resolution screens with paper-white displays to appease secretaries who used to like working with real paper. The facilities offered by some of the most sophisticated word processors rival those offered by some **desktop publishing systems** (see later), and typical screen shots from some modern word-processor packages can be seen in Figure 22.1.

Most modern word processors operate using the **WIMP** environment (Window Icon Menu Pointer). This means that the majority of operations can be performed by using a mouse to point at various menu options. These type of word processors also have the advantage that they are **WYSIWYG**. This simply means 'What You See on the screen Is What You Get on the printer'. This is shortened to '**What You See Is What You Get**'. However, with a few word processors it's still a case of what you see on the screen is almost what you get on the printer! To get a 'true' rendition you would need a more-advanced word processor or a fully blown desktop publishing system. However, the most recent trend is for most word processors to be able to cope with true WYSIWYG – the distinction between packages that are called 'word processor systems' and 'DTP packages' is becoming blurred, perhaps because of a marketing ploy? People often say to the sales people in the shops that 'they only want a simple word processor' – if the 'DTP' package is called a word processor, then the masses will be more likely to go out and buy it! The term document processor is also now being used to add to the confusion of terms.

One advantage of **WYSIWYG** and the **WIMP** environment is the ability to introduce alternative character sets with ease. For example, Greek letters may be placed anywhere in the document by pointing the mouse at an 'α', 'β' or 'γ', etc on an on-screen menu. Indeed, an entire customised keyboard could be used to more easily type the whole document in Greek. Such attention to detail when considering the user interface has played a great part in the ease of use of these new systems, and the mighty Chinese language is now finally being produced by word-processing methodology.

Many advanced word processors offer the ability to work with **multiple documents** at the same time, mainly due to the **multi-tasking** ability of the **operating system** (see page 374). This idea is very useful as you can use the clipboard to transfer or copy a block of text from one document to another. A further useful ability is to be able to work with multiple columns in the same document. This gives the system the ability to produce newspaper-like columns of text which can automatically flow from one column into the next. Many systems now have a graphics ability such that the results are up to the standard of some desktop-publishing systems.

The major facilities offered by most word processors can be summarised as shown in the next few sections.

Editing facilities

These facilities typify operations which can be carried out on blocks of text, or on individual words or characters. Most word processors would have the ability to **Search** (Find), **Replace**, **Move**, **Copy** and **Cut** etc. **Merge** two or more documents, **format** paragraphs or the entire document, and generally move around the document in very efficient ways. In addition to this, one can usually do things like insert the **current date**, **time**, **page number**, **chapter number** and **expand abbreviations** into the fully-blown versions.

Layout facilities

The ability to create page layouts is fundamental to any word processor system, it is usual to have a house style in most companies in which the company logo is placed at the top of the letter. Certain styles (see next section) would be automatically applied, and this would include layout parameters such as **Tabs**, **Indents**, **Line spacing**, **Rulers**, **Justification**, **Headers**, **Footers** and **Automatic page numbering** etc.

Style controls

A style alters the appearance of the text – it's the **font** which is used (see **DTP systems** on page 523), together with other attributes which may include Underline, **Bold**, Light, Superscripts and Subscripts, *Italics* or *combinations of some of these*, for example. (The last style here is underlined italic bold superscript!) You should be warned that over use of text effects and styles leads to documents which look unprofessional. Bear this in mind when you are undertaking work for your written project report.

Preview facilities

Although one now takes it for granted, it is only in the last few years that it has been possible to see on the screen exactly what will come out on the printer. The ability to see where the page breaks will occur, the ability to see the styles in the exact form, and the ability to alter the magnification of the document to get an overall impression means that word-processor operatives can now get it right first time. This is an obvious advantage and saves both time and money in the longer term.

Spelling checkers and thesauri

Spelling may be checked in just part or all of the document. It may be checked in one go, or as you are entering the text at the keyboard. **General dictionaries** are usually supplied, but **foreign language** or **specialist dictionaries** can often be added. There is usually the facility to build up your own **supplementary dictionaries** in which you can add to the total number of words contained in the main dictionary. I have known many English teachers who bemoan the fact that the puny 80,000-word computer dictionaries are not adequate for their vocabulary – but the recent addition of the *Oxford English Dictionary* on CD-ROM, containing well over 5,000,000 excerpts from English literature, a selection of over 1,800,000 quotations, plus technical, slang, obsolete and archaic entries has now blown this argument well and truly out of the window!

Most word processors now also come with a **thesaurus**, and the power of this combination can't be overestimated. Before the advent of the computer thesaurus it was a hassle to walk over to the library, find the thesaurus, look up the appropriate word, and then probably lose track of what you were doing because you got carried away by some other word which caught your eye. When using a computerised thesaurus, a click of the mouse will instantly bring up the appropriate set of alternatives. Add to this the ability to wander through the dictionary at will, and be able to back-track through the previous history, and you start to get an idea of the improved opportunity for increasing your vocabulary with relative ease. Many computers now also have **reverse dictionaries** and **reverse thesauri**, which means that you can find all the definitions containing your chosen word!

Grammar checking

In my opinion most of the grammar checkers which I have seen still fall short of what I, and probably what most other people require. Even so, considerable progress has been made in the last few years. For example, if you have the sentence:

I feel that the propose grammar-checking feature is not adequate.

The computer, using a menu-type system familiar to most users who have spell-checking and thesaurus facilities, would probably respond with something like:

Suggest you change above sentence to the following

I feel that the proposed grammar-checking feature is not adequate.

Such facilities are useful to say the least, but many obvious errors are not trapped by most of the current systems. Nevertheless, just a few years ago the thought of useful grammar checking accompanying standard word processors and DTP systems would have been in the realms of pure fantasy – the software developers should be congratulated on the progress which they have made to date.

Mail merge

Mail merging is the important ability to produce a standard letter, and then merge it with different names and addresses etc to produce 'personalised' letters for each person on the name and address list. It's a little like getting the letters through from the Readers Digest, for example, which might start off 'Dear Mr Jones, you have come through to the last stage of our grand draw competition . . .'! It produces the appearance of a personalised letter, but has obviously been produced automatically. One should not underestimate the importance of mail merging, and the amount of junk mail that arrives with the more-interesting letters one receives in the post shows its current popularity. Although we might put most of the junk mail in the bin, most companies are happy if just a few percent of the people that receive the mail actually reply to the advertising. However, what a waste of paper – it would be more environmentally friendly to use electronic mail. However, don't confuse mail merge with electronic mail!

Communications

Most modern word processors have facilities for electronic mail. This is very useful for internal communications via a LAN, or for national and international communications making use of MANs, WANs or the standard telephone system. Don't forget that this communication process is two way. Opportunities exist to get information from world-wide databases into your word processor back at the office. With the proposed information superhighway (see page 534), we will soon have the ability to send audio data, computer data, pictures and real-time video too – this fact alone will probably lead to the demise of the fax machine in the medium to long term – so if you have shares in a fax company – it might be best to transfer them into electronic mail instead!

Miscellaneous

There is a whole host of other facilities including things like counting up the total number of words, pages and other statistics, import and export facilities to other systems (vitally important these days), and automatically generating contents and indexes etc. In fact the ability to transfer text and pictures together with appropriate styles and layouts etc across different platforms will be important for some time to come. The ability to send **ASCII** text (see page 266) only is no longer regarded as adequate and **RTF (Rich Text Format)** now looks quite promising.

Mathematical text-processing systems

Some of the worst problems in word processing occur when **mathematical formulae** have to be produced. Only the best word processors and DTP systems are able to typeset mathematical formula without too much hassle – try producing the following on some word processors and you will be well and truly stuck!

$$\Phi(x) = \sum_{t \le x} \frac{\binom{r}{t}\binom{s}{n-t}}{\binom{r+s}{n}} \qquad \int_G \int f(x,y)dG = \lim_{\substack{n \to \infty \\ \Delta G_i \to 0}} \sum_{i=1}^{n} m_i \Delta G_i$$

However, look at any excellently typeset maths book, and you will find a wealth of styles and sizes for every single character. There is almost an infinite variety. Subtle rules have been used to get the most pleasing presentation possible. It takes a highly-skilled typesetter to produce a professional layout when dealing with mathematically-related text. Nevertheless, the most-recent word processors and many of the good DTP systems have now tackled this area too, and unskilled operators can now produce professional looking mathematical and chemical equations.

One of the best and most long-established mathematical text-processing systems available that can compete with the world's best manual mathematical typesetting systems is Donald Knuth's T_EX. This is able to produce exceptionally high quality technical manuscripts. Interestingly enough, this product is about as far from WYSIWYG as you can get! Applications such as these, therefore, go against the current trends for normal text processing. Figure 22.2 shows a typical input string, and the output from T_EX.

\[\underbrace {a + \overbrace {b + \cdots + y} ^ {24} + z}_{26} \]

$$\underbrace{a + b + \cdots + y + z}_{26}^{\overbrace{}^{24}}$$

What has to be typed in!   The result

Figure 22.2

You should now realise that two people's opinion of text processing could be very different, even if the same applications package is used. As shown above, a mathematician's secretary would have very different requirements indeed from that of a normal office secretary. They would probably need to make use of very different types of text processing systems.

Other useful hardware

Sometimes, type-written text can be scanned by a special **document scanner** (see page 228), and then **imported** into a **word processor**. This is a great advantage if there is much text to enter that has already been typed onto paper. Special OCR (Optical Character Recognition) software that accompanies this hardware can be used to recognise the patterns of text and import these patterns as ASCII text (often together with the styles) so that the text does not have to be re-typed. Great advances in text-pattern recognition over the last few years have been made in this particular area, and we are now in a position where text can be scanned in from many documents with great precision, often needing only a quick spell check before the text is in a useable state. Some of the latest software can deal with a range of styles on the same page, ignore the pictures that accompany the text and flag any errors that might be encountered during the scanning process.

Integrated software packages

Most word processors have the ability to import data from other packages such as spreadsheets and databases. Indeed some **integrated software packages** are now offering **spreadsheet** and **database** facilities from *within* the **word processor**. Unfortunately, many of these integrated packages mean simply that the individual word processing, spreadsheet and database facilities are inferior to those offered by the dedicated word processors, spreadsheets and databases. The import and export facilities of stand-alone applications is now very much more sophisticated, and much data in many different forms can be transferred with little difficulty between different systems.

Disadvantages

From the above you may very well think that a combination of word processors in the office would be an excellent idea, indeed, it probably would be. However, as with the introduction of any new technology, there is a need for **training of the personnel** who will make use of it. There is nothing guaranteed to put people off computers more quickly, than to suddenly realise they have lost a hundred hours work because they have pressed the wrong button, or a disk has become corrupted. You will also find that, as productivity is increased, you will need to make use of **fewer typists**. Sometimes people who have worked in an office environment for many years are **reluctant to change** from their old systems and make way for the introduction of word processors.

Desktop publishing systems

Desktop publishing, as *opposed* to **word processing**, is the ability to manipulate any characteristic of **text and graphics** on the printed page. This includes printing out the text in any style, shape, size and orientation etc. Add to this the potential to produce the output on many different printers including laser and Linotronic (a professional printing press), to output in true 24-bit in colour, and you should easily see why DTP systems have *revolutionised* the way in which the printing industry operates. However, don't forget that the distinction between DTP and word processing is becoming fuzzy, and top-of-the-range word processors can often do more than a cheap DTP system. In addition to all of this, DTP has given smaller companies and individuals the ability to produce professional-quality in-house publications, and a typical example of output from a good DTP system is shown in Figure 22.3.

PC Power Users Know QEMM 7 is the number one productivity-enhancing utility in the world—removing memory incompatibilities that slow your work. And for game players, it provides maximum memory for smooth, fast action. See your favourite dealer.

As Compute Magazine's reviewer said: *"If you're a power user who wants to play with the monster games... you'll need Quarterdeck's QEMM 7 memory manager utility, which not only will free up more than enough memory but will even optimize parts of your multiply-configured system."*

Figure 22.3

The early DTP systems were not used for the original composition of text, as they were too slow to keep up with the speed of a professional typist. However, as computers have become more powerful, DTP systems are able to do all that word processors can do in terms of real-time text composition, and often very much more.

Reasons for using DTP

Presenting information in a professional way is important in a modern business. If vital information is presented in a shoddy way, then it will not have the desired impact on customers. Would *you* buy equipment from a company that gives you a 'badly-laid-out poorly-typed sheet' for their publicity material? It creates the impression, (which could be entirely wrong!), that the product is likely to be of the same low standard. DTP documents can, therefore, be used to give your customers the appropriate perception that you are marketing a high quality product, or that the facilities your company provides are likely to be of a high standard. (Again this may be entirely the wrong impression!)

Basic concepts

Many of the concepts explained in the next few sections can also be applied to top-of-the-range word processors, but they have been left to this section for convenience. To understand DTP involves an understanding of some printing jargon, and this is best done by considering the text shown in figure 22.4.

The word '**Computer**' is shown in a **typeface** called **Times**, and '**Science**' is in a typeface called **Helvetica**. You can, therefore, see that a *typeface is the characteristic design of the text*, i.e. the shapes and curly lines that give the text its special appearance. **Desktop publishing systems** give you complete control over the text by altering certain attributes such as the **typeface, point size** and **leading** (pronounced 'ledding'). Figure 22.4 shows some different point sizes. 72 point and 36 point have been

Figure 22.4

compared here, but the diagram has been reduced in size to make it fit in the available space. The word **point** is a printing term that represents one twelfth of a **pica**. A **pica** is another printing term representing one sixth of an inch – you can, therefore, work out that a single point would be about $1/12 \times 1/6 = 0.0138$ inches, giving us 72 points in one inch.

Leading is the name given to the spaces between lines. It derives from the old printing term that was used when the printers put extra pieces of lead in between to make the lines further apart. Therefore, you have precise control over how far apart each line of text will be from the previous line. The leading is simply the distance between the two **baselines** as shown in figure 22.4. The terms **ascenders** and **descenders** should be obvious from looking at the diagram. As with a word processor, you can change the style of the text to give **bold** or *italic* etc. When combined with the name of the **typeface** you would have names such as Times-bold or Times-italic. The name given to a particular set of characteristics like these is called a **font**.

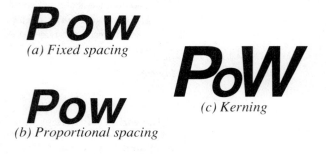

Figure 22.5

Most DTP systems offer a choice of spacing between the characters that make up some of the fonts. These are usually fixed spacing, proportional spacing and, in addition, kerning. Figure 22.5 illustrates all three ideas. Figure 22.5(a) shows 'boring old' **fixed spacing** – it's the sort of output you'd expect from a **mechanical typewriter**, but it still has its uses – e.g. program listings – proportional spacing makes them look neater. Figure 22.5(b) shows **proportional spacing**, and this is supported by most word processors – it spaces out the letters so that the *overall effect* is much more pleasing. However, some letters can't get close enough for maximum effect, especially if they are printed out at *very large* **point sizes**, and so, **kerning** is used, as shown in figure 22.5(c). This allows the letters to be *placed much closer together*. In fact the next letter can even encroach on a previous letter's space (i.e the two letters can effectively 'overlap').

Pages and frames

There are several alternative strategies, but the two main ones revolve around the concept of a **page**, and a **document**. One system uses the page as the single most-important unit, and the other considers the whole document. Both systems make use of what is called a **frame**. Typical frames are shown in figure 22.6.

As can be seen from the following sections, The **frame** is used as a **guide** for the *insertion* of all *text* and *graphics*. For consistency of style a **master page** usually

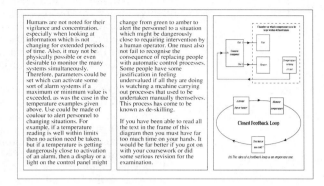

Figure 22.6

defines the standard positions of the frame on each page, with local variations being altered on each page to suit.

Text imports

The **frame** represents the borders where the text (often called a story) will fit onto the page. It can be regarded as the 'newspaper columns' before the newspaper stories are fitted into them. Long stories may take up many different frames. The DTP system would automatically spill over the text from one frame to the next frame of your choice, as can be seen from figure 22.6. If the stories to be loaded into the frames were previously produced on a word processor prior to importing them into the DTP system, then you have the option of getting the DTP system, not the word processor, to control exactly how the text will appear on the page.

Notice that preparing the text beforehand using a word processor enables many different people to write up stories for inclusion in the same document. These stories may then be exported to the DTP system by using a disk, or making use of a network system. Via international LHNs, it's easily possible for a story to be electronically transmitted and be included in a newspaper within a matter of seconds. Pictures may also be processed in a similar way as described below.

Graphics imports

The **frames** can also be used to place graphics in their appropriate position on the page. Such graphics might be produced by a **pixel-based art package** (see page 566), an **object-oriented CAD package** (see page 539), or straight from a hardware device

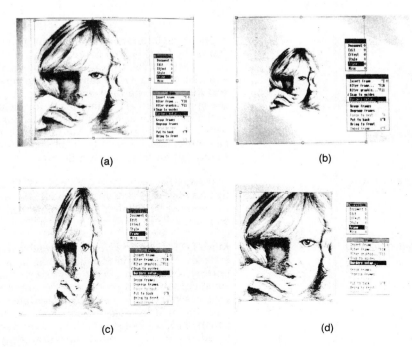

(a)   (b)

(c)   (d)

Figure 22.7

such as a **scanner** or **video digitiser** (see in a moment). On some systems these video-quality images can be produced in full colour. After importation of the image, it can be re-sized, cropped or distorted by altering the size of the frame which now contains the picture. A typical frame containing a picture is shown in figure 22.7(a). Figure 22.7(b) shows the same picture re-sized, figure 22.7(c) shows a distorted picture and figure 22.7(d) shows the original picture after it has been cropped.

Colour comes of age

Computer Concepts' 'Impression Publisher and Impression Style DTP systems', for example, on the Acorn's RISC PC range of computers, allows you to produce full coloured text, graphics, digitised and scanned images. The colours can be altered in a convenient number of ways, (including 24 bit – see page 242) making use of three different systems. These techniques are useful for people with different backgrounds such as computer personnel, printers and artists. For example, **computer specialists** will be very familiar with the **RGB (Red, Green, Blue)** model for displaying colours, whereas an **artist** is usually more familiar **with the HSV (Hue, Saturation and Value)** model which can be directly related with the more familiar terms such as **Hues**, **tints** and **tones** etc. In addition to this, there is the **CMYK (Cyan, Magenta, Yellow, Key)** model favoured by those in the commercial **printing industry**, and this is explained in detail on page 254.

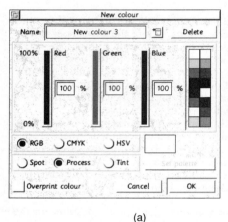
(a)

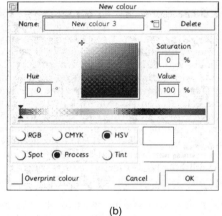
(b)

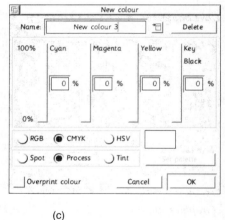
(c)

Figure 22.8

The three different types of colour menus can be seen in figure 22.8. Figure 22.8(a) shows the RGB model, figure 22.8(b) shows the HSV model and figure 22.8(c) shows the CYMK model. In some systems, by making use of a **video digitiser** circuit board, you can point a **video camera** at the image you require, and you can then see a **real-time** image on the screen. When the picture is just right, you can import it into the appropriate DTP frame ready for inclusion in your document! As video is used as the standard, this means that you can take images off the **TV** or any **video recorder** with a video output. You can also import images from **CD-ROM**s, from national and international networks (many photo libraries are now starting these services) or simply get an image from a floppy disk.

Digitised images

A **scanner** (see page 228) enables the DTP system to digitise an image that is obtained by **scanning a picture** or **document**. For example, you could put a photograph into the scanner then, after the machine had scanned the picture, it would be in the correct form for importation into a DTP frame.

Printed output

Most DTP systems give an impressive variety of printout options. This normally includes printing out the document in many different **scales** and **orientation**, i.e. **portrait** or **landscape** in different sizes. These facilities are available because, unlike some types of word processors, the entire DTP page is treated as a **graphics image**, or is described by using a **page description language** (see in a moment). There's not much point in having a superb DTP system if the final printout is not up to an equally professional standard. For most purposes, a **24-pin dot matrix printout** would be adequate only for obtaining a **draft copy**, indeed, some 24-pin dot matrix printers are capable of producing in excess of 300 dots per inch when printing out in hex-density mode. However, even though the quality is quite good, this method usually means that a page could take anything up to ten minutes to print! A typical laser printer can normally produce about 8 to 12 pages per minute. This usually gives a resolution of about 300 dots per inch, but some 600+ dpi (dots per inch) systems have now appeared on the market, and the more expensive 1200 dpi versions are becoming available.

For really professional publications (e.g. text books etc.) 300 dpi will not be enough. If this is the case then special **linotronic** printing processes giving resolutions of 1200 dpi are needed. However, the linotronic printing technology for this application is very expensive and is only usually found in professional printing establishments.

The adoption of a **page description language** called postscript (see page 253) has meant that it's often possible to take your disk to a professional bureau, and get them to print out the copy on their expensive photo-typesetter machines. A page description language allows an application such as a DTP system to send out a description of how the page (i.e. text and graphics etc.) will be printed. It describes text fonts and other associated information. Postscript was originally conceived by the Adobe Corporation for the Apple Laser writer (Apple's laser printer) but has since been adopted as *the* page description language. Many laser printers today operate making use of the postscript language, and therefore most good DTP systems will allow you to print out to a postscript laser printer, or produce a postscript file on disk.

There are now affordable **colour postscript laser printers**, and images produced on these devices are now so good that it's referred to as **NPQ** or **Near Photographic Quality**. Compare this to **NLQ** (**Near Letter Quality**). It should be noted that typical DTP printing systems are not intended for mass production. If this is the case, then you would send off your desktop published work to the printers so that thousands of copies could be printed if necessary. It would take far too long to do long print runs on dot matrix or LASER printers found in most offices and factories.

What are the alternatives?

Newspapers, magazines and books used to be compiled by using a combination of **cutting and pasting**. (Options that are available from within a DTP system.) This literally meant that you had to cut out the pictures and paste them into the appropriate position on the page. The text then had to be manually fitted around the pictures. This process is a time consuming task. It also takes a skilled operator to get the document to look professional. This produces what is called the 'camera ready copy'. It is then ready to be used as a master page for the final printing process.

As you can see from the above, the equivalent manual processes go through several different stages, and could take many people to produce the required results. A skilled operator on a DTP system may be able to produce the same sort of results in a couple of hours.

The right system for the job in hand

As with any computer system, some people make inappropriate use of the technology. You don't really need to use a DTP system to send an internal office memo! It would be far simpler to use a simple word processor or text editor, make use of electronic mail, or simply write it out using pencil and paper – what's that?

The future

It's likely that, in the next ten to 15 years, word processors and DTP systems with the ability to translate natural language will be with us, and the ability to interpret speech will probably be taken for granted. More intelligent systems with superior grammar checking as well as spell checking should be possible, and are indeed starting to appear on the market now. During the lifetime of many computer science students it's probable that the keyboard may be secondary to what is likely to become the most common data entry method for PCs – that is voice.

The word processors of the future may well combine real-time voice-to-text with optional language translation. If you think that this is a little far fetched, don't forget that it's predicted by some people that the power of a latest Cray supercomputer of today will be common in the pocket calculators of tomorrow! Indeed, in 1994, a company called MIPS, which specialises in RISC-based microprocessors, released the R8000 64-bit micro chip, which is claimed to have the *same performance* as a Cray Y-MP supercomputer – however, before you rush out and buy one, the price of the microcomputer system based on this particular chip is about £110,000 – even so, this is much less than the price of an actual Cray.

If you feel a little sceptical about this rate of progress, think for a moment. The processing power of a computer of thirty years ago, which weighed five tons, needed a mass of electricity to operate, and took up the space of a large semi-detached house, is **now literally available** on a piece of silicon 1cm^2 in area and a 'tenth of a mm' thick. This is always a sobering thought!

Spreadsheets

A **spreadsheet** is now universally associated with computers, although *the original idea of a spreadsheet was simply a piece of paper on which people added up columns and rows of numbers* to help them plan their budgets. Although the computerised spreadsheet is basically the same idea as the paper one, the facilities offered bear little resemblance to the original paper concepts. To consider a spreadsheet as a simple mechanism for carrying out tedious operations which could have been done manually would be missing the point by several miles. The computerised **spreadsheet** *has literally revolutionised the way in which many businesses operate*, but in addition to this, there are many other uses to which spreadsheets can now be put, and some of these will be mentioned later on in this chapter.

The basic ideas

Facts and figures form the basis of most company financial management strategies. In businesses, columns of figures have been added up and manipulated for many years, and the name '**spreadsheet**' was originally used because the figures were literally *spread* out on a *sheet* of paper. Computerised spreadsheets give modern businesses the powerful ability to create vast spreadsheets without the tedium of having to manually perform any of the arithmetical or other operations. With a large spreadsheet, the computer screen acts as a window through which some of the cells (see in a moment) can be viewed. Some systems allow you to view multiple parts of the spreadsheet at the same time.

At the simplest level a spreadsheet consists of a two-dimensional arrangement of cells as shown in figure 22.9. These **cells** are referenced by looking at the **intersection of the row and column numbers and letters** respectively. The cells C4 and D2 are shown highlighted in figure 22.9 However, as we shall see later, computers have also given businesses the ability to think in more than two or even three dimensions.

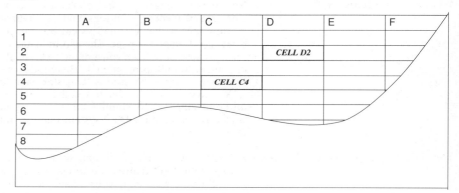

	A	B	C	D	E	F
1						
2				CELL D2		
3						
4			CELL C4			
5						
6						
7						
8						

Figure 22.9

Normal text can be typed in almost anywhere, and is very much like using a word processor. However, the power of a spreadsheet stems from the fact that it is easily able to **manipulate formulae** based around the **cell references**. As a simple example, the number in cell C3 could be added to the number in cell C4, and the result put in cell C6. In this way, figures are worked out automatically because the computer has done the adding up for you. This does not sound too amazingly useful, until you start to think of a **large spreadsheet** having **thousands of numbers, hundreds of rows** and **columns**, and some **very complex interrelated data**.

Think of the cells as being interrelated by very complex mathematical functions, needing to be put into some pre-determined order based on some obscure relationships, or complex date-related calculations involving leap years and the like – and you will start to appreciate just a small part of the overall problem – change even one important number, and several thousand other numbers which may depend on the one just altered can be automatically updated.

Spreadsheet functions

The **range of functions** available on most spreadsheets are limited only by your imagination and programming ability: standard mathematical functions such as *trig*, *statistical*, *matrix*, *complex*, *logs*, *ints* and *mods* etc., **financial functions** such as *future values of investments* and *net present value of cash flow*, **statistical functions** such as *mean*, *mode* and *standard deviation*, **date functions** to help sort out data based on dates, a whole host of **database functions**, **time functions**, and *many others* too numerous to mention. Indeed, you can invent your own functions and **macros** (see in a moment), and many spreadsheets are now providing a language like **BASIC** as the macro language for the development of user-constructed or third-party routines. For example, Microsoft's Excel 5 Spreadsheet has Visual BASIC as its Macro language, or Acorn's 'Schema' has BBC BASIC V as its macro language. This means the users can write BASIC programs which can then be used to control the spreadsheet. Virtually anything that can be done via BASIC can therefore be used to control the sheet. This makes programming the spreadsheet for simulations much easier, as new esoteric macro languages no longer have to be learned from scratch.

It's absolutely essential that you are familiar with a spreadsheet, as **it's literally one of the most important computer-based applications**, and one of the most interesting pieces of software once you have mastered the basics. A typical screen from a demo of the 'Fireworkz spreadsheet' is shown in figure 22.10.

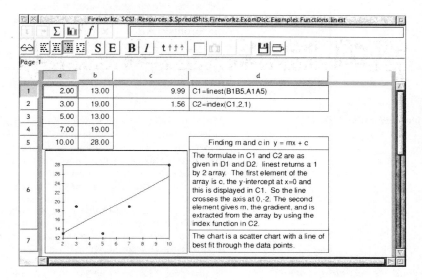

Figure 22.10

Why all the fuss about spreadsheets?

A sophisticated spreadsheet can be built up to represent **very complex relationships between a huge number of variables**. Doing the same thing by hand could literally take many hundreds of hours work – if the boss then came up to you and said 'What if we change several things from our original specification', you would probably rather resign than go through the tedious and time consuming task of having to manually re-calculate the effects on all aspects of the business! However, with a computerised spreadsheet modelling the problem, the variables could be altered and the spreadsheet would automatically re-calculate all the implications for you. Therefore, the boss can get his or her answers to the '**what if**' questions straight away (see next page).

Editing functions

It's easily possible to do a large range of editing comparable in sophistication to some word-processing systems (see page 519). You can mark entire blocks of cells so that they may be moved, copied and deleted etc. In addition to this, there are commands to insert and delete rows, put individual cells in rows or columns, and virtually every other manipulation of the data within the sheet that you can think of.

Macro functions

Macros give you the ability to make up your own sophisticated procedures by using a combination of many of the functions described above. It's usual to be able to save the **macro (list of commands)** on disk, so that the effects can be carried out simply by specifying the name of the macro. In addition to being able to write complex macros in a high-level language like Visual BASIC, for example, there is often a record-macro facility which puts the computer into a mode where data entered from the keyboard and movements with the mouse etc. are recorded so that complex or tedious combinations of events only have to be repeated just once. Next time the macro can be called, the computer can be instructed to process the new data in ways identical to those which it was previously shown.

It's sometimes tremendous fun to look at the computer automatically working through a macro, and this is one of the easiest ways to impress non-specialists in the office, at school or at college. Some teachers, for example, who know little about spreadsheets, seldom fail to be impressed when they see this package picking names and examination data off a disk, putting the names and data into alphabetical order and printing out a list on the printer, then automatically working out the examination statistics, re-ordering the names to produce another list in descending numerical order, assigning grades depending on the marks awarded, and then passing the data over to a DTP system ready for the teacher to produce their reports. Indeed, you can even get the system to produce the reports for you – but that would be giving away too many trade secrets!

'What if' questions

Ordinary data, mathematical and other relationships can be changed very easily with a spreadsheet. At the touch of a button you could ask yourself, '**What if we increase the price of our goods and sell less?**', '**What if we reduce the price of our goods and sell many more?**', 'What will be the likely effect of each of these strategies on our profits?' After the analysis has been performed by a spreadsheet, you can make use of the **charting section** of the sheet, or **export** the data into a separate **presentation graphics package** (see page 531). With a well-set-up spreadsheet, you can test out a hypothesis, generate the graphics and fax the results through to another country within minutes – that's the power of these new spreadsheet and other integrated systems.

Integrated spreadsheets

Most spreadsheets can now easily **integrate** with **word processors** and **databases**, and indeed some spreadsheets have word processors and database functions built in. However, as we have seen elsewhere in this book, such packages are called **integrated software packages**, and it's most unlikely that the facilities offered by such an integrated package would equal those of three separate specialist packages – this is why it's so important to ensure that the spreadsheet that you use can **import data** from other packages such as databases and word processors. As mentioned in other parts of the book, the OLE system (Object Linking and Embedding) helps to create links between different applications. If you have packages which support OLE, then a click or two with the mouse is all that is necessary for selected data to be transferred from the spreadsheet to a DTP system or vice versa, for example.

Beyond the second dimension

Some spreadsheets now have the facility for **three dimensions or more**. These are called **multi-dimensional spreadsheets**, but large spreadsheets in many different dimensions obviously take up pots of memory and require a powerful computer if the results are to be obtained by the end of the coffee break! Lotus, for example, manufacture a system called 'Improv' which although not a spreadsheet in the strictest sense can model data in 12 dimensions. Some modern spreadsheets now also have the ability to refer to a particular cell by name instead of by row and column. This is particularly useful if multiple spreadsheets are being used at the same time. Such spreadsheets are known as **relational spreadsheets**.

Other uses of a spreadsheet

It was mentioned near the beginning of this section that spreadsheets are very versatile, and by having a high-level language such as BASIC as the macro language you should appreciate this point only too well. Spreadsheets are not just limited to financial and business data, and anything at all which can be expressed algorithmically can be programmed into a spreadsheet. This means that *scientific and engineering simulations as well as business simulations can be carried out with ease.* Spreadsheets can be most useful in mathematics for helping to visualise and analyse number patterns, they are useful for modelling simulations based on random numbers of the type shown on page 195, and are particularly useful for solving numerical equations of the type shown on page 177. They are extremely useful as tools for demonstration of **recursion** and **iteration**, and can often be used to convert data from virtually any form into virtually any other – you really are limited only by your imagination, and this is why the spreadsheet probably reigns supreme as the most versatile applications package – an accolade it quite rightly deserves.

Never underestimate the power of a spreadsheet. Thousands of microcomputers are sold each year simply for their ability to run a spreadsheet. Apart from the word processor, it is probably *the* most popular piece of business software.

Graphical presentation packages

These packages either work in close co-operation with, or, are sometimes part of **spreadsheet packages** (see page 528). However, integrated office packages which include DTP systems, spreadsheets and a database often have a presentation package as part of the suite. For example, Microsoft's Office has a presentation package called PowerPoint. The primary purpose of these charting packages is to accept numerical data, then produce a variety of graphs and charts of the form shown in figure 22.11.

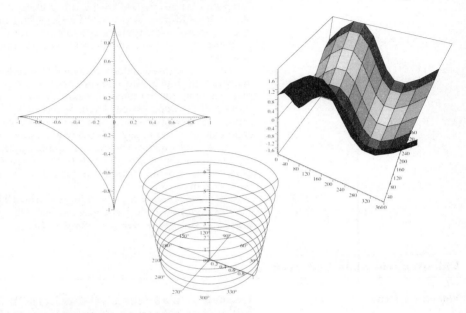

Figure 22.11

The level of sophistication of some of these packages and the range of graphs capable of being produced is now more than adequate for virtually all purposes, with horizontal, vertical, 2D and 3D colour representations in literally hundreds of different graph types being the norm.

The variety of graphics-presentation packages is quite large, with applications such as Harvard graphics being typical of what is at or near the top of the range. More general graphics packages such as CORELDRAW, for example, also have extensive charting and presentation capabilities, often with hundreds of different fonts and tens of thousands of different suitable clip-art back drops to give the presentations more panache. Such packages can act as a professional introduction to full multi-media presentations, including the use of animated techniques (see page 563).

Data can usually be transferred to and from other packages by making use of standard transfer protocols such as **CSV (Comma Separated Variables)**, or, entered manually directly into the business-graphics package. The systems are very versatile as they work out all the tedious details to ensure that the graphs are scaled properly.

Some packages, such as Stanford Graphics, for example, enables you to undertake much in terms of the analysis of the data before it is presented. Indeed such packages start to encroach on other application areas such as statistical analysis packages, or packages such as MathCAD, for example, which often keep advanced mathematicians amused for hours on end, and provide the mathematical equivalent of a Computer Aided Design package – hence the name.

The presentation of statistical data should not be underestimated in today's modern society. Not only are charts useful for showing statistics in ways which are more easily digested, they are useful for presenting arguments which may help to sway opinion one way or another. With a suitable colour printer, very slick presentations can be made. It's often possible to transfer the images to Overhead Projection transparencies, (OHP), transfer them directly to a machine that will produce 35mm slides, or export the graphics in a form that can easily be understood by DTP systems.

As with other systems, it's usual for companies to adopt some sort of general standard when it comes to graphics presentation. Consistency in style will produce a more professional looking document, and information presented by different personnel will be easier to assimilate because styles of graphics presentation are similar.

Database systems

Databases and business go hand in hand, for databases were first developed as a computerised alternative to the office-filing-cabinet system. Therefore, most (if not all) of the information contained inside office filing cabinets can now be represented in the form of a computerised database. Both textual and pictorial information can be handled with ease, and the more-recent multimedia databases can handle audio and video too.

The computerised database gives unprecedented opportunities for searching and analysis, and much information about a company, far too tedious to even contemplate carrying out by manual means becomes routine if a database package is used. Indeed, the computerised database has now become so important in many organisations that without it the company would not be able to run efficiently. Indeed, it is no exaggeration to say that many companies would literally not be able to operate at all. All information about the company, from the names and addresses of the customers and suppliers through to the detail of the thousands of financial transactions that are being carried out each day are all stored on the computerised database system.

A database is such a large application area that a small section in an applications chapter could do little justice to the important principles involved. Therefore, **databases are covered in detail in chapter 20**.

Videotex, viewdata and network systems

Videotex systems

Videotex, or **viewdata** as it is still sometimes known, is the name given to the systems in which the **public telephone network**, usually in combination with a **microcomputer**, **modem** and **appropriate communications software** is used to gain access to **information databases** such as the **Prestel** database set up by **British Telecom**, or the similar Bildschirmtext database in Germany, or Telidon database in Canada. Other countries such as Australia, France and the USA, for example, have set up their own similar systems, but other systems, such as the **Internet** which is based around a **WAN** and a huge number of **international bulletin boards**, are now extremely popular, and these are covered a little later in this chapter.

The main thing about the videotex systems is that they are **interactive** i.e. **two-way communication** is possible. (Compare this to the **teletext** system which is **one-way only**.) Prestel is a huge database and, more recently, other databases have merged with Prestel so that clients can benefit from the increased facilities. Information put onto the database is **provided** by **companies** who advertise or give other services. These are known as **Information Providers**, or **IPs**. Due to the restricted bandwidth (see page 490) of the telephone system, it's only possible to transmit low-resolution graphics of the sort that you get from the teletext services, and some typical screens are shown in Figure 22.12. However, clever compression (not used on these databases yet) can get over the low-bandwidth problem (see page 563).

As with Teletext, Prestel is based on a system of page numbers. However, there are a vast number of pages, numbering well over half a million during the 1990s. Many of these pages are free to be viewed by anyone who is a member of Prestel, (or a member of one of the associated systems such as **Campus 2000**), but there are other pages which are closed to all but the people with special access. These would include special business pages, or pages that are used exclusively by travel agents etc.

Many pages are free, but some incur a charge before they can be viewed. If this is the case, then it's brought to your attention *before* you are invited to view the information. The database can be thought of as a hierarchical structure based on following a set of menus.

Being interactive, this means that you can book things like theatre tickets, order crates of wine, or carry out other transactions – usually by quoting a credit-card number. Information can be requested and sent via snail mail (the normal post!) to your business or home address, or you can communicate by **E-Mail** if you have an appropriate mail box on the system. Via Prestel and an appropriate gateway, you

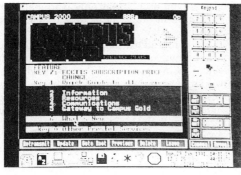

(a)   (b)

Figure 22.12

can branch out into other networks, such as the British Telecom directory enquiries database, which is 'free' to users of the system. You can also gain access to internationally connected networks such as the French Minitel Videotex system.

Charges for the service include an annual subscription for Prestel, charges for viewing certain pages, and the phone bill to the local node computer housing the database.

The teletext system

Teletext is the name given to the system that makes use of part of the normal TV signal. Normal TV signals are transmitted using a total of 625 lines that make up one screen of information. Not all 625 lines are used for picture information. The rest are used for engineering information, for remote transmitters and, more importantly for us, the digital data that is used to transmit the information on Teletext. If you alter your TV screen picture so that it's too far down the screen (assuming that you have a vertical hold button), then you will be able to see the digital data at the top of the picture. Most people will be familiar with the methods of getting the information, and a typical screen is shown in figure 22.13.(a).

Some **LAN**s now have facilities which include a **Teletext server**. This means that Teletext data, obtained via a suitable receiver can be re-transmitted over the LAN. This enables all the functions of the normal teletext system to be available at each station on the network. However, in addition to this, menu-driven systems enable data to be extracted from the screen in computer-readable form. For example, a teletext page could be frozen, then the stocks and shares prices could be extracted in ASCII format and saved to disk. It could also be imported into a word processor or DTP document, or sent to a spreadsheet ready for later analysis. Given that the system is essentially free, this is a wonderful way to build up data on which you can try out your statistical analysis packages. A system based on Acorn's RISC PC running on an Ethernet network can be seen in figure 22.13(b). Here the contents of a teletext screen is being saved 'as is' to a disk file. In addition to this particular feature, the screen itself can be saved in a variety of other formats.

(a)   (b)

Figure 22.13

Some systems, like the **Prestel** videotex system, for example, are intended almost exclusively for the business-type user. It has only marginally caught on in education, and has never really caught on in the home. Other systems like those used by travel agents and airline companies etc. also provide a specialist business-type service. Specialist systems also exist for education, with **ECCTIS**, the careers information service for higher education courses, and **NERIS**, the specialist curriculum-information database for teachers, being particularly good examples. However, in the last few years public networks have grown up on the back of systems set up by individuals in academic research institutions, with **Internet** being the most stunningly successful example. Indeed, Internet has grown from a rather obscure 'computer hackers' image, to one of the major contenders for the **information-superhighway** title in a very short space of time. It reminds me of the old transport-cafe joke – 'Eat at Joe's . . . ten thousand flies can't be wrong!' Well, over 10 million users of Internet can't be wrong either? – it certainly *is* a global communications network of networks.

The Internet

Internet is a **wide-area network**, or more specifically a *huge collection* of many **packet switched networks** (see page 505) that are all connected together by what are called **gateways** – these make the system act as if it were one large network. Many networks in *industry*, *business*, *higher education* and *government institutions* are all connected via these spiders-webs of international communications networks, although anybody can now get connected to the system with the appropriate hardware and software, and access to a UK provider to get them physically connected to the system (see in a moment). Networking in general is such a vast topic that Chapter 21 concentrates on all of the technical details of network communication and protocols. Here we will concentrate more on this vast network from a business-applications point of view.

Internet started out as a 'general chat system' for academics exchanging research information, and other similar types of users in government and industry. It has, however, grown enormously, and you now have access to literally thousands of different subjects ranging from 'home brewing' and 'Madonna' (the pop singer) to 'unidentified flying objects' to name but a few of the more printable ones. In the mid 90s it was often difficult to navigate the net, requiring an intimate knowledge of esoteric commands such as 'ftp.nau.edu', for example, which in this particular case happens to be the address of a Northern Arizona University in the USA. However, there are now more user-friendly communications methods making use of menus in the more familiar WIMP-based environment, and one service called CompuServe provides this windows-based front end if you subscribe with them. There is a whole host of other useful utilities and tools which allow you to browse through the net without the navigational nightmares described above. A **GOPHER** is one such tool which allows you to browse with relative ease.

Internet also has many conventional uses, including the ability to send E-mail (see in a moment) via the system to anyone in the world who has an E-mail address connected to the Internet. Indeed, its recent success stems from the fact that many businesses are finding that it's cheaper to use the Internet system for electronic mail than going via some of the more conventional and established private computer networks which can be rented from the telecom companies. Thousands of local **bulletin boards** are also setting up satisfying the needs of local users in a particular locality, such as a school or a local community for example.

Major network problems

Being available to everybody with the appropriate equipment and other resources, Internet has mushroomed in size, with all the consequent problems such as censorship, and illegal transmission of material such as child pornography, or information about drugs and bombs etc. There are now facilities to encrypt information on the net (see page 605), but this only adds to the problems as illegal material can now be transmitted across the network without anybody being able to tell that it's illegal! The USA have suggested a solution to the problem whereby all data must be **encrypted** making use of keys (see page 606) available to those who are bonafide receivers, but being arranged such that members of the government will always be able to decipher any message on the net! This has obviously got huge social implications, and these are discussed in detail in chapter 26.

To get connected to the Internet you obviously need a computer, a modem (see page 500) and some communications software. You will also need access to a company or institution which provides all the connections to the international computer network. This facility is sometimes provided to schools by local universities or large businesses with the appropriate connections (pun intended!). However, companies now advertise in computer magazines which can provide suitable connection services to anyone willing to pay the subscriptions and phone bills. Such companies offer facilities such as global E-mail and FAX, Network discussion groups as outlined above, and special software to make access to the system easier.

In addition to **E-mail**, one major advantage for computer users is that it's possible to gain access to companies like Microsoft or Novell, which can then provide support via E-mail, which could include **downloading** software and patches. If you've ever tried to get Microsoft on the phone then you'll realise what a huge benefit this is!

Electronic mail

Electronic mail (or **E-Mail**) is much more than simply sending a few letters typed out on a word processor. Indeed it can form the **backbone of both internal and external communications for a company**, depending on the sophistication of the networks involved. Indeed, most network systems provide appropriate software to set up electronic-mail facilities. You can normally specify that a message to be sent is for a **single person**, or you can specify a **group of people**. Memos for the board meeting can easily be sent electronically to all members of the board – wherever they happen to be – they can easily gain access to their E-mail box with just a lap-top computer and a phone line – there is no reason why the same system could not send out the message to one of the directors via their portable fax machine (see in a moment) whilst they are travelling along in their car, for example.

The mail system works on the principle that everybody has an **electronic mail box which** is usually a file on a suitable file server, either internally within the company or externally via a system such as Internet, for example. This mail box is where the **current messages** are stored. In this way the system is exactly like real mail – you do not have to be 'in' to receive it – you just have a look at it when you feel like it. However, when you log on, your computer system can automatically bring to your attention the fact that there is some **unread mail** in your **mail box**. Indeed, many internal systems are capable of **interrupting** whatever you are doing on your computer to bring to your attention the fact that an **urgent message** has arrived. Other systems give you the facilities to **remind** you that you have **not responded to a communication** after a certain period of elapsed time. After reading the message, you are usually given the option of **discarding** or **filing** the message. You can obviously send an immediate reply if this is necessary.

One should not underestimate the potential for E-Mail systems to change the face of working and human interaction as we know it today. Thousands of people already work from home by making use of their micros, and E-Mail their work back to the 'office'. Indeed, as is explained on page 608 in the social-implications chapter, working from home is becoming an increasingly attractive proposition. With appropriate networks and small video cameras, you can have eyeball-to-eyeball communication with several people either locally, nationally, or internationally. For example, JANET, the Joint Academic NETwork used to connect universities and other institutions on a world-wide basis is being developed into what's called SuperJANET – this is a version of a computer communication network which handles data needed for research with ease. Audio, video and computer data can be sent via SuperJANET – it's a far cry from the crude text-only systems available several years ago.

Fax

Fax is short for **facsimile**. It is the method where **output from a computer** or, a **scanned document** can be sent over the **standard telephone network**, and then be **reproduced** on a **fax machine** at the receiving end of the line. The computer is not a necessary requirement to send a document by fax, but as you can appreciate, it would be a waste of time to print out the document and then get the fax machine to scan it if the computer could send out the appropriate codes that could be interpreted by the receiving fax machine. Most computers now have fax cards produced which can perform all the necessary technicalities to communicate with standard fax machines and other computers with fax cards attached. If there is a fax card at both ends of the communication medium, then no paper is involved in the process at all.

Exercise 22.1

1. Some people feel that computers have brought only limited advantages to the business community. Giving two or three different examples, outline some useful or essential tasks which would be impractical to carry out without the aid of computerised systems.

2. Outline some **advantages** that *text processing by the use of word processors and DTP systems* have given to the office of today. Are there any **disadvantages**?

3. Why are **grammar checkers** still relatively awful in comparison to the extremely powerful **spell checkers** and **thesauri**?

4. Outline the *main reasons* why DTP systems have revolutionised the printing industry. If DTP systems are so versatile, why do we still need specialist printing companies?

5. Explain how a **spreadsheet** could be used to model different scenarios of the future for a company or small business, making clear reference to 'what if' analysis in your answer.

6. Making use of a **spreadsheet** that you have at your school or college, solve the following problems.
   (a) Draw the graph $y = -3x^2 - 2x + 10$ over the range x= –5 to x = +5.
   (b) Arrange a column of names, typed in at random, into alphabetical order.
   (c) Investigate the value of the function $n/(n+1)$ for increasing values of n.

7. *If* you have a **presentation** or **charting package**, extract the data from question 6(c), and superimpose a suitable backdrop behind the graph ready for use in a presentation to young children about number patterns.

8. Explain the difference between the **videotex** and **teletext systems**.

9. Outline the advantages that a **teletext server** has on a **computer network**.

10. Outline some typical facilities provided by the IPs on a database such as Prestel.

11. The **Internet** is a vast international network of networks. What do you need to get connected to such a system, and what sort of facilities are currently being provided?

12. The **Internet** has now become so large that illegal activities are obviously taking place. Should access to such a network be restricted? If not, how can we curb the activities of criminals using the net?

End of chapter summary

- There are so many **applications** of computers that it's only possible or necessary to concentrate on the most important and most common ones.
- A **general knowledge** of *many important application areas* leads to a high level of computer literacy.
- It is *not possible* to have an appreciation of all application areas – concentrate on the important and more-common ones such as those outlined in this book.
- **Computers** *are needed* for **business data processing** due to the vast quantities of data being processed each day.
- Efficient use of **business data processing** means that companies can have information that hitherto would have been too tedious to gather and analyse by hand.
- **Word processing** is now common in most offices – it has largely replaced the mechanical and electronic typewriters.
- **Word processors** enable text to be efficiently edited, particularly with reference to the layout and the insertion and deletion of text.
- When *text is in word-processed format* it can be processed electronically in an infinite number of ways, including sending E-Mail to local or remote destinations.
- **Spell checking**, **thesauri** and **grammar checking** are now common on many word-processor systems.
- **Word processors** can now be linked to other systems such as databases, for example, so that mail-merge facilities can be carried out with ease.
- **Mail merge** is the ability to extract data from a suitable source and combine it with word-processed text to produce standard letters of the 'Reader's Digest' variety.
- *Most* word processors and DTP systems today are WYSIWYG, but some maths-typesetting packages are an exception to this rule.
- **WYSIWYG – What You See Is What You Get** – a system which makes on-screen output appear identical to that which will be produced on the printer.
- **DTP stands** for **DeskTop Publishing** – a system whereby any attribute on the printed page, including pictures, may be processed to the user's requirements.

- **DTP systems** have revolutionised the printing industry, and put great power and flexibility into the hands of the individual and small publishing companies.
- **Text** may be imported into DTP and word-processor systems from a variety of sources, including, scanner (OCR), machine-readable source documents and E-mail etc.
- **Pictures** may be imported into DTP or word-processor systems by means of scanners or video cameras, or obtained from local or international clip-art directories.
- It's becoming *increasingly difficult to tell the difference between* top-of-the-range **word processors** and **DTP systems**.
- **Colour DTP systems** are now the norm with 24-bit colour being increasingly available to give top-quality NPQ images.
- **NPQ** – Near Photographic Quality
- Most DTP and word-processor systems make use of **outline fonts** or **true-type fonts**. Thousands of different fonts and styles are available.
- A **font** is a set of characteristics for a given style of text, e.g, 9 point Times Roman.
- A **style** of text, in addition to the basic font, may have other attributes such as underlined or superscript etc.
- Some word processors and DTP systems accept **speech input**, but this form of input is still in its relative infancy, although great strides have been made.
- **Charting or graphics presentation packages** produce a huge variety of graphical output from numerical data, possibly obtained from spreadsheets or other systems.
- Together with **DTP systems** and **word processors, charting packages** help to produce the professional presentations needed by today's businesses.
- A **spreadsheet** is a tabular arrangement of rows and columns into which data can be typed to model a huge variety of scenarios such as the company business transactions, scientific investigations or mathematical models.
- **Spreadsheet** operation is based around cells which contain numerical and other data. Functions may be applied to these cells to produce other data for other cells.
- Most spreadsheets have a huge variety of functions which include most mathematical and statistical functions, date functions and database functions etc.
- Many **spreadsheets** are now starting to use the high-level language **BASIC** as the **macro language**. This is easier than using many different macro languages.
- A **macro** is a set of instructions which is usually called up by name.
- **Macros** may also be **recorded** to allow the user to carry out set sequences of operations which can be built up by using the keyboard and mouse.
- Some **spreadsheets** work in *more than two dimensions*, with up to 12 different dimensions or more available on some micro packages.
- **Spreadsheets** are useful because they can model possible scenarios of the future, and answer the all-important 'what if' type questions.
- **Spreadsheets** are just as useful for scientific and engineering applications, they are useful for mathematical simulations, for use in education and a whole variety of other situations – they are one of the most versatile computer-software packages.
- **Databases** are used extensively in most businesses, and this important business application is covered in chapter 20.
- **Videotex** and **viewdata** systems make use of the *telephone*, a *modem*, a *microcomputer*, and *communications software* to access databases such as Prestel.
- The people who provide the information on databases such as **Prestel** are called **Information Providers** or **IP**s.
- **Videotex** systems are two-way systems involving interaction with the host computer system.
- **Teletext** is the system making use of the 'unused' TV lines to broadcast information along with the TV signals – it is a one-way-only communication system.
- Some **LANs** now have **teletext servers** connected which enable all the workstations to receive teletext signals and process the data in different ways.
- The **Internet System** is **many packet-switched WANs connected by gateways** such that it acts as a large international public-service network.
- There are many **specialist user groups** on the Internet, as well as E-Mail and a whole host of other facilities. CompuServe is a typical example.
- Specialist tools such as **GOPHERS** allow you to browse through the Internet with relative ease.

- ■ **Electronic Mail** or **E-Mail** involves having a mail box on some local or remote computer onto which mail can be stored. You can then log onto the system to read and process your mail.
- ■ **E-Mail**, fax and other facilities are available internationally via systems such as Internet and Prestel.
- ■ **JANET** – The Joint Academic NETwork is a system which links all British universities.
- ■ **SuperJANET** has been developed to allow video and audio information as well as text to be transmitted. This is ideal for conducting remote research on a global basis.

23 Scientific applications

Introduction

This second major-applications' chapter concentrates on the scientific, technical and engineering applications of computers. Although the business applications considered in the last chapter have probably got a higher profile in the public's mind, due to the majority of people's contact with word processors, spreadsheets, databases, and the like, in the fields of engineering and science, computers have had just as great an impact for an even longer period of time. Don't forget that it was in these fields that computers were first used, and their use has been continuing at an unabated pace ever since. From **Computer Aided Tomography** (the **CAT** scan) used in medicine to generate three-dimensional images of the internal organs of the body, to simulation of the entire structure of the known universe, scientific and technical applications will no doubt continue to grow at an ever increasing pace.

Computer aided design (CAD)

Computer Aided Design, or, **CAD** for short, used to be taken to mean the production of technical drawings for use by engineers and architects etc. However, as we shall see later in this chapter, it is now *very much* more than this. Nevertheless, CAD has its roots in the production of technical drawings, and it is to this important sub-section of CAD that we will turn to start our journey through the powerful and wonderful design facilities that are now available to engineers in the modern industrial world.

Technical drawings

Firstly, it's important to realise the difference between the type of drawings required by a graphic designer or artist, for example, and the type of drawings required by an engineer or an architect. Most of the time a **graphic designer** or **artist** might be engaged in the *production of drawings of the sort shown in figure 23.1(a)*, whereas an **engineer** might be involved in the *production of a totally different type of drawing similar in nature to that shown in figure 23.1(b)*.

Figure 23.1(a) shows an artistic-interpretation of a car, and is the sort of diagram which gives an excellent overall impression of what the finished artefact might look like. However, we would not expect to be able to manufacture the car from such a diagram. To do this more technical operation, thousands of diagrams of the sort shown in figure 23.1(b) would be required. Such diagrams show the *exact physical dimensions*, and the *detail of where holes are to be drilled*, and *the material* out of which the component is to be made etc.

Object-oriented techniques

In general, the type of **artistic diagram** shown in figure 23.1(a) is typically based on a **pixel-based art package** (see page 566), whereas the type of diagram shown in figure 23.1(b) is typically based on a **precise mathematical description of the picture**, in which each object (such as the lines and circles etc.) is represented not by a group of pixels (dots on the screen), but by the **mathematical equation of the object itself**. This later method, ideal for technical and engineering-type diagrams is called an **object-oriented diagram**, and the package which produced it is called an **object-oriented CAD package**.

Astute readers will notice that the last paragraph started off with the words 'in general'! In computing, progress continues at an unabated pace, and diagrams of the type shown in figure 23.1(a) can indeed now be done by advanced object-oriented packages. Powerful systems now have the ability to render surfaces to make them appear to be shiny metal, wood, plastic, leather, woven material or indeed anything

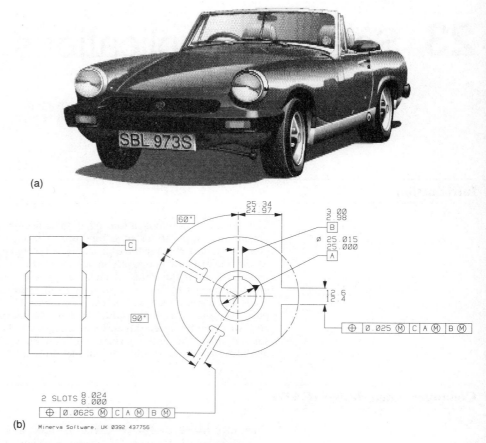

(a)

(b)   Minerva Software, UK 0392 437756

Figure 23.1

under the sun. Therefore, *at the professional end of the spectrum*, it's becoming increasingly difficult to tell just by looking at the end result which type of package has been used for the production of a particular diagram. With the increasing use of 24-bit colour (see page 242), very high resolutions and solids-rendering techniques, it's also getting impossible to tell the difference between computerised output and professional air-brushing techniques – in the 1990s, graphics packages are now this good.

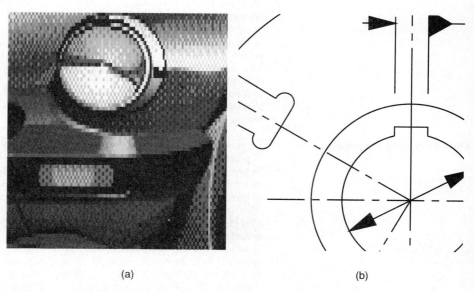

(a)   (b)

Figure 23.2

There is a *world of difference* between what can be accomplished with an image produced on a **pixel-based art package**, and the same image produced on an **object-oriented CAD package**. With a pixel-based art package, for example, zooming into a section of the diagram will reveal larger and larger pixels, as shown in figure 23.2(a). However, zoom into an object-oriented diagram, and you can observe more detail – the idea is shown in figure 23.2(b).

In this section, from this point onwards, we will concentrate entirely on object-oriented CAD techniques, and investigate the tremendous potential for the complete integration of the design and manufacturing processes.

Being able to zoom into the diagram to see more detail is particularly useful, because an engineer can build up infinitely-complex diagrams that would be too detailed to commit to a single sheet of paper. A good example here would be the city maps used by the services and utilities departments of large city corporations. For example, it's possible to have the water, electricity, gas, telephones, cable TV and the like all mapped out in different colours on the same diagram for a city the size of Birmingham, if necessary. The engineer may then call up a utility such as sewage, and zoom into a particular street to see how the storm-drain system is connected to a particular house. The equivalent system without using an object-oriented CAD package would be to make use of tens of thousands of diagrams in which each street and house in the city would all be mapped out on different pieces of paper. Any alterations to a major system would need many diagrams to be altered, but with an object-oriented CAD package, one change carried out in a few minutes would instantly update all information. This means that any zoomed-in image is automatically updated too.

There are many **other advantages** to **object-oriented CAD** which are not too obvious unless you have made extensive use of such systems. For example, if you have put all the dimensions onto a diagram, then suddenly decide to reposition a critical part in relation to others, the computer can automatically recalculate the dimension so that by the time you have moved the object, the new-position dimensions are correct – try doing this manually, and you would probably spend a few hours cursing whoever decided to move the object!

As all the objects are defined mathematically, this gives us **the ability to perform mathematical operations on the objects**. For example, if we wish to calculate the area or volume of an object – then this is no problem. Similarly if we know the volume of material and the price/unit volume, then the CAD package can calculate the materials cost of the component being manufactured – it could then be linked directly to a **database system** which holds information regarding suppliers of the appropriate materials. As all the data regarding every attribute of the component is held in the CAD package, this data can be sent to **CNC machines** (see page 545) or automatically used to give instructions to the robots to manufacture the product – object-oriented CAD systems are already this powerful, and it's even possible to carry out these operations in the technology department of many colleges and some schools – in fact, manufacturing industry has been doing just this for very many years.

Object-oriented CAD packages are ideally suited to processing complex pictures with little memory used for storing the actual picture. However, there are disadvantages in that a **lot of mathematical processing** has to be undertaken to re-draw the picture from a different view. This is why powerful workstations or powerful microcomputers with **maths co-processors** are often used. (A maths co-processor is a special chip that is used for number crunching, i.e. intensive numerical computations). It performs the maths by using hardware which, in general, is much faster than the equivalent software algorithms doing the same job. Indeed if you are thinking of buying a CAD package such as AutoCAD 13, then it's often the case that you will need a maths co-processor, and a 'top-of-the-range graphics interface card' and a decent **hi-res multisync monitor** (see page 243) for the application to work satisfactorily.

Some CAD facilities

In the next few sections we briefly list just a few of the features that are common on many CAD packages. You should note that it takes hundreds of hours to learn how to use these packages to the full, and the instructions manuals, often several thousand pages long bear witness to the complexity and versatility of such systems.

A creative design tool

Engineers and designers make extensive use of drawings to visualise their ideas. It is often tedious and time consuming to hand draw different ideas to see if they would work. By making use of a CAD package, it's usually possible to check out an idea more quickly. You can get the computer to check out the dimensions to see if it is physically possible to manufacture. You are also more likely to experiment if changes can be made at the flick of a switch. This aids the creative process and usually means that people are more likely to experiment until near perfection is reached.

On some of the CAD systems still under development, it's possible to interface the computer to a machine that actually manufactures a 3D physical model of the design in the computer! This is done by making use of special materials which are scanned by laser beams. After much processing, the 3D model can be extracted from the machine. This gives the engineer or artist a much better idea of what the component or model looks like. It is very much quicker than manufacturing a prototype by hand.

Accuracy

It should be obvious that the **CAD software** and computer, together with the **associated peripherals** such as **plotters** or **laser printers**, can produce *more accurate drawings* than by using a hand drafting method (i.e. making use of a ruler and pencil). Indeed many CAD systems offer facilities such as automatic dimensioning. This is a tedious and error-prone task if carried out manually. If the computer deals with all the dimensions, then it is a relatively easy task to get the CAD package to work out all the statistics automatically. Other associated parameters can then be obtained from these figures.

Editing

If you have ever attempted any really complicated technical drawing, then you will readily appreciate an application which allows you to make many changes without leaving marks on the paper where you have been continuously rubbing out. Even so, you would be even more impressed with the other, more advanced facilities.

Powerful editing features are usually provided which enable you to change one or more parts of the drawing. Of particular use is the system which allows the generation of similar objects in different parts of the main drawing. If one of these parts needs altering, then you can instruct the computer to change all the other parts as well if necessary.

Libraries of parts

When an architect designs a house they are usually making use of an extensive range of parts such as windows and doors etc. Most of these parts are standard and it would seem a waste of time to have to draw them from scratch. Most CAD packages allow the use of extra **libraries**. With an architect's library loaded, this would enable the designer of a house to position the appropriate components in place on the drawing of a building. The same ideas are also used for electronic components in the electronics industry and many others.

Repetitive tasks

There is often the need to draw many **similar shapes** or parts on a diagram. For example, you may be drawing a diagram which represents 100 pigeon holes which will be used as a storage system. You could also instruct the CAD system to automatically insert numbers 1 to 100 in the appropriate place in each pigeon hole. Indeed, you would use the same type of system to generate the 100 pigeon holes in the first place. Processes such as these are unbelievably tedious if carried out by hand.

Integration with other systems

Suppose that you're producing a mechanical drawing of an engine. It's obvious that this consists of many different parts. Indeed there would almost certainly be many people working on different parts of the engine at the same time, and CAD makes an ideal base from which to join all their work.

It's usually a requirement to have a parts list generated. This is simply a list of parts that go into making a particular component such as an engine. Each of these parts would probably have a number that is used to uniquely identify it. Many of the parts would be brought in from other factories to be assembled at the factory which is making the engine. Each part would therefore have to be ordered, and the part-number information which is used in the CAD package can be sent off to a **database** (see chapter 20) that deals with the ordering of the components required.

Each part would have an associated cost, and this information, (gained from the part number), can be used to generate statistics from a financial package. Even the ordering can be done automatically. If the stock control system decides that stocks of certain part numbers are running low, then the goods can be ordered automatically from the warehouse. Any paperwork needed (what's that!) can then be produced from the database and printed out making use of a report facility.

Indeed some high-tech companies now operate a totally integrated system as described above. They do not carry much stock, and order the components as and when necessary. This saves much money because you don't have expensive warehouse systems tied up in storing a vast stock. If the suppliers are geared up with the same sort of systems, then, by using networks for the interconnection, the computer in the manufacturing company can order direct from the computer in the supplier's company.

Such extensive systems are in use today. The **CAD package** contains much of the information that is needed to start off the incredible chain of events that go into the manufacture of some products. If all these processes were carried out by hand, then you would need an army of people to perform these tasks. The time between the perceived need for a component and its actual ordering would often take days or weeks. By making use of extensive computerisation, this is often reduced to minutes. Managers are also in a position to have an instant analysis about the state of any job being done within the company.

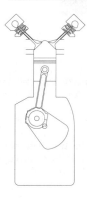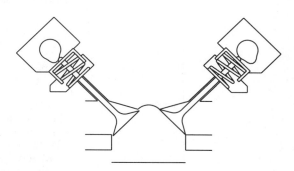

Figure 23.3

Parametric CAD packages

Some **CAD packages** allow you to define relationships **parametrically**. This means that special parameters are used which show the relationship between one part of the diagram and another. One example of a parametric CAD package has been created by Oak Computers, and a typical example is shown in figure 23.3. Here a two-cylinder internal combustion engine is simulated.

All the geometric relationships between the various parts of the diagram have been established making use of the parametric CAD software, and when the parts of the diagram have been drawn in the appropriate place, amazing relationships then exist – you have the ability to generate different positions of the mechanism by specifying different angles, i.e. by varying the parameters. If you create several appropriate pictures, you can build up a movie of the mechanical linkage. Yes, it really moves! Indeed, with enough time and practice, complete **animation sequences** can be generated. This gives you a powerful ability to visualise moving parts on the computer screen before they are actually built. It is also a great aid in educational institutions where mechanics and physics are taught.

The user interface

The **human computer interface** or **HCI** is of particular importance when considering applications. Just as the mouse has revolutionised the **WIMP environment**, so the puck and graphics tablet makes data entry into a CAD package much simpler.

Figure 23.4

Figure 23.5

A typical **CAD package template** for use on a digitiser tablet is shown in figure 23.4. It is the template that is used with the Autocad package made by Autodesk Inc.

Various settings can be chosen by placing the cursor on the puck over the appropriate position on the template and pressing one of the buttons. The buttons are similar to a mouse, but, due to the construction of the graphics tablet (see page 223), the cross-hair cursor keeps its relative position even if the puck is removed completely from the tablet and then replaced. Some superb effects are now possible making use of sophisticated CAD processes, and an example of a wire frame image can be seen in figure 23.5.

Mini, micro or mainframe?

Most of the facilities shown above are available on **powerful microcomputer systems**. However, some very advanced facilities, such as the **3D modelling system** mentioned earlier could only be achieved by using powerful **mini** or **mainframe computers** as mainframe and mini computers obviously offer more facilities than even the most powerful micro. Such facilities would include the ability to multitask with very complex drawings (i.e. carry out more than one task at the same time). This is useful if you wish to display several drawings on the screen at the same time. This may sound extravagant, but is often useful if you wish to edit one drawing whilst looking at part of another. They also offer advantages in terms of **great speed**, especially when complex 3D modelling is required. However the popularity of CAD packages has really taken off with the advent of the powerful micros.

Disadvantages of CAD

CAD was never designed for the initial doodles that help to form concepts in people's minds. It can't replace the ease of use and convenience of a pencil and paper for the early stages. It was also not designed for a simple one-off diagram. The following scenario is only too typical.

Sometimes people are so impressed with CAD that they go overboard in using it to do things that can often be done better in other ways. This is, unfortunately, a particular problem with students at school and college. They will often spend a long time learning about a particular CAD package merely to include some fancy diagrams in their project reports. Often it is done in a hurry because the reports are due to be handed in, and mistakes are therefore made. This leads to a high degree of frustration and discontent with the application being used. Another student may have produced an acceptably neat diagram in five minutes by making use of pencil and paper! The obvious solution to this particular problem is to use a simpler CAD package and leave enough time to do the diagrams properly. (See chapter 28 on writing up your projects.)

Top-of-the-range CAD packages usually take hundreds of hours to learn to use properly. There is a large investment both in terms of hardware and time. It would be silly not to make extensive use of the system after such training and commitment. If this is not the case, then a CAD system is probably not needed.

Computer aided manufacture (CAM)

Computer Aided Manufacturing, or **CAM** as it is known is the entire process of getting computers to aid many or all of the stages in a production process. It is done

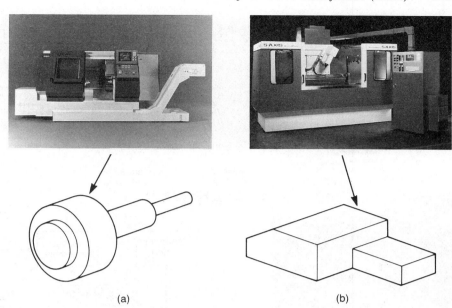

Figure 23.6

Figure 23.7

by using a variety of **Numerically Controlled (NC)** machine tools, or **Computer Numerical Control (CNC)** and **robots.** (See page 549.)

Typical machines used in the manufacturing industry would be **lathes** – to turn materials into components such as those shown in figure 23.6(a), **milling machines** – to produce components like those shown in figure 23.6(b), **drilling machines** – to drill the holes, and a whole host of other more specialist equipment. For example, there might be a specialist robot that inserts the electronic components into a printed circuit board, and this is shown in the detailed example that follows.

Traditionally, these machines were controlled by operators (people) who would carefully wind the knobs and dials on the machines so that the right amount of metal was cut off, or the right size drill was inserted into the machine so that the appropriate hole could be drilled in the component. Although a great deal of skill was needed to operate these machines, the processes were essentially 'many simple steps performed one after the other'. This is especially true for the repetitive tasks on the production line when thousands of the same type of objects were to be manufactured in the same batch.

As long ago as the 1950s, it was realised that groups of numbers could be used to give the machines instructions. It was identical in principle to machine code (see page 70) used for computers. In the early days, paper tape (a long reel of paper with holes punched into it) was used to control these machines, but now, they are more likely to have special computers **embedded** into the system (see page 547 for an explanation of **embedded systems**). The name '**numerical control**' is, therefore, derived from the fact that **machine-code type numbers** are used to **control the machines**. Instead of the operators winding the knobs, electric motors would be controlled by making use of special computer interfaces (see page 573).

A typical numerically-controlled machine is shown in figure 23.7.

These machines may be used in stand-alone mode, i.e. by themselves, or, more usefully, be integrated with other computer systems to produce what is known as **CAD/CAM**. (See in a moment.) If a machine is used by itself, then, just as assembly languages and high level languages (see page 103) have been developed to make machine code programs easier to write on computers, special assembly languages would be used on the machines to help the operators more easily describe what is necessary to manufacture and assemble the components. (This gives a whole new meaning to assembly language!)

CAD/CAM techniques

It's a natural consequence of computerisation that, if the **data** for a component's manufacture exists in a **CAD package**, and if the machine that produces or assembles the components can be controlled by **machine code**, then all you have to do is to *translate the numbers from one system to the other*, and then you have an **integrated design and manufacturing base**.

Circuit

Circuit
design

Circuit
analysis

PCB
design

BRIGHT
IDEA!

Engineer

Finished
product

Centralized
database

CNC
drill

Artwork

Computer
testing

Robot
assembly

Drilling
process

Chemical
processing
of boards

Soldering

Electronic
components

Figure 23.9

Figure 23.8

In some factories it's literally possible for the designer to produce all the information which can control an automated factory. A typical example can be found in the electronics industry. Here it can be taken several stages further and figure 23.8 shows a diagram of some of the typical processes that might be involved.

The initial concepts

The designers of a particular system would be given a specification for some particular electronic process. They would then apply their knowledge to designing an appropriate circuit. Note that for very advanced systems, an **expert system** (see page 557) may be used to help or even completely carry out this initial design process.

Computer aided design of circuit

The designer converts his or her designs into an electronic circuit and, with the aid of a computer, draws the circuit. The next stage might be to get a special **Electronic Circuit Analysis Program** to run tests on the circuit to see if it performs to specification. It's possible, by holding theoretical models inside the computer of each component used in the circuit, to *predict exactly what effect the overall design will have before any prototypes have been built*. Such techniques are extensively used in the aircraft industry, where planes now take to the air on computer simulation alone. It's no longer necessary to build up an expensive mechanical mock up to see if the beast will fly.

Computer aided design of PCB

Information about each component (e.g. its physical size, what legs of the chips have to be connected where etc) is already held in the computer system. As the electrical connections are already known from the circuit diagram, then it's a relatively easy matter to get a different computer package to design the **Printed Circuit Board (PCB) layout**. Sophisticated systems can now cope with up to 27 different layers of copper track used to connect up all the chips. Get your teacher to show you a modern printed circuit board if you have not seen one before, you will then appreciate what's happening in great detail.

Production of the artwork

Artwork for the production run of the **PCBs** is produced by getting the PCB design system to plot out the appropriate pattern. This can then be fed into the machines so that the physical boards containing the copper tracks are produced.

A **numerically-controlled drilling machine** can get data from the **PCB layout** so that all the appropriate holes to put the wires through are drilled in each board.

Computer-controlled drilling

A special **robot**, see figure 23.9, is next used to place the appropriate components onto the PCB. The components are then ready to be soldered on by the next process.

Flow soldering	This stage involves all the components being soldered onto the board by automatically passing the board over a flow solder bath.
Computerised testing	A **numerically-controlled testing machine** can now be used to perform hundreds of measurements on the completed system to ensure that the original specification is met.
Other links to the CAD/CAM process	There are other spin-offs which may not be immediately obvious from reading the above. For example, a components and parts list could be automatically generated from the initial design on the computer. This list could be used, together with the potential orders to automatically generate the orders for the parts required. This could then be tied up with the stock control systems. There is no reason why a **database system** similar to that described on page 476 could not be used as the *main hub of the organisation* of which these **CAD/CAM** methods form a part. A natural extension to this would then be the extensive use of national and international networks to connect the company with its subsidiaries and component suppliers.

Data logging and control

There are many instances where a **computer system** could be used to *monitor and log data automatically*, and to control extra peripheral equipment attached to the computer. However, the range of this type of application is vast, and would include, for example, weather monitoring stations, pollution monitoring systems and grabbing data with great speed from the results of scientific experiments. **Due to the enormous importance of this topic in today's modern industrialised society chapter 25 has been entirely devoted to it.** Nevertheless, we will take a brief look at the importance of embedded-system technology in the domestic environment in the next section, due to its importance as a technical application of computing.

Applications using embedded systems

An **embedded system** is a system which is dedicated to one specific task. Examples of embedded systems are shown in figure 23.10, and further examples can be found in chapter 25.

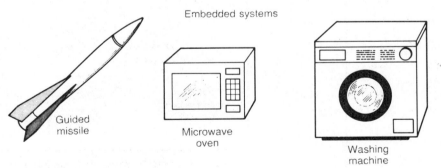

Embedded systems

Guided missile

Microwave oven

Washing machine

Figure 23.10

Here you can see a missile guidance system, a microwave oven and a washing machine. What all these systems have in common is that one or more microprocessors have been hard wired to do a very specific task. Hard wired simply means that the systems have been wired such that (unlike a normal computer system), they can't be reprogrammed to be used with anything else. The programs would probably be stored in **ROM**, and there would be a range of associated input and output chips to *control* a wide variety of dedicated **peripheral devices**.

A microwave oven example	To understand **embedded systems** more clearly we will use the **microwave oven** as an example. We can start off by making a list of what a typical microwave oven might reasonably be expected to do, some of which is shown in figure 23.11.

Typical microwave oven control features

● *Monitor key presses on the oven's control panel.*
● *Control the display that lets the user know what's happening.*
● *Adjust the power levels to the microwave transmitter.*
(Or adjust the length of time for which it is switched on.)
● *Control the safety features,i.e.*
(a) Make sure that the door can't be opened at the wrong times.
(b) Make sure that the inside of the oven does not overheat, thus causing a fire hazard.
● *Turn the table at the appropriate speed*
(Or adjust the direction of microwaves.)
● *Operate the bell which calls the attention of the cook when the food is done.*
                  etc.

Figure 23.11

It's obvious that we could program a microcomputer to do all of these things, but this would be very inefficient. For example, you would not make use of the full ASCII keyboard, nor would you want a disk drive or a full colour monitor! An embedded microprocessor system is, therefore, a microprocessor system which has the minimum of peripherals and support chips to do the job in hand in the most efficient and cost effective way. In the case of a missile, or a machine in an intensive care unit in a hospital ward, then reliability might override the cost-effective part of the system. For example, in an aircraft, there may be much redundancy built into the microprocessor systems so that, in the event of one system failing, the others could take control without catastrophic results.

A block diagram for the inside of the microwave oven system might look like that shown in figure 23.12.

A simple microwave-oven example

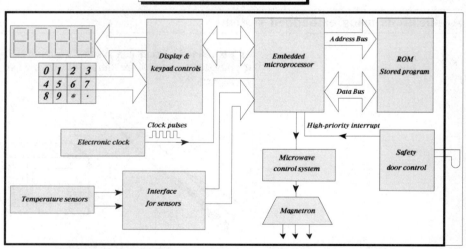

Figure 23.12

On power up, there would probably be a ROM-based program which is run that puts the microwave oven into a sensible mode. This might mean that the display would flash zeros indicating that the correct time has not yet been set. The system might also be expecting an input from the key pad before it allows you to cook any food.

Consultation with the manual might show that, once you have entered the correct time, and pushed the appropriate 'enter' button, then the display will stop flashing and display the correct time. The embedded system may then be put into a mode which is expecting the cooking instructions. This could be in the form of a power level from one to ten, followed by the time for which the food is meant to be cooked.

After a sensible combination of key presses, and assuming that the door is closed, the microwave system will be activated. During the cooking process both the time and temperature would be monitored so that the system can be automatically switched off at the appropriate time. The power level would also be continuously monitored so that it corresponds to the correct setting at the start of the cooking time. In addition to the above, a special switch on the front of the oven might cause the processor to be interrupted so that the cooking session can be suspended, or the door allowed to be opened to inspect the 'cordon-bleu' meal.

General principles

As you can see from the above, an **embedded system** is a (usually) **microprocessor-based system** that is *placed within* **dedicated consumer electronics devices** such as **video recorders** and **cameras,** in *domestic equipment* such as **cookers**, in *military equipment*, *specialised scientific equipment* and many other areas. In fact an embedded system can be found anywhere where set tasks have to be carried out automatically, or equipment has to be controlled.

Industrial robotics

Industrial robotics as a science is a far cry from the *sci-fi images* portrayed in books and some of the popular press, which unfortunately tend to have views more akin with the robot cartoons as used in this book! However, the early application of industrial robots stems from an extension of the numerically-controlled machine tools still found in operation today. As we have seen in this chapter, these **CNC (or Computer Numerical Control)** machines are devices such as drills, milling machines and lathes etc. and can be observed carrying out automated processes in many modern industrialised plants. It was the automobile industry, where these automation processes were proceeding at an unprecedented pace, which acted as a spur for the development of these specialised robots. They were often seen manufacturing a particular part of a car component, helping with the work on the assembly line or spraying paint onto the cars. Parts also had to be moved from one process to another, and a mechanical arm similar to that shown in figure 23.13 was ideal for this purpose. You should note at this stage that the detailed interfacing of these robotic devices is considered in chapter 25 where computer-controlled systems are considered in much more·detail – in this chapter we are concerned more with the effects and use of this particular scientific application of computers.

(a)

Figure 23.13

Interestingly enough, the distribution of robots throughout the world is certainly not uniform. For example, at the time of writing, Japan has somewhere in the region of just over half a million robots working in industry, but the USA, the next-largest user of robotics, has only about 100,000 – just 20% of the number being used in Japan! The UK comes a long way behind Germany and some other industrialised countries, with the car and electronics industries leading the way. These trends tend to reflect political and other issues in addition to reasons of a more technical nature. For example, in the Far East, where many workers tend to have jobs for life, robots, even the non-human looking ones, are viewed as having their own personalities and being a 'friendly help' in the work place. In the industrialised West, they are often viewed as a threat to job security.

At present, **robots** tend to be able to do **very specific tasks** *very well*. For example, a robot such as that shown in figure 23.14(a) represents the heavy high-power end

(a)   (b)

Figure 23.14

of the market. It has been designed specifically for lifting huge weights – a task that hitherto would have needed a human in conjunction with a crane. At the other end of the spectrum, personal robots such as that shown in figure 23.14(b) have appeared on the market. This is more like the image that the public has of a robot, but unfortunately, the technology to implement all the expectations from such a 'human-looking' machine is not at a sufficient stage of development. Nevertheless, researchers in Japan are actively working on domestic robot technology which will literally be able to do the cleaning around the house. However, don't hold your breath waiting, they are unlikely to be ready for retail purchase until the middle of the next century. In between the heavy and light end of the market are a wide variety of applications which include remote-controlled robots such as those used to deal with bombs, automatic vehicles such as those found moving stores from one part of the factory to another, medical applications such as artificial limbs, robots able to perform hip replacements, educational robots and many others.

Robot technology revealed

At the heart of most of these **robotics-based systems** is usually one or more dedicated **microprocessor-based computer control systems** as explained in great detail in chapter 25, but for the purposes of this chapter, the main sub-systems of a robot can be thought of as follows.

- Systems of movement
- Sensors
- Control systems
- Interfacing

Systems of movement

Most **robot arms** have associated with them what are called **degrees of freedom**. This is simply the name given to each **axis of movement**. One common system uses six degrees of freedom (ways of moving) as shown in figure 23.15 The movements of each axis may be controlled by **electric motors, hydraulics** (oil-based systems) or **pneumatics** (air-based systems). Whichever system of movement is used, the movements can be initiated by sending the correct digital information from the command computer to the interfacing electronic systems.

Robots may operate in what is called **open-loop mode** or, more likely, **closed loop mode** (see chapter 25 section on **feedback**). This is simply the way in which the **feedback systems** that control the system of movements operate. If, for example, the robot is working in open loop mode, then no check is made on the actual position of its arms. Let's suppose that the computer instructs the robot's wrist to move to the 3D-coordinate (234, 076, 512), then it will assume that, after the execution of this command and a suitable time delay, the wrist will take up this new position – irrespective of what actually happens e.g. something may be in the way and the arm could be physically obstructed. However, when in **closed loop mode**, a system of

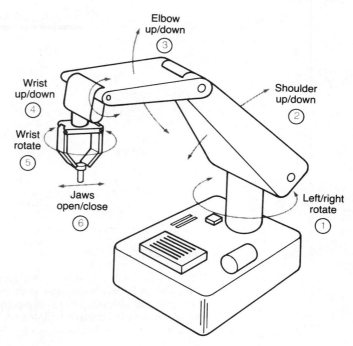

Elbow
up/down
③

Wrist
up/down
④

Shoulder
up/down
②

Wrist
rotate
⑤

Jaws
open/close
⑥

Left/right
rotate
①

Figure 23.15

feedback *is* used. This involves **sensors** (see in a moment) being placed at strategic points on the robot, which then feed back electrical signals to the computer which indicate the exact position of the robot. These signals are usually compared with the desired position and action is taken by the computer until the desired and actual positions of the robot are the same, otherwise an error condition is **flagged** indicating that it's not possible to obey this particular command. Other sensors can also stop the robot if they detect that something is wrong such as an object being in the way. This is the technique that is used, for example, when robots move goods around on the factory floor. Feedback sensors would sense if the robot has bumped into anything and, if a collision is detected, the systems will be shut down and an alarm may ring.

Sensors

Much of what a robot can do depends not only on its ability to move efficiently, but also on its ability to sense the environment. Sensors may range from a simple microswitch that can be activated if the robot bumps into something, to complex sound and vision analysis undertaken in conjunction with powerful mainframe computers. Many different types of sensors are covered in chapter 25, but here we will take a very brief look at some of the ways in which a robot can simulate the human senses. You must also not forget that robots fitted with appropriate sensors can have more than the five (six?) human senses, because quantities such as *magnetism*, *radiation* and many others can be sensed by appropriate electronic devices.

Touch

There are electrical components called **strain gauges** which can respond to small changes in pressure – actually they respond to bending, and hence to a change in shape, but the result is the same. The resistance of a strain gauge changes when pressure is applied to it. This resistance change can be converted into an analogue voltage and fed via an **A to D converter** (see page 577) before being analysed by a digital computer. Sensitivities of these systems are such that they may deal with weights of just a few grams or many tonnes.

If the robot has many sensors such as those described above, then it can perform quite delicate operations without damaging fragile components – it's possible, for example, for a robot to pick up an egg without cracking it. Indeed one of the more amusing applications of robotics is the automatic sheep-shearing machine developed by the Australian Wool Corporation. Touch sensors prevent the sheep from having too close a shave! – this remarkable device is shown in figure 23.16.

Figure 23.16

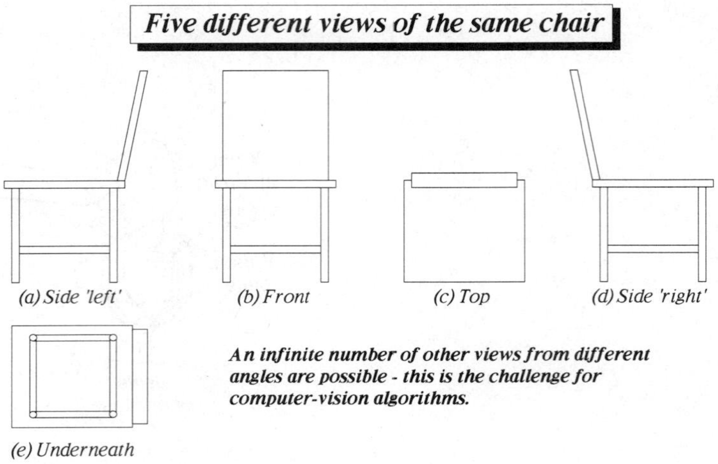

Five different views of the same chair

(a) Side 'left'   (b) Front   (c) Top   (d) Side 'right'

An infinite number of other views from different angles are possible - this is the challenge for computer-vision algorithms.

(e) Underneath

Figure 23.17

Sight

The ability to see is one of the greatest assets possessed by a human being, and although it is relatively easy to make a **robot see**, (i.e. connect a **video camera** to it), it is the **analysis of the complex images** produced that is *the* major stumbling block. A simple example will demonstrate just some of the problems involved. Let's assume that the robot observes a simple 'chair' as shown by the first view in figure 23.17(a).

Now programming the computer to recognise the image in figure 23.17(a) is reasonably simple, and should be within the grasp of an 'A' Level student, for example, but even the *same chair* can present an infinite variety of different shapes to the camera – different possibilities are shown in figures 23.17(b) to 23.17(e). There are, however, an infinite number of different viewing positions – add to this the fact that an infinite number of different backgrounds are also possible, and you should now start to see the enormity of the task facing the image-analysis software.

At present it *is* possible for **mainframe computers** to do simple versions of such image analysis, but it will be some time before enough computing power and speed can be packed into a micro, even when more efficient algorithms become available. The 64-bit micros now available would be a minimum requirement, and even these would need the addition of some **maths co-processors**, and, preferably many **transputers** to perform the complex analysis. Therefore, at present we must be content with a different perception of what is meant by 'robot vision', and be content with the robot detecting movement, colour and easy shapes or shapes from familiar angles, i.e. simple pattern recognition compared to human visual analysis. Nevertheless, these pattern-recognition robots have been developed with some success, and are able to sort out different-shaped objects on production lines – and **neural-network technology** (see page 555) is also bearing fruit.

It does not need too much of an advance for pattern recognition software to have very many commercial applications. Reading typed or handwritten text, the ability to analyse weather patterns from satellite pictures, analysis of radar and sonar patterns in the military, and detection of cancerous cells under a microscope are good examples of commercially-lucrative markets in which pattern recognition software is already being used.

Speech

Speech can be divided into two sections: first the **production of speech**, and second, the infinitely more complex task of **interpreting human speech** to initiate some desired course of action. More information on computer speech can be found in the input and output peripherals chapters 11 and 12.

Speech production

Speech production can itself be divided into subsections, according to whether the human voice has been recorded in any form for the computer to use, or whether a speech sound has been generated by using digital patterns within the computer. The first method involves digitising a **prerecorded human voice**, and storing the sound as a digital pattern within the computer. Using this method the vocabulary is limited to the number of pre-recorded words. The second method is more flexible, and relies on what are called **phonemes**. This is simply the name given to all the sounds that go to make up a particular language. Any word can be built up by joining the phonemes together. However, the speech does sound slightly unusual if this method is used, and much progress still needs to be made if we are to get away from the awful sounding and obviously artificial machine-generated voice.

Another problem with computer speech is the way in which the words are used – without the natural feeling that would be put into them when spoken by a human, the robot's speech tends to be a little monotonous – the feelings of frustration, excitement and nervousness, for example, all add to our experience of what speech ought to be like in different situations.

Speech recognition

Speech recognition suffers from similar, (but far easier to solve) problems to those of robot vision. The problems here are the endless **variety of sounds** that can be produced by different people even when speaking the same word. Also, *the same word spoken by the same person may not sound the same* – for example, they may have a cold. However, these variations do not present an insurmountable problem, and much work has gone into computer analysis of the 'spoken word' with a reasonable degree of success.

Most systems have to 'learn' the words that may be said before being used in earnest. This usually involves the people who are going to speak to the system sitting down with the computer and speaking the words into the machine. Each word is usually spoken several times and a mathematical model of each word is then stored inside the computer's memory.

When the computer is ready to be used, after a word has been spoken, it will compare the mathematical analysis of the spoken word with the models that it has inside its memory. When the best match has been found, (determined by the closest correlation), then the computer will choose the word that it 'thinks' you have said.

There are major problems still to be overcome – for example, there are many words that sound very similar, e.g. dog, fog and log etc will be very difficult to distinguish using these techniques. These problems will obviously not be solved until they can be combined with powerful real-time context-sensitive grammatical analysis of the spoken word – this is still some way off, but great progress has been made in this area and limited vocabulary context sensitive speech analysis systems are now available with an acceptable speed of operation for some applications.

Smell

Smell, in a limited sense, *is* being used by robots in industry today. These applications are usually connected with the detection of gas leaks, and indeed robots are boldly going where no robot has gone before, in an attempt to sniff out leaks in hostile environments. Special sensors are all that is needed, but **real-time chemical analysis**, needed for more advanced smell-type systems, is not yet possible. Nevertheless, chemical analysis by smell is being used with great effect in some applications (see page 237).

Taste

There are four basic types of taste – namely **sweet**, **sour**, **salty** and **acidic**. Some of these are easier to deal with than the others. Currently under development, are what are called biosensors. For example, at Imperial College, London, some biotechnologists have introduced the idea that computers can taste and smell. Indeed, this is not so far fetched as it may seem. For example, salt can be measured by electrical conductivity, and acidity can be measured easily using a pH meter. In several years time we may see robots developed to give their opinion of the Beaujolais Nouveau, and computers *are* already being used to determine the quality of various Champagnes.

Other sensing devices

There are many other sensing devices which can be connected to robots to detect heat, magnetic fields, radiation, ionisation etc. When the technology has been developed over the next few decades, robots will be able to detect many more changes in their environments than an unaided human (i.e. a human just relying on their own senses).

Control systems

At the heart of any robot system is the computer which is used to control it, and the specialised interfaces that are used to connect the robot with the ports on the computer. However, these important concepts are covered separately in chapter 25 when computer control is considered in detail.

Nano technology

No section on robots would be complete without a brief mention of **nano technology**. Nano technology derives its name from the fact that devices are built up on a **nano-meter scale, i.e. 1×10^{-9} m**! Unbelievable though it may sound, small devices, including motors and gears, have been designed and developed at this very small scale. This opens up possibilities for sending robots inside restricted areas such as the human body, for example – imagine a robot which is able to move along inside your veins and cut away the cholesterol! Such robots are indeed being developed, although there are many problems, most noticeably, and not surprisingly with the materials. For example, in 1995, the nano-technology gear wheels are so small that they wear out in a matter of seconds!

If and when advances in nano technology can be made, then much invasive surgery may become a thing of the past – computer controlled robots might be able to be injected into the blood stream and carry out various operations. Other applications for this technology are just as astounding.

Artificial intelligence (AI)

After taking a very brief look at some of the possibilities that robotics can achieve, it is worthwhile considering one of the sciences that is closely linked with robotics – that of **Artificial Intelligence** or **AI**. Indeed, AI is so closely linked that robotics itself is often classified as part of AI.

In determining whether or not a machine can think we are usually walking on 'thin ice', and expect to get much flak from non-scientists and philosophers. An excellent example of this type of philosophy is called Tesler's law which defines artificial intelligence in a way which ensures that machines will never be able to think – no matter what properties they might eventually exhibit. Tesler's law states:

'Artificial intelligence is that which machines cannot do.'

However, I think that this law might be more usefully modified to read:

'Artificial intelligence is that which machines are not very good at – YET!'

If we are to investigate whether a machine can exhibit intelligence, then we must first agree on a set of conditions about what is meant when intelligence is exhibited, and this is obviously not easy, and perhaps even impossible. It might be argued that activities such as 'learning', 'inference', 'understanding natural language', 'visual perception' etc. are all things that would obviously require intelligence if carried out by a human being. This fascinating topic is also explored at the end of the social implications chapter 26, where work carried out by Professor Roger Penrose is looked at in a little more detail. However, here we will concentrate on the scientific application of AI.

Master chef?

In the past we have all been used to the idea that it is people who are in control, and most adults have grown up with the idea that machines are simply an extension of man's muscle – but *not* an extension of his thought processes, i.e. it's the people who do the thinking and it's they who control the machines. However, consider an interesting example regarding the preparation of a gourmet meal – if a chef creates a masterpiece of culinary delight by putting in just the right ingredients, and then cooking the dish to perfection, we would not say that the oven or the cooking utensils etc. have created the dish! It was obviously the intelligence, skill and manual dexterity of the chef. But the chef was probably following a precise set of instructions that were laid down by the person who originally created the recipe. Suppose now that a robot does the cooking, using suitable microprocessor-controlled equipment. If the results turn out just the same – what has exhibited the intelligence, skill and manual dexterity this time? The machine? Surely not! – it must have been the original creator of the recipe. Do we therefore give no credit to the cook as we obviously did in the first part of this example? In the second case it was definitely a machine that did the cooking. If cooking requires any intelligence at all, then the machine must possess at least enough of it to do this particular task, or we must conclude that cooking requires no intelligence. Perhaps we are back to Tesler's law which implies that people need intelligence to do particular tasks, but machines carrying out identical tasks have no intelligence.

Artificial learning

AI is concentrating on one of the most exciting areas of software development. In the past it was usual to supply the computer with a predetermined task, and then program it with a set of specific instructions on how that task was to be performed. Imagine instead, that the computer can be programmed in such a way that it can learn and reason. If it is now given a specific task, then the system constructs the algorithm whereby this particular task can be accomplished.

Does the above example mean that the computer is going through a set of thought processes? In a limited sense this must obviously be true, for the computer must analyse the task such that it decides on one set of actions rather than another in a totally logical and non-random way. It must decide on the possible outcome if it instigates a certain set of actions. If it does not know the outcome of such actions, then it must learn by performing these actions and analysing the result. In this way, the computer *is* learning in a very similar way to that in which a child learns. Indeed, some of the research is getting so sophisticated that the computer models are actually helping us to understand the ways in which children learn and better ways of teaching may therefore be devised.

A typical example of the way in which computers can learn from experience is the way in which some chess programs get better the more games are played. It is literally a case of remembering things like 'If I make that mistake again then the consequences will be that I will lose, therefore, if there is an alternative, I will make that move, if not, I will concede the game and analyse any previous moves that caused me to get into this situation.' This is learning by experience in the true sense of the word. The physical processes that are going on inside the machine and the human may be entirely different, but they are both achieving exactly the same end result.

In 1990, Anatoly Karpov was beaten by a computer chess program. This was the first time that a grand master had been beaten by a machine. Computers do have an advantage over humans in that they have an infinitely larger memory capacity, and the ability to correlate related facts in seconds, i.e. no such bad luck as the 'I've got it on the tip of my tongue but can't quite remember what is was' syndrome. It is possible that computers will eventually exceed man in what we currently think of as intelligence and logical thought, but this is indeed a long way off, and some people think that it may never be achieved.

As advanced-level students you should be very open minded about the whole issue, and realise that today's computers and algorithms are indeed a long way from achieving anything like the thought processes that can be achieved by human beings. However, you should also realise that much progress has been made, and appreciate that human beings have taken several million years to evolve into what they are today – computers have been evolving for just over 50 years – a sobering thought! Although you may be polarised one way or the other on philosophical or religious grounds, don't forget that the frontiers of science are being continually pushed forward, and many things which in the past have been thought of as totally impossible have become probable.

Neural networks

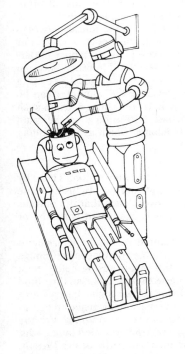

These are *nothing to do with actual computer networks*, but are related to the way in which the human brain can be mimicked by a machine. It must be realised that, at the time of writing, the current technology for this is only in its infancy – there is no way that in the immediate future we are likely to equal the parallel processing power of the human brain, and this is just one of the reasons why **AI** is held back from achieving its true potential. However, the ideas are great fun and some university degree courses are now offering biological cells as one of the options in their computer science degrees. This theory is indeed taken very seriously, and has already had tremendous spin-offs in the field of artificial intelligence, especially with learning to recognise visual images. It is likely that this may be a possible solution to the problems discussed when dealing with robot vision systems on page 552.

To understand the principles involved with neural networks it's probably best to start off by considering a *simple model* of a neuron inside the **human brain**. A simplified form is shown in figure 23.18.

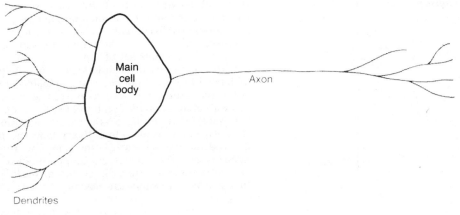

Main cell body

Axon

Dendrites

Figure 23.18

The basic logic device inside the human brain can be considered to be the neuron as shown in figure 23.18. The inputs to this basic logic element are via the **dendrites**. i.e. it is the dendrites that carry the input logic signals to the main cell body. A typical **neuron** inside the human brain might have an average of **1000 dendrites** feeding in signals. (Most students think that a 12-input AND gate has a lot of inputs!) The outputs from the system are obtained from one or more axons. It's most important to realise that we are no longer dealing with electronic logic which is described by Boolean algebra (see page 436), but are dealing with organic material that works on threshold logic levels, i.e. if the inputs together make up a large enough signal, then the system might give an output. It is, therefore, more like an analogue system rather than a digital one. However, as we shall see in a moment, it's possible to simulate neurons on a digital computer. (Isn't it possible to simulate almost everything?)

To make life even more complex, there are **two types of neural connections**. These are called **excitatory** and **inhibitory connections**. An excitatory connection is one which tells a neuron to fire a signal if the threshold level described above is exceeded. An inhibitory connection is prevented from firing if the input threshold is exceeded. Inside the human brain, these neurons are interconnected by what are called synapses.

The above sounds tremendously complex, but in practice, it is really quite simple. Basic electronic circuits called summing amplifiers can be used to simulate directly the situations shown above. (These devices appeared in the first edition of this book but were removed from the 'A' level computer science syllabuses!) Also, via algebraic relations we can simulate these neurons on a digital computer. For example,

Output = 1 if (Sum of the inputs) > Threshold level

Output = 0 otherwise

It's *easily possible* to **model an individual neuron** using more elegant relationships than the simple one shown above, but these ideas are enough to get you going at an elementary level. Indeed, you may be surprised to learn that even simple neural networks simulated on standard micros using just a few hundred neurons can start to exhibit pattern-recognition and other capabilities. However, what is impossible, using present day technology, is to approach anywhere near the number of parallel connections in the human brain – the brain has many millions of neurons such as those described above.

Faced with such a daunting task you might think that pursuing neural networks is a waste of time, but nothing could be further from the truth. Using digital simulations with a more realistic number of neurons, it's been possible to make some outstanding discoveries. Interestingly enough in the past few years neural networks have had a reasonable degree of success in helping out in unexpected ways. For example, it's possible to teach a neural network the difference between a busy underground-station platform and an empty one, or teach it to tell the difference between a traffic jam and free-running traffic. These examples are just two typical ones in a vast application area of image analysis. It is important because the computer can be taught not to recognise a particular image, but to be able to recognise a trend such as empty or busy, for example. This information can then be fed back to the main system and appropriate action may be taken by the machines which are controlling the traffic.

Consequences of neural nets

A neural network starts off by being connected up in a random fashion. Then, by stimulating the inputs, and then monitoring what the outputs are (i.e. by using some appropriate feedback paths), it's possible to model the network such that the outputs will eventually generate the required results. Each output is associated with one or more of the possible set of inputs.

If the above sounds a little vague, then a specific example will make it easier to understand. If, for example, you stimulate the system with a particular visual image (via some appropriate interfaces such as a matrix of tiny light-sensing cells), then this will set up a complex pattern of paths through the network based on the threshold logic levels that you have assigned to the various neurons i.e. we might be trying to simulate an electronic retina. Every time you present this particular visual image to the system, you wish to get the same, or, very similar associated outputs. Varying numbers of visual images can be presented to the system, and, via feedback paths, the threshold logic levels can be automatically programmed to get the desired result. In this way the system can literally learn to recognise a number of different visual images.

Even better is the ability of a neural network to recognise partial visual images and be able to associate these with previously stored visual images. This means that a neural network, just like a human being, can recognise an object if it is partially covered. For example, you would be able to recognise that the object which you are observing is a foot, even if you were presented with just the toes. You are doing this by comparing similar previous visual experiences with the one you are currently viewing, i.e. you are using your past experience to interpret the new stimuli.

Another outstanding feature of neural networks is their **tolerance to faults**. If, for example, several of the connections get completely destroyed, then the network still functions perfectly, or, at least, relatively well. This is the ultimate in parallel distributed processing. Compare this to the current electronic circuits, most of which will collapse completely if there is the slightest fault inside a chip – a single bit at fault in 16 Mbytes of RAM, for example, causes faults to occur, even though only $100/(16 \times 1024*1024)$ – or just 0.0000007% of the total memory is actually affected.

This neural-network advantage should not be too surprising, as it's a network that has been modelled on the human brain, and people loose thousands of brain cells every day! Therefore, neural networks have a tremendous potential for the future. They can be constructed by the new micro-miniaturisation techniques called wafer scale integration, or, just as likely, make use of genetically engineered protein which has been specially grown for the purpose. If this is done, then we would literally see the start of living material forming part of a computer system. These processes are also called organic molecular electronics and biocomputers.

In addition to the hardware mentioned above, a language such as **Prolog** (see page 167) allows for a high degree of parallel processing. Combine this with the fifth generation of computers and heuristic programming (see in a moment) and you have a very exciting, but perhaps turbulent future ahead.

Expert systems

These are applications which, over the past few years, have developed into amazingly useful and commercially successful systems. An alternative name for an **expert system** is a **knowledge-based system,** for reasons soon to become obvious. Such systems are best described by means of an example.

Consider the problem of diagnosing a particular illness that a patient may have in hospital. After tests have been carried out on the patient, the results are analysed and, together with the experience of the doctors, a probable diagnosis is made. Now the processes that have gone on are simply the gathering of facts, using one's experience of previous similar cases, and, together with a mountain of text-book knowledge, the doctors come up with the likely cause of the illness. Indeed, before a final conclusion is made, further tests and analysis may be necessary to follow one particular train of thought.

The processes that have just been described can be broken down into sorting through a mass of relevant (and irrelevant) data, until the results and symptoms fit most closely to the diagnosis – a task that's ideally suited to a computer.

The reason why such systems are called **expert systems** is that it is usual for a **team of experts** such as doctors and surgeons etc. to feed their knowledge into the computer so that the computer will eventually be able to diagnose the illnesses better than the individuals who fed in their knowledge. This is not really surprising, as the computer can sift through the facts very much faster than humans, and is less likely to forget some obscure point that may occur if an illness is very rare indeed. The new term that has recently been used for this process is called **mind mining**! Some people may think that this is sinister, but it is simply having the 'knowledge of a team of specialists' together with a 'very large medical library' that can be searched in seconds rather than in hours or days. Such systems have been in operation for some time with outstanding results. If a patient is lying on their deathbed because no one can diagnose the disease quickly enough, then a computerised system would certainly be a great help and get my vote.

One other area where expert systems have had remarkable success is in the oil and mineral exploration industry. Details of probable deposits can be fed into the computer, and, together with information from satellite pictures and drilling holes etc, can be processed by the expert system. After the computer has analysed many potential sites, it comes up with the site where the greatest probability of finding the resources occurs. Models have proved very reliable in the past, and have indeed pointed out finds in places which geologists did not think particularly likely. One example of such a system is called Prospector, and was developed at Stanford University.

Expert systems – the next generation

The expert systems available at the moment are primitive in comparison to those which are predicted when fifth generation technology becomes a reality early in the next century. It has long been realised that knowledge and its application to computers is not something that can be compartmentalised very easily or based on a set of formal rules. (At least not for a very long time until very sophisticated theories might be developed.) Therefore, **heuristic programming** has become a common technique when dealing with knowledge engineering, i.e. the process of getting an expert's knowledge into a computer system.

A **heuristic approach** means to develop a set of '**rules of thumb**' i.e. things that have proved useful in the past, based on previous experience. These rough rules will probably be continuously modified and moulded in the light of new experience, and, in this way, the answers that you get from the systems get nearer and nearer to those that would be given by the human expert. It's interesting to note that, many years ago, the science fiction writer Arthur C Clarke, wrote about a computer called HAL in the film 2001. **HAL** is shorthand for **Heuristic ALgorithm!**

The expert systems available now are examples of specialised knowledge; they are obviously useless if they are asked questions outside their sphere of influence. For example, the medical expert system would not even be able to determine that the reason a car might have stopped was because it had run out of petrol! Generalised systems are being developed in a limited way that enable people to have 'conversations' with the computer. However, with the current state of the art, it will not be long before you realise that you are talking to a machine rather than another human being.

The Turing test

Alan Turing (a prominent mathematician) developed a simple test to determine if a computer possessed intelligence. It runs along the following lines:

> A computer and a person are placed behind a screen so that a second person can't see either of them. Let's call the person in front of the screen, A, the person behind the screen, B and the computer behind the screen C, as shown in figure 23.19.

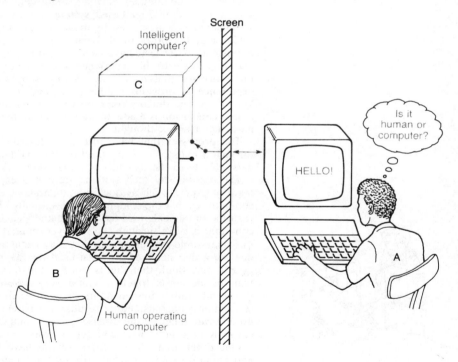

Figure 23.19

It is the task of A to ask any question of either the computer or the person behind the screen. However, there is the twist – either the computer or the person behind the screen can lie! It is the job of A to determine which is the computer.

Although this test was developed a long time ago (1950) it is a test which has still not been passed by the latest generation of machines, although some systems are reasonably convincing until you realise what they are doing. The famous Eliza program is a good example of this. Eliza is a system developed by Joseph Weizenbaum which mimics the conversation that could be had with a psychotherapist. (No insult is intended to budding psychotherapists here.) The following is a typical extract:

ELIZA	Hi I'm Eliza do you have a problem?
PERSON	I am feeling worried.
ELIZA	Did you come to see me because you were feeling worried?
PERSON	Yes I did. I thought that you may be able to help me.
ELIZA	Why do you think that I can help you.
PERSON	I just need someone to talk to.
ELIZA	You now have me to talk to.
PERSON	I think that the whole of my life is just crushing down on top of me.

One of the tricks from the above extract is that the computer locks onto key words in each sentence, and makes a reasonable response which it is hoped will be sensible in the context currently being used. You have already seen from the work in chapter 10 that one of the main problems encountered is that of getting the computer to be able to analyse natural languages such as English, and you should now appreciate just a small fraction of the potential problems involved. Perhaps neural networks might change this state of affairs in the next few years when pattern recognition in speech might be possible, just as the pattern recognition systems for images are starting to be solved.

Exercise 23.1

1. Outline the effects which **CAD** has had on **manufacturing industry**, with particular reference to *efficiency, versatility, employment and working practices*.

2. Taking **motor-vehicle manufacture** as a specific example, outline possible ways in which a CAD package might integrate with the following applications.
   (a) CAM techniques.
   (b) A spreadsheet.
   (c) A database.
   (d) A DTP system.
   (e) An expert system.

3. When would it be *more prudent* to use pencil-and-paper techniques in preference to CAD?

4. Outline the *advantages* that **CAD/CAM** techniques might have over *manual* manufacturing. Many parts of the world still don't make use of these efficient techniques – why might it be more efficient for these countries to carry on as they are?

5. Suggest how a **parametric CAD package** might be used to advantage in producing a demonstration lecture for young children explaining the principles of the internal-combustion (petrol) engine.

6. What is **CNC** and why have these machines become important in modern industrial plant?

7. Today's industrial robots are generally far removed from the stereotypes held in the general public's imagination. Outline the *differences between these two views* and comment on the limitation of today's technology to deliver this stereotyped image.

8. By using a **game of ches**s as an example – outline the difference between a robot with and without feedback moving the pieces on a standard chess board. What sensors might be useful in helping the robot with feedback to move the pieces more efficiently?

9. *Briefly outline* some problems which might arise in getting a computer system to carry out the following human-type activities.
   (a) Hearing.
   (b) Seeing.
   (c) Smelling.
   (d) Touching.
   (e) Tasting.

10. What is **AI**, and why is the subject controversial?

11. Suggest how an **expert system** might be used in helping a car mechanic to repair a fault in a car with which he or she is unfamiliar. What other technology might also be helpful in this situation?

12. **Neural networks** are trying to simulate the human brain. They have been very successful in limited areas, and their ability to solve previously-insoluble problems is remarkable. What factors are currently limiting the power of neural networks?

13. In your opinion will a computer ever be able to pass the **Turing test**? Explain.

End of chapter summary

- **Computer applications** in the **scientific**, **technical** and **engineering** fields probably account for the biggest diversity of applications – it is a vast area.
- **CAD** is an acronym for **Computer Aided Design**. It is the use of computers to help in the design stages of ideas or products.
- **CAD packages** can be divided into two broad categories, namely **object-oriented packages** and **pixel-based packages** – however, it's becoming increasingly difficult to tell the difference between the two packages by viewing the end result.
- An **object-oriented package** is one in which each part of the diagram is stored and processed as a mathematical relationship.

- A **pixel-based package** stores the picture information as a large number of tiny pixels. These packages tend to be less versatile for engineering and science.
- **Object-oriented packages** are **ideal for zooming in** to reveal greater amounts of detail, as none of the information is lost for sensible zoom ranges.
- Some **object-oriented packages** have surface and other rendering capabilities which give effects that only used to be possible with pixel-based packages.
- **Advantages of CAD packages** include the ability to **edit the pictures** an infinite number of times, have access to **libraries** and **clip art**, and **merge pictures** etc. The processes are also inherently **more accurate** than manual techniques.
- **CAD** can link to other related processes such as **CAM**, **databases**, **spreadsheets** and many other **analytical tools**.
- **Top-of-the-range object-oriented CAD packages** often require the most powerful micros, or access to mainframe computers if they are to be fast enough to be useful.
- **Parametric CAD packages** enable animated models to be created of engineering systems such as mechanical linkages.
- **CAD packages** should *not be used* to replace initial doodles with a pencil and paper – this would be like cracking a nut with a sledgehammer.
- **CAM** is an acronym for **Computer Aided Manufacture** – computer data, usually generated from a CAD package can be used to control the CNC machines which manufacture the goods.
- **CNC** stands for **Computer Numerical Control** – it is an adaptation of machine tools such that they can be controlled from numerical data generated from a computer.
- **CAD/CAM** systems are often used to help produce what can be thought of as automated factories in which the design data from the CAD package can be used to order materials, work out costs, and generate the numbers for the CNC machines.
- Together with **data logging** and **control**, **embedded microprocessor systems** can carry out constant monitoring of the manufacturing processes to ensure first-class quality control in a computer controlled integrated manufacturing environment. These processes are explained more fully in chapter 25.
- **Robotics** in practice is *far removed from the popular sci-fi image*. Today's industrial robots have looks which are determined by the specialist functions which they perform.
- **Embedded systems** are usually used for the control of robots.
- Most robots operate in **closed loop feedback mode** – which means that various sensors are used to monitor what's happening and help to control the robot.
- **Sensors** attached to the robots help them to perceive their environment – all of the human senses can be simulated, and others such as detection of *magnetism* and *radiation* are also easily possible.
- **Sight**, **smell**, **touch**, **taste** and **hearing** can be built into robots, but interpretation of information, especially visual information, is still a major problem.
- **Neural networks** are beginning to be a tremendous help with the analysis of patterns and visual information as they have the ability to learn from experience.
- A **neural network** can either be special hardware or can be simulated using software. It mimics the basic processes inside the human brain.
- At present **neural networks** are only a very small fraction of the complexity of the human brain.
- **Neural networks** have a certain degree of tolerance towards faults, and this might lead to exciting new possibilities in the future.
- **Expert systems** or **knowledge-based systems** are the names given to systems in which human experience is programmed into the computer.
- **Expert systems** have been particularly successful in the medical and oil exploration fields. However, they can be used almost anywhere.
- **Expert systems** and neural networks give machines apparent (or even real!) intelligence. Much debate rages as to where these developments may lead in the future, and whether machines will ever be able to think.
- The **Turing test**, one of the **benchmarks** of machine intelligence has not been passed, even by today's most powerful AI systems running on supercomputers.

24 Further applications

Introduction

This final chapter on computer applications completes the three chapters on standard applications. Here we will concentrate on further interesting and useful applications which don't quite fit into the 'business' or 'scientific and engineering' categories, although many of them could be used extensively in either of these contexts. You must also not forget that new applications are appearing on the market on an almost daily basis. With this in mind, you should try to keep right up to date by reading the magazines and newspapers suggested on page 6. In chapters 22, 23 and 24 we have concentrated on major applications – you are obviously not expected to be familiar with too many minor applications. Also, don't forget that your examination papers are written months before the final exam. Therefore, any new earth-shattering applications are unlikely to be in the exam paper! Nevertheless, you should *always* try to impress the examiners in a modest way with your up-to-date knowledge of the latest developments in computer science.

CD-ROM based systems

CD-ROM based systems are covered from a technical point of view in chapter 13, where the ins and outs of their operation are considered in some detail – here they will be covered because of their increasingly common and sophisticated use in many different application areas.

Over the last few years CD-ROMs have revolutionised the ways in which data and software can be distributed, and more importantly, they have revolutionised the actual amount of information that can be stored locally at a sensible cost. Extensive computer-based networks in the form of the **information superhighway**, or **floptical drives** might eventually lead to the demise of the **CD-ROM**, but until that happens they will play an *increasingly* important role. When the second edition of this book was being written just a few years ago, only a few CD-ROMs were on the market – they often cost in the region of £100, and a limited range was available – mainly of the encyclopaedic variety. Today hundreds of Mbytes of data on CD-ROMs are given away 'free' on computer-magazine covers! Tens of thousands of different CD-ROM titles are available on almost any topic under the sun, and *small companies and individuals* can now produce their own **CD-ROM masters**. This is the measure of the increase in the popularity of these systems in the space of just under five years.

Students are often amazed by the fact that the humble compact disc which they have at home is capable of storing hundreds of Mbytes of data. It sounds most impressive when compared to a maximum of about 72 minutes of pop music. In fact, there is little difference between these two requirements, and this can be shown easily by considering how the pop music is converted into bits.

Music is sampled digitally about 44,000 times a second! This high sampling rate is necessary to reproduce the audio frequency spectrum to the required fidelity. Each sample consists of about 16 bits. (Analogue to digital converters actually perform this sampling, and are covered on page 577.) Therefore, for 72 minutes of music, we would need:

$$72 \times 60 \times 44000 \times 16 \text{ bits} = 3041 \text{ Mbits}$$

Now there are 8 bits in one byte, therefore, we need about 3041/8 = 380 Mbytes to store 72 minutes of music.

If from the above, you rightly think that more music could actually be put onto the disc, don't forget that there is also a mass of other data stored on the disk to undertake operations such as **error checking** and **synchronisation**, and *extra* information to control the displays on the CD player etc. In practice about 600 Mbytes of data can be put onto a standard-size **CD-ROM**, although **compression techniques** (see page 563) and the possibility of **blue lasers** (see page 274) are able to extend this range very considerably.

Textual information storage

Most schools and colleges now have at least one CD-ROM based system, and many students should have first-hand experience of the ways in which data can be handled by these systems. As Advanced-Level students it's essential that you have a play with these systems at some stage in your course, and you *should* be using them for helping to find out general information anyway! CD-ROM drives are now starting to appear as standard equipment on many new computers, and bottom-of-the-range drives can be obtained for considerably less than £100 – far less than the cost of some of the original CD disks! Now 600 Mbytes, in some cases together with suitable compression algorithms, provide an adequate base on which to store many different types of useful textual database. Don't forget that even when uncompressed, this means that it's the equivalent of about eight hundred 800k floppy disks! For example, a years supply of the **Times newspapers**, including the **Sunday Times** fits onto a *single* **CD-ROM** if you don't include most pictures and the adverts. Also, each fitting onto a single CD-ROM would be the **Complete Works of Shakespeare**, the **Standard Oxford English Dictionary**, the **Bible**, **library catalogues** and *thousands of other suitable reference materials* – on many there is even enough space left for some suitable pictures and perhaps some speech or music too (see in a moment).

The power of these systems lies with the software which accompanies the information on the CD-ROM. It is usual to provide a system which allows searching for the information in ways similar to those described in chapter 20 on databases. The sophisticated software which controls such a system is sometimes called a **knowledge retrieval system**, and this makes the whole operation simple, powerful and easy to use, especially when undertaken within a standard windows environment.

At the simplest level, you could use a suitable general encyclopaedia to search for a 'word' or 'group of words'. For example, suppose that you type in:

'*Never in the field of human conflict*'.

Ask the computer to do a search, and within a few seconds you have probably identified an article on Winston Churchill. The system is most impressive in it's ability to find facts by typing in related information such as that shown above. You must obviously be specific, asking the computer to search for 'man', for example, would probably show thousands of different articles. From the physics of gluons, via ancient Hebrew, classical Greece and little known artists – it's possible to come up with useful information on most topics with an appropriate CD-ROM in the drive.

Often there are various options available such as 'finding words in an article' or 'making sure that the words you are looking for are all in the same paragraph' or 'do the words you are looking for have to be in the exact order?' etc. There are also some other special relations and functions. With a printer attached to the system, users can easily print out the information they require, often together with a list of other references which they can then use as a bibliography in their college libraries.

The above scenario sounds marvellous until teachers realise that complete essays could be produced by pupils in a few minutes! All the pupils have to do is type in a sensible combination of searches, then transfer the relevant parts of the articles to a suitable file. Unsuspecting members of staff would then think that the essay had been produced by the pupil on a word processor – it takes hours to achieve the same results with a pen and paper – the way that some of your teachers had to do it in the old days!

Computer data can also be used to represent pictures (see page 563), and therefore pictorial information in 'still' or 'movie' form can be stored on and retrieved from CD-ROM based systems. A *good example* of pictorial information is Microsoft's **National Portrait Gallery** – which can store all pictures hanging in the National Portrait Gallery on a single CD-ROM, making use of 256 colours and VGA resolution for each picture. In addition to this there is space for the history of each of the artists, and some other useful information too. *Without* compression, relatively few pictures can be stored on CD-ROM, and real-time moving images of good quality would only be sustainable for a limited period of time.

A typical CD-ROM based information-retrieval system is shown in figure 24.1. Here you can see a version of Microsoft's Encarta running under Windows 3.1. This particular version of Encarta is based on the 29 volume Funk and Wagnalls New Encyclopedia. This screen shot shows various types of guitars, together with an explanation of the history and other facts about each instrument.

Figure 24.1

Sound too can obviously be stored on **CD-ROM**s as the discs were originally invented for this purpose. Indeed buttons may be clicked to produce each of the distinctive guitar sounds in the above example. Add to this the still or moving images, text and computer data, and you have all the ingredients for the multimedia systems covered in the next section.

Multimedia systems

Figure 24.2

Multimedia seems to mean different things to different people, but an ordinary micro with the addition of a **CD-ROM drive**, a **sound card** and some **stereo speakers** is the *minimum* acceptable set up. The only current 'spanner in the works' is the relatively slow data-retrieval times for single-speed CD-ROM drives. It's not too bad if the data is contiguous as is the case with the movies mentioned in the last section, but random retrieval of data can be painfully slow, even on double-speed drives. Triple-speed and quad-speed drives have now appeared on the market, and are rapidly diminishing in price, but until faster drives become a reality at a sensible cost, you may have to wait for more than a few seconds for the data to be extracted from disk. This process does not sound too painful, unless you are trying to do a demonstration in front of an audience – in which case it's positively embarrassing. Some computers are now being produced with multimedia in mind, and a reasonably good multimedia computer at the time of writing is Apple's Centris 660AV, and this is shown in figure 24.2. Notice how the CD-ROM drive and space-age speakers are now an integral part of the base-design of the system. This is a much better solution than having a Heath-Robinson arrangement of wires and boxes all over the desk.

Production of CD-ROM material

With the plethora of hardware you need some sort of system which can bring it all together to produce your blockbuster presentation, programme, animation sequence or whatever with relative ease. Disparate **video clips, clip art, DTP documents** and **sound** etc., will do little or nothing for the all-important company image *unless* they can be seamlessly moulded together. If, for example, you start to 'play around' with the transfer of **images** from one system to another, then you'll find out what a mess the computer-data industry is in with regard to the *transfer* of seemingly-innocuous files – and *these problems occur even on the same hardware platform*! Don't forget that video, audio and other pictorial data takes up pots of memory, so they often have to be **compressed** if large numbers of images and sound are to fit on a single CD-ROM drive or magnetic disk. If you then go on to the next stage and expect your computer to get data from *and* also control, the **CD-ROM drives**, **video-cassette recorders**, **video cameras** and **scanners** etc. which are connected to it, then you are entering a proverbial mine field. In addition to this, you will need a powerful computer with a healthy chunk of RAM (preferably 32Mbytes or more) and a large hard disk (more than 1Gbyte) if you are intending to master your own CD-ROMs from video, audio and computer-data sources. Fortunately, the majority of people who are simply going to view your CD-ROM masterpiece can get away with a relatively ordinary computer specification.

Moving-image standards

Many hardware systems are now supporting most of these multiple standards and are currently being relatively successful in this awkward role. The **MPEG** standard is one of the emerging stars in the mid 1990s for multimedia, and this is an **ISO standard** designed for moving images. MPEG stands for the **Moving Picture Experts Group,** and is a recognised system for being extremely good at **compression** *and* **storage** of video and animation material.

Unlike conventional compression utilities (such as **JPEG** – see in a moment) which take similar areas in a scene to avoid sending identical information over and over again (see page 564), **MPEG**, or more specifically **MPEG 1**, uses the information in the frame (video clip) at the beginning of a sequence of clips as a reference. It then uses this reference frame, together with a vastly-reduced amount of information in the next few frames which describe *only those parts of the video picture that move*. If, for example, you were looking at a moving-video sequence in which the background remains static, (in practice many do – have a look the next time you watch the television!) but an object or person is moving in the foreground, then only enough information to generate the moving bits are sent in the next few frames. Now the original video frame can't remain a reference for too long (unless it's a very boring video!), therefore, another reference frame must be sent, and the next few frames in the sequence are referenced to this new one – and so it goes on. The system does not give a perfect image if most of the information in the scene is moving rapidly, and this manifests itself as an image with softer (slightly fuzzy) edges. However, MPEG are constantly working on problems like this and are rapidly finding solutions.

The above makes MPEG sound easy, but you try developing the algorithms to do it! Using this incredibly-complex technique, a massive amount of compression can take place, and it is this which enables us to fit a full-length movie onto just one or two CD-ROMs – about 74 minutes of Full-Motion Video (**FMV**) of VHS quality per disc. It's also this system which enables us to send full-motion video down an analogue phone line designed in the middle ages! One advantage of the **MPEG** standard is that it can cope with *real-time encoding* and *decoding* – this means that the computer system is fast enough to be able to extract the data from a CD-ROM, decode it and display it to get real-time video images and stereo sound on the monitor or TV set – an amazing technological feat. It is also fast enough (just) to encode moving-computer images as they happen and store them onto recordable CD-ROM. You may recall from page 276 that Philips have been producing different coloured 'books' as standards for CD-ROMs – the latest CDs encoded with MPEG conform to what is known as the white-book standard. There are also many other formats such as **VideoCD**, **AV-I**, **PhotoCD**, **CD-Audio** (for sound), and **CD-i** etc. – and these do not include some of the computer-games console formats.

Still-image standards

Still images and 'ordinary' computer graphics have their own set of standards too. **TIFF**, for example, stands for **Tag Image File Format**, and is one of the standard ways to store and exchange bitmapped-graphics files across different platforms. The popular TIFF format was originally designed with scanning in mind. **GIF** – the **Graphics Interchange Format** was developed for compressing graphics when making use of the on-line network services such as those found on the **Internet** (remember the threat to CD-ROMs from the networks?). **JPEG**, the **Joint Photographic Experts Group** is another compression format for graphics files, but is not as successful because the uncompressed data is not always a first class representation of the original!

In addition to all these standards you have the **PCX** format which is a popular graphics-file format for bitmapped images stored on the PC, and like TIFF, was also developed for handling scanned images. The PCX format is useful because most DTP systems accept it. **EPS**, or **Encapsulated PostScript** format is also useful to transfer graphics images between applications, because, like **Postscript** (see page 253) itself, the resolution of the graphic depends simply on the printing device. There are many other formats, such as **PIC**, **PICT** and **PICT2** (Apples's graphic-file format), **RLE** and **TGA** etc. – this only goes to outline what was echoed in the previous section – it makes multimedia systems extremely complex to implement in practice.

Authoring tools

One of the positive consequences of all the above is that it's now possible, at a cost of about £5,000 (*and falling*), for educational establishments and small businesses to purchase the computer hardware and software necessary to produce their own training videos, corporate advertising presentations or electronic reference books etc. on their own CD-ROM in house – a scenario that could only have been carried out at great expense by major publishing or broadcasting companies just a few years ago.

Software packages called **multimedia authoring tools** are currently being developed to enable ordinary users to efficiently manage these multimedia-type presentations. These packages, often supporting many of the multiple standards currently in operation, help to organise your multimedia presentation in a logical and easy-to-use way. The sheer logistics of organising the source material is staggering. For example, it's not unusual to have tens of thousands of clip-art images – how do you view them and locate the one you require? Some sort of database system is obviously the answer, but then this too has to integrate with all the other systems mentioned so far! The task of a multimedia authoring tool can be likened to writing a computer program. Indeed, some of the systems make use of high-level-language type programs or 4GLs to help build the presentation, training package, information retrieval system or whatever else it is that you are trying to accomplish. Others make use of a pictorial-type interface in which flowcharts, menu selections or other graphics form the method of communication between the user and the system – most systems make use of a combination of methods, with the appropriate method being chosen according to the complexity of what you are trying to do.

The windows-based environments of today are ideal for presenting the front ends of multimedia authoring packages. For example, making use of Oak Solution's Genesis Professional package on Acorn's RISC PC, the screen shown in figure 24.3 is typical of what an end user might see from a window which was created from the package.

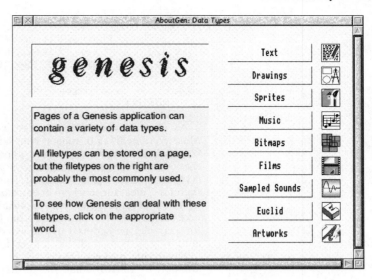

Figure 24.3

Notice how a user-friendly environment has been created in which the end-user can simply point a mouse over the appropriate box and click the button. What happens next is entirely dependent on the program controlling the multimedia application. For example, a double-click over the raised '3D music icon' could cause the current window to close, a new window may then open, giving the user an option to play various types of music. A click with the mouse over an appropriate icon on the next screen could then cause the stereo sound to come blasting out of the speakers.

To create such screens you have a large variety of menus in which tools are used for options such as creating backdrops, creating links to other pages (windows) and loading files etc. One of the menus containing the backdrop-linking tools for the Genesis Professional package is shown in figure 24.4. Here you can see various options such as the 'type of mouse click' to activate the desired action, time delays and whether any messages should be displayed etc. In addition to accepting the standard features of which there are many, you can write your own commands making use of the Genesis Script language – a BASIC-like language which can control the entire system. The following is a very small portion of a typical part of a script language.

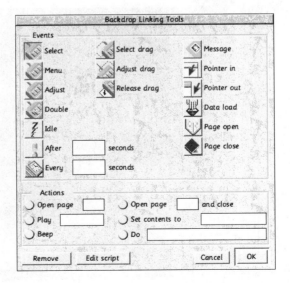

Figure 24.4

```
SET Page TO 0
WHILE Page <= LASTPAGE
            PRINT WHOLE OF PAGE Page PORTRAIT RETAINING SHAPE COPIES 1
            IF Page <> PAGE THEN
                TELL PAGE Page TO CLOSE
            ENDIF
            SET Page TO Page + 1
ENDWHILE
```

As you can see it's exactly like writing your own high-level language program. Most multimedia-authoring-system languages are so powerful that you can literally create your own windows-based applications. It obviously won't be anywhere near the lightning speed of a custom-written C++ application, but with a very fast micro, competent users can create professional looking and useful applications. These are, therefore, ideal for teachers in education or trainers in business. Even so, the amount of time it takes to create such applications is considerable, and you should not undertake such a task without realising the full implications. Some advanced level students, for example, are seduced by the wonderful things that can be done with multimedia authoring systems and they forget that it's going to take them ages to produce a fully-working package. However, if you set your sights more modestly, and don't attempt to mirror what the professionals are producing, then highly suitable computer-science projects can result, especially if you have delved into the authoring package's programming language.

More advanced multimedia packages are available (at a price!) and Authorware Professional on the PC , for example, typifies the top end of the professional market. However, you don't get much change out of £4,000 for this particular piece of software.

Pixel-based art packages

These software packages are primarily intended for **graphic designers** and **artists** who have to create images for inclusion in magazines, graphics images for inclusion in video productions such as those seen in the TV advertisements, or for retouching photographic input etc. They should be *compared and contrasted* with the **object-oriented CAD packages** (see page 539) used by engineers to produce industrial designs for machinery and architectural plans etc.

Readers should already be very familiar with the production of **bit-mapped images**, the theory of which is covered when **graphics displays** are explained on page 243, and a typical bitmapped image (from Photodesk by Spacetech running on Acorn's RISC PC) is shown in figure 24.5. In this chapter we will concentrate on typical

Figure 24.5

facilities offered by these impressive image-manipulation programs, some of which offer conversion between the different graphics-image standards mentioned in the multimedia section of this chapter.

There are also an enormous variety of packages for the PC and Apple Mac, which is obviously most famous for it's deserved reputation in the graphic-design field. Nevertheless, the most recent packages on the PC such as Micrografx Picture Publisher 4, Adobe's Photoshop and Photostyler, or Letraset's Fractal Design Painter 2.0 are equally as impressive as the best. Most art packages, especially those with 24-bit colour capability (see page 242), on all platforms now provide an enormous range of features for the professional user.

Most microcomputer-based packages offer very similar facilities, and just a fraction of the more common ones are outlined in the next few paragraphs.

Basic drawing facilities

A range of **colours** may be chosen, then applied to the screen by making use of a selection of tools such as **pencils, paintbrushes, rollers, spray cans, air brushes** and other assorted facilities. The ways of choosing from a palette of 16,777,216 colours are now getting quite ingenious, but 256-colour images can be satisfactory for run-of-the-mill work even at modest resolutions.

Shapes

A range of **basic shapes** such as **squares, triangles, ellipses, circles, polygons, sectors** and **segments** etc. are usually available, plus the ability to design your own brush and air-brush shapes. You can also create various shaped **masks**, such that you can literally use the computer-generated air-brushes in ways identical to those which you would use in a manual air-brushing environment. The secret of good air-brushing techniques is actually in clever design and use of the masks – it's a very skilled operation, even with a computer art package to help out.

Editing facilities

It's usually possible to **zoom** in and edit the picture on a pixel-by-pixel basis. Individual pixels can be placed exactly. It's also usual to have facilities such as magic wands where you can paint certain coloured areas without affecting other colours, or a variety of ways of **distorting** images into a diversity of amazing user-defined shapes. There are also facilities to **wash** areas of the screen – an effect that would normally be produced by dipping a paintbrush in water and then gently rubbing it over an area to create a washed-out effect or blend two or more adjacent colours. It's also possible to fade the paint brush as the stroke is lightened, just like the real thing, although a pressure-sensitive graphics tablet (see page 223) would be needed to carry out this operation effectively.

Cut and paste

The ability to cut and paste all or parts of the image can lead to a variety of interesting scenarios, including the creation of multiple images with ease. The author remembers creating a video cover for his school in which an unfortunately-positioned camera had to be edited out of the shot and replaced with curtain material of the exact same texture and colour as that which was next to the camera in the original picture. The adjacent curtains were cut out (a section copied) and carefully pasted so that the video camera was obscured. It then looked as if the curtains were pulled across the entire area. A feat that took just a few minutes on an art package.

More advanced facilities

The list of specialised features is now too enormous to mention. Letraset's Fractal Design painter package even allows you to use a brush style so that you can paint in the appropriate style of the grand masters like Van Gogh and some others. However, I don't think that my version of the Mona Lisa will end up hanging anywhere other than on the wall of the 'Loo gallery' in my house!

Who will make use of these packages?

In general, most fine artists have not been completely won over just yet, but many are now interested in computer-generated art as an alternative medium which can be seriously explored. The latest full-featured packages can no longer be ignored by the professional artistic community, and in a few years I think computer art will become accepted and common place. Even so, most artists tend to *like* working with paint brushes and canvas, and, just like the poet who feels that they are in more intimate contact with their work when they are actually applying the ink to the paper, it is unlikely that all artists will make use of a micro – and what a boring world it would be if they did!

Autostereograms

Computers are finding much use in graphic art such as advertising and animation of cartoon films etc. and there are obviously some things which are virtually impossible to do in art without a computer – with the 3D **autostereograms** being a good case in point. Can *you* read the **hidden message** in figure 24.6?

There can be few people in the country who have not encountered these images, and there are several ways of successfully viewing the image, two of which are:

(1) Stick a piece of glass over the image, look into the glass and focus, not on the image itself, but on the reflection of your face in the glass, which is actually behind the image – you should see parts of the image start to produce a stunning 3D effect.
(2) Stick your nose on the page just in front of the image, but don't focus on the image. Gradually move the image away from your eyes while still not focusing on the actual image – you should eventually see a 3D image, in which case stop moving your nose.

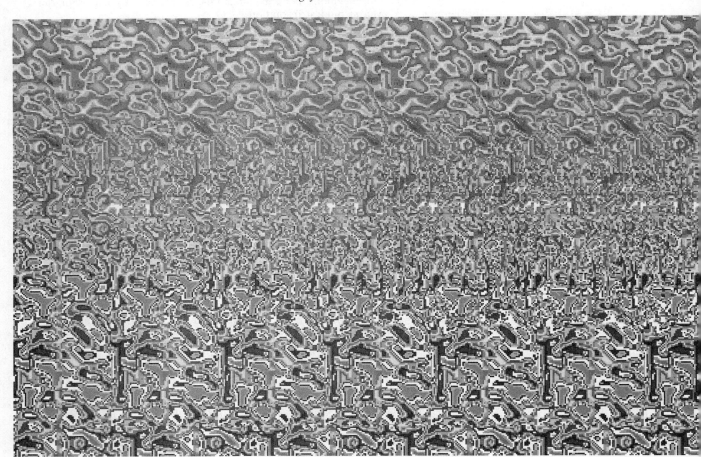

Figure 24.6

If you have defective sight in one eye, then you unfortunately will not be able to see the image. Also, some people find it difficult if not impossible to see, and think that those who can actually see it are pulling their leg!.

The people who really benefit from these art packages are the *majority* of the population who find it difficult to produce a professional quality image. Even moderately good packages allow people to experiment with ideas. **Art packages** give you *infinite flexibility*, and you can rub out your artwork thousands of times without leaving a mark or rubbing a hole in the paper. However, put one of these art packages in the hands of a talented and computer-literate artist, and the results can literally be stunning. It's not true what some people say about computer art packages taking the creativity out of the production of art work. They just give very talented people another dimension in which to operate.

Ray tracing

As can be seen from figure 24.7, some of the best computer images are possible by making use of **ray tracing**. It has long been the goal of computer scientists to generate mathematically-created images that look as if they are real. Indeed, over the last few years, the techniques have been getting better and better. However, the actual method of producing these images is *anything but* art. Indeed billions of mathematical calculations are often necessary and, even on a **64-bit microcomputer**, it may take several hours to do enough calculations to generate a single image. Powerful **mainframes** can produce stunning images in a fraction of this time, as their processing ability is many orders of magnitude higher. Indeed, the **Cray supercomputer** has generated some of the best graphics seen on computers to date, and **mainframes** or **supercomputers** *are still useful* for generation of a sufficient quantity of high-quality ray-traced images to produce a short movie. **Ray tracing** is based on a method which involves the **physics of optics (light)**. Rays of light are shone onto a mathematically generated scene, and the **shadows, reflections** and **refractions** etc that would occur in real life are painstakingly worked out point by point.

Figure 24.7

The ideas are based on **rays of light (photons)** being emitted from a light source and then, by complex or simple paths, finding their way to the viewer's eye. The idea is shown in figure 24.8.

It would be impossible, even for a supercomputer, to calculate all possible light paths. However, this would not be necessary as few of the light paths would hit the

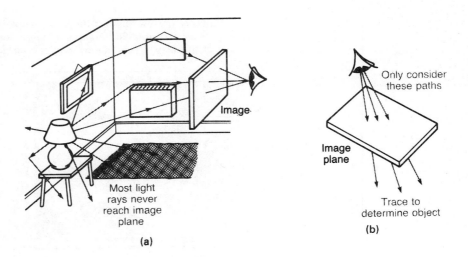

Figure 24.8

viewer's eye anyway. Therefore, a technique known as **backwards ray tracing** is used. This is where the rays are traced backwards from the viewer's eye to determine the objects from which the photons might have emerged. The idea is shown in figure 24.8. Even with this massive reduction in calculations required, it still takes a huge amount of computing power.

The techniques for generating ray traced images are now well established. However, computer scientists often ask themselves if the images they have created look real enough. Almost all of the time the answer is no, and therefore they have to ask what is the difference between the mathematical images that they have created, and the real objects which they are trying to simulate. Various techniques such as texture have now been added to increase the realism of these pictures. It's relatively easy to generate textures such as metallic objects (even with all the reflections) and matt objects and materials such as cloth, but it's still very difficult to generate all the subtle skin tones of a human being. However, it is being worked upon and will, I am sure, be simulated with great realism in the next few years. Couple this with the use of these images in a VR system (see page 258), and the human imagination may reach hitherto unknown areas.

Morphing

Another computer-art based technique which would be virtually impossible without a computer is that of **morphing**. Morphing got its name from the term metamorphosis – changing from one thing into another. There are now a large number of morphing packages available, but they have yet to be included in most standard computer art packages – no doubt they will be one day. One package called **Morpheus** by Oregan Developments for Acorn's RISC PC has a demonstration created by Henning Hansen, in which a picture of a girl, shown on the left of figure 24.9, is turned into the picture of a Tiger, shown in the right of figure 24.9. Just one of the intermediate stages is shown in the middle of figure 24.9.

Figure 24.9

To carry out morphing with a suitable package is quite simple. It revolves around importing two suitable bitmapped images for the start and end frames, then making use of a grid which is placed over the images as shown in figure 24.10.

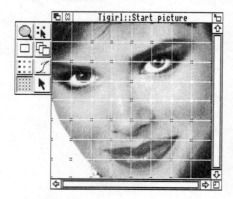

Figure 24.10

Figure 24.11

Next the grid has to be altered from the default shape in figure 24.10 so that salient points on the start grid can be mapped to salient points on the end grid. As you can see from the example shown in figure 24.11, the points around the eyes, ears and nose are very important in this particular transformation. Points at the intersection of the grid on the first image are mapped to the new positions of these same intersections on the final grid. It's up to the user of the package to interpret creatively the start and end positions of the grid to get the best effects.

Wonderful fun can be had with **morphing packages**, as any image, created from a **computer**, **video camera**, **video cassette recorder**, images pulled off of **bulletin boards** or loaded from **CD-ROM** etc can all be used as the source files, and converted into a suitable form for the morphing application by an art package. The TV and film advertising companies have recently taken to morphing in a big way.

Exercise 24.1

1. Outline some of the reasons why **CD-ROM based systems** have recently taken on much prominence in the computer industry.

2. What **hardware** poses a potential threat to the future success of CD-ROMs, and how is research and development of **CD-ROM technology** fighting back?

3. Taking a **CD-ROM based information system** with which you are familiar, outline the sort of things that can be accomplished with the system, specifically concentrating on comparisons with previous *manual methods* of carrying out the same or similar tasks.

4. Outline some of the problems when trying to integrate video, audio and computer data in practice. What is being done to overcome these problems?

5. Just a few years ago the bandwidth of the conventional telephone system was not wide enough to transmit still images with any significant speed. Without increasing this bandwidth we are now able to transmit real-time full-motion video – explain why this is so.

6. Suggest some applications which the use of MPEG 1 and standard telephone technology might bring about in the future.

7. Outline what can be achieved with a **multimedia authoring package**.

8. Why is the addition of a **high-level control language** *useful* in a multimedia authoring package?

9. Choose a *particular feature* of an **art package** with which you are familiar and outline some advantages that this feature has over manually-based techniques.

10. Is it likely that **computer art packages** will ever be able to create any sort of image that artists require? Comment.

11. How is it that **ray tracing** can produce very realistic looking images from a mathematical model?

12. Explain the basic principle of **morphing**. If you have a morphing package use it to create a suitable metamorphosis.

End of chapter summary

- ■ **CD-ROM**s form the basis of many **knowledge-retrieval systems** in which *textual* and *other information* can be extracted from a suitable CD-ROM.
- ■ **Database**-type software which accompanies most of the information-based CD-ROMs enables sophisticated queries to be extracted by **SQLs** or **QBEs**.
- ■ Other systems such as **magneto-optical disks** and powerful international networks could challenge CDs in this role in the future.

- There are currently *many thousand* **CD-ROM based titles** on the market, and it's now cost effective for small companies or educational institutions to produce their own CD-ROM masters.
- Typical **CD-ROM titles** would include **encyclopaedias**, the complete works of **Shakespeare**, the **Bible**, **The Times newspapers** and many others.
- About **600 Mbytes** of **uncompressed data** can fit onto a **CD-ROM**, but increasingly-powerful **compression algorithms** effectively pack in much more than this.
- **Fractal compression** and other similar techniques currently enable whole feature-length films including stereo sound to fit on one or two CDs.
- **Multimedia systems** enable video, audio and computer data to be integrated to produce presentations, training or advertising material.
- Multimedia computers are usually those with an integral CD-ROM drive, sound card and speakers, but more comprehensive hardware and software is needed to manage and produce your own CD masters.
- Many different multimedia standards exist for pictorial and sound data, and most systems try to cope with a variety of standards.
- **MPEG** is emerging as one of the *de facto* standards for video and animation, although other standards are used and supported.
- **MPEG** stands for the Moving Picture Experts Group.
- **MPEG 1** has allowed full-length movies to be encoded onto 1 or 2 CD-ROMs, and full-motion video to be transmitted over the standard telephone line.
- **Still graphics images** have their own plethora of standards, and this adds to the confusion of graphics-file transfer from one system to another.
- **TIFF** is a popular graphics format for *interchanging bitmapped graphics*, but many others exists such as **GIF** and **EPS**, for example.
- **EPS** Encapsulated PostScript.
- **GIF** – Graphics Interchange Format was designed to download graphics from *bulletin boards* on systems such as the **Internet**.
- **Multimedia authoring packages** are software applications which enable end users to create their own multimedia applications, presentation or training packages etc.
- **Multimedia authoring systems** work in a windows environment and can be controlled by menus or by a script language similar to a high-level language.
- A **pixel-based art package** is an application ideally suited to graphic design and artists. It's based on bitmapped-image technology, and should not be confused with object-oriented CAD packages which are more suitable for engineers.
- A *vast range of tools* are available including **brush** and **spray cans**, a range of facilities including **flood fills** and **graduated fills** and **distortion**, and a range of other features such as **cut** and **paste** etc are available on most **art packages**.
- **Art packages** are useful for doing things like **autostereograms** which would otherwise have to be accomplished by writing your own algorithms or drawing the picture by hand – a task which is almost impossible.
- **Art packages** are useful tools for allowing the *non-artistic* to produce **acceptable images**, but in the hands of a *talented artist* the results can be **stunning**.
- **Computer art packages** can be used to create artistic images that would be impossible by hand, with **autostereograms** being a good example.
- **Ray tracing** is a technique for generating realistic-looking scenes mathematically. It takes an enormous number of calculations and hence a long time, even on advanced computers to carry out this task – mainframes and supercomputers are often used.
- **Morphing** is another technique that would be extremely difficult to do without a computer. It is where one image can be transformed into another.

25 Computers in control

Introduction

Control is a vast area of computing which ranges in size from the small micro-processors **embedded** inside modern electronic equipment such as video recorders, via control of complex lighting rigs such as those found in some theatres, to the control of entire industrial plants such as those found in the chemical industry. In fact, virtually *any* process which can be controlled by a machine can in turn be controlled by a computer. This is due to the enormous variety of **sensors** available which convert physical quantities into electrical signals, and the huge variety of control equipment and **actuators** such as relays and valves etc., which can be used to switch external devices on and off, or cause things to move. *In these systems it is the computer or microprocessor which acts as the decision-making element under the guidance of a set of instructions or program which controls the process.* There is much to be considered here in terms of the **sensors, feedback systems** and **interfaces**, but one should not forget the important role played by the operating systems (see chapter 17) when computers are used in control. **Real-time operating systems** will therefore be considered in detail later in this chapter.

Some basic ideas

We start by considering the humble micro as a vehicle for our first examples – as the concepts of control are very similar irrespective of whether the process is being controlled by a microprocessor, microcomputer, mini or a mainframe.

To **interface** with the outside world, wires (or fibre-optics, radio or infra red connections etc.) must be brought out from the computer system to connect to an external device. One can easily appreciate this concept by reflecting on the fact that printers or keyboards, for example, are devices which are external to the main parts of a computer system. However, here we are thinking more in terms of devices such as **motors** and **solenoid valves** which could be used to switch the flow of a fluid on or off, **light bulbs**, **magnetic door locks** or **heating elements** etc. All these are examples of **output devices**, as the computer is controlling what happens to them. For example, is the motor going round or not? If it's rotating then is it going backwards or forwards? Is the heater element switched on or off? Is the door open or closed? More correctly, these devices are referred to as **transducers**, or more specifically **output transducers**.

Transducers

A **transducer** is the name given to any device that *converts energy from one form into another*. Therefore, a **motor** is an example of an **output transducer** which converts electrical energy into rotary motion. A light bulb would be an example of an output transducer which converts electrical energy into light.

Input transducers are equally important, for without them the computer system would have *no idea* of what is actually going on. These input transducers are the 'eyes' and 'ears' of the computer system, and typical examples would be **heat sensors** which convert temperature into an electrical signal, or **alternators** and **generators** which convert rotary motion into electrical signals.

Interfacing

Signals from the **input transducers** *must be converted into a form* which the **computer** can understand. Similarly, **signals from the computer** *must be converted into a form* suitable for driving (operating) any particular **output transducer**. Occasionally the signals coming from or going into the computer are compatible with the transducers, but most often it is necessary to have extra electronic circuits which perform the necessary conversions. These **electronic circuits** are called **interfaces**.

Some **interfaces**, such as those necessary to drive printers, for example, are usually incorporated into the main computer system itself – as most people require a printer on their system. One typical standard for printers is the **centronics parallel port**, but most computers also have other **ports** (see in a moment), such as the **RS 232 or RS 423 serial ports**, which can be used to interface many devices such as **MODEMs** and **data loggers**, for example. However, if we wish to drive *any transducer* or receive *any signal from a variety of sensors,* then a special interface of a more-general nature is usually needed (see later).

You should already appreciate that signals inside the computer are in **binary form** – where a '**zero**' represents a signal being '**off**' and a '**one**' represents a signal being '**on**'. Many computers work with 5 V representing 'on' and 0 V representing 'off'. Therefore, if you were to connect a voltmeter between two appropriate points at the back of your computer, you could observe whether a signal is 'on' or 'off' by measuring the voltage between the appropriate output pin and the GND (Ground or Earth) line inside the computer. These simple ideas are shown in figure 25.1(a), and form the basis of many control system principles.

You will need special software to control whether a particular pin is on (high) or off (low), and this software aspect of interfacing will be considered later on in this chapter. For the moment we will assume that we can simply switch the appropriate signals on and off at will.

Computer ports

A **port** is the name given to the place on the periphery of the computer system where you can extract control signals from the computer or put control signals into the computer. Consider, for a moment, the **centronics parallel port** mentioned above. In practice, all you will probably see at the back of your computer is a 25-pin socket into which you could put a plug from the device being controlled (i.e. it's *the* place where you would plug in a standard printer). Inside this socket are tiny pins which represent the places where the signals come into or go out from the computer system. Observant students will probably notice that the plug which goes into the printer itself is usually bigger – on most systems it has 36 pins! Obviously, most parallel printer ports at the back of microcomputers do not use the full compliment of facilities that are available at the printer end. All the pins at the *printer end* are shown in figure 25.1(b).

Thirty six pins is quite a lot, but fortunately, for our purposes, many of them can be ignored. However, *the* thing to note is that there are **8 data lines** available on pins 2 to 9 inclusive, and a convenient means for connecting the other end (0 V or

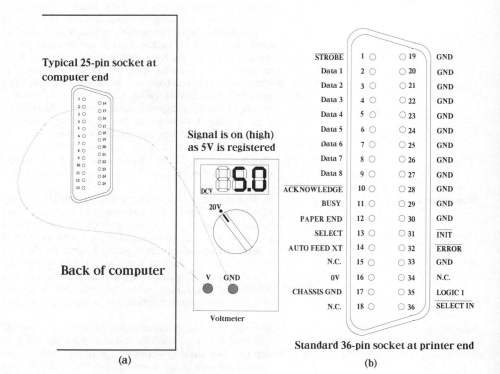

Figure 25.1

GND) of the signal or signals. In fact these 8 data lines correspond to an **8-bit data bus** along which the ASCII characters, for example, could be sent to the printer. Being a specialist printer interface, control signals such as 'select' on pin 13, for example, tell the computer that the printer is on-line and ready to go.

At the computer end, the eight data lines are available at pins 2 to 9 inclusive, and pins 17 to 25 provide the 0V or GND connections. If your computer has this interface then inside the computer special electronics generate the appropriate signals, and inside the printer appropriate electronics receive the signals. Therefore, to control a standard printer involves connecting up an appropriate lead making sure that the connections go to the correct places at each end. All the hard work of interfacing has already been done for you at both ends by the manufacturers of the computer and printer systems.

Inside your computer it would be the job of a special piece of **software** called a **printer driver** to drive the appropriate printer when it is connected to your computer system. However, *there is no reason why you could not use these outputs to control devices other than printers if you so wished* – assuming that you have the appropriate interface electronics connected between the centronics port and your own devices.

The whole point of going through the above scenario is to show you that *most computers are already acting as control systems*, therefore, it's a simple and logical extension to consider other interfaces which operate on very similar principles, but do a very different range of jobs.

Other types of interface

External disk drives, audio inputs and outputs, video inputs and outputs and a variety of other devices all need to be plugged into computer systems for various purposes. Therefore, a variety of special interfaces have been designed to cope with the variety of different specifications. For example, **SCSI** (Small Computer-Systems Interface), **SCSI 2**, **IDE** (Integrated Drive Electronics) and enhanced **IDE** interfaces are typical of the types of **port** needed to connect many devices such as disk drives and CD ROMs to your computer system. However, special **general-purpose interfaces** designed to enable the **user** to interface almost any device to the computer are also available. After dealing with serial and parallel communications, *it is these general-purpose types of interface that will be considered for the rest of this chapter.*

Expansion slots and user ports

Most **special** and **general-purpose interfaces** enable external devices to be connected to the **address bus**, **data bus** and **control bus** of the **CPU** (see page 51). Indeed, most modern microcomputer systems enable extra boards (special electronic circuits) called **expansion cards** to be plugged into the system. These electronic circuit boards provide the connections to the appropriate busses inside the computer, *and* provide suitable sockets into which a variety of different external devices can be plugged. The principles are similar to that of the centronics printer interface considered earlier, and many different standards of interface have been designed since the centronics printer port was devised over a couple of decades ago.

Serial and parallel data transmission

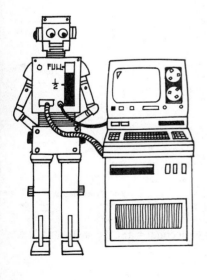

As computers become more powerful there is a need to transmit data at ever increasing rates. Therefore, the number of pins on many modern interfaces is considerably in excess of the 36-pin centronics example considered above. 16, 32 and even 64-bit data busses are now common on some types of interface, enabling more data to be sent in parallel at the same time. You should note that the difference between different bus systems *is not trivial* – indeed, it can make or break an entire computer system. If your particular computer system does *not* support a bus system which becomes popular, then most of the wonderful new devices being developed will not be able to be used with your particular micro – a potentially disastrous situation for some computer manufacturers.

Before going on to consider computer control in more detail, it's important to understand the fundamental differences between transmitting data in **serial** and **parallel** mode.

If more than one binary digit can be sent *simultaneously*, (as was the case with the centronics printer port), then data is said to be sent in **parallel**. To send data at the same time in parallel, more than one data line is needed. The printer port covered earlier can send up to 8 bits *in parallel* because it has *8 different and independent data lines* available at the output. Some of the more-powerful interfaces mentioned in the last section can send 16, 32 or 64 bits in parallel because they have up to 64 data lines available. Up to 128 data lines are not unheard of when considering powerful processors, and more will definitely be used in the future.

It is not always practical to send so many bits at the same time, not least because of the expense involved in needing so many wires simultaneously connected between the computer and the device which the computer is controlling or monitoring. Therefore, an alternative and cheaper method is to send the binary digits, one bit at a time, over a single wire from the source to the destination. This is called **serial transmission of data** and is ideal for long distances, or where single fibre-optic, infra-red or radio signals are used. However, it should be appreciated that the highest data transfer rates are only obtainable with parallel data transmission. **Parallel data transmission** is used almost exclusively *inside the computer* because of the bus systems, but **serial data transmission** is normally used when the distance between the transmitter and receiver is *greater than a few metres*, or if transmission media such as a standard telephone line are required. From reading the above you should *not jump to the conclusion that serial data transmission is always slow* – when fibre optics are used, the data transfer rate can be 100 Mbits/sec – far faster than conventional parallel transmission of data in some practical systems.

Timing and synchronisation

Whenever data is transmitted or received by a computer system it's of paramount importance to get the two devices in **synchronisation** with each other or vital data could be lost or corrupted. Inside the computer this is no problem as the **clock signals** can keep everything in step (see BORIS on page 53). In the case of the centronics printer port mentioned earlier, the printer can signal the computer that it is ready to receive data. If the printer were not switched on, indicated by no signal on the appropriate pin, then it would be silly for the computer to send the data down the wires to the printer or the data would be lost.

From reading the above you should appreciate that some serial links will need extra control lines, and therefore, even when the data itself is sent along just one line, you will often find that several lines are used in the actual connection of a serial port. In fact, the full RS-232 serial standard contains 25 pins!

There are often times when no synchronising information can be sent by separate wires at all, and you are down to a single wire or radio signal, for example. In this case it is necessary to control carefully the **rate** at which the binary digits are sent, and to add some extra information to alert the receiving device that some data is about to arrive. The *rate at which the data is being sent* is measured in **Baud**, and is a measure of the data transmission rate in **bits/sec**. Therefore, *if* all the bits being sent represent data, then 800 Baud would be 100 bytes/sec of data being transmitted. This is typical of the figures quoted for serial devices such as MODEMs, which transmit their information down a telephone wire. Sometimes the data is sent and received at different rates, as is the case with a Prestel terminal, for example. However, under these conditions we must obviously make sure that the transmitting Baud rate has been set up differently from the receiving Baud rate.

Not all bits being sent necessarily represent data – extra bit patterns called **control bits** are often sent to indicate the **start** *and* **stop points** in a typical group of bits of

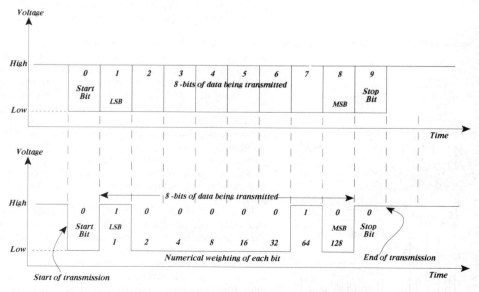

Byte of data being sent is 01000001 binary = 65 decimal = ASCII code for 'A'.

Figure 25.2

data. Figure 25.2 shows a typical case in which extra information is sent to help control synchronisation between the serial transmitting and receiving devices. Note that the start bit is used to 'wake up' the receiving device. In practice this bit would be used to synchronise the clock inside the receiver. As the Baud rate at the receiver has been set up to be exactly the same rate as the Baud rate at the transmitter, then the next 8 bits are clocked into the system and read at exactly the right moments in time so that the levels for each bit are correctly interpreted. After the data has been clocked in at the receiver, the stop bit is used to signify the end of this byte of data. (Note that the **start bit** changed the 'no data transmission' level of the line from *high to low*, but the **stop bit** has ensured that the level *goes back high again* before the next start bit can arrive.) This level then remains high until the next start bit is received which indicates that the next byte of data is whizzing down the line. If the Baud rate of the transmitter and receiver are not set up to be the same, then this method of transmission will obviously fail as all the bits will arrive at the wrong times and be misinterpreted. You will probably be familiar with this situation if you have made extensive use of MODEMs, as garbage is produced when the Baud rates are incorrectly set.

The standard outlined in figure 25.2 is one of those defined in the RS 232 system, and in this case has transmitted the letter 'A' with no parity, one start bit and one stop bit. You will appreciate that *if* this system is used, then the actual data transfer rate (i.e. bytes/sec) is less than the transmission rate because of the extra bits used for the start and stop bits. Therefore, if the transmission rate were set to 800 Baud, only 80 bytes/sec of data (ASCII code in this case) is actually sent, and not the 100 bytes/sec of data that might be implied by reading the specification of the system.

Analogue and digital signals

The signals considered so far have all been **digital** – i.e. **on** or **off**, **high** or **low**, **1** or **0**, or one or a defined number of states. Nevertheless, many signals which need to be monitored are of a very different nature. **Temperature**, **humidity** and **pressure**, for example, are *all* **continuously variable** or **analogue** in nature. A signal which can vary **continuously** between two values is called an **analogue signal**, and a typical example is shown on the left of figure 25.3.

It's currently *impossible* for a computer to deal directly with analogue signals and therefore a **special interface** called an **analogue-to-digital converter (A to D converter)** is required to change the continuously variable analogue signal into a digital form which can be interpreted by the computer. This analogue-to-digital conversion process *must* take place if the analogue signal is to be transmitted along the data bus and stored in the memory of the computer.

Figure 25.3 shows the simple principles of analogue-to-digital conversion.

Consider the analogue signal shown at the left-hand-side of the diagram. The level (**magnitude**) of this analogue signal is being measured (**sampled**) at *frequent intervals* (see in a moment), converted into an appropriate digital value by the A to D converter, then stored in the computer's memory ready for processing – all this is supposed to be happening in **real time**.

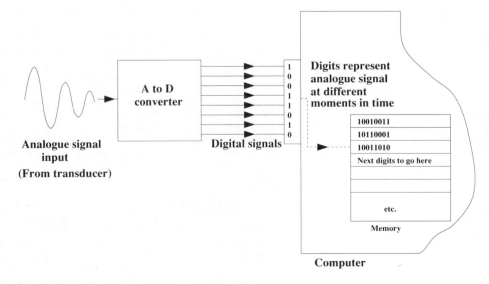

Figure 25.3

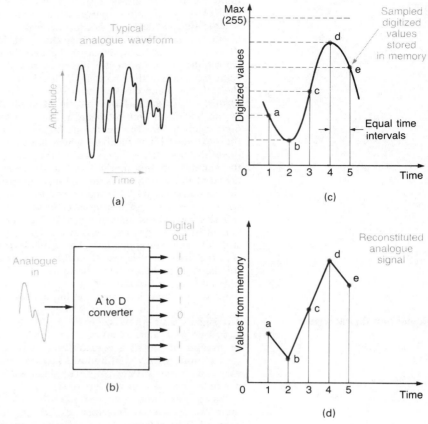

Figure 25.4

The **input signal range** needs to be *split up* into a number of *discrete levels*. This process is called **digitisation** or **quantisation**. The number of discrete levels determines the level of **resolution** with which the original analogue signal can be faithfully reproduced or analysed. The idea is shown in figure 25.4(a). With an 8-bit A to D converter, for example, 256 different levels (2^8) are possible. However, with a 16-bit A to D (2^{16}) we can get 65,536 different levels. Although it is possible to get more levels than this, the cost of the A to D converter circuits become prohibitively high. If we try to reconstruct the original analogue signal from the stored data, then the result would be as shown in figure 25.4(d). This is not as bad as it looks, because we need not assume that the points are joined by straight lines. On audio systems, for example, the straight-line graph would naturally be smoothed out by the electronics. We could also use other techniques to make the reproduction more like the original if this is regarded as being important in a particular application.

The next thing of importance to note is the **frequency** with which **samples** of the analogue input signal are taken. If this rate is too slow then important events which might happen to the analogue input signal could be lost. On the other hand, if this rate is too high, then much memory will be wasted by storing unnecessary bit patterns that give us no extra information. (See compression techniques in a moment.) **Nyquist** developed a system which states that *the sampling rate must be at least twice as high as the highest frequency component in the signal being investigated.* Therefore, if the input signal varied at a maximum rate of 10 kHz, or had important harmonics at this frequency, then a sampling rate of 20,000 samples per second would need to be made.

The audio frequency spectrum for good hi-fi systems is generally regarded to be between 10 Hz and 20 kHz – it's not surprising, therefore, to find that the A to D converters used inside audio compact disc systems sample at a rate of just above 40 kHz – about twice the maximum important frequency in the audio spectrum.

It should be realised that huge amounts of memory can be eaten up when sampling high frequency analogue signals. If, for example, a 16-bit A to D is used and if the sampling rate is set to 40 kHz, then $40,000 \times 16 \times 60 \times 3 = 115,200,000$ bits or 14.4 Mbytes of memory would be needed to store a 3 minute piece of music!

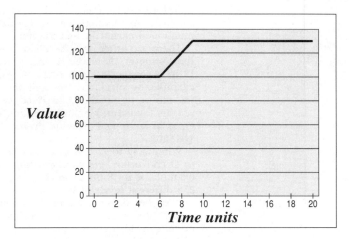

Figure 25.5

Compression techniques

From reading the above you should be able to appreciate the problems associated with A to D conversion techniques. However, there are methods for reducing this huge memory overhead which have been used very successfully indeed to compress the huge amount of data generated into more manageable proportions. Consider the signal shown in figure 25.5.

Let's assume that we're going to change this **analogue signal** into **digital values** using A to D techniques, and the sampling frequency can be determined from the arbitrary time slots shown on the horizontal axis. Now if a sample is taken at each time slot and converted into an *8-bit binary number*, then the following data shown in figure 25.6 would be generated.

Time slot	Data (Decimal)	Data (Binary)
0.00	100.00	01100100
1.00	100.00	01100100
2.00	100.00	01100100
3.00	100.00	01100100
4.00	100.00	01100100
5.00	100.00	01100100
6.00	100.00	01100100
7.00	110.00	01101110
8.00	120.00	01111000
9.00	130.00	10000010
10.00	130.00	10000010
11.00	130.00	10000010
12.00	130.00	10000010
13.00	130.00	10000010
14.00	130.00	10000010
15.00	130.00	10000010
16.00	130.00	10000010
17.00	130.00	10000010
18.00	130.00	10000010
19.00	130.00	10000010
20.00	130.00	10000010

Figure 25.6

From the above list we can see that the 21 readings (0 to 20) are encoded as $21 \times 8 = 168$ bits. Let's now use a different approach. We only need to send data *if a change* occurs. Therefore, once some specific data has been sent, the receiving end need only be notified if the data has changed. If we were to store this data in RAM or on disk, then an extra number, usually associated with the number of digits which have stayed the same, is stored along with the data. Therefore, 100,500 might be the decimal representation for storing the value of 100 – 500 times. We have therefore used a much more efficient storage technique. You will be surprised how similar many readings can be, especially from the data logging and monitoring systems mentioned earlier in this chapter.

There are other devices called **D to A converters** which take a digital output from the computer, then convert these digital values into an appropriate analogue voltage. D to A converters are often necessary to control the speed of a d.c. motor, for example, by varying the **magnitude** (an analogue value) of the voltage placed across the motor terminals. D to A converters are necessary to drive a range of **output sensors (actuators)** including audio (loudspeakers), varying the light intensity of many types of lamp, and accurate positioning using conventional servo-mechanism control systems.

When a D to A converter has been used it should be understood that, as with A to D converters, *the number of bits used determines the resolution of the system*. For example, if an **8-bit D to A** is used to control the brightness of a bulb, then only **256 different levels of brightness** would actually be available. Whether this is important or not depends upon the application. If we are using this to dim lights in a theatre, for example, then working through all values from 255 (representing) full brightness, to 0 (representing off) would convince most people that the brightness of the lamp is being faded very gradually in a smooth way. This is just one of the many reasons why computers are so useful in controlling the light and sound for professional theatre productions.

Sensors (input transducers)

Many quantities which may be measured are **analogue** in nature, and just a small selection of typical sensors which are available might include the following.

Resistance	Voltage	Current	Temperature
Pressure	Light intensity	pH	Sound intensity
Colour	Humidity	Rotational speed	g force
Radiation	Capacitance	Inductance	Magnetic-field strength
Strain	Wind speed	ECG monitor	EEG monitor

Each of the these transducers converts the appropriate quantity into an **analogue voltage** which can then be fed into an **A to D converter** so that the **digital values** may in turn be fed into a computer system as shown in figure 25.3.

A study of the physical principles of many of the above transducers is not required by computer-science courses. However, we will need to know about the range of the output voltage from a particular transducer, and then translate these numbers into appropriate digital values which could then be used to control the display on a computer monitor, or produce an appropriate data file on disk, for example.

An example

Take the case of a typical temperature sensor. This would probably contain an electronic component which is sensitive to temperature, such as a thermistor. Now the resistance of the thermistor changes with temperature, and we will assume for simplicity that extra electronics have been added which ensures that this resistance change produces a linear voltage between defined levels. (A simple chip is available to do this.) Let's assume that 0 V represents 0 degrees centigrade and 2.55 volts represents 100 degrees centigrade. (Unlikely, I know – but it makes the maths easier!) Let's also assume that we have an 8-bit A to D converter. We therefore have 256 different outputs from our A to D which represent the voltages between 0 and 2.55 inclusive. Therefore, 00000000 out from the A to D means a temperature of 0 °C, and 11111111 out from the A to D means a temperature of 100 °C. Anything inbetween will be represented to the nearest level. Therefore, a reading of 00001111 would represent:

Temperature = 15 / 255 which is approximately 5.9 °C.

Note that we *can't quote* temperatures between 5.9 °C and 5.5 °C (the nearest output corresponding to 14/255), not because our temperature sensor is not capable of representing this temperature, but because our 8-bit A to D *has not got the appropriate* **resolution.** Note also that it would be silly to quote 5.89 °C and 5.49 °C for the temperatures stated above as it is *not possible* to justify two decimal places with the resolution from an 8-bit A to D. One final point worthy of note is that **accuracy** is another thing entirely, and depends upon the accuracy of the original temperature transducer and interfacing electronics (which is making the output linear).

You will recall that we are using a chip to remove the non-linearity of the temperature-sensing device – we could easily get rid of any non-linearity by accepting whatever readings we get from the A to D converter, and then having a **look-up table** inside the computer which converts the values received into actual temperatures.

Indeed, it is the ability of the computer to do this that often makes computerised interfaces considerably cheaper and easier to develop than their pure-electronic counterparts, any 'bodges' to the readings which are necessary can be catered for in the software!

Transducer control

It is very easy to say that a digital signal can switch an electric motor on and off, but I hope that few students would dream of connecting a d.c. motor across the output terminals of a typical port at the back of any computer! Although the computer *is* supplying the signal to switch on the motor, it obviously can't supply the required current (and hence power) needed by the motor. Therefore, an external power supply (or battery) needs to be used. We effectively use some electronics to interface the low-power output from the computer to the higher-power motor as shown in figure 25.7(a).

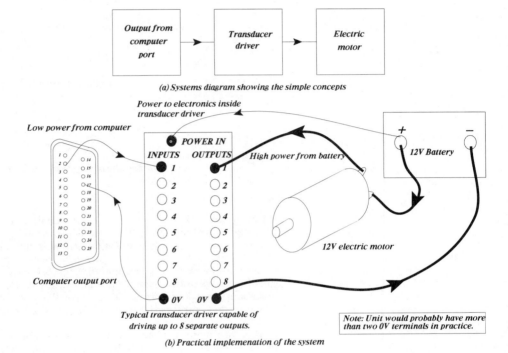

(a) *Systems diagram showing the simple concepts*

(b) *Practical implementation of the system*

Figure 25.7

You should note that the system diagram shown in figure 25.7(a) is the most easy to draw and understand, and it is *this type of diagram* that will be used in preference to the more-practical diagram shown in figure 25.7(b). However, if you wish to actually connect up a system and make it work, then you will have to get used to wiring up the arrangement in a similar way to the practical wiring layout.

Most microcomputer ports designed to enable the user to extract signals from the system are capable of outputting a current of a few mA at about 5 V. However, make use of a transducer driver and you will probably have the capacity to drive transducers such as motors up to 0.5 A or even up to 1 or 2 A if you have a beefy unit. Don't forget to follow the manufacturers instructions carefully, or if you are building your own – then make sure that you know what you are doing!

Feedback

We have seen how signals can be fed into a computer system and stored in the computer's memory, and have also seen how to monitor signals, via an A to D converter if necessary. We can achieve a more-comprehensive control system if we combine *both* the **monitoring** *and* **control functions**. For example, the temperature of a chamber or room could be monitored, and a heater switched on if it is too cold, or a motor-driven fan switched on if it is too hot. It is the role of the computer, or more-specifically the software which controls the computer to act as the decision-making element in the system.

The system described above makes use of an important control concept called **feedback**. The fan or the heater being controlled by the computer alters the temperature,

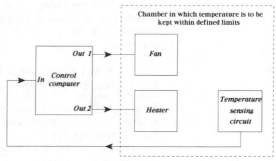

(a) Simple computer-control system with feedback

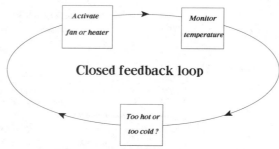

(b) The idea of a feedback loop is an important one

Figure 25.8

which, in turn is being monitored by the computer system which again affects what is happening at the output. The idea is shown in figure 25.8.

Notice how the fan or heater modifies the temperature – which is itself monitored to modify the behaviour of the fan or heater – which in turn modifies the temperature etc. Any system which modifies it's behaviour in this way makes up what is called a **closed loop system** and employs **feedback**. Feedback means that information about what is happening to a particular process is **monitored**, **fed back** to the computer and can then be used to *modify the behaviour* of the system being monitored.

There are many instances of feedback systems in real life. For example, incubators in hospitals, some traffic-light systems, and ABS (Anti-lock Braking Systems) on some cars. In an incubator system, temperature and a whole host of other quantities are measured and acted upon. In the traffic-light system the number of cars passing over sensors are monitored to modify the behaviour of the lights. In the ABS system, whether or not the wheels are locked is monitored and, if they are starting to lock, a pumping-action on the brakes is initiated which automatically helps to stop the wheels locking and the car skidding, and thus makes the car easier to control. There are also many natural examples of feedback such as the temperature control system in the human body – if we get too cold we shiver, or if we get too hot we sweat – we don't have to think about doing this, it happens automatically because of the **biological feedback mechanisms** inside our bodies.

The decision-making element

Although many types of control system can be accomplished by wiring together a few electronic components, *making use of a microprocessor or using a computer gives us the ability to solve more-complex problems in ways which are extremely cost effective.* Also, the behaviour of the systems can be modified more easily as software changes are inevitably easier than rebuilding parts of the electronic circuits. Most modern installations of any complexity make use of programmable systems as the decision-making element within the complete control system environment.

Embedded systems

Some systems, such as the control systems found in washing machines, microwave ovens and video recorders, for example, have purpose-designed microprocessor chips which, together with other chips perform all the necessary control functions. The detailed functions of these devices are usually programmed by the manufacturer and can't be altered by the users of the system. These are examples of what are commonly referred to as **embedded microprocessor systems**.

Although it is possible to rip out the existing control system from your washing machine, connect up your computer and operate the machine in this way, it would be a waste of money to have a VDU, full qwerty keyboard, disk drives and printer performing such a limited range of functions! However, the idea is not so silly as would appear at first sight. For example, in industry, computers *are* connected up to electronic devices such as video recorders to help find faults in the system, or to monitor the progress of certain parts of the video machine during the development and manufacture of new models. Automatic testing and generation of statistics about the systems being monitored are commonly gathered making use of these methods.

Stepper motor systems

The motors considered so far have been **dc motors** in which the *speed* is usually *proportional to the magnitude of the voltage* placed across the terminals. If **speed control** is required on these systems, then **D to A converters** (see page 580) would normally be employed to give the necessary alteration in voltage amplitude required to match any given speed. Complex **feedback mechanisms** (see page 582) would also be needed if we are to have any idea of the positional information of the output shaft of the motor, and extra equipment is needed if the direction of the motor is to be reversed.

A very different system of *speed, direction* and *positional control* is obtainable by making use of what are called **stepper motors**. Indeed, these devices are *so appropriate* for computer control – they could almost have been invented with the computer borne in mind. However, these motors have been controlled by digital electronics (not necessarily associated with computer systems) for at least 25 years. The ideas on which a stepper motor is based are simple, and the ease with which they can be controlled from a computer is extremely convenient to say the least.

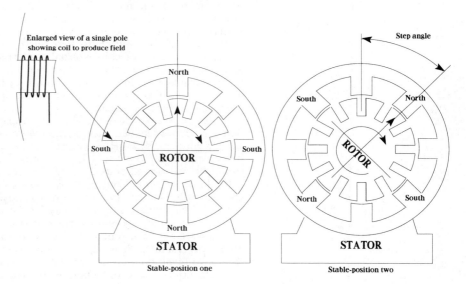

Figure 25.9

Figure 25.9 shows a section through the insides of a simple stepper motor. In practice more poles (the bits that stick out from the stator) would be present, but this diagram illustrates the principles well. A series of coils of wire (not shown on the main diagram but one is shown in the top left-hand corner) are wrapped round certain poles of the stator which produce patterns of north and south poles. The arrangement on the left shows one particular pattern, and the rotor (the bit that goes round in the middle) takes up a stable position held solid by the magnetic-field pattern. Next a different pattern is produced by another coil wrapped round a different set of poles, and this produces a different magnetic pattern as shown in the second part of the diagram. Being unstable in the old position, the rotor now moves round to the new position. This is a new stable state, and the motor has **stepped** round, in this case by about 45 degrees. If we made a different pattern the motor could be made to step round another 45 degrees – eventually the rotor would get to a position in which the original pattern would move the rotor a further 45 degrees. If the appropriate pattern repetition is carried out fast enough then the motor would appear to go round continuously. Typical stepper motors would have

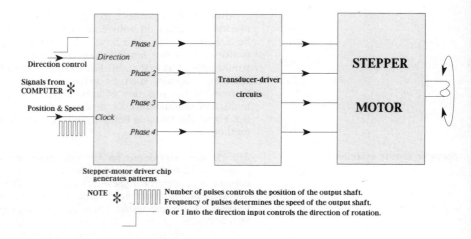

Figure 25.10

steps of about 1.8 degrees depending on price – the more expensive motors have smaller steps.

You should note that the magnetic pattern chosen was such that the motor would move round in a clockwise direction. A different pattern would cause it to move anticlockwise. Therefore, the signals which drive the motor determine the direction, the geometry of the motor determines the step angle (it's also possible to drive the motor in different ways to get what are called half steps), and the rate at which the patterns are changed determines the speed.

A typical motor would have four sets of coils which are wound around different poles, and each set of coils is usually referred to as a different phase. It's convenient to use a proprietary chip which generates these patterns for you, and the idea for a four-phase stepper motor is shown in figure 25.10. As can be seen from this diagram, control of position, direction and speed of the motor can all be obtained from just two binary signals.

If motors with small step angles are employed then very small amounts of rotation can be programmed, making these motors ideal for use inside peripheral devices such as **plotters**, **disk drives** and **printers** etc. They are also ideal for robotics, and indeed anywhere where speed, position and direction need to be controlled from a computer or from an embedded system (see page 582).

It should be noted that *very accurate positional* information is possible **without the use of feedback**. However, this assumes that the motor does not stall, and is actually doing what it's told! It may be, for example, that the inertia of the motor and the mechanical system to which it is connected keeps the shaft rotating after the pulses have been removed. Therefore, the practical use of stepper motors is a little more complex than might appear from reading the last section. Nevertheless, they have revolutionised the computer industry, enabling more complex and sophisticated control systems to be built with relative ease. Larger versions of these motors are very expensive, and therefore these output devices are usually found in precision control systems, with the original d.c. motors and feedback systems being used to move much larger loads like trains or the Jodrell Bank telescope, for example.

Having seen some of the many devices that it's possible to 'simultaneously' connect to a computer, you may be under the impression that an enormous number of different bus systems are needed. However, you will probably recall from the computer-architecture chapter that different devices are all connected to the *same* computer bus. It does not matter if we are dealing with getting data from a CD-ROM drive or controlling a stepper motor – the same data bus will probably be used for each device – apparently simultaneously.

Tri-state buffers

To understand how this is carried out in practice is relatively straight forward. It involves the use of a chip called a **tri-state buffer**. We have already encountered the term **buffer** on many occasions, but in this context, the buffer is referring to *carrying out some form of isolation so that the signals in one part of the circuit do not affect the signals in others*. Consider the data-bus system shown in figure 25.11.

We can see from figure 25.11 that *two* **stepper motors** are connected simultaneously to the computer system, but the principles we are discussing can be applied to *any number* of **input** or **output** devices connected at the same time. Data on the

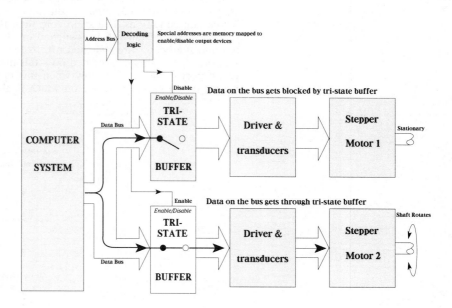

Figure 25.11

bus is usually intended for one device only, and so it has to be routed through the 'computer highways' so that it ends up in the right place. If data is placed on the data-bus or address-bus system then it 'instantly' (see page 51) appears at all points on the bus. It's then possible, for example, to open a 'gate' to let the signals through, or close a 'gate' so that the signals can't get through. If many of these gates are attached between the computer's bus and the peripheral devices, then only one gate need be opened at any one time, thus routing the data from and to the correct place.

Circuits which perform this 'gate' function are called **tri-state buffers** – this is because, unlike most digital chips inside the computer, these chips can have **three stable states**. The inputs and outputs on the tri-states can be either a '1' or a '0' just like any of the other circuits, but if the chip is disabled then it goes into what's called a **high-impedance state**. This can be thought of as being equivalent to little switches inside these devices being opened and closed – one switch would be necessary for each line on the bus, but only a single switch is shown in figure 25.11 for the sake of simplicity.

Some tri-state chips are uni-directional, as shown in figure 25.11 when driving the stepper motors, but others are bi-directional, thus allowing data to be controlled in either direction. Of course, these bi-directional chips would have to have an extra control input with a binary digit controlling the direction. We can see that these ideas are virtually identical in principle to those used when **multiplexing** is considered on page 503. Indeed, the arrangement in figure 25.11 could be used as a multiplexer circuit to drive two stepper motors at the same time – the data for each motor would be switched very fast between one motor and the other, the tri-states making sure that the right data gets to the right place. Of course, this assumes, that the software driving the system is capable of responding fast enough to drive the two motors simultaneously.

Control software

It's the job of the **software** *inside* the **computer** or **embedded-microprocessor system** to form the **decision-making element** of the control system. There is nothing difficult about this – the majority of readers of this book should be able to write suitable software already – assuming that you have an appropriate high-level or low-level language which can be used to monitor signals from, or output signals to a suitable port on the computer.

Let's take the case of the temperature-control system outlined in Fig 25.8. A typical flowchart for this particular system might be as shown in figure 25.12. From the flowchart you can see that most of the time is spent going round loops and checking for certain conditions. If it's too cold then the heater will be switched on, or if it's too hot then the fan will be switched on. If the temperature is OK, then both the fan and the heater are switched off. Note that it does not matter if you switch off a device that is already switched off – this means that the output pin from the appropriate port remains off or low when this operation is carried out. It also does not matter if you switch a device on which is already on.

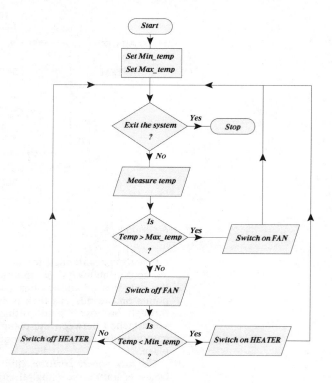

Figure 25.12

There may be some conditions under which the control system can't cope. For example, if the chamber being monitored gets damaged, then it might not be possible for the heater to heat up the chamber to a sufficient temperature, even if the heater is on all the time. Under these conditions it would be possible to activate an alarm if the temperature does not reach a desired level in a set period of time. An alarm can easily be connected to a third output from a suitable port of the computer.

Most control systems, no matter how complex, are variations on the simple themes described above. **Feedback** is constantly being monitored to provide the necessary data for the control system to be able to make decisions. Alarms can be activated or systems shut down if continuation with a particular process would be unsafe. Real-time clocks (usually the one set up inside the computer system) can be used in conjunction with the data to provide further analysis. Statistics may be produced such as a graph of temperature against time at five-minute intervals throughout the night if this was thought to be necessary. Salient points at which the fan or heater was brought into play could be plotted on the graph too. You are limited by your imagination only.

Real-time systems

Real-time systems must generate some sort of response (this may be action such as 'switching on a heater or a fan', for example) in relation to what's happening to some **external event** (such as the rise or fall of temperature, for example). Most of the real-time systems in operation today must act quickly, or extremely quickly, but this is *not* necessarily so for a system to be classified as 'real time' (see in a moment).

From reading the above paragraph you can easily see that real-time systems are of obvious importance in control, for it is in this type of environment in which a response is required from the controlling computer, often under the most stringent of time constraints. A typical example of *the* most stringent of real-time control-system constraints would be an **embedded microprocessor system** required to guide an anti-missile missile to its target. If a surface-to-air missile is launched from a ship, for example, sometimes only a few seconds are available for the missile just launched to lock onto, track and destroy the incoming target. The author knows of an ex marine, who used to be a chaplain at Tonbridge school, who owes his life to a real-time system such as the one being described. It is obviously no fun sitting in a frigate thinking that you have about twenty seconds to live before an incoming missile is about to strike. The microprocessors embedded into the anti-missile defence systems must act as quickly as possible on all the information being received from its **sensors** (the **input transducers**), make the appropriate decisions (guided by the software) and activate the appropriate guidance systems (the **output transducers**).

The designers of such systems must ensure that the best communication systems are available and that none of the vital incoming data is missed or misinterpreted – you get no second chance in some of these life-threatening situations. A *large* amount of **redundancy** is usually built into this type of **embedded system**, both in terms of processing power and duplication – sometimes triple-fail-safe systems ensure that reliability is extremely good. Often embedded systems costing tens of thousands of pounds or more do absolutely nothing for most of their life – but when a missile containing the system is launched, all hell breaks loose and the system bursts into action for a few seconds – and then it's blown to pieces! Nevertheless, hopefully the missile has done its job, a ship has been saved from sinking, tens of millions of pounds of equipment has been saved, but, most important of all, several hundred lives may have been saved too.

You will probably be pleased to know that real-time systems aren't only used in life-threatening situations. For example, when considering industrial and scientific instrumentation, it may be necessary to continuously monitor some readings and shut down a process if the safety of the plant or personnel are compromised, or if the specification for the product being manufactured is not within tightly-controlled limits. Therefore, for this particular system, although not necessarily lightning fast, the readings *must* be taken at appropriate intervals, or the system has failed to perform to specification, and some damage or loss of money may result.

Real time or not real time?

There have been many arguments in the computer world as to what actually constitutes a real time system – an airline booking system, for example, might be able to respond within a few seconds, as it is the wish of the airline company to make sure that booking a flight is not a lengthy and time-consuming process. In this case nothing drastic will happen if the response takes a few seconds longer, but it is obviously not performing to specification if a longer-than-acceptable delay should happen. Very long delays when booking airline tickets are not practical, and so this type of system is correctly referred to as real time. However, if this sort of argument is pursued to the limit, then a system which took 6 months to respond – *as long as this is acceptable in terms of the response time*, must be a real time system! This may be so, but it would usually defeat the object of what is intended when real-time systems are used in the modern world.

Most people today agree that real-time systems are, in general, ones in which the response must be very quick, but it's now becoming common to include parameters like **reliability**, and special requirements such as the *recovery* from possible **fault conditions**. Having worked through the rudiments of control systems you will appreciate that failure to respond quickly or reliably in many situations could literally result in a catastrophe. Failure of the control system in a nuclear power plant, for example, would be unacceptable. Just like the missile system considered earlier, double or triple redundancy is often built into these systems, with fail-safe devices acting as a backup in the event of a total failure of the computer system which is in control.

There can be no totally-safe system which is 100% reliable, but reliability factors of 1 failure in every 100,000,000 landings, for example, might be typical of acceptable figures for the computerised control systems on large civilian aircraft such as Jumbo Jets, or for those systems employed in air-traffic control systems. *Real time systems therefore encompass most of the conventional requirements of ordinary systems, but with added design requirements with regard to time constraints and reliability being dictated by the events being controlled.*

Real-time operating systems

From reading chapter 17 you will be well aware of the pivotal role played by the operating system inside a computer, and from reading the first part of this chapter you will also be aware of the fact that synchronising and reacting to **real-time events** which are happening in the outside world is the essence of a real-time system. Therefore, the designers of real-time computer systems have one of the most difficult tasks to date in terms of time-critical and reliable software and hardware design.

You will recall that conventional operating systems make use of interrupts to sort out priorities and get things done in the most efficient way, and although the same techniques can be used in real-time systems, it may be that conventional software or hardware restraints prevent the system from responding in real time. For example, is the data bus wide enough to get the required amount of data from point A to point B in an acceptable time given the current clock rate inside the computer? If not, then either a new bus system needs to be designed or the clock rate needs to be increased. If the clock rate is increased then different and more expensive electronics are needed for the system. Is the memory fast enough? Is the communication of data from the sensors to the computer at an acceptable Baud rate? Also, and most importantly, given the constraints of the hardware just mentioned, are the software routines in the operating system capable of operating at a speed sufficient to process the data in time?

After reading the above one might be tempted to give up and go and do anything other than be a real-time-systems engineer. However, remember that most computer systems have been designed as a compromise on cost, speed, reliability and convenience of use. Although we obviously can't say that money is no object, most people would agree that the enormous defence budgets in the West have financed the most sophisticated of computer systems, and the most speedy of critical or real-time systems. No longer must we be content with building a general purpose computer for a couple of thousand pounds which will appeal to the business and personal-computer market. Most real time systems of the sort being discussed in this chapter have large budgets for their implementation. In this case the designers of such systems can afford to make use of the fastest hardware available if this is necessary.

When writing real-time operating systems the advantage usually comes from the fact that you are designing the system to accomplish one purpose only – *that of getting a very specific and specialised job done in a time which is acceptably quick*. An operating system that is purpose designed for one application only will perform its job very quickly indeed. For less time-critical applications off-the-shelf real-time operating systems can be purchased – as this is less hassle than attempting to write one from scratch.

It is often the case that most of the unacceptable delays are created because of the complex and time-consuming processing that must be undertaken during the decision-making part of the system. The software being run on a real-time system is often working through many lines of code, and much effort is usually put into cutting down the lines of code, and performing the same functions in the most time-efficient way.

In addition to responding to interrupts in the ways described on page 378, real time systems *must* process interrupts within a specified time scale, irrespective of the number of other interrupts which may actually be happening at a particular moment in time. If this were not the case then valuable input data may be lost altogether. As with most operating systems, higher-priority interrupts may cause an interrupt to occur while the computer is mid way through processing one or more other interrupts. The use of very fast buffers (see page 384) is often incorporated into the system so that interrupts awaiting service can be processed with the maximum speed. Also, critical parts of the program which process the interrupts are often kept in high-speed cache memory. The code must also be written such that there are very few routines which *must* be completed before an interrupt can be serviced. If there are any non-re-entrant routines of this sort, then they should be kept as short as possible.

There are several **real-time high-level languages** available, of which **Ada** (see page 168) is the most notable. This language was developed by the American military for **real time control** purposes of the sort considered in this chapter.

The performance of many real-time systems can obviously be enhanced with parallel processing making use of several independent microprocessor systems (see page 64). Nevertheless, it is still often necessary to wait for the results from one processor before another can start on a new task which requires this information. Simple algorithms for parallel processing are covered on page 65.

Many **embedded systems** don't have an operating system at all, but are written directly in the low-level language of the particular processor being used. Although extremely tedious to write, these programs obviously offer the highest speed advantage for specialised systems. Also, for simple embedded systems such as those found in washing machines and video recorders, an operating system is totally unnecessary, with simple machine-code (or washing-machine code!) routines controlling simple functions such as monitoring and controlling transducers.

Industrial control systems

Many industries make extensive use of computerisation to monitor and control various production processes. From the control of large chemical complexes to the control of a small CNC milling machine in a school or college, computer control of previously-manual processes is now common. It's the computer's ability to be able to monitor what's happening 24 hours a day, seven days a week, and the precision with which it is possible to work which has lead to the demise of these often boring and tedious chores being carried out by manually-operated machines. The overriding factor is, of course, an economic one. If it were more cost effective to use manual labour in the industrialised world then computers would not have been introduced in the great profusion which we find today. There is also the safety aspect to consider, and the fact that most people today would not, in most cases, want to spend all of their time watching dials and taking down readings at frequent intervals.

Computers also have the edge when it comes to speed and efficiency. It would be impossible, for example, for a person to take readings at a rate of 1,000 per second – this is, of course, no problem for a computerised system. It would be tedious in the extreme for a person to take readings at half-hourly intervals for a period of six months – again, for a computerised system, this is not a problem. Computers don't get tired or bored, and can go on for years without deviating from the task which they have been set. This is not to say that computers never go wrong – far from it. We have to make sure that the systems fail safe when we consider the design of any process that was previously carried out by human beings.

Before going into further detail regarding a particular system, it's worth making a few observations about the many factors which may have to be taken into consideration when designing computerised control systems. All of the principles being investigated here are applicable to a wide variety of computer-control scenarios. Anything from monitoring the stresses and strains caused by the traffic going over a bridge – to looking after babies in intensive care units can be considered in similar ways.

Control systems analysis

Modern systems-analysis techniques have already been extensively covered elsewhere in this book, and the majority of the advice and methods outlined apply here too. However, to cut a long story short, we will list some of the main points to be considered when control systems in particular are being designed.

The purpose of the system

Some detailed objectives will be required and may include areas such as 'an increase in the level of safety' for some particular process, or an 'increase in efficiency' which might be expressed as a consequent increase in production or a reduction in costs, the ability to work 24 hours a day seven days a week, or the ability to monitor and control environmentally dangerous places. The extraction and production of statistics regarding a particular process or plant, for example, is also usually important. These objectives *must* be defined carefully or there can be no measure of the degree of success or failure of the project. *Quantitative and measurable parameters for each system are essential* (see the widget example in a moment).

Inputs and outputs

If a specific project is being undertaken, from an analysis of the quantitative objectives you should be able to determine what inputs and outputs are required. For example, in an **SCBU (Special Care Baby Unit)**, we might be measuring heart rate, blood pressure, temperature, oxygen content of the blood and a whole host of other important parameters. Parameters like these effectively define what **input transducers** would be necessary for the particular project. However, in practice we need to be much more specific than this – for example, if we are monitoring temperature in the SCBU – then over what range should this temperature be monitored? What resolution is necessary? What about the accuracy? A better specification might be 25 °C to 45 °C with a resolution of 0.1 degree and no deviation beyond ± 0.25% over this critical range.

What outputs are necessary? How should these outputs be presented? What form of display would best be suited to the conditions under which the system is to be

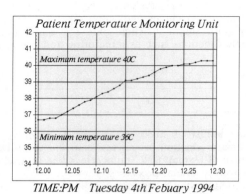

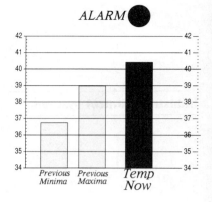

TIME:PM   *Tuesday 4th Febuary 1994*

Figure 25.13

used? Do we make use of a standard computer screen, or would an oscilloscope screen, LED or LCD screen (see page 245) be more appropriate? A computer screen might be appropriate for a permanent set up, but a small LCD screen would probably be more appropriate for a portable SCBU device which may be used on the move in an ambulance.

Do we need **hard copy** of what's been happening to the system? If so, over what time period do we need to have continuous readings available, and how frequently should these readings be taken? Should readings only be taken when an abnormal situation occurs? Is a standard printer acceptable or would a small thermal printer be ideal if the equipment were to be portable? If hard copy is *not* required, how should the output on the screen be presented – in the form of a graph, as a table of values, or some other more-specialised form of output such as a simulated control panel? Some alternative ideas for the representation of temperature in an SCBU are shown in figure 25.13. The first diagram shows an historical record of the patient's temperature for a half-hour period. The second diagram shows the previous maximum and minimum temperature, perhaps over the last hour, and the actual temperature now. In both cases it can be seen that the desired maximum temperature has been exceeded, and in the second case an alarm has also been automatically sounded. There are a whole variety of alternative representations, each having their strengths and weaknesses. For example, from the first graph it's possible to determine the *rate* of rise in temperature – this may be important. The second graph shows that an alarm has been activated – this also might make a sound until attention has been given to the unit controlling the device, in which case the system can then be reset.

Is the standard QWERTY computer keyboard the most appropriate form of input for the person who is controlling the system? It's likely that a concept keyboard (see page 223) with a special overlay would be more appropriate in many cases. Indeed, special keyboards *are* usually an essential part of most modern control systems. If no specialist keyboard is used then extensive use is sometimes made of the **soft keys** or **function keys** on a standard keyboard.

The human computer interface (HCI)

If a first-class systems analysis has taken place then we should have considered a *range* of possible output presentations and input possibilities for the system making full use of our knowledge of **Human-Computer Interaction (HCI).** (Also called the **Human-Computer Interface.**) It should be ergonomically sound and the presentation of the data should be in a form which can be easily understood and digested given the level of technical competence of the people who will be operating the system. One must always bear in mind that most of the systems will be operated by people who are *not* computer experts. Also, if we are dealing with systems such as the SCBU mentioned above, then a quick glance at the system's output for a fraction of a second might be all that can be managed before some life-saving techniques have to be carried out under conditions of great emotional and physical stress.

There is a whole science (art!) devoted to **human computer interaction**. For many years psychologists have been studying how humans react to the information presented to them by the computer in many different forms, and how it is best for humans to put information into the computer. Indeed, it was through the 'psychology of HCI' that interfaces like **windows** were developed. As far as the control systems being considered in this chapter are concerned, we are interested mainly in the clarity of information regarding its interpretation by the people who operate the control-systems. For example, an analogue display is usually best for an instant idea of the magnitude of a signal compared to its maximum allowable level, and a digital display is usually best for taking a specific reading. The development of pointing devices like the **mouse**, the use of **touch-sensitive screens**, **speech input** and **output**, and more recently hardware like the **data glove** are giving us new perspectives on how we can relate to computer systems in ways which increase productivity, creativity and safety. All of these devices and many others too are considered in the chapters on input and output systems covered elsewhere in this book.

Humans are not noted for their vigilance and concentration, especially when looking at information which is not changing for extended periods of time. Also, it may not be physically possible or even desirable to monitor the many different systems simultaneously. Therefore, parameters could be set which can activate some sort of alarm system if a maximum or minimum value is exceeded, as was the case in the temperature examples given above. Use could be made of colour to alert personnel to changing situations. For example, if a temperature reading is well within limits then no action need be taken, but if a temperature is getting dangerously close to activation of an alarm, then the display or a light on the control panel might change from green to amber to alert the personnel to a situation in which close and attentive human intervention is highly desirable. One must also not fail to recognise the consequence of replacing people with automatic control processes. Some people have some justification in feeling undervalued if all they are doing is watching a machine carrying out the processes that used to be undertaken manually by themselves. This process has come to be known as **de-skilling**.

Activation of alarm systems may actually lead to confusion if too many alarms are going off at the same time. When controlling large and complex processes such as those found in a nuclear power station or a sheet-steel rolling mill, for example, then one fault in one part of the system can, and often does, lead to faults in many other parts of the system if the original fault is not identified and corrected quickly – often within a few seconds of the fault occurring. Confusion can be compounded if operators misinterpret what's happening and this, in turn, can compound the confusion. It's fortunate that scenarios like this don't happen too often, but the underlying message is that when things do go wrong, if the principles of HCI have not been properly considered and applied, then the humans trying to deal with the situation will often not be able to cope efficiently. One must also not forget the compounding effects that a fault in the control system could have. A faulty indicator or sensor, for example could lead to the wrong action being taken. This is why the reliability of safety-critical plant must be as high as is cost-effectively possible.

Automatic monitoring

If the process being monitored or controlled is completely automatic, as might be the case with an industrial-control monitoring station, for example, then automatic shutdown of the process in the event of some particular parameter being exceeded might be the most appropriate course of action. For **remote control** and **data logging** situations such as the types used to constantly monitor weather parameters, an automatic phone call could be made alerting the on-duty operator so that appropriate remedial action can be taken as soon as is thought necessary.

Remote interrogation of systems via a phone line or network might be extremely useful for systems such as the weather stations or pollution-monitoring systems. Data could be changed into an appropriate form *before* being sent over the telephone to a computer which may be some distance from the logging or control station. In this way data from many remote stations may be automatically logged and correlated.

Signal conditioning

Are the signals being monitored in an appropriate form to be fed into the computer system? Will any **A to D** or **D to A converters** be necessary? If the analogue signals are too small then electronic amplifiers will be needed to boost the signals to acceptable values for the A to D converters to handle. Are any analogue signals too large? Special attenuation circuits might be necessary to reduce the amplitude of these signals to a sensible value that can be handled by the A to D converter circuits. Are the signals available in **parallel** or **serial** form? If they are in the wrong form then either **serial-to-parallel** or **parallel-to-serial** conversion may be needed. If there are too many signals to plug into the computer at the same time then some form of **multiplexing** might be necessary (see page 503). In practice, for systems like the SCBU mentioned above, many specialist interfaces would need to be designed for both the input and output systems.

Software for the system

Are we going to use a microcomputer, minicomputer or an embedded microprocessor system? The **software** available for each might be very different indeed. For large control systems there will probably be a combination of many of these smaller systems, perhaps communicating with each other via a suitable network. For **embedded systems**, it's likely that the software is *developed and tested* on a separate computer-based system, then **compiled** into the appropriate **machine code**, and finally blown into a suitable **ROM**-based memory chip ready to be plugged into the final controlling or monitoring device.

Widget quality assurance control

All aspects of good software development and design covered elsewhere in this book apply equally to the development of software for control systems. However, the extra conditions of time constraints when reacting in real time usually makes the software more difficult to develop.

Specialist languages such as **CORAL (COmmon Real-time Application Language)** provide the software designers of **real-time control systems** with a language that is particularly suited to the control of industrial plant. This language has been used extensively in the control industry by companies like Ferranti, and, as is the case with many long-established high-level languages, a wealth of **library routines** exist which can be incorporated into typical control-system application programs. Other languages, such as **FORTH**, have been specifically designed for control systems making use of microcomputers.

Besides being able to control the industrial plant the software routines must also cater for things like routine maintenance. For example, part of the plant may have to be cleaned once per week. It may be that production quotas will have to be reduced during this period of cleaning and the software might allow the manual re-routing of the process to alternative parts of the plant while parts of the production line are out of action.

It's probable that self-diagnostic routines would be implemented and run periodically to check that the plant is functioning within the parameters that have been set. For example, actual sets of data can be read from the industrial process under known conditions and compared with expected sets of data held inside the computer's data bank. Indeed, it may be that these auto-calibration routines are run automatically at set intervals if they do not require the processes being carried out to be stopped. The software would also probably allow the manual operators of the system to interrogate any part of the system at any phase during the process. You can therefore see that controlling what's going on is only one of the major parts of the whole package which is designed to help control, maintain, and run industrialised processes in cost effective, efficient and safe ways.

Specialist control languages such as CORAL are ideal for the control parts of the system, but one must not forget that it's probable that a major statistical analysis of the plant and an analysis of the cost effectiveness etc. will also be required. Therefore, more conventional languages will probably be used to analyse the data gathered from the sensors by other parts of the system. Specialist applications packages will also play their part too when it comes to the more-conventional data-processing aspects of the business.

After looking at the major aspects of computerised-control-system technology, we will now look at a more specific problem involving the production of widgets.

Let's assume that we are to design a computerised system to help in the testing of a widget – an electronic device which is a top-secret component for use in a more-complex radar system on a new aircraft. We will concentrate on the quality-assurance phase of the manufacturing process, namely, that of testing that the widget performs to the most stringent requirements laid down by the aviation industry.

As far as our system is concerned, we can view the widget as being a 'black box' into which two analogue voltages called V_{in1} and V_{in2} are fed, and an output which is precisely defined by the following formula.

$$V_{out} = 3.5V_{in1} + 1.6V_{in2}$$

The idea is shown in figure 25.14.

The test conditions

Let's assume that the input voltages to the widget may be allowed to vary over the range 2 V to 5 V with a tolerance of $\pm 1\%$. For each value of input voltage, there would be an acceptable range of values of output voltage. Taking one specific pair of values for the input voltages as an example, if both V_{in1} and V_{in2} were '5 V', then each could actually be within the range $\pm 1\%$ of 5 V, namely between 4.95 V and 5.05 V. This would therefore give rise to a range of outputs between two possible values from the widget under this particular pair of input conditions. This range

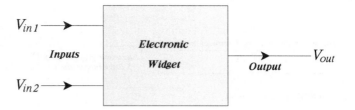

$V_{in1} \longrightarrow$

Inputs

Electronic Widget

Output $\longrightarrow V_{out}$

$V_{in2} \longrightarrow$

Figure 25.14

would have the following maximum and minimum values.

$$V_{out(max)} = 3.5 \times 5.05 + 1.6 \times 5.05 = 25.755 \text{ Volts}$$
$$V_{out(min)} = 3.5 \times 4.95 + 1.6 \times 4.95 = 25.245 \text{ Volts}$$

Generation of the data

If, for the sake of argument, the output voltage from the widget is not allowed to deviate outside of this range by more than 0.01 of a volt, the maximum acceptable output voltage from the widget under these conditions is 25.756 V, and the minimum output voltage is 25.244 V. Test data can easily be generated and programmed into the computer system such that the range of acceptable output is available for different combinations of input voltages.

The aviation industry has specified that tests must be carried out on the widget under different temperatures, pressures, humidities and vibration conditions, over extended periods of time in an environmental chamber. The output voltage from individual widgets must not vary by more than the specified range for each test condition, and an individual 'widget certification' in the form of graphs is required with the guarantee that accompanies each widget. The basic ideas shown in the cartoon are not too far from the truth *before* computerisation of these processes was undertaken – several groups of people had to work day and night to ensure that the dials were set to the appropriate points and readings were constantly monitored.

Controlling the test procedures

After consideration of just a small part of the specification we can see that test rigs would have to be designed in which an individual or group of widgets are placed, and the input and output voltages carefully monitored and recorded for each test condition. It would take too long to go into detail for all the test conditions, therefore we will concentrate only on the general set up and overall system requirements.

Vibration testing

*If anything fails in here it'll probably be **US**!*

`WIDGET TESTING`

Let's concentrate first on the **vibration testing** of the widget. We could easily set up a platform onto which each widget is bolted making use of the actual mounting facilities designed for the aircraft. The idea is shown in figure 25.15. Here you can see that the widget has been rigidly bolted to the surface of the test bed. The two voltages V_{in1} and V_{in2} are controlled from the computer software and fed via D to A converters and amplifier systems into the widget being tested. The output from the widget is attenuated, fed into an A to D converter and monitored by the computer software in real time.

In addition to the monitoring of the widget the computer controls the vibration of the bed in terms of amplitude, frequency and the times for which these conditions are to be set up. An accelerometer system is used so that the computer can monitor the g force being experienced by the unit under test.

As can be seen from figure 25.15, the computer control system has a variety of inputs and outputs, one of which is multiplexed. Multiplexing (see page 503) is often used if many inputs or outputs are required to be 'simultaneously' connected to the computer system. For example, if eight widgets are to be tested at the same time, then this would generate a further 56 inputs and 56 outputs! As long as the computer is able to process all the data at a fast enough rate, then multiplexing is one way of cutting down on a ridiculous number of input and output lines that would be required – and this is just for the vibration testing, we have not yet looked into the temperature, pressure and humidity requirements, all of which will require several more input and output systems.

The temperature tests

The temperature systems would be very similar in principle to the temperature-control systems outlined earlier in this chapter. However, for the aviation industry, more extreme temperature profiles would probably be required. Let's suppose that the widgets must perform to specification over the temperature range varying from –60 °C to +300 °C. First we will need an environmental chamber capable of

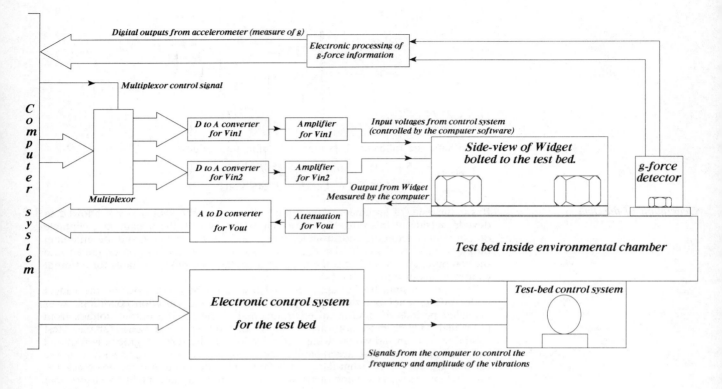

Figure 25.15

reproducing these temperatures, and, if the entire testing process is to be automated, we will need the computer system to be able to monitor and control the temperature of the chamber. For convenience we will assume that we have a single chamber that can cope with the required temperature range.

Pressure and humidity

Humidity could be controlled by a system which extracts moisture from the air (by heating and ventilation) or injected moisture into the chamber, and the pressure would be controlled by pumps to either increase the pressure or reduce the pressure inside the chamber. Humidity sensors and pressure sensors would generate analogue voltages which would also need A to D converters to condition the signals before feeding them into the computer system. The pressure, humidity and temperature control systems are shown in figure 25.16.

In practice there would probably be a few extra safety features such as automatic shutdown of the system if the pressure got so high that it would damage the test equipment inside the chamber, for example. For clarity these extra safety systems have not been shown on this diagram.

Setting up the test conditions

A suitable set of test conditions must be arranged. For example, we might make sure that the temperature is at –60 °C, then vary the input voltages from 2 V to 5 V over a two-hour period. We might then follow this with an increase in temperature over a 20-minute period to 300 °C, during which time the inputs are varied from 2 V to 5 V and back again at one-minute intervals. The temperature might then remain at 300 °C for the next 12 hours, during which time the inputs are varied at hourly intervals and the g force experienced by the unit is increased to 10 g under conditions of 90% humidity etc.

In practice these test conditions would be laid down by the aviation industry and would simulate the harsh conditions which could be experienced by the widget when it is placed on an aircraft which is flying in extreme temperatures and g-forces. These test conditions can be set up by writing the appropriate software schedules for each of the tests. It really is little more complex in principle than the simple flowcharts considered in figure 25.12. Here we are just dealing with more inputs and outputs, and have introduced an element of real time in the system if the specifications laid down by the aviation industry are to be met.

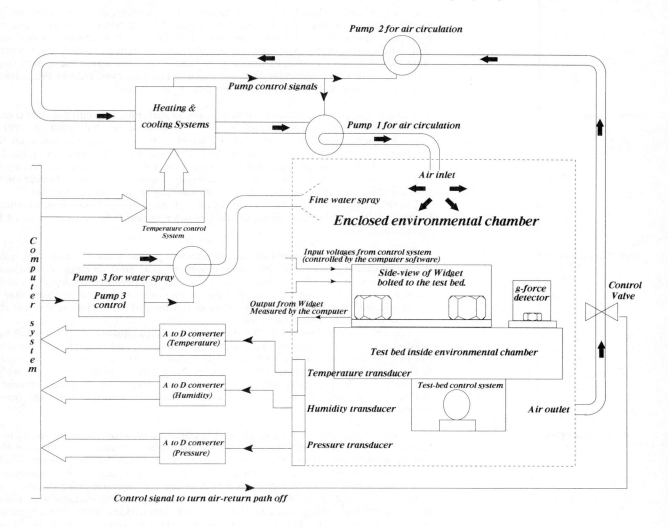

Figure 25.16

At the start of each test cycle one or more completed widgets (more in practice, but we will assume just one for the sake of argument) would be wired up to the system and the control-software sequence initiated. In practice, the operator of the system would probably have several options, one of which might be to calibrate the system. This option might ensure that a small number of tests are carried out on the test rig itself to ensure that the devices used to monitor and control the system are operating effectively. It would be a waste of time if there were a fault in the system as this would render the data collection process useless.

Checks that might be made would probably include calibration of the instruments under carefully controlled conditions, checks that the widget itself is powered up correctly and working, checks on the connections to the computer system and obvious checks on the readiness of the computer system such as 'Is there enough disk space to store the new data for a continuous automatic test?'

Specific software modules

The software can easily be split up into several important modules, with the important ones being shown in the following list.

> *Scheduling*
> *Signal conditioning*
> *Sensor monitoring*
> *Alarm systems*
> *Data collection*
> *Diagnostics*
> *Control*

Each area will be briefly looked at to explain its function in terms of the widget-testing control software, but it should be noted that it's possible to write general-purpose software for this particular environmental chamber. Indeed, if this were done with a generalised environmental chamber, there might be several other controllable parameters such as light intensity, radiation or radio waves etc. which might not be used in these particular tests for the widgets. However, change the software and other pieces of equipment could be tested just as easily.

Scheduling

The scheduling software controls what happens in real time. It would not only control what actuators and sensors should be active to achieve specific results at specific times, but would also be responsible for effective memory management such that incoming data from the sensors is not lost. It would be responsible for outputting data to disk, when necessary, printing messages on a printer, if required, driving the displays on the computer screens and generally ensuring that the schedule of the tests and the operation of the test rig is proceeding in an efficient manner.

The scheduling software would control all aspects of the test unless automatically interrupted by an alarm situation or manual intervention from the keyboard of the computer system.

Signal conditioning

The vast array of information from the sensors will probably not be linear. Therefore, the actual digital values received at the computer's port must be mapped onto actual parameters such as g-force reading in m/sec^2, or temperature in degrees Celsius. Look up tables, mathematical equations or combinations of these methods may be applied to the incoming data before it is stored on disk to represent the test data for later analysis by other software.

Similarly, parameters used by the programs to express quantities like 5 g will have to be converted into voltages which represent amplitude and frequency of the vibrations of the test bed. In this particular case the differential of the amplitude against time graph of the test bed will be related to the g force experienced by the widget at a particular frequency. It would be the job of the signal conditioning software to ensure that the correct information in the correct form is output from the correct computer port.

Sensor monitoring

Most sensors will probably be monitored irrespective of what's actually meant to be happening in the chamber. In this way the controlling software can be alerted to any unforeseen danger such as a build up of heat – perhaps the relay which switches the powerful heater on has got stuck even though temperature is not supposed to be playing a role with some particular part of the test at some point in time.

The sensors will probably be monitored and compared with maxima and minima set by the program being run, and also set for the safe maxima and minima regarding the environmental chamber. It's no use getting the controlling software to attempt to heat up a widget to 800 °C if this sort of temperature would melt some of the monitoring equipment inside the chamber, or cause damage to the chamber itself. Under extreme conditions such as this it would probably be necessary to have a safety cut out which is *not* under the control of the computer software. All potentially dangerous systems such as heat, pressure and 'g force' etc. should have cut out systems that fail safe in the event of an apparent malfunction of the computer system.

Alarm systems

The alarm systems, not shown in the control-systems diagrams on the previous pages would activate either under the control of the software when certain parts of the tests need individual attention, or under the direct control of the fail-safe systems mentioned in the last section. The fact that the alarm has gone off will probably be recorded by the software so that some diagnostic routines may be run at a later stage.

Data collection and analysis

The data from the tests can be used to generate a wealth of statistics from which it can be decided whether the widgets under test have passed or failed. If a widget has passed then the serial number can be automatically printed onto pre-prepared stationary along with the salient points from the test and any graphical output which has been calculated from the accumulated results.

If a widget has failed a test, then that part of the test (e.g. vibration or temperature etc.) should be printed out in detail, together with the reasons why the test has failed. For example, it might be that the output voltage from the widget exceeded the stated parameters by 5% under forces of 9g and temperatures of 275 °C after 5 minutes 3 sec. The widget can then be sent back to production and the faulty component inside may be identified and replaced, so that this widget may be subjected to the same tests at a later date.

Diagnostics

There should be some self-diagnostic routines in the software so that the test rig may be checked before any test is carried out. If there is a potential fault in any part of the system then the diagnostic routines on the computer system should help the engineer conducting the test to identify the fault with a minimum of delay. Any time that the environmental chamber is not testing widgets because of some fault condition is wasting money for the company that is producing the widgets.

Control

It should be possible for the operator of the system to interrupt the system at any time, irrespective of what's happening. In this case the control program should be able to override the scheduler, and the system automatically brought into a safe mode of operation under manual control. Of course, this control system should not be able to override the automatic safety features not under the control of the computerised parts of the system.

The manual control system should have the option of continuing with the test or stopping the test at any point in the schedule of operation if it were safe to do so. For example, the door of the environmental chamber must *not* be allowed to be opened if release of the pressure at a high temperature inside the chamber would cause an accident to the operator who has just opened the door. Again, this part of the system should not be able to be overridden by a manual control from the computer console.

Exercise 25.1

1. What is a **transducer** and *how is it used* in a computer control system?

2. Interfacing is an important concept in computing. Explain what is meant by an **interface**, giving some typical examples.

3. What is the purpose of a **port** on the back of a computer?

4. Make a list of *five* different **input transducers** and *five* different **output transducers** stating whether each deals with analogue or digital electrical signals.

5. Explain the main difference between **serial** and **parallel transmission** of data in computer systems. Under what conditions is each system ideal?

6. When using serial data transmission **synchronisation** between the transmitting and receiving devices is essential. Explain how this is achieved in practice.

7. Explain the difference between **analogue** and **digital** signals giving an example of each.

8. Explain the principle of **digital to analogue (D to A) conversion** with reference to a **12-bit D to A converter**. Your answer should include why **resolution** is important and you should calculate the number of different levels available from the analogue output of this particular 12-bit D to A.

9. **Feedback** is particularly important when the **safety** of computer control of an industrialised plant is being considered. Explain *what* is meant by the term **feedback** and *why* it is so important *from a safety point of view*.

10. What is the difference between an **embedded control system** and a **computer-controlled system**. Give some examples of each and outline some *advantages* and *disadvantages* of each method of control.

11. Stepper motors are ideal for control via a computer system. Explain what is meant by a stepper motor, and compare and contrast this motor with computer control using conventional d.c. motors.

12. Explain why tri-state buffers are needed inside most computer systems. Give an example of how tri-state buffers could be used to handle data going to a printer, and going to and coming from a disk drive.

13. Most control systems work is **real time**. Give an example of a real-time system and explain why it is more difficult to design these systems than conventionally-based computer systems.

14. Real time control systems often have to react extremely quickly to outside events. Outline a typical scenario in which this is the case and state *what other factors* need to be considered besides speed of operation.

15. What is meant by HCI and why is the science of HCI so important to the design of computerised control systems?

16. Design a computerised control system to make the perfect cup of coffee. You may assume that you have coffee, water, milk and sugar dispensers operated by valves. A water heater, appropriate fluid-flow measuring devices, and a set of six mugs on a carousel which is controlled by a motor. Draw a diagram similar to those for the widget environmental chamber on page 595. State any assumptions that you may have to make.

End of chapter summary

- A **computer control system** may range in size from **embedded systems** to the control of **entire industrial processes** involving a mini or mainframe computer.
- Control systems usually have **input** and **output transducers** which must be correctly **interfaced** with the computer.
- An **interface** *converts* the signals into a form which the computer system can handle, or changes computer signals into a form which can operate the transducers.
- **Input transducers** convert physical quantities such as light or temperature into an electrical signal.
- **Output transducers** convert electrical signals into other forms of energy such as rotary or linear motion, heat, light or sound etc.
- Signals coming from or going into the computer can be in **serial** or **parallel** form.
- **Serial interfaces** are ideal for communication over long distances.
- **Parallel interfaces** are ideal for *internal* computer communications (e.g. the **bus system**) or over distances up to a few metres.
- A **port** is the name given to the part of the interface to a computer where the signals come into or go out from the computer.
- There are many different connection **standards** for computer interfacing of which the **centronics** (parallel) and **RS232** (serial) are two common examples.
- Most computers are already controlling a variety of devices such as printers, or disk drives, for example. Larger control systems operate on similar principles.
- **General-purpose interfaces**, often called **user ports** or **special-purpose expansion cards** enable the bus systems inside the computer to be interfaced to the outside world.
- **Bus systems** are *important* when considering the connection of external devices. Compatibility versus changing requirements is often a problem.
- When information is transmitted from point A to point B **synchronisation** and **timing** are *essential*.
- When transmitting data in **parallel** the **clock system** provides **synchronisation**.
- When **serial transmission** is used, **stop** and **start bits** provide help with **synchronisation**.
- When data is being transmitted **serially**, the **Baud rate** must be the same at each end.
- The **Baud rate** is the number of **bits/sec**. It is *not necessarily* the same as the **information data transfer** rate because of the **start** and **stop bits**.
- Two types of signal are common – **analogue** and **digital**.
- An **analogue signal** is one which is **continuously variable** between two limits.
- A **digital signal** can have only two states – **on** or **off**.
- Computers deal with digital signals, and circuits called **analogue to digital (A to D) converters** are needed to change the analogue signals into digital form.
- **A to D converters** work by **sampling** the analogue signals at (usually) frequent intervals and producing a **digital value** for **each sample**.
- The **number of bits** in an **A to D converter** determines the **resolution** with which the original **amplitude** of the analogue signal can be represented.
- The process of converting an analogue signal into a digital value is called **digitisation** or **quantisation**.
- **Nyquist's criterion** states that an analogue signal must be sampled at twice the highest frequency component present in it *if* it is to be faithfully reproduced.
- Many different **sensors** are available which can convert quantities like **pH**, **light intensity**, **radiation**, **pressure** or **velocity** etc. into appropriate electrical signals.
- The processing power inside a computer is often used to convert **non-linear readings** from **inexpensive transducers** into more-useful numbers. The ability of the computer to do this often makes computer interfacing versatile and relatively cheap.
- Power to drive transducers like motors and lights etc. is *not* taken from the computer's port, but from external power supplies.
- Signals which are **fed back** into the computer system to provide information for the computer such that it can make effective decisions are called **feedback signals**.
- A system which *both* **monitors** *and* **controls** functions *and acts upon the information received* such that more effective control is exercised is called a **closed-loop feedback system**.
- **Feedback** means that information about what is happening to a particular process

is **monitored**, **fed back** to the computer and can be used to *modify the behaviour* of the system being monitored.

■ The use of **computers** or **microprocessors** in a control system is often very cost effective.

■ A **microprocessor** used in a **control system** is called an **embedded microprocessor system**.

■ **Embedded microprocessor systems** are typically found in devices ranging from **washing machines** to **guided missiles**.

■ A **stepper motor** is ideal for computer control because position, speed and direction can all be controlled from digital signals.

■ **Stepper motors** are used in **disk drives**, **plotters**, **printers** and many other peripheral devices.

■ A **tri-state buffer** is an *electronic* circuit which has **three states**, namely '1', '0' or a high-impedance state which is *equivalent to being switched off.*

■ **Tri-state buffers** are *used to steer electronic signals around the computer*, making sure that they go from and to the correct places.

■ The **control software** inside an embedded system or computer-controlled system is similar in principle to all other software.

■ **Response** in **real time** is often important in control systems if damage or a disaster is to be averted.

■ **Real time** is taken to mean that the response from the system is *fast enough to deal with the information coming in, process it, then give a suitable response before a set deadline.* This is *usually* taken to mean a **very fast response**, but real time *does not have to be* fast on some systems.

■ A **real time system** often has a **high reliability factor** built in, and much **redundancy** is often incorporated to ensure that reliability is as high as is cost-effectively possible.

■ A **real time operating system** is one specifically designed for **fast response** and **high reliability**. Other factors, such as efficient use of processor time and convenience of use, for example, prominent in conventional operating systems *don't usually apply* to real-time operating systems.

■ Most real time systems are **single-purpose** only – *that of getting a very specific and specialised job done in a time which is acceptably quick.* Other operating systems are often general-purpose in nature and are therefore a compromise.

■ **Small embedded systems** often have no operating system, but rely on simple machine-code programs to execute a small sequence of instructions.

■ Some languages are designed for real time operation. **Ada** and CORAL are typical examples.

■ **Cost cutting** and **increased efficiency** are major factors in implementing computerised control of industrial processes.

26 Some social implications

Introduction

The **social implications** of computers should *not be considered in isolation* from the rest of this book. Indeed, it is only by *understanding* a considerable proportion of the work at this level that you are in a position to argue rationally at a good intellectual standard about these implications. There are some topics on which the majority of the populace consider themselves to be experts, and social implications of computers is, unfortunately, usually one of them. Irrational fears which are based on ignorance, misconceptions which are usually perpetuated in science-fiction movies, and sensationalised exaggeration in the popular press go a long way to reinforce these jaundiced views. As **computer science students** *you are expected to be able to transcend this morass, and to apply rational arguments based on current technological facts and likely possible future scenarios*. You will get *few* marks in an examination if you follow the herd mentality and write bland statements such as 'Computers seem to be taking over the world' or 'Big brother is watching you', for example.

A balanced point of view

It's *essential* to be able to **perceive both sides of an argument** and produce plausible presentations for either side. Few things in computing are wholly good or bad, and misuse of technology designed for other purposes usually provides you with the converse of any particular assertion. Typical social implications are considered in this chapter, but it's also essential to keep up to date by reading appropriate newspapers, technical magazines, by listening to the radio and watching suitable TV programmes (see page 6) if your arguments are to have the added thrust of topicality. I would suggest that you choose a few controversial topics, and prepare an argument for and against in each case. You've already got a large arsenal of possibilities – with **artificial intelligence**, **neural networks**, **virtual reality**, **expert systems**, **robotics** and **global networks** to name but a few. If your teacher agrees, then this type of classroom activity can be highly enlightening, and help to prepare you for examination questions on this sort of topic.

Computer crime

Computer crime has only recently been taken *very* seriously. Surprisingly, at the time of writing the third edition of this book, most police officers in the UK still have no formal training in the use of computers, or in the ways in which computers are being used by today's high-tech criminals. However, the government is, at last, slowly starting to address this particular problem, and there is a special computer crime unit at New Scotland Yard. You may be amazed by the statement at the beginning of this paragraph, but not too long ago most computer criminals were regarded as little more than misguided and curious boffins who hacked into systems to satisfy their intellectual curiosity – unfortunately, some teachers at school still accept this childish-prank mentality when students attempt to hack into their systems too. Nevertheless, internationally, hundreds of millions of pounds lost each year to computer fraud in the commercial world has rapidly changed these ill-advised perceptions. There are many aspects to computer crime, with theft of money or information, infection with viruses, destruction of stored information and fraud to name but a few. In the next few sections we will briefly investigate some of the main areas, but information regarding actual cases can easily be obtained by searching the CD-ROM databases of newspapers such as the Times and Sunday Times, for example.

Financial gain

Although most commercial computer fraud involves financial gain, here we are referring specifically to fraud involving the mishandling of money on the computer system itself. How this might be done in practice depends upon the access that a particular individual has got to a computer system. For example, bank employees who are programmers *may* have the ability to alter figures on their own or somebody elses account. Don't forget that it's these programmers who write the error detection and correction routines which would flag such errors when financial checks are performed automatically by the system! One would be stupid to attempt to transfer large sums of money in this way, but a famous example involved a programmer who rounded down interest payments due to customers to the nearest penny, then transferred the odd fractions of a pence to one of his own accounts. Now a fraction of a penny does not sound very much, and the customers would obviously not complain if they are 0.5 pence short, for example, on the interest paid by the bank, especially if this trivial amount is part of a larger payment involving hundreds or even thousands of pounds. Nevertheless, over a few years, and with millions of customers involved, the amount grew into tens of thousands of pounds – and nobody was ever going to complain!

The hole-in-the-wall gang

More money is lost each year from hole-in-the-wall Automatic Teller Machines (ATMs) than through the archetypal bank robbery hold ups. It's not difficult to gain access to machines which can program magnetic stripes on cards, as many companies and academic institutions now produce their own identity-card systems for in-house use. If you know the encoding methods used by a particular bank, (some employees obviously do), then all that is needed is an account number *and* a PIN number to gain illegal access to an account via an ATM. Criminals have been known to observe other people entering their PIN numbers, then to pick up a carelessly discarded receipt on which an account number may be present. Armed with this information the criminal can then use the portable machine to code the account number, a fictitious daily credit allowance and PIN number into the magnetic stripe of a newly created illegal ATM card. The criminal then takes this card to a variety of machines, merrily removing the cash, taking particular care not to let other people see him or her using an obviously blank card on which a magnetic stripe has been encoded – to other members of the public this individual is going about his or her normal business. Unfortunately, it's then up to the customers to pay the bill as the bank rightly thinks that it's their card which has been used. As far as the bank is concerned phantom withdrawals don't take place – and in this particular case it's true – the bank is right in thinking that a customer's card and PIN *have* been divulged, and the customers are 'right' in thinking that they have not used their cards or told anybody about their pin numbers. That will teach people not to drop litter after they have used the ATM machine! It should also teach them to make sure that nobody else is close enough to look over their shoulder during any transactions which they may be undertaking – you have been warned.

Management embarrassment

Commercial organisations such as banks and insurance companies are often reticent about publicising computer fraud. Just think of the panic that would ensue if a particular bank admitted that 1 million pounds a week, for example, is being lost though computer system fraud! Apart from being made a laughing stock, the negative publicity would probably cause more financial loss through legitimate customers withdrawing their money, as these customers would perceive it to be unsafe if left in this particular system. No company wants to admit that their computer system has inadequate security.

Forged documentation

DTP systems are good – in fact they're so good that together with a decent laser printer it's getting difficult to tell the difference between real documentation and a forgery. Many pupils at school now have access to high-quality image creation systems, and it would be an unusual school in which some of the pupils have not, at some time in the past, attempted to forge documentation such as birth certificates or other ID cards. This is serious in itself, but when one considers the potential for creating false examination certificates, false receipts for the tax man or false tickets and passes etc, then one is into very serious criminal activities which involve major fraud if carried out on a large scale. Colour laser printers with the ability to print on different coloured card adds to the authenticity of documentation. With many hundreds of different fonts (see page 524) currently available it's becoming possible to be able to recreate exact duplicates of almost any desired documentation. The only things left which are still outside the range of all but the most determined criminals are holographic inserts, or in the case of forging money – metal stripes inside the paper and getting special paper which passes the UV reflection test.

Computer viruses

Typical viral infection symptoms

Practice safe hex!

The cost of a viral infection

Computer viruses are now commonplace, or so the viral-protection advertisements would have us believe! Unfortunately, viruses *are* becoming more common, and at the time of writing, the Computer Crime unit at New Scotland Yard had identified 135 different computer viruses in the UK. Many different viruses are unfortunately obtainable from questionable bulletin boards over the Internet (see page 534), and some joker has even produced a CD-ROM to distribute 4,000 different strains of all types of virus! Therefore, prudent companies must obviously take serious measures to protect themselves against this potentially disastrous threat. A **computer virus** is an **illegal program** which usually *propagates itself* and *modifies* or *destroys* other programs. At best it can cause annoying messages to be displayed on the screen, and at worst it can ruin a business through massive losses of essential data. There are hundreds of known computer viruses, with some of the most common having names like **Michaelangelo**, the **Trojan horse** and the **worm**, for example.

The **Michaelangelo** virus is a particular example of one type of virus called a **logic bomb** or a **time bomb**. This is a disastrous virus which usually wipes data off your hard disk on some *predetermined date*. This is often **Friday the 13th**, or in this particular case **March 6th** which happens to be the great artist's birthday.

The **Trojan horse** is an example of a **virus** *which appears to do something legitimate but at the same time actually does something illegal*. For example, whilst generating some data for transfer to a disk, an illegal copy of the data can be made and placed in an unauthorised place. This illegal copy could then be used at a later date for blackmail or other extortion purposes.

The **worm** is an example of a virus that replicates itself and takes over computer memory. Therefore, software that would normally run with no problems at all on a particular computer eventually won't be able to run properly because of lack of memory due to multiple infections of the same virus. Viruses usually propagate themselves by attaching to and modifying a **boot file** (see page 390) used when the computer starts up, and others append themselves to memory-resident modules by intercepting and diverting pointers via the virus to the original location for the module.

Many viruses cause error messages to be generated which apparently come from the operating system. Therefore, users spend some time trying to rectify errors which don't actually exist! Others link to applications and then cause these applications to fail to run on certain days (a non destructive but equally annoying variation on the Michaelangelo virus theme). One particular virus on the Acorn Archimedes computer called DataDQM causes the screen to judder by increasing amounts on Thursdays!

Some viruses display nasty messages on the screen – for example, after sixteen infections of the CeBit virus you get the message 'From the Devil, The lord of Darkness'. A virus will often load itself into an illegal area of memory and thus cause the computer to crash because routines normally resident at this point in the **memory map** (see page 392) may not be there. Others might do something as simple as change an **ASCII code** from one value to another, thus causing errors in certain documents or, even worse, in the source code of some of your programs or applications. Some viruses attempt to protect themselves in particularly nasty ways. For example, if you attempt to delete some types of virus you can actually activate a logic bomb or time bomb effect, thus causing more damage than the original manifestation.

Some software pirates also provide an extra bonus for purchasing or obtaining software which has been illegally copied by them. One such system allows you to start up the software and use it in the normal way for a period of time, then it displays the message 'Software piracy is theft – your system is DOOMED', and then proceeds to format your hard disk – I suppose that's some sort of rough justice for the person who received the pirated software in the first place!

If you work only on stand-alone computers (i.e. *no* network connections), don't share data with any of your colleagues or friends, don't use public domain software or shareware, and buy only legal original copies of software from bona fide suppliers, then all your hexadecimal data on your disks will almost certainly be safe from infection by a virus! Unfortunately, in the real world, people do have to share data, illegal or pirated software is used, shared databases are often accessed over local and international networks, and workers with malicious attitudes do deliberately infect systems with viruses, therefore, there will always be a need for protection software.

It's difficult to put precise figures on the cost of being infected by a computer virus, but conservative estimates put the total cost in the region of tens of millions of pounds each year. The real cost of data loss could be astronomic, and lead to the eventual collapse of a company if insufficient backup procedures are in place. Even if no physical damage is actually done, it's extremely time consuming to remove viruses from a computer system, especially if the viral infection is via a network. For example, a single worm virus sent out on the Internet system infected about 6,000 different computer systems – the cost of removing the virus from this number of computers is obviously not trivial. From reading the section on typical viral-infection symptoms you will be aware that a variety of different infection methods exist, making it difficult to track down by following set patterns. Random names for the same virus, random positions in memory and boot files, and random effects after a random number of infections all conspire to make sure that removing a virus is an extremely tedious, time consuming and costly business. Don't forget that the level of technical expertise to remove a virus from an infected computer is very great – and people with this level of technical expertise don't come cheap. You also have the added cost of diverting these people from their normal day to day operations.

Besides removing the virus one must obviously include the cost of loss of time and business opportunities while the system is down, or while users are unable to run copies of essential software. For example, word processors, databases, spreadsheets and the like may not be able to be used in a company until a worm has been removed from the system, thus releasing sufficient memory for the software to be able to run.

Anti-virus software

It's obviously far more efficient not to get infected with a virus in the first place, and many viral-detection and viral-killer programs are available on a variety of different platforms. Once a particular virus is known about then software can be written to detect and therefore remove it from the system. It's usual to get frequent updates of any inoculation software so that your system is protected against the latest known viruses. Most viral protection schemes are indeed excellent, and millions of pounds have probably been saved by the appropriate use of viral-protection software. Nevertheless, no viral detection and protection scheme can guarantee protection and is therefore not a substitute for rigorous and efficient procedures to re-establish data in the event of a viral or any other type of disaster.

Software piracy

Software piracy is an enormous problem – worldwide it has been estimated that it costs the industry in excess of 1 billion pounds each year through loss of royalties, and loss of profit to bona fide shops and distribution warehouses. Complete black-market industries have grown up around pirated software, especially in places like Russia, the Middle East and the Far East where pirated software is blatantly on display on market stalls together with photocopied versions of the original manuals! Software which usually costs several hundred dollars is on sale for about ten dollars!

Software theft is now so widespread that it's not economically possible to prosecute all but the most blatant offenders. As can be seen from reading the above it's even becoming 'acceptable' in many parts of the world. Nevertheless, this huge loss of income does have a deleterious effect on everyone, as the software companies do not receive the full revenue, some of which could be ploughed back into an increased development strategy for even better software. Internationally it's difficult to get all countries to stop such practices as software piracy forms a significant proportion of the local economy in some areas! In the industrialised world customs and excise officers are hard pushed to enforce the law, and in many other countries officials turn a blind eye. Along with other counterfeited goods like clothes and perfumery, pirated software is going to be a major problem for some considerable time to come.

It's the end users who eventually suffer – there's obviously no guarantee with pirated software, no after sales service, no technical support, no bug fixes from the company and no upgrade paths to the next version. However, in my opinion, the software distribution chains and shops are not totally blame free – when identical software is on sale in the USA for half of the price in the UK, one starts to ask oneself who is making all the profits? Good deals are usually also available for educational establishments, but when major producers of network software and spreadsheets, for example, require tens of thousands of pounds for the pleasure of a few hundred pupils being able to use their software, then most schools are unable to afford such high prices to run multiple copies of business-standard software legally.

Security measures

We have seen how literally billions of pounds can be lost each year through various types of computer misuse. It is not surprising, therefore, to find that enhanced security measures are needed at almost every stage of the proceedings from the guard at the factory gate through to the screening of employees before granting them a position with the company. These increased security measures help to prevent considerable financial loss, but ever-tighter security measures make increasing intrusions into the private and confidential side of people's lives – this is why we are considering this particular aspect in the social implications chapter.

Possible security breaches can be split up into two different aspects – physical security of the buildings and plant, and software security to prevent illegal access over a network, or to prevent illegal access to the systems once potential criminals are inside the building. We will concentrate first on the physical-security aspect.

Most establishments are not quite at the stage of the retina-scan security systems as portrayed in films about high-tech military systems, but finger-print, palm-print and voice recognition systems *are* now available for ordinary PCs at only a few hundred pounds each. Few systems employ these as standard procedure in the mid 90s, but it's now *very likely* that **smart cards** or preferably **smart keys** *are* employed to gain access to even modest security sites like academic institutions or small businesses, for example. One such system is manufactured by EMOS, and a general idea can be obtained by looking at the system in figure 26.1.

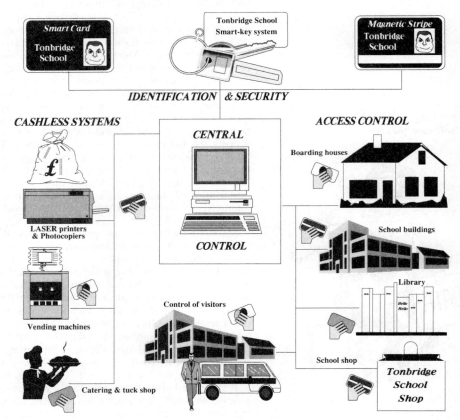

Figure 26.1

The diagram shows a possible system, part of which *is* actually installed in some schools and colleges throughout the UK, but it's easily possible to extend the systems to make them exactly as shown, or even to extend them considerably further.

As far as the security of the computer systems are concerned, assuming that an intruder has got into the grounds, the smart-key operated doors deter them from entering buildings during out-of-school hours. The beauty of the smart key or smart card system is that it's still possible to let staff or students enter any building at any time of the day or night according to their programmable security status. For example, students might have access to their own boarding house, the library and perhaps the main computer room until 10pm. The same smart cards or keys can be used to purchase goods from the school shop, food from the catering establishments, drinks from the vending machines or to loan books from the library. They can either be used on a debit or credit basis, with a cash top up machine being housed in the Porter's lodge. This means that students could insert their card into a special machine, insert a couple of ten-pound notes, for example, and then get electronic credit on their cards for use with the school photocopiers, laser printers and vending machines.

Big Brother might be watching you!

Coming back to the system security for the moment, it *is possible* to log what happens where and when, but implementation of such a system in a school context is neither desirable nor necessary. In a higher-security environment it would be possible to build up a complete dossier of staff and students' movements, according to entry and exit points including dates and times, it would be possible to extend the system to registration at the beginning and end of the day, and to increase the system security still further; PIN numbers in addition to the smart-key system could also be used. At Cambridge University they have gone a little further – voluntarily, of course – enabling pupils to know the exact whereabouts of computing staff at certain times during the day. A monitor on the wall shows where the duty staff are located inside the computing building because of electronic tags worn by members of the computing staff during these particular times.

Such systems are of obvious importance in industry, especially when one considers the enormous amounts of money lost through pilfering and fraud. Nevertheless, physical security is not enough, as some crimes are committed by the very workers who are issued with the smart cards and PIN numbers. Therefore, extra system security is needed in addition to the above physical security.

System security

Let's assume that an intruder has got past the security guard, gained access to the building by kidnapping one of the employees and using their finger prints, smart card and PIN number, got in through some locked doors and gained access to a terminal connected to the main system. (It would have been far easier to get to this stage by using a MODEM and phone line!) What extra measures can now be taken to prevent further unauthorised access to the precious computer system?

Firstly, a bona fide user must log onto the system using an appropriate **user name** and the all-important **password**. The network control software should monitor and make a note of *all attempts* to log on. *If* a **user** has tried several times to log on and failed, then the system should lock out that particular terminal or MODEM link and raise the alarm. If a genuine user has forgotten their password – tough – they should see the computer manager as soon as possible and get it reallocated. Such inconvenience is necessary as special software can easily be written which tries thousands of different passwords in a relatively short space of time. Any high-security system which lets a user log on after many different password attempts have been tried is useless in the extreme.

Passwords

Passwords should be relatively long so that they are unlikely to be stumbled upon quickly by chance or intelligent guesswork. For example, if all 128 ordinary ASCII codes may be used in a 20-character password, then 128^{20} or 1.38×10^{42} password combinations are possible – that's a lot of guessing! Even at a rate of one million guesses each second, it would take 4.4×10^{28} years to cover all the possibilities – and this is assuming that the software does not lock you out for repeated unsuccessful attempts at access. It's far more likely that some inside knowledge might be used to guess the actual password much more quickly than this. Some idiots, for example, use their telephone number, bank-account number, car registration number or their girlfriend's name. This is suicidal – you must always ensure that passwords bear no resemblance whatsoever to any information relating to your personal life or a particular project on which you are working. Institutions should have a policy of frequent password changes, and make sure that appropriate passwords are changed each time an employee with access to the system leaves or is sacked.

Let's now suppose that the appropriate password has been guessed – what other measures can be taken now? There are just a few other options now available, with further password protection of the sort described in the database-security section on page 482 being the most obvious – even if you have successfully logged onto the system, you should not have access to all data, unless you have gained access at the highest level of security – that of the system manager or DBA (see page 476).

Cryptography

One final and highly-successful method of security is that of applying the 'science' of **cryptography** or **data encryption**. Even after gaining access to the building,

breaking through the password security, successfully logging on at the computer terminal and negotiating your way to the source of the data – if you can't actually make sense of what you are looking at then the whole criminal exercise has been pointless. Cryptography is a study of the techniques for keeping data secret, and the simple ideas behind it are shown in figure 26.2.

The system shows how a **cleartext** or **plaintext** message 'Hi there!' could be transmitted over a communication link as 'gobbledygook' called **ciphertext**, then re-established as **cleartext** at the receiving end by making use of the all-important **key**. Without having access to the key, deciphering the text is very difficult or almost impossible. The link does not have to be a communication link, but could be the interface through which the encrypted data held on disk can be viewed, i.e. without the right software package *and* key the data can't be decoded because it's not in straight ASCII or EBCDIC form etc. Most computer-science students will probably be aware that it's possible to type out any file on disk as ASCII data and make some sense of the contents – if the data is encrypted then this is not possible.

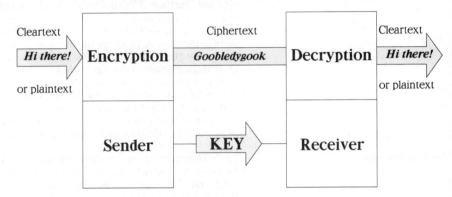

Figure 26.2

One particularly simple method of encryption makes use of a substitution table in which letters of the alphabet, for example, are replaced with others. A simple combination for one type of key is shown in the following table of figure 26.3.

Letter	Replace	Letter	Replace	Letter	Replace
A	M	J	F	S	C
B	V	K	I	T	S
C	O	L	B	U	D
D	P	M	A	V	J
E	Y	N	Z	W	E
F	G	O	X	X	K
G	R	P	Q	Y	N
H	L	Q	W	Z	U
I	H	R	T		

Figure 26.3

Therefore, the message 'HI THERE' would be encrypted as follows.

H →L, I →H, T →S, H →L, E →Y, R →T, E →Y

HI THERE → → → → → LH SLYTY

Unfortunately, assuming the language is English, for example, then known frequencies of occurrence of certain letters together with well-known combinations of other letters can help the bad guys decipher this text reasonably easily. Criminals would employ people known as cryptanalysts to try to break the codes. Governments do this too when trying to analyse international secret communications such as hot lines between different nations! The most famous code-breaker to date is probably the **Colossus** computer (see page 619) used to decipher Hitler's messages to his generals during the 2nd-world war. If you're interested in code cracking and the history of computing in particular, then a reconstruction of Colossus can be seen in the Museum of Computing at Bletchley Park near Milton Keynes in Buckinghamshire.

A more-complex method than that shown above would be needed if a secure link is to be maintained, or if highly-sensitive data is to be stored safely on disk. One such method is to supply a **repeating key** and use the positions of the letters in the key and the cleartext to determine the position of a letter in the final alphabet. For example, using the repeating key ABCDABCDABC... etc, and applying it to the message HI THERE, we get the following.

A	B C D A B C D	Repeating KEY
H	I T H E R E	Cleartext (Message)
I	K C X I G U I	Ciphertext

H→I because H (the *8th* letter in the alphabet), is added to A (the first part of the repeating key which is the *1st* letter in the alphabet) to get I (the *8th* plus the *1st* which gives us the *9th* letter in the alphabet). Similarly, B goes to K because we get (B) the 2nd plus (I) the 9th to give us K the 11th. Modulo 26 (see page 194) is used so that we wrap round to the beginning of the alphabet if necessary. The longer the repeating key the more secure the message. If the repeating key is as long as the message itself, then this would be extremely secure indeed, as the crypt-analyst has no alternative but to try all possible combinations to try to decipher the message – an impossible task for messages of reasonable lengths.

Various arithmetical methods have also been developed, and are more convenient in practice because a long key does not have to be used to decipher the message. The positions of the letters in the alphabet or the ASCII code can be used to change the letters into numbers, then an arithmetical algorithm can be applied to generate a new series of numbers representing the ciphertext. At the deciphering end an arithmetical method can be used to get back the original numbers, which can then be used to decode the message in the normal way. Such methods are used in the banking system where Electronic Funds Transfer (EFT) takes place on a routine basis.

It's the people that count

As you can see from the above, any security measures are only as good as the honesty and integrity of the people who run the system. The most complex of ciphers, impossible to crack with the fastest supercomputers would prove no problem to a 10-year old if the repeating-key sequence were known. As can be seen from the previous few sections, there are plenty of unsuitable employment opportunities for computer criminals – and this leads us nicely into the debate about computers and their effect on employment.

Computers, employment and privacy

IT in the office environment

You will need to appreciate the effects of computerisation in more general terms, and as computer science students you will be expected to produce balanced arguments as to whether the introduction of computers and information technology has had a beneficial or detrimental effect on employment in general – it depends on your perspectives, on the part of the world in which you live, on the work which you do and on your perception of progress.

Few, if any, workers remain unaffected in some way or other by the introduction of information technology. IT has permeated its way into helping with decision making at the highest levels of management, in helping to increase office efficiency by several orders of magnitude, and with the automation of manual processes on the shop floor. There will be many people who have had their jobs replaced by auto-mated systems, and many more previously sacrosanct job descriptions will probably fall prey to increasingly sophisticated technology. We will now look in a little more detail at some of the effects caused by this rapidly increasing evolutionary trend.

Historically, offices have been undergoing transformations for a great many years. Twenty years ago, for example, masses of personnel were employed in what was called the typing pool – literally hundreds of girls used to pound away on mechanical typewriters, making carbon-copy duplicates for the filing cabinets, and re-typing anything that needed re-drafting. Electronic typewriters, and increasingly sophisti-cated word processors in some industries, especially those which make use of large chunks of standard text such as the legal professions, for example, have now made a single employee as productive as about 10 to 15 old-style employees with their mechanical machines. Therefore, for each person employed in a new-style office, about ten jobs have been lost, ten salaries have been saved and the productivity output has remained very similar – an obvious and necessary increase in efficiency for any profit-motivated company. Work carried out by many people in the typing pool can now be handled by a handful of trained word-processor operatives.

Extensive national and international networks together with MODEM links now give us the option of not going into the office at all – office workers can receive and edit their work via the network or normal post, and send their completed work down the network back to the central 'office' – which may literally be hundreds or thousands of miles from their home. Such arrangements are obviously ideal for mothers with children, for example, as the hours worked may be tailored to suit the needs of the child. If, for example, the child wakes at some ungodly hour, thus ensuring that the mother is awake half the night, then some work could be done during this period of insomnia – if the mother wishes to sleep through the next morning then this is no problem. There is also a significant saving on the fares or petrol needed for transportation to the conventional office, and the consequent saving in pollution of the environment because less travelling needs to be done. There are also numerous advantages for the company too – less office space is needed (if any at all!), therefore, there are savings on initial building costs, building taxes, insurance and heating.

There are, however, some obvious disadvantages from a human point of view. For example, people have lives to live and have needs in which human interaction plays a very important role. One linchpin of society revolves not just around the work which people do at the office, but around the social interactions which people experience at work with their colleagues. People meet other people at the office, a large part of their social life is organised around people they encounter at the office – social interaction with other people would be cut drastically if people worked at home in ways which are possible because of this new technology. The introduction of new technology will continue unabated – this is obvious because of the increased efficiency and reductions in cost, but we will also have to look at the social consequences of the ways in which the technology is currently being employed if people are to have meaningful lives and remain mentally healthy.

It may be that people will go to the office, not because they have to, but because they want to. Video conferencing is now possible, and is used extensively in multinational companies. However, most people still like to do important business by having eyeball-to-eyeball contact with their potential customers. Compromises will probably be made, not for technological but for sociological reasons. Nevertheless, is it up to companies to pay for the sociological and emotional needs of their employees? Should it be the responsibility of a company to provide an office, not to get work done in the most efficient manner, but to provide a meeting place for the people they employ? Perhaps happy employees do better work than miserable ones who might be lonely if they do extensive work at home – perhaps there are some employees who like to work at home? There are many issues to be resolved here, and what's absolutely clear is that no one has currently got all the right answers.

My best friend's a robot!

Factory workers are not exempt from the above office-automation arguments. Increasingly sophisticated robots have been introduced over the last couple of decades and are currently undertaking boring and repetitive tasks that used to be carried out by an army of people. Nevertheless, no matter how dull some people may view jobs such as loading or unloading a conveyor belt, putting the same type of parts together hundreds of times during the day, or pushing the same monotonous sequence of buttons, for example, this, to the people who undertook these tasks, was a job – it gave them some purpose in life, and during tea breaks, lunch breaks and after work in the factory club or pub they met with other people who did the same type of job. It was a better alternative for them than being unemployed. More importantly, the jobs were often of an unskilled nature and therefore needed little training or qualifications.

Present day robots are extremely good at doing repetitive tasks over long periods of time. They don't get bored or tired, don't need tea breaks and can work 24 hours a day, seven days a week. However, some tasks, no matter how simple they may appear to us, are still not susceptible to solution by modern robotics and computer technology. For example, recognition of 'duff chocolates' on a confectionery production line is still undertaken by humans who sit down all day watching the chocolates go by and manually pick out the mishapes. This boring and repetitive task (unless you're a chocaholic!) is still not possible automatically because there are no efficient algorithms to determine subtle differences in the shape of a chocolate (see page 552). One must not forget that we are indeed a long way from producing robots like 'R2D2' in 'Star Wars' or 'Data' in 'Startrek', for example. The industrial robots employed today are not humanoid, they are for specific tasks only, and are not usually good if things start to go wrong or part of the production line breaks down. The present generation of technology must go through many more stages of metamorphosis before we begin to approach human recognition capabilities.

Your perspective of technological progress will probably depend on the part of the world in which you live. In the Industrialised West, for example, we make use of robots *because* they are cheaper and more efficient than employing people to do the same work. It is also becoming increasingly socially unacceptable to expect anybody to spend 8 to 10 hours a day on mindless tasks. However, in parts of the third world, where social security payments and the national health service do not exist, many people will literally do anything for a very small 'wage' indeed. Just 30p per day is not unheard of for a 12-hour shift in a factory – the alternative is starvation or crime. If there are thousands of people who are prepared to do menial tasks for a pittance – then who needs robots – it's much more profitable for the company to employ child labour instead, for example. Goods made in these sorts of situations are on sale throughout much of the industrialised world – some of the pirate software mentioned earlier in this chapter and many other types of counterfeit goods are produced in these sorts of factories.

You should also realise that robots are capable of doing much more than mediocre tasks. For example, a human brain surgeon working with a scalpel is capable of removing about 98% of most brain tumours – a robot currently being developed is reported to be able to remove 99.9% of the tumour. One leading surgeon has been quoted as saying that at some time in the future it will be regarded as barbaric if one human takes a knife to perform surgery on another – most surgery will be carried out by robots under the guidance of computers. With information about the inside of a body from various scans, computers can build up 3D images of organs in incredible detail and remote-controlled robots can make use of this information to perform better corrective surgery in a much less invasive fashion.

Retraining opportunities

There are literally hundreds of categories besides factory workers and office staff where we could easily have organised convincing arguments as to why jobs are becoming automated. However, if these people are not to be sacked then the only sensible alternative is to retrain them so that they can be usefully employed elsewhere. If these opportunities are not available within an organisation then government-run training schemes, if they exist, should be used to make sure that vital human resources are not wasted. One must not lose sight of the fact that many new jobs are created by the introduction of new technology, but these jobs tend to be of a higher skill level than the previously manual tasks which many of the workers would probably have undertaken. The opportunities for small businesses and individual companies have grown tremendously since the introduction of the personal computer. Individuals now have technology available at a sensible cost to run their own typesetting or publishing businesses, for example. Many individual companies now act as service industries developing software and hardware products for the ever increasing arsenal of PC-related goods.

Privacy

More information has been stored about individuals in the last decade or so than in all of previous history put together. A couple of decades ago, assuming you did not have a criminal record, the only available information was to be found on birth certificates, marriage certificates, driving licences, death certificates and the like. Correlation of this information was either difficult or impossible, as the computer systems of the day could not communicate with each other. Today nothing could be further from the truth – each time an individual takes out an insurance policy, applies for a financial loan, opens a bank account, receives a new credit card or, in some cases, applies for a new job, the information super highway is put into top gear. Information on some of these systems is quite revealing – for example, financial status, medical details, criminal prosecutions, current salaries, tax details, financial transactions including dates and times, and many others too numerous to mention.

The role played by the computer

If all of the above information were to be stored in tens of thousands of filing cabinets, and *if* these manual filing systems were to be processed by an army of tens of thousands of people with similar intentions to the role played by the KGB before the break up of the Soviet Union, then this massive amount of activity would pale into insignificance compared with the data processing ability of today's networked computer systems. It is only legislation such as the data protection act (see page

483) which is hopefully preventing unscrupulous people and organisations from building up comprehensive dossiers on peoples' private lives. Already many companies make extensive use of some of these computer systems to filter out potential customers by profiling for receipt of mail shots. For example, if your income is above £40,000 per annum, if you are in the 40 to 60 year age group and if you go on holiday regularly, then these criteria might be used by a company to send you details about particular world cruises on their liners, for example – this is far more effective advertising than targeting the population at random, many of whom would not be able to afford the services which the company has to offer.

From reading the above you may be starting to think that George Orwell's vision of the future is a little nearer than anticipated. However, there are tremendous advantages also. For example, if you are applying for a loan then a computer check can be made quickly and a suitable loan granted almost instantly. Credit transfer such as salaries being paid into bank accounts or clearance of cheques within days would not be possible without extensive computerised networks, and correlation of seemingly irrelevant information by bona fide organisations can have unexpected and useful spin offs to society. For example, on 19th May 1994, Robert Black, the serial child killer was sentenced to ten life sentences. He was convicted on the basis of the evidence created by the use he had made of a credit card to buy petrol in various BP garages. The dates and times of the transactions, held on BP's main computer at head office confirmed that he was in all the areas in which the children were murdered over a number of years – a very powerful use of seemingly harmless information stored on just one of the thousands of different computer systems throughout the UK.

Computers in education, training and the home

Powerful interactive multimedia systems are now a reality. The potential for education and training is inevitably enormous, especially when these systems become available on high-powered machines at a sensible cost. Complete customised training sessions can be developed making use of multimedia packages such as Hypercard on the Mac or Genesis Professional on the Arc, for example (see page 565). It is now possible to place a person in front of a machine and put them through a complete interactive training schedule with few, if any, training personnel needed. Menu-driven systems let the user explore various avenues, tests of material just learned can steer the machine through appropriate diagnostic areas, real-time audio, video, and eventually VR systems (see page 258) will add to the realism of the training experience. If you think that this might sound a little far fetched, in Germany they are already training surgeons with the help of VR techniques – student surgeons don their VR helmets, and weald a scalpel in their data-gloved hand. It's very effective training – they're even getting to the stage of simulating virtual blood spurting out of the virtual body when the virtual cut has been made.

The power of these multimedia systems should not be underestimated – in the computer industry, for example, equivalent high-standards of training carried out by professionals within a normal classroom environment often costs a couple of hundred pounds per person per day – if a company invests several thousand pounds in a multimedia system, then the cost can often be recouped within a few weeks. Indeed, training packages, based on multimedia interactive demonstrations could actually make money for the company in the longer term. Authoring packages such as those described above make wonderful projects for computer-science students, assuming that there is a script language which accompanies the system which is fully programmable – both in terms of full interaction with the operating system, various high-level languages and other applications – you are limited only by your imagination, but see the cautionary note about authoring packages and advanced-level projects on page 566.

The consequence of the educational use of cyberspace is mind boggling. For example, what's the point of talking to astronaut trainees about what it must be like to walk on the moon when pupils can don their VR helmets, put on their VR suits and physically and emotionally experience what it is like to virtually walk on the moon? Imagine you are there – turn your head and look back at the far away Earth – experience this for too long on your own and you will probably start to feel incredibly isolated – perhaps this particular emotion would not have been experienced if one was trying to convey these images by the spoken word.

If we take these developments further then one can begin to appreciate that they could and probably will have an impact on education itself. Imagine a scenario in which information about virtually any topic is almost instantly available to any depth that is required by the user of the system. What skills should now be possessed by the students at school? Perhaps the recall of facts will play a less prominent role than at present. The ability to manipulate data to extract the required information so that appropriate conclusions can be drawn might become paramount. If such a scenario is to exist in the future then, as in the past, we will probably have to redefine what is meant by education – these ideas could be as fundamental as this. Some teachers may throw their hands up in horror at the thought of what is being implied here, but we have only to look back at history to see that such fundamental changes have happened in the past – from the invention of language itself, the availability of books in quantities large enough for everybody to use, the invention of television to the introduction of microcomputers and video recorders – they have all played their part. The political, moral and philosophical directions taken by entire nations can be influenced by the use of such technologies – one has only to see the effect that satellite systems have had in less developed areas of the world. Visit some of the poorest areas, and you might see a shack with no sewage system, no windows or doors, and the people with only just enough food to survive – but you will probably notice the satellite dish on the roof feeding a TV signal into their home!

Multimedia and VR packages are obviously not the be all and end all of a student's educational experience, and high-quality packages are obviously time consuming and expensive to develop. The potential market for such systems has to be huge if they are to be successful, and this has obvious implications. We might arrive at a situation in which too many people have exactly the same experience. This may not be good from an educational perspective, even if a particular experience is excellent from an individual's point of view. Just think of the potential for indoctrination! There is obviously a need for a balanced approach involving the use of high technology where it can be shown to be useful, but using conventional human interaction where this is most appropriate. There is a mine field of opposing philosophies here, and arguments will no doubt rage for many years to come. However, if we do not address the problems which are posed by the introduction of these new technologies, or if opposition is based purely on a Luddite philosophy, then we will be doing the next generation of children a grave disservice.

Computers in the home

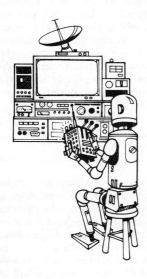

One might be forgiven for thinking that the home-computer revolution experienced in the 1980s has come and gone. The introduction of very cheap micros such as the ZX81, the ZX spectrum and the early BBC computers, for example, certainly had an impact, and these computers were launched in a blaze of publicity raising both a public awareness of and unrealistic expectations from the use of these simple 8-bit microprocessor technologies. In reality the public were initially impressed, but then they became rapidly disappointed. In their favour it must be said that these machines were an innovative use of the technology at the time, and represented the cutting edge of technological development – along with the Research Machines 380Z they can rightly claim their place as being *the* machines which got computer awareness off the ground in the primary and secondary education sectors within the UK. However, apart from the dedicated few who were prepared to learn how to program these machines in detail, and apart from the dedicated games fanatics, there was little quality software available for any of these machines until relatively late in their evolutionary cycle. Non-technical members of the public therefore quickly became disillusioned, and machines at home (and in some schools!) sat idle in the cupboard.

Some educationalists were probably over optimistic about the capabilities of these machines, and when the technology could not deliver the doubtful promises being made in some quarters, the home computer revolution was dismissed as a flash in the pan. More powerful games machines have been developed as offshoots from later generations of technology. However, the likelihood of a computer in every home now seems a remote prospect in the eyes of most of the public – but nothing could be further from the truth. Most people have little perception of the impact of the next generation of home technology – the integration of computers, broadcasting and communication systems.

Microprocessor-controlled TVs

Most households have a TV set, and many have more than one. The video has also made an impact in the homes of over half of the UK population. Imagine now the joining together of the telephone, the microcomputer, the television, video and CD-ROM technologies, all incorporated into the next generation of TVs, and you will begin to appreciate the next most likely domestic onslaught. Such systems will probably succeed during the next decade because of the vast amounts of money to be made by many parts of industry such as communications, retailing, and the service and information-dissemination sectors.

The biggest advantage of the new TV systems will be in the two-way communication processes. You no longer have to be a passive observer of what is being transmitted to your box. Via cable, satellite or the ISDN telephone system (see page 487), audio, video, text, and computer-related material can all be processed. This will allow you to send back messages to central computers linked to retail outlets, for example, from which you can instantly order a variety of goods. Quote your credit card number, perhaps a PIN number, answer a few questions and within a few hours the goods are being despatched to your home.

All the above will be possible because of the use of digital techniques, and the consequent ability to perform a massive amount of data compression (see page 563). For example, MPEG (The Motion Picture Experts Group) have defined new standards for cable, satellite and normal TV channels in which the quality of pictures and the potential for extra information is quite remarkable. Indeed, if broadcasts are compressed, then you can transmit them faster than real time! For example, it might only take half an hour to transmit 12 hours of TV signals. This means that you could load, store and selectively watch any programme in any order, you no longer have to wait for it to be broadcast at an appropriate time. Many people's lives revolve around what's being broadcast on the television, and so this, like the introduction of the video recorder before it, may further revolutionise the way that many people organise their lives in the future.

VR will probably play a part too. We are starting to see computer games in which sequences can be generated in real time by incredibly powerful arrays of microprocessor chips. With the current generation of interactive systems pre-determined video images are stored on CD-ROM and used to determine the view of cyberspace perceived by the user of the system. Interactive movies are now available, but the different possible scenarios are limited. However, with the ability to generate video-quality images in real time, we effectively have an infinite number of possible scenarios based on mathematical models of the virtual world, rather than on pre-set realities created beforehand. This new version will therefore react to the user in more realistic ways, and allow a much greater number of scenarios to take place.

The above is an obvious couch potato's dream – imagine sitting in front of the television, not having to walk down to the video shop to get your video because you can download it from a suitable database, ordering your take away pepperoni pizza and having it delivered to your door, and being able to buy any commodity from the remote-keypad terminal attached to the television. We could presumably get exercise in cyberspace – assuming that one could exercise in the virtual world! This future may sound pretty awful to some, and indeed, the vast majority of the population may actually like shopping in the conventional way. Nevertheless, the interactive nature of the TV systems could be essential technology for the disabled or housebound, could provide a significant help to people with busy schedules, and if used properly could be a sensible alternative retail outlet for many companies.

The thinking machine?

Computers have already proved their worth in a huge variety of situations ranging from undertaking boring and repetitive tasks to the simulation and modelling of many different physical and theoretical scenarios. However, philosophical arguments have raged for a number of years, and will probably continue to do so for a good deal longer regarding the possibility of building computers which are able to think for themselves. Much of the argument revolves around the issues relating to the fact that all the computers invented so far, and those yet to be invented are based around the algorithmic approach to solving problems. From reading this book you will all be aware of the fact that an algorithm is a step-by-step sequence of instructions to solve a particular problem, and you will all realise how computers can achieve spectacular results at lightning speed by the application of suitable algorithmic methods. It was a brilliant mathematician called Turing who first proposed the idea of an idealised algorithmic machine which can be used to solve any computable problem in the form of an algorithm. Indeed, if you study computer science at degree level, you will cover details of these abstract machines when you cover the theory of automata – however, the long and short of all this theory is that, based on our current levels of understanding, all machines built out of any physical devices such as mechanical bits and bobs, electronics or light, for example, must all obey the consequences imposed by this theoretical model of the Turing machine – that is all computers solve their problems by following a linear sequence of events. Very large sequences of events may be cleverly disguised in terms of recursive algorithms (see page 185), or may be considerably speeded up by splitting up the problems into many parallel sequences (see page 65), but following algorithms is essentially all that the current computers and computers in the foreseeable future can do.

Algorithms and religion

Learning, for example, can be simulated on algorithmic machines by the use of neural networks (see page 555), and pattern-recognition capabilities are getting surprisingly realistic. But what about the more human characteristics such as insight, confidence and a greater awareness to experience emotionally moving events such as music or dance, for example? Our perception of these and other emotions such as anger or love can't possibly be programmed into an algorithmic-based computer – or can they? On the one hand there is the powerful materialist philosophy which states that we are all just made out of different physical materials – that all these materials interact within the laws of nature – that we have not yet begun to understand very much about the interaction between the sensors our bodies use to perceive what's happening to us, and the relaying of this information to our brains where it is then processed to produce other signals relating in some way to such useful outcomes as emotion, and eventually to perceptions of understanding. At the other end of the spectrum there are the religious beliefs of people who argue that the mind and the body are indeed separate, and that the spiritual part of us is what makes us different from machines – a less-rational but nevertheless equally powerful argument based on convictions of people who know that such theories can't be disproved scientifically on the current basis of our knowledge.

The materialist philosophy is an argument based on scientific rationale, and assumes that if we are able to simulate the exact working of the brain in all its intimate detail – a feat that might be possible within the next few generations, then this simulation will be no different from the real thing, because it would be the real thing! The behaviour of such a system will act as though it has all the characteristics of a human because it has got all the physical characteristics of a human brain. Nevertheless, Roger Penrose, a professor of mathematics at Oxford University provides us with an alternative argument as to why computers won't ever be able to think – this is because of a strong argument that some problems, which can easily be solved by children, for example, are *not* computable by algorithmic means. Penrose feels that any problem which can't be expressed algorithmically can never be solved by a computer, and further goes on to argue that much of human intuition is based on solving problems which are not based on algorithmic methods.

At one level the brain can be considered to be a complex interconnection of neurons and synapses as explained on page 556. It is entirely possible to simulate this complex network in the form of an algorithmic computer, and this is what happens in a neural network, whether it be simulated electronically or in software. Biologists have also found a further sub-structure deep within the brain, far below that of the neural networks which seems to operate on quantum-mechanical phenomena. This network too is entirely computable and therefore reproducible on an algorithmic machine. However, Penrose believes that there is an as yet undetermined interaction between this quantum-mechanical level and the classical level of the operation of the neurons that is not computable, and therefore impossible to simulate on an algorithmic based machine – Q.E.D. so to speak. However, if this quantum mechanical level and the classical level of the brain physically exist – which they do – then perhaps one day it may be possible to build a different type of computer such that the same interaction takes places because of the actual presence of the other two systems – who knows? Professor Minosky, at Cambridge University is one of the current experts developing nanotechnology systems (see page 553). He believes that one day it may be possible to develop machines with intelligence.

What is exciting is that people will go on trying to achieve what is perhaps impossible – this, at least, is what history tells us if we are to put faith in human nature. For if we did not go on trying to understand our universe in greater and greater depth, and if we do not go on building better machines then there would be nothing more left to achieve in these important and major areas of human endeavour – many humans need to move forward on the scientific end technological frontier. If it's possible to build a thinking machine at some time in the distant future, then with insight and ability for original thought coupled together with an algorithmic logical processing capability we would indeed have built up a formidable device. I am not sure whether it would be used for the good of humanity or otherwise – or as is the case with all previous human achievements, it would be used for both!

Exercise 26.1

1. If you have a suitable database such as the **CD-ROM version** of *The Times* newspapers, for example, find and extract some suitable articles on criminal activities regarding the use of computers.

2. The **Internet** is a vast *international communication network* of networks in which people linked to computer systems can have conversations in real time or via E-Mail, or download virtually any type of information. Write a short essay in which you outline a number of points, both for and against the proliferation of such networks.

3. **Bulletin boards** have been set up internationally for the distribution of illegal software. For example, pornographic material, pirated versions of software, information about how to make bombs and a whole host of other politically sensitive or racially-motivated material is available to anyone who dials into one of these systems.
   (a) Suggest ways in which such systems can be controlled.
   (b) Is it possible to monitor peoples' access to such systems without compromising their human rights?
   (c) Should Bulletin boards be banned?
   (d) Would the banning of bulletin boards solve the social problems posed here?

4. It's possible that at some stage in the future **virtual reality systems** will be so effective that some people may be in danger of being unable to tell the difference between real life and 'life' within their virtual worlds. Such a state of mind is potentially dangerous to say the least.
   (a) Comment on the technical possibilities of this scenario occurring.
   (b) VR will probably be a force for both good and evil – explain.
   (c) How could VR help scientists to understand more about the real world?
   (d) Suggest some uses for VR within the context of the educational environment.
   (e) It was suggested in this chapter that couch potatoes may be able to exercise in a virtual world. What other interfaces to the computer would be needed to make this scenario a reality?

5. Some people think that machine intelligence will never be able to approach that of a human brain. Others think that, given time, this may be possible.
   (a) What factors are in favour of either argument?
   (b) If it were possible, suggest some uses for such a device.
   (c) Suppose it is possible, what are the potential dangers?

6. Explain how it's possible to protect computer data from **physical damage**, **theft**, and **misuse**. What techniques are currently available which prevent unauthorised access to computer systems.

7. A **worm virus** is suspected of infecting a computer. What are the symptoms and how would it be possible to eradicate the virus? What should be done in the future to increase the level of protection? Are your protection methods foolproof?

8. A **Michaelangelo virus** has been detected on your system. You do not have the technical knowledge to irradicate it and no viral-killer software is available – what sensible precaution can be taken?

End of chapter summary

- You should be able to argue rationally on many different social issues backed up by sound reasoning making use of your technical knowledge of computer systems.
- **Computer crime** may be split up into many crimes involving **financial gain**, **forged documentation**, **injection of viruses** and **deliberate destruction of data**.
- **Interconnectivity of computer systems** enables seemingly harmless information to be collected together to build up comprehensive dossiers on people's private lives.
- **Legislation** such as the **data protection act** and **computer misuse act** are intended to curb misuse of data.
- Practice **safe hex** to avoid being infected with a virus.
- The cost of large systems being affected by a virus is often enormous.
- Software piracy is an increasing problem which is difficult to irradicate as it's often tolerated in certain parts of the world.
- Security measures on computer systems involve both physical security and software-protection schemes.
- **Physical security** involves **smart card** and **keys** etc., **palm print** and **fingerprint scans**, **physical locks** and **PIN numbers**, and conventional burglar alarms.
- **System security** involves things like passwords, and cryptography.
- **Cleartext** or **plaintext** is the *input* to a **cryptographic system**.
- **Ciphertext** is the **encrypted text** which, without a suitable key is gobbledygook.
- **Cryptographic techniques** involving **long repeating key sequences** are *almost impossible* to **decipher**.

- Any **security system** is only as good as the *integrity of the people who operate it.*
- **Computers** have had an *enormous impact* on **office** and **factory** environments.
- Computers pose many extra threats to privacy of the individual if misused.
- Education and training will probably undergo major changes in the future due to increasingly sophisticated technology being available.
- **Microprocessor-controlled** TVs in conjunction with **communication systems** via **cable** and **satellite** will *revolutionise information systems in the home.*
- The **thinking computer** *has not yet been built* – it may yet prove impossible to build given our current level of understanding.
- Many **religious** and **philosophical** problems revolve around the possibility of building a computer which one day might be able to do as well if not better than a human being.

27 History of computing

Introduction

Although this is a very minor topic at this level, and indeed is not examined by most boards, it is interesting to have a little background knowledge of the history of computing. Only when armed with this knowledge can you make an objective judgement about the amazing developments that have happened over the past years.

The author has found that in his experience, the history of computers only becomes interesting when you have studied enough computing to appreciate the significance of each development. This is the main reason why this chapter appears at the end rather than at the beginning of this book.

An evolutionary approach

The modern computer was developed as a natural progression from the early calculating aids. Indeed this has had the effect of making many people still look on today's computers as complex number-crunchers. However, in most cases this could not be further from the truth.

As the computer was developed from calculating machines it is along this line that we will have to trace the family tree of modern computers.

Early calculating aids

One of the earliest calculating aids was the **abacus.** Most people are familiar with the abacus, which is a device consisting of rods upon which beads can be moved up and down. The abacus has been around for nearly 5000 years. It was later developed by the Chinese and is still in practical use today. A skilled operator can usually work out sums using the four rules faster than most people with an electronic calculator. The author knows of a little Chinese restaurant in Surrey where the abacus is still used to work out the bill. Beads seem to fly in all directions and the waiter might say '£18.60 please'!

Very many years passed between the development of the abacus and the next documented development of a useful calculating aid. The next significant development came in 1617 when **John Napier** invented what came to be known as **Napier's bones.** These were simply rods on which numbers were marked. These numbers enabled the user to work out the answers to a restricted set of the multiplication tables. The idea is shown in figure 27.1

Figure 27.1

The numbers to be multiplied are located on the top row and the left hand column. The answer is obtained at the intersection of these two. The method which Napier pioneered is still sometimes used as a curiosity in maths lessons at school.

Although Napier invented the bones it was perhaps **logarithms** which made him most famous. Tables of logarithms were developed which enabled multiplication and division to be carried out very simply by addition and subtraction. Logarithms were so popular that they became the standard method for working out tedious calculations in many industries right up until the pocket calculator took over just a few years ago.

The invention of logarithms and the bones led to the invention of a device called a **slide rule** by **William Oughtred.** This is a device in which a cursor is moved up and down various scales to perform multiplication and division using the principles of logarithms. This device was equivalent to the pocket calculator of today, and again was used until only several years ago (the author still has his slide rule in the drawer!).

Mechanical calculating machines

In 1642 **Pascal** invented a remarkable device (hence he has been honoured by the naming of a high-level language after him). Indeed the device would have been remarkable had it been invented over a hundred years later. Although only capable of addition this device had many of the techniques which have survived until the present day. For example, numbers were entered on dials that were on the front of the machine (equivalent to the keyboard). The answers to the additions appeared in little windows at the top of the machine (equivalent to the LED display). Perhaps this was the start of the **input, processing, output** cycle. Pascal's machine can be seen in figure 27.2.

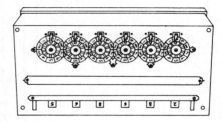

Figure 27.2

Another significant contribution to mechanical calculators was made by **Gottfried Leibnitz,** in 1617. He produced the first mechanical calculator that was capable of doing multiplication. In fact, his method, which made use of toothed gears, was so successful that it was used with little modification for many years after. Leibnitz's machine was one stage nearer to the concept of input, processing and output. The numbers were input on the dials. The processing was carried out by the gears when a handle was turned, and finally the numbers appeared at the output, in this case another set of dials.

From calculating devices to computers

As we can see from the above brief introduction the early calculating devices had a profound impact on the way in which computers were developed. However, a couple of hundred years later came the person regarded by many people as the father of computing. This was **Charles Babbage** and the time was around the 1820s when his **difference engine** was being developed.

The term difference engine was used because it is based on a mathematical method called **differences**. The machine was originally devised to assist in working out better tables of logarithms. One of the biggest problems that Babbage encountered was that the technology of the time was incapable of making the parts for the mechanical machine to the required degree of accuracy. Therefore, the difference engine could not be made. However, undaunted, Babbage continued to develop an even more complex machine called the **analytical engine.** This was such an advanced machine that it was at this point that the concept of the modern computer was realised.

Babbage's machine closely resembled modern machines in the following ways:

1. It had a part of the machine that was dedicated to performing the calculations (the **arithmetic unit** in a modern computer).
2. Part of the machine ensured that the sequence of operations was carried out in the correct order (equivalent to the **control unit** in a modern machine).

3. A complex series of cogs ensured that numbers were not presented until they were required in the calculation (the **store** in present-day machines).
4. As with the other early computers, Babbage's machine contained parts that could easily be identified as **input** and **output**.

It is no small tribute to Babbage that many of the above principles have been employed even in the latest generation of computers.

Joseph Jacquard also played an important part in the development of computing as the idea of **punched cards** was developed from his early **weaving loom.** These cards were used for the first time in the early 1800s to control the patterns of the weave. The loom became much easier to use as the complex setting of the patterns no longer had to be done by hand. In fact it was Jacquard's idea of using punched cards that was transferred and used as part of the control system in Babbage's **analytical engine.** Instead of controlling the weaving patterns, the cards controlled what mathematical calculations would take place inside the machine.

The punched card again came to the rescue in the later 1880s. America had a problem with processing census data. In fact, if the census data had been processed by hand, then it would have taken so many years to process the results that the next census would have been due before the data from the last one could have been put to good use. A competition was held to determine a way to process the data more quickly and the winner was **Herman Hollerith** who produced what became known as **Hollerith's tabulating machine.** This is shown in figure 27.3.

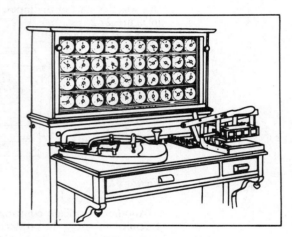

Figure 27.3

Although the cards still had to be input by hand the process was considerably faster than manual processing. In fact this was probably the first true data processing machine that was built.

The next few decades

During the next thirty years many developments were made but most were variations on making faster and more efficient mechanical calculators. In fact, although technology had now reached a point where Babbage's mechanical analytical engine could be made, people began to realise that more and more complex mechanical machines were increasingly cumbersome, difficult to make and maintain, and very awkward to use. Interest therefore centred around the newly discovered ways to make use of electricity.

The electrical machine

The use of electricity to control the flow of information within a machine made great strides. First the invention of the **relay** (an electromechanical switch) meant that electrical signals could be switched on and off and routed through the machine.

As information can be transmitted by making use of the binary system, the ability to switch these electrical signals on and off rapidly was of paramount importance. An early version of computers based on this electromechanical technology was the **Harvard MKI** (automatic sequence controlled calculator). This was one of the first machines to be built which realised the potential of Babbage's machine designed so many years earlier.

The invention of the **valve** meant that the switching operations could now be carried out more quickly, and electronic versions of machines were then developed.

However, they were still very large and cumbersome and consumed enormous amounts of energy because of the heaters that were necessary in each valve (for the process of thermionic emission).

In the 1940s computing developed at an unabated pace owing to the requirements of the military during the Second World War. This was mainly due to the ability of computers to help crack secret codes and thus enable intelligence information to be gathered. A good example of one of these code-cracking computers was called **Colossus**.

In 1946 a machine called ENIAC (Electronic Numerical Integrator Automatic Computer) represented the state of the art at the time. It performed the calculation

$$97\,367 \times 97\,367 \times 97\,367 \times 97\,367 \times 97\,367$$

in less than half a second. This was an amazing feat for the time and certainly was most impressive. However, to be able to do that the machine needed 18,000 valves, used over 200 kW of electricity and had to be housed in a fairly large hall!

A major development in software

As well as the increasing sophistication of the hardware, a most significant development was made by **von Neumann** in 1945. This was the idea that the program as well as the data should be stored inside the computer. This has led to the idea of the **stored program concept** that is still in use in machines today. Before the stored program concept was introduced, it was a massive task to program the computer to do many different things. However, after this concept was introduced, a great leap forward in the versatility of computers was attained.

The first computer to run a stored program was in fact the Manchester MK1, developed at Manchester University. Also, during the late 1940s many developments in software were taking place. In particular the Cambridge University Computer EDSAC (Electronic Delay Storage Automatic Computer) and later in America EDVAC (Electronic Discrete Variable Automatic Computer) were significant developments which worked on the modern idea of the stored program concept.

In the commercial and business environments great strides were being made and LEO (the Lyons Electronic Office) was a milestone when, in 1953, it became the first computer to be used for commercial purposes. A representation of the LEO computer can be seen in figure 27.4(a).

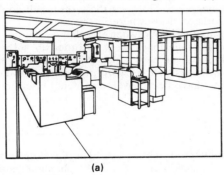 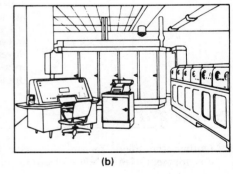

(a)   (b)

Figure 27.4

During the early 1950s another significant development took place when the Univac company developed a computer system which paved the way for the layout of present day computers. Hitherto all computers had a unique layout which made them difficult to use by all but the most specialised engineers and scientists. However, Univac paved the way for the **operators console** (inevitably a teletype machine). The **central processing unit** and **main store** were housed in a cabinet, the **printer** was housed in a separate cabinet and **magnetic tape** was used as the medium for both input and output. A stylisation of the Univac machine is shown in figure 27.4(b).

Electronic component developments

Throughout the 1940s and 1950s the **electronic valve** (the component used as a switch) ruled supreme and was used in what has come to be known as the **first generation computers.** However, in 1948, a team lead by **William Shockley** invented a tiny electronic component called the **transistor.** Over the years the transistor was developed into a device which could perform the same function as a valve (as far as computing was concerned) but consumed much less energy and occupied a fraction of the space taken up by the valve. Transistors therefore revolutionised both the size and energy requirements of complex computer systems. The road to micro-miniaturisation had begun. Never before in the history of mankind has such a tiny device had such a profound impact. The technology not only used less electricity and was smaller, but was faster and more reliable at the same time. Couple this with the tremendous advantage of costing only a fraction of the previous technology and you have some idea of the revolution that was to begin. The transistor gave birth to what has become known as the **second generation** of computers.

Much effort went into the development of this new technology. The early germanium transistors were not reliable enough to be used in guided missiles and did not work to specification if they became reasonably hot. Much research and development found that transistors made from silicon performed much better and were more reliable. Also, new techniques were being developed which enabled several transistors to be put on to a single chip of silicon. This increased the packing density and, because fewer external connections were necessary than when connecting together the discrete transistors, was inherently more reliable. Again, increases in speed were obtained simply because the components were closer together.

When several transistors (and other components) were joined together on a single base they became known as an **integrated circuit** or **silicon chip.** Computers based on this first generation integrated circuit technology became known as the **third generation** of computers.

Impressive developments were made in integrated circuit manufacture. In the early 1960s it was possible to put only a few transistors into an integrated circuit package. Today well over a million are possible. The increasingly complex functions that could be carried out on a single chip led to the development of the **microprocessor** (a single computer on a silicon chip). However, it is obvious that to make use of the power of a microprocessor, many external connections have to be made. Similarly, to turn a microprocessor into a microcomputer, devices such as a keyboard and screen have to be added.

As well as the development of microcomputers, other larger computer systems became more powerful because of the complex functions that could be carried out by the chips that they used. The current generation of chips has led to the development of what is called the **fourth generation** of computers.

Many techniques such as multiprocessing (see page 62) or parallel processing (many processors working in parallel to speed up the effectiveness of the CPU) have been developed. These have led to the current generation of mainframes being called **supercomputers.** However the term is still applied when considering the **fifth generation** discussed elsewhere in this book.

During the period when the above generations were being developed, many other important milestones were recorded in **software development.** These include the development of better high level languages, more efficient operating systems and user packages such as word processors and databases. However, all of these developments have been covered in detail elsewhere in this book.

Exercise 27.1

1. Outline the major factors that have influenced the development of the modern electronic digital computer.

2. ENIAC weighed 30 tons and contained 18,000 valves. Some of today's integrated circuits of just a few square centimetres are very much more powerful. What single development started the microminiaturisation race, and what developments have since contributed to it?

   Why is it necessary to have such small and highly densely packed circuits?

3. The development of software is just as important as the phenomenal developments that have been made in hardware. What aspects of software development have been important and what, in your opinion, is the most exciting development that is likely to affect the future?

28 Computing projects

Introduction

Project work forms a major part of many computing courses. At 'A' level it is usual to allocate about one third of the marks for this important component. In other courses project allocation and marks can be of a similar or even greater order of magnitude. Many other subjects at this level require you to undertake 'projects', but only a few insist that you carry out one extensive project over a significant period of time. It's very easy for some students to think of their computer-science projects in the same light as projects in some of their other subjects, and *this often leads to the mistaken impression that the project can be researched and completed within a few weeks – this is not so.*

The nature of computing projects

Computing projects fall into a very different category indeed from most other projects at this level. Many students are used to cramming – they believe that *extremely hard work* over a *limited period of time* will produce good results. They are used to this mode of operation because they usually write their essays or do other short-term research or examination revision in this particular way. An intense couple of days spent researching and writing an essay, for example, does work with many students – but with computer science projects, even the brightest and best-intentioned students often damage their chances considerably by applying the same overall philosophy to their computing work. They are assuming that they can learn complex packages or languages in a couple of days, they are assuming that the algorithms they chose to solve their problems will work first time, they are assuming that the computers on which they are working will be faultless in operation and work exactly as expected, and they are also assuming that nobody else will be using the facilities when they decide that it's time for them to spend a long session at the computer! *They are usually mistaken on all counts.*

Although it's human nature not to start things until the very last minute, you *must* be well disciplined and start to work hard on your project really early on, at least two terms before it's due to be handed in. If, for any reason you complete it early, then so what! You will have some extra time on your hands which will usually prove to be invaluable in a period when mock examinations and shorter but more intense projects in other subjects are taking place. With the introduction of modular 'A' levels, GNVQs and other courses, you must manage your time effectively and plan your workload many months in advance.

It's also advisable that you should not go to the other extreme of working ridiculously hard on your project over such a long time that your other work starts to suffer. Many students do get carried away with their projects because interesting projects can and indeed do become addictive, especially if they are going very well. If you start to feel that you are falling into this all-to-familiar trap, then you have probably chosen a project which is too complex, or one that is too long – both are inappropriate if it means that you have to spend a disproportionate amount of time on your project.

There may be other reasons for wanting to spend several hundred hours on a project, but don't blame it on your 'A' level course if you have chosen to do this! – it is not a requirement of the course, nor of any course. Some students may feel that the time spent is justified because they may be entering their project into a national competition, may be writing a project which they intend to develop into a saleable item, or may be thinking of starting up their own software house – all these things have been done under the umbrella of a computing project for advanced level!

From the examination point of view you should realise that most of the effort should be put into a thorough understanding of the theory papers, as this is the most effective way of spending your time if you are aiming to maximise your marks. For example, a very good project might score about 80%, whereas a superb project might score about 90% or more. Now we are arguing about 10% of the marks in a component of the examination which represents about 30% of the total, therefore, this huge difference in effort put into your project is only getting you about 10% of 30% which is 3 marks in the final examination! This type of mark could easily be achieved by learning an extra couple of facts and writing about them in the exam – a process which might take only a few minutes – a sobering thought! However, don't go to the other extreme, and hand in a project into which little or no effort has been put, because you think that you might well be able to score about 70% from the rest of the theory papers – you are gambling on doing exceptionally well, and this attitude to life will probably mean that you will have many problems later on when it comes to undertaking work in your chosen career which, in your opinion, might not be so important. The best idea is to strike a balance between doing little and working too hard, but always err on the side of hard work – if you have a bad day when doing the examination you will be glad of all the project marks that you can muster.

Where to begin?

This is often the hardest part of your project – deciding what to do! I give advice to my students by telling them to think up about half a dozen totally different possible projects, and then start to think about each one in more depth, by starting to analyse the problem as described in the project-analysis section, on page 624. Sometimes you will find that apparently very good ideas fizzle out because you can't start to think about them in the detail required, they become boring or tedious, too complex or too simple, you can't find out enough information, the computers you have at school or college don't support the sort of project you are envisaging, or the idea has been done so often before that your teacher will probably be sick in a bucket if another of his students decides to hand in yet another dating-agency database, for example. Other ideas, which might seem slightly silly at the start often bear fruit in unexpected ways, especially if you talk to other people who might be experts in your chosen project area. It's essential that you have an extended talk with your teacher or lecturer regarding your final choice, and it's most important that whatever is chosen fits exactly into the mark scheme (see next section) that you will be using.

Sometimes you will find it profitable to combine your computer-science project with other 'A' levels, so that the project you are doing for computing can be used to provide the data for the other subject. This is an apparently good idea as much of the research done might go towards two different 'A' levels! However, there are great dangers if you are not careful – it's most unlikely that any single project would satisfy two different 'A' levels, although hardware in a technology 'A' level together with software in a computer science 'A' level is one example of an exception. Different aspects of your project will usually be irrelevant as far as each subject is concerned, and you need to be skilful if you are to satisfy all criteria for both examinations – obviously we are not envisaging the same project report being submitted for both projects, but a detailed analysis of how the computer was used to solve a problem would be irrelevant, for example, in a geography 'A' level report – and similarly, a detailed analysis of the geographical interpretation of data would be irrelevant on the computer-science side. Also, don't forget that projects usually have to be chosen at different times for different subjects, and you need to plan well ahead if you are thinking of going down this particular route.

It's obviously an advantage to try to solve a real-life problem. Indeed, I think that it's almost essential that you do so. Solving real problems makes the specification sections of the project easier to write, gives you something definable to achieve, and usually produces something that might be useful in the end. However, **you must not commit yourself to producing any fully working system for anyone**. Some people get excited because they are having a pet project undertaken by an 'A' level computer science student – they look forward to having some utility, application or program which will enable them to solve their particular problem – unfortunately, the truth is more likely to be that the project will never be working completely! You must remember that you can't put in the time and effort needed to fully support some future system. You should be concerned with the all important work of getting your project to a standard good enough for your examination – you are not in the business of sorting out the many problems which may arise due to the implementation of your newly-written system. You must explain to the people concerned that if the project works perfectly then this is a bonus, you will probably be leaving school soon after the project is finished, and there may be no support for continued use of the project after you have gone. When people view projects in this light it removes the pressure from them that so often leads to the scenarios outlined earlier in this section.

It's absolutely essential that you choose a project in which you are interested. There are bound to be many projects which fall into this category – if you can think of none, then I suggest that you might be doing the wrong 'A' level! There will be times when you feel like throwing your project out of the window in frustration, and if there is no real interest in what you are trying to achieve then you will become disillusioned, not only with your project, but with computer science as a subject – choosing an interesting and appropriate project is this essential – it will affect your attitude to your work over an extended period of time. There is no recipe for choosing the right project for you particularly, but some of the projects which have been done at my schools in the past include the following.

1. Fire brigade tender evaluation program.
2. Nuclear bomb casualty calculations.
3. An analysis of stocks and shares.
4. Controlling a quadrophonic sound stage for a theatre.
5. A heart-rate monitoring system.
6. Wire-frame image manipulation.
7. An aid for mountaineers to find routes up a mountain.
8. Medical database for a boarding school sanatorium.
9. Hotel billing system from remote computers via a network.
10. A scuba-diving self-teaching guide.

Another golden rule is that you should not usually try to do something that can be done more easily in other ways, unless there is a compelling reason, such as not being able to afford a particular package. A typical illustration of this scenario would be the student who wrote a picture-drawing package in BASIC – with it you are able to draw squares, lines, circles, ellipses etc and build up pictures making use of these basic shapes – but why bother? – even the simplest of CAD packages in the public domain undertake these tasks very well – the whole object of the exercise seems so pointless – it is for reasons like this that it is suggested that you solve a real-life problem – you are less likely to fall into this particular trap!

The marking scheme

It is most important that you adhere strictly to the scheme which is going to be used for marking your particular project. Get your teacher or lecturer to photocopy the scheme if this is permissible, and *use it at all stages* of your project. For example, the 1996 project-marking scheme for the UCLES board involves the following headings.

A. Selection, analysis and formulation of a problem.
B. Selection and design of the method of solution.
C. Quality of implementation.
D. Testing and evaluation of the complete system.
E. Overall scope and quality of the project.

Each section is allocated a mark between 0 and 20, and ranges from describing how 'demanding problems have been clearly identified and desired outcomes have been achieved' to 'there is no work of the appropriate standard'! Students should know how the scheme will be applied, and be particularly vigilant regarding all the known requirements. For example, expressing an opinion that your project is working is unlikely to get you any realistic marks in the testing section – even if your project supervisor has seen a completely working perfect project! You must realise that the moderator only usually sees the written project report, and it is this alone which determines your marks. If you have not written down that you have tested the system, have not backed up your claim to test the system with suitable data and test results, then you will probably get no marks at all, *even if your system is working perfectly* – a sobering thought and one which outlines the importance of adhering exactly to your particular marking scheme.

The written report

This is the single most important piece of evidence to support your project. It is usually this piece of written work alone which will be the biggest determining factor regarding your final grade for the project. The application used or the program you have written is almost of secondary importance to the written report. Obviously your program or the application you have used will need to be undertaken in depth or you will have nothing to write about – but it's the analysis, design, testing, documentation and the like which accompanies your written report which will be important, not only in its ability to impress the moderator, but in conveying what you have done, how you have done it and the results which you have achieved. The importance of this written report can't be overestimated – a satisfactory project with a well-written and presented report will earn the student more marks than a superb project with a badly written or mediocre report. Don't forget it is the written project report which explains most of the work you have carried out – not the lines of code which constitute your actual project. You must, therefore, not spend so long trying to get your actual project working that you leave insufficient time to write the report. It's far better to stop your project altogether and concentrate on the report a few weeks before your project is due to be handed in. It's far better still to actually write up the report as you are going along – in this way you are less likely to forget why you have decided that things should be done in particular ways.

Project analysis

This important stage is an example of the detailed thought which should be put into your project, *some of which should be undertaken before making the final commitment* to any particular project. It is only by carrying out such analysis that you are able to determine the feasibility of your project, how complex it's likely to be, whether it will involve the sorts of things that you are able to do, and whether it's got enough scope to keep you interested for six months or more. These are important considerations, and time spent undertaking this analysis will be time well spent, even if you come to the conclusion that you will need to change your choice of project rapidly!

When you have decided on a particular project then much more analysis needs to be done before you sit at the computer and start to do any practical work. The best way to get marks on your project is to analyse it in detail, then do some more analysis until you think you have covered every aspect – and finally, do some more analysis! Your analysis should include the HCI (see page 590), and a detailed investigation into the existing practices which might currently be carried out in some manual version of your project. If you can compare your proposed system with an inferior manual system then you can pick up a good many marks later on. However, if you can't make your system better than an existing manual one, then there's not much point in trying to proceed any further with your project – choose another. A classic case here, for example, would be the setting up of a database which gives no advantage over the same information presented in a book. Indeed, I have known situations where the information presented in a book is preferable, because a computer was not always available when the people who were to operate the system needed to use it!

Don't forget to have a detailed look at the **'Corpus-Crumbly'** systems analysis of a library in chapter 18, and the **'Drive-you-mad' car company** in chapter 16. Both of these systems-analysis examples are worth reading before doing your own systems analysis on your project – they provide you with typical ways of tackling many different problems of the sort which you are likely to encounter.

The method of solution

The analysis part of your project can and indeed should be written up as you go along. Why bother to wait until you have got the thing working – much of the analysis will not change that much – and if it does, then this will give you ample opportunity later on to discuss in detail why you have made these changes. This all adds to the interest of the project and will enable you to score very highly when you come to do an overall assessment of what you have accomplished.

You must not forget the extensive range of analytical techniques covered in chapter 7. Use a large variety of appropriate techniques, and *make sure that your analysis is well structured and above all modular.* There will probably be many times throughout your project when you come to a dead end, loose inspiration or find that you lack information to carry on with some particularly detailed section. If you have modularised your project then you can concentrate on another part, sure in the knowledge that it will interface with all the others. You can then go back to the part that was causing you problems at a later stage.

You must also not forget to analyse the project in terms of data structures as covered in chapter 14, and think up a suitable strategy for the testing of individual modules at an early stage. It's far easier to think up suitable tests before you have written the modules. Many students get their modules working and then decide on a suitable test strategy! – they then go on to wonder why testing is needed at all – they say that the module obviously works, then promptly throw away marks that would have been awarded by the mark scheme for a suitable test strategy!

There are many techniques covered throughout this book, and you would be well advised to apply them to appropriate parts of your project where necessary. It does not matter if you have not covered a particular topic if it is needed for your project.

Read about it, learn it and use it. Indeed, there will probably be some techniques which you will never cover in class – don't worry, this is the whole point of undertaking projects – to enable you to do some further research, and to apply appropriate techniques. By doing this you will score highly for your methods of solution. However, don't forget to acknowledge the source of all routines or algorithms used in your project, it's unlikely that you have thought up some wonderful new ways of solving a particular problem – your project supervisor will probably have seen these methods before, and he or she will not be fooled into thinking that it's your original work!

Testing the system

This is often the weakest section in the report. Even able candidates with wonderful projects throw away marks at this important stage. With no sensible test strategy you have probably limited yourself to about 80% of the marks, assuming that you have produced a project which is perfect in all other respects – a stupid waste of time and energy.

Don't forget that you should devise suitable test data, and look out for unusual as well as usual situations regarding data entry. Don't forget the **validation**, **verification**, **CRCs**, **hashing** and all the other paraphernalia which go into making sure that data entry, recovery or transmission is carried out correctly. So many students fail to apply what they have learnt in the theory lessons – a sure way to loose valuable marks.

Documentation

This is essential and should be split up into two parts for most systems. First there is the **user documentation**, and this refers specifically to the instructions needed to operate the system. It should be as non-technical and easy to follow as possible. Secondly there is the **technical documentation**, of which much of your project report will form a major part. It is intended to enable a competent person to be able to correct any errors in or modify your project in your absence! This is difficult for students at school or college to adequately cover due to lack of time. However, with well structured analysis and design sections, and with a well documented program listing, there should be few problems in practice.

Does it work?

In many cases the answer will be no! However, you will probably not fail because of this, assuming that you have taken the advice outlined in this brief chapter. Don't forget that you have a deadline to meet. It can't be extended, or you will not get the project report completed in time for marking! This is a very unrealistic scenario – in real life an extension of a month or two on a project might be all that is needed to get the system fully working. Your teachers and the board realise these problems and the mark schemes are arranged accordingly so that students who have worked hard and undertaken all the correct procedures will get high marks in the project work, even if the overall project is not working. However, don't use this as an excuse for starting the project too late – there is a big difference between laziness and lack of completion due to other problems. Your lecturer will take this into account based on his or her intimate knowledge of how you have conducted yourself throughout the duration of the project.

Presentation

Finally, a word is in order about the presentation of the written report. Do use a DTP system or powerful word processor to produce your final report. Tatty handwritten documentation is really no longer acceptable from 'A' level standard computer science students. All students should be capable of a professional standard of documentation without too much effort. Indeed, if you follow the advice given earlier in this chapter, then you will already have a lot of text on the computer which has been produced as you are going along. The final report should, therefore, consist of a collating exercise, with added notes and diagrams. Indeed, do the diagrams on the computer as you are going along too – CAD packages should also be familiar to students at advanced level. Hand-written documentation is usually an indication that the project was completed in a rush, probably at home in the Easter holidays before the report was due to be handed in!

Don't forget also that the moderator is a busy person – it is essential that he or she is able to find things quickly. If you hand in a well-written and presented report, complete with an appropriate index which shows all relevant sections which relate exactly to the marking scheme (i.e. analysis, testing, user documentation, conclusions etc.) then you are more likely to be viewed sympathetically when it comes to the allocation of marks. Moderators are not going to spend a disproportionate amount of time trying to find some esoteric information buried deep in a poorly-produced document. If they can't find information after a reasonable amount if time then they will realistically assume that it's not there – a stupid waste of your time as you will, in effect, be throwing marks down the drain. As with most things to do with projects, forward planning and steady work over a long period of time are the key to success in this vitally important area.

End of chapter summary

- **Projects form a major part of most computing courses** – they should be taken seriously because they account for about 30% of the final marks.
- **Computing projects are of a different nature to the majority of other 'A' level projects** – a single project is usually carried out over an extended period of time.
- **Don't wait until the last moment before starting your project** – cramming and hard work over the space of a week or two will not be sufficient.
- **Don't spend a disproportionate amount of time on your project** – no course demands that you spend hundreds of hours making sure that your project is perfect.
- Although you need to do a good project, **the difference between an excellent and a very good project is often not worth the extra effort** – you would be far better to concentrate a similar effort on the theory papers.
- **Choosing a project may not be easy** for many students. Start off by thinking up half a dozen, then start to analyse each one in depth and decide on the best.
- **Computing projects may be combined with other subjects at 'A' level,** but you can't use the same report for each, and some parts will be irrelevant to the other.
- **Solve a real-life problem if possible** – it's easier to be objective about what you are trying to achieve, and easier to measure the results of your progress.
- **Don't promise anyone that you will produce a fully working project which will solve their problem**. The chances are high that it won't – simply through lack of time.
- **Try not to emulate things that can be done in much easier ways** – unless there is some compelling reason to do so.
- **Get a copy of the marking scheme and get to know it well**. Make sure that all required sections are covered in the detail required by the examining board.
- **The written report is the most important single piece of evidence which represents your project**. Often it's the only part that the moderator will see.
- **Analyse your project making use of all the analytical techniques that have been used in the book** – plus others if you find them to be useful.
- **It's virtually impossible to carry out too much analysis in the initial stages of project design**. All the hard work done then will pay huge dividends later.
- **When explaining your chosen methods of solution make sure that the methods are structured and modularised**. Don't forget to include test procedures before designing the modules – they're much easier to think about then.
- **The Corpus Crumbly Library and Drive-you-mad car company cases are essential reading before starting** the analysis of your project,
- **Testing the system is of paramount importance**. Most students lose marks on this aspect of their project – use abnormal as well as sensible data, and validate, verify and use CRCs etc where it is a good idea to do so.
- **Appropriate documentation** should accompany the project.
- **User documentation** should be non technical and simple.
- **Technical documentation** might be needed in addition for parts of the report – for example, an explanation of some particular method not usually associated with computing.
- **Much of your report, including any programs should be self documenting** if written in appropriate ways, and should form part of the technical documentation.
- **When doing an appraisal of your system be honest** (most of the time!). The examiners will realise that you are learning the subject, that with hindsight you would have probably done it differently, and above all don't expect the project to work perfectly. If it does then that's an added bonus.
- **Hand in a neat and well-documented report** – it should include a contents list which relates to all sections required in the marking scheme.

29 Examination questions

Answer a selection of questions

1. Using only NAND gates show how a two input OR gate can be implemented. [2 marks]
(NEAB, Paper I, 1992)

2. Describe **two** particularly relevant features you would expect to find in a high level language designed specifically for use in each of the following:
(i) commercial data processing,
(ii) scientific computing. [4 marks]
(NEAB, Paper I, 1992)

3. For each of the following, explain what it is and describe a suitable application:
(i) Optical Character Recognition (OCR),
(ii) Magnetic Ink Character Recognition (MICR),
(iii) Bar code scanning. [6 marks]
(NEAB, Paper I, 1992)

4. An on-line information retrieval system holds confidential personal data.
(a) What precautions should be taken to
(i) minimise unauthorised access,
(ii) detect unauthorised access? [4 marks]
(b) Why might different users be given different access privileges? [2 marks]
(c) Explain how the data should be recovered after corruption. [4 marks]
(NEAB, Paper I, 1992)

5. (a) Distinguish between a compiler and an interpreter and explain their relative advantages and disadvantages. [6 marks]
(b) A typical compilation process is organised into three phases: scanning (lexical analysis and symbol table construction), syntax analysis and code generation. Explain the purpose of each of these phases and illustrate your answer by briefly describing the outcome when applying each phase to the statement:
a: = sqrt(b + c); [8 marks]
(note: sqrt is a standard function)
(c) Explain what is meant by an assembler, clearly indicating how it differs from a compiler. [4 marks]
(d) A typical assembler supports macros and subroutines. Distinguish between these two facilities and explain their relative advantages and disadvantages. [16 marks]

(NEAB, Paper II, 1992)

6. A manufacturer is designing a microprocessor-controlled tumble drier. The drier is fitted with
– a motor which can rotate the drum clockwise or anticlockwise
– a heater
– a temperature level switch which is operated by the user to signal whether the drier is to operate in 'warm' mode or 'hot' mode
– a digital temperature sensor which senses the temperature within the drier. The temperature reading is passed as a 3-bit value with 000 produced at room temperature, 100 produced when the 'warm' setting is reached and 111 is produced when the 'hot' setting is reached.

All these components are connected to the microprocessor's 8-bit control port as shown in Figure 1.

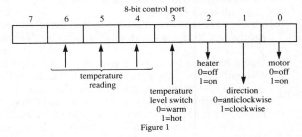

Figure 1

(i) Throughout the operation of the drier the drum follows a sequence of operations where the drum is rotated clockwise for 15 seconds and stopped for 1 second, then rotated anticlockwise for 15 seconds and stopped for 1 second.
Given the procedure *pause(n)* which pauses for 'n' seconds, write an algorithm for the procedure *cycle* which carries out the above sequence of drum rotation operations **once only**. [6 marks]
(NEAB, Paper II, 1992)

7. A programmer is considering using either the linear (serial) search or the binary search method to locate an item within an array containing numeric data.
(a) Describe both methods of searching the array and, in each case, explain how the absence of the required item can be detected. [4 marks]
(b) Under what conditions would each method be used? [2 marks]

(NEAB, Paper I, 1991)

8. Clearly distinguish between batch and real-time processing. [2 marks]
Describe an application that is suitable for batch processing. What are the advantages and disadvantages of batch processing for this application over real-time processing? [4 marks]
(NEAB, Paper I, 1991)

9. Outline briefly the purpose of normalisation
(a) of data in a database
(CCEA, Paper 2, 1993)
(b) in the binary representation of real numbers
[4 marks]

10. Show, with the aid of examples, the difference between precision and accuracy in the representation of numeric values within a computer. [4 marks]
(CCEA, Paper 2, 1993)

11. "The primary aim of the operating system of a large computer system supporting a number of multi-access users is to manage the resources of the computer system effectively."

(a) Describe the major resources of such a computer system.   [6 marks]

(b) By means of examples, indicate the need for effective management of these resources.   [6 marks]

(c) Describe, with the aid of examples, how this management process might utilise
 (i) interrupts
 (ii) a system of priority.   [12 marks]

(d) Explain how the priority of a process might be determined.   [6 marks]

12. (a) Explain why languages such as BASIC, COBOL, and Pascal are often referred to as
 (i) third generation languages (3GLs)
 (ii) high-level languages.   [4 marks]

(b) Distinguish between the terms *procedural* and *non-procedural* in the context of programming languages.   [6 marks]

(c) Computer-based tools have become important elements in the development of information systems.
 (i) List the stages in the system life cycle in the order in which they normally occur. [4 marks]
 (ii) Identify those aspects of the system life cycle for which software tools are available.   [6 marks]
 (iii) Various tools can be integrated into a single system known as an Integrated Program Support Environment (IPSE). Describe the benefits of using such an integrated system   [6 marks]

(d) There is increasing use of the term Computer Assisted Software Engineering (CASE) in software development. Explain briefly what is meant by software engineering.   [4 marks]

(CCEA, Paper 2, 1993)

13. A particular computer stores two's complement floating-point numbers in 32 bits allocated in three parts as follows:

bit 0 (the least significant bit) – sign bit
bits 1 to 23 – normalised fraction mantissa
bits 24 to 31 – exponent

Explain the purpose of each of these components.

[6 marks]

(CCEA, Paper 2, 1994)

14. Two models of microcomputer have identical specifications except that one has a 25 MHz clock while the other has a 33 MHz clock. State the purpose of a microprocessor clock and outline the way in which these different clocks will influence the microcomputers' performances.   [3 marks]

15. Explain what is meant by a *cylinder* on a magnetic disk pack and indicate how this concept can influence the efficiency of reading data from the disk pack.   [6 marks]

(CCEA, Paper 2, 1994)

16. (a) A register contains the ASCII characters "A" and "B" as follows:
 0100000101000010
Explain how shift operations can be used to:
 (i) reverse the order of the characters in the register and   [2 marks]
 (ii) replace the first character in the register with

eight zeros leaving the second character unchanged.   [2 marks]
 (iii) Show how masking can be used to achieve this second result.   [4 marks]
 (iv) If the above binary pattern is interpreted as a twos complement integer, show how shifting can be used to perform simple multiplication and division.   [4 marks]

(b) Indirect and indexed (or modified) are two modes of addressing found in assembly languages.
 (i) Describe, with the aid of examples, how each of these addressing modes differs from direct addressing and state **one** reason why each is required.   [8 marks]
 (ii) Explain briefly what is meant by the fetch-execute cycle.   [2 marks]
 (iii) Explain the operation of the decode part of the fetch-execute cycle and describe how it proceeds for an instruction containing an indirect address and one containing an indexed address.   [8 marks]

(CCEA, Paper 2, 1994)

17. The following EBNF definitions describe a simplified motor vehicle registration number:
 <reg_no> : : =<code>' '<number>.
 <number> : : = <pos_digit> [<digit>|<digit><digit>|
    <digit><digit><digit>.
 <pos_digit> : : = '1'|'2'|'3'|'4'|'5'|'6'|'7'|'8'|'9'.
 <digit> : : = '0' |<pos_digit>.
 <code> : : = 'LI'|'BI'|'IX'.

State whether each of the following is a valid or invalid registration number giving brief reasons for your answer.

(a) IX 34   (b) IX 034   (c) BI 90909   [6 marks]

18. A database application package designed for use by a single user is currently being used on a number of stand-alone microcomputers. It is now proposed to modify the package for use by a number of users over a local area network.

(a) Explain what is meant by a local area network.   [4 marks]

(b) With the aid of examples, describe two different local area network topologies and explain the communication protocols used in each.   [8 marks]

(c) Identify the problems which are likely to arise when a number of users wish to use the same software package and outline how these problems might be addressed in the network version.   [12 marks]

(d) When the network version of the package is implemented an important component will be a password security system in which the user must enter a correct password before being permitted to log on. Failure to key in the correct password in three attempts will result in permission to log on being denied. Stating clearly any assumptions you are making, design an algorithm for the processing of a user's attempts at keying in the correct password.   [6 marks]

(CCEA, Paper 1, 1993)

19. (a) Explain what is meant by the terms
 (i) hashing algorithm,
 (ii) hash table.   [4 marks]

(b) Describe an application where the use of a hash table would be appropriate.   [4 marks]

(c) (i) Explain what can cause a collision when a hash table is used.

(ii) What steps can be taken in such an event? [4 marks]

(WJEC, Paper A2, 1993)

20.(a) Give an algorithm for a routine which will simulate the throwing of two dice (each numbered 1 to 6), returning on each call the sum of the scores on the two dice. You may make use of a pseudo-random number generator but you should explain how it is used. [2 marks]

The game Two-Dice is played by two players, each of whom starts with **thirty** tokens. The players (called Ali and Bronwen) toss a coin to decide who will throw the dice during the game (Ali in this description).

The game proceeds as a series of turns, ending when one player needs to put a token on the table but has none left. The other player is the winner.

(In the unlikely event that both players run out of tokens the game is replayed from the start.)

Every turn starts with each player putting one token on the table. Ali then throws the two dice.

If the score is 7 or 11, Ali wins and takes both tokens from the table.

If the score is 2, 3 or 12, Bronwen wins and takes both tokens from the table.

Any other score is called the 'point' and is noted. Each player puts a further token on the table and Ali then throws the two dice again. This process is repeated until either the score is the same as the point, in which case Ali wins and takes all the tokens from the table, or the score is 7, in which case Bronwen wins and takes all the tokens from the table.

(b) Write down, in pseudocode or other suitable form, an algorithm to simulate the playing of the game Two-Dice. [8 marks]

(c) An addicted player has suggested that the player who throws the dice has an advantage. How would you test this suggestion? [2 marks]

(WJEC, Paper A2, 1993)

21. Syntax diagrams and BNF can be used in the definition of a programming language. Assuming that the symbols <letter> and <digit> are already defined,

(a) draw a syntax diagram to define a signed integer (i.e. a sign followed by one or more digits), [2 marks]

(b) write down the BNF rules to define a standard variable name (i.e. a string of letters and/or digits, starting with a letter). [3 marks]

(WJEC, Paper A1, 1993)

22. A sequential file held on magnetic tape has the following characteristics.

500 000 records.

Variable length records, average 100 bytes, maximum 255 bytes.

Each record preceeded by one byte containing the record length.

Records ordered on a key field of length 12 bytes.

The file is to be reorganised as an indexed sequential file with a multi-level index held on disc as follows.

Data blocks of 1024 bytes. For example (the numbers indicate the number of bytes in each part)

| 1 | 12 | 67 | 1 | 12 | 113 | ... | 1 | 12 | 58 | 1 | 278 |

record length | key field | other fields | | | | more records | | | terminator (value 0) | | free space

The records in a data block are in order of key field value. No record is split between two blocks. The blocking factor is set so that initially at least 220 bytes of free space are present in each data block. Index blocks of 1024 bytes.

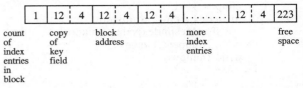

| 1 | 12 | 4 | 12 | 4 | 12 | 4 | .... | 12 | 4 | 223 |

count of index entries in block | copy of key field | block address | | | | more index entries | | | | free space

There is one low level index entry for every data block in the file, containing a copy of the key field value of the first record in the data block together with the data block address. The same blocking factor is used. The next level of index is similarly organised. It contains one entry for each low level index block, consisting of a copy of the key field value in the first entry in the low level index block together with the low level index block address. The hierarchy of indexes continues in this form, up to the high level index which contains only one block. The last four bytes of the high level index block contain the block address of the first block in a list of free blocks.

(a) Calculate, showing your workings,

(i) approximately how many data blocks will be needed when the indexed sequential file is initially created;

(ii) approximately how many index blocks will be needed when the indexed sequential file is initially created;

(iii) how many levels of index will be needed when the indexed sequential file is initially created. [5 marks]

(b) Describe in outline the algorithm which will be followed when searching for a record with a given key value (denoted by KVAL). [4 marks]

(c) Usually when a new record is to be inserted into the file there will be sufficient space for it to take its place in the relevant data block. However, sometimes the insertion of a new record will cause the relevant data block to overflow, requiring half of its contents to be moved to a new data block (taken from the list of free blocks), with consequent changes to the index.

Describe the changes that might be needed to the index. [5 marks]

(d) An exceptional situation occurs, when a new record to be inserted, is one whose key field value is lower than any currently in the file.

Explain what needs to be done in this situation. [3 marks]

(e) When a record is to be deleted from the file it is removed and not just marked as deleted. Outline the actions that need to be taken to do this. [3 marks]

(WJEC, Paper A2, 1992)

23.(a) The program below is written in a structured programming language. It reads a sequence of real values and finds the location of the minimum value.

```
program mini
declare
    real array: values {1..50}
    integer: minpos, quantity, index
begin
    read (quantity)
```

```
        if quantity < 1 or quantity > 50
            fail ('invalid data')
        else
        for index from 1 to quantity
            read (values[index])
        minpos : = 1
        for index from 2 to quantity
            if values[index]values[minpos]
                minpos: = index
        write (minpos)
    end
```

Describe in general terms how the lexical analyser of a compiler would process this program to convert it into lexical form and how it would use a symbol table during the process. [10 marks]

(b) (i) Explain why reverse Polish is often used during the operation of a compiler or interpreter. [2 marks]

(ii) Write down the reverse Polish form of this assignment statement.
a : = b - c / d * (e + f) - g   [3 marks]

(iii) A particular interpreter works by first translating all the statements of the program into reverse Polish and then executing them one by one as required. Explain in general terms how the interpreter could execute the reverse Polish form of the assignment statement in (ii).   [5 marks]

(WJEC, Paper A2, 1992)

24. A letter which is stored at each node of a binary tree is printed as the tree is traversed. If the tree consists of just three nodes with the letter D stored at the root, the letter A at the left leaf node and the letter E at the right leaf node, what will be printed when the traversal is
(i) in-order?
(ii) pre-order?
(iii) post-order?   [3 marks]

(AEB, Paper 2, 1993)

25. Two centuries ago the industrial revolution brought about fundamental social changes in Britain. In particular, instead of the majority of the people living and working on the land, they moved into town and cities to work in factories and offices. It is said that Britain is now in the midst of an *information revolution* brought about by computing technology.

Briefly describe **two** of the social changes expected from this revolution and suggest **one** parallel between peoples' attitudes today and the widespread concern of the British people in the late eighteenth century for their jobs and their futures.   [3 marks]

(AEB, Paper 1, 1992)

26. What is a *local area network* (*LAN*)?

Any LAN can be used for sending *data packets*. These are often messages from one network user to another. What are the main components of a *data packet*?   [3 marks]

(AEB, Paper 1, 1992)

27. The operating system of a large computer has a number of functions, and supports a range of facilities for the user. Explain what is meant by each of the following facilities and outline how they are implemented.
(a) A multi-programming environment.   [3 marks]
(b) Time sharing.   [4 marks]

(c) Spooling.   [5 marks]
(d) Virtual memory.   [4 marks]

(AEB, Paper 1, 1992)

28. The binary number 1001 0111 0011 can be interpreted in a number of different ways. State its value in denary if it represents:
(i) an unsigned binary integer;
(ii) a binary coded decimal integer;
(iii) a twos complement floating point number with an eight bit mantissa followed by a four bit exponent.   [4 marks]

(AEB, Paper 2, 1992)

29. A spooler program on a multi-user system, maintains a table of files to be printed. Files are given a priority rating from 1 to 5 with rating 1 being given top priority. A new file will be printed immediately after all previous files with equal or higher priority have been printed.
(i) Explain why a spooler program is used to print files.   [3 marks]

(ii) Suggest two distinct reasons for assigning a high priority to a file.   [2 marks]

(iii) The table contains for each file its name, its start address on disc, its priority rating and a pointer to the position in the table of the next file to be printed. Assume that the table is initially empty and that the printer is not yet on-line. Files are entered in the table in the order of their arrival. Copy and complete the following table after the following files have been placed in the spooler buffer for printing.

Position	Name	Rating	Address	Pointer
1	SP0001	3	00105	
2	SP0002	5	00210	
3	SP0003	2	17654	
4	SP0004	1	28513	
5	SP0005	3	76412	
6	SP0006	2	43143	
7	SP0007	3	38159	
8	SP0008	1	58765	

HEAD POINTER = 4   [4 marks]

(iv) The spooler program is written in a high level language. Name and describe a suitable data structure for this table.   [2 marks]

(v) The owner of a particular spooled file decides that the file no longer needs printing. Describe the changes to the table.   [4 marks]

(vi) Users may wish to know which files will be printed prior to their own file. Write an algorithm which will print out the names of these files given that the target file name has been entered. State any assumptions you have made.   [5 marks]

(AEB, Paper 2, 1992)

30. State **two** uses of bar codes in a factory data collection system.

Give **two** reasons why bar codes are preferred to magnetic stripe in this system.   [4 marks]

(AEB, Paper 1, 1992)

31. What is meant by *artificial intelligence* (AI)? With reference to **one** example, give one advantage and one disadvantage of an AI approach.   [5 marks]

(AEB, Paper 1, 1992)

32. Describe **four** different data types, giving for each an example from a high-level programming language with

which you are familiar. [12 marks]
(O&CSEB/UCLES, Paper 1, 1992)

33. Describe the essential differences between the hardware that is required for the following computer systems:
(a) the simulation and modelling of an engineering problem such as the design of a motor car or the construction of a building;
(b) the control of a missile;
(c) the production of management information for a large commercial enterprise. [12 marks]
(O&CSEB/UCLES, Paper 1, 1992)

34. (a) Distinguish between *a stack* and *a queue* in terms of the processing operations defined on these data structures. [9 marks]
(b) The sequence 'ab+' is known as the *postfix* form of the expression 'a+b' which is said to be in *infix* form. The postfix form for an expression can be found from the infix by inputting the latter characters and storing the operators on a stack until they are needed. That is, for the string 'a+b' we would input and output 'a', stack '+', input and output 'b' and finally unstack and output '+' to give the string 'ab+'.
(i) By processing the following string of characters from left to right, show how a stack can be used to convert the infix sequence 'a*b + c/d' into postfix form. Assume the normal priorities for the order in which mathematical operations take place in this expression. [9 marks]
(ii) How do you think brackets within expressions could be handled? [7 marks]
(O&CSEB/UCLES, Paper 1, 1992)

35. (a) Consider a number of data records held in a file on disc storage. Describe a hashing procedure that enables these records to be stored and accessed in a random manner. [7 marks]
(b) A particular firm has a large number of these files that represent the data within a large data base. These data are continually up-dated and are vital to the functioning of the firm. Describe a policy for back-up of these data that would go some way to ensure that the firm can continue in business despite computer faults and other possible catastrophes. [11 marks]
(c) What steps could be taken to ensure that the files retain their integrity on a change of hardware in the system? [7 marks]
(O&CSEB/UCLES, Paper 1, 1992)

36. (a) In computer control, a transducer converts signals from one form of energy to another. Transducers can be classified into sensors and actuators.
(i) With reference to particular devices, describe briefly each of these types of transducer. [8 marks]
(ii) Describe a practical situation in which each device you describe can be used. [7 marks]
(b) Many devices controlled by a computer work with analogue signals. Describe briefly a method for digital to analogue conversion of electrical signals. [10 marks]
(O&CSEB/UCLES, Paper 1, 1993)

37. (a) Robots can vary from simple devices to humanoid simulators. Discuss **three** features that characterise a robot and distinguish it from simpler controlling devices. [12 marks]
(b) By reference to a car production line, or some other automated production activity, describe three different uses of robots in the processes. [13 marks]
(O&CSEB/UCLES, Paper 1, 1993)

38. The core hardware of a modern personal computer can be categorised into processing, fast access memory and input/output units. The processing unit contains further registers, arithmetic and logical components. All units are connected by a bus that can transfer both data and instructions.
(a) Draw a diagram to illustrate the interconnections between these units, showing the major components and registers within the processing unit. [10 marks]
(b) Describe the flow of data during the execution of an arithmetic operation, such as the addition of two numbers stored in the memory. [10 marks]
(c) Explain briefly how control can be modified as a result of a conditional branch instruction. [5 marks]
(O&CSEB/UCLES, Paper 1, 1994)

39. (a) Distinguish between
(i) *a feasibility study*,
(ii) *a system analysis*,
(iii) *a system design*. [12 marks]
In particular, identify the documents, and their purpose, that would be produced by the end of each of the above activities.
(b) During the systems analysis of a new computer project, it is possible to identify parts of the system that it would be inappropriate to computerise. For example, bank users still hand write cheques rather than input codes and values via terminals. What criteria would you use in helping you decide which parts of a proposed system should be computerised? [8 marks]
(O&CSEB/UCLES, Paper 1, 1994)

40. A library may use a paper-based record-keeping system, a conventional computer file system or a database management system.
(a) Describe what is meant by a database and explain the role of a database management system. [5 marks]
(b) Outline the advantages of using a database management system in an application such as a library. [3 marks]
(UCLES/O&CSEB, Paper 1, 1992)

41. A program is required which will read a piece of text and find each word in it. It will make a list of the words in the text together with counts of how many times each occurs. It will then print in alphabetical order the resulting list of words with the counts.
(a) The program will need to make use of a data structure to hold the words and counts. A linked list and an array have both been suggested, with each entry containing a string and an integer. Discuss the relative merits of these two data structures, taking into account the operations which the program will need to perform. [5 marks]
(b) Write down, using pseudocode or another suitable form, an algorithm for the program, assuming the use of the data structure you identified as better in (a).

Note that for the purposes of the program a word is defined as a sequence of letters which has a non-letter before and after it. The start and end of the text, and any return characters, are all counted as non-letters. You can assume that the letters are all in lower case. [8 marks]

(c) The program is to be used to carry out some research on books by different authors. A book typically has around 100 000 words in total, and may contain several thousand different words. Discuss the merits of using a more sophisticated data structure for the program, such as a hash table or a tree. [5 marks]

(UCLES/O&CSEB, Paper 1, 1992)

42. When data is stored on a particular backing storage medium, each byte is represented by eight data bits and one parity bit. The resulting nine-bit code has odd parity (i.e. the number of ones is odd).

(a) Describe in detail an algorithm suitable for a routine which takes a byte of eight data bits (in the form of an integer in the range 0 to 255) and returns the value of the parity bit. [4 marks]

The data is stored in blocks which contain 1024 data bytes (each with its parity bit) and one parity byte (also with its own parity bit). This parity byte acts as a 'longitudinal' parity check. This means that taking the most significant bit of each data byte in the block, together with the most significant bit of the parity byte, gives an odd number of ones, and that the same applies for each of the other eight bit positions in the data bytes, including the parity bits.

(b) Outline how your algorithm for (a) could be modified to take a sequence of 1024 data bytes and to generate the parity byte. [4 marks]

(c) When a block of data is read from the backing storage medium, the parities for each data byte and for the complete block are checked. Describe the various possible results of these checks and in each case state the action which should be taken by the system [4 marks]

(UCLES/O&CSEB, Paper 1, 1992)

43. At a particular instant during the operation of a multi-access system the situation is as follows.

(a) One program is in main store and is being processed.

(b) One program is being transferred by the disc controller from main store to backing store; this operation was initiated earlier by the processor and the disc controller will interrupt the processor when the transfer is completed.

(c) Several other programs are also in main store waiting to be processed when a time slice is given to them by the scheduler.

(d) Some programs are held in backing store but could continue if loaded into main store and given a time slice.

(e) Some more programs are also held in backing store and are unable to continue until some external activity (e.g. reading a line of data from a keyboard) is completed.

(f) The main store includes between the programs a number of areas which are not currently in use; these vary in size but most are too small to contain any of the programs waiting in backing store.

Starting from the situation described, suggest the kinds of activity which might subsequently take place and describe in general terms the operation of the multi-access system

in handling these activities. You should cover the role of the scheduler, the handling of interrupts, and the management of swapping and of the main store. [10 marks]

(UCLES/O&CSEB, Paper 2, 1992)

44. A two-dimensional array contains integer data as follows.
$X[1,1], X[1,2], ... X[1,n]$ is a list in ascending order.
$X[2,1], X[2,2], ... X[2,n]$ is a list in ascending order.
.

.

.
$X[m,1], X[m,2], ... X[m,n]$ is a list in ascending order.
Describe in general terms an efficient algorithm for a routine to merge these m sorted lists to form a single sorted list of the integers in the array $Y[1], Y[2], ... Y[m*n]$. [8 marks]

(UCLES/O&CSEB, Paper 2, 1992)

45. (a) Define the term *blocking factor* in the context of transferring computer data to a disk. [2 marks]

(b) Briefly explain why, when a file is initially created on a disk, it is often convenient to leave spaces in it, both in the data area and, if relevant, in the index. [2 marks]

(ULEAC, Paper 1, 1993)

46. A particular computer with a 16-bit word, stores floating point numbers in the following form:

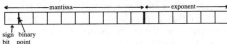

The 10-bit mantissa is stored in sign and magnitude representation.

The leftmost bit is the sign bit.

The binary point is immediately to the right of the sign bit.

The exponent occupies six bits and is represented as an integer in 2's complement form.

A number is said to be normalised when the bit immediately to the right of the binary point has the value 1.

(i) State the value represented by the binary word
0 1 1 0 1 0 1 1 0 0 0 0 0 0 1 1

(ii) The decimal number 0.2 corresponds to the recurring binary fraction
0 . 0 0 1 1 0 0 1 1 0 0 1 1 ...
Show how this number would be stored as accurately as possible. [5 marks]

(ULEAC, Paper 2, 1993)

47. (a) Describe the following types of file organisation and in each case give an example of its use.

(i) serial file

(ii) indexed sequential file;

(iii) random file.

(b) Explain why a multi-level index may be used in an indexed-sequential file. Describe how a record is accessed when such a file is used [8 marks]

48. User interfaces have gradually become more and more oriented to the needs of users over recent years.

(a) Briefly describe three features of user interfaces which have been developed and explain how each has benefited the user. [3 marks]

(b) Describe *two* ways in which user interfaces need to be developed further to make computers more accessible and friendly to untrained users. [2 marks]

(ULEAC, Paper 1, 1994)

30 Glossary of terms used in this book

NOTE: Important terms in each definition which appear in **bold type** are also defined in the glossary.

Absolute address – A number used to fix an **address** in **memory** without the need to be modified.

Access time – Time taken to locate a particular item of data.

Access time (disk) – **Seek time** + **Search time** + **read/write time**.

Accumulator – A **register** inside the **CPU** in which temporary **data** is stored.

Accuracy – the difference between the actual and computed value.

Acorn – British-based computer company (now owned by Olivetti) – manufacturer of the Archimedes and **RISC PC**. First company to bring **RISC**-based computing to the general public in the UK.

Acoustic coupler – A device used for sending information down a telephone line making use of a standard handset.

Activity (file) – The percentage of the **file** processed in any one **run**.

Ada – relatively recent **high-level language** developed with the US military and ideal for **real-time** and or **embedded applications**.

Address – A number used to locate a position in **memory** or some other device.

Address bus – The lines (wires or copper tracks on a PCB) along which the **address** signals travel.

Address modification – Used in **machine code** and **assembly language** programming where an address is transformed into another e.g. **relative addressing**.

Addressing modes – The different ways in which a **microprocessor** is allowed to calculate an **address**.

AI – **Artificial Intelligence**. That which all good computers have!!

ALGOL – ALGOrithmic Language – an early **high-level language** from which other languages such as **FORTRAN** and **Pascal**, for example, are derived.

Algorithm – A set of instructions or procedures for solving a problem.

ALOHA – This is Hawaiian for hello, and is the **radio-based computer network** that links the Hawaiian islands. **Radio networks** are becoming increasingly popular for permanent connection to **networks**.

Alpha testing – Testing a new product in a laboratory setting before being released for **beta testing**.

ALU – **Arithmetic Logic Unit**. Part of the **CPU** that performs **arithmetical** and **logical operations**.

Analogue – Something pretending to be something else.

Analogue signal – A continuously variable signal – contrast with a **digital** signal (varies in discrete steps).

AND gate – A **logic gate** whose output is '1' only if all inputs are '1'.

ANSI – The American National Standards Institute.

APL – A Programming Language – a high-level language used in engineering and science.

Apple – American-based computer company – the first to establish **windows** in the commercial world.

Application layer – The top level in the **ISO OSI model**.

Applications package – **Software applications** such as **DTP**, **CAD** & **Spreadsheets** etc.

Applications programmer – The person who writes the code to produce applications such as word processors or spreadsheets etc.

Archimedes Computer – **Acorn**'s 32-bit **RISC computer**.

Arithmetical operations – Add, subtract, multiply, divide etc.

Arithmetical shift – **Bits** move left or right but the sign is preserved.

ARM – Acorn's Risc Machine – now called Advanced Risc Machines.

ARPANET – Advanced Research Projects Agency NETwork. A very large **mesh network** – now part of the **global network**. It was from **ARPANET** that ideas for the **Internet** were initially developed.

Array – A series of **data** items arranged in a useful way.

Array processor – **Parallel processors** under the control of the same **CPU**.

Art package – See **paint package**.

Artificial intelligence – Use of **computers** involving 'human like' abilities such as visual perception, speech recognition, and **natural language** analysis etc. Philosophers will argue for many years as to what actually constitutes intelligence – it's not yet certain whether machines will ever be able to be intelligent.

Ascenders – Parts of the text which rise above the 'normal area' of the lower case letters.

ASCII – American Standard Code for Information Interchange. An agreed set of codes for each **character**.

Assemble editing (Video) – Assembling a sequence of automatically controlled recordings.

Assembler – Program that converts **assembly language mnemonics** into **machine code**.

Assembler directives – Pseudo operations which enable the **assembly-language** programmer to carry out operations such as calling **macros** which form part of the operating system.

Assembly language – programming making use of **mnemonics** instead of **machine code**.

Assignment operator – Usually ':=' or '=' depending on language.

Association – the type of connection between **entities** to define one of the standard **relationships**.

Associative store – Associating stored information with regard to its contents rather than with an **address**.

Asynchronous transmission – The transmission of data where the receiving and transmitting ends are not synchronised – **start** and **stop bits** are usually used.

ATM (1) – Automatic Teller Machine – 'Hole in the wall' from which you can get money with an appropriate card – used in banks and building societies etc.

ATM (2) – Asynchronous Transfer Mode – A network **protocol** which deals with data, video and voice.

A to D converter – **Analogue** to **Digital** converter. Converts analogue to digital signals.

ATOM – A smaller unit of a LIST in the language **LISP**.

atto (a) – Multiplier representing 1×10^{-18}

Attribute – Part of a **tuple**, **row**, or **record** in a **relational table** (**relation**).

Authoring language – Language used to program an **authoring system**.

Authoring system – A system to enable non-specialists to build up control systems for **interactive video** systems or **hypertext** systems and other **multimedia** presentations.

Auto boot – Running a special **program** which sets up your machine on start up.

AutoExec.BAT – A **file** which contains a **batch** of commands each of which is executed on start up.

Autostereogram – Seeing a 3D image in a 2D picture by clever arrangement of patterns and shapes.

Auxiliary store – See **secondary store**.

Back drop – Picture or other suitable material as a backing for charts or other presentation material.

Backing store – See **secondary store**.

Back up copy – Copy which is identical to the original but stored in a different place for safe keeping.

Back up store – Store used to back up information, e.g. a cassette tape or **QIC** etc.

Back up file – An identical copy of another **file** used for security purposes.

Backward pointer – A **pointer** indicating the way back to the previous **node** in a data structure.

Band printer – A **line printer** making use of a rotating metal band containing an embossed **character set**.

Bandwidth – Physical limitations imposed on a communication system – usually expressed in **bits**/sec.

Bar code – A code using lines of varying thickness to represent a unique produce code.

Bar code reader – A device for reading **bar codes**.

Barrel printer – See **drum printer**.

Base class (C++) – A **class** from which other classes may be derived.

Baseband – A method of sending a signal at its original frequency.

Baseline – A line on which text rests. Used in **DTP** and **word-processor** systems.

BASIC – Beginner's All-purpose **Symbolic** Instruction Code.

Batch entry – A method where the data to be entered into the **computer** system is entered **off line**.

Batch operating system – An **operating system** that supports **batch processing**.

Batch processing – A **system** where the **jobs** are usually submitted and **run** in **batches**, i.e. several at the same time.

Baud rate – The rate (measured in bits/sec) at which **data** can be transmitted.

Baudot – A scientist who carried out much work on signal transmission – **Baud rate** is named after him.

BCD – **Binary Coded Decimal**.

Benchmarks – A performance test for hardware or software in a **computer system**, e.g. speed etc.

Beta testing – Testing a new product on users before it's released officially.

Bezier curves – A type of mathematically-defined curve that obeys certain conditions at its end points. Useful in **art** and **CAD packages**.

Binary – A two-state system – usually expressed using the digits '0' and '1' but any two states could be used.

Binary adder – A **logic circuit** that adds **binary digits** together.

Binary code – Groups of **binary digits** to perform some specific function – e.g. **ASCII** or

EBCDIC.

Binary coded decimal – **Binary** code in which each digit is coded separately using four **binary digits**.

Binary counter – A **logic circuit** used to count up or down in binary on the application of a **clock pulse**.

Binary digit – A '1' or a '0' – also called a **bit**.

Binary pulse train – A voltage which alternates with time between the '0' and '1' levels being used.

Binary search – A **search** technique which repeatedly splits up a list into a left- and a right-hand sublist, and concentrates only on the half of the list which contains the data.

Binary tree – A **tree structure** where each **node** is allowed a maximum of two **children nodes**.

Biocomputers – **Computers** made out of organic molecular electronics. Genetically engineered protein is one example.

BIOS – Basic **Input Output System** – part of the **operating system**, usually housed in **ROM**.

Biosensors – Systems developed to enable **computers** to taste and **smell** etc.

Bistable – A circuit with two stable states. Term also used to denote a **flip flop**.

Bit – **Binary** digit.

Bit map – **Computer memory** that represents a **graphic** image or text in a **font** etc.

Bit-mapped font – **Fonts** made up from a map of **pixels** in a similar way to **bit mapping** on screen,

BLAISE – The British Library Automatic Information SErvice.

Block (1) – A data storage area on a **secondary storage** device. See **physical record**.

Block (2) – Part of a **program**.

Block structured language – A language which allows **structured programming** in **blocks**, i.e. **variables** can be declared to be valid within one block etc.

Blocking – A method which is used to increase the speed and efficiency with which **data** may be read from and written to various devices such as **disk** or **tape**.

Blocking factor – The number of **logical records** per **block**.

BNF – **Backus-Naur Form**. A **metalanguage** used to define some computer languages.

Boolean algebra – An algebra developed by George Boole for dealing with **logical expressions**.

Boolean variable – Can be only true or false (i.e. one of two values).

Booting – Synonymous with **bootstrapping**.

Boot up – Getting the computer system started – can also be used to load utilities and other software.

Bootstrap – A term used where a simple **program** starts off other bigger programs. It is usually used to **boot up** the **operating system** and some other software to customise the system or load applications.

Bootstrapping – The process of loading the **operating system** into the **computer**.

BORIS – The Beginner's Optimised Reduced Instruction Set **microprocessor**! (See page 52.)

Bottom of stack – The position of the last number on the **stack** – usually accessed by the **stack pointer**.

Bottom-up approach – Method of solving a problem by concentrating on the detail first – used for testing and **prototyping**.

bpi – **Bits** per inch – measure of storage density on **magnetic tape**.

Bps – **Bytes** per second.

bps – **Bits** per second.

Branches – The lines that connect the **nodes** on a **tree structure**.

Breakpoint – A point within a program which terminates execution so that the programmer may examine the state of any **variables** etc – used to help **debug** programs.

Broadband – A method of communication which uses different frequencies to send signals simultaneously by methods such as **FDM** – contrast with **baseband**.

Brother node – A **node** in a **tree structure** having the same **parent** – also called a **sister node**.

Bubble-jet printer – See **ink-jet printer**.

Bubble memory – A type of **memory chip** not based on **semiconductor** technology but using magnetic bubbles in a garnet crystal. Not quite **random access memory**, although still very fast.

Bubble sort – A **sort algorithm** where the sorted items float to the top of the list.

Bucket – A number of **sectors** or **blocks** on a **disk**.

Buffer (1) – An area of **memory** used to temporarily store data. Usually used to match devices that work at different speeds, such as **CPU** and **disk**.

Buffer (2) – Some extra **memory** inside a **peripheral device** such as a **printer** – see (1) for reason for use.

Buffer (3) – A **logic circuit** that can be used to isolate signals from the **bus system**.

Buffer (4) **(file)** – The area of **memory** where a **physical record** from a **file** is stored.

Bug – An **error** in the **program** or an 'undocumented feature' if it does anything remotely useful!

Buggy – A small robot which is usually controlled by a micro – runs around on wheels.

Bulletin board – A **computer** set up to receive and distribute **E-Mail** over a **network** or phone system.

Bus – A parallel group of wires, usually 8, 16, 32 or 64 bits wide.

Business data processing – Use of computers for accounting and stock control etc.

Business graphics package – Changes numerical data into graphs and charts etc.

Bus network – A **network topology** described by a main spur with computers connected at various points.

Byte – Eight **binary digits**.

C – A popular **high-level language** suitable for complex **systems programming** because it has much low-level language support.

C++ – A popular **object-oriented high-level language** which is a superset of **C**.

Cache – A very fast expensive **semiconductor memory** (faster than **main memory** if **SRAM** is used).

Cache (disk) – An area of **main memory** set up to hold **data** which would normally be accessed on **disk**.

Cache (internal) – An area of **memory** inside a **microprocessor**. Used to save the time in accessing **RAM.**

Cache (main) – An area of **memory** making use of **SRAM**.

Cache memory – a very high-speed **memory** used to store the most-often accessed instructions.

CAD – **Computer Aided Design**. **Object-oriented graphics package** that is ideal for design engineers and architects etc. The data is often exported to support **CAM** and **CIM**.

CAD/CAM – The integration of the **CAD** and **CAM** processes.

CAFS – **Content Addressable File Store** (see **associative store**).

CAL – **Computer Aided Learning** (or Computer Assisted Learning).

CALL – Statement used to **call** a **subroutine** or **procedure** etc.

CAM – **Computer Aided Manufacture**. The use of computers in all stages of manufacturing (e.g. numerically controlled machine tools etc.).

Campus 2000 – Schools-based external database supporting a variety of information and giving access to the wider information on systems like Prestel etc. Via a gateway many other services can be accessed.

Canonical parsing – A mechanistic way of getting a **machine** to carry out **parsing**.

Caret – The flashing **cursor** indicating where typed input is to be placed.

Carrier – The radio wave which carries the **computer data** over a satellite or other microwave link.

Carry flag – A **flag** inside the **flag register** used to show that a carry has been generated.

CAS – **Content Addressable Store**. (See **associative store**.)

CASE – **Computer Aided Software Engineering** – **software** to help with **systems analysis** and design.

Case statement – An alternative to nested **if-then statements**.

Case study – A (usually) detailed **systems analysis** or study made on a specific system.

Cassette tape – A **tape** used for **backup store** on some **microcomputers**.

Cartesian product – If we have two sets called X and Y, then the Cartesian product is the set of all ordered pairs – a nice way to think of this is that if each set is the set of real numbers, then the Cartesian product of these two sets is the set of all Cartesian co-ordinates on a piece of graph paper of infinite size.

CCD – **Charge Coupled Device**.

CD – Compact Disc.

CD-DA – Compact Disc – Digital Audio. The original CD.

CDI – Compact Disc Interactive. One standard for **interactive video systems**.

CD-R Compact Disc – Recorder. Enables the user to record information on a special CD which can then be played back on a normal CD player.

CD-ROM – Compact Disc Read Only Memory. An **optical disk** which can store video, audio and computer data.

CD-ROM-XA – The Extended Architecture version for the PC.

CD-ROM master – Master **CD-ROM** disc from which copies can be made.

CELL (1) – The name sometimes given to the **record** in a **file** – used when dealing with **pointer systems**.

CELL (2) – The intersection of a row and column in a **spreadsheet**.

Centralised network – All communications go via a central **node**.

Centronics parallel port – a common **interface** standard for connection of a **printer**.

CGA – Colour Graphics Adaptor – IBM PC adaptor standard.

Character (1) – A letter, number or symbol which goes to make up a **character set**.

Character (2) – The smallest unit of **data** that can exist in a **file**.

Character code – A **binary code** such as **ASCII** or **EBCDIC**.

Character font – The style for a particular **character set** e.g Gothic or Times Roman.

Character graphics – system such as that used to create **teletext**-type images and text.

Character set – A set of characters e.g. alphabet (upper and lower case) plus numbers.

Character variable – See **string variable**.

Charge coupled device – An **MOS** device similar in principle to **bubble memory**.

Charting package – Application to produce **charts** and graphs from numerical data.

Check digit – See **check sum**.

Check sum – Extra data, derived by applying some suitable **algorithm,** is sent along with the message as a check on the **integrity** of the received message.

Chief systems analyst – The person in charge of the **systems analysis** team.

Child node – A **node** in a **tree structure** that has a **parent node**.

Chip – An alternative term for an **integrated circuit**.

CIM – Computer Integrated Manufacture – all the data from the design via the construction of artifacts to stock control etc is processed and carried out by a centralised **database**.

Ciphertext – The **encrypted** text which can't be **deciphered** without a **key**.

Circuit switching – A method of sending messages where a dedicated physical path exists between the sending and receiving **computer**.

Circular list – a list whose **pointers** are arranged such that the **header** is joined onto the **footer**.

Circular wait state (OS) – A **deadlock** condition where two tasks are competing for the same resources.

CISC – **Complex Instruction Set Computer**. Contrast with **RISC**.

Clashes – See **collision**.

Cleartext – Also called **plaintext** – the input to a **cryptographic system**.

CLI – **Command Line Interpreter**.

Clip Art – The art work that is used for **word processors** and **DTP documents**.

Classes (C++) – A group of **objects** which share a common definition.

Clock – A crystal-controlled oscillator to produce the **clock pulses** inside a computer.

Clock pulse – A **binary pulse train** used to activate some condition at a precise moment in time. It is used to control the timing of the **CPU** and other systems.

Clock rate – The speed of the clock in **Hz**.

Clones – A computer manufactured by a third party which performs in ways identical to (or better than) those computers manufactured by the original maker of the system.

Closed loop mode – A type of **feedback** in which the output is monitored to modify the input.

CMOS – Complementary Metal Oxide Silicon. A fabrication technique used for silicon chips.

CMOS RAM – **Memory chips** used on **mother board** to hold **configuration** data. It's usual to hold the data in the memory by the use of a lithium battery which lasts for ages.

CMYK – **Cyan Magenta Yellow** and **Key**. Colour model used in the printing industry.

CNC – Computer Numerical Control. Drilling machines etc controlled by a computer. These ideas are central to an automated factory which makes extensive use of **CAD/CAM** and **CIM**.

COBOL – COmmon Business Oriented Language.

CODASYL – COnference on DAta SYstems Languages. The organisation which originally developed COBOL.

Codd – Edgar Codd defined conventions which, if obeyed, result in an efficient **relational database** structure. There are five basic **normal forms**.

Code – Another name for the program instructions.

Coding – Expressing a problem using a computer language.

Collision – A **hashing function** generating the same **address** for different **data**.

Colour correction – Compensation for incorrect colour rendition in a video or computer-based image.

Column by column mapping – A method of representing a two-dimensional **array** in **store**.

Combinational logic – A **logic circuit** in which the output depends only on the current combination of inputs – compare with the **sequential logic circuit**.

Commissioning – Installing and setting up a new **computer system**.

COM – Computer Output on **Microfilm**.

COM reader – A machine which can read computer output on **microform**.

COM recorder – A machine which transfers data from the **computer system** (disk etc.) onto **microform**.

Command.COM – The command processor – it controls the 'system prompts' and interprets commands from the **keyboard**.

Command line interpreter – Part of the operating system which interprets commands typed in at the keyboard.

Comments – Text added for **documentation** purposes – they are ignored by the **compiler** or **assembler**.

Communications controller (OS) – The system used to control communication between a **mainframe** or **mini** and the **terminals** trying to access the system. On a **mainframe** it's called a **front-end-processor**.

Communications package – **Software** to drive a **MODEM** for communication with **databases** and **bulletin boards** etc.

Compaction (Disk) – The gathering together of unused **sectors** into a contiguous space on the **disk**.

Compaction (OS) – Gathering together bits of unused **memory** in a **dynamic-memory partitioning** system.

Compilation – The process of changing the **source code** into the **object code**.

Compilation error – An error which has been detected during the **compilation** of a program.

Compiler – A **program** which **translates** a **high level language** into **machine code**.

Complementation – One way of representing negative (and positive) numbers using the **binary** system.

Complex Instruction Set Computer – A **computer** based around a **CISC microprocessor** which has a complex (very large) **instruction set** for its **assembly language**. Contrast with RISC.

Complex number – A number having a real ('ordinary') and an imaginary part. The imaginary part is plotted at 90 degrees to the ordinary part. A typical number would be written as x + iy.

Compression techniques – Techniques used to fit a quart into a pint pot! – often used to increase the data capacity of **disks** and get over the problems of limited **bandwidth** on **network systems**. Various standards exist such as **JPEG** and **MPEG** etc.

CompuServe – One of the companies providing facilities to access the **Internet**.

Computer – A processor of **information**. Processed information forms the basis of knowledge itself.

Computer Aided Design – Use of **computers** to aid design and other related processes.

Computer Aided Learning – Special **interactive** teaching packages.

Computer Aided Manufacture – Use of **computers** to design and build artifacts.

Computer Aided Software Engineering – **Software** to help with **systems analysis** and design.

Computer crime – The process of using a computer to carry out criminal activities.

Computer operator – A person who controls the day-to-day operation of the **computer** such as loading programs or putting paper in the printers – it's a term usually associated with minis and mainframes.

Computer program – A set of instructions which tells the computer what to do.

Computer misuse act – Legislation introduced in 1990 to curb misuse of computers e.g. injecting **viruses** and other forms of **hacking** etc.

Computer Services Department – The **data processing** personnel for a small company.

Concept keyboard – A **keyboard** which can have specialised overlays to perform functions with specialist **software**, e.g. pictures can be used on the keyboard etc.

Concurrency (OS) – Carrying out different operations at the same time or within a specified period (usually quite short).

Concurrent – tasks being carried out at the same time.

Concurrent Pascal – Version of **Pascal** which supports **parallel processing**.

Conditional jump – **Jump** to another part of a **program** on a condition such as an **overflow**, for example.

Configuration – The way in which a **system** has been set up, e.g. 8 Gbyte disk – **SVGA** mode etc.

Constant – A value that does not vary.

Construct – A **syntactic** structure used in a language, e.g. a **conditional** or **loop construct**.

Content Addressable Store – See **associative memory**.

Continuous variable – A **variable** that can have any value between various limits.

Control bus – The lines along which the control signals travel.

Control character – A character which is not printed but causes some other action to take place.

Control software – **Software** used to manage a **control system**.

Control structure – structures such as **if-then**, **case** and **do-while** etc.

Control system – The integration of a **computer** and other **peripherals** to control machinery and plant.

Control Unit – Part of the **CPU** – it controls the timing and routing of signals inside the **CPU**.

Conversational mode – an **interactive system** in which the **computer** and **user** are 'talking', e.g. an **interpreted BASIC** environment.

CORAL – COmmon Real-time Application Language – used for **real-time control systems**.

Core store – A form of **primary storage** in which tiny doughnut-shape ferrite rings are used as the means of storage – now mostly out of date – also (rarely) the name given to **primary store**.

CPA – **Critical Path Analysis**.

CPU – **Central Processing Unit**.

cps – **Characters** per second.

Crash (1) – The system has unfortunately gone wrong and you will have to reset the machine!

Crash (2) – The disk heads have gouged a path through your valuable data stored on the surface of the disk – You will have to make use of the backup copy which you recently made!

CRAY – A computer manufacturer specialising in making ultra-fast supercomputers, e.g. the Cray 1, Cray 2 and Cray XM/P (500 to 1500 Megaflops!).

CRC – **Cyclic Redundancy Check**.

CRISC – Complex Reduced Instruction Set Computer (**Pentium** term!) . A combination of **RISC** and **CISC**.

Critical Path Analysis – A time and resource management technique for large projects.

Cross assembler – One which produces assembly-language code that is to be run on another **machine**.

Cross compiler – One which produces high-level-language code that is to be run on another **machine**.

CRT – Cathode Ray Tube. The main screen in a computer monitor.

Cryptographic system – A system which uses **cryptography**.

Cryptography – the art of data **encryption** and **decryption** – keeping transmitted messages secret.

CSO Colour Separation Overlay (Video). Used for trick shots with false backgrounds, e.g. making superman appear to fly.

CSV – Comma Separated Variable. A format for passing data between packages.

Cursor – The movable mark on the **VDU** that indicates your current position on the screen.

Cursor keys – Special keys which control the direction of the **cursor**.

Cyan – The 'turquoise blue' colour obtained when Green and Blue light are mixed.

Cybernetics – The science of **robotics** and **AI**, particularly to do with mimicking human characteristics.

Cyberspace – name for the space created by a **VR system** – the environment in which one is virtually present. Also used as a general name describing the electronic world of information.

Cyclic redundancy check – A mathematical **error**-checking technique for transmitted data.

Cylinder – Concentric **disk tracks** (one on top of the other) form a **cylinder** on a **disk pack**.

Cylinder number – Each **cylinder** within a **disk pack** has a unique number.

Daisy wheel – The daisy shaped wheel around which the characters are embossed.

Daisy wheel printer – A high-quality printer using a daisy-wheel mechanism as found in typewriters.

DAT – Digital Audio Tape. One method of tape backup used on micros.

Data – The raw material in which the **computer** deals.

Database – A (usually complex) system containing many different but interconnected **files** from which complex information can be extracted, usually by means of a **query language (SQL)** or **DML**.

Database Administrator (DBA) – One who looks after and maintains a **database**.

Database Management System – A complex piece of software which enables the DBA to maintain and manage the **database**.

Data bus – The lines along which the data signals travel.

Data capture – The general term for gathering data together to be fed in to the computer system.

Data compression – See **compression**.

Data controller – Person in charge of the **data-control staff**.

Data control staff – The people who make sure that all the jobs to be entered by the data entry staff (clerks etc.) are in the correct place with nothing missing etc.

Data Description Language – A language used to describe the data in a database. It describes the data at various levels of abstraction.

Data dictionary – Holds the definitions of the descriptions of the data within a **database**.

Data encapsulation (C++) – **Objects** contain both **data** and **functions**.

Data encryption – See **encryption**.

Data entry staff – People in a **data processing** department who look after and enter the data into a computer system.

Data export – See **export**.

Data file – A **file** consisting of **data** that is usually used by a **program file**.

Data flow architecture – One of the techniques of **parallel processing**.

Data flow diagrams – special diagram to show interaction between **data** and processes.

Data flow graph – A technique of splitting up a problem ready for solution by **parallel processing**.

Data glove – A **virtual-reality** input device worn on the hand and used to control **virtual worlds**.

Data hiding (C++) – Only **member functions** have access to private data within their own **class**.

Data integrity – Making sure that the **data** is correct.

Data import – See **import**.

Data link layer – See **link layer**.

Data logger – A device (and software) for interfacing a **computer** to specialist input devices such as **pH sensors**, for example.

Data logging – The automatic capture of data by using a **data logger**.

Data preparation – Entering the **raw data** into the system (usually in machine readable form).

Data preparation supervisor – The person in control of the **data entry staff**.

Data processing (DP) – The arrangement of **raw data** into a form that is useful for other purposes.

Data processing manager – The person in charge of the **DP department**.

Data protection act 1994 – The government act that lays down guidelines for personal **information** stored in **computer systems** – it gives people the right to see stored data which affects them.

Data types – Different types of **data** in a **high-level language** e.g. **array**, **boolean**, **character** etc.

Data security – Making sure that data is not misused or observed by the wrong people.

Data structures – The organising of **data** in special ways so that efficient processing may take place.

Daughter board – An accessory board such as a sound or video card which plugs into the **mother board**.

DB2 – IBM's powerful **relational database** system for **mainframes**.

DBA – **The DataBase Administrator**.

DBMS – **DataBase Management System**.

DBOMP – **DataBase** Organisation and Maintenance Processor. A **network database** for a **mainframe**.

DDE – Direct Data Entry, e.g. the use of a **key-to-store** system.

DDL – **Data Description Language**.

Deadlock (OS) – A resource being requested by one **task** is held by another.

Debuggers – Special **software** that helps you to **debug programs**. They often allow you to single step through a **machine code program** and see the effects on each **register** etc.

Debugging time – Empirical rule stating that **debugging time** = programmer time × (number of lines of code)^2.

Debugging – Removing **errors** from **systems** or **programs**. Also applies to **hardware**.

DEC – The Digital Equipment Corporation. A major computer manufacturer.

Decimal system – Base ten – using the digits 0,1,2,3,4,5,6,7,8,9.

Deciphered – The **encrypted** text is decoded.

Decision tables – A tabular arrangement of conditions and actions.

Decision trees – A sideways **tree structure** showing conditions and actions – an alternative to using d**ecision tables**.

Declaration – Declaring **variable** types at the beginning of a **program**.

Declarative language – A type of language where you do not have to state explicitly how the output is to be derived from the inputs. Used in **fifth generation languages** like **Prolog**, for example.

Decode (1) – Extracting the original data from an **encoded** message.

Decode (2) – Term used to indicate when a **machine-code instruction** is being analysed to determine its function.

Decoder – A **logic circuit** that changes a code from its **encoded** form back to its original form.

Decryption – changing a gobbledygook message back into ordinary text making use of a suitable **algorithm** and a **key**.

Default values – Sensible values chosen by the computer in the absence of other information from the **user**.

Demodulation – Changing a signal back into its original form.

De-Morgan's law – A useful law in **Boolean algebra** for helping to simplify **logical functions**.

Denary – The name for the decimal system.

Dependency – A **relationship** in which the existence of one thing depends on the existence of another.

Derived class (C++) – A **class** that exhibits all the characteristics of the **base class** and some others in addition.

Descenders – Part of the text which goes below the **baseline.**

Design structure diagram – A BS6244 alternative to basic **flowcharts**.

Desktop computer – A **microcomputer** such as the **PC**.

Desktop publishing – **Software** that gives a **computer** the power to manipulate virtually any characteristic of **graphics** and text on the screen.

Despooling – The process that extracts all the **spooled data** from **disk** or **tape** and carries out the appropriate processing such as printing, for example.

Device address – The **address** which, when put on the **bus**, causes the device to be active.

Device handler (OS) – A **program** which handles communications between the **operating system** and different devices such as the **keyboard** etc.

Dhrystones – A **benchmark** test for general instructions.

Diagnostics – General name for **debugging tools** and the like for helping to find **bugs** in the **system**.

Dictionary (1) – A list of **variables** and other useful information **compiled** during the **syntax analysis** phase.

Dictionary (2) – A word list used to check the spelling in a **WP** or **DTP** system.

Dictionary (3) – Data about the data stored in a database – called the data dictionary.

Differentiation (maths) – The process of finding the derivative which is essentially the gradient of a graph at some particular point.

Digital – Varies in discrete steps.

Digital computer – A **computer** that operates on **digital** signals, i.e. almost all computers.

Digital plotter – A **plotter** which works on an absolute (x,y) co-ordinate system, e.g. move to 234,5678.

Digitisation – See **quantisation**.

Direct addressing – A mode of **addressing** in which a **memory location** is used to directly specify an **address**.

Direct access – Any item of **data** can be found without having to go **sequentially** through the entire list.

Direct access files – See **Random access file**s.

Direct access secondary storage – **Storage** where the **data** can be accessed directly – e.g. **disks**.

Direct entry – A method where **data** is entered into the **computer system on line**.

Directive – A special instruction to an **assembler**. See **assembler directives**.

Directory – Information about the **files** stored on **magnetic disk**.

Directory file structure – See **hierarchical file**.

Disassembler – Software which attempts to extract the **object code** from the **source code**. It's often impossible to get a correctly disassembled output.

Discrete variable – A **variable** that can only have a discrete set of values.

Disk – A **direct access storage** device.

Disk cache – **Semiconductor RAM** used to speed up **disk** access.

Disk cartridge (1) – Mainframe. A single (removable) 14in-disk housed in a plastic container.

Disk cartridge (2) – Micro. A removable hard disk drive such as the **SCSI** cartridge system.

Disk drive – The **peripheral storage device** which houses the **magnetic** or **optical disk**.

Disk pack – A large **hard-disk system** using a stack of 14in disks on a common spindle and accessed by at least one **read/write head** per disk surface. **Data** is stored in **cylinders**.

Distributed network – A **network** with many independent interconnections.

Distributed processing – Different **computers** handling their own work, but also helping to manage common resources on the network.

Divergence (iteration) – The actual solution gets further away from the theoretical solution.

DMA controller (OS) – A special **microprocessor** used to handle Direct Memory Access.

DMA – Direct Memory Access. Access to memory not under the direct control of the main processor.

DML – Data Manipulation Language. Language used to access data in a database.

Documentation – **Information** written about **programs** or **applications** etc. Ranges from simple manuals through to a complex technical description.

DOS – Disk Operating System.

Dot matrix printer – A **printer** which fires tiny pins through a ribbon thus forming the characters by dots.

Double buffering – A technique of using two **buffers** to speed up input/output.

Double precision – Using a double **word length** to increase the **precision** of calculations.

DP – Data Processing.

dpi – dots per inch. A measure of print quality.

DQL – Data Query Language.

Draft copy – copy used to check work before the final copy is made. Often a lower-quality output would be used, e.g. a 300 dpi laser printout to check a book which will be typeset at 1200 dpi.

DRAM – Dynamic Random Access Memory. The most common type of **RAM**.

Drum plotter – A device in which a pen moves across a rotating drum to produce **graphics** output.

Drum printer – A type of **line printer** that utilises a revolving drum.

Dry run – The process of working through a program *by hand* to see what the answers should be.

D to A converter – A **digital** to **analogue** converter. Converts **digital** to **analogue** signals.

DTP – DeskTop Publishing.

Dumb terminal – A **keyboard** and **VDU** with little or no processing power. The processing has to be carried out by the computer to which the terminal is connected.

Dump – The copying of a **file** to **disk** or the **printer** etc.

Duplex – A two way (only one way at a time) communication system.

Dynamic memory partitioning (OS) – Allocation of memory partition in an *ad hoc* way according to need.

Dynamic RAM – **Memory** that has to be **refreshed** to maintain its contents.

EAN – European Article Number – one type of code used with the **bar-code** system.

EAROM – Electrically Alterable Read Only Memory.

E-Mail – **Electronic mail**.

EBCDIC – Extended **Binary Coded Decimal** Interchange Code – often used with IBM tape systems.

EBNF – Extended Backus Naur Form – more versatile alternative to **BNF**.

ECONET – One of Acorn Computers' **LAN**s.

Editor – Name for the **software** which can display and edit text.

EDP – Electronic Data Processing.

EEROM – Electrically Erasable Read Only Memory.

EFT – Electronic Funds Transfer. Use of IT to transfer money from one account to another.

EFTPOS – Electronic Funds Transfer at the Point Of Sale.

EGA – Enhanced Graphics Adaptor. IBM PC video standard now largely replaced by better ones.

EIDE – Enhanced Integrated Drive Electronics. Upgraded version of the **IDE interface**.

EISA – Enhanced Industry Standard Architecture. An enhanced version of **ISA** bus system.

Electrically Alterable Read Only Memory – A **ROM** in which locations can be electrically altered without having to reprogram the whole **chip**.

Electrically Erasable Read Only Memory- A **ROM** which can be erased electrically instead of making use of UV light.

Electronic data processing – See **data processing**.

Electronic encyclopaedia – An encyclopaedia stored on **CD-ROM**.

Electronic mail – The ability to send and receive documents via suitable networks (including the telephone-**network** system).

Electronic male – One of the cartoon robots in this book!!

Element – An item in an **array**.

Embedded microprocessor – A **microprocessor** system which is dedicated to one particular task such as controlling a washing machine.

Embedded system – A **system** which contains an **embedded microprocessor**.

Emulation – One **computer** system pretending to be another.

Emulator – **Hardware** or **software** or a combination of both carrying out the emulation process.

Encode – Putting **data** into some sort of code.

Encoder – A **logic circuit** which changes the **data** into a code suitable for **machine** entry.

Encryption – Changing 'ordinary-message text' into gobbledygook using a **key** and a suitable **algorithm**.

Encryption key – What's needed to decipher an **encrypted** message.

Endless loop – See **loop, endless**.

Engine – Simply another term for a processor. (**Hardware** and **software**.)

Entity – A concrete or abstract representation of data held in a **database** which corresponds to a **record**.

Entity dependence diagram – Pictorial way of showing how one **entity** depends on others, and the **association** between each different **entity**.

Entity relationship diagram – pictorial way of showing relationships between entities. **Relationships** are usually shown in diamond-shaped boxes, and **entities** in square boxes.

Enumerated data type – a data type in which a list of data (e.g. mon,tue,wed) indicates the data set.

EOF – End Of File

EPROM – Erasable Programmable Read Only Memory.

Equivalence gate – See **XNOR gate**.

Erasable Programmable Read Only Memory – A **PROM** that can be erased using ultra-violet light.

Ergonomic keyboard – **Keyboard** specifically designed to overcome problems such as **RSI**.

Ergonomics – The relationship between humans and their interaction with systems such as computer systems, for example.

Error (1) – A mistake.

Error (2) – **(absolute relative)** – | relative error |

Error (3) – **(absolute)** – | actual error |

Error (4) – **(actual)** – (exact value – computed value).

Error (5) – **(percentage)** – relative error × 100%

Error (6) – **(relative)** – actual error/exact value.

Ethernet – An industry standard **LAN** popular for connecting **PC**s and most other machines.

European Article Number – A **bar code** for coding goods as found in the UK.

Even parity – An even number of '1s' in each transmitted code acts as a check on **data integrity**.

Exa (E) – Multiplier representing 1×10^{18} (computing alternative 1024^6).

Exclusive OR gate – An **OR gate** that does not give an output (of 1) when all inputs are at '1'.

Execute – To carry out the instructions in a **program**.

Execution error – An **error** which occurs when the **program** is **running**.

Executive – See **operating system supervisor**.

Expansion slots – places inside a **PC** which help to enable **peripherals** to be connected to the **system**.

Expert system – A specialist problem-solving **system** programmed with knowledge from a human expert.

Exponent – Indicates the power of a number, e.g. in 10^3, 3 is the exponent.

Export – Getting data from your computer system to another computer system.

Expression – Part of a language **construct** used to calculate a single value from one or more **operands**.

Extended ASCII – Making use of the **parity bit** to extend the **ASCII code**. 128 extra codes are generated.

External database – A **database** accessed via a **WAN**, often making use of the phone system and a **MODEM**, examples are **Campus 2000**, **Prestel** and **NERIS**.

External devices – Devices which are connected to the system such as **printers** and **keyboards**.

External interrupt – An **interrupt** caused by an external device.

External sort – A **sort algorithm** used when the **files** to be **sorted** are too large to fit in **main memory**.

E13B – The system of numbers used at the bottom of bank cheques for **MICR**.

Fatal error – An **error** which would terminate the **execution** of a **program**.

Factorial – A mathematical sequence of numbers such that N! = N(N-1)(N-2)(N-3)...3.2.1 and 0! = 1.

FAT (OS) – File Allocation Table. A file used by **DOS** to allocate space on a **disk** and to help locate and manage the **files**.

Father file – The name given to the current **master file** when being used in conjunction with the **transaction file** to produce the new **master file**.

Fax – Short for facsimile. Sending pictures down the telephone line. (However, it's obvious that text can also be sent.)

FDDI – Fibre Distributed Data Interface. Very high-speed **fibre-optic network**.

FDM – Frequency Division **Multiplexing**.

Feasibility study – Part of the **system life cycle** which examines possible solutions to **systems** problems.

Feedback – Part of the output signal is fed back to modify the input signal.

femto (f) – Multiplier representing 1×10^{-15}.

Fetch – Term used to indicate that a **machine code instruction** is being fetched from memory.

Fetch-decode-execute cycle – The repetitive tasks always being undertaken by a **microprocessor** when it's switched on.

Fibre optic – A cable made out of plastic or glass fibre, useful for **computer** communication systems.

Field – A group of characters that represent a single item of **data** in a **file**.

Field width – The number of **characters** stored in a particular **field**.

FIFO – First In First Out.

FIFO stack – A **stack** designed to operate on the **FIFO principle**, also known as a **queue**.

Fifth-Generation Language – **Declarative languages** such as **Prolog** and **LISP**.

File – A collection of **records** that are related in some way and are a single unit.

File creation – Setting up a new **file** so that it is ready to accept **data**.

File maintenance – Keeping the contents of **files** in an efficient state and making **backups** etc.

File manager – Part of **OS** which maps logical onto **physical-level subschema**.

File security (1) – The arrangements made to prevent unauthorised access to **files**.

File security (2) – The physical safety of **files** such as placing them in fire-proof safes.

File server – **Computer** on a **network** from which the **files** are served.

Finish pointer – A **pointer** that points to the end of a **list**.

Firmware – The **software** stored in **ROM**.

First-Generation Language – Assembly **languages** and **machine code**.

First Normal Form – **Attributes** with multiple or repeating values must be removed so that all tuples (records) in a relation (table) are of the same length.

Fixed-length field – A **field** in a **file** where the number of **characters** can't be varied.

Fixed-length record file – All **records** in the **file** are of fixed length – not necessarily the same length.

Fixed partition – A section of **memory** of fixed size, usually used in **multi-user systems**.

Fixed point number – The decimal point can't be altered by an **exponent**.

Fixed spacing – Text as would be produced on a mechanical typewriter.

Flag – A **bit** inside a **register** which is set if a particular event has happened, e.g. the **overflow flag**.

Flag register – A **register** whose contents are made up of many **bits**, all acting as **flags**.

Flat-bed plotter – A device which controls a pen moving over a flat piece of paper (x,y, co-ordinates).

Flip flop – A **sequential logic circuit** which is used as a **storage** element and is found in **counters** and **shift registers**.

Floating point accelerator – See **maths co-processor**.

Floating point number – A number with a **mantissa** and an **exponent**. Contrast with **floating point**.

Floppy disk – A small flexible version of a **disk**, mainly used on **microcomputers** – there are several formats, and the size of floppy in use today is mainly 3.5 in.

Flops – FLOating Point operations per Second. A measure of a computer's processing speed.

Flowchart – Pictorial representation of an **algorithm**. Different types exist e.g. **program flowcharts**, **systems flowcharts** and **design structure diagrams** etc.

FMV – Full Motion Video. Used to describe VHS-quality movies encoded using **MPEG** 1 onto a **CD-ROM**.

Font – The name given to a **style** of text when combined with **typeface** and other characteristics such as **point size** etc., e.g. Times Roman 30pt.

Font card – The smaller version of the **font** cartridge found in **printers**.

Font cartridge – A plug-in module used for extra **fonts** on a **laser** or **dot-matrix printer**.

Footer (1) – A **pointer** that points to the end of a **list**.

Footer (2) – The line of text at the bottom of a document (below the main body of text).

For loops – **Loop structure** based on a counter which controls how many times the loop is executed.

Formal language – Unambiguous **context-free language** used on current generations of **computers**.

Format – The layout of a document or file etc.

Formatting – Preparing a **disk** ready for storing data.

FORTH – **High-level language** suitable for **control**.

FORTRAN – FORmula TRANslator. A **high-level language** suitable for maths, science and engineering applications.

FORTRAN 90 – A modern version of **FORTRAN** which supports **concurrent** programming.

Fourth-Generation Language – Languages used in **spreadsheets** (macros) and **databases** (SQLs) etc.

Forward pointer – A **pointer** indicating the way forward to the next **node** in a data structure.

FPU – Floating Point Unit. Same as a maths co-processor – hardware used to speed up numeric calculations.

Fractal – A simple unit that is used to build up other, more-complex units.

Frame – A guide for the text in a **DTP system**.

Free-storage pointer – A **pointer** used to indicate the next free location.

Frequency – Cycles per second. Measured in **Hz**.

Front-end processor – Another **computer** used to control the input/output operations of a larger system.

Full adder – A **logic circuit** that adds two **binary digits** that can cope with a carry from the previous bit.

Full duplex – A simultaneous two-way communication system.

Fully dependent – See **functional dependency**.

Function – Something which is used to call up a **subroutine** during **compilation**, e.g. 'sin' (sine), 'sqr' (square root) or 'eof' (end of file), for example.

Functional dependency – A unique association **one-to-one relationship** only.

Functional language – A **paradigm** based on **parameters** being passed to **functions**.

Gantt charts – Calendar-type charts which show the proposed or actual progress of a project using horizontal bars.

Gate – **AND**, **OR** and **NOT gates** etc. built up from electronic circuits. They control the actions of digital signals presented at the inputs to these gates. The output depends on the combination of inputs.

Gateway – A **computer** that is used to connect different **networks** together so that larger networks may be formed. For example, the **Internet** is formed by the interconnection of many other networks.

G code – The code consisting of numbers and letters used to control a **CNC** machine.

General-purpose register – A **register** that is not assigned to any particular task, although it may be used for special purposes when some instructions are being carried out.

GIF – Graphics Interchange Format. A **compression** standard for **graphics files** developed for use when downloading files from **bulletin boards** on **networks** like the **Internet**.

Giga (G) – Multiplier representing 1×10^9. (Often-used alternative in computing $1024 \times 1024 \times 1024$.)

GigaFlops – 10^9 **Flops**.

Global communications network – A world-wide connection of **computers** such that **computer data** can be transmitted from any **machine** to any other **machine**.

Global variable – A variable which is available to all of the program. Contrast with **local variable**.

GOPHER – An **Internet** tool designed to help navigate and browse through the **network**.

GOTO – An unconditional **jump**.

Grammar checker – Accessory for **WP** and **DTP systems** – still in relative infancy.

Grandfather-father-son – A method of **backing up** in which three generations of **files** are kept.

Grandfather file – A **master file** two generations old.

Graphics – A picture that can be manipulated on the **computer**.

Graphics tablet – A device to transfer a picture into the computer by moving a pen across the tablet.

Gray code – A code where only one digit changes between transitions when the code is used for counting.

Grey-scale image – A 'black and white' image made up from many shades of grey.

GUI – Graphical User Interface. **WIMP**-based computer interface, e.g. **windows**.

Hacker – A person who illegally breaks into or tampers with computer systems.

Hacking – The unauthorised use of computer equipment.

Half adder – A **logic circuit** which adds two **binary digits** but can't cope with a carry from the previous column.

Half duplex – Two way communication, but only one way at any one time.

Handshaking – A **protocol** used when communication with **peripheral** equipment is taking place.

Hard copy – A printout, usually on a piece of paper.

Hardware development – The process of developing new **hardware**.

Hardware test programs – **Programs** that are run to diagnose a fault in the **computer hardware**.

Hard wired – A **system** which is programmed by the hardware (e.g. wire links etc.) and can't be altered.

Hash table – A table which contains data stored by means of a **hashing function**.

Hash total – See **check sum**.

Hashing – See **hashing functions**.

Hashing functions – A set of rules that generates a storage **address** – usually applied to a numeric **key field** or by using some numeric relationship such as **ASCII** or **EBCDIC** etc on a **string field**.

HCI – Human Computer Interface – the art of human interaction with a **computer**.

HDCD – High Density Compact Disc.

Header (1) – The line at the top of a page in a **DTP system** (above the main body of text).

Header (2) – A **pointer** that points to the beginning of a **list**.

Header (3) – **Digital data** that contains **information** such as the destination etc. for a message transmitted over a **network**.

Header label record – The **record** of the beginning of the **tape** which identifies the **tape**.

Heat-sensitive printers – **Printers** which use special heat-sensitive paper brought into contact with hot pins.

Hertz – Cycles per second.

Heuristic programming – A programming method based on rules of thumb and learning from previous experience.

Hex – Short for **hexadecimal**.

Hexadecimal – Base sixteen. Uses the characters 0, 1, 2, 3, 4, 5, 6, 7, 8, 9, A, B, C, D, E and F.

Hierarchical database – A **database** built up on a **hierarchical data structure**.

Hierarchical data model – The **tree**-type **data structure** model.

Hierarchical data structure – The structure that is derived from the principles involved in a family tree.

Hierarchical file – A file based on **hierarchical data structures**.

High-level languages – English-like language such as **COBOL, Pascal** or **BASIC**, for example.

High-resolution graphics – Computer pictures with a lot of detail.

HIPO chart – Hierarchical Input Output Processing. A form of **structure diagram**.

Hollerith code – The code used on 80-column punched cards.

HRG – High Resolution Graphics.

HSV – Hue Saturation Value. A colour model used by artists making use of hues, tints and tones, used on some **DTP systems**.

Human Computer Interface – See **HCI**.

Human readable – **Data** that is in a form that can be read by humans.

Hypermedia – A **system** making use of **computer data**, video and audio etc.

Hypertext – A sub-set of **hypermedia** where textual information can be set up by associating parts of the data with other ideas – useful for research that needs carrying out on the text.

Hz – Abbreviation for **Hertz**, or cycles per second.

I/O – Input/Output

IAS – Immediate Access Store. The **primary** or **main storage** inside a **computer**.

IBG – Inter-Block Gap. Gaps inbetween the **blocks** of data on a **tape system**.

IBM – International Business Machines (affectionately known as 'Big Blue'). The largest computer company in the world.

IC – Integrated Circuit. The alternative name for a **silicon chip** – also called a **chip**.

ICL – International Computers Ltd. A British based manufacturer of computer equipment.

Icons – The pictures used in the **WIMP environment** to help with selection of various actions.

IDE – Integrated Drive Electronics. A **disk-interface** standard.

Identifier – One or more **characters** which are used to identify an element in a **high-level language**.

IDMS – Integrated Data Management System. A **network database** for a **mainframe.**

Immediate access store – Same as **primary store** or **main store**.

Immediate addressing – A mode of **addressing** in which an **address** is specified by an immediate **operand** (a number immediately after the **Op code**).

Immediate mode – Execution of a command from outside a program, e.g. typing in a command from the keyboard which can then be directly **interpreted** by the **operating system**.

IMP – Interface Message Processor.

Impact printer – Any **printer** relying on a hammer or pin etc. impacting on a ribbon to produce a **character**.

Imperative languages – Ones in which sequences of instructions called **imperatives** are given to the computer. Typifies telling the computer *how* to do something. Also called **procedural languages**.

Import – Getting data from another computer system into your computer system.

IMS – IBMs Information Management System database on a **mainframe computer.**

IMS/R – Relational version of IMS.

Incremental plotter – A **plotter** which works on co-ordinates which are relative to the last position.

Index (1) – A number, usually held in an **index register**, that represents an offset.

Index (2) – A reference used to help locate **records** and **files** on a **disk** or **CD-ROM** etc.

Indexed addressing – An **addressing mode** in which several **registers**, including an **index register** are combined to produce the actual **address** – it's useful for setting up **stacks** and **queues** etc. The **absolute address** is a base address plus an **index**.

Indexed sequential file – A **sequential file** in which the **records** are pointed to by **pointers** held in an **index**.

Indirect addressing – An **addressing mode** in which an **address** is calculated indirectly, usually by specifying a **memory location** and a **register**.

Infix notation – Normal algebraic notation where the operator appears in between the operands, e.g. P + Q.

Information – **Data** + **structure**.

Information providers – Companies that provide information for database systems such as **Prestel**.

Information superhighway – A **global network** which will eventually transmit computer data, audio and video etc.

Information Technology – Applying computer technology to the solution of a wide variety of problems.

Inheritance (C++) – Passing on characteristics from a parent class to a child class.

Initialise – Making sure that all **variables** and **constants** etc are set up correctly before the rest of the program is run.

Ink-jet printer – Printer technology which squirts ink from a nozzle to form the text or **graphics**.

Inorder traversal – A method for traversing (moving around) a **tree structure**, visiting the left-hand, **root** and right-hand subtrees in that order.

Input – **Data** to be entered into the **computer system**.

Input peripherals – Devices such as **keyboards**, **mice**, **scanners** or other data-input technology.

Insert edit (video) – Inserting a new video image into the middle of an existing recording.

Insertion sort – A simple and straightforward **sort algorithm**, items of data inserted in the correct place.

Instruction pointer – See **program counter**.

Instruction register – A **register** which contains the current instruction being **executed** by the **program**.

Instruction set – A set of **assembly language mnemonics** which represent the machine code of a particular **computer**, e.g. instructions for Motorola's 68000 or Intel's 80 × 86 range of microprocessors.

Integer – A whole number.

Integrated Circuit – Same as **IC** or **silicon chip**.

Integrated software package – **Software** which usually has a **word processor**, **database** and **spreadsheet** integral in the same system. Now being replaced by single **packages** with **OLE**.

Integrated system – A **system** in which it is easy to pass **data** between one part and another.

Integration (maths) – The process of finding the area 'under' a graph between two given points.

Integrity – Making sure that transmitted **data** or **data** entered into a system is correct.

Intel – A large-scale manufacturer of **chips** and **microprocessors**. Inventors of the famous 80×86 range of processors and the **Pentium** etc.

Intelligent terminal – A **terminal** that is capable of doing much local processing.

Interactive – The user can **interact** with the system – contrast with **batch**, for example.

Interactive video – Video based on a **CD-ROM** system in which the **user** can **interact**.

Inter-block gaps – The gaps between **blocks** on a **tape system**.

Interface (1) – Special electronic circuits to help connect different **peripherals** and other devices like **transducers** to the **computer system**.

Interface (2) – The interaction between people and **computers**, e.g. the **HCI** that an **operating system** might present to the user.

Interface Message Processor – Another name for a **node computer** on a **network**.

Internal sort – A **sort** that can be accomplished by using the **main memory** in a **computer system**.

Internet – A **global network** of other **networks** which forms one basis of the **information super-highway**. It is a **packet-switched network** consisting of many small **networks** interconnected via **gateways**.

Interpreter – A **program** which **translates** a **high-level language** into **machine code** in an **inter-active** environment. It is slow as each line is **translated** each time it is encountered.

Inter-record gaps – The gaps between **records** on a **tape system**.

Interrupt – The **CPU** is interrupted from what it is doing so that something else may receive attention.

Interrupt disabled – The **CPU** pays no attention to **interrupts** when they occur.

Interrupt enabled – The **CPU** pays attention to the **interrupts** when they occur.

Interrupt flag register – A **register** in which the **bit** patterns are used as **flags** to represent the state of many operations, e.g. **overflow** or **underflow**, **carry** generated etc.

Interrupt handling routine – The **software** which has been written to take control once an **interrupt** has been initiated.

Interrupting device – The device which has caused the **interrupt**, e.g. the **disk** or the **printer** etc.

Interrupt priorities – The priority assigned to different **interrupts** in the **system**. There may be devices which have high priority and others which have a low priority.

Interrupt request – A device has requested an **interrupt**.

Interrupt servicing – The process of handling an **interrupt**.

Interrupt vector – A **pointer** used to point to the place where the **interrupt** handler resides in **memory**.

Inverter – See **NOT gate**.

IP – **Information Provider**.

IRG – **Inter-Record Gap**.

ISA – Industry Standard Architecture. A 16-bit bus system for the IBM PC and its clones.

ISDN – Integrated Services Digital Network. A fast transmission system which can handle audio, video, computer and other forms of data.

ISO – The International Standards Organisation.

ISO OSI model – The ISO model for Open-Systems Interconnection. A seven-layer model for the standardisation of **network** interconnection.

IT – **Information Technology**.

Iteration (1) – **Looping**.

Iteration (2) – A mathematical method of solving problems by **numerical analysis**.

JANET – The Joint Academic NETwork. A large **PSN** in the UK used by universities and industrial research establishments to communicate via computer and send **E-Mail** – now part of **Internet**.

Jackson Structured Programming – A method developed by Jackson to show sequence, **itera-tion** and selection on a structure diagram.

JCL – Job Control Language. The language in which a **job-control program** is written.

J-K flip flop – A versatile **flip flop** used in electronic **counters** and **shift-register** circuits.

Job – The name given to a **program** (or set of work which can be regarded as a single unit) which is to be **run** on a **computer system**.

Job Control Language – The language in which the **job-control** **program** or **job-control commands** are written.

Job-control program – A sequence of **job-control commands** used by the machine operator to **run** a **batch** or **jobs** and do other **tasks**, usually on a **mainframe computer**.

Joystick – A device to control the **cursor** or other functions by waving a stick in two (or 3) dimensions. Useful for computer games, flight-simulators and **VR** etc.

JPEG – The Joint Photographic Experts Group. One method for storing and compression of coloured graphics images. It's not as effective as some of the other systems.

JSP – **Jackson Structured Programming**.

Jump – Transfer of control from one part of a program to another.

Justification – Term used to denote alignment in WP and DTP systems, e.g. left or right justi-fied text.

Just-in-time – Production techniques where components arrive just in time to be used in the factory.

k – short for **kilo**. Multiplier representing 1×10^3. (Often used computer alternative 1024.)

Karnaugh maps – A pictorial way of simplifying certain types of **Boolean functions**.

Kernel (OS) – An alternative name for the nucleus of an **operating system**. It's the part of the operating system which performs the most basic of operations.

Kerning – A term for altering the gap between text by small amounts. Useful for large point sizes.

Key (1) – The pattern needed to unlock **ciphertext**.

Key (2) – The information for totally-black text in the **CMYK colour model** used by printers.

Keyboard – Device for entering text manually into the **computer system**. English keyboards are of the QWERTY type. A variety of different keyboards now exist for overcoming **RSI** problems.

Key field – The most-important **field** which uniquely identifies a **record**.

Key-to-disk – A machine to get data from the **keyboard** to a disk without using the main machine.

Key-to-store – General name for a machine to get data from the keyboard to a storage device such as **disk**, **tape** or **CD-ROM** etc without using the main machine – ideal for **batch processing**.

Key-to-tape – A machine to get data from the keyboard to a tape without using the main machine.

kilo (k) – Multiplier representing 1×10^3 (Often-used alternative in computing 1024.)

kilobyte – 1024 bytes.

Knowledge-based system – See **expert system**.

Label – A means of identification used in a program, e.g. JUMP to the label 'Next'.

Landscape – A sideways document in which the longest side is at the top.

Laptop – A portable computer.

LASER – Light Amplification by the Stimulated Emission of Radiation.

Laser disk – Name for the 12 in version of the **CD-ROM**. Largely superseded by the 12 cm **CD-ROM**.

Laser disk player – Name for the machine which handles the 12 in optical laser disks.

Laser engine – The name given to the part inside a laser printer which gives it its characteristics.

Laser printer – **Page printer** based on laser technology.

Laser scanning mechanism – System to read bar codes at **EFTPOS** terminals.

Latency – See search time.

LCD – Liquid Crystal Display. Screen used mainly on portable equipment.

Leading (DTP) – Space between the lines on a document.

Leaf node – **Terminal node** on a **tree structure**.

Least significant bit – The **binary digit** at the end of a **binary** number having the least place value.

LED – Light Emitting Diode. A semiconductor which emits light – used for displays, especially 7-segment LED displays as used in control panels to display numbers.

Lexical analysis – The first stage during **compilation**.

Linear structure – One set of instructions carried out one after the other in a linear sequence.

Light pen – A pen-shaped device which enables you to 'write' directly on the **monitor** screen.

Line editor – A simple text editor which can handle only one line of text at the same time.

Linear congruential method – A method of generating **pseudo-random numbers** with very long cycle lengths.

Linear list – A one-dimensional **array**.

Linear search – The most simple **search algorithm**.

Line printer – A printer which prints 'one line' at a time, e.g. chain or drum printer.

Link layer – The second layer in the **ISO OSI network model**.

Linked list – A **list** whose structure is defined by **pointers** and not physical locations.

Linking loader – A **loader** that is able to link together programs that have been assembled separately.

Linotronic printing – Professional printing system (often 1200 dpi resolution) used for books etc.

LIPS – Logical Inferences Per Second. A **fifth-generation** measure of computer performance.

LISP – A **high-level computer programming language**.

List – A set of **data** arranged into some order.

Literal – A **symbol** (**lexical** unit) in a **programming language** which is itself used as **data**.

Liquid crystal – A crystal in a liquid or solid state which can be altered by an electrostatic field.

Liveware – Silly term for people who use the system – compare with **software**, **hardware** and **firmware**.

Loader – A **program** that loads part of the **operating system** or other previously-assembled program into **memory**.

Local Area Network (LAN) – A **network** in the same building or the same locality (up to about 1 km).

Local variable – A **variable** which is recognised only within a **procedure** or a **block**.

Logical error – An error in the logic of a program – compare with **syntax** and **execution errors** etc.

Logical operations – **AND, OR, NOT, NAND, NOR, XOR** and **XNOR**, Shift left and Shift right etc.

Logical record – A **record** viewed from a **software** point of view.

Logical shift – **Bits** are moved right or left with zeros filling the vacated spaces.

Logic bomb – A type of catastrophic computer **virus**.

Logic circuit – A circuit made up from **logic gates**.

Logic gate – An electronic circuit designed to perform a specific function such as **AND, OR** and **NOT** etc.

Logo – A **high-level language** used extensively by children to create patterns, and thus learn to program the computer. However, it's also a powerful **high-level language** in its own right

– most famous for it's turtle graphics.

Log off – The process of signing off from a computer system so that the logical connection is severed.

Log on – The process of identifying yourself to a **computer system**.

Long Haul Network – an alternative term for a **WAN**.

Look up table – A table in which a value is given depending on the value of some other variable, e.g. conversion of a bank account number onto a customer name could be done with a look-up table.

Loop – Part of a **program** which may be executed many times.

Loop, endless – See **endless loop**.

Loop network – A physical **ring network**.

Lower case – Small letters (not capitals).

Low-level language – **Machine code** or **assembly language**.

LSB – Least Significant **Bit**.

LSI – Large Scale Integration – between 500 and 20,000 transistors per chip.

Machine – Alternative name for the **computer**.

Machine architecture – The way in which the inside parts of a particular **machine** are organised.

Machine code – The **binary** or **hex digit**s used to **program** the machine at a fundamental level.

Machine language – Same as **machine code**.

Macro – A single instruction which is replaced by a group of other instructions.

Macro assembler – An assembler that supports **macros**.

Macro instruction – See **macro**.

Magenta – The 'crimson' colour obtained by mixing red and blue light.

Magnetic bubble memory – See **bubble memory**.

Magnetic disk – **Data** is recorded on concentric tracks on both sides of a rotating magnetic surface. See **floppy disk** and **Winchester disk**.

Magnetic media – Media such as **magnetic disks** and **magnetic tapes** etc.

Magnetic tape – A **serial-access** medium on which a large amount of **data** can be stored cheaply. Many different **tape** formats exist, and tapes are used for **serial files** and **backup** purposes.

Magneto-optical drive – Technique to increase **data** storage making use of **lasers** in conjunction with magnetic media.

Mail box – A place on a **disk** (usually on a **file server** or other **computer**) where **E-mail** can be stored.

Mail merge – Combining standard letters with database information to produce 'personalised' letters.

Mainframes – The largest of **computer** installations.

Main memory – See **primary store**.

Main store – The computer's **RAM**. See **primary store**.

Maintenance – Keeping a system up to scratch after it has been installed. (Software and hardware.)

MAN – Metropolitan Area **Network**. Longer than a **LAN** but shorter than an **LHN** or **WAN**.

Mandelbrot – IBM mathematician who discovered the Mandelbrot set.

Mandelbrot set – An analysis of the boundary of a mathematical function using complex numbers. Worlds of infinite complexity may be explored using colours and a computer.

Mantissa – The numbers representing the fractional part of a **floating point number**.

MAR – **Memory Address Register**.

Mark-sense reader – A machine capable of reading a source document on which marks are made with an HB pencil. Used for marking multi-choice examination material.

Masking – The ability to prevent alteration of certain **bits** inside a **register** when the rest of the **register** is being updated.

Master control program – See **operating system supervisor**.

Master disk – **Disk** containing the original copy of **software**.

Master file (1) – A **file** of information which is used in conjunction with a **transaction file** to produce a **new master file**.

Master file (2) – A **file** used for reference only or the **original file** from which copies are made.

Master tape – **Tape** containing original material.

Mathematical typesetting package – A text processing system designed for maths and chemical formulae.

Maths co-processor – A bolt-on number crunching chip to carry out high-speed maths. Some powerful processors already have these facilities built in.

Matrix – A rectangular **array** of elements.

M/c – An abbreviation for **machine**, i.e. the **computer**.

MDA – Monochrome Display Adaptor. An IBM PC adaptor for single-colour text.

MDR – **Memory Data Register**.

Media – The name for the disks and tapes or paper etc. on which data can be stored.

Mega (M) – Multiplier representing 1×10^6 (Often-used alternative in computing 1024×1024)

Megabyte – 1,048,576 bytes (1024×1024).

Member functions (C++) – Functions which are members of a particular **class**.

Memory – See **primary storage**.

Memory Address Register – A **register** holding the **address** of the most-current **instruction** or **data** taken from or put out to **memory**.

Memory Data Register – A **register** holding the most-recent **data** taken from or put out to memory.

Memory location – One of the 'pigeon holes' in which data can be stored.

Memory management – The name given to the techniques used to manage the **memory** when more than one **task** is being undertaken.

Memory map – A diagram showing how the computer's memory is split up to hold different programs or parts of the **operating system** etc. It's a map of the memory utilisation.

Merging – The joining of two **data** sets.

Mesh network – See **distributed network**.

Message switching – A permanent path is set up between two node computers which can be used for short-duration messages, these paths are then instantly available for other traffic. Compare with the circuit-switching systems used for the public telephone networks.

Meta assembler – An assembler which **assembles** code for many different **instruction sets**.

Metalanguage – A language used to describe another language, e.g. **BNF**.

Metal Oxide Silicon – One of the fabrication techniques used in the manufacture of **silicon chips**.

Meta symbols – The symbols used in a **metalanguage**.

Michaelangelo – A virus which is activated on March 6th, but also used as a generic name for other viruses of this type.

MICR – Magnetic Ink Character Recognition, e.g. the **E13B** character set at the bottom of bank cheques.

MICR Reader – A device used to read **MICR** documents. Bank cheques are the best example.

micro – Same as **microcomputer**.

micro (μ) – Multiplier representing 1×10^{-6}.

Micro-code – A further level below conventional machine code used to customise your own instructions.

Microchip – Same as chip.

Microcomputer – A **computer** which is built up around a **microprocessor** as the main **CPU**.

Microfiche – A rectangular photographic card on which frames of information are stored.

Microfilm – A photographic technique of reducing documents in size and storing them on film.

Micro-instruction – See **micro code**.

Microsoft – The largest software company in the world. Authors of **MS-DOS**, **Windows**, **Excel** and other best-selling blockbusters.

Microform – A collective term for **microfilm** and **microfiche**.

Microprocessor – Most of what's required to implement a computer system on a **single chip**.

Microprogramming – Programming making use of **micro-code** – several of these micro-code instructions would make up a machine-code instruction.

MicroProlog – A version of the **high-level language Prolog** for **micros**.

MIDI – Musical Instrument Digital Interface. A standard for connection of instruments to a computer system.

Mid-product method – A method for generating **pseudo-random numbers**.

Mid-square method – A type of **hashing function**.

milli (m) – Multiplier representing 1×10^{-3}.

Mind mining – The process of putting human knowledge into an **expert system**.

Mini – Same as **minicomputer**.

Minicomputer – A computer half way between a **micro** and **mainframe** in terms of performance and facilities. The term is getting more difficult to apply as micros become more powerful.

MIPS – Millions of Instructions Per Second – A **computer benchmark** measurement.

Mirror-reflecting gray code – A type of **gray code** used to generate the numbers for **Karnaugh maps**.

Mnemonic – An aid to the memory. Usually used for **assembly language instructions**.

MODEM – **MO**dulation–**DEM**odulation. A device used for sending and receiving data using the phone line. It converts data into audible tones so that the ordinary telephone lines can be used.

MODULA II – A high-level language which is derived from Pascal – ideal for concurrent processing.

Modular programming – Breaking up larger programs into smaller modules.

Modulation – Changing a signal into a form suitable for transmission.

Modulo arithmetic – clock arithmetic where the numbers go round in cycles e.g. MOD 4 would be 0,1,2,3,0,1,2,3,0,1 etc.

Monitor (1) – **Computer VDU**.

Monitor (2) – The **operating system supervisor** of a **microcomputer**.

Morphing – Changing one **computer graphic** into another in a defined way.

Motorola – A large scale **chip** manufacturer. Famous for the 68000 range of Apple Mac processors.

Monte-Carlo method – Method used for finding an area under a graph making use of **pseudo-random numbers**.

MOS – Metal Oxide Silicon. A fabrication techniques used for **silicon chips**.

Most Significant Bit – The **binary digit** at the end of a **binary** number which has the largest place value.

Most significant digit – Same as **Most Significant Bit**.

Mother board – The main **PCB** inside a **microcomputer**.

Mouse – Pointing and switching device for computer input – ideal for a **windows** environment.

MPEG – The Moving Pictures Experts Group. A standard for the **compression** and storage of video and computer-animation material.

MSB – Most Significant Bit.

MS-DOS – MicroSoft's **Disk Operating System**.

MS-DOS Shell – MSDOS system to provide simple **GUI** and **multitasking** from **DOS**.

MSI – Medium Scale Integration. Between 10 and 500 transistors per chip.

Multi-access – More than one **user** having access to a **system** at the same time.

Multimedia – The buzz word indicating the amalgamation of text, computer data, audio, video and anything else that you can think of into a single system.

Multi-mode operating system – An **operating system** which supports more than one mode of operation, e.g. **batch** and **multi-access**.

Multiple buffering (OS) – Use of two or more **buffers** to speed up communication between the **processor** and **peripheral** devices.

Multiple bus systems – A system in which two or more **bus systems** operate in parallel to speed up data transmission.

Multiplexing – A process of sending many signals down the same line at the same time or apparently at the same time.

Multiplexer – A device that carries out **multiplexing**.

Multiprocessing – More than one **CPU** is used inside the **computer** at the same time.

Multiprogramming – More than one **program** can be operated on at the same time or apparently at the same time. (Depends on whether the system has more than one **CPU**.)

Multiprogramming operating system – An **operating system** that supports **multiprogramming**.

Multiscan monitors – See **multisync monitors**.

Multisync monitors – A **VDU** with a variable (and usually higher) range of scanning frequencies controlling the **raster** scan display.

Multitasking (1) – **Micro.** Doing more than one thing at the same time or apparently at the same time.

Multitasking (2) – **Mainframe** and **mini**. Many users' data being serviced by the *same* program.

MVS – Multiple Virtual Storage. An **operating system** developed for **IBM mainframes**.

NAND gate – A **logic gate** which is **NOT(AND)**.

nano (n) – Multiplier representing 1×10^{-9}.

Nanotechnology – Technology carried out at nano-metre scale, e.g. small **robots** can be constructed so that they may be injected into the human body.

Nassi-Schneiderman diagram – One type of **structure diagram**.

Natural language – A context-sensitive language such as English or French.

Navigator – A program which helps to use the **CompuServe** front end to the **Internet**.

Near Letter Quality – A technique used to improve the output from **dot-matrix printers**.

Near Photographic Quality – The highest quality associated with the best colour **laser printers**.

NERIS – National Educational Resources Information System. **External database** of educational resources.

Nested if-then – If-then statements within other **if-then statements**.

Nested loop – Loops within other loops – don't forget that certain rules must be obeyed.

Network (1) – Many **computers** linked together and sharing the same resources such as **file servers, teletext servers** and **printer servers** etc.

Network (2) – A **data structure** that enables any relation between **nodes** to be implemented.

Network architecture – See **network topology**.

Network database – A **database** built up using a **network data model**.

Network data model – A **data structure** in which any **node** can be connected to any other.

Network layer – The 3rd level of the **ISO OSI network model**.

Network operating system – An **operating system** that supports the use of a **network**.

Network topology – The various physical layouts of the **networks** from a **topological** point of view.

Neural network – Circuits or **software** set up in ways similar to a simplified operation of the human brain.

Newton – Apple's **PDA** computer with **pen-based input**.

Nibble – Half a **byte**, i.e. four **bits**.

NIC – Network Interface Card (IBM PC).

NLQ – Near Letter Quality.

Node (1) – The name given to the **record** in a **data structure**.

Node (2) – A point at which different **networks** are interconnected.

Node computer – A **computer** placed at the **node** of a **network** to handle communications.

Non-equivalence gate – See **exclusive OR gate**.

Non-impact printers – Printers such as **laser** or **bubble** jet which don't have hammers or pins.

Non-interactive processing – Processing that does not require **user** intervention.

NOR gate – A **logic gate** which is **NOT(OR)**.

Normal form – A set of rules regarding Codd's relational database system.

Normalisation (1) – Putting a **floating point number** into **normalised form**.

Normalisation (2) – Setting up a **database** to Codd's **normal forms**.

Normal form (1) – See **first, second** and **third normal** forms of a **relational database**.

Normal form (2) – A **floating point number** after it has been **normalised**.

Normalised – Changing something into a form which is more efficient.

NOS – Network Operating System.

NOT gate – A **logic gate** which has an output which is the inverse of the input.

NPQ – **Near Photographic Quality**.

Numerical analysis – Building up complex **numerically-based models** so that a variety of mathematical tasks may be accomplished, e.g. **numerical integration** or **differentiation**, finding roots etc.

Numerical integration – The process of finding areas under a graph.

Numeric control – The computer control of drills, lathes and milling machines etc. (see **CNC**).

Numeric data – **Data** consisting of numbers only.

Numeric keypad – Part of the keyboard used specifically for entering numbers.

Nyquist's criterion – Sample at twice the highest rate of the frequency of interest when **digitising analogue** signals.

Object code – The **machine code** ready to be **executed** on a computer.

Object Linking and Embedding – A **system** which can transfer data backwards and forwards between packages at the flick of a mouse button. Useful for getting a diagram from a **DTP package** into a **CAD package**, then editing it and putting it straight back into the **DTP package**, for example.

Object oriented (1) – The use of **objects** to perform **tasks**.

Object oriented (2) – **CAD package** technique representing **objects** by mathematical equations.

Object-oriented programming – A complete programming methodology in which **objects** form the basis of many operations.

Object program – The output from an **assembler** or **compiler**.

Objects (C++) – A **data object** – a strictly-controlled **data structure** which makes it easier to develop complex systems.

OCR – **Optical Character Recognition**.

Octal – Base eight – uses the digits 0,1,2,3,4,5,6,7.

Odd parity – An odd number of 1s in the transmitted code as a check on data **integrity**.

OEM – The Original Equipment Manufacturer – company that makes the equipment that could be used by other companies in their products.

Off line – Not under the control of the **computer**.

OHP projection – Device placed on top of the OverHead Projector to project a computer image on a standard OHP screen.

OLE – **Object Linking and Embedding**.

OMR – Optical Mark Reader – same as **mark-sense reader**.

Ones complement – One less than the **twos complement**.

Onion diagram – Means of viewing the layers of **operating system software** and other applications.

On line – Under the control of the **computer**.

OOP – **Object Oriented Programming**.

Op code – short for **operation code**.

Open-loop mode – No **feedback**.

Operand – Something on which an operation is performed, e.g. in SQR(4) = 2 – '4' is the **operand**.

Operating system – The extremely complex **software** which controls a **computer**, and provides the interface between the **user**, **programs**, **applications** and the **hardware**.

Operating system supervisor – The **software** that controls the organisation of the **operating system**.

Operational research – The use of mathematical and scientific methods to help manage decision making.

Operation code – The **binary** code which represents a **machine-code** operation.

Operations manager – The person in charge of a **data processing department**.

Operator – The person who is operating the computer – same as **user**.

Optical Character Recognition – (1) A device to read carefully prepared hand written documents or typed text into the computer and change it into **ASCII** or other text.

Optical Character Recognition – (2) A device to read special characters on a source document. Sometimes used on **turnaround documents**.

Optical disk – A **disk** in which **data** is read by a **laser** – **CD-ROM** is the best example.

Optical methods – Methods making use of light to perform their primary function.

Optical wand – See **bar-code** reader.

Optimisation – Producing the most efficient output from a **compiler** or **assembler**. It rarely equals hand-optimised code.

Order – The size of a **matrix** in rows and columns, e.g. (4,3).

OR gate – A **logic gate** whose output is 1 if any of the inputs are 1.

OS – **Operating System**.

OSI – Open Systems Interconnection. An **architecture** for the interconnection of **computer networks**.

OS/2 – An **operating system** developed by **IBM** for their personal computers.

Outline font – Maths definitions used to create infinitely-scalable **fonts**. (Also called true-type fonts.)

Output – The **data** from a **computer system**.

Output peripherals – Devices such as **printers** and **plotters** which output **data**.

Overflow – A number too large to be represented by the **computer system** has occurred.

Overflow flag – A **flag** inside the flag register indicating that an **overflow** has been detected.

Overflow table – A method of dealing with **collisions** when using a **hashing function**.

Package – See **software package**.

Packet – A defined chunk of data used on a **message-switching network**.

Packet switching network – A **message**-switching **network** in which messages are split up into convenient packet-sized chunks ready for transmission. Contrast with **circuit-switching networks**.

Paddle – A one-dimensional **joystick**.

Page – A **block** of **memory**.

Page-description language – A language which describes every attribute on the printed page. Used for some types of **laser** and other **printers**.

Page printer – A **printer** where a page is apparently printed all at the same time, e.g. a **laser printer**.

Paint package – A **pixel based art package**. Some **object-oriented packages** can now produce similar effects.

Palette – The range of colours normally available on the computer at any one time.

Paradigm – Organising principles used in the design of **high-level languages** or other systems.

Parallel adder – A **logic circuit** which adds together two **binary** numbers in parallel.

Parallel data – **Data** in which several **bits** are sent simultaneously along different communication channels.

Parallel processing – **Architecture** enabling more than one thing to be done at exactly the same time. Need more than one **processor** to accomplish this.

Parallel transmission – Several signals are sent simultaneously.

Parallelism – The art of doing more than one thing at the same time.

Parameter – A **variable** that has temporarily assumed a constant value for the purposes of being passed on to a **subroutine** or **procedure** etc.

Parametric CAD – **CAD package** which allows diagrams to be expressed in terms of **parameters**, which express relationships between parts of the diagram. Animation is possible using **parametric CAD**.

Parent node – A **node** in a **tree structure** which has **children**.

Parity – A method used to ensure the **integrity** of received **data**. **Errors** can be detected and a retransmission requested – 2D parity can theoretically correct data which has been incorrectly received.

Parity check – Making use of **parity** to check **data integrity**.

Parity bits – Same as **parity digits**.

Parity digit – The extra **parity bit** added for the purpose of **parity** checking.

Parity track – A **track** on **magnetic tape** used to hold the **parity bits**.

Parsing – Seeing if the rules of **syntax** have been obeyed.

Partition – Part of **memory** set aside to hold set **data** or **programs** etc.

Partition sort – See **quick sort**.

Pascal – **High-level language** named in honour of the mathematician Blaise Pascal.

Passing by reference – Value of the **variable** gets changed as the actual variable is referenced and is therefore irrevocably altered by the **procedure**.

Passing by value – Value of the **variable** used to pass the **parameter** to the **procedure** is *not altered* because a copy (i.e. a different variable) has been used to receive the information.

Password – A code which is checked for **integrity** on entry to a secure system.

Patch – A bug fix to get round an error in a program until the next version is reached. Also used as a term which applies to slight modification of the original code for some specific user requirement.

PC (1) – Personal Computer – used to be **IBM PC** or compatible, but now a generally used term for a micro.

PC (2) – **Program Counter**.

PCB – **Printed Circuit Board**. A fabricated board to hold and connect the **chips** and other electronics.

PCI – **Personal Computer Interface**. A 64-bit bus system for the IBM PC and its clones.

PCM – **Pulse Code Modulation.**

PCMCIA – The Personal Computer Memory Card International Association. The standard for the credit-card-size interface for **modems**, **faxes**, **disk drives**, **network** adaptors etc which plug into **portable computers** – it's so small that normal connection leads won't fit into it!

PD – Public Domain.

PDA – Personal Digital Assistant, e.g. **Apple's** Newton.

PDL – Page Description Language, e.g. **PostScript**.

PDS – Public Domain Software. Software you don't have to pay for.

Pen Input – Use of a pen as the main input medium instead of a **keyboard** – ideal for **PDAs**.

Pentium – Intel's 80586 processor, called the **Pentium** to overcome copyright problems.

Peripherals – Devices connected to the main **computer** such as **disks**, **keyboards**, **printers** etc.

PERT chart – A chart showing events and activities, times and resources enabling **critical paths** to be evaluated.

Peta (P) – Multiplier representing 1×10^{15}. (Computing alternative 1024^5.)

pH – Numerical scale depicting acidity or alkalinity (7 is neutral).

Phoneme – A basic unit into which speech can be split up.

Photo CD – Developed by Kodak – a system used to store still images on CD.

Physical layer – The most basic layer of the **ISO OSI network model**.

Physical record – A **record** whose size is convenient from a **hardware** point of view. Several **logical records** will probably fit into a **physical record**. Also called a **block**.

pica – measure used by typesetters. 1 pica is 12 **points** – 72 points is 1 inch.

pico (p) – Multiplier representing 1×10^{-12}.

PIN – Personal Identification Number.

Pipeline architecture – A technique of **parallel processing** where different instructions are **fetched**, **decoded**, and **executed** at the same time.

Pipelining – See **pipeline architecture**.

Piracy – illegal theft of **computer software**.

Pixel – A picture element – often the smallest element which goes into making up a picture.

Plaintext – See **cleartext**.

Plated-wire store – 'Bullet proof' storage used in harsh military environments and black boxes on aircraft.

Platform – term used to describe a **hardware** or **software** environment, e.g. an **Intel** platform or a **Unix** platform.

Plotter – A device that produces high-quality **hard copy** for **CAD packages**. Large sizes and hence cost effectiveness are the only advantage these devices have over the current colour **laser printers**.

Pointer (1) – The contents of a **register** or **memory location** which is used to point to some other location.

Pointer (2) – The **icon** on the screen that's moved around by the **mouse**.

Point Of Sale Terminal – A **computer terminal** specifically designed for use in a shop. It will probably have integral bar **code readers**, links to a **computer** and links to the phone system etc.

Point size – A measurement used for the size of text in a **DTP system**. There are 72pts in 1 inch.

Polish notation – Prefix notation in which **arithmetical operators** appear before the **operands** e.g. + P Q means P+Q in 'normal' terminology.

Polling – Taking a poll to see if any **peripherals** need attention.

Pop – Terminology for removing a **data** item from a stack.

Port – A connection on the periphery of a **computer** in which signals can be fed into and/or extracted from the system.

Portable (1) – A portable computer.

Portable (2) – Being applicable to more than one **computer system**, e.g. a **high-level language**.

Portrait – A document view with the shortest side at the top.

POS – **Point Of Sale**.

Postfix notation – see **reverse Polish notation**.

Post-order traversal – A method for traversing (moving around) a **tree structure** visiting the left and right **sub trees** and then the **root**.

PostScript – A popular **page-description language**.

Pot – Same as potentiometer.

Potentiometer – An electronic component used to vary an analogue voltage.

Power open system (OS) – An operating system developed for the Power PC-based machines.

PowerPC – A collaboration between **Apple**, **IBM** and **Motorola** to produce a range of **RISC**-based **machines** based around the PowerPC chip.

Power user – Someone who is a very advanced and technically-competent user of the **system**.

PPM – **Pulse Position Modulation**.

Pragmatics – Other aspects (besides **syntax** and **semantics**) of a language implementation such as efficiency, practicality and ease of use etc.

Precedence – The order of priority in evaluation of an **arithmetical** or **logical expression**.

Precision – A term usually associated with **word length** – something can be expressed with great **precision** but need not necessarily be **accurate**.

Predicate – A logical relationship.

Prefix notation – See **Polish notation**.

Pre-order traversal – A method of traversing (moving around) a **tree structure** visiting the **root** first, followed by the left and right-hand **sub trees**.

Presentation layer – The sixth layer of the **ISO OSI network model**.

Presentation package – **Applications package** to produce presentations using a mixture of text, graphics, charting, back drops, audio and video data.

Prestel – British Telecom's **database** accessed via the phone system.

Primary key – the key by which a **table** in a **relational database** is best described – the primary key may contain several **attributes** if **normalisation** is to be achieved in practice.

Primary storage – The main **semiconductor storage** inside a **computer system**. This is usually very fast **RAM** but **cache** is often quicker still, being made up of **SRAM**.

Printer – A device for obtaining **hard copy**.

Print head – That part of the **printer** which is the actual printing mechanism.

Priorities (1) – The **computer operator** can assign a **priority** to a **job** so that it can override **operating-system** scheduling procedures. The operator's pay cheque program has the highest priority in this mode!

Priorities (2) – The **operating system** can assign **priorities** to tasks to maximise the efficiency of the system in terms of resources being efficiently used etc.

Priorities (3) – **Interrupting devices** may have **priorities** assigned according to the urgency with which the interrupts must be serviced.

Probability – A number between 0 (which represents impossible) and 1 (which represents certainty).

Procedural languages – Languages like **BASIC** or **Pascal** which make use of **procedures** or groups of statements.

Procedure – A separate section of the **program** designed for some specific purpose. Unlike a **function** it can receive and return multiple values.

Process control – Using **computers** to monitor industrial tasks such as a chemical works.

Private (C++) – **Data** which is only associated with a particular **class**.

Productions – Rule definitions define syntax using **BNF** or **EBNF**.

Program – A set of **instructions**.

Program Counter – A **register** to keep track of the current position in a program. Same as **sequence control register**.

Program documentation – **Documentation** which accompanies the program to explain how it works at a technical level.

Program execution – Running the **program** so that it may carry out it's instructions.

Program file – A **file** which is literally a **program**. As opposed to a **data file**, for example.

Program flowchart – A **detailed flowchart** which outlines how a **program** works and can hence be used to help develop the **program**.

Programmable Read Only Memory – A **chip** that can be permanently programmed to the **users** requirements.

Programmer – The person who codes the **programs** from the information provided by the **systems analyst**.

Programmer time – 'Average' time taken for a programmer to do a 'job' – Good programmers have smaller values for programmer time.

Projection TVs – Large screen projection of computer and other images.

Prolog – PROgramming in LOGic – A **fifth-generation language**.

PROM – **Programmable Read Only Memory**.

Prompt – A **character** used to prompt the **user** of an **interactive system** to input **data**.

Proportional spacing – Variable gaps between the characters in text – generally looks better than fixed spacing, but fixed spacing is good for program listings.

Protection – The prevention of unauthorised access to the **computer system**.

Protection ring – A **ring** which must be placed on a reel of **tape** if data is to be written to it.

Protocol – A set of rules for communication between different devices.

Prototyping – Making a mock-up of parts of the system for early evaluation and possible modification.

Pseudocode – A **high-level language-like** code used to help develop **algorithms**.

Pseudo operations – See **directive**.

Pseudo random numbers – A number pattern that repeats itself every so often. The secret is to make the pattern so long that nobody notices it – it therefore looks like a real random number.

PSN – **Packet Switched Network**.

PSS – Packet Switched System – same as a **PSN**.

Public (C++) – **Data** which is available to all **classes**.

Public domain – Software which is free!

Puck – Input device for use on a **graphics tablet**.

Push – Term used to denote an item of data being put onto the **stack**.

PWM – **Pulse Width Modulation**.

QBE – Query By Example – an alternative to **SQL** for **database queries**.

QIC – Quarter Inch Cartridge – system of tape **backup** used on **micros**.

Quantisation – the process of converting to discrete levels when converting an **analogue** signal to a **digital** one.

Query – Requesting information from a **database** – usually in the form of an **SQL** or **Query By Example**.

Queue (1) – A **FIFO stack**.

Queue (2) – **(OS)** – The **batch** of **jobs** waiting to be processed in a **batch** environment.

Queueing theory – A **simulation** technique for analysing **data** associated with **queues**.

Quick sort – A special sort **algorithm** which is quick for long lists of data.

Quinkey – A special **keyboard** design for one-handed data entry.

QWERTY – The English and American keyboard layouts – look at the letters along the top row. Not all keyboards are alike – France uses the AZERTY keyboard and the Chinese keyboard can only be imagined!

Radio networks – A **computer network** making use of radio waves as the carrier of the information.

Radix – Another name for a **number base**.

Radix conversion – One type of **hashing function**.

RAID – Redundant Array of Inexpensive Drives – used to increase reliability of **file servers** – A mirror image of the data is stored on one or more backup disks.

Raster scanning – Mechanism used in most conventional **computer monitors** to drive the electron beam in the **CRT** to make up the picture.

RAM – **Random Access Memory**.

Random access – The time taken to access any location is not dependent on position.

Random access files – Any **record** may be read without having to read all the previous **records**.

Randomisation algorithm – An **algorithm** used to determine the **physical address** at which the **data** can be stored.

Random numbers – A number sequence in which the next number chosen does not depend on the previous number, and all numbers are equally likely to occur.

Range – The difference between the largest and smallest values.

Raw data – **Data** that has been collected but not processed in any way.

Ray tracing – A technique of generating realistic-looking images by following paths of light reflected from the objects in the picture.

RDBMS – **Relational DataBase** Management System.

Read – Term used to get access to data stored in memory or some other suitable storage device. The act of reading does not destroy the data but makes a copy of it.

Read head – The part of a **tape** or **disk** which reads data from the magnetic surface.

Reading – The process of accessing **information** from **memory** or a **file** etc.

Read Only Memory – **Data** is permanently stored inside the **chip**. It can't be removed.

Read/Write – The control signal used with a memory chip to determine whether a Read or Write operation is to take place.

Read/Write head – The same head is used for the read and write operations.

Read/Write time – The time taken for a read or write operation to take place.

Real number – A 'normal' number.

Real time – A **system** which can respond in an appropriate amount of time – usually very quickly, but not necessarily so. Modern definitions are now including reliability together with response speed.

Real-time clock – An electronic circuit which keeps the time of day. This information may be used by software to display clocks or activate **control systems** etc.

Real-time operating system – An **operating system** that supports this mode of operation.

Record – A self-contained part of a **file**, usually made up of several **fields**.

Recursion – A programming technique where a routine is written such that it may call itself.

Recursive algorithm – One that can call itself.

Reduced instruction set – The **assembly language** consists of fewer simple instructions taking only a few **clock cycles**. The very-complex complex instructions common on **CISC** processors are removed.

Refresh – The process of topping up **DRAM** with charge – contents would leak away if this is not done.

Register – A special electronic circuit (highest access speed) where data can be stored for a specific purpose. **Registers** are usually inside the main **CPU**.

Register addressing – An **addressing mode** making use of **registers** to specify the **address**.

Relation – A *two-dimensional* **table** in a **relational database**. **Tuples** or **rows** correspond to **entities** or **records**, and each *subsection* of a **tuple** corresponds to a **field**. The **table** corresponds to a **file**.

Relational algebra – An algebra which deals with relations using operations with sets.

Relational calculus – A branch of mathematics which deals with the generation of new relations from existing ones. It is the link to the idea of a tuple in Codd's relational database theories.

Relational database – A **database** built up on a set of **relational tables**.

Relational data model – A **data structure** making use of a set of **tables**.

Relational operator – '=', '<', '>', '**AND**', '**OR**' etc.

Relational spreadsheet – A **spreadsheet** which has the facility to reference **cells** by name.

Relational table – A 2-dimensional **table** in a **relational database**.

Relationship – A link, or some sort of **dependency** or **association** between two or more **attributes**. One-to-one, one-to-many, many-to-one and many-to-many relationships are common.

Relative address – An **address** calculated by adding a number to a base **address**.

Relocatable code – **Programs** that can run in different parts of the **memory**.

Remote access – Getting access to a computer system from a place removed from the main installation.

Repeat until – Statements in loop are **executed** and **Boolean** condition checked at the end.

Report – The output to the screen or a file from a **database query**.

Report generator – A program that allows non-specialist users to generate reports from a database.

Research and development staff – The staff who do research into the **computer systems** of tomorrow.

Reserved word – A **key word** used in a **high-level language** to perform a specific function.

Reset – Make a bit = 0.

Resistor – An electronic component used to alter the current or voltage.

Resolution (1) – A measure of how closely one can get to some ideal, e.g. **high-resolution graphics** are more realistic than low-resolution graphics.

Resolution (2) – The number of discrete levels when **digitising** an **analogue** signal.

Resolution (3) – The magnitude of the difference between the last two **bits** representing a number.

Return – Instruction to return from a **subroutine**.

Reverse Polish notation – **Postfix notation**. Operator appears after the operands e.g. P Q + means P + Q.

RGB – Red, Green and Blue. One of the additive colour models used in a computer system.

Ring – A loop of cable which is used in some types of physical **ring networks**.

Ring list – See **circular list**.

Ring network – A **network** based on a circular loop of cable. A **token-ring network** is not necessarily wired as a physical ring network.

RISC – Reduced Instruction Set Computer. Complex instructions removed from the instruction set.

RISC computer – A **computer** based around a **RISC microprocessor**.

RISC microprocessor – One which has a **reduced instruction set** as its **assembly language**.

Robot (1) – Device used to carry out specialist function, usually in an industrial environment.

Robot (2) – Device intended to mimic human-like qualities – still some way into the future.

Robotics – Intelligent **computer control** of mechanical machines.

Rogue value – A value which can't possibly be interpreted as being part of a data set – used to terminate the execution of some particular part of the program.

ROM – Read Only Memory.

ROM cartridge – A cartridge containing a **ROM** which can plug into a **micro** or games machine.

Root (maths) – The solution to an equation expressed as $f(x) = 0$.

Root directory – The base **directory** in a hierarchical **data structure**.

Root node – The first **node** in a **hierarchical data structure**.

Rounding error – The **error** due to **rounding up** or **rounding down**.

Row – Same as a **tuple** from a **relational table** – corresponds to a record in a **relational database**.

Row-by-row mapping – A method of representing a two-dimensional **array** in **main store**.

RSI – Repetitive Strain Injury. Problems due to excessive periods at badly-designed **HCIs**.

RS 232 and RS 423 – Serial port interfacing standards.

RTF – Rich Text Format – one way of getting text together with styles and tab settings etc from one word processor to a different type of word processor.

Run – The term used to denote that a **program** or other **job** is being carried out.

Sampling frequency – The rate at which **analogue data** is sampled for conversion in an **A to D converter**.

Scanner – A hand-held or desk-top device used to **scan** images and text into a **computer**.

Scheduler – Operating system software which determines the **schedules** for a **job**.

Scheduling – The techniques used by the **operating system** to allocate **CPU** time in a **multi-tasking** or **multi-programming multi-access** environment, e.g. **time sharing**.

Schema – The logical definition of a **database**.

Scratch file – File used for temporary storage of **data**.

SCSI – Small Computer Systems Interface. An **interface** standard for **microcomputers**.

SCSI 2 (or SCSI II) – A faster and higher-specification version of SCSI.

Searching – Finding a specific item of data from a **list**.

Search length – The average number of **data** comparisons that must be made to **search** for an item of **data**.

Search time (disk) – The time taken for the head to move and the disk to rotate until the head is over the required data.

Search time (searching) – The average time taken to find an item of **data** in a **list**.

Secondary store – Storage for **data** that is not needed so quickly, e.g. **disk**, **tape** and **CD-ROM**.

Second-Generation Language – Unstructured **high-level languages** such as early versions of **BASIC** or **FORTRAN**.

Second normal form – All **attributes** in an **entity** must be **functionally dependent** on the **primary key**.

Sector – Disk track is split into sub-sections called **sectors**.

Sector number – Each **sector** has a unique number associated with it.

Seeds – The numbers used to start off a **pseudo-random-number** sequence.

Seek time (disk) – Time taken for the **head** to move to the right track.

Semantics – The meaning applied to a language.

Semiconductor – A material having an electrical conductivity half way between that of an insulator and a conductor. Specially treated semiconductors are used to manufacture **silicon chips**.

Semiconductor store – Same as **RAM** or **main store** or **primary store**.

Senior programmer – The person in charge of a programming team.

Sensors – See **transducers** (input).

Sequence control register – Same as the **program counter**.

Sequential access – The complete list of **data** must be searched until the required item is found.

Sequential access file – **File** in which **records** are stored, one after the other in some pre-determined order.

Sequential logic circuit – A **logic circuit** whose outputs depend on previous inputs.

Sequential search – See **linear search**.

Serial access file – A **file** in which **records** are stored one after the other with no regard to order.

Serial adder – A **logic circuit** which adds **binary digits** together **serially**.

Serial data – **Data** which is treated one **bit** at a time.

Serial data transmission – The transmission of **data** along the same line, often using a single channel only.

Serial file – A **file** which is not in any special order.

Serial operating systems – see **batch operating systems.**

Serial printer – A **printer** which prints one **character** at a time.

Serial transmission – One **bit** of **data** is sent at a time.

Session layer – The fifth layer of the **ISO OSI network model**.

Set – Make a bit = 1.

Shell – A layer of an **onion diagram**.

Shell sort – A sort **algorithm** developed by Donald Shell.

Shift leader – A person who leads a team operating a **mainframe computer** on a shift.

Shareware – A method of distributing software where you are supposed to pay for it if you like it and use it.

SID – Standard Idiot Test. Getting an 'idiot' to test your **programs** – normal people are usually just as effective!

Sign and magnitude – Method of representing positive and negative **binary numbers**.

Silicon – A **semiconductor** material.

Silicon chip – An electronic component containing **transistors** and other components made from silicon and other materials, and housed inside a small package called an **integrated circuit**.

Silicon disk – RAM used as though it were acting as a hard disk.

Simplex – Communication in one direction only.

Simulation – The **computer** acting as a model to determine some particular **system** performance.

Sister node – See **brother node**.

SLSI – Super Large Scale Integration. More than 100,000 transistors per chip.

Smalltalk – An **object oriented programming language**. Still going strong – a popular alternative to **C++** for some people.

Smell input – Gas detectors used as input devices interfaced to an appropriate **computer system**.

Smart cards – A credit card device which contains a simple **computer**.

Smart key – A device which looks like a key, but carries a **microchip** such that it can carry out the same functions as a **smart card**. Often used in high-security buildings.

Smart terminal – One which has some local processing ability.

Soft copy – The output on a **VDU** screen.

Soft keys – The **function keys** or user-defined keys on a **keyboard**.

Software – The **programs**.

Software development – The process of developing new and better **software**.

Software engineering – Methodology which embraces **documentation**, **maintenance**, **testing**, **debugging**, and development of a **system** making use of a variety of **software engineering** tools (**CASE**).

Software houses – The companies that develop **software**.

Software packages – **Applications packages**.

Son file – The latest generation of **master file**.

Sorting – Putting **raw data** into some pre-determined order, e.g. alphabetical.

Soundex – A 'sounds like' search on a **database**.

Source document – A document on which the source data to be entered into the **computer** may be found.

Source program – **Program** before being **assembled** or **compiled**.

Speech input – **Data** entered by means of the human voice.

Spell checker – Usual accessory on most **WP** and **DTP systems**. Unfortunately not context sensitive.

Spooling (1) – Sending several **files** to the **printer** so that the main **processor** is relieved of the task.

Spooling (2) – A process which gathers together **jobs** to be **run** and puts them on a fast access medium ready for **batch processing**.

Spreadsheet – An **applications package** to model financial, mathematical and other scenarios.

Sprite – A picture made up of **pixels**.

SQL – **Structured Query Language**.

S-R flip flop – A **logic circuit** with set and reset inputs.

SRAM – **Static Random Access Memory**. The fastest type of **RAM** which does not need to be **refreshed**.

SSI – Small Scale Integration. Less than 10 transistors per chip.

Stack – An area of **memory** used to contain temporary data.

Stack pointer – A number (usually inside a **register**) used to maintain the **stack**.

Star topology – A fast and secure method of connecting computers on a **network**.

Start bit – Extra bit sent as an aid for synchronisation purposes in a **serial** transmission link.

Start pointer – A **pointer** used to indicate the beginning of a **list**.

Statement – A **high-level language** program instruction.

State transition diagram – A diagram to show physical or logical states in a system, and the possible transitions between them.

Static RAM – See **SRAM**.

Status register – See **flag register**.

Stepper motor – A motor that moves a set angle in response to a pulse from a **digital** system.

Stop bit – A bit used to indicate the end of a group of bits in a **serial** link.

Storage – Same as **memory**.

Storage partitioning – A form of **memory management**.

Store – See **primary store**.

Story – A text file in a **DTP system**.

String – A set of alphanumeric **characters** and other punctuation etc.

String variable – A **variable** that can consist of a string of **characters**.

Structure diagram – A better alternative to **flowcharts** to establish pictorially a structure for many types of **algorithm**.

Structured programming – A methodology used to ensure good programming style, which in turn maintains understandability and maintainability etc.

Structured Query Language – A language by which information in a **database** may be accessed.

Stylus (pen input) – A device used to write on the screen. Often no more than a pointer.

Subroutine – A self-contained part of a **program** usually designed to accomplish a specific task.

Subschema – The conceptual, logical and physical levels into which a **database** may be split up.

Subscripted variable – **Variable** used to describe a **vector** or an **array**, e.g. position (3,2,4).

Subtree – **Tree structure** that consists of **parent** and **children nodes** extracted from a larger tree structure.

Supercomputer – The fastest and most powerful computers available. Used to carry out maths-intensive applications such as forecasting the weather or creating realistic **ray-traced** images.

SuperJANET – A higher **bandwidth** and more versatile version of **JANET**.

SVGA – An enhanced version of the **Versatile Graphics Array (VGA)**. 256 to full 24-bit colour depending on hardware available.

Switching algebra – An algebra which helps to realise **logical functions** making use of switches.

Symbolic address – The use of **symbols** (characters) to represent an **address**, e.g. a label.

Symbol table – A table used by **compilers** and **assemblers** which stores the relationships between the **symbolic addressing** used by the programmer and the **machine addresses** on the actual **machine**.

Synchronous transmission – The transmission of data where the sending and receiving ends are in synchronisation.

Synonyms – See **collision**.

Syntax – The rules which govern the structure of a language.

Syntax analysis – The stage during **compilation** when the rules of the language are being checked for a particular program.

Syntax diagram – Pictorial alternative to **BNF** and **EBNF** for describing the **syntax** of a language.

Syntax error – A breach of one of the rules of **syntax**.

System – The **computer system** as a whole.

System life cycle – The classic stages of **systems analysis**.

Systems analysis and design – The **analysis**, **design**, **testing**, correcting and **maintenance** of a system.

Systems analyst – The person who carries out the **systems analysis** phase.

Systems flowchart – A **flowchart** with extra systems-type **symbols**.

Systems programmer – The person who writes code for **operating systems** and the like.

System software – **Software** such as the **operating systems** and **utilities**.

Table – **Rows (tuples)** and columns containing **attributes** which represent a **relation** in a **relational database**.

Taligent – The code name for an **object-oriented operating system** developed jointly by **IBM** and **Apple**.

Tape cartridge – A small **cassette**-type **tape** system used for **backup** on **micros**.

Tape library – The name given for the store of **tapes**, usually associated with a **mainframe**.

Tape streamer – **Tape system** used for **backing** up **hard disks**, usually on a **micro**.

Target machine – The **machine** on which the code is intended to **run**.

TCP/IP – Transmission Control **Protocol / Internet Protocol**. A popular interconnection between **LANs** and **WANs**.

TDM – Time Division **Multiplexing**.

Technical documentation – Detailed documentation to enable other programmers to modify the system.

Teleconferencing – See **video conferencing**.

Teleprinter – A special **machine** with an integral **keyboard** and **printer** for sending and receiving messages.

Teletext – **Data** transmitted along with conventional TV signals – **decoded** and displayed on TV screen, local **microcomputer**, or via a **teletext server** on a **computer network.**

Telex – A system of communication making use of **teleprinters**.

Teraflops – 10^{12} flops. A **fifth-generation** performance measurement.

Tera (T) – Multiplier representing 1×10^{12}. (Often-used alternative in computing 1024^4.)

Terminal – Special **hardware** or more commonly a **microcomputer** running **terminal-emulation software** which enables it to communicate with a **mainframe** or external **database**.

Terminal-emulation software – **Software** that enables a standard **micro** to act as a **terminal** for external communications.

Terminal node – A **node** in a **tree structure** which has no **children**.

Test data – **Data** used to test input to a **system** – care and thought need to be put into the choice of **data**.

T$_E$X – Donald Knuth's mathematical **typesetting** package.

Text editor – A simple **word processor** used to construct **source code** for **high** or **low level languages**, or to create documents for **E-mail** etc.

Thesaurus – Usual accessory to **WP** and **DTP** system containing synonyms.

Third-Generation Language – Structured languages such as later versions of **BASIC** and **Pascal** etc.

Third normal form – There should be no **functional dependencies** existing between **attributes** that could not be used as an *alternative* to the **primary key** – these are called **transitive dependencies**.

Third party – A supplier, other than the original manufacturer of the system who supplies **software** or **hardware** for the system.

Thrashing – An unfortunate consequence of using a **virtual-memory system** whereby code is continually being brought in and sent back to the **disk**.

Throughput – The amount of work being done by a **system**.

TIFF – The Tag Image File Format – A popular **graphics** interchange format originally designed to handle **scanned** images.

Time division multiplexing – A technique which sends more than one signal down a communication line by allocating time slots to each signal.

Timer interrupt – A **job** has **run** out of time on the **CPU** – usually by getting stuck in an **infinite loop**.

Time sharing system – Each **job** or **user** is allocated a fixed amount of time, usually on a rotating basis.

Time slice – An amount of time allocated to a **user** in a **time-sharing system**.

Token (1) – An electronic **token** (special message) used in a **token-ring network**.

Token (2) – The smallest independent part of a **program** which has some meaning.

Token ring network – A **computer network** in which an electronic **token** has to be grabbed before communication is possible.

Tokenising – Replacing **high-level language** code by more efficient tokens.

Top-down approach – Method of designing a solution to a problem by splitting it up into sub-problems.

Top-down design – Same as **top down approach**.

Top of stack – The first number on the **stack**.

Topology – Properties in terms of the shape and interconnections etc. The London underground map is a topological representation of the underground system, for example.

Toolbox – That part of the screen of an application which displays the tools which are available within a particular application, e.g. a **CAD toolbox** would have special shape-drawing tools etc.

Touch screen – A **VDU** in which criss-crossing infra red beams may be broken by pointing a finger at the screen. Often used for easy selection of on-screen menus.

Tournament sort – A sort **algorithm** making use of a **binary tree**.

Trace – A system to help find out in what order a **computer** is **executing** a **program**.

Track (1) – Concentric **tracks** on a **floppy** or **hard disk**.

Track (2) – Continuous spiral on a **CD-ROM disk**.

Track (3) – Linear track on a **tape**.

Trackball – A device in which a ball is rotated to move the **cursor** on the screen. An upside-down mouse!

Track number – The number assigned to a **track** on a **disk**.

Transactions – Generally used to denote new business information ready to be input to the **system**, e.g. things sold in a shop or factory or stock brought into the warehouse on a certain day etc.

Transaction file – A **file** of **transactions** used to update the **old master file** to produce the **new master file**.

Transducer (input) – A device which converts a physical quantity into an electrical signal.

Transducer (output) – A device that converts an electrical signal into a physical quantity.

Transducer – A device that converts energy from one form into another.

Transducer driver – Circuit which boosts an electrical signal to drive outputs like motors, solenoids and heating elements etc.

Transistor – A tiny electronic component used as a fast switch inside a computer.

Transitive dependencies – If A is dependent on B and B is also dependent on C, then A is dependent on C and a transitive dependency is said to exist. It can often lead to unintentional deletion of data in a database.

Translator – **Software** which converts one language into another, e.g. a **compiler**, **interpreter** or **assembler**.

Transport layer – The fourth layer in the **ISO OSI network model**.

Transputer – A special **microprocessor** or an arrangement of **microprocessors** for **parallel processing**.

Traversal – Moving around a **data structure**.

Tree – A **hierarchical data structure**.

Tree sort – See **tournament sort**.

Tree structure – A **data structure** making use of a **tree**.

Tri-state buffer – An electronic circuit which is used for routing. It has three states – '0', '1' and 'off'.

Trojan horse – One type of computer **virus**.

True-type fonts – See **outline fonts**.

Truncation error – An **error** due to 'chopping off' some of the 'less-significant digits'.

Truth table – A list of the relationships between the outputs and inputs of a **logic circuit**.

TTL – Transistor-Transistor Logic. One type of fabrication technique used in logic **chips**.

Tuple – The correct term for a **row** or **record** from a **relational table**. Called a **tuple** because it's the *correct term* from relational calculus and relational algebra from which **relational databases** are derived.

Turing – A mathematician who did much pioneering work in computing.

Turing test – A test to see if a computer has intelligence.

Turnaround document – A document, output from a **computer system**, which is intended to be fed back into the system at a later stage.

Turtle – A little **robot** which acts as a plotter when doing turtle **graphics** in Logo.

Turtle graphics – Drawing pictures using the **high-level language Logo**.

Twos complement – a method of representing positive and negative numbers in **binary**.

Two-way linked list – A **list** which has both **forward** and **backward pointers**.

Typeface – The characteristics of machine-generated text, e.g. Times, Helvetica etc.

Ultrix – DECs version of Unix.

Unconditional jump – A forced **jump** to another place in the **program** with no pre-conditions.

Underflow – A number too small to be represented by the **system** has been encountered.

Universal Product Code – The American equivalent of the **EAN bar-code system**.

Unix – A popular and long-lasting operating system used in the professional world for **micros, minis** and **mainframes**.

Updating – Changing information (especially in a **file**) for more-recent information.

Upgrade – Changing parts (or all!) of the **hardware** or **software** for later and hopefully better versions.

Upper case – Capital letters only.

UPC – Universal Product Code. The American equivalent of the **EAN bar code** system.

UPS – Uninterruptible Power Supply. Used to prevent **volatile RAM** losing its contents in the event of a power failure – most systems will not allow you to keep on computing – it only lasts a few seconds.

User – You!

User-defined keys – Special **keys** on the **keyboard** which can have effects programmed by the **user**.

User documentation – The manuals (usually non technical) for the **users** of the system.

User friendly – A computer system that is supposed to be easy to use, e.g. a windows-based system.

User interface – That part of the **system** which interacts with the **user**. See **GUI, WIMP** and **HCI**.

Utilities – **Software** such as disk **formatters**, **viral** killers and parts of the **operating system**.

Validation – **Data** is checked to see if it is sensible in the context in which it is being used, e.g. a date is not entered as 31/2/96.

Variable – A **data** item that can take on a range of different values.

Variable-length field – A **field** in which the width depends on the number of **characters** entered.

Variable-length file – The **file** length depends on the number of characters entered into it. Compare to a **fixed-length file** in which dummy **data** is used to create the maximum-length file from the start.

Variable partition – A portion of the **memory** which is varied in size by the **operating system**.

Variable type – The type of variable such as **integer, floating point, enumerated** or **string** etc.

VAX – Virtual Address eXtension. **DECs** range of **minis**.

VCR – Video Cassette Recorder.

VDU – Visual Display Unit. Same as a **monitor**.

Vector (1) – A one-dimensional **array**.

Vector (2) – A pointer used to hold the address of a routine which is resident somewhere else.

Vectoring – System used to transfer control from one part of the program to another by an **address pointer** which is called a vector. The **vector** can be altered so that the routines may be held in different parts of the memory for different operating system versions, for example.

Vector processor – Special **hardware** for calculations on **vectors**.

Verification – A check to see if data has been entered correctly, e.g. name Clark might be Clarke.

VESA – Video Electronics Standards Association. A group of PC manufacturers who have set a standard for HRG and video adaptors.

VGA – Versatile Graphics Array. One type of graphics standard (several actually!) on an **IBM** compatible PC. 256 colours in low resolution or 16 colours in high resolution – **SVGA** is better.

Video adaptor – A circuit generating all the signals required to generate text and/or pictures on the computer's **raster display**.

Video conferencing – Eyeball-to-eyeball communications via a **computer network**.

Video digitiser – Video camera linked to a computer to **digitise** an image.

Video phone – Sound and **real-time** vision via the telephone or other network.

Videotex – Interactive system in which text and low-resolution **graphics** etc. can be exchanged via a **network**.

Viewdata – Same as **Videotex**.

Virtual machine (1) – A **machine** that utilises **virtual-memory techniques**.

Virtual machine (2) – The **user's** perception of a **machine** that is remote from the actual **hardware**.

Virtual memory – Use of **disk** to give the illusion that you have lots more **RAM**.

Virtual peripheral – A **peripheral** that is shared by many **users**, e.g. a **printer server**.

Virtual Reality – A computer-simulated world interacting with the **user** via **data gloves** and special **helmets** etc.

Virtual world – The illusion created by **VR**.

Virus – **Software** which is illegally injected into a system which often has annoying or even catastrophic results. It is designed to propagate itself and infect other computer systems too.

Visual Display Unit – The name for a computer screen, monitor or VDU.

VLSI – Very Large Scale Integration – between 20,000 and 100,000 transistors per chip.

VMS – **Virtual Memory System**.

Voice input – Human voice used to control a **machine**.

Voice output – Synthesised human speech.

Volatile store – **Memory** that looses its contents if the power is removed from the system.

Volatility (file) – The frequency with which updates are performed.

von Neumann – A mathematician who did much pioneering work on computers.

von-Neumann bottleneck – The queueing up of all the instructions waiting to be processed.

von-Neumann concept – The cycle of **fetching**, **decoding** and **executing** instructions one at a time.

VHS – Vertical Helical Scan. *The* most popular format for video tapes in the 1990s.

VR – **Virtual Reality**.

VRAM – Video RAM – RAM used for the display of video information – usually incorporated on a graphics display adaptor card.

VTR Video Tape Recorder.

WAN – **Wide Area Network**.

Wand – Also called optical wand – device to read **bar codes**.

What-if analysis – Modelling scenarios on a **spreadsheet**.

Whetstones – A **benchmark** test for **floating-point operations**.

While loop – checks **Boolean** condition before executing loop statements.

Wide Area Network – A long-range network making use of public lines such as the telephone system.

Wildcard – A character which can be used to replace a group of other characters – usually used in a search.

WIMP – **Windows Icons Mouse Pointer**. The familiar **desktop** operating environment.

Winchester disk – A **hard disk** making use of **Winchester** technology.

Window – A part of the screen through which you can see either a separate application or some other scene such as a **directory**.

Windows 3.1 or **95** – A **windows**-based **operating system** for the **PC**.

Windows NT – Windows New Technology. Another windows operating system for the **PC**.

Wire-frame modelling – Building up 3D images just using the outline edges.

Word – The number of bits that can be handled by the **CPU** at any one time. Usually 8, 16, 32, 64 or 128.

Word length – The number of **bits** capable of being handled by a computer at any one time, e.g. how many bits can be transferred from **memory** to the **CPU**.

Word processor – An **applications package** used for the creation of documents.

Working tape – Tape used to store current data.

Workstation (1) – Name used for high-performance **microcomputer**.

Workstation (2) – Name used for a terminal on a network.

WORM – Write Once Read Many times. One type of **optical disk**.

Worm – A type of **computer virus**.

WP – **Word Processor**.

Write – Term used to make a record of **data** in **memory** or on some suitable storage **media**. The act of writing data will usually destroy (overwrite) any data that used to be stored in the same place.

Write head – The part of the **disk** or **tape** which writes the **data** to the magnetic media.

WYSIWYG – What You See Is What You Get. Screen contents reflect what would be printed out.

Xerographic printer – **Printer** making use of the Xerox photocopying techniques.

XNOR gate – A **logic gate** which is a **NOT(XOR)** gate.

XOR gate – A **logic gate** which is similar to an **OR gate** but excludes the situation where all inputs are 1, which in this case gives a 0 out.

4GL – **Fourth-generation language**.

68000 – The range of **microprocessor chips** from **Motorola**.

80x86 – The range of **CISC microprocessor chips** from **Intel**.

31 Answers to exercises

Answers to exercises

To cut down on the enormous amount of space that would be required the answers given here have been kept *very brief* indeed – students **should expand considerably on the given information when answering examination-type questions or doing their own work**. One or more page number references are also provided where the relevant extra information can be found in the chapter being studied, and other relevant and related chapter and page references are also given. Additional reference material is sometimes quoted along with the answers to enable students to investigate the subject further if necessary. Some questions are of the open-ended research type and therefore have no answer in the following sections.

Answers to exercise 2.1

1. (a) **Input**, **processing** and **output**. The computer system and sub-sections of it can be categorised for analysis in separately-identifiable chunks. Division between **hardware** and **software** also important.
   (b A **compiler** – it is **software** – *the rest* are examples of **hardware**.
2. **Information** is obtained from **raw data** after some suitable **structure** has been applied to it.
3. Examples only are given – your answers will depend on your own systems.
   (a) RISC PCs, Apple Quadra, PowerPC, PowerMac, Gateway P5-60 Multimedia, Sinclair ZX80 etc.
   (b) VisualBASIC, BASIC V, Pascal, Turbo C, Borland C++, COBOL 85, Logo, FORTH, Prolog etc.
   (c) AUTOCAD 13, Microsoft Office, Impression Publisher, Lotus Improv, DataEase v4.53, ClarisWorks, Pagemaker v5, CorelDraw 5, WordStar v7, Vector, Snippet, CompuServe InfoMan etc.
   (d) Varies between 2Mbyte and 32 Mbyte or more, depending on micros.
   (e) Windows 3.1, Windows 95, System 7, RISC-OS 3.5, Unix, Ultrix, Novell, OS/2 etc.
   (f) Ethernet – 10 Mbits/sec, Econet – 200 kbits/sec, FDDI – 100 Mbits/sec etc.
4. 1st – valves, 2nd – transistors, 3rd – SSI, 4th – VLSI, 5th – knowledge-based machines with AI.
5. (a) Micro – desktop, few peripherals, single user, cheap, easy to use etc.
   (b) Mini – size between micro and mainframe, multi-user, expandable, £10,000+, floor or large desktop etc.
   (c) Mainframe – large – floor standing, lots of peripherals, many users, £100,000+ etc.
   (d) Laptop – very small, portable, often has the power of a desktop micro, battery limitations at present.
6. A processor/s in which more than one thing can be achieved at the same time.
7. Any information can be coded into binary e.g. 10011000 might mean the colour red or 10111001 might mean 'switch on the coffee pot'. By following coded instructions in binary, and with the appropriate peripherals attached, it's possible for a computer to do many different tasks.
8. Candidates for possible consideration would be VR (see page 236), AI (see page 554) or nano technology (see page 553), for example.

Answers to exercise 3.1

1. (a) (i) 10 (ii) 40 (iii) 127 (iv) 1339
   (b) (i) 11011 (ii) 10000000 (iii) 1100010101 (iv)101011001011111011
2. See page 24 for the method of repeated division. Note; no marks would be awarded in an examination if these sums were worked out any other way.
   (a) 1101 (b) 1111111 (c) 101100101
3. (a) 1101 (b) 11001 (c) 1010001 (d) 10111000 (e) 1010 (f) 101 (g) 110100
4. (a) 1111 (b) 11110010 (c) 110010 (d) 100011110 (e) 1001 (f) 1111 (g) 101011
5. (a) 208 (b) C3B2 (c) 13A (d) 131 (e) 8B6F (f) 8C13C9 (g) 17
6. (a) 253 (b) 2554 (c) 60752 (d) 3
7. (a) AB (b) B2 (c) F0 (d) 9954 (e) 16 (f) 55
8. (a) 101100000 (b) 1001111001 (c) 1111111101100000 (d) 111110111111111 1
9. (a) 1110000 (b) 10111101 (c) 1010011100 (d) 111101011001
10. (a) 1201 (b) 173673 (c) 125715 (d) 10000
11. (a) 1D9 (b) 40 (c) DB1 (d) E38

12. Note: Convert each number into decimal first.
 (a) 0100/0010 (42decimal)
 (b) 0100/1000/0110 (486 decimal)
 (c) 0010/0110/0011/1001 (2639decimal)

Answers to exercise 3.2

1. (a) 0.01 (b) 0.00001 (c) 1.1 (d) 1111.011 (e) 1101.1001 (f) 1000011.000011
2. (a) 11111100 (b) 11110011 (c) 10111011 (d) 10000101
3. (a) (i) 1111110110 (ii) 1111001000 (iii) 1001110110
 (b) (i) 1111110111 (ii) 1111001001 (iii) 1001110111
4. (a) 000010000000 (b) 100000110010 (c) 100011000100
5. (a) 11000000.1100 (b) 11101110.0110 (c) 10001110.1101

Answers to exercise 3.3

1. (a) See pages 33 and 35. (b) See page 35. (c) See page 36.
2. (a) 2047 (b) 1 (c) –1 (d) –2048
3. (a) $1 - 1/2^9 = 1 - 0.001953125 = 0.998046875$ (b) $1/2^9 = 0.001953125$
 (c) 0.001953125 (d) –0.998046875
4. (a) 0.1000000 0001   (b) 0.1001000 0100
 (c) 1.0100000 0010   (d) 1.0001000 0101
 (e) 0.1000000 1110   (f) 1.0000000 1010
5.   *.*********/*******
 (a) Max positive   0.111111111/011111 i.e. $(1 - 1/2^9) \times 2^{31}$
 (b) Min positive   0.100000000/100000 i.e. $(1/2 \times 2^{-32})$
 (c) Smallest mag neg. 1.011111111/100000
   (twos comp of mantissa is 0.100000001) i.e. $-(1/2 + 1/2^9) \times 2^{-32}$
 (d) Largest mag neg.   1.000000000/011111 i.e. $1 \times (2^{31})$
6. See pages 35 and 39.
7. See page 40 for explanation of following:

          sign
          bit
 (a)   0 1 1 0 0 0 0   (+48)
         +   1 1 0 0 0   (twos comp of 8)
                 ─────────────
   bit   (1)   0 0 1 0 0 0 0   Worked, set bit(1) = 1
   lost +   1 1 1 0 0 0   shift right 1 place
                 ─────────────
   bit   (1)   0 0 0 0 0 0 0   Worked, set bit(2) = 1
   lost +   1 1 1 1 0 0 0   shift right 1 place
                 ─────────────
                1 1 1 1 0 0 0   Not worked, set bit(3)= 0

 Hence answer = 1 1 0

 (b)   0 1 1 0 0 1 1   (+51)
         +   1 0 1 0   (twos comp of 6)
                 ─────────────
                0 0 0 0 0 1 1   Worked, set bit(1) = 1
         +   1 1 0 1 0   shift right 1 place
                 ─────────────
                1 1 0 1 0 1 1   Not worked, set bit(2) = 0
         +   0 0 1 1 0   Restore
                 ─────────────
                0 0 0 0 0 1 1
         +   1 1 1 0 1 0   shift right 1 place
                 ─────────────
                1 1 1 0 1 1 1   Not worked, set bit(3) = 0
         +   0 0 0 1 1 0   Restore
                 ─────────────
                0 0 0 0 0 1 1
         +   1 1 1 1 0 1 0   shift right 1 place
                 ─────────────
                1 1 1 1 1 0 1   Not worked, set bit(4) = 0
         +   0 0 0 0 1 1 0   Restore
                 ─────────────
                0 0 0 0 0 1 1 . 0   shift right 1 place
         +   1 1 1 1 1 0 1 . 0
                 ─────────────
   Bit   (1)   0 0 0 0 0 0 0 . 0   Worked, set bit(5) = 1
   Lost

 Hence answer = 1 0 0 0 . 1
                 (i.e. 51/6 = 8.5).

Answers to exercise 3.4

1. (a) Any deviation from the theoretically correct value.
 (b) See page 44.
 (c) See page 44.
 (d) 5/7 = 0.714286 (6 decimal places) = 0.714 (3 decimal places).
   Relative error = (5/7 – 714/1000)/(5/7) = 0.0004.
 (e) Actual error = 13.4442 – 13.44 = 0.042.
   Relative error = 0.042/13.4442 = 0.00312 (3 sig fig.)
 (f) 0.0005

2. $0.05/108.3 - 0.05/29.1 = -1.26 \times 10^{-3}$
3. Max absolute error in 31.8 is 0.05, max abs error in 2.16 is 0.005. Therefore max abs error in answer will be 0.055. Therefore, answer will lie between $33.96 + \text{or} - 0.055$, i.e. between 33.905 and 34.015.
4. Actual value $3.2 \times 3.2 - 2.8 \times 2.8 = 2.4$ (exactly). m/c works to 2 sig. fig.
   First method: $3.2 \times 3.2 - 2.8 \times 2.8 = 10 - 7.8 = 2.2$.
   rel %error $= (2.2 - 2.4)/2.4 \times 100\% = 8.3\%$
   Second method: $3.2 + 2.8 \times 3.2 - 2.8 = 6 \times 0.4 = 2.4$.
   rel %error $= (2.4 - 2.4)/2.4 \times 100\% = 0\%$. i.e. exact.

Answers to exercise 4.1

1. (a) The chip at the heart of a micro system which executes the m/c code instructions (see page 49).
   (b) M/c instructions are **fetched** from memory, **decoded** and then **executed** (carried out) (see page 49).
   (c) The Central Processing Unit. (Often the same as the microprocessor in a small micro.)
   (d) The Arithmetic Logic Unit. That part of the CPU which carries out these operations.
   (e) A register inside the CPU which keeps track of which instruction is currently being executed.
   (f) An electronic circuit which acts as a temporary store for binary data (see pages 54 and 454).
   (g) A parallel group of wires along which binary data can be sent (see pages 50 and 51).
   (h) The main place inside the computer in which binary data is temporarily stored (see pages 150 and 262).
2. To generate timing signals and to instruct the microprocessor to get on with the next part of the cycle. The output from the clock is an electronic periodic signal consisting of a train of pulses (see page 50).
3. Stored as **binary data** but often accessed as **hex data** (see pages 23 and 27).
4. **Address bus** – to generate memory and other device addresses. **Data bus** to carry the data from one part of the computer to another. **Control bus** to generate control signals such as read/write etc. (see page 262).
5. Each device is mapped onto the system making use of a unique address – data can be shared using the same data bus – in this way data can be sent to or got from different devices on the system.
6. A memory map is needed so that everybody can agree as to where in memory programs can be run or where in memory special routines can live safely without being inadvertently disrupted (see pages 52 and 392).
7. (a) Acts as the electronic control inside the CPU which routes and controls movements of data.
   (b) A register for the accumulation (temporary storage) of results (see page 53).
   (c) A register to store the contents of the memory location which was last accessed (see page 54).
   (d) The Current Instruction Register holds the op code for the current instruction (see page 54).
   (e) The bus or busses actually inside the microprocessor chip itself.
   (f) A register which is used to hold the current address of the memory location being accessed.
8. A special code is chosen by the microprocessor manufacturers which can be decoded by the microprocessor so that appropriate action is taken. These codes are called operation (op) codes.
9. It does not! It's up to the programmer to get the program arranged and interpreted correctly.
10. Assume numbers are in memory locations 100 to 104 inclusive. Assume answer to be put into loc. 105. The diagram shows the five original numbers *before* execution of program – zeros have been assumed in loc. 105. Program shown is typical, result is shown on R.H.S. of the diagram.

Typical assembly-language mnemonics

Address 100	00000111		LOAD,A	(100)	Address 100	00000111	
101	00001001		ADD,A	(101)	101	00001001	
102	00000111	Binary code for	ADD,A	(102)	102	00000111	Binary code for
103	00001001	original numbers	ADD,A	(103)	103	00001001	original numbers
104	00001001		ADD,A	(104)	104	00001001	
105	00000000	Reserved for answer	STORE,A	(105)	105	00101001	Answer is placed here
Memory map before			NOTE: (100) means the contents of location 100		Memory map after		

A refers to Accumulator, therefore LOAD,A (100) means load the Acc with the contents of memory location 100. ADD,A (101) means add to the Acc, the contents of memory location 101, and place the result into the Acc. Finally, STORE,A puts the contents of the Acc into memory location 105.

1. **Parallel processing** is the ability to do **more than one thing simultaneously**. It is *not* the same as multitasking (see page 374), and needs special hardware consisting of either a special CPU, or more than one CPU. If software is written to take advantage of parallel processing then a significant increase in speed is possible (see page 65).
2. Pipelining can fetch, decode and execute different instructions at the same time (see page 61).
3. Some results needed for future processing may not be ready yet. Special software which splits up the processes into separate tasks is necessary (see page 65).
4. It is the maximum rate at which data can be transferred along the bus measured in bits/sec. Physical limitations of the bus construction and electronics determine the maximum rate (see pages 63 and 490).
5. Fast cache memory acts as an interface to the faster processors (see page 63).
6. Increase the width or upgrade the electronics and increase the clock rate.
7. Spreadsheet and CAD package because of intensive calculations that are necessary.
8. Independent parts of the problem can be passed over to different processors. If problem is not coded in this way one or more of the processors could be idle for significant periods of time (see page 65).
9. (a) Holds number of m/c code instructions in memory to cut down on fetch-execute times.
    (b) Holds chunks of data in this area of cache to save fetch-execute times.
    (c) Wide data bus for higher bandwidth.
    (d) Pipeline architecture can be operating on different instructions simultaneously.
    (e) Hardware to speed up the maths. (Saves accessing software routines in memory.)
    (f) Fast clock rate makes processor work extremely fast.
    (g) A benchmark indicating that 100 million instructions can be processed each second. Refer to detailed specification sheets on the Pentium processor from Intel.

1. M/c code is the binary or hex code, assembly language is the mnemonics (see page 71).
2. The m/c code is *different* for each type of machine. It's possible if **emulation** is used. (Software to make a program appear to be running on the target machine.)
3. These aids to the memory make life very much easier and less tedious for the programmer. The **four parts** of the instruction are **LABEL, OP CODE, OPERAND** and **COMMENT** (see page 74).
4. Op code is the mnemonic representing the operation like ADD or SUB etc. The operand is the data to be operated on, and a comment is for documentation purposes.
5. Different modes of addressing allow programmers to code different data structures more effectively, e.g. the implementation of an array, for example (see pages 77, 114, 287 and 293).
6. Put *very* simply, general purpose registers allow the programmer to have more freedom; however, specific registers are helpful for implementation of many standard operations (see page 72).
7. A flag register is used to flag (i.e. bring to the attention of the programmer) certain conditions such as arithmetic overflow and underflow, carry set, or the fact that an interrupt has occurred (see page 78).
8. Using **80×86 Assembler**:   **MOV**   **DL,05H**
                                 ADD   **DL,0AH**
   The method used here is called **immediate addition** because the *constant* numbers 5 and 10 (in hex in the above program) appear immediately after the register. 5 is **MOV**ed into the DL register and 10 is **ADD**ed to it so that the result is held in the DL register. Flags indicate if the result is too big – positive or negative etc.
9. Suppose original byte is 10101011. Use 10101011 AND 11100011 + 000111000. Use mask 111000111 to *reset* the middle digits so that 00011100 can be added *without altering other digits* – try it and see!
10. Arithmetic shift preserves sign, logical shifts don't (see pages 80 and 81).

Original number		1 1 1 1 0 0 0 0 1 1 1 1 0 0 0 0
(a)	LSL 3	1 0 0 0 0 1 1 1 1 0 0 0 0 0 0 0
(b)	ASL 3	1 0 0 0 0 1 1 1 1 0 0 0 0 0 0 0
(c)	LSR 3	0 0 0 1 1 1 1 0 0 0 0 1 1 1 1 0
(d)	ASR 3	1 0 0 1 1 1 1 0 0 0 0 1 1 1 1 0

11. Carried out in bitwise mode, e.g. 11 AND 10 = 10, and 11 OR 10 = 11 etc (see page 79).
12. Using 80×86,
    An unconditional jump is   JMP NEXT;   Jump to label next unconditionally
    A conditional jump is   JNO NEXT;   Jump to label next if NO overflow
13. It is used to point to an area of memory called a stack. Helps the programmer to implement a stack data structure. (See pages 84 and 288.)
14. An assembler is software which converts assembly language mnemonics into m/c code. It has many advantages over hand assembly or writing directly in m/c code (see page 89).
15. Different types of assembler support different facilities, e.g. a cross assembler produces object code for a different target m/c etc. Other types – macro assemblers and meta assemblers etc. (See page 88.)
16. Loads the assembled program into memory and links to libraries etc (see page 89).
17. Macro assembler supports macros (generation of code from a single instruction) (see page 88). Library routines are code which can be called up by name (often written by others) and inserted into your programs.

18. Printing out the contents of registers to compare with manually-calculated values.
19. You can use pre-written operating-system routines to perform common but useful tasks like 'get a character from the keyboard' or 'save a block of data to disk', for example.

Answers to exercise 6.1

1. Makes the machine easier to use. Complex problem-oriented solutions as opposed to machine-oriented solutions are possible. Software development is significantly easier and faster.
2. No single language can cope with the vast range of requirements from embedded system control (see page 547) via advanced mathematics to business administration etc. – the language would be too cumbersome.
   (a) Typifies telling the computer how to do something by using instructions called imperatives.
   (b) Typifies telling the computer what to do (not exactly how to do it).
   (c) Typifies languages expressed in terms of functions or procedure calls.
   (d) Makes use of objects which are classes describing both data and operations.
   N.B. Most languages contain one or more of the above paradigms.
3. It's a whole design philosophy approach to programming and systems analysis (see page 426).
4. (a) 3rd (b) 1st (c) 2nd or 3rd depending on version (d) 5th (e) 2nd (f) 4th.
5. **BBC BASIC V** used for *all* examples.
   (a) A **variable** is an *identifier* which can take on a range of different values – but only one at a time!
       Variable name examples – x, fred, Name$, x_value, radius_of_circle.
   (b) An **identifier** is a set of *one or more characters* used to identify a data element such as a **variable**, an **array** or a **function** etc.
       Identifier examples – stock(n), 45.3, balance_of_account, 3.141592654, y12.
   (c) **Reserved words** are key words which can't be used for identifiers – however, BBC BASIC V allows this if lower-case letters are used.
       Reserved word examples are – COUNT, VOICES, PLOT, FILL, SOUND.
   (d) Built-in maths functions are identifiers that call up pre-written functions.
       Maths-function examples are COS, SQR, LOG, EXP, TAN etc.
6. (a) A diagram which defines the syntax of a language pictorially – as opposed to using techniques such as BNF or extended BNF etc (see page 203).
   (b) BNF – Backus Naur Form (see page 203).
7. Different data types give rise to different characteristic sets of possible values. Explicit data types might be INTEGER or STRING – only rules applying to that data type may be applied – it thus gives a more rigorously enforced structure to the program.
8. **BBC BASIC V** is used for the following definitions.
   (a) for loop
       FOR <variable> = <expression> **TO** <expression> **[STEP** expression]
           Valid statements
       NEXT <variable>
   (b) while loop
       WHILE <expression>   (Never executed if expression is false)
           Valid statements
       ENDWHILE
   (c) repeat-until loop
       REPEAT   (Always executed at least once, even if expression is TRUE)
           Valid statements
       UNTIL <expression>
9. **BBC BASIC V** used for the following examples.
   (a) Data types are   NUMERIC – Integer, Floating point.
       BOOLEAN, STRING, ARRAYS (Subscripted variables), FILE (Simple pointer)
   (b) Range of numeric data types are
       INTEGER –2147483648   to +2147483647
       Floating point -1.7×10^{38} to $+1.7 \times 10^{38}$
10. (a) **Boolean** – used for TRUE/FALSE values only.
    (b) **Integer** – Numeric values, whole numbers only, limited range but good accuracy.
    (c) **Real** – Numeric values, large range, limited accuracy if floating point is used.
    (d) **String** – Alphanumeric character storage, limited length, can't do arithmetic on numbers but can concatenate strings, search for characters, used to help sort data into alphabetical order etc.

Answers to exercise 6.2

1. A list of values that the variable can assume, e.g. Tom, Dick or Harry.
2. **BBC BASIC V** – DIM structure(5,3) would define a two-dimensional array named structure. To access the element in the 2nd row and the 2nd column use the variable structure(2,2).
3. The pointer data type holds a number which can be used to point to a memory location, an element within an array, an element within a record or a file, or a position within a string etc. By changing the pointer number we can access different data items set up using the rules of a number of different structures.
4. A condition, such as the value of a variable, for example, is tested, and if the condition is TRUE (Boolean function) then a JUMP to a different part of a program is carried out. For example, using **BBC BASIC V** – IF test >= maximum THEN PROCreset – calls

the reset procedure if test >= maximum.

5. WHILE is never executed if the condition is FALSE, whereas REPEAT – UNTIL will always be executed at least once, *irrespective* of whether the condition is **TRUE** or **FALSE**.

6. Loops can only be nested within themselves, they can't overlap (see page 123).

7. Excessive use of the GOTO can lead to unwieldy and unreadable programs. It's often extremely difficult to follow the logic of a program which is liberally sprinkled with GOTOs. Use only on error conditions.

8. Case structures are more readable, and are easier to use when constants are used for the test condition, nested IF-THEN statements are more versatile, unless the language supports ranges within case structures.

9. A **function** is used as a subroutine that returns the value of a *single variable*, a **procedure** is a subprogram which can have many parameters passed over to it and returned from it.

10. Using **BBC BASIC V**
```
INPUT "Radius of circle";rad
Area = FNArea_of_circle(rad)
PRINT "Area of circle of radius";" ";rad;" is";Area
END
DEF FNArea_of_circle(radius)
= PI * radius^2
```

11. **BBC BASIC V**
```
DIM x(5)                          DEF PROCaverage
PRINT "Input five numbers"        LOCAL Total, count
FOR count = 1 TO 5                  Total = 0
   INPUT x(count)                 FOR count = 1 TO 5
NEXT count                          Total = Total + x(count)
PROCaverage                       NEXT count
PRINT "The average is ";average   average = Total/5
END                               ENDPROC
```

12. The scope of a **local variable** is defined and recognised only locally by a unit of the program such as a procedure, a **global variable** is recognised and can be altered by *any part* of the program.

13. Passing by value means that the variable being used to transfer the value to the procedure does not get altered itself, only its **value** is **passed**. Passing by **reference** means that the variable being used to pass the parameter does get **referenced** and therefore *irrevocably altered* by the procedure.

14. It makes the program much easier to understand for both the programmer and any people who have to modify the program at a later stage. It adds to the self-documenting nature of structured programming.

Answers to exercise 7.1

1. (a)

1. (b)

1. (c)

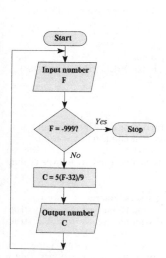

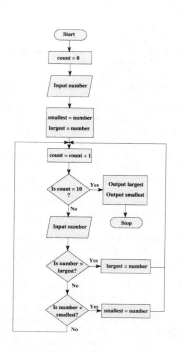

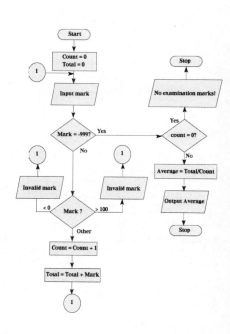

1. (d)

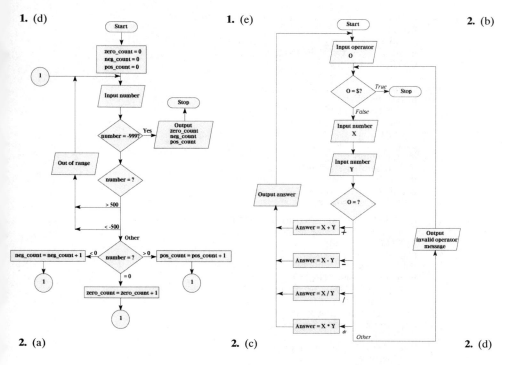

1. (e)

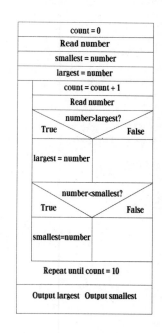

2. (b)

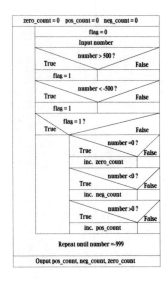

2. (a)

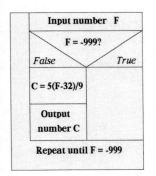

2. (c)

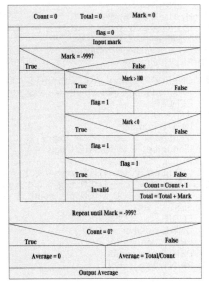

2. (d)

2. (e)

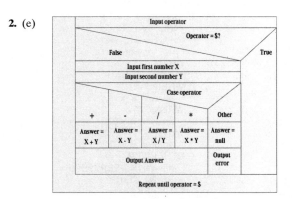

3. Pseudocode algorithms can easily be derived from the final code in question 4.

4. (a)
```
REPEAT                    NB All code in BBC BASIC V
INPUT f
c = 5*(f-32)/9
IF f<> – 999 THEN PRINT c
UNTIL f = –999
```

(b)
```
count = 1
INPUT number
smallest = number
largest = number
REPEAT
count = count + 1
INPUT number
IF number>largest THEN largest = number
IF number<smallest THEN smallest = number
UNTIL count = 10
PRINT largest,smallest
```

(c)
```
ON ERROR PRINT ERL,REPORT$:END
count = 0: Total = 0: mark = 0
REPEAT
flag = 0
INPUT mark
IF mark <> -999 THEN
  IF (mark > 100) OR (mark <0) THEN flag = 1
    IF flag = 0 THEN
      count = count + 1
      total = total + mark
    ELSE
      PRINT "Out of range"
    ENDIF
  ENDIF
UNTIL mark = -999
IF count = 0 THEN
  average = 0
ELSE average = total/count
PRINT average
```

(d)
```
ONERROR PRINT ERL, REPORT$ : END
zero_count =0: pos_count =0: neg_count =0
REPEAT
flag = 0
INPUT number
IF number > 500 THEN flag = 1
IF number < -500 THEN flag = 1
IF flag <> 1 THEN
  IF number = 0 THEN zero_count = zero_count +1
  IF number < 0 THEN neg_count = neg_count +1
  IF number > 0 THEN pos_count = pos_count +1
ELSE
ENDIF
UNTIL number = -999
PRINT pos_count
PRINT neg_count
PRINT zero_count
```

(e)
```
REPEAT
INPUT operator$
IF operator$ <> "$" THEN
  INPUT x
  INPUT y
  CASE operator$ OF
  WHEN "+"
   answer = x + y
  WHEN "-"
    answer = x – y
  WHEN "/"
    answer = x/y
  WHEN "*"
    answer = x * y
  OTHERWISE
    answer = –99999999
    PRINT "Error"
  ENDCASE
  PRINT answer
ELSE
ENDIF
UNTIL operator$ = "$"
```

5. Top down for splitting up the problems into sub-sections ready for coding, bottom up for testing each part before its use with the next stage in the hierarchy of the problem.
6. Objects can be built up independently, then used in a similar way to 'Lego bricks' to build up a larger module. Due to the nature of the objects, unforeseen unintentional interaction between the many different modules is unlikely if programmers obey all the appropriate rules.

Answers to exercise 7.2

1. JSP is particularly suited to structured programming because good structured code production is a natural consequence of following the JSP diagram.
2. Sequence, selection and iteration making use of JSP are shown in the following three diagrams.

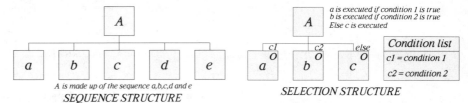

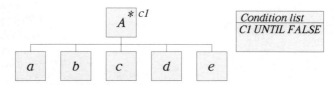

3. One possible JSP structure is shown in the following diagram

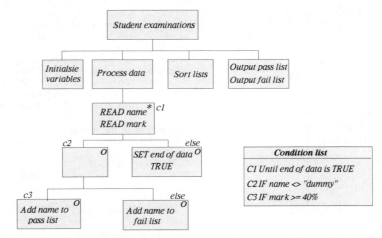

4. Relationships between elements of a system may be more easily emphasised.
5. The data-flow diagram for your teacher-marked assignments could be as follows.

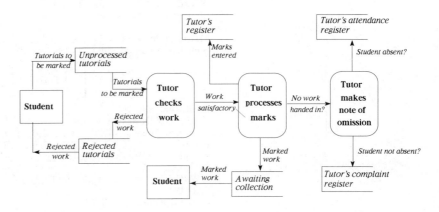

6. In general, problems where cycling through set sequences is necessary. Typical problems involve defining states of any electronic hardware, but more importantly, from a software-analysis point of view, different problems might include the **analysis of possible moves in a game**, **defining rules for computer languages** and expressing **control-system algorithms** (i.e. what can and can't be done when the system is in a particular state).

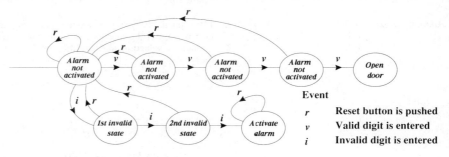

		r		
		Event		
	r	Reset button is pushed		
	v	Valid digit is entered		
	i	Invalid digit is entered		

7. Decision table for the delivery charges is as follows:

Conditions	1	2	3	4
Price >= £1,000	Y	N	Y	N
Delivery >100 miles	Y	Y	N	N
Actions				
Free delivery			X	
5% delivery charge	X			X
10% delivery charge		X		

8. A chart showing horizontal bars in which project activity is plotted against weeks, days or months etc. according to the overall schedule of the project. They give an instant visual indication as to the nature of the schedule, but aren't very versatile if situations change rapidly on a day-to-day basis.

9. Time-critical management problems involving 'latest start' and 'earliest finishing times' for whole or parts of projects. An example could be undertaking construction work on a building. Materials need to be delivered such as glass for the windows, tiles for the roof, bricks for the walls and paint for the decorations etc. All these resources have to be scheduled and a hold up in any one resource such as bricks for the walls will obviously delay the roof being started etc. The critical path through the project is the path which effectively dictates the completion time, any critical activity within this path may have extra resources allocated to it to cut completion time if this is thought to be important.

Chapter 8 FORTRAN 90 –
student activities (page 155)

(1) Calculation of the average
```
PROGRAM Average
REAL::x,total=0.0
INTEGER::number=0
WRITE(*,*) "Please type in positive numbers terminating with -999"
DO
  READ(*,*) x
  IF(number=-999) EXIT
total = total + x
number = number + 1
END DO
ave = total/number
WRITE(*,*) "The average is ,ave
END PROGRAM Average
```

(2) Matrix multiplication
Sum being carried out is   x   *   y   =   z

$$\begin{bmatrix} 1 & 2 & 3 \\ 4 & 5 & 6 \\ 7 & 8 & 9 \end{bmatrix} * \begin{bmatrix} 9 & 8 & 7 \\ 6 & 5 & 4 \\ 3 & 2 & 1 \end{bmatrix} = \begin{bmatrix} 30 & 24 & 18 \\ 84 & 69 & 54 \\ 138 & 114 & 90 \end{bmatrix}$$

```
PROGRAM MATRIX
REAL, DIMENSION(3,3)::x,y,z
x = RESHAPE( SOURCE = (/1,2,3,4,5,6,7,8,9/), SHAPE = (/3,3/)
y = RESHAPE( SOURCE = (/9,8,7,6,5,4,3,2,1/), SHAPE = (/3,3/)
z = MATMUL(MATRIX_x,MATRIX_y)
DO count = 1,3
  WRITE(*,*) z(1,count),(2,count),(3,count)
END DO
END PROGRAM MATRIX
```

Chapter 8 COBOL 85 –
student activities (page 160)

(1) VAT at 17.5%
```
IDENTIFICATION DIVISION.
PROGRAM-ID. VAT-CALCULATION
DATA DIVISION.
WORKING STORAGE SECTION.
77 PRICE              PIC 999V99.
77 INCLUSIVE-PRICE    PIC 9999V99.

PROCEDURE DIVISION.
VAT-CALCULATION.
ACCEPT PRICE.
MULTIPLY PRICE BY VAT GIVING INCLUSIVE-PRICE.
DISPLAY "Without VAT " PRICE "With VAT" INCLUSIVE-PRICE.
STOP RUN.
```

(2) Compound interest program.
The following program makes use of the standard compound interest formula as follows

Final capital = (Initial amount of money) x $((1 + \text{Interest Rate}))^{\text{Number of Years}}$

```
IDENTIFICATION DIVISION.
PROGRAM-ID. COMPOUND-INTEREST.
DATA DIVISION.
WORKING STORAGE SECTION.
77 INITIAL-AMOUNT     PIC 9999V99.
77 INTEREST-RATE      PIC 99V99.
77 NUMBER-OF-YEARS    PIC 99.
77 CAPITAL            PIC 99999.99.

PROCEDURE DIVISION.
COMPOUND-INTEREST-CALCULATION.
DISPLAY "Please type in the initial amount of money ".
ACCEPT INITIAL-AMOUNT.
DISPLAY "Please type in the rate of interest".
ACCEPT INTEREST-RATE.
DISPLAY "Please type in the number of years".
ACCEPT NUMBER-OF-YEARS.
COMPUTE CAPITAL = INITIAL-AMOUNT*(1 + INTEREST-RATE/100)**
                                        NUMBER-OF-YEARS.
DISPLAY "At the end of your term you will have" CAPITAL.
STOP RUN.
```

Chapter 8 Pascal – student activities
(page 160)

(1) Insertion sort
```
PROGRAM insert_sort(input,output);
VAR current_position, pointer_position, maximum, temp, count :INTEGER;
VAR n : ARRAY[0..20] of INTEGER;
BEGIN
  maximum :=20;
  FOR count :=1 TO maximum DO
    BEGIN
      WRITELN('Please type in number');
      READLN(n[count]);
    END;
  WRITELN('Original list is');
  FOR count :=1 TO maximum DO
    BEGIN
      WRITELN(n[count]);
    END;
  current_position :=1;
  REPEAT
    current_position := current_position + 1;
    pointer_position :=1;
    WHILE pointer_position <= current_position DO
      BEGIN
        IF n[pointer_position] > n[current_position] THEN
          BEGIN
            temp := n[current_position];
            FOR count:= current_position DOWNTO pointer_position + 1 DO
              BEGIN
                n[count] := n[count -1]
              END;
          END;
          pointer_position := pointer_position + 1
      END;
  UNTIL current_position = maximum;
```

```
                    WRITELN('Sorted list');
                    FOR count := 1 TO maximum DO
                      BEGIN
                        WRITELN(n[count])
                      END;
                  END.
```

(2) Factorials based on recursion

```
PROGRAM factorial(input,output);
VAR n, answer, actual_time, start_time, stop_time : INTEGER;

  FUNCTION factorial(n: INTEGER) : INTEGER;
    BEGIN
      IF n <=1 THEN
        BEGIN
          factorial :=1
        END
      ELSE
        BEGIN
          factorial := n*factorial(n-1)
        END
  END;

  BEGIN
    WRITELN('Please type in a number');
    READLN(n);
    start_time := time;
    answer := factorial(n);
    stop_time := time;
    actual_time := stop_time – start_time;
    WRITELN(answer);
    WRITELN('It took just', actual_time,'centiseconds');
  END.
```

Note: On fast computers the above routine might take less than 10 msec for the computer to evaluate the highest possible factorial before arithmetic overflow occurs.

Chapter 8 BASIC – student activities (page 162)

(1) The following makes use of BBC BASIC V on the Archimedes and RISC PC.

```
INPUT "Please type in a sentence using lower-case letters";sentence$
consonants = 0:vowels = 0:words = 1
FOR count = 1 TO LEN(sentence$)
  Flag = FALSE
  Letter$ = MID$(sentence$,count,1)
  CASE Letter$ OF
      WHEN "a","e","i","o","u" : vowels = vowels + 1:Flag = TRUE
  ENDCASE
  IF (Flag = FALSE) AND Letter$<>" " THEN consonants = consonants + 1
  IF Letter$ = " " THEN words = words + 1
NEXT count
PRINT "There are ";vowels;" vowels"
PRINT "There are ";consonants;" consonants"
PRINT "There are ";words;" words"
```

(2) The following makes use of BBC BASIC V on the Archimedes and RISC PC.

```
MODE 116:REM Very high resolution mode
GCOL 0,1
side = 80:x_offset =50:y_offset = 50
x = -1*(side + x_offset):y= -1*(side +y_offset)
FOR vertical_loop = 1 TO 17
  y = y + side + y_offset
  x = -1*(side + y_offset)
  FOR horizontal_loop = 1 TO 22
    x = x + side + x_offset
    RECTANGLE FILL x,y,side,side
  NEXT horizontal_loop
NEXT vertical_loop
```

Chapter 8 C++ – student activities (page 167)

(1) The following is written using Microsoft's C++ compiler.

```
//Square Root evaluation program making use of a library function
#include <iostream.h>
#include <math.h>
void main()
```

```
{
double number, root;
cout << "Please type in a number";
cin >> number;
root = sqrt(number);
cout >> "The square root of your number is"
        << root << endl;
}
```

(2) The following is written using Microsoft's C++ compiler.

```
//Generate a given number of specified characters on a single line
#include <iostream.h>
void repeatchar(char, int); //Declare function repeatchar

void main()
{
char inputchar:
int inputnum;

cout << "Please enter character to be repeated";
cin >> inputchar;
cout << "How many times to repeat?";
cin >> inputnum;
repeatchar(inputchar,inputnum);            //Call function repeatchar
}

void repeatchar(char chin, int numin); //Define function repeatchar
for(int x=0; x<numin; x++);
    cout << chin;
cout << endl;
}
```

Answers to exercise 8.1

1. Each language has particular strengths and weaknesses because it's not yet possible or efficient to design a language which copes with all requirements. Special languages such as COBOL are ideal for business-type data processing, FORTRAN for mathematical and scientific work, and C++ for application and systems development etc.
2. Historically FORTRAN has been taught on scientific and engineering degree courses – therefore a huge range of experience at this level has been built up. A massive library of pre-written functions exist – if any other language is used then this vast amount of effort would need to be re-coded.
3. True parallel processing means having the hardware to do more than one thing at the same time – usually by using multiple processors. Without appropriate hardware support concurrent algorithms would not run on some machines – until all machines with compilers can support parallel processing there would be an incompatibility problem and the code would not run on single-processor machines.
4. C++ naturally splits up programs into parts which are protected from influencing other parts – this is ideal for parallel processing operations.
5. BBC BASIC coin-tossing program

```
FOR toss = 1 TO 100
  coin_1 = RND(2)
  coin_2 = RND(2)
  IF coin_1 = 1 AND coin_2 = 1 THEN TT = TT + 1
  IF coin_1 = 1 AND coin_2 = 2 THEN TH = TH + 1
  IF coin_1 = 2 AND coin_2 = 1 THEN HT = HT + 1
  IF coin_1 = 2 AND coin_2 = 2 THEN HH = HH + 1
NEXT toss
Combined = TH + HT
PRINT "There were ";TT; "pairs of tails"
PRINT "There were ";Combined; "combined pairs"
PRINT "There were ";HH; "pairs of heads"
```

6. BBC BASIC V – very simple spelling checker. The ten dummy words are the numbers one to ten in lower case only. If you have time expand the ideas to deal with upper and lower case, and accept strings of text. Perhaps you can find a better checking method too!

```
REM Spell checker
DIM word$(10)
REM Read dictionary
FOR count = 1 TO 10
  READ word$(count)
NEXT count
DATA one,two,three,four,five,six,seven,eight,nine,ten
FOR count = 1 TO 10
```

```
   PRINT word$(count)
NEXT count
REM User input
INPUT "Word to be checked";check$
Flag = FALSE
FOR count = 1 TO 10
  IF check$ = word$(count) THEN Flag = TRUE
NEXT count
IF Flag = TRUE THEN PRINT "Correct" ELSE PRINT "Incorrect"
```

7. The following FORTRAN program has very rudimentary output – it can be considerably improved. You could also program the system to get a distance-time graph – have a go if you have the time and appropriate facilities on your computer system.

```
PROGRAM Missile
REAL::U,time,S
U = 3
t = 0
WRITE(*.*) "Time       Distance"
Loop: DO WHILE S>0
          time = time + 0.1
          S = U*time – (1*9.81/2)*time**2+10
          WRITE(*,*) time, S
       END DO Loop
END PROGRAM Missile
```

8   Pascal Fibbonacci numbers

```
PROGRAM Fibbonacci(input,output);
VAR sum, number, next, current, count :INTEGER;
BEGIN
  number:= 0;
  next:= 1;
  sum := 0;
  FOR count :=1 TO 25 DO
    BEGIN
      WRITELN(number);
      sum := sum + number;
      current := number + next;
      number := next;
      next := current;
    END;
END.
```

9.   Pascal date conversion – only a simple layout and simple validation techniques have been used.

```
PROGRAM Date_conversion(input,output);
VAR day, month, year : INTEGER;
BEGIN
  WRITELN('Please type in the date in the form dd, mm, yyyy');
  READLN(day,month,year);
  IF (day < 0) OR (day > 31) THEN WRITELN('Invalid date')
    ELSE WRITE(day,' ');
  IF (month <0) OR (month > 12) THEN WRITELN('Invalid date');
  CASE month OF
      1: WRITE('January');
      2: WRITE('February');
      3: WRITE('March');
      4: WRITE('April');
      5: WRITE('May');
      6: WRITE('June');
      7: WRITE('July');
      8: WRITE('August');
      9: WRITE('September');
     10: WRITE('October');
     11: WRITE('November');
     12: WRITE('December');
  END;
  IF (year < 0) THEN WRITELN('Invalid date')
    ELSE WRITE(year);
END.
```

10.   This question is dependent on the chosen language.

Answers to exercise 9.1

1. Using BBC BASIC V

```
REM Estimation of root 5
N = 5
xn=2
WHILE ABS((xn*xn)-5)>0.000005
  xn=0.5*(xn + 5/xn)
  PRINT xn
ENDWHILE
PRINT xn
```

2. From the following diagram you can see that

$$\frac{\pi r^2}{2r \times 2r} = \frac{Number\ of\ points\ within\ circle}{Total\ number\ of\ points}$$

Therefore, $p = 4 \times$ Number of points within circle/Total number of points. BBC BASIC V program to evaluate Pi is as follows.

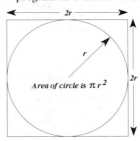

Area of circle is πr^2

```
REM Generate approximation for PI
REM assume square with a side of 1
INPUT"How many random numbers";number
FOR count = 1 TO number
  x=RND(1):y=RND(1)
  IF SQR(x^2+y^2)<1 THEN hit = hit + 1
NEXT count
pi=4*hit/number
PRINT pi
```

3. Iteration is a simple idea, but recursion usually leads to elegant and more efficient solutions. Recursion may place heavy demands on storage as each call to a recursive procedure usually involves placing data on a stack.

4. BBC BASIC V implementation or recursive function.

```
REM Count down from integer n
INPUT "Please type in an integer";n
PRINT "All integers preceding this number"
PROCcountdown(n)
END
DEF PROCcountdown(n)
  IF n > 0 THEN
    PRINT n;
    PROCcountdown(n-1)
  ENDIF
ENDPROC
```

5. BBC BASIC V implementation of recursive function.

```
REM Summing all positive integers <= n
INPUT "Please type in an integer";n
PRINT "The sum of all positive integers up to and including this number is";
PROCsum(n)
PRINT sum
END
DEF PROCsum(n)
  IF n > 0 THEN
    sum = sum + n
    PROCsum(n-1)
  ENDIF
ENDPROC
```

6. BBC BASIC V implementation of recursive algorithm.

```
REM Recursive reverse string
INPUT "Please type in a string";test$
PROCreverse(test$)
END
DEF PROCreverse(test$)
  IF LEN(test$) > 0 THEN
    PRINT RIGHT$(test$);
    PROCreverse(LEFT$(test$))
  ENDIF
ENDPROC
```

7. BBC BASIC V implementation of chip-shop simulation.

```
PROCinitialise
FOR minute = 1 TO 120
 PROCinitialise
 PROCcust_arrive
 PROCcust_serve
 PROCanalyse
NEXT minute
END
DEF PROCinitialise
  customers = 0
ENDPROC
DEF PROCcust_arrive
  Arrive = RND(1)
  IF Arrive < 0.2 THEN new_customers = 0
  IF (Arrive >= 0.20) AND (Arrive < 0.45) THEN new_customers = 1
  IF (Arrive >= 0.45) AND (Arrive < 0.70) THEN new_customers = 2
  IF (Arrive >= 0.70) AND (Arrive < 0.85) THEN new_customers = 3
  IF (Arrive >= 0.85) AND (Arrive < 0.95) THEN new_customers = 4
  IF Arrive >=0.95 THEN new_customers = 5
ENDPROC
DEF PROCcust_serve
  Serve = RND(1)
  IF Serve < 0.35 THEN customers_served  = 1
  IF (Serve >= 0.35) AND (Serve < 0.60) THEN customers_served = 2
  IF (Serve >= 0.60) AND (Serve < 0.80) THEN customers_served = 3
  IF (Serve >= 0.80) AND (Serve < 0.95) THEN customers_served = 4
  IF Serve > 0.95 THEN customers = 5
ENDPROC
DEF PROCanalyse
  customers = customers + new_customers
  PRINT "In minute number ";minute;"   ";new_customers;" have arrived"
  IF customers-customers_served > 0 THEN customers = customers – customers_served
  PRINT "At the end of minute number ";minute;" There are "; customers;
" waiting"
ENDPROC
```

After running the above analysis several times, it is very rare indeed to get 6 or more customers waiting. Therefore, Barry Ramsden does appear to have enough staff.

8. Different mathematical relationships with long sequences can be used to generate pseudo-random numbers. There is no known algorithmic method to generate truly random numbers. See page 195.

Answers to exercise 10.1

1. (a) To change the code into machine-code form that will run on the target machine.
    (b) Compilers, interpreters and assemblers.
    (c) **Compiler** – translation of high-level language into machine code with all code being processed at the same time.
        Interpreter – translation into machine code just one line at a time – run in an interactive environment.
        Assembler – changing assembly-language mnemonics into machine code.

2. (a) **Lexical analysis** – split up the source code into smaller chunks with individual meaning such as PRINT, for example.
    (b) **Syntax analysis** – determine whether the string of input code forms valid 'sentences' etc.
    (c) **Code generation** – necessary for generating the final code on the target machine.

3. **Object program** – the final code suitable for execution.
    Source program – the program ready to be input to the translation process (usually a text editor).
    Tokens – a representation of part of the source code which has some individual meaning.
    Parsing – the syntax analysis phase of the translation process.
    Dictionary – a list kept by the compiler of variables in the program.
    Terminal symbols – the final characters that must make up the source code like '1' or 'A' etc.
    Optimisation – carrying out further processing on the code so that it is more efficient in terms of speed of execution or size etc.

4. (a) Identifier (using Pascal).

    <identifier> ::= <letter> | <combination>
    <combination> ::= <letters><digits> | <digits><letters> | <combination>
                                                                <letters>

    <letters> ::= <letter> | <letter> <letters>
    <digits> ::= <digit> | <digit> <digits>
    <letter> :: = A|B|C|D|E|F|G|H|I|J|K|L|M|N|O|P|Q|R|S|T|U|V|W|X|Y|Z
    <digit> ::= 0|1|2|3|4|5|6|7|8|9

(b) String (using BASIC)

<string> ::= "" | " <any character except ">"

(c) Unsigned real number (using Pascal).

<unsigned real> ::= <decimal number> | <decimal number> <exponent>
| <digits> <exponent>

<exponent> ::= E <digits> | E <sign> <digits>
<decimal number> ::= <digits> . <digits>
<digits> ::= <digit> | <digit> <digits>
<sign> ::= + | –
<digit> ::= 0|1|2|3|4|5|6|7|8|9

5.

Using Pascal:

Identifier

String

Unsigned real number

6.

<directory entry>	::=	<surname><title><initials>,<number><street><street/town><town><telephone no.>
		|<surname> <title> <initials> , <street> <street/town> <town> <telephone no.>
		|<surname> <initials>, <number> <street> <street/town> <town> <telephone no.>
		|<surname> <initials>, <street> <street/town> <town> <telephone no. >
<surname>	::=	<letters>	
<title>	::=	<DR.> | <REV.>	1
<initials>	::=	<group>	2
<group>	::=	<letter> | <letter>,<group>	3
<street>	::=	<letters> l <part>,<street>	4
<part>	::=	<letters><space>	5
<space>	::=	< >	6
<town>	::=	<letters>	7
<letters>	::=	<letter> l <letters><letter>	8
<telephone no.>	::=	<number>	9
<number>	::=	<digit>|<digit><number>	10
<letter>	::=	A|B|C|D|E|F|G|H|I|J|K|L|M|N|O|P|Q|R|S|T|U|V|W|X|Y|Z	11
<digit>	::=	0|1|2|3|4|5|6|7|8|9	12
<street/town>	::=	.|.<street/town> (Separates street from town)	13

(a) Note: position is vitally important (or town and surname definitions could easily be confused).

Note also that some of the very obvious sub-stages such as a group of single letters becoming a group of multiple letters has not been shown.

Brown	Y.,	271	Kingsway	....	Exeter	736442
<letters>	Y.,	271	Kingsway	....	Exeter	736442
<surname>	Y.,	271	Kingsway	....	Exeter	736442
<surname>	<letter> .,	271	Kingsway	....	Exeter	736442
<surname>	<group>,	271	Kingsway	....	Exeter	736442
<surname>	<initials>	271	Kingsway	....	Exeter	736442
<surname>	<initials>	<number>	Kingsway	....	Exeter	736442
<surname>	<initials>	<number>	<letters>	....	Exeter	736442
<surname>	<initials>	<number>	<street>	....	Exeter	736442
<surname>	<initials>	<number>	<street>	<town/street>	Exeter	736442
<surname>	<initials>	<number>	<street>	<town/street>	<letters>	736442
<surname>	<initials>	<number>	<street>	<town/street>	<town>	736442
<surname>	<initials>	<number>	<street>	<town/street>	<town>	<number>
<surname>	<initials>	<number>	<street>	<town/street>	<town>	<telephone no.>
			<directory entry>			

(b) Zoe   P.J.,   274   ....   Bognor 817325
     \<letters\>   P.J.,   274   ....   Bognor 817325
     \<surname\>   P.J.,   274   ....   Bognor 817325
     \<surname\>   \<letter\>.\<letter\>.,   274   ....   Bognor 817325
     \<surname\>   \<group\>,   274   ....   Bognor 817325
     \<surname\>   \<initials\>   274   ....   Bognor 817325
     \<surname\>   \<initials\>   \<number\>   ....   Bognor 817325
     \<surname\>   \<initials\>   \<number\>   \<street/town\>   Bognor 817325

Answers to exercise 10.2

1. (a) P Q * R S – T * + .(b) M N + O P – * .   (c) A B C D / x + .
       (d) x y z / + u v – /

2. (a) (A + B) × C. b) X – (Y / Z × S) + T. (c) (x + y) * (r – s) * x / t
       (d) A + B – 3 * (F – G) / H – K * (F – G)

3. (a)   9   placed on stack   9
             3   placed on stack 3 9
             –   sign encountered   6   (9 – 3)
             2   placed on stack 2 6
             /   sign encountered   2   Answer = 20

       (b)   12   placed on stack   12
             9   placed on stack 9 12
             –   sign encountered   3   (12 – 9)
             16   placed on stack 16 3
             20   placed on stack 20 16 3
             –   sign encountered   ....   –4 3   (16 – 20)
             *   sign encountered   ....   –12   (3 * –4) Answer = –12

       (c)   11   placed on stack   11
             3   placed on stack 3 11
             2   placed on stack 2 3 11
             ↑   sign encountered   ....   9 11   (3 ↑ 2)
             +   sign encountered   20   (9 + 11)
             7   placed on stack 7 20
             6   placed on stack 6 7 20
             3   placed on stack 3 6 7 20
             /   sign encountered 2 7 20   (6/3)
             –   sign encountered   ....   5 20   (7 – 2)
             /   sign encountered   4   (20/4)

Answers to exercise 11.1

1. (a) Standard method is to use a **mark-sense reader** and appropriate source documents (see page 224).
       (b) CAD – Any GUI-friendly device such as a **mouse**, **trackball** or **light pen**. However, a **puck** in combination with a **graphics tablet** is probably *the* most versatile, especially when part of the tablet is set up as a **concept keyboard**. (See pages 221, 220 and 223.)
       (c) The **data glove** is probably the most common but part or **whole body suits** are being developed which can monitor movements of any part of the body, and place the body with respect to some co-ordinate system operating within the computer (see pages 236 and 258).
       (d) **Bar codes**, **LASER scanners**, **magnetic stripe cards** and **smart cards** all have a part to play in using computer-input peripherals for control of **Electronic Funds Transfer at the Point Of Sale**. Some new radio-tag systems can now tot up the contents of the trolley without removing the goods!
       (e) A **flat-bed scanner** can scan text and pictures into the computer as a **bit-mapped image**. Special software can then analyse the textual parts of the scanned image and turn it into ASCII text, bit-mapped or true-type fonts ready for production of CDs.
       (f) **Flat-bed scanners** or **high-quality video digitisers** are *both* capable of producing the required image quality, with expensive flat-bed scanners being the highest quality possible.
       (g) Any **MIDI-based keyboard** together with an appropriate **MIDI interface** and **suitable software** would be able to capture data played by the musician in real time and output the music in an appropriate form. For example, the Sibelius software for the Arc, Mac and the range of PCs.

2. Due to the increased awareness regarding **RSI**, **ergonomic keyboards** are becoming more popular.

3. **Turnaround documents** such as those used for *electricity-meter reading*, for example, can be used to input the readings either as a mark in a box or neatly-written characters which can be recognised by the computer.

4. A concept keyboard could be configured to respond to picture overlays placed on top of the keyboard – when a child pushes one of the pictures the computer can be made to respond in an appropriate way.

5. Electronic Funds Transfer at the Point Of Sale – 'cash' transactions are carried out electronically. Advantages are shops do not keep so much money that can be stolen, fraud is less likely, it's often quicker and more convenient for the customer etc.

6. (a) Different types of keyboards to be considered in your explanation are ergonomic,

Maltron and other different layouts, different language keyboards and concept keyboards.

(b) Mouse and trackball input devices have made GUIs much easier. Alternative 'use of the cursor keys' is less satisfactory. Ease of use for graphics-based input, art packages, menu selection, more intuitive interface, less command-driven input and hence computers easier to use etc.

(c) Pressure-sensitive graphics-tablet based input is an alternative for getting hand-sketched material into the computer system. Artists find the medium reasonably intuitive, good accuracy to less than 0.1 mm is possible, handwriting input handled, strokes of stylus (pen) combined with extra buttons make for a large set of alternatives such as deletion, colour, change of thickness etc.

(d) Video card together with a single video recorder and powerful computer can now replace an entire edit suite. Video processing possibilities only limited by software and can thus be upgraded without change of hardware. Non-linear editing possible, no degradation on multiple edits etc.

(e) Need multiple sensors capable of detection of chemicals in the wine which give it its characteristic taste. (See chapter 25 for interfacing these devices.) Algorithms to relate good and bad wines to chemical content necessary to analyse results.

7. Terminal emulation software turns a micro into a terminal which is linked to a mainframe. Although micro facilities are powerful, this software allows users to share information which is held on the mainframe or to get access to information stored on the mainframe.

8. **For** – most people can speak faster than they can type, easier form of input, more natural form of input, ideal input medium for some disabled people, ideal input if hands are occupied with other tasks at the time (e.g. both hands might be fully occupied with a computer-control system).

Against – noisy in an office environment (imagine 20 people shouting at their computers!), many different words sound the same, people might have a cold, thousands of people are already trained to type, some operations would be incredibly tedious with voice-only input – imagine telling a word processor to put text into underlined-and-centered-bold-italic Times in 22.5pt! Pointing and clicking would be far easier.

9. PDAs, such as Apple's Newton, for example, make use of pen-based input and are thus ideal pocket-sized communication and data processing centres. Note pads, diaries, simple databases, simple spreadsheets and word processors all fit neatly into this category, along with specialised software for business personnel. Fax, video communication links and computer communications will connect this device to the information super highways of the future. PDAs of tomorrow will be doing what micros are doing today.

10. Smart cards and smart keys (see page 604) are least susceptible to tampering and are thus more secure. They are also more versatile and robust. Smart keys can hold sophisticated programs giving access to a wide range of different areas. PIN numbers, finger print, voice print or retina scans could add to security.

11. Office PCs tend to be low-volume data, often entered by hand directly into an application. Mainframes tend to be large-volume data entry, often carried out in batch processing mode (see page 371). Office PCs tend to be stand-alone or networked, mainframe input tends to be via terminals, micros acting as terminals or via a network.

12. A bit-mapped image stores the image as many tiny pixels associated with a co-ordinate position on the page. Each pixel has an associated colour. When viewed at normal size an illusion of a picture is created. To get text into a form understood by a computer complex algorithms have to be applied to the probable text outlines and correlation with previous images representing the patterns of the text is undertaken. If the correlation is high the text is assumed to be of a particular character and font.

13. Sensors are available and others can be developed which convert limited movement into an electrical signal which can be interpreted by a computer system. Such input techniques are discussed in chapter 25. Appropriate software displaying menus can activate choices based on what's happening to a pointer on the screen, what noises are being made, or what buttons may have been pressed on a special input unit.

Answers to exercise 12.1

1. Computer monitors – high quality, high-resolution, non-interlaced. Domestic TVs, 'low' quality, less resolution, usually interlaced raster scan. Monitors are also low radiation, multisync touch screen etc.

2. A system which uses 1 byte per RGB colour thus having 3 bytes or 24 bits giving 16,777,216 colours.

3. Each memory location in video RAM contains bits which are used to describe the grey scale or colour of a pixel on the screen. Each memory location is mapped to a physical position on the screen (see page 224).

4. CRT – very high quality, bright, high resolution, uses much energy. LCD, usually small, not so bright, less resolution, uses far less energy. CRT mainly for desktops – LCD mainly for portables.

5. Touch-screen useful for pointing finger at screen when making a choice from a menu. More user friendly and ideal for shopping malls and the like – a mouse would probably get stolen!

6. Typewriter – slow, manual operation only – dot matrix printers together with WP replace typewriter, able to do graphics. Laser printers able to do high quality work, colour now possible etc.

7. A bit-mapped font uses a map of pixels to generate the shape, outline fonts use maths definitions.

8. They are extremely fast for high-volume output.

9. See colour model on page 254. Cyan, Magenta, Yellow and Black toners are combined to produce a range of colours which can be used to produce 24-bit or 32-bit (+ 8 for the black) images.

10. A5 paper size is 8.27 in by 5.23 in. At 300dpi this gives $300 \times 300 \times 8.27 \times 5.23 = 3,892,689$ dots. Monochrome image would take $3,892,689/8 = 486,586$ bytes. Coloured image $= 3 \times 486,586 = 1,459,758$ bytes. The black image (assuming the CMYK model is used) will need another 486,586. Therefore just over 2 Mbytes would be needed.

11. Skilled typesetters have been replaced by DTP operators. More scope for small publishing companies. Very much more scope for individuals with computers to publish documentation.

12. For up to A3 size probably. Larger than this probably not, due to the enormous expense of the laser printer. Architects often use A2 and A1 sizes or larger, plotters go considerably larger than this, and can be the size of a small room.

13. Still popular in libraries and garages etc. as they save vast amounts of space on information storage and are also very cheap.

14. (a) Plotter (b) Linotronic (c) Laser or bubble jet (d) Laser or bubble jet
    (e) Thermal or dot matrix.

15. Can save memory by specifying white space in alternative ways. Can make use of lower-bandwidth networks, save money on phone or satellite bills if information can be sent in less time.

16. (a) Voice output. (b) Braille output – can be used with suitable interface.

Answers to exercise 13.1

1. Cheap, fast and plenty of it!

2. A **pigeon-hole** concept is used as a description of primary storage where each *unique* physical memory location has an **associated address**. The **word length** determines the number of bytes held in each location, and the data bus is usually of sufficient width to make sure that the contents of a single memory location may be transferred in one go. The width of the address bus determines the memory capacity. (See page 264.)

3. The program currently under execution is held in primary storage. The fetch times for each instruction have a significant effect on the execution speed of a program. Cache memory can be used if necessary.

4. RAM – Random Access Memory, used for primary storage (see page 263). ROM – Read Only Memory used for Operating Systems and other programs which don't change (see page 390). Embedded systems (see page 582) would probably be ROM only. Few, if any systems these days are RAM only, as manual code would have to be typed in to boot the system (see page 582).

5. **Volatile** means that the contents of the memory will be lost if the power is removed. Use an Uninterruptible Power Supply (UPS) if important data might be lost (see page 265).

6. **SRAM** – Static Random Access Memory. Common use is for cache memory as it's faster than DRAM.

7. A memory map maps out important parts of RAM and ROM used for specific purposes. Without it important areas of memory could be inadvertently overwritten for other purposes.

8. **EPROM** – Erasable Programmable Read Only Memory. Used for experimentational software development, ideal for small batch production and testing of operating-system ROMs before being committed to blowing a real ROM. Ideal for development of embedded systems. (See page 582.)

9. **ASCII** – The American Standard Code for Information Interchange. A code developed to allow different computers to share information by recognition of a common code. Compare with EBCDIC, and extended ASCII. (See pages 278 and 266.)

10. **Backing store** such as **tapes**, **magnetic disks** and **optical discs** etc.

11. **Direct** and **sequential** access modes of operation.

12. Your answer should address the problems of physical disk sizes, different disk formats, different operating systems and different data storage mechanisms used by different applications.

13. Floppies have less expensive and simpler mechanisms and are open to the atmosphere, therefore the track density is far less than for a Winchester, for example, which is housed in a hermetically-sealed unit free from dust, smoke and other debris.

14. Number of surfaces, track density, sectors/track and bytes/sector. Bus parameters (e.g. width and speed) and interface electronics limit the computer's ability to extract data from the disk at the maximum rate. Also the disk's physical parameters such as seek time and read/write access time plus the speed of rotation etc.

15. CD-ROM discs are very cheap, made even cheaper by the popularity of compact-disc audio systems. A large amount of data can be stored on each disc, therefore ideal for the distribution of software. Users can try before they buy (see page 268).

16. Speed of access is the biggest problem, and writable CD-ROM systems are currently expensive (but getting cheaper). Data storage capacity is also going to be a problem at some time in the future. Multiple spin speed drives (e.g. quadraspin) are beginning to overcome the data-transfer speed problem, and blue lasers will eventually quadruple the storage capacity. Compression is currently used to pack in more data.

17. As usual in the computer world different manufacturers develop different systems inde-

pendently. The problems with CD-ROM drives are quite bad because they are also used for home entertainment and other systems – and all these need to be compatible if multi-media systems are to take off.

18. Disks may be quite fast, but compared to CPU speeds they are painfully slow. Therefore, an area of memory acting as a buffer significantly decreases data access times if the appropriate parts of the disk are stored in the cache memory.

19. Tapes are still the cheapest storage medium in terms of cost/byte. Vast quantities of data are currently stored on tape, and the medium is ideal for batch processing.

20. The **physical records** stored on the secondary storage media are such that the *most efficient transfer size* to the *physical media* is set up. The **logical record** used within an application or a program etc. will not usually relate to the size of the physical records. Therefore, a buffering system is used to translate the physical access requirements to the logical (application or program's) requirements.

21. Tapes on micros are generally used for backup purposes. Tapes on mainframes are usually used for batch-processing and sequential file handling operations (see page 340).

Answers to exercise 14.1

1. (a) A one-dimensional array – there is usally no regard to the order of the data.
   (b) A system in which the end of the list is automatically linked to the beginning of the list by pointers.
   (c) Stack – a list set up and accessed by pointers such that there is a 'top' and a 'bottom' – LIFO Last In First Out – FIFO First In Last Out. Stack pointers are used to identify the position of data within the stack.
   (d) Queue – a FIFO stack.
   (e) Array – ordered set of data elements accessed either row-by-row or column-by-column. Any number of dimensions is possible.

2. (a) (i) A list in which each node is linked to another by means of a pointer system.
   (ii) A data element which indicates the position of another data element, e.g. alphabetical pointer or exam-order pointer etc.
   (iii) Backwards and forwards pointer systems set up to enable navigation of the list in either direction.
   (b) See page 299.

3. A hierarchical data structure based on the idea of a family tree – most data can be expressed in the form of a tree structure.
   (a) A sub-ordinate part of the tree consisting of parents and children.
   (b) A specific data item which may also contain one or more pointers.
   (c) **Terminal node** – most sub-ordinate node in the tree structure. **Child node** – one which has a parent node. **Parent node** – one which has one or more children nodes. **Sister node** – one in which other nodes have the same parent. **Root node** – the node at the top of the tree structure.
   (d) Virtually anything can be expressed in this way, but typical examples include *parts for a component* or *pupils in a school*.

4. Parent can have a maximum of only two children. Alphabetical names (see page 307).

5. Preorder .... a, b, d, h, i, e, j, k, c, f, l, m, g, n, o.
   Inorder .... h, d, i, b, j, e, k, a, l, f, m, c, n, g, o.
   Postorder .... h, i, d, j, k, e, b, l, m, f, n, o, g, c, a.

6. Tree is hierarchical, network is complex. See page 311.

7. (a) See page 312. (b) See page 313.

8. Hierarchical structure making use of pointers (forward, or forward and backward if you need to make sure that you can go up as well as down in the directory).

Answers to exercise 15.1

1. (a) To make processing more efficient e.g. external merge sort. See page 350.
   (b) See page 318. (c) See page 319.

2. See pages 318, 32, 324.

3. See page 330.

4. 7, 3, 9, 1. (7 and 3 compared and swapped).
   3, 7, 9, 1. (7 and 9 compared no swap).
   3, 7, 9, 1. (9 and 1 compared and swapped).
   3, 7, 1, 9. (swaps were necessary, start again).
   3, 7, 1, 9. (3 and 7 compared no swap).
   3, 7, 1, 9. (7 and 1 compared and swapped).
   3, 1, 7, 9. (7 and 9 compared no swap).
   3, 1, 7, 9. (swap necessary, start again).

   3, 1, 7, 9. (3 and 1 compared and swapped).
   1, 3, 7, 9. (3 and 7 compared no swap).
   1, 3, 7, 9. (7 and 9 compared no swap).
   1, 3, 7, 9. (swap necessary, start again).

   1, 3, 7, 9. (1 and 3 compared no swap).
   1, 3, 7, 9. (3 and 7 compared no swap).
   1, 3, 7, 9. (7 and 9 compared no swap).
   1, 3, 7, 9. (no swaps necessary. List is in order).

5. Data that covers the entire range and multiple values.

6. Split files up into smaller parts. Sort the smaller parts and store on disk. Then do merge sort. See page 350.

1. (a) See following tree:

									1000
1st search								500		500
2nd search						250		250		
3rd search					125		125			
4th search				63		62				
5th search			31		32					
6th search		15		16						
7th search	7		8	Note: Only one part of the subtree shown.						
8th search	3	4								
9th search 1	2		Worst case is when data is at a terminal node.							
Final search. 1	1									

2. See page 334.

1. (a) The smallest possible element of a file.
  (b) The smallest self-contained subsection of a record.
  (c) A set of fields treated as a single unit of a file, e.g. information on one particular customer.
  (d) A set of related information, split up into records and fields.
2. (a) Organised with no attention to order of records.
  (b) Organised with regard to some pre-determined order, e.g. alphabetical.
  (c) A record may be accessed without going through all previous records.
  (d) One or more indexes added to a sequentially-organised file.
3. (a) Creation of the appropriate structure in memory or on a secondary storage device.
  (b) Altering records in the file structure, but can also cover addition and deletion of records.
  (c) Combining two files into one, usually in some pre-determined order.
  (d) A special marker which is used to denote the end of a computer file.
4. A number used to point to a specific record within a file in memory or on disk etc.
5. A field by which the record is usually identified, e.g. customer account number.
6. (a) A system of pointers establishing links which enable parts of the file to be accessed quickly.
  (b) An area in memory or on disk used to enable new data to be inserted into an indexed sequential file without completely rewriting the file, i.e. a useful method of updating.
  (c) A set of pointers which enables special paths to be followed through the file data structure.
7. A new master file is produced from a sequentially-arranged old master file and a sequentially arranged transaction file (see page 351).
8. An address is generated from some key item of data by applying a suitable algorithm (see page 312).
9. (a) A copy of a file for purposes of data security in the event of an accident or disaster.
  (b) A file which is accessed by means of a suitable hashing algorithm.
  (c) A file structure based on a hierarchical structure such as a binary tree, for example (see page 305).
  (d) A file containing temporary data which can be erased after use.
10. A logical record is based on a suitable data structure whereas a physical record is based on a unit of physical storage used on devices such as disk or tape, for example. It's often the case that several logical records fit into a single physical record, and this number represents what's called the blocking factor.
11. Making sure that files are kept up to date, that backup copies are made and general house-keeping etc.
12. Buffers allow for the transfer of larger chunks of data from the secondary storage medium than would normally be the case. Thus processing of the records kept in the buffer is very quick.
13. Pascal code is as follows. **(For simplicity temporary files (i.e. not saved to disk) have been used.)**

```
PROGRAM createfiles(input,output,integer,positive,negative);
VAR integer,positive,negative : FILE OF real;
    item : real;
    count,total : 1..maxint;
(*CREATE FILE OF INTEGERS*)
BEGIN
  write('How many integers will be entered? ');
  readln(total);
  rewrite(integer);                        (*Creates integer file*)
  FOR count := 1 TO total DO
    BEGIN
      readln(item);
      integer^ := item;
      put(integer);
    END;
(*READ FILE OF INTEGERS and CREATE positive and negative files*)
  reset(integer);                          (*Reset pointer to beginning*)
  rewrite(positive);                       (*Creates positive file*)
  rewrite(negative);
```

```
        WHILE NOT EOF(integer) DO
          BEGIN
            read(integer, item);                    (*Creates negative file*)
            IF item > 0 THEN
            BEGIN
              positive^ := item;
              put(positive);                        (*Puts positive numbers in pos. file*)
            END
            ELSE
            BEGIN
              negative^ := item;
              put(negative);                        (*Puts negative numbers in neg. file*)
            END
          END;
      (*READ and print out positive and negative*)
        writeln('Here are the positive numbers in the integer file');
        writeln;
        reset(positive);
        WHILE NOT EOF(positive) DO
          BEGIN
            item := positive^;
            write(item);
            get(positive);
          END;
        writeln('Here are the negative numbers in the integer file');
        writeln;
        reset(negative);
        WHILE NOT EOF(negative) DO
          BEGIN
            item := negative^;
            write(item);
            get(negative);
          END;
    END.
```

14. The algorithm required is described in detail on page 350 – it is the same algorithm that reads the sorted master and transaction files to produce a new master file, although the file names will obviously change.

15. Pascal code is as follows. **(For simplicity, temporary files (i.e. not saved to disk) have been used.)**

```
    PROGRAM Hamburgers(input,output,data);
    VAR data : FILE OF integer;
        code, quantity, Hamburger, Cheese_burger, Egg_burger : integer;
        count,total : 1..maxint;
    (* CREATE the code and quantity file*)
    BEGIN
      write('How many values will be entered? ');
      readln(total);
      rewrite(data);
      FOR count := 1 TO total DO
        BEGIN
          write('Please type in code followed by quantity ');
          readln(code,quantity);
          data^ := code;
          put(data);
          data^ := quantity;
          put(data);
        END;
      Hamburger := 0;
      Cheese_burger := 0;
      Egg_burger := 0;
      reset(data);
      WHILE NOT EOF(data) DO
        BEGIN
          read(data,code);
          read(data,quantity);
          CASE code OF
            1 : Hamburger := Hamburger + quantity;
            2 : Cheese_burger := Cheese_burger + quantity;
            3 : Egg_burger := Egg_burger + quantity;
          END;
        END;
      writeln('Hamburgers ', Hamburger);
      writeln('Cheese Burgers ', Cheese_burger);
      writeln('Egg Burgers ', Egg_burger);
    END.
```

16. Pascal code is as follows. **(For simplicity temporary files (i.e. not saved to disk) have been used.)**

```
PROGRAM checkfiles(input,output,fileA,fileB);
VAR fileA,fileB : TEXT;                        (*Special text file in Pascal*)
    word, wordA, wordB : char;
    count, total : 1..maxint;
    flag : boolean;
BEGIN
(*Create first simple text file*);
write('How many words? ');
  readln(total);
  rewrite(fileA);
  FOR count := 1 TO total DO
    BEGIN
      readln(word);
      writeln(fileA,word);                     (*Write word to text fileA*)
    END;
(*Create second identical text file*);
  write('type in the data again');
  writeln;
  rewrite(fileB);
  FOR count := 1 TO total DO
    BEGIN
      readln(word);
      writeln(fileB,word);                     (*Write word to text fileB*)
    END;
(*Compare both files and flag if in error*);
  RESET(fileA);
  RESET(fileB);
  count := 0;
  flag := FALSE;
  WHILE NOT EOF(fileA) OR NOT EOF(fileB) DO
    BEGIN
      readln(fileA,wordA);                     (*Read word from fileA*)
      readln(fileB,wordB);                     (*Read word from fileB*)
      count := count + 1;
      IF wordA <> wordB THEN
      BEGIN
        writeln('Entry ',count,' is not the same');
        flag := TRUE;
      END;
    END;
    IF flag = FALSE THEN writeln('Both files are identical');
END.
```

Answers to exercise 17.1

1. Without an OS the computer would be far too complex and tedious to use. Most of the fundamental things we take for granted are carried out by the OS.
2. MVS, Unix and Ultrix.
3. See onion diagrams on pages 370 and 389.
4. The OS simulates the interface with the user, and thus the picture that the end-users see is not that of hardware, but of the virtual world produced by the OS.
5. Usually by information entered at a terminal in terms of sequences of job-control commands or other commands to perform specific actions such as terminating a series of events etc (see page 372).
6. A batch of jobs is automatically run one after the other during the same session.
7. On a micro, both terms mean the same thing! However, on a mini and mainframe, multi-programming means two or more different programs running at the same time, but multi-tasking means two or more users making use of the same program at the same time, e.g. 10 users may be using the same COBOL compiler.
8. Look at the scheduling diagram on page 379, but think of your own specific example.
9. Interrupts are constantly being executed so that the processor can move between one task and another that requires attention. More important tasks have higher-priority interrupts, peripherals operate extensively using interrupts.
10. Hardware interrupts – e.g. key pressed on keyboard or disk drive not ready etc. Software interrupts – program suspends operation and causes another routine to be run – program times out etc.
11. Important events may be missed if lower-priority things get done instead.
12. Fixed – far less complicated, but less versatile. Variable – more efficient but extremely complex to run. Both systems have many advantages and disadvantages. (See pages 380 and 381.)
13. Virtual memory makes use of disk space as an effective extension of semiconductor RAM. With efficient memory management, virtual-memory systems can be very effective (see page 381).

14. Tasks being continually taken out of and brought back into memory which leads to gross inefficiency.
15. Each user is allocated a small time slice – if it's managed properly the service for each user comes round quickly enough such that they do not notice any gap in processing ability of the computer being used. Multiprogramming may be implemented by allocating each program a separate time slice.
16. More than one processor is needed to share the enormous load, especially with the communication problems for many users accessing the same CPU. Reliability can be increased if more than one main processor is used as a larger amount of redundancy is built in.
17. Buffers and communications controllers or front-end processors.
18. Direct-Memory Access. Releases the processor from managing block-memory transfers.
19. To cope with the horrendous processor-intensive activity that would have been taken up with handling the communication between all the users and the main machine.
20. Distributed – many computers with shared network resources. Centralised – one main machine with many terminals.
21. Some micros now have more power than some of the mainframes used to have in the 70s and 80s.
22. Passwords, data encryption (see page 605).

Answers to exercise 17.2

1. More powerful chips have led to user-friendly operating systems based on the WIMP environment.
2. To run different software packages at apparently the same time. Useful for transfer of data between CAD and DTP, for example.
3. Enables different software platforms to be run on the same micro. RISC PC or PowerPC are examples.
4. OS written using an OOP language such as C++. Large systems can be developed with more chance of working properly.
5. A Basic Input-Output System, that part of the operating system which controls Input and Output.
6. Boot files are used to load other parts of the operating system or customise the computer. OS is often not committed to ROM because of frequent updates and bug fixes etc.
7. See the FAT explanation on page 391.
8. It maps out the function of all the blocks of memory, e.g. graphics, I/O etc.
9. A peripheral device may request some processor time to perform a special function. This is usually achieved by means of an interrupt. See page 394 and chapter 5 page 85.
10. Cache memory is usually 'fast SRAM', it can be used in preference to ordinary DRAM for most-frequently needed parts of the current program.
11. Long sequences of esoteric commands do not have to be remembered, you can point at an icon instead.
12. Using a special boot file created by the user to load certain programs and utilities etc. It saves the user having to go manually through a large number of operations to set the machine up to an individual specification.
13. An error such as disk full, for example, can be detected by the part of the operating system which determines if there is sufficient space to save the data. If not, an error message is produced.
14. A network interface card and a network operating system.
15. Most software is written for these particular platforms – it gives a degree of standardisation which helps to share information. RISC PC, PowerPC and PowerMac are attempting to change this mold.
16. Making sure users do not have access to other people's work.
17. The operating system is transparent because it's often quite simple to use.
18. Incompatible physical and logical data formats. The network could provide a common communication protocol and ASCII data can be transferred via the network interface.
19. There is no method to guarantee correctness of programs because of the enormous number of different paths through the system. Send patches which can be added on to the existing operating system.
20. Virtual-reality OS, international information superhighway, speech input and output, possibly thought control in the far future – your guess is as good as mine!

Answers to exercise 18.1

1. A set of rules which have proved to be very useful in making sure that development of a project is steered through to a successful conclusion. As modern software and techniques have become available, other strategies such as prototyping and altering of the original specification are now generally acceptable (see page 402).
2. Customers often don't know what they want as they are not computer specialists. Prototyping helps to point the way or to develop systems in more heuristic ways.
3. Program flowcharts are too detailed – use systems flowcharts for describing more-complex systems.

4. (a)

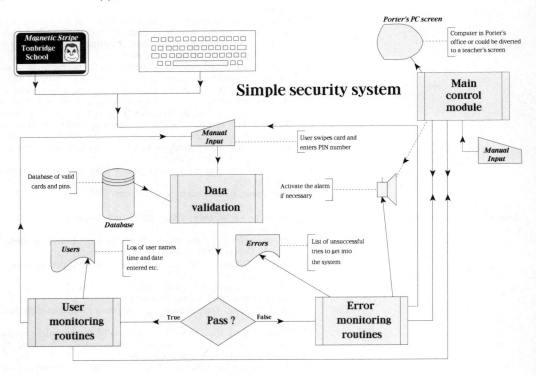

Simple security system

4. (b)

Electronic registration system

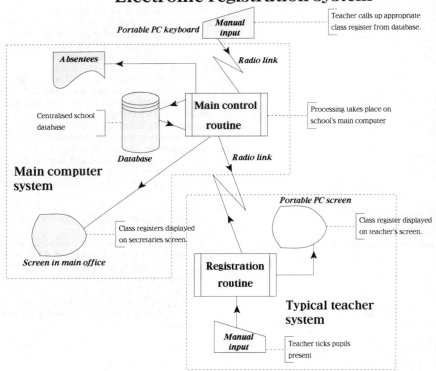

4. (c)

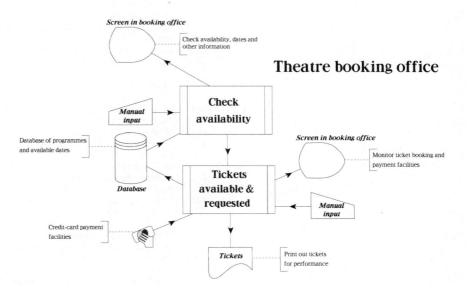

4. (d)

Local newsagent shop (delivery processing)

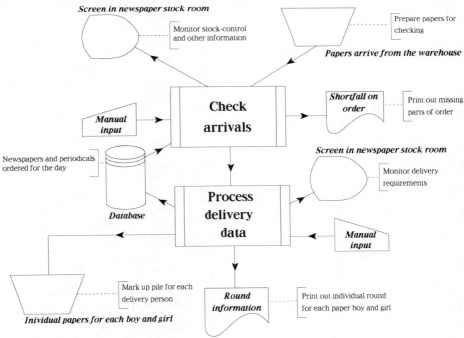

5. (a) List is not exhaustive – some general pointers are shown.
  (i)   More efficient patient care and better statistics about the operation of the surgery.
  (ii)   Less waiting time than with a manual system.
  (iii)   Automatic production of prescriptions.
  (iv)   Better management of medical records.
  (v)   Better accounting in terms of drug purchase and distribution.
  (vi)   Better information dissemination and communication between doctors.
  (vii)   Etc. etc.
  (b) List is not exhaustive – some general pointers are shown.
  (i)   Types of software available.
  (ii)   Key word search such as DTP, CAD or PERT etc.

        (iii)   Location of appropriate manuals.

        (iv)   Where to get expert help.

        (v)   Hardware and OS platform for software.

        (vi)   Any extra special peripherals needed such as scanners or graphics tablets etc.

        (vii)   Etc. etc.

  (c) List is not exhaustive – some general pointers are shown.

        (i)   Achieve a reduction in running costs compared to manual operation of the system.

        (ii)   Determine most efficient zone in terms of usage, e.g. daytime and evening use, for example.

        (iii)   Determine the best places for automatic monitoring of temperature.

        (iv)   Automatic shutdown in the event of a system or power failure.

        (v)   Manual override to alter setting if necessary.

        (vi)   Summer and winter timetables – special timetables for weekends etc.

        (vii)   Etc. etc.

  (d) List is not exhaustive – some general pointers are shown.

        (i)   Achieve greater efficiency in terms of information distribution to pupils and staff.

        (ii)   Allow for instant emergency distribution of notices.

        (iii)   Allow automatic cycling through screens.

        (iv)   Allow some degree of user choice of screen from each display terminal.

        (v)   Text and pictures should only be altered by staff with appropriate authority.

        (vi)   Multiple levels of user gaining access to a hierarchy of information.

        (vii)   Etc. etc.

6. (a) List is not exhaustive – some general pointers are shown.

        (i)   Awkward transition from the manual to the automatic system.

        (ii)   Staff need to be trained on how to use the system.

        (iii)   What happens in the event of a power cut?

        (iv)   Patients might need to be reassured about privacy of information.

        (v)   How is the information in the computer transferred to another surgery when a patient moves?

        (vi)   Etc. etc.

  (b) List is not exhaustive – not so many here as the system is less critical.

        (i)   Database needs to be available on all software platforms!

        (ii)   Staff and pupil training will be needed to make full use of the system.

        (iii)   Etc. etc.

  (c) List is not exhaustive – some general pointers are shown.

        (i)   Staff training needed – system will be more complex to use than manual system.

        (ii)   Change over to automatic system will have to be done in the summer.

        (iii)   Extensive trials will be needed to make sure it operates effectively and safely.

        (iv)   Etc. etc.

  (d) List is not exhaustive – some general pointers are shown.

        (i)   Staff training – people will have to get used to finding a computer to distribute a notice.

        (ii)   Cycling through the system on screen might be annoying if too many pages are used.

        (iii)   Pupils might find it a novelty to keep changing the screen while others are looking at it.

        (iv)   Etc. etc.

7. (a) List is not exhaustive – some general pointers are shown.

        (i)   Data protection act must be observed – build this into system.

        (ii)   Levels of password protection will be needed if information is to be viewed by different staff.

        (iii)   Possible to encrypt sensitive data.

  (b) List is not exhaustive – some general pointers are shown.

        (i)   No problems in security here – database will probably be read-only.

  (c) List is not exhaustive – some general pointers are shown.

        (i)   Ensure that no unauthorised person has access to the programmable part of the system.

        (ii)   Ensure that appropriate personnel may activate manual override if appropriate.

  (d) List is not exhaustive – some general pointers are shown.

        (i)   Password protection to make sure staff have access only to their particular parts of the system.

        (ii)   Make sure power and monitors etc. can't be switched off at notice board end.

8. (a) Many purpose-built systems exist – these need investigation and would probably be more cost effective than writing your own software.

  (b) Use database package – not much point re-inventing the wheel for a standard application.

  (c) Probably need to write customised software – however, market should be investigated.

  (d) Probably best to use a multi-media package, but if teletext type system is required then a teletext editor and some sort of carousel-type communications package would be useful.

9. (a) Check on patients appointments and booking system – after extensive stand-alone testing, run in parallel with existing manual system until you are satisfied that the manual system is no longer needed.
    (b) Check that many of the key-word searches find the expected items of software. Check that unusual input does not crash the system. Check validation routines when inputting standard queries.
    (c) Check that the software recovers from a power failure by removing the power from the system – check that the battery back-up system has kept real time, and that the boot system has restarted properly.
    (d) Check that the carousel system continues to function for several cycles. Check that any page being displayed can be interrupted by appropriate controls at the monitors – check security by attempting to break into files.

10. Gantt charts and PERT charts to keep project on schedule – CASE aids such as modelling and simulation, debuggers and trace routines to help check program modules etc.

11. Checksums and check digits check integrity of entered data, CRCs and hashing check integrity of batches of data. (See pages 512, 312 and 423.) All help with data validation checks.

12. Validation – getting machine to check if data is sensible in the context it is being used. Verification – getting a machine or person to check if data is correct. (See page 423.)

13. (a) Different user manuals for the doctors, receptionists, and nurses etc. General guide for practice managers and GP fund holders. Technical manuals for personnel who will maintain the system. More technical manuals for programmers who may have to alter the system.
    (b) User guide for the pupils and staff. Technical guide for system manager to maintain the database.
    (c) User guide for the caretakers or boiler personnel. Technical installation guide including the location and operation of the specialist peripherals. Technical manual for people who will maintain (program) the system on a day-to-day basis. Highly technical manual for both software and specialist hardware implementations – allow software and hardware engineers to modify the system.
    (d) User guide for staff who will write the notices. Simple guide for the users of the system. Technical guide for personnel who will maintain the system.

14. CASE – Computer Aided Software Engineering. Modern techniques for helping manage project from initial conception to completion (see page 426).

Answers to exercise 19.1

1. See page 430.
2. See page 430.
3. (a) See page 431. (b) See page 436 . (c) See page 435.

Truth table for four input NOR gate									
Inputs				NOR output	Inputs				NOR output
A	B	C	D	X	A	B	C	D	X
0	0	0	0	1	1	0	0	0	0
0	0	0	1	0	1	0	0	1	0
0	0	1	0	0	1	0	1	0	0
0	0	1	1	0	1	0	1	1	0
0	1	0	0	0	1	1	0	0	0
0	1	0	1	0	1	1	0	1	0
0	1	1	0	0	1	1	1	0	0
0	1	1	1	0	1	1	1	1	0

4. (a) NAND gates only (see page 434).   (b) NOR gates only (see page 434).

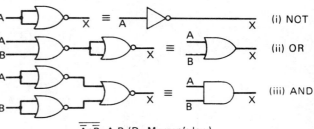

$\overline{A.B}=A+B$ (De Morgan's law) $\overline{A+B}=A.B$ (De Morgan's law)

5.

X	Y	$\bar{X}$	$\bar{Y}$	X.Y	$(\overline{X.Y})$	X.$\bar{Y}$	$(\overline{X.Y}) + (X.\bar{Y})$	$\bar{X} + \bar{Y}$	$\bar{X} + Y$	$(\overline{\bar{X} + Y})$	$(\bar{X} + \bar{Y}) + (\overline{\bar{X} + Y})$
0	0	1	1	0	1	0	1	1	1	0	1
0	1	1	0	0	1	0	1	1	1	0	1
1	0	0	1	0	1	1	1	1	0	1	1
1	1	0	0	1	0	0	0	0	1	0	0

(Note: very easy to show using De Morgan's law.)

7. (a) $A.\bar{B} + A.\bar{C} + A.D + B.\bar{C}.D$

(b)   Let function be X.
$\bar{X}$ from Karnaugh is $A.\bar{B}.C.\bar{D}$. Therefore $\bar{A} + B + \bar{C} + \bar{D}$ is simplified expression. (De Morgan's law.)

(c)   B

8.

A B C D	Ā B̄ C̄ D̄	Ā.B̄.C.D	Ā.B.C̄.D	A.B.C̄.D	A.B̄.C.D.	Ā.B.C.D	A.B.C.D	X
0 0 0 0	1 1 1 1	0	0	0	0	0	0	0
0 0 0 1	1 1 1 0	0	0	0	0	0	0	0
0 0 1 0	1 1 0 1	0	0	0	0	0	0	0
0 0 1 1	1 1 0 0	1	0	0	0	0	0	1
0 1 0 0	1 0 1 1	0	0	0	0	0	0	0
0 1 0 1	1 0 1 0	0	1	0	0	0	0	1
0 1 1 0	1 0 0 1	0	0	0	0	0	0	0
0 1 1 1	1 0 0 0	0	0	0	0	1	0	1
1 0 0 0	0 1 1 1	0	0	0	0	0	0	0
1 0 0 1	0 1 1 0	0	0	0	0	0	0	0
1 0 1 0	0 1 0 1	0	0	0	0	0	0	0
1 0 1 1	0 1 0 0	0	0	0	1	0	0	1
1 1 0 0	0 0 1 1	0	0	0	0	0	0	0
1 1 0 1	0 0 1 0	0	0	1	0	0	0	1
1 1 1 0	0 0 0 1	0	0	0	0	0	0	0
1 1 1 1	0 0 0 0	0	0	0	0	0	1	1

AB

CD \	00	01	11	10
00	0	0	0	0
01	0	1	1	0
11	1	1	1	1
10	0	0	0	0

from Karnaugh map:

$X = C.D + B.D = D.(C + B)$

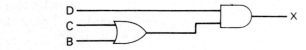

9.

$$X = 0\ 1\ 0\ 1\ 1\ 0\ 0\ 1 \qquad X = 0\ 1\ 0\ 1\ 1\ 0\ 0\ 1$$
$$Y = 1\ 1\ 0\ 0\ 1\ 0\ 0\ 1 \quad \text{NOT } X = 1\ 0\ 1\ 0\ 0\ 1\ 1\ 0$$
$$X \text{ AND } Y = 0\ 1\ 0\ 0\ 1\ 0\ 0\ 1$$

$$X = 0\ 1\ 0\ 1\ 1\ 0\ 0\ 1$$
$$Y = 1\ 1\ 0\ 0\ 1\ 0\ 0\ 1$$
$$X \text{ NOT equiv } Y = 1\ 0\ 0\ 1\ 0\ 0\ 0\ 0$$

10. (a) $\overline{(A . (B + C))} \quad = \quad \bar{A} + \bar{B}.\bar{C}$

$\overline{(A . (B + C))} \quad = \quad \bar{A} + \overline{(B + C)}$

| Need to show this, therefore,
| De Morgan's law with A and (B + C) as elements.

$\qquad\qquad\qquad = \quad \bar{A} + \bar{B}.\bar{C}$ De Morgan's law on last term with B and

i.e. $\overline{(A.(B + C))} \quad = \quad A + \bar{B}.\bar{C}$ C as elements.

(b)

				X =	Y = B, C same but diff. from A	Z = B, C Both 0	
A	B	C	D	A is 0			
0	0	0	0	1	0	1	
0	0	0	1	1	0	1	
0	0	1	0	1	0	0	
0	0	1	1	1	0	0	
0	1	0	0	1	0	0	Expressions for each part
0	1	0	1	1	0	0	
0	1	1	0	1	1	0	$X = \bar{A}$
0	1	1	1	1	1	0	
1	0	0	0	0	1	1	$Y = \bar{A}.B.C + A.\bar{B}.\bar{C}$

1	0	0	1	0	1	1	$Z = \bar{A}.\bar{B}.\bar{C} + A.\bar{B}.\bar{C}$
1	0	1	0	0	0	0	
1	0	1	1	0	0	0	
1	1	0	0	0	0	0	
1	1	0	1	0	0	0	
1	1	1	0	0	0	0	
1	1	1	1	0	0	0	

Valid decimal digit $= X + Y + Z = \bar{A} + \bar{A}.B.C + A.\bar{B}.\bar{C}. + \bar{A}.\bar{B}.\bar{C} + A.\bar{B}.\bar{C}$
Hence valid decimal digit $= \bar{A}. + A.\bar{B}.\bar{C}$
Z is redundant as both of its conditions are covered by parts X and Y; see above truth table.

(c)

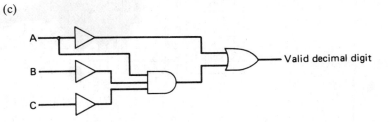

Valid decimal digit

Answers to exercise 19.2

1. BCD to 7 segment decoder.

Karnaugh maps to each segment:

BCD input A B C D	7 segments a b c d e f g
0 0 0 0	1 1 1 1 1 1 0
0 0 0 1	0 1 1 0 0 0 0
0 0 1 0	1 1 0 1 1 0 1
0 0 1 1	1 1 1 1 0 0 1
0 1 0 0	0 1 1 0 0 1 1
0 1 0 1	1 0 1 1 0 1 1
0 1 1 0	1 0 1 1 1 1 1
0 1 1 1	1 1 1 0 0 0 0
1 0 0 0	1 1 1 1 1 1 1
1 0 0 1	1 1 1 0 0 1 1
1 0 1 0	x x x x x x x
1 0 1 1	x x x x x x x
1 1 0 0	x x x x x x x
1 1 0 1	x x x x x x x
1 1 1 0	x x x x x x x
1 1 1 1	x x x x x x x

(a)
CD \ AB	00	01	11	10
00	1	0	x	1
01	0	1	x	1
11	1	1	x	x
10	1	1	x	x

(b)
CD \ AB	00	01	11	10
00	1	1	x	1
01	1	0	x	1
11	1	1	x	x
10	1	0	x	x

(c)
CD \ AB	00	01	11	10
00	1	1	x	1
01	1	1	x	1
11	1	1	x	x
10	0	1	x	x

CD \ AB	00	01	11	10
00	1	0	x	1
01	0	1	x	0
11	1	0	x	x
10	1	1	x	x

CD \ AB	00	01	11	10
00	1	0	x	1
01	0	0	x	0
11	0	0	x	x
10	1	1	x	x

CD \ AB	00	01	11	10
00	1	1	x	1
01	0	1	x	1
11	0	0	x	x
10	0	1	x	x

Note: x denotes code can't happen
(inputs are invalid)

CD \ AB	00	01	11	10
00	0	1	x	1
01	0	1	x	1
11	1	0	x	x
10	1	1	x	x

From the above Karnaugh maps:
$a = A + C + A.D + \bar{B}.\bar{D}$
$b = A + B + C.D + \bar{C}.\bar{D}$
$c = A + B + \bar{C} + D$
$d = A.B + \bar{B}.\bar{D} + A.C + \bar{B}.C + C.\bar{D} + B.\bar{C}.D$
$e = A.B + A.\bar{D} + C.\bar{D} + B.\bar{D}$
$f = A + B.C + B.\bar{C} + \bar{C}.\bar{D}$
$g = A + B.\bar{C} + \bar{B}.C + C.\bar{D}$

	BCD Inputs				7 segment display						
	A	B	C	D	a	b	c	d	e	f	g
0	0	0	0	0	1	1	1	1	1	1	0
1	0	0	0	1	0	1	1	0	0	0	0
2	0	0	1	0	1	1	0	1	1	0	1
3	0	0	1	1	1	1	1	1	0	0	1
4	0	1	0	0	0	1	1	0	0	1	1
5	0	1	0	1	1	0	1	1	0	1	1
6	0	1	1	0	1	0	1	1	1	1	1
7	0	1	1	1	1	1	1	0	0	0	0
8	1	0	0	0	1	1	1	1	1	1	1
9	1	0	0	1	1	1	1	0	0	1	1
—	1	0	1	0	x	x	x	x	x	x	x
—	1	0	1	1	x	x	x	x	x	x	x
—	1	1	0	0	x	x	x	x	x	x	x
—	1	1	0	1	x	x	x	x	x	x	x
—	1	1	1	0	x	x	x	x	x	x	x
—	1	1	1	1	x	x	x	x	x	x	x

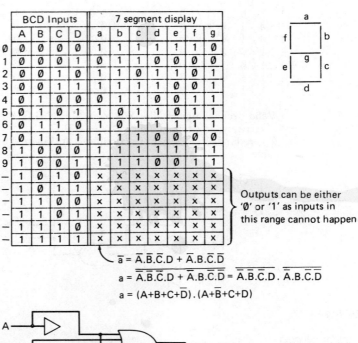

Outputs can be either '0' or '1' as inputs in this range cannot happen

$$\overline{a} = \overline{A}.\overline{B}.\overline{C}.D + \overline{A}.B.\overline{C}.\overline{D}$$

$$a = \overline{\overline{A}.\overline{B}.\overline{C}.D + \overline{A}.B.\overline{C}.\overline{D}} = \overline{\overline{A}.\overline{B}.\overline{C}.D} . \overline{\overline{A}.B.\overline{C}.\overline{D}}$$

$$a = (A+B+C+\overline{D}).(A+\overline{B}+C+D)$$

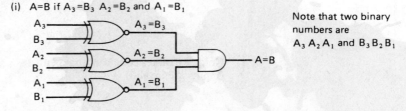

Note: Only (a) is shown in this example,
         (b) to (g) are left to the reader!

2. See page 452.

3. See pages 434, 449 and 451. Serial addition, not so many circuits needed, but slow. Parallel addition, more circuits needed, but fast.

4. See page 454.

5. See page 454. Arrange most significant bit to be clocked, and feed through clock pulses in the opposite direction, counter must also start off in the 1111 state.

6.

Considered in three stages

(i) $A=B$ if $A_3=B_3$ $A_2=B_2$ and $A_1=B_1$

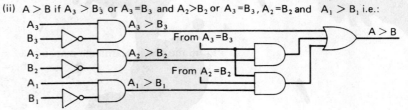

Note that two binary numbers are $A_3 A_2 A_1$ and $B_3 B_2 B_1$

(ii) $A > B$ if $A_3 > B_3$ or $A_3=B_3$ and $A_2>B_2$ or $A_3=B_3$, $A_2=B_2$ and $A_1 > B_1$ i.e.:

(iii) A<B if A_3<B_3 or A_3=B_3 and A_2<B_2 or A_3=B_3 and A_2=B_2 and A_1<B_1 i.e:

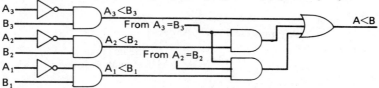

7.

A	B	C	Odd parity bit
0	0	0	1
0	0	1	0
0	1	0	0
0	1	1	1
1	0	0	0
1	0	1	1
1	1	0	1
1	1	1	0

Parity = $\bar{A}.\bar{B}.\bar{C}+\bar{A}.B.C+A.\bar{B}.C+A.B.\bar{C}$ i.e:

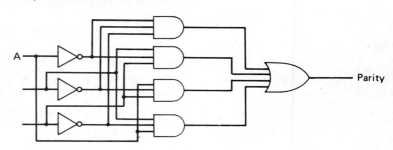

A	B	C	P	Check
0	0	0	0	Illegal
0	0	0	1	O.K.
0	0	1	0	O.K.
0	0	1	1	Illegal
0	1	0	0	O.K.
0	1	0	1	Illegal
0	1	1	0	Illegal
0	1	1	1	O.K.
1	0	0	0	O.K.
1	0	0	1	Illegal
1	0	1	0	Illegal
1	0	1	1	O.K.
1	1	0	0	Illegal
1	1	0	1	O.K.
1	1	1	0	O.K.
1	1	1	1	Illegal

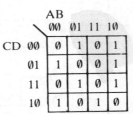

AB

CD		00	01	11	10
	00	0	1	0	1
	01	1	0	0	1
	11	0	1	0	1
	10	1	0	1	0

Can't simplify Karnaugh map.

Check = $\bar{A}.\bar{B}.\bar{C}.P + \bar{A}.\bar{B}.C.\bar{P} + \bar{A}.B.\bar{C}.\bar{P} + \bar{A}.B.C.P + A.\bar{B}.\bar{C}.\bar{P} + A.\bar{B}.C.P +$
$A.B.\bar{C}.P + A.B.C.\bar{P}$

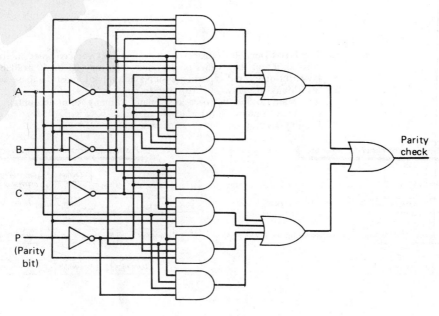

8.

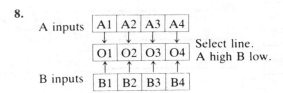

A inputs

A1	A2	A3	A4

O1	O2	O3	O4

Select line.
A high B low.

B1	B2	B3	B4

B inputs

The circuit will consist of four identical elements. Consider the A1, B1 and O1 lines:

IF select = 1 THEN O1 = A1 OR IF select = $\emptyset$ THEN O1 = B1

Select	A1	B1	O1
$\emptyset$	$\emptyset$	$\emptyset$	$\emptyset$
$\emptyset$	$\emptyset$	1	1
$\emptyset$	1	$\emptyset$	$\emptyset$
$\emptyset$	1	1	1
1	$\emptyset$	$\emptyset$	$\emptyset$
1	$\emptyset$	1	$\emptyset$
1	1	$\emptyset$	1
1	1	1	1

A1 B1

	00	01	11	10
Sel 0	$\emptyset$	1	1	$\emptyset$
1	$\emptyset$	$\emptyset$	1	1

From Karnaugh:

O1 = A1 . Sel + B1 . $\overline{\text{Sel}}$

Similarly:
O2 = A2 . Sel + B2 . $\overline{\text{Sel}}$
O3 = A3 . Sel + B3 . $\overline{\text{Sel}}$
O4 = A4 . Sel + B4 . $\overline{\text{Sel}}$

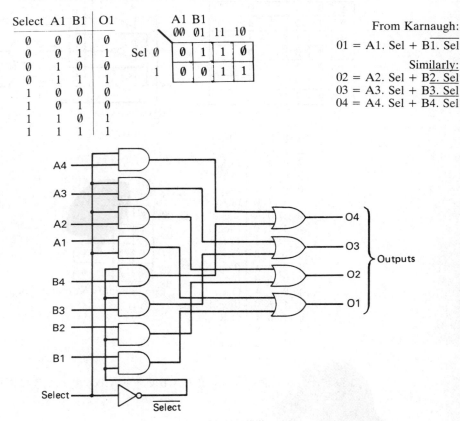

Answers to exercise 20.1

1. The DBMS enables efficient organisation and very complex interactions to take place. Also, different data views of the same data may be made available for different users. Powerful query and reporting systems accompany most database software.

2. (a) Many to many.   (b) One to one.
(c) Many to one, but occasional many to many (joint accounts).
(d) One to many.   (e) Many to many.

3. Possibly arrange on Dewey as shown.

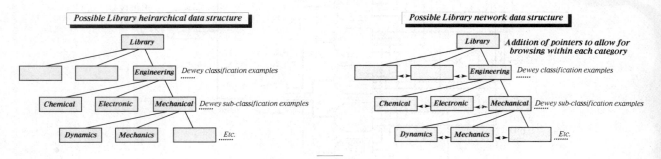

4. Techniques of inorder traversal (see page 307) can be used on the following hierarchical structure.

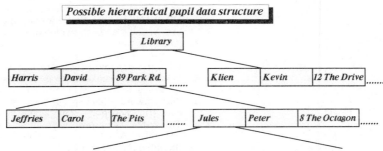

5. It's based on a mathematical relation expressed as a 2D-table, and not on a structure diagram like the hierarchical and network databases.

6. (a) An entry in a cell on a relational table – equivalent to a field in a record.
    (b) A tuple or row in a relational table – equivalent to a record in a file.
    (c) A 2-D table in a relational database – it's *not* the same as a relationship.
    (d) The key (attribute) by which a relational table is best known.
    (e) A row from a 2-D relational table.
    (f) Altering the relations to conform to the set of Codd's rules.

7. Functional dependency – a one-to-one relationship only exists between the attributes which are to be functionally or fully dependent. Transitive dependency – if one attribute is functionally dependent on another, which is also functionally dependent on a third, then the first is also functionally dependent on the third.

8. A record in which multiple-field entries are allowed so that the overall length of the record can grow. Eventually record would not be able to get bigger than (say) the buffer size – also does not conform to the first normal form.

9. Possible arrangement of data in **first normal form** (i.e. no attribute in either table can have multiple values). Therefore, all records in each table are of the same length.
    Student (Student name, <u>Student ID</u>, Address, Home phone, Company, Company phone)
    Subject (<u>Subject code</u>, Subject name, Student ID, Grade, Teacher, Department)

Possible arrangement of data in **second normal form** (i.e. all attributes in each table can be uniquely identified just by using the primary key). Note that a composite primary key is needed for Subject grade, as 'Student ID' or 'Subject code' alone could not uniquely identify the grade.
    Students (Student name, <u>Student ID</u>, Address, Home phone, Company)
    Company (<u>Company</u>, Company phone)
    Subject (<u>Subject code</u>, Subject name, Teacher, Department)
    Subject Grade (<u>Student ID</u>, <u>Subject code</u>, Grade)

Third normal form (i.e. no functional dependency on attributes that could *not* act as alternative primary keys).
Student – 'Student name', 'Address' and 'Home phone' could all act as alternatives to the primary key due to strong relationship with student ID. However, 'Company' could *not* be used as a primary key, but as it's the only non-identifying attribute there can't possibly be a relationship between company and another non-identifying attribute.
Company – obviously no problems.
Subject – 'Teacher' and 'department' are both non-identifying attributes, a teacher uniquely identifies a Department, and therefore a functional dependency exists between these two non-identifying attributes. This will have to be altered to get the data in third normal form. Change to the following.
    Subject (<u>Subject code</u>, Subject name, Teacher)
    Teacher (<u>Teacher</u>, Department)
    Subject grade – again obviously no problems.
The complete set of relations for the database in third normal form is, therefore, given by the following.
    Students (Student name, <u>Student ID</u>, Address, Home phone, Company)
    Company (<u>Company</u>, Company phone)
    Subject (<u>Subject code</u>, Subject name, Teacher)
    Teacher (<u>Teacher</u>, Department)
    Subject Grade (<u>Student ID</u>, <u>Subject code</u>, Grade)
Possible problem – Teacher may not be unique – therefore, invent a teacher ID.

10. Declarative query makes use of non-procedural SQL commands, user friendly HCI uses a graphical interface or pre-set queries structured by the DBA.

11. Physical, and software security measures must be taken – see page 482 to page 484.

12. Depends on the database which you have at your school or college.

1. **LAN** – Local Area Network – up to about 1 km/network although multiple networks may be connected by bridges. Under control of individual institutions.
MAN – Metropolitan Area Network – usually FDDI – up to about 100 km. Individual or national control depending on the size of your estate!
WAN – Wide Area Network – making use of public service networks from BT or Mercury etc. National and international in scope.

2. Access to wide range of external databases – E-mail facilities. Disadvantages – few, but security problems may arise or viruses could be caught from bulletin boards etc.

3. Data transfer rate is too slow if usage is heavy.

4. Possible to download software at same time in a school environment. Add local hard disk controller to act as shared-resource server (see page 491).

5. Star network – high speed, high security, high cost! Bus network – less secure but lower cost. Ring network – same as bus network.

6. The system has grown up in an *ad hoc* way with different manufacturers all doing their own thing. Also, as systems evolve, different standards have to be adopted to cope with the different requirements.

7. It acts as a modulator at the transmitting end and a demodulator at the receiving end. Converts computer data into audible tones to be transmitted over a normal telephone network.

8. (a) Parallel one wire/binary digit – usually 16, 32 or 64 bits sent at the same time. Serial – data sent down a single wire (often a few in practice) or a single channel radio, laser or infra-red link – it is converted into a form in which each bit arrives one after the other.
   (b) Baud rate – number of bits/sec. Information transmission rate – (baud rate – overheads)bits/sec, where overheads are things like parity bits or CRC bits etc.
   (c) Changing computer data into a form to be transmitted over the appropriate medium.
   (d) Sending more than one signal down a communication at the same time or apparently at the same time depending on the method of multiplexing being used.
   (e) A message is routed along a line which can't be used 'simultaneously' by other users.
   (f) Frequency Division Multiplexing – broadband multiplexing techniques have been used.
   (g) A check carried out by a mathematical algorithm which derives a set of bits which can be inserted together with the transmitted message.
   (h) Fibre Distributed Data Interface – one current standard for fibre optic networks.

9. Packet switching uses the node computers to route packets of data over any link. Can be used by other users at the 'same time'. Telephone – exclusive use of a single line for the duration of the call.

10. Baseband – single frequency only. Broadband – use of FDM to send signals simultaneously at different carrier frequencies.

11. Important so that different systems can communicate with each other internationally. It's a convention to which many vendors can make sure that their individualised systems conform.

12. A drastic effect because it will open up paths for easy communication on a global scale.

13. It defines the guts of the hardware – therefore, it's the only hardware-only layer.

14. It's one type of level 2 and 3 protocols which have become very popular indeed. The IP is the protocol used by the ever-growing Internet system.

15. Parity and CRCs – see page 510 and 512. Too complex, and not good at correcting a really badly messed-up message. It's simpler to re-transmit the message.

16. Students and staff! Hacking, fire, flood, electromagnetic interference, disk failures on the file servers, computer viruses, you name it – it has probably happened.

1. Possibilities could be: **better information management systems** making use of spreadsheets, databases and DTP systems; **better communications** making use of E-Mail, local, national and international networks; **better presentation** in terms of advertising, company brochures, catalogues etc. All these systems are usually cost effective – a major criteria for any company.

2. Ease of editing and merging of work, same text may be used in many different forms, e.g. transfer from WP to spreadsheet or database, ease of communication using networks, automated error checking in terms of spelling and grammar etc. **Disadvantages** – staff need to be trained in new technology, more potential for error if information not managed properly, greater potential for fraud or misuse of information in the system.

3. Rules of English grammar are still much too complex for today's technology – rules of spelling are simple in comparison. Competent grammar checking will take a few more years yet.

4. De-skilled the job of laying out text – relatively cheap equipment now produces professional results etc. Specialist printers still needed for high-quality colour and high-volume work.

5. Anything that can be expressed in terms of relationships with numbers can be modelled on a spreadsheet. This includes anything from simulating queueing through database-type work to nuclear power-station evaluation. For example, 'what if' we put an extra checkout at the supermarket – what would be the likely effect on the lengths of the queues at the checkouts? (See 'Chippy' example on page 199.)

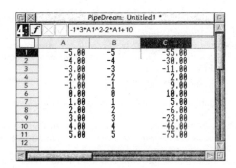
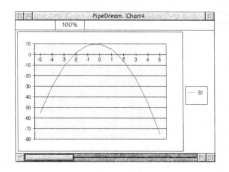

6. (a)   Graphs produced on Acorn Archimedes using Pipedream 4.

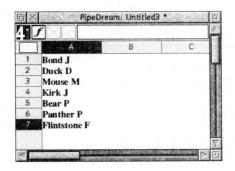
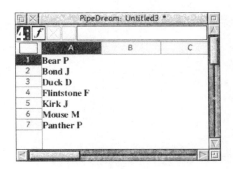

(b)   Original list on left – list after a block sort on the right.

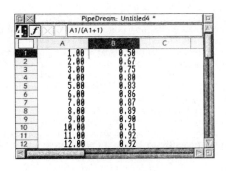
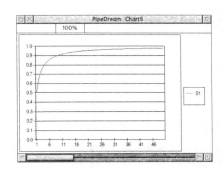

(c)   For convenience only part of the data is shown on the left. Chart for 100 values is on right.

7.   Any suitable backdrop will do.

8.   Videotex – 'two way' making use of communications package, modem, micro and WAN – Teletext one way making use of unused TV signals (see page 533).

9.   Able to download and save page data in a variety of formats ready for computer processing.

10.   What's on in London, Travel information, Campus 2000 education information, E-Mail etc.

11.   Modem, micro, communications software, and a third party to provide connection via their gateway. Also need to pay subscriptions, and have information about how to navigate and use the network. Hundreds of thousands of different interests are catered for.

12.   No – restricted access to this would lead to many disadvantages for business and bona fide personal users, and the criminals would find other ways of distributing their information. Possible to make use of encryption as suggested by the USA (page 605).

Answers to exercise 23.1

1.   All future processes from parts lists via control of CNC machines and automatic testing can be controlled from original CAD-package data. More accurate than manual techniques – infinite editability. Less people needed, therefore detrimental effect on employment. (See pages 545 and 607.)

2.   (a)   CAD data used to control CAM process (see page 544).

(b)   CAD data exported to spreadsheet for numerical analysis and modelling.

(c)   CAD data exported to database for parts information – link to suppliers and stock system.

(d)   CAD data exported to DTP system for help with the production of catalogues.

(e)   CAD data exported to expert system to help build up a diagnostic database for testing purposes.

3.   At the initial-ideas stage.

4.   All processes more rigorously controlled – automated – less people needed etc. In some countries labour is so cheap that it's more cost effective to use people – also, they may not have skills or factories etc.

5.   Model 4-stroke cycle to show operation of cylinders, valves and spark plugs etc using animation.

6.   CNC – machines controlled by computer-generated data. Data can be got from CAD details.

7.   Specialist robots are designed for the task in hand, not to look humanoid. Today's hardware and software is not yet capable of human-like robots – perhaps in a few tens of years time.

8.   With feedback – can tell if pieces have fallen over, can tell if a piece has been grabbed properly etc. Without feedback robot is operating blind. Strain gauges, light sensors, video cameras etc.

9.   (a)   Background noise – miscellany of sounds generated from speech.

(b)   Interpretation of visual input – variety of background views etc.

(c)   Real time chemical analysis of gasses is still very difficult and expensive.

(d)   Few problems, but many sensors would be needed if we are to simulate the human skin.

(e)   Few problems, but again real-time chemical analysis of acidity and salt etc. is difficult.

10.   Artificial Intelligence. Difficult to define intelligence – powerful and emotional religious arguments – many scientists on both sides of the fence, each with theories to back their arguments.

11.   CD-ROM based video and audio images can be relayed to mechanic to help with repair. VR helmet could also be useful with head-up display type projection.

12.   Interconnectivity of parallel processing elements is limited to far less than the billions of connections in the human brain.

13.   Probably! The Turing test will not necessarily be passed for several tens of years, but I think that it's inevitable one day if the last 50-years progress continues at the same (or even slower) pace.

Answers to exercise 24.1

1.   Able to store a vast amount of data cost effectively. Hardware and software to operate the system now cheap and plentiful. Windows-based applications are easier to distribute on CD-ROM.

2.   Global networks containing huge databases and bulletin boards in which masses of information currently stored on disk could be downloaded. Floptical drives might also prove more cost effective eventually. CD-ROMs fighting back with blue lasers giving quadruple data storage capacity. But blue lasers could be used on flopticals too!

3.   *The Times* and *Sunday Times* newspaper articles. For example, searching for all information on South Africa from 1991 to 1995. Try doing this by hand – searching through 5 years of newspaper articles!

4.   Major problems are incompatibility between masses of different hardware and software standards, particularly regarding images. Trouble is that things have developed so fast, and the quality and amount of information is getting better and better, that we have not stood still sufficiently to create a definitive standard. MPEG seems to be almost there – but who knows what's round the corner?

5.   Compression techniques have done wonders in the last few years – compressed computer data takes up far fewer bits, and therefore 'more' information can be sent down the phone line using the same bandwidth.

6.   Better video phones – therefore, ability for experts such as doctors to examine patients remotely, pictorial information available from worldwide databases, interactive TVs making use of the phone etc.

7.   Creation of presentations, videos or CD-ROMs etc. containing a mixture of still and moving images and sound, all interacting with the user by customised menu systems. Ordinary users can create their own applications in ways hitherto impossible.

8.   It enables very sophisticated control of the interactive environment between the user and the computer. It also enables the programmer of such a system to customise parts of the package to interact with the computer in imaginative ways.

9.   It's incredibly easy to type in text in a desired font, then get the package to make 3D letters from the typed-in text. The text can then be distorted into almost any shape, and control points on the image can be altered until it's just right. Doing this by hand is painfully slow and takes a great degree of artistic skill.

10.   In the future most art packages will be able to re-create virtually anything that can be done with manual techniques. However, it's unlikely that people will want to get computers to generate oil paintings on large sheets of canvas, for example. Each method belongs to a different set of requirements.

11.   The techniques used are exactly the same as those which are used by the human eye to perceive an image.

12.   A start and stop computer graphic each of which has an identical grid superimposed on it. The user alters the grids so that points on the start image may be mapped to identical

points on the final image. A number of different intermediate stages are chosen to produce an animation effect.

Answers to exercise 25.1

1. A device to convert one form of energy into another – specifically, for computer systems either physical quantities into electrical signals, or electrical signals into physical quantities.

2. A device which is used to convert signals from any form into a form that the computer can understand, or to convert computer signals into any other suitable form, e.g. disk-drive interface, printer interface, sound or video card, network interface etc.

3. To connect a range of peripheral devices.

4. Input – pH sensor, light sensor, microphone, gas detector, temperature sensor. Output – loudspeaker, motor, light bulb, solenoid, buzzer. Solenoid is digital – rest are analogue, but may be operated digitally in special circumstances, e.g. motor or bulb can be on or off, but they are analogue devices in nature as they can be gradually increased in speed or brightness.

5. Serial – data is sent one bit after another down the same transmission medium – ideal for long distances. Parallel – two or more bits sent simultaneously down different wires or other media – ideal for communication inside the computer, i.e. short distances.

6. Start and stop bits, and transmitting at a given baud rate – see page 576.

7. Digital – varies in discrete steps, e.g. logic-gate output. Analogue – continuously variable, e.g. sound.

8. 12 bit – hence 4096 discrete levels for quantisation of analogue signal. Resolution determines how closely we can simulate the intended analogue signal (see page 578).

9. Feedback – paying attention to what is actually happening by monitoring suitable signals derived from input transducers – without this ability, safety may be compromised as wrong assumptions about what is actually happening could be made, e.g. the computer might have switched off a motor but it's still going!

10. A computer-control system has a fully-blown micro, mini or mainframe controlling the process, whereas an embedded system has only a microprocessor with memory etc. dedicated to a particular task. Examples of embedded systems are video recorders and cameras, examples of micro-controlled systems could be PCB drilling machine or CNC milling machine. PC control more versatile – embedded is cheaper.

11. Stepper motors can move in discrete steps under the control of a digital signal. Ideal for computer control. Ordinary d.c. motors require analogue voltage for speed control.

12. Tri-state means on, off or high impedance. Used to route signals along the bus system – tri state can prevent data for disk drive from reaching the printer, can also determine the direction of data (see page 584).

13. Real time – system must respond quickly enough to react to some external event. Engine management system in a car is a good example. Software routines have a limited time for execution and may be too slow.

14. A critical temperature is reached inside a nuclear reactor. The shut-down procedure must be activated immediately. Data integrity (correctness) and reliability are just as important as raw speed.

15. HCI – Human Computer Interface. People often form an integral link in a control system, and speed of reaction and interpretation of data by the human operators is important. The design of the interface should ensure that smooth and stress-free operation is possible.

16. Perfect Coffee maker is *as shown in diagram on next page* – assume that milk is put into the cup before the coffee is added, sugar is added last.

Answers to exercise 26.1

1. You will have to find your own *The Times*-database CD-ROM articles!

2. Allows mass communication – formation of user groups on any subject on a worldwide basis – access to massive databases on a worldwide basis – could form the basis of the information superhighway – means of bypassing censorship – i.e. any information, legal or otherwise can be transmitted without detection, unless a big-brother society is set up in which all information is monitored! – data may be encrypted to avoid detection, governments might make this action illegal if they can't 'see' what's going along the wires themselves – the range of possible topics here is vast.

3. (a) Making it illegal to set up bulletin boards with undesirable material – only fool-proof way is for the authorities to tap the phone lines!

   (b) No.

   (c) Fortunately the good bulletin boards outnumber the bad by many orders of magnitude. Only way to stop bad bulletin boards is to monitor and shut down. On balance they should not be banned.

   (d) No, some other methods would be used instead, e.g. distribution by floppy or CD-ROM etc.

4. (a) Very likely – VR methods are already real enough to train pilots, surgeons and many others.

   (b) The same arguments exist here as for video, except with a frightening added degree of potency. Just as video can be a good or bad influence, so too can VR.

   (c) Exploring micro-worlds, e.g. inside the body.

Automatic coffee-making machine

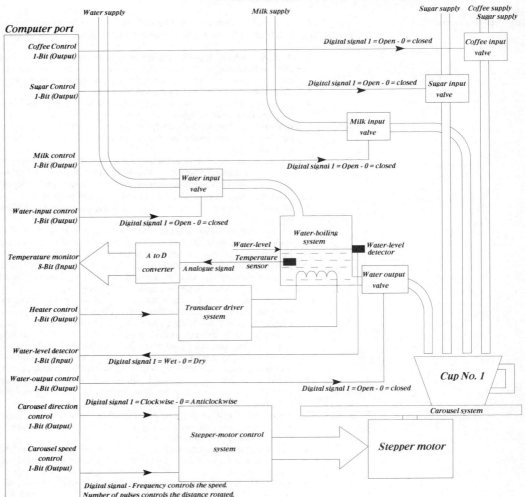

(d) Feeling that you are present at some historical event, being able to create dangerous experiments with complete safety, etc.

(e) An exercise bike, for example, could act as a vehicle for getting muscle power to move you around inside the VR world.

5. (a) **Against** – Penrose with his mathematical arguments which state that some problems can never be solved by algorithmic technology, and it's specifically these problems which relate to what makes the human brain different; religious beliefs; conviction that humans are inherently different etc.

   For – Research into different ways of using conventional and unconventional computers; biochips making use of protein (living computers?); early research into neural nets suggests that computers can dream; research into an understanding of how computers can learn etc.

   (b) **Potential uses** – Try to help solve problems too complex for humans to consider? Great potential for inventing better machines which could not be conceived of by man etc.

   (c) **Potential dangers** – Would man still be in control of such machines? How would humanity control the direction in which the machine intelligence would lead?

6. Physical damage – fire-proof safe, keep away from magnets, bomb proof site!! etc. Theft – high-security entry systems etc. Misuse – scrutiny of personnel etc. (See page 604.)

7. Having less and less spare computer memory when running your normal programs. Eradicate by use of a virus killer if possible. It's not possible to have a foolproof system.

8. Alter the date, if necessary, so that it will never be Michaelangelo's birthday!

Index